Walt WHITMAN, 1838-1939

a reference guide

A
Reference
Guide
to
Literature

Hershel Parker
Editor

Walt WHITMAN, 1838-1939

a reference guide

SCOTT GIANTVALLEY

G.K. HALL &CO.

70 LINCOLN STREET, BOSTON, MASS.

Library of Congress Cataloging in Publication Data

Giantvalley, Scott, 1949-
  Walt Whitman, 1838-1939 : a reference guide.

  Originally presented as the author's thesis (doctoral
—University of Southern California)
  Includes index.
  1. Whitman, Walt, 1819-1892—Bibliography. I. Title.
Z8971.5.G5 1981 [PS3238] 016.811′3 81-6538
ISBN 0-8161-7856-9   AACR2

This publication is printed on permanent/durable acid-free paper
MANUFACTURED IN THE UNITED STATES OF AMERICA

Contents

The Author vi

Preface vii

Introduction xi

Works and Editions xv

Abbreviations xvii

References Cited in the Text xix

Writings About Whitman, 1838-1939 1

Appendix 413

Addenda 415

Introduction to Index 421

Index 423

The Author

Scott Giantvalley teaches English at Golden West College, Huntington Beach, California, and serves as West Coast Managing Editor for <u>Quarterly Review of Film Studies</u>. He received his Ph.D. in American Literature from the University of Southern California in 1979, with an earlier version of this reference guide as his dissertation. He received his M.A. from California State University Northridge in 1975 and his B.A. from Occidental College in 1970. He is the author of a collection of poetry, <u>Apricot</u>, and his mock-Jacobean tragedy, <u>The Fair Lady Abroad</u>, has been performed in Los Angeles. He has had articles published in the <u>Walt Whitman Review</u>, the <u>James Joyce Quarterly</u>, <u>Opera Journal</u>, <u>Studies in American Fiction</u>, and <u>Pacific Coast Philology</u> (forthcoming).

Preface

Few literary figures during their lifetimes have received the high acclaim and categorical rejection accorded to Walt Whitman. His career, largely because of this disparity, naturally sparked much discussion, often relating to the very nature of his reception. Although this reception has been traced many times before, the present reference guide for the first time assembles in one place not only the bibliographical information on all significant known commentary on Whitman published in English from the earliest discovered mention of him in the press in 1838 through 1939, but also annotations to allow readers to judge whether a particular item is likely to be worth their further attention. Thousands of items hitherto not included in published bibliographies, many unnoted by any previous commentators on Whitman, are here listed and annotated. Some items, previously identified incompletely, have been located and provided with specific dates and other information; for other items, bibliographical information as presented in previous bibliographies has been silently corrected. Thus, where discrepancies exist between an earlier bibliography and this entry, it may be assumed that this entry contains the corrected information.

A mammoth job like compiling a comprehensive bibliography of material written about Walt Whitman and then locating each item in order to read and annotate it for use in this reference guide must have a beginning, even if no conclusion is possible other than an open-ended one, as with Whitman's poetry itself. Thus, the the bibliography must allow for the possible discovery of additional items and indeed encourage an active search for them, in an effort to make the list of known discussions of Whitman as complete as possible.

Such a job began simply enough by consulting the standard bibliographies of Whitman for the period under study, up through 1939. These major sources were the bibliographies of Oscar Lovell Triggs in the Complete Writings of Whitman (1902), Emory Holloway and Henry Saunders in the Cambridge History of American Literature (1918), Gay Wilson Allen in Twenty-Five Years of Walt Whitman Bibliography (1918-1942) (1943), and Index to Early American Periodical Literature, 1728-1870: No. 3, Walt Whitman (1941). I also consulted indexes to the New York Times, the New York Tribune, and the Critic, as well as the Reader's Guide to Periodical Literature and the National Union Catalogue. Key books devoted to Whitman which provided other material were the major recent biographies by Gay Wilson Allen, Roger Asselineau, and Justin Kaplan; Joseph Jay Rubin's study of Whitman's journalistic days, The Historical Whitman; and two book-length examinations of Whitman's reputation, Harold Blodgett's Walt Whitman in England and Charles Willard's Whitman's American Fame.

Willard's heavy reliance on Henry Saunders's collection of Whitmaniana at Brown University for many discussions of Whitman in newspapers and obscure magazines prompted me to visit Brown, where I pored through well over a hundred scrapbooks of secondary material relating to Whitman, mostly articles clipped from newspapers and magazines from the late 1800s through the early 1940s, large numbers of them not included in any bibliographies. Many of these items were from readily available periodicals, but many came from newspapers and magazines hardly well-known, including some from England and British Commonwealth nations. For many of these items the date was given only in Saunders's handwriting rather than as part of the clipping. However, for items which I have verified further by seeking them elsewhere after having learned of their existence in his collection, I have found Saunders's accuracy to be excellent, so I feel secure in listing the dates and periodical titles which he provided.

Saunders's collection also contains his typescript bibliography upon which the Cambridge History of American Literature bibliography was based. It includes many items which were omitted from the published version because of spatial limitations. From this I discovered many books containing essays on Whitman, reminiscences, textbook introductions to him, as well as periodical articles unlisted elsewhere, many of which appeared in his scrapbooks. Also providing information on many items was a lengthy typed list with annotations of periodical items of major and minor significance, chiefly from 1918, 1919, and 1920, not listed or presented elsewhere. Items noted as having only incidental mention of Whitman have not been included, whether actually seen or not, unless the writer himself or herself is significant. Items from either the typescript bibliography or the annotated listing which I have not personally seen are cited in the text as being "Reported in Saunders Supplement."

The process of tracking down items was often frustrating and often frustrated, as my symbol * indicates.

Items thus marked have not been seen by me, some because of their rareness and the difficulty of borrowing or copying them from various libraries across the country, some because of the impossibility of locating them through standard reference sources; others, as I note, have not been found in the periodical of the date listed or in other possible dates checked.

My search for items naturally began at the University of Southern California, where I was pursuing my doctoral studies. I then proceeded to other local research centers, the University of California at Los Angeles, the Los Angeles Public Library, and the Huntington Library in San Marino. Farther afield, besides consulting Brown University's collection, I visited the public libraries of San Francisco, Brooklyn, and New York (particularly its Oscar Lion collection of Whitman material), and the libraries of the University of California at Berkeley and Stanford University. Items not available at those libraries were requested through the interlibrary loan system.

A number of items have been found not through any bibliographer or commentator but simply through playing hunches, checking out likely authors, periodicals, and dates for possible reviews of Whitman's work or comments on him. A major source for mention of Whitman during a significant segment of this period is the Conservator, the journal Horace Traubel founded in 1890 as an organ of progressive political, social, and religious thought and gradually (after Whitman's death) as a vehicle for the promulgation of Whitman's ideas and spirit and the advancement of his reputation. The listings of items from the Conservator are numerous during the thirty years of its publication, up to June 1919, when it ceased publication due to Traubel's sudden death, rather effectively symbolic of the end of an era: The acceptance of Whitman evident in the vast number of centenary tributes to him and his recognition as a founding father of the modernist movement precluded the need for any more of Traubel's tireless efforts in his behalf. The Conservator's pages are filled with Whitman's name, and no attempt has been made to include all references, but the significant discussions and interesting incidental mentions are present.

The most noticeable omissions from this reference guide are items in languages other than English, except for those translated or discussed in other articles during the period under discussion. Those interested in exploring Whitman's reputation in other countries, which was certainly significant in the late nineteenth century and increasingly so in the early twentieth century, should consult Gay Wilson Allen's New Walt Whitman Handbook, which devotes a long section to Whitman's critical reception globally, with extensive notes for further references.

In the present reference guide, items are listed by year of publication, with two divisions per year, one for books, arranged alphabetically by author, one for periodicals, arranged chronologically beginning January 1. Quarterly publications precede the month beginning that quarter (spring before April, etc.). Items with the same date are arranged alphabetically by author, with anonymous articles alphabetically arranged according to the name of the publication, and the city of publication for a newspaper considered part of the title. Items from newspapers generally provide both page number and, after a colon, the column number(s) in which an item appears. These have not always been easily ascertainable, since many items were photocopies received through the interlibrary loan system or found in Saunders's scrapbooks of clippings, with pages unidentified; therefore, pages and column numbers are often missing.

Information is also provided as to subsequent reprints of items, using cross-reference numbers consisting of the year followed by the number of the item within that year (e.g., 1855.7 is the seventh item in 1855). This system also serves as the means of indexing. Numbering begins with books and continues (not starting over again) with periodicals. An occasional item will be listed as a reprint of an item which is listed after it. Such is the case when a book, listed naturally in the first section of the year, reprints an article published in a periodical that same year and consequently listed in the second section. More confusing, perhaps, is the case when a newspaper at the end of August, for example, reprints an article from the September issue of a magazine; but since magazines generally appear before the actual date of issue, an article might actually be reprinted before the publication date appearing on the original item.

Annotations will not be evaluative but will simply provide information as to the content of an item, using quotation and paraphrase to indicate the author's estimate of Whitman and his work. Abbreviations are used, according to the lists which follow the introduction, for the titles of Whitman's works referred to and for references cited in the text either as sources for bibliographical items or as sources for reprinted items.

The index provides a means for locating items by particular authors, in various publications, and on various subjects (including people, biographical information, other countries and cultures in relationship to Whitman, and themes of Whtiman's work, although with regard to the latter it cannot pretend to be complete). The format is explained in the heading to the index.

At this point I would like to thank a number of people for their valuable assistance during my pursuit of as complete a collection of Whitman items as could be presented.

First must come Norma Chalfin, for her much appreciated help in preparing the initial working bibliography from which I began and branched out.

The sine qua non of my pursuit has been the staff of the reference department of the Doheny Library at the University of Southern California, particularly interlibrary loan librarian Linda Edgington, who has helped in tracking down numerous obscure publications. Also contributing to the progress of my work were Barry Sell and Christine Gladish of the reference department and Heddy Richter of Doheny's American literature collection.

Aother significant debt is to Rosemary Cullen, special collections librarian of the Harris Collection of Brown University's John Hay Library, who not only facilitated my examination of the extensive Saunders Collection of Whitmaniana, but also provided me later with photocopies of many hard-to-locate items.

Also to be thanked are various Whitman scholars, including Roger Asselineau, Gay Wilson Allen, Harold W. Blodgett, and Jerome Loving, who have responded promptly to my queries regarding obscure items; likewise numerous librarians across the country and in Great Britain, Canada, Australia, and New Zealand, who responded to requests for items through the interlibrary loan system. The following librarians corresponded directly with me regarding particularly difficult items, and their help is most appreciated: Dr. Neda M. Westlake of the University of Pennsylvania's Charles Patterson Van Pelt Library; John Martin of the Duke University Library; Francis X. Scannell, state librarian of Michigan; Davis Erhardt of the Long Island division of New York public libraries; Dennis R. Laurie, of the American Antiquarian Society of Worcester, Massachusetts; Anthony J. Kostreba of the Library of Congress; and Eugene D. Decker, State Archivist, Kansas State Historical Society.

I have been in immediate personal contact with, and am deeply grateful for the assistance of, the staffs not only of the University of Southern California libraries, but also of the Huntington Library in San Marino, the central branch of the Los Angeles Public Library, the public libraries of New York, Brooklyn, and San Francisco, the Long Island Historical Society, and the university libraries of Stanford and the University of California at Berkeley, Los Angeles, and San Diego.

After the gathering of items and the making of annotations, the next stage involved marshaling these thousands of annotations into proper chronological and alphabetical order within each year; for their help in this task I thank Gordon Blitz and my parents, J. R. and Meredith Giantvalley. In the final stages, my dissertation committee at the University of Southern California, Ronald Gottesman, Hershel Parker, and Lynn Ross-Bryant, offered profitable suggestions and welcome support, and William White gave me valuable encouragement after looking over the manuscript in this earlier incarnation of the present book. The book as published adds to the items included in the dissertation not only items from the years preceding 1855 and the two decades following 1919 but also a number of items more recently discovered and annotations for other items which I had not been able to locate before the dissertation.

A final note of particular gratitude goes to Hershel Parker for involving me in this fascinating project, which has not ended with the publication of this book but which will continue, through a yearly update in the Walt Whitman Review, as I find items presently not annotated or hitherto unlisted.

In the end, I can only follow Whitman's advice, as it appears in his final version of "Song of Myself" (section 38), perhaps added because of his increasing realization that his task and that of his "eleves" (including future bibliographers?) was endless: "Continue your annotations."

P.S.: I continued by annotations because of some recent publications citing other items from this period. These are included in the Addenda, since these publications appeared too late for me to include these items in the text itself (or in the index). I am glad at least that they could be incorporated in this form.

Introduction

The combination of appreciation and disapproval which greeted <u>Leaves of Grass</u> in its first review in the <u>New York Daily Tribune</u> of 23 July 1855 sounded the keynote for Whitman criticism throughout much of the eighty-five years to follow. Some reviewers expressed only disapproval; others, as if to counter them, expressed ecstatic and unqualified approval for the poet whose personality and poetic thought had inspired them. Yet from the beginning Whitman found readers who were willing to recognize in him a poet of worth even if they, unlike some of his apologists, could not accept uncritically everything he wrote. This balanced view, always present in Whitman criticism, increasingly prevailed. The history of Whitman's reputation may be regarded as the eventual emergence of criticism from the straits between denunciation and hero worship, for the various items through the years reveal such judicious criticism to be the true savior of Whitman's reputation, always present but constantly struggling against too vehement proponents as well as opponents.

When the 1855 edition appeared, early readers were startled by poetry with no rhyme or consistent meter, poetry which used the common language of the people and spoke frankly of the poet as a particular man and of the human body in its less poetically respectable functions. Some could not see beyond their initial shock and often disgust at the presumed "violation of decency" in Whitman's vocabulary and subject matter (which displayed much "libidinousness" and "Phallic worship"), the "audacious egotism," and the formlessness ("an impertinence towards the English language"), shrinking from the book without a second look and seeing Whitman as a lunatic or a subject for "the public executioner's whip." Yet others found much of value in it, pointing to such familiar poetic qualities as "original perception of nature, " "effective description," "a large sense of the beautiful," "a rare felicity of diction," "a lofty purpose," and "bold, stirring thoughts." Such critics may have had some qualms regarding Whitman's mixed diction, need for polish, or occasional indecencies, but their attitude was quite constructive and open-minded. Whitman was early perceived as a wholly American product and a descendant of transcendentalism, whether these qualities were regarded as positive or negative. Although the strongest proclamations of Whitman's importance may have come from Whitman's own hand, he already had gained a number of sympathetic readers, notably several who, through Emerson's recommendation of the book to them, would later become active advocates, like Franklin B. Sanborn and Moncure Daniel Conway.

Controversy over Whitman continued, spurred on by a number of negative reviews, with wide attention given to him in late 1859 and early 1860 as he moved toward a new edition. The responses to his new poems followed already familiar lines, although praise (beyond Whitman's own) was more extensive. Moreover, frequent parodies of his work appeared, not only in New York, Boston, and Philadelphia, but in less likely cities like San Francisco and New Orleans; many of these items were reprinted in the pages of the New York <u>Saturday Press</u>.

While a figure of fun, Whitman was also taken quite seriously as a significant and appropriate voice for America, young, vital, and rebellious, like America herself in the mid-nineteenth century before the disillusionment of the Civil War. However, he remained largely ignored by major literary magazines like <u>Atlantic Monthly</u> and <u>Harper's</u>. They would not enter the fray, even to render criticism, until later, particularly after British praise and accusations of Americans' neglect of Whitman, notably in 1876.

One might wonder whether the literary establishment was more offended by Whitman's style, considered as a failure to create something truly poetic, by his openness in dealing with physical matters, or by his focus upon himself (particularly in the originally untitled opening poem of the first edition, whose later titles, "Walt Whitman" and finally, in 1881, "Song of Myself," brazenly proclaimed an egotistic concern). All three matters were cause of great consternation, even into the twentieth century. It may well be the explicitness which most struck nineteenth-century readers, since a tone of revulsion rather than mere criticism pervades so many of these early commentaries. This quality in Whitman's first edition may have poisoned his later work for reviewers, for <u>Drum-Taps</u>, though devoid of the "indecencies" which filled <u>Leaves</u>, was also faulted, though in this case only for its formlessness.

But even bad reviews were good for keeping Whitman's name before the reading public, which became increasingly familiar with his name and style, whether or not they had ever read his book. His personality and life further contributed to this recognition, with various controversies during his lifetime furthering his notoriety. His dismissal from the Department of the Interior by Secretary James Harlan in 1865 had one happy result: The Good Gray Poet (1866.2), William Douglas O'Connor's extensive defense of the poet which described Whitman's worth as a man and as a writer. It also gave Whitman his enduring, if essentially misleading, sobriquet, which contributed to his transformation in the public eye from the New York "rough" and "loafer" to the kindly gray figure who served the wounded during the war.

The next significant year was 1868, when William Rossetti published his retitled and rearranged Selections from Whitman, who then received considerable acclaim in England for these poems as well as for those which Rossetti had not included because of their potentially controversial nature. While Whitman owed much of his reputation in England to the endeavors of such significant literary figures as Rossetti, Robert Buchanan, Swinburne, and Edward Dowden, he also received favorable attention from anonymous reviewers, a fact which disproves the theory of William Bates (1883.1) that the aforementioned writers presented this formless poet to the British public as a literary hoax.

Buchanan sparked a heated controversy in 1876 when he condemned America's literary establishment for neglecting Whitman and letting him suffer in poverty. Even such adverse responses as Bayard Taylor's in the New York Tribune and J. G. Holland's in Scribner's, however, helped to feed Whitman's new image as the Sage of Camden, struck down by poverty and ill health, persisting in his work against all odds. And even Holland would admit that Whitman had created some true poetry, although he could not grant that name to most of what Whitman wrote.

A significant breakthrough in America occurred when Century Magazine (formerly Scribner's) published E. C. Stedman's extensive appraisal of Whitman. Not only was this the first major American periodical to devote so much space to Whitman, but the review was highly favorable (though retaining the standard doubts about Whitman's treatment of sex).

A year later, when the author's final edition appeared, critical reaction remained mixed or worse. Perhaps the persistence, in the face of repeated criticism, of those qualities that had been deplored at Whitman's first appearance made the critics of 1881 and 1882, now more numerous than in previous years, generally harsher as well. Whitman had not only set "all the ordinary rules of criticism at defiance," as the Brooklyn Daily Eagle had remarked in 1855; he also seemed to have simply ignored the suggestions of his critics over the past quarter-century, however constructive they may have been, choosing to continue stubbornly in his own way. Critics could not help but resent this discounting of their presumably valuable advice.

For the most part, readers were better prepared for accepting Whitman in 1881 since he had been around for so long and his form and manner were no longer so new and startling. Thus, there was less emphasis on the sexual aspects of his work (at least until suppression efforts by the Boston district attorney and the Massachusetts attorney-general in May 1882). Concern focused on Whitman's form, even though, as the Atlantic reviewer fairly pointed out, Stedman had given ample evidence that this form was no mere novelty and ought to be regarded as valid poetry. Reviewers were quick to praise "O Captain! My Captain!" and other more regular poems as happily inconsistent with Whitman's poetic theory. His prevailing formlessness, however, was heavily deplored: A little freedom to experiment, such as Emerson and Longfellow had toyed with before Whitman, might be accepted, but persistence in this undisciplined method suggested an obstinate, blatant rejection of the accepted conventions of the craft that some of the reviewers themselves (Holland for one) had so meticulously mastered. In such a period when poetic form outweighed content Whitman could hardly win wide appreciation.

A few months after the 1881 edition appeared, censorship reared its ugly head (in Boston, not surprisingly) and the matter of sex was brought to the forefront as pens and periodicals went to battle over a few lines, particularly "To a Common Prostitute." Whitman had his supporters, largely among such contemporary radical publications as Liberty and the Truth Seeker, besides such die-hard friends as O'Connor and John Burroughs, but his poetry was not forgotten, even if he had become a cause célèbre. Various periodicals and newspapers proceeded to publish his occasional poems and prose, and his activities were frequently reported. When Swinburne in 1887 published "Whitmania" (1887.63), an insulting retraction of his earlier enthusiasm, he was trounced by journalists. After all, Whitman had become a grand old man of American letters, and his house on Mickle Street in Camden, New Jersey, was already the destination of literary pilgrimages.

Critical reception of Whitman's later works, Specimen Days (1882), November Boughs (1888), and Good-Bye My Fancy (1891), continued to be mixed, generally more favorable in England than at home, with reviews of the latter two books even bemoaning the senility of the author.

Whitman's death in 1892 did not change attitudes suddenly: when retrospective reviews were required, the Independent merely revised its wholly negative review of the 1881 edition; Thomas Wentworth Higginson, writing for the New York Evening Post and the Nation (1892.60), did the same, extending his criticisms considerably, including the attribution of Whitman's debility to the "drench of passions" in Whitman's youth, but concentrating on his lack of form and consequent inability to win immortality.

The opinion of Higginson was not, however, that of the majority. Whitman's themes, ideas, and spirit were much more often praised highly, sometimes as giving his work value in spite of his form, sometimes in close conjunction with his form. Some publications, like the Californian, simply praised his life as his greatest poem, suggesting that his poetry could never rank with that of Lowell, Longfellow, and Whittier. Others, most persistently his faithful friend Burroughs in several commentaries throughout 1892 and the following years (most being incorporated into his book-length study of Whitman [1896.2]), emphasized the value of Whitman's personality, not merely as exemplified in his life, but as revealed through his poetry, a personality compounded of vigor, spirituality, nationalism, and democratic breadth of sympathy.

Whitman as a poet was too often lost from sight by many avid followers in the decades to come. His thought was expounded in relation to socialism, women's rights, and labor, his personality was recollected by those who had known him (even in a short visit), and pages of such discussion filled the Conservator, founded in 1890 and edited by Horace Traubel, Whitman's friend and documenter. Occasionally one finds among the entries a discussion of Whitman's poetry, explaining, for example, how a poem developed from Whitman's manuscripts or sources or comparing Whitman with another writer, but the Conservator was interested less in literature than in what literature could be used to accomplish. Traubel was a man who knew and loved Whitman intimately, but he was also seeking to change American society in the direction of justice and brotherhood; hence he emphasized Whitman the man and his personality, as well as Whitman's hopes for the betterment of mankind, two central concerns of the Walt Whitman Fellowship, which he founded in 1894 and which included as members most of the men and women whose articles appeared in the Conservator.

In addition to these personal and social-economic-political concerns, the third major emphasis of the Fellowship was not literary but religious, owing to another influential voice: that of Richard Maurice Bucke, the Canadian physician who found in Whitman, man and poet, a new spirit which enlightened his own life. A true disciple, he gave testimonials to Whitman's influence upon him and tried to spread the word, most notably in his authorized 1883 biography of Whitman (which Whitman himself contributed to and revised) and in his extensive analysis of the "cosmic consciousness" Whitman's personality and poetry revealed (1901.3). Bucke's religious focus paved the way for writers of various progressive faiths during the late nineteenth and early twentieth centuries, including spiritualists, theosophists, and even Methodists. Whitman was quoted and expounded upon from the pulpit, to the great consternation of one Methodist minister, W. V. Kelley, who edited the Methodist Review and was appalled in 1897 that right-thinking people, including ministers of the gospel, could favor such an atheistic, immoral, unpoetic charlatan.

To consider Whitman's poetry as poetry one generally had to look beyond the Conservator. Notable early discussions were William Sloane Kennedy's inadequately titled Personal Reminiscences of Walt Whitman (1896.9) and Oscar Lovell Triggs's "The Growth of 'Leaves of Grass,'" originally published in the Conservator (1897.127), and reprinted with additions in the 1902 Putnam edition of Whitman's Complete Writings. Major explanations of his prosody eventually followed with Fred Newton Scott's article in Journal of English and Germanic Philology (1908.31) and Basil De Selincourt's book-length study (1914.5). Writers on poetics in general, such as George Saintsbury and Brander Matthews, were also discussing Whitman's form at the beginning of the century, sometimes favorably, sometimes not, but at least acknowledging it as sincerely intended and not the mere fumblings of an untalented crank. The first decade of the twentieth century was hardly too early to be accepting free verse as an entirely valid vehicle for successful poetry, with the imagists, Masters, Oppenheim, and Sandburg only a few years away. Traubel himself, whatever may be said of his own efforts at poetry, had staunchly persisted in expressing his ideas in free verse, at least keeping the form breathing until the early moderns (American as well as French and German) gave it vibrant life in new, quite un-Whitmanesque ways and often for un-Whitmanesque purposes. Writings by Robinson, Masters, Sandburg, and the quasi-American Lawrence early demonstrated Whitman's impact on modern poetry, although frequently the moderns felt the need to quarrel with him in a poetic rite of passage indicating a break with the Great Gray Father in order to assert their own identity, as Pound suggested in "A Pact" (1913.34): "I have detested you long enough."

Fortunately biography has nothing to do with prosody. Nor is it necessary for a study of the ideas and feelings expressed in a poet's work, but in Whitman's case, their divorce was made well-nigh impossible due to to Whitman's identification of himself with his book ("Camerado, this is no book, / Who touches this touches a man") and to the frequent assertion by others that he embodied the ideals expressed in his work. Particularly in the interpretation of sexual aspects of a literary work, biography and criticism almost inevitably (and often dangerously) merge, one being made to reflect the other.

The sex in "Children of Adam" had certainly caused much dismay during the nineteenth century, with assumptions made about Whitman's character because of the sexual explicitness of his poetry. Interestingly, however, the "Calamus" poems had raised few eyebrows in early years, perhaps because homosexual content was so unheard of as to go quite unsuspected, perhaps because homosexuality was a topic that reviewers were too modest to mention, although an occasional writer, while otherwise approving, might find the physical expression of Whitman's notion of friendship "simply disgusting" (Arthur Clive in 1875.16). Those nineteenth-century writers who did perceive homosexual content were chiefly men like John Addington Symonds and Edward Carpenter who recognized in Whitman's poetry their own homosexual feelings. Knowing nothing about the author as a man when they first read his work, they responded to the words and images on the page rather than to any biographical facts.

In the early twentieth century, the question of Whitman's homosexuality, as observed in his life and personality as well as his works, became more openly discussed, whether with acceptance (Carpenter, Havelock Ellis), revulsion (Eduard Bertz, Harvey O'Higgins), or denial of the idea (Henry S. Saunders in a privately circulated typescript, Whitman's French biographer Léon Bazalgette, and the American-French poet Stuart Merrill in the pages of the Mercure de France, 1913-14). The homosexuality of a major American writer was hardly something to be accepted readily, so literary historians and centenary reviews ignored the matter. No biographer until Edgar Lee Masters in 1937 admitted Whitman's homosexuality as worthy of careful analysis, although it was discussed by certain nonbiographical commentators and mentioned in Holloway's biography (1926.13).

Homosexuality was only one of the problem areas facing Whitman biographers, for the legend that Whitman himself helped create through his three chief disciples, Bucke, Burroughs, and Traubel, involved a romanticized image of his life and ignored or consciously suppressed many of his early writings, both journalistic and literary. The Bucke and Burroughs books, part biography, part literary analysis, relied primarily on Whitman's own accounts; the 1896 books by Kennedy and Thomas Donaldson focused on the Camden years of their own acquaintance with Whitman. The first attempts at scholarly biography were made by Binns (1905.1) and Perry (1906.13). Until the appearance of Holloway's book in 1926 other biographers broke no new ground, drawing almost entirely from their predecessors (with the exception of Traubel's exhaustive transcriptions of Whitman's conversations in his last years, which he began publishing in 1906). However, Holloway's and Masters's books did benefit from the extensive research that had in the meantime been done on Whitman and which resulted in a number of collections and editions of Whitman's early writings.

By Whitman's centenary in 1919, he was widely acknowledged, not only as a primary force behind modernism but as one of American literature's three or four chief figures. Harriet Monroe's centenary estimate in Poetry (1919.135), while noting certain "limitations of perspective and range," cited his vast contributions to modern poetry: insistence on freedom of form, rejection of traditional poetic diction, and "reassertion of the ancient conception of the poet as prophet, and of poetry as religion, as an ecstatic expression of faith." Louis Untermeyer termed him "father of the American language" and the stimulus for America's significant contemporary writers. Such centenary estimates appeared not only in the more intellectual and literary publications, but in scores of newspapers throughout America and the British Commonwealth as well. They tended to be reasoned and admiring, if often critical of "the Whitman cult" for its extremism in the pursuit of recognition for Whitman and its perpetual appropriation of the poet to various causes. Occasional faults in Whitman were admitted, but his strengths and positive qualities received primary emphasis: his sympathy, vitality, optimism, naturalness, originality; the worth of his poetic theory and artistry; his patriotic, mystic, epic, and contemporary qualities. His often criticized egotism and his catalogues were defended and explained. Stuart P. Sherman in the New York Evening Post (1919.270) was typical in finding Whitman's work of permanent value because it raises man to an awareness of himself as a moral being and of his great destiny.

However, in the great centenary concert of voices praising the poet-prophet of democracy and the self a few discordant notes were heard. The Times Literary Supplement (1919.201) attributed Whitman's method to laziness and considered his ideas inadequately demonstrated. The disapproval expressed in a sarcastic article in the New York Sun (1919.229) outweighed its favorable comments; its judgment of Whitman is indicated in the designation of "O Captain! My Captain!" as the only poem known by the man in the street and "the one that is most likely to live forever." This was a familiar judgment throughout Whitman's lifetime and afterwards, but not so common among more perceptive and thoughtful critics who considered "Out of the Cradle Endlessly Rocking" and "When Lilacs Last in the Dooryard Bloom'd" as the pinnacles of his poetic achievement, or the daring few who appreciated "Song of Myself."

Nevertheless, the prevailing tone during the centenary year was approving, with widespread recognition of Whitman's greatness as poet and prophet. Henry Seidel Canby emphasized both of these roles in his extensive analysis of Whitman (1931.6), although other commentators often chose to focus on one or the other: John Bailey, an Englishman, preferred to concentrate on Whitman as poet (1926.1), while Americans like Lewis Mumford (1926.22) and Vernon Parrington (1930.17) emphasized socially prophetic aspects.

Whitman's secure position at this time did not preserve him from attack but seemed rather to encourage a backlash—not mere critical carping and rejection of his claims as a poet but exertion of considerable effort to prove him unworthy of the esteem he had been shown. William Barton (1928.3) sought to place Whitman's wartime service in a considerably dimmer light; Harvey O'Higgins (1929.48) deplored Whitman's pose as a masculine man, and Esther Shephard (1938.17), his pose as an original, uncultured writer; Mark Van Doren (1935.29), while generally acknowledging Whitman's greatness as a poet, found his homosexuality to be his chief, hidden motivation, thus invalidating his democratic ideas. These writers raised a number of valid points, but they did little to diminish the continued prestige of Whitman.

Perhaps the most significant development in Whitman commentary during the 1930s involved the socialist interpretation: while earlier radicals like Emma Goldman, Eugene Debs, and writers for Comrade had heartily welcomed Whitman to their cause, influenced largely by Traubel's own socialism, depression era leftists like Michael Gold, Granville Hicks, and Newton Arvin found Whitman's economic stance naive and not valid for the contemporary situation, although they considered his heart as being generally in the right place.

The 1930s also saw the birth of American Literature, the key organ for serious Whitman criticism and scholarship until the founding in 1955 of the Walt Whitman Newsletter (subsequently the Walt Whitman Review). Examinations of Whitman's prosody, thought, and sources appeared here and in university publications and scholarly journals as Whitman scholars pored through old newspapers, periodicals, manuscripts, and letters. By the end of the 1930s the bulk of Whitman's published work had been collected and republished; most of his surviving manuscripts were now in print, as were many of his letters; a number of specific poems had been explicated; all important aspects had, at least to some degree, been examined. There was still work to be done in reading Whitman closely, in analyzing his life and his work in the light of psychoanalytic theory, in piecing together many facts of his life before Leaves of Grass, in preparing accurate texts, and in exploring Whitman's poetic development through the many changes of his book, but the work already done indicated the significant position Whitman had attained, a preeminence in American poetry which shows little sign of abating.

Works and Editions

1842   Franklin Evans

1855   Leaves of Grass (first edition)

1856   Leaves of Grass (second edition)

1860   Leaves of Grass (third edition)

1865   Drum-Taps and Sequel to Drum-Taps

1867   Leaves of Grass (fourth edition)

1868   Poems by Walt Whitman (W. M. Rossetti's English selection)

1871   After All, Not to Create Only

       Democratic Vistas

       Leaves of Grass (fifth edition)

1875   Memoranda During the War

1876   Leaves of Grass (Author's Centennial Edition)

       Two Rivulets

1881-82   Leaves of Grass (sixth edition)

1882   Specimen Days and Collect

1888   November Boughs

       Complete Poems and Prose of Walt Whitman

1891   Good-Bye My Fancy

1891-92   Leaves of Grass (reprint of sixth edition, with annexes)

1892   Complete Prose Works

1897   Leaves of Grass (reprint of 1891-92 edition, with "Old Age Echoes")

       Calamus (letters)

1898   The Wound-Dresser (letters)

1899   Notes and Fragments

1900   Leaves of Grass (variorum edition, D. McKay)

1902   Complete Writings of Walt Whitman (Putnam's Sons)

Abbreviations

Titles of poems used throughout will generally be those of the 1891-92 edition, although another title may be used in the item itself. If reference is made to a particular passage from a longer poem like "Song of Myself," the annotation will use the form "Myself" 21 to indicate the twenty-first numbered section of that poem.

"Adam" ("Children of Adam")

"After All" ("After All, Not to Create Only," later called "Song of the Exposition")

"Answerer" ("Song of the Answerer")

"As a Strong Bird" ("As a Strong Bird on Pinions Free," later called "Thou Mother with Thy Equal Brood")

"As I Lay" ("As I Lay with My Head in Your Lap, Camerado")

"Astronomer" ("When I Heard the Learn'd Astronomer")

"Banner" ("Song of the Banner at Daybreak")

"Bivouac" ("By the Bivouac's Fitful Flame")

"Body Electric" ("I Sing the Body Electric")

"Broad-Axe" ("Song of the Broad-Axe")

"Brooklyn Ferry" ("Crossing Brooklyn Ferry")

"Captain" ("O Captain! My Captain!")

"Cradle" ("Out of the Cradle Endlessly Rocking")

"Dalliance" ("The Dalliance of the Eagles")

"Dirge" ("Dirge for Two Veterans")

"Ethiopia" ("Ethiopia Saluting the Colors")

"Exposition" ("Song of the Exposition")

Good-Bye (or "Good-Bye") (Good-Bye My Fancy--book or poem)

Leaves (Leaves of Grass, preceded by year of edition, if necessary)

"Lilacs" ("When Lilacs Last in the Dooryard Bloom'd")

"Lo, Victress" ("Lo, Victress on the Peaks")

"Locomotive" ("To a Locomotive in Winter")

"Man-of-War-Bird" ("To the Man-of-War-Bird")

Memoranda (Memoranda During the War)

"Myself" ("Song of Myself")

November (November Boughs)

"Occupations" ("A Song for Occupations")

"Once I Pass'd" ("Once I Pass'd through a Populous City")

"One Hour" ("One Hour to Madness and Joy")

"Ontario" ("By Blue Ontario's Shore")

"Open Road" ("Song of the Open Raod")

"Passage" ("Passage to India")

"Pioneers" ("Pioneers! O Pioneers!")

"Prayer" ("Prayer of Columbus")

"Prostitute" ("To a Common Prostitute")

"Redwood" ("Song of the Redwood-Tree")

"Rise O Days" ("Rise O Days from your Fathomless Deeps")

"Rolling Earth" ("A Song of the Rolling Earth")

"Rolling Ocean" ("Out of the Rolling Ocean the Crowd")

"Salut" ("Salut au Monde!")

Specimen (Specimen Days)

"Spider" ("A Noiseless Patient Spider")

"Spirit" ("Spirit that Form'd this Scene")

"Square Deific" ("Chanting the Square Deific")

"Terrible Doubt" ("Of the Terrible Doubt of Appearances")

"There was a Child" ("There was a Child Went Forth")

"Thou Mother" ("Thou Mother with Thy Equal Brood")

"Trumpeter" ("The Mystic Trumpeter")

"Unfolded" ("Unfolded Out of the Folds")

"Universal" ("Song of the Universal")

"Vigil Strange" ("Vigil Strange I Kept in the Field One Night")

Vistas (Democratic Vistas)

"Weave In" ("Weave In, My Hardy Life")

"Whispers" ("Whispers of Heavenly Death")

"With Husky-Haughty Lips" ("With Husky-Haughty Lips, O Sea!")

"Woman Waits" ("A Woman Waits for Me")

References Cited in the Text

References will be cited in the text by last name of the first or only author (and identifying date if the author has more than one item), unless otherwise indicated.

AN&Q. Abbreviation for American Notes and Queries.

Allen, Gay Wilson, ed. The Merrill Studies in Leaves of Grass. Columbus, Ohio: Charles E. Merrill Publishing Co., 1972.

Allen, Gay Wilson. The Solitary Singer. New York: New York University Press, 1967.

_____. Twenty-Five Years of Walt Whitman Bibliography (1918-1942). Boston: F. W. Faxon Co., 1943.

Asselineau, Roger. The Evolution of Walt Whitman: The Creation of a Personality. Cambridge, Mass.: Harvard University Press, Belknap Press, 1960.

Barrus, Clara. Whitman and Burroughs Comrades. Boston and New York: Houghton Mifflin Co., 1931.

Bergman, Herbert. "Walt Whitman Parodies." American Notes and Queries 8 (August 1948), 74.

_____. "Whitman in June, 1885: Three Uncollected Interviews." American Notes and Queries 8 (July 1948), 51-56.

_____. "Whitman on His Poetry and Some Poets: Two Uncollected Interviews." American Notes and Queries 8 (February 1950), 163-66.

_____. "Whitman on Politics, Presidents, and Hopefuls." American Notes and Queries 8 (May 1948), 19-26.

Blodgett, Harold. Bibliography in Walt Whitman in England. Ithaca: Cornell University Press; London: Humphrey Milford, Oxford University Press, 1934, pp. 223-34.

Bradley, Sculley, and Blodgett, Harold W., eds. Leaves of Grass. Norton critical edition. New York: W. W. Norton & Co., 1973. Cited as Bradley/Blodgett.

Bucke, Richard Maurice. Walt Whitman. Philadelphia: David McKay, 1883.

_____. Walt Whitman's Autograph Revision of the Analysis of Leaves of Grass. New York: New York University Press, 1974. Reprint of part of Bucke (1883).

Cameron, Kenneth Walter. Emerson, Thoreau, and Concord in Early Newspapers. Hartford: Transcendental Books, 1958.

_____. "Roden Noel, Poet and English Defender of Whitman." American Transcendental Quarterly 12 (Fall 1971), 67-98.

CHAL. Abbreviation for Holloway and Saunders.

Dowden, Edward. Walt Whitman, by Richard Maurice Bucke. To Which Is Added English Critics on Walt Whitman Edited by Edward Dowden. Glasgow: Wilson & McCormick, 1884.

Fabre, Michael. "Walt Whitman and the Rebel Poets." WWR 12 (December 1966), 88-93.

Frenz, Horst, ed. Whitman and Rolleston: A Correspondence. Indiana University Humanities Series, no. 26 (1951), 109-17.

Frey, Ellen Frances, comp. Catalog of the Whitman Collection in the Duke University Library Being a Part of the Trent Collection. Durham, N.C.: Duke University Library, 1945. Cited as Trent.

Funnell, Bertha H. Walt Whitman on Long Island. Port Washington, N.Y.: Kennikat Press, Ira J. Friedman Division, 1971.

Gathering. Abbreviation for Rodgers and Black.

Glicksberg, Charles I. "Charles Godfrey Leland and Vanity Fair." Pennsylvania Magazine of History and Biography 62 (July 1938), 309-23.

_____. "Walt Whitman Parodies: Provoked by the Third Edition of 'Leaves of Grass.'" American Notes and Queries 7 (March 1948), 163-68.

Gohdes, Clarence, and Silver, Rollo G., eds. Faint Clews and Indirections. Durham, N.C.: Duke University Press, 1949.

Hendrick, George. "Newspaper Squibs About Whitman." Walt Whitman Birthplace Bulletin 4 (April 1961), 7-9.

Hindus, Milton, ed. Walt Whitman: The Critical Heritage. London: Routledge & Kegan Paul, 1971.

Holloway, Emory, ed. The Uncollected Poetry and Prose of Walt Whitman. Garden City, N.Y., and Toronto: Doubleday, Page & Co., 1921. Cited as Uncollected.

Holloway, Emory, and Adimari, Ralph, eds. New York Dissected By Walt Whitman. New York: Rufus Rockwell Wilson, 1936.

Holloway, Emory, and Saunders, Henry S. Whitman Bibliography in Cambridge History of American Literature. Vol. 2. New York: G. P. Putnam's Sons, 1918, pp. 551-81. Cited as CHAL.

Holloway, Emory, and Schwarz, Vernolian, eds. I Sit and Look Out: Editorials from the Brooklyn Daily Times by Walt Whitman. New York: Columbia University Press, 1932.

Hubach, Robert R. "A Kansas City Newspaper Greets Walt Whitman." Notes and Queries 185 (18 December 1943), 365-66.

_____. "Three St. Louis Interviews of Whitman." American Literature 14 (May 1942), 141-47.

_____. "Western Newspaper Accounts of Whitman's 1879 Trip to the West." WWR 18 (June 1972), 56-62.

Hubbell, Jay B., ed. American Life in Literature. New York and London: Harper & Bros., 1936.

Imprints. Abbreviation for Leaves of Grass Imprints.

In Re. Abbreviation for Traubel, Bucke, and Harned.

Index to Early American Periodical Literature, 1728-1870: No. 3, Walt Whitman, 1819-1892. New York: Pamphlet Distributing Co., 1941.

Jones, Joseph. "Emerson and Whitman 'Down Under': Their Reputations in Australia and New Zealand." Emerson Society Quarterly, no. 42 (1966), 35-46.

KTO. Abbreviation for Literary Writings in America.

Kennedy, William Sloane. The Fight of a Book for the World. West Yarmouth, Mass.: Stonecroft Press, 1926.

_____. Reminiscences of Walt Whitman. Paisley, Scotland, and London: Alexander Gardner, 1896.

Knox, George. The Whitman-Hartmann Controversy. Frankfurt and Munich: Peter Lang; Bern: Herbert Lang, 1976.

"Leaves-Droppings." In 1856 Leaves of Grass, Brooklyn.

Leaves of Grass Imprints. Boston: Thayer & Eldridge, 1860. Cited as Imprints.

Literary Writings in America: A Bibliography. Millmore, N.Y.: KTO Press, 1977, pp. 10405-33. Cited as KTO.

Long Islander, Annual Whitman Supplement. See Whitman Supplement.

Loving, Jerome. Walt Whitman's Champion: William Douglas O'Connor. College Station, Tex., and London: Texas A & M University Press, 1978.

Mabbott, Thomas Ollive, and Silver, Rollo G. A Child's Reminiscence by Walt Whitman. Seattle: University of Washington Book Store, 1930.

Martin, Willard E., Jr. "Whitmaniana from the Boston Journal." WWR 23 (June 1977), 90-92.

McLeod, A. L. Walt Whitman in Australia and New Zealand. Sydney: Wentworth Press, 1964.

McMullin, Stanley E. "Walt Whitman's Influence in Canada." Dalhousie Review 49 (Autumn 1969), 361-68.

McMullin, S[tanley] E. "Whitman and the Canadian Press 1872-1919: A Brief Survey." WWR 20 (September 1974), 132-40.

Miller, Edwin H., ed. A Century of Whitman Criticism. Bloomington: University of Indiana Press, 1969.

Moulton, Charles Wells, ed. The Library of Literary Criticism of English and American Authors. Vol. 8. Buffalo, N.Y.: Moulton Publishing Co., pp. 129-53.

Moyne, Ernest J. "Folger McKinsey and Walt Whitman." WWR 21 (December 1975), 135-44.

_____. "Walt Whitman and Folger McKinsey, or Walt Whitman in Elkton, Maryland: A Study of Public Taste in the 1880's." Delaware Notes 29 (1956), 103-110.

Murphy, Francis, ed. Walt Whitman: A Critical Anthology. Middlesex, England, and Baltimore: Penguin, 1969.

Neilson, Kenneth P. "A Discovery Rediscovered in the Search for Walt Whitman Music." WWR 19 (September 1973), 114-18.

Page, Curtis Hidden, ed. Bibliography in The Chief American Poets: Selected Poems. Boston, New York, and Chicago: Houghton Mifflin Co., 1905, pp. 647-50.

Pearce, Roy Harvey, ed. Whitman: A Collection of Critical Essays. Englewood Cliffs, N.J.: Prentice-Hall, 1962.

Peattie, R. W. "Postscript to Charles Kent on Whitman." WWR 15 (June 1969), 107-11.

Pizer, Donald, ed. <u>Theodore Dreiser: A Selection of Uncollected Prose</u>. Detroit: Wayne State University Press, 1977.

Rodgers, Cleveland, and Black, John. <u>The Gathering of the Forces</u>. New York and London: G. P. Putnam's Sons, 1920. Cited as <u>Gathering</u>.

Rubin, Joseph Jay. <u>The Historic Whitman</u>. University Park: Pennsylvania State University Press, 1973.

Rubin, Joseph Jay, and Brown, Charles H., eds. <u>Walt Whitman of the New York Aurora</u>. State College, Pa.: Bald Eagle Press, 1950.

Rupp, Richard H., comp. <u>Critics on Whitman: Readings in Literary Criticism</u>. Coral Gables, Fla.: University of Miami Press, 1972.

Saunders, Henry S., ed. <u>Parodies on Walt Whitman</u>. New York: American Library Service, 1923.

Saunders, Henry S. <u>Whitman in Fiction</u>. Toronto: H. S. Saunders, 1928. Cited as Saunders <u>Whitman in Fiction</u>.

Saunders Supplement. Abbreviation for the typescript bibliographies in the Henry S. Saunders Collection of Whitmaniana at Brown University (see Preface).

Schwab, Arnold T. "Huneker on Whitman: A Newly Discovered Essay." <u>American Literature</u> 38 (May 1966), 208-18.

Traubel, Horace. <u>With Walt Whitman in Camden</u>. Vol. I, Boston: Small, Maynard, 1906. Vol. II, New York: Appleton, 1908. Vol. III, New York: Mitchell Kennerley, 1914. Vol. IV, edited by Sculley Bradley, Philadelphia: University of Pennsylvania Press, 1953. Vol. V, edited by Gertrude Traubel, Carbondale: Southern Illinois University Press, 1964.

Traubel, Horace L., Bucke, Richard M., and Harned, Thomas B., eds. <u>In Re Walt Whitman</u>. Philadelphia: David McKay, 1893. Cited as <u>In Re</u>.

Trent. See Frey.

Triggs, Oscar Lovell, comp. Bibliography in <u>The Complete Writings of Walt Whitman</u>. Vol. 10. New York and London: G. P. Putnam's Sons, 1902, pp. 139-233.

<u>Uncollected</u>. Abbreviation for Holloway, <u>Uncollected Poetry and Prose</u>.

<u>WWR</u>. Abbreviation for <u>Walt Whitman Review</u>.

Wade, Allen, ed. <u>The Letters of W. B. Yeats</u>. London: Rupert Hart-Davis, 1954.

Wallace, James K. "Whitman and <u>Life Illustrated</u>: A Forgotten Review of <u>Leaves</u>." <u>WWR</u> 17 (December 1971), 135-38.

White, William, ed. <u>The Collected Writings of Walt Whitman: Daybooks and Notebooks</u>. New York: New York University Press, 1978.

Whitman Supplement 1972 (<u>Long Islander</u>), edited by William White. "Whitman at Dartmouth."

Whitman Supplement 1978 (<u>Long Islander</u>), edited by William White. "Whitman in the Long Islander."

Whitman Supplement 1979 (<u>Long Islander</u>), edited by William White and Scott Giantvalley. "Reminiscences of Walt Whitman."

Willard, Charles B. <u>Whitman's American Fame: The Growth of His Reputation in America After 1892</u>. Providence, R.I.: Brown University, 1950.

Writings About Whitman, 1838-1939

<u>1838</u>

<u>BOOKS</u>--None

<u>PERIODICALS</u>

  1 [SPOONER, ALDEN.] "The Long Islander." <u>Long Island Star</u> (14 June), 2:4.
        Announces founding of <u>Long Islander</u> with Walt Whitman as editor and publisher; wishes it success.

 *2 ANON. "Another Newspaper in Suffolk County." <u>Hempstead Enquirer</u> (16 June).
        Quoted in Funnell.
        Notes debut of <u>Long Islander</u> "in a very graceful and easy manner." Whitman, its publishers, "has spared no pains to make it acceptable to the reading community."

<u>1839</u>

<u>BOOKS</u>--None

<u>PERIODICALS</u>

 *1 ANON. Note. <u>Long Island Farmer</u> (August or September).
        Quoted in Rubin.
        Complains of a young spaniel (Whitman) on the <u>Long Island Democrat</u> who "is a dirty cur at best."

<u>1840</u>

<u>BOOKS</u>--None

<u>PERIODICALS</u>

 *1 BUCKEYE [pseud.]. Letter. <u>Long Island Farmer</u> (6 October).
        Reprinted: 1937.40.
        Criticizes Whitman's part as "a well-known locofoco of the town" and "champion of Democracy" in a political debate with the Whigs; warns him against making false accusations.

<u>1841</u>

<u>BOOKS</u>--None

<u>PERIODICALS</u>

 *1 ANON. Report of Whitman's speech. <u>New Era</u> (30 July).
        Reported in <u>Uncollected</u>.

  2 ANON. "The Great Anti-Bank Meeting in the Park Last Night." <u>New York Daily Tribune</u> (30 July), 2:2-5.
        Extensively quotes and summarizes Whitman's speech at political meeting.

  3 ANON. "The Meeting in the Park." New York <u>Evening Post</u> (30 July), sec. 2, 2:1.
        Quotes speech by "W. Whitman Esq. of Suffolk" at meeting protesting Whig actions.

  4 ANON. "The Great Anti-Bank Meeting in the Park Last Night." New York <u>Herald</u> (30 July), 2:1-4.
        Quotes Whitman's speech.

<u>1842</u>

<u>BOOKS</u>--None

<u>PERIODICALS</u>

  1 ANON. "Our Weekly Gossip." <u>Brother Jonathan</u> 1 (26 February), 238.
        Notice of the essay "Boz and Democracy" in this issue, which "bears the initials of as true and honest a democrat [Whitman] as the editor of the Globe, or any of the correspondents of that paper."

  2 [BRYANT, WILLIAM CULLEN.] "<u>Democratic Review</u>." New York <u>Evening Post</u> (5 March), 2:1.
        Review of current issue of <u>Democratic Review</u>: "Walter Whitman's tale of the 'Last of the Sacred Army' is a very neat and fanciful performance."

 *3 [HERRICK, ANSON, and ROPES, JOHN F.] Editorial note. New York <u>Aurora</u> (28 March), 2.
        Reprinted: Rubin; Rubin and Brown.
        Announces that the <u>Aurora</u>'s new editor is "Mr. Walter Whitman, favorably known as a bold, energetic and original writer," whose accession will enable the publishers to establish "a sound, fearless and independent daily paper."

1842

4 ANON. "The Aurora." Brooklyn Eagle (30
   March), 2.
       Reprinted: Rubin and Brown.
       Editorial note: "A marked change for
   the better has come over this spirited
   little daily since the accession of Mr.
   Whitman to the 'vacant chair.' There is,
   nevertheless, a dash of egotism occasionally."

*5 [HERRICK, ANSON, and ROPES, JOHN F.] Editorial
   note. New York Aurora (16 May).
       Reprinted: Rubin; Rubin and Brown.
       "Mr. Walter Whitman desires us to state
   that he has been for three or four weeks
   past, and now is, entirely disconnected
   with the editorial department of the Aurora."

*6 _____. Editorial note. New York Aurora (29
   August).
       Reprinted: Rubin and Brown.
       Notes appearance of an abusive article
   reprinted in Whitman's Evening Tattler, "a
   small, 'obscure daily' now under the control
   of a 'pretty pup' once in our employment;
   but whose indolence, incompetence, loafer-
   ism and blackguard habits forced us to kick
   him out of office." Quotes with ironic
   comment Whitman's reasons stated therein
   for leaving the Aurora.

7 ANON. "Literary Notices." New York Daily
   Tribune (3 September), 1:5.
       Notes appearance in Democratic Review
   of Whitman's story "The Army of Tears,"
   which "betrays a good, healthy tone of
   thought and feeling, but is decidedly inferior in point of grace and taste to
   previous papers by the same author."

8 ANON. "Friends of Temperance, Ahoy!" New
   World 5 (5 November), 305.
       Reprinted: Uncollected; 1929.10.
       Advertisement of Franklin Evans, to be
   published in the New World extra on November
   23, "By a Popular American Author," and
   which "will be universally read and admired." "It was written expressly for the
   NEW WORLD, by one of the best Novelists in
   this country," its incidents "wrought out
   with great effect," with an excellent moral
   and "beneficial influence."

9 ANON. "The Newspaper Writers of New York."
   New York Herald (9 November), 2:2.
       Lists fifty-two newspaper writers of
   Manhattan (including "Wm. Whitman"), whose
   biographical sketches will be presented to
   show their genius and talent. (These biographies never appeared.)

10 ANON. Paragraph review of Franklin Evans.
   New York Daily Tribune (23 November), 1:2.
       The novel's message of temperance is
   important. Being a novel and not a tract,
   it may do much good, and it is recommended
   "to the novel-reader for its exciting
   scenes, and to all for its intrinsic interest

and worth."

11 ANON. Note. Brother Jonathan 3 (26 November),
   378.
       "'Franklin Evans, or the Inebriate,' is
   the title of a clever story for the Wash-
   ingtonians, just issued from 30 Ann st, in
   the modern style of Novels. Price 12½
   cents." (Entire item.)

*12 ANON. "American Literature." New York Herald
   (27 November).
       Reported in Rubin, but not located on this
   date.
       Review of Franklin Evans and books by
   James Fenimore Cooper and Cornelius Mathews:
   all will be read widely, but Cooper writes
   like a finished workman while "the others
   are mere apprentices, having just shed their
   feathers as penny-a-liners."

*13 ANON. Review of Franklin Evans. Brooklyn
   Eagle (last week of November).
       Reported in Rubin but not located.
       "The known quality of Walter Whitman is
   sufficient guarantee of its high character.
   If successful now the author promises to
   'try again.'"

*14 ANON. Review of Franklin Evans. New York
   Aurora (last week of November).
       Reported in Rubin.
       The fiction is worth more than the
   price.

1843

BOOKS--None

PERIODICALS

1 ANON. Headnote to Walter Whitman's poem
   "Death of the Nature-Lover." Brother
   Jonathan 4 (11 March), 290.
       "The following wants but a half hour's
   polish to make of it an effusion of very
   uncommon beauty."

1845

BOOKS--None

PERIODICALS

1 [POE, EDGAR ALLAN.] "The Magazines." Broadway
   Journal 1 (3 May), 285.
       Whitman's "Richard Parker's Widow" in
   the Aristidean is admirable.

2. _____. "To Correspondents." Broadway Journal
   2 (22 November), 311.
       "Many thanks to W. W."

3 ED[ITOR] B[ROADWAY] J[OURNAL] [Edgar Allan
   Poe.] Footnote to Whitman's "Art-Singing
   and Heart-Singing." Broadway Journal 2
   (29 November), 318.
   Quoted in Uncollected.

Explains the author's admission to "no
scientific knowledge of music," and announces agreement "with our correspondent
throughout."

1846

BOOKS--None

PERIODICALS

1 ANON. "Fourth of July!" Brooklyn Eagle (30
   June), 2:5.
      Quoted in Neilson.
      Announces Walter Whitman as writer of
   one of the odes to be sung at the Independence Day celebration.

2 ANON. "City Intelligence." Brooklyn Eagle
   (1 July), 2:3.
      Quoted in Neilson.
      Announces that odes by Whitman and
   Rev. T. B. Thayer will be sung at the
   Fourth of July celebration.

*3 [LEES, HENRY A.] Note. Brooklyn Daily
   Advertiser (1 September).
      Quoted in Rubin.
      Whitman intended "ere long, to abandon
   politics, theatricals, transcendentalism,
   and Leggett-ism for the higher and more
   dignified position of Literary Reviewer."

4 ____. "More 'Criticism.'" Brooklyn Daily
   Advertiser (2 September), 2:3.
      Quotes New York News on the ridiculous
   dramatic criticisms of the Eagle's otherwise
   sensible editor; suggests that these
   criticisms "are beginning to be appreciated
   at last."

*5 ANON. "Whitman, Spare That Tree!" New York
   Mirror (3 September).
      Quoted in Rubin.
      Comic poem on Whitman's criticisms of
   Ellen Tree in the Eagle, following an
   earlier prose criticism of him (quoted in
   Rubin, but undated).

6 ANON. "A Complaint without a cause." Brooklyn
   Daily Advertiser (3 December), 2:3.
      Whitman described his own earnings when
   he wrote the day before of "a very fair
   American writer who receives only five
   dollars a month for contributing to a certain magazine." Actually, the publishers
   and readers are the ones "entitled to sympathy and commiseration."

1847

BOOKS--None

PERIODICALS

1 ANON. "Which Is the Monkey?" Yankee Doodle 1

(23 January), 182.
   Quoted in 1939.23.
      Response to article (by Whitman) in the
   Brooklyn Eagle, "Monkeyism in Brooklyn,"
   criticizing its over-nationalistic stance
   in putting down those who adore Byron and
   Scott.

*2 ANON. Note. Brooklyn Daily Advertiser
   (3 April).
      Quoted in Rubin.
      Dares anyone to deny "that the editor
   of the Eagle was a Whig some few seasons
   before he was hired to write locofoco editorials for the Eagle."

*3 ANON. Note. Brooklyn Daily Advertiser (5
   April).
      Quoted in Rubin.
      Demands to know Whitman's allegiance in
   the summer of 1841 and whether he did not
   later bitterly oppose Silas Wright's guber-
   natorial nomination. Whitman is accused of
   being a political apostate because of his
   contributions to the Whig American Review.

4 ANON. "Celebration of the 4th of July in
   Brooklyn." Brooklyn Daily Eagle (9 June),
   2.
      Notes "Walter Whitman" as on the com-
   mittee of three planning the Fourth of July
   celebration.

*5 [NOAH, MORDECAI.] Headnote to reprinting of
   Whitman's "Shirval: A Tale of Jerusalem."
   New York Sunday Times (10 October).
      Quoted in Rubin.
      This is a "touching and ingenious
   sketch."

1848

BOOKS--None

PERIODICALS

1 ANON. "Editorial Change." New York Daily
   Globe (21 January).
      Criticizes Whitman's dismissal as editor
   of the Eagle because of the Conservatives
   now controlling the Brooklyn party.

2 [BRYANT, WILLIAM CULLEN.] "Democracy in Kings
   County, L.I." New York Evening Post (21
   January), 2:2.
      Reprinted: Uncollected.
      Quotes from Brooklyn Star on Whitman as
   a Barnburner being forced off the Eagle
   "because the 'Old Hunkers' wanted one of
   their own men there." But a new paper is
   likely to emerge for the radicals, with
   Whitman expected to engage in it.

3 [GREELEY, HORACE?] "A Barnburner Paper." New
   York Daily Tribune (21 January), 3:3.
      A new paper is to be started by the
   Barnburners, with "Mr. Walter Whitman, late
   of the EAGLE," in charge.

1848

4   [VAN ANDEN, ISAAC.] Editorial comment. Brook-
    lyn Daily Eagle (21 January), 2.
    Quoted in Gathering; Rubin.
        Response to the meddling of the New
    York Globe (1848.1), defending the Eagle's
    rights to dismiss "one of its editors" as
    it pleases.

5   ANON. Two editorial paragraphs. New York
    Daily Globe (22 January).
        Notes Eagle's response (1818.4). "We
    know Mr. Whitman, the discharged editor,
    to be strong in favor of free territory,
    and free white labor in such territory as
    we may acquire from Mexico, and have been
    informed that this was the principal cause
    of the dismissal."

6   ARISTIDES [pseud.]. "Brooklyn Affairs." New
    York Atlas (23 January), 3:1.
    Quoted in Rubin.
        Whitman's bold anti-slavery stance has
    led to his dismissal. This "young man of
    fine literary attainments, fearless, ener-
    getic," is better fit for pursuits not
    connected with party strife and not requir-
    ing prostitution of his talents.

7   ANON. "Impromptu Address to the Editor of the
    Advertiser." Brooklyn Daily Eagle (17
    February), 3:1.
    Reprinted: Gathering.
        Humorous six-line verse on Whitman's
    departure and the Advertiser's meddling in
    the Eagle's affairs.

8   ANON. "The Crescent." Brooklyn Daily Eagle
    (14 March), 2:1.
    Quoted in Gathering.
        The New Orleans Crescent seems to be a
    "fearless, independent sheet," revealing
    Whitman's "handy work in several of its
    editorials." "We trust that both will
    flourish."

*9 [LEES, HENRY A.] Note. Brooklyn Daily
    Advertiser (23 June).
    Quoted in Rubin.
        Announces meeting Whitman upon his
    return from New Orleans, with his "brown
    face smiling," and with plans for a paper
    which would oppose Hunkerism. It should
    lead to "fun" in Brooklyn.

*10 ANON. Article. Brooklyn Daily Eagle (19
    July).
    Quoted in Holloway (1932), but should be
    1849 (see 1849.3).

11 ANON. "Free Soil Meeting." New York Evening
    Post (7 August), 2:3.
        Whitman is listed as a Brooklyn dele-
    gate to the convention in Buffalo.

12 [GREELEY, HORACE?] "'The Freeman.'" New York
    Daily Tribune (1 November), 2:7.
        The Freeman will resume publication,
    "edited and published by Walter Whitman,

Esq. who manfully opposes Hunkerism in all
its forms."

*13 ANON. "The Freeman." Long Islander (17
    November).
    Reprinted: Funnell.
        Whitman has emerged from the misfortune
    of the Freeman office fire "with a spirit
    no wise daunted" and is publishing again,
    with "much taste in arrangement." If his
    paper is not supported, "it will not be
    from want of energy and ability on his
    part."

1849

BOOKS--None

PERIODICALS

*1 ANON. Paragraph on Whitman. Brooklyn Daily
    Advertiser (7 February).
    Quoted in Holloway (1932).
        Notes current activities of "our modest,
    amiable, and unobtrusive friend Whitman" as
    editor and operator of a printing office.

2   ANON. Paragraph. Brooklyn Evening Star (26
    April).
        Describes the editor of the Freeman
    (Whitman) as "an enthusiastic Free Soiler,"
    "a vigorous and independent man." He is
    wished success in his enterprise.

3   ANON. "The Advertiser." Brooklyn Daily Eagle
    (19 July), 2:1.
        A paragraph quoted from the Advertiser
    (unlocated) says that Whitman's rupture
    with the Eagle was due to his determination
    that the paper "not be the organ of old
    hunkerism" and to an occasion on which,
    "when personally insulted by a certain
    prominent politician, Mr. Whitman kicked
    that individual down the editorial stairs."
    The Eagle rejects the Advertiser's favoring
    of Whitman, whom the Eagle knows as "indo-
    lent, heavy, discourteous and without steady
    principles." His subsequent newspaper en-
    deavors were owing to the friendship of
    other Brooklyn and New York newspapers but
    were not noteworthy.

4   [BRENTON, JAMES J.] Paragraph. Long Island
    Democrat (18 September), 2:4.
        Announces Whitman's severance from the
    Freeman and wishes him well.

*5 ANON. Note. Long Island Star (19 September).
    Quoted in Rubin.
        Whitman is "the Abdiel of his party" in
    holding out against the alliance of the
    Hunkers.

*6 ANON. "Sketches of Distinguished Animals."
    Brooklyn Daily Advertiser (22 September).
    Quoted in Rubin.
        Promises to devote an entire piece to
    "Editor Whitman, that transcendentally fast

politician, far ahead of his day and generation."

7 ANON. "City News & Gossip." Brooklyn Daily
Eagle (24 September), 3:1.
Paragraph on Whitman puffing himself in
the Sunday papers, as when he left the
Eagle, although he has since been kicked
out of other newspapers he has worked on.

8 ANON. "Sketches of Distinguished Animals. By
One of 'em. No. VIII. The Editor."
Brooklyn Daily Advertiser (4 October),
1:7-2:1.
Three paragraphs on a recent Brooklyn
editor (Whitman). "Full of egotism," he
assumes "to be a literary genius--one of
the shining lights" of the century. He is
"a civilized but not a polished Aborigine,"
possibly descended from some Indian tribe.
His appearance, activities, and politics
are described.

*9 ANON. Announcement of Brenton's book (1850.1).
Long Islander (23 November).
Reprinted: Whitman Supplement 1978.
Whitman is listed among the journalists
covered.

*10 ANON. Note. Williamsburgh Times (21 Decem-
ber).
Quoted in Rubin.
"Our talented friend Walter Whitman,
Esq., late of the Brooklyn FREEMAN, is con-
nected with the NEWS."

1850

BOOKS

1 BRENTON, JAMES J., ed. Voices from the Press:
A Collection of Sketches, Essays, and Poems,
by Practical Printers. New York: Charles
B. Norton, p. xix.
Two-paragraph sketch of Whitman's
career under "Notices of Contributors,"
focusing on his newspaper work and his
sketches, beginning with "Death in a School
Room," "very popular." He "is an ardent
politician of the radical democrat school"
and established the Brooklyn Freeman "to
promulgate his favorite 'Free Soil' and
other reformatory doctrines." His story
"The Tomb Blossoms" is anthologized in this
collection.

PERIODICALS

2 ANON. "Animal Extraordinary." Brooklyn Daily
Eagle (29 May), 3:1.
Announces the arrival of "'the man in
the high-held shirt collar'" (Whitman); a
reporter will try to discover more.

*3 [LEES, HENRY A.] Note. Brooklyn Daily
Advertiser (22 June).
Quoted in Uncollected.
Quotes a stanza of Whitman's "The House
of Friends," "a queer little poem in one of
the New York papers," as representing

Whitman derogatorily addressing his former
Democratic political cronies, with whom he
worked while at the Eagle.

1851

BOOKS--None

PERIODICALS

1 WHITMAN, WALTER. "Art and Artists. Remarks
of Walter Whitman, before the Brooklyn Art
Union, on the evening of March 31, 1851."
Brooklyn Daily Advertiser (3 April), 1:6-8.
Prints Whitman's address.

*2 ANON. "The Salesman." Long Islander (6 June).
Reprinted: Whitman Supplement 1978.
Announces debut of the Salesman under
Whitman's editorship. This old friend, to
whom the Long Islander is indebted for its
"initiary steps in the art of Print-orial,"
is wished success.

1852

BOOKS--None

PERIODICALS

*1 ANON. Headnote to "Visit to the People's Bath
and Wash House--A New Era." Williamsburg
Times (4 May).
Quoted in Rubin.
The article following is "from the pen,
we judge, of our friend Walter Whitman."

1854

BOOKS--None

PERIODICALS

*1 ANON. Headnote to "Sunday Restrictions"
(letter by Whitman). Brooklyn Evening Star
(20 October).
Reported in Uncollected.
Explains receipt of this memorial from
its author, Walter Whitman.

1855

BOOKS--None

PERIODICALS

1 ANON. Advertisement. New York Daily Tribune
(6 July), 1:2.
Announces Leaves, on sale at Fowler and
Wells.

2 [DANA, CHARLES A.] Review of Leaves. New York
Daily Tribune (23 July), 3:2-3.
Reprinted: Bucke; Holloway (1936); Hindus
(without extracts).
In the "extraordinary prose" of the
Preface (quoted), this "nameless bard"
presents his poetic theory, anticipated by
Emerson. His poems follow no model but his
own brain. His indecent language comes
"from a naive unconsciousness rather than

1855

from an impure mind." His work is "full of
bold, stirring thoughts," "effective description," often "a rare felicity of diction"
though marred by "eccentric fancies." Extracts are printed under invented titles.
Beneath its "uncouth and grotesque embodiment" is "much of the essential spirit of
poetry."

3 ANON. Review of Leaves. Life Illustrated
(28 July).
Reprinted: Wallace.
This curious book contains a portrait
of the unknown author (a perfect loafer,
though a thoughtful, amiable, and able one),
a remarkable preface in the Emersonian
manner, and a series of utterances in
rhythmical prose. The discerning reader
will find much in it to please him.

*4 ANON. Advertisement. Life Illustrated (4
August and 11 August).
Reprinted: Wallace.
Leaves, "A Poem," is on sale at Fowler
and Wells.

5 [WHITMAN, WALT.] "Walt Whitman and His Poems."
New York Evening Post (24 August), 1:3-4.
Reprint of 1855.7.

6 [NORTON, CHARLES ELIOT.] "Walt Whitman's
Leaves of Grass." Putnam's Monthly 6
(September), 321-23.
Reprinted: 1856.2; Imprints; 1928.18;
Miller; Hindus.
This "curious and lawless collection of
poems" is written "in a sort of excited
prose." The writer's vocabulary strays
from polite standards. But his Preface
(quoted) reveals new principles, applied in
poems that are "a compound of the New England transcendentalist and New York rowdy,"
fused "with the most perfect harmony." He
reveals "an original perception of nature,
a manly brawn, and an epic directness" like
no other Transcendentalist. Extensive
extracts are quoted. Whitman's labeling
himself "an American" is certainly to be
believed.

7 [WHITMAN, WALT.] "Walt Whitman and His Poems."
United States Review 5 (September), 205-12.
Reprinted: 1855.5; 1855.8; Imprints; In
Re; Hindus; Murphy.
"An American bard at last!" Whitman
represents the start of a truly American,
"athletic and defiant literature." He
recognizes no literary precedents, for the
new poets must declare their independence
from traditional poetry. His verses have
"the sweeping movement of great currents of
living people," such as this review presents in long prose listings. Nature and
sensations provide Whitman's true poetic
inspiration. He proclaims the beauty of
sex. Perfection for him is no dream. He
has interest in all aspects of life, poetry
being only part of the whole. "He is the
largest lover and sympathizer" in literature. He announces poets to succeed him.

8 ANON. "A Pleasant Quiz." Albion n.s. 14 (8
September), 429.
Prefatory remarks to reprint of 1855.7:
"We take it to be a smart satire upon the
present tendency of authors to run into
rhapsody and transcendentalism; and therefore its main fault in a literary point of
view--that it suggests the notion of a man
reviewing his own work--is not of much
importance."

9 ANON. "Book Notices. 'Leaves of Grass'--An
Extraordinary Book." Brooklyn Daily Eagle
(15 September), 2:2-3.
Reprinted with deletions and change of
"Walter" to "Walt": Imprints; Hindus.
This book "sets all the ordinary rules
of criticism at defiance," as a staggering
compound of "transcendentalism, bombast,
philosophy, folly, wisdom, wit, and dulness
[sic]," a reproduction of the inner being of
its author. Extensive extracts from the
Preface reveal the ideas behind his poetry,
"the free utterance of an untrammeled
spirit": rejection of the artificial and
the established, appreciation of all.
"Myself" 6 (quoted) is unsurpassed in
interpreting nature. Some grossness bars
the poem from reading in mixed company.
"It is an extraordinary book, full of
beauties and blemishes, such as Nature is
to those who have only a half-formed acquaintance with her mysteries."

10 [WHITMAN, WALT.] "Walt Whitman, a Brooklyn
Boy." Brooklyn Daily Times (29 September).
Reprinted: Bucke; also in facsimile:
Bucke (1974). Revised: 1856.2; Imprints;
In Re; Hindus; Bradley/Blodgett.
The poet will appear "very devilish to
some," "very divine" to others, in his rude
and vital American qualities. He "celebrates natural propensities in himself" and
thus "celebrates all," seeking to present a
new type of character as example "for the
present and future of American letters and
American young men." Whitman's appearance,
personality, and habits are described; his
phrenological chart is quoted, showing "the
begetter of a new offspring out of literature, taking with easy nonchalance the
chances of its present reception, and,
through all misunderstandings and distrusts,
the chances of its future reception."

11 _____. "An English and an American Poet."
American Phrenological Journal (October),
90-91.
Abridged: 1856.2; Imprints; In Re; Hindus;
Murphy.
Review of Leaves and Tennyson's Maud.
The current state of poetry is to be deplored. British feudal themes are not
applicable to America. Tennyson is the best
of the current poets. But Whitman startles
with his strangeness, shunning old models
and the refined life, "a prodigal user of
his own land" and all the sciences, par-
taking personally of the life around him,
as is evident in the many activities (here
listed) in which he participates through

his poetry. "Every sentence and every passage tells of an interior not always seen." The greatest poet's aim should be to touch the reader with the actual spirit of life. Whitman will prove "either the most lamentable of failures or the most glorious of triumphs, in the known history of literature."

12 EMERSON, RALPH WALDO. "'Leaves of Grass.'" New York Daily Tribune (10 October), 7:1. Reprinted: 1855.13; 1856.2; Imprints; Hubbell; Miller; Murphy; Hindus; Bradley/ Blodgett; Rupp; and in most biographies and many critical articles.

Emerson's letter to Whitman, according to a headnote, views Whitman's "original and striking collection of poems" from "a more positive and less critical stand-point" than the Tribune's recent review (1855.2). The letter, printed in full, praises Leaves as "the most extraordinary piece of wit and wisdom that America has yet contributed," with "courage of treat-ment" and "large perception" and "incom-parable things said incomparably well." "I greet you at the beginning of a great career, which yet must have had a long fore-ground somewhere for such a start."

13 _____. "Personal and Literary." Life Illus-trated (20 October). Reprint of 1855.12.

Headnote to Emerson's letter remarks that "we were among the first to commend" this work.

14 [GRISWOLD, RUFUS W.] Review of Leaves. Criterion 1 (10 November), 24. Reprinted: Imprints; Hindus. Extract reprinted: Bucke.

Emerson's endorsement of this book is to be questioned, although the book does show "a certain transcendental kind of thinking." "This poet (?) without wit, but with a certain vagrant wildness, just serves to show the energy which natural imbecility is occasionally capable of under strong excitement." This book is a symptom of lack of respect for delicacy, virtue, and modesty. The laws "must have power to suppress such obscenity." The disagreeable contents should be exposed, but there is hardly a newspaper so vile as to print them.

15 ANON. "Annihilation of Walt Whitman." Life Illustrated, N.S. 1 (15 December), 53. Reprinted: Holloway (1936).

The Criterion's unfair review (1855.14) concentrates on indecency, although Emerson found the book congenial.

1856

BOOKS

1 "KATINKA" [pseud.]. Abbie Nott and Other Knots. Philadelphia: J. B. Lippincott &

Co.

Preface consists of three lines from "Myself" 20.

2 WHITMAN, WALT. Leaves of Grass. Brooklyn. "Leaves-Droppings," pp. 345-84.

At the end of this second edition are printed Emerson's letter (1855.12) and the following reviews, most undated: 1856.8, 1855.10, 1856.3, 1855.6, 1855.11, 1856.11, 1856.10, 1856.19, 1856.16.

PERIODICALS

*3 ANON. Review of 1855 Leaves. Christian Spiritualist. Reprinted: 1856.2; Imprints; Hindus.

This new author has "a wild strength, a Spartan simplicity," but shows more promise than performance. His genius accepts the whole nature of man and all men as his brothers. "Conservatives regard him as a social revolution." "His style is everywhere graphic and strong," in a new idiom which "serves his purpose well," as extracts show. Proceeding through the volume, the poet becomes :more serenly elevated." His sympathy is with man, not convention. His work demands study "as a sign of the times," evidence of "a new era."

*4 ANON. Review of Leaves. Monthly Trade Gazette. Reprinted: Imprints.

Leaves displays a far-reaching grasp of Titantic thought, boldly, manfully, and appositely expressed." The rejection of metrical rules seems valid. It is America's "most considerable poem" to date.

5 ANON. "Studies Among the Leaves." Crayon 3 (January), 30-32. Reprinted in part: Imprints.

Tennyson's Maud is compared with Leaves, one representing art at its most refined, the other being "rude and rough, and heed-less in its form--nonchalant in everything but its essential ideas," which are grand and vigorous but chaotic. Both poems are irreligious and somewhat morbid; "a higher seeing of Nature would have shown Walt. Whitman that all things in Nature are not alike beautiful, or to be loved and honored by song." Both poets could use more "grace and symmetry of construction." Though with a wonderful vigor of thought and power not often found, Leaves has no ideality or purpose but is barbarous and undisciplined. The Preface (quoted) contains his "creed of the material" which ignores the ideal. Whitman sees art as "merely reproduction." However, various quoted passages show that "he has felt the beauty of the material in full measure."

6 HALE, EDWARD EVERETT. Review of 1855 Leaves. North American Review 83 (January), 275-77. Reprinted: Imprints; Hindus; Murphy; Bradley/Blodgett; WWR 5 (June 1959), 31-33.

1856

Whitman, in a sort of poetry, succeeds in his attempt to speak with the insouciance of animals. The best thing in the volume may be the Preface, with "freshness, simplicity, and reality," as an extract shows. This "collection of observations, speculations, memories, and prophecies, clad in the simplest, truest, and often the most nervous English," recreates the extent of Whitman's experience in real scenes from many aspects of life. But some of his lines are not fit for women, although the book is not meant to "attract readers by its grossness." It is worth going to the bookstore to buy, even if one has trouble finding it.

7 ANON. "Notes on New Books." Washington Daily National Intelligencer (18 February), 2:1-2.
    Review of 1855 Leaves, "a singular volume." Whitman's "punctuation is as loose as his morality." His portrait matches his self-description as representative of the "roughs." The title and the grass metaphor in "Myself" 6 are examined. Whitman is clearly a pantheist, even a Spinozist or Platonist, without really knowing these philosophers, and a fatalist. He seeks to live among the animals, but Apuleius's Golden Ass, though like him "in its freedom from any thing like sentimental refinement or prudish delicacy," might make him appreciate the human state. This book fulfills the expectations of unintelligibility and esoteric meanings that Emerson's praise of it aroused. His "transcendental sinuosities of thought" are difficult to follow, but he has "wonderful powers of description and of word-painting."

8 [HOWITT, WILLIAM?] or [FOX, WILLIAM J.?]
    Review of 1855 Leaves. London Weekly Dispatch (9 March), 6.
    Reprinted: 1856.14; with change of accidentals and "Walter" to "Walt": 1856.2; Imprints; Hindus; Murphy.
    This strange, audacious book lacks the usual conditions of poetry, but its pieces achieve "a singular harmony and flow" in "their strength of expression, their fervour, hearty wholesomeness, their originality, mannerism and freshness." Whitman has a "large sense of the beautiful" and a clear conception of true "manly modesty." His poems "will become a pregnant text-book" full of quotations for every aspect of life.

9 ANON. "Leaves of Grass." Saturday Review 1 (15 March), 393-94.
    Review of 1855 Leaves, quoting Emerson's letter (1855.12) and extracts from the favorable reviews (Whitman's own) sent with the volume. "Myself" is quoted to explain Whitman's subject, title, theory of humanity, theological creed. But after such matter, Whitman "suddenly becomes exceedingly intelligible, but exceedingly

obscene. If the Leaves of Grass should come into anybody's possession, our advice is to throw them instantly behind the fire."

10 ANON. Review of 1855 Leaves. Examiner, no. 2512 (22 March), 180-81.
    Abridged: 1856.2; Imprints; Hindus.
    Whitman writes like "a wild Tupper of the West," maddened by reading Emerson and Carlyle. His purpose, "to assert the pleasure that a man has in himself" and "the harmony in which he should stand, body and soul, with fellow-men and the whole universe," might have been achieved without so much obscenity. Passages reveal "a speciality of personal reference" new to literature. Most of the book reads like auctioneer's catalogues, says the reviewer, who then puts an actual auctioneer's catalogue into Whitmanesque lines as a parody (reprinted in Saunders).

11 ANON. Review of Leaves. Critic (London) 15 (1 April), 170-71.
    Reprinted: 1856.2; Imprints; in part: Bucke; Murphy; Hindus; in facsimile: Bucke (1974).
    The man and the book are "rough, uncouth, vulgar," as extracts show. He deserves "the public executioner's whip" for indecencies like "Body Electric" 5. His inartistic "copy-book" lists merely reveal the old theme of universal sympathy. Such "free language" and "audacious egotism" can hardly be real poetry.

12 ANON. "Walt Whitman's Article." Life Illustrated, N.S. 1 (12 April), 188.
    Reprinted: Holloway (1936).
    Brief article calling attention to Whitman's article, "America's Mightiest Inheritance," with a brief introduction to him. "He expresses the very soul of democracy." He has ideas, knowledge, experience, and "more than considerable talent."

13 FERN, FANNY. "Fresh Fern Leaves. Peeps from Under a Parasol.--No. 3." New York Ledger (19 April), 4.
    Reprinted: Holloway (1936).
    Describes with admiration Whitman's appearance and rich, deep voice.

*14 HOWITT, WILLIAM. "Wm. Howitt upon Walt Whitman." Life Illustrated, N.S. 1 (19 April), 197.
    Reprint of 1856.8. Reprinted: Holloway (1936).

15 ANON. "A Strange Blade." Punch 20 (26 April), 169.
    "An American Rough, whose name is WALT WHITMAN, and who calls himself a 'Kosmos,' has been publishing a mad book under the title of Leaves of Grass. We can only say that these Leaves of Grass are fully worthy to be put on a level with that heap of rubbish called Fern Leaves, by FANNY FERN, and similar 'green stuff.' The fields of American literature want weeding dreadfully."

*16 ANON. Review of 1855 <u>Leaves</u>. Boston <u>Intel-</u>
<u>ligencer</u> (3 May).
Reprinted: 1856.2; Bucke; Hindus; Murphy.
The author of "this heterogeneous mass
of bombast, egotism, vulgarity and nonsense"
must be a lunatic, deserving "the lash for
such a violation of decency."

17 FERN, FANNY. "Fresh Fern Leaves. 'Leaves of
Grass.'" <u>New York Ledger</u> (10 May), 4.
Reprinted: 1856.18; Holloway (1936).
Review of 1855 <u>Leaves</u>. It is fresh
and delicious. "The effeminate world"
needed such "a 'Native American' of thorough, out and out breed," who would dare
to "speak out his strong, honest thoughts."
Charges of coarseness and sensuality should
be applied to more insidiously sensual
works. Critics are repenting their failure
to see beauty, strength, and grace in
<u>Leaves</u>. Short extracts are quoted with
praise, notably ones showing Whitman's
commendable attitude toward women as equals.

18 _____. "Fanny Fern's Opinion of Walt Whitman."
<u>Life Illustrated</u> N.S. 2, (17 May), 20-21.
Reprint with changes of accidentals of
1856.17. Reprinted: Holloway (1936).

19 [LEWES, GEORGE H.?] or [OLLIER, EDMUND?]
"Transatlantic Latter-day Poetry." <u>Leader</u>
7 (7 June), 547-42 [sic, should be 548].
Reprinted with some changes and deletions:
1856.2; 1856.21; <u>Imprints</u>; Holloway (1936);
Hindus; Murphy.
Review of 1855 <u>Leaves</u>. Whitman is one
of the amazing creations of the modern
American mind, but he "is no fool, though
abundantly eccentric, nor is his book mere
food for laughter." The Preface is quoted
to give insight into the book's "character
and objects." His form is "startling, and
by no means seductive, to English ears."
Also staggering is his dominant "all-
attracting egotism," his soul being present
in all things and typifying all human souls.
His aberrations, especially his plain-
speaking, are regrettable in view of the
"many evidences of a noble soul" in these
pages. "Myself" 33 is quoted to show "the
vividness with which Walt can paint the
unhackneyed scenery of his native land."

20 ANON. "Notes and Queries." <u>Life Illustrated</u>
n.s. 2 (14 June), 54.
Response to H.M.A. and H.Q.: the price
of <u>Leaves</u> "prepaid by mail," is $1.25.

*21 [LEWES, GEORGE H.?] or [OLLIER, EDMUND?]
Review of 1855 <u>Leaves</u>. <u>Life Illustrated</u>
n.s. 2 (19 July).
Reprint of 1856.19. Reprinted: Holloway
(1936).
Editorial note introduces this as "the
nearest approach to fair treatment" Whitman
has received in England.

22 ANON. "Leaves of Grass." <u>Life Illustrated</u>

n.s. 2 (16 August), 124-25.
Reprinted: Holloway (1936).
A new edition of <u>Leaves</u> is about to
appear, "with amendments and large additions."
It has found admirers, despite its peculiar
style and somewhat repellent matter. "The
first edition of a thousand copies rapidly
disappeared." Whitman has "become a fixed
fact," his message "worthy of regard."
<u>Leaves</u> must be included among those produc-
tions which could have sprung up only in
America.

23 [WHITMAN, WALT.] "New York Dissected. V--
Street Yarn." <u>Life Illustrated</u> n.s. 2 (16
August), 125.
Reprinted: Holloway (1936).
Paragraph describing the appearance of
Whitman, "the sturdy, self-conscious micro-
cosmic, prose-poetical author of that in-
congruous hash of mud and gold," <u>Leaves</u>.

24 ANON. Review of 1856 <u>Leaves</u>. <u>Christian</u>
<u>Examiner</u> 61 (November), 471-73.
Reprinted: <u>Imprints</u>; Hindus.
<u>Leaves</u> is "an impertinence towards the
English language" and "an affront upon the
recognized morality of respectable people."
"To its pantheism and libidinousness it
adds the most ridiculous swell of self-
applause." Although some discern "a vein
of benevolence," Whitman's philanthropy
actually "cares as little for social rights
as for the laws of God." Emerson's commendation was wrongly used to support a
different edition. This volume is being
noticed here only because "a sister Review"
praised it.

25 W., D. Review of 1855 <u>Leaves</u> and W. E. Aytoun's
<u>Bothwell</u>. <u>Canadian Journal</u> n.s. 1 (Novem-
ber), 541-51.
<u>Leaves</u> is a startling volume, breaking
the laws of poetry which <u>Bothwell</u> follows
so strictly. Though much of it might be
quoted to look ridiculous and deletions are
necessary before reprinting any passages,
much is suggestive and poetic, if needing
the artist's polishing. Extracts and part
of a review (1855.11) included with the
volume are quoted.

26 [SWINTON, WILLIAM.] Review of 1855 and 1856
<u>Leaves</u>. <u>New York Daily Times</u> (13 November),
2:1-3.
Reprinted: <u>Imprints</u>; Hindus; Allen (1972).
Whitman is a mass of contradictions.
His hand is apparent in two of the published
reviews, suggesting a dishonesty inconsistent
with his refreshing poetic philosophy. He
seems ahead of his time. Notice is made of
his transcendental egotism, descriptive and
expressive skills, dilution of these with
"nakedness of speech" and "Phallic worship"
although he is motivated by "a lofty purpose." Extracts are presented under invented
titles. He is truly, uniquely western, and
could have cured his flaws through more
cultivation and contact with intellectuals.

1856

Using Emerson's praise for a different edition is "a literary fraud," but Whitman's work retains "a singular electric attaction," novel in manner though not in thought, with "manly vigor." "We are much mistaken if, after all, he does not yet contribute something to American literature which shall awaken wonder."

*27 ANON. "New Publications." Brooklyn Daily Times (17 December).
   Reprinted: Imprints; Holloway (1932).
   Review of 1856 Leaves. This work is "an assertion of a two-fold individuality for the author: of himself personally, and of himself nationally." Whitman's style is described, with his "frequent instances of all-important and majestic thought" rather than sentiment, revealing "lessons of the highest importance." "The poems improve upon a second reading." The work is slightly Emersonian, but more "unbridled."

1858

BOOKS--None

PERIODICALS

*1 [SHEPARD, GEORGE?] "Leaves of Grass." Long Islander (10 December).
   Reprinted: Whitman Supplement 1978.
   Whitman "has generally been considered by his acquaintances as a man of more eccentricity than genius or practical talent." Leaves bears out that reputation, being a "poem with variations," "the loudest and lustiest specimen of egotism." Whitman's singing of "Walt" as a type of universal manhood is described, "patriotic, loving, idle, loafing and independent." Leaves recalls Ecclesiastes. "But with all its merits--its wonderful use of the English language, its endless hints of knowledge, its evidences of minute and extensive observation, its powers of fancy, satire and sarcasm, and its often sublime and exquisite touches of poetry--it is a repulsive and nasty book."

1859

BOOKS

*1 ANON. Fourteen Thousand Miles Afoot.
   Reprinted: Imprints; Bucke; Hindus.
   The "tabooing" of Leaves recalls the "innate vulgarity" and "unchastity of heart" of the American people, for "there is not an indecent word, an immodest expression, in the entire volume." Its "fragrance of nature" and Eden-like innocence make it "the healthiest book, morally, this century has produced."

PERIODICALS

2 ANON. "Personal." New York Tribune (23 March), 7:1.
   A correspondent of The New-Haven Journal reports Whitman driving a Broadway omnibus.

2a ANON. "Personal." New York Daily Tribune (25 March), 7:1.
   Reprinted: Imprints.
   Quotes Boston Courier's opinion of Whitman's omnibus driving: "it seems that his natural indolence has conquered his poetic inspirations."

2b ANON. "Personal." New York Daily Tribune (26 March), 6:4.
   A correspondent denies that Whitman drives omnibuses, though he chooses to ride on the stage-box rather than inside, and "he might drive a trip or two just to oblige a driver friend."

*3 ANON. "An Omnibus Driver or Not?" New York Constellation (not located on 4 July, the single issue published).
   Reprinted: Imprints.
   Whitman can drive an omnibus if he likes.
   Whitman can be an omnibus driver if he desires.

4 ANON. "On-Dits in Sporting Circles." Spirit of the Times 29 (2 April), 90:1.
   Reprinted in facsimile: WWR 11 (September 1965), back cover, and (December 1965), 105.
   Same material as 1859.2b.

5 [WHITMAN, WALT.] Brief note. New York Saturday Press (24 December), 2:2.
   Reprinted: Mabbott.
   Comment on Whitman's new poem, "A Child's Reminiscence" ["Cradle"], on p. 1 of this issue. This "wild and plaintive song," with an effect like that of music, "will bear reading many times."

*6 ANON. Note. Brooklyn City News (24 December).
   Reprinted: Imprints; Hindus.
   Notes the appearance of "A Child's Reminiscence," a "curious ballad" following Whitman's "same rude and mystical type of versification." A straightforward explication is given, with extracts, although it must be read in its entirety, and several times.

*7 ANON. "Walt Whitman." Brooklyn Daily Times (24 December).
   Reprinted: Holloway (1932).
   Notes the appearance of "A Child's Reminiscence," "a new and characteristic poem" by Whitman, "who shot up so suddenly into the literary heavens three years ago, and sent 'his barbaric yawp over the roofs of the world.'"

8 ANON. "Walt. Whitman's New Poem." Cincinnati Daily Commercial (28 December).
   Reprinted: Imprints; 1860.2; Mabbott; Hindus.

"The author of 'Leaves of Grass' has perpetrated another 'poem,'" which the Saturday Press (1859.5) praised more than such drivel deserves. The poem is mere chaos and nonsense, although not as coarse as his previous work, which displayed "far worse sins of morality than of taste" in dragging love "down to the brutal plane of animal passion." This "unclean cub of the wilderness" lacks any "spark of the poetic faculty" and has not learned "the first principle of art."

1860

BOOKS

1 ANON. Leaves of Grass Imprints: American and European Criticisms on "Leaves of Grass." Boston: Thayer & Eldridge, 64 pp.
Reprints reviews and other journalistic extracts concerning Whitman, as advertising for the 1860 Leaves. Dating is usually only by year, and often in error. Contents: 1856.6; 1856.24; 1855.7; 1856.5; 1856.26; January Searle [George Phillips?], "A Letter Impromptu," poem in hexameters praising Whitman and his work (unlocated); 1856.8; 1855.10; 1856.3; 1855.11; 1856.11; 1856.10; 1856.19; 1856.27; 1856.4; 1859.1; 1855.9; 1855.14; 1859.8; 1859.6; 1860.6; 1860.5; 1859.2a; 1859.3. The inside covers print Emerson's letter (1855.12) and current advance notices (1860.15; 1860.16).

PERIODICALS

2 ANON. "Walt Whitman's New Poem." New York Saturday Press (7 January), 1:1-2.
Reprint of 1859.8.

3 [WHITMAN, WALT.] "All about a Mocking-Bird." New York Saturday Press (7 January), 3:2-3.
Reprinted: Mabbott.
This mocking-bird will sing much in the future: a fuller Leaves will soon appear. Readers must respond to Whitman with the soul rather than the intellect. His method of construction is that of Italian opera, which is also strange to many but to which one must also yield oneself. America needs a stronger poet, more suitable than foreign bards, a voice for today: Whitman may be the one.

4 CLARE, ADA. "Thoughts and Things." New York Saturday Press (14 January), 2:6.
In contrast to William Winter's much-praised poem in last week's Saturday Press, Whitman's "Child's Reminiscence" "could only have been written by a poet, and versifying would not help it. I love the poem."

5 UMOS [pseud.?] "Waifs from Washington.--VI. . . . Walt Whitman's Yawp." New York Saturday Press (14 January), 2:4-5.
Abridged: Imprints.
Describes his impressions of "Child's

Reminiscence": Whitman seemed to be "on his musical skates for the first time." It seems like a lot of jumbled type set up in lines of unequal length. But this writer's wife confessed "she didn't think it trumpery--she thought there was something in it."

6 SAERASMID [pseud.?]. "Yourn and Mine, and Any-Day (A Yawp, after Walt Whitman.)" New York Saturday Press (21 January), 1:1.
Reprinted: Imprints; 1860.48; Saunders.
Parody of "With Antecedents" (Saturday Press, 14 January).

7 _____. "'Poemet.'--(After Walt Whitman.) With Parentheses, Analytical, Aesthetical, Philosophical, and Explanatory." New York Saturday Press (11 February), 1:1.
Parody of "Of Him I Love Day and Night" (Saturday Press, 28 January).

*8 ANON. Article on Whitman. New York Leader (3 March).
Reprinted: Glicksberg (March 1948).
Describes Whitman's appearance but acquits him of "intentional oddity"; describes his character and social behavior, his interest in drivers, the purity of his private relations, his possession of "a genial appreciation of nature, a profound admiration of the sublime, and a heartiness and thoroughness of temper." Some of his lines and phrases "are destined to endure" despite his grotesque form, which can produce no changes in American literature. Leaves has "original creative power," despite "a strange incoherent tendency." "Each poem contains a redundance and unmanageable surplus of imagery, strung together so loosely and in such confusion, as to conceal the continuous thread in 99 out of every hundred words."

9 ANON. "Ages of American Authors." Vanity Fair 1 (10 March), 172.
Quoted in Glicksberg (1938).
This whimsical piece notes that "the author of Leaves of Grass is 81 (his youthful appearance may be attributed to vegetable diet)."

10 ANON. "Counter-Jumps. A Poemettina.--After Walt Whitman." Vanity Fair 1 (17 March), 183.
Reprinted: Saunders.
Parody with caricature.

11 SAERASMID [pseud.?]. "Autopatheia." New York Saturday Press (17 March), 1:1.
Parody.

12 [HOWELLS, W. D.] "Bardic Symbols." Columbus Daily Ohio State Journal (28 March), 2:3-4.
Whitman has come upon the scene again, after the "wonderful" Leaves, "with a poem more lawless, measureless, rhymeless and inscrutable than ever." "Bardic Symbols" (in the April Atlantic) is summarized,

1860

though its full meaning remains unclear, except in occasional passages. Tennyson's "Break, Break, Break," "full of 'divine despair,'" may sum up its meaning. Whitman has erred in discarding forms and laws, "for without them the poet diffuses," being "spent before he reaches the reader's heart through his bewildered understanding."

13 ANON. "The Model Statesman." Vanity Fair 1 (14 April), 243.
Quoted in Glicksberg (1938).
Incidental comparison of Senator Wigfall to Whitman, whose "slabs of wisdom are all in a crumble compared with the granitic chunks that fall from Wigfall!"

14 ANON. "A True 'Barbaric Yawp.'" Vanity Fair 1 (14 April), 251.
"The milkman's morning cry." (Entire comic item.)

15 ANON. "Walt Whitman in Boston." Boston Saturday Evening Gazette (21 April), 2:5.
Reprinted: Imprints; Hindus.
Brief note on Whitman, now in Boston overseeing "a much larger and superior collection of his tantalizing 'Leaves,'" which, after running the gauntlet of the United States and Great Britain, and receiving divers specimens of about the tallest kind of indignant as well as favorable criticism, seem to have arrived at a position where they can read their title clear to be considered something." Once the volume is received, its quality may be determined.

16 [PHILLIPS, GEORGE S.?] "Literary Gossip on Books." New York Illustrated News 1 (5 May), 394.
Reprinted: Imprints; Hindus.
Announcement of new edition of Leaves. Although Whitman's speech seems at first "wild, rude and barbaric," "his sentences resound with the primordial music of nature." He reveals "marvelous insights and truths," and is "the first true voice which has been spoken of America." He can ignore the critical snobs and look forward to his words becoming part of the common speech of America.

17 ANON. "New Publications. The New Poets." New York Times (19 May), Supplement, 1:1-2.
Review of Leaves, "more reckless and vulgar" than before, without the genius or grace of Rabelais but with "evidence of remarkable power" in Whitman's human sympathy, intensity, use of epithet, earnest purpose, love of nature, recognition of deity in everything. Some of the finer and the grosser passages are pointed out. His work is like a rough diamond. He needs to become civilized.

18 [CLAPP, HENRY?] or [WHITMAN, WALT?] "Walt Whitman--Leaves of Grass." New York

Saturday Press (19 May), 2:4-6.
Reprinted: Mabbott; in part: Hubbell.
Review of Leaves, its leading idea the supremacy of the human soul and its divine harmony with the body. Contemporary rhyming poets ignore the real life of the present, whereas the form in Whitman's poems is determined by the thought or passion of the poet, which may produce "sweet and thrilling music," despite some prosy elements and defects in philosophy, art, taste, and style. Long extracts are quoted appreciatively, and the North American Review (1856.6) in part.

19 ANON. "Leaves of Grass." Momus (24 May).
Reprinted: Holloway (1936).
Eight-line poem attacking the "obscene productions" of Whitman, "the dirtiest beast of the age."

20 ANON. "New Books." Boston Saturday Evening Gazette (26 May), 2:2.
Reprinted: WWR 25 (June 1979), 77.
Parody review in Whitmanesque lines of 1860 Leaves, which is "full of good thoughts, naughty thoughts, noble thoughts," "incomprehensible, insane, inexpressive, impure, invigorating, infuscatable, and infoliate."

21 [PHILLIPS, GEORGE S.] "Literature. Leaves of Grass--by Walt Whitman." New York Illustrated News 2 (26 May), 43.
Reprinted: 1860.40; Mabbott.
Review of Leaves. Whitman's message comes not from books but is "alive with God," meant for the "brave, truthful reader." He is America's first native poet. His oriental perception of the miracle of all existence is the book's great charm. His phallic passages mar an admirable book. It is a genuine piece of autobiography, but his personal pronouns must not be misinterpreted, for they often speak for the race. This book has more true poetry than most modern volumes.

22 [WHITE, RICHARD GRANT.] Parody. Albion 38 (26 May), 249.
Reprinted: 1860.27. Revised: 1883.26; Saunders.
Parody in many numbered sections, with Whitmanesque paradoxes and mixed diction, following which an editorial remark admits that some of Whitman's poetry reveals "sympathy with and close observance of external nature." Although nine-tenths of his book is incoherent and sometimes indecent, "a confused mass of folly, feculence, and falsehood," the remaining tenth makes the book worth reading and keeping.

23 ANON. "Literature." Banner of Light 7 (2 June), 4.
Review of Leaves. Most people have by now heard of Whitman, whose originality no one can question. He reveals culture, even when seeming to spurn it. Few writers today

"have so seized hold of the <u>spirit</u> of
things." His strength is welcome in contrast to "literary poodles" and snobs. His
verse forms "the truest illustration, if
not representative, of the real American
Age that is, and is to be." His poems,
"alive with power," show a living soul, "a
grand interpreter," "the very child of
nature." Readers should know his "wonderful
productions" and the soul behind them.

24 ANON. "Walt Whitman." <u>New York Illustrated
News</u> 2 (2 June), 60.
Reprinted: Holloway (1936).
This issue's new cover portrait of
Whitman is described. The new edition is
bringing him forward "as one of the most
remarkable men of this day." Biographical
informaion; publication history of <u>Leaves</u>;
Emerson's letter (1855.12) quoted. Whitman
"has risen from the case to become one of
the great lights and leaders of litera-
ture--a poet whose broad and vigorous power
and uncommon felicity of illustration is
acknowledged wherever the English language
is spoken." The success of this edition
"has already been great, and must be
enormous."

25 ANON. "Note of the Week." New York <u>Saturday
Press</u> (2 June), 2:6.
Calls attention to the review of <u>Leaves</u>
(1860.26), evidence of the <u>Press</u>'s openness
to printing every variety of opinion.

26 BEACH, JULIETTE H. [actually by Mr. Beach].
"Leaves of Grass." New York <u>Saturday Press</u>
(2 June), 2:6.
The "Adam" section is disgusting in its
presentation of man's brutal aspects in
sexual relations. Whitman has elements
which might make a great poet--strength and
beauty--but "he has no soul."

27 [WHITE, RICHARD GRANT.] Parody. New York
<u>Saturday Press</u> (2 June), 4:3-4.
Reprint of 1860.22.

28 HEENAN, ADAH ISAACS MENKEN. "Swimming against
the Current." New York <u>Sunday Mercury</u> (10
June, though cited as 3 June in Allen), 2:2.
Incidental paragraphs on Whitman, "the
American philosopher," "centuries ahead of
his contemporaries," clearly understanding
the past, hearing the divine voice, wielding
his pen for liberty and humanity. He
retains his conviction despite criticism.
Headnote by editor Robert Henry Newell
disclaims responsibility for this "eulogium
of that coarse and uncouth creature."

*29 ANON. Review of <u>Leaves</u>. New Orleans <u>Weekly
Mirror</u> (9 June).
Reported in Allen (1967), p. 263.

30 ANON. "A New American Poem." <u>Southern Field
and Fireside</u> (9 June), 20.
Whitman's work certainly ends the lack
of a distinctly American voice in literature, but he "glories in materialism of the
most degraded kind," more so in this edition
than in his first. This edition is not
worth notice **exc**ept for the fact that it
has been widely advertised and praised.
This "poet of prize-fighters" and "minstrel
of muscle" may find admirers among some for
his "apotheosis of brute strength."

31 CHILTON, MARY A. "'Leaves of Grass.'" New
York <u>Saturday Press</u> (9 June), 3:4-5.
Whitman is an "apostle of purity," the
teacher of divine truth, refusing with
"child-like innocence" to recognize "such
distinctions as 'decency and indecency' in
the human structure," believing that the
body and its functions are to be admired.

32 [CLAPP, HENRY?] "Correction." New York
<u>Saturday Press</u> (9 June), 2:3.
A note from Mrs. Juliette H. Beach has
informed the editor that the article printed
by error above her name (1860.26) was actually written by her husband.

33 THABAB, BABBAGA [pseud.?]. "The Song of
Dandelions. (After Walt Whitman.)" New
York <u>Saturday Press</u> (9 June), 1:1.
Parody reprinted from Philadelphia <u>City
Item</u> (unlocated).

34 ANON. "Book Notices." <u>New York Illustrated
News</u> 2 (16 June), 91.
<u>Leaves</u> has sold well "because it <u>is</u> a
queer book." "It is superbly printed," as
permanent literature (which it will prove
to be) should be.

35 ANON. "'Leaves of Grass'--Smut in Them."
<u>Springfield Daily Republican</u> (16 June).
"A more scandalous volume we never
saw"; some pages could not be read aloud
to a decent assembly. Its danger lies in
the claims to respectability and purity
made for it by such as Chilton (1860.31,
quoted). Whitman regards nothing as unclean, no passions as degrading, although
they should only be hallowed in the context
of marriage.

36 LELAND, HENRY P. "Walt Whitman." New York
<u>Saturday Press</u> (16 June), 1:2.
Reprinted: 1860.40.
From the Philadelphia <u>City Item</u> (unlocated). Whitman gives American poetry a refreshing infusion, even if shocking. "He
is Consuelo for the poor man, the friend-
less, the outcast," being "the people's
Poet," direct and frank. People are urged
to discover what he is getting at. He is
lacking chiefly in the all-important attri-
bute of making money.

1860

37 A WOMAN [Mrs. Juliette H. Beach?]. Letter.
New York Saturday Press (23 June), 3:2.
Quoted in 1860.40.
    Defends Whitman as an embodiment of the
new "National Genius." Leaves will be "the
standard book of poems in the future of
America," with its "grand sublimity and
boldness" and the writer's spirit "raised
beyond everything else."

38 P., C. C. "Walt Whitman's New Volume." New
York Saturday Press (23 June), 1:5.
    This woman opposes the attacks on
Leaves, having found in it no poem to make
her blush, "no sentiment which might not be
expressed by a pure man." Whitman's measure
fits "the first distinctive American bard
who speaks for our large-scaled nature, for
the red men who are gone, for our vigorous
young population." He reveals proper openness about the body, "the greatness of my
destiny," the balance of the universe,
"the boundless love brooding over mankind."
Episodes in "Myself" are praised.

39 ANON. "Walt Whitman and His Critics." Leader
and Saturday Analyst (30 June), 614-15.
Reprinted: 1860.54.
    Review of Leaves. Early Whitman critics
attributed roughness and sensuality "to the
individual writer, and not to the subjective
hero supposed to be writing," ignoring the
learning which is evident throughout, particularly a knowledge of "Kant's transcendental method" and perhaps others of the
German school, at least through Emerson
and French interpreters. These Leaves are
not a marvel, but "the most natural products of the American soil," asserting "the
fullest American freedom." Certain passages
are "not meant for obscenity, but as scientific examples." The style, in the manner
of Tupper and Warren's "Lily and the Bee,"
is rhythmical but disjointed. The volume
should succeed because there are many fools
in the world who will be drawn by prurient
interest but who may possibly be made wise
by the book.

40 ANON. Advertisement for Leaves. New York
Saturday Press (30 June), 3:5.
Reprinted: Mabbott.
    Includes reprints of reviews 1860.21
and 1860.36, and extract from 1860.37.
This volume, "full of humanity's life-blood
and magnetism," is assured of "a quick sale
for every copy." (The complete advertisement is reprinted in the next two Saturday
Press issues and abridged for subsequent
issues.)

41 ANON. "Walt Whitman and American Art." New
York Saturday Press (30 June), 2:3-4.
    In contrast to so much art, mere
"effect, ornament, and sentiment," Whitman
provides "the first extended picture of
our life as we live it in America." "His
red-flannel shirt" is a pretension of

his own, and he sometimes descends into
nonsense and vagueness, but such an antidote is needed against current dogmatism.
He does not preach or ornament, and "is
never prosaic, for one who has breadth
through all his catalogue of particulars
to keep the thread of his thought."

42 ANON. "Leaves of Grass." Crayon 7 (July),
211.
    Review of Leaves. Whitman's mind shows
no signs of capacity except as "a mental
reservoir" into which he has tumbled "all
the floating conceits his brain ever gave
birth to," with "no trace of judgment,
taste, or healthy sensibility." This
"poetry (!)" is characteristic of our
abundant country and may please "twenty-one
year old [sic] statesmen and philosophers,
and people who pride themselves more in
being able to read and write than able to
think."

43 [HERRICK, ANSON.] "Walt Whitman." New York
Atlas (1 July), editorial page, col. 5.
    Note on Whitman's "Broadway Pageant"
in the New York Times: "incomprehensible,
egotistic twaddle" from this "rough, shaggy,
pea-jacketed individual." He is commended
for taking over for a sick Broadway stage-
driver. "Whitman's poetry is very bad, and
so are his garments--but his heart is sound
enough."

*44 ANON. Review of Leaves. Lancet (7 July).
Reported in Blodgett, but not found in this
issue.

45 ANON. "Leaves of Grass." Literary Gazette,
n.s. 4 (7 July), 798-99.
Reprinted: Bucke; Hindus.
    Review. This work should be titled
"Stenches from the Sewer" or "Squeals from
the Sty." Whitman writes like a fool or
madman. His "peculiarly coarse materialism"
emphasizes worship of his own body, in "a
tone of consistent impurity." He is "the
most silly, the most blasphemous, and the
most disgusting" of all writers.

46 ANON. "Leaves of Grass." Saturday Review 10
(7 July), 19-21.
Reprinted: 1860.57.
    Review. It is odd that Whitman should
be so indecent in a country which stresses
decency and euphemism. He illustrates "the
effect of the secondary Carlylism of Emerson
on a thorough American rowdy." His pantheism, occasionally rhythmical versification
on the model of Tupper, use of slang, choice
of language similar to public speaking commonplaces are described. Much of his book
reveals "very vivid imagination," with
"Myself" 21 being more like true poetry than
anything else in the book.

47 [WINTER, WILLIAM.] "The Torch-Bearers [sic].
A Paean for the Fourth of July. (After

Walt Whitman.)" New York Saturday Press
(7 July), 4:1.
Reprint of 1860.48.

48 _____. "The Torch-Bearer. A Paean for the
Fourth of July. (After Walt Whitman.)"
Vanity Fair 2 (7 July), 23.
Reprinted: 1860.47; 1920.81.
Parody.

49 ANON. Review of Leaves. Critic (London) 21
(14 July), 43-44.
There is scarcely "a single consecutive
sentence or expression out of which a meaning can be cudgelled." Leaves shows resemblance to Tupper. Passages from "Myself"
are quoted mockingly, some pages like "a
manual of surgery," others not quoted "for
decency's sake," although "this pure unmitigated trash is read and admired by not
a few persons in America," where he has
earned "a poet's crown." Whitman believes
in his "poetical infallibility," but poetry
cannot exist without "sense, grammar, and
metre."

50 ANON. "Walt Whitman." New York Saturday
Press (14 July), 1:1.
Parody reprinted from New Orleans
Delta (unlocated).

51 ANON. "Leaves of Grass." Spectator 33 (14
July), 669-70.
Review. Though some acclaim Whitman as
the fulfillment of the quest for an American poet, his is a "gospel of lewdness and
obscenity," with a "free and easy" form
meant to supersede the "effete theories
and forms" still popular in the old country. His egotism is "twofold--swaggering
and brutish by virtue of his rowdyism, all
conglomerating and incomprehensible by
virtue of his pantheistic transcendentalism." All things are equally good to him
and therefore equally fit as poetic subjects, merely placed in "compendious in-
ventories." "With Antecedents" is placed
in parallel columns with its parody
(1860.6) for comparison. But besides
"nonsense, coarseness, and filth," Whitman
has "strong perceptive faculties and a
vivid imagination, and he can express his
human sympathies in language that becomes
a man."

52 [HOWELLS, W. D.] "New Publications."
Ashtabula (Ohio) Sentinel 29 (18 July), 4.
Reprinted: 1860.58.
Whitman is full of contrasts, being
sublime and beastly, with "a wonderful
brain and an unwashed body." However, "he
has told too much" for one to want to know
him. The secrets of the soul, but not of
the body, may be revealed, but Whitman is
shameless.

*53 HARTE, FRANCIS BRETT. "San Francisco--After
Walt Whitman." Golden Era 8 (22 July).

Reported in KTO. Reprinted: 1860.59.
Parody.

54 ANON. "Walt Whitman and His Critics." New
York Saturday Press (28 July), 2:4-5.
Reprint of 1860.39.

55 [CONWAY, MONCURE D.] Review of Leaves. Dial
(Cincinnati) 1 (August), 517-19.
"Whitman has set the pulses of America
to music," as may be sensed when one reads
him outdoors or surrounded by human activity. Extracts are quoted to reveal "that
quintessence of things which we call
Poetry," although "in some of these pages
one must hold his nose whilst he reads."
But one should not lose these great utterances. Whitman "is never frivolous, his
profanity is reverently meant, and he
speaks what is unspeakable with the simple
unreserve of a child."

*56 ANON. Review of Leaves. Boston Cosmopolite
(4 August).
Extract reprinted: Bucke; Hindus.
"In no other modern poems do we find
such a lavish outpouring of wealth,"
although its "rude state" may shock us.
In treating nature "without fig-leaves"
Whitman displays sincere, not immoral,
motives, resembling the Hebrew scriptures.
"The style is wonderfully idiomatic and
graphic." He displays sympathy, wonder,
freedom in treating "the commonest daily
objects and the most exalted truths of the
soul." The spirit of music and poetry is
in his verse, which fuses "elements hitherto
considered antagonistic in poetry."

57 ANON. "Leaves of Grass." New York Saturday
Press (4 August), 4:1-2.
Reprint of 1860.46.

58 [HOWELLS, W. D.] "A Hoosier's Opinion of
Walt Whitman." New York Saturday Press
(11 August), 1:3.
Reprint of 1860.52.

59 [HARTE, FRANCIS BRETT.] "San Francisco. After
Walt Whitman." New York Saturday Press
(18 August), 4:1.
Reprint of 1860.53.

60 [CURTIS, GEORGE W.] "Editor's Easy Chair."
Harper's New Monthly Magazine 21 (September),
555.
Quotes and comments upon "A Broadway
Pageant," which reveals Whitman's descriptive power and skill of observation, and
which "says fine and striking things, often
with cadence, never with the essential
melody of song."

61 ANON. "The Song of the Barbecue. Not by Walt
Whitman, nor Professor Longfellow." Vanity
Fair 2 (29 September), 168-69.
Comic poem in short unrhymed lines.

1860

62 ANON. Review of Leaves. Westminster and
Foreign Quarterly Review 74, n.s. 18 (1
October), 590.
        This book, full of "obscenity and
profanity," would be unworthy of notice
were it not published so respectably.
Whitman's "Hegelian morality" (though his
"direct acquaintance" with German philosophers is doubtful) regards man as his own
god. His shameless defense of "the emancipation of the flesh" indicates "a moral
disorganization" in America. His versification is like Tupper's "English Humdrum,"
with an occasional "poetical expression"
such as a savage might hit upon by chance.
"These 'Leaves of Grass' are the symptoms
of a moral fermentation in America, which
no doubt will result in a broader and
clearer life--but the progress is painful
and the yeast nauseous."

63 [WHITMAN, WALT.] "A Brooklynite Criticised."
Brooklyn City News (10 October).
Reprinted in facsimile: Bucke (1974).
Abridged: Bucke; 1936.51.
        Notice of Imprints, explaining the
publication history of Leaves. The poem
itself, "a compact unity," is "the Song of
the sovereignty of One's self--and the Song
of entire faith in all that Nature is,
universal and particular--and in all that
belongs to a man, body and soul."
Whitman's egotism speaks for every reader
as "the gospel of Democracy." His work,
new in form and spirit, contradicts established canons of criticism, demanding new
standards. Leaves is to be "absorbed by
the soul," "returned to, again and again."
It has permanency and "a peculiar native
idiomatic flavor," that of "the celebrated
New York 'rough.'" For Whitman, the sexual
relations are "the most beautiful and pure
and divine of any," his indecency merely
that of biblical writers and innocent
youth. Some of the Imprints criticisms
are amusing.

64 WINTER, WILLIAM. "Before Him. A Picture.
(After Walt Whitman.)" New York Saturday
Press (20 October), 2:6.
Reprinted: 1864.2; 1933.17.
        Parody.

65 ANON. "French Appreciation of 'Leaves of
Grass.'" New York Saturday Press (17
November), 3:4-5.
        From October Bibliographie Imperiale.
Passages are quoted from the translation
due in January, Brins d'herbe, to show
"how thoroughly the poems of Walt Whitman
may take root in the French language," for
"poetry is not a matter of words, it is
all in its ideas." A change in language
cannot detract from Whitman's power or
sweetness.

66 ANON. Incidental mention. Vanity Fair 2 (17
November), 252.

Quoted (with error) in Glicksberg (1938).
        The author notes, in looking for an
appropriate poet for his subject, that
unfortunately "Walt Whitman is engaged, or
else the world should see a lyric of despair which would drive to raving lunacy
the infant in the cradle, and the crow on
the housetop."

67 ANON. "The City. Not by Walt Whitman." New
York Saturday Press (24 November), 4:1-2.
        Parody reprinted from New Orleans
Sunday Delta (unlocated).

68 [DEL VECCHIO, JAMES.] Editorial. Brooklyn
Standard (24 November), 2:1-2.
Reprinted: Holloway (1936).
        Whitman is de facto Brooklyn's poet
laureate. His genius gives him "a sublime
way of saying queer things, and a queer
way of saying sublime things." His intentions are good. Leaves is to be liked, not
criticized. Whitman's usual activities
around town are described.

*69 ANON. Review of Leaves and O'Connor's novel
Harrington. Boston Wide World (8 December).
Reprinted: WWR 9 (September 1963), 63-64.
        "These 'poems' (prose run crazy) are
the veriest trash ever written, and vulgar
and disgusting to the last degree. There
never was more unblushing obscenity presented to the public eye than is to be
found in these purient [sic] pages."

1862

BOOKS--None

PERIODICALS

1 [WHITMAN, WALT?] "Bath Oriental." Vanity
Fair 5 (12 April), 183.
        Parody in Whitmanesque lines and diction
on the Turkish bath.

2 QUICK, TOM. "The Old Sports of New York.
Fast Men of the Past & Present." New York
Leader (16 August), 3:4.
        Anecdote of Whitman (whom this writer
knows) taking the place of a sick driver,
whom he admired, for a week, getting "his
eye blacked for the compliment." He "can
write books with pretty pieces in, and
drive an omnibus for a friend."

1863

BOOKS--None

PERIODICALS

1 F[ULTON], W. A. C[HANDOS-]. "A Walk Up Fulton
Street." Brooklyn Standard (7 February),
1:5.
        Quoted in Holloway (1936).

Describes attractive appearance of a
medium-sized man who seemed unsophisticated
but with a vigorous, original mind. Later
the writer learned that this was Whitman,
author of Leaves.

2 ANON. "Walt. Whitman in Washington." Brooklyn
Standard (28 February), 2:4.
Reprinted: Uncollected, vol. 2.
Quotes Washington correspondent of the
Times (not found in New York Times) about
Whitman's arrival in Washington after being
robbed of fifty dollars, his engagement in
the hospitals, anecdote of his being
stopped during carnival time by a watchman
who suspected his beard was part of a mask.

1864

BOOKS

1 FARNHAM, ELIZA W. Woman and Her Era. New
York: A. J. Davis & Co. Vol 1, pp. iv,
72; vol. 2, pp. 19, 241-44, 282, 314-16,
464, 465.
Quotations from Whitman reveal his
"grand confidence" in pursuing "the struggle
of Progress" and his "courage and clear
moral vision" in defeating the idea of
"'ethical perdition.'" Whitman's supreme
feeling for the "sacred and excellent
beauty" of art has nowhere else been
"expressed in language comparable" to his,
regarding the true qualities of woman. He
provides "the written speech of which the
Pre-Raphaelite pictures are the color-
language."

2 NICHOLS, Dr. THOMAS L. Forty Years of American Life. Vol. 1. London: John Maxwell &
Co., pp. 299-302.
Revised: 1874.1.
Reprints Winter's "Before Him"
(1860.64), on Prince Edward's visit to New
York, "written in an original style of
poetry invented by Walt Whitman, a New
York political loafer, not destitute of
genius, and patronized by Emerson." This
poem, "by a pupil and imitator, has been
thought a trifle satirical, but will,
perhaps, repay a cursory perusal."

3 TAYLOR, BAYARD. John Godfrey's Fortunes;
Related by Himself. A Story of American
Life. New York: G. P. Putnam's, Hurd &
Houghton, pp. 278, 326-27, 329-30, 394,
452.
Smithers, a Bohemian, is presented in
this novel spouting Whitman-like sentiments
of the admiration of common men. He has
written "'Edda of the Present,' a heroic,
muscular poem, in irregular metre," in
which another character accuses him of
exploiting his sailors and longshoremen.
Another character says, "I celebrate myself."

PERIODICALS

4 [CHANDOS-FULTON, W. A.] "The Local Press.
IX." Brooklyn Standard (22 October), 1:3.
This history of the Brooklyn Daily
Eagle notes Whitman's brief editorship of
the Eagle and its concurrent loss of ground.
His previous newspaper and writing exper-
ience (as "author of several novelettes")
is mentioned.

5 _____. "The Local Press. X." Brooklyn
Standard (5 November), 1:2-3.
Notes Whitman's 1858 editing of the
Brooklyn Daily Times. Traces history of
Brooklyn Freeman; Whitman was chosen as
editor because he was a Free Soiler; he
did all the writing. He remained until
1849 when he decided to travel. Notes his
other journalistic and literary activities;
his driving a Broadway stage. An extensive
note provides biographical information on
his hospital work and illness, the printing
and selling of the first three editions of
Leaves.

6 EMERSON, RALPH WALDO. "Mr. Emerson's Lectures
on 'American Life.' V. 'Books.'" Boston
Commonwealth (31 December), 2:1.
Reprinted: 1932.10.
Incidental mention in the discussion
of journalism as "the type of American
literature": "No Tennyson, no Shakespeare,
no Bacon, but rather Walt Whitmans, Parson
Brownlows, extravagant and eloquent Western
orators, half song-thrush, half alligator."

1865

BOOKS

1 THOREAU, HENRY D. Letters to Various Persons.
Edited by R. W. Emerson. Boston: Ticknor
& Fields, pp. 141-42, 146-48.
Reprinted: 1894.16; Miller; Hindus; Murphy;
Rupp; Hubbell; and in Essays and Other
Writings of Henry Thoreau, edited by Will H.
Dircks (London: Walter Scott, [1891]),
pp. 228-29, 232-33.
Letters to Mr. B[lake] dated 19 November and 7 December 1856 describe Thoreau's
visit to Whitman and his responses to the
1856 Leaves. "He is apparently the greatest
democrat the world has seen." A few pieces
are "simply sensual," but people should be
so pure as not to understand them. Leaves,
unequalled for preaching, is primitive,
oriental, exhilarating, encouraging. "He
occasionally suggests something a little
more than human." (See 1935.27 for manuscript draft of the 19 November letter.)

PERIODICALS

2 ANON. "Washington. . . . Dismissal of Clerks
in the Interior Department." New York
Herald (4 July), 4.

1865

Notes recent quiet commotion among some clerks in the Interior Department because of the dismissal of several of their number, with "Walter Whitman" and others among "those with whose services Mr. Harlan has concluded to dispense."

3 ANON. "Morality in Washington." Brooklyn Daily Eagle (12 July), 2:2.
Discusses Whitman's dismissal. Though "personally a good-hearted fellow, with some ability," "he was bitten with the mania of transcendentalism." He was, however, too much a child of nature for Emerson's patronage, going to dine with him at the Prescott House in New York wearing a red shirt and pilot jacket, his "invariable costume." Except for the impropriety of its language, Leaves might have been accepted as a burlesque on Emerson's thought and style, but Whitman mistook nastiness for the simplicity of nature.

4 ANON. Advertisement for Drum-Taps. New York Daily Tribune (28 October), 2:4.
Advertises Drum-Taps, published this day, with list of partial contents.

5 ANON. "Personal." Round Table 2 (4 November), 135.
Announces upcoming publication of Drum-Taps by Bunce and Huntington, "written in the same uncouth and lumbering but strikingly idiomatic style."

6 ANON. "Drum-Taps--Walt Whitman." Watson's Weekly Art Journal (4 November), 34-35.
Review of Drum-Taps. Whitman in literature, like Ward in art, expresses our "New-World self-assertion," presenting facts, springing from our American life. Whitman's artistic looseness is consistent with his mood. Drum-Taps reveals greater regard for beauty of form than Leaves. "Pioneers" is reprinted with praise.

7 H[OWELLS], W. D. "Drum-Taps." Round Table 2 (11 November), 147-48.
Reprinted: Miller; Murphy.
Review of Drum-Taps. Unlike Leaves, Drum-Taps contains no indecency, although the artistic method remains mistaken. The American people seek not an expression "more rude and formless than that of the savagest tribes" but rather "the highest, least dubious, most articulate speech," as Whitman's unpopularity proves. These poems derive from his noble part in the war, and in many the pathos brings tears to the eyes. "But they do not satisfy," because Whitman is content with suggestion, rather than expression of true poetic thoughts. His "rich possibilities" and thorough absorption of "the idea of our American life" suggest that he may yet write without demanding the reader to form the poem himself.

8 [JAMES, HENRY.] "Mr. Walt Whitman." Nation 1 (16 November), 625-26.
Reprinted: 1908.9; Miller; Hindus; Murphy.
Review of Drum-Taps. These poems "of an essentially prosaic mind" lack the "visible goal" of rhyme, much like Tupper's, and differ from prose because of the strange vocabulary. Whitman believes wrongly that his substance is more important than style; this book is "an offence against art," although pretending to touch the feelings. He talks too much about himself, for art requires subordination of the self. He has only "flashy imitations of ideas." His own personal qualities, however worthy, are irrelevant for singing truly the nation's battles and glories.

9 ANON. "Walt Whitman's Drum Taps." New York Times (22 November), 4:6.
Review of Drum-Taps. Whitman compares poorly with Praed. His "poverty of thought" and lack of standard versification prove him no poet. His wartime service will be remembered long after Leaves and Drum-Taps are gone.

10 ANON. "Literary. 'Drum-Taps.'" Brooklyn Daily Union (23 November), 2.
Whitman has done noble service in the war, but he is not a poet, for poetry needs music and imagination, not only the strong feeling and appreciation of nature which Whitman has. His fervent patriotism has produced only commonplace work, despite "occasional sonorous lines and frequent thrilling passages." He sins in assuming himself to be the most original and authoritative critic of this world.

11 [CURTIS, G. W.] "Editor's Easy Chair." Harper's New Monthly Magazine 32 (December), 123-24.
Those who question the placement of Drum-Taps next to the poems of Tennyson and others here reviewed should consider whether there is no poetry in "Captain" and "Beat, Beat, Drums!" (here reprinted with comment).

1866

BOOKS

1 GUROWSKI, ADAM. Diary: 1863-'64-'65. Washington: W. H. & O. H. Morrison, p. 128.
Entry of 5 March 1864 cites Whitman, "the incarnation of a genuine American original genius," who "alone in his heart and in his mind has a shine for the nameless, for the heroic people."

2 O'CONNOR, WILLIAM DOUGLAS. The Good Gray Poet. A Vindication. New York: Bunce & Huntington, 46 pp.
Reprinted: Bucke; 1927.17; Loving.
Abridged: Miller; Hindus.

Defense of Whitman occasioned by his dismissal from the Interior Department by Secretary Harlan, who told an eminent government official that he dismissed Whitman because he had written a book "'full of indecent passages'" and was "'a very bad man,' a 'Free-Lover.'" Included are physical descriptions of Whitman, opinions by Alcott, Thoreau, and Lincoln, and testimonials to his good character. He loves music and art, is indebted to the Bible, and is a "laborious student of life." Only eighty lines out of nine thousand are in question and have been misread. Examples from classical literature which deal with sex more blatantly are cited. Leaves is "purely and entirely American" but transcends mere nationalism, emphasizing the wholeness of the human being, the sacredness of the body, the divinity of all things. It is a masterpiece, even with its faults, commendable for its meter ("flexible, melodious, corresponsive to the thought," similar to nature's, incomparable to Tennyson's) and its use of the English language. Various poems are praised as "examples of great structural harmony as well as of the highest poetry." "Lilacs," "unique and solitary in literature," will remain "the chosen and immortal hymn of Death forever." His contemporaries "are but singers; he is a bard," ranking with Shakespeare, Dante, and others. He seeks to remedy contemporary morbid attitudes toward sex. Time will memorialize him and his war-time service. The wrong done him demands redress, affecting all literature.

PERIODICALS

3 [WHIPPLE, E. P.] "'The Good Gray Poet.'" Boston Evening Transcript (17 January), 2:2.
   Review of O'Connor (1866.2), full of "mental bombast." The "mere loss of an office is not a fit occasion for such an apotheosis of the victim." Indeed, since a clerkship is so small a place for a "'Kosmos'" like Walt, "his removal from it might be taken as a tribute to his genius."

4 [STODDARD, R. H.?] or [HOWELLS, W.D.?] Review of O'Connor (1866.2). Round Table 3 (20 January), 37.
   Though justice has not been done Whitman, O'Connor's praise of him is extravagant. Whitman is "a man of unquestioned talent, not to say genius," but has written passages with "a very rank odor." He "will be a Great Name" who has truly written literature only when the great writers to whom O'Connor compares him are forgotten.

5 ANON. Editorial. Chicago Republican (25 January), 4.
   Notes appearance of O'Connor's defense of Whitman. Is he "in danger of being

ousted from his place in Parnassus" just because he has been dismissed from his office? Besides, such a clerkship should be taken by a disabled soldier, not an able-bodied man like Whitman.

6 ANON. Review of O'Connor (1866.2). Nation 2 (25 January), 118-19.
   O'Connor's cause is trivial in this exaggerated "'vindication,'" with its "fulsome laudation" of Whitman. Harlan may dismiss whom he chooses. O'Connor is damaging his own reputation as a writer.

7 F. "'Drum-Taps.'" New York Saturday Press (27 January), 3.
   Review of Drum-Taps. Whitman's two great ideas--"the omnipresence of the soul, and the sacredness of the individual--lie at the roots of poetry and civilization." His claim to be a great poet lies rather in "a picturesqueness of phrase unsurpassed in literature, and a powerful rhythm, whose long musical roll is like that of the waves of the sea." His "passion for individuals is so strong that it continually wrestles with and overthrows his belief in the universal." "If he clung closer to realities and less tenaciously to appearances, he would be the greatest poet of our day."

8 LANMAN, CHARLES. "The 'Good Gray Poet.'" Round Table 3 (27 January), 61.
   Reprinted: Bucke.
   This letter from "a friend of Secretary Harlan" corrects implications in review (1866.4). Whitman was discharged not for religious opinions but for "two satisfactory reasons: he was wholly unfit to perform the duties which were assigned to his desk; and a volume which he published and caused to be circulated through the public offices was so coarse, indecent, and corrupting in its thought and language as to jeopardize the reputation of the department."

9 ANON. "Secretary Harlan Playing Cato the Censor." Boston Commonwealth (3 February), 2:5-6.
   Describes O'Connor's defense of Whitman (1866.2) and supports him against Harlan, questioning Washington morality, citing literary precedents. Whitman "is a person of too much genius to be treated otherwise than with respect."

10 O'CONNOR, WM. D. "Walt Whitman and Mr. Harlan." Round Table 3 (3 February), 76.
   Reprinted: Bucke.
   Denies Lanman's assertions (1866.8) and thanks reviewer (1866.4) for agreeing that the dismissal is an "insult to literature."

11 H[INTON], R. J. "Why Walt Whitman Left the Interior Department." Milwaukee Sentinel (9 February), 2:4-5.
   Corrects misconceptions about Whitman

arising from the Sentinel's reprinting of
Lanman's letter (1866.8). Lanman is editor
of the Congressional Biographical Dictionary. O'Connor's statements (1866.2),
quoted, are vouched for by the writer's
own "long acquaintance" with Whitman.

12 [PIATT, J. J.] "From Washington. Literature
in Political Harness." Columbus Morning
Journal (12 February), 1.
     Describes Whitman's appearance; notes
various praises of him; recalls seeing him
going to the White House, where he met
with Lincoln; deplores his dismissal, but
criticizes O'Connor's strong language in
1866.2.

13 [STRANGFORD, VISCOUNT.] "Walt Whitman." Pall
Mall Gazette (16 February), 10.
     Reprinted: 1869.1. Abridged: 1866.15.
     While it is foolish to fire Whitman
for poems written years ago, he is indeed
outrageously and defiantly obscene and
opposed to conformity. His ideas resemble
Eastern thought, following the pantheistic
strain in American transcendentalism.
Although he could hardly have known Persian
poetry, he comes close to its accent and
might benefit from careful study and translation of it to save himself from dreary
platitudes, occasional bathos, and "epi-
curean autolatry."

14 [SANBORN, F. B.] "Literary Review. Walt
Whitman's Drum Taps." Boston Commonwealth
(24 February), 1:6-7.
     Review of Drum-Taps. Describes
Whitman's war work and his trouble getting
published and noticed, in contrast to
writers far less worthy. "Captain"
(reprinted) is "the most touching dirge"
yet written for Lincoln, "perhaps the most
effective entire poem in the book." Other
extracts show Whitman's power. But he is
great and pleasing only at intervals.
This volume, free from earlier coarseness,
will help remove the prejudice against
Whitman and "secure him that place in
literature during his lifetime which he is
sure to hold in the next age." The following review notes the contrast between
Whitman's choliambics" and the Sewell
family's smooth prose, but "both are good
in their way, and both are needed."

15 [MORSE, SIDNEY?] "Walt Whitman's Drum-Taps."
Radical 1 (March), 311-12.
     Review of Drum-Taps. Whitman has more
of the essence of poetry than many of his
contemporaries, for to him all the world
glows with poetic beauty. He touches our
soul and can make his own rules. Drum-Taps
reveals no new characteristics but omits
the sexual aspects. The mystery associated
with Whitman in his war work is described,
his vivid word-painting noted.

*16 ANON. Review of Drum-Taps. London Times (8
March).
     Reported in Kennedy (1926) and Blodgett,
but not located on several dates checked.

17 C[ONWAY], M. D. "Correspondence. London."
Round Table 3 (17 March), 171.
     Notes Whitman's fame in Europe,
arousing "something far other than ridi-
cule--namely, a genuine belief that he has
genius, and a curiosity to know something
about him." London is concerned over his
dismissal. Extracts from Strangford
(1866.13) are quoted.

*18 ANON. Review of Drum-Taps. London Review
(8 June).
     Reported in Blodgett, but there is no issue
on this date and several other dates checked
presented nothing.

19 BENSON, EUGENE. "About the Literary Spirit."
Galaxy 1 (15 July), 491.
     Incidental. Criticizes contemporary
men of letters, in looking for a vital
contemporary American literature: "If they
have reacted against formality and hypocrisy
like Walt Whitman, like him, also, they are
devoid of the literary spirit."

20 ANON. Review of Melville's Battle-Pieces.
Albion 44 (15 September), 441.
     Incidental: Melville lacks Whitman's
power of placing us in rapport with the
events he writes about.

21 [LOWELL, JAMES RUSSELL.] Review of Howell's
Venetian Life. North American Review 103
(October), 611-12.
     Reprinted: 1920.20.
     Howells "was a natural product, as
perfectly natural as the deliberate attempt
of 'Walt Whitman' to answer the demand of
native and foreign misconception was perfectly artificial. Our institutions do not,
then, irretrievably doom us to coarseness
and to impatience of that restraining precedent which alone makes true culture
possible and true art attainable."

22 CONWAY, MONCURE D. "Walt Whitman." Fortnightly Review 6 (15 October), 538-48.
     Reprinted: 1866.25; 1882.10.
     Whitman offers "the most interesting
illustration" of the current oriental
tendency in American letters. Emerson's
response to Whitman is explained. Much
of Leaves may repulse the ordinary mind,
but from such matter American thought must
be built. Conway's first meeting with
Whitman is recalled: his appearance,
anecdotes, biographical sketch, war work
(serving over a hundred thousand men).
"Captain," a touching dirge for "his warm
friend and admirer," Lincoln, is printed.

24 ANON. Paragraph. Round Table 4 (27 October),
212.

"Mr. Walter Whitman is said to be preparing something for the press." "We are
not partial to his verse," which bears "the
same relation to poetry that an auctioneer's
catalogue does to a bit of genuine description." When such books as Whitman's are
considered additions to our literature,
"chaos will have come again."

24 B[URROUGHS], J[OHN]. "Literary Review."
Boston Commonwealth (10 November), 1:7-2:1.
Reprinted: WWR 6 (September 1960), 46-48.
    Review of 1867 Leaves. Whitman's work
here approaches completeness, revealing
that what he has been building is a man,
"a new democratic man, whom he believes to
be typical of the future American, and of
whom he perpetually uses himself as the
illustration." "Myself" reveals "how a
man is made," and is "a search after
power." "Adam" reveals the animal nature
as the basis of all else, though it is not
unduly emphasized at the expense of moral
and aesthetic qualities. "Calamus" celebrates a more mature feeling. "Salut,"
"Brooklyn Ferry," and "Open Road" are
described, as is the new arrangement.
"Drum-Taps" is sanctifying, revealing
Whitman as surpassing others in tenderness
and love as in rude force and virility,
with "a benevolence such as was never
before the inspiration of poems."

25 CONWAY, MONCURE D. "Walt Whitman." Every
Saturday 2 (17 November), 580-83.
Reprint of 1866.22.

26 BURROUGHS, JOHN. "Walt Whitman and his 'Drum
Taps.'" Galaxy 2 (1 December), 606-15.
Reprinted in part: Murphy.
    Review of Drum-Taps. Whitman remains
serene despite persecution. His life,
career, reception, and plan for a religious
section in his book are described. His
"most enthusiastic champions" are "young
men, and students and lovers of nature,"
with many women also accepting him. His
book expresses fully "a perfectly healthy,
unconventional man," as model of the
American of the future. He is cultivated,
but a student of men and things rather
than of books. He made acquaintance with
Emerson's writings only after publishing
his first edition. His personality and
recent hospital work are described. His
"entire sympathy with nature" differentiates
him from the rest of modern literature,
his gravity and primitivism contrasting
with "our profuse sentimentalism" and melancholy. The solemnity of Drum-Taps contrasts strongly with the exultation of
Leaves. Whitman regards peace rather than
war as the permanent condition of modern
society. He shows appropriate democratic
concern for the individual, not the army.
Long extracts are quoted and commented on,
particularly from "Lilacs," which uses the
indirect method of nature. Material from

this article is used in 1867.1; 1877.1;
1896.2.

27 O'C[ONNOR], W. D. "Current Literature. Walt
Whitman." New York Times (2 December),
2:1-5.
    Editor [Henry J. Raymond] prefaces the
article with denial of responsibility for
these opinions: some of Whitman's postwar
poetry has value, but he also contains
"indecency and filth." O'Connor explains
his acquaintance with both poem and poet.
The new edition presents Whitman's plan to
greater advantage. Leaves is the "only
book in our literature which aims at a
distinctively national character." Centering his book on himself, as did Dante and
Montaigne, Whitman makes himself "a representative embodiment" of the complete human
being. Extracts show his belief in women's
equality. His verse is not "unpoetical,"
but corresponds to nature, music, biblical
writers, and American life. His war poems
abstain from "any vindictiveness during
the struggle, any note of exultation over
the vanquished," emphasizing rather war's
tragic aspects, comradeship, and national
unity.

1867

BOOKS

1 BURROUGHS, JOHN. Notes on Walt Whitman, as
Poet and Person. New York: American News
Co., 108 pp. No index.
Reprinted: 1871.1. Extract reprinted:
1926.4.
    Describes his first acquaintance with
Leaves (1861) and with Whitman (1863); the
various editions and their reception. The
1867 edition (here concentrated on) completes Whitman's work, although he may wish
to express further "the religious aspira-
tional elements." Major poems and sections
are explicated; they combine to form one
poem, paralleling nature's unity. More
than Wordsworth, Whitman accepts nature
completely, with its force. He is not
ignorant of the resources of literary composition, for his lines have poise and
grace and he avoids abstractions in favor
of "flesh-and-blood reality." He has some
satiric talent. He will lead to a nobler
school of criticism, but he shows no concern for immediate approval. While he
rightly emphasizes the worth of the body,
his spirituality cannot be denied. Sketch
of Whitman's life, character, hospital
work (described through Whitman's letters)
is presented. Drum-Taps is discussed
(largely as in 1866.26), "the vital and
distinguishing memento through literature
of the late war," commemorating not battles
but human pain. "Lilacs" needs no plot
development, displaying dramatic interplay
between images.

1867

PERIODICALS

2 [HILL, A. S.] Review of Drum-Taps and Sequel.
   North American Review 104 (January), 301-3.
      Drum-Taps, since it lacks the impro-
   prieties of Leaves, "can be judged on its
   intrinsic merits," although it too lacks
   the formal restraints a true artist requires.
   Along with "the extravagance, coarseness,
   and general 'loudness' of Bowery boys,"
   Whitman possesses their better traits as
   well: acceptance of his body, candor,
   sensitivity to the beauty of nature and
   man without sentimentality, a "braggart
   patriotism" which proved genuine during the
   war. The merit of these poems depends not
   on Whitman's hospital work but on their
   "almost photographic accuracy of observation," "masculine directness of expression,"
   and "tenderness of feeling," with frequent
   original epithets. Extracts are quoted,
   especially from the "remarkable" "Lilacs."

3 ANON. "Book Table." Independent 19 (10 January), 2.
      Review of Melville's Battle-Pieces,
   noting Whitman's influence on these poems.

4 C. "The Aldrich-Swinburne Controversy."
   Round Table 5 (19 January), 41.
      This letter uses Whitman as an illus-
   tration in its discussion of frequent
   charges of plagiarism against poets. It
   would be easy to prove that, even though
   "Whitman had perhaps never read a line of
   Catullus," "the address To a Common Prostitute owes the inspiration of its subdued
   indecency to the more blushing obscenity
   of Catullus's atrocious Clarmen [sic] 32
   Ad Ipsithillam." However, pointing that
   out would be fruitless except for the possibility of Whitman's "or his prochain
   [sic] amie's probably able reply."

5 W[ILLIAM D. O'CONNOR]. "'C.' on Walt Whitman."
   Round Table 5 (16 February), 104.
      Long letter arguing against the charge
   in 1867.4 that Whitman might not know
   Catullus and the comparison to a poem of
   "gross lust." Whitman's poem expresses
   tolerance, human love and faith, the spirit
   of the modern age and of Christianity. The
   prostitute's significance in modern literature is described. Whitman's uplifting
   lines are quoted, making with the prostitute
   a "direct appointment for the superior
   life."

6 C. "Catullus and Whitman." Round Table 5
   (23 February), 121.
      Short letter in response to 1867.5,
   explaining that he read the poem "fresh
   from the chaste rhapsodies of the Enfans
   d'Adam, which possibly colored my construction." "W." misconstrued his meaning, for
   he believes in Whitman's originality.

7 MONADNOCK [Moncure Daniel Conway?]. "Affairs
   in England . . . Walt Whitman." New York
   Times (18 March), 1:3.
      "A column of genial and appreciative
   criticism" of Whitman in a recent London
   Sunday Times (unlocated) predicts for
   Leaves a prominent place in American literature, although it is for individual rather
   than family reading. Whitman is national
   in the fullest sense, and particularly Man-
   hattanese, combining "the freedom and
   coarseness of Rabelais, the poetry of
   Ossian, and the philosophic flavor of
   Emerson." This review may induce some publisher to bring out an inexpensive edition.

8 BENSON, EUGENE. "Literature and the People."
   Galaxy 3 (15 April), 875-76.
      It is uncertain whether Whitman's is
   the direction in which America can find a
   national expression, although we can honor
   him for his poetry and its liberating qualities, similar to those of Emerson, Godwin,
   and Beecher. Whitman's work "cannot be
   truly estimated yet."

9 ANON. "Literary." Public Opinion (London) 11
   (25 May), 581.
      Quotes New York Times (unlocated) about
   Whitman preparing a new edition. "If he
   could so far yield to what he regards as
   the prejudices of the public as to omit a
   few of the poems included in former editions,
   he would readily not only achieve a wide
   popularity, but make known some of the
   finest and noblest strains in the English
   tongue to persons who probably will otherwise never see them."

10 ANON. "Walt Whitman." New York Tribune (20
    June), 6:2-4.
       Review of Burroughs (1867.1). Because
    of his "earnest conviction," Burroughs
    demands a hearing for his attitude toward
    Whitman, who "must possess some elements of
    manliness which the public at large has not
    recognized." Burroughs presents many sug-
    gestions to help "in forming an impartial
    estimate" of Whitman's writings. Whitman
    corrects the false attitudes toward nature
    prevailing in most merely beautiful modern
    verse. But does he really merit comparison
    with Tennyson and Browning?

11 ANON. Paragraph review of Burroughs (1867.1).
    New York Evening Post (21 June), 1:1-2.
       Burroughs's account of Whitman is the
    fullest yet published, interesting for "the
    freshness of its facts and the honesty of
    the writer's purpose." Whitman's life is
    briefly traced, his "striking eulogy" of
    Lincoln noted. What Burroughs says "of the
    good heart and the unquestioned talent of
    the man is just."

12 O'C[ONNOR], W. D. "Walt Whitman." New York
    Times (30 June), 3:1-4.
       Review of Burroughs (1867.1), the "first

adequate, intelligent and truthful presentation" of Whitman, as either person or writer, with great value "as a key to the works and personal character of a misunderstood and slandered poet," and also as commentary on the true aims of art and criticism. Extensive extracts from Burroughs.

13 R[OSSETTI], W. M. "Walt Whitman's Poems."
    London Chronicle (6 July), 352-54.
    Reprinted: 1867.15; 1867.16. Revised:
    1868.2.
         Whitman's poems, mixing prose with
    poetry, have a powerful rhythmical sense.
    His life and appearance are described (from
    Burroughs, 1867.1). "Whitman is, far more
    than any of his contemporaries, a man of
    his age, an initiator in the scheme and
    structure of his writings, and an individual
    of audacious personal ascendant [sic],
    incapable of compromise of whatever kind."
    His flaws include gross or inappropriate
    words, obscurity, detached lists, boundless
    self-assertion (though intended as representative). Leaves must be read as a whole.
    Combining personality and democracy, it is
    "the essentially modern poem," also echoing
    the old Hebrew poetry. Whitman is a realist and an optimist, but not a materialist.
    He is entirely original, with a certain
    influence on future poetry.

14 ANON. "Notes: Literary." Nation 5 (25 July),
    64.
         Paragraph summarizing and quoting
    1867.13, which has a stronger impact because
    more temperate than criticisms from Whitman's
    other admirers. Rossetti's description of
    Whitman's style suggests why Emerson felt
    such an affinity for him.

15 [ROSSETTI, W. M.] "Walt Whitman." New York
    Times (28 July), 2:5.
    Reprint in part of 1867.13.

*16 ROSSETTI, W. M. "Walt Whitman's Poems." New
    York Citizen (10 August).
    Reprint of 1867.13. Reported in Kennedy
    (1926).

17 [ARNOLD, MATTHEW.] "Theodore Parker." Pall
    Mall Gazette (24 August), 12.
    Reprinted: Essays, Letters and Reviews by
    Matthew Arnold. Edited by Fraser Neiman.
    Cambridge, Mass.: Harvard University Press,
    1960.
         Like Parker, Whitman "is as a poet a
    genuine American voice, not an echo of
    English poetry," although their admirers
    make more of this Americanism than it is
    worth. Whitman's response to a soldier's
    question about his religion is quoted as
    appropriate to Parker as well.

18 ANON. "The Magazines for September." Nation
    5 (29 August), 168.
         Notes the appearance of "Carol for
    Harvest" in September Galaxy: the "charm

in the mere rehearsal of the autumnal aspects of nature" gave the reader "an impression of poetry somewhere" but generally this was "like all other performances of Mr. Whitman's: ejaculatory, extremely vocative, incoherent; it expresses no ideas, and suggests mere emotion; it is in no sense a worthy celebration of the first great peace-harvest after our years of war."

19 ANON. "Some American Verse." Saturday Review
    24 (21 September), 383.
         Review of John W. Montclair's Themes
    and Translations, which is typical of
    American verse in resembling English verse
    and ignoring the vastness of America and
    the energy of her people. Whitman is the
    notable exception to this generalization.

20 ANON. "Editorial Department." Northern
    Monthly Magazine 1 (October), 598-99.
         Whitman, "an eccentric literary
    prophet," has "recently had greatness
    thrust upon him, by way of a joke, we fear,
    through several laudatory reviews in the
    English magazines." "His respect for moral
    teachings is not remarkable." "Mentally
    he is of the brute brutish." "His last
    published what-d'-you-call-it, he calls A
    Carol for Harvest, for 1867, and we strongly
    suspect was originally intended for an agricultural catalogue." Why does he bother
    with any conventions of verse, like capital
    letters? Apparently "English undefiled is
    not suited for the expression of Mr.
    Whitman's great thoughts." He is compared
    to Ossian.

21 ANON. "Literariana." Round Table 6 (12 October), 248.
         Notice of 1867.19. Whitman receives
    from the English a regard higher than he
    has received from any equal literary authority at home. Such praise may yet make
    Americans take notice of him, but posterity
    will determine his true rank.

22 BENTON, M. B. Review of Burroughs (1867.1).
    Radical 3 (November), 189-91.
         Burroughs is suited to this task.
    Whitman is compared to Homer, singing the
    divine impulses of our day. The future will
    determine whether he has written today's
    epic memorial.

23 BUCHANAN, ROBERT. "Walt Whitman." Broadway
    Magazine 1 (November), 188-95.
    Reprinted: 1867.25; 1868.1.
         Review of 1867 Leaves and Drum-Taps.
    Much abused over the years, Whitman has
    become a "sacer vates" with a message for
    the future of personal liberty, universal
    equality, "the divine functions of the
    body." His verse shows biblical influence.
    In "Myself" he uses himself as "the cosmical
    Man." "Adam" may be coarse but its message
    is important. His language is "strong,
    vehement, instantaneously chosen," "sometimes

1867

even rhythmical," although "he sometimes
talks rank nonsense." He lacks "artistic
sympathies" and taste. Some of his lines
are monotonous and prose-like, although
there is "absolute music" in Drum-Taps and
"Lilacs," "in proportion to the absence of
self-consciousness, and the presence of
vivid emotion." Whitman is "the clear
forerunner of the great American poet."

24 ANON. "Literariana." Round Table 6 (2 November), 296.
        Notice of 1867.23. "In common with
almost every late English writer on Walt
Whitman's poems, Mr. Buchanan praises them
warmly for qualities which have hitherto,
by the majority of American critics, been
considered the reverse of commendable."

25 BUCHANAN, ROBERT. "Walt Whitman." Washington
Sunday Morning Chronicle (10 November).
Reprint of 1867.23.

26 HIGGINSON, T. W. "Literature as an Art."
Atlantic Monthly 20 (December), 753.
        Incidental: "It is no discredit to
Walt Whitman that he wrote 'Leaves of Grass,'
only that he did not burn it afterwards."

27 ANON. "The Magazines for December." Nation 5
(5 December), 453.
        Notes the appearance of "Democracy" in
December Galaxy as being "without form and
void," with matter and manner similar to
Whitman's poems.

28 ANON. "Walt Whitman's Utopia." Round Table
6 (7 December), 370-71.
        Whitman's "Democracy" presents a fit-
ting answer to Carlyle's "Shooting Niagara"
in Macmillan's, although lacking Carlyle's
"grim humor." Whitman's "views have a
larger scope," although he is "the more
incomprehensible." Whitman's ideas on
democracy are analyzed, with criticism.

29 ANON. "Notes: Literary." Nation 5 (12 December), 472.
        Review of January Putnam's, noting
O'Connor's story (1868.5), which glorifies
Whitman "as the grand incarnation of
friendliness and brotherliness" he may well
be. However, the displays of physical
affection between men in the story are
disgusting. Yet the story is powerful and
true, and worth the price of the magazine.

30 WAYNE [pseud.?]. "Democracy, Carlyle, and
Whitman." Round Table 6 (21 December),
413-14.
Reprinted: 1868.9.
        Long letter in response to the Whitman
and Carlyle essays. Neither writer is
"intelligible to a majority of his admirers." Wayne criticizes Whitman's condemnation of American literature, his "servile
and not altogether successful" imitation
of Carlyle's style, his "undigested"

thoughts. Though sentimental, Whitman's
ideas on democracy are superior to Carlyle's,
but he "is too certain of its permanence."
In prophesying and not reasoning, he typifies
the national folly. Concluded 1868.7.

1868

BOOKS

1 BUCHANAN, ROBERT. David Gray, and Other
Essays, Chiefly on Poetry. London:
Sampson Low, Son, & Marston. "Walt
Whitman," pp. 203-20.
Reprint of 1867.23.

2 ROSSETTI, WILLIAM MICHAEL, ed. Prefatory
Notice and Postscript to Poems of Walt
Whitman. London: John Camden Hotten,
pp. 1-27; 402-3.
Revision of 1867.13. Revised: 1886.8;
1926.25.
        The bulk of the preface is a summary of
1867.13, adding quotations from Conway
(1866.22) and a letter regarding Whitman
from a friend [Swinburne] criticizing
Whitman's bluster but admiring him.
Rossetti also prints his letter of October
1867 to William Bell Scott in gratitude for
introducing him to Leaves. The preface
includes comments on the broadness of
Whitman's perspective, his perception of
deeper realities, his similarity to
Swedenborg, the different editions, and
explanations of the means of selection for
this volume and the title choice. "Myself"
was unfortunately, but necessarily, sacri-
ficed. Whitman's startling language errs
on an aesthetic, not a strictly moral basis.
He is of the order of great poets, with a
unique position as founder of a new poetic
literature. Readers should ask, not if he
is like other poets, but: "Is he powerful?
Is he American? Is he new? Is he rousing?
Does he feel and make me feel?" Postscript
emphasizes that Whitman had no part in the
selection, notes his plan for new pieces
on death and immortality, and calls for a
complete English edition.

3 SWINBURNE, ALGERNON CHARLES. William Blake.
London: J. C. Hotten, pp. 300-304.
Reprinted: Hindus.
        Blake and Whitman share a passion for
sexual and political freedom, similarity
to "the Pantheistic poetry of the East," a
selfless love which has made them both
martyrs and prophets, and some of the same
shortcomings. Whitman is less profound
but "more frank and fresh." Blake has no
sustained work to equal "Cradle" or "Lilacs"
("the most sweet and sonorous nocturn ever
chanted in the church of the world"), but
their "breadth of outline and charm of
colour" recall Blake.

4 TRENCH, RICHARD CHENEVIX, D. D. Note in A
   Household Book of English Poetry. London:
   Macmillan & Co., p. 414, includes "Come Up
   from the Fields, Father," 359-61.
      Contrary to Rossetti, American poetry
   does not begin with Whitman, for his old
   ideas would not have been heeded "if he
   had not put it more uncouthly than others
   before him." His message is simply the
   lack of distinction between higher and
   lower, holy and profane. But Whitman has
   "one little poem which I could quote with
   real pleasure." (The next edition of this
   anthology, however, drops the Whitman
   poem.)

PERIODICALS

5 O'CONNOR, W. D. "The Carpenter. A Christmas
   Story." Putnam's Magazine 1 (January),
   55-90.
   Reprinted: 1891.9.
      The title character in this story is a
   Whitman-like figure who visits a troubled
   rural family during the Civil War. Christ-
   like, he understands their problems and
   encourages them to solve their difficulties
   through love, such as he has shown in his
   hospital service, where he came to know the
   family's two sons, serving in opposing
   armies.

6 [DENNETT, J. R.] "Literature Truly American."
   Nation 6 (2 January), 7-8.
      Whitman may be indecent in speech and
   deficient in art, but his heartily expressed
   conviction of the "greatness of mere manhood" and of human equality reveal him as
   "a preacher of democracy," though the poet
   of democracy is still to come.

7 WAYNE [pseud.?]. "Democracy, Carlyle, and
   Whitman." Round Table 7 (11 January),
   22-23.
      Concludes 1867.30. Criticizes
   Whitman's ideas of democracy by counter-
   posing his own. Prophecy is not needed
   when the people should be concerned about
   rescuing "imperilled liberty."

8 [CONWAY, MONCURE D.] Review of Swinburne
   (1868.3). Fortnightly Review 9 (February),
   216-20.
      Notes Swinburne's comparison of Blake
   and Whitman. Blake's spirit is evident in
   Whitman's "large and free genius." Whitman
   ignores theological language and form and
   celebrates nature and life "without regard
   to lines of good and ill." However, he
   lacks Blake's "theological defiance."

9 [WAYNE.] "Democracy, Carlyle, and Whitman."
   New Eclectic Magazine 1 (February), 190-94.
   Reprint of 1867.30.

10 ANON. "The Spiteful Letter." Fun (1 February),
   217.
   Reprinted: 1868.11; 1904.20; Saunders.

      A parody of Whitman is included in
   these responses to the question "Who sent
   the spiteful letter to Alfred Tennyson?"
   (evoked by his poem "Lines on Receiving a
   Spiteful Letter"). The editor notes of
   the parody that many manuscript pages are
   omitted, though the reader still remains
   in doubt as to Whitman's answer.

11 ANON. Parodies from Fun. Every Saturday 5
   (29 February), 287.
   Reprint of 1868.10.

12 H[INTON], R. J. "The Poet Walt Whitman--His
   Fame and Fortunes in England and America--
   His Present Position." Rochester Evening
   Express (7 March).
      Overview of Whitman's life, career,
   critical reception. Whitman the man is
   described from the writer's personal acquaintance. The forthcoming edition "has attained
   far more perfect proportions, even than the
   edition of 1867," with "the new part devoted
   to the poetical expression of worship, and
   of the religious faculty in man," nearly
   ready to complete Whitman's plan and volume.
   His work is "beginning to be understood" as
   "founded on ethic intentions, and animated
   by a devout and religious spirit."

*13 ANON. Review of Rossetti (1868.2). Academia
   no. 12 (21 March), 277-79.
   Reported in Trent. Extracts reprinted:
   1868.25; Peattie.
      Whitman's music is bigger and louder,
   requiring judgment by means other than
   scanning. "His pages teem with thought"
   at a level seldom reached and "never so
   long maintained." He is "the most original
   product of his time," the total expression
   of America, "divinely human in his sentiments, Hebraic and heroic in the assertion
   of his personality, intensely fervid in his
   patriotism," universal in his love and
   brotherhood.

14 ANON. "Walt Whitman." London Review 16 (21
   March), 288-89.
      Review of Rossetti (1868.2). Though
   mystical and sometimes incoherent, Whitman
   is a man of power, "the Turner of poets."
   Much is subject to ridicule, but only
   because he is so far from commonplace.
   Though realistic, Whitman insists on "the
   mystic transmutation of spirit," perceiving
   himself as representative. Rossetti provides an excellent means of knowing a writer
   who cannot be overlooked.

15 ANON. "Table Talk." Round Table 7 (21 March),
   187.
      Whitman "has nearly completed a final
   edition of his poems, which, as many of our
   readers who have had occasion to look for
   them are aware, are not easily to be found."
   This edition includes many new pieces and a
   new part which practically fulfills his
   "long-nourished design" of completing his

1868

work by depicting the personality's religious element.

*16 ANON. Review of Rossetti (1868.2). London
Sunday Times (29 March), 7.
Quoted in Peattie.
The excisions will not be offensive to
the haters of expurgated editions. It is
a model as "a book of extracts."

17 BURROUGHS, JOHN. "Before Genius." Galaxy 5
(April), 423-24.
Revised: 1877.1 (with Whitman mention
deleted).
Incidental mention of Whitman and
Emerson as the only advance in American
literature "beyond the merely conventional
and scholastic."

*18 ANON. Review of Rossetti (1868.2). London
Morning Star (6 April).
Quoted in Peattie.
The complete Whitman contains passages
"which no intelligent mind could regard as
immoral; but which undoubtedly adopted a
Biblical plainness of speech such as our
manners today cannot tolerate," and which
Rossetti has omitted to ensure acceptance
of Whitman, the tendency and tone of whose
poems is "pure and noble." He is truly
American, perhaps "founder of a new poetic
dynasty"; he is to be welcomed and understood.

*19 KENT, CHARLES. "Walt Whitman's Poems."
London Sun (17 April), 31490.
Reprinted: WWR 11 (March 1965), 9-19.
Review of Rossetti (1868.2). These
poems, a revelation, were read with pleasure. Although the apparently tainted ones
were deleted, these poems are not emascu-
lated. They have "startling, intense, and
absolute originality," yet are always
rhythmical in their own way, with charm,
grace, pathos, suggestiveness, genius. If
one concedes Whitman's difficulties (form,
"terse but never bald realism," "exotic
verbiage," disregard of syntax), one feels
his magician's spell, as in several passages quoted with comments on their "word-
painting." Whitman's work reveals a wide
philosophy and comprehensive humanity, his
wonder and his exultation in death. Each
poem must be viewed in its entirety.
"Lilacs" and the even finer "Cradle" are
explained. Like other poets, Whitman has
chosen his own emblem, the lilac.

20 ANON. Review of Rossetti (1868.2). Examiner,
no. 3142 (18 April), 245-46.
Quoted in Peattie.
Whitman is well worth studying on both
sides of the Atlantic. He displays both
the wisdom and the folly of contemporary
American thought. His life is traced, with
his shaping out of the past and present a
philosophy that is his own yet is shared
with many great thinkers of the past.

Though Rossetti's selection is suitable for
schoolgirls, the omissions detract from the
book's value as a philosophical study and
his rearrangements and new titles detract
from the poems' accuracy as illustrations
of the temper of a man. These poems "are
the unadorned utterances of a strong man's
strong thoughts," "often highly poetical,"
often not at all, with a "mode of word-
heaping in which there is no style at all."
Whitman denies creeds and urges man's oneness with life, combining the materialism of
Comte with the spiritualism of Swedenborg;
his modern gospel finds favor with many.
"Lilacs" is "the most poetical thing in the
book, judged by the ordinary rules of
poetry," but "Captain" is quoted, being
shorter.

*21 ANON. Review of Rossetti (1868.2). Lloyds
Weekly London Newspaper (19 April), 8.
Quoted in Peattie.
This reviewer read the poem "with great
interest" and "deep gratification." "One
reading is quite insufficient, and time is
required in order that the strangeness of
the beauty may be absorbed and assimilated."

22 ANON. Review of Rossetti (1868.2). Athenaeum,
no. 2113 (25 April), 585-86.
Extract reprinted: 1868.34.
Although some poems rely on mere lists,
certain entire poems and occasional passages
triumphantly reveal the essentials of poet-
ry--emotion and imagination--most outstandingly "Cradle," explicated and quoted as an
example of Whitman's fine "unconscious power
of symbolization." His beliefs are worthy,
except "that he cannot recognize the possibility of goodness" in an aristocrat;
they reveal him "a wide, sincere, and passionate thinker," with no new ideas but "a
new combination of separate views."

23 ANON. "Walt Whitman." Living Age 97 (25
April), 251-52.
Reprint of 1868.14.

24 ANON. Notice of April Galaxy. Round Table 7
(25 April), 268.
"The paper which will probably attract
most notice is the second of Walt Whitman's
remarkable yawps," entitled "Personalism."
It surpasses his former article about democracy "in incoherency and bombastic unreason."
Its "gist" is summarized.

25 ANON. "Table-Talk." Round Table 7 (25 April),
269.
Extract reprinted from 1868.13.
The Round Table writer suggests that
English critics may be favoring Whitman's
celebration of "lusty nature" out of disgust
at "the very artificiality of their native
poets."

26 ANON. "Walt Whitman's Poems." Saturday Review
25 (2 May), 589-90.

Reprinted: 1868.33; 1868.35; Hindus.
Review of Rossetti (1868.2). Rossetti's
regret at eliminating so many poems is
appropriate, for he suppresses significant
evidence, such as "Myself," a key to understanding Whitman, who may attract some by
his novelty, unconventionality, and obscurity. Perhaps Rossetti regards him as
an antidote to the feebleness and sentimentality of much modern poetry. If a poem
like "Visages" (quoted) is poetry, we need
another word for what Shakespeare wrote.
In response to the questions in Rossetti's
preface: yes, Whitman is American, like
"certain forms of rowdyism and vulgarity";
he has no new thought; his unconventionality is cheap. He will have no influence
on American or English poetry.

27 S[MALLEY], G. W. "Great Britain," New York
Tribune (9 May), 1:2.
Paragraph criticizing the Athenaeum
(1868.22) for regarding Whitman's work as
poetry. He is much discussed in private
but favorably so by only one source, not a
competent one. "Carlyle likens him to a
buffalo, useful in fertilizing the soil,"
but mistaken in supposing that "the world
desires to contemplate closely" such contributions.

28 ANON. "Carlyle on Whitman." Washington
Evening Star (13 May), 1:4.
Quotes from 1868.27. Whitman's Ameri-
can admirers will hardly relish Carlyle's
characterization of his productions as
"Buffalo Chips."

29 ANON. Review of Rossetti (1868.2). Public
Opinion (London) 13 (16 May), 505-6.
"We really are at a loss to understand
how any man of intelligence and judgment
can honestly applaud the productions of
Whitman." He is not a poet, his scribblings
"entitled to unmitigated contempt." "He
shrieks and wails in the most incoherent
manner," "deals in barbarous and hideous
verbiage," with ideas jumbled together
carelessly, full of "bombastic doggerel."

30 ANON. Paragraph. Round Table 7 (16 May), 316.
Comments on Whitman's political opposition to Carlyle. Association with his intellectual inferiors has led Whitman to use
his "natural powers" only to produce "such
inconceivable drivel as his pseudo-political
articles" in Galaxy. His notion of democracy is hardly to be admired.

31 ANON. "Mr. Swinburne's Essay on Blake."
Broadway Magazine 1 (June), 728-30.
Review of 1868.3, noting the comparison
of Blake to Whitman. Rossetti's edition
(1868.2) will give a false impression,
lacking "some of his strongest and best
things," which are "outspoken rather than
indecent." Unlike other transatlantic
poets, he is "an original and thoroughly

American genius," though a prophet rather
than a poet. While the metrical promise
of his initial lines is seldom fulfilled,
his writings have "a strange sort of rough
music." The discipline of rhyming might
make him less repetitious. His work has "a
fresh, healthy, physical glow" and "hearty
sympathy," reflecting his actual life. He
shows biblical influence "though his language is more nineteenth-century and vernacular."

32 [WHITE, RICHARD GRANT.] Review of Swinburne
(1868.3). Galaxy 5 (June), 792.
Incidental: "It is not surprising that
Mr. Swinburne finds in Blake a great likeness to Walt Whitman." But this theme is
not of interest to ordinary readers.

33 ANON. "Walt Whitman's Poems." Living Age 97
(6 June), 637-40.
Reprint of 1868.26.

34 ANON. "A Word Out of the Sea." Living Age 97
(13 June), 702-3.
Extract reprinted from 1868.22.

35 ANON. Review of Rossetti (1868.2). New
Eclectic Magazine 2 (July), 371-75.
Reprint of 1868.26.

36 FREILIGRATH, FERDINAND. "Walt Whitman." New
Eclectic Magazine 2 (July), 325-29.
Reprinted: 1868.38; Miller. Retranslated:
1892.191; 1897.84; 1915.33.
Translated from the Augsburg Allgemeinen
Zeitung (24 April). For his admirers,
Whitman is the only American poet, derived
from the soil, expressing his age. Adverse
criticism does not trouble him. His verses
seem rugged and formless but are "not devoid
of euphony." His language is "homely,
hearty, straightforward," the tone is
"rhapsodical, like that of a seer." He is
quite uneven. His "I" is part of America,
the earth, mankind, the all. Everything
for him is symbolic of a spiritual fact.
He makes ordinary verse-making seem childish.
Is this the poetry of the age to come? "Is
Walt Whitman a greater [sic] than Richard
Wagner?" Biographical sketch is given from
Rossetti (1868.2); extract from Conway
(1866.22).

37 ANON. "Walt Whitman." Chambers's Journal of
Popular Literature, Science, and Art 45
(4 July), 420-25.
Review of Rossetti (1868.2). Despite
the extravagant praise, Whitman is noteworthy, "the first characteristic poetical
writer that the United States have produced."
His very faults are national; he is "Yankee
to the backbone" in his independence and
originality. The present edition, bowdler-
ized for the Old Country's "squeamish
tastes," is suitable for ladies. His prose
is akin to Emerson's, his poetry to no one's.
An extract from the 1855 Preface, quoted,

1868

is "a fine lay-sermon." His titles are
"almost always affected or unmeaning."
Long extracts are quoted, especially from
"his most characteristic poem," "To Think
of Time." His influence will be great and
may produce pupils surpassing him. His
"picturings" are often "too prolonged,"
though vivid and "expressed with power."
His poems have humor, though perhaps un-
intentionally. Rossetti (1868.2) and
Conway (1866.22) are quoted.

38 FREILIGRATH, FERDINAND. "Walt Whitman."
Boston Commonwealth (4 July), 4:3-4.
Reprint of 1868.36.

39 TOWNSEND, GEORGE ALFRED. "Letter from George
Alfred Townsend." Cleveland Leader (23
September).
Describes Whitman's appearance while
walking the streets; a conversation with
him, in which he explains his rejection of
rhyme and measure because they are not the
way of nature. Whitman, "boatswain's
whistle to the ship Optimist, a sort of
John Baptist to the Great American Poet
coming," is "really an earnest man," though
fettered to his character. He has only
"the vague apparition of a great poem," for
he is too barbaric, but he is fascinating
for America and has "devouter admirers"
than Whittier or Longfellow.

40 [LOWELL, JAMES RUSSELL.] Review of John James
Piatt's poems. North American Review 107
(October), 661.
Reprinted: 1920.20.
Discusses the projected American poet,
who requires universal, not merely provincial traits. "Of the sham-shaggy, who have
tried the trick of Jacob upon us, we have
had quite enough, and may safely doubt
whether this satyr of masquerade is to be
our representative singer."

41 ANON. "Minor Topics." New York Times (1
October), 6:6.
Describes Whitman's appearance again on
Broadway, as an individual figure who
attracts attention; his recent edition; his
reception; the remarkable endurance of his
book despite attacks on "the appearance in
our easy-going, imitative literature of an
obstinate, tenacious, determined living
American man." Vistas is anticipated.

42 BENSON, EUGENE. "Democratic Deities." Galaxy
6 (November), 663.
Incidental: Whitman represents not an
average man but "a superb illustration" of
the better and higher man that democracy
can produce. He "may tenderly and gravely
celebrate his humanity and comprehensive
solicitude," but we need specific individual
men to provide us with positive examples of
merit as our writers and preachers.

43 ANON. Paragraph. Round Table 8 (7 November),
312.
Whitman "is said to have been for a
long time 'engaged in a poem, or series of
poems, intended to touch the religious and
spiritual wants of humanity,'" with which
he proposes to finish off Leaves. His
summer work has included Vistas, "a small
prose work," and "several papers for London
magazines."

*44 POORE, BEN: PERLEY. "Waifs from Washington.
Personal." Boston Journal (20 November).
Quoted in Martin.
Whitman's "imposing figure and cheery
face" have been seen on Pennsylvania Avenue
as he returns from work.

45 ANON. "Table Talk." Once a Week (London)
n.s. 2 (12 December), 496.
Reprinted: Saunders.
Parody: "I am W*lt Wh*tm*n."

1869

BOOKS

1 STRANGFORD, Viscountess, ed. A Selection from
the Writings of Viscount Strangford. Vol. 2.
London: Richard Bentley. "Walt Whitman,"
pp. 297-300.
Reprint of 1866.13.

PERIODICALS

*2 [WHITMAN, WALT.] Note. Washington Star (18
January).
Quoted in 1929.60 and Bradley/Blodgett.
Note on "Proud Music" in Atlantic
Monthly (February 1869): "a long poem from
his sturdy pen, and one of the very best,
to our notion, that he has yet written."

3 ANON. "Walt Whitman." Washington Sunday
Chronicle (9 May).
Describes Whitman's current situation,
habits, and physical condition as he approaches his fiftieth birthday. A late
German critic has termed him "'the most
radically Christian and Socratic poet of any
modern writer,'" for his emphasis on friendship and inner light and his attitude toward
material things as the gateway to spiritual
existence. A revised collection of his
verses will be printed next summer, along
with Vistas. Whitman is quoted in philosophical response to the accusations made
against his character. Recent fine portraits
are noted.

4 [AUSTIN, ALFRED.] "The Poetry of the Period:
The Poetry of the Future." Temple Bar 27
(October), 314-27.
Reprinted: 1870.1.
Whitman's four themes, appropriate to
the present age of which he claims to be the
bard, are America, democracy, personality,

and materialism. He recognizes no distinctions between persons as to degree or virtue, or between the body and the soul. His poems, resembling "the improvising of savages," contain much nastiness. Contrary to the opinion of his admirers, his "grotesque, ungrammatical, and repulsive rhapsodies" have nothing in common with the Bible or any other honored literature. Whitman's "revolt with a vengeance" was necessary considering contemporary poetry, which is dependent on feudalism and gentility and "deficient in all masculine and lofty qualities."

1870

BOOKS

1 AUSTIN, ALFRED. The Poetry of the Period. London: Richard Bentley. "The Poetry of the Future," pp. 192-223. Reprint of 1869.4.

2 STILES, HENRY R. A History of the City of Brooklyn. Vol. 3. Brooklyn: Published by subscription, pp. 890, 935, 938.
Notes Whitman's association with the Brooklyn Freeman (first published 25 April 1848) and the Eagle (his editorship beginning 26 February 1846).

PERIODICALS

3 H[OWITT], W[ILLIAM]. "The Poems of Walt Whitman." Spiritual Magazine, n.s. 5 (January), 34-40.
Along with much verbiage and Yankee brag, Whitman has bright new thoughts and tender sentiments. His thought is true spiritualism, emphasizing joy and sympathy and "the eternal springs and streams of primal being," as no mere poet of the world (like Browning or Swinburne) has done. Extensive quotations support these assertions.

4 [GILCHRIST, ANNE.] "A Woman's Estimate of Walt Whitman (From Late Letters by an English Lady to W. M. Rossetti)." Radical 7 (May), 345-59.
Reprinted: 1887.6; In Re; 1918.9.
Abridged: Bucke; Miller; Hindus.
Rossetti introduces the essay as "about the fullest, farthest-reaching, and most eloquent appreciation of Whitman yet put into writing," and "the most valuable" because from a woman's point of view. The essay consists of three letters (22 and 23 June, 11 July 1869), with additions: Whitman's poems were like "electric streams," uniquely rewarding, fresh like nature. Poetry must accept him "as equal with her highest" or else "stand aside, and admit there is something come into the world nobler, diviner than herself." He fearlessly deals with reality and the

present, conveying his brotherhood and love in "Calamus," "Drum-Taps," his hospital work, and his admission of the darkness within himself. His enumerations are "necessary parts of the great whole." He rejects poetic diction in favor of words taken "from the varied experiences of life." He cannot, even in the complete edition, corrupt women readers, for he reveals that shame in the act leading to parenthood is not in accord with God's will, soul and body being one. His poetry follows the path that science has already laid out. He is an appropriate poet for the greatness of the American land.

5 ANON. "The National Capital . . . Personal." New York Times (16 August), 1:4.
Notes the appearance in the Washington Star (unlocated) of an item about Whitman, "a treasury clerk, recently called the poet of Democracy," receiving an invitation from Tennyson to his home.

6 BURROUGHS, JOHN. "More about Nature and the Poets." Appletons' Journal 4 (10 September), 315-16.
Incidental discussion: Whitman alone of recent poets reaches deeply into nature as "a bard certainly aboriginal and virile enough," "thoroughly Greek in his attitude toward man," treating nature in a new way, considering her grandest facets and her lowliest, absorbing modern science in the spirit of religion.

7 SIGMA [pseud.?]. "Washington Gossip. . . . Walt Whitman at the Latest Dates." New York Evening Mail (27 October), 1:1-2.
The Washington papers have all noted Whitman's return to town. He is well-known by sight to all citizens since he lives so much out of doors. Description of his appearance, habits, interest in the news, political stances (domestic and foreign). Washington's qualities make this a fit place for him, "both in his personnel and what his works represent." O'Connor and Burroughs are also described.

8 ANON. "New Publications." New York Times (11 November), 2:2.
Paragraph review of Leaves, Vistas, Passage. Whitman cannot be recommended to the general reader, his books fit only "for those who make researches in literature not suited to family reading." Knowledge of the man is needed to know his work.

1871

BOOKS

1 BURROUGHS, JOHN. Notes on Walt Whitman, as Poet and Person. New York: J. S. Redfield, 126 pp. No index.
Reprint of 1867.1, with "Supplementary

1871

Notes," pp. 109-26.
The discussion is brought up to the
1871-72 Leaves, according to Whitman
the final edition. The new poems are
explicated, showing the new volume to be
a clearer expression than before "of that
combination in which Death and the Unknown
are as essential and important to the
author's plan of a complete human Personality as Life and the Known." Whitman,
following the German idealist philosophers,
uses the material as a door to the spiritual realm. Leaves depicts the nineteenth
century. Whitman is a sane model for his
readers, though not without faults. He
balances his "enormous sense of objective
nature" with an "equally enormous egoism."
Recent commentary on Whitman is quoted.

2 FORMAN, H. BUXTON. Our Living Poets: An
Essay in Criticism. London: Tinsley
Bros., pp. 11, 302-3, 370.
Incidental comparisons of Whitman's
work to poems by Swinburne and William Bell
Scott. Whitman reveals "the true artist's
unlimited sympathy with all animate and
inanimate nature" in "the intensest form
it has ever yet taken."

3 SWINBURNE, ALGERNON CHARLES. Songs Before
Sunrise. London: F. S. Ellis. "To Walt
Whitman in America," pp. 143-49. Includes
epigraphs from Whitman on frontispiece and
p. [xii].
Extract reprinted: Legler.
Poem in rhymed stanzas urging Whitman,
as representative of the American spirit,
to bring new life to Europe. Direct references only in title and stanzas one and
three.

PERIODICALS

4 [DOWDEN, EDWARD.] Review of Leaves, Vistas,
and Passage. Westminster Review 96 (July),
33-68.
Reprinted: 1878.3. Abridged: Miller;
Hindus; Murphy.
Whitman is unlike his American predecessors, who are closer to the European
than the American mentality. His literature of democracy differs from the exclusive and stylistically rigid literature of
aristocracy. He seeks "the recognition of
new forces in language," "creation of a
new manner of speech," and music without
syllable counting. Inclusive in his sympathies, he makes "the people itself, in
its undiminished totality," appear in his
poems; hence his democratic catalogues.
Rather than an individual hero, he celebrates himself "as a man and an American,"
his epic hero being the American nation as
leader of the human race. He recognizes
the flaws of America, but without despair.
His portrayal of sex, though offensive to
some, is "in a spirit as remote from base
curiosity as from insolent licence." His

unique presentation of comradeship, an
equal love between men, makes us love the
man for this "power capable of counter-
balancing the materialism, the selfishness,
the vulgarity of American democracy." His
grass is an appropriate democratic symbol.
He uses the pathetic fallacy not out of
egotism, but to share with the world his
emotions. His faith in the future leads
him occasionally to deny evil, but his
concern with personal qualities requires
the preference of the virtuous over the
vicious. Whitman's purpose is to stimulate
the reader to "go upon his own way."

*5 POORE, BEN: PERLEY. "Waifs from Washington."
Boston Journal (28 March).
Reprinted: Martin.
"Whitman's friends are enjoying an
obituary notice of that true-hearted poet,
who is not aware that he has been killed
by a railroad accident at the North. . . ."

6 ANON. "Americanisms: A Study of Words and
Manners." Southern Review 9 (April), 318-
19.
The end of this article discusses
Whitman as "the writer who is supposed now-
a-days to express most clearly and originally
the texture of American thought." However,
his "proclivity for filth" appears even
when he treats the most ordinary themes.
Passages from "Myself" are quoted, revealing
"great power and tenderness," "real and
genuine poetry, of a very high order, originality, thought, and a flush of young
imagination," although its "unbridled
license of speech" makes it rough and reckless. "Yet, this is the poetry of the
future,--the culmination of American culture!" Concluded 1871.7.

7 ANON. "Americanisms: A Study of Words and
Manners." Southern Review 9 (July), 533,
558.
Concludes 1871.6. Whitman is used
incidentally as an example of America's
gaining her own literature.

8 FOUNTAIN, LUCY. "An Evening with Swinburne."
Galaxy 12 (August), 233-34.
Records conversation with Swinburne
regarding Whitman, whom he reads much and
ranks second to Hugo among living poets.
He praised "Cradle" and "Lilacs," but
criticized the catalogues, despite this
writer's defense of them. He read his ode
dedicated to Whitman, before its publication.

9 R[ICHARD], H[INTON] J. [sic]. "Washington
Letter. Walt Whitman Personally, Poetically
and Prospective." Cincinnati Commercial
(26 August), 1-2.
Describes Whitman's relation to his
job, his ability to put all his efforts
into writing rather than work, his dress,
appearance, personality; traces his reputation and recognition by important literary

figures. The author recalls his own stay in the hospital when Whitman ministered to him.

10 ANON. "Walt Whitman Recognized." Springfield Daily Republican (4 September), 2:1-3.

Traces history and reception of Leaves, largely negative despite classic precedents for the "ithyphallic passages." Emerson's eulogy of Thoreau is quoted, with the explanation that Whitman is the person "'not known to this audience'" of the three men Emerson cites as significantly influencing Thoreau. Whitman's war experiences are described. His latest book reveals use of some old Greek meters.

11 ANON. "The American Institute. Inauguration of the Fair. The Opening Exercises--Poem by Walt Whitman." New York Commercial Advertiser (7 September), 3:1-2.

Prints "After All" as delivered by Whitman, "the national poet," who was greeted on appearance "with loud and prolonged applause." His recitation "seemed to fully meet the expectations of his auditors, and his poem was declared on all hands to be an appropriate and marked feature of the opening exercises."

12 ANON. "The American Institute Fair." New York Evening Post (7 September), 4:8.

Describes Whitman's reading of his poem for the institute, which showed him "a good elocutionist."

13 ANON. "The Fair of the American Institute. Walt Whitman's Poem." New York Evening Post (7 September), 2:5-6.

Headnote to the printing of "After All" calls his recitation of this poem "the most novel feature" of the fair.

*14 ANON. "Our Great Poet." New York Globe (7 September).
Reprinted: Traubel I.

Editorial. Tonight the "one man who is recognized in the Old World as a great poet" from America will deliver his poem at the fair. "What other American poet has ever been honored like this?" He is the best choice for the job. His appearance and habits are described as similar to Horace Greeley's. His life is briefly described. "He is a whole-souled fellow" and worth hearing.

15 ANON. "American Institute Fair." New York Times (8 September), 2:1-2.

Headnote to "After All" calls it "a characteristic production," fit for the occasion. Whitman's delivery of it is described as "constrained" and modest. Few could hear him because of the size and noise of the room and his soft voice, but those who heard applauded frequently.

16 ANON. "The American Institute." New York Tribune (8 September), 2:1.

Describes the fair and prints extracts from "After All." Whitman was received by applause.

17 ANON. "A Whitmaniacal Catalogue." New York World (8 September), 4:5.

The managers of the fair made an appropriate choice in Whitman if they wanted a catalogue of the objects on exhibit, since that is what he is noted for. He evidently based his poem on "those two great American works, 'What I Know About Farming' and 'Essays upon Political Economy,'" with "a confusion of mind never before paralleled." His poem (though it cannot be called so "merely because a muse is violently dragged into it") is summarized.

18 ANON. "Poetry and Ploughs . . . Barbaric Yaup [sic] from Whitman." New York World (8 September), 8:1-3.

Headnote to printing of "After All," Whitman's delivery of which "no one among the meeting-house benches could have heard," although the managers (provided with copies of it) applauded where appropriate.

19 [TAYLOR, BAYARD.] "The Battle of the Bards." New York Tribune (9 September), 4:6.
Reprinted: 1876.4; Saunders.

The necessary omission for reasons of space of parts of Whitman's "remarkable poem" (1871.16) is regretted. But an extract has been retrieved and is here quoted: "Who was it sang of the procreant urge" (a parody). Parodies of other poets on the theme of the fair follow.

20 K., E. "An Anecdote of Walt Whitman." New York Evening Post (11 September), 1:3.
Quoted in Hendrick.

Describes Whitman having his portrait done by a lady and liking the color of a deep flush upon his face, though someone thought the portrait one of a drinking man.

21 ANON. Editorial. New York Sun (11 September), 2:3.

The critics have decried Whitman's new poem, but he anticipated their objections. "He is too rude in his contempt for the juggling artifices of ordinary rhymesters, and too audacious in his disregard of established literary usages ever, [sic] to be tolerated by those who admire literary millinery as the proper outfit of a poet. But among poets themselves he will not fail of due recognition; and the greater the poet the more cordial will be his admiration for this vigorous and genuine son of the soil." No American man of letters is more highly thought of by Tennyson, Browning, Arnold, and others. His most marked quality is his Americanism, "large, masculine, free from humbug." He is patriotic, "democratic, human, and unconventional." His poetry has

1871

more immortal qualities than common poets'
"soft sentimentalities."

22 ANON. "Walt Whitman as a Speaker." Washington Chronicle (11 September).
Reprinted: Whitman, After All, Not to
Create Only (Boston: Roberts Bros., 1871).
Quotes a letter from New York on
Whitman's institute poem, describing the
scene, his delivery, the poem's occasionally playful but predominantly serious tone,
his favorable reception, although his real
audience came only with the poem's publication in most of the New York and Brooklyn
dailies.

23 NOEL, Hon. RODEN. "A Study of Walt Whitman,
the Poet of Modern Democracy, I." Dark
Blue 2 (October), 241-53.
Revised: 1886.4. Reprinted: Cameron
(1971).
Whitman, "American democracy incarnate,"
is more prophet than artist so that he may
convey the intense sense of personality.
His expression is often but not always
deficient, returning poetry to an emphasis
on content. He reveals an influence more
oriental than biblical. He is sometimes
coarse but never prurient. "Lilacs" reveals
his ability to create "a simple, beautiful
whole," matching language to idea, in contrast to the frequently fragmented quality
of the exuberant catalogues. Drum-Taps is
praised. Concluded 1871.26.

24 ANON. "Table-Talk." Appletons' Journal 6
(7 October), 415.
Commentary on "After All," sometimes
striking, more often amusing. Whitman's
philosophical stance errs in praising labor
to the denigration of the intellect. He
ought not reject the past but offer it to
the laborer, who should be elevated through
his imagination.

*25 POORE, BEN: PERLEY. "Waifs from Washington.
Literary Notes." Boston Journal (7 October), Supplement.
Reprinted: Martin.
Tennyson has invited Whitman to visit
him: "it is feared that the latter intends
to read aloud to the unfortunate Laureate
that catalogue of American products and
trades which he picked up in the American
Institute and blindly labeled a poem," to
be published by Roberts Brothers "for the
dementation of the American public."

26 NOEL, Hon. RODEN. "A Study of Walt Whitman,
the Poet of Modern Democracy, II." Dark
Blue 2 (November), 336-49.
Revised: 1886.4. Reprinted: Cameron
(1971).
Concludes 1871.23. "Calamus" is discussed, its ideal of manly friendship
strongly opposed to modern isolation.
Whitman's doctrine of equality is flawed,
for the average man should not be the

measure of the whole universe.

*27 POORE, BEN: PERLEY. "Waifs from Washington."
Boston Journal (12 December).
Reprinted: Martin.
Notes Whitman as "one of the leading
promenaders" on Pennsylvania Avenue.

1872

BOOKS

1 ALLIBONE, S. AUSTIN. A Critical Dictionary of
English Literature and British and American
Authors. Vol. 3. Philadelphia: J. B.
Lippincott & Co., p. 2700.
Brief listing of biographical data,
works, and reviews, noting conflicting
opinions. Negative English criticism may
indicate a national jealousy for the fame
of Shakespeare, Milton, and Spenser, "and
there is a good deal in Whitman that will
be found in neither of these."

2 BUCHANAN, ROBERT. The Fleshly School of Poetry
and Other Phenomena of the Day. London:
Strahan & Co. "Walt Whitman," pp. 96-97;
also 89.
Reprinted: Hindus.
Although often condemned like the
"fleshly" Rossetti and Swinburne, Whitman
is not an imitative singer like them, but
"a Bard, outrageously original and creative,"
a "spiritual person" and "colossal mystic."
His fifty lines of indecency, unnecessary
and silly like some by Shakespeare and
others, are forgivable because surrounded
by "spotless love and chastity." He could
hardly have been "a man of strong animal
passions" because "an epicure in lust" would
have avoided the "frightful violence in his
expressions." Buchanan disclaims sympathy
with Whitman's pantheism but admires Whitman
for his wealth of knowledge, vast conceptions,
noble and practical teaching. His style
relates prose cadence and metrical verse,
coming close to "perfect speech," and is
"his greatest contribution to knowledge."

3 DRAKE, FRANCIS S. Dictionary of American
Biography. Boston: James R. Osgood & Co.,
p. 978.
Brief paragraph of biography and editions.

4 HART, JOHN S. A Manual of American Literature:
A Text-Book for Schools and Colleges.
Philadelphia: Eldredge & Bro., pp. 376-78.
Whitman "is the most singular instance
on record of a successful poetical iconoclast." His verse may not scan, but the
lines are rhythmical; out of vulgar and
prosaic subjects he creates "forms of delicacy, grace, and beauty." Sketch of his
life and character. He rejects the past
and applies American freedom to art, with
democratic sympathies. "His diction is extremely terse and idiomatic," his thought

"unimpeded." Whether a true poet or only "a poetic nature," he will endure for having "aroused the public from dull conventionality and imitation, and set us upon independent thinking."

5 ROSSETTI, WILLIAM MICHAEL, ed. Preface to <u>American Poems</u>. London: E. Moxon, Son & Co., pp. xxiv, xxvi-vii.

Whitman is the greatest American poet. He is not insensible to grace or art but works on a massive scale of intuitions, sympathies, and observations. Over ninety pages of Whitman's poems are here anthologized.

6 SWINBURNE, ALGERNON CHARLES. <u>Under the Microscope</u>. London: D. White, pp. 45-56. Reprinted: Murphy.

As apparent in several poems, the poet in Whitman often yields to the formalist, too rigid in his poetic and democratic doctrines. Swinburne criticizes his catalogues and his doctrinaire rejection of rhythm. Whitman is best when arousing the reader. He is original but will found no school of poetry.

7 UNDERWOOD, FRANCIS H. <u>A Hand-Book of English Literature. Intended for the Use of High Schools</u>. Boston: Lee & Shepard, p. 461. Reprinted: 1893.13.

Headnote to "Come Up from the Fields, Father" and "Dirge," pp. 462-64: inaccurate biographical sketch; description of <u>Leaves</u> which contains "pictures of marked originality and unquestionable power," as well as some indefensible passages. Whitman's form appears strange, but reading aloud reveals him a poet, with "the poet's incommunicable power to touch the heart." His lines are "diamonds in the rough," lacking appropriate form, yet "he has set down some of the most striking thoughts and sketched some of the most vivid scenes to be found in modern literature" and is "less indebted to others for his ideas and for his power of illustration than almost any American writer."

PERIODICALS

8 ANON. "Recent Literature." <u>Atlantic Monthly</u> 29 (January), 108-9.

Criticizes the inclusion of a laudatory introduction in the volume presenting <u>After All</u>, "one of his curious catalogues of the American emotions, inventions, and geographical subdivisions."

9 ANON. "Book Reviews." <u>Canadian Monthly and National Review</u> 1 (March), 279.

Review of Forman (1871.2), over-worshipful of Whitman, "the Nemesis of an over-refined and artificial school," whose work may refresh readers whose brains are racked with Browning, but it is hardly poetry and perhaps "merely rampant bestiality."

10 [TAYLOR, BAYARD.] "Diversions of the Echo Club. Night the Fourth." <u>Atlantic Monthly</u> 29 (April), 451. Reprinted: 1876.4.

Incidental: in his life, N. P. Willis "was as natural a democrat as Walt Whitman."

11 ANON. "By Mail and Telegraph." <u>New York Times</u> (27 April), 1:4.

Paragraph on the appeal Whitman has made in the Washington papers for "immediate pecuniary assistance for a man of genius" (himself), who was once a bright star in literature but now is poor and ailing.

12 ANON. "Walt Whitman." <u>Once a Week</u> 26 (1 June), 501-5.

Whitman is "peculiarly an American production," his poems "filled with an American spirit." He will shock the ordinary reader of poetry but will be appreciated by those who regard "true poetry as something more than fine words." A letter from Whitman on his purpose is quoted, as are extracts showing him as "the true prophet." "Old Ireland" presents an "intensely human" picture. Biographical information is presented from O'Connor (1866.2) and Rossetti (1868.2). His hospital service entitles him to the love and respect of every right-thinking person.

13 ANON. "Dartmouth College. The Exercises Marred by the Inclement Weather--Walt Whitman's Poem." New York <u>Herald</u> (26 June), 3:4.

Whitman is to recite a poem, here printed, at the Dartmouth commencement.

*14 [WHITMAN, WALT.] "Walt Whitman's Poem Today At Dartmouth College." Washington <u>Evening Star</u> (26 June). Reprinted: Whitman Supplement 1972; <u>WWR</u> 1972.

Account of Whitman's reading of the poem, which "needs full perusal and careful study," like all his works, and which echoes his fervid patriotism and reveals his belief in new forms and disapproval of contemporary writers. Extracts are quoted.

15 ANON. "Dartmouth College. Walt Whitman at the Commencement Exercises--The Recitation of His Poem, as Published in the Herald, Creates Quite a Sensation." New York <u>Herald</u> (27 June), 5:5.

Describes Whitman, his delivery of the twenty-five-minute poem, his voice's "vitality and elasticity," his "outward quiet" and "interior magnetism," his poem, containing "eloquence and poetry of the highest class," a celebration of his country like those of classical poets but seeing grandeur in the future of his country, not the past.

16 STRAHAN, ALEXANDER. "Norman Macleod." <u>Contemporary Review</u> 20 (July), 303.

Incidental application to Macleod of

1872

the refrain of "For You, 0 Democracy," "by one of the truest poets of our time" (unnamed).

17 [TAYLOR, BAYARD.] "Diversions of the Echo Club. Night the Eighth." Atlantic Monthly 30 (July), 83-84.
Reprinted: 1876.4. Parody reprinted: Saunders.
     As part of an ongoing literary discussion, several imaginary characters discuss Whitman's form, language, sympathies, occasional irregular rhythms, "modern, half-Bowery-boy, half-Emersonian apprehension of the old Greek idea of physical life." One offers the parody "Camerados."

*18 BENTZON, Mme. [Thérèse]. "A French Opinion of Walt Whitman." New York Spectator and Weekly Commercial Advertiser (19 July).
Reported in Asselineau.
     Translation of article from Revue des Deux Mondes (1 June 1872).

19 SWINBURNE, ALGERNON CHARLES. "Victor Hugo: L'Année Terrible." Fortnightly Review n.s. 12, o.s. 18 (1 September), 246n.
     Note quotes "0 Star of France" by "the greatest of American voices," "the first poet of American democracy," citing Whitman's praise of Byron and Hugo in Vistas.

20 HINTON, RICHARD J. [by WALT WHITMAN?] "Walt Whitman in Europe." Kansas Magazine 2 (December), 499-502.
     Describes Whitman's appearance and works. Whitman intends to let Leaves "stand as his poetic expression of American individuality," while Vistas and other later pieces will be put into a new volume as "an expression of nationality." European criticisms are cited. Bentzon (see 1872.18) expressed amazement and terror at Whitman but praised his portrait of war in Drum-Taps. Fore Ide og Virkelighed (June 1872) examined Leaves and Vistas from the literary, communistic, and spiritualistic points of view. Despite neglect, Whitman has spent the best years of his life "illustrating the idea that the true greatness of New World democracy is not to be best attained in political freedom or geographical magnitude or general worldly prosperity," but in founding a native poetic literature.

1873

BOOKS

1 SYMONDS, JOHN ADDINGTON. Studies of the Greek Poets. London: Smith, Elder, & Co., p. 422n.
     "Walt Whitman is more truly Greek than any other man of modern times. Hopeful and fearless, accepting the world as he finds it, recognizing the value of each human impulse, shirking no obligation, self-regulated by a law of perfect health, he,

in the midst of a chaotic age, emerges clear and distinct, at one with nature, and therefore Greek."

PERIODICALS

*2 WOODHULL, VICTORIA C. "Victoria C. Woodhull's Address." Woodhull & Claflin's Weekly (25 January), 3-7, 14-15.
Reprinted: The Victoria Woodhull Reader, edited by Madeleine B. Stern (Weston, Mass.: M & S Press, 1974).
     This address criticizing puritanical attitudes toward sex cites Whitman's dismissal by Harlan, who misread "the sublimest passages of inspiration, with the bleared ignorance of uncultured stupidity." Whitman, "the distinguished poet and philanthropist," "the most representative and characteristic of American poets," was well defended in O'Connor's book (1866.2, quoted), "the most exhaustive display of the freedom which has been accorded to genius, in this direction, which is to be found anywhere in literature."

*3 POORE, BEN: PERLEY. "Waifs from Washington. . . Personal." Boston Journal (29 January).
Reprinted: Martin.
     Notes Whitman's "slight stroke of paralysis."

4 DENT, JOHN C. "America and her Literature." Temple Bar 37 (February), 396-406, passim.
     Most of American literature "might have been written by Englishmen," but "a purely American literature" is taking shape with Whitman, Twain, Miller, and Harte, Whitman being "imcomparably the most original." He shares with Wordsworth contemporary abuse, "passionate susceptibility of feeling," "depth of philosophic meditation," "homeliness of expression," and "disregard for, and contempt of, classic precedents." Whitman will not achieve popularity in his lifetime, but merits his country's favor for his deeds. "He is the very incarnation of American democracy: fresh, hopeful," and self-reliant. One should read him for oneself (although Rossetti's edition omits "Myself," "the author's masterpiece").

5 R[ICHARD], H[INTON] J. [sic]. "New York Letter. . . . Walt Whitman." Cincinnati Commercial (25 February), 2.
     Describes Whitman's praiseworthy devotion to the wounded soldiers; recalls accompanying him on his rounds, the soldiers' love for him. "Walt had little to give," but "he gave more than any other man I knew."

6 KERR, ORPHEUS C. "The Poets' Airing; or, The Rejected Balloon Ballads." New York Daily Graphic (2 August), 222.
Reprinted: Saunders.
     Among the parody poems memorializing the transatlantic balloon trip is one by

"W-lt Wh-tm-an," "Aeriform Aermica," which
has "too much of the practical character"
and "is unsingable, save to Wagner's music."

7 ANON. "Walt Whitman." New York Times (20
   August), 5:3.
        Paragraph on Whitman now living in
   Camden, recovering from his stroke, according to his letter to a New York friend
   (quoted).

8 BURROUGHS, JOHN. "The Birds of the Poets."
   Scribner's Monthly 6 (September), 567-68,
   574.
        Reprinted: 1877.1.
        Whitman's treatment of the bird in
   "Cradle" (quoted) is "entirely ideal,"
   "eminently characteristic," "altogether
   poetical," its free translation of a bird-
   song "unmatched in our literature." The
   use of the bird in "Lilacs" is also praised.

9 LE BARON, MARIE. "Walt Whitman at Home.
   Visit of a Lady to the Poet--His Personal
   Appearance--His Illness and Convalescence."
   New York Daily Graphic (3 September), 434
   [should be numbered 442].
        Pleasant personal account of Whitman's
   physical condition, surroundings. "He
   works slowly, and his poetical sentences
   are altered and rewritten many times."

10 ANON. "Walt Whitman." New York Daily Graphic
   (25 November), 162.
        Describes Whitman, close to death but
   prevailing through "his herculean constitution": his appearance, activities,
   personal history.

11 MATADOR [pseud.]. "A Real American Poet.
   All about Walt Whitman and His Poetical
   Labors--The Meaning [,] the Strength, the
   Beauty, and the Melody of His Poetry."
   New York Daily Graphic (25 November), 165.
   Abridged: Bucke; Hindus.
        Describes from personal experience the
   seven-year process of coming to appreciate
   Whitman's poetry after initial ridicule.
   Extracts are quoted "to show that Whitman's
   poetry is original, strong, beautiful, and
   melodious." His descriptive powers give
   "a vague mystery of hinted color" in the
   method of tone poets and musicians. His
   treatment of love is "that of a strong,
   passionate man." His prosody is analyzed.

1874

BOOKS

1 NICHOLS, T. L. Forty Years of American Life.
   London: Longmans, Green, & Co., p. 495.
   Revision of 1864.2. Reprinted: 1937.12.
        Deletes Whitman material from 1864.2.
   In "Additamenta," includes a quotation
   from "Walt Whitman, whom I knew, a journey-
   man printer."

PERIODICALS

2 ANON. "Walt Whitman on Oxford." Shotover
   Papers, or, Echoes from Oxford 1 (16 May),
   79-80.
   Reprinted: Saunders.
   Parody.

3 B. V. [James Thomson]. "Walt Whitman. I."
   National Reformer (26 July), 50-51.
   Reprinted: 1892.14; 1910.19.
        Primary and secondary sources are
   listed: Burroughs (1871.1), O'Connor
   (1866.2), Gilchrist (1870.4), Rossetti
   (1868.2), Conway (1866.22). Whitman's life
   is traced to 1856, with his negative reception, especially for "Adam." Continued
   1874.4.

4 _____. "Walt Whitman. II." National Reformer
   (2 August), 67-68.
   Reprinted: 1892.14; 1910.18.
        Continues 1874.3. Describes Whitman;
   his praiseworthy hospital work which demanded
   compassion as well as more courage than
   fighting did. Continued 1874.5.

5 _____. "Walt Whitman. III." National Reformer (9 August), 82-83.
   Reprinted: 1892.14; 1910.19.
        Continues 1874.4. Describes Whitman
   after the war; Harlan's dismissal. Continued 1874.6.

6 _____. "Walt Whitman. IV." National Reformer
   (16 August), 100-101.
   Reprinted: 1892.14; 1910.19.
        Continues 1874.5. Whitman's magnificent
   body deserves celebration, but he has also
   a potent brain, heart, and personality.
   Burroughs (1871.1) is quoted. Continued
   1874.7.

7 _____. "Walt Whitman. V." National Reformer
   (23 August), 124-125.
   Reprinted: 1892.14; 1910.19.
        Continues 1874.6. Emerson is quoted
   from 1855.12 and a lecture in January 1871;
   his statement that Whitman has not fulfilled
   his promise is denied, for most of the later
   pieces are quite worthy of his first ones.
   The 1855 Preface is quoted to explain
   Whitman's quest for an American literature.
   "Myself" is quoted. Continued 1874.8.

8 _____. "Walt Whitman. VI." National Reformer
   (30 August), 135.
   Reprinted: 1892.14; 1910.19.
        Continues 1874.7. Whitman's verse has
   audacity, "a roaring exultation," biblical
   cadences and natural rhythms. Swinburne
   (1868.3) errs in comparing Whitman with
   Blake, for Whitman embraces the common
   world of reality as Blake never does.
   Whitman's themes are approvingly described.
   He is compared with Burns, Spinoza, Heine,
   Melville. Concluded 1874.9.

9 _____. "Walt Whitman. VII." National Reformer (6 September), 148-49.
Reprinted: 1892.14; 1910.19.
    Concludes 1874.8. Whitman's projection
of himself into all realms of nature and
humanity, his belief in union, democracy,
and liberty are described. His wonderful
chants "seem less works of art than immediate outgrowths of nature." "Lilacs" may
stand beside Shelley's "Adonais." Whitman
is interesting for his character, not his
opinions. He is commended to all readers,
especially the young, still susceptible to
such influence. Even his faults may be
"sanative" because of his greatness. Postscript notes his present condition and
recent work.

10 SAINTSBURY, GEORGE. "Leaves of Grass."
Academy 6 (10 October), 398-400.
Reprinted in part: 1935.1; Miller; Hindus;
Bradley/Blodgett.
    The section headings in the new Leaves
(1871 edition) give little idea of their
content; sections are not clearly related.
The incorporation of "Drum-Taps" and changes
in individual poems are improvements.
Leaves has unity and must be studied as a
whole. Whitman's gospel of brotherhood is
summarized. His treatment of sex has no
pruriency, but a Socrates-like comradeship
is regarded even more highly. Praise is
given Whitman's universality (the reason
behind his catalogues), descriptive faculty,
biblical form, political fairness. He
exalts the Yankee but his language is "not
offensively American." Leaves is America's
most original production, "if not the most
unquestioned in excellence."

11 H[ALE], P[HILIP]. "Walt Whitman." Yale
Literary Magazine 40 (November), 96-104.
    Whitman set himself the task of being
the poet of democracy that America needed,
but only lately has he been recognized as
founder of a new literary epoch. Leaves,
a wonderful book, has high aspirations for
America of building personalities and joining them through adhesiveness. Whitman
views the body as clean and wonderful. He
is nature's long-lost poet. His cheerful
faith is one of his chief glories. His
verse represents the tendency away from
rhyme, using nature's rhythms. "Myself"
shows him as "democracy incarnate."
"Whitman through his book becomes yourself."

12 [REID, WHITELAW.] Editorial. New York
Tribune (26 December), 4:6.
    Notes a Camden newspaper's castigation
(unlocated) of the country's press for
speaking lightly of Whitman's poetry.
Whitman is nevertheless truly respected
for his "patriotic and charitable character" during the war, whatever may be
thought of his poetry; his current sickness
is the result of his work; he is wished a
peaceful old age.

BOOKS

1 BURROUGHS, JOHN. Winter Sunshine. New York:
Hurd & Houghton, pp. 10, 205.
Reprinted: 1895.3.
    Minor incidental references and quota-
tion.

*2 DOWDEN, EDWARD. Shakespeare, A Critical Study
of His Mind and Art. London: H. S. King.
Reprinted: 1881.5.

3 HORNE, RICHARD HENGIST. Cosmo de' Medici, An
Historical Tragedy and Other Poems. 3rd
ed. London: George Rivers. "A Star over
Niagara," p. 157.
Reprinted: Dowden.
    Poem presenting an exchange between
Blake, who asks Whitman for "more form,"
and Whitman, who rejects "echoes of sham-
psalms" from "half-born poets."

4 N[ICHOL], J[OHN]. "American Literature."
Encyclopaedia Britannica. 9th ed. Vol. 1.
p. 733.
    Whitman displays "an uncouth power."
Some good descriptive passages redeem
Leaves from absolute barbarism. Drum-Taps
is less objectionable, giving vigorous
pictures of the war; "Lilacs" has the qualities of a noble elegy, with some of his
usual flaws.

5 STEDMAN, EDMUND CLARENCE. Victorian Poets.
Boston: James R. Osgood & Co., pp. 402-3.
Revised: 1887.11.
    Whitman "well and boldly avows himself
the mouthpiece of our democratic nationality," as Swinburne has stated, although he
should give credit to other American poets
as well. But Whitman's "unconscious for-
malism" injures his poems.

PERIODICALS

6 MAYER, S. R. TOWNSHEND. "Leigh Hunt and
Charles Ollier." St. James's Magazine,
n.s. 14 (January), 407-9.
Reprinted: David Bonnell Green, "Charles
Ollier: An Early English Admirer of Walt
Whitman," Walt Whitman Newsletter 4
(December 1958), 106-8.
    Includes letter of February 1856 from
Ollier to Hunt, describing Whitman, who has
given the world "the most original book
ever composed," his purpose "the universal
reconcilement of things." His mode of
utterance, all-embracing philosophy, imagery,
descriptions, and wordcraft are praised.
He must not be judged too harshly for sometimes stressing the carnal aspect. He is
profound, though sometimes obscure and
vulgar. Few pieces in English literature
equal some of his passages, "ever fresh and
surprising." "Walt is a great poet--almost
a prophet. His poem is about nothing,

because it is about everything." Ollier's son Edmund is writing a review of Leaves for the Leader.

7 S[COVEL], J[AMES] M. "Walt Whitman. His Life, His Poetry, Himself. 'The Good Gray Poet' Self-Estimated." Springfield Daily Republican (23 July), 3:1-3. Reprinted: 1875.8.
   Describes Whitman from personal acquaintance with him; his condition, lineage, publication history, friendship with Tennyson, Emerson's changing opinions (prints 1855.12), upcoming work, conversation concerning his purpose (quoted). A local paper's account of recent Camden meeting of Walt Whitman Club is quoted, noting Whitman's reading of "Trumpeter." Though much praised abroad, Whitman is neglected and rejected by publishers. His works cannot be procured, "though the demand is steady and not inconsiderable."

8 [SCOVEL, JAMES.] "Walt Whitman. His Health and His New Book--What He Thinks of His Own Poems--His Relations with Tennyson." New York Tribune (24 July), 7:5. Reprint of 1875.7.

9 [JAMES, WILLIAM.] "German Pessimism." Nation 21 (7 October), 233.
   Review of Pfleiderer's Der Moderne Pessimismus. Incidental: "As far as the outward animal life goes, the existence of a Walt Whitman confounds Schopenhauer quite as thoroughly as the existence of a Leopardi refutes Dr. Pangloss"; hence optimism is as true as pessimism.

10 HARPER, OLIVE. "Walt Whitman in Private Life. A Visit to His Quiet Country Home--Personal Review of His Works." New York Daily Graphic (6 November), 53.
   Whitman is the "glorious representative of America, worthy poet of a new and rugged yet grand theme." Leaves powerfully presents life in an appropriately unclothed state, revealing his personal respect for the body. He is an "indefatigable" reviser. His egotism is justifiable because of the worth of his works. He impressed this interviewer with his personality, warmth, and greatness.

*11 [WHITMAN, WALT.] "Walt Whitman at the Poe Funeral." Washington Evening Star (18 November), 2:1. Reprinted: Complete Prose Works (with minor changes); 1875.12; 1935.17.
   Describes Whitman's presence at the unveiling of the Poe monument in Baltimore; reports brief interview with him on his attitude toward Poe.

*12 _____. "Walt Whitman and the Poe Celebration." Boston Journal (22 November). Reprint of 1875.11. Reported in Martin.

13 CONWAY, MONCURE D. "A Visit to Walt Whitman." Academy 8 (27 November), 554.
   Whitman is neglected by book publishers, magazines, and anthologies. His upcoming Two Rivulets reveals a greater personal interest than any of his previous work, with "graphic outlines of the scenery" and "sympathetic appreciation of the spirit of old Virginia" in Memoranda. Whitman is described as "a man cast in the large mould, both as to heart and brain," in every sense "the greatest democrat that lives."

14 ANON. "Walt Whitman." Cope's Tobacco Plant 1 (December), 834.
   Quotes Joaquin Miller's tribute to Whitman from the New York Tribune (unlocated): the colossal mind that has written great books is "dying desolate" though still looking "like a Titan god!"

15 [BAYNE, PETER.] "Walt Whitman's Poems." Contemporary Review 27 (December), 49-69. Reprinted: 1876.6; Hindus.
   The praise of Whitman's "atrociously bad" poetry by reputable English critics must be a hoax. His newness is superficial, his pompous truisms borrowed. His high regard for the animals is "a wild caricature of Darwin's teaching." His immoral egotism passes beyond admiration for man's divinity to become "crude self-worship." He has "mental vision and descriptive grasp" but generally produces "auctioneer catalogues." Mere originality, for which Dowden and Rossetti praise him, is not art. Even his best passages largely "deal with sensational subjects and fierce excitements," like inferior writing, although occasionally he approaches "the perspicuity, compression, vividness and force of good writing." Discrimination from his critics would have obviated the need for such a piece as this. His method is "a literary trick," his political philosophy chaotic.

16 CLIVE, ARTHUR [Standish O'Grady]. "Walt Whitman, the Poet of Joy." Gentleman's Magazine, n.s. 15 (December), 704-16. Reprinted: 1918.14; 1919.83. Extracts reprinted: Bucke; Dowden; In Re; Miller.
   Modern literature is melancholy, but Whitman is "gay, and fresh, and racy," suggesting "something enormous," sensing the supernatural world all around him. Against modern literature's "intellectualism," Whitman sets the physical and the common as subjects. Despite his supposed condemnation of education and culture, it is the cultivated classes who recognize him. He is like Shakespeare in exalting passionate friendship, but his depiction of the physical aspects of this friendship "appears simply disgusting," for "the emotion does not exist in us." Unmatched since Shakespeare, Whitman's breadth of vocabulary is exactly right for the melody of his verse. Thoroughly enjoying the

1875

world, Whitman has what Wordsworth lost. "He is the noblest literary product of modern times, and his influence is invigorating and refining beyond expression."

17 EDITOR. Response to letter entitled "The Neo-Pagans." Nation 21 (2 December), 355.
This discussion of moral sensibility in criticism, in response to a letter complaining of Saintsbury's favorable commentary on Baudelaire, notes Saintsbury's recent notice of Whitman (1874.10), which "picked out for special glorification all the most spurious-sounding passages," as in examples given.

1876

BOOKS

*1 BUCHANAN, ROBERT. Faces on the Wall. London. "Walt Whitman."
Reprinted: 1880.10; Bucke; 1901.2; Legler.
Sonnet of tribute.

2 ELIOT, GEORGE. Daniel Deronda. Edinburgh and London: William Blackwood & Sons, vol. 2, p. 223; New York: Harper & Bros., vol. 1, p. 332.
Two lines from "Vocalism" 2 form the epigraph to Chapter 29.

3 RIPLEY, GEORGE, and DANA, CHARLES A., eds. The American Cyclopaedia: A Popular Dictionary of General Knowledge. Vol. 16. New York: D. Appleton & Co., p. 610.
Brief biographical sketch of Whitman and mention of some of his works.

4 TAYLOR, BAYARD. The Echo Club, and Other Literary Diversions. Boston: James R. Osgood & Co., pp. 154-55, 157-58, 168-70. Includes reprints of 1871.19; 1872.10; 1872.17. Extracts reprinted: Hubbell.

PERIODICALS

5 ANON. "Joaquin Miller." Dublin University Magazine 87 (January), 90-95.
Only Miller and Whitman may be considered "fitting exponents of characteristic American thought, unimitative painters of American life and scenery," though contrasting in their themes and convictions, with Whitman glorifying democracy and looking toward a magnificent future for mankind, and Miller reverting to Indian history with small sympathy for revolution. They alone of American writers have "shown such strength of passion, such depth of pathos, such energy, ardour, and originality, in short, such indisputable poetic greatness." Miller lacks Whitman's multiformity, "rapturous buoyant aspirations," and "democratic fervour," but has the advantage of "greater simplicity and

lucidity" without "the rambling and sometimes chaotic unrhymed lines of the greatest American poet."

6 [BAYNE, PETER.] "Walt Whitman's Poems." Littell's Living Age 128, 5th ser. 13 (8 January), 91-103.
Reprint of 1875.15.

7 V., B. [James Thomson]. "Whitman and Swinburne; or, Democracy and Freethought in England and America." Secularist (8 January), 29-30.
Account of a well-received lecture of that title by Mr. Foote, discussing Whitman as the poet of American democracy, through the tracing of his life. His mother was influential in his reverence for woman. Foote explained Whitman as spokesman "not only of the soul, but also of the body; not only of the good and happy, but also of the bad and miserable," championing the oppressed and being a brother to all.

7a [PERRY, THOMAS SERGEANT.] Long paragraph. Nation 22 (13 January), 28-29.
Describes with dismay English adulation of Whitman and his "'Blades of Grass,'" which "most people found themselves unable to read." Bayne's article (1875.15) was needed, even if he overlooks "many of the less faulty passages of Whitman, where the poetical feeling, which he undoubtedly has, is not diluted by his wild and barbaric fervor of expression."

8 SAINTSBURY, GEORGE. "Mr. Saintsbury and the 'Neo-Pagans.'" Nation 22 (13 January), 27.
Letter in response to 1875.17, with incidental reference to Whitman, whom he has praised (1874.10) "in spite of the fact that if there is one thing in the world which is distasteful to me it is democracy."

9 ANON. "Walt Whitman." Springfield Daily Republican (18 January), 4-5.
Whitman is receiving more attention abroad than at home because non-Americans must try to fit him to his surroundings, while that is obvious for his countrymen. But he must now be given due honor. Articles by Bayne (1875.15) and Clive (1875.16) are discussed. While he receives some honor in America, biographical sources and encyclopedias ignore him. Although his savings are currently depleted because of his illness (described), he hopes to live on his writing income. The soon-to-be-published Leaves and Two Rivulets should exceed the hundred-copy edition planned.

10 [WHITMAN, WALT.] "Walt Whitman's Actual American Position." West Jersey Press (26 January).
Reprinted: Uncollected; 1928.10. In part: 1876.11; 1876.22.
His country's rejection of his work has wrecked Whitman's life, which is

described before <u>Leaves</u> and during the war. Despite trouble with publishing houses and magazines, he perseveres, with new volumes soon to come out. His "artist feeling for deep shadows, streaked with just enough light to relieve them, might find no greater study than his own life."

11 ANON. "Personal." <u>New York Tribune</u> (29 January), 6:6.
Whitman "is living quietly in Camden, working steadily and unobtrusively, and occasionally appearing in public for some charitable object," as at a recent reading for the benefit of the poor; 1876.10 is quoted.

12 BARLOW, GEORGE. "Walt Whitman; or, The Religion of Art." <u>Human Nature</u> 10 (February), 49-76.
"This startling American singer" has been deplored by some but regarded by others as "the very incarnation of the poetic religion of the future." The bulk of the article presents the voice of Whitman explaining through rhapsodical prose proclamations the religion of art for which the world is not yet ready, based on love, wholeness, human liberty, and the movement toward perfection.

13 BURROUGHS, JOHN. "A Word or Two on Emerson." <u>Galaxy</u> 21 (February), 258-59.
Reprinted: 1877.1.
Incidental explanation of Emerson's response to Whitman, which perceived in him "too much of the whooping savage."

14 ANON. "Personal." <u>New York Tribune</u> (10 February), 4:5.
"A gentleman of Philadelphia has sent Walt Whitman a present of $100."

15 ANON. "Walt Whitman's Poems. Extracts from 'Two Rivulets.'" <u>New York Tribune</u> (19 February), 4:3-5.
Presents extracts of poetry and prose with brief introductory and transitional comments, including explanation of the title.

16 ANON. "Walt Whitman. A Glimpse at a Poet in His Lair. What the Author of 'Blades of Grass' Says About Newspapers and Publishers. Interesting Reminiscences of Washington Triumphs." Philadelphia <u>Times</u> (24 February), 2:1-2.
Quoted in 1876.17.
This journalist extensively describes his visit the day before to Camden to talk with Whitman, noting Whitman's appearance ("young in his old age," seeming quite the poet), his living quarters, the imminent publication of his book, his difficulties publishing in magazines. Reporter describes Whitman's activities in Washington in 1871-72; Whitman was an intimate friend of Grant, acquainted with nearly every member of Congress.

17 ANON. "Personal." <u>New York Tribune</u> (25 February), 4:5.
Extract reprinted from 1876.16.

*18 ANON. Article on Whitman. <u>The Hour</u> (March).
Reported in Asselineau.

19 ANON. "John Burroughs's 'Winter Sunshine.'" <u>Scribner's Monthly</u> 11 (March), 750.
This review of Burroughs (1875.1) notes a positive influence from Whitman in his way of looking at things, a negative influence regarding some inaccurate grammar and almost coarse expressions.

20 [HOWELLS, W. D.] "Recent Literature." <u>Atlantic Monthly</u> 37 (March), 373.
Incidental mention in review of Browning's <u>The Inn Album</u>: "Our own Mr. Walt Whitman is a poet who has carried neglect of the form to its logical conclusion, and has arrived at a sort of literary resemblance to all out-doors, and is much such a poet as a summer morning is, or an alarm of fire, or some unpleasant smell which he would personally prefer to prayer."

21 ANON. "Editor's Table." <u>Appletons' Journal</u> 15 (11 March), 343.
Whitman's theory of poetry (quoted) involves breaking down the barrier with prose. He should cease posing as a poet and "hereafter print his prose as prose."

22 ANON. "Walt Whitman." <u>Athenaeum</u>, no. 2524 (11 March), 361.
To clarify the controversy over Whitman's "literary and worldly well-being" a news item "authenticated by Whitman's own words" (quoted) verifies Whitman's poverty (1876.10 reprinted in part).

23 ANON. "New Work by Walt Whitman." London <u>Daily News</u> (11 March), 5:6-6:1.
In America Whitman enjoys respect and affection for his genuineness and "rough honesty" and the "wild sort of sweetness in the strange man's character." However, his poetic reputation has been declining, although it had been favorable due to British acclaim. Fortunately he is not suffering from extreme poverty as reported recently, but he has fallen into a mood of sorrow, as evident in <u>Two Rivulets</u>, from which characteristic extracts are printed, pre-publication, with brief comments.

24 BUCHANAN, ROBERT. "The Position of Walt Whitman." London <u>Daily News</u> (13 March), 2:7.
Reprinted: 1876.26.
Whitman's rejection by the orthodox literary figures of America, to whom he is far superior, is deplorable. Attention is called to his condition, as described in 1876.22, and a subscription is proposed to ease his poverty by distributing his little-read works "to many a poor and struggling

1876

thinker." His poetry will prove "a living scripture to the world."

25 AN OBSCURE AMERICAN. "Mr. Walt Whitman's Poems." London Daily News (14 March), 6:4.
Letter satirically deplores Buchanan's opinion of American literary figures (1876.24). The English public will judge Whitman on his own merits, despite Buchanan's "efforts to raise a new idol on the ruins of old reputations."

26 ANON. "Great Britain. . . . Aid for Walt Whitman." New York Times (14 March), 7:3.
Paragraph on Buchanan's appeal, quoting from 1876.24.

27 ROSSETTI, WM. MICHAEL. Letter. London Daily News (14 March), 6:4.
Whitman's poverty is confirmed. Admirers of "this powerful and moving poet" are urged to support the subscription in hopes that his countrymen will be "encouraged or shamed" into helping him.

28 ANON. Editorial. London Daily News (16 March), 5:1-2.
Reprinted in part: 1876.35.
Whitman merits support for his "honesty, truth, and purity," but Americans should not be criticized for ingratitude or lack of appreciation, having never asked that such poetic experiments be made. It was to be expected that he claim to be what had long been sought, America's national poet. Some of his work reveals the power and feeling of a true poet, not a mere "accomplished maker of verses," but much of his potential remains unfulfilled. He brings no particular revelation to the world. His rebellion against convention derives from Rousseau and Diogenes. His idea that poetry should be free from the bonds of rhythm is like asking a painter to abandon colors and outlines.

29 BUCHANAN, ROBERT. "Mr. Walt Whitman." London Daily News (16 March), 6:1.
Letter responding to 1876.25, showing admiration for the works of Lowell and Longfellow but not for their neglect of Whitman. The subscription is defended, having the support of businessmen, who appreciate, like Whitman, the value of work.

30 AUSTIN, ALFRED. Letter. London Daily News (16 March), 6:1.
Buchanan has "clouded a question of benevolence with untimely literary fervour." Whitman deserves support, whatever the quality of his efforts, because anyone devoting himself to being a poet is worthy of praise. Besides, his fine service in war is worth "more than to have composed all the poetry that was ever written."

31 BUCHANAN, ROBERT. "Walt Whitman." London Daily News (17 March), 3:6.
Letter denying that the subscription is for "benevolence" as Austin says (1876.30); it is rather a means for Whitman's admirers to recognize his talent. The editorial (1876.28) is "a single reader's opinion." It is not America in general but her literary class that is being criticized.

32 ANON. "Walt Whitman." Saturday Review 41 (18 March), 360-61.
Reprinted in part: 1876.36; 1876.42; in full: 1926.20.
The repudiation of Whitman for his "shameless obscenity" indicates the American public's strong moral sense. Despite current interest in him, he has shown no gain in popularity over twenty years. "His name would be a taint to any respectable periodical," for "apart from his scandalous eccentricities, his writings are poor stuff, and the affectation of deep philosophy is easily seen through." Such work of "a sort of psychological monstrosity" does not demand the implicit approval of support.

33 [DANA, CHARLES A.] "A Shot from the Other Side." New York Sun (19 March), 4:1-2.
Editorial in response to Buchanan's criticisms (1876.24). Whitman is a humane man with a democratic spirit, but not the "rude man" his English admirers believe, for he began his career like many literary young men, with sentimental tales, taking up his "rude measures" as an afterthought which proved successful. Buchanan does a service, as does Whitman, in taking literature out of the hands of the emasculating literary coteries, for we need a literature more virile than that produced by poets like "Tupper [i.e., J. G.] Holland."

34 S[MALLEY], G. W. "Anglo-American Topics." New York Tribune (28 March), 1:4.
Reports the Daily News controversy; criticizes Buchanan (1876.24) for his accusations of American writers.

35 [TAYLOR, BAYARD.] "In Re Walt Whitman." New York Tribune (28 March), 4:3-4.
Editorial in response to Buchanan (1876.31), agreeing with editorial (1876.28, quoted); other letters are quoted (1876.27, 1876.25). Lord Houghton has claimed that Whitman lived simply but not in discomfort. Emerson regretted his letter's use to support something inappropriate for women or youth. Whitman was certainly respected in Washington, especially for his war services, whatever people thought of his poetry.

36 ANON. "Literary Notes." New York Tribune (30 March), 6:2.
Reprint in part of 1876.32.

37 [TAYLOR, BAYARD.] One-paragraph editorial. <u>New York Tribune</u> (30 March), 4:5.
  Comment on Buchanan (1876.31) and <u>Saturday Review</u> (1876.32). Contrary to Buchanan's assertions, American authors (notably Stedman) helped Whitman in Washington after he was dismissed from one position.

38 STEDMAN, E. C. "Walt Whitman's Clerkship." <u>New York Tribune</u> (31 March), 5:4.
  Corrects misconception of 1876.37, giving the credit to O'Connor. Whitman's fellow American writers would support him without a "transatlantic sentimentalist" to remind them, for they "have a sincere regard for the man," even when they do not agree with the extreme claims of Whitman's disciples.

39 ANON. "Walt Whitman." <u>Boston Evening Transcript</u> (1 April), 6:1.
  Corrects Buchanan's impressions of the attitude of the literary class (1876.24); Whitman, rather, "is simply not mentioned," like other indecent things; he evokes such a response, even from many "who half believe that he is possessed of poetic insight and power." He should not fly in the face of the inherited sensibilities of civilization. The <u>West Jersey Press</u> (1876.10) is quoted as more accurate than Buchanan's account.

*40 ANON. Article on Whitman. Camden <u>New Republic</u> (1 April).
  Reprinted: Bucke.
  Criticizes <u>Tribune</u> (1876.35) for erroneous insinuations. Whitman's works are beginning to claim serious judgment, while the <u>Tribune</u> offers only "frivolous slurs."

41 ANON. "Personal Gossip." <u>Frank Leslie's Illustrated Newspaper</u> 42 (1 April), 63.
  Notes Buchanan's appeal to help Whitman, whose countrymen do not seem to buy his works "with sufficient zeal to give that poetical Hercules a comfortable subsistence."

42 [STODDARD, R. H.?] "Editor's Table." <u>Appletons' Journal</u> 15 (1 April), 437-38.
  Reprinted in part: Bucke.
  Opposes Buchanan's slur on American literature (1876.24) and the British adulation of Whitman, whose life (traced here) shows him "a mere trickster." After his early commonplace, respectable work, he sought notoriety with "unparalleled audacity" in a loose living and writing style, a pose, though he was considered "the original genius of Nature itself." "He entered upon the <u>rôle</u> of loafer, dressed up accordingly, vulgarized his name, and wrote a book filled with drivel and indecency."

43 SWINTON, JOHN. "Walt Whitman." New York <u>Herald</u> (1 April), 8:2.
  Reprinted in part: Bucke; 1887.13.
  Letter. Whitman is not in danger of starvation but merits Buchanan's proposed assistance because of his illness. His life and works are commendable, especially his war work (described), worthy to be admired whatever is thought of his poetry.

44 ANON. "Walt Whitman's Want--A Public." New York <u>Herald</u> (2 April), 8:5-6.
  Editorial. "Blatant, coarse and sensual as his song is," Whitman cannot approve of Buchanan's "drumhead" efforts. His writings have a certain quality "not overlooked or underestimated in this country--namely, his bold belief in the great destiny of the United States." But his "uncouthness" and "catalogue tediousness" remove even his least objectionable work from interest. He outdoes Swinburne in "unfiltered filth and naked nastiness." His "incoherent exulting yells" may sound like the new voice of democratic aspirations to the English, but not to Americans.

45 ANON. "Walt Whitman." <u>Frank Leslie's Illustrated Newspaper</u> 42 (8 April), 84. Illustrated with W. Kurtz's photograph (as engraving).
  Biographical sketch, noting his appearance at the mechanics' club in Camden, quoting his views on poetry.

46 [TAYLOR, BAYARD.] "American vs. English Criticism." <u>New York Tribune</u> (12 April), 4:4-5.
  The usually restrained English appreciated the change Whitman's "barbaric yawp" provided, but Americans seek harmony for their "unresolved elements" and need not bow to the English verdict. One can acknowledge his "rudimentary genius," yet miss "the developed poetic intelligence," because his work is "a chaos, pierced here and there by splendid phrases," a mixture of "the old Greek reverence for the human body," "Emerson's democratic philosophy," and "the slang, coarseness and aggressive <u>insouciance</u> of the New York Bowery boy."

47 BURROUGHS, JOHN. "Walt Whitman's Poetry. An Estimate of Its Value." <u>New York Tribune</u> (13 April), 6:1.
  Letter in response to editorial (1876.35): the <u>Daily News</u> editorial (1876.28) is not representative. Whitman gives something better than mere literature, something "bracing and masculine" which speaks to a man and to a nation. If Whitman does not fit current concepts of poetry, new terms may be necessary. His form is that of nature. Though poor and ill, he is a philosopher, accepting his condition cheerfully.

48 ANON. "The Scribner Magazines." <u>Springfield Daily Republican</u> (19 April), 5:1.

Holland (1876.56) "does sound justice" to Whitman, "showing that where he succeeds in being the poet he was meant to be, it is by the old means of rhythmic emphasis which he claims to discard."

49 [SANBORN, FRANK.] "Walt Whitman. A Visit to the Good Gray Poet." Springfield Daily Republican (19 April), 4:5-6; 5:1.
Reprinted: 1876.50.
Criticizes Bayne's abuse of Whitman (1875.15) because Whitman's portrayal of sex is more ideal than Swinburne's or Martial's. He has broader range than Burns but can never be a popular writer, though popular in his instincts and topics, because he lacks poetic form and melody. He cannot be criticized as a moralist. The writer recalls his first acquaintance with Whitman, at his [Sanborn's] trial in 1860. Whitman's life in Camden is described. His best poems were inspired by the war, as quoted extracts show; his "lament for Lincoln" is praised. His mission is to celebrate comradeship and idealize democracy.

50 _____. "Walt Whitman. A Visit to the Good Gray Poet." Springfield Republican (21 April).
Reprint of 1876.49.

51 HOLLAND, J. G. "Walt Whitman." Boston Evening Transcript (22 April), 6:3.
Extract reprinted from 1876.56.

52 O'CONNOR, W. D. "Walt Whitman. Is He Persecuted?" New York Tribune (22 April), 8:1-3.
Reprinted: Loving.
Affirms Whitman's poverty; objects to recent negative comments; cites American admirers; describes his first reading of Leaves, "the vast charm of their sea-like lines and superb imagination," the "apt and agreeing rhythms," with no "impure thought or indecent word." Whitman deserves respect during his lifetime, that he may enjoy the reputation which the future is sure to accord him.

53 PERRY, NORA. "A Few Words About Walt Whitman." Appletons' Journal 15 (22 April), 531-33.
Explains the controversy, citing American and British defenders and favorable reviews. Whitman's audience is growing. Carlyle is quoted as calling Whitman "a man furnished for the highest of all enterprises--that of being the poet of his age" (quoted from Frank Leslie's where it accompanied an engraving of Whitman [unlocated], though according to Barrus, Carlyle did not say this of Whitman). If he is not to every critic's taste, his purpose is noble, though his method may be objectionable. A friend of Perry's who found that Whitman needs to break the silence about certain subjects is quoted. He has indeed a sense of reverence.

54 [TAYLOR, BAYARD.] "Intellectual Convexity." New York Tribune (22 April), 6:5.
Editorial mocking Burroughs (1876.47) and O'Connor (1876.52) for advancing Whitman as a voice of nature and exalting chaos into a literary ideal. Whitman wisely holds himself aloof from such "aggressive championship."

55 [DANA, CHARLES A.] Editorial paragraph. New York Sun (28 April), 2:5.
Criticizes Holland (1876.56). Whitman's lack of the regularity of "Tupper Holland" is no reason to say his work is not poetry, for Ossian and the Bible have similar rhythms. But this writer disclaims any "great admiration" for Whitman's work such as his English friends show.

56 [HOLLAND, J. G.] "Is it Poetry?" Scribner's Monthly 12 (May), 123-25.
Reprinted: 1882.5.
Whitman is neglected because editors regard his form of expression as illegitimate, unpoetic but "too involved and spasmodic and strained to be respectable prose." Passages from Emerson and Carlyle are printed in Whitmanesque lines to show his similarity to them; actual passages from Whitman are quoted as "possibly inferior to them in quality," although Whitman "has a strong individuality, and is more robust than Emerson." "Locomotive" shows Whitman "capable of poetry" with its strong, rhythmical conclusion. Whitman is wished well, his earlier grossness ignored. But he is wrong, "a literary eccentric" in his theories and performances, and will have no following.

57 ANON. "Pauper Poets." Independent 28 (4 May), 14.
Criticizes Buchanan's charges (1876.24). Whitman "is perfectly well understood and appreciated at his full value" in America. He assumed his pose and indecencies when he found his ordinary essays and poems would not bring him notoriety. He has been well rewarded for his labors and is free to work, like other American poets.

*58 ADAMS, ROBERT DUDLEY. "Walt Whitman, the American Poet." Sydney Evening News (20 May).
Reported in Asselineau.

59 S. J. F. "Walt Whitman. The Athletic Bard Paralyzed and in a Rocking Chair. His Explanation of His Verse and His Condition." New York World (21 May), 1:1.
Records visit to Camden. Whitman's persisting cheerfulness explains "the affectionate interest" most people take in him. Though tired of speaking of it, Whitman responds to query about his poetic plan. He would have liked to stop the publication of Buchanan's letter (1876.24). He pays his own way at his brother's. His

health is described; also his new collection, for which five dollars is "not too
big a price."

60 [WHITMAN, WALT.] "Walt Whitman." West Jersey
Press (24 May).
Describes the controversy, contradict-
ing the denials by the American press that
Whitman has been mistreated by press and
public. Yet he has continued to live up
to "his own ideal," "in deed and print."
Though sick, he is not in such a sad estate
as supposed; he gives to the needy more
than he spends on himself. "His life and
book are the most signal example on record
of perseverance" and resolution. "Captain"
(reprinted) might be applied to him now.

61 [CURTIS, G. W.] "Editor's Easy Chair."
Harper's New Monthly Magazine 53 (June),
141-42.
Contradicts Buchanan regarding the
neglect of Whitman, a literary conspiracy,
and the jealousy of American writers.
Publishers are not interested in his works
because people will not buy them. America
cannot be scolded into admiration.
Whitman's fine character is acknowledged.
Appreciation may not come in a poet's lifetime, but that is not the public's fault.
Americans would respond to an appeal for
help if Whitman or his friends made it.

62 ANON. "Personal." Harper's Weekly 20 (10
June), 463.
Quotes Whitman's recent letter to a
friend on not being deprived of any physical
thing he needs, though he is poor.

63 GOSSE, EDMUND W. "Walt Whitman's New Book."
Academy 9 (24 June), 602-3.
Review of Two Rivulets, which throws
much light on Whitman's "brave and self-
sacrificing" character. He demands a
different criticism in order to recognize
his excellent intentions and primitive
truths which he expresses, at his best, in
"a kind of inarticulate poetry," perhaps
because of his purpose of portraying the
normal man's daily life. "Lilacs,"
"Myself," "Ox-Tamer," "Locomotive,"
"Redwood," "Prayer" (close to blank verse)
are praised; criticized are "Eidólons" and
the Centennial songs (their catalogues
being inferior to those depicting the
body). Whitman's prose style is "heavy
and disjointed," but the intrinsic interest
of his content transcends this. His principle of the love of comrades, carried out
in the deeds Memoranda describes, will last
the longest of his themes.

64 RICHARDSON, CHARLES F. "Walt Whitman."
Independent 28 (29 June), 1.
Response to 1876.57. Whitman's character is not discreditable. His form is
legitimate and likely to be a boon for his
successors. "Lilacs" and "Captain,"

Whitman at his best, may please the most
exacting ear. Few other poems sustain the
power of individual expressions; hence he
is of the second rank, below the New
England poets. He is gross and cannot be
compared with writers of other eras which
had different standards.

65 BURROUGHS, JOHN. "What Makes the Poet?"
Galaxy 22 (July), 57, 59.
Incidental references, praising quotations from Whitman. Reading him conveys a
sense of power and passion, especially
"Myself," "an operatic launching forth of
the voice to its utmost."

66 ANON. "Robert Buchanan and Walt Whitman in
Court." New York Tribune (13 July), 2:5.
Quotes Buchanan's remarks during the
trial of a libel charge he filed against
the Examiner. After hearing some of
Whitman's poems read, he admitted they were
"exceedingly unclean and animal," dealing
with things which "ought not to be written
about at all," although the main tone of
Whitman's writings is "healthy and pure,
and not sensual."

67 ANON. "Burial of Little Walter Whitman."
Philadelphia Ledger (20 July), 4:9.
Reprinted: Bucke.
Brief account of funeral of Whitman's
nephew, less than a year old. Whitman
remarked to a little girl there: "You
don't know what it is, do you, my dear?
We don't either."

68 HAGER, J. C. "An Only Child's Tea Party."
Christian Register (2 September), 4.
Poem.

69 DODGE, MARY MAPES. "The Two Mysteries."
Scribner's Monthly 12 (October), 888.
Reprinted: 1879.5; 1904.8.
Rhymed poem on death, quoting Whitman
anecdote (1876.67) as epigraph.

70 PERRY, THOMAS SERGEANT. "George Sand."
Atlantic Monthly 38 (October), 447.
Incidental: "At times George Sand
seems to have drunk at the same spring with
Walt Whitman when he is wildest in his rapturous cries; for time, space, and elementary
truths all roll in confusion throughout
these pages."

71 [McCARTHY, J. H.] "Songs Oversea." Examiner,
no. 3586 (21 October), 1191-93.
Review of Two Rivulets, which reveals
a still vigorous power ("Locomotive"),
evidence of Whitman's love for the sea and
nature, "virtues and strength sufficient
for claiming laureateship of the great
American nation." The "splendidly dramatic
and grandly descriptive" account of the
assassination (quoted) suggests that Whitman
could become "America's first historian."

1877

1877

BOOKS

1 BURROUGHS, JOHN. <u>Birds and Poets with Other
Papers</u>. New York: Hurd & Houghton. "The
Flight of the Eagle," pp. 213-63 (reprinted:
1886.22); also reprints of: 1873.8, pp.
17-21, 46; 1876.13, pp. 196-97, 201-2;
1868.17, p. 167 (the Whitman reference
being deleted); also Preface and p. 173.
　　Whitman's sympathy with nature frees
art by his "very abnegation of art," with
an "interior, spontaneous rhythm" based on
an operatic outpouring, achieving its own
form. Americans, spoiled by sweets, need
an infusion of his "heroic stamina." His
method is "to show rather than to tell."
His catalogues are full of action and
historic value for the future. He views
sex with "a scientific coldness and purity"
and an "alive and sympathetic" quality as
well. He reconciles the modern sciences
to poetry, religion, and life, placing man
back at the center of things but fully
including the earth. His prose is like
Carlyle's but "much more vascular and
human." His poems are solidly "clothed
with rank materiality," yet "he never fails
to ascend into spiritual meanings." On
p. 212 is Arran Leigh's poem "To Walt
Whitman" ("They say that thou art sick,
art growing old"), reprinted in Bucke and
Legler.

2 <u>Kottabos</u>, 2. Dublin University: Trinity
College. "Poems Written in Discipleship.
VII. Of the School of Walt Whitman. A
Proem," by J[ohn] T[odhunter], pp. 14-16;
"On Walt Whitman's 'Leaves of Grass,'" by
T. W. H. R[olleston], pp. 294-95.
　　Todhunter's poem disclaims parodic
intention, using Whitmanesque lines in an
Irish context. Rolleston's rhymed stanzas
praise the various aspects of Whitman's
poetry, which will eventually succeed.

3 SAVAGE, MINOT. <u>The Religion of Evolution</u>.
Boston: Lockwood, Brooks, & Co., p. 228.
　　Incidental: "Poetry is one: is therefore Shakespeare no higher or more divine
than Tupper or Walt Whitman?"

PERIODICALS

4 BENTON, JOEL. "John Burroughs." <u>Scribner's
Monthly</u> 13 (January), 337, 340-41.
　　Praises Burroughs's work on Whitman
(1867.1) without sharing his enthusiasm.
For Burroughs, Whitman was a stimulating
force that helped him.

5 MILLER, JOAQUIN. "Walt Whitman." <u>Galaxy</u> 23
(January), 29.
Reprinted in part: Bucke; in full:
Legler.
　　Poem of tribute in five quasi-Spenserian
stanzas.

6 ANON. "Walt Whitman on Tom Paine." <u>New York
Tribune</u> (29 January), 2:5-6.
　　Whitman spoke at a meeting in Philadel-
phia honoring Paine; his words are quoted.

7 ANON. "A Reception to Walt Whitman." <u>New
York Tribune</u> (6 March), 5:5.
　　Briefly describes a reception for
Whitman at John H. Johnston's house, list-
ing guests and recitations by Whitman and
others.

8 JUNE, JENNIE. "Our New York Letter. Jennie
June's Weekly Jottings." <u>Baltimore American
and Commercial Advertiser</u> (10 March), 2:4.
　　Personal description of Whitman; Mr.
Waters's plan to paint him.

9 _____. "Our New York Letter. Jennie June's
Weekly Jottings." <u>Baltimore American and
Commercial Advertiser</u> (17 March), 2:4.
　　Reports a dinner for four including
Whitman; provides her genial impressions of
him, his current activities, his ideas on
the roles of men and women in civilization.

*10 [WHITMAN, WALT.] "Walt Whitman." <u>Camden Post</u>
(29 March).
Reprinted: Bucke; White.
　　Describes Whitman's visit to New York,
his welcome by society, his fraternizing
with bus drivers and boatmen, his new book
in progress.

11 ANON. Review of Burroughs (1877.1). <u>Atlantic
Monthly</u> 40 (July), 114.
　　Burroughs's eloquent defense of Whitman
is one of the best pieces, honoring Whitman
"as the only thorough-going exponent of a
dignified, poetic, prophetic democracy whom
our literature can yet show." This should
help those who can regard Whitman only with
impatience.

12 ANON. "John Burroughs's 'Birds and Poets.'"
<u>Scribner's Monthly</u> 14 (July), 407-8.
　　Burroughs derives enthusiasm but not
inspiration from Whitman. He quotes beautiful passages, and Whitman has "written in
his peculiar impassioned prose some fine
things, and in real versified poetry some
of the best war lyrics we possess; but we
cannot bring ourselves to admire him as a
whole in the generous way of Mr. Burroughs."
Whitman is far from being the scientific
poet Burroughs claims.

13 MARVIN, JOSEPH B. "Walt Whitman." <u>Radical
Review</u> 1 (August), 224-59.
Reprinted in part: Bucke.
　　Emerson's idea of the American bard was
fulfilled by Whitman. Biographical sketch.
Whitman is a universal, not merely national,
poet, the first to regard the average man
as interesting to the imagination. His
emphasis on more than political freedom,
his democratic depiction of all aspects of
life and America, treatments of sex and

manly friendship, and "long-drawn cadence" are praised.

*14 [WHITMAN, WALT.] "'The Old Gray' under a tree." Camden Daily Post (2 August). Reprinted: White.

Reports on Whitman's health, considerably improved. The Washington Evening Star (unlocated) says that he contemplates a visit soon to Washington. Lately he has been at the Staffords' farmhouse at Timber Creek, where Herbert Gilchrist has been painting him.

15 CLIFFORD, W. K. "Cosmic Emotion." Nineteenth Century 2 (October), 420, 428. Reprinted: 1879.3.

Quotes passages from Whitman incidentally to exemplify aspects of the cosmic emotion, showing that our experience is only "part of something larger."

16 [LATHROP, GEORGE?] "The Contributors' Club." Atlantic Monthly 40 (December), 749-51.

Contrasts Whitman's later pieces with his earlier work, by which most people judge him, although stressing its nastiness over its fine lines. Several passages, examined in terms of the way sound and metrics contribute to meaning, show him to be "one of our very first masters of verbal melody and harmony." His treatment of both human topics and modern machinery is praised.

1878

BOOKS

1 ADAMS, W. DAVENPORT. Dictionary of English Literature. London, Paris, and New York: Cassell Peter & Galpin, n.d., p. 687.

"Whitman, Walt, American poet (b. 1819), has published numerous volumes of 'poems.'" Extract from Buchanan (1867.23) is quoted.

2 CALDER, ALMA. Miriam's Heritage: A Story of the Delaware River. New York: Harper & Bros., pp. 7, 24, 163.

Quotations from "Redwood," "Think of the Soul," and "So Long!" are used as epigrams for the first, last, and one other chapter.

3 DOWDEN, EDWARD. Studies in Literature. London: C. Kegan Paul & Co. "Walt Whitman," pp. 468-523. Reprint of 1871.4.

There are a few minor deletions and additions in footnotes providing more recent quotations from Whitman and information on his health.

4 LINTON, W. J. Poetry of America. London: George Bell & Sons, pp. x, 371. Frontispiece portrait.

Note to seventeen pages of extracts from Whitman's poetry (as compared to

eighteen pages each of Lowell and Whittier) explains the general retention of Whitman's punctuation because his "manner is altogether his." "The Dresser" is worth printing not only as poetry but "as a record of his own noble life."

5 RICHARDSON, CHARLES F. A Primer of American Literature. Boston: Houghton, Osgood & Co., pp. 90-91. Revised: 1884.11.

Whitman's work is rhapsody rather than poetry, "pervaded with a love of liberty," blemished by catalogues and affectations, but with "many strong and fine lines." "Captain" and "Lilacs" are praised.

6 ROSSETTI, WILLIAM MICHAEL. Lives of Famous Poets. London: E. Moxon, Son, & Co., p. 391.

Last sentence in book, at end of essay on Longfellow: "The real American poet is Walt Whitman--a man enormously greater than Longfellow or any other of his poetic compatriots."

7 SYMONDS, JOHN ADDINGTON. Many Moods: A Volume of Verse. London: Smith, Elder, & Co. "The song is to the singer" is quoted on title page.

PERIODICALS

*8 ANON. "Walt Whitman for 1878." West Jersey Press (16 January). Reported in White.

9 WAGER-FISHER, Mrs. MARY E. "Poets' Homes. No. XVI. Walt Whitman." Wide Awake 6 (February), 109-15. Three portraits. Reprinted: 1879.7. Abridged: 1881.28.

Introduction for young readers with biographical sketch noting Whitman's wide range of experience, interest in lower classes, career problems, war service, illness, anecdote of his nephew's funeral (see 1876.67). He has made "the most thrilling and powerfully descriptive record" of the war. The quality, if not the quantity, of Whitman's praises implies an unparalleled popularity. His appearance, personality, personal and literary habits are described. He is understood to be "leisurely engaged on a third volume to be called 'Far and Near at '59.'" One should judge Whitman's work for oneself, for there is always more in it than may first appear. Extracts of his poetry are quoted.

10 ANON. "The Contributors' Club." Atlantic Monthly 41 (March), 391-92.

Incidental reference to Whitman as an example of how invisible the boundary is between prose and poetry.

11 ANON. Editorial on Bryant's death. London Times (14 June), 9:5-6. Quoted in Bucke.

Incidental references: "Unless WALT
WHITMAN is to be reckoned among the poets,
American verse from its earliest to its
latest stages seems an exotic, with an
exuberance of gorgeous blossom, but no
principle of reproductions." "WALT
WHITMAN, even without the repulsive eccentricities of his moral tone, must have sunk
into obscurity among his countrymen from
the want of mannered and borrowed polish
which is his special distinction."

12 ANON. "William Cullen Bryant." New York Sun
(15 June), 3:3.
Account of Bryant's funeral. "The man
most looked at was the white-haired poet,
Walt Whitman, who presented a Homeric picture, in which were combined the easy good
nature of Grandfather Whitehead and the
heroic build of an antique statue." He
"smiled acquiescence in the eulogy."

13 ANON. "Current Literature." Dublin University
Magazine 92, n.s. 2 (July), 111-12.
Review of Dowden (1878.3), which gives
Whitman fair treatment and "makes us feel
the freedom and lovingness and simple
greatness of the man who is the outcome
and truest representative of his age and
nation."

14 [SEDGWICK, A. G.] "Swinburne's New Volume."
Nation 27 (18 July), 45-46.
Incidental reference, noting how recent
English preference for form over matter has
led to praise for Whitman, "the chief characteristics of whose verse was [sic] an indecency which should long ago have brought
him under the eye of the Society for the
Suppression of Vice." He wrote "prose
without knowing it." This poetry was not
moral and had no purpose.

15 ANON. "The Contributors' Club." Atlantic
Monthly 42 (September), 368.
Response to 1878.10. Prose and poetry
are indeed distinct, "although Isaiah,
Ossian, or Walt Whitman are poetic in their
universified language."

16 [HOLLAND, J. G.] "Our Garnered Names."
Scribner's Monthly 16 (October), 895-96.
This discussion of the stature of
American literature, occasioned by Bryant's
death, concludes by predicting the eventual
forgetting of Poe, Thoreau, and Whitman.
It is a mystery "how an age that possesses
a Longfellow and an appreciative ear for
his melody can tolerate in the slightest
degree the abominable dissonances" of
Whitman. America has too much "morbid
love of the eccentric."

17 STEVENSON, ROBERT LOUIS. "The Gospel According
to Whitman." New Quarterly Magazine 10
(October), 461-81.
Reprinted: 1882.11; 1900.17. Abridged:
Miller.

No one can deny the value of Whitman's
matter and spirit. He rejects the literature of the past in favor of a contemporary
democratic ideal, seeking to portray the
average American and himself as faithfully
as possible. Against the more fashionable
melancholy, Whitman counterpoises "a certain
high joy in living" and an "outdoor atmosphere" which parents should offer as a
cure "for the distressing malady of being
seventeen years old." Whitman's wonder at
life allowed him to embrace all of it. He
emphasized the equal importance of self-
assertion and sympathy, a spirit of "ultra-
Christianity." His morality stresses the
positive rather than negative virtues,
while not ignoring "the existence of temporal evil." His life exemplifies his
theory. His seemingly "formless jottings"
of wartime memoranda are perhaps "the best
and the most human and convincing passages"
in his work. His style is "a most surprising
compound of plain grandeur, sentimental affection, and downright nonsense," sometimes recalling the Old Testament. A fine
critic, he must have known better. He was
not the man to treat that "most indelicate
of subjects," fatherhood. He attracts
attention like "a Bull in a China Shop."
His philosophy, sometimes contradictory, is
often "startlingly Christian." No one can
"get evil from so healthy a book," which is
"simply comical" when falling short of
nobility.

BOOKS

*1 BUCKE, RICHARD MAURICE. Man's Moral Nature:
An Essay. New York: G. P. Putnam's Sons,
p. v.
Quoted in "Whitman and Man's Moral Nature,"
by Artem Lozynsky, WWR 21 (March 1975), 36.
"I dedicate this book to the man who
inspired it--to the man who of all men past
and present that I have known has the most
exalted moral nature--to WALT WHITMAN."

2 BURROUGHS, JOHN. Locusts and Wild Honey.
Boston: Houghton, Osgood & Co., p. 85.
"I admire immensely this line of Walt
Whitman:--'The slumbering and liquid trees.'"

3 CLIFFORD, WILLIAM KINGDON. Lectures and
Essays. Vol. 2. Edited by Leslie Stephen
and Frederick Pollock. London: Macmillan
& Co. "Cosmic Emotion," pp. 269, 282-83.
Reprint of 1877.15.

*4 de SALAMANCA, FELIX. The Philosophy of Hand-
writing. London: Chatto & Windus, pp. 149-
50.
Quoted in Saunders Supplement.
Analysis of Whitman's handwriting: not
pleasing, but having more vigor, originality,
and "masculine beauty" than conventional
manuscript like Bryant's or Whittier's.

5 DODGE, MARY MAPES. Along the Way. New York: Charles Scribner's Sons. "The Two Mysteries," pp. 15-17. Reprint of 1876.69.

6 [LEECH, Dr. WILLIAM.] The Obliviad: A Satire. New York: James Miller; London: B. Quaritch, pp. 204-6. Quoted in 1933.13.

This poem in couplets criticizes Whitman for being inscrutable and writing "crippled prose," comparing him to Francis Saltus, with explanatory notes on Whitman's life.

7 [WAGER-FISHER, Mrs. MARY E.] "Walt Whitman." In Poets' Homes. Pen and Pencil Sketches of American Poets and Their Homes, by Arthur Gilman et al. Boston: D. Lothrop & Co., pp. 35-59. Reprint of 1878.9.

PERIODICALS

8 [FORNEY, JOHN W.] Paragraph. Progress, 1, No. 21 (5 April), 1.

Praises Whitman whose work appears in this issue; notes English interest in him.

9 ANON. "A Poet on the Platform. Walt Whitman as a Lecturer." New York Tribune (15 April), 2:3-4.

Describes Whitman's start as a lecturer last night in New York. His speech on Lincoln's death is described and printed.

10 ANON. "Abraham Lincoln." Harper's Weekly 23 (3 May), 342-43.

Incidentally notes Whitman's lecture on Lincoln and reading of "Captain," "one of the most striking and touching of all the memorial poems of that time." Whitman's paper with its vivid touches is described.

11 JAMES, WM. "The Sentiment of Rationality." Mind 4 (July), 317, 345. Reprinted: 1897.10.

Quotes extracts from Whitman as words that are valid for us regarding the sufficiency of the present moments and mystical perceptions.

12 BATHGATE, HERBERT J. "Walt Whitman." Papers for the Times 2 (1 September), 155-64.

Explanation of Whitman's value: his faith in man, his large-scale, painful intensity due to his sympathy, joyous intoxication with life, almost Christ-like teachings. His style derives from the Bible and Homer. He occasionally "degenerates into a mere maker of catalogues," but his lyrical poems indicate his delicacy, distinction, and the "sweet strangeness which poets alone possess." He is "America's first Great Bard." His poetry is extensively quoted.

*13 [MUMFORD, MORRISON?] Note. Kansas City Times (2 September). Quoted in Hubach (1943, 1972).

Whitman is scheduled to come "celebrate himself" at the Kansas Celebration and read a poem for the Old Settlers Reunion on 15 September.

*14 _____. "Walt Whitman." Kansas City Times (6 September). Quoted in Hubach (1943, 1972).

"The renowned cosmical poet of America" will give Kansas "a treat such as has seldom been presented."

*15 ANON. Note. Kansas City Daily Journal (11 September). Quoted in Hubach (1972).

Whitman is among the "Big Guns" who will speak at Lawrence.

*16 ANON. Note. Lawrence Daily Journal (11 September). Quoted in Hubach (1972).

Announces Whitman's coming to Kansas City by train.

17 ANON. "Personal." New York Tribune (11 September), 4:5. Quoted in 1879.22.

Whitman, "still suffering from partial paralysis," will "attend the Kansas celebration on condition that he shall not be called upon to make any public speeches or eat any public dinners."

*18 [MUMFORD, MORRISON?] Note. Kansas City Times (11 September). Quoted in Hubach (1943, 1972).

Kansas might have to be quarantined against Whitman.

*19 ANON. "Walt Whitman, the Poet." St. Louis Globe-Democrat (13 September). Reprinted: Hubach (1942).

Interview with Whitman upon his arrival, "an oddity in appearance as in his writings." Whitman tells of his reasons for coming, his literary labors, his love for meeting people, his praise for American boys.

20 ANON. "Two Visitors. Each Widely Known, Stopping Briefly in the City. Col. Forney, the Journalist, and Walt Whitman, the Poet." St. Louis Missouri Republican (13 September), 3:7. Reprinted: Hubach (1942).

Describes arrival of Forney and Whitman to take part in Kansas quarter-centennial; briefly describes Whitman's appearance and travel plans.

*21 ANON. Note. Kansas City Daily Journal (14 September). Quoted in Hubach (1972).

Announces program for the Kansas Celebration, including a poem by Whitman. He and Forney should help fill Lawrence to overflowing.

1879

*22 [MUMFORD, MORRISON?] Note. Kansas City Times
    (14 September).
        Quoted in Hubach (1943, 1972).
            Cites Tribune (1879.17) on Whitman's
        paralysis and requirements.

*23 ANON. Note. Kansas City Journal (16 Septem-
    ber).
        Quoted in Hubach (1972).
            Notes Whitman's white beard.

*24 ANON. Note. Lawrence Daily Journal (16
    September).
        Quoted in Hubach (1972).
            Account of where Whitman stayed and
        his feeble health, which may keep him from
        reading the poem as expected.

*25 ANON. Note. St. Louis Globe-Democrat (16
    September).
        Quoted in Hubach (1972).
            Whitman's appearance at the celebration
        made him "the cynosure of all eyes," es-
        pecially attracting the society of young
        people.

*26 [MUMFORD, MORRISON?] Note. Kansas City Times
    (16 September).
        Quoted in Hubach (1972).
            The "illustrious trio" of Whitman,
        Forney, and Edward Everett Hale, who have
        just arrived, is described.

*27 ANON. Note. Atchison (Kansas) Champion (17
    September).
        Reported in Hubach (1972).
            Describes Whitman.

*28 ANON. Note. Kansas City Journal (17 Septem-
    ber).
        Quoted in Hubach (1943).
            Whitman visited the newspaper head-
        quarters at the fairgrounds at Bismarck
        Grove near Lawrence.

*29 ANON. Note. Kansas City Times (17 September).
        Reported in Hubach (1943).
            Whitman visited the Times headquarters
        at the fairgrounds.

*30 ANON. Note. Kansas Tribune (17 September).
        Quoted in Hubach (1972).
            Thatcher's appearance nearly made the
        crowd forget their disappointment at not
        hearing Whitman.

*31 ANON. Note. Topeka Commonwealth (17 Septem-
    ber).
        Reported in Hubach (1972).
            Whitman's interest in Kansas and
        activities there are described.

*32 ANON. Note. Topeka Daily Blade (17 Septem-
    ber).
        Reported in Hubach (1972).
            Announces Whitman's presence and
        expected appearance with Forney at the
        latter's lecture that evening.

*33 ANON. Note. Topeka Daily Blade (18 Septem-
    ber).
        Reported in Hubach (1972).
            Reports Whitman's departure for Denver.

*34 ANON. Note. Denver Rocky Mountain News (20
    September).
        Reported in Hubach (1972).
            Notes Whitman's presence.

*35 [WHITMAN, WALT.] Interview with Whitman.
    Denver Daily Tribune (21 September?).
        Reprinted: 1938.23. Cited in Hubach (1972).
            Describes Whitman's appearance, his
        opinions of the West and Denver.

*36 ANON. Note. Sterling (Kansas) Rice County
    Gazette (26 September).
        Quoted in Hubach (1972).
            Notes Whitman's visit, his being im-
        pressed with the mountains and plains.
        "We hope Mr. Whitman will embody these
        impressions in some of his elegant poetry."

*37 ANON. Paragraph. Sterling (Kansas) Weekly
    Bulletin (26 September).
        Reprinted: Hubach (1972).
            Notes Whitman's stopping in Sterling
        and his delight with the city.

*38 ANON. Note. Ottawa (Kansas) Gazette (27
    September).
        Reported in Hubach (1972).
            T. D. Thatcher explained that Whitman
        was unable to write or deliver a poem for
        the celebration.

*39 [MUMFORD, MORRISON?] Note. Kansas City Times
    (27 September).
        Reprinted in Hubach (1943).
            Whitman visited the races in Kansas
        City but did not bet or "indulge in any
        poetic gush over the Exposition."

*40 ANON. Article. Atchison (Kansas) Globe (30
    September), 1.
        Reported in Hubach (1972).
            Notes Whitman's improved health, his
        interest in going into the Lyceum field as
        a lecturer and reader of his poems.

41 ANON. "Walt Whitman. His Ideas About the
    Future of American Literature. The Religion
    and the Politics of the New Nation. Some
    Original Thoughts from a Most Original
    Thinker." St. Louis Post-Dispatch (17
    October), 2:4.
        Reprinted: Hubach (1942); 1932.27.
            Interview with Whitman, who prophesies
        the greatness of the central states and an
        American literature "entirely new, entirely
        different." He comments favorably on a few
        writers, unfavorably on several other con-
        temporaries; describes his purpose.

42 SYMONDS, J. A. "Matthew Arnold's Selections
    from Wordsworth." Fortnightly Review 32
    (1 November), 699-700.

Incidentally quotes Whitman's "severe
verdict" on English poetry from Vistas.
Whitman surely knows the American people
better than the refined students of Boston
do, and finds that English poetry has
little to contribute to their forward
movement. He would, however, have perceived Wordsworth as an exception.

43 BURROUGHS, JOHN. "Nature and the Poets."
    Scribner's Monthly 19 (December), 293-94.
    Reprinted: 1881.1.
    No poet has studied American nature
    more closely than Whitman or sought more
    carefully the right descriptive phrases.
    He is not merely local. He dwells upon
    life, not simply nature, discovering its
    meaning for humanity.

1880

BOOKS

1 DALTON, J. G. Lyra Bicyclica: Forty Poets
   on the Wheel. Boston: Published for the
   author. "Poem of the Ride. A Parody-
   Mosaic. By Walt Wheelman," pp. 104-10.
   Revised: 1885.3.
   Parody, taking off on various lines
   from Whitman's poems.

1a TODHUNTER, JOHN. Study of Shelley. London:
    C. Kegan Paul & Co., pp. 1-3.
    "This age has produced three great
    poets of Democracy," Shelley, Hugo, and
    Whitman. Whitman, "the idealist of real
    life," sets "pulses beating with intenser
    life," making us feel the golden age in
    the present. His expression of the rela-
    tions between the sexes is "full of the
    savage sensuality of an unprogressive
    naturalism."

PERIODICALS

2 WALTERS, FRANK. "Walt Whitman." Papers for
   the Times, 2d ser. (1 January), 47-63.
   Abridged: Bucke.
   "America has found voice" in the power
   and beauty of Whitman's poems, which "are
   one with nature." "He interprets your soul
   to you." His poems "are the man himself."
   Whitman sees the world as God's poem,
   denies the dualism of matter and spirit.
   His poems are sensuous but never sensual.
   He is pagan but also "intensely Christian"
   in his sympathy. His "Religion of Humanity" points toward progress.

*3 [WHITMAN, WALT?] "Walt Whitman Home Again."
    Camden Post (7 January).
    Reprinted: Bucke.
    Notes Whitman's return from his travels,
    his admiration of the West, his gratitude
    for his improved health.

4 ANON. "Brief Comments." Literary News, n.s.
   1 (March), 47.

Ruskin has just sent a request to
Whitman for five complete sets of Leaves.
He says in a letter that Whitman's works
excite "such furious criticism" because
"they are deadly true--in the sense of
rifles--against all our deadliest sins."

5 [PENNYBACKER, ISSAC R.] "Walt Whitman."
   Philadelphis Press (3 March), 5.
   Reprinted: 1880.6. Quoted in Bergman
   (1950).
   Account of visit with Whitman at his
   home on Stevens Street. His recent trip
   West gave him pleasure because he had
   accurately depicted the West although he
   was previously unfamiliar with it. Biographical information is given, somewhat
   inaccurately. Whitman's intentions are to
   deal with common men and things. He changed
   an erroneous line about whales when corrected by an old whaler. He says that Tennyson,
   Longfellow, and Whittier write too much
   like saints. He clings to rhythm. He
   comments on Bryant, Longfellow, and Whittier
   as great writers, with Emerson ahead of
   them; also comments on Bayard Taylor. His
   method was certainly not adopted merely to
   gain fame in England by being different.
   The "rugged thought" of "Myself" 32 and 18
   surpasses much contemporary verse. Prose
   from Two Rivulets is quoted.

6 _____. "How Walt Whitman Writes." New York
   Tribune (7 March), 3:4.
   Reprint of 1880.5.

7 ANON. "Literary Gossip." Athenaeum, no. 2734
   (20 March), 378.
   Report of same quotation as 1880.4.
   Reprinted: 1908.15.

8 WHITE, W. HALE. "The Genius of Walt Whitman."
   Secular Review (20 March), 180-82.
   Commentary on Two Rivulets, little
   recognized but containing perhaps the best
   recent defense of democracy as well as the
   truest poetry and insight. Extensive
   quotations reveal Whitman's ultimate faith
   in democracy, shaped by the war. His poetry
   makes most modern poetry seem "nothing but
   jingle." It has "the charm of the picture,"
   not sentimental but concerned with the
   present, though not despairing, as seen in
   "Prayer." "He sings the sweetness of common
   occupations."

9 FAWCETT, EDGAR. "Americanism in Literature."
   Californian 1 (April), 332-37.
   Whitman is acclaimed in England as the
   emancipator of American letters because he
   represents untrammeled impulses of which
   Americans do not need to be reminded. His
   lack of form and art is a pose, not coming
   from the democratic spirit of the people,
   who prefer rhyme and meter. He can create
   poetically beautiful and powerful lines;
   his "barbaric yawp" does not represent the
   true direction of American poetry.

1880

10 BUCHANAN, ROBERT. "To Walt Whitman." Progress
    2 (3 April), 463.
    Reprint of 1876.1.

*11 [WHITMAN, WALT.] Account of Whitman's Phila-
    delphia lecture on Lincoln. Camden Post
    (16 April).
    Reported in White.

12 THOMSON, JAMES. "Walt Whitman, I." Cope's
    Tobacco Plant 2 (May), 471-73.
    Reprinted: 1910.19.
        Biographical information from Burroughs
    (1871.1). Defense of Whitman against
    charges of smut, Emerson against charges
    of hasty judgment on Whitman in his letter
    (1855.12). Continued 1880.17.

*13 BUCKE, RICHARD MAURICE. "The Good Gray Poet."
    Philadelphia Press (7 May).
    Reported in CHAL and White, but not
    located on this date.

14 ANON. "Ingersoll's Audacity." Philadelphia
    Press (26 May), 1:1-4.
        Describes and prints Ingersoll's
    lecture on religion, noting Whitman's
    presence there and quoting his occasional
    interpolated "Amen" during the course of
    the speech.

*15 B[UCKE], R. M. Letter to editor. Philadel-
    phia Press (26 May).
    Reprinted in Bucke, but not located on this
    date.
        It was a person next to Whitman, not
    Whitman himself, who uttered the "Amens"
    punctuating Ingersoll's lecture (see 1880.
    14).

*16 _____. Letter to editor. Camden Post (28
    May).
    Reported in White. Reprint of 1880.15.

17 THOMSON, JAMES. "Walt Whitman, II." Cope's
    Tobacco Plant 2 (June), 483-85.
    Reprinted: 1910.19.
        Continues 1880.12. Whitman's poems on
    the war are "immeasurably greater and
    nobler" than anything by other Americans
    on the subject, and lack bitterness. He
    surpasses the Boston school, though their
    prose is more scholarly. His faith in demo-
    cracy does not ignore doubt or despair.
    Continued 1880.25.

*18 ANON. Interview with Whitman. London
    (Ontario) Advertiser (5 June).
    Quoted in McMullin (1974); AN&Q 3 (June
    1943), 35-36.
        Describes Whitman's appearance, "full
    of animation." He is "a reverent man with
    no suggestion of irreverence or pruriency
    in his talk." To the material in 1880.19
    are added remarks on a local clergyman's
    disapproval of Whitman's work and Whitman's
    remarks on his idea of giving expression
    to nature as we find it, on his form and

retention of rhythm rather than melody, and
on other authors writing too much like
saints.

19 ANON. "Walt Whitman. Interview with the
    Author of 'Leaves of Grass.'" London
    (Ontario) Free Press (5 June).
        Whitman talks of writing the first
    Leaves, his supporters (including Zola),
    his opinions of fellow-writers, his life.
    This writer terms him the ideal poet.

20 MACLEAN, Mrs. KATE SEYMOUR. "Walt Whitman
    and His Poems." Rose-Belford's Canadian
    Monthly and National Review 5 (July), 29-34.
        Whitman's "more enlightened religion"
    and moral code meet near-universal antagon-
    ism because he rejects literary orthodoxy,
    although he includes poetic touches when
    they come to his power naturally. He has
    "vivid pictures," a profound reverence for
    nature and humanity. Extracts show his
    fitting of expression to subject. He
    achieves directness and simplicity of ex-
    pression more successfully than any book
    save the Bible. One should approach him as
    one approaches religion or philosophy, not
    superficially. "His sins of grossness and
    coarseness of style" do not detract from
    his healthful nature. "America has found
    at last a poet of hew own."

21 MULVANY, CHARLES PELHAM. "Round the Table.
    Walt Whitman." Rose-Belford's Canadian
    Monthly and National Review 5 (July), 94-
    95.
        At first dissenting from Maclean's
    estimate (1880.20), Mulvany then read the
    full edition and discovered Whitman as "all
    that Tupper is not,--a poet, original, full
    of force and fire, ebullient with sympathy for
    human life, and for all life. His poetry finds
    one" through his worthy political and religious
    philosophy. His form has precedents in various
    religious poetry and is suited to his rush
    of fancies. He treats sex incidentally
    but outspokenly, making "short work of con-
    ventional pruderies like the Hicksite icono-
    clast that he is."

22 THRALL, ANTHONY [John Vance Cheney]. "Satin
    Versus Sacking." Californian 2 (July),
    35-44.
        Fawcett's arguments (1880.9) are contra-
    dictory; his verse, not Whitman's, is arti-
    ficial. Whitman is full of fascination with
    life, as extracts show. He has something
    to say, with "faith, earnestness, sympathy,"
    and "acute powers of perception and a pecu-
    liar gift of language." He provides welcome
    relief from such poetry as Fawcett's.

23 ANON. Editorial. Toronto Mail (29 July), 2:4.
    Extract reprinted: 1880.26.
        Whitman's ideas, individuality, and
    "comprehensiveness of human sympathy" are
    praised. Though breaking from conventions,
    his verses retain a rhythm "particularly

their own," no mere "melodious jingle."
Despite his lack of general popularity,
he may be the greatest of contemporary
American poets. Like Tennyson or Longfellow,
he should be judged by his best, not his
worst, compositions.

24 ANON. "Literary Miscellany." Literary News,
n.s. 1 (August), 201.
    Comments on Whitman's visit to Canada,
quoting his interview (1880.19).

25 THOMSON, JAMES. "Walt Whitman, III." Cope's
Tobacco Plant 2 (August), 508-10.
Reprinted: 1910.19. Extract reprinted:
1889.8.
    Continues 1880.17. Record of Whitman's
war service from Burroughs (1871.1) and
O'Connor (1866.2). Whitman's conduct and
style in describing it are exemplary. Continued 1880.29.

26 ANON. "Canadian Estimate of Walt Whitman."
New York Times (1 August), 10:4.
Extract reprinted from 1880.23.

*27 ANON. "Concord Conversations." Springfield
Republican (2 August).
Reprinted in facsimile: Cameron (1958).
    Whitman had been invited to the Concord
school and would have gone if he were not
in Canada and going down the St. Lawrence.

28 [HOPPS, Rev. JOHN Q.] "A Study of Walt
Whitman's Genius and Poetry." Truthseeker
(London) (September), 194-203.
    Whitman is the most truly American
poet, belonging to the soil and the backwoods, stressing "a life fresh, free, and
energetic." Some "positively awful passages
in praise of even the fiercest bodily passions" make his complete works impossible
for everyone to read, but he belongs to a
purer world where such openness and abandon
might be possible. He is a poet of childlike wonder and surprise, of daily life, of
sympathy with all. Even his catalogues
have a charm. He concurrently identifies
with all and lives the life of an onlooker.
Extensive quotations. Concluded 1880.31.

29 THOMSON, JAMES. "Walt Whitman, IV." Cope's
Tobacco Plant 2 (September), 522-24.
Reprinted: 1910.19.
    Continues 1880.25. Describes and
quotes Memoranda extensively; comments on
Whitman's "Three Young Men's Deaths"
(Cope's, April, 1879). Whitman aptly
presents the horrors of war, necessary to
make readers come to shun it. Concluded
1880.38.

30 DAVIS, SAM. "Walt Whitman Again." Californian
2 (October), 385-86.
    Response to Thrall (1880.22). Whitman's
thought is clothed "in cheap, badly fitting
garments." He dismisses absolutely the
art a reader expects. The passages Thrall

cites are prosaic or absurd. Few readers
are willing to dig so hard to find beauties
in Whitman.

31 [HOPPS, Rev. JOHN Q.] "A Study of Walt
Whitman's Genius and Poetry." Truthseeker
(London) (October), 225-29.
    Concludes 1880.28. Long passages are
quoted to reveal Whitman's sympathy and
aspirations. Rhyme and "artificially
measured feet" are not missed, especially
because "these poems are alive and throbbing, as few poems are, with a strong vivid
personality," "one of the greatest, most
pathetic, and most vivid revelations of
human passions, instincts, affections, and
aspirations the world has ever known."

32 ANON. "Notes and News." Academy 18 (2 October), 238.
    "Walt Whitman will shortly give in one
of the London magazines his estimate of the
leading English poets of the nineteenth
century."

33 STEDMAN, EDMUND C. "Walt Whitman." New York
Tribune (17 October), 8:3.
Extract reprinted from 1880.35.

34 ANON. "Sadie! Bernhardt's Banquet." Puck 8
(27 October), 122.
Nine-line parody reprinted: Saunders.
    Among the speakers whose parody address-
es are quoted is Whitman, whose poem "was
in progress when PUCK's reporter departed
from the festive scene."

35 STEDMAN, EDMUND CLARENCE. "Walt Whitman."
Scribner's Magazine 21 (November), 47-64.
Revised: 1885.6. Extracts reprinted:
1880.33; 1880.36.
    "As a lyric and idyllic poet," Whitman
is, "when at his best, among the first of
his time." He applies the Concord philosophy to daily life, but with suspicion "of
all save the masses." Stedman recalls the
strong impression Whitman's work made on
him when read in the Putnam's review
(1855.6). Whitman's purposes were "to
assert the 'Religion of Humanity,'" "to
predict a superb illustration of this
development in 'These States,'" "to portray
an archetypal microcosm" in himself, and
"to lay the groundwork for a new era in
literature." His reception is traced to
deny the professed neglect. Whitman robs
sex of its appeal by treating it openly
rather than with nature's "half-concealment."
His style, with Greek and Hebrew affinities,
is "capable of impressive rhythmical and
lyrical effects," although blank verse
might have helped him avoid some tediousness. "His diction, on its good behavior,
is copious and strong, full of surprises,"
using words of the people, slang, foreign
words, new senses for common verbs and
nouns. His mode seems suited only to himself, no other poets having used it success-

1880

fully. His vivid pictures are due to his
knowledge of America and her people. His
poetry proclaims a glorious future but his
prose portrays a corrupt nation. Though
the people prefer Whittier, Whitman yet
may reach them. His self-assertion is
bracing, except when it "seems to be
'posing.'" But the "extravagance of
genius" is allowed to great poets like
Whitman.

36 _____. "Walt Whitman's Naturalism." New
York Tribune (7 November), 8:3-4.
Extract reprinted from 1880.35.

37 DUSENBURY, V. HUGO. "His Warning to Autograph-
Hunters." Puck 8 (10 November), 156.
Reprinted: Saunders.
Quotes what Whitman (among others)
would offer a prospective autograph-hunter
in a long parody.

38 THOMSON, JAMES. "Walt Whitman, V." Cope's
Tobacco Plant 2 (December), 558-59.
Reprinted: 1910.19.
Concludes 1880.29. Quotes Memoranda
and 1855 Preface, with comments.

1881

BOOKS

1 BURROUGHS, JOHN. Pepacton. Boston: Houghton,
Mifflin & Co. "Nature and the Poets,"
pp. 122-24.
Reprint of 1879.43.

2 CHAINEY, GEORGE. The Infidel Pulpit: Lectures by George Chainey. Vol. 1. Boston:
George Chainey, n.d. "Lessons for To-day,
from Walt Whitman," pp. 91-97; "True Democracy," pp. 98-104; also quotations, pp.
111, 113.
Reprints of 1881.22 and 1881.23.

3 CONWAY, MONCURE D. Thomas Carlyle. New York:
Harper & Bros., p. 100.
Despite Conway's attempts "to make him
admit the merit of certain passages" in
Whitman, Carlyle said, "I cannot like him.
It all seems to be, 'I'm a big man because
I live in such a big country.' But I have
heard of great men living in very small
corners of the earth."

4 COOKE, GEORGE WILLIS. Ralph Waldo Emerson:
His Life, Writings, and Philosophy.
Boston: James R. Osgood & Co., pp. 233-34.
Revised: 1900.5.
Explains Emerson's opinions of Whitman's
poetry, favoring Whitman's earlier work
over his less coarse recent poems of
spiritual power.

5 DOWDEN, EDWARD. Shakspere: A Critical
Study of His Mind and Art. 3d ed. New
York and London: Harper & Bros., pp. 35,

284, 292, 357-58, 381-82.
Revision of 1875.2.
Incidental references to Whitman: he
is among this century's spiritual teachers
who are adding a modern element to
Shakespeare's positivism; Vistas is quoted
on Shakespeare's feudalism; lines from
"Calamus" are quoted as a motto for the
sonnets, on a similar theme.

6 [SANBORN, F. B.] "Holmes." In The Homes and
Haunts of Our Elder Poets. New York:
D. Appleton & Co., pp. 159, 160.
Incidental comparisons of Holmes to
Whitman: Holmes "dwells upon his personal
history microscopically, where Thoreau and
Whitman would have done it telescopically."
Next to Whitman's, Holmes's personal
sketches "seem rather petty, though more
refined and well-mannered."

7 [STODDARD, R. H.] "Longfellow." In The Homes
and Haunts of Our Elder Poets. New York:
D. Appleton & Co., p. 96.
Incidental reference: "If the English
had not so settled it, would we ever have
found out for ourselves what great national
poets we have in Mr. Walt Whitman and Mr.
Joaquin Miller?"

PERIODICALS

8 ANON. "American Poetry." The American 1
(29 January), 249-50.
Summary of and response to Whitman's
"The Poetry of the Future" in the January
North American Review: Whitman overemphasizes democratic and American functions of
poetry; he seems to tend to "disregard the
poetical quality of his work in comparison
with its aboriginality," sometimes neglecting his undoubted poetical sensibility when
he merely lists things.

9 KENNEDY, WILLIAM SLOANE. "A Study of Walt
Whitman." Californian 3 (February), 149-58.
Beyond "his magnificent originality as
an interpreter of nature" and "the unparalleled grandeur of his poems of immortality
and death," Whitman is "the first great
poet of democracy," spokesman for the
masses through the "grossness" and "swagger"
of his early writings and his "almost
wholly Saxon" language. His democracy,
novel idea of friendship, and individual
personality are explained; his egotism is
offensive. He has "titanic strength,"
amplitude, but a dangerous optimism and
lack of discrimination. He insists on the
vital necessity of religion.

*10 ANON. Account of Whitman's lecture in Boston.
Boston Daily Advertiser (16 April).
Reprinted: 1881.14.
Notes prominent citizens present at
Whitman's Lincoln lecture.

11 ANON. "The Martyr President." Boston Evening Transcript (16 April), 2:2.
     Account of Whitman's Lincoln lecture at the Hawthorne rooms, its content, the historical significance.

*12 ANON. Editorial leader. Boston Evening Traveller (16 April).
     Quoted in 1881.20.
     Account of Lincoln lecture, a memorable occasion with the audience paying homage "to one who is already fast being regarded as the typical citizen of the republic," though "scorned as a barbarian rhymester." He read "his grandly pathetic lament," "Captain."

*13 ANON. "Walt Whitman: How He Related His Reminiscences of Abraham Lincoln." Boston Journal (16 April).
     Reported in Martin.

14 ANON. "Walt Whitman in Boston." New York Times (18 April), 2:4.
     Reprint of 1881.10.

15 [BAXTER, SYLVESTER.] "Walt Whitman. His Second Visit to the New England Metropolis. A Cordial Welcome in Literary Circles. Sketch of His Life and Poetic Characteristics." Boston Herald (18 April), Supplement, 1:1-2.
     Reprinted in part: Bucke.
     Account of Whitman's Lincoln lecture, his popularity in Boston, life (slightly inaccurate), appearance, and character. He put much of his individuality into his work, forming "a poesy inspired by the nineteenth century, by the broad American continent." Stedman (1880.35) failed to grasp Whitman's true significance.

16 PORTER, LINN B. "Walt Whitman." Boston Evening Transcript (18 April), 6:1.
     Reprinted: Bucke; Legler.
     Sonnet praising Whitman's personal power, felt from his presence at the lecture even more than from his works.

17 ANON. "Walt Whitman." New York Tribune (21 April), 4:4-5.
     Editorial. Whitman writes of contemporary matters "in an antique spirit and an almost archaic phraseology." His independence from literary conventions is his appeal; he is himself, unspoiled by his literary coteries. At first shocking, his work is "in demand and read still."

18 ANON. "News and Notes." Literary World 12 (23 April), 153.
     An eyewitness account of Whitman's Lincoln lecture of 15 April; description of his other Boston activities, a planned future visit.

19 ANON. "Table Talk." Literary World 12 (23 April), 152.
     Letter criticizes Literary World for its high ranking of Whitman.

20 ANON. "Walt Whitman's Late Lecture in Boston." Progress (30 April), 391.
     Reprinted with minor changes: Bucke.
     Notes Whitman's lecture on Lincoln and his two previous deliveries of it, quoting Boston Evening Traveller (1881.12); other Boston activities; his significant callers; return to Camden; impressions of Boston.

21 BUNNER, H. C. "Bric-a-Brac. Home, Sweet Home, with Variations. VI. As Walt Whitman might have written all around it." Scribner's Monthly 22 (May), 159-60.
     Reprinted: 1884.4; 1904.20; Saunders.
     Parody.

22 CHAINEY, GEORGE. "Lessons for To-Day from Walt Whitman." The Infidel Pulpit 1, no. 12 (21 May), 1-7.
     Reprinted: 1881.2.
     No heart but Whitman's "beats so full and respondent to the life of the living present." This "poet of the future" emphasizes lessons for today, not from the past, in contrast to other literature, the church, and other institutions. He sought his truth from nature, his style from the sea. "Shakespeare was the Pacific, while Whitman is the Atlantic" without the Pacific's romance. Chainey describes his love for Whitman's "thought-provoking, mysterious, symbolic, vague, and often tantalizing words" though without a full understanding, as with nature. Whitman calls for the surrender of the church, though some of his beliefs seem at one with it. He must wait to come into his own. His words must be heeded regarding the body and passion. Much of this lecture is used in The Gnostic (1885.21).

23 _____. "True Democracy." The Infidel Pulpit 1, no. 13 (28 May), 1-7.
     Reprinted: 1881.2.
     Whitman's ideas and words are used as text for this sermon: Whitman "chants the glory of the future that is to blossom out of the heart of the people," and is thus "superior to every other modern writer," truly democratic, as our country needs, in contrast to the aristocratic Carlyle.

24 ANON. "American Literature." Critic 1 (18 June), 164.
     George Woodberry's article on American Literature in Fortnightly Review ignores all American poetry but Longfellow's: "Is it by accident that Walt Whitman was born in America?"

25 BURROUGHS, JOHN. "Nature in Literature." Critic 1 (16 July), 185.
     Reprinted: 1882.4; 1902.6.
     Unlike earlier writers, Whitman regards nature "mainly in the light of science," viewing modern conditions as well as "the highest regions."

1881

26 STEDMAN, EDMUND C. "Poetry in America. First Article." <u>Scribner's Monthly</u> 22 (August), 544n.
    Incidental reference to Whitman as one of the "many true poets" whose almost simultaneous appearance in American literature Stedman seeks to explain. Concluded 1881.35.

27 ANON. "Walt Whitman in Huntington." <u>Long Islander</u> (5 August), 2.
    Reprinted: Whitman Supplement 1978.
    Account of Whitman's and Bucke's visit to Long Island this past week; his ancestors; list of their visitors and homesteads they visited.

28 WAGER-FISHER, Mrs. MARY E. "Walt Whitman." <u>Long Islander</u> (5 August), 2.
    Abridged from 1878.9.

29 ANON. "Literary Notes." <u>Critic</u> 1 (13 August), 221.
    Announces Whitman's return from his Long Island visit, his upcoming edition, and Bucke's preparation of his book, to be half biography, half criticism.

30 ANON. "'The Good Gray Poet.'" Boston <u>Daily Globe</u> (24 August), 2:3-4.
    Reprinted in part: Bucke; Bergman (1950).
    Interview with Whitman while he is in Boston looking over the proof-sheets of his new edition which completes the plan he had in mind from the beginning of his work. His theory, he says, "is to give a recognition of all elements compacted into one." People have had difficulty understanding him, thinking his early work represented the whole building rather than the mere foundation. His theories of poetry are described. He is quoted on comradeship, his opinions of writers, his changes (made for the purposes of conciseness, not censorship), the war's significance to his work. His war activities, visit to Long Island, recent publishings, and Bucke's upcoming book are described.

31 [O'REILLY, J.B.] "Walt Whitman's Poems." The <u>Pilot</u> 44 (27 August), 5:3.
    Whitman is in town supervising the upcoming publication of <u>Leaves</u>, now recognized by a well-known publishing house which has agreed to publish it without expurgations. He claims his work now achieves "completeness and relative proportion."

32 B. "To Walt Whitman." <u>Liberty</u> 1 (17 September), 4.
    Sonnet rejoicing in Whitman's acceptance by the literary elite.

33 ANON. "Literary Notes." <u>Critic</u> 1 (24 September), 264.
    Paragraph on Whitman's current visit with the Emersons in Concord.

34 [HOLLAND, J. G.] "Literary Eccentricity." <u>Scribner's Monthly</u> 22 (October), 945-46.
    Whitman's new form has been too eagerly accepted by the English as characterizing the new American literature, but it is not imitated.

35 STEDMAN, EDMUND C. "Poetry in America. Second Article." <u>Scribner's Monthly</u> 22 (October), 823, 826, 827.
    Concludes 1881.26. Whitman's charm lies in his "fresh, absolute handling of outdoor nature," not his "method and democratic vistas." Stedman defends his <u>Scribner's</u> essay (1880.35) and praises Whitman's artistry and democracy.

36 [WHITMAN, WALT?] "A Poet's Supper to his Printers and Proof-Readers." <u>Boston Daily Advertiser</u> (17 October), 8.
    Account of Whitman's informal reception for his printers from Rand & Avery's upon their completion of the setting up of <u>Leaves</u>. Whitman told about his life as a printer and his political views of tolerance and the progress made in "fraternizing." He read "John Anderson, my Jo."

37 ANON. "Personal." <u>Boston Evening Transcript</u> (22 October), 3:3.
    "Walt Whitman has been invited to visit Mr. Swinburne, the poet, and will leave for Europe in a few months."

37a JARVES, JAMES JACKSON. "Art and Poesy in Italy. Walt Whitman Held Up as a Model to Italian Poets." <u>New York Times</u> (24 October), 2:1-2.
    Approvingly quotes Enrico Nencioni in the <u>Fanfulla</u> regarding Whitman as an antidote to the "piddling realism and hot-house sensationalism" of modern Italian and European literature.

38 [BAXTER, SYLVESTER.] "'Leaves of Grass.' The Complete Poems of Walt Whitman. As Published by a Famous Boston House. A Friendly Characterization of the Poet's Work." Boston <u>Sunday Herald</u> (30 October), 3:5-7.
    Review of 1881 <u>Leaves</u>. Brief account of the history of <u>Leaves</u>; Emerson's letter (1855.12) reprinted. There will be much opposition to Whitman's work as it becomes more well-known, but its place is secured. It is now more complete with a more comprehensive patriotism. It is truly "poetry of the noblest kind," "fresh and beautiful," with "rhythmic swing," "clearness of vision," "large and magnificent tolerance," and "the ecstasy of being." His lines could not be cut into equal lengths; his cataloguing provides "a mosaic picture" of the people and nation; his foreign phrases "depict unassimilated fragments floating on the life-current of the nation." "The want of artistic grace in form is compensated for by the artistic picturesqueness of

form." The first person is used not literally but to show how "everyone is to
himself the central point of the world."
Whitman, as poet of evolution and prophet
of modern science, "conjoins materialism
with ideality." "Myself" is like "a noble
drama." Themes of the poems are listed;
passages are quoted with praise, including
comments on some new poems ("Spirit,"
"Italian Music in Dakota"). "Captain" is
"already established as a popular American
classic." Stedman (1880.35) missed the
point that Whitman had to include all, not
write what was only partially true. There
is no more evil in Whitman than in nature.

39 ANON. "Supplementary Notes." Literary News,
n.s. 2 (November), 379.
    Among Osgood's recent publications is
"Walt Whitman's new edition of his characteristic Leaves of Grass ($2)."

40 ANON. "Personal." Boston Evening Transcript
(2 November), 1:2.
    Notes Bucke's preparation of "a book
to be called 'Contemporaneous Notes of Walt
Whitman,' which is intended to collect as
much as possible about the poet, especially
biographical matters, personal anecdotes
and traits, and bibliographical items,
while they can be yet authenticated, and
while he is 'yet in the flesh.'"

40a ANON. "Whitman's 'Leaves of Grass.'" Critic
1 (5 November), 302-3.
Reprinted: 1882.4; Hindus.
    Review of 1881 Leaves. The changes are
generally good. Only lovers of poetry have
penetrated and rejoiced in Whitman's work.
His doctrines have been misconstrued; he is
enthusiastic about the wonders of the body,
not lewd. He has lack of taste, monotonous
expression, but great power. "Drum-Taps"
and Memoranda are praised. He represents
America.

*41 ANON. Interview with Whitman. Philadelphia
Press (6 November).
Reported in 1928.36.

42 ANON. "Our Boston Literary Letter." Springfield Daily Republican (10 November),
3:1-2.
Extracts reprinted: Bucke.
    Whitman, John Brown, and Lincoln are
three great figures America has produced
in one generation. "The immense landscape
of Whitman's teeming and unharvested imagination" is praised. Leaves captures the
picture of his mind through its broad unity,
suggesting the utterance of the early gods.
He is unmatched in capturing the spirit of
the Civil War. Without Emerson, Whitman
might not have written, yet his "unformed
and almost lawless paragraphs, this broad
range over the most prosaic elements of
life" could not be further from "the Emersonian mode."

43 ANON. "Personal." Boston Evening Transcript
(11 November), 3:3-4.
    Quotes Whitman's impressions of Boston,
New York, and Philadelphia from his interview in the Philadelphia Press (1881.41).

43a ANON. "New Publications. Walt Whitman."
New York Tribune (19 November), 6:1.
Reprinted in part: Bucke.
    Review of 1881 Leaves. Whitman is
celebrated more than he is read. He has
genius and some real poetry, but the indecent elements still present represent art's
"last degradation."

44 ANON. "Walt Whitman's Poems." Literary World
12 (19 November), 411-12.
    Review of 1881 Leaves. Whitman cannot
be regarded as our representative American
poet because of his war on poetic tradition
and our ideas of decency and purity. His
form is "a chaos of monotonies," not diverse
like the elements. His powers of observation are acute, but he fails to grasp "the
inner spiritual lessons." "American he is,
of the ruder and more barbaric type." His
religion "is curiously Asiatic." He has
gleams of great things ("Captain," "Singer"),
but he cannot be considered a real poet.

45 M[ITCHELL], E[DWARD] P. "Walt Whitman and the
Poetry of the Future." New York Sun (19
November), 2:5-6.
    Review of 1881 Leaves, which allows
Whitman's work to be judged as a whole.
He has not compromised by cancelling any
objectionable line. His work is justifi-
ably full of "an egotism that reaches the
verge of sublimity." His versification is
his most superficial distinction, actually
a "reversion to a primitive mode of poetic
expression," comparable to passages quoted
from Psalms and Ossian, never becoming
monotonous. Whitman reacts against romanticism, showing the modern man in relation
to nature and modern society. His portrait
of himself falls short in being part ideal
and part real, but no more so than any
other writer's attempts. His democratic
philosophy is not clearly thought out. He
presents like no other poet the range of
human activity.

46 ANON. "Literature. Walt Whitman's Claim to
Be Considered a Great Poet." Chicago
Tribune (26 November), 9:3-4.
    Review of 1881 Leaves. Whitman's
poetry is not enjoyed by the people but
requires "a peculiarly cultured taste."
His work might be better as prose. Nothing
that Swinburne wrote compares with the foulness of some of Whitman's verses. His work
is imaginative but lacks form, suggesting
not a new art but "a great art in its most
degraded form." His "extraordinary nature"
reveals "rugged strength," "active, brilliant imagination," and "far-reaching enthusiasm," with command of language and

1881

inexhaustible vocabulary, but "these qualities do not make him a great poet"; if he
is a great poet, then others were "but
'pitiful rhymers.'"

47 ANON. "'Leaves of Grass.'" Liberty 1 (26
November), 3.
Review of 1881 Leaves, which has not
lost Whitman's "original native simplicity, freshness, and vigor," "outspoken
independence," and "naked truthfulness
and purity." Whitman is the poet of innovation and evolution, quivering with
life. "Ontario" (quoted) reveals Whitman's
mission, at one with Liberty's.

48 ANON. "A 'Symposium' on 'Leaves of Grass.'"
Literary World 12 (3 December), 446.
Reprinted: Bucke.
Comments from three readers support
the Literary World's stand against Leaves
(see 1881.44), "the dirtiest unsuppressed
book ever published in this country."

49 ANON. "Literary Notes." Critic 1 (3 December), 339.
"Walt Whitman informs us that there is
no truth in the report that he is about to
visit England."

50 ANON. "Notes of New Books." Philadelphia
Times (3 December), 6:3.
Review of 1881 Leaves, which should
"win the world's wider attention." Brim-
ming with Whitman's personality, it retains
his "undimmed, immortal" sight, with "the
mad turbulences hushed a little," though
it remains "green and vital as ever." He
is strong to retain his personal eccentricities (as in dress) in a strait-laced
world. He has many lines that "breathe
and bristle with power, that sparkle and
flash with beauty," though with occasional
eclipses. "It is life, seen and recorded,"
with the "intense splendor of his own
being," unlike the writers of other ages
but appropriate to this generation:
"gigantic, rude, loud, prosy, mechanic,
conceited. Whirling, unsettled, abounding
in vitality, extent and power."

51 SHOEMAKER, W. L. "To Walt Whitman." Literary
World 12 (3 December), 446.
Sonnet urging Whitman to clothe his
thoughts, which "are strong, and many fair
and sweet," in "befitting dress" of meter
and rhyme.

*52 ANON. Review of Leaves. Pioneer Press (12
December).
Reported in Asselineau.

53 [HIGGINSON, T. W.] "Recent Poetry." Nation
33 (15 December), 476-77.
Extract reprinted: 1881.54.
Review of 1881 Leaves, which makes
even poor poetry in other volumes here
reviewed look good. Whitman's "somewhat

nauseating quality remains in full force."
His love lacks personal emotion, is animal-
istic. "Drum-Taps" rings hollow. His one
fine poem, "Captain," overthrows his whole
poetic theory and suggests that Whitman
may yet recognize the value of form. Only
an occasional phrase, not a complete work,
will be remembered. He should be compared
to Ossian, once praised, now ignored.

54 _____. "Mr. Walt Whitman's Obscenity."
Washington Post (19 December), 2:4.
Extract from 1881.53 (quoted from New York
Evening Post, but same as Nation).

55 ANON. "Walt Whitman's 'Leaves of Grass'
Redivivus." Independent 33 (29 December),
10.
Revised: 1892.70.
Review of 1881 Leaves. "Much of this
book is a loud and long-winded replication
of Emerson's egoistic pantheism." We may
fall for a while into Whitman's movement,
then he falls into prose. "The diction is
repulsive," retained although he became
more decent in Drum-Taps. He will appeal
only to a few critics, not to "the general
voice of the sane."

1882

BOOKS

1 BALDWIN, JAMES. An Introduction to the Study
of English Literature and Literary Criticism. Vol. 1. Poetry. Richmond: B. F.
Johnson Publishing Co., pp. 558-60.
Whitman is "an American disciple of
the pre-Raphaelite school," with few admirers in America. "Spirit" is cited as
"a fair specimen of his best style."
Opinions of Whitman are quoted. The last
fifteen lines of "Myself" are given: it
is "difficult to discover what poetry there
is in such spasmodic utterances."

2 CONWAY, MONCURE DANIEL. Emerson at Home and
Abroad. Boston: James R. Osgood & Co.,
pp. 360-61.
Emerson admired Whitman's "Oriental
largeness and optimism," and said one should
not be too squeamish when reading him. The
Bohemians told a story, here described, of
Whitman's effect on Emerson.

3 COTTERILL, H. B. An Introduction to the Study
of Poetry. London: Kegan Paul, Trench &
Co., pp. 21-24.
Reprinted in part: Dowden.
Quotes and analyzes passages from
"Broad-Axe," one of the finest examples of
the "faculty of exciting an emotional feeling by mere association with material
things," revealing Whitman's tendency upward from appearances toward an ideal,
showing him a great poet in this, though
"he may not be one of the greatest."

4 [GILDER, JEANNETTE, ed.?] Essays from "The
Critic." Boston: James R. Osgood & Co.
Includes reprints of 1881.25 and 1881.40
and two essays by Whitman.

5 HOLLAND, J. G. Every-Day Topics: A Book of
Briefs. 2d ser. New York: Charles
Scribner's Sons. "Is it Poetry?", pp. 126-
34.
Reprint of 1876.56.

6 LELAND, CHARLES G. The Gypsies. Boston and
New York: Houghton, Mifflin & Co., pp.
235, 283.
Recalls a visit to the New Jersey
gypsies and meeting Whitman on the way.

7 NICHOL, JOHN. American Literature, An Historical Sketch 1620-1880. Edinburgh:
Adam & Charles Black, pp. 207-14.
Reprinted in part: Hindus.
Whitman, though a writer of great
force, "is ruined as an artist by his contempt for art," notwithstanding his revisions. Lacking humor, he has perpetrated
absurdities, but his perception of natural
beauty exhibits some genius. His positive
moral values are his democratic philanthropy, confidence in a new world, and
intense sympathy. "Lilacs," "Captain,"
and "Reconciliation" represent his highest
mood.

8 PARKE, WALTER. Lays of the Saintly, or, The
New Golden Legend. London: Vizetelly &
Co., n.d. "St. Smith of Utah," pp. 68-74.
Reprinted: Saunders.
Story of Joseph Smith told in a
Whitmanesque parody.

9 SANBORN, F. B. Henry D. Thoreau. Boston:
Houghton, Mifflin & Co., pp. 186, 188.
Mentions Thoreau's writings on Whitman
and his meeting with him.

10 SHEPARD, WILLIAM [William Shepard Walsh], ed.
Pen Pictures of Modern Authors. New York:
G. P. Putnam's. "Walt Whitman," pp. 161-
77.
Two articles on Whitman are reprinted:
Conway (1866.22) and "Bohemians in America"
from Danbury News (unlocated), by "Jay
Charlton," who recalls Whitman, before the
war, reading aloud his poems, which were
failures. He "would have served the world
better had he stuck to the printer's case
and left poetry alone." Whitman's quarrel
with George Arnold over secession is described.

11 STEVENSON, ROBERT LOUIS. Preface to Familiar
Studies of Men and Books. London: Chatto
& Windus, pp. xvii-xix; also "Walt
Whitman" (reprint of 1878.17), 91-128;
"Thoreau," 166-67.
Preface explains Stevenson's need to
qualify his admiration for Whitman in
1878.17 in order "to explain him credibly

to Mrs. Grundy," although he would have
liked to speak more strongly in Whitman's
favor. The essay on Thoreau compares him
with Whitman, his disciple, bawling the
same doctrine that Thoreau whispered; but
"one pursues Self-improvement" churlishly
while the other follows happiness, loving
others, helping us to live.

PERIODICALS

12 HEYWOOD, ANGELA T. Leaflet Literature.
Princeton, Mass.: Word office.
Two undated single-sheet articles from
the Houghton Library at Harvard University.
The first traces the suppression by the
"lascivious Idiots" of the Vice Society
and prints the district attorney's letter
to Osgood, the list of passages to be ex-
punged, Whitman's response. The August
Word (unlocated) published "Prostitute"
and other lines to be deleted. Purity or
impurity is in the eye of the beholder.
The second article presents Emerson's
letter (1855.12) and "An Open Letter to
Walt Whitman," by Ezra H. Heywood, dated
5 November, noting the suppression of the
Word for publishing Whitman's lines, mentioning other radical Whitman supporters
(including Benjamin Tucker), recalling
Heywood's own reading of Leaves from
Theodore Parker's pulpit to an Anti-Slavery
Society meeting in 1861, noting Dr. J. H.
Swain's reading of the suppressed poems at
the Free Love Convention in May. "Human
language contains no finer type of manly
sympathy for the supposed 'fallen,' no more
impressive portraiture of the divinity of
motherhood than is apparent in these two
'obscene' poems." Heywood is sustained by
Whitman's inspirations. He published extracts from a Philadelphia paper regarding
Leaves in the November Word (unlocated).

13 [ALDEN, HENRY MILLS.] "Editor's Literary
Record." Harper's New Monthly Magazine 64
(January), 313.
Among the new volumes of poetry here
acknowledged is Leaves, "a congeries of
bizarre rhapsodies, that are neither sane
verse nor intelligible prose."

14 ANON. Review of 1881 Leaves. Atlantic
Monthly 49 (January), 124-26.
Whitman's offensive passages are no
more characteristic than "the fresh, strong,
healthy presentation of common things in a
way that revivifies them, the genuine aspiration, the fine sympathy with man and
nature, the buoyant belief in immortality."
Debate over his form is no longer necessary.
The imagination informing the whole of one
of his poems transcends the weakness of
any parts, such as vocabulary, although
many of his epithets are vivid and apt.
"Pioneers," "Lilacs," "Cradle," "Man-of-
War Bird," and "Locomotive" are praised,
as is his aim "to increase virility in

manners, thought, and writing." But he can have no wide influence because his method breaks natural laws and degrades the body by depriving it of its spiritual attributes.

*15 ANON. Review of 1881 Leaves. Toledo Journal (January).
Reported in Gohdes and Silver.

16 [BROWNE, FRANCIS F.] "Briefs on New Books." Dial 2 (January), 218-19.
Reprinted: Hindus.
Review of 1881 Leaves. To accept Whitman's poetic revolution would mean dropping all distinctions between poetry and prose. Whitman ironically may be better remembered for his fine regular poems "Captain" and "Ethiopia" and such near-metrical ones as "Lilacs," as well as occasional lines and passages. His freedom and virility are primitive, his democracy sentimental. His crudeness, though not extensive in this volume, is due to his general lack of taste, selectivity, and "the sense of poetic fitness."

17 ANON. "New Publications." Detroit Free Press (7 January), 3:3.
Review of 1881 Leaves. Whitman's genuineness and self-confidence are not to be doubted. However, this work is scarcely poetry, although as prose it would be "grandiloquent, sonorous, rhetorical," sometimes imaginative, almost always "egotistical." "Adam" is indecent.

18 ANON. "Walt Whitman on Aesthetic Poetry." Philadelphia Times (11 January), 3:2.
Paragraph on Oscar Wilde's upcoming visit to Whitman, who says he has not read a line of Wilde's poetry or of much other contemporary poetry, though he is "disposed to give the poetry of aestheticism a fair chance."

19 BALL, B. W. "Two American Poets." The Index (12 January), 332-33.
Whitman and Bryant both reflect their environments. Whitman is indeed one of the roughs, sometimes charming, sometimes repulsive. Marvin (1877.13) is quoted.

20 ANON. "'The Poetry of the Future.'" New York Examiner 59 (19 January), 1.
Review of 1881 Leaves, "blasphemous and obscene" and worthy of prosecution. Whitman "wallows in vice and crime at every opportunity," and is all the worse because according to his friends he has not the excuse of "a depraved and bestial nature." "Myself" 21 is "poetically expressed," passages from "Cradle" and "Lilacs" are exquisite, with an occasional sublime truth set in beautifully fitting words. He is a poet (although not a great one), but "has written very little poetry." He will be remembered only for "Captain," "the most

stirring lyric" of the Civil War. "He is the 'Bowery Bhoy' in literature." He can paint nature and has "a certain rough power," but he is narrow, "uncouth and barbaric," with bathos more often than pathos, "a dithyrambic Emerson," "a prose Swinburne run mad," "an obscene Ossian," "a poetical Zola."

21 ANON. "Wilde and Whitman." Philadelphia Press (19 January), 8:1.
Reprinted: 1935.20; 1936.17.
Interview with Whitman on his favorable impressions of Wilde who visited him the day before. Whitman admires the aesthetes' break from convention. Wilde has admired Whitman since childhood.

22 M., G. E. "Whitman, Poet and Seer. A Review of His Literary Scheme, Work, and Method." New York Times (22 January), 4:5-7.
Review of 1881 Leaves, which shows in Whitman's work "a harmony and an intellectual completeness" hitherto absent. Whitman stands for democracy, "the spiritual and material evolution of man," teaching that the purpose, not merely the act, may be immoral. Whitman's intentions are better than his work, for he equates the ability to discriminate with mere technical dexterity. Though too primitive, his work does remind us of America's creative spirit. "Adam" is "over-Whitmanish," only questionably moral. "Myself" is "a healthy expression of vigorous humanity and imaginative egotism," its contradictions intentional. The "Songs" present him "at his best, free of verbiage and pretension." "Drum-Taps" shows a strong spirit of manhood. These poems are significant as a whole rather than individually, for Whitman fails in the poet's chief work, use of language. His value lies in his modernity and individuality.

23 ANON. Commentary on Leaves. New York Evangelist (26 January), 2:6.
Whitman owes his short-lived fame to "the sedulous puffings of a few admirers" and the "ridicule of judicious critics." The Examiner (1882.20) is quoted.

24 COOK, CLARENCE. "Wilde and Whitman." New York Tribune (29 January), 4:6.
Extract reprinted from 1882.26.

25 ANON. "Leaves of Grass." Catholic World 34 (February), 719-20.
Review of 1881 Leaves. "Enfans d'Adam" would be more truly titled "Enfans de la Bête," since Whitman acts "free from all conscious restraint, young and lusty." He is "a more recent and more genuine outcome of transcendentalism," "more a creature of his instincts," than Emerson, whose Calvinistic heritage Whitman lacks. But man should act in accord with rational laws, not with opinions like Whitman's, so degrading to man.

26 COOK, CLARENCE. "Some Recent Poetry."
International Review 12 (February), 222-24.
Review of 1881 Leaves. Wilde's latest
volume (also reviewed here) reveals
Whitman's influence in his titles but lacks
Whitman's "call to sing." Whitman merely
enlarges Emerson's earlier ideas, but in
an original way. His work is not impure
but lacks taste and humor. The 1855 Leaves
had "a rudimentary good taste," a unity and
expression that the new edition lacks, and
will remain a real contribution to American thought. "Captain," "Banner," and
"Cradle" are unforgettable. Whitman is
not really a true American, but he and
Emerson are America's only poets so far.

27 H[IGGINSON], T. W. "Unmanly Manhood."
Woman's Journal 13 (4 February), 1.
Though "called 'manly' poetry," the
work of Wilde and Whitman is immoral.
"Drum-Taps" seems hollow since Whitman,
though fit and available, failed to join
the army in the war.

28 ANON. Editorial. New York Times (13 February), 4:6.
Brief biographical sketch, since
Whitman "has never had a biographer in
the real sense of the term."

*29 ANON. Interview with Oscar Wilde. St. Louis
Globe-Democrat (26 February).
Quoted in 1936.17.
Quotes Wilde's praise for Whitman,
whose picture he owns.

30 ANON. "Literary Notes." Boston Commonwealth
(18 March), 2:8.
Whitman is preparing his prose writings
for publication.

31 ANON. "Among Books." Mace 3 (21 March), 2-3.
Review of 1881 Leaves. At last the
modern poet appears in the person of
Whitman, "the first authentic message from
the New World to the Old." "At once the
most egotistic and most universal of bards,"
he includes and accepts all subjects and
religions, evil as well as good. He makes
readers think for themselves. (Errors in
this essay regarding Whitman's current age
and the recency of his stroke may indicate
a composition date around 1876.)

32 ANON. Editorial on Longfellow's death.
London Times (25 March), 11:4.
Quoted in Bucke.
One cannot point to a worthy successor
of the Boston group now gone, though
Whitman's "rough, barbaric, untoned lines
full of questionable morality and unfettered by rhyme" may be "the nucleus of the
literature of the future," "a real American
literature" to mirror American life and
"no false ideal."

33 ELLIS, HENRY H[AVELOCK]. "The Two Worlds."
Modern Thought 4 (April), 129-30.
Whitman has "masculine breadth and
power," "a coarse healthfulness, a hearty
world-embracing sympathy" similar to that
of Rabelais and Rubens. His occasional
"outbursts of lyric song" are scarcely
surpassed by those of Heine. Like Heine,
Whitman strives to express the two worlds
of the real and the ideal, the prosaic and
the poetic; he is hardly conscious of the
discord between these worlds and unable to
harmonize them. He lacks humor. Nothing
is too commonplace for his attention, hence
the contempt he has received. His lists,
not without charm, recall Milton's.

34 CHAINEY, GEORGE. "The Clergy." This World 3
(1 April), 10.
Incidental: "We need some of the
gospel of Walt Whitman, who grandly and
heroically dares to say. . . ." ("Myself"
quoted).

35 ANON. "Emerson." New York Times (28 April),
4:3-4.
Editorial on Emerson's death: "He had
none of the superabundant robustness of
WHITMAN," who is his opposite but "full of
Emerson."

*36 BUCKE, RICHARD MAURICE. "Walt Whitman."
Family Circle (May).
Reported in CHAL.

37 ANON. "British Estimates of Emerson." Boston
Daily Advertiser (10 May), 2:2.
Reprinted in facsimile: Cameron (1958).
Pall Mall Gazette (unlocated) is quoted:
"Certainly Walt Whitman is a poor substitute
for Longfellow."

38 ANON. "'Leaves of Grass.' An Interview with
the Author at Camden, N.J. The Correspondence With His Boston Publishers. The
Effort of Attorney-General Marston to Suppress the Book." Boston Daily Globe (22
May), morning ed., 1:5; evening edition,
1:6.
Massachusetts Attorney General Marston
is going to suppress the publication of
Leaves. Whitman's exchange with Osgood
regarding expurgation, which he refused,
is reported. Whitman denies any negative
feelings.

39 ANON. "Walt Whitman." Boston Evening Transcript (22 May), 4:3.
Abridged: Bucke.
Editorial describing the prosecution
of Leaves, which are permanently wilted
now, it is hoped. Certainly no one ever
bought the book for mere "literary enjoyment." Whitman was welcomed by enthusiastic
critics because he came at a time when American poetry lacked vigor. "It would be
exaggeration to say that Whitman has written
nothing of poetic merit, but it would not

be exaggeration to say that every line from his pen worthy of preservation could be crowded within the limits of half a dozen pages." No one ever owed more to his friends for his reputation. The New York critics will surely take this opportunity to support Whitman against Boston prudery.

40 ANON. "Whitman's 'Leaves of Grass.' Its Publication Suspended by Order of the Attorney-General of Massachusetts." New York Times (22 May), 1:4.
Reprinted: 1882.42.
Announces Marston's action; traces troubled history of Leaves.

41 ANON. "'Leaves of Grass' Condemned." New York Tribune (22 May), 5:5.
Announces Marston's action; the responses of Osgood and Whitman.

42 ANON. "A Blur at a Poet." Philadelphia Press (22 May), 1:7.
Reprint of 1882.40.

*43 [WHITMAN, WALT?] Camden Post (22 May).
Reprint of 1882.44.
Reported in White.

44 _____. Editorial. Philadelphia Press (22 May), 4:1-2.
Reprinted: 1882.43.
Deplores Marston's action. Whitman's work should be accepted as literature; his possibly offensive lines lack the "subtle impurity" of other works. This action will not hurt Whitman, whose fruitful career may look forward to greater glories.

45 BUCKE, R. M. "'Leaves of Grass' Suppressed. An Indignant Protest Against the Act and an Earnest Plea for the Book." Springfield Daily Republican (23 May), 2:6.
Reprinted: Bucke.
Whitman's book is "the most honest, pure, religious and moral of this or of almost any other age," advocating nothing immoral but seeing all elements in the physical world, including sex, as "the work of a wise and good God," teachings which are sacred like Christ's own.

46 ANON. "Dirt in Ink." Boston Daily Advertiser (24 May), 4:3-4.
Editorial supporting Marston's action and the limitation of a completely free press. Whitman and Leaves are not mentioned.

47 ANON. "Men and Things." Boston Herald (24 May), 4:1.
Quotation from New York Sun (unlocated): Whitman pursues his theory of realism in literature to extremes, but he is still a man of genius, with some "magnificent, peerless" pieces.

48 O'CONNOR, WILLIAM D. "Suppressing Walt Whitman." New York Tribune (25 May), 3:1-2.
Reprinted: 1882.60; Loving.
Deplores America's first suppression of "an honest book, the work of a man of great and admitted genius." The passages pronounced obscene are described to show their humanity and literary precedents. Emerson (1855.12, reprinted) showed a "cool, deliberate judgment" which he never retracted, notwithstanding "invented anecdotes." Important admirers of this sanest, most splendid and enduring literary product of the "Celto-Saxon race" of today are listed.

49 ANON. "Literary Notes." Boston Commonwealth (27 May), 2:8.
Summary of the history of the 1881 edition up to Osgood's decision not to publish it any longer.

50 [TUCKER, BENJAMIN R.?] "Obscenity and the State." Liberty 1 (27 May), 2.
Ironic editorial rejoicing that the government guards the private moral natures from the "hell-born nature" of Whitman (who has been admired by the "most competent critics living"). Perversion of physical passion is more dangerous than perversion of moral passion by the government.

51 ANON. "'Leaves of Grass.'" Boston Daily Globe (28 May), 4:7.
Marston and Comstock are mocked for taking up "the task of emasculating the literature of today." It is shameful that Massachusetts is so puritanical as to suppress poems "that have met with the approval of the clearest, purest intellectuals of the nineteenth century."

52 [HASKELL, E. B.?] Editorial. Boston Sunday Herald (28 May), 6:5.
Reprinted: Bucke.
The regrettable suppression reveals "prurient prudery."

53 CHADWICK, JOHN. "Emerson and Whitman. The Rev. John W. Chadwick Replies to Mr. W. D. O'Connor." New York Tribune (28 May), 7:1.
Chadwick admirers Whitman and most of O'Connor's defense (1882.48), but finds some of Whitman "simply nasty and disgusting," though purely intended. Whitman's account of his talk with Emerson is quoted to show Emerson's disapproval of certain elements in the poetry.

54 ANON. Editorial. New York Times (2 June), 4:6.
Marston's action is generally considered "foolish and pernicious." Modern readers can censor literature such as "Adam" for themselves. Though impure, Whitman deserves free expression.

55 [ABBOTT, EDWARD?] "The Suppression of Walt
Whitman." Literary World 13 (3 June), 180.
"Public sentiment will sustain the
authorities" in suppressing Leaves, which
demands moral as well as literary judgment.
No author has the right to publish such
"downright indecencies" for anyone to read.

56 ANON. Interview with Oscar Wilde. Boston
Herald (3 June), Supplement, 5:5-6.
Wilde defends Whitman, citing the 1855
Preface as evidence of Whitman's noble
attitude to life and poetry. He must be
read as a whole, with no lines taken out
of context. In fifty years he will be
considered one of America's greatest
writers. Wilde agrees with Whitman in
seeing much grace in American machinery.

57 ANON. "Literary Notes." Critic 2 (3 June),
154.
Extracts from current defenses of Whitman.

58 ANON. "The Massachusetts Dogberry." Critic
2 (3 June), 152.
The law in Massachusetts is foolish to
prosecute a twenty-year-old book. Pointing
out its corrupting "nude passages" will
simply "make it highly prized by those who
hope to find it 'spicy.'" The prosecution
merely calls attention to its own "filthy
view of the book" and its own impurity and
makes Whitman "a social martyr" rather
than letting his book be considered as a
work of art. Some passages in Longfellow's
Christus are as wicked as anything in
Leaves.

59 G[ERE], T[HOMAS] A. "Walt Whitman. Some
Recollections of the 'Good, Gray Poet' from
One of the Old Sentimental 'Roughs.'" New
York World 22 (4 June), 9:1.
Reprinted in part: Bucke.
Recalls Whitman riding on the East
River steamboat on which this writer
worked. Whitman taught the boatmen about
politics and the arts while learning from
them about the boat and the river. Contrary to charges of eccentricity, Whitman
disliked show or sham in dress. He never
uttered an "impious thought" or "unchaste
sentence."

60 ANON. "A Revival of Puritanism." Truth
Seeker 9 (10 June), 360.
O'Connor's letter (1882.48) is reprinted
in full, showing up the outrage in true
color. Censorship brought about by religion's political influence in this country
is protested.

61 ANON. "This Is a Poem." Cambridge Meteor
(14 June), 128-29.
Extract reprinted: Saunders.
Parody.

62 CHAINEY, GEORGE. "Keep off the Grass." This
World 3 (17 June), 3-9; Supplement prints

"Prostitute."
This lecture (delivered 11 June) condemns District Attorney Stevens's suppression of Leaves. Its title conveys its
"grandest idea" of representing "the common, unpoetic realities of every-day life."
It is no mere copy of European books but is
distinct, like the American continent.
Whitman is a poet because he has something
to reveal, truth that transcends "mere
beauty of form or expression." Though
appearing contradictory, he has "the higher
logic of nature." The "first poet of true
democracy," he emphasizes the self and
human sympathies. "Prostitute" is chaste
and pure, sympathetic toward the woman that
society has produced, yet the poem has
harmed his reputation. He regards nothing
related to the body as vulgar, treating sex
openly in contrast to many who indulge in
"smutty yarns" in private. Emerson (1855.
12) and O'Connor (1882.48) are quoted.
Much of this material is used in The
Gnostic (1885.21).

63 O'CONNOR, WILLIAM D. "Emerson and Whitman.
Mr. O'Connor Replies to the Rev. Mr.
Chadwick." New York Tribune (18 June),
4:4-5.
Reprinted: Loving.
Chadwick's letter (1882.53) is insulting. Emerson remains Whitman's friend,
basing his request not on moral but on
literary considerations.

64 SIGMA [R. H. Stoddard?] "Judging the Case on
Its Merits. The Mistake of Trying to
Reform Society by Abolishing Clothes--
Emerson's Qualifications of His Approval of
Whitman." New York Tribune (18 June),
4:5-6.
Response to O'Connor (1882.48).
Whitman's work can hardly celebrate "chaste
love," since it lacks the context of marriage. Erotic themes in other writers do
not demand such "glorification of the
animal man." Whitman can hardly be called
a poet, despite "many fresh, noble and
elevated sentiments" amid much that is
trivial and repulsive. The suppression was
a mistake but is not unique.

*65 ANON. "Emerson and Walt Whitman." Boston
Index (22 June).
Reported in CHAL but not located in this
volume of the Index.

66 SLENKER, ELMINA D. "Elmina at the 'Hub.'"
Truth Seeker 9 (24 June), 398.
Account of Chainey's lecture (11 June)
on "Suppression of the Sale of Whitman's
'Leaves of Grass' as an Obscene Book"
(printed in 1882.62), a fine defense for
such "a grand and noble work." "Myself" 2
and 3 (quoted) "show the true spirit of the
author and his nearness to the great heart
of nature and the universal oneness of
truth and perfection."

1882

67 ANON. "William Douglas O'Connor on the Suppression of 'Leaves of Grass.'" Foote's
Health Monthly 7 (July), 17.
Quotes O'Connor's scorching but valuable letter (1882.48), though he seems
unaware of the Vice Society's past out-
rages.

68 ANON. "Whitman and Emerson." Critic 2 (1
July), 177.
Quotes Chadwick-O'Connor exchange
(1882.53, 1882.63). O'Connor fails to see
Emerson's later reticence regarding
Whitman.

69 ANON. "Occasional Notes." Pall Mall Gazette
(1 July), 4.
Describes Whitman's "striking article"
on Poe (Critic, 3 June), criticizing a
phrase therein: "as if a barbarous jargon
of this sort could make originality out of
commonplace."

70 CHAINEY, GEORGE. "A New Joshua." This World
3 (1 July), 2-4.
Editorial describing Chainey's troubles
with Boston Postmaster Tobey regarding the
printing and mailing of This World with
the Whitman lecture and poem in it (1882.
62). He prints letters to himself from
Whitman and O'Connor and announces his own
perserverance against censorship and tyranny.

71 DEUCEACE [pseud.?] "Eastern Notables. Walt
Whitman, Rhapsodist and Loafer. A Bard of
an Iconoclastic Kind--Some Specimens of His
Originality Run Mad--His Eminent Admirers--
How He Loafs and Invites His Soul." St.
Louis Globe-Democrat (2 July), 18:1-2.
Consideration of Whitman's status as
poet. Despite his admirers, he will not
be popular, because of his difficulties.
His poems are not obscene but deliberately
natural with "a Biblical plainness." His
poetry has touches of "deep humanity, evidences of aspiration, but hardly any picturesqueness, or passion, or beauty, or
music." His life reveals strong personal
magnetism.

72 ANON. "Not Objectionable Mail Matter." New
York Times (9 July), 7:5.
The postmaster-general has reversed
the decision of the Boston postmaster to
prohibit the mailing of Leaves, so that it
may now be circulated through the mails.

73 ANON. Editorial. New York Times (13 July),
4:7.
Notes and agrees with the "brief and
acidulous reference" to Whitman in 1882.69.

74 ANON. "Whitman's 'Leaves of Grass.'" New
York Tribune (15 July), 5:4.
Account of the new movement to suppress
Whitman in Philadelphia. Rev. Mr. Morrow
of the Tabernacle Methodist Episcopal

Church is quoted extensively, praising
Whitman's work as "robust and virile, but
not obscene," not immoral but needing to
be read truly. He would, however, expur-
gate the book for his daughter, for it
demands mature minds.

75 ANON. "Walt Whitman's Work." Philadelphia
Press (15 July), 1:7.
Quotes Rev. James Morrow, who supports
Whitman (see 1882.74).

76 ANON. Editorial. Philadelphia Press (22
July), 4:5.
Whitman's first edition has sold out;
thus good comes for Whitman out of a high
official's mistake.

77 ANON. "'Leaves of Grass' Not Obscene."
Truth Seeker 9 (22 July), 459.
Quotes This World and letter from James
H. Marr, Assistant U.S. Postmaster-General,
about allowing Leaves to be mailed.

78 TUCKER, BENJAMIN R. Letter to Stevens and
Marston in advertisement for Leaves.
Liberty 1 (22 July), 4.
Offers Leaves on sale to anyone; challenges the district attorney and attorney
general to find a jury "sufficiently
bigoted" to believe with them that his
sale of Leaves is an unlawful act. This
advertisement appears in subsequent issues
as well.

*79 ANON. "Old Obscenity Comstock." Washington
Sunday Capital (23 July).
Reported in Asselineau.

80 [HEARN, LAFCADIO.] "'Leaves of Grass.'" New
Orleans Times-Democrat (30 July), 4:2-3.
Reprinted: 1929.9.
Review of 1881 Leaves. The beauties
claimed for this "eccentric, tiresome,
flatulent, raw, [sic] volume of rhapsodies"
are not apparent. "Adam" poems would condemn Whitman. Lacking artistry, he is "an
American Naturalist," as reckless as Zola
and Maupassant but "infinitely less talented." "Body Electric" is coarse, erring in
terming unappealing parts of the body the
soul. There is some philosophy in the book,
"pages of force and rough beauty," "originality, depth, strong feeling," showing
Whitman is honest though rude and eccentric.
Leaves, though lasting awhile through curiosity, "will crumble away."

81 ANON. "'Leaves of Grass.'" Foote's Health
Monthly 7 (August), 12.
Questions the extent of freedom in
America if a work like Leaves can be sup-
pressed by the Vice Society.

82 ANON. "Vandals Still Treading on 'Leaves of
Grass.'" Foote's Health Monthly 7 (August),
11-12.
Cites Rev. Mr. Morrow's approval of

Leaves (see 1882.74). Reading Whitman, as
so many now will do, will stimulate discussion on whether art dealing with the
body's varied functions should be considered obscene.

83 CON AMORE. "Leaves of Grass." Philadelphia
Press (4 August), 5:2.
Letter offering an impressionistic
appreciation of Whitman's work.

84 ANON. "Literary Notes." Philadelphia Press
(5 August), 5:3.
Paragraph reporting the status and
value of editions of Leaves.

85 ANON. "Whitman's 'Leaves of Grass.' The
Book Sold Freely in This City." New York
Tribune (6 August), 8:4.
Reprinted: 1882.86.
A reporter, exploring bookstores to
determine how Leaves is selling, interviews
a salesman who affirms that the proceedings
have helped sales. Comstock is also inter-
viewed, commenting on the postmaster general's order against Leaves and announcing
his intention of suppressing Leaves in New
York.

86 ANON. "Whitman's 'Leaves of Grass.'" Philadelphia Press (7 August), 3:4.
Reprint of 1882.85.

87 ANON. "Walt Whitman's Complete Volume. The
Condemnation of the Unedited Book." The
American 2 (12 August), 282-83.
Review of 1881 Leaves. Some of the
pieces present "only the animalism of the
male"; some are unpoetic physiology.
Whitman should have expurgated because
much of the book is valuable for its simplicity, individuality, courage, naturalness, and truthfulness.

88 GORDON, T. FRANCIS. "Walt Whitman's Complete
Volume. The Realism of Walt Whitman."
The American 2 (12 August), 282.
Whitman's emphasis on the physical,
falsely proclaimed as new, strips passion
of "all imaginative charm" and higher
emotion. Occasional bursts of something
like poetry call for submission to the laws
of poetic art. His egotism and self-assertion are admired in Europe as typical of
the New World. His "insistent realism" is
generally condemned from an artistic rather
than an ethical viewpoint.

89 ANON. "Post Office Censorship." New York
Times (13 August), 6:2-3.
Reprinted in part: 1882.107.
Editorial opposing censorship, using
Leaves as a case in point. It is not a
book "from which the public morals would
suffer, even were it possible to say of it
with a nearer approach to positiveness
that it transgresses the bounds of decency."

90 ANON. Paragraph. New York Tribune (15
August), 4:5.
J. A. Galbraith, Fellow of Trinity
College, Dublin, has removed Leaves from
the library shelves out of disgust; he
supports Marston.

91 ANON. "Literary Notes." New York Tribune
(16 August), 6:1.
"Mr. W. M. Rossetti quotes Trelawney
as saying concerning Whitman's 'Leaves of
Grass' that he found in it the materials of
poetry, but not poetry itself."

92 AGNOSTIC [pseud.]. Letter. Truth Seeker 9
(19 August), 522.
Criticizes Chainey's promotion of
atheism, changing from that course only to
give readers "some of Walt Whitman's nas-
tiest productions."

93 [TUCKER, BENJAMIN R.?] "On Picket Duty."
Liberty 1 (19 August), 1.
Notes cowardice and stupidity of
Marston and Stevens in refusing to respond
to his challenge (1882.78).

94 O'CONNOR, WILLIAM D. "Mr. Comstock as Cato
the Censor." New York Tribune (27 August),
5:5.
Reprinted: Loving.
Explains the post office difficulties.
The virtuous character of Leaves is shown
by the support of Morrow, W. J. Fox, Ruskin,
Thoreau, Freiligrath, and Emerson. Comstock
is dared to try to stop its circulation.

95 ANON. "Benjamin R. Tucker to the Front."
Foote's Health Monthly 7 (September), 13.
Reprints Tucker's letter (1882.78);
explains the facts regarding the Postal
Department's refusal to interfere with the
circulation of Whitman's poems; quotes from
a private letter describing the sell-out of
the first Philadelphia edition within two
days. Leaves "will be one of the most
extensively read volumes that has been
issued from the American press, notwithstanding the fact that it had been about
thirty years before the public with only
here and there a reader among the literati!"

96 ANON. "Late Publications." Boston Commonwealth (1 September), 1:6.
Brief review of 1881 Leaves. Much of
Whitman's work seems "the baldest of prose,"
yet there are many passages which bear much
rereading. The "'fleshly' pieces" are
merely "beatific adorations of the great
gift of maternity" but might be eliminated
because society is not ready for them.

97 ANON. "Leaves of Grass. By Your Honor's
Permission?" Man (1 September), 6-7.
Protests the suppression, particularly
the trouble Chainey has had with the publication of This World for printing "Prostitute."

98 MOLLOY, FITZGERALD. "Leaders of Modern
 Thought." Modern Thought 4 (1 September),
 319-26.
  Extract reprinted: Dowden; Hindus.
    Whitman is "America's representative
 poet," a "man of the poeple." Various
 criticisms are quoted; poems are quoted
 extensively. Whitman's character is
 defended. He is "a recognised Leader of
 Modern Thought."

99 ANON. "New Books." Philadelphia Press (11
 September), 7:3.
    Brief review of 1881 Leaves. An ex-
 purgated edition should be brought out for
 people (including youth) who should not be
 deprived of Whitman's other ideas, even
 though the offending passages are integral
 to Whitman's purpose. This book is worth
 anyone's reading.

100 G., A. E. "Walt Whitman's 'Fleshly Pieces.'"
 Liberty 1 (16 September), 1.
  Reprinted: 1882.105.
    Contrary to the Commonwealth's sug-
 gestion (1882.96), Whitman's works should
 not be expurgated, for keeping the sexual
 pieces from the public would perpetuate
 their ignorance.

101 ANON. "Correspondence. Whitman, Zola, Etc."
 Boston Commonwealth (23 September), 1:4.
    Whitman's book is "harmless," for
 prurience depends upon the buyer.

102 ANON. Editorial paragraph. Critic 2 (23
 September), 254.
    Rees Welsh & Co., the new publishers
 of Leaves, treat it trivially in their
 advertising in the Press: "'Leaves of
 Grass,' by Walt. Whitman, is not an agri-
 cultural book, in the haymaker's parlance;
 but it's a daisy, and don't you forget it."

103 ANON. "Literary Notes." Critic 2 (23 September), 256.
  Extract quoted from 1882.108.

104 BURROUGHS, JOHN. "English Nature." Critic 2
 (23 September), 249.
    American nature has "glimpses of a
 grace and beauty, not to say sublimity,"
 that are to English nature "as a line of
 Emerson or Whitman is to a couplet of Pope
 or Thomson."

105 G., A. E. "Walt Whitman's 'Fleshly' Pieces."
 Boston Commonwealth (23 September), 1:3-4.
  Reprint of 1882.100.

106 ANON. "Arts and Letters." Springfield Daily
 Republican (24 September), 4:6.
    Deplores the vulgar advertising of
 Leaves (see 1882.102), inappropriate for
 such a noble work, which looks ahead into
 eternity rather than back into the past.
 The trivial person may misunderstand
 Whitman's use of the first person, not

realizing that it "represents the essential
 man."

107 ANON. "The Post-Office Redeemed." Foote's
 Health Monthly 7 (October), 13-14.
    Quotes extensively New York Times
 (1882.89), approving their opposition to
 censorship.

108 FROTHINGHAM, O. B. "The Morally Objectionable
 in Literature." North American Review 135
 (October), 323-38, passim.
  Extract reprinted: 1882.103.
    The "disgusting things" in Whitman's
 poetry are not corrupting but are part of
 his high aim, which involves "moral enthusiasm," "aspiration of human brotherhood,"
 and "faith in progress." Whitman regards
 the soul as sovereign over sense. His
 coarse elements, although the theory behind
 their inclusion is not to be endorsed, have
 been unduly emphasized, giving Leaves an
 undeservedly bad name.

109 WARD, SAM. "Lines to Walt Whitman. Being a
 Plea Against the Good Gray Poet's Lawless
 Paces." New York World (2 October), 2:3.
  Reprinted: 1882.116.
    Poem in nine rhymed stanzas: all things
 have rhyme and meter, so why should poetry
 avoid them?

110 ANON. "Literary Notes." Critic 2 (7 October),
 270.
    Rees Welsh says that the person res-
 ponsible for the advertisement (see 1882.
 102) no longer has charge of that department.

111 ANON. "New Publications." New York Tribune
 (14 October), 6:2.
    One-paragraph review of Specimen.
 Whitman's prose may come nearer his intrinsic quality than the "wilder and less
 genuine strains" of his poetry. This prose
 has "freshness and individuality," but
 little new to say.

112 ANON. "Whitman's New Book." Boston Sunday
 Herald (15 October), 9:3-4.
  Reprinted in part: Bucke.
    Review of Specimen, which is "more
 directly comprehensible to the understanding
 of the multitude than the greater and more
 famous work," but has the same characteristics: "grand healthiness of tone, largeness of view, universal reach, and, at the
 same time, delicate perception and sensitiveness, and identity with Nature." The
 portrayal of the war is vivid and unmatched.
 Specimen, though Whitman (quoted) has
 called it a "jumble," would establish him
 as a great poet even without Leaves, being
 "pregnant with Whitman's personality" and
 "the working of a poet's mind." Contents
 are described, with notice of "a vein of
 playfulness, and a humor--if it may be
 called so--probably different from anything

yet in literature." The Poe essay reveals "the best critical powers." Since Leaves was transferred to the Philadelphia publisher, four editions have been exhausted, with a fifth in progress.

*113 ANON. Summary of Chainey's lecture the night before. Chicago Herald (16 October). Reprinted: Bucke.
This lecture is presumably the same as that printed in This World (1882.62).

114 ELMINA [D. SLENKER]. "'Leaves of Grass.'" Truth Seeker 9 (21 October), 663.
Letter announcing her ousting as president of the Snowville, Virginia, Woman's Reading Club "because the preachers' wives could not bear the odium of my owning, reading, and circulating that horrid book," Leaves, which she finds full of strong, vigorous, pure, and wholesome truths and now offers for sale.

115 ANON. "'Leaves of Grass' Again." Washington Post (27 October), 1.
E. H. Heywood has been arrested for "sending obscene matter through the mails," including extracts from Leaves.

116 ANON. "Whitman's Music and the Lute." Liberty 2 (28 October), 4.
In response to Ward (1882.109, reprinted), "Lines to Sam Ward" mocks mere rhyme and measure.

117 ANON. "Letters in America." Scottish Review 1 (November), 39-40.
Whitman, preaching unity and universal sympathy, is too large for the world's measures. His form is "highly effective." His catalogues merely impart the names of many things rather than their common significance, but he adopted such methods for his own reasons; we shall accept them because of his nobility.

118 CONE, HELEN GRAY. "Narcissus in Camden." Century Magazine 25 (November), 157-59. Reprinted: 1885.1; Saunders.
Parody of Whitman and Wilde in dialogue form depicting their exchange upon Wilde's visit to Whitman (see 1882.21).

119 ANON. "All About Walt Whitman." Literary World 13 (4 November), 372-73.
Review of Specimen. Whitman's prose is better than his poetry because it is clean, sane, intelligible. His life is traced through description of the contents. The Civil War reminiscences reveal familiar incidents in unconventional terms. A few passages are here printed in verse lines to demonstrate the interchangeability of Whitman's prose and poetry. His prose reveals his pleasanter side.

*120 ANON. "Talks with Trelawney." Truth Seeker 9 (4 November).

Reported in White, but not located in this issue or elsewhere in the year.

121 [BENNETT, D. M.?] "E. H. Heywood Again in Prison." Truth Seeker 9 (4 November), 697.
Heywood has been indiscreet to send indecent matter by mail, selecting Whitman's "most objectionable poem" ("Prostitute"). Though generally grand and containing the genius of true poetry, Whitman's poems are not all necessarily "desirable to spread over the land."

122 G. "Vice-Suppressing Societies." Truth Seeker 9 (4 November), 698.
Letter: "The obscenity complained of by vice-suppressing societies and Boston's prosecuting attorneys, [sic] is in their own minds and not in Walt Whitman's poems."

123 HILLER, J. H. Letter. Truth Seeker 9 (4 November), 700.
Disapproves of Elmina's notice of Leaves (1882.114) and the general approval liberals give Leaves, the 1860 edition of which he finds obscene. Whitman cannot be pure-minded since he constantly talks about prostitutes.

124 [FORNEY, JOHN W.] "Walt Whitman's Late Illness." Progress, 5 (11 November), 2-3. Reprinted in part: Bucke.
Describes Whitman's recent recovery from illness due to his wartime labors; notes his perseverance though opposed by critics and little read; quotes "a late lecture" by Bucke on how to read Leaves.

*125 ELMIRA, "THE QUAKER INFIDEL." "Suggestions and Advice to Mothers." Iconoclast (Indianapolis) (11 November). Reported in Asselineau.
Mothers should make their children read Leaves because Whitman sang the body with admirable purity.

126 SLENKER, ELMINA D. "The Bright Side, as Elmina Sees It." Truth Seeker 9 (11 November), 711.
Explains her materialist point of view, quoting Whitman to show the dark side of nature ("Salut") and the bright side ("Open Road").

127 ANON. "Notes and News." Academy 22 (18 November), 362.
Paragraph corrects publishers' names from Dowden's review (1882.128) and notes the selling out of the first edition before it was issued. An English publisher should publish Whitman.

128 DOWDEN, EDWARD. "Specimen Days and Collect." Academy 22 (18 November), 357-59.
Review of Specimen, "sweet and sane and nourishing," with the feel of fresh air, although from an invalid. Whitman provides fine criticism, with "keen perception of the limitations of Emerson's genius." Some

1882

early pieces have been printed now "to
avoid the annoyance of a surreptitious
issue which had been announced." Whitman's
many English admirers are named, in hopes
that Whitman will pay a visit to England.

129 [BENNETT, D. M.] "Claiming Too Much." Truth
Seeker 9 (25 November), 744.
    Deplores Heywood's questionable taste
in circulating indecent passages from
Whitman, which could only damage him, as
should not be done.

130 WALKER, E. C. "Words in Brief." Truth Seeker
9 (25 November), 746-47.
    Response to Hiller (1882.123):
Whitman's poems are indecent only to those
with vile ideas of sex. His noble candor
will drive away such attitudes. The editor
(see 1882.121) should not consider Whitman's
poems obscene. But Heywood's act was unjust to Whitman since this Christian-raised
people might misjudge such poems.

131 ANON. "Among Books." Mace 4 (27 November),
2-3.
    Review of Specimen, which exceeds
Whitman's poems in their own remarkable
originality, strength, and beauty, making
him one of the nineteenth century's "very
greatest writers in prose and poetry." He
is a trenchant modern prophet, taking up
Carlyle's mantle, adding new point to his
and Emerson's texts. He is "a man of vast
reading" and "immense pliability of intellect." His ideas on democracy, particularly
from Vistas, in which he is at his most
eloquent, are quoted; also two war sketches
revealing "nervous strength."

132 MACAULAY, G. C. "Walt Whitman." Nineteenth
Century 12 (December), 903-18.
Reprinted: 1883.10. Extract reprinted:
Dowden; In Re; Hindus.
    Review of 1881 Leaves, noting changes
from earlier editions. Whitman sells well,
despite his poor taste, slang, neglect of
syntax, disregard of meter, incoherence,
egotism. His unmatched power of passionate
expression, depth of grief, and sympathy
with nature are praised. His religion is
pantheism; his "poetical optimism continually leads him to assert immortality."
"His own claim to be the poet of America
is based on other than pure literary
grounds."

133 ELMINA [D. SLENKER]. "Leavs [sic] of Grass."
Truth Seeker 9 (2 December), 765.
    Quotes Whitman to show liberals "how
he echoes your most daringly bold venture
toward the new life of universal self-hood."
He is defended against Hiller (1882.123).
His vast array of topics is unparalleled
in a volume of less than four hundred
pages. Various opinions of Whitman are
noted; Whitman is quoted regarding "Prostitute."

134 ANON. "New Publications. Walt Whitman's
Prose." New York Times (18 December),
2:6-7.
    Review of Specimen. Whitman's prose
manner is "a kind of cultivated affectation,"
best when "most free from the writer's
word-torturings." His works on nature
reveal mastery in picturesque word-painting.
He sees the world in a way new to literature. His comments on American poetry show
that he does not reject it, although he
might have commented on such eminent American verse-writers as Lowell, Stedman,
Aldrich, and Stoddard. Whitman's theory of
utter frankness in literature is interesting,
but would abolish "mystery in social relations." Because of his belief in science,
progress, and America, Specimen is "an
important contribution to our literature."

135 ATLANTIS [pseud.]. "American Celebrities.
No. 1. Walt Whitman." Life (London) 5
(21 December), 1068-69.
    Describes Whitman's life, how he looked
and dressed in New York twenty-five years
before, the controversy over his work, his
own reviews of himself, his financial problems with publishers and the Partons, his
living off of other people, his quarrel
with George Arnold over not joining the
army, his trip West, his present Camden
residence.

1883

BOOKS

1 BATES, WILLIAM. The Maclise Portrait-Gallery
of "Illustrious Literary Characters" with
Memoirs. London: Chatto & Windus, p. 99n.
    Among the impostures bringing disgrace
upon the sacred name of poetry is "the
'Walt Whitman' hoax," perpetrated upon the
gullible public by Rossetti and his friends,
who dug up "an American 'poet' who had
never written a word of poetry in his life."
What he wrote was "barbaric, coarse, conceited, and irreverent, or generally mean-
ingless," but was declared "the noblest
Transatlantic 'tone' yet heard." His vogue
continues. His book is worth having as a
literary curiosity.

2 BLIND, MATHILDE. George Eliot. London: W. H.
Allen & Co., p. 210; Boston: Roberts Bros.,
p. 279.
    Incidental: Eliot, when a friend
recommended she read Whitman, "hesitated
on the ground of his not containing anything spiritually needful for her, but,
having been induced to take him up, she
changed her opinion and admitted that he
did contain what was 'good for her soul.'"

3 BUCKE, RICHARD MAURICE. Walt Whitman. Philadelphia: David McKay, 236 pp. Illustrated.
No index.

Reprinted: 1884.3.

Part One, 1. "Biographical Sketch": Chronology of Whitman's life, based on his own notes. The leading fact in his life and book is "moral elevation." His family background, natural environment, education from people and worldly experience are traced.

2. "The Poet in 1880.--Personnel, Etc.": Accounts (published and unpublished) are quoted of personal acquaintance with Whitman from different periods. Helen Price contributes a seven-page character study. His heroism in hospital work and sickness is emphasized. His central teaching is the greatness of the common-place.

3. "His Conversation": Whitman's own words are used to help explain his various philosophic and poetic ideas.

"Appendix to Part 1": Reprints O'Connor (1866.2) with a new, lengthy intro-duction in which O'Connor defends his book and Whitman himself against specific re-viewers' criticisms, praising Whitman's ideals and poetry. Leaves is "the poem of the embodied soul." Also reprinted are 1866.8 and 1866.10.

Part Two, 1. "History of Leaves of Grass": Account of its reception, the more successful 1860 edition, later difficulties.

2. "Analysis of Poems, Etc.": In treating the intellectual side of democracy, the prose complements the poetry. Leaves is "the image of his real work, which was his life itself." "Myself" is explicated as "perhaps the most important poem that has so far been written at any time, in any language." The "Calamus" emotion is defended against O'Grady (1875.16). Other major poems are explicated. Whitman's later work moved toward greater polish but less power.

3. "Analysis of Poems, Etc., Continued": Bucke describes his own response to Leaves, initial and subsequent. Leaves is different for each reader, "the bible of Democracy." Whitman carries in himself the history of the country from Washington through the rejoining of the states.

"Appendix to Part II. Contemporaneous Criticisms, Etc., 1855-1883": Compendium of critical remarks on Whitman, some com-plete, some extracted; includes Leonard Wheeler's sonnet "O pure heart singer," reprinted in Legler.

Walt Whitman's Autograph Revision of the Analysis of Leaves of Grass (New York: New York University Press, 1974) reprints Part Two (2, 3, and appendix), with manu-script facsimiles, showing the large part Whitman played in writing and revising this book. Whitman also contributed the opening chapter.

4 EMERSON, RALPH WALDO. The Correspondence of Thomas Carlyle and Ralph Waldo Emerson 1834-1872. Vol. 2. Boston: James R. Osgood & Co., p. 251.

Reprinted: Bucke; 1884.6.

Letter of 6 May 1856 suggests that Carlyle should read Leaves, "a nondescript monster which yet had terrible eyes and buffalo strength, and was indisputably American," though it "wanted good morals." "If you think, as you may, that it is only an auctioneer's inventory of a warehouse, you can light your pipe with it."

5 LANIER, SIDNEY. The English Novel and the Principle of Its Development. New York: Charles Scribner's Sons, pp. 44-62, 118-19. Reprinted with changes: 1897.14. Abridged: Miller.

Whitman errs in thinking that the poetry of the future must be "democratic and formless." Like Wordsworth, he has professed to write for the people but has failed to appeal to them. None of America's great statesmen or poets fits Whitman's des-cription of the great democrat; his muscular ideal is no picture of true manhood, but represents the worst kind of aristocracy, rejecting the weak. His "dandyism" is everywhere apparent; his "detailed descrip-tion of the song he is going to sing" is "the extreme of sophistication in writing." He is too naive regarding the simplicity and contentment of the animals. (See 1933. 29.)

6 MEREDITH, GEORGE. Poems and Lyrics of the Joy of the Earth. London: Macmillan & Co. "An Orson of the Muse," p. 173.
Sonnet to Whitman.

7 PELLEW, GEORGE. Jane Austen's Novels. Boston: Cupples, Upham, & Co., pp. 47-48.
Incidental: "Whitman expresses the reaction against conventionality in poetry; Zola, that against conventionality in novels and the drama; and, though neither writer is able in his practice to avoid the ex-cesses he condemns, we may believe that the art and fiction of the future will gradually be brought into ever closer relation to the facts of experience."

8 SOUTHWICK, ALBERT P. Short Studies in Litera-ture for The Use of Schools. Philadelphia: Eldredge & Bro., p. 120.
"Miscellaneous Writers of this Age" simply lists Whitman as "the author of Leaves of Grass, and Drum-Taps."

PERIODICALS

9 ANON. "Walt Whitman's New Book." Critic 3 (13 January), 2-3. Portrait and manuscript facsimile.
Review of Specimen. The word "Ensemble," which gives Whitman's work its chief value and grandeur, is explained. Whitman is "a Democratic Prometheus." He is impressed most by his country's size. He is a poet's poet. Wanting to depict everything, he "fails magnificently." The patriotism and

nature notes here are welcome; "his fearlessly egotistical account" of his background will help readers of Leaves.

10 MACAULAY, G. C. "Walt Whitman." Eclectic
    Magazine, n.s. 37 (February), 252-62.
    Reprint of 1882.132.

*11 ANON. Review of Emerson-Carlyle letters
    (1883.4). Philadelphia Press (18 March).
    Reprinted: Bucke.
        Quotes Emerson's letter to Carlyle
    (1883.4), a valid first impression, but
    Emerson's insight is apparent in his letter
    to Whitman (1855.12), observing "the coming
    power looming great through the mist of
    forms strange and new in literature."

12 [AITKEN, ROBERT M.] "Among Books." Mace 4
    (19 March), 2-3.
        Review of Sanborn (1882.9). Incidental:
    in Whitman "we have a world entirely
    American--infinite ares, the very wanton-
    ness of physical strength, a proud sense of
    inexhaustible reproductiveness, the in-
    calculable might of the mass."

*13 ANON. "American Freethought and Freethinkers."
    Sydney Evening News (21 March).
    Reprinted in Bucke.
        Describes Charles Bright's lecture on
    American Freethought, including his remarks
    on Whitman, "the grandest and best man in
    every sense, morally, intellectually, and
    physically, he had ever met in his life--a
    prophet poet" in advance of his contempo-
    raries.

14 BAKER, MAY COLE. "Walt Whitman. A Woman's
    Criticism." The Republic 7 (24 March),
    88-90.
        Describes the positive responses of
    people to whom she quotes Whitman. His
    language, however, is not for the common
    people but for his peers. His best work
    has a subtle rhythm with accent replacing
    quantity. His poetic method is that of the
    Old Testament and the Koran. Familiarity
    is necessary to appreciate him. The 1855
    Preface is necessary to judge his work.
    His skill at epithet is sometimes "combined
    into a long swell of melody" with "sym-
    phonic power" as in "Myself" 21. He loves
    nature and portrays her with fidelity. In
    his war writings "he has reached nearer the
    vital force of the American people than any
    other writer," with "exquisitely tender"
    songs for the dead. Concluded 1883.15.

15 ____. "Walt Whitman. A Woman's Criticism.
    II." The Republic 7 (31 March), 104-5.
        Concludes 1883.14. Praises Whitman's
    love of liberty and stance toward woman's
    equality. He treats sex with no vile in-
    tent but has erred in presenting it in
    common speech. Science is important to his
    role as poet. His unique message of renewed
    hope and courage is necessary for America.

Passages from Tennyson's "In Memoriam" are
compared with Whitman's poetry. Despite
his detractors, Whitman's work cannot be
ignored.

16 STEDMAN, EDMUND C. "Emerson." Century Maga-
    zine 25 (April), 877, 879, 882.
        Incidental references to Emerson's
    influence on Whitman and his modification
    of his early praise of Leaves, due to his
    artistic taste and his New England distaste
    for the unsavory rather than to prudery or
    censorship. Emerson's "Mithridates" is
    "the key-note and best defense of Whitman's
    untrammeled, all-heralding philosophy."

17 [WINTER, WILLIAM?] "Literary Notes." New
    York Tribune (9 April), 6:2.
        Announces Bucke's upcoming "Study of
    Walt Whitman," "a dissertation for which it
    might be said by the irreverent there is no
    deep yearning on the part of the literary
    world."

18 ANON. "Sidney Lanier on the English Novel."
    Critic 3 (19 May), 228-29.
        Review of 1883.5. A university lec-
    turer should be tolerant enough to accept
    someone like Whitman as a fact and seek to
    explain rather than belabor him. Lanier
    fails to see the "stagnant milieu" that
    made Whitman what he is. Lanier, with
    "almost womanly instincts" and lofty atti-
    tudes toward the women of his time, naturally
    turns away from Whitman, who has "hinted
    pretty broadly that even his great faith in
    American democracy is shaken when he thinks
    of America's Women." Lanier strains in
    calling Whitman affected; his own affecta-
    tion merely appeals to different tastes.

*19 ANON. "A Piece of the Family History." Long
    Islander (25 May).
    Reprinted in part: Whitman Supplement
    1978.
        Traces history of the Long Islander
    from Whitman's founding of it in 1836 [sic],
    describing its status under his editorship
    and his sale of it.

20 KENNEDY, WILLIAM SLOANE. "The Obsolescence of
    Barrel-Organ Poetry." Critic 3 (26 May),
    239-40.
        This explanation of the modern trend
    away from rhymes and fixed meters inciden-
    tally notes the fatigue man complained of
    when "a certain American poet" burst away
    from the fetters of the rhymesters "and
    soared clean beyond their range."

21 [MISS H.] "New Publications. The Apotheosis
    of Walt Whitman." New York Tribune (8
    June), 6:1.
        Review of Bucke: "enthusiasm so pro-
    found, praise so lavish, are hardly within
    the pale of reasonable criticism."

22 [GILDER, JEANNETTE?] "'Walt Whitman.'"
   Critic 3 (9 June), 266-67.
      Review of Bucke. Most who read Whitman
   carefully, without bias, may be classified
   as his admirers. Whitman's life and personality are described, presented plainly
   by this book, which does not let such intimacy detract from Whitman's true dignity.

*23 ANON. Note. Camden Mirror (16 June).
      Quoted in Bergman (May 1948).
      "Walt Whitman is the favorite poet of
   Grover Cleveland, of New York."

24 ANON. "Walt Whitman in Russia." Critic 3
   (16 June), 278-79.
      Abstract with quotations (translated)
   of Popoff's article on Whitman in Zagranichny Viestnik, which has been suspended
   for the rest of the year for publishing the
   essay. Popoff praises America, its energy,
   and its "heroes of labor" whom Whitman sang
   in his best poems like "Broad-Axe" and
   "Pioneers." Popoff notes the mission
   Whitman sees for America, perceiving
   Whitman as a "microcosmos."

25 ANON. Review of Specimen. Westminster Review,
   n.s. 64 (July), 287-91.
      Traces Whitman's life, as in Specimen.
   His "energy, good sense, and cheerful
   patience" are praised. "The thought is
   often highly poetic, and always wholesome
   and unconventional." But his style is
   flawed by excess, redundancy, and want of
   definiteness. His criticism shows great
   insight, but his enthusiasm for the democratic as against the fedual is too perva-
   sive. The length of this review is defended
   by the inherent importance of this work.

26 WHITE, RICHARD GRANT. "Mr. Washington Adams
   in England." Atlantic Monthly 52 (July),
   106-9.
      Reprinted: 1884.14.
      Includes a discussion of Whitman by a
   Yankee and some Europeans. Although,
   according to some, he represents the humbler
   people, only "the fastidious aristocracy
   and literary bric-à-brac hunters of the
   intellectual world" care for him. He lapses
   only rarely into common-sense and human
   feeling. His book, including its title,
   is written in an unknown jargon. The
   Yankee reads a piece that Whitman has
   "never published yet" (parody reprinted
   from 1860.21, as White's note suggests).
   The Europeans find it universal and "all-
   inspiring," "all-embracing," the true
   philosophy of the New World.

*27 ANON. Note. Boston Weekly Transcript (10
   July).
      Quoted: Hendrick.
      After Grover Cleveland called Whitman
   his favorite poet, "it is thought by the
   Brookline Chronicle that the governor's
   chances for the presidency have reached
   the vanishing point."

28 ANON. "Walt Whitman's Prose Works." Spectator
   56 (12 July), 933-35.
      Review of Specimen. Whitman's "egotis-
   tical mouthing of sentiments either trite
   or untrue" is admired so greatly because he
   is a nonconformist. Passages are quoted as
   "trite reflections, dressed up in a sledge-
   hammer style, and constantly interrupted by
   trivial personal parentheses." Reading a
   few is equivalent to reading all. Whitman
   appears in a pleasanter light than in his
   poems. Passages like the war memoranda
   have power and insight, without the vulgar
   personal element. He should have served
   as a soldier. His writings lack "any real
   and permanent significance." "Captain" is
   "his one successful lyrical poem." His
   grammar, slang, original vocabulary, ignorance, "animalism," and use of Emerson's
   letter are criticized. Emerson presents a
   higher form of Whitman's democratic faith.

29 THAYER, WILLIAM R. "A Dangerous Disciple."
   The American 6 (14 July), 219.
      Review of Bucke, a book comic in its
   earnest exaggerations of Whitman's merit,
   failing to explain or support its mystic
   assertions.

30 ANON. Notice of Pellew (1883.7). Nation 37
   (19 July), 55-56.
      Contrary to Pellew's assertions,
   Whitman and Zola represent "the reaction
   against love of form and beauty in art."
   Whitman is a pioneer, not in reacting
   against conventions, but in teaching
   "equality between beautiful and ugly, clean
   and dirty, foul and pure."

31 ANON. Review of Bucke. Nation 37 (26 July),
   84.
      This book's author has little culture
   or critical ability. The first stage of
   Whitman's career was not promising, the
   next revealed nothing original or distinctively American except for the "singular
   shape" of Leaves. Whitman mistook "uncontrolled feeling for soaring thought,"
   caring only for impressions and ignoring
   the progress of modern thought. He lacks
   the "transfiguring devotion to one woman."
   But the war improved him with patriotism,
   "a broader, more sympathetic humanity,"
   and a higher imagination. Yet he retains
   the grosser parts of Leaves, carrying individualism to the point of "extremest selfishness."

32 ANON. "Walt Whitman." Toronto World (29
   August), 2:2-3.
      Review of Bucke. Though knowledgeable
   about his material, Bucke does not succeed
   in analyzing Whitman's "Titanic utterances,"
   but gets lost in vagueness. Yet he will
   help readers understand the more obvious
   aspects of Whitman's philosophy. The book's
   physical features and its collection of
   criticisms are excellent. "The pass-key to

1883

Walt Whitman is a proper apprehension of his broad, boundless humanity, his bold self-reliance, his confidence in the future of the human race, his tender love for his kind, his pity for the downtrodden and unhappy."

33 LANIER, MARY DAY. "Mr. Sidney Lanier's Judgment of Walt Whitman." Nation 37 (30 August), 183.
Reprinted in part: 1897.14.
Letter presenting a paragraph omitted from 1883.5 by Dr. William Browne, the editor: Lanier admits disagreements with Whitman but praises "Captain" and the "bigness and naivety" of some passages.

34 ANON. "Walt Whitman." Scottish Review 2 (September), 281-300.
Reprinted in part: 1884.3.
Traces history of Leaves and its reception. Whitman's prose, though with intense realism and much to admire, is not equal to his verse. His charm and force work gradually on the reader, who may be repelled at first. Leaves is "an Epic of Life." Whitman is one of America's most notable figures, with lofty purposes for the nation, democracy, and the literature which gives them expression. He is deficient in artistic ability and effort, having earlier failed in the standard forms, achieving rhythm and melody only in rare poems like "Cradle," "Lilacs," and "Captain." Whitman's frankness is an error of taste, not of morals. "His manner, style, and spirit are entirely his own," distinctively American, democratic, and modern. His verse is universally human and does not disdain the past or other writers. In evocative power he ranks with the foremost poets.

35 DOWDEN, EDWARD. Review of Bucke. Academy 24 (8 September), 156.
Bucke writes "as a lover intoxicated by Whitman's presence," for he over-praises, yet he tells much about Whitman and reveals the spiritual quality behind Whitman's writings. Whitman is both a mystic and a keen observer.

*36 ANON. "Letter from Walt Whitman." Long Islander (21 September).
Reprinted: Whitman Supplement 1978.
Quotes letter from Whitman to the Long Islander; notes receipt of a copy of Specimen for the Huntington Public Library.

37 [ALDEN, HENRY MILLS.] "Editor's Literary Record." Harper's New Monthly Magazine 67 (October), 798.
Review of Lanier (1883.5), noting his "refutation of the crude theories of imaginative art advanced by Walt Whitman and Emile Zola."

38 THOMAS, G. WALTER R. "To Walt Whitman." The Index (20 December), 297.
Sonnet of tribute.

1884

BOOKS

1 ADAMS, OSCAR FAY. A Brief Handbook of American Authors. Boston: Houghton, Mifflin & Co., p. 178.
Brief factual entry, listing references and publishers of Whitman. "His style is rhapsodical and his expressions frequently coarse and repellant [sic], while his descriptions often sink to the level of a catalogue." "Captain" is perhaps his best poem.

2 BACKUS, TRUMAN J. Shaw's New History of English Literature; Together with a History of English Literature in America. Rev. ed. New York and Chicago: Sheldon & Co., pp. 466-67.
"Captain" shows that Whitman can use rhyme, although he chose a poetic theory which eschewed it, depending rather upon the stress of feeling and the truth of sentiment. His work seems rather the rough material of poetry than the finished article. Despite many a Shakespearean phrase and burning thought, his lack of form is often an insuperable obstacle to his recognition.

3 BUCKE, RICHARD MAURICE. Walt Whitman. To Which Is Added English Critics on Walt Whitman Edited by Edward Dowden. Glasgow: Wilson & McCormick, 255 pp. Illustrated. No index.
Reprint of 1883.3, with additions, pp. 237-55.
Presents in approximate chronological order extracts from commentary on Whitman by various English critics and literary figures, including some private letters.

4 BUNNER, H. C. Airs from Arcady and Elsewhere. New York: Charles Scribner's Sons. "Home Sweet Home: VI. As Walt Whitman might have Written all around it," pp. 68-73.
Reprint of 1881.21.

5 BURROUGHS, JOHN. Fresh Fields. Boston: Houghton, Mifflin & Co., p. 30.
Quotes a line from "Rise O Days" by "our poet."

6 EMERSON, RALPH WALDO. The Correspondence of Thomas Carlyle and Ralph Waldo Emerson 1834-1872. Vol. 2. Boston and New York: Houghton Mifflin Co., p. 283.
Reprint of 1883.4.

7 FAITHFULL, EMILY. Three Visits to America. Edinburgh: David Douglas, pp. 89-91.
Recalls "delightful hours spent in the society of this most eccentric genius" in

Philadelphia at the Robert Pearsall Smiths'; describes his Socrates-like appearance and magnetism; quotes him on American cities. He is "certainly a cultured man," "a deep thinker and an able talker," but he should have taken Emerson's advice about pruning Leaves.

8 GRIDLEY, C. OSCAR. Notes on America. London: Printed for private circulation, J. Gaskill, printer, 24 pp., passim, especially 5-8.

Gridley's visit to America made him realize even more "the depth and grandeur of Whitman's spirit" as related to the continent. Whitman's philosophy is explained as related to his hopes for democracy. His universal sympathy and trust in man is poetical and almost God-like. His genius is truly American, with a repulsive exterior but loving heart. Gridley describes his visit to Whitman just after he had moved to Mickle Street: his personality, appearance, opinions. A parody from Norristown Herald (unlocated) is reprinted, pp. 12-13 (reprinted in Saunders). Whitman is quoted throughout in relation to various aspects of America.

9 HATTON, JOSEPH. Henry Irving's Impressions of America: Narrated in a Series of Sketches, Chronicles and Conversations. Boston: James R. Osgood & Co., pp. 211-12.

Records Irving's meeting with Whitman; describes Whitman's resemblance to Tennyson, although with "a milder face, and less rugged in its lines."

10 LANIER, SIDNEY. Poems of Sidney Lanier. New York: Charles Scribner's Sons. "Memorial," by William Haynes Ward, pp. xxxvii-xxxviii.

Although Lanier found something refreshing in Whitman, he rejected Whitman's lawlessness in art, writing in his notes: "Whitman is poetry's butcher. Huge raw collops slashed from the rump of poetry, and never mind gristle--is what Whitman feeds our souls with." Whitman's argument seems to be "that, because a prairie is wide, therefore debauchery is admirable, and because the Mississippi is long, therefore every American is God."

11 RICHARDSON, CHARLES F. A Primer of American Literature. New and rev. ed. Boston: Houghton, Mifflin & Co., pp. 91-92. Revision of 1878.5.

To the brief discussion of 1878.5, commentary is added on Whitman's indecency and omission of "the 'upward look.'" "The world's great poets have been morally in advance of their times; Whitman lags behind."

12 ROBERTSON, JOHN. Walt Whitman, Poet and Democrat. Round Table Ser. 4. Edinburgh: William Brown, 52 pp. No index.

Two poems preface the discussion: a sonnet by A. A. ("Strong poet of the sleep-less gods that dwell") and a poem in rhymed dactylic hexameters presumably by Robertson ("Have we not hailed them great"), both praising Whitman. English readers demand "a new and autochthonic poetical product." Appropriately for his time, Whitman manifests "the force which is democracy; the typical self-asserting individual." His diatribe against American literature is unfair, forgetting Hawthorne, Poe, and Emerson, but Whitman must be "didactically inconsistent in order to be consistently prophetic." He is generally too earnest to perceive the humorously incongruous. His attitudes toward sex merit attention. His prose, less shocking, might be read first as a way into his poetry, distinguished from the prose by its lilt and passion. He is no barbarian in art but is familiar with more literature than was supposed earlier. "Lilacs," not "Captain," should be cited as an example of his real verse. He has grown away from his early flaws and aggressive quality toward more delicate perceptions in his later, more recognizably poetic work. His poetic theory is discussed here as part of the movement of artistic expansion Wagner embodies. His style "moves the sensibilities as potently as do its teachings" of a forward-looking optimism.

13 WATSON, WILLIAM. Epigrams of Art, Life, and Nature. Liverpool: Gilbert G. Walmsley. 82, "To Walt Whitman." Reprinted: 1884.3; Legler.

Quatrain: some "find thee foul," but "Thou followest Truth."

14 WHITE, RICHARD GRANT. The Fate of Mansfield Humphreys. Boston: Houghton, Mifflin & Co., pp. 102-9. Reprint of 1883.26. Extract reprinted: 1884.23.

PERIODICALS

*15 ROLLESTON, T. W. "Walt Whitman Abroad." Translated by Horace Traubel. Camden Post (13 February). Reprinted: Frenz.

Translates part of T. W. Rolleston's discourse in Dresden on Whitman (other parts appearing in In Re): Whitman wrote "the most astounding literary work of the present era." His poetry concerns the conduct of our lives and requires our self-examination. His is explained as "the greatest poetical Representative of German Philosophy." He portrays the relation between the human soul and the whole outer and inner world, emphasizing cultivation of the complete man. He represents "the first appearance in poetic literature of a real Democratic mind." His work combines the effects of a mind, poetry, and a "personal, physical influence." Traubel adds a note at the end mentioning Rolleston's use of classical illustrations and the subsequent discussion of Leaves among the professors.

1884

16 STURGIS, JULIAN. "A Mad Parson." Longman's
    Magazine 3 (April), 614-35, passim.
    Parody ("Covent Garden Market," p. 630)
    reprinted: 1888.3; Saunders.
        The old man, Ferdinand, goes through
    the story voicing Whitman-like sentiments
    about the open-air life and involvement
    with people of all kinds. His preachings
    are ridiculed by another character in this
    parody of Whitman's style and thought.

*17 ROBERTS, CHARLES G. D. "Notes on Some of the
    Younger American Poets." The Week (24
    April), 328.
    Quoted in McMullin (1974).
        Whitman, "the most prominent figure in
    American poetry," has genius and "elemental
    strength" which transcend his flaws (vocab-
    ulary, egotism, catalogues).

*18 BENSEL, JAMES BERRY. Article on Longfellow
    and Whitman. Lynn (Massachusetts) Saturday
    Union (24 May).
    Quoted in 1884.19; Kennedy.
        Whitman sent Longfellow a letter asking
    to dedicate Leaves to him, but Longfellow
    refused unless he omitted certain lines,
    which Whitman refused to do. Leaves and
    Whitman are praised.

19 ANON. "A Fabulous 'Episode.'" Critic, n.s. 1
    (31 May), 258.
        Summarizes 1884.18, "a very kindly and
    eulogistic notice" of Whitman, though wrong
    about the interchange between him and
    Longfellow, as Whitman claims.

*20 [WHITMAN, WALT.] "Whitman's Birthday." Phila-
    delphia Times (31 May).
    Reported in White.

21 KENNEDY, WALKER. "Walt Whitman." North
    American Review 138 (June), 591-601.
        There is occasionally the "gleam of the
    diamond in this mass of rubbish" of "un-
    couth chants, the mixed metaphors, the
    hirsute style, the ragged similes, and the
    rickety grammar." Whitman's deficiencies
    in clarity, consistency, art, and common
    sense, blatantly exemplified in passages of
    "Myself," represent the antithesis of the
    democratic spirit. His egotism represents
    "the delirium of self-conceit." In exalting
    the flesh he ignores the morality that
    literature should teach.

22 ANON. "Notes." Critic, n.s. 1 (28 June), 311.
        Quotes response by Bensel to Whitman's
    denial of sending Leaves to Longfellow
    (1884.19). Vouches that Longfellow did
    indeed tell such a story, as related by
    Bensel in a newspaper letter several years
    ago (to the San Francisco Chronicle, un-
    located), which Longfellow saw but which
    no one at that time denied.

23 WHITE, RICHARD GRANT. "A Poem that Walt
    Whitman Never Published." Literary World

15 (28 June), 212-13.
    Extract reprinted from 1884.14, with intro-
    ductory comment.

24 BELLOW, FRANK. "Recollections of Ralph Waldo
    Emerson." Lippincott's Magazine, n.s. 8
    (July), 45-50.
        Describes his conversations with Emerson
    in 1855 about Leaves and Whitman; Emerson's
    initial excitement; his surprise at his
    letter's publication ("I should have en-
    larged the but very much"); account of his
    presence at a reading of Leaves by a minister
    who did not suspect its contents.

25 ANON. "A Poet on Politics." Philadelphia
    Press (30 October), 8:3.
    Reprinted in part: Bergman (May 1948).
        Interview with Whitman who speaks on
    his political views, especially regarding
    Blaine and Cleveland. His writing activities
    are noted. He "is a man who does not seem
    to age rapidly."

26 ANON. "The Office Boy's Mother in America."
    Judy 35 (10 December), 277.
    Reprinted (with changes): Saunders.
        Parody in which the poet ("The Office
    Boy's Mother") discovers that she need not
    use rhyme but should follow Whitman's various
    examples.

27 ANON. "Walt Whitman on Cleveland. He Denounces
    Blaine and Speaks Warmly of the President-
    Elect." New York World (31 December), 1:3.
    Quoted in Bergman (May 1948).
        Whitman is quoted extensively in two
    long paragraphs addressed to a reporter,
    discussing Blaine's defeat and Cleveland's
    victory.

1885

BOOKS

1 CONE, HELEN GRAY. Oberon and Puck: Verses
    Grave and Gay. New York: Cassell & Co.
    "Narcissus in Camden. A Classical Dialogue
    of the Year 1882," pp. 110-17.
    Reprint of 1882.118.

2 CROSS, J[OHN] W. George Eliot's Life as re-
    lated in her Letters and Journals, Arranged
    and Edited by her Husband. Vol. 3. New
    York: Harper & Bros., pp. 200-201, 247.
        Quotes Eliot's letter of 18 April 1876
    to John Blackwood regarding her concern
    that she did not omit the Whitman epigraph
    in Daniel Deronda (1876.2): "not because
    the motto itself is objectionable to me--it
    was one of the finer things which had clung
    to me from among his writings--but because,
    since I quote so few poets, my selection of
    a motto from Walt Whitman might be taken as
    a sign of special admiration, which I am
    very far from feeling."

3 DALTON, JOSEPH G. Lyra Bicyclica: Sixty Poets
    on the Wheel. 2d ed. Boston: E. C. Hodges

& Co. "Poem of the Ride. A Parody-Mosaic. By Dalt Wheelman" (reprint with minor change and added closing lines of 1880.1), pp. 142-48; "Chanting the Round Mirific. By Dalt Wheelman," pp. 149-53.

The added parody is followed by a pair of rhymed stanzas praising "Wild Walt whom nature greatly leads" over the more effeminate "soft poets of the period."

4 HOLMES, OLIVER WENDELL. Ralph Waldo Emerson. Boston: Houghton, Mifflin & Co., pp. 325-26, 344-45.

Although Emerson did not confound the prosaic with the poetical, his followers such as Whitman have done so. Whitman "enumerates all the objects he happens to be looking at as if they were equally suggestive," making the reader select. Whitman's comments on Emerson in 1881 are quoted.

5 "PUCK" [pseud.] "Choice Selections from the Works of W_lt Wh_tm_n," Puck's Annual for 1885. New York: Keppler & Schwarzmann, p. 13.
Reprinted: Saunders.
Parody.

6 STEDMAN, EDMUND CLARENCE. Poets of America. Boston and New York: Houghton, Mifflin & Co. "Walt Whitman," pp. 349-95; also passim per index.
Revision of 1880.35.

Minor revisions required by changes in time; additions regarding Whitman's vision of the destiny of his land and people as guiding the future of the world; references to Whitman as a truly American poet throughout the volume.

7 THOMAS, JOSEPH. Universal Pronouncing Dictionary of Biography and Mythology. New ed. Philadelphia: J. B. Lippincott, p. 2463.
Brief biographical paragraph of Whitman's early career and writings.

PERIODICALS

*8 ANON. Account of Gosse's visit to Whitman. Camden Post (7 January).
Reported in Barrus and Asselineau.

*9 ANON. Account of Gosse's visit to Whitman. Camden Post (8 January).
Reported in Asselineau.

10 SELWYN, GEORGE [Walt Whitman]. "Authors at Home. VII. Walt Whitman at Camden." Critic 6 (28 February), 97-98.
Reprinted: 1888.6; 1898.18; 1902.24; Uncollected.
Sketches Whitman's life at various residences; describes extensively his home in Camden, where "to my household, wife and family, he has been an honored and most cherished guest." Dr. Drinkard's opinion

of Whitman is quoted: "the most natural man I have ever met." The sources of Whitman's work include his experiences and printing background. His "public sociability" is described. Despite his hardships, his spirits remain "vigorous and radiant."

11 ANON. "Mr. Irving's Second Tour in America." The Theatre, n.s. 5 (1 April), 178-79.
Describes Whitman's appearance, home, conversation, simple life. His prose must be admired, whatever is thought of his poetry. The 1872 Preface is quoted for its description of America "with rugged originality" and an ideal of her mission. But the poetic forms Whitman despises will not soon disappear.

12 ANON. "Walt Whitman." New York Daily Graphic (31 May), 4.
Brief biographical and physical account of Whitman on the occasion of his birthday, illustrated by portraits, facsimiles, drawings of Whitman scenes by A. Feraud. He absorbed the city and country of New York, both interior and exterior. Long Island was a fitting background for Leaves, influencing his work as did the opera. "His aim was to give expression to nature as we actually find it in the American laborer, boatman, mechanic." "Myself" 32 is quoted as representing "his philosophy of life, his hatred of cant, his revolt against arbitrary power."

13 ANON. "Pen Pictures of Authors." Literature and Life 3 (June), 164.
Paragraph describes Whitman's physical appearance, his simple but "scrupulously neat and clean" dress, his "clear and firm" voice.

14 GILCHRIST, ANNE. "A Confession of Faith." To-day, n.s. 3 (June), 269-84.
Reprinted: 1887.6; 1900.8; 1918.9.
Whitman is an unacclaimed innovator like Wordsworth. He may be termed the "Poet of Democracy" for proclaiming a profoundly religious faith in man. His book is not the mere biography of a man but "his actual presence." For him, the Civil War verified America's greatness, although he regards contemporary America with an anxious eye. He is a pioneer into a New World literature, making a beginning with the "vitality, initiative, sublimity" of his poems.

*15 ANON. Interview with Whitman. New York World (5 June).
Reprinted in part: Bergman (July 1948), but not located on this date.
Quotes Whitman on various writers (including Hugo and Tennyson); notes that he is still without a publisher.

16 [SCOVEL, JAMES.] "Walt Whitman. The Author of 'Leaves of Grass' at Home." Springfield

Daily Republican (16 June).
Extensive description of Whitman's
current situation, his hard times, his
earnings from writing. His dexterity in
writing has increased rather than decreased
with age, as evidenced in the way he wrote
his recent poem on Grant. Whitman's
letter of 1876 to Rossetti regarding his
situation is printed, as is a letter to
Whitman describing a review of Leaves from
Dresden which discusses Whitman's philosophical significance. The responses of
the publishing houses Ticknor & Fields and
Lee & Shepard are quoted upon Trowbridge's
urging that they publish Whitman. The
over-enthusiastic quality of some of the
criticism on Whitman is due to the vehemence
of the opposite side as well as to his
personal magnetism. His desire to have as
much published about him as possible is due
to his quest for understanding.

*17 ANON. Interview with Whitman. Marietta
(Ohio) Register (19 June).
Reprinted in part: Bergman (July 1948).
Describes Camden, Whitman's neighbor-
hood and house; quotes his remarks on
American poets (the four chief ones being
Emerson, Whittier, Bryant, and Longfellow--
who visited Whitman in Camden), on Hugo,
on defining poetry.

18 BALLOU, WILLIAM H. "Walt Whitman." Cleveland
Leader and Morning Herald (28 June), 4:5-6.
Reprinted: 1885.19; 1885.22. Reprinted
in part: Bergman (July 1948).
Account of his visit to Whitman in
Camden, his house, appearance, hope of
visiting Tennyson soon, happy condition,
freedom from want. He is quoted on progress,
present and future poetry (especially American), his ranking of the chief American
poets (Bryant, Emerson, Whittier,
Longfellow), the West as an important force
in literature (including his own), his
attitudes toward politics, religion, science,
tobacco, nature: "I am an old bachelor who
never had a love affair. Nature supplied
the place of a bride with suffering to be
nursed and scenes to be poetically clothed."
Whitman doubted the interview "as a vehicle
of communication" until assured that his
words would be taken "verbatim et punctuatim
et literatim."

18a [_____.] "Talk with Walt Whitman." New York
Sun (28 June), 10:5.
Reprint (with minor changes) of 1885.18.

*19 _____. Interview with Whitman. Washington
Post (28 June).
Reprint of 1885.18. Quoted in Bergman
(July 1948), but not located on this date.

20 ANON. "Walt Whitman's Style." Literary News,
n.s. 6 (July), 220.
Quotes Burroughs on Whitman as giving
something "better than mere literature or
art."

21 [CHAINEY, GEORGE.] "Walt. Whitman." The
Gnostic 1 (July), 1-8.
Much of this lecture is drawn directly
from 1881.22 and 1882.62. Favorable and
unfavorable commentary is quoted, including
Leonard Wheeler's whole sonnet. Whitman
rejects religion and politics as currently
practiced. His gospel is practical, "though
he believes more firmly than any one in the
soul and its immortality," regarding which
Chainey has spoken with him. He recognizes
the importance of "at-one-ment between
body and soul." His supreme service is
"his lofty defiance of the prurient tastes
and immodest modesty of this conventional
age," his readers being at fault if they
cannot recognize Leaves as "a sacred and
inspired book." Whitman said that Chainey's
publication of the condemned passages in
1882 "had done more than anything else" to
help the sale of Leaves.

*22 BALLOU, WILLIAM H. "Walt Whitman." Camden
Post (3 July).
Reprint of 1885.18. Reported in Kennedy.

23 ANON. "Notes and News." Academy 28 (7 July),
28.
Announces list of subscribers supporting
Whitman.

24 ANON. Review of Burroughs (1884.5). Nation
41 (9 July), 36.
Incidental reference: Burroughs recognizes as a man only someone like "Whitman
in puris naturalibus."

25 ANON. "Whitman on Grant. The Tribute of the
Poet Laureate of Democracy to the Great
Soldier." Philadelphia Press (26 July),
2:4-5.
Reprinted in part: Bergman (May 1948).
Interview with Whitman, describing
Camden's friendly attitude toward him, his
home, his physical appearance (including a
scar from a fall). This "student of nature
whose inimitable verses are honored abroad
even more highly than at home" praises
Grant and Lincoln as appropriate heroes for
America and quotes his poem on Grant.

*26 ANON. "Lofty Actors Withdraw. (A Thought of
Walt Whitman's Amplified, Versified and
Elucidated.)" Ingersoll Chronicle and
Canadian Dairyman (30 July).
Quoted in Bergman (August 1948).
Parody on Whitman's poem on Grant.

27 BUCHANAN, ROBERT. "Socrates in Camden, with
a Look Round." Academy 28 (15 August),
102-103.
Reprinted: 1901.2.
Long rhymed poem recording his visit to
Whitman, comparing him to Socrates and
Christ, asking him to revive the over-
refined American literature of the present.
(CHAL errs in saying this is reprinted in
1887.3.)

28 URNER, BENJ. "Grant. July 23d, 1885. (After Walt. Whitman.)" John Swinton's Paper (16 August), 2:2.
    Poem on Grant in Whitmanesque verse.

29 ANON. Paragraph. Athenaeum, no. 3017 (22 August), 241.
    Reprinted: 1885.31.
    Notes free-will offering from England to Whitman; prints his letter of 1 August to Herbert Gilchrist accepting the gift although his condition is not so needy as thought.

30 STEDMAN, EDMUND C. "The Twilight of the Poets." Century Magazine 30 (September), 794, 799.
    Incidental references: contemporary poetry is "less suggestive of changes and results" than Leaves or other earlier American poetry; an autochthonous verse is needed, a verse not proffered by earlier poets, unless by Whitman.

31 ANON. "Whitman's English Friends--From the London Athenaeum." New York Times (4 September), 5:3.
    Reprint of 1885.29.

*32 ANON. Note on Whitman's receipt of a phaeton. Camden Post (15 September).
    Reported in Kennedy.

33 ANON. "A Surprised Poet." Boston Herald (16 September), 2:7.
    Describes Whitman's reaction to the gift of the horse and phaeton when they were delivered on 15 September. The friends who contributed money for the gift are listed.

34 ANON. "Walt Whitman Surprised." New York Times (16 September), 5:3.
    Describes Whitman's receipt of the gift, while he was talking with Tom Donaldson's son.

35 ANON. "A Poet on Wheels. Admiring Friends Present a Modern Pegasus to Walt Whitman." Philadelphia Press (16 September), 5:1.
    Describes Whitman chatting with a visitor when the horse and phaeton (described) were driven up; his delighted reaction; list of the donors.

*36 [BOCOCK, JOHN PAUL?] or [BRAINERD, ERASTUS?]. "Out of Harness at Last." Philadelphia News (21 September).
    Reprinted: Saunders.
    Parody in free verse occasioned by the mistaken theft of Whitman's horse's harness.

37 ANON. "A Camden Lyric. A Poet's Presumed Lament Before the Recovery of his Lost 'Harness,' September 21, 1885. Not by Walt Whitman." Philadelphia Press (23 September), 4:6.
    Comic poem in five quatrains on Whitman's loss of the harness.

38 ANON. Note. Literary World 16 (3 October), 344.
    Notes what Whitman has received from the sales of his works.

39 ANON. Note. Literary World 16 (17 October), 370.
    Further describes Whitman's receipts from sales.

40 POWERS, HORATIO N. "Mr. Stedman on the Poets of America." Dial 6 (November), 172-74.
    Review of 1885.6: Stedman's chapter on Whitman is just, but Whitman does not have the poetic eminence to merit a separate chapter. "Half of his verse might be eliminated without injury to his fame or to the interests of literature."

*41 [McKINSEY, FOLGER.] Account of Pythian Journalists' Club banquet. Cecil Whig (5 December), 3.
    Quoted in Moyne (1975).
    McKinsey read letters from Whitman and Joaquin Miller, honorary members, and praised them, noting his own friendship for Whitman, this country's greatest poet.

*42 _____. "Studies--In Literature and Biography. Whitman To-day." Cecil Whig (19 December), 3.
    Quoted in Moyne (1975).
    Account of his visit to Whitman on 12 December 1885. Whitman, "the perfect embodiment of the chosen poet," with great wisdom, "has made the times" and "predicted America." He is not vulgar or incoherent, but "only sensuous as nature is sensuous." His notions of the poet, of man as a god, and of the importance of the soul are explained. He is poet of the soul more than of the mind.

1886

BOOKS

1 BURROUGHS, JOHN. Signs and Seasons. Boston and New York: Houghton, Mifflin & Co.
    "A Salt Breeze," pp. 166-67, 173, 175-77.
    Poems revealing Whitman's knowledge of the sea and his various sea-like qualities are quoted.

2 KENNEDY, WM. SLOANE. The Poet as a Craftsman. Philadelphia: David McKay, pp. 13-20.
    In his most finished poems, Whitman's art follows the laws of nature and symphonic music. Like Hugo he struggles for poetic reform but with less acceptance. His lines correspond to the natural length of the thoughts and echo Homer's hexameters. He often suspends the main thought of a poem until the close.

3 LATHROP, GEORGE PARSONS. Introduction to Representative Poems of Living Poets, Amer-

1886

ican and English, Selected by the Poets
Themselves, edited by R. W. Gilder. London:
Cassell & Co., p. xxii.
  Whitman's "faults of art and judgment
are on a scale commensurate with his original genius," which sometimes attains a
strange harmony in his long swinging lines
yet is often prosaic. "Eidŏlons" and
"Spirit," here anthologized, are commented
on. Whitman is always "meditative, moralizing, introspective; seeing all other
objects and persons in himself, and himself
in all other persons and objects." Also
included (pp. 650-57) are "Patrolling
Barnegat," "Ox-Tamer," and "Ashes of
Soldiers."

4 NOEL, Hon. RODEN. Essays on Poetry and Poets.
London: Kegan Paul, Trench & Co. "A Study
of Walt Whitman," pp. 304-41.
Revision of 1871.23 and 1871.26.
  Changes include some condensation,
revision of the "Calamus" discussion, and
some additions, particularly at the end
(reprinted: Cameron [1971]). Whitman's
rich humanity, with its abundance of the
Christ-spirit, is praised, yet he can also
discern what is evil, especially in Vistas.

5 POSNETT, HUTCHESON MACAULAY. Comparative
Literature. New York: D. Appleton & Co.,
pp. 32, 68-69, 71, 364, 372, 388-89.
  Whitman exemplifies the modern tendency
to present "the corporate life of men" and
combines democracy and personality. He is
the culminating embodiment of the union of
"social sympathies, individual consciousness, Nature's life, all on a scale of
greatness never before approximated."

6 PROWELL, GEO[RGE] R. The History of Camden
County, New Jersey. Philadelphia: L. J.
Richards & Co., pp. 332-33.
  Biographical sketch of Whitman "from a
late book, by Allen Thorndike Rice," unlocated; notes imminent appearance of
November, Whitman's present residence and
appearance, his living "in a very plain
and democratic manner," with his works read
more abroad than in America.

7 RHYS, ERNEST. Introduction to Leaves of Grass:
The Poems of Walt Whitman, Selected.
London: Walter Scott, pp. ix-xxxix.
  Biographical sketch from O'Connor
(1866.2), Burroughs (1867.1), Bucke (1883.
3), and Specimen. Whitman's new form is
not a freakish eccentricity but the genuine
outcome of a new, vastly extended apprehension of contemporary life and letters,
returning to a Burns-like use of contemporary idiom and concern after decades of
archaic and cultured poetry. Others will
follow his new poetic mode but will need to
avoid his mannerisms. Although he is a
mystic like Hegel, he requires only emotional, not academic, equipment. A beginning reading order is outlined. Besides

his literary excellence, Whitman exerts a
strong personal magnetism, "potent for
moral elevation," especially for the young.
Due to the limitations of average readers,
poems that have been criticized are here
omitted (notably "Myself," "Adam," "Salut,"
"Passage," "Sleepers"); otherwise the
selection, following Whitman's order, is
fairly complete.

8 ROSSETTI, WILLIAM MICHAEL, ed. Preface to
Poems by Walt Whitman. A New Edition.
London: Chatto & Windus, pp. 1-22.
Reprint of 1868.2. Reprinted: 1926.25.
  This edition merely resets 1868.2, with
a brief paragraph appended to the preface
noting Whitman's illness and recent works.

9 SANBORN, KATE. The Vanity and Insanity of
Genius. New York: George J. Coombes,
pp. 92-95, 178.
  Whitman is "our chief egotist," his
conceit surpassing belief, as shown in
quoted passages. To critics he is either
an eagle or a harpy.

10 TUPPER, MARTIN FARQUHAR. My Life as an Author.
London: Sampson Low, Marston, Searle, &
Rivington, p. 150.
  No reference to Whitman in this book,
but Tupper quotes a review (by Whitman) of
his Probabilities, an Aid to Faith from the
Brooklyn Eagle.

11 WILKIE, JAMES. The Democratic Movement in
Literature. Walt Whitman. Cupar-Fife,
Scotland: Printed in the Fifeshire Journal
office, 44 pp.
  Impressionistic introduction to Whitman.
After a long discussion of democratic
ideals and literature, Wilkie presents
Whitman as the great poet sought by the
modern world, even though he is not recognized by public or critics. He is of a
different, more democratic mould than
Longfellow and looks toward a hopeful future
with more certainty than Tennyson. His
theme is the love of comrades; Leaves is "a
working out in the light of other years" of
David's lament for Jonathan. He does not
lull with mere beauty but urges toward
action and greatness. His life is briefly
described from Bucke (1883.3) and O'Connor
(1866.2). Writings of a man with such
devoted war service cannot be evil. He
must be read.

PERIODICALS

12 ANON. "Stedman's Poets of America." Atlantic
Monthly 57 (January), 131.
  Review of 1885.6. "American democracy
is not yet red-shirted, and Whitman remains
to the public mainly a curiosity."

13 HAWEIS, Rev. H. R., M. A. "A Visit to Walt
Whitman." Pall Mall Gazette (13 January),
1-2.

Reprinted: 1886.14; 1886.29; 1896.7.
Extract reprinted: 1886.23.
      Account of his December 1885 visit to
Whitman, who speaks of Emerson, Tennyson,
Browning. His revolt against rigid form
resembles Wagner's, seeking a more adequate
method for conveying the interior changes
of the soul. Such a poem as "Whispers"
reveals Whitman's insight and genius. His
broad sympathy is typical of America.

14 _____. "A Visit to Walt Whitman." Pall Mall
      Budget (14 January), 12.
      Reprint of 1886.13.

*15 ANON. Account of meeting of the Pythian Jour-
      nalists' Club. Cecil Whig (16 January), 3.
      Quoted in Moyne (1975).
          A letter from Whitman to the club is
      read.

16 THOMPSON, WILLIAM. "Mr. Haweis and Walt
      Whitman." Pall Mall Gazette (16 January),
      2.
          Corrects Haweis (1886.13) in ascribing
      the English edition of Whitman to Dante
      Gabriel Rossetti and in implying that those
      poems were expurgated.

*17 ANON. Note. Cecil Whig (23 January), 3.
      Reported in Moyne (1975).
          Announcement of Whitman's upcoming
      appearance in Elkton, Maryland, to deliver
      his Lincoln lecture.

*18 [JOHNSTON, GEORGE.] "Local Department. Minor
      Locals." Cecil Whig (23 January).
      Quoted in Moyne (1956).
          Announces Whitman's upcoming lecture
      on Greeley for the Young Men's Lecture
      Course; citizens would do well to see and
      hear this renowned man, regarded as Amer-
      ica's best poet.

*19 QUILP [George Johnston]. "Walt Whitman at
      Home. A Visit to the Good Gray Poet of
      Camden." Cecil Democrat (23 January).
      Reprinted: Moyne (1956).
          Describes "the poet par excellence of
      the nineteenth century," a "hoary-headed
      poet and priest" with a perspective into
      the future; his warmth and suggestions of
      the inner man; his room; a visit to Whitman
      from some young ladies. Whitman's conver-
      sation is quoted (he prefers writing for
      himself to writing for posterity), often
      "as hard to comprehend as his poetry." His
      thought and his purity and goodness as a
      man are described.

*20 ANON. Announcement. Elkton Appeal (27 Jan-
      uary).
      Quoted in Moyne (1956).
          Whitman's lecture on Greeley is an-
      nounced. Though he "has written consider-
      able poetry which ordinary folks have not
      been able to understand," his reading of
      several of his pieces may help make it plain.

*21 ANON. Note. Cecil Democrat (30 January).
      Quoted in Moyne (1956).
          Correction of Whitman's subject in
      upcoming lecture (see 1886.18): He is to
      speak of Lincoln, with whom he was sitting
      at the assassination. His description of
      it is "one of the finest specimens of word
      painting," highly commended by Boston
      critics in 1881.

*22 BURROUGHS, JOHN. "Essays--Moral, Scientific,
      Historical." Cecil Whig (30 January), 1.
      Reported in Moyne (1975). Reprint (the
      first of three installments) of "The Flight
      of the Eagle" (1877.1).

*23 HAWEIS, Rev. H. R. "A Visit to Walt Whitman."
      Cecil Whig (30 January), 1.
      Reported in Moyne (1975). Extract reprinted
      from 1886.13.

*24 [McKINSEY, FOLGER.] "Local Department." Cecil
      Whig (30 January), 3.
      Quoted in Moyne (1975).
          Announces Whitman's lecture and reading
      of "the touching and beautiful poem,"
      "Captain."

*25 _____. "Poet, and Martyr President. Walt
      Whitman to Describe the Shooting of Lincoln
      Before an Elkton Audience." Cecil Whig
      (30 January), 3.
      Reported in Moyne (1975).
          Detailed account of Whitman's upcoming
      lecture.

*26 ANON. Review of Whitman's lecture. Cecil
      Democrat (6 February), 3:4.
      Reprinted: 1936.34. Quoted in Moyne (1975).
          Whitman's lecture in Elkton, Maryland,
      on 2 February pleased those who could ap-
      preciate "his peculiar, though by no means
      eloquent style." The audience seemed in-
      adequate to it. Whitman, who has been
      termed the Homer of America, is not the only
      poet who has failed to be appreciated by
      his country.

*27 [McKINSEY, FOLGER.] Account of Whitman's
      lecture and reception. Cecil Whig (6
      February), 3.
      Reprinted: Moyne (1975).
          Whitman's lecture is praised, his de-
      livery and appearance described. At the
      reception George Johnston praised him as
      "the Homer of America" and "originator of
      the American school of poetry."

*28 ANON. Brief note. Elkton Appeal (10 February).
      Quoted in Moyne (1956).
          Notes "some diversity of opinion as to
      the merits" of Whitman's lecture.

29 HAWEIS, Rev. H. R. "A Visit to Walt Whitman."
      Critic, n.s. 5 (27 February), 109.
      Reprint of 1886.13.

1886

30 ANON. "Greville and Whitman. Two Interesting
Lectures by Well-known Authors. . . . 'O
Captain! My Captain.' Walt Whitman's
Lecture on the Death of Abraham Lincoln."
Philadelphia Press (2 March), 5:4-5.
Description of Whitman and his reading
at Morgan Hall last night. To hear him
many braved a storm, filling the house and
showing that Whitman is not without honor
in his own region, Camden. The lecture
and "Captain" are quoted; his reading was
free from an elocutionist's artificialities.

*31 ANON. Report on Whitman's Lincoln lecture in
Camden. Camden Coast Pilot (6 March).
Reported in Barrus.

32 [COSTELLOE, MARY D. SMITH.] "Whitman for the
Drawing Room." Papers for the Times, no.
22 (April), 181-85.
Review of Rhys (1886.7). Rhys's introduction ignores Whitman's real advance,
his attitude toward death. People who
seek to appear respectable but secretly
enjoy immoral jokes and deeds will be disappointed in Whitman's work, which is
"cleanly minded." "Myself" and "Singer in
Prison" are unfortuantely omitted, but
"City Dead House" and "Dalliance" are
happily included.

33 GOODALE, DORA READ. "To Walt Whitman."
Lippincott's Monthly Magazine 37 (April),
363.
Rhymed poem of tribute.

34 ROWLANDSON, H. "'Towards Democracy.'" Dublin
University Review 2 (April), 319-28.
Review of Edward Carpenter's Towards
Democracy, noting his debts to Whitman,
whose place is as assured as that of any of
his contemporaries. His method remains
unexhausted for such disciples as Carpenter.
Whitman's poetic principle is analyzed and
considered sound though not always satisfactory in practice. He felt rhythm should
reinforce the meaning, hence his long lines.
Both poets reject "the proprieties" and
shock "modern notions of delicacy."

35 DOWDEN, EDWARD. "The Interpretation of Literature." Contemporary Review 49 (May), 704,
709.
Whitman is mentioned incidentally as
typical of unaccepted writers who at last
came into their own.

36 ANON. "Walt Whitman's Birthday." New York
Times (4 June), 2:4.
Describes Whitman's quiet lifestyle,
the financial status of his works, his
health. He gave his lecture on Lincoln
four times this spring.

37 [GILDER, JEANNETTE.] "The Lounger." Critic,
n.s. 6 (3 July), 7.
Describes the sale of a first edition
and an autograph letter of Whitman which

explained that he set some of the type for
it and had 800 copies printed.

38 [BARROWS, SAMUEL J.] "An Editor's Farewell."
Christian Register 65 (12 August), 499.
Much of Whitman reads like a plagiarized
"auctioneer's catalogue." The ease of
writing such raw poetry is shown by a
parody, "Adieu!"

39 KENNEDY, WILLIAM SLOANE. "The Precession [sic]
of the Poets." Critic, n.s. 6 (4 September),
109-10.
Incidentally mentions Whitman as example
of orchestral (as opposed to organ) harmony
in verse, especially evident in his sea-
chants.

40 ANON. "Notes." Critic, n.s. 6 (18 September),
144.
J. B. B. writes to correct the assertion
of Haweis (1886.29) that Whitman was present
at Lincoln's assassination.

41 ANON. "Poets and Poetry of America." Quarterly Review 163 (October), 363-94, passim.
Reprinted: 1887.21.
Whitman's "attempt to represent the
large ideas, the concrete realities of
multiform activities, the panoramic pageant
of moving life--the great heart of the
democratic Republic--was rather prophetic
of the future than descriptive of the
present." He seeks a new literature for
democracy, free in form and subject.
"Lilacs" and "Cradle" prove him "a lyric
genius of the highest order," first among
American poets for "creative force and imaginative vigour." His theory is defensible,
not for seeking "to render poetry inartistic," but for seeking to reproduce in verse
the pulse of nature. His language is
praised. He echoes Emerson's thought as a
transcendental evolutionist. His lists are
powerful in expressing vastness. His fanat-
icism is his strength and weakness. The
future lies with him, not for his form but
for his depiction of personality (which in
him displays comradeship, sympathy, an open-
air quality) and concrete reality.

42 C., J. F. "Portfolio." Yale Literary Magazine, 52 (November), 75-76.
Whitman's democratic spirit and good
heart, if not his writings, are loved by
the common people he associated with. He
sought inspiration by lying in the sun,
especially at Coney Island.

43 LATHROP, GEORGE PARSONS. "The Literary Movement in New York." Harper's New Monthly
Magazine 73 (November), 823-24.
Of all the poets of New York, only
Whitman "has attempted to reproduce its
elements in a shape suggesting their mass
and variety, and with a spirit responding
to and interpreting them." His method,
alternating "dull prose with gleams of
splendid poetry," may be fit to express the

actual city, through his large grasp and native tone.

44 SALT, H. S. "Henry D. Thoreau." Temple Bar 78 (November), 382.
Incidental discussion of the "natural affinity and fellowship" between Thoreau's genius and Whitman's. Whitman, "a leviathan among modern writers," is "the very incarnation of all that is free, healthy, natural, sincere." He proclaims his "glorious democracy" rather than teaching or rebuking, as Thoreau does.

45 HUGHES, H. D. "Walt Whitman.--The Old Gray Poet." Leisure Moments 1 (December), 266-71.
Whitman discarded ordinary verse forms in favor of an original blend of the prose of Bacon, Carlyle, and others, and the poetry of Shakespeare, Milton, Homer, and Hugo. Through chaos he attains a kind of order, with a compass and harmony greater than the accepted and more elegant poets because of his "towering magnetic presence." Leaves is a dramatic poem of man in his relation to the outward world. The war pictures of Drum-Taps are described. "Cradle" and "Lilacs" are compared, praised, explicated. One reaches Whitman's atmosphere only after repeated readings. His style is a "mass movement" of details which gather as the sentence moves along. His titles give evidence of his skill in epithets.

46 J., S. B. "Poetical Occultism. Some Rough Studies of the Occult Leanings of the Poets. III." The Path 1 (December), 270-74.
Explains the doctrines of meditation, karma, and reincarnation, showing how Whitman exemplifies them.

47 ANON. "A Poet in Penury." London Daily News (16 December), 5:2.
Editorial quotes from a letter circulated by Mr. Underwood, U.S. consul at Glasgow, describing Whitman's need. Lovers of poetry here and abroad should help him. "He does not so much write poetry, as throw out, in a curious unworked form, ideas, many of which would have been the stuff of noble poetry had he been a poet," especially his passage on the death of Lincoln. They are "pensées" rather than poetry, his cataloguing being a major fault. But they show his great "nobility and manfulness of character."

48 ANON. "Occasional Notes." Pall Mall Gazette (16 December), 3:2.
Paragraph proposing that money be raised as a Christmas gift for Whitman to ameliorate his living conditions. His poverty is a discredit to Americans "with a taste for letters," since his life cannot last much longer although his work will be discussed as long as the language survives.

49 ANON. "Walt Whitman." London Daily News (17 December), 5:5.
Quotes the Evening Post (unlocated), whose reporter visited Whitman to find him healthy and comfortable, contrary to the Glasgow appeal letter. Whitman says he is grateful to his English friends and will not decline the gift, but he is not in want.

50 ANON. "Walt Whitman's Purse." New York Times (17 December), 5:2.
Report of Glasgow appeal (see 1886.47). J. H. Johnston claims that if Whitman were in need, plenty of American friends would help him. High prices being paid for his works are noted. A paragraph from the Philadelphia Call (unlocated) is quoted reporting Whitman's own claims of good health and denials of poverty.

51 ANON. "Walt Whitman at Home." Pall Mall Gazette (17 December), 6:2.
Quotes Evening Post (see 1886.49).

52 ANON. "Occasional Notes." Pall Mall Gazette (18 December), 3:2.
List of donors of money and their kind words on Whitman. Whitman's need is certain, although it has been exaggerated, and the gift is well-deserved because his hand has been stretched out in "actual help" as well as in "poetical salvation."

53 ANON. "Occasional Notes." Pall Mall Gazette (20 December), 3.
Reports more contributions.

54 ANON. "Occasional Notes." Pall Mall Gazette (22 December), 3.
Reports more contributions.

55 ANON. "Occasional Notes." Pall Mall Gazette (23 December), 3.
Reports more contributions.

56 [COSTELLOE, MARY D. SMITH.] "Walt Whitman at Camden. By One who has been there." Pall Mall Gazette (23 December), 1-2.
Describes Whitman's surroundings, writing habits. He is not in want; his writing and lectures provide for "an unexacting and simple life."

57 ANON. "Occasional Notes." Pall Mall Gazette (24 December), 3.
Reports more contributions to the gift for Whitman.

58 [GILDER, JEANNETTE.] "The Lounger." Critic, n.s. 6 (25 December), 319.
Literary England's tone toward Whitman is amusing. He is not starving as they suppose. His response to British concern is frank, typical of his "bland and childlike nature."

1887

1887

BOOKS

*1 ARNOLD, EDWIN. Death and Afterwards. London: Trübner & Co.
Reported in Blodgett. See Addenda (1892).
Quotations from Whitman are used.

2 BEERS, HENRY A. An Outline Sketch of American Literature. New York: Chautauqua Press, pp. 232-39, bibliography, p. 239.
Revised: 1891.3.
Some of Whitman's verse may offend, but it is appropriate to his "strong, masculine joy in life and nature" in all aspects. His prosaic attempts to get everything into his verse are offset by lines "often unsurpassed for descriptive beauty and truth." His ideas are not many, individualized humanity finds small place, but "one likes to read him because he feels so good," with his confidence in immortality and man's future.

3 BUCHANAN, ROBERT. A Look Round Literature. London: Ward & Downey. "The American Socrates," pp. 341-46; also 354, 382, 384, 385.
Whitman is outlawed in his country, like Socrates, while lesser poets are praised. Buchanan describes his visit to Whitman in March 1885: how Whitman lives, with little income from his poetry, neglected by editors because considered dangerous. In personality he is akin to Socrates and Christ. He is unconcerned with praise, fame, or wealth, having spoken his message and lived his life. He is "supreme in his power of conveying moral stimulation." (CHAL errs in calling this article a reprint of 1885.27.)

4 CORELLI, MARIE. Thelma. London: Richard Bentley & Son. Vol. 2, p. 208; vol. 3, pp. 173-74.
The title character wonders at "cloudy-eyed eccentrics" who admired Whitman's "common-place sentence-writing." Another character later laughs at Whitman's favor among the English, quotes "Ox-Tamer" mockingly.

5 F[ORMAN], H. B[UXTON]. "Walt Whitman." In Celebrities of the Century, edited by Lloyd C. Sanders. London: Cassell, pp. 1046-48.
Biographical sketch, showing Whitman's preparation for preaching the gospel of democracy and the natural man. He may be termed a prophet, the most absolute optimist, more at one with the external universe than perhaps anyone whose writings are extant and possessing firmer faith about the soul. "His perfectly primeval outspokenness" and "want of attention to form" must be accepted as part of his religion.

6 GILCHRIST, HERBERT HARLAKENDEN. Anne Gilchrist: Her Life and Writings. London: T. Fisher Unwin, 368 pp., passim. No index.
Contents: Author's preface, prefatory notice by W. M. Rossetti (both discussing Whitman's relationship with Anne Gilchrist), biography, essays (reprints of 1870.4 and 1885.14). Gilchrist's life is largely narrated through letters (to and from Gilchrist herself, Rossetti, Whitman, others). Her relationship with Whitman is traced, as is the development of her essay (1870.4) and its publication. Extensive transcriptions by her son Herbert of Whitman's conversations record his comments on or anecdotes about Emerson, Joaquin Miller, Jenny Lind, Count Gurowski, Thoreau, Tennyson, Eliot, Scott, Shakespeare, Henry James's essay on Sand.

7 GISSING, GEORGE. Thyrza: A Tale. Vol. 3. London: Smith, Elder, & Co., pp. 172-73, 177-82, 210.
Reprinted: 1927.19.
A character writes a letter describing his experience of Whitman and urges his correspondent to read him. His music, force, and value help in becoming "a sound and mature man." "Song of Joys" is praised and described. Whitman is "all spirit," speaking with "the very voice of Nature" and of "the healthy, unconscious man."

*8 HUNT, THEODORE W. Representative English Prose and Prose Writers. New York: A. C. Armstrong & Son, p. 295.
Reported in Moulton.
"To endorse, in any valid sense, much of the tenor of modern opinion as to the poetic merit of the school of Whitman, is altogether impossible, though the oracle of Delphi order it." (The book was searched, but no reference to Whitman was found.)

9 MORRILL, JUSTIN S. Self-Consciousness of Noted Persons. Boston: Ticknor & Co. "Walt Whitman," p. 43.
Whitman's poems "are not winning all the gratitude" Americans owe them. Only Whitman among American poets offers "lusty self-appreciation." He never fears to take a reader into his confidence.

10 MORRIS, CHARLES. Half-Hours with the Best American Authors. Vol. 2. Philadelphia: J. B. Lippincott, p. 489.
Headnote to "Redwood": Whitman's poetry is "never likely to become popular," being rarely above the level of prose. Though frequently "full of imaginative fervor," "with many passages of fine power," it exalts "the grosser bodily element," without the spiritual element. "Redwood" "has a deeper and more elevating significance than is usual" with him; "if judiciously pruned," it might rank high in the poetic world.

11 STEDMAN, EDMUND CLARENCE. <u>Victorian Poets</u>.
   Cambridge: Riverside Press, pp. 402, 424,
   428, 450.
   Revision of 1875.5.
        Incidental references to Whitman in
   relation to Swinburne and Austin and to
   his "Hebraic chant, often vibrating with
   rhythmical harmony," as "the outcome of a
   belief that rhymes are hackneyed and
   trivial."

12 STEVENSON, ROBERT LOUIS. Selection in <u>Books</u>
   <u>Which Have Influenced Me</u>. London: printed
   in the <u>British Weekly</u> office, pp. 7-8.
   Reprint of 1887.44.

13 UNITED STATES CONGRESS. HOUSE COMMITTEE ON
   INVALID PENSIONS. <u>Walt Whitman; Report to</u>
   <u>Accompany H. R. 10707</u>. Washington: U.S.
   Government Printing Office.
        H. B. Lovering's proposal to provide
   Whitman a pension of twenty-five dollars
   a month is supported by quotations regarding
   his hospital work from 1866.2; 1876.43; a
   letter from a woman to Bucke; Dr. D. W.
   Bliss; the Philadelphia <u>Progress</u> (unlocated).
   Whitman's current sickness and poverty are
   emphasized, with no reference to his poetry.
   Committee recommends passage of the bill.

14 WHIPPLE, EDWIN PERCY. <u>American Literature and</u>
   <u>Other Papers</u>. Boston: Ticknor & Co., pp.
   112-14.
        Whitman "might have been styled the
   marvellous 'b'hoy.'" His disregard for all
   convention should have been modified regarding the relations of the sexes. His
   latest books are not so objectionable, but
   <u>Leaves</u> would still, "if thoroughly cleaned,"
   be considered his ablest and most original
   work. Such an innovator, after such high
   praise, may have to suffer some unjust
   neglect.

PERIODICALS

15 WILLIAMS, FRANCIS HOWARD. "To Walt Whitman."
   <u>Lippincott's Monthly Magazine</u> 39 (January),
   132.
   Reprinted: 1894.19.
        Sonnet of tribute: "Bold innovator in
   the realm of thought. . . ."

16 ANON. "Notes." <u>Public Opinion</u> 2 (1 January),
   247.
        Two sentences on the money sent Whitman
   from Europe.

17 ANON. Paragraph. <u>Critic</u>, n.s. 7 (8 January),
   12.
        Quoted from <u>The World</u> (unlocated):
   Whitman is described when a "handsome
   youth." Captain Simon Cooper has compared
   Whitman and saltwater.

18 ANON. "Measure Before Congress . . . A Bill
   to Pension Walt Whitman." <u>New York Tribune</u>
   (18 January), 2:5.

   Paragraph notes the bill introduced by
   Mr. Lovering of Massachusetts, initiated
   not by Whitman but by his friends in that
   state.

19 ANON. Editorial paragraph. <u>Springfield</u>
   <u>Republican</u> (18 January), 4.
        Whitman and his services should be
   honored through private beneficence rather
   than the proposed public pension.

20 WHITMAN, WALT. "The Walt Whitman New Year's
   Gift." <u>Pall Mall Gazette</u> (25 January), 11.
        Letter thanking <u>Gazette</u> for the recent
   funds sent him, with an extract printed in
   facsimile.

21 ANON. "Poets and Poetry in America." <u>Critic</u>,
   n.s. 7 (29 January), 56-58.
        Reprint of final part of 1886.41 (preceding
   two <u>Critic</u> issues have reprinted the earlier
   part of the article).

22 BURROUGHS, JOHN. "Mere Egotism." <u>Lippincott's</u>
   <u>Monthly Magazine</u> 39 (February), 301.
   Reprinted: 1889.2.
        Incidental reference explaining his
   debt to Whitman, among others: Whitman
   offered "a certain liberalizing influence,
   as well as a lesson in patriotism," human
   sympathy, and "a sense of a living, breathing man" throughout his poems.

23 HUGHES, HARRY D. "Walt Whitman's Prose Works."
   <u>Leisure Moments</u> 2 (February), 17.
        Discussion of Whitman's prose, with
   comparisons to the great classical prose
   writers in English. Even without his poetry,
   he would rank "as an English prose classic,"
   his style "such as only the largest and
   most Titanic workman could effectively use,"
   his personality and patriotism expressed
   more strikingly than in his poems.

24 ANON. "Minor Notices." <u>Critic</u>, n.s. 7 (5
   February), 65.
        Brief review of Knortz's book on
   Whitman (1893.11, in German): "a clear and
   impartial <u>view</u>" of Whitman "as he appears
   to a German," dealing with all his important
   aspects, since he is a man who can no longer
   be ignored.

25 ANON. Paragraph. <u>Literary World</u> 18 (5 February), 40.
        Quotes an English characterization
   (unlocated) of a certain controversial
   American poet: "He is a Hebrew bard translated to the American backwoods, where he
   has turned himself inside out, thence going
   on to study pantheism on the quays of New
   York."

26 H[IGGINSON], T. W. "Women and Men. War Pensions for Women." <u>Harper's Bazar</u> 20 (5
   March), 162.
        The same arguments put forward to sup-
   port a pension for Whitman as a war nurse

1887

(a duty he chose over the field despite his "conspicuously fine physique") might apply to the women who also served, but neither poets nor women should receive pensions, which have already been much abused.

27 ANON. "Literature. Notes." Public Opinion 2 (12 March), 485.
     Notes Whitman as the principal speaker at the last meeting of the Contemporary Club in Philadelphia, where he read "Trumpeter" and "Cradle," "a boyish reminiscence read by the old man with deep feeling."

28 ANON. Review of Gilchrist (1887.6). Athenaeum, no. 3100 (26 March), 409-10.
     Incidental: Whitman has unfortunately kept back Gilchrist's letters, though surely for a worthy purpose. Most people will think her worship of Whitman excessive, but its effect on her was beneficial.

29 ANON. "Personal." Harper's Bazar 20 (26 March), 215.
     Whitman is preparing a character study of Quaker evangelist Elias Hicks. "It will be the most considerable piece of prose" he has recently done.

30 HIGGINSON, THOMAS WENTWORTH. "Sidney Lanier." Chautauquan 7 (April), 417-18.
     Reprinted: 1899.8.
     Lanier's criticisms of Whitman, "a literary spirit alien to his own," are quoted approvingly from 1883.5. Among the grounds for his disapproval would be Whitman's choice of civilian work during the war, in contrast to Lanier's own military service.

31 ANON. "Notes." Critic, n.s. 7 (9 April), 184.
     Paragraph announces Whitman's upcoming New York lecture on Lincoln, a fine way to contribute to his support, which the British are helping through collections.

*32 ANON. "An Old Poet's Reception." New York Evening Sun (15 April).
     Reprinted: White.
     Account of the reception at the Westminster Hotel the previous evening after Whitman's Lincoln lecture in the afternoon. Whitman's comments on riding stages and knowing drivers are quoted. The stream of visitors (some described in anecdotes) includes E. C. and Arthur Stedman, Joseph, Jeannette, and Mrs. Richard Gilder, H. H. Boyesen, Frank R. Stockton, Wyatt Eaton, Burroughs, Joel Benton, Major Pond, Pearsall Smith, Mrs. General Custer, E. S. Nadal, John Fiske, Lawrence Hutton, J. H. Johnston, Alexander, Professor Ritter, and Stuart Merrill (unnamed, but see 1922.15).

33 ANON. "The Good Gray Poet Is White Now. Walt Whitman's Welcome by his Friends in Madison Square Theatre." New York Sun (15 April), 1:4.
     Account of Whitman's vivid lecture on Lincoln, his appearance, the audience.

34 ANON. "A Tribute from a Poet." New York Times (15 April), 8:1-2.
     Account of Whitman's lecture, with quotations, his appearance, the audience, the reception.

35 ANON. "Hearty Cheers for Whitman. He Speaks on Abraham Lincoln." New York Tribune (15 April), 5:2.
     Account of the setting and audience for Whitman's lecture, where Howells took tickets at the door; Whitman's appearance, speech, backstage visitors, reception, guests.

36 ANON. "Notes." Critic, n.s. 7 (23 April), 211.
     Carnegie, unable to attend the lecture, gave Whitman a liberal donation. Whitman's essay on Hicks is announced.

37 ANON. "Walt Whitman on Lincoln." Critic, n.s. 7 (23 April), 206-207.
     Account of Lincoln lecture on 14 April, with extracts.

38 ANON. "Personal." Harper's Bazar 20 (23 April), 291.
     Describes St. Gaudens's plans to make a bust of Whitman.

39 ANON. "Personal." Harper's Weekly 31 (23 April), 291.
     Cites Whitman's recent praise for Sir Walter Scott, who nourished him more than American poets or contemporary foreign poetry; Whitman's growing faith in immortality; his recent visit to New York and popularity with some young boys; several artists painting him.

40 [GILDER, JEANNETTE.] "The Lounger." Critic, n.s. 7 (23 April), 207-8.
     Describes Whitman's naturalness while sitting for a photograph by Cox, who never had a better subject.

41 ANON. "Notes." Public Opinion 3 (30 April), 71.
     Paragraph on Whitman's upcoming lecture in Boston: Holmes and C. E. Norton are furthering the enterprise.

42 ANON. "Literary and Art Notes, Etc." Pall Mall Gazette (6 May), 3.
     Americans, including George W. Childs and Andrew Carnegie, are ready to help Whitman, following the Gazette's subscription.

43 [GILDER, JEANNETTE.] "The Lounger." Critic,
n.s. 7 (7 May), 232.
    Corrects a New York correspondent who
claimed Howells took tickets at Whitman's
lecture when he was not even present (see
1887.35).

44 STEVENSON, ROBERT LOUIS. "'Books Which Have
Influenced Me.' No. VIII." British Weekly
2 (13 May), 18.
Reprinted: 1887.12; 1905.16; Hindus.
    Leaves is among the books which in-
fluenced Stevenson: it "tumbled the world
upside down for me" and brought back "all
the original and manly virtues." But it
is only for those with the gift of reading,
for some books are too powerful for the
average man.

45 ANON. Review of Buchanan (1887.3). Critic,
n.s. 7 (14 May), 242-43.
    Buchanan's book is rather biased; he
gives Whitman "his most enthusiastic
praise."

*46 ANON. Article on Whitman. Camden Courier
(19 May).
Reported in Kennedy (1896).
    Account of the visit Whitman has
received from John Newton Johnson of
Alabama.

47 ANON. "Walt Whitman." Boston Herald (24 May),
4:1-2.
    Editorial calling attention to the
Rev. Dr. Bartol's proposal (1887.48) and
urging support for this plan to build
Whitman a summer house near Timber Creek.
There is hope for completion by midsummer,
so that Whitman may be free from the city
heat and "live surrounded by the natural
beauties which he has done so much to show
the world in their deeper meanings."

48 BARTOL, C. A. "Walt Whitman. Friends of the
Poet Propose to Build Him a Summer Cottage."
Boston Herald (24 May), 6:8.
    Letter asking support for America's
most original writer, praising "Captain"
and "Myself" 35. His "plainness is purity."
"No author among us is so little a bor-
rower." His conception of the world as a
burial place is finer than that of
"Thanatopsis."

49 ANON. "Summer Plans of Literary Workers."
Critic, n.s. 7 (28 May), 265.
    Paragraph on Whitman, his health, pre-
paration of the Hicks essay, and alterna-
tives of visiting Bucke in Canada or
traveling abroad.

50 GOULD, ELIZABETH PORTER. "Whitman Among the
Soldiers." Critic, n.s. 7 (28 May), 268-69.
Reprinted: 1889.4.
    Whitman's descriptions of his hospital
work in Specimen become more vivid as the
years go by and add to the reality of his

poems. Whitman's actions, spiritual insight, and faith are described.

51 ANON. Review of Gilchrist (1887.6). Nation
44 (2 June), 476.
    Incidental: Gilchrist's writings on
Whitman "show a quick sentiment and a comprehension of the great lines along which
his feelings and ideas move; but they cannot be looked upon as criticism." Her
advocacy of him seems to be regarded as
one of her most notable acts; but Americans
would disagree.

52 ANON. "Walt. Whitman at Sixty-eight." Pall
Mall Gazette (2 June), 7.
    Quotes London Daily News correspondent
(unlocated) on Whitman's birthday, citing
Whitman's diary.

53 LEWIN, WALTER. Review of Specimen. Academy
31 (4 June), 390-91.
    Whitman has immense self-assurance but
does not consider the reader, who may nevertheless be instructed and charmed by this
singular miscellany. Whitman's nature
notes recall Thoreau's, but Thoreau was "a
disinterested student of nature" while
Whitman is more concerned with relating
nature to himself. He offers "his thought,
not an echo," urging us to be ourselves.

54 ANON. "Personal." New York Tribune (5 June),
4:5.
    Whitman has been invited to England
and to Canada, but his feeble health may
prevent either trip.

55 ANON. "A Cottage for Walt Whitman." New York
Times (11 June), 4:7.
    The Boston Post (unlocated) reports
John Boyle O'Reilly's surprise at being
appointed treasurer for the fund raising
money for Whitman's seaside cottage. Much
money has been collected, so Whitman may
soon have the house.

56 ANON. "Mr. Stevenson's Literary Studies."
Literary World 18 (11 June), 179-80.
    Review of 1882.10. The Whitman essay
is "even-handed" but for the most part
kindly. The chief value of Whitman's works
is "expression of individuality."

57 ANON. "A Walt Whitman Society." Boston Daily
Advertiser (30 June), 4:3.
Reprinted: Knox.
    Describes efforts to raise money for a
cottage for Whitman, a just expression of
regard for him, although the "fulsome
eulogy" from abroad is ludicrous, since
much he has written "is not even good
prose." At his best, however, he is
"grandly and truly poetical--a great seer-
bard." A Whitman society such as Sadakichi
Hartmann proposes might dissipate the unjust criticism rendered Whitman and would
also preserve all the literature about him.

58 ANON. Paragraph. Literary World 18 (9 July), 216.
> Notes plans for Whitman society; quotes Advertiser (1887.57).

59 [GILDER, JEANNETTE.] "The Lounger." Critic, n.s. 8 (23 July), 43.
> Notes Swinburne's criticism (1887.63) of Whitmania, a disease from which Emerson, Lowell, and Stedman seem to suffer.

60 _____. "The Lounger." Critic, n.s. 8 (30 July), 55.
> Quotes from Hartmann's circular regarding the Whitman society: it does not appeal to her, despite her admiration for Whitman; a society is not necessary to appreciate him.

61 [SCUDDER, HORACE E.] "Anne Gilchrist." Atlantic Monthly 60 (August), 275-81.
> Review of 1887.6. Gilchrist used Whitman to enlarge her conception of human life, but she was wrong, for naturalism is not enough. The English sought in American art the expansion of the human spirit which Americans were seeking to control by practicing perfection of form. Her writings on Whitman were not strictly critical.

62 SWINBURNE, ALGERNON CHARLES. "Whitmania." Library Magazine, 3d ser. (August), 308-14. Reprint of 1887.63.

63 _____. "Whitmania." Fortnightly Review, n.s. 42 (1 August), 170-76.
> Reprinted: 1887.62; 1887.82; 1894.18; 1926.29; Miller; Hindus.
> Whitman displays "a just enthusiasm, a genuine passion of patriotic and imaginative sympathy, a sincere though limited and distorted love of nature, an eager and earnest faith in freedom and loyalty," and a manful, rational tone regarding duty and death. He says wise and noble things but is original in neither thought nor manner. He should not be ranked with the greatest world poets, as the "Whitmaniacs" rank him. "Drum-Taps" reveals no higher literary quality than rhetoric. "Captain" fails at rhythm and cadence, not rhyme. The poet, if he is not a singer, must be a maker, but Whitman only accumulates words. He has not descended to Zolaesque realism, but resorts to animalism in treating sex. He might have made a good orator but scarcely can be considered a major poet.

64 ROSSETTI, W. R. Editorial paragraph. Boston Evening Transcript (4 August), 4:4.
> Reprinted: 1887.66.
> Letter announcing Rossetti's support for a Whitman society, praising Whitman as "a man of great nature, who has spoken a great message to the world."

65 KENNEDY, W. S. "Boston's 'Walt Whitman Society.'" Critic, n.s. 8 (6 August), 67.
> The use of Kennedy's and others' names was unauthorized, although the idea of a Whitman club is good and is being pursued by other admirers of Whitman, including those abroad, many of whom have agreed to join.

66 ROSSETTI, W. R. "Personal." Boston Evening Transcript (8 August), 1:2.
> Reprint of 1887.64.

67 ANON. "Walt Whitman Will Not Answer." New York Times (11 August), 1:2.
> Despite the request of the North American Review's editors that he respond to Swinburne (1887.63), Whitman refused, making no comment other than that he was surprised at the outburst but wouldn't pass final judgment until he had read it. He continues "bright and cheerful despite his infirmities."

68 [GILDER, JEANNETTE.] "The Lounger." Critic, n.s. 8 (13 August), 79.
> Whitman needs to be defended from his friends, particularly the Whitman Society: "his independent soul revolts at the idea of being the pensioner of a private organization." Art work begun or planned on Whitman is announced.

69 ANON. "Laus Veneris vs. Leaves of Grass." Public Opinion 3 (20 August), 407.
> Paragraph from Philadelphia Telegraph (unlocated) on Swinburne (1887.63) which may mean the end of the Whitman cult in England. "Whitman's method is marked neither by Sappho's divine sublimity of fascination nor Titian's transcendent supremacy of actual and irresistible beauty."

70 [GILDER, JEANNETTE.] "The Lounger." Critic, n.s. 8 (20 August), 91-92.
> Whitman's refusal to answer Swinburne (see 1887.67) shows his good sense.

71 ANON. "Books and Authors. Some Prose-Poems." Boston Daily Advertiser (25 August), 2:4.
> Sadakitshe [sic] Hartmann's poetry (quoted) shows him a follower of Whitman in method, although he denies knowing whether Whitman is a poet or not. Prejudice against such verse as Whitman's must be stifled. Hartmann's "Walt Whitman" is quoted, a tribute to Whitman's work as "the grandest lessons of my life."

72 ANON. "Books and Authors. Some Literary News and Notes." Boston Daily Advertiser (26 August), 2:2.
> Quotes Critic (1887.70) as saying the right thing about Swinburne's attack.

73 ANON. "Bombastes Swinburneoso." Critic, n.s. 8 (27 August), 91-92.
> Quotes Pall Mall Gazette (unlocated) summarizing Swinburne (1887.63) with a few

comments; notes Whitman's response to him (see 1887.67).

74 LEWIN, WALTER. "'Leaves of Grass.'" Murray's Magazine 2 (September), 327-29.
Reprinted: 1887.81.
Leaves grows with Whitman as a transcription of his life and varied experience, "a biography of the human soul," but lacking "concentrative force." His portrayal of sex seems necessary as a release preceding the rest of the book. He enjoys nature for its health-giving and sensuous qualities. His themes are modern, American, commonplace. He is the first to treat man working as a subject for poems. Leaves must be read as a whole, revealing the wonderful life of the world and the brotherhood of all, with ideals of unity, beauty, and progression.

75 SYMONDS, JOHN ADDINGTON. "A Note on Whitmania." Fortnightly Review, n.s. 42 (1 September), 459-60.
Response to Swinburne (1887.63), agreeing that Whitman is "not a poet in the technical sense," arguing that Whitman's portrait of woman is hardly equal to Swinburne's accusations but rather a "clean and healthy" ideal. His glorification of "natural reciprocity between the sexes" (if somewhat repulsive in his presentation) is misrepresented by Swinburne, who should regret what he has written.

76 ANON. "Whitman in London. (Adapted from the American.)" Punch 93 (3 September), 101.
Reprinted: Saunders.
Parody.

77 [BAXTER, SYLVESTER.] Long editorial paragraph. Springfield Republican (9 September).
Commentary on the cottage subscription, the Whitman Society, the responses of Whitman and Swinburne to each other. Perhaps Swinburne had heard of Whitman's opinion of his work as not genuine with all its decorative elaboration and therefore reacted in "Whitmania" (1887.63).

78 ANON. "'Caviare to the General.'" Critic, n.s. 8 (17 September), 144.
Quotes St. James's Gazette (unlocated): the Whitmanites push Whitman to little effect; his prose surpasses his poetry.

79 HUNEKER, JAMES. "Wagner and Swinburne." American Art Journal 47 (1 October), 370.
Incidental: Whitman's "frank outspoken utterances are too healthy to come under discussion."

80 ANON. "Current Notes." Lippincott's Monthly Magazine 40 (October), 611-12.
Criticizes Swinburne's surprising essay (1887.63) which reveals "the conservatism that attends advancing age."

*81 LEWIN, WALTER. "'Leaves of Grass.'" Library Magazine, 3d ser. (October).
Reprint of 1887.74. Reported in Blodgett.

82 SWINBURNE, ALGERNON CHARLES. "Whitmania." Eclectic Magazine, n.s. 46 (October), 454-58.
Reprint of 1887.63.

83 ANON. "Notes." Public Opinion 4 (22 October), 48.
Reprint of 1887.84.

84 ANON. "Current Notes." Lippincott's Monthly Magazine 40 (November), 762.
Reprinted: 1887.83.
It was recently announced that Whitman would umpire a baseball game in Camden, and many of his admirers came, eager to see him "in a new and difficult rôle." However, he did not appear, since the announcement had been made without his authority or even his knowledge.

85 NOEL, RODEN. "Mr. Swinburne on Walt Whitman." Time 17 (December), 653-58.
Response to Swinburne (1887.63), who implies that Whitman is not a thinker; he is rather a seer, his style "appropriate to his vigorous and original idiosyncrasy" while Swinburne himself claims only pretensions to being a thinker and stylist. Whitman's rhythm is praised; likewise his depiction of lovers, who are not lecherous as suggested. He is "ultra-Pantheistic," opposes convention and asceticism, and "makes us feel the organic soundness of this universe." Swinburne's attack is "aristocratic spleen." Whitman's love is Christ-like.

86 WILLARD, CYRUS FIELD. "A Chat with the Good Gray Poet." American Magazine 7 (December), 217-22.
Account of his visit to Whitman and of Whitman's remarks (rejecting notions of a theory in his poetry, commenting on socialism). His poetry may be a bit rough but it conveys "finer fervor and more rhythmical delight" than Milton's blank verse. "Lilacs" and "Captain" are praised, making a mockery of the Boston Public Library's restricted circulation of Leaves. A long, good-humored, parodic ode, written recently by an admirer, "America's Greeting to Walt," (reprinted in Saunders), ends the article.

87 TENNYSON, ALFRED. Letter to Whitman. Critic, n.s. 8 (10 December), 306.
Friendly letter of 15 November 1887 is printed.

88 ETYMOLOGIST. "'Yonnondio.'--A Word-History." Critic, n.s. 8 (17 December), 317.
Corrects Whitman as to the true meaning of the title of his "affecting elegy" printed in the 26 November Critic.

1888

BOOKS

1 DAVIDSON, JAMES WOOD. <u>The Poetry of the
   Future</u>. New York: J. B. Alden, pp. 110-13,
   146-47.
      Whitman and Adah Menken are right in
   dropping meter and stanza, but failed in
   dropping rhythm as well. Whitman has
   written "some genuine poetry," "a good deal
   of mere prose," and much "twaddle and
   stuff." His thoughts are mostly prosaic
   and ought to have been separated from his
   few poems, which should have sustained
   their rhythm more fully. "If the matter of
   his writings have merit even as prose or as
   what-not, he will live; but his rank <u>as a
   poet</u> cannot well be greater in the future
   than it is in the present." "Myself" is
   quoted and partially scanned.

1a ELLIS, HAVELOCK, ed. Preface to <u>The Pillars
   of Society, and Other Plays by Henrik
   Ibsen</u>. London: Walter Scott, n.d., p. xx.
   Reprinted: 1890.3.
      Incidental: In his belief that the
   realization of democracy is possible only
   by the creation of great men and women,
   "Ibsen is at one with the American, with
   whom he would appear at first sight to have
   little in common." "Broad-Axe" is quoted.

*2 GREG, THOMAS T. <u>Walt Whitman: Man and Poet</u>.
   Warrington, England: n.p.
   Reported in <u>CHAL</u>.

3 HAMILTON, WALTER. <u>Parodies of the Works of
   English and American Authors, Collected
   and Annotated by Walter Hamilton</u>. Vol. 5.
   London: Reeves & Turner, pp. 103, 256-62.
      Reprints various parodies, preceding
   them with introductory remarks and extracts
   from "Myself" and other poems unfamiliar
   to English readers, since Whitman's "mannerisms are far more familiar to most
   English readers than the vigour of his
   poetry" and many of his finest thoughts
   have been omitted from English editions
   due to editors' mock-modesty. Whitman is
   "emphatically a poet for <u>men</u>," not for
   "tinkling rhyme."

4 RICHARDSON, CHARLES F. <u>American Literature
   1607-1885</u>. Vol. 2. New York and London:
   G. P. Putnam's Sons, pp. 268-81.
      Whitman equals the Genteel poets in
   ability, but he attracted attention by
   "magnifying the physical and the crudely
   spontaneous." He has "strength without
   artistic power." His prose is pleasant
   and fresh but inelegant in style and of
   little value. His poetic plan to present
   a complete picture of his times and of an
   individual man is not adequate, for he
   omits man's spiritual development. His
   treatment of sex is not peculiarly shameful, but sex "is not <u>per se</u> a poetic theme."

His unity is mere conglomeration. His
choice of verse form is appropriate and
often pleasing, though seldom a true "art-
product." He is most successful in dealing
with sympathy, the eternal, and nature. In
a century he will no longer be seen as the
prophet he claims to be. His world is
incomplete and poor next to Emerson's.
Whitman is the fittest of Lincoln's laureates and merits the name of poet for the
Lincoln poems and such others as "Brooklyn
Ferry" and "Broad-Axe."

5 ROBERTS, CHARLES G. D., ed. <u>Poems of Wild
   Life</u>. London: Walter Scott, p. 238n.
   Reprinted: Moulton.
      Paragraph note to "Redwood" and "From
   Far Dakota's Cañons": Whitman, "a force
   in modern poetry," seeks to give "new and
   striking expression to what is distinctive
   in American life" by breaking with standard
   poetics. In spite of his contempt of form,
   he has proved himself a great poet with
   "his profound humanity, his breadth,
   strength, and insight."

6 SELWYN, GEORGE [Walt Whitman]. "Walt Whitman
   in Camden." In <u>Authors at Home: Personal
   and Biographical Sketches of Well-Known
   American Writers</u>, edited by J. L. and J. B.
   Gilder. New York: Cassell & Co., pp. 335-
   42.
   Reprint of 1885.10. Revised: 1902.24.

PERIODICALS

7 SEMPERS, CHARLES T. "Walt Whitman and His
   Philosophy." <u>Harvard Monthly</u> 5 (January),
   149-65.
      Traces his own gradual understanding of
   <u>Leaves</u> as "a living cosmos" coming out of
   "seeming chaos." Whitman is a true singer,
   with a religious conception of the world
   and nature. Though serious of purpose, he
   is not devoid of humor. He has a true
   historic consciousness, a sense for spiritual significance. He is compared to
   Spinoza. He has communicated his enthusiasm for the ordinary to recent fiction
   writers. His prose and lack of distinctions are criticized. Poems are suggested
   for reading.

8 ANON. "Thomas Hughes on American Literature."
   <u>Critic</u>, n.s. 9 (7 January), 11.
      Quotes letter from Hughes, Q. C., in
   which he incidentally notes his inability
   to understand Whitman's ideas and "cataract
   of big words," as well as his dislike of
   portions of some poems, "as bad in morality
   as in taste," although he respects Whitman's
   character and career.

9 [HOWELLS, W. D.] "Editor's Study." <u>Harper's
   New Monthly Magazine</u> 76 (February), 478-79.
      Whitman has finally done justice to
   Emerson's still valid exceptions to him,
   in manners, not morals; Emerson sympathized

with Whitman's aesthetic revolt. Whitman and Tolstoy, "at opposite poles morally, are the same in aesthetic effect." Whitman's rebellion was itself a confession of literary consciousness.

10 P[AIN], B[ARRY] E. O. "The Poets at Tea." <u>Cambridge Fortnightly</u> (7 February). Reprinted: 1888.3; 1904.20; Saunders. Parodies of poets, including Whitman.

11 ANON. "Mixed with New Poetry. Edgar Fawcett Startling the Nineteenth Century Club People." <u>New York Times</u> (8 February), 4:7. Quotes Rhys's lecture on today's poetry, inferior to that of Shakespeare's day and needing to be more in accord with that of Whitman. Fawcett responded that he found Whitman dull; his kind of poetry could never be ideal poetry. Rev. William Lloyd attacked Whitman, confessing that he could not understand him. Maria Brace embraced Whitman warmly.

12 ANON. "Notes." <u>Critic</u>, n.s. 9 (11 February), 73. Announces and describes Kennedy's <u>Walt Whitman the Poet of Humanity</u>, soon to be published by Frederick W. Wilson & Brother of Glasgow.

13 ANON. "Literary Notes." <u>New York Times</u> (13 February), 3:2. Reprint of 1888.12.

14 ANON. Account of Rhys's lecture "The New Poetry." <u>Independent</u> 40 (16 February), 204. Notes the disagreement over Whitman (see 1888.11). "We agree with him [Rhys] in thinking that a great poet must be a poet of the people and must have sympathies as broad, as free, and as simple as Nature. But we part company with him when he asserts that Walt Whitman has these qualifications pre-eminently, and that the spirit of 'Leaves of Grass' is the spirit that is to animate the new poet."

15 ANON. "Notes." <u>Critic</u>, n.s. 9 (25 February), 97. Whitman's verse appears in the New York <u>Herald</u> for the purpose of relieving his poverty, according to a reputed arrangement with Mr. Bennett, whose terms are liberal even for him.

16 ANON. Note. <u>Book Buyer</u> 5 (March), 63. "Walt Whitman prefers to write on a tablet placed on his knee, rather than on a table or desk."

17 MUNGER, Rev. T. T. "Personal Purity. II." <u>Christian Union</u> 37 (1 March), 267. Incidental: "Do not suffer yourself to be caught by the Walt Whitman fallacy that all nature and all processes of nature are sacred and may therefore be talked

about. Walt Whitman is not a true poet in this respect, or he would have scanned nature more accurately. Nature is silent and shy where he is loud and bold."

18 ANON. "A Whitmanese Waif." <u>New York Commercial Advertiser</u> (3 March), 6:3. Reprinted: Saunders. Parody.

19 ANON. "The Listener." <u>Boston Evening Transcript</u> (6 March), 4:5. Account of Rhys's lecture on "The New Poetry," with quotations: Whitman "has dared to face the whole nineteenth century world, boldly, unflinchingly." Though admitting the need for form in poetry, Rhys "at least credits Whitman with an honest attempt to answer the need of the time." The English approve of him for his "pure humanity." His new means of expression is "endlessly suggestive." Rhys and the writer quote Whitman's "magnificent lines," "Years of the Modern." Mrs. Spaulding spoke in praise of Whitman. Despite the meeting's overall approval of Whitman, he would not be so well regarded by the people, except for "Captain." He falls short of the New Poet they want but anticipates the coming of that poet.

20 THOMPSON, MAURICE. "Literary Sincerity." <u>Independent</u> 40 (8 March), 291-92. Response to Howells's citation (1888.9) of Whitman, Zola, and Tolstoy as three figures of absolute sincerity. His tribute is "the first monument to the spirit of rottenness" and pruriency ever erected in America, the result of realism. Howells intimates that it is to Whitman's discredit "when he winces now and again at his own nastiness."

21 ANON. "The First Blizzard." New York <u>Herald</u> (14 March), 4:4. Reprinted: Saunders. Parody in four free-verse lines of "The First Dandelion" (<u>Herald</u>, 12 March), whose publication coincided with the blizzard.

22 ANON. "Served Him Right." New York <u>Herald</u> (15 March), 4:4. Reprinted: Saunders. Four rhymed lines on the poet singing of spring but being stopped by the blizzard (see 1888.21).

23 R., C. F. "Questions." <u>Critic</u>, n.s. 9 (7 April), 174. Asks for location of a Whitman statement about writing only the human part of his "double-poem." The answer: <u>Specimen</u>, p. 281.

24 MOULTON, LOUISE CHANDLER. "Three Very Famous People. Mrs. Cleveland, George W. Childs and Walt Whitman. Words of Washington and Philadelphia. Poet Who Wrote of the Birds

1888

on Paumanok's Shore." Boston <u>Sunday Herald</u>
(29 April), 20:1-2.
    Recalls her visit with Talcott Williams
to Whitman, "the most essentially American
of our poets," "a growth of the soil,"
whose poetry she admires, especially
"Cradle" (here described), a favorite with
Philip Bourke Marston and Rossetti, who
used to recite it. Whitman is like his
poems, friendly and dignified. He and his
verse lack affectation, though his theories
seem "fitter for a larger, more sincere,
less complex time than ours." He represents "plain living and high thinking."

25 ANON. "The Literary Creed of Emile Zola."
    <u>Time</u>, n.s. 7 (May), 564.
        Incidental: Zola believes that a great
    change in poetry is due. "In Walt Whitman
    we might perhaps suspect a representative
    of this change, a transition-link between
    the poetry of the past and the poetry of
    the future, but M. Zola descends to no such
    concrete illustration."

*26 [BONSALL, HARRY.] Account of Whitman's birth-
    day dinner. <u>Camden Post</u> (1 June).
    Reported in Traubel I.

*27 ANON. "Walt Whitman Enters the Seventies."
    Philadelphia <u>Times</u> (2 June).
    Reprinted: Traubel I.
        Describes Whitman's condition of in-
    creasing infirmity but good spirits and
    mental brightness; notes his work on
    <u>November</u>, due this fall.

28 KENNEDY, W. S. "Fraudulent 'Leaves of Grass.'"
    <u>Critic</u>, n.s. 9 (2 June), 272.
        Calls attention to the pirated editions
    using the 1860 plates.

29 C., V. S. "The Good Gray Poet." <u>New York</u>
    <u>Daily Graphic</u> (2 June), 105; illustrations,
    103.
        Extract reprinted: 1888.44.
        Notes Whitman's birthday; traces the
    controversies involving him; describes his
    current life, early life, occasional pub-
    lishing.

30 [GILDER, JEANNETTE.] "The Lounger." <u>Critic</u>,
    n.s. 9 (9 June), 283.
        Notes Whitman's birthday, health, work
    on <u>November</u>, money earned from writing; he
    is making nothing from the fraudulently
    published <u>Leaves</u>.

31 WILLIAMS, FRANCIS HOWARD. "The Poetry of
    Walt Whitman. (First Paper.)." <u>The</u>
    <u>American</u> 16 (9 June), 119-20.
        Whitman fulfills the true role of art,
    interpreting the whole of nature, avoiding
    half-truths, describing what he himself
    has seen, bringing us into contact with
    fundamental passions as they really are,
    with no exaggeration of fact. Many find
    <u>Leaves</u> unfit for the very young, but it

was not meant for them. Concluded 1888.
38.

32 ANON. "Walt Whitman Seriously Ill." <u>New</u>
    <u>York Times</u> (11 June), 1:2.
        Short account of his health.

33 ANON. "Walt Whitman Better." <u>New York Times</u>
    (12 June), 4:7.
        His health is improved but he is "going
    steadily down hill."

*34 ANON. Report of Whitman's health. Camden
    <u>Courier</u> (14 June).
    Reported in Traubel I.

35 ANON. "Walt Whitman's Illness." <u>New York</u>
    <u>Times</u> (15 June), 5:2.
        Whitman has suffered a severe relapse.

36 ANON. "Notes." <u>Critic</u>, n.s. 9 (16 June),
    298.
        Describes Whitman's recent attack of
    paralysis and his holding out against it.

37 COMPENDIUM. "Current Criticism." <u>Critic</u>,
    n.s. 9 (16 June), 298.
        Includes quotation of 1888.25 and
    Julian Hawthorne from <u>America</u> (unlocated):
    That Whitman revolted against formality and
    artificiality is praiseworthy and to be
    emulated, but his method was self-conscious
    and became grotesque.

38 WILLIAMS, FRANCIS HOWARD. "The Poetry of
    Walt Whitman. (Second Paper.)." <u>The</u>
    <u>American</u> 16 (16 June), 135-36.
        Concludes 1888.31. Whitman's form is
    a further evolution of freedom from highly
    artificial poetry. He rejected established
    forms as inadequate for expressing his
    thought, which often required more syllables
    than standard English meters could put in
    a line; he preferred to keep each thought
    a unity. The opening of "Lilacs" is put
    into blank verse but such attempts to
    "'improve'" Whitman would destroy his in-
    dividuality.

39 MORRIS, CHARLES. "The Poetry of Walt Whitman."
    <u>The American</u> 16 (23 June), 151.
        Response to Williams (1888.31 and 1888.
    38). Morris has read little of Whitman's
    poetry, but he seems merely "an industrious
    catalogue-maker," falling to earth when he
    should soar. A poet should do more than
    simply reproduce nature. His rhythmic
    method may have merits but it lacks attrac-
    tiveness, denying the ear's expectations.

40 ANON. "The Poet Walt Whitman." Detroit <u>Free</u>
    <u>Press</u> (24 June), 18:3.
        Whitman's death will bring sorrow to
    all, though he is wholly incomprehensible
    to most readers. His life is a model phys-
    ically and psychically, through his content-
    ment and simple habits. His individuality
    as a poet is a virtue, showing strength,

though it makes him too little understood.
However, that situation may improve, as
with Wagner. But "he has succeeded in
impressing his personality upon the literature of America."

41 LEWIN, WALTER. Review of Democratic Vistas,
and Other Papers (Walter Scott Camelot ed.).
Academy 33 (30 June), 441-42.
Whitman's complete prose should be
published by Scott, particularly his best
piece, the 1855 Preface, here omitted,
although this volume has "plenty of excellent matter." His essays are jottings,
rarely stylistically polished but valuable
for their thought, though he may explain
himself a bit more than necessary. Whitman,
"faithful, honest, uncompromising," is a
"much-needed teacher" for a time when many
utter not their own thought but only echoes.

42 M[cPHELIM], E[DWARD] J. "Walt Whitman."
America 1 (30 June), 6-7.
Extract reprinted: 1888.47.
Whitman, "the Jack Cade of American
literature," rebelled against convention
and represented the masses, but of his
cause only his name will remain. The
Chicago Public Library withholds from public inspection the 1855 Leaves. Though
genuinely impelled to sing democratic
ideals, Whitman took on his pose as the
prophet of democracy deliberately and ex-
travagantly, with the eye of a seer but not
the selectivity of an artist. Though not
obscene, his choice of subjects was poor.
"Captain" is among the world's great
elegies; "Death Carol" has the "luxury of
language" of Shakespeare. His measure can
be sublime or obscure. He erred in thinking that American poetry could be determined by conscious design. A brief conversation between Whitman and Henry Ward
Beecher is quoted. Whitman, with a poet's
soul and love for his country, "will grow
in stature among American poets."

43 BECKETT, REGINALD A. "Whitman as a Socialist
Poet." To-day, n.s. 10 (July), 8-15.
Whitman is the poet who has come nearest
to expressing socialist ideas, with his
faith in natural processes and evolution,
his expression of all aspects of contemporary life, his gospel of comradeship
requiring social equality. His thought
has been courageously pursued. His idea of
love revives Christianity's essence. He
fuses Hebraic and Hellenic tendencies, the
mystical and the realistic, and reveals
their identity.

44 [C., V. S.] Paragraph. Current Literature
1 (July), 14.
Extract quoted from 1888.29.

45 WINTER, WILLIAM. "Matthew Arnold. A Speech
by William Winter." Boston Evening Transcript (3 July), 6.

Reprints speech Winter made in London,
incidentally referring to Whitman: Many
in England "have accepted, and have extolled
even to the verge of extravagance, one of
our authors--a very worthy man--for little
or no better reason than because he has
discarded all versification, and all prose
as well, and furnished in their places an
unmelodious catalogue of miscellaneous
images, generally commonplace and sometimes
unfragrant."

46 MORRIS, HARRISON S. "The Poetry of Walt
Whitman." The American 16 (7 July), 183-84.
Whitman has passages equal to any in
our literature "for landscape description"
and "the happy epithet," but he has stronger
claims to recognition as a thinker. By
birth a poet, he falls short of the canons
of art, except in moments of great emotion.
Seeking like Wordsworth to be philosopher
and poet at the same time, he falls short
of both. He must be praised for his adventurous course of candor. Smacking of the
soil, his poetry seems intended to record
America in her youth for future races to
know and understand.

47 [McPHELIM, EDWARD J.] "Notes." Critic, n.s.
10 (14 July), 23.
Extract from 1888.42.

48 REPPLIER, AGNES. "Workmanship in Art." The
American 16 (28 July), 231-32.
Extract reprinted: 1888.53.
Workmanship, not choice of subject,
makes a poet, and much of Whitman is merely
prose, disregarding the self-restraint of
true greatness and staining fair thoughts
with "sensual indulgence" and "unsavory
images." His license in form extends to
morality. "He has wasted riotously the
patrimony of genius."

49 ANON. "Walt Whitman's November." Philadelphia
Press (29 July), 8:1. Illustration of
house.
Account of Whitman's recovery from his
attack in June, his habits, attitudes, work
on November.

50 ANON. "Walt Whitman. Partial Recovery from
His Illness." New York Times (30 July),
2:4.
Account of Whitman's health and work in
progress.

51 CLEVELAND, PAUL R. "Is Literature Bread-
winning?" Cosmopolitan 5 (August), 315.
Whitman and other authors are discussed
as to how they earned their livings: "a
kind of modern Elijah," Whitman let others
support him, "a serene, sagacious, optimistic vagabond whom no one can dislike," "more
philosopher than poet," his character as
original as his verse, belonging to the
future rather than to any prior time. He
has never earned much money for himself,

1888

proving that "the true bard need not be burdened with his own self-support."

52 ANON. "An Old Song by New Singers." Presbyterian Journal 13 (2 August), 4.
From Chicago News (unlocated): parodies on "Mary Had a Little Lamb" include "Walt Whitman's Way," five long lines, descriptive and abstract.

53 [REPPLIER, AGNES.] "Is it Poetry?" Public Opinion 5 (4 August), 381.
Extract from 1888.48.

54 LUDERS, CHARLES HENRY. "A Matter of Form." The American 16 (11 August), 264-65.
Kennedy (1886.2) is wrong regarding Whitman's line divisions, but for certain subjects as in "Cradle" and "Lilacs," "the Whitmanesque form is excellent." However, Whitman errs in often leaving nothing to his reader, providing no artistic selection. His form gains in being distinctive but loses in tending to monotony.

55 [STODDARD, R. H.?] "Poetical Fads." Independent 40 (6 September), 1131.
Reprinted: Traubel II.
The strange veneration for Whitman continues in England. "Old Age's Lambent Peaks" (in September Century) is quoted and commented upon, as being original only in its construction and obscurity. The promotion of poets by cliques is criticized.

56 WILLIAMS, FRANCIS HOWARD. "The Poetry of Walt Whitman: A Rejoinder." The American 16 (15 September), 345-46.
Takes issue with the critical standards of Charles Morris (1888.39) and Harrison S. Morris (1888.46): Whitman's purpose is remedial, not unclean or immoral. He leans toward beauty and is not merely the poet of democracy.

57 ANON. "Some New Books." New York Herald (17 September), 9:5.
Whitman is full of surprises, not dying three months ago as expected, but going on to produce a new book, November, ready for publication. Its essay on Hicks is quoted.

58 ANON. "Walt Whitman's Words. He Thinks Bryant America's Greatest Poet. Optimistic Old Age. He Agrees with Darwin. Yet Seeks a Loftier Theology." New York Herald (23 September), 8:3.
Recalls first meeting Whitman in June 1885. This article chiefly records information and Whitman's words from two uncredited sources, Scovel (1885.16) and Ballou (1885.18).

59 ANON. Review of Olive Schreiner's Story of an African Town. New York Home Journal (26 September), 2:5-6.
Quoted: Traubel II.

Incidentally cites a passage which is "an exquisite poem, which Walt Whitman might be proud to own among the best of his rhymeless rhythms."

60 ANON. "The Magazines." Critic, n.s. 10 (6 October), 170.
Whitman's vivid piece in the October Century, "Army Hospitals and Glimpses," is "one of the most stirring memoranda of the War, and will outlast thousands of such papers by eye-witnesses of inferior literary skill."

61 [GILDER, JEANNETTE.] "The Lounger." Critic, n.s. 10 (6 October), 166.
The Herald piece (1888.58) is full of discrepancies and unfairly criticizes Stedman. It is odd that it should have been sent by telegraph.

62 HARDING, EDWARD J. "Matthew Arnold: Paralipomena." Critic, n.s. 10 (6 October), 161.
Incidental: some of Arnold's descriptions remind one of Whitman's best work. Although they differ greatly, "the movement of life suggests itself alike to both as a theme of song."

63 ANON. "The Good Gray Poet Still Cheerful." New York Times (7 October), 20:6.
Quotes a letter from Whitman to Karl Knortz and a post card from Rolleston, both of whom were involved in bringing out Leaves in German, "in which can be rendered the peculiar phraseology and style of Walt Whitman better than French or Italian." Whitman's style is adopted by George Moore in his new novel.

64 [KENNEDY, W. S.] "Whitman's New Volume." Boston Evening Transcript (17 October), 5:5.
Review of November. Many of the poems show Whitman's "full power," others "show marks of the advancing lethargy of age," but the whole is remarkable coming from a sickroom, Whitman "exhibiting an astonishing tenacity of grip on life," his brain clear as ever. His life at this time is described, with faithful friends like Traubel attending him.

65 SUMMERS, WILLIAM, M. P. "A Visit to Walt Whitman." Pall Mall Gazette (18 October), 1-2.
Reprinted: 1888.69.
Account of meeting Whitman in September 1888, his conversation on his health and life, the Irish question, American politics. He is "one of the most striking personalities and one of the most typical and representative characters" American has yet produced.

66 [PHILLIPS, MELVILLE.] "The World of New Books. Some Extracts from Walt Whitman's 'November

Boughs.'" Philadelphia Press (21 October),
18:1. Illustrated.
   Review. These sad last words of
Whitman will appeal to every reader. Every
book-lover will want this book as "souvenir
of the man or last link in his ruggedly
wrought work." Contents are described,
particularly the "disjointed" Hicks essay
which includes Whitman's "most brilliant
bit of prose."

67   ANON. "Books and Authors." New York Home
Journal (24 October), 2:6.
   Brief review of November, proof "that
advancing age does not necessarily imply
decay of intellect." "Some of these poems
might have been written in the full vigor
of manhood." His current situation is
noted.

68   ROGERS, GEORGE. "Walt Whitman Again. Another
Volume By the Good Grey Poet, and Some
Thoughts On His Writings Suggested By Its
Appearance." Philadelphia North American
(25 October).
   Review of November. Amid the controversy over Whitman's merit, Rogers takes a
middle view of Whitman as "a man intoxicated
with a single idea, that of the incomparable
importance of the bare, the naked fact," a
man with the virtues of sincerity and originality, unlike many writers. However,
since he rejects the ornaments of rhetoric
(understandably, since he is concerned
about possible distortions of his thought),
he may be considered "a great writer, a
profound philosopher, a pregnant essayist,"
but not a poet at all. "Whitman expects
too much of his readers," insisting they
"share in the throes of his intellectual
parturition," while they would rather have
the work done for them. The ideas of
"Backward Glance" are examined and doubted.

*69   SUMMERS, WILLIAM, M. P. "A Visit to Walt
Whitman." Pall Mall Budget (25 October).
Reprint of 1888.65. Reported in Kennedy
(1926).

70   ANON. "The Latest Books . . . Walt Whitman
on 'Leaves of Grass.'" Philadelphia Times
(27 October), 4:6.
   Review of November. "Backward Glance"
reveals something pathetic in Whitman's
recognition of his failure in the world.
His intentions are described and quoted
from the essay. He "does not deny, but
courageously avows that 'Leaves of Grass'
is a song of sex and amativeness," and
stands by his genius to the end. The
volume is indispensable to every owner of
Leaves and every student of Whitman's
claims as a poet.

71   ANON. "Walt Whitman's 'November Boughs.'"
Philadelphia Evening Bulletin (30 October),
8:1.
   Review. Whitman's works defy criticism,

for his literary creed insists he follow
his own standard. The preface is "a noble
composition." "Sands at Seventy" cannot be
called poetry, but shows "occasional flashes
of poetic light, which gleam through an
excess of big-wordiness." His "stout,
tough Americanism" is admirable. The book
is affecting and will produce thought,
particularly the various essays (briefly
described).

72   [HOWELLS, W. D.] "Editor's Study." Harper's
New Monthly Magazine 77 (November), 967.
   Review of volumes of poetry by Charles
Leonard Moore and W. E. Henley, which "have
the same claim through the same divine
art--the art of John Keats, the art of Walt
Whitman--to the world's attentive regard."

73   WOOLSON, CONSTANCE FENIMORE. "A Pink Villa."
Harper's New Monthly Magazine 77 (November),
845.
   A character in this short story murmurs,
"Pioneers! oh, pioneers!", "half chanting
it." "None of the Americans recognized his
quotation."

74   GARLAND, HAMLIN. "Whitman's 'November Boughs.'"
Boston Evening Transcript (15 November), 6.
   Review of November, with praise for
"Backward Glance" and Whitman's choice of
titles. This volume reveals how calm and
philosophical Whitman really is. His life
is commendable, as is the motive behind
the objectionable passages. It is "un-
reasonable to hold a prejudice against a
most remarkable outpouring of exalted passion, prophecy, landscape painting, songs
of the sea and, above all, calls for deeper
love for Nature and for men." He should be
honored while still with us.

75   ANON. Review of November. The American 17
(24 November), 91.
   Whatever is thought of Whitman's form,
his poetry has "a vital spirit, poetical
in its nature." These pieces show "less
force, less ruggedness, less of the extreme
Whitmanesque individuality, while they in-
cline more to retrospection, and a vein of
chastened sadness." The prose sketches
are "all notable in style and matter, and
some extremely vivid and striking." "Backward Glance" deserves a careful consideration. "This is a very important addition
to the list of Whitman's works."

76   ANON. One-paragraph review of November.
Independent 40 (29 November), 1538.
   "An interesting miscellany"; the prose
has value as "reflections of the author,"
"the most altogether pleasing" piece being
that on Father Taylor (who is briefly discussed).

77   HALL, Rev. GEORGE. "Walt Whitman." Monthly
Magazine (Barnsley, England) (December),
4-5.

1888

Quotes letter from recent visitor to
Whitman, "now becoming a power for good
with English thinkers." Specimen is
"breezy and sunshiny." Leaves exhibits a
rare combination of "wholesome self-posses-
sion" and "a most tender and magnetic
affection." His aim is to further all
humanizing influences in social and domestic life. He offers readers an influx of
vigor, moral ardor, spiritual faith and
human sympathy, and a wholesome and elevating optimism rare in this realistic age.

78 ANON. "Whitman's November Boughs." Literary
World 19 (8 December), 446-47.
Review. Whitman is valuable for his
personality, his prophecy of the new era of
comradeship and the ideal democracy, and
his break with "the outworn mold," even if
he has failed in his attempt to construct
a new technique in verse. Pre-eminent
among moderns, he "sounds the note of
revolt against universal self-indulgence
and boredom," providing "a bracing tonic"
for the mind. His poems are suggestive,
stimulating because inspired by optimism.
We can thank him for revealing candidly his
inmost thought.

79 ANON. Review of November. New York Tribune
(9 December), 14:2-3.
The poems of "Sands at Seventy" display
Whitman's characteristic strengths and
weaknesses and "a curious stability of
quality." His exaggerated realism and
departure from accepted methods are due to
narrowness rather than to a radical spirit
of reform. These poems, however, display
less crudeness and more melody. But
Whitman should realize the flaws in his
convictions, apparent through the people's
failure to respond to him, for his most
successful poems are those least following
his eccentric method.

*80 ANON. Paragraph. Philadelphia Press (15
December).
Reprinted: Traubel III. Not located on
this date.
Notes the marked change for the better
in Whitman's condition.

81 ANON. One-paragraph review of November.
Nation 47 (20 December), 502.
This volume merely presents the "infinitely sad spectacle" of Whitman's sickly
old age, following which the "cooler atmosphere" of a new edition of Sidney provides
welcome relief.

82 ANON. "Books of the Week. Walt Whitman
Unbosoms Himself About Poetry." New York
Herald (23 December), 7:5.
Review of November, "as varied in contents as its author's own mind," with everything in it interesting, especially his
commentary on his literary purposes (extensively quoted).

83 GOODALE, Mrs. D. H. R. "Concerning Old and
New Books." Springfield Republican (25
December), 3:4.
In his new book (November), Whitman
emphasizes "the old manly (self) assertion
of individual will and freedom, and testifies to the immeasurable value of life,--
still looking and longing for that brotherhood of man in which each shall live and
work to share all good with his fellows."
However he is ultimately judged, "we owe
him much for the sincerity, earnestness and
vigor with which he has insisted upon human
and vital realities as the only true ground
of art," a high standard to follow.

*84 [WHITMAN, WALT.] Paragraph. Camden Post (27
December).
Reprinted: Traubel III.
Traces Whitman's health history; praises
his doctors.

*85 ANON. "Whitman's Complete Works." Long
Islander (29 December).
Reprinted: Whitman Supplement 1978.
Notes receipt from Whitman of his com-
plete works; praises his "good big heart"
and his "'Ode to Lincoln.'"

1889

BOOKS

1 ANON. Harper's Fifth Reader: American Authors.
New York, Cincinnati, Chicago: American
Book Co.; Harper & Bros., p. 509.
Note to "Captain" (printed p. 432):
brief biography and explanation of "Captain."

2 BURROUGHS, JOHN. Indoor Studies. Boston and
New York: Houghton, Mifflin & Co., pp. 23,
70, 71, 140, 208, 246-47, 249.
Brief references, including reprint of
1887.22. Whitman is probably distasteful
to most of his countrymen because of his
mass and strength.

3 EMERSON, EDWARD WALDO. Emerson in Concord: A
Memoir Written for the 'Social Circle' in
Concord, Massachusetts. Boston and New
York: Houghton, Mifflin & Co., p. 228n.
Quoted in Traubel IV.
Describes Emerson's response to the
promise of Leaves and his later disappoint-
ment. "He used to say, 'This catalogue-
style of poetry is easy and leads nowhere,'
or words to that effect."

4 GOULD, ELIZABETH PORTER. Gems from Walt
Whitman. Philadelphia: David McKay, 58 pp.
Contents: "To Walt Whitman," Gould's
poem in fourteen long lines with some rhyme
(reprinted: Legler); "Biographical and Bibliographical Note," brief sketch; "Fac-simile
'Of Life Immense,'" Whitman's manuscript;
"Gems from Leaves of Grass," excerpts and
short poems; reprint of 1887.50.

5 RICKABY, JOHN, S. J. The First Principles of
Knowledge. New York: Benziger Bros.,
pp. 214-15, 412.
Quotes lines from "various 'poems'"
regarding Whitman's incoherent view of evil
as nonexistent or equal to good and his
acceptance of all ideas, lines which the
context cannot explain. His truest line
is: "I have not understood anything."
"One reason for insisting on the First
Principles of Knowledge [i.e., the knowledge
of faith] is to prevent men like Walt
Whitman from becoming the poets either of
the future or of the present."

6 SHARP, WILLIAM, ed. Introduction to American
Sonnets. London: Walter Scott, p. xxiv.
Incidental: "Walt Whitman, stricken
in years and health, but as serene as of
yore, still alert to all the infinite possibilities of his own soul and of mankind
in general, still oblivious of the irre-
deemable commonplace of so much of his
barbaric chant."

7 SYMINGTON, ANDREW JAMES. "Walt Whitman." In
Appleton's Cyclopaedia of American Biography. Vol. 6. Edited by James Grant
Wilson and John Fiske. New York: D.
Appleton & Co., pp. 485-86.
Biographical sketch. Leaves "is a
series of poems dealing with moral, social,
and political problems, and more especially
with the interests involved in nineteenth
century American life and progress."
Whitman's style, though preventing his
popularity, utters "musical thoughts in an
unconventional way which is entirely his
own." (This sketch provided, almost verbatim, the material for many of the obituary
articles in 1892).

8 THOMSON, JAMES. Selections from Original Contributions by James Thomson to "Cope's
Tobacco Plant." Cope's Smoke-Room Booklets,
no. 3. Liverpool: Published in the Cope's
Tobacco Plant office. "Walt Whitman,"
pp. 50-51.
Extract reprinted from 1880.25.

9 TRAUBEL, HORACE L., ed. Camden's Compliment
to Walt Whitman: May 31, 1889: Notes,
Addresses, Letters, Telegrams. Philadelphia: David McKay, 74 pp.
Following a quotation by Whitman and a
poem, "To Walt Whitman," by Ernest Rhys
(revised: 1894.13 and Traubel II), Traubel
describes the birthday banquet and projects
Whitman's fame: he is now a prophet
honored in his country, by literary and
nonliterary figures, for he himself and
his works are nonliterary. "He has rung
the alarum for behoof of humanism in literature." The addresses are printed, as
follows:
Samuel H. Grey: Whitman is honored as
worthy man and as poet.
Thomas B. Harned: Whitman's person is

greater than his book, for he consistently
follows his teachings (equality, humility,
serenity).
Herbert Gilchrist: Whitman's influence
is spreading among the masses, artists, and
scholars in the United Kingdom.
Francis Howard Williams: Whitman, the
revolutionary, is inevitably misunderstood
as infidel, sensualist, materialist.
John Herbert Clifford: Considers
Whitman's philosophy and the necessarily
corresponding seriousness and lack of humor.
Charles G. Garrison: Whitman is not
lawless but offers a true philosophy.
E. A. Armstrong: Emphasizes New
Jersey's pride in Whitman.
Richard Watson Gilder: Praises Whitman's
magnificent, inimitable form, his appreciation of the duality of existence, his role
as a picture of our times.
Julian Hawthorne: Praises Whitman's
sympathy as man and poet, encompassing his
friend Lincoln as well as the prostitute of
his poem.
Hamlin Garland: Describes Whitman's
principal messages, "Optimism and Altru-
ism--Hope for the future and Sympathy toward
men." He is "the strongest, most electric,
most original of modern poets."
Henry L. Bonsall: On Whitman's well-
regarded work and personality.
Lincoln L. Eyre: Whitman stands for
what is best in American life, the fittest
representative of an indigenous literature.
Translated extract from Eduard Bertz's
article in Deutsche Press (2 June 1889).
"Letters: Over-Sea--Over-Land":
Tributes and regrets from Hallam Tennyson,
W. M. Rossetti, Sarrazin, Rolleston, William
Morris, Dowden, Costelloe, Schmidt, Edward
Carpenter, John Hay, R. Pearsall Smith,
Burroughs, Bucke, Kennedy, Sidney Morse,
E. C. Stedman, F. B. Sanborn, Howells,
Whittier, Sylvester Baxter, T. B. Aldrich,
Felix Adler, Horace Howard Furness,
George W. Childs, Twain, Will Carleton,
William Salter, J. W. Chadwick, George H.
Boker, John A. Cockrill, Julius Chambers,
G. W. Curtis, Jeannette Gilder, John
Habberton, William C. Gannett, H. D. Bush,
R. J. Hinton, J. F. Garrison, describing
the value Whitman has had for them and
personal memories of their acquaintance
with Whitman or Leaves.
"By Wire: Then, Postscript": Telegrams
in honor of Whitman from Henry Irving,
Ingersoll, Jefferson Whitman, Mrs. A. H.
Spaulding, Mrs. Fanny Taylor, Felix Adler,
T. B. Aldrich, J. H. Gilman. Last-minute
letters on Whitman from Forman, Brinton,
Symonds. Translated extract from Sarrazin
(see 1893.11). For further accounts of
banquet, see 1889.48-1889.59.

10 WILLARD, FRANCES E. Glimpses of Fifty Years:
The Autobiography of an American Woman.
Chicago and Philadelphia: H. J. Smith &
Co., Woman's Temperance Publishing Associa-

tion, pp. 541-42.
Reprinted: Whitman Supplement 1979.
Recalls meeting Whitman at the Smiths'
in Philadelphia, "the mildest, most modest
and simple-hearted man I ever saw," contrary to her expectations. He came alive
when nature was the topic. "His sense of
God, Nature and Human Brotherhood" seemed
"raised to such a power, and fused in such
a white heat of devotion, that they made
the man a genius." (For another account
of this evening, see 1915.18.)

PERIODICALS

11 ANON. "The Newest Books." Book Buyer 5
(January), 584; portrait from November,
p. 585.
Brief review of November, describing
it, especially "Backward Glance," which
throws valuable light on Leaves. Much in
the shorter papers is "vigorous in expression and full of suggestiveness."

12 B[UCKE], R. M. "Walt Whitman." Magazine of
Poetry 1 (January), 15.
Biography; publications. Whitman's
fame will rest not on his prose but on
Leaves, in structure "rhythmic prose," in
force and meaning "poetry of a high if not
the highest order," its subject always
"himself treated as the typical man, not
so much as being better than others, but
as seeing more clearly the divinity that
is in every human being." Whitman's personality is presented with vividness and
vitality in his work. Six pages of poems
and extracts follow, with two portraits.

13 IMAGE, SELWYN. "A New Book by Mr. Whitman."
Hobby Horse, no. 13 (January), 37-39.
Review of November. "Backward Glance"
gives it "its greatest, its unique value,"
as Whitman's "own clear summary" of his
work and is quoted to show its suggestiveness, simplicity, noble tone, and pathos.
Asks us to clasp the hand Whitman extends
to us, "to receive that blessing, with
which he bids us be of good cheer and go
forward."

14 [BAXTER, SYLVESTER.] "Whitman's Complete
Works." Boston Herald (3 January), 4:6-7.
Review of Whitman's Complete Works,
which "combines the homely democratic simplicity associated with Whitman's name with
the essential features of a handsome book--
a worthy garment for the great thoughts
presented." The 1855 Preface, "a masterpiece of composition in the grand style,"
and Vistas, "one of the greatest essays
ever written concerning America," are
praised and described. The new sections
are described and quoted. "Sands" "are
like the voice of an old friend," like the
words of all old poets whose "great harvest
has been gathered," "fragmentary utterances"
but showing no decline in Whitman's "terse

and vivid delineations with a word or
phrase that both depicts and suggests."
This complete edition is "monumental in our
literature." His new work is "pervaded by
the healthy personal feeling, lofty patriotism and deep spirituality inherent in
Whitman."

15 ANON. "'November Boughs.'" San Francisco
Chronicle (13 January), 7:8.
Review. Except for "a few sonnets and
prose articles," most of the book will be
tedious to all but his admirers, for whom
Whitman can do no wrong. He regards himself too highly (though he seems honest) in
his attempt here to justify Leaves again.
But he cannot be regarded as representative
of Americans, with such un-American traits
as his acceptance of gifts from friends and
lack of ambition. "He has many genuine
poetic ideas, even in his old age," but they
"seldom find adequate expression," his mannerisms forbidding perfect development.

*16 ANON. Review of November? Boston Traveller
(17 January).
Quoted in Asselineau.
"If there are readers who find intellectual greatness and spiritual uplifting
in Walt Whitman, we can only say that for
those who enjoy this kind of 'poetry', it
is poetry that they will enjoy . . . ."

17 [HARRISON, Prof. W. H. or W. M.] "Walt
Whitman's 'November Boughs.'" Critic, n.s.
11 (19 January), 25.
Review. November "is a preparation for
the long sleep--a touching ave et vale,"
but also with the luxuriance and bloom of
spring, with all Whitman's essential beliefs
and practices and "wonderfully graphic tab-
leaux of memoranda." "Backward Glance" is
the "most remarkable part"; other pieces
reveal "marvellously nervous prose," and an
"egotism not as an abstraction but as an
intensely concrete, kindled, personal
necessity of modern democratic verse asserting itself triumphantly." The book is "full
of the unction and eloquence of a most sweet
personality."

18 [WILDE, OSCAR.] "The Gospel According to Walt
Whitman." Pall Mall Gazette (25 January),
3.
Reprinted: 1908.18.
Review of November. Whitman's work is
the record of a human soul--not tragedy,
because there is joy and hope, but rather a
drama of spiritual development. He is at
his best when analyzing his own work, as in
this volume, or looking to the poetry of the
future, for literature to him has a social
aim, which may be his chief value rather
than his poetic performance. In rejecting
art, he is an artist.

19 ANON. "Books and Authors." Echo (London),
no. 6263 (26 January), 1:5.

Paragraph review of November, "imbued with the sanguine, generous faith in man which characterised his youth," "a fascinating and most suggestive record of the history of a mind," with some delightful and haunting passages and expressions. Orthodox critics may reconsider their judgment of Whitman after reading his explanation of how his choice of theme determined the form of expression. "You may or may not call Whitman a poet--the Poet of Democracy--but, if not a poet, he is a prophet of the new time."

20 [HOWELLS, W. D.] "Editor's Study." Harper's New Monthly Magazine 78 (February), 488.
Reprinted: Miller; Bradley/Blodgett.
Review of November. While Whitman is still with us, we should admit that "his literary intention was as generous as his spirit was bold, and that if he has not accomplished all he intended, he has been a force that is by no means spent." He did not quite liberate poetry from meter and rhyme, but he allowed poetry to be more direct and natural. His "gospel of nudity" is unnecessary. November is innocent, meditative, and reminiscent, with prose that is more poetic and full of pathos and the love of truth than his poetry.

21 ANON. "Authors New and Old." Philadelphia Times (17 February), 11:5.
Reprinted: Traubel IV.
Paragraph on Whitman's "partiality for postal cards," easier for him to use for his correspondence, though a well-known literary gentleman was disgusted at Whitman's so casual response to his letter. Whitman's correspondence habits are described, including his refusal to give autographs.

22 ANON. "Walt Whitman Still Sick." Philadelphia Times (17 February), 6:2.
Paragraph on Whitman's recent severe illness and feeble condition, though "his intellect is as keen and his words as cheery as of yore," and a small group of friends visits him frequently.

23 LEWIN, WALTER. Review of November. Academy 35 (23 February), 127.
For the uninitiated, this volume "offers little to attract and at the same time little to repel," but Whitman's admirers will welcome it. Interesting prose pieces and poems of varying merits are pointed out. Whitman has bravely "lived to celebrate his triumph" in compelling attention and winning regard, without compromise. These pages present a note of sadness, but still "the same hopeful, cheery, affectionate, and great-souled man and poet," his heart untouched by age.

24 [PORTER, CHARLOTTE?] "The Library." Poet-Lore 1 (March), 145-47.

Review of November, which provides large glimpses of its subjects, revealing Whitman's breadth, democratic kindliness, and homespun sense. "Backward Glance" helps us understand his poetry.

25 [WALSH, WILLIAM S.] "Book-Talk." Lippincott's Monthly Magazine 43 (March), 445.
Review of November. Whitman is not for those who love shams and conventions, order and the past; he is part of "the great unconquered chaos that surrounds us." He reveals our own vague feelings to us. "Backward Glance," "his excellent preliminary essary," is quoted for its illuminating thought.

26 ANON. "November Boughs." Saturday Review 67 (2 March), 260-61.
Review. There is nothing controversial here; Whitman is "singularly modest" in "Backward Glance." His critics have failed to distinguish between flaws in his premises and his actual poetic ability and achievement. His flaws include democratic enthusiasm, portrayal of personality without passing "every personal emotion through the sieve of the universal," diction, overfrankness, some of his rhythmic theory. "Death Carol" and "Sea-Shore Memories" (his "next best") represent his true poetry. He is one of America's "remarkably few poets."

*27 ANON. Article on Rhys. Boston Evening Transcript (6 March).
Reported in White, but wrong year: see 1888.19.

28 ANON. Editorial paragraph. New York Herald (12 March), 6:3.
Reprints Whitman's "The First Dandelion" with confidence that it will not be so inappropriate as on its first appearance last year, when the blizzard came.

29 ANON. "Echoes of the Streets." Philadelphia Press (13 March), 4:7.
Quoted in Traubel IV.
"Whitman is not without a keen sense of the humorous." When a young poet brought his tragedy "Columbus" to Whitman, Whitman replied, "I've been paralyzed once."

30 ANON. "Profits of Professions. . . . The Profession of Letters." Philadelphia Press (17 March), 20:1.
Quoted in Traubel IV.
Incidental: "It is said that Walt Whitman of late years has earned about $300 annually with his pen."

31 ANON. "Books and Authors. . . . Walt Whitman in German." New York Home Journal (27 March), 1:9.
Paragraph quoting Ernest Rhys from Boston Evening Transcript (unlocated) on Whitman's growing fame in Europe and

1889

Rolleston's "'very excellently well done translation,'" a remarkable addition to Germany's literature.

32 CARPENTER, EDWARD. "'November Boughs.'" Scottish Art Review 1 (April), 334-35.
    Review. Carpenter describes his visit to Whitman several years ago. "Sands at Seventy" contains work comparable to Whitman's best, with the same "acceptance of ordinary facts," "direct gaze into the spiritual world behind them," egotism, yearning love, jagged lines, emotional passages. His poetry's power lies in its expression of nature.

33 PAYNE, WILLIAM MORTON. "Recent Books of Poetry." Dial 9 (April), 323-24.
    Review of November, in which Whitman's thought and language fit his character and mood. His honesty and stylistic genius will ensure his influence and permanence. Several extracts are quoted with praise.

34 ANON. "Personal Intelligence." New York Herald (13 April), 6:5.
    "Walt Whitman's odd fancies in conversation have been written for tomorrow's Herald by the young German poet, C. Sadakichi Hartmann."

35 MORRIS, HARRISON S. "'The Revolution against Taste.'" The American 17 (13 April), 409.
    Taking off from Gosse's discussion in the last Forum of contemporary attitudes toward the great poets, Morris explains that these attitudes are frequent among Whitman's admirers, who fail to understand that he appreciates "the finer intricacies of art," although they were not made for him.

36 ANON. "Walt Whitman." New York Herald (14 April), 16:4-5.
    "Whitman is the most interesting figure in American literature to-day," no one else being so widely loved or hated. A revolutionary, he expects and forgives detraction from the conservatives, whose right to their opinions he respects. His opinions on his contemporaries, "given freely and frankly in the course of conversation," quoted on another page (1889.37), "are of world wide interest."

37 HARTMANN, C. SADAKICHI. "Notes of a Conversation with the Good Gray Poet by a German Poet and Traveller." New York Herald (14 April), 10:6.
    Reprinted: 1893.17; Knox; Walt Whitman Birthplace Bulletin 3 (October 1959).
    Presents quotations from Whitman on his fellow writers (Bryant, Holmes, Emerson, Hawthorne, Stedman, Whittier, Lowell, Stoddard, Poe, Rousseau, Byron); epigrammatic statements; comments on great statesmen, cities, his poetic ideas.

38 HINTON, RICHARD. "Walt Whitman at Home--An Interesting Visit to the Famous Poet's Humble Sick-Room." New York World (14 April), 28:1-3.
    Reprinted: 1889.69.
    Account of his visit with Whitman, the power of Whitman's personality over people, their first meeting in 1855. The 1855 Leaves is described, its opening lines "the keynote of democracy." The meaning of his poetry becomes plainer with more readings. His poetry seems egotistical but his life is not, revealing rather a strong faith in himself. "Lilacs" is the most sane and spiritual poem of death in English.

39 ANON. "Walt Whitman." Literary News, n.s. 10 (May), 180-81.
    An idea of Whitman's life (here summarized) is necessary to understand the work of this most subjective of writers. "Backward Glance" is quoted to give a sense of his purpose. He found unsuspected virtues in the people. His writing "presupposes trained intellect," "wide experience and reading, and individual thinking." His themes of freedom, the sacredness of all, his sense of purpose and criticisms of the age are described. He urges readers to use their "mental strength." His earnest call is too little heeded now.

40 EATON, WYATT. "Recollections of Jean François Millet." Century Magazine 38 (May), 99.
    Incidental: Whitman reminded him of Millet "in his large and easy manner."

41 ANON. "'Authors at Home.'" Critic, n.s. 11 (4 May), 218.
    Review of 1888.6. "Much is told us by an intimate friend of Walt Whitman, whose head of silver and heart of gold gleam in these sympathetic pages as seldom before."

*42 ANON. "A Camden Compliment--On Walt Whitman's 70th Birthday--An Imposing Celebration--Morgan's Hall has been secured for dinner which will be attended by prominent literary characters." Camden Post (10 May).
    Reported in Asselineau.

43 BUCHANAN, ROBERT. "Imperial Cockneydom. A Rejoinder to Critics." Universal Review 4 (15 May), 78, 82.
    Incidental references: Cockneydom rather than cosmopolitanism is spreading abroad, so that "young men have given no ear to the 'barbaric yawp' of Whitman, know not even the name of Herman Melville."

44 BLATCH, HARRIET STANTON. "Stepniak at Home." Boston Evening Transcript (18 May), 5:1-3.
    Quoted in Traubel V.
    Stepniak, Russian nihilist interviewed in London, said that Leaves was a favorite of his, by "an author who is not sufficiently appreciated in his own land."

45 ANON. "Notes." Critic, n.s. 11 (25 May),
    264.
        Notes Whitman's upcoming birthday.
    Reaction against the negative treatment of
    Whitman's work is growing, for many "great-
    ly admire his writings, though without
    thinking them the be-all and the end-all of
    American poetry." His personality is also
    warmly admired.

*46 HUNEKER, JAMES. "Walt Whitman." New York
    Home Journal (29 May), 8.
    Reprinted: Schwab. Revised: 1891.50.
        A reaction against the negative criti-
    cism given Whitman has begun. His appear-
    ance and life (from Burroughs) are de-
    scribed. His book is at first bewildering,
    "a voice primal and fresh" for "this intro-
    spective and self-tormented age," with a
    positive but not rose-colored attitude
    toward life and people. He is moral, with
    biblical simplicity of speech in "Adam,"
    with pervasive mysticism and praiseworthy
    ideals of woman and friendship. "He is
    nature herself humanized." His form is
    majestic, not harsh, with an immense vocab-
    ulary used artistically. His book is the
    epic of America. Through egotism he pro-
    jects himself into all. Significant poems
    are noted. He is one of the grandest
    forces in American literature, with an
    invigorating influence.

47 RHYS, ERNEST. "The Portraits of Walt
    Whitman." Scottish Art Review 2 (June),
    17-24. Illustrated.
        Describes the photographs and oil por-
    traits, with some factual errors.
    Whitman's personal references in "Calamus"
    reveal his ideal of manly beauty as not
    conventional. His outdoors natural life
    has resulted in a noble physical presence
    in old age.

*48 [BONSALL, HENRY L.] "Camden Honors Him--Poet
    Whitman's 70th Birthday." Camden Post
    (1 June).
    Reported in Asselineau.

49 ANON. "Walt Whitman's Birthday." New York
    Times (1 June), 4:7.
        Account of birthday dinner, listing
    leading guests, quoting Whitman's few
    trembling words and letters from absentees
    Whittier (who praises only Whitman's war-
    time services), Howells (who calls him a
    "liberator"), and George H. Boker (who
    regards Whitman highly as "poet and as a
    noble example of manhood"). See 1889.9.

50 ANON. "Walt Whitman's Birthday." New York
    Tribune (1 June), 7:1-2.
        Account of birthday dinner, quoting
    Grey, Whittier, Howells (see 1889.49), and
    Twain (who notes the vast changes that
    Whitman has lived through). "No poet,
    certainly no innovator in poetic methods,
    was ever in higher honor in his own

country." Whitman's personal qualities as
well as originality make him "a National
figure in literature," his name known
wherever English poetry is studied.

51 ANON. Editorial paragraph. Philadelphia
    Inquirer (1 June), 4:2.
        The birthday tribute "must have been
    extremely gratifying to the old poet."
    His physical state makes doubtful any
    further public appearances, "but his mental
    energy is unimpaired."

52 ANON. "A Tribute to a Poet." Philadelphia
    Inquirer (1 June), 2:1-2.
        Extensive account of birthday dinner,
    describing the guests, Whitman, and his
    behavior during the evening, quoting and
    summarizing addresses as well as Whitman's
    words to the company.

53 ANON. "Whitman at Seventy." Philadelphia
    North American (1 June).
        Editorial paragraph. Whitman is highly
    regarded in the world of letters if not by
    the general public, who prefer melody in
    their poetry and would rather not think
    for themselves, as Whitman's poetry demands.
    But Whitman's appreciation by the minority
    who have the habit of thought augurs well
    "for the growth and endurance of Whitman's
    influence and fame."

54 ANON. "Whitman's Natal Day." Philadelphia
    North American (1 June), 1:4.
        Extensive account of birthday dinner,
    describing the guests and speeches, quoting
    some speeches and greetings as well as
    Whitman's response (worded differently from
    that quoted in 1889.52). "It was a great
    night for Camden."

55 ANON. "The Old Poet's Birthday." Philadelphia
    Press (1 June), 5:3.
        Extensive account of birthday dinner,
    quoting some speakers, including Whitman
    (as quoted in 1889.54), listing those
    present.

56 ANON. "Walt Whitman's Birthday." Philadelphia
    Times (1 June), 4:6.
        Account of birthday dinner, a tribute
    rendered deservedly to Whitman's "kindly,
    genial personality," quoting some addresses
    and letters, including Whitman's response,
    listing the members of the committee that
    planned the dinner.

57 ANON. "Walt Whitman's Seventieth Birthday."
    Critic, n.s. 11 (8 June), 287-88.
        Account of birthday dinner, quoting
    letters from Howells, Whittier, Twain, and
    Burroughs.

58 ANON. "The News of Camden." Philadelphia
    Press (27 June), 3:5.
    Quoted in Traubel V.
        Paragraph on the presentation to

Whitman by the Camden dinner committee of "$125 in gold, the balance from the sale of the tickets, after all expenses had been met."

59 ANON. "Notes and News." Poet-Lore 1 (July), 348.
Records Whitman's pleasant comments at the birthday dinner.

60 ANON. Review of November. Scottish Review 14 (July), 212-13.
Describes contents, the most interesting being "Backward Glance." The papers on Shakespeare and Burns are suggestive but not new.

61 DE KAY, CHARLES. "George Fuller, Painter." Magazine of Art 12 (September), 349-54.
Fuller admired and was influenced by Whitman, sharing with him a New York City background, interest in commonplace subjects, and failure to appeal to the common people both valued. Whitman "is a poet for writers, for strong natures loving the unconventional, and for readers weary of much verse." Impressionism is important for both.

62 ANON. "Sir Edwin Arnold Here." New York Times (15 September), 1:5.
Interview with Arnold upon his arrival in New York yesterday. He describes his pleasant interview with Whitman, "one of the greatest of your American writers," whose poetry has "nothing impure in it," contrary to the claims of "prudish people."

*63 ANON. "Arnold and Whitman." Philadelphia Press (15 September).
Reported in Asselineau, but not found on this date.

64 ANON. "Arnold and Whitman." Philadelphia Times (15 September), 4:5.
Interview with Whitman, who claims that the dinner for him at Morgan's Hall gave him new life. His activities are described. Arnold's letter from New York of 12 September is printed, greeting Whitman from Tennyson, Browning, and Rossetti, and asking permission to visit him. Arnold's visit with Whitman the previous afternoon is described, with their conversation quoted; Whitman recited a poem by Arnold after Arnold recited from Leaves.

65 ANON. Editorial. New York Times (16 September), 4:2.
Objects to Arnold's claim that Whitman's poetry is not impure (1889.62). His admirers may prefer such dirt, but that poetry should not be called pure. Impurity is not a quality of good art.

66 [GILDER, JEANNETTE.] "The Lounger." Critic, n.s. 12 (28 September), 153.
Describes Arnold's visit to Whitman,

who could not reciprocate by quoting Arnold's poems when Arnold quoted his, for he is not "a great reader of general literature" and has not discussed with this writer (Gilder) the writers of the day. His appearance is striking and demands a portrait, which Alexander should complete from the studies he has so far made of Whitman.

*67 ARNOLD, Sir EDWIN. Letter to Whitman. Boston Traveller (5 October).
Reported in White.

68 [GILDER, JEANNETTE.] "The Lounger." Critic, n.s. 12 (12 October), 178.
Describes the Gutekunst portrait of Whitman and his sitting for it.

69 [HINTON, RICHARD.] "Walt Whitman at Home--An Interesting Visit to the Famous Poet's Humble Sick-Room." Dublin Evening Telegraph (19 October).
Reprint of 1889.38.

*70 ANON. "Honor in His Own Country." Philadelphia Press (30 October).
Quoted in Hendrick.
Whitman has given his name to a cigar.

71 ANON. "Walt Whitman." Illustrated London News 95 (16 November), 634.
Describes Whitman's personality, outlook, optimism, democracy, knowledge of profound ethical truths. "His writings are effusions" rather than careful in form or style; his nonecstatic moods show much common sense. The wholesome purpose of Leaves is described. He cannot be recognized as a great author but is valuable for his sincerity, love of nature and human nature, patriotism and love of freedom, individuality, and benevolent spirit. His works, except for Specimen, need time to ripen for the reader.

72 MORRIS, HARRISON S. "A French Critic on Walt Whitman." The American 19 (16 November), 89-90.
Extract reprinted: 1889.75.
Summary, with quotations (in translation), of Sarrazin's essay on Whitman from La Renaissance de la Poésie Anglaise 1798-1889: Whitman's joyful and vital pantheism, Whitman as above art and unique in letters, outside any conventions, deserving the name of bard rather than poet or philosopher. No other review of Whitman has shown "so complete a mastery of the subject, both philosophical and literary." For a translation of Sarrazin, see In Re (1893.11).

*73 ANON. Full-page portrait of Whitman. Illustrated London News, Supplement (30 November).
Reported in Blodgett.

74 [GILDER, JEANNETTE.] "The Lounger." Critic,
n.s. 12 (21 December), 312.
Describes Alexander's portrait of
Whitman, which "has all the strength of
his face, and at the same time all of its
sweetness."

75 MORRIS, HARRISON S. "Current Criticism.
Whitman's 'Indescribable Masculinity.'"
Critic, n.s. 12 (21 December), 319.
Extract reprinted from 1889.72.

*76 ANON. Paragraph. Camden Post (26 December).
Reported in White.
Describes Whitman driving to Harleigh
Cemetery to pick a burial lot.

1890

BOOKS

1 ANON. Echoes from the Oxford Magazine: Being
Reprints of Seven Years. London: Henry
Frowde. "The Innings. Dedicated to Walt
Whitman," by [R. W.] R[aper], pp. 56-60;
"Behold! I Am Not One That Goes to Lec-
tures," by [A. T.] Q[uiller-Couch], 63-64.
Reprinted: Saunders.
Parodies.

2 BARLOW, GEORGE. From Dawn to Sunset. London:
Swan Sonnenschein & Co. "Walt Whitman,"
pp. 428-30.
Poem in rhymed stanzas: tribute to
Whitman as a poet speaking for his country.

3 ELLIS, HAVELOCK. The New Spirit. London:
George Bell & Sons. "Whitman," pp. 89-132.
Extract reprinted: Bradley/Blodgett.
America's figures of world significance
are Emerson, Thoreau, and Whitman.
Whitman's growth during the war, his Greek
spirit, and his energy are described. From
his early emphasis on the unity of matter
and spirit, with morality being "the normal
activity of a healthy nature," he moved to
a stronger spiritual emphasis. His religion
is strenuous rather than mystical. Love is
central for him, and personal. He "opened
a fresh channel of Nature's force into
human life--the largest since Wordsworth,
and more fit for human use." Ellis's
essay on Ibsen is a reprint of 1888.1a.

4 HERRINGSHAW, THOMAS W. Local and National
Poets of America. Chicago: American Publishers' Association. "Walt Whitman,"
pp. 193-94. Portrait.
One-paragraph biographical sketch preceding extracts. Leaves is "a record of
the author's thoughts, in song--solely of
America and to-day."

5 HOLMES, OLIVER WENDELL. Over the Teacups.
Boston and New York: Houghton, Mifflin &
Co., pp. 234-38.
Reprint of 1890.43.

6 INGERSOLL, ROBERT G. Liberty in Literature:
Testimonial to Walt Whitman, An Address
Delivered in Philadelphia, October 21,
1890. New York: Truth Seeker Co., 77 pp.
Portrait.
Same as 1890.55. Extracts printed: 1890.
52. Reprinted: 1892.7.
Discarding customs and rules, Whitman
spoke his true thought, proclaiming the
gospel of the body and denying human depravity. Leaves, like the Bible and
Shakespeare, cannot be judged only by a few
lines. Whitman believes in democracy and
liberty, paints vivid pictures, uses no
rhyme and meter but rather the true essence
of poetry, symbols. He finds revelation
everywhere, not in narrow creeds. "Cradle"
and "Lilacs" are explicated. Whitman is
the poet of childhood, youth, manhood, and
old age. He has lived his philosophy,
accepted life, "voiced the aspirations of
America"; "above all, he is the poet of
Love and Death." One becomes part of all
life through Leaves.

7 JOHNSTON, J[OHN]. Notes of Visit to Walt
Whitman, etc., in July, 1890. Bolton: T.
Brimelow & Co., 46 pp.
Reprinted: 1898.11. Revised: 1917.6;
1918.12.
Describes Whitman, his home, habits,
conversation, opinions, sympathy, magnetism,
keen senses; Johnston's visit to Brooklyn
and West Hills to see Whitman's early
friends and home. Andrew Rome describes
Whitman as he knew him. John Y. Baulsir,
a ferry pilot Johnston met by chance, recalls with fondness Whitman and his book.
Sandford Brown, a former student of Whitman,
recalls him favorably, describing his habits
and thinking. Visits to Herbert Gilchrist
and Burroughs are described. Whitman's
personality offers the tonic influence of
nature and personifies camaraderie.

8 SYMONDS, JOHN ADDINGTON. Essays Speculative
and Suggestive. Vol. 2. London: Chapman
& Hall. "Democratic Art. With Special
Reference to Walt Whitman," pp. 30-77.
Revised: 1893.9.
Whitman exemplifies democratic art,
cherishing the art and literature of the
past but looking ahead, seeking in the
people themselves a robust character. He
realizes America's spiritual inadequacy.
Of contemporary figures, only Millet and
the Russians would meet Whitman's approval.
Extensive quotations, especially from
Vistas.

9 WOODBURY, CHARLES J. Talks with Ralph Waldo
Emerson. New York: Baker & Taylor Co.,
pp. 62-63, 128.
Includes reprint of 1890.11.
Adds description of Emerson's disapproval of Whitman coming to dinner without
his coat ("though undoubtedly he enjoyed
the unrestrained man and democratic poet,
despite the odour his verses perspire").

1890

PERIODICALS

10 ANON. "Walt Whitman Cheerful." New York
       Times (26 January), 1:4.
       Quoted in 1890.12.
          Interview with Whitman, who speaks
       rather jovially of his attitude toward
       death and his life-expectancy, of Boker's
       death as disturbing him, of his many
       friends, and of his activities.

11 WOODBURY, CHARLES J. "Emerson's Talks with a
       College Boy." Century Magazine 39 (Feb-
       ruary), 625.
       Reprinted: 1890.9.
          Records his conversations with Emerson
       in the late 1860s, quoting his praise for
       Whitman "'until he became Bohemian,'" and
       his explanation of Thoreau's interest in
       Whitman.

12 ANON. "Notes." Critic, n.s. 13 (1 February),
       60.
       Extract quoted from 1890.10.

13 [HOWELLS, W. D.] "Editor's Study." Harper's
       New Monthly Magazine 80 (March), 646.
          Incidental: "though we have now passed
       the time in which our great cycle of poets
       flourished, we still have Holmes, Whittier,
       Lowell, Whitman, Trowbridge, and Stoddard
       among us," as well as the younger poets.

14 ANON. "'Gems from Walt Whitman.'" Critic,
       n.s. 13 (15 March), 126.
          Review of Gould (1889.4). Whitman
       spills over attempts to sample him, for one
       prefers his "full roar and torrent" without
       pruning, "winsome, humane, tender, optimis-
       tic." He solved the ancient controversy
       "between classic tintinnabulation and the
       great movement that fills the world,"
       matching rhythm of ideas to that of words.
       His work's quality varies according to one's
       mood, so selecting passages of "a constant
       and perpetual beauty" is difficult, but
       such change, like nature's, is his charm.
       These excerpts are fine for popularizing
       him, but are really only "a pretty trifle."

15 ELTON, OLIVER. Review of Ellis (1890.3).
       Academy 37 (5 April), 231.
          Ellis shows discrimination in choosing
       Whitman, Ibsen, and Tolstoy to deal with as
       significant contemporary figures, for "their
       spirit is younger and concerns us more than
       that of many writers who are their junior."
       Though neglected, "Whitman keeps his faith
       in the faithless people unshaken." "Ellis's
       account of this great poet is probably the
       best that has been supplied by anyone ex-
       cept the poet himself." Though "the in-
       cidental nakedness of his writing" cannot
       be harmful, many of his poems fall short
       in art. His capacity for inspiration and
       prophecy is ahead of his literary sense,
       except for an occasional "immortal flower
       of verse" like "Captain." Ellis emphasizes

Whitman as prophet, but Whitman must still
be considered as a poet.

16 ANON. "Walt Whitman Ill. Too Much Spring
       Air Has Given the Poet the Grip." New
       York Times (6 April), 1:6.
          Quotes Whitman on his condition and
       the spring day.

17 [WHITMAN, WALT.] "Walt Whitman Tuesday Night."
       Boston Evening Transcript (19 April), 5:5.
       Reprinted: Complete Prose Works.
          Account of Whitman's Lincoln lecture in
       Philadelphia, quoting the new paragraph he
       has added. It is believed to be his thir-
       teenth delivery of it. His appearance and
       weak condition are described.

18 ANON. Two-paragraph note. The American 20
       (26 April), 31.
          "Tennyson stated that Walt Whitman was
       certainly one of the greatest, and probably
       the greatest of living poets," according to
       a private letter from a friend of Tennyson's
       to whom Tennyson addressed the remark and
       who is himself not an admirer of Whitman.
       This shows that "a prophet is not without
       honor, save in his own country."

19 [GILDER, JEANNETTE.] "The Lounger." Critic,
       n.s. 13 (26 April), 210.
          Account of Whitman's Lincoln lecture in
       Philadelphia. Though feeble, "his voice
       has lost none of its charm and his manner
       none of its magnetism." His reading of
       "Captain" is "an experience never to be
       forgotten"; he is "seen and heard at his
       best" when commemorating Lincoln's death.

20 BUCKE, RICHARD MAURICE. "'Leaves of Grass'
       and Modern Science." Conservator 1 (May),
       19.
       Reprinted: In Re.
          Whitman, no trained scientist, "dips
       into all conceivable subjects" without
       striking a false note. Might his "inner
       light" serve him as accurately in those
       areas where we cannot check him?

*21 GUTHRIE, WILLIAM NORMAN. "The Apostle of
       Chaotism." University of the South Maga-
       zine (May).
       Reprinted: 1897.7 (pp. 343-48).
          Whitman's best work is truly poetry,
       but his mannerisms, here enumerated, are
       deplored. Explanations are given of his
       "Nihilistic Theology," "Chaotistic Ethics,"
       "Pan-Fetichism," "Neo-phallicism," all un-
       representative of America.

22 SANTAYANA, G. "Walt Whitman: A Dialogue."
       Harvard Monthly 10 (May), 85-92.
       Reprinted: Murphy.
          Two young collegians argue over Whitman,
       his use of English, his style. One finds
       in him a new sensation, the other says he
       does not use the language as men use it.
       One says he is to be read for inspiration,

not style, "an attitude, a faculty of appreciation," not a theory; he sees things in their intrinsic nature and is not a charlatan or immoral as the other claims; rather, he is only a spectator.

23 ANON. "Notes." Critic, n.s. 13 (10 May), 242.

Quotes Whitman's remarks used to preface his Lincoln lecture in Philadelphia on 15 April.

*24 ANON. Comment on Whitman. The Week (16 May), 375.

Quoted in McMullin.

Whitman is not even original or improper, "simply dull."

*25 BROWN, JOHN HENRY. Sonnet to Whitman. The Week (16 May), 376.

Quoted in McMullin. Reprinted: 1892.1; 1897.101.

Tribute to Whitman: "Great democrat, great poet, and great man!"

26 RANDOM, RODERICK [pseud.]. "Letters to Men of Note. To Walt Whitman, in America." Wit and Wisdom (17 May).

Addressed to Whitman: Your philosophy is easier "for simpletons like Thoreau and Walt Whitman" than for people with "knowledge of Mayfair." You have Milton's reforming fervor and sweeping vigor but not his antique grace or "majestic and mellifluous roll," despite many beautiful and tender lines and couplets. "You are not so much a singer as a prophet and exhorter," helping us to "freedom of spirit."

27 ANON. "Notes." Critic, n.s. 13 (31 May), 276.

Whitman's birthday is to be celebrated by a dinner. His health remains the same.

28 ANON. "Walt Whitman's Birthday." New York Times (1 June), 5:2.

Account of dinner, including Whitman's discussion with Ingersoll of the question of immortality, which remarks Whitman revised and Traubel printed in In Re.

*29 ANON. "The Old Poet Talks Across Table on Immortality with the Agnostic." Philadelphia Press (1 June).

Reported in Asselineau, but not located in this issue.

30 [WHITMAN, WALT.] "Honors to the Poet. Walt Whitman's Friends Help Him Celebrate His Birthday." Philadelphia Inquirer (1 June), 1:4-5.

Reprinted: White.

Account of Whitman's birthday banquet in Philadelphia. Ingersoll's address is quoted: Whitman is the first true poet of democracy and the common, teaching Americans the dignity of manhood and womanhood, providing for future historians a full

picture of America. Other speakers and guests are listed; Dr. S. Weir Mitchell recalled reading Leaves to his six-year-old son. Whitman's refutation of Ingersoll's doubts about immortality is quoted.

31 ANON. "Walt Whitman Honored." Camden Post (2 June).

Brief note on the birthday dinner, listing some guests.

*32 [WHITMAN, WALT.] "Ingersoll's Speech." Camden Post (2 June), 1.

Reprinted: Prose Works 1892. Quoted in White.

Account of the birthday celebration "and the late curious and unquestionable 'boom' of the old man's wide-spreading popularity and that of his 'Leaves of Grass.'" Ingersoll's address is praised as great oratory and a "flattering summary" of Whitman. The account of Whitman's response is taken from the end of the Inquirer article (1890.30).

*33 ANON. "Walt Whitman's End--It seems to be approaching rapidly now." London (Ontario) Free Press (4 June).

Reported in Asselineau.

34 ANON. "Walt Whitman on Himself--He had a mission to perform and he has performed it." New York Times (8 June), 1:4.

Reports his activities, his ideas on his work, his attitude to God.

35 ANON. "Notes." Critic, n.s. 13 (28 June), 326.

The Philadelphia Press (unlocated) announces Whitman's choice of a burial place, which is described.

36 ANON. "Books of the Month." Atlantic Monthly 66 (July), 143.

Review of Gould (1889.4). Excerpts from Whitman would not be as objectionable as those from less fragmentary poets, but these lines give an unfortunate impression of him, exaggerating "the Tupper element" and the spasmodic quality of the lines.

37 ANON. "Literary Miscellany." Literary News, n.s. 11 (July), 221.

Describes the spot Whitman has chosen for his grave, "characteristic of the man."

38 KENNEDY, WILLIAM SLOANE. "The Quaker Traits of Walt Whitman." Conservator 1 (July), 36.

Reprinted: In Re. Also used in 1896.9.

Whitman, empowered by the spiritual inner light from his Quaker background, exhibits such Quaker traits as tolerance, plainness, sincerity.

39 TRUMBULL, JONATHAN. "Walt Whitman's View of Shakespeare." Poet-Lore 2 (July), 368-71.

Whitman reveres Shakespeare's works but

1890

believes them "inadequate as applied to
America." Shakespeare tells nothing about
himself; Whitman tells all that he can,
but leaves much to conjecture. Heroism is
only "part of the great message of humanity" in each writer.

40 ANON. "Literary Notes." <u>New York Tribune</u>
(21 August), 8:1.
Quoted in 1890.47.
Paragraph questioning Whitman's meaning
in a sentence from "Old Man's Rejoinder"
(<u>Critic</u>, 16 August).

41 ANON. "A Talk with Whitman. The Old Poet's
Reminiscences of Famous Literary Men.
Interesting Political Views." Philadelphia
<u>Times</u> (25 August), 4:4.
Reprinted: 1890.44. Reprinted in part:
Bergman (May, 1948).
Interview with Whitman, who describes
his health and activities; denies Woodbury's
idea (1890.9) that he appeared without a
coat; recalls Emerson, J. Boyle O'Reilly,
Joaquin Miller, Edwin Arnold; notes his
admiration for James G. Blaine, criticism
of President Harrison; praises the old age
of Whittier and Tennyson.

42 T[RAUBEL], H. L. "Walt Whitman's Birthday."
<u>Unity</u> 25 (28 August), 215.
Account of birthday celebration and
guests, quoting Whitman's comments.

43 HOLMES, OLIVER WENDELL. "Over the Teacups.
X." <u>Atlantic Monthly</u> 66 (September), 388-
90.
Reprinted: 1890.5.
Whitman may claim to have introduced
literary independence to America because
of his undiscriminating acceptance of all
words and subjects into his poetry and the
originality of his specimens of a new literature. "No man has ever asserted the
surpassing dignity and importance of the
American citizen so boldly and freely as
Mr. Whitman." But some restraint is preferable to "lawless independence."

44 ANON. "Whitman's Reminiscences--The Old Poet
Talks Entertainingly--His Contempt for
Harrison." <u>New York Times</u> (1 September),
3:4.
Reprint of 1890.41.

45 ANON. "Whitman on Harrison." <u>Boston Herald</u>
(3 September), 4:1.
Paragraph quoting Whitman on Harrison
from the Philadelphia <u>Times</u> (1890.41) and
a similar remark he made to a young Boston
friend.

46 ANON. "Notes." <u>Critic</u>, n.s. 14 (6 September),
124.
Quotes Whitman on activities and health
from the Philadelphia <u>Times</u> (1890.41).

47 FINLEY, KATE BARCLAY. "Walt Whitman Interpreted." <u>Critic</u>, n.s. 14 (13 September),
133.
In response to the <u>Tribune</u> (1890.40),
she explains Whitman's meaning as to the
false forms of literature, art, and religion, calling him "a great poet because he
keeps ever near the mighty pulsating heart
of the people, never forgetting his mission
to it, in the minor considerations of poetic
form and diction."

48 HORTON, GEORGE. "An Old Man Once Saw I."
Chicago <u>Herald</u> (18 September), 5.
Reprinted: <u>In Re</u>.
Poem on an old man meeting the female
embodiment of fame.

49 BUCKE, R. M. "The Case of Walt Whitman and
Col. Ingersoll." <u>Conservator</u> 1 (October),
59.
Typical of the nation's plight is the
prejudice against Whitman, her "one great
poet," and Ingersoll, her "supreme orator."

50 ANON. "Refused to Col. Ingersoll--Walt
Whitman's testimonial benefit cannot be
held in the Academy--Horticultural Hall
chosen." Philadelphia <u>Press</u> (5 October),
1:4.
Ingersoll's address on Whitman must be
given somewhere else.

51 ANON. "A Testimonial to Walt Whitman." <u>New
York Times</u> (22 October), 2:6.
Account of Ingersoll's oration, hailing
Whitman as "the greatest of living poets."

52 ANON. Account of Ingersoll's oration.
Philadelphia <u>Press</u> (22 October), 11:3-4.
Most of the article quotes Ingersoll's
speech (see 1890.6), ending with Whitman's
brief "hail and farewell" speech at the
oration's close.

53 ANON. "Notes." <u>Critic</u>, n.s. 14 (25 October),
210.
Brief account of Ingersoll's oration at
the testimonial for Whitman.

54 ANON. "Give It to the Bard?" <u>Punch</u> 99 (1
November), 215.
Humorous note regarding Ingersoll's
address (1890.55): a few of his statements
might be construed in a sense negative to
Whitman and his reputation.

55 INGERSOLL, ROBERT G. "Testimonial to Walt
Whitman. Let Us Put Wreaths on the Brows
of the Living." <u>Truth Seeker</u> 17 (1 November), 690-93, 700.
Same as 1890.6.
Quotes the description of the event
from the <u>Press</u> (1890.52). The speech is
expanded from Ingersoll's address at the
birthday dinner (see 1890.30).

56 ANON. "Walt Whitman." Public Opinion 10
     (8 November), 116.
          From Chicago Inter-Ocean (unlocated):
     Our views of poetry have changed since
     Whitman was the fad, but although we can
     form a truer assessment of him now and
     recognize in him some high poetic thoughts,
     he has not really contributed to a change
     in poetry, which still seeks art, subtlety
     of thought, and rhythm (if not rhyme).
     Yet, as Ingersoll has recently suggested,
     Whitman is truly "a picturesque figure" as
     he waits for death.

57 [TUCKER, BENJAMIN.] "On Picket Duty."
     Liberty 7, no. 15 (15 November), 1.
          Briefly praises Ingersoll's "senten-
     tious force and penetration" in his char-
     acterization of "one of the greatest qual-
     ities" of Whitman and his work: "In every-
     thing a touch of chaos."

57a MERCER, EDMUND. "Walt Whitman." Great
      Thoughts, n.s. 5 (22 November), 336-40.
      Portrait on front page and p. 337.
          Though joy is his keynote, Whitman is
      not without recognition of the darker side
      of life. His life is traced (with some
      error). Leaves is "one complete work," to
      be read "from beginning to end, as a philo-
      sophical treatise." His work is moral (if
      not wholly for general reading). He por-
      trays camaraderie, "free, glorious manhood
      and the sweetest womanliness," a depth of
      feeling for humanity. His religion takes
      the best from all religions, finding God
      in nature and trusting in death. A poet
      of a high class, he fulfills Arnold's
      definition of poetry as a criticism of
      life, which he treats in all its aspects.
      His work is vast, like his scenery, and
      soul-stirring. Concluded 1890.59.

58 ANON. "Of Making Many Books." Critic, n.s.
     14 (29 November), 282.
          Good-Bye is announced; it will contain
     Ingersoll's address (1890.55) and transla-
     tions of Sarrazin and Rolleston (see In
     Re). Whitman's health, activities, prepar-
     ation of preface to O'Connor's stories
     (1891.9) are described.

59 MERCER, EDMUND. "Walt Whitman." Great
     Thoughts, n.s. 5 (29 November), 351.
          Concludes 1890.57a. "A forerunner
     into a new and vaster realm of poetry,"
     Whitman was not understood, but appreciation
     for his truth is increasing, his democratic
     literature spreading (though he is not the
     pioneer in this, but shows the influence
     of Plato). His courage and integrity are
     evident in his confession, "Prayer."

60 ANON. "A Poet's Judgment on Poets." Review
     of Reviews 2 (December), 581.
          Précis of Whitman's "characteristically
     Whitmanesque" article in November North
     American Review. One passage (quoted),

"if cut up into irregular lengths, would
probably pass muster with much of his
poetry."

1891

BOOKS

1 ANON. Twenty Modern Men, from the National
    Observer. London: Edward Arnold. "Walt
    Whitman," pp. 36-41.
         Whitman's career and work are full of
    contradictions. He offended from wrong-
    headedness, not prurience. He believes
    the fallacy that laws of art must vary with
    political and social changes. But "he
    leads you into the open air," and offers a
    new rapture in approaching death. "Cradle"
    and "Lilacs" outweigh the rest of his work
    and are unequalled in America "for passion
    and depth and nobility of thought." "He
    will live as the singer of the old eternal
    themes--Friendship and Love and Death."

2 ARNOLD, Sir EDWIN. Seas and Lands. New York:
    Longmans, Green, & Co., pp. 75-79; in 1892
    London ed., 78-84.
         Account of his visit of September 1889
    to Whitman, whom he eagerly sought out as
    "one of the chief personages of American
    literature in his own strange and unre-
    strained, albeit most musical and majestic
    style." He explains his admiration for
    Whitman's art and truth.

3 BEERS, HENRY A. Initial Studies in American
    Letters. New York: Chautauqua Press,
    pp. 176-81; also 126, 183.
    Reprint with minor changes of 1887.2.

4 HARDY, THOMAS. Tess of the D'Urbervilles: A
    Pure Woman. Vol. 2. London: James R.
    Osgood, McIlvaine & Co., chap. 25, p. 46.
         The character Angel Clare views and
    apostrophizes "the absorbing world without,"
    using a quotation from Whitman ("Brooklyn
    Ferry").

5 HAWTHORNE, JULIAN, and LEMMON, LEONARD.
    American Literature: An Elementary Text-
    Book for Use in High Schools and Academies.
    Boston: D. C. Heath & Co., pp. 261-66.
    Reprinted: 1896.83.
         Whitman's peculiarities were determined
    not so much by conscious conviction as by
    egotism and ignorance. He rejected form
    because he could not achieve it, yet his
    method is much more "laborious and cramp-
    ing," imitating Isaiah and Jeremiah but
    replacing their eloquence with vulgarity.
    His writings are not consistent with his
    philosophy: he is "not a democrat" or "free
    from prejudice," remaining the fad of "the
    aristocracy of culture." Yet as a human
    being he reveals a harmonious nature, large
    sympathies, with an occasional lyrical im-
    pulse ("Captain"), suggesting that his

1891

value for literature lies in his portrayal
of emotion rather than thought.

6 LOMBROSO, CESARE. The Man of Genius. London:
Walter Scott, pp. 7, 318.
    Whitman is an example of insane artists
who pioneer in originality: he created "a
rhymeless poetry, which the Anglo-Saxons
regard as the poetry of the future," with
"strange and wild originality."

7 LYNCH, ARTHUR. Modern Authors: A Review and
a Forecast. London: Ward & Downey, 189
pp., passim, especially 41-44, 85-87, 101,
110, 117-21, 123-27, 171-72. No index.
    Whitman is the only American writer
discussed in this study of what literature
should do. He is "the only immortal" among
contemporary poets, with a sense of values
truer than mere artificial training and
conventions, with "his broad, free, flowing
discourse of life" which finds "harmony in
the succession of ideas themselves," not in
mere formal meter alone. Reading him is
refreshing, with his native atmosphere of
greatness and open air. Even in using the
first person, he shows a more objective
regard of himself than his friends do.
His poetry comes from his own experience
and character. His morality and his musical ear (which suits his meaning) are explained.

8 MALET, LUCAS [Mary St. Ledger Harrison.]
Wages of Sin. London: Swan Sonnenschein
& Co. Vol. 1, pp. 77-78; vol. 2, pp. 17,
147; vol. 3, pp. 126, 133, 185, 195, 210.
    This novel quotes Whitman's poetry
frequently, presenting characters who
admire him, particularly his attitude
toward the open road and "delicate Death."

9 O'CONNOR, WILLIAM DOUGLAS. Three Tales.
Boston and New York: Houghton, Mifflin &
Co. "The Carpenter," pp. 211-30.
Reprint of 1868.5 (Whitman wrote the pref-
ace for this volume).

10 SMITH, G[EORGE] J[AMES]. A Synopsis of
English and American Literature. Boston:
Ginn & Co., p. 98.
    The typeface chosen for the brief
Whitman entry indicates a middle ranking
for him, out of a range of five. He is
"a singular 'poetical iconoclast'; graceful, tender."

11 S[TEPHEN], J[AMES] K. Lapsus Calami. Cambridge: Macmillan & Bowers. "Of W. W.
(Americanus)," p. 43.
Reprinted: 1891.24; 1904.20.
    Parody: Whitman-like lines describing
sounds.

12 STRONACH, A. L. Simple History of English
Literature. London: Thomas Nelson & Sons,
p. 165; "Captain," 260-61.
    "WALT WHITMAN writes much that is hard

to understand. He is almost more a prophet
than a poet. One might call him the
Browning of America." (Entire item.)

PERIODICALS

13 ANON. "'The Good Gray Poet.'" No Name Magazine 2 (January), 45-47.
    Whitman "has succeeded in hoodwinking
thousands." He believes in the leveling
tendencies of socialism, the instincts of
the passions, universal equality, and himself. His verses are biblical in form but
with "prurient assumptions," glorifying
the meanest bodily functions as well as
himself. He is an eccentric without morals.

14 MERLIN [pseud.]. "To Walt Whitman." The Week
(16 January).
    Poem praising Whitman's qualities of
nature, referring to particular poems.

15 [GILDER, JEANNETTE.] "The Lounger." Critic,
n.s. 15 (24 January), 47.
    Quotes a postcard from Whitman.

16 ANON. Portrait of Whitman and facsimile of
autograph postcard. Review of Reviews 3
(February), 163.

17 KENNEDY, WILLIAM SLOANE. "Dutch Traits of
Walt Whitman." Conservator 1 (February),
90-91.
Reprinted: In Re.
    The Dutch traits in Whitman outweigh
the Quaker, in terms of his physical appearance and energy. His "profound spirituality" and "mystical philosophy" differentiate him most from his ancestors. Used
in 1896.9.

18 TRAUBEL, HORACE L. "Walt Whitman: Poet and
Philosopher and Man." Lippincott's Monthly
Magazine 47 (March), 382-89. Portrait.
Reprinted: In Re.
    Whitman is American literature's "one
unique influence." The effects of his
early life and ancestry, the impact of his
creative individuality, his sympathy, intentions, and reputation are explained.

19 ANON. "Magazine Notes." Critic, n.s. 15 (21
March), 154.
    Calls attention with favor to Whitman's
pieces in Lippincott's (March), which show
his unimpaired literary faculty. His article in North American Review (March) is
briefly summarized.

20 CURTIS, WILLIAM O'LEARY. "Whitman's Defects
and Beauties." The Month 27 (April), 527-
36.
    Whitman's works may not be poetry at
all. Because present taste is improving,
"literature will produce no more Whitmans."
His admirers are becoming fewer. His
philosophy is unsafe: he never gets beyond
the earth his egotism leads him to prepos-

terous conclusions about man and God.
America has still no great national poet.

21 [WHITMAN, WALT.] Editorial paragraph. Camden
   Post (16 April).
   Reprinted: Prose Works; Good-Bye.
      Whitman came out into the sun yesterday
   after four months in his room while sick.
   He has a book forthcoming.

22 TRAUBEL, HORACE L. "Walt Whitman at Date."
   New England Magazine, n.s. 4 (May), 274-92.
   Revised: In Re.
      Physical description; phrenological
   chart reprinted; personal qualities and
   appeal; illness; habits, personal and
   literary; lack of depression; preference
   for spontaneity; many anecdotes; his books,
   reading, attitudes toward contemporary
   writers; friends; portraits; room. His
   message: literature "is not to tell a
   life, but to be one."

23 ANON. "Jottings." Boston Evening Transcript
   (7 May), 4.
      "The Epictetus saying, as given by
   Walt Whitman in his own quite utterly
   dilapidated physical case--(and Whitman is
   particular about verbalism and even commas)
   is, 'a little spark of soul dragging a
   great lummux of corpse-body clumsily to and
   fro around.'"

23a TRUMBULL, M. M. Editorial paragraph. Open
    Court 5 (7 May), 2800.
       Quotes a letter from Whitman in the
    February Review of Reviews: "I am totally
    paralysed from the old secession war time
    overstrain." This should silence those
    who sneer at his pension, even though "he
    did not overstrain himself enough to go to
    the war." He need not pretend in order to
    gain sympathy, for all will pity a poet in
    distress; "and if his poems entitle him to
    a pension, let him have it, for poetry, and
    not for a 'war time overstrain.'"

24 ANON. "Lapsus Calami." Spectator 66 (9 May),
   664.
      Review of J. K. S. (1891.11), quoting
   the Whitman parody and wondering whether
   Whitman "could have written anything bringing out so effectively the intolerable in-
   flation and prolixity of his own flat enthusiasm."

25 D[OLE], N[ATHAN] H[ASKELL]. "To Walt Whitman."
   Literary World 22 (9 May), 160.
   Reprinted: 1891.42.
      Poem of friendly praise in short free-
   verse lines.

26 [HUNEKER, JAMES.] "The Raconteur." Musical
   Courier 22 (13 May), 482.
      Incidental: "Of individualities living
   among us we still have dear old Walt
   Whitman, who represents a primal force but
   in the best of whose work, despite its

rugged sincerity, there is always an unfinished quality."

27 [TUCKER, BENJAMIN.] "On Picket Duty."
   Liberty, 8, no. 2 (16 May), 1.
      Criticizes General Trumbull (1891.23a)
   for sneering at Whitman's services during
   the war. "It is more manly work to help to
   save men's lives than to help to destroy
   them as Gen. Trumbull did."

27a ANON. "Minor Notices." Critic, n.s. 15 (23
    May), 275.
       Brief review of Ingersoll (1890.6),
    whose exaggerated praise of Whitman is
    offensive and neither needed by nor worthy
    of Whitman.

28 ANON. "Walt Whitman: His Opinions By an Old
   Friend and Neighbor." Review of Reviews 3
   (June), 533-34.
      Quotes extracts from Traubel (1891.18),
   who "describes with the faithfulness of a
   Boswell" Whitman's daily life.

29 ANON. "Walt Whitman's Birthday." New York
   Times (1 June), 1:6.
      Whitman's birthday was celebrated at
   his Camden home, with letters received from
   Tennyson, Stedman, R. W. Gilder, and others.

*30 [WHITMAN, WALT?] Account of birthday cele-
    bration. Camden Post (2 June).
    Reported in White.

31 ANON. "Walt Whitman's Birthday." Pall Mall
   Gazette (2 June), 3.
      Account of Whitman's birthday activities
   from a telegram sent to Dalziel: he received
   callers, entertaining them with selections
   from his own works; congratulatory letters
   are noted.

32 ANON. "Notes." Critic, n.s. 15 (6 June),
   306.
      Brief account of Whitman's birthday
   celebration.

33 MORRIS, LEWIS. "Some Thoughts on Modern
   Poetry." Murray's Magazine 10 (July), 4.
      Whitman will be remembered for emanci-
   pating verse from the rules of rhyme and
   even rhythm, after the controversies over
   his plain speaking or even the fine universalist spirit of his writings shall have
   ceased to interest. He may pursue emancipation more than is desirable, but his more
   moderate poems should make any sensible
   reader realize "that with him a new power
   has been born into the English-speaking
   world with which we shall have to deal very
   largely in future."

33a TRAUBEL, HORACE L. "Walt Whitman as Pensionée."
    Open Court 5 (2 July), 2864-65.
       Commends Tucker's response to Trumbull
    (1891.27). Whitman never sought a pension.
    Praises Whitman's long years of "outlawry,"

1891

"non-recognition and outrageous assault";
he persevered even through paralysis. Why
should he be ashamed of gifts from friends?
"He gave all he had; he labored to free
literature from thralldom" and democracy
from old ideas.

33b TRUMBULL, M. M. "Nurse and Soldier." Open
Court 5 (2 July), 2865.
Accepts Traubel's criticism (1891.33a),
although a newspaper account led him to
believe Whitman received a pension. Though
neither nurse nor soldier should receive a
pension, it would be better given to the
soldier. Is the plan to give Whitman a
pension now still afoot?

33c [GILDER, JEANNETTE.] "The Lounger." Critic,
n.s. 16 (4 July), 7-8.
Quotes and corrects 1891.31; notes
misconceptions about "The Midnight Visitor,"
a poem actually by Murger, which Whitman
put into rhymed verse after others had
translated it. His failure in rhyming is
evident in "Captain," though it is one of
his most praised works.

34 [TUCKER, BENJAMIN.] "On Picket Duty."
Liberty, 8, no. 7 (25 July), 1.
Long paragraph on Traubel's letter to
Open Court (1891.33a) urging a pension for
Whitman; General Trumbull (1891.33b) has
suggested that only soldiers, if anyone,
should be awarded pensions.

34a ANON. Editorial note to "Walt Whitman's
Last." Lippincott's Monthly Magazine 48
(August), 256.
Whitman only wrote the explanation of
his purpose (here printed) "after considerable persuasion on the editor's part."
Good-Bye "is his last message," and though
much will be said of it, nothing will be as
interesting as Whitman's own "characteristic utterance" upon it.

35 TRAUBEL, HORACE L. "Walt Whitman's Birthday.
May 31, 1891." Lippincott's Monthly Magazine 48 (August), 229-39.
Reprinted without the omissions Traubel
notes here: In Re.
Account of the celebration in dialogue
form, "made up from the direct work of a
stenographer and liberal notes kept by the
writer." Letters honoring Whitman are
quoted, along with his comments. Bucke
notes the diversity of opinion as to
Whitman's major theme. Whitman's contradictory impulses and reasons for never
marrying are discussed.

36 T[RAUBEL], H. L. "Over-Sea Greeting. Walt
Whitman's Fame Abroad." Camden Post (1
August).
Account of the Lancashire group and
Johnston's visit (see 1890.7). Letters
are printed from Johnston and Wallace to
Whitman, and from Bucke to Whitman describ-

ing his visit with them in England. A song
praising Bucke and Whitman is quoted.

37 ANON. "Notes and News." Academy 40 (8
August), 114.
Bucke is in England arranging for the
publication of Good-Bye, upon which Whitman
is quoted. The birthday celebration is
noted.

38 ANON. "Whitman's Farewell. A Melancholy
Book." New York Tribune (16 August), 14:2.
Review of Good-Bye. Whitman's faith
in his work's endurance should not be disturbed at this point in his life; this book
seems meant to satisfy his mind. Some of
the attempts at prose are unintelligible.

39 [GILDER, JEANNETTE.] "The Lounger." Critic,
n.s. 16 (29 August), 108.
A journalist recently printed a line of
Whitman with "whatever" written out rather
than contracted as originally, thus spoil-
ing the rhythm.

40 ANON. Review of Good-Bye. Literary News,
n.s. 12 (September), 282.
From Commercial Advertiser (unlocated).
This final book "from our old original individualistic American poet" shows him "in
good fettle and equal to himself," particularly interesting in "his recollections
of persons once famous." "Long, Long
Hence" is reprinted, "a shadowing forth of
a half comprehended entity in thought."

41 ANON. "The New Books. . . . Walt Whitman."
Review of Reviews 4 (September), 227.
Brief review of Good-Bye, one of the
month's most interesting books.

42 D[OLE], N[ATHAN] H[ASKELL]. "To Walt Whitman."
Literary News, n.s. 12 (September), 260.
Reprint of 1891.25.

43 MORSE, SIDNEY. "The 'Second Annex to "Leaves
of Grass."'" Conservator 2 (September),
51-52.
Review of Good-Bye, like all Whitman's
writings an expression of his personality,
fortunately lacking the polish which so
many miss in him. Even the lesser pieces
contain the magnetism of his best work.

44 ANON. Review of Good-Bye. Critic, n.s. 16
(5 September), 114.
Whitman's soul shines through. His
"beliefs in future personality, identity,
immortality, a merciful and loving God,
progress, consciousness," and his "protest
against materialism" compare with those of
Tennyson and Whittier. Optimism and the
benignity of death prevail.

45 ANON. Review of Good-Bye. Independent 43
(10 September), 1355.
This book is the work of a worn-out and
diseased mind and makes one pity Whitman,

without disagreeing with the justness of
his treatment by editors. "It will be well
for the world when his writings disappear
and are as little talked of as they always
have been little read."

46 ANON. "Goodbye My Fancy." Literary World
22 (12 September), 305.
Review. This "definitive leave-taking"
is "pathetic and courageous." Whitman's
poetic manner pleases more in his prose
than in his chants. This volume fitly
closes "the literary career of a poet who
has with pride and fidelity obeyed his own
genius, and who has sought to collect
within himself, and to understand and
speak--in his oracular, strange voice--the
experiences of common humanity."

47 HIGGINSON, THOMAS WENTWORTH. "Emily
Dickinson's Letters." Atlantic Monthly 68
(October), 446.
Letter reprinted: 1924.2; 1936.16.
In response to Higginson's questioning
her about several writers then much dis-
cussed, Dickinson replied (April 1862):
"You speak of Mr. Whitman. I never read
his book, but was told that it was dis-
graceful."

48 ANON. "'The Midnight Visitor.'" Critic,
n.s. 16 (17 October), 201.
Traubel describes Whitman's connections
with this poem; he put in shape what someone translated for him from Murger.

49 [HOWELLS, W. D.] "Editor's Study." Harper's
New Monthly Magazine 83 (November), 962-66,
passim.
The English assume there is no American
literature because we all don't write like
Whitman. He seems to have exhausted the
resources of his formlessness. He fails
ultimately to embrace beauty itself, although moving in the right direction. He
is "suggestive if not representative of
America," for there are moods other than
his.

50 HUNEKER, JAMES GIBBONS. "Walt Whitman." New
York Recorder (1 November), 26:3-4.
Quoted in Schwab. Revision of 1889.46.
The original article has been condensed
and slightly qualified. Whitman's recent
volumes are "but radiating sparks from the
central hub of his early ideas." Recognition is coming for his new language as a
possible poetic dialect.

51 ANON. "Day with Walt Whitman. How the Venerable Poet Spends His Lagging Leaden
Hours." New York World (8 November), 26.
Account of a visit with Whitman: his
room ("characteristic of a literary man"),
his appearance, "the same rugged personality, the same terseness and broadness of
expression that have characterized him all

through life." Whitman describes his
habits, eating, mental state, philosophy,
ideas on current poetry.

52 HILL, S. McCALMONT. Review of Arnold (1891.2).
Academy 40 (14 November), 425-26.
Incidentally notes and quotes the
pretty picture of the poets Arnold and
Whitman gathering for sympathetic talk.

53 [GILDER, JEANNETTE.] "The Lounger." Critic,
n.s. 16 (29 November [should be 28 Novem-
ber]), 307-8.
Account of her visit with Whitman, his
clear mind, his cluttered room, his posing
for a photograph for her.

54 TRUMBULL, JONATHAN. "The Whitman-Shakespeare
Question." Poet-Lore 3 (December), 626-29.
Whitman is beginning to be recognized
as a stage in the evolution of verse, more
distinctive and original than Shakespeare,
suggesting what is needed for an American
poetry. Whitman clubs may help propagate
his work, as clubs have generated interest
in Browning and Shakespeare.

55 ANON. "Walt Whitman's Good-bye." Pall Mall
Gazette (12 December), 3.
Review of Good-Bye with extensive
quotations. The volume has "the interest
of last words," but Whitman is wished a
long life.

56 ANON. "Walt Whitman Dying." New York Times
(21 December), 2:6.
Brief account of Whitman's condition.

57 ANON. "No Hope for Walt Whitman. The aged
poet may live three or four days longer."
New York Times (22 December), 1:3.

58 ANON. "Walt Whitman Slowly Dying." New York
Times (23 December), 4:7.

59 ANON. "Walt Whitman Still Alive. He has
given up the struggle for life and is willing to die." New York Times (24 December),
1:3.

60 ANON. "The Poet's End Very Near. An unfavorable turn in the condition of Walt Whitman."
New York Times (25 December), 4:7.

61 ANON. "Walt Whitman's Condition." New York
Times (26 December), 1:2.

62 [GILDER, JEANNETTE.] "The Lounger." Critic,
n.s. 16 (26 December), 376.
Quotes dispatch on Whitman's dying
condition.

63 ANON. "Walt Whitman Still Sinking." New York
Times (27 December), 4:7.

64 ANON. "Walt Whitman Still Lingering." New
York Times (28 December), 1:2.

1891

65 ANON. "Walt Whitman About the Same." New
    York Times (29 December), 1:5.

1892

BOOKS

1   BROWN, JOHN HENRY. Poems: Lyrical and Drama-
    tic. Ottawa: J. Durie & Son. "To Walt
    Whitman," p. 65.
    Reprint of 1890.25.

2   CHRISTIE, JOHN. Poems and Prose. Auckland:
    Bowring & Lusher, p. 197.
    Reprinted: McLeod.
        Whitman and America are "large, live,
    full of power, and teeming with wonderful
    potentialities." His poetry and prose are
    more invigorating than anything in modern
    literature. He was no "analyser of life"
    in its secondary details. His benign
    optimism anticipated the future.

3   CLARKE, WILLIAM. Walt Whitman. London: Swan
    Sonnenschein & Co.; New York: Macmillan &
    Co., 132 pp. No index.
        This is "written as an exposition
    rather than as a criticism" of Whitman's
    works. "His Personality": His early life,
    with much outdoor experience, prepared him
    to be the poet of the body. His democratic
    bearing is gentle, not coarse, combining
    New World, pagan, and Christian qualities.
    "His Message to America": He is America's
    representative voice, depicting her more
    fully than other writers. He recognizes
    America's shortcomings but fails to provide
    a serious solution. Yet he tries to help
    America find her soul behind all the mate-
    rialism and hypocrisy. "His Art": His
    formlessness allows readers to arrange his
    material for themselves. His catalogues,
    though indiscriminate, are meant to show
    participation in the breadth of life. His
    inability to distinguish between verbiage
    and inspiration in his work is partly due
    to the lack of intelligent, sympathetic
    criticism from his compatriots. His treat-
    ment of sex, though physiological, avoids
    the usual slyness. He is forward-looking
    in form and theme, a sacer vates. "His
    Democracy": His idea of democracy is
    neither entirely collectivist nor individ-
    ualist. His "dash of barbarism" would be
    healthy. "His Spiritual Creed": He accepts
    evil as leading eventually to good and be-
    lieves in spiritual solidarity and individ-
    ual immortality.

4   CONWAY, MONCURE DANIEL. The Life of Thomas
    Paine. Vol. 2. New York and London:
    G. P. Putnam's Sons, pp. 422-23.
        Quotes Whitman's conversation on Hicks
    and Paine, defending Paine's character
    according to Colonel Fellows's testimony.

5   FOSS, SAM WALTER. Back Country Poems. Boston:
    Potter Publishing Co. "Walt Whitman," pp.
    251-52. Photograph.
    Reprinted: 1893.24; 1900.13.
        Poem of tribute.

6   HARRISON, CLIFFORD. Stray Records; or Personal
    and Professional Notes. Vol. 2. London:
    Richard Bentley & Son, pp. 198-202.
        Account of his own appreciation of
    Leaves since boyhood. Whitman reveals one's
    own thoughts and experiences, although some
    regard his simplicity as "almost pointless
    and foolish." If a part seems hard to
    understand or inconsistent, the fault is
    probably in the reader rather than in
    Whitman, because he is such a great artist.

7   INGERSOLL, ROBERT G. Walt Whitman. An
    Address. Truth Seeker Library no. 21.
    New York: Truth Seeker Co., 86 pp.
    Reprint of 1890.6 with the addition of the
    funeral address (1892.15).

8   MABIE, HAMILTON W[RIGHT]. The Memorial Story
    of America. Philadelphia: John C. Winston
    & Co., pp. 589, 773; photograph, p. 592.
        Whitman, with "the iconoclastic, self-
    assertive, sanguine characteristics of the
    masses, . . . is virile, but not always
    rational," without nice distinctions of
    thought. He has "something of mob violence
    about him, but also much mob power and
    vehemence, . . . the power and extreme of
    his class."

9   MINTO, W., ed. Autobiographical Notes of the
    Life of William Bell Scott. Vol. 2. New
    York: Harper & Bros., pp. 32-33, 267-69.
        Letters from Rossetti and Thomas Dixon
    are quoted, showing the introduction of
    Leaves into England, through American
    traveling bookseller James Grindrod, and
    describing their appreciation of Whitman.

10 SMITH, WILLIAM, F. S. A. S. A Yorkshireman's
    Trip to the United States and Canada.
    London: Longmans, Green & Co., pp. 173-78.
    Illustrated.
        Brief account of his visit to Whitman
    on 9 May 1891, when Whitman was unable to
    converse much. Smith had difficulty with
    Whitman's writings when he first read them
    twenty years or so before but has since
    gained admiration for them. Whitman's life
    is traced through extensive quotation of
    Great Thoughts (1890.57a).

11 [STEDMAN, ARTHUR, ed.] Editor's Note to Auto-
    biographia or The Story of a Life by Walt
    Whitman, Selected from His Prose Writings.
    New York: Charles L. Webster & Co., pp.
    v-vii.
        Whitman approved making the selection,
    but the editor is responsible for the selec-
    tions made. Whitman's prose style is de-
    scribed as "conversational and loosely
    written or elaborately involved."

12 ____. Editor's Note to Selected Poems by
Walt Whitman. New York: Charles L.
Webster & Co., pp. vii-viii.
This edition, with the selection of
which Whitman had nothing to do, concentrates on the poems "most nearly in harmony
with the poetic era (though really they
have a character quite apart from it)."
Whitman may be recognized here as "wonderfully rhythmic."

13 STEDMAN, EDMUND CLARENCE. The Nature and
Elements of Poetry. Boston and New York:
Houghton Mifflin Co., pp. 35, 38, 129, 158,
195-96, 252-53.
Whitman's fidelity to nature and America is his greatest achievement. "His
theory of unvarying realism" is in error.
Like Lanier, Whitman moves toward "an
escape from conventional trammels to something free" in rhythm. His cosmic power
has affinities to Bryant.

14 THOMSON, JAMES. Poems, Essays and Fragments.
London: Bertram Dobell. "Walt Whitman,"
pp. 148-95.
Reprint of 1874.3-1874.9. Reprinted:
1910.19.

15 TRAUBEL, HORACE, ed. Good-bye and Hail Walt
Whitman: At the Graveside of Walt Whitman.
Philadelphia: Billstein & Son, 39 pp.
Includes reprints of 1892.82, 1892.162,
1892.181. Reprinted in part: 1892.204;
1893.11.
Prints in order the readings (by F. H.
Williams) and addresses at Whitman's funeral,
with opening and closing extracts from
Whitman's work and E. C. Stedman's poem
"Good-bye, Walt" (reprinted: 1892.118,
1892.123, 1892.125) and Harrison S. Morris's
sonnet "He was in love with truth" (reprinted: 1894.8), both reprinted in Legler.
Thomas B. Harned: Praises Whitman's
life as consistent with his teachings.
Daniel G. Brinton: Whitman leaves his
message of individuality and freedom in his
legacy of verse.
Richard M. Bucke: Whitman was great in
personality, understanding, spirit, faith.
He still lives, sustaining us by his
strength.
Robert G. Ingersoll: His fame is secure
as "the poet of humanity," sympathy, human
rights, America, democracy, life, love, the
natural, death. "He has uttered more supreme words than any writer of our century,
possibly of almost any other." He was
above all a man. He absorbed all religions
and transcended them. His frankness and
self-reliance will eventually be praised.
Gratitude is due him. (Reprinted: 1892.7;
1892.144.)
John Burroughs (present at the service
but not speaking): Whitman would have
enjoyed the crowds of common people at his
funeral. He does not ignore the idea of
excellence, for he "would lift the average

man to a higher average," without losing
the universal qualities.
"Sprigs of Lilac: Clipt from Sundry
Letters": Letters or extracts honoring
Whitman from Tennyson, Symonds, W. Rossetti,
H. Forman, E. Carpenter, Rolleston, R.
Schmidt, J. W. Wallace, John Johnston,
Ellen O'Connor, Elizabeth Fairchild,
Herbert Gilchrist, Sidney Morse, J. H.
Clifford, W. S. Kennedy, H. Garland, S.
Baxter, T. B. Aldrich, I. Newton Baker,
John H. Johnston, Percival Chubb, H. L.
Bonsall, Dr. Longaker, Harry D. Bush, R. W.
Gilder. (For further accounts of the
funeral, with quotations from addresses,
see 1892.63-1892.74.)

PERIODICALS

16 HALSEY, JOHN J. "Walt Whitman." Dial 12
(January), 317-19.
Whitman, appropriately for an American,
departs from "old-world proprieties and
poetics" to use a primitive mode of song,
full of rapture and prophetic imagination,
despite occasional flaws. In "Universal,"
"that superb ode," he impersonates "a universal Zeit Geist." He has "complementary
ideas of personality and universality,"
"divine compassion," mastery over the truths
of evolution, intolerance of only wrong-
doing. He is "the positive constructive
expression" of Shelley's "negative and
destructive spirit," "a John the Beloved
among men, an Isaiah among seers." His
"best expression will hereafter share the
laurel-wreath only with the words of Emerson
and of Lowell."

17 TRAUBEL, HORACE L. "Lowell--Whitman: A Contrast." Poet-Lore 4 (January), 22-31.
Appreciation of Lowell, followed by
impressionistic appreciation of Whitman,
whose work is of the elements and not of
books, moving the soul, singing life, emancipating literature, asserting immortality.
Whitman is quoted on his purposes.

18 WATTS, D. G. "Walt Whitman." Arena 5 (January), 228-36. Portrait as frontispiece.
Whitman, "the ugly duckling of American
literature," stands for national and spiritual freedom. His consistently unrewarded
nonconformity is admirable, in literature
as in his attitude toward the body. His
poems are discussed in divisions: "Descriptive (miscellaneous) poems," "poems of
nature," "poems of the war," "poems of Democracy and man." Whitman merits recognition for what he can offer America.

19 ANON. "Notes." Critic 17 (2 January), 15.
Paragraph on Whitman's condition, noting
Arena (1892.18).

20 ANON. "Walt Whitman." Harper's Weekly 36 (2
January), 2-3.
At the time of Whitman's current illness,

his "simple, manly character" and "cheerful and self-relying heartiness" are
praised, making him universally well-
regarded. O'Connor's sobriquet for Whitman
was suggested by Tennyson's address to
Wellington ("O good gray head. . . ."). As
a writer, he "will probably be regarded as
an interesting oddity, not as a great poet
or master," having no followers or well-
known phrases. An unidentified critic and
friend of Emerson is quoted from November
1855, criticizing Emerson's praise for
Leaves, "a book without a law, an offence
and an affront."

21 ANON. "Walt Whitman." Illustrated American
9 (16 January), 391-95. Illustrated.
Although Whitman may repel at first,
his moral intention becomes clear, to
"bring men back to sound ways of thinking
and feeling." His syntax and language
pose problems, but he achieves profound
moments of passionate expression. Life
sketch; quotations from critics and poems,
notably "Cradle" and "Lilacs," which mark
him as "inferior to few, if any, of our
time in strength of native genius." He
holds religion as above all. His central
belief is health for body and soul.

22 YOUNG, JOHN RUSSELL. "Men and Memories. Walt
Whitman, 'The Good Gray Head That All Men
Knew'--Whitman as He Was in the War Days--
His Silent, Modest Heroism--His Theology
and Politics--Reminiscences by John Russell
Young." Philadelphia Evening Star (16
January), 5-6.
Reprinted: 1901.17.
Recalls his early admiration for
Whitman's writings and personality, noting
Whitman's flaws and significant influence
on literary style. Various works are
praised, notably "Banner" and "Lilacs,"
"the high water mark of American poetic
genius." Concluded 1892.27.

23 ANON. "Personal." Boston Evening Transcript
(18 January), 5:1.
"Walt Whitman is improving steadily,
and Sunday was able to read the newspapers
for a short time."

24 K[ENNEDY, W. S.] "Walt Whitman." Boston
Evening Transcript (18 January), 6:2.
Letter to editor: Whitman's "pluck and
bull-dog tenacity of life" is worthy of his
Dutch and English ancestry. He is still
sending out a few gift copies of his latest
edition. Few creative artists have been
able so to see the satisfactory completion
of their work, supervising its mechanical
reproduction in the most minute particulars.

*25 ANON. Editorial. Toronto Mail (23 January).
Reported in Willard.
On Whitman's recovery from his attack
last month.

26 [GILDER, JEANNETTE.] "The Lounger." Critic
17 (23 January), 55.
Notes Whitman's condition; quotes a
letter from Burroughs.

27 YOUNG, JOHN RUSSELL. "Men and Memories.
Further Recollections of Walt Whitman--The
Interview with Sit Edwin Arnold--The Message
from Tennyson--Whitman's Lesson to Mankind--
Reminiscences of John Russell Young."
Philadelphia Evening Star (23 January), 5.
Reprinted: 1901.17.
Concludes 1892.22. Quotes Whitman's
comments on Longfellow, Tennyson, Emerson,
Poe. Whitman's faith is more than paganism.
His great work will long endure without
parallel for its depiction of democracy and
"the Dignity of Man and the Divinity of
Love."

28 ANON. "The Good Grey Poet." Christian Leader
11 (4 February), 110.
Biographical sketch, noting Whitman's
editing of various country papers. His
hospital work gave him "not more than two
nights' sleep in the week" for five years.
"In the richest country in the world, its
greatest and most original genius has never
made more than workman's wages or lived in
a house bigger than a cottage." Authors
present at the 1887 Lincoln lecture are
listed. A description of Whitman from a
visitor to Camden is quoted. Whitman is
the prophet of a new age and country, requiring his own means of expression and
freedom from authority. "Captain" proves
him "a great lyric poet," but generally he
is more concerned with accuracy of a descriptive word than with lyric fervor or
form, though at best his lines have an
oceanic sweep similar to that of the Hebrews.
His religious views have modified to "the
hopefulness of a mystic Christian faith."

29 BURROUGHS, JOHN. "Mr. Howells's Agreements
with Whitman." Critic 17 (6 February),
85-86.
The writer and critic must derive principles from nature and life, not from accepted works. Whitman is not merely on the
way to the way, as Howells says (1891.49),
but is on the way itself--toward realization
in art through actual life. Despite flaws
in Whitman's work since his stroke in 1873,
"his work as a whole constitutes one of the
master poetic currents of the world." His
revolution will be accepted.

30 [GILDER, JEANNETTE.] "The Lounger." Critic
17 (6 February), 87.
Notes Young's interesting account
(1892.27), quoting Whitman's remarks on
writers. Notes a corrected typo in the
Burroughs article (1892.29).

31 MORRIS, HARRISON S. "Philadelphia Letter."
Literary World 23 (26 March), 109.
Comments on Gilchrist's portrait of

Whitman, the upcoming publication of
Selected Poems (1892.12), the fund-raising
for Whitman's sickbed.

32 ANON. "Walt Whitman Dead." Buffalo Morning
Express (27 March), 1:2-4.
Account of Whitman's death, life
(largely in his own words), writing career,
with quotations from "that wonderful"
"Myself," "Captain" (which moved Stedman
to tears), "A Midnight Visitor" (one of his
best later poems), "A Twilight Song."
Vistas is his least satisfactory work.
"Worst of all, he violated the poetical law
of suggestion" in his frankness.

33 ANON. "Walt Whitman Passes Away"; "Sketch of
the Poet's Life." New York Herald (27
March), 16:1-3.
Account of Whitman's life (noting his
early days in New York) and death. Examples
of his verse and a Herald interview are
quoted. His poetry will always be a sealed
book to the masses, although the beauty and
pathos of "Cradle" may be universally appreciated, and Two Rivulets contains "poetic
prose and noble verse" with no objectionable
features.

34 ANON. "Walt Whitman Dead." New York Recorder
(27 March), 6:2; also p. 1.
Editorial tribute to "an American of
Americans," now joined with Lincoln.

35 ANON. "Obituary. Death of Walt Whitman."
New York Sun (27 March), 2:3-4.
Account of death, final illness. The
subject of controversy, he died a poor man.
Life sketch. Leaves, "a volume of rhapsodical poems," deals especially with the
American life and progress of the time and
includes everything (however small or
secret). "Of late years the bitter attacks
on Whitman have ceased, and he has been
admitted to be indeed a poet." A disappointment in early life is said to be his
cause for never marrying.

36 ANON. "Death of Walt Whitman--Peaceful End of
the Old Gray Poet at Camden." New York
Times (27 March), 4.
Account of Whitman's death scene, final
days, illness, tomb.

37 ANON. "Walt Whitman's Career--His Was a
Striking and Most Singular Figure--A Remarkable and Original Literary Character--
A Poet Who Was Little Careful of Rhythm and
Had the Courage to Speak Out." New York
Times (27 March), 10:1-3.
Reprinted: Bradley/Blodgett.
Extensive discussion of Whitman's
career, life, and largely negative reception, due to "two or three indecencies"
which would cause less scandal today, as
well as to technical innovations and egotism, though these qualities were exhilarating to some readers. Even the United
States was too restricted a theme for him

as he tried to express the human being in
all its aspects. His poems remain unappreciated by most people except for some of
"Drum-Taps" and poems "free from physiolog-
ical themes" like "Cradle," "which ranks
with the greatest productions of genius in
English." Perhaps future readers will be
drawn by the exaltation with which he embraced all humanity. Whitman is compared
to other writers and artists.

38 ANON. "Walt Whitman Dead." New York Tribune
(27 March), 5:1-2.
Account of life (taken from Burroughs,
1867.1), death, career, with list of works
and writings about him.

39 ANON. "Walt Whitman Is No More." New York
World (27 March), 5:1-2.
Account of life, death, works. To the
biblical parallels of his innovations,
Whitman successfully added a discordant
aspect of his own (although his verse might
have been equally successful as prose paragraphs). The high regard in which he is
held as a man should be granted him as a
poet, although his poetry should be admired
more for its sincerity than for its form.
"Cradle," "Sail Out for Good, Eidólon Yacht,"
and "Old Ireland" are praised. There is
much that is exalted in Whitman, but his
egotism intrudes on his patriotic verse.

40 ANON. "Whitman's Voice Forever Stilled."
Philadelphia Inquirer (27 March), 1:8,
3:7-8. Illustrated.
Extended account of Whitman's last
hours and history of his illness. Brief
account of the career of "decidedly the
most unique American poet of the nineteenth
century." Leaves "deals with moral, social
and political problems," with many poems
personal and "a love of liberty in conscience and politics" pervading all.

41 ANON. "Walt Whitman." Philadelphia Press
(27 March), 4:2-3.
Editorial. Whitman is America's most
significant figure and most picturesque
personality, uttering democracy, the secrets
of nature, the revelation of the spiritual.
Innovative writers take time to be accepted,
but although Whitman was generally disapproved of or ignored, except abroad, he is
well-loved for his personality.

42 ANON. "Walt Whitman Dead"; "The Poet's
Career." Philadelphia Press (27 March),
1:4-5, 2:3-6. Illustrated.
Detailed account of Whitman's end. Extensive account of his life and career.
His poetic revolt may be due to his late
start, in contrast to other great English
poets, although his verse is full of the
life of youth. He loved people and interested the world's great men by his words.
Whitman is quoted on his ideas; translations
and criticism are cited.

1892

43 ANON. "Walt Whitman Dead. End of the Long
 Career of the Poet. His Noble Services
 During the War. His Ideas of Poetry and
 Life--Reflections on Death in His Old Age";
 "A Sketch of His Career. Life and Traits
 of the Poet of the American People." San
 Francisco Chronicle (27 March), 14:1-2.
  Account of life, death, career. One of
 Whitman's last letters is quoted. He is
 "a genuine poet, but his poetical ideas
 were never more than half wrought out." He
 relied on himself, reasoning that the ordi-
 nary man could perceive all possible ideals.
 His style sometimes juxtaposes the highest
 sentiment with "a dozen lines of rubbish."
 "Captain" is praised.

44 ANON. "Past Three Score and Ten. Walt
 Whitman Dies Calmly at His Camden Home."
 Boston Herald (28 March).
  Account of life, death, controversy.
 "With few examples, the younger class of
 writers, both in America and England, are
 his enthusiastic admirers, regarding him as
 one of the few great poets of the world."

45 ANON. "Death of Walt Whitman." London Times
 (28 March), 7:2-3.
 Reprinted: 1896.1.
  Account of death. Whitman's "uncouth
 style," departure from norms of prosody,
 and freedom of language preclude his general acceptance. However, for his earnest
 optimism and freshness of thought his influence upon future American literature is
 sure, although he was better received
 abroad. He "despised the veneer of modern
 society, and advocated a return to the
 original simplicity of character in man,
 with a love of nature and the external
 universe."

46 ANON. "'A Great and Original Genius.' Walt
 Whitman as the London Press Views Him--The
 Funeral." New York Evening Telegram (28
 March), 1:5. Illustrated.
  Quotes London papers on Whitman. The
 funeral of "America's great poet" will be
 one of the most notable such events of
 recent years.

47 ANON. "Walt Whitman's Place." New York
 Evening Telegram (28 March), 4:2.
  Editorial. Whitman's death may reverse
 the prevailing American attitude toward
 "one of the most unique of her literary
 products," the product "of American Bo-
 hemianism--which means, of New York cosmopolitanism."

48 ANON. "Walt Whitman." New York Times (28
 March), 4:4.
  Whitman was not a great poet because he
 failed to give valid form to his fine poetical sensibility, which was particularly
 attuned to the value of common people and
 things. His titles and occasional lines
 and fragments are more poetical than most

of his complete pieces. He was not a
founder of a new poetic school; his picturesque personality was of more interest.

49 ANON. "Walt Whitman's Funeral." New York
 Times (28 March), 2:2.
  Announces funeral and the results of
 the autopsy to which Whitman had agreed:
 his organs were discovered to be "in a
 state of disease that should by all the
 laws of medicine have killed him years ago."

50 ANON. "The Poet of Democracy." Pall Mall
 Gazette (28 March), 1.
  Whitman's philosophy and poetic experiments are based on democracy. "Prayer"
 symbolizes his purpose. "He dignifies 'the
 common and the unclean' by his firm grasp
 of the essential and the elemental." The
 "Whitmanesque frame of mind" his poetry
 requires is only a mood of mid-century
 America; he will be better remembered for
 such prose as Vistas, which gives America
 a needed sense of dignity, and Specimen.

51 ANON. "Walt Whitman. A Memoir of the Poet."
 Pall Mall Gazette (28 March), 3.
  Account of his life, works, earlier
 Gazette references to him. Though certain
 readers projected the coarse naturalism of
 some of his passages upon Whitman himself,
 others saw in Leaves "strength, colour,
 love, and knowledge of nature and the
 utterances of a genuine poet."

52 ANON. "Walt Whitman." Philadelphia Inquirer
 (28 March), 4:3-4.
  Editorial. Whitman's admirers should
 appeal to time and simply assert for the
 present that Whitman "filled an honest and
 a unique position in modern literature."
 Only a few lines of his may be considered
 poetry, for novelty is not poetry; otherwise "we are on the verge of a revolution
 in poetic appreciation." He is mourned as
 a man with great love, but not as founder
 of a poetic school.

53 ANON. "An Autopsy Made on Whitman's Body."
 Philadelphia Press (28 March), 2:1-2.
  Report of funeral plans, visits by his
 brother and by Eakins, Murray, and O'Donovan
 making casts and masks of Whitman's body in
 preparation for sculpting. The reasons for
 the autopsy and its findings are described.

54 ANON. Editorial. San Francisco Chronicle
 (28 March), 4:3.
  "Had it not been for his open warfare
 on religion and on conventionality Whitman
 would have enjoyed a far larger measure of
 popularity, for no one can read him without
 being struck by his vigor, his originality
 and his love of nature." Despite such
 faults as excessive cataloguing and occasional coarseness, he is to be admired for
 his proud independence and wholesome nature.
 We need a selection of his best work.

55 ANON. "Walt Whitman, 'The Only One.'" Springfield Daily Republican (28 March). Reprinted: 1892.125.

Tribute to Whitman as "messenger of democracy" and "a great poet." His life and career are sketched, with particular discussion of the 1876 edition and his periodical publications, and with praise for Vistas and various poems.

56 [CHAMBERLIN, JOSEPH E.] "The Listener." Boston Evening Transcript (28 March), 4.

Whitman was unequalled in "his sublime optimism, his splendid faith in the health, the goodness, the divinity of the earth and of humanity." His writings will take care of themselves, fully expressing him. Since he was a great man, the world will eventually discover his great message.

57 C[HAMBERLIN], J[OSEPH] E. "Walt Whitman. 'The Good Gray Poet' Is Dead." Boston Evening Transcript (28 March), 6.

Traces Whitman's life and work. Anecdotal impressions of Whitman from the Pfaffians are quoted. Whitman made his life serve his ideals.

58 CONWAY, M[ONCURE] D. "Walt Whitman." Manchester Guardian (28 March), 8:3-4.

Whitman incarnated American democracy, scorning the restraints of verse and monarchy. His poetry had an order of its own. Visits with Whitman and Emerson are recalled. Whitman was not such a rough as he presented himself to be. His later editions show little decline from his earlier vigor, sincerity, largeness, and freedom. Inaccurate account of Whitman's dismissal by Harlan.

59 [FORMAN, H. B.] "Death of Walt Whitman." London Daily Chronicle (28 March), 3:5-7.

Whitman's life and work (traced extensively) are remarkable for vitality. His wide experience was appropriate for his work in "depicting a huge peopled landscape" in "a series of spiritualised realistic studies," in form and expression "less indebted to previous literature than any productions of a literary kind which have survived." He has been subject to much misunderstanding. Though his work is appropriately placed under a single title, "several of the most important fresh poems" written since 1855 "have thus been deprived of the advantage of challenging attention as new books under fresh titles." "Death's Valley" (described) has been kept back for some time by Harper's, waiting for a fitting time which should be now for this "noble legacy from the poet." Whitman's thought and qualities suggest "some primeval Titan" seeking to save the human race, a task which seems possible through this work since Whitman has suffered yet affirms life. His words to Mary Davis on death are quoted. The "great doctrine" of this great

optimist is set forth. The plot chosen for his grave is described.

60 [HIGGINSON, T. W.] "Walt Whitman. His Death on Saturday Evening--His Life and His Literary Place." New York Evening Post (28 March), 11:1-3. Reprinted: 1892.120. Extract reprinted: 1892.102. Revised: 1899.8.

Brief life sketch. The English find "picturesque and novel" Whitman's "vague sentiment of democracy" which "is to us comparatively trite and almost conventional." His works gained attention "by his superb and now blighted physique," the exaggerated acclaim of his hospital services, and their role as curiosities. The earlier revolts against form by Tupper and Ossian are poorly regarded now. His flaws diminish in his later work, with shorter lines and better-defined rhythms, as in "Darest Thou Now, O Soul?" However, his admirers usually place "Captain" first. Morbidly concentrating on sex, he lacks the sentiment of individual love and the ideal side of passion. This writer testifies to Whitman's "bad influence" on many young men. His senility, "the retribution for 'the drench of the passions' in youth," compared unfavorably with the old age of Bryant and Whittier. Whitman is gifted in occasional strains and in his choice of titles, e.g., "When Lilies last in Dooryard Bloomed" [sic], but he is affected in using foreign phrases and talking of labor and war. He has such ingredients of a poet's nature as sympathy and a keen eye but lacks form, "and without form there is no immortality." There follow favorable quotations on Whitman from London Standard (unlocated), 1892.45, 1892.50.

*61 ANON. "Walt Whitman." Sydney Morning Herald (29 March), 8. Reprinted: McLeod.

Public opinion on Whitman may change with his death, but his popularity and recognition during his lifetime "have not been nearly so cordial in England as in his own country," because of his treatment of sex and "his rhythmic extravagances." Sketches Whitman's life. Notes his ability to encourage thought in his readers, his sympathy with nature, and his skill in portraying impressions. His art, though appealing to those "tired of the smooth vapidities and empty jingles of most modern verse," is of less interest than his vigorous, free, and manly thought, which speaks for the American continent; English readers remain unsure.

62 TRAILL, H. D. "Walt Whitman." St. James's Gazette 24 (29 March), 4-5.

Whitman's claims to being a poet cannot be left to posterity to decide, as recent commentators suggest, for his unpoetic lines have already determined that he is not.

1892

The chief praise he has received has been
for his power and thought, which prose
writers may have as well. Even his ideas
are not so original, though he has some
striking phrases and passages, like "the
noble apostrophe to Death," "a solemn and
moving strain of reflection."

63 ANON. "Whitman." Camden Post (30 March), 1.
Account of the funeral today, printing
the speeches of Harned, Bucke, and Ingersoll
(see 1892.15).

64 ANON. "'Good-by, Walt! Good-by from All You
Loved on Earth!' Walt Whitman at Rest in
the Cyclopean Tomb Which He Built for Himself. Simple and Impressive Funeral Services. Notable People Gathered at This
Marriage Feast of Death." New York Evening
Telegram (30 March), 1:1-2. Illustration.
The ceremony earlier today was "a
funeral without tears, and yet a funeral
more full of love than are most funerals."
"Lowly working men and women, white men and
colored, rubbed elbows with men whose names
are known to fame. There was affection in
the low voices. That which lay before them
had once framed the personality of a sweet
and tender and sympathetic friend, and they
knew it." Harned and Bucke are quoted (see
1892.15).

65 ANON. "Walt Whitman's Bequest." New York
Evening Telegram (30 March), 4:2.
In a recent interview in the Telegram
(unlocated), Whitman said that "behind all
things is 'the human critter,'" inspiring,
as were many of his thoughts. The world
should remember the debt it owes "this rare
genius."

66 [BONSALL, H. L.] Editorial. Camden Post (30
March).
Quoted in 1923.57.
Whitman was strongly the poet of the
people, of "virile democracy and universal
comradeship," and the people love him,
whatever the literary quidnuncs are de-
ciding about "his 'unique position' in the
world of letters." His tomb will be the
destination of many pilgrims in the future.

67 H[INTON], H[OWARD]. "The Poet's Carol to
Death." New York Home Journal (30 March),
4:1.
Quotes the "lovely" "Death Carol," with
praise for "Lilacs," apt words now for
Whitman, "the greatest and most original
poet" of America, who, "beyond all others,
has voiced the new life of the New World."
He "speaks directly from personal experience of life and immediate contact with
the soul," with Homeric simplicity and
strength. No contemporary poet has more
phrases and lines that send a thrill through
the reader's soul. His fame will grow until he is regarded as "the first spokesman
of that newer and larger life which animates
the New World democracy."

68 TILLING, A. E. "Walt Whitman. In Memoriam."
Bristol Times and Mirror (30 March).
Rhymed poem of tribute: "O voice of
hope, thy songs are sung." Leaves "shall
still be green," though Whitman is called
by "The Master."

69 WHITMAN, WALT. "A Hitherto Unpublished Poem
by Walt Whitman." New York Home Journal
(30 March), 4:2.
Reprinted: Uncollected.
Prints for the first time verses "New
Year's Day, 1848," verses Whitman wrote "in
the album of a lady, . . . interesting as a
specimen of his early essays in verse."

70 ANON. "Walt Whitman." Independent 44 (31
March), 439.
Revision of 1881.54.
Whitman wrote "the noisiest, noisomest
stuff ever called poetry," with coarse
catalogues; lack of structure, music, and
imagination; "strained and repulsive" diction. Nothing good can be said of one who
has added nothing good to our literature.

71 ANON. "Walt Whitman Laid at Rest." New York
Times (31 March), 3:7.
Account of funeral, quoting Ingersoll
(see 1892.15).

72 ANON. "Walt Whitman Burial." New York Tribune
(31 March), 6:6.
Account of funeral, quoting Stedman's
poem and much of Ingersoll's address (see
1892.15).

73 ANON. "Thousands Mourn for Walt Whitman."
Philadelphia Inquirer (31 March), 1:6-7,
5:7. Illustrated.
Extended account of the funeral, a
tribute worthy of Whitman's life, showing
the respect of many for "his love of humanity and his deathless song", the democratic
throng viewing his body and attending the
funeral, floral tributes, trip to the cemetery, significant mourners (including a
representative from Twain), addresses,
burial, the crowd taking flowers from the
stage at the end as mementos. Ingersoll's
address is quoted (see 1892.15).

74 ANON. "Whitman Buried as He Wished." Philadelphia Press (31 March), 1:6-7, 2:5-6.
Illustrated.
Extended account of the funeral, including Ingersoll's eulogy in full and quotations
from Harned and Bucke (see 1892.15). The
crowds at Whitman's house are described,
the great number of women and children
present proving that he "was a great favorite with women and tenderly loved by
children." The springtime scene at the
tomb, described, fit nature's poet.

75 CLAUDIUS CLEAR [pseud.]. "The Correspondence
of Claudius Clear: Walt Whitman." British
Weekly 11 (31 March), 373.

Though opinion will remain sharply divided over Whitman, some readers will always consider him "a great and original writer, a true poet, and one whose conception of the universe was in the end large, pure and pitiful." He fights against "the anti-Christian notion that the universe is common and unclean," and embraces night and death, as in "Death Carol," his finest poem.

76 ANON. "The 'Good Gray Poet' Gone." Literary News 13 (April), 115.
    Obituary, emphasizing his eventual status, probably "among the 'immortals,'" if only for "Lilacs." "Cradle" also ranks "with the great products of genius" and justifies the praise given him.

77 ANON. "Notes and News." Poet-Lore 4 (April), 229-30.
    Whitman's death reminds us of his message and all that his life will represent to the world. With his inclusiveness, he was the first writer to express intentionally democracy in literature. His style "was not only the man, it was also the message." His importance "in the evolution of poetry and spiritual thought is very great."

78 CRAWFORD, ANNIE LAZIERE. "Why We Read." Vassar Miscellany 21 (April), 349.
    Whitman is listed incidentally among writers whose perceptions and sympathies help us better to understand life.

79 HAIGHT, B. H. "'Whitman's Legacy.'" Vassar Miscellany 21 (April), 369-72.
    Whitman "writes his inmost thought in plainest words," with a freedom of expression based on natural rhythm and spontaneous emotion rather than fixed laws. He glories in the divinity of his manhood. His catalogues are endowed with keen sympathy. The world has yet to accept the legacy of himself as representing modern man.

80 JOHNSON, WILLIAM H. "Whitman and Jesus." Conservator 3 (April), 12.
    Whitman and Jesus were both powerful personalities. To deify either is to wrong humanity in the name of religion.

*81 PARKER, GILBERT. "Walt Whitman." Literary Opinion 2 (April), 1-6.
    Reported in CHAL.

82 [TRAUBEL, HORACE, ed.] "At the Graveside of Walt Whitman." Conservator 3 (April), Supplement.
    Reprinted: 1892.15.
    Prints the readings and speeches from the funeral as well as Burroughs's essay.

83 ZUBOF, ROMAN I. "Walt Whitman in Europe." Writer 6 (April), 63-65.

A forward-looking American, Whitman recognized "no beauty higher than creative nature." Zubof records his personal experience with the Dublin library's refusal to purchase Whitman's immoral book. Readers discover in Whitman's work a force, sentiment, and moral passion that amply compensate for occasional roughness or looseness of expression.

84 ANON. Note. Philadelphia Inquirer (1 April), 4:4.
    "This for Walt Whitman: His was a poet's heart, whatever were his lines."

85 ANON. "Walt Whitman." Black and White (2 April), 424, 426.
    Sketch of Whitman's life. With occasional indecencies, he is great in spite of his theories of formlessness and democracy and most impressive when he simply confronts nature. The good in him will survive in anthologies.

86 ANON. "Walt Whitman." The Graphic (London) 45 (2 April), 418, 424.
    Whitman may not be considered a poet, lacking "the power of rhythmic utterance in the highest sense," but he was an important writer. His central thought is that in each human being is "the germ of great qualities." Hence, he opposed mere conventionality. Though his ideas are not really original, he expressed them in his best work "with so much freshness and vigour that it had at first an air of novelty" and a strong influence. He acted on his precepts, with joy in common things and his inner world. His optimistic writings are a refreshing contrast to the generally pessimistic tone of contemporary literature. Biographical, character, and career sketch with Sarony portrait on p. 424.

87 ANON. "Death of Walt Whitman." Illustrated London News 100 (2 April), 415. Illustrated. Photograph by Sarony, p. 433.
    Whitman's life corresponds to "his work as the poet of the common human life." In some respects he is a typical American. His life and work are traced, including his "splendid poetry" on the war and his unsparing realism in "Adam."

88 ANON. "Walt Whitman." Newcastle (England) Weekly Chronicle (2 April), 4:3.
    Editorial. Whitman's life, with its diversified pursuits, was his most memorable poetry, for his lines often have little music or philosophy. He will be remembered not as a poet but as a preacher of a lofty though impossible creed of universal freedom.

*89 ANON. Unpublished fragment by Whitman. New Orleans Item (2 April).
    Quoted in Uncollected.
    Prints a fragment of a poem by Whitman

1892

(actually a parody), "unprinted until now,"
written a year ago while he was in Duluth,
a city which impressed him. (See 1931.60.)

90 ANON. "Walt Whitman." Public Opinion 12 (2
    April), 659.
        From Philadelphia Inquirer (unlocated
    in issues between Whitman's death and this
    publication date): account of the dispute
    over Whitman's verse, "deliberately harsh,
    purposely unmetrical," lacking the musical
    expression, domestic emotions, and dramatic
    element which so many readers seek.
    Whitman's merit was that he tore away arti-
    ficial covers to show "the real man without
    adornment or disguise." His appeal for
    those in the "hotbeds of culture" lies in
    his naturalness and "plain, unvarnished
    humanity that is likely to make his verse
    enduring."

91 ANON. "Walt Whitman." Saturday Review 73
    (2 April), 378-79.
        Whitman was truly sui generis. He
    stood up against English and American
    criticism for many years, until eulogists
    "extolled his crazy and childish politics,"
    "palliated his marine-store catalogues,"
    and "went mad over his daring imitation of
    the naughty little boys." Eventually his
    true genius became recognized, despite his
    small intellectual power and defects in
    morals, politics, and aesthetics. Unlike
    any American but Poe, he possessed "the
    three things indispensable to the poet--a
    poetic phrase, a poetic rhythm, and a
    poetic imagination," evident "even in his
    most perverse and prosaic moods."

92 ANON. "The Good Gray Poet." Sheffield Weekly
    Independent (2 April), 9:3-4.
        Obituary article. Americans have grad-
    ually joined the English in honoring "the
    laureate of their national aspirations, the
    singer of the ideal democracy." Whitman's
    method of writing, on scraps of paper later
    pinned together, explains his irregular
    rhythms.

93 ANON. "What the 'World' Says." Sheffield
    Weekly Independent (2 April), 9:5.
        A paragraph in this column describes
    the writer's visit nineteen years ago to
    Whitman's Washington attic, where they
    spoke of English and American poets.

94 ANON. "What 'Truth' Says." Sheffield Weekly
    Independent (2 April), 9:5.
        A paragraph in this column notes that
    Whitman, "a worthy and estimable old gen-
    tleman," was no poet, writing "very muddled
    prose." John Bright replied to this
    writer's questioning of Bright's high regard
    for Whitman by expressing doubts as to
    whether the writer could appreciate Whitman
    with any amount of explanation.

95 BURROUGHS, JOHN. "Walt Whitman The Poet of
    Democracy." Christian Union 45 (2 April),
    636-37.
        Whitman was the first to depict fully
    democratic thoughts in literature. "He is
    more akin to the climate overhead and to
    the geology under foot than to any conscious
    traits and tendencies of the people." "He
    projects the America of the future," cor-
    recting its present tendencies. Europe
    appreciates him as the first American poet
    because of his new spirit. He stresses
    equality of the sexes, sacredness of the
    common people, an all-accepting religious
    spirit, identity of body and soul. He
    rejects notions of the ridiculous and the
    decorous, permitting no curtains of art
    between himself and his reader.

96 _____. "Walt Whitman 30 May 1819-1892 March
    25 [sic]." Critic 17 (2 April), 199-200.
    Portrait by G. Kruell.
        The disapproval of such men as Lowell
    and Matthew Arnold may be significant, yet
    Whitman is highly regarded by other major
    figures, including Europeans whose poetic
    standard is presumably more highly developed
    than ours. Whitman's culture, sympathetic
    nature, and physical presence are vouched
    for. Burroughs quotes his diary entry
    regarding Whitman's response to Swinburne's
    attack (1887.63). Whitman is the first to
    embody himself in literary composition. He
    will endure not for his ideas but for his
    poetic emotion and the spirit behind his
    work, too often misunderstood. Later works
    like "Prayer" and "Redwood" are inferior to
    such earlier works as "Drum-Taps." His
    democratic ideal is not to level all men
    but to present the above-average man. There
    follow accounts of Whitman's life, death,
    and contributions to the Critic, and a re-
    print of Emerson's letter (1855.12), pp.
    201-2.

97 C., L. C., and A MAN OF LETTERS. "Walt Whitman
    and Mr. Watts." Pall Mall Gazette (2 April),
    2.
        L. C. C.'s letter comments on Watts's
    criticism (1892.109) and Whitman's supposed
    indecency, since quotations from Whitman
    "figured very largely in the action about
    the Slang Dictionary." "A Man of Letters"
    complains of the cruel remarks by Watts on
    "this sweet old man." It is not surprising
    that he should be unintelligible to many,
    just as "startling originality and absolute
    large-heartedness" always are "to the pedant
    and the cynic."

98 [CAMPBELL, W. W.?] "At the Mermaid Inn."
    Toronto Globe (2 April).
    Quoted in McMullin (1975).
        Whitman is a great poet, truly the
    singer of America, with unparalleled "simple
    and unaffected egotism," enjoyment of life,
    interest in America, despite much that jars
    the sensitive mind. Lincoln and Whitman

are both representative, "grotesque and rude as was the age," unique in world history.

99 CRINKLE, NYM [Andrew Carpenter Wheeler.] "Whitman's Moods. Nym Crinkle Writes of the Dead Poet's Characteristics. What His Optimism Caused." New York Commercial Advertiser (2 April), 5.

Recollections of Whitman watching the stream of life in New York, 1856; by the sea; in the Partons' home. Whitman's quality was cognitive rather than creative, "a magnificent, simple realism which pondered and wondered, but never tried to reconstruct." He did not have the masculine drive to struggle and overcome, but rather the feminine endurance, being not a great character but a great poet. The decline of the contemplative in him and the growth of the reflective parallel the decay of his magnificent physical powers. His reading of Isaiah was an influence on him.

100 DUNCAN, JAMES G. "Walt Whitman." Bolton Journal (2 April).

Obituary tribute to Whitman, his cheerful personality and appearance, his unselfish and pure life "in keeping with the Greek idea of morality." He is a poet of the open air, not the drawing room, seeking perfect liberty and unconventionality. His philosophy, owing much to Hegel, is described, as are his new attitudes toward death, morality, sex. He represents the culmination of the influence of Emerson and Thoreau. Some poems contain "a wonderful rushing and throbbing." "Broad-Axe" is "worthy of Isaiah in parts." "Drum-Taps" is "the finest collection of martial and camp songs that have ever appeared." "As a moral teacher, as a figure in the world's history, as a feature of the nineteenth century, Whitman has already been accepted by those who are capable of correct judgment." However, a future poet may join Whitman's naturalness and vigor with Tennyson's beauty and grace.

101 [GILDER, JEANNETTE.] "The Lounger." Critic 17 (2 April), 202.
Reprinted: 1892.116.

Describes and protests the squalor of Whitman's room which was not emphasized adequately in her prior description (1891. 53).

102 [HIGGINSON, T. W.] "Obituary. Walt Whitman." Literary Digest 4 (2 April), 614.
Extract reprinted from 1892.60.

103 [MABIE, HAMILTON.] "Walt Whitman." Christian Union 45 (2 April), 632-33.
It is now time to judge Whitman fairly, appreciating his later meditations as nobler than his early cruder work. He was a striking personality and fortunate in expressing himself. He must be approached

with an open mind toward his "work of very uncommon force." He has simple, primitive instincts and a prophetic view of democracy. His imagination surpasses that of most contemporary American poets. His physical frankness was an error, though void of impurity. His form may be prosaic or have "the spontaneity and breadth of the older primitive poetry." He will live through "the poems which came glowing from his imagination" ("Captain," "Lilacs," "Singer in Prison," "Cradle"), rather than "the longer and more elaborate works which betray effort and artifice."

104 Φ. "Walt Whitman." The Speaker 5 (2 April), 403-4.
Recollection of his last visit with Whitman, noting Whitman's optimism, magnetism, nobility in simple living, ability to deal with the common people. Though more characteristically American than Lowell, he may have more admirers in England than in America. He was unlike the average American and lacked "the nervous American restlessness" which Higginson admires. His ideal was "the perfect union in man of a superb physique with a transcendently noble spirit." He became increasingly less nationalistic. His opinions on English and European writers are cited. He was most influenced by Carlyle.

105 PHILLIPS, BARNET. "Walt Whitman's Way." Harper's Weekly 36 (2 April), 318-19.
After a discussion of the methods of other writers, Harrison Morris is quoted on Whitman's method of writing. His verse "pulsates with strong life" and "erosive power," but he was not rapid in composition. With regard to the Murger poem ("Midnight Visitor") which he used to recite, it is noted that "he knew no French."

106 R[HYS, ERNEST?] "Recollections of Walt Whitman." Illustrated London News 100 (2 April), 418.
Although Whitman accepted death, his loss is great to those who knew him. A visit to Whitman shortly before Christmas 1887 is recalled, with description of Whitman's impressiveness, serenity, message to the young. A letter is printed in facsimile.

107 R[OLLESTON], T. W. "Obituary. Walt Whitman." Academy 41 (2 April), 325-27.
Reprinted: 1892.167.
Whitman's book grew "not by mere addition, but by an organic process of growth." Sketch of Whitman's life, with praise for his unprotesting death, in accord with the mood of his poetry. He saw the divine in the ordinary, like Wordsworth, but surpassed him in proclaiming the whole body and accepting all, thus becoming perhaps the first truly democratic poet and a strong example for future native poetic growth. The power,

1892

sincerity, and "uplifting tide of elemental
life" in Whitman's poetry are praised.

108 WATROUS, A. E. "Walt Whitman." Harper's
Weekly 36 (2 April), 317-18. Illustrated.
The question remains "whether his contempt for the arts of poetry has not deprived him of the power of leading others
as close to nature's shrine as he always
dwelt." He sang the greatness of America,
its people and their possibilities. His
war poems were a great public service.
Leaves suffered suppression because of
concern for propriety, for there never was
any question as to its morality. His
spirit remained innocent and optimistic to
the end. His lack of popularity may be due
his failure to appeal to women.

109 WATTS, THEODORE. "Walt Whitman." Athenaeum
99, no. 3362 (2 April), 436-37.
Reprinted: 1892.170.
It is regretted that Whitman never came
to London, because he had "the genius of a
magnetic personality," although no one
would credit him with poetic genius. He
was so highly regarded in England only
because he was an American. Watts admits
earlier ridicule of Whitman but praises him
now as "a fine and manly soul." Such lyrics
as the poems about Lincoln and about death
are "almost sublime," revealing his poetic
sensibility. He should have paid more
attention to meter and grammar, although
biblical rhythm may yet come into its own.
Whitman's ideas are rather muddle-headed;
his indecency is harmless.

110 ANON. "Her Point of View." New York Times
(3 April), 12:1.
Account of a woman who saw a face
through a train window about the time of
Whitman's death. Upon reading a newspaper
account of the death, she recognized
Whitman's face as the one she had seen
through the window.

111 BARRON, ELWYN A. "Whitman." Chicago Inter-
Ocean (3 April).
Long poem in free verse: those readers
who recognize the power throughout nature
should acclaim Whitman's poetry.

112 F[REDERIC], H[AROLD.] "A Fine Bismarck
Boon . . . Walt Whitman's Death the Great
Literary Sensation." New York Times (3
April), 1:6.
Reprinted: 1892.122.
Paragraph from London on the wide
coverage of Whitman's death in the English
press. "The English discovered the virile
characteristic note in Whitman when we
ourselves seemed deaf to it. It is not
improbable that his future place in American estimation will be largely based upon
the reflection of British admiration back
to our own shores."

113 HABBERTON, JOHN. "The Good Gray Poet. Walt
Whitman's Life Quarter of a Century Ago."
Chicago Sunday Tribune (3 April), 25:5.
Reprinted: 1892.171.
Recalls knowing Whitman in his New York
days, mentions his habits of dress and
hairy chest. "His general appearance suggested burned-out paganism complicated with
rum and abhorring the bathtub." His book
is "the outcome of a course of determined
and gross indulgence which all of the
author's decent friends deplored." His
mind and enviable physiology were "permanently weakened by excesses committed in
his prime," for his later work did not
fulfill the promise of his earlier work.

114 S[MALLEY], G. W. "The News of Europe." New
York Tribune (3 April), 1:3.
Reprinted: 1892.122.
Paragraph on the honor England is paying
Whitman, more than he is receiving in America, due to his homage from Tennyson and
Swinburne, who "liked something else in
him than his formlessness and chaotic
method." "He is discussed as an individuality rich in temperment, and of a very considerable intellectual force and originality," but his lack of poetic form "removes
him from the list of true poets."

115 ANON. "Walt Whitman's Will." New York Times
(4 April), 5:2.
Briefly notes the general terms of
Whitman's will, read last night.

116 [GILDER, JEANNETTE.] Paragraph. Elmira Daily
Gazette and Free Press (4 April).
Reprint of 1892.101.

117 SCHUMAKER, J. G. "Reminiscences of Walt
Whitman. An Early Novel from His Pen Mentioned." New York Tribune (4 April), 8:2.
Recollections of Whitman from Schumaker's
first acquaintance with him in the 1840s,
knowing Whitman's family, Whitman's meeting
with General Garfield, seeing Whitman after
Lincoln's assassination, which he interpreted as "'a type of the Rebellion'"; his
drinking of gin cocktails while writing
Franklin Evans; his arrest and trial for
assault when a young man.

118 ANON. Editorial. Independent 44 (7 April),
479-80.
Many letters were received approving
the recent estimate of Whitman (1892.70).
Stedman's "Good-bye, Walt" is printed with
John B. Tabb's Whitmanesque parody of it in
slangy free verse.

119 CONWAY, MONCURE D. "Walt Whitman. My Little
Wreath of Thoughts and Memories." Open
Court 6 (7 April), 3199-3200.
Recollections of a thirty-six-year
acquaintance with Whitman, his appearance,
childlike humility and delight in approval,
funeral, visits to him in 1855 and shortly

before his death, lack of prurient intention, feeling toward democracy, poetic pioneering.

120 [HIGGINSON, T. W.] "Walt Whitman." Nation 54 (7 April), 262-64.
Reprint of 1892.60 with minor change.
Revised: 1899.8.

121 ANON. "Walt Whitman's Will." New York Times (8 April), 4:7.
Describes briefly Whitman's estate; the plan to raise money to preserve his house for future visits by admirers.

122 ANON. "The Battle Not Yet Ended." Critic 17 (9 April), 216.
Summarizes and quotes recent newspaper comments on Whitman's death.

123 ANON. "The Funeral." Critic 17 (9 April), 215-16.
Account of funeral; Stedman's poem "Good-bye, Walt"; comments on Whitman's poem "Death's Valley" in Harper's (April).

124 ANON. "New York Notes." Literary World 23 (9 April), 126.
An old friend from Whitman's New York days has called him "the most genial and the kindest of fellows," clean in mind, body, and speech. His titles are often some of the best things he wrote, with "many a brilliant gem."

125 ANON. Obituary. Literary World 23 (9 April), 132-33.
Reprint of 1892.55 and Stedman's poem (see 1892.15).

126 ANON. "Walt Whitman." Literary World 23 (9 April), 126.
Whitman "may be called the Columbus of the spirit of the New Continent," with "extraordinary grasp" of all, not only the higher emotion and thought of the people which Whittier and Longfellow portrayed more wisely. He aimed to express "the infinite fraternity of things" but fell short because of his artistic flaws and contempt for the natural reserves of soul and body. "A great and unique poet," he will long be remembered for such work as "Captain" and "Cradle."

127 ANON. "Was Walt Whitman a Poet?" Public Opinion 13 (9 April), 21.
From Brooklyn Citizen (unlocated): Ingersoll in his funeral address should have pointed out some of the supreme words Whitman has supposedly uttered in greater number than any other recent writer. His personality may be admirable, without contributing much poetry, for poetry requires "expression as well as comprehension, form as well as matter," and "Whitman's mind was essentially tuneless," a quality he came to regard as an excellence. His works may be referred to for the next century

as expressing "certain temporary aberrations in the literary development of this century, but otherwise he is not likely to fill much of a place in the mind of posterity."

128 ANON. "Walt Whitman." Punch 102 (9 April), 179.
Reprinted: 1892.151; 1893.11; 1905.11; Legler.
Poem of tribute in rhymed couplets: "'The good gray Poet' gone! Brave, hopeful WALT!"

*129 ANON. "Walt Whitman: An American Poet, Recently Deceased." Sydney Town and Country Journal (9 April), 19.
Reprinted: McLeod.
Whitman was a "perfectly original" and "most remarkable" figure. His poetic theory, rejecting the artificial and conventional, is not hard to understand. His life is sketched. His reputation has gradually taken firm root in England. His positive personal influence is noted.

130 BURROUGHS, JOHN. "Walt Whitman, After Death." Critic 17 (9 April), 215.
Letter in response to the Evening Post obituary (1892.60), denied publication by the editor. The allegations of Whitman's debauched life are denied, "Adam" representing not Whitman's own experience so much as the male generating principle. He is admired not by British lovers of Artemus Ward and Josh Billings but by such men of culture as Symonds, whose letter on Whitman is quoted.

131 CAVAZZA, E. "Walt Whitman." Literary World 23 (9 April), 126.
Short rhymed poem of tribute.

132 COLLINSON, JOSEPH. Letter. Newcastle (England) Weekly Chronicle (9 April), 5:4.
Cites Maclise (1883.1) as source for calling Whitman's acclaim a hoax. However, Whitman has two poems unequalled in America for passion, depth, and nobility of thought, "Cradle" and "Lilacs." Whitman will survive as the singer of the eternal themes of friendship, love, and death. (Ideas identical to those in 1891.1.)

133 EDGAR, PELHAM. "Walt Whitman. A Thoughtful Essay on His Personality and Genius." Toronto Mail (9 April), 12.
Whitman extends the poetic message of the early years of the century, revolting against literary conventionalism. His religious attitudes, friendship, egoism (a factor of strength), democratic spirit, and mystic quality are summarized. His verse is "its own magnificent apology."

134 PATTERSON, JAMES. Letter. Athenaeum 99 (9 April), 470.
Explains Whitman's introduction into England via Thomas Dixon.

1892

135 S[TEAD, W. T.?] "Walt and Watts. (An
    Explanation.)" Pall Mall Gazette (9
    April), 3.
       Reprinted: 1892.174.
       Rhymed poem on Whitman not writing in
    meter and therefore being rejected by Watts
    (1892.109).

136 ANON. "Adieu, Walt Whitman!" Frank Leslie's
    Illustrated Weekly 74 (14 April), 183.
    Photographs of funeral, p. 189.
       Ingersoll's "exaggerated eulogy was
    characteristic of its object." Though the
    subject of much controversey, Whitman was
    greatly loved, as evidenced by the crowds
    and many kinds of people at his funeral.
    "He was the peer of the greatest, the
    friend of the most lowly, the sympathizer
    with the degraded and suffering, and the
    champion of the oppressed."

137 THOMAS, Prof. CALVIN. Letter. Nation 54 (14
    April), 286.
       Response to Higginson (1892.60) cor-
    recting him on the origin of the phrase
    "God-intoxicated man."

138 ANON. Letter. Athenaeum 99 (16 April), 504.
       Correspondence from Philadelphia de-
    scribing Whitman's funeral, his face
    (beautiful in death), his welcome of death.

139 A READER. "Walt Whitman." Newcastle Weekly
    Chronicle (16 April), 5.
       Whitman was an original force in art
    who made his own way. His revolt resem-
    bled Wordsworth's, but with a much wider
    range, rejecting artificial technique and
    morality. His intentions excuse his exag-
    gerations and mistakes. He is "the first
    indication of the new world possessing any
    power to produce a literature entirely its
    own." He suggested that the literature of
    the future should be of use, not a mere
    plaything.

140 ANON. "Personalia." Critic 17 (16 April),
    231-32.
       Data on Whitman's estate; commentary on
    Emerson's displeasure at Whitman's use of
    his letter; compendium of English and Amer-
    ican comments on Whitman's death.

141 ANON. "Walt Whitman." Illustrated American
    10 (16 April), 388.
       Whitman was certainly great, formed in
    the mould of seers, sympathizing with all.
    His contempt for conventional restraints
    was probably a mere mannerism rather than
    a manifestation of style and communion with
    nature. He was capable of exquisite deli-
    cacy, which might have become more pro-
    nounced if his early life had been spent
    in harmony with nature rather than the
    city. He is not only American, but sang
    the song of all humanity.

142 ANON. "A Whitman Enthusiast." Radical Review
    (London) (16 April), 44.
       Paragraph on John Johnston's relation
    with Whitman, whose photograph was reproduced
    in the Radical Review a fortnight earlier
    (unlocated).

143 BUCHANAN, ROBERT. "Walt Whitman." Great
    Thoughts (16 April), 256.
       Reprinted: 1901.2.
       Poem in six rhymed quatrains ("One
    hand-shake, Walt!") reprinted from The
    Echo (unlocated).

144 INGERSOLL, ROBERT. "Walt Whitman.--Ingersoll's
    Eulogy." Pall Mall Gazette (16 April), 7.
       Reprint of funeral address (see 1892.15).

145 MONROE, HARRIET. "A Word About Walt Whitman."
    Critic 17 (16 April), 231.
       Reprinted: Hindus.
       The masses do not appreciate Whitman
    because he too accurately presents rude
    reality; they prefer more refined poets
    like Longfellow and Bryant. European
    readers meanwhile appreciate Whitman's
    vigorous qualities, representative of the
    young democracy. Whitman does not fulfill
    the artist's tasks but he gives us speci-
    mens from nature.

146 WALFORD, [Mrs.] L. B. "London Letter."
    Critic 17 (16 April), 228.
       Whitman is currently a popular topic in
    England, but many, such as an ex-Lord Chan-
    cellor of the columnist's acquaintance,
    haven't read him. Whitman is an acquired
    taste which the mother country will probably
    never acquire. His claims "as a powerful
    and original plain-dealer with facts" are
    now sure, but his rugged mode and lack of
    reticence are jarring.

147 THERRELL, DAN MacLAUGHLIN. "A Plea for Walt
    Whitman." New York News (19 April).
       Defense of Whitman and his verse against
    recent superficial criticism; explanation
    of the philosophy behind his treatment of
    sex. His sins against syntax and English
    grammar support what he expresses. His
    work is no worse than such works of other
    "manly poets" as "Venus and Adonis," "Don
    Juan," "Faust."

148 C. "Walt Whitman." Nation 54 (21 April), 301.
       Letter defending Whitman from accusa-
    tions of indulgence (1892.60), explaining
    Whitman's egotism and outspokeness. His
    formal faults are insignificant: "good
    technique is common in the world; insight
    and inspiration are rare."

149 ALDRICH, CHARLES. Letter. Critic 17 (23
    April), 245-46.
       Testifies to Whitman's situation as
    described in 1892.101. Whitman's American
    friends who helped support him were fewer
    than his English ones.

150 ANON. "Walt Whitman." Critic 17 (23 April),
245.
Quotes various current comments on
Whitman.

151 ANON. Reprint of 1892.128. Critic 17 (23
April), 245.

152 L. Commentary. Toronto Globe (23 April).
Comments upon Watts (1892.109) and
Saturday Review (1892.91). The intense
differences of opinion regarding Whitman
are due to the strength of personality in
his work, greater than that in other
writers.

153 RAFFALOVICH, ANDRÈ. Sonnet. Critic 17 (23
April), 245.
Tribute to Whitman from The Hawk (un-
located).

154 ANON. "New Publications. Walt Whitman."
New York Tribune (26 April), 8:1.
Review of Selected Poems (1892.12).
Whitman's early offensive barbarism is now
recognized as specifically modern. His distinctive experience of democracy and love
of humanity, with a true poetic spirit, are
apparent in this selection of his best work,
which is sure to endure, though his other
work, often rigid and infelicitously expressed, may not.

155 RANKIN, President J. E. "Walt Whitman as a
Poet." Independent 44 (28 April), 577.
Response to 1892.70: Whitman is supported for his Americanism (evident in his
catalogues), his poetic conceptions (evident
in his titles), his occasionally thought-
fitting form ("In Cabined Ships at Sea").
He will have influence because he has left
crude materials for future poets. His
great poetry includes "Lilacs" and "Captain."

*156 WHITMAN, WALT. "Isle of La Belle Rivière."
Cincinnati Post (30 April).
Reprinted: Uncollected.
Publication of one of Whitman's early
poems, written in 1849 while on his trip
down the Ohio Valley and left with his
host, Farmer Johnson. The poem's discovery
is explained.

157 ANON. "News Notes." Bookman (London) 2 (May),
38-39, 42.
Cites various current commentaries on
Whitman and his death: the American opinions are more guarded than those of the
English; the Nation writer (1892.102) does
not seem really familiar with Whitman's
poetry.

158 ANON. "New Books." Californian Illustrated
Magazine 1 (May), 669.
Memorial tribute to Whitman, whose life
was "his greatest poem." The controversy
over his worth still rages, because he has

produced both rare and crude thoughts, but
public sentiment does not now rank him with
Longfellow, Whittier, and Lowell, and probably never will.

159 ANON. "Book Inklings." Poet-Lore 4 (May),
286-87.
Review of Leaves with Lowell and
Meredith volumes of poetry. "The poet of
human selfhood, ordinarily supposed to be
less weighted with the love of libraries
than Lowell, less subtly introspective
than Meredith, supposed to be, indeed, only
an untutored child of Nature herself, seems
yet to have written in his 'Leaves of
Grass'--for example, in his praise of mind-
images he call 'Eidōlons'--of all the songs
of thought's supremacy the most unequivocal."

160 ANON. "An Estimate of Walt Whitman." Overland
Monthly, 2d ser. 19 (May), 551-57.
Describes Whitman's personality, which
attracted some, repelled others. Whitman's
first volume was tedious, too often prosaic.
His obsession with his version of a philosophy is typical of men who are "neither
of the illiterate nor the educated class,
well-read and slightly trained." He cari-
catures transcendentalism and reverts to
indecencies which American literature has
been outgrowing. He is an outsider, writing
unnecessary patriotic verse, ignoring romantic love. He displays powerful grasp of
thought, strength in expressing various
themes and moods, a feeling for outdoor
nature, "recurring gleams of real poetry" in
"a good chanting measure," "rich in telling
phrases," some of which have entered the
vernacular.

161 BURROUGHS, JOHN. "The Poet of Democracy."
North American Review 154 (May), 532-40.
Americans have been shocked by Whitman's
frankness in speaking in the democratic
spirit. In contrast to the New England
poets, he reveals the unconscious America,
in attempting to spiritualize modern materialism. He involves the reader with himself and his thought. He measures himself
by the largest standards in an effort to
raise the average.

162 COMPENDIUM. "Sprigs of Lilac for Walt
Whitman." Conservator 3 (May), 18.
Reprinted: 1892.15.
Letters and tributes to Whitman. Con-
cluded 1892.181.

163 GARRISON, WILLIAM H. "Walt Whitman."
Lippincott's Monthly Magazine 49 (May),
623-26.
Recollection of his twenty-year acquaintance with Whitman in Camden, describing
Whitman's conversation, mixed vocabulary,
dignified demeanor, insistence on accuracy
in his published work, the power of his
personality.

1892

164 M., D. S. "Aspects of Walt Whitman." Harvard
      Monthly 14 (May), 125-26.
           Whitman is "a great phenomenon, though
      not a great poet." He receives the uni-
      verse ecstatically if not always articulate-
      ly. Despite his imagination and ideas, he
      lacks art and selection.

165 McCULLOCH, H., Jr. "Aspects of Walt Whitman."
      Harvard Monthly 14 (May), 122-25.
           Whitman stands for a pastoral America,
      which might have been but can never be
      now. His universal brotherhood and belief
      in individuality and equality were voiced
      before the days of "undesirable immigrants."
      His blatant Americanism might be preferable
      to the present borrowings from Europe. The
      life he advocates is that of the frontier,
      tinged by "a faint idealism." He cannot be
      judged by existing standards.

*166 PENNELL, ELIZABETH R. "Reminiscences of Walt
      Whitman." Literary Opinion 2 (May), 57-60.
      Reported in CHAL and Trent.

167 R[OLLESTON], T. W. "Obituary. Walt Whitman."
      Eclectic Review 118, n.s. 55 (May), 693-97.
      Reprint of 1892.107.

168 ROOSE, PAULINE W. "A Child-Poet: Walt
      Whitman." Gentleman's Magazine 272, n.s.
      48 (May), 464-80.
           Whitman retained "the vision of his
      infancy" throughout life, answering all
      questions with the easy assurance of a
      child, retaining delight and wonder, loving
      heart, and interest in himself. His de-
      pressions are merely reflections of others'
      moods. His imagination, fresh observations,
      sense of fun are described. He contains
      both the giant and the child.

169 WALSH, WILLIAM S. "Walt Whitman." Lippincott's
      Monthly Magazine 49 (May), 621-23.
           Whitman's single-eyed vision which
      ignored all external distinctions gave him
      poetic insight but denied him the more
      worldly gift of humor. Perhaps he aban-
      doned too soon the quest for a proper
      vehicle of expression which would reach the
      masses. "Captain," his most ordered poem,
      is perhaps his greatest. He went to nature,
      not art, for his cadences.

170 WATTS, THEODORE. "Walt Whitman." Eclectic
      Review 118, n.s. 55 (May), 690-93.
      Reprint of 1892.109.

171 HABBERTON, JOHN. "Walt Whitman's Youth. Mr.
      Habberton Says that the Poet Dressed Shab-
      bily and Lived Loosely." New York World
      (1 May).
      Reprint of 1892.113.

172 ANON. "Walt Whitman--Life Chronicle."
      Arcadia 1 (2 May), 16-17.
           Obituary notice and examination of
      Whitman's work, seeking a middle course
      between "Whitmaniacs and Whitmanglers."

He is far below the masters of song, lacking
affinity and respect for rhyme and meter.
His thoughts extended only to the common
details of human existence. His lack of
decency is criticized. Samuel Warren's
earlier free verse and catalogues in "The
Lily and the Bee" (1851) are noted. However, Whitman does have some poetry.

*173 ANON. "Walt Whitman--By One Who Knew Him."
      Illustrated Australian News (2 May).
      Reprinted: McLeod.
           Explanation of Whitman's candor regard-
      ing sex; recollection of an evening spent
      with Whitman about ten years ago in Camden
      and his conversation regarding expurgation.
      Whitman was a great poet because his life
      was also great. Comradeship, which he
      actively practiced, is the central note of
      his democracy.

174 ANON. "Walt and Watts. (An Explanation.)"
      Critic 17 (7 May), 268.
      Reprint of 1892.135.
           Critic also calls attention to other
      Athenaeum items on Whitman (1892.134, 1892.
      138) and notes that a volume in the English
      Dilettante Series will be devoted to
      Whitman.

175 ARGUS [pseud.?]. Letter. Critic 17 (7 May),
      268-69.
           Praises Monroe (1892.145), criticizes
      Walford (1892.146): Whitman is appreciated
      in England by "full-grown men." He is "the
      only American American poet."

176 ANON. "Traits of Walt Whitman--Even His
      Friends Sometimes Misunderstood Him--His
      Curious Simplicity and Freedom from Affecta-
      tion--An Interesting Conversation between
      the Poet and Colonel Ingersoll." New York
      Times (8 May), 17:1.
           Describes Whitman's unassuming person-
      ality, his simplicity as his quality most
      influential on literature, various anecdotes,
      his lack of humor and of interest in poli-
      tics, his disagreement with Ingersoll over
      immortality.

*177 NIQUELL [pseud.?] "Walt Whitman, a Study."
      North British Review (Edinburgh) (21 May).
      Reported in Kennedy (1926). Concluded
      1892.179.

178 MURRAY, JOHN. "The Most 'American, American
      Poet.'" Critic 17 (28 May), 305.
           Response to 1892.175, proposing Whittier
      for the title: clean and beyond suspicion,
      as well as American.

*179 NIQUELL [pseud.?]. "Walt Whitman, a Study."
      North British Review (28 May).
      Concludes 1892.177.

180 ANON. "The Contributors' Club. An Impression
      of Walt Whitman." Atlantic Monthly 69
      (June), 851-54.
           Recollection by a woman of an 1883

visit and other meetings with Whitman,
noting his curiosity and harmonious nature,
quoting his conversation on Homer,
Wordsworth, Bryant, the importance of the
physical life. His reading of "Cradle"
revealed him as a true ancient bard.

181 COMPENDIUM. "Sprigs of Lilac for Walt
Whitman." Conservator 3 (June), 26-27.
Reprinted: 1892.15.
Concludes 1892.162.

182 LANIER, C. D. "Walt Whitman." Chautauquan,
n.s. 6 (June), 309-313.
Traces Whitman's life, love for comrades
of all kinds. His work, reminiscent of
Hindu and Hebrew translations, has strength,
fire, charm, and "deep, weird rhythm," whatever its limitations as literature. His
acclaim by the English has had an adverse
effect on American readers. He combines
genius and fatuity. "Ox-Tamer" (described)
is ignored but is one of his best pieces.
Whitman's democracy narrowly rejects the
upper class. He will be remembered as a
seer, not a poet, with Leaves only a literary curio.

183 PAYNE, WILLIAM MORTON. Review of Stedman
(1892.12). Dial 135 (June), 55.
In such a selection, much needed,
Whitman's work will live as long as anything hitherto produced in our literature,
because presented without "cacophonous
catalogues" and "vague and vaporous philosophy."

184 [SCUDDER, HORACE E.] "Whitman." Atlantic
Monthly 69 (June), 831-35.
Whitman's "magnificent physical
presence" may be felt even in a poem like
"Myself." His work is distinctly literary,
"a deliberate attempt at an adequate mode
of expressing large, elemental ideas." He
is best when celebrating the sensuous man.
"Captain" is his most accepted work because
of its restraint in a moment of deep emotion. "Sea-Drift" contains the best examples of rhythm divorced from rhyme. The
patriotic 1855 Preface is praised. Whitman
generally lacks universality.

185 ANON. "Notes." Public Opinion 13 (4 June),
221.
From Illustrated American (unlocated):
describes Whitman's belief in "a floral
prototype" for every individual. He used
to place before each friend's picture the
flower or leaf which symbolized that personality.

186 [GILDER, JEANNETTE.] "The Lounger." Critic
17 (4 June), 316.
Paragraph describing a batch of seven
hundred letters and three hundred post-
cards Whitman wrote to one man, "a very
intimate friend," proving him a prolific
letter writer, since he had other intimate
correspondents as well. His writing was

legible, his punctuation and capitalization
a bit eccentric.

187 ANON. "Boston Letter." Critic 17 (11 June),
330.
Note on celebration of Whitman's birthday in Kennedy's home.

188 ANON. "Whitman's 'Selected Poems.'" Critic
17 (11 June), 323.
Review of 1892.12, a good selection.
Whitman's place is yet to be decided. His
work may contain the foundations of a new
system of poetry.

189 ARGUS [pseud.?]. "The 'American' Poet."
Critic 17 (11 June), 331.
Letter in response to 1892.178. The
American poet is one who rejects the imita-
tion of European models, as only Whitman
does. Europeans find only him, as prophet,
and Poe, as poet, to be new voices in
America.

190 ANON. Review of Clarke (1892.3). Literary
World (London), n.s. 45 (17 June), 577-78.
Clarke's socialism helps him understand
Whitman, though he is great as a prophet,
not for mere politics.

191 FREILIGRATH, FERDINAND. "Walt Whitman."
Translated by Sadakichi Hartmann. Liberty 8,
no. 44 (18 June), 3-4.
New translation of 1868.36.

192 ANON. "Magazine Notes." Critic 17 (25 June),
352.
Atlantic (1892.184) gives a low estimate
of Whitman's poetry, accusing him of formlessness, although Whitman's method of
writing was far more suitable to the scythe
than to garden scissors for cutting modest
posies.

193 ANON. "Walt Whitman." Review of Reviews 5
(July), 738-39.
Extracts from current commentary on
Whitman, including a reprint of Whitman's
account of writing Leaves in Frank Leslie's
Popular Monthly.

194 TRAUBEL, HORACE L. "Walt Whitman's Birthday,
May 31st." Conservator 3 (July), 36.
Account of the celebration, noting
papers read, quoting conversations, including
comments by Eakins on Whitman's awareness
of form in art.

195 ANON. "The Poet as Dreamer and Seer."
Spectator 69 (2 July), 14-15.
Philosophical discussion taking off
from discussion of Whitman. Clarke's book
(1892.3) is praised. Whitman lacks "the
sense of historical perspective" and the
"gift of melodious lyricism." Revolt from
tradition represents an "anti-poetic, because essentially anti-humane and illiberal
spirit," for "the 'poetry of democracy' is
strident." The poet who lives entirely in

1892

the future is necessarily "of most partial and fragmentary vision."

196 ANON. "Brief Notices." Public Opinion 13 (7 July), 123.
    Review of Stedman (1892.12). Whitman certainly "had a strong, rugged, picturesque nature," giving birth "to phrases and brief characterizations which are powerful." "Captain" is praised. His work will not stay before the public very long.

197 ANON. "Walt Whitman Again." Literary World 23 (16 July), 243.
    Brief favorable review of Clarke (1892.3), who recognizes Whitman's rudenesses and his chant's chaotic shapelessness and admires his great sympathy and tremendous egotism, which is not without some justification.

198 TRAUBEL, HORACE L. "Walt Whitman's Last Poem." Once a Week 9 (16 July), 3.
    Account of finding among Whitman's papers "A Thought of Columbus" and verifying that it was his last poem. His conversation with Whitman during his last sickness is quoted.

199 BAXTER, SYLVESTER. "Walt Whitman in Boston." New England Magazine, n.s. 6 (August), 714-21.
    Recollection of Whitman and his activities during his April 1881 visit to Boston, which Baxter originally wrote up in 1881. 15.

200 BLACK, GEORGE D. "Walt Whitman." New England Magazine, n.s. 6 (August), 710-14.
    Account of the effect of Whitman's poetry on him; the varieties of his biographical experiences; Whitman as "radical democrat"; his appropriate rhythm, poetic skill, spiritual perception, Greek-like love of life, oriental reverence for death.

201 GAY, WILLIAM. "Walt Whitman: Poet of Democracy." Australian Herald (August), 220-22. Reprinted: 1893.4; McLeod.
    Whitman exemplifies the principle that poetry should induce in the reader a feeling similar to the feeling of the writer from whom it originated. In American literature he is even greater than Emerson, "for with equal insight he has a larger heart," strengthening readers through his personality. His magnetic power and spiritual insight lead to a new poetry, "of the free individual man."

202 HARTE, WALTER BLACKBURN. "Walt Whitman's Democracy." New England Magazine, n.s. 6 (August), 721-24. Photograph, p. 725.
    Whitman will survive for his spirit of democracy, if not for his poetry, which is uneven. His work did not appeal to the masses because they prefer sentimental commonplace to the eternal. "Cradle" reveals a true poetic imagination. He is best when appealing to the heart with vivid pictures and descriptive phrases; when appealing to the minds, he produces incoherent philosophy. Through his egoism he seeks to arouse readers to awareness of their true selves rather than the false fronts displayed in public.

203 BURROUGHS, JOHN. "A Boston Criticism of Whitman." Poet-Lore 4 (August-September), 392-96.
    Responds to Atlantic (1892.184). The major key of Leaves is appropriate for the poetry of power. Whitman's work is not unrestrained but, "true to itself, follows its own law," rejecting the traditional advantages of poetic art. His egotism is not narrow but the egotism of democracy. He offsets the belittling of men by specific disciplines.

204 [TRAUBEL, HORACE.] "Notes and News." Poet-Lore 4 (August-September), 461-70.
    Quotes funeral ceremonies, recitations in full, addresses in part (1892.15).

205 ANON. "News and Notes." Literary World 23 (27 August), 297.
    Quotes M. de Wyzega from Revue Bleue on American poets: Whitman, "the magnificent and noble old man," was "every inch a poet." London Daily News (unlocated) is quoted on American literature's necessary qualities: American writers "cannot all be Walt Whitmans, a circumstance which we would be the very last to regret. One vast Walt is enough for a century." Howells (1891. 49) is quoted.

206 BOUGHTON, WILLIS. "Walt Whitman." Arena 6 (September), 471-80.
    Whitman's words have more encouragement regarding death than what was said at his funeral. He is a fresh force in our literature. Vistas helps one understand Leaves. His ambition to create an American poem and sing the modern man is a grand conception worthy of a great literary man. The perplexing "Myself" is explained. Whitman may be criticized for "Adam" and for inattention to art, but he created such true poetry as "Cradle" and "Spider." He wrote for the people but they are not yet ready to understand him.

207 ANON. "Briefer Mention." Dial 13 (1 September), 150.
    Short favorable review of Clarke (1892. 3).

208 ANON. "Walt Whitman." Critic 18 (3 September), 116.
    Favorable review of Clarke (1892.3). Whitman leads the reader along in his optimism and exuberance; thus, one overlooks the "artistic atheism" of his lines because of their rhythm of the heart to which anyone can respond. They are readily translated. He appeals to those who consider essence more important than form.

209 [TUCKER, BENJAMIN.] "On Picket Duty." Liberty 9, no. 4 (24 September), 1.
　　　Recalls his earlier suggestion (unlocated) that Whitman regretted his lines praising Emperor William, which Liberty condemned at their first appearance. J. William Lloyd and Traubel said this surmise was incorrect. If so, Whitman's poem is "an indelible stain upon a great life-work." Traubel reports Whitman as saying, "'William [O'Connor] and Tucker didn't understand me.'" Traubel's explanations of Whitman's attitude are not consistent with the language of the poem.

*209a GAY, WILLIAM. "To Walt Whitman." Australian Herald (October).
Reported in Jones. Revised: 1894.4.
　　　Sonnet of tribute: "Thou who didst take the world in thy embrace."

210 TRIGGS, OSCAR L. "Robert Browning as the Poet of Democracy." Poet-Lore 4 (October), 481-90.
　　　Incidental: Whitman, "the supreme bard of democracy," is in direct accord with Browning "in all really vital matters," fighting "for freedom and the souls of men." Whitman, Browning, and Wagner are equally profound as thinkers and in their chief characteristic, "the deep emotional element."

211 ANON. "An American Visits Tennyson." Boston Evening Transcript (6 October), 6:5-6.
　　　Prints with headnote a letter to Whitman [from Bucke] describing a visit to Tennyson: "None of the Tennysons, I imagine (I had hardly any talk about 'Leaves of Grass' except with Hallam, who spoke very freely and pleasantly on the subject) have read you so as to understand you or what you are after, but have read you enough to know in a more or less vague way that you are a great force in this modern world."

*212 MILLER, JOAQUIN. Article. San Francisco Chronicle (8 October).
Quoted in Wagner (1929.26), but not located on this date.
　　　The little wits only recently were mocking Whitman. Whitman had tears in his eyes when he read to Miller Tennyson's invitation to his home. Tennyson was thus defying all America.

213 [GILDER, JEANNETTE.] "The Lounger." Critic 18 (15 October), 213.
　　　Describes the soon-to-be-published In Re (1893.11).

214 ANON. "Walt Whitman as Revealed in His Prose Writings." Dial 13 (16 October), 249.
　　　Brief review of Autobiographia (1892. 11). To know Whitman thoroughly one must know his prose, here readily available. "These pages, so full of the subjective revelation of self" and "a poet's joy in nature," resemble Thoreau's.

215 ANON. "Whitman's 'Autobiographia.'" Literary News 13 (November), 333.
　　　Review of 1892.11, which provides "a consecutive and most interesting account" of Whitman's picturesque life, "told in his own rugged yet distinctive language," so that the book seems all too short. It is like "a roughly jotted diary, instinct with the personality of the writer and the more attractive to a large proportion of readers for its conversational and graphic style." It will give a pleasant and "close acquaintance with one of the most remarkable of American writers."

216 PIATT, JOHN JAMES. "To Walt Whitman, the Man [Washington, May, 1863.]" Cosmopolitan 14 (November), 118.
　　　Poem recalling Whitman telling of his hospital experiences and praising him for his embodiment of Charity and Good-Comradeship.

217 D[ONALDSON, THOMAS?] or D[OUGLAS, Lord ALFRED?] "Walt Whitman (I.)." Spirit Lamp 2 (4 November), 39-44.
　　　Whitman is praised as the voice of democracy and individualism, relying not on the past but on experience and the heart. His love extends to all. His greatness lies in what he does with the eternal themes of love and death. His acceptance of death as an element of life encourages emphasis on the present. Concluded 1892.220.

218 ANON. "Autobiographia." Literary World 23 (5 November), 391.
　　　Review of 1892.11, praising Whitman's prose as poetic and revealing of himself.

*219 WALLACE, JAMES W. "Prophets of Democracy." Labour Leader (10 November).
Reported in Blodgett.

220 D[ONALDSON, THOMAS?] or D[OUGLAS, Lord ALFRED?] "Walt Whitman (II.)." Spirit Lamp 2 (18 November), 82-88.
　　　Concludes 1892.217. Whitman's work is truly poetry of genius, with "an infinitely varied music and rhythm," "intensity and penetration," though "a certain lack of restraint and compression" makes him "not an artist in the strict sense." Through his suggestiveness he seeks to awaken readers' powers to see and hear for themselves. He is genuine, rejecting outworn traditional poetic machinery. His war poems may be his greatest, particularly "Vigil Strange," presenting his actual intense emotions. He has widened the range of human sympathies and set the human relations in a new light, opening up a fresh field for poetry, as Wordsworth did with a similar moral enthusiasm but less engagement with the world.

221 ANON. Review of "Autobiographia" [1892.11]. Public Opinion 14 (26 November), 193.

1892

These writings show him "in everyday naturalness," giving insight into his character and style. Most interesting is his Washington diary.

222 ANON. "Notes and News." <u>Poet-Lore</u> 4 (December), 646-47.
Describes soon-to-be-published <u>In Re</u> (1893.11).

223 HABBERTON, JOHN. Brief review of "Autobiographia" (1892.11). <u>Godey's Magazine</u> 125 (December), 642.
The eccentric poet's life could not be better expressed than here.

224 SALMON, EDWARD. "Walt Whitman." <u>London Society</u> 62 (December), 588-600.
Whitman is probably the last quarter-century's "most interesting, because the most extraordinary, figure," "a remarkable product of intellectual democracy" and America. His egotism was personal and national, with democracy his principal theme. His creed seems to be "Christianity in alliance with Pantheism and Pantheism modified by Positivism." An English newspaper correspondent's interview of a few years ago with Whitman is quoted. He is the poet of antithesis. The war's beneficial influence on his work is explained, with several <u>Drum-Taps</u> poems. "Captain" surpasses "Lilacs" in "passionate plaintive beauty." Whitman is probably "too intensely and uncompromisingly American" to symbolize a new order in Europe, whose interest in him has been due primarily to curiosity and fascination with his work and convictions. His method will keep him from the people, yet he says much that they should know. He should be honored and studied.

225 ANON. Brief review of Traubel (1892.15). <u>Critic</u> 18 (10 December), 325.
Describes the collected tributes, all with "the golden glamor of love."

1893

BOOKS

1 BRISBANE, REDELIA. <u>Albert Brisbane: A Mental Biography</u>. Boston: Arena Publishing Co., pp. 15-16.
Brisbane's wife describes him dictating a poem to her after saying that he could write as good poetry as "Passage," which she had been reading aloud on the train after Whitman had given it to them in Washington.

2 FOOTE, GEORGE W. <u>Flowers of Freethought (First Series)</u>. London: Pioneer Press, n.d. "Walt Whitman," pp. 169-73.
Obituary tribute. Whitman's death comes as a relief for this superb specimen of physical manhood. His utterances on sex

sin against decorum, not nature; "he belonged to a less self-conscious antiquity." His admirers are cited. "Lilacs" will surely live as a great poem, though "whole masses of his poetry will probably sink to the bottom--not, however, before doing their work and delivering their message." He was "a true Freethinker," appealing to the brotherhood of all and the dignity of each. America needs his teachings.

3 GARLAND, HAMLIN. <u>Prairie Songs</u>. Cambridge and Chicago: Stone & Kimball. "A Tribute of Grasses. To W. W.," p. 116.
Reprinted: <u>In Re</u>; Legler; 1929.58; 1939. 36; 1939.47.
Poem of tribute: "Serene, vast head...."

4 GAY, WILLIAM. <u>Walt Whitman, The Poet of Democracy</u>. Melbourne, Sydney, and Adelaide: E. A. Petherick & Co., 48 pp.
Three articles reprinted from <u>Australian Herald</u> (two unlocated, tracing his life and work, and 1892.201). According to his preface, Gay seeks to vindicate Whitman's message, for his excellence overshadows his defects.

5 LAW, JAMES D. <u>Dreams o' Hame and Other Scotch Poems</u>. London and Paisley: Alexander Gardner. "A Few Words to Walt Whitman," pp. 82-86.
Poem in Scots dialect describing Law's first acquaintance with <u>Leaves</u> and gradual appreciation of it.

6 LE GALLIENNE, RICHARD. <u>The Religion of a Literary Man</u>. New York: G. P. Putnam's, pp. 80, 86, 117.
Incidental: In its recognition of everything that breathes life as holy, <u>Leaves</u> is "more helpful than <u>The New Testament</u>--for it includes more." Whitman's is among the great messages of our age that remain unheeded.

7 LELAND, CHARLES GODFREY. <u>Memoirs</u>. New York: D. Appleton & Co., pp. 258, 395, 436-37.
Leland's brother Henry sent Whitman an admiring letter which "inspired him to renewed effort" at a time when he had received no encouragement as a poet. A conversation with Tennyson is described, regarding Whitman and poetry, in which Tennyson found Whitman wanting. One covers more ground and establishes more intimacy with such men as Whitman, Tennyson, and others in only one or two interviews than with most people in many meetings.

8 RAYMOND, GEORGE LANSING. <u>The Genesis of Art Form: An Essay in Comparative Aesthetics</u>. New York and London: G. P. Putnam's Sons, pp. 20, 54.
Deplores the lack of art form, the first necessity of style, in passages from Whitman.

9 SYMONDS, JOHN ADDINGTON. <u>Walt Whitman: A</u>
<u>Study</u>. London: John C. Nimmo, 160 pp.,
plus 35 pp. on Whitman's life. Illustrated.
No index.

Whitman's immortality was assured by
1860, for nothing he wrote after that is
greater. The elements of Whitman's creed
(each expounded in a separate section) are:
"religion, or the conception of the universe; the personality or the sense of self
and sex; then love, diverging into the
amative and comradely emotions; then democracy, or the theory of human equality and
brotherhood." Whitman's religion recognized the immanence of God and the divinity
in all things; "Square Deific" explains his
thought. Sexual and comradely love are
both necessary for "a completely endowed
individuality." Whitman rejects notions of
woman as the weaker sex. "Calamus" elevates
friendship to a spiritual level, sensuous
as well but neither sanctioning nor condemning physical desire. It is a "force
for stimulating national vitality." The
democratic spirit discussion reprints much
of 1890.8, with some rearrangement and the
deletion of material not pertaining to
Whitman. Whitman chose a new attitude
toward literature as well as a new form.
His form and style as well as his content
are significant. He has produced excellent
poetry, despite such defects as lists,
sparseness of humor, "accent of swagger."
Metaphorical description of the feel of
Whitman's work; record of his own experience
reading it and its effect upon him.

10 THOMPSON, MAURICE. <u>The Aesthetics of Literary</u>
<u>Art</u>. Hartford: Hartford Seminary Press,
pp. 20, 68-69, 70-71.

Incidental references, criticizing the
coarseness of much modern literature, such
as the works of Whitman, who does not express "the deep characteristics of our
civilization as a whole" and has imported
his art-spirit from ancient Egypt. His
sincerity "is a matter of his own manu-
facture."

11 TRAUBEL, HORACE L.; BUCKE, RICHARD M.; and
HARNED, THOMAS B. <u>In Re Walt Whitman</u>.
Philadelphia: David McKay, 452 pp.
[Traubel], "A First and Last Word":
Whitman had cosmic breadth, involvement
with all men and life, absolute candor.
This book, as Whitman intended, supplements
Bucke (1883.3).

John Addington Symonds, "Love and
Death: a Symphony": Long poem on Whitman's
themes.

Reprints of 1855.7, 1855.10, 1855.11,
here ascribed to Whitman for the first
time.

Reprint of 1890.48.

Horace L. Traubel, "Notes from Con-
versations with George W. Whitman, 1893":
Transcribes George's reminiscences about
Whitman's character, habits, and attitudes

toward the family, especially earlier in
life.

Reprints of 1870.4 and 1892.128.

Richard Maurice Bucke, "The Man Walt
Whitman": One must know the man to know
his work. Considering him as a poet is a
misconception. He passed beyond his own
generation. His intellectual stature, extraordinary senses, and faith in immortality
are described.

Walt Whitman, "Letters in Sickness:
Washington, 1873": Letters to his mother
and others, reprinted in <u>Wound-Dresser</u>
(1898.3).

John Burroughs, "Walt Whitman and His
Recent Critics": Survey of memorial articles which reveal more appreciation for
the man than for his work. The comments of
a symposium on Whitman in a Chicago daily
(unlocated) are described: involved were
Maurice Thompson, James W. Riley (who "has
wrestled with him, but with very poor
results"), Mr. McGovern, Joseph Cook (a
clergyman), and Joel Chandler Harris (who
notes the importance of appreciating America
and its sweep to appreciate Whitman;
Whitman's poetry is not literary but written
for those who know nature and man at first
hand, who will find in him "the thrill and
glow of poetry and the essence of melody"
in its "rarer intimations and suggestions").
Burroughs praises Whitman's power, care
with words, vital personality. He is a
bard or prophet rather than a poet, "<u>un</u>-
artistic rather than <u>in</u>artistic." Whitman
counterposes self-assertion against the
belittling of man by the perverted prevailing notion of Christianity.

William Douglas O'Connor, "'The Good
Gray Poet:' Supplemental": An unpublished
letter to the Boston <u>Transcript</u>, dated 23
January 1866, further explaining his views
on censorship and <u>Leaves</u>.

Gabriel Sarrazin, "Walt Whitman,"
translated by Harrison S. Morris from <u>La</u>
<u>Renaissance de la Poésie Anglaise, 1798-</u>
<u>1889</u>: Whitman counteracts the pessimism of
contemporary Europe. "I. Pantheism": For
Whitman God and Nature are one. He surpasses the spirits of Renan and Hegel,
giving affirmation, not argument. "II.
The New World": "Walt Whitman is not an
artist, he is above art." Whitman reveals
correspondences between the soul and the
external world, looks toward the ideal
democracy. "III. Leaves of Grass": Extensive quotations, revealing the physical
feeling of Whitman. "IV. Walt Whitman":
Whitman is a man, associated with the
masses, manual labor, patriotism. He
preaches by example. His life is sketched
from Bucke, with note of his very American
shifting of occupations. <u>Leaves</u> is extensively quoted throughout, with many passages
presented in French translation in the
notes. Retranslated: 1899.26. Abridged:
Miller.

Reprints of 1891.17, 1891.18, 1890.38.

Albert Edmund Lancaster, "To Walt Whitman": Sonnet. Reprinted: Legler.

Karl Knortz, "Walt Whitman," translated by Alfred Forman and Richard Maurice Bucke, with deletions: Explanation of Whitman's form, his ideas in Vistas (an aid to understanding his poetry), the themes of Leaves. Whitman is the poet of identity, of the modern era, of the wholeness of the human personality. He is truly Christian in his acts.

Rudolf Schmidt, "Walt Whitman, the Poet of American Democracy," translated by R. M. Bain and Richard Maurice Bucke, with deletions: Through his verse and form Whitman produces the effects of nature and America. "Myself," "Adam," "Calamus" are explained with their democratic and spiritual purposes. Whitman brings about the feeling of life in the reader. "Salut" presents an "all-comprehending world solidarity." His struggle between pantheism and democracy and his rarely surpassed poetic gifts are discussed, his ideas in Vistas (a new literary type) explained.
Reprint of 1890.20.

T. W. Rolleston, "Walt Whitman," translated by Alfred Forman and Richard Maurice Bucke, with deletions: Whitman's work perfectly represents this age. He follows the German philosophic method of working toward the central actuality of things rather than concentrating on phenomena. The workings of his intellect, his basic principles are described. He will endure because his profound intellect is combined with a wealth of poetic power and a real personal influence. Extract reprinted: Hindus.
Reprint in a more complete version of 1891.35.
Reprint of 1893.3.

Richard Maurice Bucke, "Walt Whitman and the Cosmic Sense": Describes cosmic sense, using Whitman as an example because of his change, presumably in June 1853, described in "Myself" 5. This material is expanded in 1901.3.

Walt Whitman, "Immortality": His ideas on immortality are explained from a transcription of his conversation with Ingersoll (see 1890.28).

Thomas B. Harned, "The Poet of Immortality": Leaves is a religious book. Whitman reveals Christ-like qualities. His spiritual life was a growth, not a sudden conversion as Bucke says. Whitman's personal belief in immortality and his preference for natural over formal religion are verified through Harned's personal recollections of him.

Sidney H. Morse, "My Summer with Walt Whitman, 1887": Recalls first meeting with Whitman in 1876, his later experience while working on a sculpture of him in 1887: various anecdotes, the farmer Johnson's visit, attitude toward labor problems. Quotes what Whitman wrote (in the third

person) for Morse's notebook on his ideas, intention, situation; other material from his notebook on Whitman's conversation; an Emerson anecdote; letter from Whitman to Morse.

Daniel Longaker, "The Last Sickness and the Death of Walt Whitman": Recalls his first interview with Whitman in March 1891, Whitman's condition throughout his last year, some of his conversation, notes of the post-mortem, which revealed no traces of debauchery causing his decline.

J. W. Wallace, "Last Days of Walt Whitman": Extracts of letters from Traubel to the Bolton group and to Bucke from 21 December 1891 until Whitman's death, tracing the course of his condition to reveal "authentic glimpses" of Whitman and his "deportment and spirit"; also short letters from Whitman and Warren Fritzinger.

Francis Howard Williams, "Walt Whitman: March 26, 1892": Sonnet ("Darkness and death?"). Reprinted: 1894.19, 1900.16.

Horace L. Traubel, "At the Graveside of Walt Whitman": Reprints the funeral addresses and readings from 1892.15, with introductory note describing the throngs honoring Whitman at his house and the cemetery. Whitman "eluded the darkness" and "reappeared in us" who take up "'the burden and the lesson' eternal of life."

Throughout the volume are extracts from Whitman's correspondence with Rossetti and Dowden and from criticism, and Lanier's letter to Whitman (1896.73).

12 TRIGGS, OSCAR L. Browning and Whitman: A Study in Democracy. London: Swan Sonnenschein & Co.; New York: Macmillan & Co., 145 pp. No index.
To form a more complete notion of democracy, one must balance the individualism of Emerson and Thoreau with the notion of union, brotherhood, and love in Lowell and Whitman, who enshrined Lincoln as embodiment of this democratic faith in the "Commemoration Ode" and "Lilacs," America's chief poetic contributions to the world. Whitman is the world's most complete embodiment of the democratic sentiment, in person and poems. He is compared with Millet, Blake, Jefferies, Browning. Last of the romanticists, he does not lose himself in nature but looks for its revelations to man. For him and Browning life is a quest for "self-realisation with reference to eternity." Whitman emphasizes equality, belief in good, immortality, individuality, and community. He did for poetry what Wagner did for music; they and Browning are profound thinkers, emphasize consonants rather than vowels in their verse, and link literature with life.

13 UNDERWOOD, FRANCIS H. The Builders of American Literature. Boston: Lee & Shepard. "Walt Whitman," pp. 235-37.
Reprint of Whitman comments from 1872.7, adding recent works and death date.

14 WENDELL, BARRETT. <u>Stelligeri and Other Essays</u>
<u>Concerning America</u>. New York: Charles
Scribner's Sons, pp. 142-43.
Whitman in his form represents the
spirit that may inspire the American literature of the future. Though uncouth and
inarticulate, he can make you feel how the
New York ferries are fragments of God's
eternities. (This material is used in
1900.18.)

PERIODICALS

15 ROBINSON, CHARLES. "The Confessions of an
Autograph-Hunter." <u>Cosmopolitan</u> 14 (January), 308-9.
Whitman's "charming" reply to Robinson's
request for "a 'sentiment'" is quoted:
conclusion of "Salut."

16 ANON. "Notes." <u>Critic</u> 19 (21 January), 39.
Notes the funds raised to purchase
Whitman's home in Camden.

*17 HARTMANN, SADAKICHI. Article on Whitman.
<u>Weekly Review</u> (Boston) 3 (4 February),
174.
Reprint of 1889.37. Reported in Knox.

18 TRAUBEL, HORACE L. "Walt Whitman the Comrade."
<u>Conservator</u> 4 (March), 7-8.
Impressionistic account of Whitman's
impact on the reader. His book is a lesson,
centering on love, equality, freedom. "He
offers you yourself."

*19 HARTMANN, SADAKICHI. Article on Whitman's
house. <u>Weekly Review</u> (Boston) 3 (4 March),
308.
Reported in Knox.
Account of recent visit to Whitman's
Camden house, which should be left as when
he lived there if it is to become a museum
faithful to him.

20 BURROUGHS, JOHN. "Whitman's and Tennyson's
Relations to Science." <u>Dial</u> 14 (16 March),
168-69.
"Whitman and Tennyson were fully abreast
with science," but responded differently,
Tennyson with his intellect, Whitman with
his imagination. Whitman, rather than
Tennyson, will reveal new meaning to every
age. (Most of this article is incorporated
into the "Science" chapter of 1896.2.)

21 CHENEY, JOHN VANCE. "Walt." <u>Californian</u>
<u>Illustrated Magazine</u> 3 (April), 553-61.
Reprinted: 1895.4.
A slangy, informal estimate of Whitman,
whose aura of wildness is necessary for
his teachings, such as "the forgotten fact
that we are not born with our clothes on."
He describes not contemporary America but
an earlier America, "the raw period before
literature was," requiring the reader to
fashion the poem for himself. Admiration
for "Lilacs" has been confused with patri-

otic sentiment, for it has no great merit
as verse. His ideas on death and democracy
have been better stated elsewhere, but he
gives us the stuff of life and a fresh outlook.

22 LOCKWOOD, DeWITT C. "The Good Gray Poet. (A
Biographical Sketch.)" <u>Californian Illustrated Magazine</u> 3 (April), 579-86.
Popular sketch of Whitman's life and
reception, based on Bucke. His theme was
man, thoroughly perceived and portrayed.
The real reason he never married was "his
inability to find that 'right person.'"
Recollection of seeing Whitman for the last
time at his 1887 Lincoln lecture in New
York.

23 ANON. Brief review of Triggs (1893.12).
<u>Critic</u> 19 (8 April), 217.
Notes Triggs's belief in Whitman's
importance. The book will have interest
for admirers of either poet, though it is
flawed.

24 FOSS, SAM WALTER. "Walt Whitman." <u>Book News</u>
<u>Monthly</u> 11 (May), 402.
Reprint of 1892.5.

25 P[ORTER, CHARLOTTE.] "Browning Books of the
Year." <u>Poet-Lore</u> 5 (May), 278-79.
Review of Triggs (1893.12). "Browning
is the dramatist of the Whitman principle."
Triggs reveals the correspondences between
"these most modern of poets." Whitman's
world-wide significance and relation to
other American poets are noted.

26 ANON. Review of Symonds (1893.9). <u>Literary</u>
<u>World</u> (London) n.s. 47 (5 May), 403-4.
Praises Whitman and the book.

27 ANON. "Notes." <u>Critic</u> 19 (6 May), 301.
Quotes Philadelphia <u>Record</u> (unlocated)
on Whitman's brain being examined by the
Anthropometric Society.

28 BURROUGHS, JOHN. "A Glance into Walt Whitman."
<u>Lippincott's Monthly Magazine</u> 51 (June),
753-58.
<u>Leaves</u> moves through the trappings of
the reader's mind to touch his sense of
real things. It gives the impression not
of art but of nature and life at first hand.
Whitman has freshness, objectivity, "a disregard for details," "an atmosphere of
health and sanity," especially in relation
to sex. His criticism is affirmative rather
than destructive. His preference for the
laboring man over the gentleman meets the
needs of "a highly refined and civilized
age."

29 PORTER, CHARLOTTE. "A Talk on American Patriotic Poems." <u>Poet-Lore</u> 5 (June-July), 351-
53.
"Banner" is quoted as "a wonderful,
mystical, many-folded national flag-song"
which nobody seems to know.

1893

30 TRIGGS, OSCAR L. "Walt Whitman." Poet-Lore
5 (June-July), 289-305.
   Whitman's life, early reading, influences are traced. His work was "absolutely
modern," sounding "the joys of virile manhood and womanhood." Leaves is praised for
its vastness and the nobility of its practical philosophy, pantheistic without denying the worth of the individual. Whitman's
"transcendental point of view" emphasizes
unity rather than dualism. His faith in-
corporates modern science. His form is
between pure speech and pure song, meant to
bear both thought and emotion, not merely
"a spurious form of 'prose-poetry'" but "a
new harmony" like Wagner's. Whitman is the
American representative of European romanticism. His poetry appeals beyond art
because of his personality and truth to
nature. His greatest artistic contribution
is the sense of wonder regarding life. "He
is the poet of joy." "Lilacs" is comparable
with the great elegies, presenting death as
leading to life. His lessons lead the soul
on to its own lessons and poems.

31 ANON. "In Memory of Walt Whitman." New York
Times (1 June), 5:3.
   Account of the New York birthday dinner,
speeches, letters read.

32 ANON. "Walt Whitman's Birthday Celebrated."
New York Tribune (1 June), 10:2.
   Account of birthday dinner, people
present and speaking.

33 ANON. Commentary on readers' poll. Critic 19
(3 June), 357.
   In the tabulation of votes for the
most popular American work, Whitman makes
a very poor showing.

34 BURROUGHS, JOHN. "A Poet of Grand Physique."
Critic 19 (3 June), 372.
Extract quoted from 1893.28.

35 CROCKETT, S. R. "Literary Vignettes. I.
Walt Whitman, Compositor, Hospital Nurse,
and Comrade." Christian Leader 12 (22
June), 590-91.
   Quotes Johnston (1890.7). "There was
always something epical and primeval" about
Whitman, "one of the greatest and most
genuine of the singers of the people."
"Pioneers" is praised for its noble, manly
comradeship. Whitman had broad sympathies.
Even in selections one perceives "the broad
majesty of his thought and message," his
"Titanic rhythm," "a strong, forceful soul"
standing out in American literature.

36 ANON. "Studies of Democracy in Poets." Dial
15 (1 July), 20-21.
   Brief review of Triggs (1893.12), explaining his suggestive thesis.

37 ANON. "An English Critic of Walt Whitman."
Critic 20 (22 July), 49.

Review of Symonds (1893.9), "the most
complete presentation yet made of all phases
of Whitman's many-sided philosophy."
Symonds indicates how Whitman could inflame
cultivated Englishmen, much as Socrates did
his disciples, with a remarkable influence
on contemporary English thought.

38 BLOCK, LOUIS JAMES. "Walt Whitman." Poet-
Lore 5 (August-September), 422-23.
Reprinted: 1895.1.
   Poem in seven unrhymed but metrical
stanzas, paying tribute to Whitman's voice,
vision, and strength.

*39 ANON. Article. Philadelphia Times (1 August).
Reported in Willard.
   University Extension students from the
University of Pennsylvania went on a pil-
grimage to Camden sites, where Harned and
Traubel spoke to them.

40 LEWIN, WALTER. Review of Symonds (1893.9).
Academy 44 (2 September), 185-87.
   At last "an adequate estimate" of
Whitman. Significant works on Whitman are
surveyed, Symonds's discussion summarized.
Symonds goes to extremes in explaining what
Whitman did not mean regarding the passionate
element of friendship and in explaining
Whitman's motives as scientific. Whitman's
temperament was more artistic than scientific or theological, more religious than
artistic. Leaves is a biography of the
human soul, hence the need to include sex.
Symonds does not pay sufficient attention
to Whitman's artistic concerns, evident in
his continual revisions. He includes all
aspects of life, ignoring any coherent system. His candor is refreshing, his craving
for affection understandable. His role as
prophet was somewhat self-imposed, but his
personal influence is abundantly proved.

41 ANON. "Walt Whitman." Temple Bar 99 (October),
252-59.
   Whitman's "paean to Democracy," in a
new and national literary form, "throbbed
with the lusty life of America." His life
is sketched with some exaggeration. "His
splendid egotism" sustained him until he
won national regard and affection, more for
his life than for his works. He transforms
his flaws into triumphs. His form displays
careful work and admirable consistency. The
1855 Preface is perhaps his noblest poetry.
He will be significant to future poets and
to America and the world.

42 GARLAND, HAMLIN. "Literary Emancipation of
the West." Forum 16 (October), 165.
Reprinted: 1894.3.
   Incidental references to Whitman, who
announced the period of literary breaking-
away in America, "but could not exemplify
it in popular form. He voiced its force,
its love of liberty and love of comrades,
but he was the prophet, not the exemplar.

He said well that the real literature of America could not be a polite literature."

43 TRAUBEL, HORACE L. "Walt Whitman's 'Artistic Atheism.'" Poet-Lore 5 (October), 498-505.
Whitman views the old forms as appropriate to their time but seeks a freer measure for his needs and those of democracy. He seeks art in nature rather than from other artists. Like Wagner, he has been criticized according to old criteria which he has surpassed, not merely to gain temporary success as Stoddard has claimed, because his style, though appearing simple, is "the most difficult of styles." Leaves is a complete book, the first poem coming full-circle to meet the last. His book has subtlety, like the individual. His conversations with Traubel regarding his intentions are quoted, showing him as "criticism's august master, not its slave."

44 TRAUBEL, HORACE L.; BUCKE, R. M.; and HARNED, THOMAS B. "Walt Whitman in War-Time. Familiar Letters from the Capital." Century Magazine 46 (October), 840-50. Engraved portrait of 1863.
Reprinted: 1898.3.
Explanatory note prefaces letters from an upcoming volume entitled "Hospital Letters" (actually Wound-Dresser, 1898.3), published not for literary merit but for light on Whitman's "expansive personality." The letters, from December 1862 to June 1864, are primarily "direct confessions of son to mother, couched in all the simple verbal beauty of manly love and reverence."

45 BURROUGHS, JOHN. "Mr. Gosse's Puzzle over Poe." Dial 15 (16 October), 214-15.
Incidental references to Whitman in comparison with Poe, who lacks the mental and spiritual food and the relation to his fellows that Whitman offers.

46 HABBERTON, JOHN. Brief review of Symonds (1893.9). Godey's Magazine 127 (November), 623.
Symonds takes Whitman too seriously, as most English critics do; Americans hardly recognize poetry in him. The reasons he offers for terming Whitman a great genius are "too indefinite to win many to his way of thinking."

47 C[HADWICK], J. W. "Literature. Walt Whitman." Christian Register, 72 (2 November), 698.
Review of In Re, a disservice to Whitman, who does not need such defending. One has only to pick up his work to escape from this atmosphere of excessive adulation and appreciate Whitman for oneself.

48 SANBORN, F. B. "Thoreau and His English Friend Thomas Cholmondeley." Atlantic Monthly 72 (December), 750, 752-53.
Quotes letter of 16 December 1856 from Cholmondeley to Thoreau asking about Whitman, "who appears to be a strong man" but is writing only fragments; letter of 26 May 1857 (reprinted: 1894.16) describes his difficulty understanding Whitman, whose work Thoreau had sent him: "I find reality and beauty mixed with not a little violence and coarseness, both of which are to me effeminate. I am amused at his views of sexual energy, which, however, are absurdly false." "It is the first book I have ever seen which I should call 'a new book.'"

49 PAYNE, WILLIAM MORTON. "Whitmaniana." Dial 15 (16 December), 390-92.
Review of In Re, necessary for the student of Whitman or American literature but too eulogistic. His "fanatical devotees," praising his faults and virtues alike, keep the cultivated public from realizing his true stature. Contents are described and evaluated.

1894

BOOKS

1 BURROUGHS, JOHN. Riverby. Boston and New York: Houghton, Mifflin & Co., pp. 213-14, 248.
Incidental references and quotation of Whitman, noting his feeling for the night.

2 FISKE, JOHN. Edward Livingston Youmans. New York: D. Appleton & Co., p. 46.
Youmans met Whitman in New York in 1842 when he was editing the Aurora and Whitman wrote for it, "when he was plain Mr. Whitman, wearing a coat and necktie like other people." Youmans later maintained "that Walt was an arrant humbug," his "yawp" and "obtusive filthiness" "assumed purely for pelf, after he had found that polite writing would not pay his bills."

3 GARLAND, HAMLIN. Crumbling Idols: Twelve Essays on Art Dealing Chiefly with Literature, Painting and the Drama. Chicago and Cambridge: Stone & Kimball, pp. 9, 11, 39, 45, 73, 117, 189.
Reprint of 1893.42 with other minor references.

4 GAY, WILLIAM. Sonnets and Other Verses. Melbourne: E. A. Petherick & Co. "To Walt Whitman," p. 10.
Sonnet.

5 JOHNSON, LIONEL. The Art of Thomas Hardy. London: Elkin Mathews & John Lane; New York: Dodd, Mead & Co., p. 10.
Though Whitman felt that democracy and America justified his rejection of metrical law, he is "most a poet, when, forgetting the imagined new needs of his time and country, he chaunts simple, heroical things, with a 'large utterance,' almost Homeric."

1894

6 LINTON, W[ILLIAM] J[AMES]. <u>Threescore and Ten</u>
   <u>Years 1820 to 1890: Recollections</u>. New
   York: Charles Scribner's Sons, pp. 216-17.
   Reprinted in 1895 as <u>Memories</u> (London:
   Lawrence & Bulley).
      Recalls seeing Whitman in Washington
   and Camden, and his fondness for the "fine-
   natured, good-hearted, big fellow," "a true
   poet who could not write poetry." Brief
   comment on his war work and recognition for
   it.

7 MITCHELL, S. WEIR. <u>When All the Woods Are</u>
   <u>Green: A Novel</u>. New York: Century Co.,
   pp. 274-75.
      Several characters discuss Whitman,
   one "thankful for what he does" and recalling him as "the most innocently and
   entirely vain creature I ever knew." One
   character's friend once sent Whitman a
   check for an autographed copy of "Captain,"
   which Whitman sent. Poems that a young
   girl might read are suggested.

8 MORRIS, HARRISON S. <u>Madonna and Other Poems</u>.
   Philadelphia and London: J. B. Lippincott.
   "Walt Whitman," p. 187.
   Reprinted from 1892.15. Reprinted: 1900.
   16.

9 NORTON, CHARLES ELIOT, ed. <u>Letters of James</u>
   <u>Russell Lowell</u>. Vol. 1. New York: Harper
   & Bros., pp. 242-43.
   Reprinted: 1928.18.
      Letter to Norton (12 October 1855) in
   response to his of 23 September (see 1913.
   14) recalls Whitman at the <u>Democratic</u>
   <u>Review</u>, disagrees with Norton over Whitman's
   worth, stating that an artist needs not
   mere power but self-restraint as well and
   should not aim at originality.

10 OSTRANDER, STEPHEN M. <u>A History of the City</u>
   <u>of Brooklyn and Kings County</u>. Vol. 2.
   Brooklyn: Published by subscription, p.
   89; facsimile, facing p. 90.
      Whitman is mentioned as editor of
   <u>Brooklyn Eagle</u> and in other connections
   with Brooklyn. His letter to Charles M.
   Skinner of 19 January 1885 is printed in
   facsimile.

11 RAYMOND, GEORGE LANSING. <u>Art in Theory: An</u>
   <u>Introduction to the Study of Comparative</u>
   <u>Aesthetics</u>. New York and London: G. P.
   Putnam's Sons, pp. 28-29.
      "Our American representative of the
   exclusively romantic tendency is Whitman,"
   generally devoid of meter, aesthetic subjects, picturesque phraseology. His virile
   and suggestive matter and manner are a
   force for good in literature, but his works
   cannot be considered poetry.

12 _____. <u>Rhythm and Harmony in Poetry and Music</u>
   <u>together with Music as a Representative</u>
   <u>Art: Two Essays in Comparative Aesthetics</u>.
   New York and London: G. P. Putnam's Sons,

pp. xxi-xxii, 111.
   Whitman is being praised by those who
earlier worshipped other poets for form.
His works have not even a suggestion of
such excellence in form which his admirers
once considered the only standard of poetic
merit. The laws of sound apply equally to
poetry and to music, though Whitman's admirers might deny it.

13 RHYS, ERNEST. <u>A London Rose & Other Rhymes</u>.
   London: Elkin Mathews & John Lane; New
   York: Dodd Mead & Co. "To Walt Whitman on
   His 70th Birthday," p. 84.
   Revised from 1889.9 and from Traubel II.
   Reprinted: Legler.

14 ROBERTSON, J[AMES] LOGIE. <u>A History of English</u>
   <u>Literature for Secondary Schools</u>. New York:
   Harper & Bros., p. 336.
      Summary paragraph on Whitman, "the most
   original and national of American poets;
   originator of a unique style, which is
   neither prose nor verse, yet is not wanting
   in a wild kind of rhythm, and is often
   highly poetical."

15 RUTHERFORD, MILDRED. <u>American Authors: A</u>
   <u>Hand-book of American Literature</u>. Atlanta:
   Franklin Printing & Publishing Co., pp.
   322-27.
      Whitman is "a coarse poet" and "appeals
   to the worst part of our nature, not the
   best." American writers and editors
   honored his genius but not his coarseness.
   Brief life sketch; Whitman's comments on
   his intentions. Positive and negative
   opinions are quoted from F. H. Williams,
   Thomas Hughes, and others.

16 SANBORN, F. B., ed. <u>Familiar Letters of Henry</u>
   <u>David Thoreau</u>. Boston and New York:
   Houghton, Mifflin & Co., pp. 321, 339-41,
   345-49.
   Reprint of letters from 1865.1, which are
   reprinted: Miller; Hindus. Also reprint
   of Cholmondeley letter (1893.48).
      Notes Thoreau's gift of <u>Leaves</u> to
   Cholmondeley, whose stepfather threatened
   to throw it in the fire upon hearing some
   of it read. Thoreau's visit to Whitman is
   described, with the strong impression Whitman
   made on his life. Extracts from Alcott's
   diary are quoted regarding his visit with
   Thoreau to Whitman on 10 November 1856 (see
   corrected, complete versions in 1938.16).

17 SIMONDS, ARTHUR B. <u>American Song: A Collection</u>
   <u>of Representative American Poems, with Ana-</u>
   <u>lytical and Critical Studies of the Writers,</u>
   <u>With Introductions and Notes</u>. New York and
   London: G. P. Putnam's Sons. "Walt
   Whitman," pp. 107-9; poems (chiefly from
   "Calamus," "Sands," and "Drum-Taps"), 109-
   15.
   Quoted in 1897.49.
      Whitman's debts to Homer, Shakespeare,
   Job, Emerson are explained, with his "obser-

vation of American barbarism." He terms
America's qualities his own, "pride, care-
lessness, and generous receptivity." His
subjects and successful poems are described,
particularly the shorter ones here anthologized, which fulfill "the artistic conditions of proportion and unity" and reveal
different poetic moods. With less disdain
of literary form, he would have been a much
more important figure.

18 SWINBURNE, ALGERNON CHARLES. Studies in Prose
and Poetry. London: Chatto & Windus.
"Whitmania," pp. 129-40.
Reprint of 1887.63, with minor changes.
Reprinted: 1926.29.

19 WILLIAMS, FRANCIS HOWARD. The Flute-Player
and Other Poems. New York and London:
G. P. Putnam's Sons. "Walt Whitman (May
31, 1886)," reprint of 1887.15, p. 78;
"Walt Whitman (March 26, 1892)," reprinted
from 1893.11, reprinted in 1900.16, p. 79.

PERIODICALS

*20 CHOPIN, KATE. "A Respectable Woman." Vogue
(4 January).
Reported in "Kate Chopin and Walt Whitman,"
by Lewis Leary, WWR 16 (December 1970),
120-21. Reprinted: 1897.4.
A man quotes "Myself" 21.

21 BURROUGHS, JOHN. "Walt Whitman and His Art."
Poet-Lore 6 (February), 63-69.
Reprinted in part: 1896.2.
    Whitman's abandonment of poetic conven-
tions is equivalent to the rejection of
religious ritual, relying solely upon the
spontaneous motions of the spirit. He is
inartistic only when he is ineffective.
He conveys by suggestion, conceals the
artist. He uses art, but for the purpose
of reflecting nature.

*22 HORTON, Rev. R. F. "Walt Whitman." Great
Thoughts (February).
Reported in Saunders Supplement (with typescript copy) but not located in this issue.
    Whitman is "too American for the Ameri-
cans." "What most men consider nasty is
not nasty to him" but part of the humanity
he accepts. His primary quality is the
"power of entering into the life of the
universe and interpreting it with a human
passion," in an appropriately rhymeless
and meterless expression. "Cradle" is
compared with the poetry of Shelley and
Tennyson.

23 P[ORTER, CHARLOTTE]. "'In Re Walt Whitman'
and Other Books on Whitman." Poet-Lore 6
(February), 95-101.
    Review of Burroughs (1867.1), Bucke
(1883.3), Clarke (1892.3), Symonds (1893.
9), In Re (1893.11). Whitman's stated
purpose behind his egotism is "universal
self-reliance," which Symonds ignores.

Clarke fails to comprehend Whitman's
"pivotal idea of the claims of personality."
The variety of the contents of In Re (described) is appropriate to Whitman. Bucke
deals well with Whitman's personal development but fails to place Whitman in literary
tradition and reveal his artistic debts.

24 ANON. "Telegraphic Brevities." New York
Times (1 February), 8:6.
    Mary Davis has been awarded five hundred
dollars in her suit for five thousand dollars
against Whitman's estate.

25 THOMPSON, MAURICE. "The Sapphic Secret."
Atlantic Monthly 73 (March), 367.
    Whitman is mentioned in two paragraphs.
Greek realism rather than that of Whitman,
Ibsen, or Tolstoy is the true realism.
Whitman was not able to achieve the freedom
and heathen sincerity of ancient man because
of the "difference between original,
unconscious nakedness and a belated bluster
about 'truthfulness to nature.'"

26 BURROUGHS, JOHN. "'The Saphhic Secret.'"
Critic 21 (17 March), 177-78.
    Response to 1894.25. Whitman emulates
the Greeks by taking his place and time as
joyously and fearlessly as they did. "He
is modern and alive and forgets the past in
his absorption of the present." He brings
to America the needed "un-literary" values
the Greeks exemplify.

27 THOMPSON, MAURICE. "Again 'The Sapphic
Secret.'" Critic 21 (31 March), 211-12.
    Response to 1894.26. "Whitman did not
sing American civilization" as the Greek
poets sang the Greek, for he emphasizes an
un-American, "Greek nakedness and the
'phallic thumb of Love.'"

28 GOSSE, EDMUND. "A Note on Walt Whitman." New
Review 10 (April), 447-57.
Reprinted: 1894.32; 1896.6; 1925.5; 1928.
12.
    Because Whitman's work is "literature
in the condition of protoplasm," his critics
find in him reflections of themselves.
Every sensitive person goes through but
generally passes out of "a period of fierce
Whitmanomania." Account of Gosse's reluctant visit to Whitman in Camden, on Whitman's
invitation, in January 1885. He was taken
in by Whitman's "magnetic charm." Whitman's
theory of "uncompromising openness" strips
away social conventions; "a keenly observant
and sentient being, without thought," he
goes further than Rousseau. He provides
self-recognition for readers at a particular
crisis in their development, but is this
literary? "Myself" (described) reveals
many happy phrases as well as such flaws as
laxity of thought, brutality, toleration of
the ugly and forbidden. Whitman just misses
being one of the greatest of modern poets.

29 PLATT, ISAAC HULL. "Walt Whitman's Ethics."
    Conservator 5 (April), 24.
        Whitman's ethics proceed from his ideal
    of universal beauty and goodness and not
    from mere obedience to dogma.

30 BUCKE, RICHARD MAURICE. "Cosmic Consciousness,
    I." Conservator 5 (May), 37-39.
        Traces evolution of the mind in the
    human race, leading to cosmic consciousness.
    This discussion is based on twenty-three
    individuals, including Whitman (just men-
    tioned). The material provides the basis
    for Bucke's book of the same title (1901.3).
    Concluded 1894.33.

31 CARPENTER, EDWARD. "'Towards Democracy.'"
    Labour Prophet 3 (May), 49-51.
    Reprinted: 1922.4.
        "LEAVES OF GRASS 'filtered and fibred'
    my blood: but I do not think I ever tried
    to imitate it or its style." Carpenter's
    Towards Democracy may resemble it because of
    similar "emotional atmosphere" and because
    of Whitman's personal influence on him,
    although the two men have opposite temper-
    aments and standpoints. "Whitman's full-
    blooded, copious, rank, masculine style
    must always make him one of the world's
    great originals--a perennial fountain of
    health and strength, moral as well as phys-
    ical."

32 GOSSE, EDMUND. "A Note on Walt Whitman."
    Littell's Living Age 201 (26 May), 495-501.
    Reprint of 1894.28.

33 BUCKE, RICHARD MAURICE. "Cosmic Consciousness,
    II." Conservator 5 (June), 51-54.
        Concludes 1894.30. Describes onset of
    cosmic consciousness, quoting and citing
    Whitman and others as examples. Those with
    this faculty represent the coming of a new
    race.

34 CLARKE, HELEN A. "The Relations of Music to
    Poetry in American Poets." Music 6 (June),
    163-74.
        Describes how Whitman, among other
    poets, deals with music: his idea of har-
    mony, his historical sense regarding the
    development of art (although he tends to be
    too inclusive of all, while Emerson excludes
    all but the beautiful). He made the first
    recognition of "distinct individualities in
    music" which for him was not an abstraction
    as for the older poets. Music was important
    as his inspiration, particularly in "Proud
    Music." Concluded July 1894, with no men-
    tion of Whitman.

35 GILMAN, NICHOLAS P. "Democracy and the Poet."
    New World 3 (June), 311-28.
        Symonds's claims for Whitman (1890.8)
    neglect other democratic writers. The
    American people do not seem to care for
    Whitman's so-called democratic art. He
    emphasizes too much the bragging of the

divine average man. If his verse is formless, with no power over rhyme and meter,
"no invocation of democracy will save him
from a minor place among poets." Whittier
and Lowell better reveal "the just relations
of democracy and the poet," lifting us to
an ideal.

36 PLATT, ISAAC HULL. "The Cosmic Sense as Man-
    ifested in Shelley and Whitman." Conserva-
    tor 5 (June), 54-55.
        The concept of spirit in Whitman's
    poetry is compared with Shelley's concept
    of the "Life of Life," a spiritually tri-
    umphant force. Shelley's "precocious
    awareness" of this is matured in Whitman.

37 [TRAUBEL, HORACE.] "Walt Whitman Fellowship:
    International." Conservator 5 (June),
    60-61.
        Account of the first meeting of the
    Fellowship, 31 May 1894: founding of the
    Fellowship Papers, listing of members and
    officers, object of the group. A letter of
    greeting from J. W. Wallace is printed.

*38 SPEDDING, W. "Walt Whitman." Primitive
    Methodist Quarterly Review (July).
    Reported in Saunders Supplement, but not
    located in this year.

39 ANON. "Literary Notes." New York Tribune
    (6 July), 8:2.
        Describes founding of Whitman Fellowship
    a few weeks ago; quotes an English opinion
    of Whitman as the great standard for English
    democracy.

40 ANON. "Notes." Critic 22 (7 July), 16.
        Lists the officers of the newly founded
    Whitman Fellowship.

*41 X.X.X. [J. LE GAY BRERETON]. "Hints on Walt
    Whitman's 'Leaves of Grass.'" Hermes
    (University of Sydney) (25 July), 10-12.
    Reprinted: McLeod.
        Whitman's lack of humor prevents him
    from realizing when he is making himself
    look ridiculous. But even in his catalogues
    each line often conveys a beautiful and
    distinct picture. His poetry must be read
    as a chant. His work comes out of natural
    forces; his form is sometimes perfect. He
    forces us to use our own intelligence. He
    loves vastness but also accurately de-
    scribes all natural objects. Concluded
    1894.46.

42 A[STOR], W. W. "Walt Whitman's 'Leaves of
    Grass.'" Pall Mall Magazine 3 (August),
    709-11.
        Whitman embodies the ideal of American
    democracy. He presents "brilliant thoughts"
    and natural impressions but also "the mud
    beneath," "the freest possible relations
    between the sexes," the lack of distinction
    among religions. He is at his best when
    writing without affectation and in a senti-
    mental, retrospective vein, as in "The Dead

Tenor." He has skill at conveying meaning
concisely but also has "much vague utterance and undefined longing and vapoury
boasting." He has survived because of his
eroticism. A nine-line parody, "I am Walt
Whitman," is quoted.

*43 BUTCHART, REUBEN. "Song of the Wheel."
Toronto Saturday Night (August).
Reprinted: Saunders.
Parody. Not located in the four August
1894 issues.

44 ONDERDONK, JAMES L. "Walt Whitman--A Character Sketch." Altruistic Review (August),
64-77.
Abridged: 1901.14.
The state of American poetry into which
Whitman entered is explained, including
Whitman's forerunners in themes, purposes,
nationalism, and method. He seemed to
affect vulgarisms artificially, since "music
and melody were inherent in his soul." His
individuality is most true when he forgets
his self-imposed mission and gives rein to
his fancy, as in "Trumpeter." "Broad-Axe"
reveals his elemental grandeur. His lines
recreate nature; his attitudes toward death
and modern science are noteworthy, their
expression unsurpassed. "Passage" is
nobler than "Exposition" as a poem of
modern science. He represents the entire
republic, not a particular section.

45 WILLIAMS, FRANCIS HOWARD. "Walt Whitman as
Deliverer." Walt Whitman Fellowship Papers
1, no. 4 (August), 11-30.
Whitman points away from the myth of
antiquity by favoring the present. He
delivers one from the art myth by advancing
the growth of art; his art suffers when he
curtails his freedom of expression ("Captain," "Ethiopia"). Regarding the myth of
social convention, Whitman seeks not to
destroy but to build up, eradicating vice;
his sexual poems must be viewed as referring to an individual who epitomizes the
race.

*46 X.X.X. [J. LE GAY BRERETON]. "Hints on Walt
Whitman's 'Leaves of Grass.'" Hermes
(University of Sydney) (14 August), 8-9.
Reprinted: McLeod.
Concludes 1894.41. Whitman's personality is his theme, but it is healthy, not
morbid or egoistic, seeking affinity with
nature and one's natural impulses, accepting the interdependence of body and soul,
the absence of shame in sex, the tender and
even physical qualities of friendship ("an
indispensable element in Democracy"). His
equality, identification, ability to see
below the surface of things, belief in
eternal progress and evil's insignificance
are described.

47 BUCKE, RICHARD MAURICE. "Memories of Walt
Whitman." Walt Whitman Fellowship Papers
1, no. 6 (September), 35-46.

Account of his meeting with Whitman.
Whitman is quoted on his work. His humor
and the funeral are described.

48 SAVAGE, M. J. "The Religion of Walt Whitman's
Poems." Arena 10 (September), 433-52.
Reprinted: 1935.7.
Whitman was a truer disciple of Christ
than many modern Christians. His egotism
means that every personality is no less
wonderful than God. His optimism leads to
acceptance of the physical, although he
rejects impurity. His acceptance of death
was tested during the war. Extensive
quotations illustrate Whitman's ideals and
are compared to Old Testament poetry.

49 TRAUBEL, HORACE L. "Walt Whitman and Good
and Evil: a Discussion." Conservator 5
(September), 103-6.
Record of a conversation among Bucke
and others following a reading from Leaves:
Whitman's egotism, belief in immortality,
regard for good and evil as positive forces,
belief in cultural evolution, attitude
toward slavery. Some passages are interpreted.

50 ANON. "Literary Notes." New York Tribune
(16 September), 14:5.
Criticizes Williams (1894.45): his
enthusiasm leads him to a misguided attempt
to put Whitman into blank verse, which "is
not Whitman!"

51 ANON. "Literary Notes." New York Tribune
(23 September), 14:5.
Bucke's paper (1894.47) shows him still
"swinging the censer" in Whitman's worship.
Whitman's absurdity is evident in a proof
he offered for Bacon's authorship of
Shakespeare.

52 ANON. "Notes and News." Poet-Lore 6 (October),
526-27.
Praises and quotes Savage's appreciative
criticism (1894.48).

53 T[RAUBEL, HORACE]. "At West Hills in October."
Conservator 5 (October), 123.
Brief free-verse poem on his visit to
the birthplace of Whitman, who is referred
to only as "the child illustrious just born,
the vicissitudes and honors of the future
unsuspected."

54 TRAUBEL, HORACE L. "Walt Whitman and Murger."
Poet-Lore 6 (October), 484-91.
Prints Murger's poem "La ballade de
désespéré," a literal translation of it,
and Whitman's rhymed version, "The Midnight
Visitor," to reveal the quality of Whitman's
achievement. Comments on the poem from
Whitman and others are quoted. Whitman's
readings of his version are described.

55 ANON. "Huntington. A Hunt for Mementoes of
Walt Whitman, the Poet." New York Tribune
(13 October), 13:4.

1894

Account of visit by Traubel, Platt, and Brinton to Long Island. The Fellowship's purposes are described.

56 ANON. "Literary Notes." New York Tribune (25 October), 8:1.
Quotes extracts from 1894.54.

57 ANON. Response to Burroughs (1894.21). Poet-Lore 6 (November), 577-79.
Whitman was indeed literary, having rewritten his first draft of Leaves five times before he was satisfied. He was receptive to the past.

58 BURROUGHS, JOHN. "Whitman's Self-Reliance." Conservator 5 (November), 131-34.
Same as 1894.59. Reprinted: 1896.2.
Whitman fulfilled Emerson's ideal of the self-reliant man, remaining heroic in the face of rejection. Leaves "is a monument to the faith of one man in himself." Whitman's egotism united him to his fellows.

59 _____. "Whitman's Self-Reliance." Walt Whitman Fellowship Papers 1, no. 9 (November), 51-58.
Same as 1894.58.

60 LARMINIE, WILLIAM. "The Development of English Metres." Contemporary Review 66 (November), 730-31.
In the matter of irregular, unrhymed meters, Whitman was on the right track with his revolt, creating more musical lines than Henley and Matthew Arnold and even than writers of much orthodox rhymed verse. If he had combined culture with his great gifts and had understood his principles more clearly, he could have effected a complete metrical revolution.

61 QUINN, ARTHUR HOBSON. "Walt Whitman and the Poetry of Democracy." The Red and Blue (University of Pennsylvania) 7 (November), 33-41.
Whitman confines his attention to the lower third of the human race, but singing of the lower ranks is not new. His form fails to make his truly noble thoughts (as in "Calamus") capable of moving readers by unpleasantly mixing lines of metrical cadence with lines lacking it. He does not have a sustained poetic impulse. He cannot be the founder of the poetic school of democracy because he is not a great poet nor the first or the true exponent of democracy. He and Symonds (1890.8) are refuted: democratic art cannot be a new type of art, different from classic and romantic; Whitman is therefore a classicist in choice of subject (the familiar), a romanticist in treatment (which is strange). His productions hover on the borderline of art; thus he has done nothing for art, although his thought is valuable and true.

*62 YEATS, W. B. Letter to editor. United Ireland (24 November).
Reprinted: Wade.
In response to a recent comment on Americans not heeding British critics, Yeats claims that Whitman, "the most National of her poets," was indeed helped by Irish and English admirers who counteracted America's neglect of him because of his originality. (Signed "A Student of Irish Literature.")

63 ANON. Review of Simonds (1894.17). Poet-Lore 6 (December), 633-34.
Incidental: "Whitman is not shown reaching his highest table-lands of utter trust in the Soul, in Religion, and in Man, because his bent is still 'caviare to the general.'"

64 BRINTON, DANIEL G., and TRAUBEL, HORACE L. "A Visit to West Hills." Walt Whitman Fellowship Papers 1, no. 10 (December), 59-66.
Each in turn describes his visit to Whitman's birthplace with Platt. Anecdotes from townsfolk about young Whitman, remembered as "naturally lazy," not a churchgoer. No one had unpleasant memories of him.

65 CLARKE, HELEN A. "Walt Whitman and Music." Conservator 5 (December), 153-54.
Describes Whitman's love for opera; concept of harmony, projected to the cosmic level; habit of singing to himself as a possible basis for some poems.

66 P. A. C. [Charlotte Porter and Helen A. Clarke]. "A Short Reading Course in Whitman." Poet-Lore 6 (December), 644-48.
Reprinted: 1895.19; 1919.277 in part.
In response to subscribers' requests, poems are suggested to help understand Whitman's ideas, concentrating on Love, Democracy, and Religion.

*67 YEATS, W. B. Letter to editor. United Ireland (1 December).
Reprinted: Wade.
Though Emerson praised Whitman (as cited in an editorial response to 1894.62), other Americans hounded him from office and refused to publish his contributions to magazines. However, English writers praised him, representing "that audience, 'fit though few,' which is greater than any nation" and placing him among the immortals.

1895

BOOKS

1 BLOCK, LOUIS JAMES. The New World, with Other Verse. New York and London: G. P. Putnam's Sons. "Walt Whitman," pp. 84-86.
Reprint of 1893.38.

2 BROWN, HORATIO F. *John Addington Symonds: A Biography Compiled from His Papers and Correspondence.* New York: Charles Scribner's Sons. Vol. 1, pp. 404, 412, 413; vol. 2, pp. 15-16, 70, 130-31, 132, 134, 182, 281, 291, 331, 337.

Generally brief references from Symonds's letters and journal revealing Whitman's impact on him; some ideas were used in 1893.9.

3 BURROUGHS, JOHN. *Winter Sunshine.* Boston and New York: Houghton, Mifflin & Co., pp. 2, 105, 206.

Reprint of 1875.1.

An essay, "Autumn Tides," is added, with a quotation from Whitman.

4 CHENEY, JOHN VANCE. *That Dome in Air: Thoughts on Poetry and the Poets.* Chicago: A. C. McClurg & Co. "Walt Whitman," pp. 144-68.

Reprint of 1893.21.

5 GAY, WILLIAM. *Walt Whitman: His Relation to Science and Philosophy.* Melbourne: Mason, Firth & M'Cutcheon, 48 pp.

Reprinted: McLeod.

Whitman overestimated his poetic calling and intuition at the expense of intellectual efforts, although he recognized and accepted science, transforming it into great poetry in "Myself." Because immersed in reality, he appeals to many who find most modern poetry irrelevant. His debts to Hegel are explained. Though he wrote some poetry of the highest quality ("Lilacs," "Trumpeter," "Cradle"), he is best classed with the modern prophets like Carlyle and Emerson, stinging readers into thought.

6 HARTMANN, P. SADAKICHI. *Conversations with Walt Whitman.* New York: E. P. Coby & Co., 51 pp.

Reprinted: Knox.

Informal account of his acquaintance with Whitman in Camden, 1884-91. Their conversation is quoted, with Whitman's comments on politics and literature. His own altercation with Harned over the authenticity of his statements is described, along with his efforts to found a Whitman society and visits with Burroughs and Stedman.

7 LLOYD, J[OHN] WILLIAM. *Wind-Harp Songs.* Buffalo: Peter Paul Book Co. "Mount Walt Whitman," pp. 34-35.

Free-verse poem on Whitman's death, comparing him to a mountain.

8 NORDAU, MAX. *Degeneration.* Trans. from the 2d ed. of the German work. London: William Heinemann, pp. 230-32.

Reprinted: Hindus.

Whitman's madness, but not his genius, is undoubted. His shameless outbursts of "erotomania" made his fame. He lacks moral sense; his patriotism is sycophantic; his "hysterical exclamations" have rejected

form as too difficult. He is compared to Verlaine (as a man), to Wagner and Maeterlinck (as an artist).

9 ROSSETTI, WILLIAM MICHAEL, ed. *Dante Gabriel Rossetti: His Family-Letters.* Vol. 2. Boston: Roberts Bros., pp. 332, 348-49.

Letters to William of 1876 and 1878 support the subscription for Whitman but question his ranking with great poets or anyone not writing "sublimated Tupper." But he appreciates Whitman's "fine qualities."

10 [STEAD, W. T.], ed. *Poems by Walt Whitman.* The Masterpiece Library, The Penny Poets, no. 27. London: *Review of Reviews* Office, 60 pp.

Extract reprinted: 1896.28.

Introductory and explanatory notes for some of the poetry. Whitman's poems are now available to the average person. He believed in the world as good, although he was not blind to its miseries. He was rather unconcerned about his inconsistencies, which reflect his place and time. His egotism is explained, as are his songs of the divinity of sex as "the supreme outcome of intense affection" and his sympathy with the individual soldier in war.

11 WOLFE, THEODORE F. *Literary Shrines: The Haunts of Some Famous American Authors.* Philadelphia: J. B. Lippincott Co. "A Day with the Good Gray Poet," pp. 201-17; also 50.

Record of a visit to Whitman in Camden (date unspecified): his home, person, conversation, religious and poetic faith, readings of "Lilacs" and "Cradle," comments on fellow-writers and critics.

PERIODICALS

12 JACKSON, EDWARD PAYSON. "Whitman and Tolstoi." *Conservator* 5 (January), 165-68.

Text of his Fellowship lecture and brief summary of subsequent discussion. Tolstoy and Whitman typify different phases of the Christ-idea; both are energetic idealists, undeterred by opposition, loving mankind.

13 KENNEDY, WILLIAM SLOANE. "Suppressing a Poet." *Conservator* 5 (January), 169-71.

Traces the history of Whitman's Boston suppression; records briefly Kennedy's talks with Rev. Frederick Baylie Allen of the Vice Society and with District Attorney Stevens. Whitman, in opposition to the antinaturalistic, ascetic religion of his suppressors, has founded "a new religion, which accepts and rejoices in the body."

14 TOWNSHEND, E. C. "Towards the Appreciation of Emile Zola." *Westminster Review* 143 (January), 65.

Whitman was surprisingly unaware of

1895

Zola when he prophesied a literature of the
future. His prose and poetry ("some of
those strange rhythmic utterances where
Whitman boasts of a lofty pantheism") are
quoted as applicable to Zola.

15 COMPENDIUM. "Whitman." Conservator 5 (February), 189.
     Current periodical and book mentions
of Whitman.

16 EDITOR. "Walt Whitman." Labour Prophet 4
     (February), 17-18. Illustrated.
     We need reverence for heroes like
Whitman, not a cult but rather appreciation
of his book, which emphasizes one's self as
the source of life, joy, and truth. His
treatment of the relation of body with soul
is honest, but he falls short of the height
in failing to deal with the sacredness of
married life. "Cradle" reveals him as a
poet possessing "the beauty and pathos and
mystery of life and death and nature." He
is the poet of something greater than state
socialism: namely "the divinity of the
Body and the Soul," the private possession
of oneself.

17 FIELDS, ANNIE [Mrs. James T.]. "Oliver Wendell
     Holmes. Personal Recollections and Unpub-
     lished Letters." Century Magazine 49 (Feb-
     ruary), 511.
     Reprinted: 1896.5.
     Quotes Holmes, who thought the right
thing had not been said about Whitman:
"Emerson believes in him; Lowell not at all;
Longfellow finds some good in his 'yaup'
[sic]: but the truth is, he is in an amorphous condition."

18 KENNEDY, WILLIAM SLOANE. "The Friendship of
     Whitman and Emerson." Poet-Lore 7 (Feb-
     ruary), 71-74.
     Whitman did not know Emerson except
from magazine pieces before publishing
Leaves. His letter to Kennedy denying
prior acquaintance is printed. The two
poets truly loved each other, Emerson finding in Whitman his complement, through his
"new friendship among men." His letter
(1855.12) is reprinted. This material is
used in 1896.9.

19 PORTER, CHARLOTTE, and CLARKE, HELEN A. "A
     Short Reading Course in Whitman." Walt
     Whitman Fellowship Papers 1, no. 13 (Feb-
     ruary), 73-79.
     Reprint of 1894.66.

20 WILLIAM, FRANCIS HOWARD. "Reply to a Critic."
     Conservator 5 (February), 182-85.
     Answers the various criticisms in
Walker Kennedy's North American Review
essay (1884.21).

21 [CHAMBERLIN, J. E.] "The Listener." Boston
     Evening Transcript (9 February), 12:4.
     Describes Whitman's tomb, appropriate
for the poet "most closely in sympathy with
American democracy," yet not what this
writer would have chosen for Whitman, who
would have been better buried in the woods
or near the sea, or else cremated to unite
his body with the elements, as his works
urge.

21a BURROUGHS, JOHN. "Democracy and Literature."
     Outlook 51 (16 February), 266.
     Incidental: "Democracy in literature,
as exemplified by the two great moral democrats in letters, Whitman and Tolstoï,
means a new and more deeply religious way
of looking at mankind, as well as at all
the facts and objects of the visible world"
and means finding poetic motives in science
and the people.

22 PORTER, CHARLOTTE. Letter in "The Listener."
     Boston Evening Transcript (16 February),
     12:4.
     Response to 1895.21. The tomb did ful-
fill Whitman's plans, though contradictory
to his philosophy, perhaps showing "survival
of old conventions" and a pride in future
pilgrims to the site. This inconsistency
may comfort his disciples, since "not all
genuine Whitmanism is contained in Whitman,
but depends upon them for its fulfillment."

22a [CHAMBERLIN, J. E.] "The Listener." Boston
     Evening Transcript (20 February), 4:5.
     Prints W. S. K[ennedy]'s letter in re-
sponse to 1895.22: Whitman is buried in
the woods, and his tomb was for his family,
not only himself. He built it securely
to prohibit tomb robberies. His egotism in
building this monument to himself is understandable and deserves the gratitude of
future generations. His principles are
noted, not including repudiation of wealth
or exaltation of poverty. "The Listener"
responds, rejecting the idea that he and
Porter were criticizing Whitman's motives.
For what happens to the body is not what is
important, as lines from Whitman show.

22b CLARKE, HELEN A. "Passage to India." Conser-
     vator 6 (March), 7-10.
     "Passage" is explained as tracing the
relation of the material universe to God,
who is here given the most anthropomorphic
conception in literature.

23 P. A. C. [Charlotte Porter and Helen A. Clarke].
     "School of Literature. Poems Illustrative
     of American History: Poems of Discoveries;
     Lowell's 'Columbus' and Whitman's 'Prayer
     of Columbus.'" Poet-Lore 7 (March), 161-66.
     Both poems reveal Columbus's inward
character through a key moment of introspection. Historical information is offered
to correlate with the imaginative conceptions
in these poems. Continued 1895.26.

24 [CHAMBERLIN, J. E.] "The Listener." Boston
     Evening Transcript (2 March), 12:4.

Reprints "Of Him I Love Day and Night"
as evidence that Whitman supported "The
Listener's" and Porter's argument (see
1895.22a).

24a ANON. "'Passage to India': A Discussion."
Conservator 6 (April), 24-25.
Quotes several speakers in discussion
arising from 1895.22b; some reminiscences
of Whitman; Ernest Fenollosa on the sounds
in Whitman's poetry.

25 BRINTON, DANIEL G. "Walt Whitman and Science."
Conservator 6 (April) 20-21.
Whitman's poetry reflects the growth
of science in his age. A possible influence may be J. W. Draper's History of Civilization. Whitman's ideal man is the goal
of universal evolution.

26 P. A. C. [Charlotte Porter and Helen A. Clarke].
"School of Literature. Poems Illustrative
of American History: Discoveries: Lowell's
and Whitman's Columbus." Poet-Lore 7
(April), 218-22.
Continues 1895.23. Whitman's version
agrees with actual events. His Columbus
is a man of high spirituality rather than
intellectual grasp in contrast to Lowell's.
Both explorers look toward an improved
humanity, but Lowell's does so out of resentment, Whitman's for the sake of humanity. Concluded 1895.32.

27 TRAUBEL, HORACE L. "Walt Whitman, Schoolmaster: Notes of a Conversation with
Charles A. Roe, 1894." Walt Whitman Fellowship Papers 1, no. 14 (April), 81-87.
After a biographical sketch of Roe
(born 1829), a former student of Whitman's
at Flushing, his conversational recollections of Whitman at the time are transcribed.

28 ANON. "'Earthly, Sensual, Devilish.'"
Independent 47 (11 April), 487.
Incidental reference in this article
disapproving of Wilde's behavior and his
theory of art for art's sake: "The worship
of Whitman's vulgar animalism has found its
logical conclusion."

29 HARTE, W. B. "Dr. Nordau on Walt Whitman."
Critic 23 (13 April), 280.
Letter citing Nordau's opinion of
Whitman in 1895.8.

30 CLARKE, HELEN A. "Does Whitman Harmonize His
Doctrine of Evil with the Pursuit of Ideals?"
Conservator 6 (May), 39-43.
Whitman presents the opposing elements
of positive and negative forces, with un-
wavering faith in complete good as the end
of the process.

31 PECK, HARRY THURSTON. "Some Recent Volumes of
Verse." Bookman 1 (May), 254.
Review of Stephen Crane's The Black

Rider and Other Lines. Incidental: "In
fact, if Walt Whitman had been caught young
and subjected to aesthetic influences, it
is likely that he would have mellowed his
barbaric yawp to some such note" as that
of Crane's poems.

32 P. A. C. [Charlotte Porter and Helen A. Clarke].
"School of Literature. Poems Illustrative
of American History: Discoveries: (Conclusion.)" Poet-Lore 7 (May), 275-77.
Concludes 1895.26. Presents quotations
from Columbus's letters and log; study
questions for the two poems.

33 BUCKE, RICHARD MAURICE. "Was Walt Whitman
Mad?" Conservator 6 (June), 55-58.
Reprinted: 1895.66.
Response to Nordau (1895.8), explaining
criteria for degenerative insanity from his
background as a physician, showing that
Whitman meets none of them, being excep-
tionally sane, like others who have tran-
scended their period (Gautama, Jesus, Dante,
Shakespeare, Balzac, etc.).

34 BURROUGHS, JOHN. "Emerson's and Lowell's
Views of Whitman." Conservator 6 (June),
51-52.
Emerson was most critical of Whitman's
intentions and concepts. For Lowell, concerned with form, Whitman offended his sense
of craft.

35 CLIFFORD, JOHN HERBERT. "The Fellowship of
Whitman." Conservator 6 (June), 51.
Reprinted: 1895.68.
Two sonnets: "What life that ever
lived or died" and "O Good Gray Poet! thou
hast never died!"

36 _____. "The Whitman Propaganda is Whitman."
Conservator 6 (June), 59-60.
Reprinted: 1895.69.
Defends the Fellowship against its
detractors, emphasizing comradeship in
Whitman's faith, not mere discipleship.

37 GARLAND, HAMLIN. "Whitman and Chicago University." Conservator 6 (June), 60-61.
Reprinted: 1895.72.
Comments on Triggs's course on Whitman
(see 1895.45), in which Garland participated.

38 HARNED, THOMAS B. "Whitman and the Future."
Conservator 6 (June), 54-55.
Reprinted: 1895.73.
Explains the elements of Whitman's
philosophy relevant for the future: his
democracy, spiritual force, religious
nature, consistency with science, courage
in facing death.

39 HOWELLS, W. D. "First Impressions of Literary
New York." Harper's New Monthly Magazine
91 (June), 62-74. Illustrated.
Reprinted: 1895.40; 1900.10; Hindus;
Hubbell.

1895

Describes his warm meeting with Whitman at Pfaff's in 1860 and a later meeting in Boston. In Whitman he always found "the sense of a sweet and true soul," with "spiritual dignity." Whitman's work is valuable as a liberating force, more for intention than effect. Howells prefers Whitman's prose.

40 _____. "Walt Whitman at Pfaff's." Conservator 6 (June), 61-62.
Reprint of Whitman reminiscence from 1895.39.

41 MAYNARD, LAURENS. "For Whitman's Birthday--1895." Conservator 6 (June), 53.
Short poem in blank verse.

42 THURNAM, ROWLAND. "To Walt Whitman." Conservator 6 (June), 55.
Sonnet: "Master, across the sea there comes thy song."

43 T[RAUBEL], H. L. "Collect." Conservator 6 (June), 49-51.
Summarizes Whitman's message: man's divinity, the social bond, social reform.

44 TRIGGS, OSCAR LOVELL. "On Degeneracy." Conservator 6 (June), 52-53.
Criticizes Nordau (1895.8): Whitman's "mysticism, egotism, and emotionalism" may be taken as symptoms of insanity, but as a whole personality, Whitman embodies the higher thought and movements of the time.

45 _____. "Whitman the Most Significant and Most Universal of Modern Writers." Conservator 6 (June), 60.
Reprinted: 1895.77.
Whitman has "advanced nearly every important modern movement." Leaves is the best example of the revelation of personality in the history of art. Triggs mentions the course he is teaching on Whitman at the University of Chicago (see also 1895.37).

46 WALLACE, J. W. "The Task Left Us by Whitman." Conservator 6 (June), 60.
Urges better fulfillment of the democratic duties Whitman bequeathed.

47 MONCK, EMILY CHRISTIANA. "Greek Traits in Walt Whitman." Poet-Lore 7 (June and July), 327-32.
Whitman is Greek in the treatment of common objects, nature, the body. Like the Greeks he rejoices in life, but he also perceives the joy of death and enlarges the democratic spirit to include the lowest classes. He suggests the absence of art which is the highest art. His fidelity to himself is an emulation of the true Greek spirit.

48 ZANGWILL, I. "Men, Women and Books." Critic 23 (22 June), 453.

Quoted in 1895.61.
Incidental reference in this discussion of Maeterlinck to his "Serres Chaudes" being "akin to the metrical chant of Whitman and the Psalms."

49 ANON. "Boston Whitman Report: May 31st." Conservator 6 (July), 76.
Lists topics of the Boston Fellowship's recent papers and discussions.

50 MILLER, KELLY. "What Walt Whitman Means to the Negro." Conservator 6 (July), 70-73.
Reprinted: 1895.74.
Contrasts Whitman's treatment of blacks as equals with the patronizing attitudes of other writers. Whitman does not depreciate culture and refinement; he seeks to lift all up, not drag any down. Whitman points to a higher destiny for the blacks. He has given the largest human expression of charity.

51 PLATT, ISAAC HULL. "The Justification of Evil." Conservator 6 (July), 75-76.
Explains good and evil as relative terms, as shown in Whitman's works, which reveal his faith in the universe.

52 ABBEY, CHARLOTTE L. "Chanting the Square Deific." Conservator 6 (August), 90-91.
Uses this poem as an object lesson for the soul's growth to perfection through encountering and transcending evil.

53 BURROUGHS, JOHN. "Two Critics of Walt Whitman." Conservator 6 (August), 84-87.
Stedman's charges of narrowness and artificiality (1885.6) are outdated. Whitman may be both a critic in prose and a prophet in poetry, judging the actual and praising the ideal. Gosse (1894.28) notes appropriately the demands Whitman makes on the reader.

54 T[RAUBEL], H. L. "Collect." Conservator 6 (August), 81.
Quotes letter from J. Leonard Corning, U.S. consul in Munich, explaining why he called Whitman a saint.

55 BORN, HELENA. "Whitman's Altruism." Conservator 6 (September), 105-7.
Reprinted: 1902.2.
Egoism must precede true altruism. Whitman's life answers all allegations of selfishness through his self-sacrifice.

56 FAWCETT, EDGAR. "Two Letters Indicating the Con of Whitman." Conservator 6 (September), 103-4.
Whitman is "an excessively unrepresentative writer." His work is "repulsive and sensational; the simple recording of impressions cannot constitute literature."

57 ANON. Review of Hartmann (1895.6). New York Herald (21 September), 11:5.

Quoted in Knox.
"We have all heard of Sadakichi, but who is Whitman? Very little will be revealed to us by this book. He appears to have been a Camden (N.J.) sage and poet whom Sadakichi honored with his friendship, but who did not rise to a full appreciation of the honor conferred."

58 ANON. "As M. Maurel Sees Us." Critic 24 (28 September), 204.
Quotes opinions of baritone Victor Maurel in Le Temps: Whitman is the "greatest man-of-letters of America, his philosophical works have placed him on the level of the great minds of Europe."

59 BUCKE, RICHARD MAURICE. "The Pro of Whitman." Conservator 6 (October), 119-20.
Brief response to Fawcett (1895.56): not all readers can appreciate Whitman.

60 BURROUGHS, JOHN. "Walt Whitman Again." Conservator 6 (October), 116-19.
Response to Fawcett (1895.56): Whitman is admired by great men of letters but is a prophet rather than being concerned with mere form. He formulated his own laws for poetry, in which he did not fail.

61 COMPENDIUM. "Odd Notes on Whitman." Conservator 6 (October), 126.
Comments on Whitman from the press.

62 FOSS, SAM WALTER. "Walt Whitman." Conservator 6 (October), 116.
Sonnet of tribute: "Thou stood'st alone and sang'st thine unschooled song."

63 JAMES, WILLIAM. "Is Life Worth Living?" International Journal of Ethics 6 (October), 2-3.
Reprinted: 1897.10; Hindus.
Incidental: Describes Whitman's optimism and joy in living, as a mood that would make the question in the title of the essay unnecessary.

64 PORTER, CHARLOTTE. "Hafiz and Whitman." Conservator 6 (October), 122.
Reprint in part of 1895.65.

65 P[ORTER, CHARLOTTE]. "The Modernism of Hafiz." Poet-Lore 7 (October), 518.
Reprinted in part: 1895.64.
Hafiz is an ancestor of Whitman, his treatment of love and friendship approaching Whitman's in respect to the unity of soul and body, but he falls short of the larger sense that Whitman conveys.

66 BUCKE, RICHARD MAURICE. "Was Walt Whitman Mad?" Walt Whitman Fellowship Papers 2, no. 9 (November), 23-30.
Reprint of 1895.33.

67 BURROUGHS, JOHN. "More Whitman Characteristics." Conservator 6 (November), 131-33.

Summary of Whitman's religion: purity of man, acceptance of physical death, immortality of the ego. His faith was an expression of feeling, not a systematic philosophy; he embodied cosmic forces. His value is not as a rebel or patriot but as a great nature.

68 CLIFFORD, JOHN HERBERT. "The Fellowship of Whitman." Walt Whitman Fellowship Papers 2, no. 2 (November), 3-4.
Reprint of 1895.35.

69 _____. "The Whitman Propaganda is Whitman." Walt Whitman Fellowship Papers 2, no. 8 (November), 19-22.
Reprint of 1895.36.

70 COG, I. N., HISTORIAN [Charlotte Porter]. "The Purport of Browning's and Whitman's Democracy. Mr. Breeze's Paper: Part IV of Annals of a Quiet Browning Club." Poet-Lore 7 (November), 556-66.
At the end of this mock record of a meeting, Whitman is described as unmatched in justifying the democratic idea with an evolutionary philosophy of history. Whitman and Browning are similar in regarding the poet as leader, but differ in art and spirit: Whitman is "the seer," Browning is "the maker-see." They appeal to different audiences but all classes should respond to their message. Continued 1895.82.

71 FAWCETT, EDGAR. "Some Responses and Ruminations." Conservator 6 (November), 135-37.
Response to Bucke (1895.59) and Burroughs (1895.60), wondering how Ingersoll could agree with Whitman's attitude toward religion, explaining the importance of art, which Whitman ignores.

72 GARLAND, HAMLIN. "Whitman and Chicago University." Walt Whitman Fellowship Papers 2, no. 6 (November), 13.
Reprint of 1895.37.

73 HARNED, THOMAS B. "Whitman and the Future." Walt Whitman Fellowship Papers 2, no. 7 (November), 15-18.
Reprint of 1895.38.

74 MILLER, KELLY. "What Walt Whitman Means to the Negro." Walt Whitman Fellowship Papers 2, no. 10 (November), 31-41.
Reprint of 1895.50.

75 TITHERINGTON, RICHARD H. "The Good Gray Poet." Munsey's Magazine 14 (November), 138-46.
Illustrated.
Traces Whitman's reputation, quoting several estimates, with sketch of his life and anecdotes from J. H. Johnston. His quite unmercenary character, practical religion, and naturalness in Leaves are praised. His visit to some Indian prisoners in Kansas [1879] and their responsiveness to him are described.

1895

76 TRIGGS, OSCAR LOVELL. "Some Aspects of
    Whitman's Art." Conservator 6 (November),
    137-39.
        Response to Fawcett (1895.56):
    Whitman's form involves "rhythmic movements
    and melodic and harmonious vocalism," is
    better heard than read, and compares with
    operatic recitative. His impressionistic
    method is part of his democratic protest
    against aristocratic sacrifice. Like
    Rousseau and Wordsworth, he places truth to
    self above conformity.

77 _____. "Whitman the Most Significant and Most
    Universal of Modern Writers." Walt Whitman
    Fellowship Papers 2, no. 5 (November), 11-
    12.
    Reprint of 1895.45.

78 ANON. "Walt Whitman Fellowship Branch Meet-
    ings." Conservator 6 (December), 158.
        Describes paper by Mrs. Mary Dana Hicks
    on "The Pictorial Quality in Walt Whitman."

79 ANON. "Walt Whitman in England." Conservator
    6 (December), 155.
        Reprint of notice from Glasgow Herald
    (unlocated) of Richard Le Gallienne's new
    edition of Whitman, which is unnecessary
    unless it is complete, since the audience
    is now ready for Whitman's "plain speech."

80 HARNED, THOMAS B. "Walt Whitman and His
    Boston Publishers." Conservator 6 (Decem-
    ber), 150-52.
    Reprinted: 1902.11; 1902.12.
        Quotes letters of 1881 between Whitman
    and Osgood and other publishers concerning
    financial and publication matters. Con-
    cluded 1896.22.

81 MONCK, EMILY CHRISTIANA. "Walt Whitman in
    Relation to Christianity." Poet-Lore 7
    (December), 607-13.
        Whitman's ideas are essentially
    Christian: love (even for sinners), egal-
    itarian sympathy, pride in the soul's ex-
    altation into oneness with God, immortality,
    human divinity.

82 [PORTER, CHARLOTTE.] "Mr. Breeze's Paper
    Discussed: Part V. of Annals of a Quiet
    Browning Club." Poet-Lore 7 (December),
    619-24.
        Continues 1895.70. Includes an argument
    over Whitman's catalogues, which have "a
    more vital relation to his thought than
    Homer's catalogue of ships has to his plot,"
    says one person. Whitman's inclusiveness
    is a new kind of selection.

83 SANBORN, F. B. "Emerson in His Home." Arena
    15 (December), 16-21.
    Reprinted: 1935.7.
        Recalls Emerson giving him a copy of
    Leaves and being impressed with it anew in
    1862; the Saturday Club's rejection of
    Emerson's request to invite Whitman in 1860;

Mrs. Alcott, Mrs. Emerson, and Sophia
Thoreau's unwillingness to meet Whitman;
Whitman's 1881 visit; Emerson's recollections of meeting Whitman in 1855; his
praise in 1878 for Whitman's early but not
his later works.

1896

BOOKS

1 ANON. Eminent Persons: Biographies Reprinted
   from The Times. Vol. 5. London:
   Macmillan & Co. "Walt Whitman," pp. 226-
   29.
   Reprint of 1892.45.

2 BURROUGHS, JOHN. Whitman: A Study. Boston
   and New York: Houghton Mifflin Co., 268
   pp. No index.
   Extracts reprinted: Hindus; 1896.86 (etc.);
   1928.5.
       Explanation of Whitman's principal
   ideas and spirit, answering various criticisms. Brief sketch of his life and description of his personality, using
   Whitman's letters and commentaries by those
   who knew him. Contents as follows: "Preliminary"; "Biographical and Personal"
   (using material from 1866.26 and 1867.1);
   "His Ruling Ideas and Aims"; "His Self-
   Reliance" (including reprint of 1894.58);
   "His Relation to Art and Literature" (including partial reprint of 1894.21); "His
   Relation to Life and Morals" (including
   reprint of 1896.39); "His Relation to
   Culture" (including reprint of 1896.48);
   "His Relation to his Country and his Times";
   "His Relation to Science" (including par-
   tial reprint of 1893.20); "His Relation to
   Religion"; "A Final Word."

3 DONALDSON, THOMAS. Walt Whitman the Man. New
   York: Francis P. Harper; London: Suckling
   & Galloway, 278 pp. No index. Illustrated.
       Purpose: "to give the public an in-
   sight into the life and habits of Mr.
   Whitman, as I saw it and them," because "in
   some phases, there was more in the man than
   in his works." The period concentrated on
   is 1876-92 when Donaldson knew him, with
   extensive use of notes made shortly after
   their conversations describing Whitman's
   personality, attitudes, relationships,
   writing method. His correspondence with
   Tennyson, letters from other admirers, correspondence concerning the raising of funds
   for his hospital work, letters accompanying
   the donation of money for Whitman's buggy
   (notably from Twain, Gilder, Holmes,
   Whittier) are printed. Much biographical
   information, many anecdotes.

*4 DUER, CAROLINE, and DUER, ALICE. Poems. New
   York: George H. Richmond & Co. "Once I
   Went."
   Reprinted: Saunders.
       Parody.

5 FIELDS, ANNIE. Authors and Friends. Boston and New York: Houghton, Mifflin & Co., p. 133.
   Reprint of 1895.17.

6 GOSSE, EDMUND. Critical Kit-Kats. London: William Heinemann; New York: Dodd, Mead. "A Note on Walt Whitman," pp. 95-111.
   Reprint of 1894.28.

7 HAWEIS, Rev. H. R. Travel and Talk. Vol. 1. London: Chatto & Windus; New York: Dodd, Mead & Co. "Walt Whitman," pp. 139-45.
   Though ill-treated "because so needlessly frank and utter in his word-painting," Whitman "had a dash of peculiar genius and a sort of fearless and prophetic strength which belonged to none of his distinguished critics," in seizing "the spirit of vigorous New America." His compassionate deeds showed him truly a man; gifts given to him in old age he merely accepted without great thanks, for he had done what all true men should do. His description of Lincoln's assassination is "almost unequalled" in modern American prose, and "Singer in Prison" is "one of the tenderest, most pathetic, and most noble-souled pieces of poetry" in English. The account of his visit to Whitman is reprinted, with minor changes, from 1886.13.

8 HUBBARD, ELBERT. "Whitman." In Little Journeys to the Homes of American Authors. New York and London: G. P. Putnam's Sons, pp. 169-96. 1855 portrait.
   Reprinted: 1900.17; 1901.40.
   Slight errors in biographical details. Description of Whitman, with "the look of age in his youth and the look of youth in his age that often marks the exceptional man." Camden is described, with Hubbard's one visit to Mickle Street in August 1883 and description of Whitman's conversation and warmth. Above all poets, he is the poet of humanity and comes across in his poetry as honest, fearless, masculine, concentrating on the beauty and glory of the present.

9 KENNEDY, WILLIAM SLOANE. Reminiscences of Walt Whitman. Paisley, Scotland, and London: Alexander Gardner, 190 pp. No index.
   Extract reprinted: Hindus.
   1. "Memories, Letters, etc.": Recalls visits with Whitman, various aspects of his later life. Prints, quotes, or cites letters to, from, and about Whitman. Reprints material from 1895.18, 1891.17, 1890.38.
   2. "Drift and Cumulus": Explanation of the organization of Leaves according to Whitman's main concerns: The body, democracy, and religion, the key words being respectively joy, love, and faith. The lack of humor and the egotism are appropriate, but Whitman did have flaws. He alone among poets completely reveals

humanity, society, and the world, and particularly America in all aspects. "Eidólons" and "As I Ebb'd" are explicated.
   3. "The Style of Leaves of Grass": Whitman's Wagner-like melody demands perspective of the ear. "Lilacs" is compared to Milton's "Lycidas." Whitman's form, poetic development, flaws, and idiosyncratic words are explained. Whitman is objective and personal, letting the appropriate pictures or objects convey his emotions.

10 MATTHEWS, BRANDER. Introduction to the Study of American Literature. New York: American Book Co., pp. 224-25.
   Whitman was "an intense American," looking to the future confidently. His verse is often beautifully rhythmic. "Captain" is praised.

11 ROBINSON, EDWIN ARLINGTON. The Torrent & The Night Before. Cambridge: Riverside Press. "Walt Whitman," pp. 31-32.
   Reprinted: 1897.20.
   Memorial poem: Whitman will endure, though dead and not understood.

12 SALT, HENRY S. Life of Henry David Thoreau. London: Walter Scott, pp. 117-19, 150.
   Quotes Thoreau on Whitman from 1865.1. It is remarkable that Thoreau, "the thrifty, simple, self-complete type," should so rightly appreciate "the largely inclusive and sympathetic" Whitman.

13 _____. Percy Bysshe Shelley, Poet and Pioneer. London: Arthur C. Fifield, pp. 141, 159.
   Quoted in 1896.44.
   Shelley was as erroneously criticized in his time as Whitman and Ibsen are now. Whitman is Shelley's true successor, "the originator of a new democratic ideal, and of a new manner of expressing it."

14 SANTAYANA, GEORGE. The Sense of Beauty: Being the Outlines of Aesthetic Theory. New York: Charles Scribner's Sons, p. 112.
   Whitman is an example of one who makes chaos sublime. "Never, perhaps, has the charm of uniformity in multiplicity been felt so completely and so exclusively."

15 SEAMAN, OWEN. The Battle of the Bays. London and New York: John Lane. "Presto Furioso," pp. 71-73.
   Reprinted: Saunders.
   Parody.

16 SMYTH, ALBERT H. Bayard Taylor. Boston and New York: Houghton, Mifflin & Co., pp. 138, 248, 260, 275.
   Notes Whitman's presence at Pfaff's, "looking like the Phidian Jove"; Taylor's parody (1876.4); Taylor's poem "The Bath," which Whitman might have written, "could he by some strange miracle have been converted to art."

1896

17 SYMONDS, JOHN ADDINGTON. A Problem in Modern
    Ethics: Being an Inquiry into the Phenom-
    enon of Sexual Inversion Addressed Especially
    to Medical Psychologists and Jurists.
    London: n.p., pp. 111, 115-25, 130.
        Uses Whitman's prose and verse to exem-
    plify the emotional intensity between men
    which is an element of the homosexual's
    feelings, although Whitman's letter to
    Symonds seemed to shun suggestions of in-
    version. But his poetry neither indicates
    specifically nor rejects physical desires.
    His ideal may be the means of controlling
    and elevating the "darker, more mysterious,
    apparently abnormal appetites."

18 ZANGWILL, I[SRAEL]. Without Prejudice. New
    York: Century Co., pp. 11, 287-88, 331,
    349, 367-68.
        It is a pity that Whitman, "whose in-
    spiration came so often from synthesis,"
    did not live to see the Chicago World's
    Fair, which would have justified his inven-
    tories and his claim to be the voice of
    America with "its moral broadness and its
    material all-inclusiveness." No other
    poet has followed him with this great argu-
    ment. He kept trying to see the richness
    of life "in the most unpromising materials."
    A parody, "A Song of Advertisements. (After
    Whitman.)," is reprinted in Saunders.

PERIODICALS

19 ANON. "An Unexpurgated English Edition of
    Whitman." Conservator 6 (January), 172.
        From Glasgow Herald (unlocated):
    Whitman is a powerful personality whose
    audience is growing, due to his manly and
    healthy quality. His poetry demands a com-
    plete edition.

20 BUCKE, RICHARD MAURICE. "Mr. Fawcett's Objec-
    tions to Whitman Reviewed." Conservator 6
    (January), 170.
        Clarifies his commentary in 1895.59:
    the value of Whitman's verse rests on
    "splendid flashes of insight" and "profound
    spiritual visions" comparable to those of
    the great mystics.

21 GAY, WILLIAM. "To Walt Whitman: In His Own
    Spirit." Conservator 6 (January), 168.
        Free-verse poem accepting Whitman's
    spirit of self-reliance: "You say to me
    continually that I am as good as you."

22 HARNED, THOMAS B. "Walt Whitman and His
    Boston Publishers." Conservator 6 (Jan-
    uary), 163-66.
        Reprinted: 1902.11; 1902.12.
        Concludes 1895.80. Extracts of
    Whitman's correspondence with publishers in
    1882 with explanatory comments, including
    list of proposed expurgations.

23 SCOTT, COLIN A. "Sex and Art." American Jour-
    nal of Psychology 7 (January), 226.

Incidental quotation of Whitman on the
role of artists as answerers.

24 TRAUBEL, HORACE L. "Conversations with Walt
    Whitman." Arena 15 (January), 175-83. Two
    photographs.
        Extract reprinted: 1896.29. Reprinted:
    1935.7.
        Recalls Whitman's personality, habits,
    conversation, quoting him on religion,
    politics, social problems, his work and
    purpose. He used America in a symbolic,
    not merely national sense.

25 T[RAUBEL, HORACE]. "Poems of Walt Whitman."
    Conservator 6 (January), 174.
        Favorable review of Stead's edition
    (1895.10), quoting his reasons for omitting
    "Adam."

26 CATHER, WILLA. "The Passing Show." Sunday
    State Journal (Lincoln, Nebraska) (19 Jan-
    uary), sec. 2, 1:3.
        Reprinted: WWR 12 (March 1966), 3-5.
        Whitman had no literary ethics beyond
    those of nature. He lacked discrimination,
    particularly in diction. His poems are
    "reckless rhapsodies over creation in
    general, some times sublime, some times
    ridiculous." He has "a primitive elemental
    force," "full of hardiness and of the joy
    of life," exulting in nature and the physi-
    cal, sensual as the old barbarians were,
    though such elements do not create the
    highest poetry. His whole-heartedness and
    good fellowship give him "an undeniable
    charm." Leaves makes us realize that
    spiritual perceptions, not keen senses
    alone, make poetry.

27 COMPENDIUM. "Whitman." Conservator 6 (Feb-
    ruary), 189.
        Recent commentary on Whitman, including
    letter on the Boston Whitman Fellowship,
    describing Harry De M. Young's paper,
    "Whitman's Poems of Revolt."

28 STEAD, W. T. "Whitman." Conservator 6 (Feb-
    ruary), 190.
        Extract reprinted from 1895.10.

29 ANON. "Walt Whitman at Home." Literary Digest
    12 (1 February), 400.
        Précis with extensive quotation of
    Traubel (1896.24).

30 ANON. "Notes and News." Poet-Lore 8 (March),
    168.
        The 1855 Preface is translated into
    French by Laurence Jerrold in the January
    Le Magazine Internationale. Robert Reitzel
    has an article in Der arme Teufel on
    Whitman's poetry as proceeding from a con-
    sciousness of being one with the universe,
    "an insignificant moment in the process of
    Becoming."

31 BORN, HELENA. "Poets of Revolt: Shelley,
    Whitman, Carpenter, I." Conservator 7
    (March), 8-10.
    Reprinted: 1902.2.
        These poets are seers and reformers,
    indebted to communion with nature and the
    unseen. They are robust personalities,
    celebrating comradeship and defending
    democracy and women's rights. Continued
    1896.38.

32 COMPENDIUM. "Notes Major and Minor." Con-
    servator 7 (March), 13.
        Recent commentary on Whitman.

33 ELDRIDGE, CHARLES W. "Who Were Walt Whitman's
    'Boston Publishers'?" Conservator 7
    (March), 3-4.
        Calls attention to Thayer and Eldridge
    as Whitman's first Boston publishers and to
    the unauthorized copies made from the 1860
    plates.

34 GARRISON, CHARLES G. "Whitman and Woman."
    Conservator 7 (March), 6-7.
        Whitman presented natural laws, yet was
    reviled in woman's name. Woman contributes
    the moral impulse to the evolving world,
    as Whitman perceived.

35 KENNEDY, WILLIAM SLOANE. "Alfred Austin on
    Walt Whitman." Conservator 7 (March),
    7-8.
        Comments on the new poet laureate's
    opinion of Whitman (see 1869.4).

36 TROWBRIDGE, J. T. "Whitman Inspired and Un-
    inspired: and his 'Eroticism.'" Conserva-
    tor 7 (March), 4-5.
        The first two editions contain Whitman's
    best work; the rest represent progressive
    decline. Osgood is defended for not pub-
    lishing Whitman. Emerson was offended at
    the "gross animalism" in Whitman's later
    poems.

37 ANON. "Admirers of Walt Whitman." New York
    Tribune (8 March), 22:1.
        Account of the first dinner of the
    Whitman Fellowship, those present represent-
    ing a wide range. Some of the speakers'
    comments are noted.

38 BORN, HELENA. "Poets of Revolt: Shelley,
    Whitman, Carpenter, II." Conservator 7
    (April), 23-26.
    Reprinted: 1902.2.
        Continues 1896.31. Discussion of
    Shelley, then of Whitman, who celebrates
    all and refuses to support causes. Peaceful
    comradeship is his ideal; he favors litera-
    ture rather than politics as the force to
    alter civilization. Concluded 1896.41.

39 BURROUGHS, JOHN. "Whitman's Relation to
    Morals." Conservator 7 (April), 19-22.
    Reprinted: 1896.2.
        In his democracy and tolerance Whitman

sums up and justifies the modern world,
with the goal of universal brotherhood.
Leaves depicts the archetypal man in America.
Whitman does not deal with human love in
domestic, sentimental, and conventional
terms, or in terms of Byron's "hectic lust"
and Swinburne's "impotence."

40 WILLIAMS, FRANCIS HOWARD. "'A Woman Waits for
    Me.'" Conservator 7 (April), 26-27.
        Response to Trowbridge (1896.36):
    Whitman's works are defensible as true
    representations of nature. "Woman Waits"
    may be read as "a splendid metaphor," con-
    taining excellent poetry.

41 BORN, HELENA. "Poets of Revolt: Shelley,
    Whitman, Carpenter, III." Conservator 7
    (May), 36-37.
    Reprinted: 1902.2.
        Concludes 1896.38. Discussion of
    Carpenter with comparisons to Whitman, who
    appeals less directly to the sympathies
    than Shelley or Carpenter.

42 BUCKE, RICHARD MAURICE. "Notes on the Text of
    'Leaves of Grass,' I." Conservator 7
    (May), 40.
        Explains the factual source of the
    shipwreck in "Myself" 33.

43 ELDRIDGE, CHARLES WESLEY. "'A Woman Waits
    for Me': The Personal Relations of Emerson
    and Whitman." Conservator 7 (May), 38-39.
        Response to Trowbridge (1896.36):
    Emerson remained friendly and was not of-
    fended at the publication of his letter.
    He urged Whitman to censor the poems in
    order to achieve popular acceptance but
    never accused him of immorality.

44 SALT, H. S. "Shelley and Whitman." Conservator
    7 (May), 40-41.
        Extract reprinted from 1896.13.

45 TRIGGS, OSCAR LOVELL. "Walt Whitman: His
    Relation to Science and Philosophy." Con-
    servator 7 (May), 44-45.
        Response to Gay (1895.5): Contemporary
    forms of monism contribute more than the
    idealism of Kant or Hegel to understanding
    Whitman.

46 BRINTON, DANIEL G. "Whitman's Sexual Imagery."
    Conservator 7 (June), 59-60.
    Quoted in 1896.55.
        Whitman's use of erotic imagery is akin
    to primitive ritual symbolism.

47 BUCKE, RICHARD MAURICE. "Notes on the Text
    of 'Leaves of Grass,' II." Conservator 7
    (June), 59.
        There is a question whether Whitman
    knew French. Scraps of Rousseau in his
    literary remains may have been translated
    from the original.

48 BURROUGHS, JOHN. "Whitman's Relation to Culture." Conservator 7 (June), 51-53.
Reprinted: 1896.2.
He reveres Whitman as a personality. Whitman escaped the literary disease, moving from artificial culture to "more radical and primary sources."

49 CRONIN, DAVID EDWARD. "A Few Impressions of Walt Whitman." Conservator 7 (June), 57-59.
Recalls seeing Whitman in New York, meeting him at Pfaff's in 1857, reading Leaves early in the war. He was not "degenerate" in the medical sense of the word, but a natural, virile man.

50 KENNEDY, WILLIAM SLOANE. "A Peep into Walt Whitman's Manuscripts." Conservator 7 (June), 53-55.
Whitman constantly revised, thinking on paper a great deal. The drafts of "Come, said my Soul" are discussed. Not all of his changes, though deliberate and reasoned, were for the better.

51 PLATT, ISAAC HULL. "Shelley and Whitman: A Comparison and a Contrast." Poet-Lore 8 (June), 332-42.
Of poets in English, Shelley and Whitman have the most claim to eminence because their verse embodied their love of their fellow-man. They have the same admirers and the same revolt against conventionality and oppression but differ in character and method, "Shelley the most radical of revolutionists, Whitman the most conservative of radicals," "an evolutionist." Neither reached his immediate audience. Shelley was a dualist and fought against wrong, but Whitman saw good in everything, having faith in the absorption of evil into good. "To a Skylark" and "Cradle" illustrate their different attitudes toward nature; "Adonais" and "Lilacs" (explicated) reveal their similar attitudes toward death.

*52 THE PROPHET [Theodore Dreiser]. "Reflections." Ev'ry Month 2 (June), 2-3.
Reprinted: Pizer.
This contrast of the strong man and the weak man loosely paraphrases "Body Electric" 3.

53 STODDARD, RICHARD HENRY. "World of Letters." New York Mail and Express (20 June), 30.
Reprinted: 1896.54.
Presents "a chapter of personal reminiscences" of Whitman from Dr. D. B. St. John Roosa, a former physician at New York Hospital where Whitman frequently visited stagedrivers. Roosa recalls Whitman riding the omnibuses, his affinities for the drivers as "strong types of human character," visits with him to Pfaff's, his "extremely pleasing" personality. Stoddard appends a note praising these reminiscences as "readable anywhere," especially in the columns of "World of Letters," which "are surely broad enough to include Whitman, whatever we may think of his alleged poetry."

54 [STODDARD, RICHARD HENRY.] "Walt Whitman." Philadelphia Evening Telegraph (30 June). Reprint of 1896.53 with minor changes in Stoddard's opening remarks.

55 ANON. "Annual Meeting: Boston, May 31." Walt Whitman Fellowship Papers 3, no. 3 (July), 11.
Report of Fellowship meeting, quoting Brinton on Whitman (1896.46).

56 HARTE, WALTER BLACKBURN. "Walt Whitman and the Younger Writers: An Interview with John Burroughs." Conservator 7 (July), 69-72.
Burroughs's recollections of Whitman; explanations of his ideas (especially regarding sex), relations with women, influence on younger poets; the importance of imitating his spirit, not just his style.

57 HILL, GEORGE BIRKBECK. "Letters of D. G. Rossetti. III. 1855-1857." Atlantic Monthly 78 (July), 52.
Reprinted: 1896.60; 1897.9.
Prints Rossetti letter to William Allingham: "I have not been so happy in loathing anything for a long while, except, I think, Leaves of Grass, by that Orson of yours. I should like just to have the writing of a valentine to him in one of the reviews."

58 PORTER, CHARLOTTE. "The American Idea in Whitman." Conservator 7 (July), 73-75.
Reprinted: 1897.66.
Whitman's concept of democracy rests on oneself (individuality), the social one, or all other selves (universal opportunity), and progressive plan (selfism and altruism set in relation for the progress of all).

59 [PORTER, CHARLOTTE, and CLARKE, HELEN A.] "New Ideas in Teaching Literature." Poet-Lore 8 (July), 447-48.
Advises a comparison of three poems on death: Emerson's "Threnody," Woodberry's "The North Shore Watch," and "Lilacs" (which "suggests the old lament for Spring in its first stanza" but "takes an entirely new attitude toward Death" as "the joyful outlet to a larger life"). Other elegies might also be compared to it.

60 T[RAUBEL, HORACE]. "Whitman as He Appeared to Dante Rossetti and Allingham." Conservator 7 (July), 77.
Extract reprinted from 1896.57.

61 WALLACE, J. W. "Whitman's Expanding Influence in England." Conservator 7 (July), 75.
The upcoming unabridged English Leaves should be a great success.

62 BUCKE, RICHARD MAURICE. "Notes on the Text of 'Leaves of Grass,' III." Conservator 7 (August), 88-89.
     Explains source for the sea-battle in "Myself" 35.

*63 THE PROPHET [Theodore Dreiser]. "Reflections." Ev'ry Month 2 (August), 6-7.
     Reprinted: Pizer.
     Opening reference: "In a number of his minor poems Walt Whitman beautifully emphasizes the need of being strong, of entering the race with sturdy, fleet limbs, and flesh fair and sweet. . . ."

64 ANON. "American Independence." Christian Register 75 (6 August), 505-6.
     Quoted in 1896.66.
     Whitman, in contrast to other American writers, wrote "a mass of trash without form, rhythm, or vitality." His only real poems "are those in which he made some effort to conform to the laws of form, beauty, and decency that he persistently avoided."

64a HOMANS, NATHALIE W. "Walt Whitman." Christian Register 75 (27 August), 555.
     Reprinted: 1896.66.
     Rejects criticisms in 1896.64.

65 ABBEY, CHARLOTTE L. "Freedom and Walt Whitman." Conservator 7 (September), 106-7.
     Whitman's concept of freedom does not affirm the status quo but assumes that the individual has the means of achieving freedom. One must struggle to free oneself from the bonds of society and materialism.

66 COMPENDIUM. "Walt Whitman as a Creator of 'Trash.'" Conservator 7 (September), 108.
     Reprint of 1896.64 and 1896.64a.

67 O'CONNOR, WILLIAM DOUGLAS. "Another Recovered Chapter in the History of 'Leaves of Grass.'" Conservator 7 (September), 99-102.
     Account, originally written 16 September 1882, of Chainey's suppression for publishing Whitman's proscribed poetry.

68 TRIGGS, OSCAR LOVELL. "Whitman's Lack of Humor." Conservator 7 (September), 102-3.
     Reprinted: 1899.50.
     Whitman occasionally used satire but generally avoided humor in favor of higher aspirations. His faith allowed him to see beyond the incongruous which is the source of most humor.

69 ANON. "Americans in the Parnassian Fellowship." Conservator 7 (October), 125.
     Paragraph from Philadelphia Evening Telegraph (unlocated): Of American poets, Lanier may be ranked after Emerson, Poe, and Whitman (who did most to free American poetry from the New England school's domination).

70 BURROUGHS, JOHN. "The Poet and the Modern." Atlantic Monthly 78 (October), 565-66.
     Whitman lacks the shaping gift to deal fully and artistically with the modern world. He is centripetal, drawing all things into himself, to recast the whole country as "a sort of colossal Walt Whitman." He voices the democratic spirit, and sows the germs for larger and saner types of humanity.

71 CARPENTER, EDWARD. "Wagner, Millet and Whitman: In Relation to Art and Democracy." Progressive Review 1 (October), 63-74.
     Reprinted: 1898.5.
     These three are revolutionaries in art and commentators upon it, bringing us back to earlier, more communal and natural concepts of art. Whitman "had to enlarge the boundary of human expression" for the new things he had to say: his "intense consciousness of the Actual," his quick shifts of poetic identity. All three have an intense sense of the whole and acceptance of the universal, an intense realism and acceptance of the actual, and a prophetic sense of the life of the people.

72 KENNEDY, WILLIAM SLOANE. "To Keep Green the Memory of a Gallant Man." Conservator 7 (October), 116-18.
     Tribute to O'Connor, quoting his comments on Whitman in private letters, discussing O'Connor's treatment of Whitman in "The Carpenter" (1868.5).

73 LANIER, SIDNEY. "Whitman's Large and Substantial Thoughts: His Beautiful Rhythms." Conservator 7 (October), 122.
     Letter written to Whitman in 1878 (printed in In Re and Traubel I), disagreeing with Whitman's artistic form but declaring his love for Whitman.

74 T[RAUBEL], H. L. "A New Life and Study of Whitman." Conservator 7 (October), 125.
     Announcement of Kennedy (1896.9), which contributes new biographical material and an objective evaluation of Whitman's life.

75 BURTON, RICHARD. "Originality in Literature." Dial 21 (16 October), 212-14.
     The controversy over Whitman represents the dilemma of whether an unconventional writer's work is originality or affectation. "He conquered, so far as he did conquer, by the natural music in him sounding forth in his irregularly rhythmic, half-prosaic dithyrambs, and by the picturesque virility and the large sweep of his thought and expression." Whitman must be regarded as sincere, not a poseur.

76 COMPENDIUM. "Whitman." Conservator 7 (November), 141.
     Recent commentary on Whitman.

1896

77 KENNEDY, WILLIAM SLOANE. "Sursum Corda,
    Comrades!" Conservator 7 (November), 140-
    41.
        Acceptance for Whitman is coming. Al-
    though a Yale professor has termed J. W.
    Riley "'the real poet of American democ-
    racy,'" Riley does not measure up to
    Whitman.

78 MAYNARD, LAURENS. "Kennedy's Reminiscences of
    Walt Whitman." Conservator 7 (November),
    138-40.
        Appreciative review of 1896.9, with
    frequent quotations. Kennedy's criticisms
    are excellent, but his personal account is
    more unique.

79 TRAUBEL, HORACE L. "Julian Hawthorne's
    Several Opinions of Walt Whitman." Con-
    servator 7 (November), 136-37.
        Quotes Hawthorne's criticism of
    Whitman (1891.5) and his Camden speech
    praising Whitman (1889.9), questioning
    which is his true opinion.

80 PATTEE, FRED LEWIS. "Is There an American
    Literature?" Dial 21 (1 November), 243-45.
        Incidental references, listing Whitman
    among the important, national, "strong and
    intensely original" writers America has
    produced.

81 CROSBY, ERNEST H. "Maurice Maeterlinck the
    Mystic, II." Conservator 7 (December),
    147-49.
        Notes several similarities of
    Maeterlinck to Whitman.

82 HAWTHORNE, JULIAN. "Hawthorne-Lemmon 'American
    Literature.'" Conservator 7 (December),
    151-52.
        Response to Traubel (1896.79), defending
    the criticism in 1891.5 as his own and not
    a change of opinion.

83 _____. "Walt Whitman." Conservator 7 (Decem-
    ber), 153-54.
    Reprint of 1891.5.

84 T[RAUBEL, HORACE]. "Calamus: A Series of
    Letters Written by Walt Whitman to a Young
    Friend." Conservator 7 (December), 156-57.
        Announcement of publication of Calamus
    (1897.2).

85 TRAUBEL, HORACE L. "Hawthorne-Lemmon 'American
    Literature.'" Conservator 7 (December),
    152.
        Response to 1896.82.

86 T[RAUBEL], H. L. "Whitman: A Study." Con-
    servator 7 (December), 155-56.
        Appreciative review of Burroughs
    (1896.2), who might have included a chapter
    on Whitman as a mystic. Extensive quota-
    tion. Continued 1897.29.

87 ANON. "Books of the Week. Apotheosis of Walt
    Whitman." Chicago Daily Tribune (5 Decem-
    ber), 10:1-2.
        Review of 1896.2 and 1896.3. Burroughs,
    exalting Whitman, is interesting for his
    enthusiasm and makes the reader feel simi-
    larly toward Whitman. His friendship with
    Whitman was founded on their similar sym-
    pathies. Burroughs admires him not for
    mere revolt but for being the poet of democ-
    racy and individualism. His interpretation
    of Whitman is summarized. Whitman will
    gain "a higher niche in literature" because
    of this book. Donaldson also helps to
    round out Whitman's figure, particularly as
    a man.

1897

BOOKS

1 ADAMS, OSCAR FAY. A Dictionary of American
    Authors. Boston and New York: Houghton,
    Mifflin & Co., p. 420.
        Brief biographical data of this "poet
    regarding whose claims to the title much
    controversy has raged," and whose "rejection
    of rhyme and metre will probably always
    repel the mass of readers." His works are
    listed, with some secondary sources.

2 BUCKE, RICHARD MAURICE, ed. Calamus: A Series
    of Letters Written During the Years 1868-
    1880 by Walt Whitman to a Young Friend
    (Peter Doyle). Boston: Laurens Maynard,
    173 pp. Preface by John Addington Symonds.
    Reprinted: 1902.4.
        Introduction: The letters, representing
    a third of the total correspondence, are
    printed verbatim. Visits with Whitman by
    Bucke and Burroughs are described. Whitman's
    friendship with Doyle is typical of him, as
    shown by samples of letters to other young
    friends. Account of interview with Doyle,
    recording his comments on Whitman's habits,
    personality, reading, opinions. Summary of
    Doyle's life. Chronology of Whitman's life
    and publications.

3 BURROUGHS, JOHN. "Walt Whitman." In A Library
    of the World's Best Literature Ancient and
    Modern. Vol. 39. Edited by Charles Dudley
    Warner. pp. 15885-91. Selected poems
    follow, pp. 15892-910.
    Reprinted: 1902.5.
        The nudity of Whitman's subject matter
    and style repelled readers but the newer
    generation is coming to appreciate his
    spirit. His life is sketched. He appealed
    to our concrete everyday sense rather than
    to our abstract aesthetic sense. He aimed
    at a complete human synthesis, identified
    poetic with religious emotion. He achieves
    his own organic form. He is not didactic.
    He may not become a popular poet, but he
    will influence poets (both to become more
    American and to follow oneself) and enlarge

criticism. He is among the few major
poets.

4 CHOPIN, KATE. A Night in Acadie. Chicago:
Way & Williams. "A Respectable Woman,"
p. 394.
Reprint of 1894.20.

5 FOLEY, P. K. American Authors 1795-1895.
Boston: Printed for subscribers, pp. 307-
10.
Bibliography of Whitman's published
works.

6 GUTHRIE, WILLIAM NORMAN. Modern Poet Prophets,
Essays Critical and Interpretive. Cincinnati: Robert Clarke Co. "Walt Whitman,
the Camden Sage," pp. 244-332; also 343-48
(reprint of 1890.21).
Same as 1897.7.

7 _____. Walt Whitman (The Camden Sage) as
Religious and Moral Teacher: A Study.
Cincinnati: Robert Clarke Co., 105 pp.
Same as 1897.6.
Examines Whitman's religious thought
under the following headings: "The Religious Teacher"; "What Is Religion?" (his
Quakerism, fusion of Western and Eastern
concepts, Hegelian notion of becoming);
"Divine Pride" (egotism as uniting the soul
with God); "Worship" (significance of the
body); "The Problem of Evil" (Whitman's
five distinct meanings for evil); "Salvation and the Savior" (salvation as growth,
poet as savior); "Immortality" (related to
ideal democracy); "Personal Identity" (relation of body and soul); "Perpetuity of
Character" (the soul's growth through conflict); "'Traveling Souls' and Their End"
(Whitman's belief in many births); "Whitman's
Methods and Style" (his poetry as related
to his religion, making a poet of the
reader; his flaws as imposed from within,
organic like his strengths).

8 HIGGINSON, THOMAS WENTWORTH. Book and Heart:
Essays on Literature and Life. New York:
Harper & Bros., pp. 198-99.
Incidental reference in discussion of
cosmopolitanism as not what makes a writer
most memorable: "the American names one
sees oftenest mentioned in European books--
Emerson, Thoreau, Poe, Whitman--are those
of authors who never visited Europe, or
under such circumstances as to form but a
trivial part of their career." Those
"American writers who established our
nation's literature, half a century ago,
were great because they were first and
chiefly American."

9 HILL, GEORGE BIRKBECK. Letters of Dante
Gabriel Rossetti to William Allingham
1854-1870. New York: Frederick A. Stokes
Co., pp. 181, 183-85.
Includes reprint of 1896.57.
Adds explanatory notes quoting

Allingham's letter of 1857 regarding his
impressions of Whitman as pleasant and
suggestive but not new and not poetry.

10 JAMES, WILLIAM. The Will to Believe and Other
Essays in Popular Philosophy. New York:
Longmans Green & Co., pp. 33-34, 64, 74.
Reprints of 1895.63 and 1879.11 (with addi-
tions not concerning Whitman).

11 JOHNSON, H. HAROLD. Walt Whitman. Abertillery,
England: W. R. Haylings, 46 pp.
1. "Introductory: 'The Man and his
Work'": Explains his first negative response to Whitman, until helped to understanding by Symonds's Study (1893.9). This
book is meant as an introduction for a
difficult poet; beginners should start with
his prose prefaces. His method is that of
the artist rather than the philosopher, demanding not adherence to a system (which he
lacked) but rather the individual's own
discovery of philosophy.
2. "Self": Whitman sees the self as
part of God, the fundamental note of his
democracy. His egoism is not inconsistent
with humility.
3. "Democracy": Whitman's idea of
equality does not deny differences but
rather means equality of opportunity, with
Christ-like deeds possible for each and
religious inspiration available here and
now.
4. "Religion (1)": Whitman regarded
God as infinite and unknowable. Explications
of "Eidólons" and "Square Deific" reveal his
idea of religion and the absolute lying
behind all.
5. "Religion (2)": Whitman had a
material basis for his abstract conceptions
and believed in a contemporary basis for
religion. His view of death conveys an
atmosphere different from most current
Christianity. "Lilacs" is "the noblest
hymn to Death in our language."
Throughout the book Whitman is quoted
extensively, passages organized to convey
his ideas clearly.

12 KENNEDY, WILLIAM SLOANE. In Portia's Gardens.
Boston: Bradlee Whidden, pp. 28, 143, 152-
53, 156n, 214, 217-18.
Extract reprinted: 1897.152.
Brief references to Whitman's treatment
of nature, his omission from the Boston
Public Library's walls because of Lowell's
disapproval. "Voice of the Rain" is described briefly, offering "the most beautiful lines on the rain"; it "will bear deep
pondering."

13 KNOWLES, FREDERIC LAWRENCE, ed. Preface to
The Golden Treasury of American Songs and
Lyrics. Boston: L. C. Page & Co., p. xi.
Revised: 1901.10.
Incidental: "I am especially sorry to
leave unrepresented a writer--more imagina-
tive, possibly, than any American poet

except Poe--whose utter contempt for technique in the ordinary sense places him wholly outside my present purpose."

14 LANIER, SIDNEY. The English Novel: A Study in the Development of Personality. New York: Charles Scribner's Sons, pp. 45-47, 50-65, 121-22.
    Reprint of 1883.5 with changes.
    The changes, restorations from Lanier's original manuscripts, include admissions of some appreciation of Whitman; the paragraph from 1883.33 is included. See 1933.29.

15 MILLER, JOAQUIN. The Complete Poetical Works. San Francisco: Whitaker & Ray Co., pp. 59n, 222-23n.
    Recalls his first reading of Whitman; Whitman's visit to Boston; Longfellow's favorable commentary on Whitman and visit to him; fruitless efforts to get Whitman to write a tribute to Garfield for one hundred dollars. Miller's Whitman poem (1877.5) is not included.

*16 MILLER, JOHN. Books: A Guide to Good Reading. n.p.
    Reported in Willard.
    Vistas is recommended.

17 NEWHALL, JAMES R. The Legacy of an Octogenarian. Lynn, Mass.: Nichols Press, pp. 92, 130-35, 410.
    Recalls his acquaintance with Whitman when they worked on a daily New York paper in 1842; his style resembled that of Dickens, lacking "the rough, ragged, and sometimes uncouth features that so marred it after he had fraternized with the Bohemians." Recalls Whitman's love for walking outside, freedom from vicious habits, particular experiences. Though many rank him high as a poet, the world would probably rather lose his work than that of Bryant or Longfellow.

18 PAINTER, F. V. N. Introduction to American Literature. Boston and Chicago: Sibley & Ducker, pp. 94-95.
    "Walt Whitman (1819-1892). Printer, school-teacher, carpenter, and poet. Principal work, 'Leaves of Grass.' By some assigned a very high rank; by others scarcely regarded as a poet at all. He is highly appreciated in England, and his pieces have been translated into several modern languages."

*19 PETITT, MAUD. Beth Woodburn. Toronto: Briggs, p. 62.
    Reported in Saunders Whitman in Fiction.

20 ROBINSON, EDWIN ARLINGTON. The Children of the Night: A Book of Poems. Boston: Richard G. Badger. "Walt Whitman," p. 85.
    Reprinted from 1896.11.

21 TENNYSON, HALLAM. Alfred Lord Tennyson: A Memoir By His Son. Vol. 2. New York and London: Macmillan Co., pp. 115, 343-45, 424.
    Prints two 1887 letters from Tennyson to Whitman, 1872 letter from Whitman to Tennyson. Tennyson is quoted on Whitman's neglect of form, occasional "nakedness of expression," but fine spirit.

PERIODICALS

22 ANON. "Notes and News." Poet-Lore 9, no. 1 (Winter), 154-56.
    The original personality of Whitman polarized critics, and still does. He is not a poseur except in so far as every writer is: he "posed" in consciously aiming for a new effect in art, although it seems inevitable to the reader.

23 P[ORTER, CHARLOTTE]. "Books on Whitman." Poet-Lore 9, no. 1 (Winter), 131-37.
    Review of Burroughs (1896.2), Donaldson (1896.3), Kennedy (1896.9). Whitman's vast system eludes their attempts to organize their attempts to organize their material, and will be summed up better by the more democratic criticism of the future. Kennedy sheds fine light on Whitman's Hegelianism; he and Burroughs are suggestive in discussing Whitman's art. The worship of Whitman so common now suits an Old World mentality more than it does Whitman's democratic mind.

24 CHAMBERLIN, JOSEPH EDGAR. "Memorials of American Authors." Atlantic Monthly 79 (January), 69, 72.
    Despite his acclaim abroad, Whitman has been honored by no statue and only by gradual recognition at home. The movement to memorialize him through his "poor tenement" in Camden may be casting reproach on Whitman's contemporaries.

25 COMPENDIUM. "Morris: Whitman." Conservator 7 (January), 172.
    Includes extracts from recent articles mentioning Whitman.

26 KENNEDY, WILLIAM SLOANE. "William Shakespeare Asks Leave to Be." Conservator 7 (January), 168-71.
    Argument for Shakespeare as the author of his plays, not Bacon. Whitman is comparable to Shakespeare in lacking an educated background. Denying a common man like Shakespeare the power of writing his plays denies Whitman's philosophy. A future critic might play the same game with Whitman and explain how Emerson actually wrote his poems.

27 MIDDLETON, LAMAR. "Whitman, the Anachronism." Quartier Latin 2 (January), 171-74.
    Appreciation of Whitman, who proclaims "the gospel of brawn" and adoration of the

nation, surpasses Wordsworth, and was born
out of his time, like Wagner.

28 TRAUBEL, HORACE L. "Notes on the Text of
'Leaves of Grass,' IV." Conservator 7
(January), 171.
    Prints two drafts of "Grand is the
Seen" and Whitman's comments to Traubel
about it.

29 T[RAUBEL, HORACE]. "Whitman: A Study, II."
Conservator 7 (January), 173.
    Continues 1896.86. Quotes Burroughs
(1896.2) approvingly on Whitman's spiritual
import. Continued 1897.42.

30 COOK, GEORGE C. "Two Views of Walt Whitman."
Dial 22 (1 January), 15-17.
    Review of Burroughs (1896.2) and
Donaldson (1896.3). There are three attitudes toward Whitman: "complete non-
acceptance," "acceptance so complete that it
involves the rejection of his opposites
like Tennyson," and the simultaneous acceptance of other poets with the ability "to
love and be helped by the crude and powerful work of Whitman without being swept off
their feet." Burroughs gets swept away;
he provides insight but should recognize
Whitman as an artist only when he is "in
the height and heat of rare emotion."
Whitman absorbs the object rather than
becoming one with it, as Shakespeare did.
Donaldson's appealing presentation of the
man shows that Whitman's principles "do
not, in a strong nature like his own, lead
to evil of any kind."

31 ANON. "Trying to 'Place' Whitman." New York
Times Saturday Review (9 January), 4-5.
    Review of Burroughs (1896.2) and
Donaldson (1896.3), emphasizing the paradox
of Burroughs's possessing the very qualities
he praises Whitman for lacking. Burroughs
fails to answer adequately the perennial
questions about the reason for Whitman's
rough utterances; he overexplains Whitman's
"huge, untamed animalism." Is the vitality
of Whitman's work declining? How many
people read him?

32 TRIGGS, OSCAR LOVELL. "The Primary Condition
of Understanding Whitman." Dial 22 (16
January), 41-42.
    Response to Cook (1897.30), disagreeing
with his evaluation of the two books:
Donaldson is untrustworthy but Burroughs
has placed himself in mental and emotional
relations with his subject. Whitman created
his own audience, demanding identity from
his readers, not a cold critical view, for
his book represents life and appeals "almost
wholly to the will and the moral nature,"
as many have realized.

33 ANON. "Walt Whitman. More Talk about His
Life and Works." New York Tribune (17
January), sec. 3, 2:3-5.

    Review of Burroughs (1896.2) and
Donaldson (1896.3). Whitman's teaching is
incoherent, his poetry is not poetry, but
he had spiritual vigor with some poetic
feeling. His "simply prosaic sermonizing"
lacks the beauty of poetic tradition; the
reader must supply the magic behind the
facts, as Burroughs has done. He could not
translate his true human sympathy into
poetry; his freedom from convention and his
masculinity are somewhat affected. His
future rank seems doubtful.

34 [CHADWICK, J. W.] "Two Whitman Books." Nation
64 (21 January), 55-56.
    Review of Donaldson (1896.3), who
believes that Whitman has been taken too
seriously as a poet, and Burroughs (1896.2),
whose claims are rather exalted and need
more proof, especially regarding Whitman's
egotism. Burroughs ignores the sometimes
repellent quality of Whitman's caresses to
the soldiers themselves.

35 ANON. "Walt Whitman." Literary World 28 (23
January), 19-20.
    Review of Burroughs (1896.2) and
Donaldson (1896.3). Donaldson combines
trivial with valuable observations;
Burroughs offers poetry and enthusiasm.
Both are valuable, "for the mere outward
actions of as strong and original a personality as Whitman's are indicative of character, while so sympathetic an admirer as
Mr. Burroughs can always throw new light on
the inner meaning of the strange, inchoate
mass which Mr. Whitman left behind him."

36 ANON. "The Rambler." Book Buyer 14 (February),
24-25.
    Reprints and briefly comments on two
portraits of Whitman (from 1855 Preface and
with the butterfly).

37 ANON. "Walt Whitman: Two New Books about the
Man and His Work." Book Buyer 14 (February),
9-11.
    Review of Burroughs (1896.2), with
praises, and of Donaldson (1896.3), which
displays the typical Whitman disciple's
incoherent admiration but has interest
because Whitman's personality was his master
poem.

38 BUCKE, RICHARD MAURICE. "Notes on the Text of
'Leaves of Grass,' V." Conservator 7
(February), 185-86.
    Traces the growth of Whitman's poems
through his accumulation of jottings on
small scraps of paper. Some scraps can be
identified in published poems, some cannot.
Taken together, they would make a good-
sized volume.

39 [CARPENTER, EDWARD.] "A Visit to Walt Whitman
in 1877." Progressive Review 1 (February),
407-17.
Reprinted: 1906.5.

Account of visit to Whitman in Camden
with side trips to the Stafford and
Gilchrist homes; description of Whitman's
personality, attitudes toward nature and
life, conversation on his poetic plan,
oriental literature and people, labor.
Holmes is quoted (from Carpenter's visit to
him in Boston) on the opinions of himself,
Lowell, and Longfellow regarding Whitman.
Carpenter praises Whitman's "strange omniv-
orous egotism, controlled and restrained
by that wonderful genius of his for human
affection and love."

40 LEE, GERALD STANLEY. "Mr. Burroughs's Study
of Walt Whitman." Bookman 4 (February),
559-62.
Review of 1896.2. Whitman is "perhaps
the most heroic and gentle and immovable
figure in American letters." Burroughs
will prove to be his most effective friend
after Emerson but needs to recognize how
Whitman fell short of his ideal, never
reaching humbleness before the universe
and transcending himself. We still await
the great poet.

41 T[RAUBEL], H. L. "Collect." Conservator 7
(February), 177-78.
Criticizes Smyth's statement (1896.16):
Whitman would not have been improved by
art because he sought to inform art with
the writer's own personality.

42 T[RAUBEL, HORACE]. "Whitman: A Study, III."
Conservator 7 (February), 189.
Continues 1897.29, quoting extracts
from Burroughs with praise. Continued
1897.53.

43 COOK, GEORGE C. "'The Primary Condition of
Understanding Whitman,' and the Secondary
Condition of Understanding Anybody." Dial
22 (1 February), 77-78.
Response to Triggs (1897.32): One must
give oneself up to a poet and then be
critical. He himself has been moved by
Whitman but he recognizes other poets'
worth also, without adopting, like the
disciples, "Whitman's attitude toward
Whitman." Whitman is still "second only to
Emerson as a pure force in American literature."

44 HARPER, FRANCIS P. "The Human and the Superhuman View of Whitman." Dial 22 (1 February), 78.
Response to Triggs (1897.32), who has
not shown Donaldson to be untrustworthy,
seeming to prefer a superhuman presentation
of Whitman to Donaldson's human presentation, although Whitman would have resented
such a conception.

45 WATSON, J. "Whitman Cant vs. Criticism."
Dial 22 (February), 78.
Response to Triggs (1897.32): A reader
should not have to shut off his critical
judgment, as Triggs suggests he must.

46 ANON. "John Burroughs on Walt Whitman."
Literary Digest 14 (13 February), 457.
Review of Burroughs (1896.2), whose un-
certainty over how to describe Whitman is
apparent, for he uses much repetition.
This is not a bad introduction to "a poet
whom so many people still refuse to know."

47 ANON. Review of Burroughs (1896.2). Methodist
Review 79, n.s. 13 (March), 338-39.
If Whitman is a Messiah as Burroughs
suggests, "it is an atonement by stark
naked shamelessness." Many will simply take
Whitman at his word and put his book down,
unread. This book should have been titled
The Apotheosis of Whitman.

48 ANON. "Whitman." Conservator 8 (March),
10-11.
Favorable review of Burroughs (1896.2)
from London Chronicle (unlocated): Whitman
is the pioneer not of a new literature but
of a new, democratic view of life. The
world now accepts him as "a great and
resonant voice."

49 COMPENDIUM. "Recent Study and Criticism of
Whitman." Conservator 8 (March), 11-12.
First in a series of compendia of commentary on Whitman from newspapers, magazines, and books. Continued 1897.62.

50 GARRISON, CHARLES G. "Lucas Malet on Whitman."
Conservator 8 (March), 9-10.
Comments on Malet's novel (1891.8).

51 KENNEDY, WILLIAM SLOANE. "Notes on the
Pfaffians." Conservator 8 (March), 9.
Includes comments from the Pfaffians on
Whitman, quoted from Chamberlin (1892.57).

52 T[RAUBEL], H. L. "Collect." Conservator 8
(March), 2-3.
Such concern for Whitman's ultimate
place as evidenced in the Dial controversy
(see 1897.43) is pointless, for reputations
change. Let us acknowledge his impact on
those readers today who understand him.

53 T[RAUBEL, HORACE]. "Whitman: A Study, IV."
Conservator 8 (March), 12.
Continues 1897.42. Whitman brought to
American democracy, as to literature, a
vista wider than provincial patriotism.

54 TRIGGS, OSCAR LOVELL. "Democratic Criticism."
Dial 22 (1 March), 141-42.
Response to Cook (1897.43): Leaves
calls for democratic criticism, which
records genuine personal experience, rather
than aristocratic criticism, which estimates
literary values according to absolute standards. It is the most human book in the
world and demands that readers interact
with the poet and the objects of the universe.

55 ANON. "Notes and News." Poet-Lore 9, no. 2
(Spring), 311-12.

Adds to Cook's three attitudes toward
Whitman (1897.30) a fourth, the recognition
in Whitman of "as great a balance of power
and form as there is in Tennyson," despite
the difference in "the laws of beauty
governing them." Triggs (1897.32) is defended against Watson (1897.45) regarding
the importance of approaching Whitman with
an open mind.

56 MICHAEL, HELEN ABBOTT. "Woman and Freedom in
    Whitman." Poet-Lore 9, no. 2 (Spring),
    216-37.
    Reprinted: 1907.6.
        Influenced by the women of his family,
    Whitman appreciated woman in her various
    roles and depicted her in other than the
    standard literary roles. He believes in
    woman's freedom but generally restricts
    her to practical roles. In seeking freedom,
    Whitman emphasizes spiritual rather than
    political or economic aspirations, but he
    urges the financial independence of women.
    His poetry is dissatisfying in not present-
    ing woman as a rounded character or in-
    volving her in his notion of comradeship.
    But his emphasis on individualism will help
    the progress of both men and women.

57 P[ORTER, CHARLOTTE]. "Kipling's 'Seven Seas'
    an Atavism." Poet-Lore 9, no. 2 (Spring),
    293.
    Quoted in 1897.62.
        Whitman achieved greater success than
    Kipling in modelling modern actualities to
    artistic purpose, notably in "Passage" and
    "Locomotive."

58 ANON. "Reviews of Recent Publications."
    International Studio 1 (April), 140.
        Review of H. W. Mesdag: The Painter of
    the North Sea: the sea painted by Mesdag
    is that which Whitman described in "After
    the Sea-Ship," "a quite masterly perfor-
    mance," to which the only objection would
    be that "it is more like beautiful prose
    than beautiful poetry."

59 BUCKE, RICHARD MAURICE. "Lawyer or Actor?"
    Conservator 8 (April), 20-23.
        Incidental references to Whitman in
    this discussion of the authorship of
    Shakespeare's works: anecdote of Whitman
    reading lines which he and others assumed
    were Shakespeare's but which turned out to
    be Bacon's; denial of Kennedy's assertion
    (1897.26) that Whitman and Emerson share
    parallel lines.

60 CARPENTER, EDWARD. "Walt Whitman in 1884."
    Progressive Review 2 (April), 9-19.
    Reprinted: 1906.5.
        Account of visit to Mickle Street in
    June 1884; Whitman's conversation on his
    friends, death, the secret behind Leaves.
    Analysis of Whitman's character: obstinacy
    mixed with infinite tenderness, caution,
    and artfulness; voluminousness; contrary

moods; tolerance. Emerson's characterization of Whitman is quoted from his conversation with Carpenter. Whitman saw himself
as the typical man of a new era, his power
of love developed to an extreme, spiritual
and emotional as well as physical and
sexual. Leaves derives from his illumination, his perception of the universal har-
monized with practical experiences.

61 CLOSE, STUART. "Whitman's 'Catalogues.'"
    Conservator 8 (April), 25-26.
        The catalogues are meant "to identify
    and unify man with the universe," to glorify
    the commonplace. The reader is to work out
    the meanings and relationships of these
    lists of crude materials.

62 COMPENDIUM. "Recent Study and Criticism of
    Whitman, II." Conservator 8 (April), 27.
        Includes items by Philip Henry Savage
    from Harvard Advocate and John Trevor from
    Labour Prophet.

63 DAVIS, REBECCA HARDING. "Some Hobgoblins in
    Literature." Book Buyer 14 (April), 229-31.
        Whitman is brought up as "another Ameri-
    can whom popular prejudice has clothed with
    abnormal qualities," regarding him as either
    exemplar or devil. Though he possesses a
    seer's eye and tongue, the contradictions
    between his behavior and his professed
    ideals reveal him as "a boorish, awkward
    poseur." But his indecency was only that
    of thousands of others "who are coarse by
    nature and vulgar by breeding."

64 JACKSON, EDWARD PAYSON. "Whitman and Whittier
    as Patriots." Conservator 8 (April), 24-25.
        Whitman's patriotism is Christ-like,
    based on love for mankind, tolerance, and
    selflessness. Concluded 1897.76.

65 KENNEDY, WILLIAM SLOANE. "An Annotated Edition
    of 'Sartor Resartus.'" Conservator 8
    (April), 28-29.
        Carlyle's Sartor rather than Emerson's
    work provides some germs for Leaves. Their
    similarities are noted as hymns of labor
    and democracy, with identical spiritual
    philosophy and "Berkeleyanisms" and similar
    prose style, though Whitman remains unique.

66 PORTER, CHARLOTTE. "The American Idea in
    Whitman." Walt Whitman Fellowship Papers
    3, no. 6 (April), 19-26.
    Reprint of 1896.58.

67 SEDGWICK, HENRY D., Jr. "Bryant's Permanent
    Contribution to Literature." Atlantic
    Monthly 79 (April), 539.
        Incidental: the various American poets,
    including Whitman, "utter the common human
    feelings that enter the hearts of common
    man."

68 STODDART, MARY. "Walt Whitman." Conservator
    8 (April), 20.

1897

Poem of tribute in four rhymed stanzas:
"He pointed to men life."

69 TORREY, BRADFORD. "The Demand for an American
Literature." Atlantic Monthly 79 (April),
571.
Incidental: Whitman is "one American
poet whose literary patriotism was never
called in question," never being conservative or emulating the English.

70 T[RAUBEL, HORACE]. "Whitman and Symonds."
Conservator 8 (April), 29.
Quotes Symonds's comments on Whitman
from Brown (1895.2), which lacks description
of "the warm personal relations existing
between Symonds and Whitman."

71 BUCKE, RICHARD MAURICE. "Memories of Walt
Whitman: 2." Walt Whitman Fellowship
Papers 3, no. 10 (May), 35-42.
All who knew Whitman, and particularly
those he helped during the war, should
record their memories. Notes taken in
December 1891 during Whitman's last sickness are printed: his conversation, will,
condition.

72 BURROUGHS, JOHN. "On a Dictum of Matthew
Arnold's." Atlantic Monthly 79 (May),
715-16.
Defending subjective criticism from
Arnold's opposition, Burroughs cites the
different attitudes of Emerson and Lowell
toward Whitman, a contrast similar to that
of Symonds and Gosse.

73 COMPENDIUM. "Recent Study and Criticism of
Whitman. III." Conservator 8 (May),
43-44.

74 HIGGINSON, THOMAS WENTWORTH. "Cheerful Yesterdays. VII." Atlantic Monthly 79 (May),
676.
Reprinted: 1898.8; Whitman Supplement 1979.
Describes Whitman in Thayer and
Eldridge's shop in 1860. His own prejudice
against Whitman may be due to his reading
the unsavory passages while seasick on a
voyage. The impression of Whitman as having
"not so much of manliness as of Boweriness"
was not eradicated when he failed to fight
in the war.

75 JACKSON, EDWARD PAYSON. "A Convert to
Whitman." Walt Whitman Fellowship Papers
3, no. 8 (May), 29-31.
Describes his discovery upon actually
reading Whitman's work that it is not repulsive and that his versification is
grander than mere "jingles."

76 _____. "Whitman and Whittier as Patriots,
II." Conservator 8 (May), 36-37.
Concludes 1897.64. Following discussion of Whittier, the question is raised:
why didn't Whitman oppose slavery with
similar passion in his own work?

77 MERWIN, HENRY CHILDS. "Millet and Walt
Whitman." Atlantic Monthly 79 (May), 719-
20.
A few excellent lines and phrases notwithstanding, Whitman never mastered the
art of writing, yet he is the only writer
so far who has perceived what democracy
really means, who has appreciated the
beauty and heroism in the daily lives of
the common people. Millet's paintings
exemplify Whitman's ideas: the two have
much in common, except for Whitman's egotism.

78 SANBORN, FRANK B. "Reminiscent of Whitman."
Conservator 8 (May), 37-40.
Uses much of the same material as
1895.83. Recalls meeting Whitman in Boston;
describes his appearance and mannerisms;
cites critics.

79 TARBELL, IDA M. "A Great Photographer."
McClure's Magazine 9 (May), 559-64.
This article on photographer G. C. Cox
reprints his photograph of Whitman, than
which "what could be more characteristic,
fuller of sweetness and truth?" It has
been the foundation of other art works.
Seeing it, the actress Duse said, "But it
is his soul! How can one photograph a soul?"

80 T[RAUBEL], H. L. "Collect." Conservator 8
(May), 34-35.
Answers Jackson's question (1897.76) by
citing passages from Whitman indicating his
strong opposition to slavery, though on a
human rather than political level. Contrary
to Sanborn's suggestions (1897.78),
Whitman's verse is truly meant for the lips.

81 T[RAUBEL, HORACE]. "Whitman as Mystic." Conservator 8 (May), 45.
Favorable review of Guthrie (1897.7) on
the importance of Whitman's mysticism.

82 ANON. "Walt Whitman and Peter Doyle." Time
and the Hour (22 May).
Notice of Calamus (1897.2) with extensive quotation.

83 COMPENDIUM. "Recent Study and Criticism of
Whitman. IV." Conservator 8 (June), 60.
Includes comments by Herbert Small in
Time and the Hour and Walter Blackburn
Harte in Kansas City Lotus.

*84 FREILIGRATH, FERDINAND. "An Early Estimate of
Walt Whitman." Translated by Sadakichi
Hartmann. Art News 1 (June), 3.
Reprinted: 1897.142. Reported in Knox.
Same as 1892.191.

85 KENNEDY, WILLIAM S. "Whitman's Letters to
Peter Doyle." Conservator 8 (June), 60-61.
Review of Calamus (1897.2). The letters,
valuable for readers of Leaves but useless
for others, display Whitman's simplicity of
language and feeling.

86 MAYNARD, LAURENS. "Walt Whitman's Comradeship." Conservator 8 (June), 53-55.
Reprinted: 1898.56.
    Comradeship is Whitman's pervasive
theme in life and art, "a solvent for the
evils of our civilization," fittingly
placed between self-love ("Adam") and love
for all mankind ("Salut").

87 ANON. Review of Calamus (1897.2). Boston
Morning Herald (5 June).
    The letters are "laughable," "pretty
poor stuff," containing chiefly gossip and
requests for money and papers.

88 CARMAN, BLISS. "The Modern Athenian." Boston
Evening Transcript (5 June), 18.
    Review of Calamus (1897.2), which shows
contentment but none of the genius or wit
or philosophy expected of a poet. Whitman's
was not a trained mind. But "the riches of
his wholesome and rugged poetry" will survive, his weaker efforts being forgotten.
This book sheds light on his character.

89 ANON. "Calamus." Chicago Evening Post (12
June), 5:1-2. Illustrated.
    Review of 1897.2. "The correspondence
is commonplace in the extreme." The "attachment seems a strange one" since Doyle
does not understand Whitman's poetry. The
book is a success only as a curiosity and
of interest only to Whitman's admirers.

90 ANON. Paragraph review of Calamus (1897.2).
Boston Evening Transcript (14 June), 6:7.
    This review is presented in opposition
to the earlier notice (1897.88). This book
will delight Whitman's apostles but prove
"intolerably dull" to others. Why print
the letters at all?

91 ANON. "Walt Whitman's Letters." Boston Daily
Advertiser (15 June), 8:3-4.
    Review of Calamus (1897.2). Whitman's
executors should not publish what is no
credit to Whitman, since these letters are
"kindly, but stupid."

92 Y[OUNG], J[AMES] W[ALTER]. "Whitman's Letters."
Knoxville (Tennessee) Tribune (15 June),
4:3-4.
    Review of Calamus (1897.2): it reveals
Whitman's great capacity for "exalted
friendship," as in the series of Greek conception, the "Calamus" poems; illustrates
his "great-hearted warmth of feeling." The
more we know of the man, the better we can
understand his poetry; as a man he "was
probably greater than anything he wrote."
He represents soul rather than mind in his
style. These letters might introduce
people to the poet and correct erroneous
conceptions of him.

93 ANON. Brief review of Calamus (1897.2). St.
Louis Globe-Democrat (19 June).
    These letters add nothing to Whitman's

literary fame and have no interest for the
average reader, though praised by Bucke and
Symonds.

94 ANON. "Letters by Walt Whitman." Brooklyn
Daily Eagle (20 June), 4:2.
    Review of Calamus (1897.2), not impor-
tant as literature but as an aid to understanding Whitman better as a man who never
displays petulance or discontent and strong
longing only rarely. That Doyle once saved
Whitman's life "may account for the regard
that subsisted between this odd pair."

95 ANON. "The Book World. 'Calamus.'" Cleveland
Leader (20 June), 21:1-2.
    Review of 1897.2, with long quotations
from Doyle and Burroughs. Its principal
value is that it shows, better than any
other work, Whitman's sympathetic heart.
This book gives the impression, which there
is no reason to doubt, that "he overshadows
all idealizations of fiction."

96 HALE, PHILIP. "Whitman Again." Boston Journal
(20 June).
    Favorable review of Calamus (1897.2):
Whitman's letters, parental, brotherly,
sentimental, prove that his attitude was
not a pose.

97 ANON. Review of Calamus (1897.2). Boston
Pilot (26 June).
    Whitman's letters show him "uninstructed,
illogical"; praise for him is "mistaken
clemency." Those who claim he was a poet
should read these letters.

98 DONNAN, MAY W. "Whitman's Letters to Doyle."
Indianapolis Journal (28 June), 4:7.
    Review of Calamus (1897.2), appropriately
not the letters of a litterateur but the
frank description of personal activities
from one man to his friend, with no hint at
posing or playing the superior but showing
Whitman's keen interest and delight in
everything. Those who dislike or do not
know his work can discover the man through
these letters, childlike in simplicity,
"manly in feeling," full of human interest.

99 ANON. "New Publications." Philadelphia Public
Ledger (29 June), 7:2.
    Review of Calamus (1897.2): it reveals
"an extreme simplicity and naiveté," "the
simple practical creed of his life," his
sympathy for the unlettered. Whitman's
deep affection is a key to his magnetism.
The introduction is "a delightful and important addition to our knowledge of
Whitman's unique personality." The letters
are "pathetic in their hints of failing
powers" due to his illness.

100 WILLIAMS, FRANCIS HOWARD. "Immortality as a
Motive in Poetry." Poet-Lore 9, no. 3
(Summer), 370, 375.
    Incidental: Though the most reviled of

1897

poets, Whitman most fully expresses the truth of immortality. He believes in "the eternal supremacy of the individual and the indestructibility of the human soul," with a spiritual significance even in his supposedly most materialist poems.

101 BROWN, JOHN HENRY. "To Walt Whitman." Conservator 8 (July), 77.
Reprint of 1890.25.

102 COMPENDIUM. "The Calamus Letters of Walt Whitman." Conservator 8 (July), 77.
Reviews of Calamus (1897.2) quoted from various sources.

103 _____. "Recent Study and Criticism of Whitman. V." Conservator 8 (July), 76.

104 SALT, HENRY S. "Burroughs' Study of Whitman, I." Conservator 8 (July), 74-75.
Burroughs (1896.2) provides a justification rather than a critical study, unproductively considering whether Whitman was "a true artist." Concluded 1897.125.

105 T[RAUBEL], H. L. "Collect." Conservator 8 (July), 66-67.
Commentary on 1897.115, praising Whitman for what Chapman deplores.

106 YOUNG, JAMES WALTER. "The Poet of Conflict." Conservator 8 (July), 74.
Whitman is emancipating, leading us into struggle but giving us courage.

107 ANON. "Walt Whitman as 'Comrade.'" Chap-Book 7 (1 July), 138-39.
Review of Calamus (1897.2), very plain and not useful. Specimen gives a better idea of Whitman; the poems are a better comment on the letters than vice versa. Comradeship, of cardinal importance in Whitman's works, is evident here but does not come to full expression; Whitman's devotion is more paternal than comradely. The "Calamus" poems are among Whitman's most powerful.

108 [CHADWICK, J. W.] Review of Calamus (1897.2). Nation 65 (1 July), 19-20.
Same as 1897.111.
These letters reveal a purity of affection. Doyle's letters should have been included. Whitman's "unvarying puerility" is possibly a concession to Doyle. His kindness is evident, but there is nothing here to show his intellectual ability or poetic gift.

109 ANON. Review of Calamus (1897.2). London Daily Chronicle (6 July), 6:7, 7:1-2.
These letters provide "a charming picture" of the recently rare subject of comradeship. Doyle's picture of Whitman is vivid and sincere. Letters (quoted) reveal Whitman's genial personality, which may have suggested Ibsen's character Dr. Stockmann.

110 ANON. Review of Calamus (1897.2). Manchester Guardian (7 July), 4:8.
The extreme reactions to Whitman indicate the "elemental depth and force" of his personality. Calamus sheds interesting light on Whitman.

111 [CHADWICK, J. W.] "Literature." New York Evening Post (7 July), 4:1.
Same as 1897.108.

112 HALE, PHILIP. "Talk of the Day." Boston Journal (8 July).
Response to Nation (1897.108), defending Whitman's simplicity as more appropriate for this correspondence than the style of Vistas.

113 ANON. Brief review of Calamus (1897.2). Philadelphia Evening Bulletin (10 July), 8:3.
Calamus expresses Whitman's tenderness of heart as well as his "personal friendship for 'common people'" as have few of his published writings.

114 [SWINTON, JOHN.] "New Books." New York Sun (10 July), 7:1-2.
Review of Calamus (1897.2). O'Connor's impression of Whitman is questioned, since Whitman did not strike everyone the same way; his enthusiastic admirers are not to be trusted entirely. The grander elements of Whitman's poetic themes are hardly suggested in these letters, which are interesting, however, because not intended for publication. Letters are quoted to reveal different moods.

115 CHAPMAN, JOHN JAY. "Walt Whitman." Chap-Book 7 (15 July), 156-59.
Reprinted: 1898.7. Abridged: 1897.121; 1897.119; Miller, Murphy.
"America was solved" for English readers when they discovered Whitman as representing what they believed Americans were, but the country he writes of does not exist nor have its people read him. However, he is representative, having "given utterance to the soul of the tramp" in a "revolt of laziness." He was both poseur and "authentic creature." His belief in his mission made him "a quack poet," with an incoherent mind, despite "a few lines of epic directness and cyclopean vigor and naturalness." He had great physical enjoyment of life. "Lilacs" and his "wonderful descriptions" lack "conscious art."

116 ANON. "An Old Parody on Walt Whitman." Academy 52 (17 July), 50.
Reprinted: 1897.128; 1898.22. Parody reprinted: Saunders.
Reprints and explains background of parody, "This is a wedding," from London of 1878 (unlocated).

117 TRIGGS, OSCAR LOVELL. "The Study Table. Calamus." The New Unity (22 July).
    Brief review of 1897.2, an important event. The letters throw light upon the "Calamus" poems, superior to any commentary.

118 ANON. "Walt Whitman's Letters." San Francisco Chronicle (25 July), 4:3.
    Review of Calamus (1897.2), not poetic or literary since Whitman is adapting his language to his reader, lacking the nature observations which characterized much of his fine later writing. However, the reader will gain a warmer regard for Whitman because of his sincere love for this comrade.

119 CHAPMAN, JOHN JAY. "Walt Whitman as a Literary Tramp." Public Opinion 23 (29 July), 146-47.
    Abridged from 1897.115.

120 MABIE, HAMILTON WRIGHT. "The Literary Sympathy of John Burroughs." Public Opinion 23 (29 July), 147-48.
    Abridged from 1897.124.

121 CHAPMAN, JOHN JAY. "Walt Whitman as a Tramp." Literary Digest 15 (31 July), 400-401.
    Abridged from 1897.115.

122 ANON. Review of Calamus (1897.2). Progressive Review 2 (August), 479-80.
    These letters reveal Whitman's "genial, large, robust, tender nature," his "real affection for his brother-man," his theory of comradeship in practice.

123 KENNEDY, WILLIAM SLOANE. "Identities of Thought and Phrase in Emerson and Whitman." Conservator 8 (August), 88-91.
    Reprinted: 1927.11.
    Lists parallels between passages by Emerson (before 1856) and Whitman, as evidence not of borrowing but of the fact that two philosophers talking about life and its conduct must use similar grounds, especially when living at the same time, amid similar thought and classes.

124 MABIE, HAMILTON WRIGHT. "John Burroughs." Century Magazine 54 (August), 562-63, 567, 568.
    Abridged: 1897.120.
    Incidental references to Whitman's influence on Burroughs, whose loyal and generous advocacy of Whitman was necessitated by the "atmosphere of exasperating indifference, if not of downright antagonism." Burroughs's claims have helped bring American opinion closer to foreign opinion on Whitman, whose freshness is appealing and elemental unless considered from a merely literary standpoint.

125 SALT, HENRY S. "Burroughs' Study of Whitman, II." Conservator 8 (August), 91-92.
    Concludes 1897.104. The parallels of Whitman with Tennyson are inaccurate. Whitman "does not stand for the entire democratic concept." Despite such deficiencies due to enthusiasm, Burroughs's work surpasses other studies.

126 T., S. "New Publishers and New Editions of Whitman." Conservator 8 (August), 83.
    Describes new contract with Small, Maynard to publish Whitman's works.

127 TRIGGS, OSCAR LOVELL. "The Growth of Leaves of Grass." Conservator 8 (August), 84-88.
    Revised: 1902.26.
    Leaves must be considered as a growth, related to the author's own life process. His preparatory early works and experiences are explained as relevant. Leaves is based on Whitman's convictions of inherent human greatness, the United States as seat of a pure democracy, and the failure of literature to meet the needs of the people. These poems are records of experiences, fresh and spontaneous. Triggs explains the themes in early editions, the development of Whitman's order, his revisions.

128 ANON. "A Skit on Walt Whitman." New York Times Illustrated Magazine (1 August), 5.
    Reprint of 1897.116.

129 HALE, EDWARD E., Jr. "Walt Whitman and the Critics." Chap-Book 7 (1 August), 193-94.
    Response to Chapman (1897.115). "A good re-estimate" of Whitman is needed. Certainly he is not representative of America, nor do all English readers think so. No tramp ever had a soul like that expressed in Whitman's poetry, nor is it tramp-like save in rejecting authority. Chapman may object to some of Whitman's middle-class characteristics, but he does not account for the vitalizing power which can appeal to so many intelligent men.

130 THOMPSON, MAURICE. "Walt Whitman and the Critics." Chap-Book 7 (1 August), 194-95.
    Response to Chapman (1897.115). Whitman's American eulogists are not critics, for they focus on the man, not the literature. His sincerity is genuine, but acquired rather than spontaneous. His form shows "labored, overwrought unnaturalness." He had the poetic sense but "deliberately set out to be queer and loose," producing absurdities.

131 TRIGGS, OSCAR LOVELL. "Walt Whitman and the Critics." Chap-Book 7 (1 August), 192-93.
    Response to Chapman (1897.115): he misses the mystical meaning of Whitman's "terminology of tramping." Whitman's English admirers loved Whitman's work not for its uncouthness, but for its universal poetic greatness.

132 THOMPSON, MAURICE. "The Personal Note." Chap-Book 7 (15 August), 241-43.

This discussion of the importance of style incidentally contrasts Whitman with the Greek poets, against whom his lines ring hollowly and crudely. Like Baudelaire, he suffers from a "chronic self-deception" keeping "the real 'man himself' out of the work." He had merely superficial knowledge.

133 ANON. Review of Calamus (1897.2). Baltimore News (16 August).
The letters were needed earlier, as illustrating Whitman's concept of friendship. Comments on Whitman are cited.

134 ANON. "Walt Whitman Still a Bone of Contention." Literary Digest 15 (21 August), 490-91.
Chapman (1897.115) has "stirred up a hornets' nest," as revealed in various responses quoted.

135 ANON. Review of Calamus (1897.2). Philadelphia Press (21 August).
Can these "trifling and commonplace" letters have been praised by Symonds? Whose idea was it to publish them: Whitman's, as if to make capital only?

136 ANON. Review of Calamus (1897.2). Academy 52 (28 August), 159-60.
Reprinted: 1897.152.
Whitman's admirers are too serious; his "generous tingling message of democracy" does not need their commentary. These letters show Whitman like other men, with tremendous humanity and warmth. Doyle's picture of Whitman and his boyishness is "a piece of real literature." Whitman was drawn to young men because "he could influence them, colour their potentialities; they were frank and fresh and spirited and unaffected." "Calamus" appears quite unobjectionable after one reads these letters.

137 TRAUBEL, HORACE L. "Walt Whitman's Letters. An Explanation of How Mr. J. A. Symonds Was Enabled to Examine Them." Philadelphia Press (28 August).
Response to 1897.135: Symonds was given copies of the letters in 1891 by J. W. Wallace. Whitman himself had nothing to do with "promulgation, public or private."

138 ANON. "A Bibliography of Walt Whitman." Bookman 6 (September), 81-82.
Describes and lists editions of Whitman's works. The 1860 edition was said to be an exemplary specimen of typography. Prompt pecuniary response to the 1876 edition helped prolong Whitman's life.

139 COMPENDIUM. "Recent Study and Criticism of Whitman. VI." Conservator 8 (September), 107.
Includes material from Chicago Interior, Christian Register, and Guardian.

140 T[RAUBEL], H. L. "Collect." Conservator 8 (September), 98-99.
Protests Whitman's negative treatment by the American (1897.145), but "Whitman offers the challenge of rebellion" and welcomes dissent.

141 T[RAUBEL, HORACE]. "Whitman Interpreted." Conservator 8 (September), 109.
Brief favorable review of Guthrie (1897.7). Whitman will live because he had a message and because he was competent to communicate it effectively.

142 FREILIGRATH, FERDINAND. "An Early Estimate of Walt Whitman." Translated by Sadakichi Hartmann. Musical Courier 35 (1 September), vi.
Reprint of 1897.84.

143 JERROLD, LAURENCE. "Mr. Chapman on Whitman: An English Reply." Chap-Book 7 (1 September), 274-75.
Ironic commentary on Chapman (1897.115): Is his "naive simplicity" in passing judgment on English criticism greater than his "perverse incomprehension" of Whitman? Chapman is familiar with both methods of attacking Whitman: "to paint the man luridly" (a British method) and "to declare the book artless." Chapman disapproves of Whitman as "not a respectable member of society," although he may actually realize "how widely and how deeply the poet read life." He may resent the uncultured Whitman being considered America's greatest poet. "The British public still thinks Whitman immoral, and the French public calls him mad."

144 ANON. "Calamus." Literary World 28 (4 September), 295.
Review of 1897.2, "the plain, rugged utterances of a warm human-hearted man," to which quality "they owe their sole value," being "almost unlettered in style." "The popular idea of Whitman as a poet is certainly not assisted by reading them."

145 BAUSER, WHARTIN. "Calamus. Letters by Walt Whitman." American 27 (11 September).
Review of 1897.2, "the correspondence of an illiterate vulgarian." Whitman "Barnumized" universal ideas into a prose-verse mixture infused with ridiculous egotism.

146 ANON. "Literary Notes." New York Tribune (26 September), Supplement, 13:3-4.
Review of Calamus (1897.2), "interesting as showing Whitman in his character of cheerful adviser and constant comrade." The best part of the book is Bucke's introduction with Doyle's reminiscences, which lack literary biases.

147 M., W. E. "Whitman's Letters to Doyle." Poet-Lore 9, no. 4 (Autumn), 617-18.

Review of Calamus (1897.2), which gives
no hint "as to the workings of his vast
synthetic intellect." Its one ingredient
is Whitman's "strong feeling of love for
men," "the beautiful spirit that pervaded
the Calamus poems."

148 ANON. "Walt Whitman." Academy (October).
Reported in CHAL, but not found in any of
the October issues.

149 ABBEY, CHARLOTTE L. "Walt Whitman and His
Unsung Songs." Conservator 8 (October),
118-19.
Reprinted: 1898.50.
Whitman's evolutionary thought is
closer to the Eastern than to the Darwinian
conception. The "Sea Drift" poems enclose
the secret of spiritual evolution. His
unsung songs will be the songs of his successors.

150 COMPENDIUM. "Recent Study and Criticism of
Whitman. VII." Conservator 8 (October),
122-23.
Includes material from Boston Literary
Review, City and State, Progressive Review
(Ernest Crosby notes that Tolstoy "could
not make him [Whitman] out"), New Unity,
as well as annotated items.

151 T[RAUBEL], H. L. "Collect." Conservator 8
(October), 115.
Reprinted: 1897.154.
Notes the difficulties major writers
have with Whitman as a writer, though many,
such as Tennyson, admired the man.

152 COMPENDIUM. "Recent Study and Criticism of
Whitman. VIII." Conservator 8 (November),
139-40.

153 [KELLEY, WILLIAM V.] "The Whitman Craze in
England." Methodist Review 79, n.s. 13
(November), 952-64.
Deplores British adulation of Whitman.
Even a minister, Dr. Robert F. Horton, has
said that Whitman has part of the word of
God in him. Gosse (1894.28) alone seems to
have retained his sanity and perceived
Whitman's faults. Whitman's books "contain
the most indecent things ever put in type,"
equalling any deed Wilde ever did. Europe
was glad to regard Whitman, "the world's
most flatulent and bombastic egotist," as
the typical American. His work is often
"grotesque and monstrous in form," but
occasionally displays "a sort of swimming
majesticalness." He is hardly Greek as
his admirers claim.

154 [TRAUBEL, H. L.] "Whitman and His Contemporaries." Public Opinion 23 (4 November),
595.
Reprint of 1897.151.

155 ANON. Review of Calamus (1897.2). Independent
49 (25 November), 22 (1546).

Whitman's friends keep forcing Leaves
on the world. This book provides sure
proof of their delusion and his "lack of
poetic genius," giving "the impression of
immense stupidity joined to ignorance and
vulgarity."

156 ANON. "Leaves of Grass." Literary World 28
(27 November), 431-32.
Review of 1897 Leaves. Compared with
the 1876 edition, it is "practically a new
work based on the old." The writer refrains
from again expressing this journal's opinion
of Whitman's work but suggests that the
verse would read just as well if printed as
prose.

157 BORN, HELENA. "Personality in Whitman."
Conservator 8 (December), 154.
Describes program for Boston Whitman
Fellowship on Whitman's treatment of
"physical personality"; the discussion;
speakers. (See 1898.20.)

158 COMPENDIUM. "Recent Study and Criticism of
Whitman. IX." Conservator 8 (December),
155-56.

159 SWIFT, BENJAMIN. "The Function of Art."
Cosmopolis 8 (December), 691-704.
Reported in Triggs, but no reference found
to Whitman.

160 ANON. "A New Edition of Whitman." Public
Opinion 23 (2 December), 724-25.
Review of 1897 Leaves, praising its
physical presentation. "Old Age Echoes"
will be of interest to Whitman lovers, even
if of no great importance. Whitman's "is a
strong and clear voice that will be heard"
with widening influence. If he is rejected
as poet because he lacks regular meter,
then the Psalms are not poetry. He certainly has the emotional appeal and power
and the vitalization of ideas of great
poetry. We must divest ourselves of prejudices and receive his message. Criticisms
of Whitman's triviality and uncleanness are
answered.

161 ANON. "Walt Whitman in Every-Day Life."
Literary Digest 15 (4 December), 938-39.
Review of Calamus (1897.2), quoting
Academy (1897.136). The Doyle interview is
"far more quotable than the letters," which
"rarely touch on topics of general or
abiding interest."

162 de KAY, CHARLES. "Walt Whitman. An Appreciation." New York Times Saturday Review
(11 December), 23.
Reprinted in part: 1898.22.
Review of 1897 Leaves. Whitman is contrasted with Nietzsche: Whitman's egotism
is more human, for he includes and identifies
with all types of people and reflects the
ideals of many Americans. He holds a unique
place in American literature, "beside Poe

and Emerson, yet far apart from them."
"Last of Ebb, and Daylight Waning" is unparalleled in describing beach sounds.

163 ANON. "Whitman as Viewed by Contemporaries."
Literary Digest 15 (18 December), 1000.
Quotes 1897.151.

164 FAWCETT, EDGAR. "Men, Manners and Moods."
Collier's Weekly 20 (23 December). 18.
Reprinted in part: 1898.22.
Criticism of W. E. Henley, "plainly a
convert to the Walt Whitman school."
Fawcett's "inveterate opposition to Whitman"
is due to Whitman's failure to express the
democratic idea (not so new an idea) within
the limits of art. He was "an intention,
never an execution," bounded by Emerson,
Carlyle, egotism, and impertinence, only
"a big note-book."

1898

BOOKS

1 BARDEEN, C[HARLES] W[ILLIAM]. Authors'
Birthdays. 1st ser. Syracuse: C. W.
Bardeen. "Walt Whitman," pp. 137-81.
General introduction, quoting critics,
tracing Whitman's life. Leaves reveals
his personality, emphasizes sympathy and
immortality, achieves a vague effect of
rhythm and a musical sense like the earliest,
most spontaneous form of poetic expression.
He has genius in assimilating nature. The
affection he felt for some man (rather than
some woman) was fortunately not acted upon.
His frankness is indelicate but not corrupt. His devotion to America is too extravagant.

2 BATES, KATHARINE LEE. American Literature.
New York: Macmillan Co.; London: Macmillan
& Co. "Walt Whitman," pp. 199-202.
Shock at Whitman's egotism and perver-
sity is well-founded. "Drum-Taps" contains
his best, serious concerns. Apart from the
war, his attitude toward life is as cheerfully irresponsible as his attitude toward
art. The love of the common man is his
best quality.

3 BUCKE, RICHARD MAURICE, ed. Preface to The
Wound Dresser: A Series of Letters Written
from the Hospitals in Washington during the
War of Rebellion. Boston: Small, Maynard
& Co., pp. vii-viii.
Reprinted: 1902.4.
Describes the letters: they are not
literature, but do not have to be.

4 [BURROUGHS, JOHN?] "Whitman." In National
Cyclopaedia of American Biography. Vol. 1.
New York: James T. White & Co., p. 255.
Page-long biographical sketch, quoting
Stedman (1880.35), Dowden (1871.4), and
Stevenson (1878.17) for ideas on Whitman's

work. His recent "occasional literary
efforts evince the original and quaint
power of his earlier writings." His acts
and personality bear witness to his wholesome, charitable character.

5 CARPENTER, EDWARD. Angels' Wings: A Series
of Essays on Art and Its Relation to Life.
London: George Allen & Unwin. "Art and
Democracy (Wagner, Millet, and Whitman),"
pp. 1-24.
Reprint of 1896.71 with added introductory
paragraph.

6 CARPENTER, GEORGE RICE. American Prose:
Selections with Critical Introductions by
Various Writers and a General Introduction.
New York: Macmillan Co.; London: Macmillan
& Co., p. 383.
Slightly inaccurate biographical sketch,
noting Whitman's unequalled knowledge of
his ordinary countrymen and his "equally
penetrating and all-embracing" sympathy.
See also 1898.14.

7 CHAPMAN, JOHN JAY. Emerson and Other Essays.
New York: Charles Scribner's Sons. "Walt
Whitman," pp. 111-28.
Revision (minor) of 1897.115. Extracts
reprinted: Miller, Hindus.

8 HIGGINSON, THOMAS WENTWORTH. Cheerful Yester-
days. Boston and New York: Houghton
Mifflin Co., pp. 230-31; also p. 289.
Reprint of 1897.74.

9 HOWE, M. A. DeWOLFE. American Bookmen:
Sketches, Chiefly Biographical, of Certain
Writers of the Nineteenth Century. New
York: Dodd, Mead & Co. "Walt Whitman,"
pp. 222-41.
Reprint of 1898.23.

10 JOHNSON, CHARLES F. Elements of Literary
Criticism. New York: American Book Co.,
p. 141.
The ability to interpret the civilization
of his own day "even imparts an element of
greatness to the formless waste of words
that lies on the pages of Whitman."

11 JOHNSTON, JOHN. Diary Notes of a Visit to
Walt Whitman and Some of His Friends in
1890. Manchester: Labour Press; London:
Office of the Clarion, 151 pp. No index.
Illustrated.
Reprint of 1890.7, adding chapter titles
and photographs taken by the author.
Revised: 1917.6; 1918.12.

12 NOBLE, CHARLES. Studies in American Literature:
A Text-book for Academies and High Schools.
New York and London: Macmillan Co., pp.
253-58. Portrait.
Brief life sketch; list of works; discussion of "Man-of-War-Bird" and "Captain"
as examples of Whitman's best work, securing
his place in literature. However, his

occasional crude form and gross expression, though not intended immorally, hinder his acceptance.

13 PANCOAST, HENRY S. An Introduction to American Literature. New York: Henry Holt & Co. "Walt Whitman," pp. 294-302; study list, 302-4.

Describes unsettled controversy over Whitman; his life, which suits such a "poet of our people." Despite defects in language and style, his work has the power of a "strong if often wilfully eccentric personality." Many passages are beautiful, others prosaic or incoherent. His work is "utterly removed from the people" and most highly valued by the cultured. Study list points out his significant works and biographies.

14 SANTAYANA, GEORGE. Critical introduction to Whitman. In American Prose: Selections with Critical Introductions by Various Writers and a General Introduction, by George Rice Carpenter. New York: Macmillan Co.; London: Macmillan & Co., pp. 383-88.

Whitman's prose reveals the man and his ideas and supplements the poetry "with eloquence, clearness, and evident sincerity." Whitman perceives and describes only the surface, not the underlying structure of things, and fails to organize his material as a trained writer would do. "Full of sympathy and receptivity, with a wonderful gift of graphic characterization and an occasional rare grandeur of diction, he fills us with a sense of the individuality and the universality of what he describes." His notion of an absolute democracy ignores all distinctions and extraordinary qualities, unrepresentatively looking to the past and the primitive rather than the future. His ideas are expressed with the same passion and intuition admired in his poems, as he appeals to more than a national ideal, in a fresh escape from convention and mere intellect.

15 SCUDDER, VIDA D. Social Ideals in English Letters. Boston and New York: Houghton Mifflin Co., pp. 198-99, 203, 204, 227, 285-86, 294.

Whitman is among the major exemplars of the optimism in mid-century American literature. Echoes of Emerson's "American Scholar" "passed into laughter-compelling bravado in the extraordinary yet clarion songs of Whitman." Quotations from Whitman illustrate American ideals of individualism and democracy. He seeks "contact of the entire man with man, for full expression and reception of personality," a noble desire.

15a SHARP, R. FARQUHARSON. A Dictionary of English Authors. London: George Redway, pp. 299-300.

Biographical outline; list of works.

16 TOKE, LESLIE A. ST. L. "Walt Whitman." In Prophets of the Century, edited by Arthur Rickett. London: Ward Lock & Co., n.d., pp. 227-49; chronology and bibliography, 333-34.

Whitman's works, which reveal his rich and varied life (summarized), display "a wealth of detail, a daring realism, a tender sympathy, and a spiritual insight, unequalled in literature since the sixteenth century." Whitman is above all "the poet of Health," "physical, moral, political, and spiritual," advocating a Greek-like balance, with an attitude toward sex to be praised, not blamed. His controversial adhesiveness is based, like all forms of affection, on the sexual nature (although its manifestation is not necessarily sexual). His notion of democracy does not contradict his "militant individualism" because he regarded these as social and spiritual, not political, matters. His religious philosophy was evolutionary, "a healthy optimism based on a sane mysticism." His prose style is "irritating and obscure" with an American vernacular difficult for the English, but his poems have beauty, a distinctive music, sound contributing to their sense, and meanings beyond those perceived at first reading.

17 TRIGGS, OSCAR LOVELL, ed. Introduction and selected bibliography to Selections from the Prose and Poetry of Walt Whitman. Boston: Small, Maynard & Co., pp. xiii-xliii, 251-57 (bibliography revised: 1902.25).

Whitman was a seer, to be defined not by external experience but by spiritual experience, as revealed through his work. Leaves came to him through some inspiration and is autobiographical in a larger sense. His life is traced from Bucke (1883.3), emphasizing the qualities gained during his poetic apprenticeship and what contributed to making him poet of the soul. He connects America's two great eras--that of independence and that of love and union. The contributions of past literature and thought to his poetry are discussed, with note of his favorite works. The importance of sympathy to his character and work is explained.

18 WHITMAN, WALT. Walt Whitman at Home, By Himself. Critic Pamphlet, no. 2. New York: Critic Co., 8 pp.
Reprint of 1885.10, identifying its author as Whitman.

19 WOLFE, THEODORE F. Literary Haunts and Homes: American Authors. Philadelphia: J. B. Lippincott Co., pp. 44, 51, 68-69, 129-30, 134-36, 143-47.

Describes places on Manhattan and Long Island associated with Whitman's life and compositions, with some biographical anecdotes.

1898

PERIODICALS

20 ANON. "Personality in Whitman." Poet-Lore
10, no. 1 (Winter), 113-14.
Presents the program for the current
season (November to March) of the Boston
Whitman Fellowship, listing readings and
discussion topics for meetings concerned
with physical, emotional, moral, intellectual, and aesthetic personality.

21 P[ORTER, CHARLOTTE]. "New Editions. The New
Whitman." Poet-Lore 10, no. 1 (Winter),
140-42.
Review of 1897 Leaves. The setting is
worthy of this "historic landmark in the
literary life of the New World," of which
each leaf is "a radiation from a central
nucleus of life," with themes expanding
from the opening poems "to pursue still
wider-sweeping orbits of meaning concerning
Life and Death, the Soul and Evolution."

22 COMPENDIUM. "Recent Study and Criticism of
Whitman. X." Conservator 8 (January),
171-72.

23 HOWE, M. A. DeWOLFE. "American Bookmen. X.--
Walt Whitman." Bookman 6 (January), 427-38.
Illustrated.
Reprinted: 1898.9. Extract reprinted:
1898.28.
Popular survey relating Whitman's life
experiences to his work, which reveals him
in a double personality, as an individual
and "in his imagined life of 'the average
man.'" His care in revising and finding
the right word disproves charges of "offhand
work." The range of criticism was to be
expected for one introducing a new art form.
It is not true that Whitman must be accepted
either entirely or not at all or read to
the exclusion of other poets. His enthusiasm for mankind, his national spirit, his
faith, hope, and love will appeal to most
readers.

24 T[RAUBEL], H. L. "Collect." Conservator 8
(January), 161-62.
Notes upcoming publication of Wound-
Dresser (1898.3), of "great autobiographic
value," showing Whitman practicing his
profound camaraderie. Whitman is quoted on
his love of giving himself. No "ism" can
use his name without recognizing the value
of his personal vision.

25 ANON. "Walt Whitman Letters and 'Leaves.'"
Critic 29 (1 January), 4.
Review of 1897 Leaves and Calamus
(1897.2), which "throws all the light that
is needed upon the poet's friendship with
younger men," "a semi-physical attraction"
common among boys, young working-class men,
and savages, but rare in mature men like
Whitman. These letters show his aesthetic
enjoyment of physical pleasures. They
reveal no complaints about the inequality

he occasionally notices in America, for he
believed too much in America to "dream of
a social revolution," failing like most of
his contemporaries to think that the world
might evolve in another direction than that
toward which America wished to lead. The
new edition of Leaves shows that interest
in Whitman is not subsiding; it improves
upon prior editions.

26 ANON. "Some New and Old Verse and Worse."
The American 28 (15 January), 47.
Review of 1897 Leaves. Whitman largely
drew attention because of his "note of
nakedness," later dropped. The rest of his
work is "a mixture of rhythmical rant about
the manness of man and the Americanity of
America, with a free and easy paraphrasing
of the Hebrew prophets as to style and
sometimes in lofty sentiment," although
those originals knew poetry from prose.
Whitman repels rather than enchants, an
oddity rather than an oracle whose current
acclaim will be wondered at by future generations.

27 BUCKE, RICHARD MAURICE. "Notes on the Text of
Leaves of Grass, VI." Conservator 8 (Feb-
ruary), 183-84.
Describes and presents notes for
"Broad-Axe."

28 COMPENDIUM. "Recent Study and Criticism of
Whitman. XI." Conservator 8 (February),
186-87.
Includes interview with Richard Le
Gallienne in New York Herald (unlocated).

29 GILCHRIST, GRACE. "Chats with Walt Whitman."
Temple Bar 113 (February), 200-212.
Reprinted: 1898.54. Extracts reprinted:
1898.35.
An "appreciation from the human, and
not the literary point of view," quoting
Whitman's conversation, largely from her
brother's transcriptions, when Whitman was
fifty-eight: comments on Shakespeare, Sand,
Scott, Carlyle, Bulwer-Lytton, Tennyson,
Hugo, Heine, Symonds, beauty, education.
"He liked reading critiques on himself."

29a GOULD, ELIZABETH PORTER. "Walt Whitman and
Manhattan." Conservator 8 (February), 186.
Whitman's prophecy of the union of New
York and Brooklyn has come to pass: it
should be known by his name for it,
"Manhattan."

30 KENNEDY, WILLIAM SLOANE. "Notes on the Text
of Leaves of Grass, VII." Conservator 8
(February), 184-85.
Notes oriental traits in Whitman's
poems.

31 PROCTOR, THOMAS. "Some Personal Recollections
and Impressions of Walt Whitman." Journal
of Hygiene and Herald of Health 48 (February), 29-39.

Describes Whitman's impressive appearance on the streets of New York, three or four years before the war; meeting Whitman in Washington during the war; his circle's affection for Whitman the man and amusement at his poetry; residence in the same house where Whitman lived after the war; brief anecdotes; Whitman's personality (chaste, clean, leisurely, genial); eating, dressing, and health habits; enigmatic speech; passive listening; responsiveness to nature (witnessed in two excursions with him, described here).

32 ANON. "The Final Whitman." Chap-Book 8 (1 February), 255-56.
    Review of 1897 Leaves, "well-appointed," considering the wide range of opinion regarding Whitman's work. The new poems are commented upon as endearing.

33 HALE, PHILIP. "Music in Boston." Musical Courier 36 (2 February), 24.
    Notes Whitman's love of opera as revealed in his Wound-Dresser letters (1898.3); identifies the singers Whitman refers to and traces their careers.

34 ANON. "Notes." Literature 2 (5 February), 156.
    Gosse's estimate of Whitman's work as literature in a state of protoplasm (1894.28) is disproved by lines from "Lilacs" 13, which are "literature itself, a sonorous and triumphant song, not unworthy of a place beside the lament of David for his brother Jonathan." Nevertheless, critics should not go to such extremes of praise as the Temple Bar article (1898.29), which places him slightly below Shakespeare, for Whitman also contains "some glaring absurdity" along with his "wonderful lines."

35 GILCHRIST, GRACE. "Walt Whitman." New York Tribune (13 February), Illustrated Supplement, 18:3-4.
    Extracts reprinted from 1898.29.

36 ANON. "Whitman and War." Chap-Book 8 (15 February), 290-91.
    Review of Wound-Dresser (1898.3), describing Whitman's worthy hospital work which the book reveals. The letters are simple, without conscious poetic touches; they are human documents, with "perfect openness" but no boastfulness or religious cant. Whether a poet or not, "he was an American who believed that it was sweet and fitting to lay down his life for his country."

37 PERRY, JENNETTE BARBOUR. "Whitmania: 'Defend me from my friends.'" Critic 29 (26 February), 137-38.
    Reprinted: 1898.41.
    Whitman's admirers go to extremes in poetry that seems more a parody than an imitation. He would scarcely approve,

having asked for no school to be founded on him. The Whitmanites, as well as the anti-Whitmanites, often appear ridiculous, as Whitman himself never did.

38 GREENE, HENRY COPLEY. "A Satyr Aspires." New World 7 (March), 54-67.
    Whitman's idealist theories, developed out of contemporary influences (Hegel, transcendentalism), seem chaotic until viewed as his rejection of reason in favor of a joyful faith in intuition. He made God, the nation, and all other men after his own image. His "mystic determinism" led to "no torpid toryism" but to "progressive self-reliance." His catalogues of confusion failed to recast experience harmoniously, but his smaller subjects produced poems like impressionist pictures. He was brilliantly realistic but revealed high art in phrases rather than whole pieces. His glorification of lust was nearly justified as a protest against the mentality which persecuted him. He is almost more himself in imagined experiences, in his striving toward mysticism. He shows influences of classic and modern literature, but "Death Carol," his most beautiful work, is new. His spirit will triumph in democracy by appeal to a few strong thinkers who may lead the people on to his ideal.

39 KENNEDY, WILLIAM SLOANE. "Whitman in Italy." Conservator 9 (March), 12.
    Explains thesis of Pasquale Jannaccone's Italian study of Whitman's prosody (La poesia di Walt Whitman e l'evoluzione delle forme ritmichi, Turin: R. Frassati, 1898).

40 LE GALLIENNE, RICHARD. "Walt Whitman: An Address." Conservator 9 (March), 4-5.
    Reprinted: 1898.64. Abridged: 1898.68.
    Whitman lays bare the bosom of human nature, generalizing from himself to all modern men. Fellowship members should be true Whitmanites, not mere respectables, for Whitman urged us to bring outdoor air to indoor work.

41 PERRY, JENNETTE BARBOUR. "Recent Study and Criticism of Whitman. XII." Conservator 9 (March), 11-12.
    Reprint of 1898.37.

42 T[RAUBEL], H. L. "Collect." Conservator 9 (March), 2-3.
    Mocks Fawcett for still criticizing Whitman even while saying he is dead, typical of other Whitman opponents who are threatened by his growing reputation. Le Gallienne's address (1898.40) is praised. Whitman is not a person but a vision, admonishing us to walk free.

43 TRAUBEL, HORACE L. "Notes on the Text of Leaves of Grass, VIII." Conservator 9 (March), 9-11.
    Notes Whitman's oriental mysticism.

1898

44 ALDEN, WILLIAM L. "London Literary Letter."
    New York Times Saturday Review (5 March),
    155.
    Reprinted: 1898.52.
        Paragraph on Whitman's work being taken
    more seriously in England than in America,
    because he is regarded as typical, like
    Bret Harte's miners, although neither is
    necessarily representative of America. "I
    wonder which was really the more thoroughly
    American, Joaquin Miller's red-flannel
    shirt or Whitman's red-flannel poetry."

45 FAWCETT, EDGAR. "Men Manners and Moods [sic]."
    Collier's Weekly 20 (12 March), 18-19.
    Quoted in 1898.52.
        Criticizes Literature's praise of
    Whitman (1898.34). The passage from
    "Lilacs" quoted therein is prose rhapsody
    rather than poetry; its weaknesses are
    analyzed. Whitman's admirers show mental
    weakness, being unable to perceive his
    bombast and braggadocio. He will never
    gain a niche in the temple of fame. His
    admirers did not "flock about him while he
    lay dying." He has merely attacked art.
    His adoption of his "inexpressibly trivial"
    nickname is in itself a pose. "Captain"
    is "an effort of sophomoric quality,"
    despite devotees' attempts to offer it as
    proof of his poetic quality. Fawcett
    briefly recalls a reception for Whitman,
    whom he met there.

46 BENTON, JOEL. "Mr. Chapman's Emerson." New
    York Times Saturday Review (19 March), 186-
    87.
    Quoted in 1898.52.
        Review of Chapman (1898.7). "The
    Whitman essay is too brief." No critic
    fails to mention Whitman's egotism, but
    his words are not to be read only literally,
    applied exclusively to himself, for "his
    exaltation is mainly vicarious, and not
    merely personal."

47 BURROUGHS, JOHN. "The Secret of Whitman's
    Following." Critic 29 (19 March), 189-91.
        Response to Perry (1898.37). Whitman
    is sure now to endure, partly because "he
    contains such a world of suggestion, both
    poetic and philosophical." He is "full of
    the yeast and leaven of poetry, but the
    reader who has no grist of his own will
    find him very unsatisfactory." His work is
    significant for its focus on Whitman the
    man. His magnitude overwhelms his defects,
    and he stands independent of, rather than
    above, art.

48 ANON. "The Wound Dresser." Public Opinion
    24 (24 March), 377.
        Review of 1898.3. Whitman's contribu-
    tion to the literature of the war is second
    to none, taking a humble point of view.
    These letters, carefully edited, have a
    vigor and a more than literary interest
    through their directness, simplicity, and
    informality.

49 M., W. E. "Whitman's Wound-Dresser." Poet-
    Lore 10, no. 2 (Spring), 307-9.
        Review of 1898.3, which strengthens
    the impression of Whitman as a "big-hearted,
    wonderfully sympathetic man." Without this
    war experience, Leaves might have lacked
    "that vital and abiding element pervading
    every line." Whitman put into action
    Carlyle's ideas about work. These letters
    contain "some real bits of literature."

50 ABBEY, CHARLOTTE. "Walt Whitman's Unsung
    Songs." Walt Whitman Fellowship Papers 4,
    no. 3 (April), 7-10.
    Reprint of 1897.149.

51 BUCKE, R. M. "Walt Whitman, Man and Poet."
    National Magazine 8 (April), 34-39. Illus-
    trated.
        Traces his acquaintance with Leaves
    (from 1867) and Whitman (from 1877), and
    his early difficulty understanding Leaves;
    describes Whitman's "joyful acceptance of
    things," even up through his death. His
    family letters reveal his unselfishness.
    He is both a rebel and a heretic, as every
    great poet must be.

52 COMPENDIUM. "Recent Study and Criticism of
    Whitman. XIII." Conservator 9 (April),
    26-27.
        Includes unlocated items from Clarion,
    Christian Register, New York Home Journal.

53 DRAKE, A. B. "Symmetry in Leaves of Grass."
    Conservator 9 (April), 24-25.
        Appreciation of Whitman, explaining
    some of the qualities of Leaves.

54 GILCHRIST, GRACE. "Chats with Walt Whitman."
    Eclectic Magazine 130 (April), 451-59.
    Reprint of 1898.29.

55 GUTHRIE, WILLIAM NORMAN. "Walt Whitman as
    Poetic Artist, I." Conservator 9 (April),
    22-24.
    Reprinted: 1912.10.
        In their verse Blake and Whitman seek
    expression rather than compression like
    Shakespeare and Milton. Explanation is
    given of the new rhythm's freedom, the need
    for prosaic, inferior portions to heighten
    the great moments. Continued 1898.63.

56 MAYNARD, LAURENS. "Walt Whitman's Comradeship."
    Walt Whitman Fellowship Papers 4, no. 5
    (April), 13-19.
    Reprint of 1897.86.

56a T[RAUBEL], H. L. "Collect." Conservator 9
    (April), 17-18.
        Response to Le Gallienne (1898.40),
    asking who is the "true Whitmanite"? A
    later paragraph discusses Whitman's style
    as his own and as part of his message,
    though the free-verse line has been used
    before and may be used now by others.

57 T[RAUBEL, HORACE]. "Selections from the Prose
    and Poetry of Walt Whitman." Conservator
    9 (April), 28-29.
        Review of Triggs (1898.17), character-
    ized as simply an abridgement, not an ex-
    purgation like Stedman's book (1892.12);
    "a book adapted to the use of schools and
    colleges and for the initiation of the
    casual reader and of the skeptic."

58 TUCKER, JOHN FOSTER. "To Walt Whitman." Con-
    servator 9 (April), 25.
        Free-verse poem of tribute: "Come back,
    Walt Whitman."

59 JAMES, HENRY. "American Letter. . . . Walt
    Whitman's Letters to Peter Doyle." Liter-
    ature 2 (16 April), 453.
    Reprinted: 1898.97; Hindus; Murphy.
        Review of Calamus (1897.2), which
    appeals to the democratic sense, with
    "something of the same relation to poetry
    that may be made out in the luckiest--few,
    but fine--of the writer's other pages,"
    having no "line with a hint of style--it is
    all flat, familiar, affectionate, illiterate
    colloquy." The voice is American, filled
    with "many odd and pleasant human harmo-
    nies" and ordinary American impressions.
    The letters reveal a beautiful nature and
    "the personal passion."

60 BALL, M. V. "Whitman and Socialism." Con-
    servator 9 (May), 40-42.
        Whitman knew some economics but did not
    study the subject; nor did he appreciate
    the gravity of the economic crisis. His
    opposition to systems prevented his being
    a socialist. However, his contributions
    were large enough that he need not be forced
    into an "ism."

61 BRINTON, DANIEL G. "The Wound Dresser." Con-
    servator 9 (May), 44.
        Review of 1898.3, praising Whitman's
    "spirit of human love, compassion, in-
    finite sympathy," which disproves accusa-
    tions of his degeneracy.

62 COMPENDIUM. "Recent Study and Criticism of
    Whitman. XIV." Conservator 9 (May), 43.
    Includes unlocated items by Joaquin Miller
    and Nathan H. Dole.

63 GUTHRIE, WILLIAM NORMAN. "Walt Whitman as
    Poetic Artist, II." Conservator 9 (May),
    36-37.
    Reprinted: 1912.10.
        Continues 1898.55. Whitman was not
    indifferent to rhythm, as is evident in the
    changes he made when putting the Preface
    into poetry. "Warble for Lilac-Time" is
    analyzed as exemplifying Whitman's poetic
    principle. However, the meaning and prin-
    ciple behind his catalogues remain myste-
    rious to most readers. Concluded 1898.77.

64 LE GALLIENNE, RICHARD. "Walt Whitman: An
    Address." Walt Whitman Fellowship Papers
    4, no. 10 (May), 45-49.
    Reprint of 1898.40.

65 SMITH, GEORGE J. "Whitman: Radical or Con-
    servative?" Walt Whitman Fellowship Papers
    4, no. 6 (May), 21-37.
        For Whitman, equality is of potential
    being: he often recognizes individual in-
    equalities. He believes in the inner law
    but acknowledges the need for civil law and
    government. He looks for evolution, not
    revolution, being dependent on the past but
    seeking progress. He does not ignore the
    distinction between virtue and vice but
    pities the wrong-doer, looking for a right
    spirit in men. For him religion is not a
    creed but "an emotional attitude toward
    world and man and God," experienced every-
    where. He is both conservative and radical.

66 SMITH, WAYLAND HYATT. "Blending of Orient and
    Occident in Whitman." Walt Whitman Fellow-
    ship Papers 4, no. 7 (May), 39-40.
        Whitman is more oriental than occidental
    in his mysticism and assertion of the non-
    physical significance of being, yet he has
    more outline than the East.

67 WIKSELL, GUSTAV P. "Self-Primacy in Whitman."
    Walt Whitman Fellowship Papers 4, no. 8
    (May), 41-42.
        Testifies to the many truths Whitman
    has revealed to him; praises Whitman's
    divine power.

68 LE GALLIENNE, RICHARD. "Richard Le Gallienne
    on Walt Whitman." Public Opinion 24 (5
    May), 563-64.
    Abridged from 1898.40.

69 JAMES, HENRY. "American Letter. . . . The War
    and Literature." Literature 2 (7 May),
    541-42.
    Reprinted: 1898.93; 1900.27.
        Review of Wound-Dresser (1898.3), an
    "interesting and touching collection," "not
    such a document as the recruiting-officer,
    at the beginning of a campaign, would re-
    joice to see in many hands." These vivid
    letters convey Whitman's "admirable, original
    gift of sympathy," his pity, horror, and
    helplessness, "without unhappy verbiage or
    luckless barbarism." They deserve a place
    on the shelf of patriotic literature.

70 ANON. "Some Unpublished Letters of Walt
    Whitman." Saturday Review 85 (21 May),
    688-89.
        Review of Wound-Dresser (1898.3), which
    may prove salutary for various contemporary
    readers, particularly through its direct
    appeal to our sense of duty. The letters
    and their background are described; they
    are suited to their intended readers, not
    literary or artificial but full of pathos
    and sympathy. Whitman is truly "a martyr

to the cause of humanity," with an unquestionable "genius for affection" and a sound
patriotism.

71 ANON. "The American Soldier." Spectator 80
(21 May), 728-30.
Review of Complete Prose Works and
Wound-Dresser (1898.3). The results of
Whitman's "untiring watcher's intense
sympathy" on his health are not surprising
in light of these descriptions of his work,
"Dante-like pictures" of an inferno which
are unmatched in literature. Passages are
quoted and described extensively, one revealing the "strong sympathy with Nature"
which was "the essence of Whitman's genius."

72 ELSHEMUS, LOUIS M. "Comment and Query.
Le Gallienne and Some Others--An American
Poet's Protest." New York Times Saturday
Review (28 May), 354.
Protests the adulation rendered the
British poet Le Gallienne while American
poets, notably Whitman, are recognized only
abroad. Whitman's manly poetry and "courageous hymns to natural strength and beauty"
are ignored in favor of the "low licentiousness" of Kipling, George Moore, Hardy, and
Le Gallienne. (A full page of responses,
with scant mention of Whitman, appeared on
4 June of the Saturday Review, p. 374.)

73 ANON. "Whitman Fellowship Papers." New York
Tribune (31 May), 10:2.
Lists program of speakers at annual
Fellowship meeting in New York today. The
Boston Branch will hold its celebration in
Walden Woods, Concord.

74 BUCKE, RICHARD MAURICE. "An Open Letter to
Edgar Fawcett." Conservator 9 (June),
56-58.
Response to Fawcett (1898.45): contrary
to Fawcett's claims, Whitman's friends did
not neglect him in his later days, as Bucke
shows.

75 _____. "Walt Whitman, Man and Poet." Cosmopolis 10 (June), 687-94.
In Whitman the contrasting temperaments
of his two ancestral strains met, creating
in him all four temperaments. No self-
indulgent loafer, he was a puritan in
morality and "a persistent, untiring worker"
for his family and his intellectual pursuits.
His "extraordinary moral and emotional
equipment" combined with a great knowledge
of his country and its people to express
"an almost superhuman personality." He was
a great poet not in the sense of producing
a finished work of art but rather according
to Matthew Arnold's criteria: "poetic
largeness, freedom, insight, benignity,"
and "the high seriousness of the great
masters." He always wrote from a careful
observation of reality. His unparalleled
achievement in expressing his soul, which
one day will be understood, will contribute
to the world revolution.

76 COMPENDIUM. "Recent Study and Criticism of
Whitman. XV." Conservator 9 (June), 58-59.
Includes unlocated items from Christian
Register and New York Criterion (by Vance
Thompson).

77 GUTHRIE, WILLIAM NORMAN. "Walt Whitman as
Poetic Artist, III." Conservator 9 (June),
52-55.
Reprinted: 1912.10.
Concludes 1898.63. The accents of words
in Whitman are determined by the sense,
especially in the case of compound words.
Particular passages are analyzed for varying
accents. Whitman only used rhythmic pauses
as required by meaning. Passages are
printed with indications of accents and
pauses.

78 T[RAUBEL, HORACE]. "Collect." Conservator 9
(June), 51.
Praises Emerson's acclaim of Whitman,
though he never did anything so reckless
again. Whitman fulfilled Emerson's dreams.

79 ANON. "Talks of Walt Whitman. John Swinton
Surprises His Hearers at the Annual Dinner
of Fellowship." New York Times (1 June),
7:4.
Swinton emphasizes Whitman's lack of
intellect, seeing him as a natural man; he
attacked Whitman for not helping him in his
social work in New York slums. Other
speeches are briefly cited, defending
Whitman.

80 ALDEN, WILLIAM L. "London Literary Letter."
New York Times Saturday Review (18 June),
401.
Too many English people believe in a
rugged America as represented by Leaves,
but G. W. Cable's fiction is "far more
distinctively American than anything that
Whitman ever wrote."

81 ANON. "Walt Whitman. Selections from His
Prose and Verse--What Whitman Stands For."
New York Times Saturday Review (18 June),
402.
Review of Triggs (1898.17), explaining
Whitman's place in literature. He was a
true poet in the original Greek sense, "a
maker of messages embodying the spirit of
his time." Parallels are seen to other
innovations in form from music and literature of the past. Whitman's music is broad
and big, appropriate to his "gigantic,
passionate humanity," but he also appreciated
more polished poety, and some of his own
sensuous verse proves him not to be one-
sided, for he expresses the soul's reaches.

81a ANON. "Notes and News." Poet-Lore 10, no. 3
(Summer), 467-68.
Describes Whitman's notebooks, classified
by subject; reprints and comments on one
passage (courtesy of Traubel) concerning
his ideas for poetry.

82 KENNEDY, WILLIAM SLOANE. "To the Editors."
Poet-Lore 10, no. 3 (Summer), 451-52.
Points out parallel between Burns's
"Scotch Drink" and the blacksmith passage
from "Exposition" with its "strikingly
original" image.

83 P[ORTER, CHARLOTTE]. "School of Literature.
Human Brotherhood in Whitman and Browning:
A Topical Reading Course." Poet-Lore 10,
no. 3 (Summer), 421-24.
Suggests readings from both poets with
discussion questions for them separately
and in comparison regarding individualism,
love, leadership, role of the poet, and
world patriotism.

84 COMPENDIUM. "Recent Study and Criticism of
Whitman. XVI." Conservator 9 (July),
74-76.
Includes unlocated items from Atlanta
Constitution and New York Criterion (by
Vance Thompson).

85 MAYNARD, LAURENS. "A Few Notes on Whitman
and the New England Writers." Conservator
9 (July), 68-71.
Reprinted: 1899.45.
Describes, from their published
writings, Whitman's relations with Emerson,
Thoreau, Sanborn, Longfellow; the attitudes
toward Whitman of Lowell, Holmes, Whittier,
Higginson. The younger New England writers
lack their spirit of hostility; many acknowledge Whitman's influence.

86 T[RAUBEL], H. L. "Collect." Conservator 9
(July), 66-67.
Paragraph on Higginson's antipathy to
Whitman and his failure to regard him as a
poet; challenges him to answer this in
these columns.

87 BURROUGHS, JOHN. "Sympathetic Criticism."
Chap-Book 9 (1 July), 111-12.
Incidental references: Whitman, having
brushed classical models aside, should be
judged according to newer standards, appropriate to "the romantic and democratic
school," in which the "unique, individual
utterance, or expression of personality" is
important, and "the end is not form, but
life." Many have been guilty of intemperate
enthusiasm toward Whitman and Browning, but
admirers should make a cult of neither one.

88 SHARP, WILLIAM. "Among my Books." Literature
2 (2 July), 753-54.
Review of Jannaccone's Italian study of
Whitman. (See 1898.39.) No translation so
far has conveyed Whitman's dominant characteristic of "poetic virility." His
poetry reveals variously "long sonorous
rhythms," "sustained rhythmic utterances,"
"immense and undulant harmonies." His
"Yankee accent" appears even in translation,
though he loses "the vehement personal in-
tonation." Original and Italian versions
of "Youth, Day, Old Age and Night" and ex-

tracts from "Myself" are compared. Whitman's
poetry raises the question of whether
poetic boundaries "should be extended indefinitely."

89 [HUNEKER, JAMES G.] "Raconteur." Musical
Courier 37 (13 July), 23-24.
Recalls meeting Whitman in 1878 and
worshipping him when a young man. But
Whitman was actually a great poseur, with
some sublime lines but "his message puerile
rubbish." His "nonsense, obscenity, morbid
eroticism, vulgarity and preposterous mouth-
ings" spoil one's taste for his splendid
poems (including "Lilacs," praised as "a
threnody without parallel"), "the finest
things America has given to the nations."
He was truly a literary man; the working
man prefers Longfellow. He had much of the
effeminate in him, evident in "Calamus,"
which is "Greek, with its curious antique
profile and rank forbidden flavor." But
"the world would be poorer" without Whitman.

90 COMPENDIUM. "Recent Study and Criticism of
Whitman. XVII." Conservator 9 (August),
91-92.

91 T[RAUBEL, HORACE]. "A Visit to Walt Whitman."
Conservator 9 (August), 93.
Favorable review of Johnston (1898.11).

92 FLETCHER, A. E. "Tolstoy and Whitman." The
New Age (4 August), 260-61.
Whitman and Tolstoy share love for the
common people and the open-air life, a
similar political ideal, belief in the
ethical purpose of art. Their lives are
dissimilar, but the admirer of Tolstoy
should accept Whitman, as the New Testament
to complete the Old Testament, for Whitman
emphasizes not sin but a Christ-like love
and "vindication of the beauty and purity
of the true marriage." Both are among the
immortals.

93 COMPENDIUM. "Recent Study and Criticism of
Whitman. XVIII." Conservator 9 (Septem-
ber), 107-8.
Includes Theodore Tilton's reminiscence
of Whitman forty years ago from New York
World and an item from Brann's Iconoclast.

94 TRIGGS, OSCAR LOVELL. "Walt Whitman: A
Character Study." Conservator 9 (September), 100-102.
Reprinted: 1899.50.
Whitman affects men by his personality.
His appearance is described through quotations from various writers; also his portraits and his emotionalism and "fresh
strong human nature." Concluded 1898.98.

95 HENDRY, HAMISH. "Walt Whitman's Prose."
Saturday Review 86 (24 September), 414-15.
Review of Complete Prose Works. Apart
from the poetry, the prose suffers, for
Whitman meant to eliminate the dividing
line, as in some of the finer pieces from

1898

Specimen which frequently end "upon the highest poetical note in his compass." His portrayal of the Civil War reveals true "epical strength and completeness" in presenting the more poignant aspects. The invalid with his courage yields "a rarer note than the poet who loafed robustly in the grass." Whitman's approach to books, through the temperament rather than the mind, is valuable for its "masculine force," counteracting the current domination of "the prim and the effeminate." That he has been misunderstood and reviled, though clean, wholesome, and cheerful, is only an indication of his value.

96 KNORR, HELENA. "Selections from the Prose and Poetry of Walt Whitman." Poet-Lore 10, no. 4 (Autumn), 586-87.
    Review of Triggs (1898.17), a fine introduction to Whitman, who must be approached the right way. His prose as well as his poetry reveals his "penetrating insight" and "large sympathies."

97 COMPENDIUM. "Recent Study and Criticism. XIX." Conservator 9 (October), 123-24.
    Includes item from Boston Literary Review.

98 TRIGGS, OSCAR LOVELL. "Walt Whitman: A Character Study." Conservator 9 (October), 117-19.
    Reprinted: 1899.50.
    Concludes 1898.94. Whitman's ideal egotism is consistent with fellowship and represents ideal manhood. "He saw but he was not the 'maker-see.'" He followed the nineteenth-century tendency toward orientalism. His tolerance and good will eventually overpowered his fighting qualities. He saw life whole and expressed his deepest passion.

99 COMPENDIUM. "Recent Study and Criticism. XX." Conservator 9 (November), 137-38.
    Includes items from New York Criterion and Home Magazine.

100 ANON. Brief review of Wound-Dresser (1898.3) and Triggs (1898.17). Critic 33 (November), 399.
    Wound-Dresser sheds light on Whitman's personality and is valuable as "a graphic and truthful description, by a non-professional observer, of the state of the army hospitals during the war." He proved that "a sort of divine afflatus" proceeding from the healthy human body helps the sick better than doctor's physic. These letters prove Whitman to be the average American in his faults as well as virtues. Triggs's selections are "fairly representative" though "the rhapsodical and badly punctuated" 1855 Preface "is nothing more than a curiosity" and might be spared. This volume should be as much as the general reader "can assimilate of the great exponent of Americanism."

101 HOLBROOK, M. L. "A Psychic's View of Whitman." Conservator 9 (November), 136.
    Quotes lines from Whitman and records a psychic's answers as to their truth.

102 HUSTON, PAUL GRISWOLD. "Whitman as a Mystic." Conservator 9 (November), 133-35.
    Whitman had no great symbolic scheme like Blake, Spenser, or Dante, but used natural symbolism, going directly to inner reality. Several poems are examined for mystical analogies, perceptions, and nature worship.

103 LIVINGSTON, LUTHER S. "The First Books of Some American Authors. III--Irving, Poe and Whitman." Bookman 8 (November), 234-35.
    Describes Franklin Evans and the first and second Leaves, noting recent prices they brought. Emerson's letter and some of the opinions in "Leaves-Droppings" (1856.2) are quoted.

104 COMPENDIUM. "Recent Study and Criticism of Whitman. XXI." Conservator 9 (December), 155.
    Includes review of Wound-Dresser (1898.3) from New York Criterion; also a sermon by Minot Savage using Whitman as illustration.

105 SMITH, GEORGE J. "Whitman and Mannahatta." Conservator 9 (December), 148-49.
    Reprinted: 1899.56.
    Manhattan is an appropriate city for Whitman's optimistic attitude. Whitman's various impressions of Manhattan are quoted, showing his perceptions of the people as a great spectacle.

1899

BOOKS

1 BOTTA, ANNE C. LYNCH. Handbook of Universal Literature. Rev. ed. Boston: Houghton, Mifflin & Co., p. 535.
    Revised: 1902.3.
    "Walt Whitman (d. 1892) writes with great force, originality, and sympathy with all forms of struggle and suffering; but with utter contempt for conventionalities and for the acknowledged limits of true art."

2 BRERETON, J. LE GAY, [Jr.] Landlopers. Sidney: William Brooks & Co., pp. 29-30, 55. Quoted in Jones.
    References to his reading and quoting of Whitman while on a walking journey.

3 BUCKE, RICHARD MAURICE, ed. Editor's preface to Notes and Fragments: Left by Walt Whitman. London, Ontario: A. Talbot & Co., pp. v-vi.
    Describes contents, Whitman's manner of

attaining knowledge, his industry in learning which shows him not a loafer.

4 BUTLER, GEORGE F. Love and Its Affinities.
Chicago: G. P. Engelhard & Co., pp. 12,
52-53.
    Whitman's sexual openness may be nearer
truth and nature than the Westminster cate-
chism is. His verse might be regarded as
that of "the primitive he-goat, adorable
symbol of ancient Priapus," yet his life
and relationships "were singularly pure,"
revealing a "self-sacrificing spirit."
"This ferocious animalism appealed to men
of letters of the highest distinction,"
including Browning, "one of his sincerest
admirers."

5 COLVIN, SIDNEY, ed. The Letters of Robert
Louis Stevenson to His Family and Friends.
New York: Charles Scribner's Sons. Vol. 1,
pp. 50, 65; vol. 2, p. 24.
Revised: 1911.5.
    Stevenson describes his labor at his
Whitman essay in 1873. A letter to Symonds
in 1886 says that not even Whitman has done
justice to death as "a great and gentle
solvent."

6 DARROW, CLARENCE S. A Persian Pearl: and
Other Essays. East Aurora, N.Y.: Roycroft
Shop. "Walt Whitman," pp. 75-109.
Reprinted: 1902.9; 1902.56.
    Whitman alone seems natural in this
artificial nineteenth-century life. His
work will live or die because of his philosophy and his material. Only Whitman has
defended the Creator in everything, accepting evil for the good that may come out of
it. He reveres the body, with a healthier
version of love than in most literature.
Upon his fundamental, inclusive democracy,
which enthrones natural justice above the
law books and holds women as men's equals,
"the regenerated world will be built." He
transcends mere optimism and pessimism to
attain a serene harmony with life and death.
He was ahead of his materialistic, class-
conscious, falsely modest time.

7 FISHER, MARY. A General Survey of American
Literature. Chicago: A. C. McClurg & Co.,
pp. 350-64.
    Sketch of Whitman's life. He "was
wholly indebted to sensory impressions for
his intellectual development." He seems to
have broken Leaves into separate poems only
because of Poe's rejection of long poems.
His war work and attitude toward affliction
are commendable. Specimen, like his poetry,
lacks a true poet's imagination and power
of selection, but is also free from sentimentalizing. His admirers have turned to
him from an excess of culture. Some of his
lines "have a certain rude vigor and
rhythmic swing decidely fresh and pleasing"
("Captain," "Redwood," "Occupations," "Come
up from the Fields"), but most are "the

veriest dry bones of prose." He displays
flawed diction, cloudy ideas, mere lists.
His teaching is "a step backward."

8 HIGGINSON, THOMAS WENTWORTH. Contemporaries.
Boston and New York: Houghton Mifflin Co.
"Walt Whitman," pp. 72-84; also 96-98.
Revision of 1892.119; reprint of 1887.30.
Reprinted in part: Hindus. Revised:
1903.5.
    Higginson tempers or deletes some of
his harsher earlier statements, admits the
increasing acceptance of Whitman, and acknowledges that Whitman's later career was
purified as his sexual emphasis diminished.

9 JAMES, WILLIAM. Talks to Teachers on Psychology: and to Students on Some of Life's
Ideals. New York: Henry Holt & Co. "On
a Certain Blindness in Human Beings," pp.
248-54.
Reprinted: Miller.
    Whitman, through quotations from
"Brooklyn Ferry" and a Calamus letter
(1897.2), exemplifies "a sort of ideal
tramp," practically unproductive, but taking
time out to sense the splendor of the world.

10 LANIER, H. W. and LANIER, Mrs. SIDNEY, eds.
Letters of Sidney Lanier. New York:
Charles Scribner's Sons, p. 208.
Reprinted: 1899.60; 1933.29; Hindus.
    Letter of 3 February 1878 to Bayard
Taylor praises Leaves as "a real refreshment" when first read, despite Whitman's
"error that a thing is good because it is
natural" and his difference from Lanier in
conceptions of art.

11 LOOMIS, CHARLES BATTELL. Just Rhymes. New
York: R. H. Russell. "Jack and Jill, As
Walt Whitman Might Have Written It," pp.
68-70.
Reprinted: Saunders.
    Parody.

12 McCARTHY, JUSTIN. Reminiscences. Vol. 1.
New York and London: Harper & Bros., pp.
171-72, 199, 225-28; London: Chatto &
Windus, 196-97, 228-29, 258-61.
Extract reprinted: Whitman Supplement
1979.
    Records conversations in 1871 with
Bryant, Emerson, and Whitman. Bryant professed no great belief in Whitman. Emerson
retained his strong faith in him, although
Whitman's artistic creed made him "almost
an impossibility for ordinary social life."
Whitman's contentment in poverty as observed
on a visit to his garret-like room in Washington is described. Not anxious to explain
his theories, he seemed "one of nature's
gentlemen." Whitman and all he wrote had
"the charm of real manhood."

13 PIER, ARTHUR STANWOOD. The Pedagogues: A
Story of the Harvard Summer School. Boston:
Small, Maynard & Co., pp. 11, 32-35.

Quoted in 1899.64.

On recommendation of their teacher, adult students read Whitman to achieve "a catholic appreciation of literature." One reads it disapprovingly.

14 ROSSETTI, WILLIAM MICHAEL. <u>Ruskin: Rossetti: Preraphaelitism: Papers 1854 to 1862.</u> London: George Allen, pp. 134, 147, 159-60.

Prints letters of 1856 and 1857 from W. B. Scott to Rossetti on his discovery of <u>Leaves</u>, "somewhat like a revelation, although an ungainly and not a little repulsive one," with flaws and a similarity to the Bible.

15 [RUSSELL, MARY ANNETTE.] <u>The Solitary Summer.</u> New York and London: Macmillan Co., pp. 29-30.

She responds to what Whitman has to say "of night, sleep, death, and the stars," for the dusk is appropriate to "the beatings of that most tender and generous heart," with his great love for nature, "yearning, universal pity," and "eager looking to death."

16 SALTER, WILLIAM MACKINTIRE. <u>Walt Whitman: Two Addresses.</u> Philadelphia: S. Burns Weston, 46 pp.

Reprint of 1899.68 and 1899.74.

17 SAVAGE, MINOT JUDSON. <u>Life Beyond Death.</u> New York and London: G. P. Putnam's Sons, p. 184.

Incidental: Whitman was misunderstood. Only Jesus and Socrates "so magnificently, so calmly, so conqueringly met death. I know of nothing in all literature to match the sweet, grand things which Whitman has written about death," like "Joy, Shipmate, Joy," equalling "Crossing the Bar."

18 SEARS, LORENZO. <u>American Literature in the Colonial and National Periods.</u> Boston: Little, Brown, & Co. "Walt Whitman," pp. 348-59.

Whitman adopted original style after failing at traditional forms; he incorporated "prosy thought" and naturalistic elements. The virtues of his work include sympathy and patriotism. He was oriental in temperament and occidental in manner, a universal poet. He outgrew many faults after 1860; readers should study his poems in reverse order of composition to meet the finer work first.

19 SPEIGHT, E[RNEST] E[DWIN], ed. <u>The Temple Reader: A Reading Book in Literature for School and Home.</u> New ed., rev., enlarged, and illustrated. London: Horace Marshall & Son, pp. 243-44, 263-64.

Reported in Trimble (1905.19).

Prints several poems with critical remarks from Rossetti and Stevenson.

20 THAYER, WILLIAM ROSCOE. <u>Throne-Makers.</u> Boston and New York: Houghton Mifflin Co., pp. 314-15.

Foreigners found their expectations of the American spirit fulfilled "when Whitman, with cowboy gait, came swaggering up Parnassus, shouting nicknames at the Muses and ready to slap Apollo on the back," but he deserves attention for reasons other than such extravagances.

21 THOMPSON, VANCE. <u>French Portraits: Being Appreciations of the Writers of Young France.</u> Boston: Richard G. Badger & Co., pp. viii, 5, 23, 45, 49, 56, 59, 101, 103-4, 108, 112, 115, 118, 119-20, 141, 160, 194, 200-201, 202.

Just as Poe created modern French prose, Whitman recreated modern French verse. His law of versification is explained. The affinities of Verhaeren, Vielé-Griffin, and De Bonhélier to Whitman are discussed.

PERIODICALS

22 ANON. "Life and Letters." <u>Poet-Lore</u> 11, no. 1 (Winter), 144-50.

Lines from "Broadway Pageant" have been mistakenly used to support the establishing of American sovereignity over the Filipinos, but Whitman's suggestion of an Asian movement westward signified rather the adoption of American sovereignty over the Filipinos, cannot be considered an imperialist.

23 ANON. Parody. <u>Poet-Lore</u> 11, no. 1 (Winter), 160.

Reprinted: Saunders.

Whitmanesque parody of "Hey-Diddle-Diddle" reprinted from London <u>Clarion</u> (unlocated; earlier reprinted in 1898.62).

24 COMPENDIUM. "Recent Study and Criticism of Whitman. XXII." <u>Conservator</u> 9 (January), 170.

Commentary by Edwin Arnold; Grand Duke Cyril of Russia in New York <u>Journal</u> interview; Vida Scudder, 1898.15; <u>Springfield Republican</u>; Benjamin Tucker in <u>Liberty</u>.

25 GOSS, CHARLES F. "An Ode to Old Chronics." <u>Conservator</u> 9 (January), 168-69.

Reprinted: Saunders.

Parody.

26 SARRAZIN, GABRIEL. "Walt Whitman." Translated by William Struthers. <u>Conservator</u> 9 (January), 164-65.

Translation of the article earlier translated in <u>In Re</u> (1893.11). Continued 1899.32.

27 FICHTOR, L. C. "Questions and Answers." <u>New York Times Saturday Review</u> (7 January), 15:3.

Reprinted: 1899.60.

Seeks author of poem, a stanza of which is quoted ("Oh, he was pure! the fleecy snow"), which has been attributed to Whitman. The answer suggests that the lines are from Elizabeth Oake Smith's "The Sinless Child." (See 1902.33.)

28 BRIGHAM, JOHNSON. "Walt Whitman and the West." Midland Monthly Magazine 11 (February), 139-42.

Whitman traveled much in the West in his imagination, as is shown in many quoted allusions to the Prairie States. He "attributed to the average Western farmer greater breadth, in life as in horizon," than the average New England farmer enjoys. He appeals to scholars rather than to common people or westerners but must compel the attention of all thoughtful men and women. Continued 1899.37.

29 COMPENDIUM. "Recent Study and Criticism of Whitman. XXIII." Conservator 9 (February), 186.

Includes extensive review of Triggs (1898.17) from Criterion; comments from Liverpool Labour Chronicle; Literature (comparison of Richard Hovey to Whitman); London Chronicle.

30 CROTHERS, SAMUEL M. "The Enjoyment of Poetry." Atlantic Monthly 83 (February), 272-73.

Incidental: Whitman rejects the poetry of dreams and romance as not real, but his realistic lines are not quite poetry. However, his "marvelous dirge," "Lilacs," uses poetic suggestion to describe a mood, not an event, with "the old familiar elements" making this "real poetry."

31 KENNEDY, WILLIAM SLOANE. "Whitman's Descent from the Dutch." Conservator 9 (February), 185.

Describes a picture in the Amsterdam Rijksmuseum which reminds him of the "Whitman race stock," the Dutch.

32 SARRAZIN, GABRIEL. "Walt Whitman." Translated by William Struthers. Conservator 9 (February), 180-82.

Continues 1899.26. Continued 1899.40.

33 T[RAUBEL, HORACE]. "The Memory of Lincoln: The Words of Abraham Lincoln." Conservator 9 (February), 188.

Comments on "Captain" and "Lilacs" as tributes to Lincoln and his land.

34 VALENTINE, EDWARD A. UFFINGTON. "The Poet of Manhood." Conservative Review 1 (February), 140-46.

Review of Calamus (1897.2), 1897 Leaves, Wound-Dresser (1898.3). "Backward Glance" is a fine introduction to Whitman. His greatest poem was his own personality; a realization of this will temper condemnation of his carnal aspects. He is most impressive as a teacher with a broad and positive philosophy, but he has much true poetry as well, in the "Miltonic largeness" of

"Lilacs," the "exquisite lyrical feeling" of "Cradle," the "breadth of mentality and fervor of soul" of "Prayer" and "Trumpeter." He sought to appeal to the common people rather than to convince the cultivated critic of his artistic merit; the people at least appreciated "the rugged poem of his manliness," his lasting gift.

35 HINTON, RICHARD J. "Walt Whitman and His Friend 'Jack.'" New Voice 16 (4 February), 2.

Recalls walking with Whitman in Boston and confronting Whitman's troubled acquaintance, whom Whitman set upon the right path.

36 WOLFE, THEO. F. "Is It Walt Whitman's?" New York Times Saturday Review (18 February), 108.

Reprinted: 1899.60.

Prints stanza from poem "The Fallen Angel" (see 1899.27), which a former pupil of Whitman's believes that Whitman wrote; asks for further information, since it has not been located in the periodicals.

37 BRIGHAM, JOHNSON. "Walt Whitman's Verse." Midland Monthly Magazine 11 (March), 249-55.

Continues 1899.28. James Whitcomb Riley, in conversation with Brigham, called Whitman a fraud. Whitman's ideas and worth are represented essentially in about seventy poems. His egotism is a means for conveying his altruism. His sexual philosophy has been misinterpreted because he broke "Adam" into separate poems, thus inviting consideration of them separately. Burroughs has personally assured Brigham of Whitman's lack of impurity in thought and life. "Autumn Rivulets" section, particularly "Prostitute," is analyzed. Whitman's catalogues sometimes group meaninglessly, sometimes suggestively. His love of nature is vividly displayed; his poetry is more suitable than Tennyson's for declamation in natural settings. Concluded 1899.43.

38 BUCKE, RICHARD MAURICE. "Portraits of Walt Whitman." New England Magazine 20 (March), 33-50. Illustrated.

Extract reprinted: 1901.16.

Survey of drawings and photographs of Whitman, with brief biography. Whitman was not a student, caring little for literature; he could not read Tennyson and Browning, probably read little Carlyle. His main concern was living. His spiritual awakening is described, as well as Bucke's own, corroborating Whitman's message. Whitman is a Christ-figure, looking to a new race. (Some of this material is used in 1901.3.)

39 COMPENDIUM. "Recent Study and Criticism of Whitman. XXIV." Conservator 10 (March), 9-10.

Includes items from St. Louis Hesperian and Home Journal.

1899

40 SARRAZIN, GABRIEL. "Walt Whitman." Trans-
lated by William Struthers. Conservator 10
(March), 4-6.
Continues 1899.32. Continued 1899.49.

41 T[RAUBEL, HORACE]. "Walt Whitman as Poet
Prophet." Conservator 10 (March), 13.
Brief appreciation of Guthrie (1897.7)
for its human element and lack of doctrine.

42 BAKEWELL, CHARLES M. "The Teachings of
Friedrich Nietzsche." International Jour-
nal of Ethics 9 (April), 314.
Quoted in 1899.39.
Incidental: Nietzsche's style has "a
megalomaniacal conceit that outdoes Walt
Whitman,--who is, by the way, a curious
pendant to Nietzsche."

43 BRIGHAM, JOHNSON. "Walt Whitman's Verse."
Midland Monthly Magazine 11 (April), 371-
76.
Concludes 1899.37. Whitman's democratic
creed sought America's possibilities for
all humanity. He rejoiced in the courage
but not the bloodshed of war; "Drum-Taps"
reveal a feminine gentleness in his virile
soul. He extended comradeship to women and
men. "Lilacs" (explicated) is greater than
the universally accepted "Captain." Whitman
emphasizes the soul's progress and a glad
acceptance of death unparalleled in literature.

44 COMPENDIUM. "Recent Study and Criticism of
Whitman. XXV." Conservator 10 (April),
27.

45 MAYNARD, LAURENS. "A Few Notes on Whitman and
the New England Writers." Walt Whitman
Fellowship Papers 5, no. 5 (April), 25-34.
Reprint of 1898.85.

46 MORSE, LUCIUS DANIEL. "The Aspiring Satyr."
Conservator 10 (April), 28.
Response to Greene (1898.38): Whitman,
with his infinite sympathies and the "broadest and clearest outlook upon life," has
nothing in common with satyrs, as his life
and works show.

47 NORTH, ERNEST DRESSEL. "Notes on Rare Books."
Book Buyer 18 (April), 228.
Only recently has there been interest
in collecting first editions of Whitman,
who merits such attention "if he is our
only truly original American poet." A
careful bibliography of his work is needed;
a checklist is provided as a start.

48 ROCKELL, FREDERICK. "Three Anarchists of
American Literature." University Magazine
and Free Review 11 (April), 176-91.
Whitman, Emerson, and Thoreau, "representing the Himalaya peaks of American
literature, were each, more or less openly,
declared Anarchists." Whitman's view of
life synthesized spiritualism and material-

ism. His "beautiful word-music" and humanitarian sentiments are admirable. An anarchist rather than a socialist, Whitman puts
the individual first, not the government.
He does not deserve Nordau's charges
(1895.8). "He was the Columbus of a new
world of poetry."

49 SARRAZIN, GABRIEL. "Walt Whitman." Trans-
lated by William Struthers. Conservator 10
(April), 20-21.
Continues 1899.40. Concluded 1899.55.

50 TRIGGS, OSCAR LOVELL. "Walt Whitman: A
Character Study." Walt Whitman Fellowship
Papers 5, no. 3 (April), 7-22.
Reprint of 1898.94, 1898.98, 1896.68.

*51 [O'DOWD, BERNARD.] "Walt Whitman: His Meaning
to Victorians--Democracy v. Feudalism.
(Excerpts from a Recent Lecture by 'Gavah
the Blacksmith.')." Melbourne Tocsin (13
April), 2.
Reprinted: McLeod.
Whitman differs from the great poets of
the past in singing the heroism of the
average man. His democratic spirit and
rejection of the past's tyranny must be
embraced by Australians, on whom the article
focuses.

52 MILLS, BENJAMIN FAY. "Walt Whitman, The Man
and His Message." Twentieth Century Religion 1, no. 28 (15 April), 3-19.
Text of address. Sketch of Whitman's
life and personality. Notes current life
of Whitman's "most intimate friend" (Doyle).
Whitman's work has been criticized for form
(though "he is recognized as a prophet by
the greatest masters of style" of this century) and frankness, but Mills defends them,
deploring the narrow-minded omission of
Whitman from the Boston Public Library wall.
His use of "I" means three things: himself,
representing the average man; the average
man--anyone; and "the Universal Soul."
Mills recalls his first surreptitious purchase and reading of Leaves to show that
appreciating Whitman may take some time, as
was the case with Mayor Jones. Whitman
invites us to originality, which so many
people shrink from. He believes in progress
and growing, in all things as divine, with
great faith in death. Poems are quoted to
show Whitman's messages.

53 COMPENDIUM. "Recent Study and Criticism of
Whitman. XXVI." Conservator 10 (May), 42.

54 HARNED, THOMAS B. "Whitman and Physique."
Walt Whitman Fellowship Papers 5, no. 8
(May), 43-53.
Reprinted: 1899.58; 1902.11; 1902.12.
Largely a transcription and summary of
Whitman's various notes on health, which
suggest Whitman's hopes for the mental and
spiritual health of the perfect man, accord-
ing to which standards he lived.

55 SARRAZIN, GABRIEL. "Walt Whitman." Translated by William Struthers. Conservator 10 (May), 37-39.
Concludes 1899.49.

56 SMITH, GEORGE J. "Whitman and Mannahatta." Walt Whitman Fellowship Papers 5, no. 6 (May), 35-40.
Reprint of 1898.105.

57 CLARKE, HELEN A. "An Ideal of Character Drawn from Whitman's Poetry." Conservator 10 (June), 56-58.
Whitman's morality avoids indifference and fatalism to achieve a God-like love, although his strength of character may have made him unaware of the struggle of some souls who desire to follow evil. His poetry emphasizes the ultrahuman rather than the human will.

58 HARNED, THOMAS B. "Whitman and Physique." Conservator 10 (June), 53-54.
Reprint of 1899.54.
Concluded 1899.62.

59 SANBORN, F. B. "Whitman's Example in American Society." Conservator 10 (June), 55-56.
Whitman set an example by his sincere political activity, defense of manual labor, advocacy of brotherhood and women's rights. He contrasts with the "Oriental submission to fictitious Destiny" of modern materialistic Americans.

60 COMPENDIUM. "Recent Study and Criticism of Whitman. XXVII." Conservator 10 (July), 73-74.
Includes comments from New Voice (by Crosby) and Providence Journal.

61 _____. "Whitman in Boston: 1899." Conservator 10 (July), 71-73.
Quotes from messages to the Boston Whitman Fellowship from Julia Marlowe, James A. Herne, Samuel M. Jones, Stephen M. Reynolds, Lucius D. Morse, William Struthers, William Mountain, Bucke.

62 HARNED, THOMAS B. "Whitman and Physique, II." Conservator 10 (July), 68-70.
Concludes 1899.58.

63 PLATT, WILLIAM. "The City Dead House." Conservator 10 (August), 85.
Though he once regarded this poem as one of Whitman's masterpieces, Platt now criticizes the use of a poor, already demeaned prostitute to be further demeaned when the subject might as well have been a wealthy person. Whitman's own thought has led to this criticism.

64 T[RAUBEL, HORACE]. "Whitman in a Summer Novel." Conservator 10 (August), 93.
Quotes passage relating to Whitman from Pier (1899.13).

65 ALDEN, WILLIAM L. "London Literary Letter." New York Times Saturday Review (5 August), 518.
Whitman and Melville both need to be studied; people should not make the mistake that because both "wrote pages of unmitigated rubbish they did not also write pages of which their country should be forever proud."

66 COMPENDIUM. "Walt Whitman on the Situation." Conservator 10 (September), 105-6.
Reprint of 1899.70 and 1899.70a.

67 COMPENDIUM. "Actor: Poet: Philosopher." Conservator 10 (September), 106.
Includes comments on Whitman from periodicals.

68 SALTER, WM. M. "The Great Side of Walt Whitman." Ethical Addresses, 6th ser., no. 7 (September), 121-44.
Reprinted: 1899.16. Abridged: 1919.140.
Whitman's style is flawed, but "Captain," by which most people know him, does not illustrate the imaginative levels and range of thought that are his best claims to distinction. His catalogues reveal diversified brotherhood. He emphasizes individual significance, the body's sacredness, women's equality, the dignity of labor, true democracy, love for country, and progress, especially of souls. "Passage" culminates his thought as "a holy scripture of the new world."

69 T[RAUBEL, HORACE]. "Notes and Fragments." Conservator 10 (September), 108-9.
Review of 1899.3. These papers "throw more light upon Whitman's background, philosophy and faith than any other book except Leaves of Grass itself" and demonstrate his breadth of knowledge.

70 ANON. "Walt Whitman on the Situation." New York Sun (11 September), 6:3.
Reprinted: 1899.66.
Editorial parodying Traubel and the Conservator, which is not original but perhaps only Whitman's spirit dictating to Traubel.

70a COPELAND, Rev. ARTHUR. "The Chanter of Expansion." New York Sun (13 September), 6:7.
Reprinted: 1899.66.
Contradicts 1899.70: Whitman is an original thinker, a great bard and American, not an infidel or anti-Imperialist. The Sun's postscript agrees with Whitman's sentiments on national expansion.

1899

71 BORN, HELENA. "Whitman's Ideal Democracy."
    Poet-Lore 11, no. 4 (Autumn), 569-82.
    Reprinted: 1902.2.
        Our society is deficient in soul.
    Whitman provides the seeds for an ideal
    democracy based on liberty, equality, and
    love (in its two aspects, both ennobled).
    Whitman dislikes authority, anticipates
    contemporary notions of socialism and women's
    equality. He is poet of egoism and altruism
    equally and would include all political and
    religious creeds.

72 COMPENDIUM. "Recent Study and Criticism of
    Whitman. XXVIII." Conservator 10 (October),
    121.

73 MacMECHAN, ARCHIBALD. "'The Best Sea Story
    Ever Written.'" Queen's Quarterly 7
    (October), 126.
        In a discussion of Melville's peculiarly
    American style, he is called "a Walt Whitman
    of prose."

74 SALTER, WM. M. "The Questionable Side of Walt
    Whitman." Ethical Addresses, 6th ser., no.
    8 (October), 145-66.
    Reprinted: 1899.16.
        Whitman's celebration of the body and
    sex is inoffensive. However, this is not
    so for his celebration of sexual lawless-
    ness and his apparent denial of moral stan-
    dards, arising from his Christ-like sympathy
    for all, even the sinner (although he fails
    to reject the sin), his unmoral way of op-
    timistically looking at this universe, and
    his view of the poet's function of uttering
    all. Whitman also believed in the struggle
    for greatness in each individual. His
    effect will be for good more than evil.

75 COPELAND, ARTHUR. "Will Walt Whitman's Work
    Survive?" Self-Culture 10 (November), 250-
    52.
        "Backward Glance" is Whitman's "passion-
    less defence" of his work. Leaves "is the
    greatest incarnation since the Gospel of
    St. John," the life of a "strong, healthy,
    cosmopolitan soul," a hero. Whitman's
    poetry is evident in his titles and prose
    also. He gives a sense of real being, not
    imitation. He will survive because of his
    personality, unique yet representative, his
    deep piety, his faith in man and the victory
    of good.

76 MacCULLOCH, J. A. "Walt Whitman: The Poet of
    Brotherhood." Westminster Review 152
    (November), 548-62.
        Whitman is precursor of a new era in
    poetry which embodies the best of the past
    while providing a fresh treatment of sub-
    jects and "a new if somewhat crude style."
    The influence of Whitman's experience,
    reading, and transcendental thought is ex-
    plained. His style is discussed: its
    flaws of diction, impropriety, and lack of
    humor, its convincing rhythm and music.
    His range of vision is unsurpassed even by
    Shakespeare. He has a sympathetic imagina-

tion, vivid portrayals of nature, optimism,
brotherhood joined with belief in individual
genius and character. His prophetic vision
should appeal to all who love nature and
life.

77 MORSE, LUCIUS DANIEL. "Dr. Daniel G. Brinton
    on Walt Whitman." Conservator 10 (Novem-
    ber), 132-35.
        Recounts conversation with Brinton,
    who describes his meeting and acquaintance
    with Whitman, Whitman's "perennial cheer-
    fulness," personality, opinions (opposition
    to war, orthodox view of immortality), care-
    ful revisions.

78 COMPENDIUM. "Recent Study and Criticism of
    Whitman. XXIX." Conservator 10 (December),
    154.

79 BUCHANAN, ROBERT. "Latter-Day Leaves. No.
    9--The Last Year of the Century." Sunday
    Special (31 December), 2.
        Three great personalities influencing
    the present through their vision (Herbert
    Spencer, Dickens, Whitman) are described
    and compared as expressing and feeling the
    same joy of life and faith in man.
    Buchanan's visit to Whitman, America's "one
    great poet," is described (see also 1887.3),
    with his personality ("sublimely free of the
    slightest literary self-consciousness") and
    his high thoughts. The dream of these men--
    the perfectibility of human nature--seems
    vanished at the close of the century.

1900

BOOKS

1 BRONSON, WALTER C. A Short History of American
   Literature. Boston: D. C. Heath & Co.
   "Walt Whitman," pp. 265-73.
       Whitman's basic themes are democracy
   (or comradeship) and science (primarily
   evolution). His errors are intellectual
   and aesthetic rather than moral. His diction
   is usually dramatic and strong but he lacks
   structural power, his longer poems being
   "mere heaps." He was not a great poet but
   had "some of the bones of one."

2 BURROUGHS, JOHN. The Light of Day. Boston
   and New York: Houghton, Mifflin & Co.,
   pp. 222-24.
       The last pages, discussing the voyage
   of the spirit, quote "This Compost" and
   "Song at Sunset."

3 CARPENTER, GEORGE R. Chapters on American
   Literature. In English Literature, by
   Stopford A. Brooke. New York and London:
   Macmillan Co., pp. 319-21.
       Whitman's works have been thought
   typical of democracy because he "knew the
   life of the people," but they have not
   understood him because of his "uncouth
   words and rough thoughts." "The grandeur
   of his conception and the majestic sweep of
   his verse entitle him to a place among our

poets." He pushed to an extreme the methods of Emerson and Thoreau. Though without prominent disciples, he has led our verse toward simplicity and disregard for formal conventions.

4 CHAMPNEYS, BASIL. <u>Memoirs and Correspondence of Coventry Patmore</u>. London: George Bell & Sons. Vol. 1, pp. 387-88; vol. 2, pp. 264-65.

Letters of 1887 and 1888 refer to Whitman: "the day of all or nearly all poetry which has been hitherto written is over (that of Walt Whitman may perhaps be excepted)"; Whitman should go about with an itinerant dentist and "sing the advent of democracy between the intervals of tooth-drawing. He would certainly secure 'the thumb-mark of the Artisan' for his classical style."

5 COOKE, GEORGE WILLIS. <u>Ralph Waldo Emerson: His Life, Writings, and Philosophy</u>. Boston and New York: Houghton Mifflin Co., n.d., pp. 233-34, 387, 404.
Revision of 1881.4.

Two chapters are added as an updating since Emerson's death. Whitman is quoted regarding his visit to Emerson in September 1881 and his 1860 talk with Emerson, which largely clears up their relations. The bibliography lists three articles by Whitman.

6 de MILLE, A[LBAN] B[ERTRAM]. <u>Literature in the Century</u>. Toronto and Philadelphia: Linscott Publishing Co., pp. 297-300.

Whitman's poems lack form and art, being "the height of lawless force," except when submitting to rhyme and meter as in "Captain." His bigness was uncontrolled by any grace. He has some elements of poetry and "unbounded vitality" and "tenderness for his kind." His audience was not among the common people but among the small class which could make allowances for his failings and still appreciate his good points.

7 GENUNG, JOHN FRANKLIN. <u>The Working Principles of Rhetoric</u>. Boston, New York, Chicago, London: Ginn & Co., p. 217.

Whitman's adoption of rhythmical Hebrew parallelism might have been more successful "if he had had a better ear for rhythm of the constituent phrase." "Open Road" is quoted to exemplify Whitman's "jumble rhythm."

8 GOULD, ELIZABETH PORTER. <u>Anne Gilchrist and Walt Whitman</u>. Philadelphia: David McKay, 89 pp. No index. Illustrated.
Extracts reprinted: 1900.51.

Primarily biographical on Gilchrist and her relationship with Whitman, based on 1887.6 and 1898.29, with quotations from and commentary on George Eliot, Joaquin Miller, Rossetti, O'Connor, Carpenter, Burroughs, all in relation to Whitman. Gould recalls her own acquaintance with Whitman. Includes a reprint of 1885.14.

9 HODGSON, GERALDINE. <u>Walt Whitman: Poet and Thinker</u>. Manchester: Co-operative Newspaper Society, 88 pp. No index.

1. "Whitman's Personal Appeal": Whitman may be guilty of artistic blunders, as in his sex poems, because he wrote not for art's sake but for a moral message. He relied on direct personal appeal. His audience will grow because of his breadth, sympathy, and keen attention to detail.

2. "Whitman as a Literary Man": He was influenced by nature rather than literature, and by cultures other than English. The greatest of his lines could be changed only for the worse. From his vast vocabulary he often chooses inappropriate words, though he is entirely capable "of melodious phrasing, of apt description, of felicitous epithet."

3. "Whitman's Democracy": His democratic ideal in <u>Vistas</u> is an attitude of mind rather than a political state. Collectivism and individualism are not reduced to synonymity, but one serves and produces the other. Such may be the wave of the future, but Whitman's esteem for business energy and materialism is slightly inconsistent with his moral emphasis.

4. "Whitman's Sense of Nature": Similarities to Wordsworth are noted.

5. "Whitman's War Poetry": He falls short of inspiring men to acts of courage but succeeds in portraying the pathos and actions of war.

6. "Whitman's Philosophy": The influence of Hegel in Whitman's political philosophy and optimistic moral system is explained.

7. "Whitman in Various Lights": Defense of Whitman's egotism and notion of human divinity. He often failed to express his thoughts appropriately. His faults are those of the American race, whose virtues he also shares. Behind all his work are "his soaring indefatigable energy" and the charm of a "self-sufficing soul."

10 HOWELLS, W. D. <u>Literary Friends and Acquaintance: A Personal Retrospect of American Authorship</u>. New York and London: Harper & Bros. "First Impressions of Literary New York," pp. 67-90.
Reprint of 1895.39.

11 JOHNSON, CHARLES F. <u>Outline History of English and American Literature</u>. New York, Cincinnati, Chicago: American Book Co., pp. 522-25.

Whitman lacks art and skill but "has broad, inchoate conceptions of his own," making readers see death, nature, and the democracy of labor in new ways. Even critics who find his verse chaotic "cannot deny the power of 'When last the Lilacs Bloomed' and the 'Mocking Bird' and the 'Man of War Bird,'" though only "Captain" (here reprinted) has popular acceptance.

12 MITCHELL, S. WEIR. <u>Dr. North and His Friends</u>. New York: Century Co., pp. 13-14.

1900

Characters engage in a brief argument over Whitman, whom two of the characters knew, vouching for his vanity. Dr. North (the narrator) tells an anecdote of Whitman in the office of a physician who said that he was in Whitman's debt rather than vice versa.

13 POND, Major J. B. Eccentricities of Genius. (Memories of Famous Men and Women of the Platform and Stage.) New York: G. W. Dillingham, pp. 386-88, 497-501.

Account of Sir Edwin Arnold's visit to Whitman, at which Pond and John Russell Young were also present (see 1891.2, 1892.27). Recalls Whitman giving readings under his management; mistakenly mentions a visit to Whitman by Matthew Arnold; reprints 1892.5.

14 SANTAYANA, GEORGE. Interpretations of Poetry and Religion. New York: Charles Scribner's Sons. "The Poetry of Barbarism," pp. 166-216, primarily pp. 177-87.

Reprinted in part: Miller; Hindus; Murphy.

Today's poetry, exemplified by the admirable but limited Whitman and Browning, is a poetry of barbarism because it lacks beauty, ideals, and a "grasp of the whole reality," depicting sensations and transitive emotions without the ordering reason. For Whitman, the surface is all, though presented "with a wonderful gift of graphic characterization and an occasional rare grandeur of diction." His democracy was not merely constitutional but social and moral, with actual equality among men. He foreshadows a new literature of democracy which will ignore all distinctions, including those of genius and virtue, thus looking to the past rather than to the future with a Spencerian evolution toward differentiation and organization. Hence Whitman's desired audience rejects him, but he is welcome at times.

15 STARKWEATHER, CHAUNCEY C. Special introduction to Essays of American Essayists. The World's Great Classics, edited by Timothy Dwight, Julian Hawthorne, Arthur Richmond Marsh, Richard Henry Stoddard, and Paul van Dyke. New York: Colonial Press, p. vi.

Praising Whitman is like praising Shakespeare; the future will place him "high on the list of glorious names, the first voice of a united, crystallized, original America, a bard who sang democracy, our great citizenship, God-love, and the comradeship of the throbbing, suffering, hoping, majestic human heart." Headnote to 1855 Preface (p. 400) presents a biographical sketch and a brief estimate, noting his "clumsy, at times unintelligible" prose, which "sometimes rises to poetic grandeur," with "a rough, moving eloquence and beauty."

16 STEDMAN, EDMUND CLARENCE, ed. Introduction to An American Anthology 1787-1900. Boston and New York: Houghton Mifflin Co., pp. xix, xxiii-iv, xxv; fifteen Whitman poems

printed, 221-32; biographical notes by A[rthur] S[tedman], 830-31; reprints of Whitman tribute poems "Darkness and death?" (1894.19), 483, and "He was in love with Truth" (1894.8), 620.

Whitman shares with Bryant an "elemental quality," but differs in style and awareness of the heterogeneity of recent America. Emerson, Poe, and Whitman are now the most alive of our poets, offering the most for the Old World to learn from, because they were the most individual.

17 STEVENSON, ROBERT LOUIS. The Essay on Walt Whitman. With a Little Journey to the House of Whitman by Elbert Hubbard. East Aurora, N.Y.: Roycroft Shop, 91 pp. Frontispiece: bas-relief of Whitman profile by St. Gerome Roycroft.

Reprints of 1878.17 (with changes in wording at the beginning of each section) and 1896.8 (with minor deletions).

18 WENDELL, BARRETT. A Literary History of America. New York: Charles Scribner's Sons. "Walt Whitman," pp. 465-67; bibliography, 553.

Revised: 1904.21. Abridged: Miller; Bradley/Blodgett.

Whitman has "remarkable individuality and power" but his eccentricity produced controversy. His democracy emphasizes equality rather than simple liberty. He errs in denying inferiority and evil. He creates "literary anarchy" by juxtaposing beautiful phrases with jargon. His experience is strictly American and confined to New York's lower classes, an atmosphere pervading his work, including his "most nearly beautiful" poem, "Brooklyn Ferry." "At most he leaves you with a sense of new realities concerning which you must do your thinking for yourself." His style suggests decline. "Myself" and "Brooklyn Ferry" are "recklessly misshapen," yet we are fortunate that he did not remain silent but made attempts at utterance. His lack of literary consciousness is foreign to the American spirit, but his poetry's substance is wholly American.

19 WOLFE, THEODORE F. Literary Rambles At Home and Abroad. Philadelphia: J. B. Lippincott Co. "The Haunts of Walt Whitman," pp. 85-99. Illustrated.

Describes with appropriate biographical data and brief quotations the Camden ferry and ferryman (though "how much of his devout and optimistic master-verse was here begotten of the contemplations such objects inspired, we may never know"), the Camden streets Whitman visited, the disposal of his wheelchair to an invalid neighbor, George's house on Stevens Street, Mickle Street house ("scarcely changed since we visited him here" except for the profaning of the inside by lodgers), Mrs. Davis's home with its Whitman memorabilia, Traubel's home, Timber Creek with its changes (except for

the natural scenes which Whitman described
so vividly that they are readily recognized),
and the tomb.

PERIODICALS

20 C[ARUS], P[AUL]. Review of Salter (1899.16).
   Open Court 14 (January), 59-60.
         Salter's "impassionate" praise of
   Whitman's natural nobility is more convincing than the enthusiasm of Whitman's
   admirers. Carus objects not to his innovations of immoral tendencies but to "his
   lack of poetical strength and genuine sentiment." Whitman is psychologically interesting but lacks beauty. His "scorn for traditional rules" is praised, but most of his
   lines "are mere talk," pleasant, thoughtful,
   or trivial.

21 COMPENDIUM. "Recent Study and Criticism of
   Whitman. XXX." Conservator 10 (January),
   169-70.
         Includes commentary on Whitman by
   Henry B. Fuller (Saturday Evening Post) and
   Julian Hawthorne (North American Review),
   both unlocated.

22 T[RAUBEL, HORACE]. "Through Nature to God."
   Conservator 10 (January), 171.
         Review of John Fiske's book of that
   title, which ignores Whitman in dealing with
   the mystery of evil though Whitman could
   present the greatest tests furnished by
   literature. This book can "disarm Salter's
   ethical objections to Whitman" (1899.16).

23 COMPENDIUM. "Recent Study and Criticism of
   Whitman. XXXI." Conservator 10 (February),
   184-85.

24 KENNEDY, WILLIAM SLOANE. "On Walt Whitman."
   Conservator 10 (February), 188.
         Review of Salter (1899.16). "The con-
   founding of good and evil" in Leaves is explained by reference to Hegel. Whitman's
   true being was always "profoundly moral,"
   as his life shows.

25 COMPENDIUM. "Recent Study and Criticism of
   Whitman. XXXII." Conservator 11 (March),
   9-10.

26 SALTER, WILLIAM M., and KENNEDY, WILLIAM
   SLOANE. "Good and Evil in Whitman." Conservator 11 (March), 6-7.
         In response to 1900.24, Salter asks how
   to justify the "false notes" in Whitman on
   moral questions. Kennedy responds that
   Whitman seems to "condone licentiousness"
   but his general atmosphere is "nobly moral,"
   usually looking beyond the "petty moral
   adjustments" of society, although sometimes
   speaking from its sphere.

27 COMPENDIUM. "Recent Study and Criticism of
   Whitman. XXXIII." Conservator 11 (April),
   25-27.

Includes, among other commentary, remarks
on W. H. Bell's "Walt Whitman Symphony" from
Unity, Truth (London) and London News.

28 HUBBARD, ELBERT. Incidental note. Mind 5
   (April), 85.
         Hubbard considers Ruskin, William
   Morris, Thoreau, Whitman, and Tolstoy
   "prophets of God" and the equals of the Old
   Testament prophets.

29 STRUTHERS, WILLIAM. "An Italian Writer on
   Whitman." Conservator 11 (April), 21-22.
         Explanation of Jannaccone's discussion
   of prosody (see 1898.39), which divides
   Whitman's poems according to whether they
   have "distinctive rhyme and rhythm," "clear
   rhythmic design but no rhyme," or "rhythmic
   vagueness." Continued 1900.32.

30 BEARDSHEAR, W. M. "The Charge of a Brother
   Walt." Philistine 10 (May), 161-67.
         Proclaims Whitman's philosophy using
   only Whitman's words or a close paraphrase,
   as addressed to a potential disciple.

31 COMPENDIUM. "Recent Study and Criticism of
   Whitman. XXXIV." Conservator 11 (May),
   43.
         Includes Bliss Carman's remarks on
   Santayana (1900.14).

32 STRUTHERS, WILLIAM. "An Italian Writer on
   Whitman, II." Conservator 11 (May), 38-40.
         Continues 1900.29. Examines "Pioneers"
   as example of second type, showing Whitman's
   deliberate variation of rhythm; "Eidólons"
   and "Dirge" as examples of third type. Continued 1900.35.

33 ANON. "Personal." New York Tribune (30 May),
   8:4-5.
         Quotes from the Youth's Companion a new
   story about Whitman (unlocated): George W.
   Childs paid him to ride the streetcars and
   let him know which drivers needed new over-
   coats.

34 CLARKE, HELEN A. "The Awakening of the Soul:
   Whitman and Maeterlinck." Conservator 11
   (June), 58-60.
         Maeterlinck must be recognized as a
   successor to Whitman because "the democratic
   inclusion of all souls" pervades his poetry.

35 STRUTHERS, WILLIAM. "An Italian Writer on
   Whitman, III." Conservator 11 (June), 53-
   54.
         Continues 1900.32. Continues examina-
   tion of "Eidólons" and "Dirge." Such forms,
   "because of the dissatisfaction they instill
   into the senses and the psyche, more effi-
   caciously express intimate commotions, profound anguish, and the sweetness of sorrow."
   Jannaccone's reconstruction of "Weave in"
   according to an orthodox pattern is explained, showing "how much less forcible, how
   much less adequate, is the regulated revision

1900

than the irregular original." Continued
1900.47.

36 COMPENDIUM. "Recent Study and Criticism of
Whitman. XXXV." Conservator 11 (July),
75-76.

37 T[RAUBEL, HORACE]. "Anne Gilchrist and Walt
Whitman." Conservator 11 (July), 76-77.
Review of Gould (1900.8): no new
matter, but a good "summary of a remarkable
friendship." Gilchrist's contribution to
Whitman is praised.

38 TRIMBLE, W. H. "The Open Court and 'Leaves of
Grass.'" Open Court 14 (July), 439-40.
Response to 1900.20: "Adam" is not immoral or "written for the sake of mere
obscenity." Whitman's poetic strength and
sentiment may be seen in "Open Road," "This
Compost," "Drum-Taps." His fame is not due
to the questionable passages, for many admirers are familiar only with expurgated
versions, which America perhaps needs. His
admirers are listed.

39 WILLIAMS, FRANCIS HOWARD. "Individuality as
Whitman's Primary Motive." Conservator 11
(July), 71-73.
Whitman's primary message is not, as the
Fellowship believes, comradeship, but rather
individuality. Socialism is not yet ripe;
Whitman calls each of us to perfect our-
selves.

40 DAVENPORT, W. E. "Walt Whitman in Brooklyn--
W. E. Davenport Recalls Some Interesting
Facts About the Poet's Residence Here.
Father and Son Printers. Anxious to Become
a Platform Orator. Text of an Address
Before Brooklyn Art Union in 1851." Brook-
lyn Daily Eagle (14 July), 18:1-2.
Generally biographical information, in-
cluding Whitman's religious and personal
habits.

41 MEAD, LEON. "Walt Whitman." Conservator 11
(August), 90-92.
Whitman was suited to his age, his egotism being "merely the objective expression
of the universal man." Mead recalls conversation during his visit to Whitman with
Joaquin Miller; Whitman was moved to hear
of Longfellow's praise. Other casual
visits are recalled.

42 TRAUBEL, HORACE L. "Recent Study and Criticism
of Whitman. XXXVI." Conservator 11
(August), 93.
Traubel's article from the Philadelphia
North American (unlocated) is reprinted,
giving evidence of Whitman's "lyrical quality" from the songs written to Whitman's
words by several Philadelphia musicians,
here described.

43 ABBEY, CHARLOTTE. "The Ultimate Human Problem."
Conservator 11 (September), 106-7.

Describes Whitman's ideal woman as a
model for the modern women's movement.

44 T[RAUBEL, HORACE]. "Walt Whitman." Conservator 11 (September), 109.
Brief notice of 1900.17: "Stevenson
will not be accused of taking an extreme
position," but is more against Whitman than
for him.

45 ANON. "Anne Gilchrist and Walt Whitman." New
York Times Saturday Review (8 September),
595.
Favorable review of Gould (1900.8),
summarizing the relationship.

46 [HUBBARD, ELBERT.] "Heart to Heart Talks with
Philistines by the Pastor of His Flock."
Philistine 11 (October), 142-47.
Prints letter to him from Dr. George M.
Gould rejecting Whitman as "an old sponge
and tramp." Hubbard comments ironically on
the letter.

47 STRUTHERS, WILLIAM. "An Italian Writer on
Whitman, IV." Conservator 11 (October),
120-21.
Continues 1900.35. Summarizes
Jannaccone: Whitman's use of parallelism in "Myself,"
"phonic rhythms" in "Lilacs"; comparison to
traditional rhythms. His "most marked
characteristic is a psychic constitution
of rhythm" and "the formation of groups
through homogeneity of ideas." Continued
1900.48.

48 _____. "An Italian Writer on Whitman, V."
Conservator 11 (November), 135.
Continues 1900.47. Jannaccone compares
Greek syntonic prose with Whitman's patterns
of "stress upon segments of thought in
parallels." The "struggle between the
logical and rhythmic elements" produces enjambment and continuity of thought from
verse to verse. Whitman's work is representative of the evolution of rhythmic
patterns from ancient to modern poetry.
Concluded 1901.26.

49 BENTON, JOEL. "Walt Whitman. The New and
Enlarged Variorum Edition of his 'Leaves of
Grass.'" New York Times Saturday Review
(10 November), 772.
Review of new edition. Emphasizes the
suggestiveness of Whitman's poetry, his
egotism as universal, his all-inclusiveness
as depicted in his catalogues. His work
must be viewed as a whole rather than as
separate lyrics. Omission of "Locomotive"
is regretted. "Spider" is printed as brief
example of Whitman's poetic excellence.
"Captain" and "Lilacs" have unparalleled
pathos.

50 COMPENDIUM. "Recent Study and Criticism of
Whitman. XXXVII." Conservator 11 (December),
156.

51 GOULD, ELIZABETH PORTER. "Anne Gilchrist and Walt Whitman." Current Literature 29 (December), 702-3.
Extracts reprinted from 1900.8.

52 [HUNEKER, JAMES G.] "Raconteur." Musical Courier 41 (12 December), 38.
Praises the score of William Henry Bell's symphony "Walt Whitman," which should be performed in America, including settings from "Broad-Axe" and "Lilacs," "Whitman's noble lament." Bell is "a Whitman worshipper" though the work "is by no means revolutionary in its tendencies."

1901

BOOKS

1 BALFOUR, GRAHAM. The Life of Robert Louis Stevenson. London: Methuen & Co. Vol. 1, pp. 86, 94, 97-98, 112, 140, 173; vol. 2, pp. 162, 176, 215.
The study of Whitman was one of three main factors in his development, Stevenson said. Notes for a paper on Whitman are quoted. Mrs. Stevenson recalls her husband reading "Cradle" and "Captain," moving deeply even the skeptical ones in the audience.

2 BUCHANAN, ROBERT. The Complete Poetical Works of Robert Buchanan. London: Chatto & Windus. Vol. 1, "Walt Whitman," p. 425; vol. 2, "Socrates in Camden" and "Walt Whitman," 395-98.
Reprints of 1876.1; 1885.27; 1892.142.

3 BUCKE, RICHARD MAURICE. Cosmic Consciousness: A Study in the Evolution of the Human Mind. Philadelphia: Innes & Sons. "Walt Whitman," pp. 178-96; also passim. No index.
Reprinted: 1923.2. Extract reprinted: Miller.
Whitman's works and life (described, largely from 1883.3) show him as "the best, most perfect, example the world has so far had of the Cosmic Sense," for in him "the new faculty has been, probably, most perfectly developed." He wrote from the point of view of cosmic consciousness. "Myself" 5 depicts the moment of illumination; passages from Vistas illustrate his emphasis on "the All" and "the equal grandeur and eternity of the individual soul." His refusal to abase the old physical self to the new indicates full mastery of the cosmic consciousness. Whitman's writings are used throughout the book to explain the experiences of others, suggest similarities (as in the section on Shakespeare's sonnets), and reveal his influence. (Bucke expands upon material in 1893.11 and 1894.30.)

4 COURTHOPE, WILLIAM JOHN. Life in Poetry: Law in Taste. London and New York: Macmillan &

Co., p. 79.
Quoted in 1904.2; 1909.1.
Response to lines quoted from Whitman: "if you had anything of universal interest to say about yourself, you could say it in a way natural to one of the metres, or metrical movements, established in the English language."

5 CROSBY, ERNEST. Edward Carpenter: Poet and Prophet. Philadelphia: Conservator, pp. 2, 4-5, 6, 7, 11, 12, 17-18, 45-46.
Whitman and Carpenter share a similar view of life as "a great and transcendent unity," although Carpenter is self-conscious. Their new form and similar poetic gifts are described; also their celebration of "comradeship in terms worthy of the ancient Greeks," although "it is irrational to condemn them offhand as inverted and abnormal."

6 ELLIS, HAVELOCK. Studies in the Psychology of Sex. Vol. 2. Sexual Inversion. Philadelphia: F. A. Davis Co., pp. 24-26, 202.
Revised: 1915.11.
Whitman's notion of friendship has a strong physical content. But he must be treated not merely as an invert but as "the prophet-poet of Democracy." He apparently did not see a connection between his desire for physical contact with men and the actual sexual act, according to his letter to Symonds. Letter from "Q" is quoted presenting arguments against Whitman's claims of paternity. Whitman's notion of manly love "furnishes a wholesome and robust ideal to the invert who is sensitive to normal ideals."

7 HALSEY, FRANCIS WHITING, ed. American Authors and Their Homes: Personal Descriptions and Interviews. New York: James Pott & Co., pp. 108-9.
Quotes Howells's conversation on Whitman, comparing the poet to Columbus, who "discovered an island, instead of the continent," criticizing his lack of form except when "at a sublime height."

8 HERRINGSHAW, THOMAS WILLIAM. Herringshaw's Encyclopedia of American Biography of the Nineteenth Century. Chicago: American Publishers' Association, p. 1004.
Brief biography, list of works, "Captain" his most popular poem.

9 JONES, SAMUEL M. Letters of Love and Labor. Vol. 2. Toledo: Franklin Printing & Engraving Co. Epigraph.
Four lines from "Myself and Mine" are used as epigraph.

10 KNOWLES, FREDERIC LAWRENCE, ed. The Golden Treasury of American Lyrics and Songs. London: George Routledge & Sons, pp. ix, xi, 316.
Revision of 1897.13.
America has added "no distinctly new

notes to English poetry" beyond Poe and Whitman, who is now represented in this edition of the anthology by five selections, since no collection of American verse would be complete without him. <u>Leaves</u> reveals a noble lyrical spirit.

11 MASON, H. L. <u>American Literature--A Laboratory Method</u>. Philadelphia: Published by the author, pp. 45, 51-52, 71.

    List of poems to read from this "Chanter of Comradeship and Democracy"; study questions on Whitman in general and specifically "Cradle," "Trumpeter," "Lilacs," and "Captain."

12 MOODY, WILLIAM VAUGHN. <u>Poems 1901</u>. Boston and New York: Houghton, Mifflin & Co. "An Ode in Time of Hesitation," p. 18. Reprinted: Hubbell.

    Stanza seven calls for "some elder singer" to guide the people now: "Is Whitman, the strong spirit, overworn?"

13 NEWCOMER, ALPHONSO G. <u>American Literature</u>. Chicago: Scott, Foresman and Co., pp. 252-64, 351-52.

    Whitman's message is "only a more emphatic declaration of what was already in the prose of Emerson and the verse of Whittier and Lowell." His purpose was to depict an entire personality and suggest the individual's evolution, using himself as a typical American. He "fills a large place in the hearts of many lovers of English poetry"; his "virile, stimulating personality" cannot be omitted from American literature. His prose is valuable for depicting war and for helping to explain his poetry. His strange vocabulary is sometimes saved by a humorous intent, but his formlessness does not seem capable of "the final poem even of Democracy." He needs more artistry but has "pointed the way for a future and more able bard." He was the truest laureate of the war and Lincoln. His poetry frequently has true melody and harmony, but he was chiefly concerned with arousing the reader.

14 ONDERDONK, JAMES L. <u>History of American Verse (1610-1897)</u>. Chicago: A. C. McClurg & Co., pp. 323-39; also 179-81, 189-90, 356-57, 360.
Abridged from 1894.44.

    Incidental references include a comparison with Bryant.

15 ROSE, RAY CLARKE. <u>At the Sign of the Ginger Jar: Some Verse Gay and Grave</u>. Chicago: A. C. McClurg & Co. "Walt Whitman [A Monologue.]," pp. 45-46.

    Poem in four rhymed stanzas presenting Whitman defending his verse and inviting the reader to join him: "I am no slender singing bird."

16 RUSSELL, A. J., ed. <u>Stories of the Illumination of Walt Whitman, Tennyson, etc., copied from the Publication Society of the Liberal Christian Science Church</u>. Minneapolis: Byron & Willard. "Illumination of Whitman," pp. 12-24.
Extract reprinted from 1899.38.

17 YOUNG, MAY D. RUSSELL, ed. <u>Men and Memories: Personal Reminiscences of John Russell Young</u>. Vol. 1. New York: F. Tennyson Neely. "Walt Whitman," pp. 76-109. Reprints of 1892.22 and 1892.27.

    Also includes two Whitman poems and a parody by Young from 1888.

PERIODICALS

18 DAWSON, POLLY ERNESTINE. "Whitman." <u>Conservator</u> 11 (January), 165.

    Brief address to a reader: Purge your soul of impurity that you may read "this great-souled Whitman" truly, for he is spotless.

19 TRIGGS, OSCAR LOVELL. "A Century of American Poetry." <u>Forum</u> 30 (January), 630-40, passim.

    Review of Stedman (1900.16). Whitman exemplifies "heroic realism." He and Poe are "conspicuous among American poets for their striking originality and intensive force," conveying unique experiences, creating distinctive styles, founding schools (Whitman's being in greater evidence in Stedman's anthology).

20 CARLILL, H. F. "A Plea for a Consideration of Walt Whitman." <u>Literature</u> 8 (12 January), 25-26.

    Whitman's significant "influence on the vocabulary and syntax of English prose" demands serious criticism. "He is the most sensuous, the most realistic writer in the history of literature," unmatched in "giving the bare immediate impression." His intention is "the very denial of art," but his poetic instincts are often just right. Whatever the faults of his truly expressive and "practically perfect" style, they are part of his whole character and outlook, for his work is "intellectually one and organic."

21 CAULDWELL, WILLIAM. "Walt Whitman as a Young Man." <u>New York Times Saturday Review</u> (26 January), 59.
Reprinted: 1901.41.

    Recollection of being "quite chummy" with Whitman when about seventeen, working in the same building in which Whitman (about twenty-five) was working on the <u>Aurora</u>. Whitman's appearance, activities, and political disagreements are described.

22 COMPENDIUM. "Recent Study and Criticism of Whitman. XXXVIII." <u>Conservator</u> 11 (February), 185.

23 RATCLIFFE, S. K. "On the Alleged Importance of Walt Whitman." Literature 8 (16 February), 113-14.

Response to 1901.20. Whitman's influence on prose is doubtful, for he is more a personal than a literary force. His form is not invented, being similar to most primitive literatures. Primarily young people respond to him. His language is often absurd, except when "his imagination triumphs over his theory" and permits him to endow common words with fresh significance and beauty, like any master of speech. His one idea is merely American individualism. He has no poetical offspring. "Captain" shows that he could not work in traditional forms. His work will endure for expressing his personal spirit of fellowship. His poetic temperament is more than protoplasmic only when moulded by creative imagination, and then it meets the canons of poetry.

24 IVES, ELLA GILBERT. "The Gospel of the Open. Studies of Some of Its Preachers. Walt Whitman." Boston Evening Transcript (27 February), 13:3-4.

Impressionistic description of Whitman's identity with nature, using extracts. "Cradle" conveys brilliantly the feeling of the sea, the moment of "the boy's baptism into the poet's rapture." Whitman conveys the ethical as well as physical aspect of a scene. He knew nature well, if not scientifically.

25 MOUNTAIN, WILLIAM. "Whitman's Gift of Joy." Conservator 12 (March), 5-6.

Whitman conveys gladness through knowledge of one's own soul and the perception of the beauty and value of all other things. Not even Buddha or Christ had this unique gift.

26 STRUTHERS, WILLIAM. "An Italian Writer on Whitman, VI." Conservator 12 (March), 7-9.

Concludes 1900.48. Jannaccone examines the poetry in Whitman's Preface and Specimen. Summary of Whitman's physical rhythmics: his return to primitive forms makes the logical element prevail, but his rhythmics are distinguished from the primitive. His aesthetic effects and content are interdependent.

27 WOODHULL, MARY G. "Walt Whitman--A Memory Picture." Literary Era, n.s. 8 (March), 159-60. Butterfly photograph.

Recollection of Whitman from her childhood in Camden.

*28 SULLIVAN, LOUIS H. "Kindergarten Chats. IV. The Garden." Interstate Architect and Builder 3 (9 March).

Reprinted: Kindergarten Chats (revised 1918) and Other Writings, by Louis H. Sullivan (New York: Wittenborn, Schultz, Inc., 1947).

Incidentally quotes Whitman.

29 BEST, ST. GEORGE. "Walt Whitman." Book-Lover 2, no. 2 (Spring), 284.

A free-verse poem of tribute for Whitman's great themes, celebrating "the dawning victory of his unfettered speech."

30 CROSBY, ERNEST. "A New York Memorial to Whitman." Conservator 12 (April), 21-22.

The New York area produced what is essential in Whitman's work, although it possesses no memorial to him, a far more significant and picturesque figure than Dr. Johnson. He needs to be remembered not in the Hall of Fame but in the haunts of people; a ferryboat might be named for him, that people might hear his name and get to know him.

31 DASKAM, JOSEPHINE DODGE. "The Distinction of our Poetry." Atlantic Monthly 87 (April), 702.

Incidental: Whitman's "titanic force, that sweeping annihilation of all accepted canons, that unregulated if colossal genius," cannot be imitated because he contains too many possibilities for degeneration in his style, "a law unto itself." At his best (e.g., "Lilacs"), Whitman is "to be cherished as one of the great universal brotherhood who have risen most adequately to the expression of a deep and lofty feeling; at his worst, however, he falls to a level which is precisely the level reserved for the American of genius in his most unfortunate lapses." He is more akin to us in our failures than in our successes.

32 BARBER, EDWARD. "An American Bard and an Anglican Reviewer." Conservator 12 (May), 44-45.

Commends the London Guardian's review (unlocated) of Wendell (1900.18), which objects to his treatment of Whitman, "the man of the largest and deepest poetic vision produced by America."

33 EDWARDS, WARD H. "An Introduction to Walt Whitman." William Jewell Student 7 (June), 305-15.

Chiefly quotes various commentators praising Whitman. Whitman's life was virtuous, his work a reflection of himself, his style appropriate, as the Bible's is. His "great impetus words" include "Comradeship," "Good Cheer, Content and Hope." His major philosophic poems have a remarkable broadening influence on the reader. "Captain" is unsurpassed in English; "Lilacs" is his best and most suggestive and imaginative poem.

34 PLATT, ISAAC HULL. "Whitman and Cosmic Emotion." Conservator 12 (June), 57-59.

Cosmic emotion, the "awe which arises from viewing the universe as cosmos or order," is expressed in Whitman's poems as

1901

"the great uplifting power ennobling the human soul and thereby regenerating society," leading to love.

35 STRUTHERS, WILLIAM. "Walt Whitman: 1901." *Conservator* 12 (June), 52-53.
Reprinted: Legler.
Sonnet of tribute: "He fell asleep. . . ."

36 ANON. "Walt Whitman Fellowship Meeting." *New York Tribune* (1 June), 8:6.
Notes attendees and addresses, including one on "Whitman and American Poetry" by Edwin Markham.

37 ANON. "Walt Whitman. The Organization Named After Him Holds Its Convention in This City." *New York Times Saturday Review* (8 June), 411.
Describes speeches at the Walt Whitman Fellowship by I. H. Platt, Edwin Markham, John Swinton, Alma Calder Johnson [sic], Mrs. Richard Hovey, Mayor Samuel M. Jones, Charlotte Perkins Gilman; notes briefly other speakers and readers; notes preponderance of women present, tendency of the speakers to establish a cult.

38 BENTON, JOEL. "Whitman in Literature." *New York Times Saturday Review* (8 June), 411.
Whitman was shocking when he first appeared, but he came to be recognized as a poet with grace and beauty beneath the "chestnut burr," with meaning in his "amorphous lines." Benton praises Whitman's titles, break with tradition, vicarious egotism, faith in his own standard, power of suggestion.

39 D., N. G. "Why is Walt Whitman Unappreciated?" *New York Times Saturday Review* (8 June), 411.
Notes never having seen a volume of Whitman in ordinary homes among many volumes of popular poets, major and minor. Perhaps Whitman is therefore not a true poet.

40 HUBBARD, ELBERT. "Walt Whitman." *Book-Lover* 2 (Summer), 352-57.
Reprint of 1896.8.

41 COMPENDIUM. "Recent Study and Criticism of Whitman. XXXIX." *Conservator* 12 (July), 76.

42 _____. "Whitman: 1901." *Conservator* 12 (July), 72-73.
Various comments and greetings to the Fellowship, including ones from Stedman and Garland.

43 CROSBY, ERNEST. "The Whitman Cipher." *Conservator* 12 (July), 73-74.
Comic essay ascribing the authorship of *Leaves* to Bucke.

44 [TRAUBEL, HORACE.] "Query Anent Bacon-Shakespeare." *Conservator* 12 (July), 71.
Anecdote of Whitman looking at his pictures of Shakespeare and Bacon and saying, "I guess we'll keep our Will."

45 ANON. "Whitman's Lincoln. His 'When Lilacs Last in the Dooryard Bloomed' Superbly Issued in England." *New York Times Saturday Review* (24 August), 598.
Review of Essex House Press edition. Whitman wrote of Lincoln from personal knowledge and observations set down promptly. *Specimen* reveals war's aspects "far more convincingly and vividly" than *Red Badge of Courage* without attracting half the attention.

46 COMPENDIUM. "Recent Study and Criticism of Whitman. XL." *Conservator* 12 (September), 108.
Includes a long poetic tribute to Whitman by Adalena F. Dyer: "He walked the earth like Pan."

47 KELLEY, WILLIAM V. "The Deification of 'One of the Roughs.'" *Homiletic Review* 42 (September), 202-8.
Extract reprinted: 1901.56.
Attacks Whitman's violations of decency, which even his admirers acknowledge; scoffs at foreign tributes. It is fitting that a "professional blasphemer" (Ingersoll) spoke at his funeral. Whitman is comparable to Nietzsche in lunacy and imposture.

48 PLATT, WILLIAM. "The Modesty and Egotism of Genius." *Conservator* 12 (September), 104.
What would have become of the message of great artists like Whitman and Beethoven had they been modest, as their critics wish?

49 SCHOLES, C. W. "Walt Whitman, His Poetry and Philosophy." *Pacific Monthly* 6 (September), 141-43.
Recalls meeting Whitman and Bucke in Ontario. Whitman is a titan in his work. His philosophy emphasizes the priority of personality and the harmony of universal law. His poetry, though dissociated from rhyme and measure, is responsive to cosmic laws.

50 WATSON, E. H. LACON. "Literature Portraits.-- XVII. Walt Whitman." *Literature* 9 (7 September), 219-26.
Reprinted: 1927.23.
Whitman's poetry is "intolerable rant" at first sight, juxtaposing eloquent with ludicrous passages. Whitman, "essentially simple-minded," was most concerned with dramatic messages, secondarily with exploiting his own personality. Whitman's early life is summarized from Bucke (1883.3). His best work is *Specimen*, his worst *Vistas*; his lack of method is less disturbing in the poetry.

51 MOORE, CHARLES LEONARD. "Three Lyrical Anthologies." Dial 31 (16 September), 177.
Review of Stedman's anthology (1900.16),
among others. Incidental comparison of
Whitman to Browning, whom he "would over-
whelm and obliterate" as a lyric poet.
His meter lacks verse's advantages, but "is
a sufficiently sounding instrument." When
he writes a poem with a theme and a beginning, middle, and end, "he is very great."
"His two best pieces are large and glowing
odes," "stamped with immortality."

52 ANON. "Whitman--Some Incidents in His Career
Before He Attracted Attention as a Poet."
Philadelphia Times Saturday Book Review
Supplement (28 September).
Presentation, with quotations, of
Whitman's newspaper writings and concerns.

53 ANON. "An English View of Whitman." Current
Literature 31 (October), 482.
Précis with quotations of article from
London Guardian (unlocated): Whitman is
American literature's "great original
force." Wendell's point of view (1900.18)
is criticized. Whitman's way of looking at
things is new, American, and his own. His
faults (saying whatever comes into his mind
without editing or planning) are on the
surface. The greatest original force since
Wordsworth, he finds poetry where even
Wordsworth did not, in the seething life of
modern cities.

54 COMPENDIUM. "Recent Study and Criticism of
Whitman. XLI." Conservator 12 (October),
122.

55 [SPARGO, JOHN?] "Greeting." Comrade 1 (October), [12].
This editorial in the first number
opens with the first two stanzas of "For
You, O Democracy" as a fitting "Salutatory
to our readers," expressing this journal's
goal. "The literature of the world might
be searched in vain for anything more
beautiful, or simple, or direct, than this
Psalm of Comradeship."

56 WILLIAMS, FRANCIS HOWARD. "The Whitman Cult."
Conservator 12 (October), 119.
Response to an extract here reprinted
from Kelley (1901.47): such critics have
never understood the Gospel itself.

57 ANON. "Walt Whitman. His Early Work as
Reviewer, Poet, and Editor Before His
'Leaves of Grass' Was Published." New York
Times Saturday Review (5 October), 704-5.
Corrects Wendell (1900.18) regarding
Whitman's vagrant youth through extensive
quotations showing Whitman's keen political
concerns while writing for the newspapers.

58 COMPENDIUM. "Recent Study and Criticism of
Whitman. XLII." Conservator 12 (November), 138-39.

59 [HUBBARD, ELBERT.] "Heart to Heart Talks
with Philistines by the Pastor of His
Flock." Philistine 13 (November), 178-83.
This discussion of Burroughs includes
comments on Whitman, who did not join the
army because of his charitable instincts
and horror of war. Burroughs has made
Whitman's "fragmentary philosophy" a "practical working gospel."

*60 NORRIS, HOMER A. Review of a Whitman musical
setting. Concert Goer (November).
Reported in Willard.
Whitman gives "the most complete synthesis" of his America through his lines,
however flawed; they are the fit ways of
expressing modern thought, analogous to the
most significant modern music.

61 ANON. "A Woman's Opinion of Whitman." Book-
Lover 2 (November-December), 410-11.
Review of Gould (1900.8). Whitman has
written of all types of love but the romantic. "Gods" and "Myself" provide "two of
the noblest lines in literature" dealing
with "supermundane love, or divine love
beyond the present life." Gilchrist's
life and attitudes toward Whitman and his
work are described through quotations.

62 LONDON, JACK. "Lincoln, the Man of the
People. New Volume of Verse by Edwin
Markham." San Francisco Examiner Sunday
Magazine (10 November), 12:1-2.
Quoted in 1902.28.
Review of Markham's Lincoln and Other
Poems. Incidental: "Not forgetting Walt
Whitman's 'O Captain, My Captain,' wet with
tears and halting with half-sobs, it is not
too much to state that in Mr. Markham's
'Lincoln' the last word has been said."

63 MILLARD, BAILEY. "Edwin Markham." San Fran-
cisco Examiner Sunday Magazine (10 Novem-
ber), 12:5-6.
Incidental: Markham's tribute to
Lincoln is finer than Whitman's "superb"
"Captain."

64 ANON. "Primal Sanities." Academy 61 (30
November), 511-12.
Review of Holmes (1902.14). Critics
should be concerned with Whitman as a
spiritual force, not as to whether his
works are poems. Holmes perceives Whitman's
Hegelianism and "gusto of life." Whitman
is a single-minded rather than myriad-
minded man. He often finds "large and
classical utterance for essential human
moods."

65 CROSBY, ERNEST. "A Visit to John Burroughs."
Comrade 1 (December), 54-55.
Describes some of Burroughs's recollections of Whitman in Washington, their first
meeting, his expression in conversation of
his "strong views of the evil way in which
things were going," though "he kept all

1901

such moods out of his books." He was "a new type of man," "the typical democrat of the future, but as yet he hardly seems to have had a second." He thought once of building a home near Burroughs's Riverby. Burroughs claims that Whitman "would have been enthusiastic" for strikers.

66 DIACK, WILLIAM. "Edward Carpenter: The Walt Whitman of England." *Westminster Review* 156 (December), 655-63.
      Whitman stamped his individuality on his age, producing such disciples as Carpenter, whom some like Tolstoy regard as the greater of the two. Incidental comparisons of Carpenter with Whitman, whose music Carpenter surpasses in sweetness, although he cannot reach "the lofty grandeur" of "Lilacs" or "the breadth and vigour and boundless freedom" of "Open Road." As a modern teacher, Carpenter stands a little below Whitman, who is "a perennial fount of life."

67 DREISER, THEODORE. "A True Patriarch. A Study from Life." *McClure's Magazine* 18 (December), 136.
      The title character of this story is described: "One might take him to be the genial Walt Whitman, of whom he is the living counterpart."

68 W. "Walt Whitman--A Sketch." *Universal Brotherhood Path* 16 (December), 502-11.
      As a universalist, Whitman perceived the spirit of nature throughout the universe. His concern was to express his thought, not to make it poetic. His style, "full of the music of nature," needed no meter or rhyme. His descriptions are graphic. He does not wholly ignore sentimental love but emphasizes "the broader less personal side." His poetry suggests a new literature and will live to inspire the character. One must read him for oneself. His prophecies in "Redwood" and "Exposition" (quoted) are fulfilled by the [Theosophical] Society in Point Loma, California.

1902

BOOKS

1 ABERNETHY, JULIAN W. *American Literature*. New York: Maynard, Merrill, & Co. "Walt Whitman," pp. 426-34.
      Whitman's rhythms are not really those of nature. His strengths include "his intense Americanism," "his all-embracing faith in the future of democracy," "his contention for individualism," and his notion of comradeship uniting all classes. The war produced "his nearest approaches to poetic feeling and expression of the highest order," but his ideas are few and his sentences often unconnected. He lacks humor and emphasizes realism at the expense of ideality. "His ignorance and uncouthness must not be mistaken for primordial simplicity and hirsute strength." Yet he cannot be ignored. Reading list.

2 BORN, HELENA. *Whitman's Ideal Democracy and Other Writings*. Edited by Helen Tufts. Boston, Mass.: Everett Press, pp. xi-xxxvi, 3-19, 20-30, 31-54, 55-61, 63, 73. Includes reprints of 1899.71; 1896.31; 1896.38; 1896.41; 1895.56.
      Incidental comparisons of Thoreau to Whitman in "Thoreau's Joy in Nature." Editor's biographical sketch of Born describes Whitman's strong impact on Born.

3 BOTTA, ANNE C. LYNCH. *Handbook of Universal Literature*. 2d rev. ed. New York and Boston: Houghton Mifflin Co., p. 523. Revision of 1899.1.
      Discussion of Whitman is expanded. He was the poet of democracy, producing little verse but rather "an amorphous hybrid medium" which forcibly expressed his individualism, a rebellion provoked by "the insipid 'Correctness'" of the Knickerbocker School poets, whom Whitman will long outlive as a power.

4 BUCKE, RICHARD MAURICE, ed. *Calamus*. In *The Complete Writings of Walt Whitman*. Vol. 8. New York and London: G. P. Putnam's Sons. Reprint of 1897.2.

5 BURROUGHS, JOHN. Biographical introduction to *The Poems of Walt Whitman (Leaves of Grass)*. New York: Thomas Y. Crowell Co., pp. ix-xvii. Reprint of 1897.3.

6 _____. *Literary Values and Other Papers*. Boston and New York: Houghton Mifflin Co., pp. 4, 24, 27, 66-67, 75, 78, 99, 110, 117-18, 119, 129, 132, 155, 181, 183-85, 204, 205-6, 213-14, 223, 227.
      Comments on Whitman's imaginative use of words, his self-effacing and unadorned style, "the processional, panoramic style that gives the sense of mass and multitude." Whitman may do things that would be jarring in a more refined poet, but they are meant to challenge, not to shock. Bad taste appears in Whitman when he fails to follow his own ideal. He attains the beauty of rocks, trees, and mountains, not flowers. He should be measured by his own standards, following life, not form or beauty. His unshaken faith makes him optimistic, while other great contemporary writers are disturbed. Whitman indicates the next phase of dealing with nature and science in literature. He is the most suggestive of our poets through blending realism and mysticism. One composer says that Whitman stimulates him more than Tennyson does. He strikes the chord of death better than Tennyson.

7 CARPENTER, EDWARD. Ioläus: An Anthology of
   Friendship. London: Swan Sonnenschein &
   Co.; Boston: Charles E. Goodspeed, pp. 177-
   81.
   Reprinted: 1917.3.
       Headnote to extract from Vistas and
   three "Calamus" poems: the most intimate
   part of Whitman's message is the love of
   comrades, largely ignored since the Greek
   age but potentially part of the new era
   Whitman seeks to inaugurate "by his great
   power, originality and initiative, as well
   as by his deep insight and wide vision."

8 CHESTERTON, G. K. Twelve Types. London:
   Arthur L. Humphreys, pp. 115, 117, 122,
   143.
       Incidental comparisons of Whitman to
   Stevenson and Tolstoy. "Whitman returns
   to nature by seeing how much he can accept,
   Tolstoy by seeing how much he can reject."
   Like others, Whitman had the "faculty of
   teaching the average men as their equal,"
   without condescension.

9 DARROW, CLARENCE S. A Persian Pearl and Other
   Essays. Chicago: C. L. Ricketts. "Walt
   Whitman," pp. 43-74.
   Reprint of 1899.6.

10 HALSEY, FRANCIS WHITING, ed. Authors of Our
   Day in Their Homes: Personal Descriptions
   and Interviews. New York: James Pott &
   Co., pp. 93-94.
   See also 1902.27.
       Interview with Laurence Hutton includes
   description of his cast of Whitman's hand
   and his inscribed portrait of Whitman.

11 HARNED, THOMAS B., ed. Letters Written by
   Walt Whitman to His Mother from 1866 to
   1872. New York and London: G. P. Putnam's
   Sons, 132 pp.
   Reprinted: 1902.12.
       Prefatory note describes Whitman's
   character as revealed in these letters.
   This volume includes reprints of 1895.80,
   1896.22, and 1899.54, and a new essay,
   "Walt Whitman and Oratory," presenting
   Whitman's comments on oratory and suggesting
   their application to his writing.

12 HARNED, THOMAS B. "Letters Written by Walt
   Whitman to His Mother"; "Walt Whitman and
   Oratory"; "Walt Whitman and Physique";
   "Walt Whitman and His Second Boston Pub-
   lishers." In The Complete Writings of Walt
   Whitman, edited by Richard Maurice Bucke,
   Thomas B. Harned, and Horace L. Traubel.
   Vol. 8. New York and London: G. P.
   Putnam's Sons.
   Reprint of 1902.11.

13 HARNED, THOMAS B., and TRAUBEL, HORACE L.
   Introduction to The Complete Writings of
   Walt Whitman, edited by Richard Maurice
   Bucke, Thomas B. Harned, and Horace L.
   Traubel. Vol. 1. New York and London:

G. P. Putnam's Sons, pp. xiii-xcvi.
Extract reprinted: 1902.55.
    Primarily biographical. Whitman gained
his education mostly from life itself, with
great knowledge of men. Quotations from
Burroughs (1871.1), to which Whitman contributed much advice and revision, as he
did to Bucke (1883.3). Whitman's error in
dating his New Orleans trip is corrected.
Whitman was not indolent but preferred the
human spirit to money-making. Leaves is a
picture of America in the nineteenth century, its substance Whitman himself; each
reader must become its author. Whitman is
inclusive, not limited. His mystical qualities and humanistic philosophy are described. Recollections of a person who
knew Whitman in the early 1850s are quoted.
The war offered reaffirmation of his earlier
prophecy and thus served to complete
Leaves. Whitman appeals not to the brain
or the literary imagination but to emotion.
His admirers are often radical. His personality and life in Camden, carnival-like
funeral, confidence that he would be heard
are described.

14 HOLMES, EDMOND. Walt Whitman's Poetry: A
   Study and a Selection. London and New
   York: John Lane, 132 pp. "Walt Whitman's
   Poetry," pp. 1-76.
       Whitman is emotional, self-conscious,
   optimistic, and American. Explanation of
   his democratic purpose, messages of emancipation of self and importance of love,
   flawed materialist emphasis (particularly
   regarding women), equating of good and evil.
   His soul is aware of nature's beauty but he
   lacks the patience and self-forgetfulness
   of the true artist. His anatomical descriptions have a theoretical, not an emotional
   purpose. His affirmation of death is inconsistent and unintelligible to his desired
   audience. He is the poet of the ideal in
   spite of himself, and he recognizes injus-
   tice and misery. Poems on death and the
   sea reveal his questionings but do not
   reveal reverence or humility. He is "the
   poet of democratic equality,--and therefore
   of chaos," failing to lead to spiritual
   perfection through upward growth.

15 JAMES, WILLIAM. The Varieties of Religious
   Experience. New York: Longmans, Green, &
   Co., pp. 84-87, 395-96, 506.
   Reprinted in part: Miller; Murphy.
       Whitman is "the supreme contemporary
   example of the inability to feel evil."
   Through using the first person, Whitman expresses expansive sentiments for all men.
   He restores natural religion but is not a
   true pagan, having a conscious pride in
   his freedom and "a touch of bravado." He
   has a "vague expansive impulse" in the
   faith-state.

16 LAWTON, WILLIAM CRANSTON. Introduction to the
   Study of American Literature. New York and

1902

Chicago: Globe School Book Co., pp. 249-51, 343-44, 349, 352.

Brief estimate focusing on Emerson's strange but consistent appreciation of Whitman. Whitman's later work, especially his prose, "often expresses in inspiring fashion the exultant vigor, the generous humanity, of our national life." But he appeals neither to the masses nor to the critical few because of his formlessness and violation of good manners.

*17 LEWIS, E. C. My Book Record and Guide. Boston: Mutual Book Co., p. 156. Reported in Willard.

Leaves is listed among sixty poetry and drama books worth reading.

18 LIDDELL, MARK H. An Introduction to the Scientific Study of English Poetry. New York: Doubleday, Page & Co., pp. 95-96, 155-59, 161, 165.

Two brief passages from "Cradle," examined as typical of Whitman's poems which are essentially poetic, display rhythm through their "arrangement of thought-moments punctuated into definite sequences by emotional pulses" rather than metrical ones.

19 LLOYD, J. WILLIAM. The Natural Man: A Romance of the Golden Age. Newark: Benedict Prieth, pp. 5, 97-98.

A character cites qualities of Whitman, Emerson, and Thoreau experienced as part of the pantheistic attitude toward life; those men felt their continuity with the universe. One can feel Whitman's infinite comradeship." "Myself" 39 is quoted as epigraph.

20 LODGE, GEORGE CABOT. Poems (1899-1902). New York: Cameron, Blake & Co. "To W. W.," p. 1.

Prologue poem in free verse ("I toss upon Thy grave"), with echoes of Whitman's verse, suggesting that the book is a tribute for Whitman.

21 MacCRACKEN, HENRY M., ed. The University Encyclopedia of Twentieth Century Knowledge. Vol. 10. New York: P. F. Collier & Son, pp. 7071-73.

Sketch of Whitman's life and motivations. He was not content with mere spectatorship but shouldered the burden of his fellows and grappled with life's sternest realities. His immortality is assured by his early neglect, European recognition, gradual appreciation, and distinct style, whatever its dangers. His chants "have a peculiar, wild, stirring charm," "apt to make regular verses seem tame and insipid." Whitman sang men as men with a bolder sweep of subject and treatment than Wordsworth. He is an idealist, "a prince of impressionists in literature," to be appreciated in the same spirit he shows toward man and nature.

22 MAUDE, AYLMER. Tolstoy and His Problems. London: Grant Richards. "Talks with Tolstoy," p. 192.

Tolstoy found Whitman's chief defect was "that with all his enthusiasm, he yet lacks a clear philosophy of life. On some vital issues he speaks as if with authority, yet stands at the parting of two ways and does not show us which way to go."

23 ROSS, PETER. A History of Long Island. New York and Chicago: Lewis Publishing Co., pp. 424, 425; quotation from Whitman as epigraph, p. iii.

Brief biographical sketch of Whitman, hardly a success as editor or businessman. Brooklyn's central attraction for him was the ferry; his heart was more in Manhattan. Yet he wrote much of Leaves on Long Island, though later he was only a visitor on the island of his birth.

24 SELWYN, GEORGE [Walt Whitman]. "Walt Whitman in Camden." In Authors at Home: Personal and Biographical Sketches of Well-Known American Writers, edited by J. L. and J. B. Gilder. New York: A. Wessels Co., pp. 335-42. Revision of 1888.6.

Changes merely acknowledge the fact of Whitman's death.

25 TRIGGS, OSCAR LOVELL. Bibliography in The Complete Writings of Walt Whitman, edited by Richard Maurice Bucke, Thomas B. Harned, and Horace L. Traubel. Vol. 10. New York and London: G. P. Putnam's Sons, pp. 139-233. (Revised from 1898.17.)

Sections devoted to descriptive bibliography of Whitman's writings; biographical and critical items (including items with incidental discussion); poems (listing of alternative titles).

26 _____. "The Growth of 'Leaves of Grass.'" In The Complete Writings of Walt Whitman, edited by Richard Maurice Bucke, Thomas B. Harned, and Horace L. Traubel. Vol. 10. New York and London: G. P. Putnam's Sons, pp. 101-34. Revision of 1897.127.

Besides minor additions or deletions of quotations, a final section is added on "Method of Composition," praising Whitman's careful mechanics, typographical correctness, selection of titles. Notes for some poems and different versions of "Grand is the Seen" and "Come, said my Soul" are examined. Facsimiles are included.

27 WHITELOCK, WILLIAM WALLACE. "Edwin Markham." In Authors of Our Day in Their Homes: Personal Descriptions and Interviews, edited by Francis Whiting Halsey (New York: James Pott & Co.), pp. 77-78.

Quotes Markham: Whitman "formulated many great truths," but should not be overpraised "as the greatest man of the Christian era" and America's prophet. Despite occasional puerilities, he sometimes thrills.

PERIODICALS

28 ABBOTT, LEONARD D. "Edwin Markham: Laureate of Labor." Comrade 1 (January), 74-75.
London (1901.62) is quoted comparing Markham and Whitman. Markham says that Whitman has been a forerunner of the new democratic art.

29 COMPENDIUM. "Recent Study and Criticism of Whitman. XLIII." Conservator 12 (January), 170-71.

30 ANON. "An English Poet's View of Walt Whitman." Dial 32 (16 January), 54-55.
Brief review of Holmes (1902.14), who admires Whitman judiciously, emphasizing his artistic dualism. His selections give only Whitman's best, e.g., the great poems "Lilacs," "Cradle," and "Passage."

31 [HIGGINSON, T. W.] Review of Holmes (1902.14). Nation 74 (23 January), 75.
Brief review praising Holmes's choice of selections and his criticism.

32 CARPENTER, EDWARD. "Walt Whitman's Children." Reformer 6 (February), 87-93.
Revised: 1906.5.
Whitman's sexual statements in Leaves need not be taken literally, but apparently he did have affairs with women, and of more than casual duration. He was later equally attracted to men and women, a possible indication of "a higher development of humanity" or just "a personal peculiarity." The evidence seems contradictory, however, though we may read some poems like "Once I Pass'd" as actual experiences.

33 T[RAUBEL, HORACE]. "'The Punishment of Pride.'" Conservator 12 (February), 189.
Reprints Whitman's early poem from New World, which Charles Roe recalled Whitman reciting. (See 1899.36.)

34 TROWBRIDGE, JOHN TOWNSEND. "Reminiscences of Walt Whitman." Atlantic Monthly 89 (February), 163-75.
Revised: 1903.15.
Recalls his impressions of Leaves in 1855, his first acquaintance with Whitman in Boston, 1860. Whitman told him then that he was first struck by Emerson in 1854. Conversations with Whitman and O'Connor are recorded, including Whitman's reading of his war pieces to Trowbridge, who found them inferior to the greatly moving passages in the earlier Leaves because more refined. Emerson's and Lowell's reactions to Whitman are described. Whitman's prose, like his poetry, is uneven, but generally "he produces the effect of an art beyond art."

*35 ANON. Mention. Concert Goer (15 February).
Quoted in Willard.
"New York's existence has never been seriously disturbed by enthusiastic devotion to her greatest poet."

36 T[RAUBEL, HORACE]. "Walt Whitman's Poetry: A Study and a Selection." Conservator 13 (March), 12.
Review of Holmes (1902.14), criticizing his assumptions that Whitman has "doctrines" and lacks reverence and that he endorsed America without reservation. His democracy is yet to appear. Holmes recognizes no order or unity in Leaves.

37 HUBBARD, ELBERT. "Walt Whitman and John Burroughs." Cosmopolitan 33 (May), 110-11.
Anecdote of Whitman being robbed of money Doyle had given him, while Whitman was rooming with Burroughs, and Doyle and Bucke lived in the garret. Doyle and Burroughs are described at present. (See 1917.58 for the inaccuracies in this account.)

*38 LUFTIG, P. [Peter Airey]. "The Great City (not Whitman--but the reality)." Sydney Bulletin (17 May).
Quoted in Jones.
Parody based on "Broad-Axe."

39 COMPENDIUM. "Recent Study and Criticism of Whitman. XLIV." Conservator 13 (June), 59-60.

40 McILWRAITH, JEAN N. "A Dialogue in Hades. Omar Khayyám and Walt Whitman." Atlantic Monthly 89 (June), 808-12.
Reprinted: Saunders.
Comic dialogue between the established poet and the newcomer: Omar has trouble understanding Whitman, who shows that many of his lines echo the older poet's verses and themes. Whitman is perhaps provincial, with contradictions, but his poetry represents joy and confidence and not just in the present life as Omar's does.

41 PLATT, ISAAC HULL. "The Silence of Walt Whitman." Conservator 13 (June), 56-57.
Whitman "conveys a meaning even by what he refrains from saying," with emotion deeper than the apparent meaning of his words.

42 ANON. "Walt Whitman as a Conservative." New York Times Saturday Review (7 June), 381.
Account of Fellowship meeting, quoting Eldridge's letter recalling conversations with Whitman and the O'Connors in Washington and describing Whitman's evolutionary attitude toward reforms and disapproval of some radical movements.

43 ABBOTT, LEONARD D. "J. William Lloyd: Brother of Carpenter and Thoreau." Comrade 1 (July), 224-25.

Lloyd is a brother of Whitman and has learned from him and inherited his breadth.

44 COMPENDIUM. "Recent Study and Criticism of Whitman. XLV." Conservator 13 (July), 75.
Includes comments by L. M. Powers in Universalist Leader, from City and State (Philadelphia) and Torch of Reason (Silverton, Oregon).

45 HALSEY, FRANCIS W. "Walt Whitman and the Elemental in Books." Conservator 13 (July), 71-72.
Whitman belongs among the writers who forever deal with elemental and eternal things. Halsey chiefly discusses other immortal writers.

46 HUBBARD, ELBERT. "Corot." Little Journeys to the Homes of Eminent Artists 11 (July), 4-5.
Whitman and Corot are compared in their war services, unpretentiousness, attitude toward life. The world remains undecided whether Whitman was "simply a coarse and careless writer" or one too subtle and penetrating for most readers.

47 LEIGHTON, WALTER. "Whitman's Note of Democracy." Arena 28 (July), 61-65.
Whitman has absorbed America's landscape and humanity. He was the "foe of artificiality" and disdainful of political and social demands.

48 TRAUBEL, HORACE. "Walt Whitman as Both Radical and Conservative." New York Times Saturday Review (12 July), 470.
Response to 1902.42, recording his own understanding of Whitman's beliefs. Whitman "was not conservative because he was not radical, but because he was radical," not wishing to be associated with any particular movement but seeking to accept all.

49 SMITH, GEORGE J. "A Harvard View of Whitman." Conservator 13 (August), 85-87.
Wendell (1900.18) is inaccurate about Whitman's growth and employment and misunderstands his democratic ideal as celebration of the average rather than as equality of possibility. Concluded 1902.51.

50 T[RAUBEL, HORACE]. "Whitman's Ideal Democracy." Conservator 13 (August), 93.
Review of Born (1902.2), discussing her character; no Whitman reference.

51 SMITH, GEORGE J. "A Harvard View of Whitman." Conservator 13 (September), 102-4.
Concludes 1902.49, denying Wendell's claims that Whitman records without evaluating and that his poetry is entirely descriptive.

52 ANON. "'Walt Whitman's Children.'" Book-Lover 3 (September-October), 374-75.
Précis with quotation of 1902.32.

53 ANON. "The Matter with 'Walt.'" New York Tribune (7 September), Illustrated Supplement, 13:1-2.
Humorous account of a conversation among young men from various colleges regarding Whitman's merits. They chide his egotism and lack of form and note the contrast between Emerson, conventional and well-bred in his writing and life, and the impression Whitman's writing gives of himself.

54 [KENT, CHARLES A.] "Summer Pilgrimage to the Home of 'the Good Gray Poet.'" Chicago Sunday Record-Herald (28 September). Illustrated.
Chiefly biographical. Whitman, more prophet than poet, is contrasted with Lowell. He gave "the first real expression of the strong, self-conscious, aggressive young manhood of our cities and towns."

55 BUCKE, R. M., HARNED, THOMAS B., and TRAUBEL, HORACE. "Leaves from Whitman's Later Life." Critic 41 (October), 319-27.
Extract reprinted from 1902.13.
(Bucke, as one of the Putnam Edition editors, is listed as coauthor, but 1902.13 mentions that his death prevented his having a share in writing the introduction.)

56 DARROW, CLARENCE. "Walt Whitman." Goose-Quill 2 (October), 7-20.
Reprint of 1899.6.

57 PLATT, ISAAC HULL. "Wendell on Whitman: Criticism or Libel?" Conservator 13 (October), 118-19.
Correction of Wendell's account (1900.18) of Whitman's early life, noting his worthy associates. Wendell fails as a historian.

58 ABBOTT, LEONARD. "The Democracy of Whitman and the Democracy of Socialism." Conservator 13 (November), 136-37.
Whitman is the most democratic of men but fails to appreciate the need for socialism. He could emancipate himself as a wage-slave cannot.

59 DYER, LOUVILLE H. "Walt Whitman." Wilshire's Magazine, no. 52 (November), 76-83.
Extended appreciation: Whitman's writing represents "perfect sanity"; Leaves is "the flowering of mature manhood," an influence for life rather than a work of art. Whitman is compared to Tolstoy in work and life.

60 T[RAUBEL, HORACE]. "The Poet of the Wider Selfhood." Conservator 13 (November), 140.
Review of Maynard (1903.9), a good compendium which "creates no prejudice for or against Whitman."

61 HUNT, THEODORE W. "A Visit to 'Walt' Whitman." Book-Lover 3 (November-December), 423.

Account of visit to Whitman shortly
before his death. Whitman indicated amazement and pain at the inability of some to
understand his thought, though he was grateful to those who spoke in his favor (including Lowell). Despite Whitman's emphasis,
his prose rather than his poetry represents
his best work, offering astute remarks on
books and authors.

62 ANON. "The Good Grey Poet." Boston Evening
Transcript (26 November), 9:3-5.
Favorable review of Putnam edition
(1902.13). Extracts show Whitman as a
hard worker, an intelligent critic of
literature and America. His dominating
weakness was lack of humor, although humor
would have been destructive of his purpose.

63 ANON. "American Classics. New Editions for
the Holidays--and After." New York Tribune
(4 December), 10:3.
The final paragraph reviews the first
five volumes of the Putnam edition (1902.
13), handsome, although Traubel's opinion
of Whitman's immortality, voiced in the
introduction, is far from generally accepted
and may never be so. Concluded 1902.64.

64 ANON. "Poe and Whitman. The Putnam Editions
of Their Works Completed." New York
Tribune (17 December), 10:1.
Briefly concludes 1902.63 upon the
receipt of Whitman's final five volumes.

65 ANON. Review of Putnam edition (1902.13).
Outlook 72 (20 December), 948.
This edition adequately presents for
the first time the work of "one of the most
original and widely discussed American
writers." The introduction should have
included a more judicial appraisal. "An
interpreter of the brawniest democratic
ideas," "a lover of life in its completeness" without distinctions, Whitman has
appealed to intellectuals more than to
those he sought to interpret. He needs to
be represented only by his work of genius,
rather than by work that reveals merely
his temperament and point of view.

1903

BOOKS

1 BURTON, RICHARD. Literary Leaders of America.
New York: Chautauqua Press. "Whitman,"
pp. 264-95.
Revised: 1904.5.
Whitman is coming to be recognized as
"a force of real significance in our
national development, and the study of our
democratic ideals." He was "a kind of
inspired reporter and tramp, whose notebook
jottings turned out to be poems." His life
and democratic minglings are summarized.
His purpose was to depict fully an indiviual

within the American environment, a task
involving "an intense egoism,--not egotism."
Despite failures in taste and selectivity,
Whitman is a great poet, with "vision and
voice." He "approaches nearest to artistic
form," avoiding "prosy banalities," in such
poems as "Cradle" and "Lilacs" (here reprinted, ranking with Lowell's "Commemoration Ode" as an American threnody). Leaves
is best approached through a selected edition; his prose also merits attention.

2 CARPENTER, GEORGE RICE. John Greenleaf
Whittier. Boston and New York: Houghton
Mifflin Co., p. 262.
"Captain" is "possibly the greatest" of
"the poetry of any permanent value produced
by the war," "in that it is the most direct
and spontaneous translation of the emotion
of a people into beautiful imagery."

3 CHADWICK, JOHN WHITE. "Walter Whitman." In
Chambers's Cyclopaedia of English Literature,
edited by Robert Chambers. New edition by
David Patrick. London and Edinburgh:
W. & R. Chambers, pp. 803-8. Photograph by
Norman.
Reprinted: 1938.4.
Biographical sketch. "His theories of
versification seem afterthoughts," though
his form "was the inevitable expression of
his character" and emphasizes harmony
rather than melody, at its best suggesting
great musical compositions. He creates
vivid phrases but also bad ones (especially
in "Myself" 6), with some flaws in diction
and sound. His catalogues, often considered
a fault, contribute to his power and "sense
of elevation and expansion." Though sincere, his treatment of sex is flawed, and
"Calamus" reveals in Whitman "an invirile
strain." He seems to teach moral indifference but is valuable for his "dauntless
optimism," sympathy, and emphasis on the
individual and democracy. Extracts and a
bibliographical paragraph are presented.

4 CHESTERTON, G. K. Robert Browning. London:
Macmillan Co., pp. 21, 43, 49, 114, 165,
184.
Incidental favorable references to
Whitman, particularly as exemplifying the
modern tendency toward the simple and primeval. One or two of his poems are unsurpassed in expressing "the pure love of
humanity." Browning is "the only optimistic
philosopher except Whitman."

5 HIGGINSON, THOMAS WENTWORTH, and BOYNTON,
HENRY WALCOTT. A Reader's History of
American Literature. Boston, New York, and
Chicago: Houghton, Mifflin & Co., pp. 220-
23, 227-34, 264, 308, 315.
Extracts reprinted: 1903.19; 1903.20.
The Whitman and Lanier sections are
revisions of 1899.8. Whitman is hardly a
poet in the strict sense. Several poems
record the excitement he found in the New

1903

York metropolis, though "he was, indeed, a
person and a poet singularly detached from
place." Brief bibliography and biography
are included.

6 JAY, HARRIETT. Robert Buchanan: Some Account
of His Life, His Life's Work and His Literary Friendships. London: T. Fisher
Urwin, pp. 113, 227, 271, 272, 297-305.
    Buchanan recalls his acquaintance with
Browning. When Buchanan brought up the
subject of Whitman, Browning expressed his
"loathing and contempt," "chiefly on moral
grounds." He did not seem to have studied
Whitman at all, condemning him "simply on
the score of some miserable and possibly
garbled quotation carried to him at second
hand." Buchanan's other relations with
Whitman are traced.

7 LAW, JAMES D. Here and There in Two Hemi-
spheres. 1st ser. Lancaster, Pa.: Home
Publishing Co. "Walt Whitman," pp. 441-42.
    Reminiscence from his time of residence
in Camden, whose citizens loved Whitman,
though most had not read him. Law recalls
his visit to Whitman in 1890, Whitman's
deafness, strong language, reading.

8 MABIE, HAMILTON WRIGHT. Backgrounds of Literature. New York: Outlook Co.; New York
and London: Macmillan & Co. "America in
Whitman's Poetry," pp. 194-243. Illustrated.
Reprint of 1903.42.

9 MAYNARD, MILA TUPPER. Walt Whitman: The Poet
of the Wider Selfhood. Chicago: Charles
H. Kerr & Co., 145 pp. No index.
    1. "A Glimpse of the Man": Sketch of
Whitman's life and character, with comments
on studies by Burroughs (1896.2) and
Symonds (1893.9).
    2. "The Copious Personal Self":
Whitman's stress on man's divinity fulfills
Emerson's idea of self-reliance.
    3. "The Cosmic Self": Whitman's
ecstatic use of science and evolution.
    4. "The Eternal Self": Death is "the
guarantee of eternal meaning."
    5. "'Even These Least'": Whitman's
identification with sinners does not indicate depravity or inability to distinguish
good from evil; rather, he believes in
perfectibility.
    6. "The Larger Woman": Whitman favors
in woman not feminine but "great human
qualities," emphasizing motherhood, not
"romantic sentiment."
    7. "The Larger Man": Whitman empha-
sizes the physical man before honoring the
intellectual or spiritual man, rejecting
refinement.
    8. "Youth, Maturity, Age": Whitman
praises these ages for spontaneity, aspiration, and sublimity respectively.
    9. "Unity with Nature": Whitman may
be best when describing and interpreting
nature, but he keeps the human soul central.

"Lilacs" demands hard study to yield ever
richer returns, like all deeply wrought
art.
    10. "Democracy": It is to be found
in the future, beyond governments.
    11. "America": His ideas of America,
tested in the war, gained reality for his
later poetry. He united individuality and
social unity.
    12. "Comradeship": Whitman's love
poems are addressed "to anyone and everyone"
with a passionate, actual fervor.

10 MIMNERMUS [pseud.?]. "The Poets and Rationalism." In Agnostic Annual. London: C. A.
Watts & Co., p. 63.
    Incidental: Whitman is among the major
poets of Freethought, upon which his superb
egoism and emancipating influence are based.

11 PATTEE, FRED LEWIS. A History of American
Literature. Boston and New York: Silver,
Burdett & Co. "Walt Whitman," pp. 376-84.
    Whitman takes on every subject, produces
grand lines, startling realistic touches,
sweeping pictures as well as much that ex-
hausts the enthusiasm. His extreme democracy was new to Europe. His personality
must not be equated with his work, being
neither egotistic nor immoral. His truest
poetry is outside Leaves (Drum-Taps, the
Lincoln poems, "Man-of-War-Bird," "among
the treasures of American literature").
"Captain" is praised highly. Bibliography,
biographical sketch, reading list are included. (See 1896.10a in Addenda.)

12 ROSSETTI, WILLIAM MICHAEL. Rossetti Papers
1862 to 1870. New York: Charles Scribner's
Sons, passim per index.
    Extracts reprinted: Hindus.
    Whitman is discussed critically and the
backgrounds and reception of Rossetti's
selection (1868.2) and Gilchrist's article
(1870.4) are traced through extracts from
Rossetti's diary and various letters (mostly
to Rossetti) from Whitman, Gilchrist,
Burroughs, O'Connor, Horace Scudder, Thomas
Dixon, Hotten, Dowden, Symonds (who recalls
Tennyson's angry first response to Leaves),
W. J. Stillman (describing a visit to
Whitman in 1869), and Kenningale Cook.
Part of O'Connor's proposed "Introduction
to the London Edition" is printed. Rossetti
notes Conway's indication that Emerson
still admired Whitman and got Lincoln to
approve Whitman's hospital visits. He de-
scribes Professor Norton's comments on
Whitman during an 1869 visit.

13 SPRAGUE, LESLIE WILLIS. Syllabus of a Course
of Six Lectures on Social Messages of Some
Nineteenth Century Prophets. No. 219 (1903-
1904). Philadelphia: American Society for
the Extension of University Teaching.
"Lecture VI. Walt Whitman (1819-1892) and
the Hope of Democracy," pp. 19-22.
    Lecture outline: Whitman should be

studied in relation to the major movements
of his time rather than in relation to
merely external aspects of nineteenth-
century life. Notes on Whitman's ideas,
organization, themes. His flaws are part
of his experimentation. Topics for discussion; significant primary and secondary
readings.

14 STODDARD, RICHARD HENRY. Recollections Per-
sonal and Literary. Edited by Ripley
Hitchcock. New York: A. S. Barnes & Co.,
p. 266.
Recalls standing at the door of Pfaff's:
"I saw Walt Whitman and others inside, but
through diffidence or some other feeling,
I did not enter."

14a TRENT, WILLIAM P. A History of American
Literature, 1607-1865. New York: D.
Appleton & Co. "Walt Whitman," pp. 480-
96; also passim per index.
Whitman's transcendentalism was distinctive, being based on his absorption of
actual American life, which led to his
poetic independence. His sexual frankness,
though open to misconstruction, must have
shaken the hold of prudery. The popularity
of "Captain" makes one regret that Whitman
"did not oftener utter himself spontaneously," although it is less impressive than
"Man-of-War-Bird" and several extracts.
The modern attack on "Whitmanism as a
specially virulent form of modern decadence
seems somewhat beside the mark." His
"elemental force" is characteristic of
great Americans. Leaves contributed to the
recent increased interest in sport and
open-air life. Whitman reconciles his
poetry with modern science. His rhythm
has hypnotic effects. Such earlier defects
as his jargon disappear in his later work,
often purely descriptive poems which will
"most attract the normal reader." His
idealism transcends the description of him
as "a mere realist or naturalist." "America
has not enough genuine poets to be able to
reject Whitman," whatever his defects.

15 TROWBRIDGE, JOHN TOWNSEND. My Own Story:
with Recollections of Noted Persons. Boston
and New York: Houghton, Mifflin & Co.
"Walt Whitman--with Glimpses of Chase and
O'Connor," pp 360-401.
Revision of 1902.34.
Additions to the earlier article mostly
concern Secretary Salmon Chase and O'Connor.
Passages from Emerson and Whitman are compared. Burroughs and O'Connor are contrasted as champions of Whitman.

16 WILLIAMSON, GEORGE M[ILLAR]. Catalogue of A
Collection of Books Letters and Manuscripts
Written by Walt Whitman In the Library of
George M Williamson. Jamaica: Marion
Press; New York: Dodd Mead & Co.
Introductory note describes editions
and facsimiles. This catalogue is a de-
sciptive bibliography of Whitman's published work, with facsimiles of title pages,
manuscript poems and letters, other Whitman
items.

17 WOODBERRY, GEORGE EDWARD. America in Literature. New York: Harper & Bros., pp. 239-
43.
Whitman, an idealist, appeals because
of the "pure primitiveness" of his ideas
and his "boldness of outline." But he
distorts what Americans are, except in "a
few fine lyrics."

PERIODICALS

18 LLOYD, J. WM. "Written at Walt Whitman's
Grave." Conservator 13 (January), 165.
Free-verse poem wishing Whitman peace,
comparing him with Christ.

19 ANON. "Influence of the South." Boston
Evening Transcript (23 January), 10:3-5.
Account of Higginson's Lowell Institute
Lecture (published in 1903.5) the day
before, quoting his remarks on Whitman and
other non-Bostonian writers.

20 HIGGINSON, T. W. "Col. Higginson on Whitman."
New York Times Saturday Review (31 January),
73.
Extract from 1903.5.

21 BENTON, JOEL. "John Burroughs and Walt
Whitman." Wilshire's Magazine (February),
64-67.
Reprinted: 1903.41.
Recalls meeting Whitman in Washington
in 1868 and hearing his Lincoln lecture in
New York, at which Lowell noted Whitman's
aged appearance. Whitman, who had no
system, should not be used to support "all
the pitiable little philosophies afloat."
After reading Burroughs on Whitman, followed
by the Lincoln poems and other brief lyrics,
one will find new horizons.

22 DAVENPORT, WILLIAM E. "Identity of Whitman's
Work and Character." Conservator 13 (February), 181-84.
Leaves derives its truths straight
from Whitman's broad experience. He did
not need religious aids but attained religious force in his work and its mission,
applying his philosophy to his own life,
"a moral triumph."

23 KEMPE, EDWARD. "A Book and Its Writer.
III.--Walt Whitman's 'Drum-Taps,' and Notes
of the War." New Zealand Illustrated
(February), 377-84.
Reprinted: McLeod.
Whitman looked beyond the political and
social viewpoint to see the war as America's
heroic opportunity. His work used his own
identity as a microcosm, much like Thoreau's
writings. Whitman's character combines
"womanly tenderness" with "Yankee push and

shrewdness." His rhapsodies reveal a power
near madness. His war poems and prose,
though formless, effectively handle living
facts with a mastery inspired by intense
feeling, far different from "the false
realism of recent war literature."

24 S[PARGO], J[OHN]. Review of Maynard (1903.9).
   Comrade 2 (February), 116.
        This book is "altogether admirable,"
   especially for those who don't know Whitman,
   because Maynard loves Whitman and knows both
   what and how to read, like the friend who
   revealed the value of Leaves to Spargo, who
   had earlier regarded "'that Whitman jargon'"
   as a pose.

25 G[OULD?], E. P. "Milnes to Hawthorne about
   Whitman." Conservator 14 (March), 12.
        Prints comments from Lord Houghton's
   letter to Hawthorne praising Leaves for its
   vigorous vitality, though "destitute of
   art." Hawthorne's response is unknown.

26 PLATT, ISAAC HULL. "Whitman's Executors
   Defended." Conservator 14 (March), 6-7.
        Defends Whitman's executors from
   charges of the Philadelphia Ledger that
   they are "too worshipful to produce anything
   of critical value"; cites their significant
   papers.

27 ENDE, A. von. "Whitman's Following in Germany."
   Conservator 14 (April), 23-25.
        Describes Whitman's high esteem in
   modern Germany, his introduction there,
   various critics' viewpoints, his influence
   on contemporary poems and poets (symbolists,
   realists, Nietzscheans).

28 ANON. "Reviews of Unwritten Books. VII.
   Walt Whitman's 'Grandee Spain Succumbing.'"
   Monthly Review 11 (May), 151-57.
        Satirical mock-review of an imaginary
   annex to Leaves, quoting parody passages
   focusing on the Spanish-American War.

29 MUZZEY, DAVID SAVILLE. "The Ethical Message
   of Walt Whitman." Ethical Record 4 (May),
   147-51.
        Whitman's assertiveness is not egoism
   but an expression of his unselfish devotion
   to the mass of Americans. He is the best
   representative American poet, "the poet of
   Ethical Culture," a preacher first (as in
   "Thou Mother"). His significant terms are
   explained as related to his doctrines.

30 WILLIAMS, FRANCIS HOWARD. "Whitman." Conservator 14 (May), 40.
        Letter to Whitman Fellowship: It is
   no longer necessary to keep Whitman's name
   before the public because each year he
   looms larger in our literature. Williams
   learned from him "the nobility of individual manhood and the real meaning of immortality."

31 [HIGGINSON, T. W.] Review of Putnam edition.
   Nation 76 (14 May), 400-401.
        This edition surpasses all recent
   collections of any author's complete works,
   particularly because it appropriately includes the changes Whitman made in his
   writings, some for the sake of propriety.
   "This remarkable man" is generally allowed
   here to speak for himself, as he does with
   a becoming modesty too rarely visible in
   his work, which "atones for a multitude of
   sins."

*32 ANON. "Gum-Tree's Whitmaniac Chant after the
   Disclosures of Baker and Smith, of N.S.W.
   Technological Museum." Sydney Bulletin
   (16 May).
   Reprinted: Jones.
        Parody.

33 JAMES, WILLIAM. "Champion of the Individual."
   Boston Evening Transcript (25 May), 3:4.
   Reprinted: Cameron.
        Incidental mention in his address at
   Concord commemoration of Emerson's centenary: Emerson's "optimism had nothing in
   common with vague hurrahing for the universe
   with which Walt Whitman has made us familiar."

33a SMITH, GEORGE J. "Emerson and Whitman."
   Conservator 14 (June), 53-55.
   Reprinted: 1904.36.
        Whitman must have absorbed Emerson's
   gospel before publishing Leaves, but his
   faith in self-reliance and democracy is
   more passionate than Emerson's. His life
   and art carry out Emerson's theory, but
   Whitman was indebted to no one for "his
   power of vision, his fusion of thought with
   generous emotion," being American literature's most distinctive figure.

34 TRAUBEL, HORACE L. "Walt Whitman at Fifty
   Dollars a Volume, and How He Came to It."
   Era, n.s. 11 (June), 523-29. Illustrated.
        Describes Whitman in his old age:
   habits, interests, feelings.

*35 GREEN, H. M. "First Impressions of Walt
   Whitman." Hermes (31 July), 14-16.
   Reprinted: McLeod.
        Whitman's earnestness and love of
   humanity often redeem him from poor taste
   in form and content. He is capable of a
   sweet lyric like "Cradle," reminiscent of
   Shelley. Unfortunately he revolts from
   art as well as artificiality, descending
   into license. Along with much truth, he
   says much that is insignificant or "hyster-
   ically over-emphasized." He is "'another
   good man gone wrong.'"

36 BALL, M. V. "Whitman." Conservator 14 (August),
   89.
        Letter to Fellowship: Whitman has
   greatly influenced him and inspires us to
   be lovers of humanity.

37 KENNEDY, WILLIAM SLOANE. "Whitman." Conservator 14 (August), 88-89.
    Letter to Fellowship on his admiration
for both Whitman and Emerson, comparing
them.

38 REYNOLDS, STEPHEN M. "Walt Whitman the
Prophet-Poet of Democracy." Comrade 2
(August), 251.
    "Whitman's universal sympathy, his all
inclusive love, vast wisdom and great knowledge of men and things, gave him the
Prophet-spirit and made all he has ever
said for Democracy limitlessly interesting
to all lovers of mankind." Vistas and
poems like "Salut" express his notions of
democracy as "not fatalism," absolute
brotherhood, evolution to nearer perfection,
the significance of the individual, the
elevation of men and women "to the highest
planes of physical, mental and spiritual
happiness" through love, "the leveling
tendency upward of Democracy."

39 WOODWARD, F. L. "Walt Whitman: A Prophet of
the Coming Race." Theosophical Review 32
(August), 508-515.
    Whitman's message, embracing love,
democracy, and religion, agrees with theosophy, the Wisdom religion, filled with joy
and equanimity. He has been wrongly
accused of indecency, having immense influence for good. He represents the true
spirit in which to live and face death.

40 TRAUBEL, HORACE. "Walt Whitman's Respect for
the Body." Physical Culture 10 (September),
246-50.
    Whitman objected to formal medicine
and "contended for the whole man," opposing
asceticism, practicing moderation in exer-
cise and diet. Whitman's fight against
censorship and prudery is summarized.

41 BENTON, JOEL. "John Burroughs and Walt
Whitman." Book-Lover 4 (September-October),
375-76.
Reprint of 1903.21.

42 MABIE, HAMILTON W. "American Life in Whitman's
Poetry." Outlook 75 (5 September), 67-78.
Reprinted: 1903.8. Extract reprinted:
1903.44.
    Whitman may not reach "the heights of
spiritual vision" but he reveals "the most
inclusive human sympathy." He is primitive
as well as modern in "his resolute acceptance of the democratic order in all its
logical sequences." His defects include
egotism and lack of reticence, selection,
and self-criticism. His original contribution is the use of the America of active
life, which a greater poet may treat more
spiritually. In imagination he surpasses
the New England poets, though with much
"uninspired dullness." He reacted against
artifice, not art, for his effective
arrangements reveal artistry. He treats

the intimate relation between men and women
"as if it were a public function." His
tenderness is most notable in "his striking
and original treatment of death." His control of form was not equal to his material,
and his democratic equalitarianism failed
to include "the more highly developed types"
of humanity.

43 BAXTER, SYLVESTER. "Whitman and Emerson."
Conservator 14 (October), 120-21.
    Brief greeting to the Fellowship:
Whitman and Emerson are the only two great
poets in nineteenth-century America.

44 MABIE, HAMILTON W. "The Worth of Whitman."
Booklovers' Magazine [Appleton's Magazine]
2 (October), 442.
Extract reprinted from 1903.42.

45 RILEY, W. HARRISON. "Reminiscences of Karl
Marx." Comrade 3 (October), 5-6.
    Recalls visiting Marx and quoting lines
from Whitman with which Marx "was evidently
well pleased." Whitman, at Riley's one
meeting with him, asked him about Ruskin.
An editorial postscript by John Spargo
explains Riley's conversion to socialism
because of Leaves, which he first discovered
in Boston in 1857. Riley was "the means of
interesting Ruskin in Whitman." A letter
from Ruskin to Riley is quoted regarding
the "glorious things" in Whitman and asking
about him.

46 MATTHEWS, HORACE B. "Salut au Chauffeur
(Supposed to Have Been Written by Walt
Whitman.)." Life 42 (8 October), 339.
    Parody: a drive is described in
Whitmanesque style.

47 ANON. "Philosophy of Whitman." Boston Evening
Transcript (16 October), 10:7.
    Reports the Hon. George F. Williams's
paper for Boston Whitman Fellowship,
"Moralizing and Demoralizing Forces," based
on Whitman's philosophy ("the breadth and
democracy of his Americanism" and "the vast
horizons of his belief in man and of his
faith in the future") but focusing on contemporary economic, political conditions.

48 ANON. "English Appreciation of Walt Whitman."
Atlantic Monthly 92 (November), 714-16.
    The English respond most to Whitman's
depiction of America's newness, of which
Americans may be almost ashamed. His outdoor
feeling appeals "to men of an extremely
sensitive temperament." Most English readers
recognize his work as a great and permanent
contribution to literature in English.
Three passages from "Whispers," "Pioneers,"
and "Dirge," each "perfect in its way," are
quoted and described.

49 SKINNER, CHARLES M. "Walt Whitman as an
Editor." Atlantic Monthly 92 (November),
679-86.

1903

Account of Whitman's newspaper experience and editorials (quoted extensively,
revealing his reform-minded and democratic
ideas). This work may have confirmed
Whitman "in his frank, ungilded style, his
homely figures, his avoidance of buncombe
and fustian."

50 LACEY, MARGARET. "Hamilton Mabie on Whitman."
Conservator 14 (December), 153-54.
Criticizes Mabie's summary of Whitman's
philosophy (1903.42). Whitman's "striking
individuality of expression" did inaugurate
a new era in literature, but he shared much
with saints and seers of all time.

1904

BOOKS

1 ABERNETHY, JULIAN W., ed. Introduction,
selected critical opinions, and bibliography to Selected Poems of Walt Whitman, With
Introduction and Notes. New York: Charles
E. Merrill Co., pp. 3-12, 13-16, 17-18.
Biographical sketch notes various influences upon Whitman's poetry from life
and art; critical disapproval because of
his "rejection of all established canons of
verse and his audacious anticipation of the
gross realism of a later period." His
revolutionary poetic purpose, to express
American democracy for the people, has
failed, his most appreciative readers being
those of the highest culture. But beyond
his theory, his work has "the true colors
of eminent poetic achievement," being "most
simple and direct when his emotion dominates
his theory." His late poetry shows a subdued, more rhythmic expression. His prose
is also valuable. His faults must be
acknowledged, then his beauty and power
realized. He was not ignorant, but produced
his odd effects and seeming errors intentionally and indeed revised carefully. His
poems must be read several times, with concentration on the conception, not the expression. The notes to selected poems
(including "Cradle," "Lilacs," "Trumpeter,"
"Captain," "As a Strong Bird," "Ethiopia,"
"Patroling Barnegat") explain meaning, background, connection with other poets, earlier
versions, other opinions.

2 ALDEN, RAYMOND MACDONALD. English Verse:
Specimens Illustrating Its Principles and
History. New York: Henry Holt & Co.,
p. 431.
Reprint of 1901.4 with extracts from
Swinburne (1887.63) quoted in footnote.

3 BEERBOHM, MAX. The Poets' Corner. London:
William Heinemann.
Reprinted: 1937.27.
This book of cartoons of various poets
includes one of "Walt Whitman, inciting the
bird of freedom to soar."

4 BENSON, ARTHUR C. Rossetti. London:
Macmillan & Co., p. 173.

Quotes D. G. Rossetti's letter on
Whitman (1896.57): apparently he had not
yet read Whitman's poetry except in reviews.
However, he never actually changed his mind,
feeling that Whitman neglected the importance
of form for poetry.

5 BURTON, RICHARD. Literary Leaders of America:
A Class-Book on American Literature. New
York: Charles Scribner's Sons, pp. 264-95.
Reprint of 1903.1.
A brief bibliography is added to the
volume, pp. 317-18, with Burroughs's 1896
Study the only Whitman listing.

6 CARMAN, BLISS. The Friendship of Art. Boston:
L. C. Page & Co., pp. 9, 217, 223.
Incidental: Carman wishes Whitman's
prophecies "were heeded more generally, and
his sturdy, beautiful aspirations more
gladly accepted." While Whitman and Emerson
apparently provide simplicity after Pope,
the cadences of Leaves "are far more intricate than those of 'The Essay on Man.'"

7 CONWAY, MONCURE DANIEL. Autobiography: Mem-
ories and Experiences of Moncure Daniel
Conway. Boston and New York: Houghton,
Mifflin & Co. Vol. 1, pp. 215-19, 356;
vol. 2, p. 416.
Extract reprinted: Hubbell. Facsimile of
Whitman letter.
Recalls his first reading of Leaves on
Emerson's recommendation; prints his letter
to Emerson of 17 September 1855 reporting
his first visit to Whitman; records his
second visit in summer 1857. The comments
of Emerson, Carlyle, and Swinburne on
Whitman are noted.

8 DODGE, MARY MAPES. Poems and Verses. New
York: Century Co. "The Two Mysteries,"
pp. 7-9.
Reprint of 1876.69.

9 EMERSON, RALPH WALDO. Natural History of
Intellect and Other Papers. Boston and New
York: Houghton Mifflin Co. "Art and
Criticism," pp. 285-86.
Incidental reference in a lecture
delivered in Boston in 1859, here printed
for the first time: Whitman is the American
master of the language of the common people
"but has not got out of the Fire-Club and
gained the entrée of the sitting-rooms."

10 FINDLATER, JANE HELEN. Stones from a Glass
House. London: James Nisbet & Co. "Walt
Whitman," pp. 251-90.
General appreciative estimate, describing
Whitman's ideas, all stemming from his
belief in the spiritual nature of the universe. His method expresses his "rugged,
uncompromising nature," but "Adam" somewhat
defeated his purpose. He is modern in
portraying the wonder and beauty in the
ordinary. His poems about America and the
ideal democracy are least appealing to
English readers. His treatment of war is
unsurpassed.

11 KENNEDY, WILLIAM SLOANE, ed. Editor's preface
to Walt Whitman's Diary in Canada, With
Extracts from Other of His Diaries and
Literary Note-Books. Boston: Small,
Maynard & Co., pp. v-vi.
Reprinted: White.
Brief explanation of his obtaining the
notes transcribed in this volume from Bucke.

12 PLATT, ISAAC HULL. Walt Whitman. Beacon
Biographies of Eminent Americans. Boston:
Small, Maynard & Co., 147 pp., with chronology, pp. xi-xxii. No index.
The purpose of this biography is "to
bring into brief compass the salient features of the life," whether for those
curious about Whitman or those already
familiar with him, drawing from critics,
prior biographies, reminiscences. Platt
is largely concerned with defending Whitman
from various accusations. His failure to
win "instant applause" for Drum-Taps (unsurpassed in war literature) and "Lilacs"
(his masterpiece, here explicated) indicates
"how the public often forms its opinions of
literary work from hack critics." The last
chapter explains Whitman's purposes in
Leaves and corrects the common misconstruc-
tions regarding egotism, sex, comradeship,
composing process. Whitman does not preach
but presents an ethics of the spirit,
bristling with tangents, rather than "a
formulated system of philosophy." Bibliography of standard editions of Whitman and
important secondary sources.

13 POWYS, J. C. Syllabus of a Course of Six
Lectures on Representative American Writers.
No. 241 (1904-1905). Philadelphia: American Society for the Extension of University Teaching. "Lecture V. Walt Whitman,"
pp. 11-13.
Summarizes Whitman's pantheism and
cosmic emotion, which were anticipated by
Rabelais and Goethe. Whitman is superior
to Wordsworth and Browning, his value depending not on art but on vision and scope.
His democracy and sympathy are unique, his
philosophy Hegelian in its acceptance of
all. The underlying secret of the universe
for him is love.

14 ROBERTS, HARRY. Prefatory note to Leaves of
Grass (Selected). London: Anthony
Traherne & Co., pp. ix-xii.
Printing selections allows the deletion
of the "ridiculous or tiresome." Whitman's
form suits "his great blocks of thought."
He is to be valued for his optimism, treatment of sex and comradeship (though "an
even nobler conception" would have blended
the two), unique views of death and immortality, open-air spirit, belief in individuality.

15 SAINTSBURY, GEORGE. A History of Criticism
and Literary Taste in Europe. Vol. 3. New
York: Dodd, Mead, & Co.; Edinburgh and

London: William Blackwood & Sons.
"Whitman and the 'Democratic Ideal,'" p.
640.
Whitman's criticism is in some ways
more influential than Poe's, but his premise
is wrong, denying greatness to English literature because it is antidemocratic and
feudal. His temper is "wholesome and generous," however, with admirable expression,
as seen throughout his work.

16 SYMONS, ARTHUR. Studies in Prose and Verse.
London: J. M. Dent & Co. "What is Poetry?,"
p. 194.
Incidental: "The writer like Walt
Whitman, who seems to contain so much
material for poetry, which he can never
shape into anything tangibly perfect, is
not less disqualified from the name of poet
than a writer like Pope, who has the most
exquisite control over an unpoetical kind
of form which exactly fits an unpoetical
kind of substance."

17 TRAUBEL, HORACE, ed. Forward to An American
Primer by Walt Whitman. Boston: Small,
Maynard & Co., pp. v-ix.
Revision of 1904.30. Reprinted: White.
Expands headnote for 1904.30, adding
quotations from Whitman's conversation and
more commentary on the circumstances of the
writing and Whitman's ideas about language.
The manuscript is printed without the dele-
tions of 1904.30.

18 TRENT, WILLIAM P. A Brief History of American
Literature. New York: D. Appleton & Co.,
pp. 183-89; brief bibliography, p. 197.
Whitman gave voice to the aspirations
of the nation, yet was "sufficiently separated from the masses to form and promulgate
a philosophy of democracy and a religion of
blended egoism and socialism." "If the
outcry had been less great against his
entire work, he might possibly have seen
the futility, if not the impropriety, of
his offences against public taste," for
certain passages were at worst "only dis-
gustingly coarse." His postwar writings
were "less eccentric in form and substance,"
but his strengths as well as weaknesses
became less evident. Vistas and Specimen
reveal "a depth and range of thought and a
command of impassioned language rare in any
period of literature." His prose and such
strong poems as "Cradle" and "Passage" merit
him "a high place among American authors."

19 WALLACE, HENRY. Walt Whitman: Seer. A Brief
Study. London and Newcastle-on-Tyne:
Walter Scott Publishing Co., 55 pp.
Despite its form, Whitman's work is
poetic, the product of his personality. He
believes himself "the great characteristic
product of America," and his work "the indicative fingerprint of the new and glorious
future." His message is simplified Hegel;
comradeship is his solution to all problems.

1904

He views life as struggle and pilgrimage,
with comradeship not immediately achieved.
He assumes God's existence, is optimistic
about the universe as a whole. He celebrated life to the end. Extensive quotations from his poetry.

20 WELLS, CAROLYN, ed. A Parody Anthology. New
York: Blue Ribbon Books; New York: Charles
Scribner's Sons, pp. 219-28, 341-45, 363-
65.
Includes eight parodies of Whitman,
most reprinted in Saunders.

21 WENDELL, BARRETT, and GREENOUGH, CHESTER NOYES.
A History of Literature in America. New
York: Charles Scribner's Sons. "Walt
Whitman," pp. 371-78.
Revision of 1900.18.
This version is abridged and revised
for students, omitting "needless or debat-
able matter" and "expressions of opinion
obviously unsuitable for schools," according
to the preface. Chapter opens with a list
of references.

PERIODICALS

22 CARPENTER, EDWARD. "The Gods as Embodiments
of the Race-Memory." Hibbert Journal 2
(January), 261, 278.
Incidental reference to Bucke's sensation upon first meeting Whitman that he was
a god or more than human. Whitman is used
as an example of intimations of divinity
due to a kind of race-memory present in
our minds and occasionally coming to the
surface.

23 ENDE, AMELIA von. "Walt Whitman in Germany,
I." Conservator 14 (January), 167-69.
Whitman is a spiritual power to the
younger Germans, a corrective to militant
German nationalism. Early criticism is
described. Concluded 1904.27.

24 KENNEDY, WILLIAM SLOANE. "The germ idea of
Whitman's 'noiseless patient spider' poem."
Conservator 14 (January), 173.
Quotes a sentence from William
Rounseville Alger's The Doctrine of a Future
Life, "on which Whitman clearly built up
his extremely beautiful poem."

25 MILLER, FLORENCE HARDIMAN. "Some Unpublished
Letters of Walt Whitman's Written to a
Soldier Boy." Overland Monthly 43 (January), 61-63. Facsimile.
Describes and quotes from Whitman's
letters to an unidentified recipient; the
source for this collection is unacknowledged.
These letters reveal a loneliness which
suggests that Whitman's ideal of comradeship
was fading, perhaps having met with some
rebuff. Of major American poets, he "most
lived his poetic fancies."

26 SHARP, WILLIAM. "Walt Whitman." Harper's
New Monthly Magazine 108 (January), 192.
Reprinted: 1910.14.
Quatrain on Whitman's glorious approach
to death.

27 ENDE, AMELIA von. "Walt Whitman in Germany,
II." Conservator 14 (February), 183-85.
Concludes 1904.23. Notes tributes of
Schlaf and Federn. Whitman's democracy is
identical with the ideal society heralded
by Goethe and others. He represents healthy
religious ideals for German youth.

28 COLLINS, CHURTON. "The Poetry and Poets of
America.--III." North American Review 178
(March), 444-49, 453.
Reprinted: 1905.6.
Despite acclaim by various intelligent
readers, a natural reaction against conventionality and familiar forms, Whitman
has much of the charlatan in him, supposedly
original but using ideas from others. His
genius is evident on such rare occasions as
"Lilacs" and "Cradle," his proclamation of
an American future is moving, but he probably will not last since he "does not
respect himself" and "is not true to art."

29 TRAUBEL, HORACE. "A Fragment of Whitman
Manuscript." Artsman 1 (March), 195-97.
Whitman's manuscript "Agitations,
Dangers in America," presented in facsimile,
is preceded by Traubel's explanation quoting
Whitman's words on the passing of war eras.
A couple of days later he turned over to
Traubel these four small sheets of paper he
had just found, which are even more true
now than when they were written.

30 _____. "An American Primer." Atlantic Monthly
93 (April), 460-70.
Revised: 1904.17.
Headnote introduces Whitman's notes on
language as "a challenge rather than a
finished fight," not planned for publication
in their present state but intended first
as a lecture when he worked on them in the
1850s. While parts of his important message
here expressed found their way into his
poetry and prose, "the momentum gathered
and brought to bear upon the subject in the
manuscript now under view was nowhere else
repeated."

31 ANON. "Posthumous Whitman." New York Times
Saturday Review (2 April), 226.
"Primer" (1904.30) is certainly char-
acteristic of Whitman but of doubtful value.
His lack of form is due to laziness, a poor
artistic practice.

32 BARKER, ELSA. "To Walt Whitman." Walt Whitman
Fellowship Papers 10, no. 5 (May), 27-34.
Same as 1904.37.
Long ode of tribute in stanzas of ir-
regular rhyme and length.

33 KNAPP, ADELINE. "A Whitman Coincidence."
Critic 44 (May), 467-68.
Notes source for "Man-of-War-Bird" in
a description by Jules Michelet, suggesting
how the little-educated Whitman may have
gained much of his amazing knowledge of
nature.

34 MONAHAN, MICHAEL. "Some Remarks to the
Whitman Fellowship." Walt Whitman Fellowship Papers 10, no. 6 (May), 35-38.
Emphasizes the value of the spirit of
fellowship, which is a truer means of
emulating Whitman than merely dressing like
him.

35 SCOVEL, Colonel JAMES MATLACK. "Walt Whitman
As I Knew Him." National Magazine 20 (May),
165-69.
Extract reprinted: Whitman Supplement 1979.
Recalls his twenty-five-year acquaintance with Whitman: Whitman's character,
response to the attempted suppression,
refusal to write tribute poem for Garfield
under the pressure of money; various anecdotes, including dinners and drinks at his
house with Whitman; a Boston woman's offer
of love and aid.

36 SMITH, GEORGE J. "Emerson and Whitman." Walt
Whitman Fellowship Papers 10, no. 3 (May),
13-22.
Reprint of 1903.33.

37 BARKER, ELSA. "To Walt Whitman." Conservator
15 (June), 52-54.
Same as 1904.32.

38 T[RAUBEL, HORACE]. "Long and Short Editions
of Leaves of Grass." Conservator 15 (June),
60.
Defends the incorporation of "Old Age
Echoes" into the Putnam edition as Whitman's
probable wish. Before buying, know whether
your edition is complete, if the bookseller
claims so.

39 BURROWES, PETER E. "The Walt Whitman Fellowship." Comrade 3 (July), 215.
Account of New York birthday commemoration, "full of promise for that philosophy
of the inclusive life which Whitman stands
for," as shown by the wide variety of people
represented and the various aspects of
Whitman they admire. The "firm strokes of
his great verses" leave "pictures more like
stone carvings than written memories." The
addresses are described, likewise the inappropriate polished walking stick of
Whitman's which was passed around.

40 HERRON, GEORGE D. "Whitman as a Spiritual
Liberator." Conservator 15 (July), 71-72.
Testifies to Whitman's power over him,
teaching the meaning of freedom, the way
to "serve a cause, or a brother," the way
to realize spiritual potential. But Whitman
is less a teacher than a spirit.

41 MONAHAN, MICHAEL. "The Whitmanites." Papyrus
3 (July), 1-4.
Recounts experience of attending Fellowship meetings, with sarcasm.

42 GAMBERALE, LUIGI. "The Life and Works of Walt
Whitman, translated by William E. Davenport
from an article in Revista d'Italia."
Conservator 15 (September), 103-6.
The identity of Whitman's life and
works; his absorption of nature and city
life; his vision of humanity as one, as
evidenced during the war. His vague democratic ideal shows little faith in the
reader's intelligence. His artistic defects
are the absence of the individual person in
his poetry and his incapacity for the artistic delicacy Tennyson embodies. "He is
not always a great artist yet often a great
poet and unfailingly a great heart."

43 GLASIER, J. BRUCE. "An Incensed Whitmanite.
His Diatribe and Philosophy." Comrade 3
(September), 254.
From Labor Leader (unlocated): Quotes
conversation with another Englishman who
deplores the "hypocrites and respectables"
claiming to follow Whitman while hoarding
up wealth with no concern for the struggling
poor. Whitman's greatness is evident from
the condemnation he aroused. He became
"one of the immortal Titans of literature"
without education or dramatic circumstance
to gain him attention.

44 CROSBY, ERNEST. "Whitman the Lover." Conservator 15 (October), 121.
Emerson left the lover out of his
Representative Men; he should have recognized
that quality in Whitman. Leaves is "one
long love letter to mankind."

*45 ANON. "Punch and the Navvy Fiend: 'A Song of
the Open Road.'" London Daily Mirror (5
October).
Reprinted: Saunders.
Parody.

46 R., J. G. Paragraph review of Platt (1904.12).
Yale Literary Magazine 70 (December), 118-
19.
Platt is faithful but gray, ignoring
Whitman's eccentricities and picturesqueness; Whitman "was distinctly more active,
more brilliant" than here shown.

47 T[RAUBEL, HORACE]. "Whitman." Conservator 15
(December), 153-54.
Review of Platt (1904.12), well-organized,
complete, "one of the best of historians"
compared to Whitman's other biographers.

1905

1905

BOOKS

1 BINNS, HENRY BRYAN. A Life of Walt Whitman.
London: Methuen & Co., 369 pp. Index.
Illustrated.
Sources beyond published material include unpublished manuscripts and information from Whitman's personal acquaintances,
as acknowledged in footnotes. Throughout
the book, the contemporary American scene
and spirit are described as necessary for
understanding Whitman. His character had
an early tinge of puritanism. A romance
in New Orleans is conjectured from various
evidence, including "Once I Pass'd" and
Whitman's letter to Symonds. Whitman
recognized science and philosophy as
"essential, not hostile, to poetry." His
progressive integration of character and
his mystical experience are described. His
message was "rather of self-assertion, than
of self-surrender." His various works are
explained as they appear, with his unique
religious emotion, self-reviews, perception
of everything as symbolic, notion of comrades, Quaker traits, ambivalence toward
war, friendships. After its culmination in
the 1860 Leaves, Whitman replaced his self-
assertion with "helpful love." Vistas is
discussed as "a scathing attack upon American complacency," with a contrasting faith
in "the heroic character of the people."
The poems of the "Passage" period reveal an
interest in formal perfection, although
they are less elemental than the earlier
poems. Whitman is related to literary and
philosophical predecessors and contemporaries, especially Carlyle, Mazzini, Emerson,
Thoreau, Browning, Tolstoy, William Morris,
Nietzsche, George Fox. He was neither
socialist nor individualist, but sought a
"society of Comrades" which required simultaneous development of social consciousness
and individual independence. Of the two
orders of poetry, "the song of the Night-
ingale" and "the flight of the Eagle,"
Whitman lacks the former's allusive grace,
but only the very greatest poets of all
time can unite and reconcile the two. His
funeral is described through Doyle's responses. Appendices present information on
Whitman's maternal grandmother's family and
Traubel's letter to Carpenter regarding
Whitman's allusions to his having children.

2 BURROUGHS, JOHN. Introduction to Lafayette in
Brooklyn, by Walt Whitman. New York:
George D. Smith. [5 short unnumbered pages].
Recalls Whitman telling the incident described in the article, which is printed
from an undated manuscript, unpublished
though prepared for the printer. When
Lafayette embraced Whitman, "the French
democrat of the eighteenth century, as
exemplified by the life and character of
one of its most noted representatives,

embraced and caressed the heir of the new
democracy of the nineteenth century--its
future poet and most complete and composite
embodiment." Hence Whitman felt warmly
toward France. The volume's last page has
brief explanatory notes for the article.

3 _____. Ways of Nature. Boston and New York:
Houghton Mifflin Co., p. 206.
Incidental quotation of Whitman.

4 CARMAN, BLISS. The Poetry of Life. Boston:
L. C. Page & Co., pp. 9, 57, 133, 138, 156-
57, 162-63, 209, 255.
Whitman's qualities are praised throughout the book. He and Emerson are "the most
novel and significant of American poets,"
being approached only by Dickinson. "When
he gave free play to his genius, he spoke
with the tongue of a seraph," but when he
tried to imitate himself and "put in practice certain notions of his own as to what
poetry ought to be, he failed."

5 CHESTERTON, GILBERT K. Heretics. New York
and London: John Lane, p. 111.
Incidental: "Dionysius and his church
was grounded on a serious joie-de-vivre
like that of Walt Whitman."

6 COLLINS, JOHN CHURTON. Studies in Poetry and
Criticism. London: George Bell & Sons.
"The Poetry and Poets of America," pp. 63-
71, 77, passim per index.
Reprint with minor changes of 1904.28.

*7 GUTHRIE, KENNETH S. The Spirit Message of
Literature. Medford, Mass.: Prophet Pub-
lishing Co., pp. 59, 71.
Quoted in Willard.
Attacks the "hideous, unblushing deprav-
ity" of this obscene "satyr."

8 HIGGINSON, THOMAS WENTWORTH. Part of a Man's
Life. Boston and New York: Houghton,
Mifflin & Co., pp. 2, 25, 164, 193-97.
The dead should be honored with "not
the mournfulness of old-time epitaphs, but
rather the fine outburst of Whitman's brief
song of parting, 'Joy, Shipmate, Joy.'"
Whitman, like other leading American literary
figures, was "sunshiny and hopeful, not
gloomy." Leaves, because first encountered
on a sea voyage, "inspires to this day a
slight sense of nausea, which it might,
after all, have inspired equally on land."
Specimen is quoted, describing a butterfly:
here, "our most wayward American poet, reverting for once unequivocally to the prose
form, has given the best and the most
graphic butterfly picture easily to be
found in that shape." Critics of Whitman's
poetic form may find their conviction
strengthened "by the peculiar attraction of
this outdoor reverie in prose."

9 HUTTON, LAURENCE. Talks in a Library with
Laurence Hutton. Recorded by Isabel Moore.

New York: G. P. Putnam's Sons, pp. 214-15, 223-24.

Recalls Whitman's personal magnetism, "his wonderful physical beauty" like that of Michelangelo's Moses and more appealing than his verse. When he saw Whitman riding an omnibus before the war, he recognized him as "a unique figure in American life." He recalls his first visit to Whitman in 1877, under the auspices of Mary Mapes Dodge.

10 IRWIN, MABEL MacCOY. _Whitman, The Poet-Liberator of Woman_. New York: Published by the author, 77 pp.

One must be reborn "into the life of conscious unity with the race" before understanding Whitman. He perceived woman's subordinate position in his time and extended his message of freedom to women and to men. He regards love of the sexes and love of comrades as distinct, equally supreme, necessary to human fulfillment. He heathily perceives both sexes as equals in sexual fulfillment, and never dissociates sex-function from parenthood. He believes sex problems should be dealt with openly. Mabie (1903.8) was wrong about Whitman lacking chivalry. "Adam" praises the beauty of the body and translates it "into the substance of the soul." "Woman Waits" justifies itself in portraying the woman that should someday appear. Woman must have full freedom.

11 MACPHAIL, ANDREW. _Essays in Puritanism_. Boston and New York: Houghton, Mifflin & Co. "Walt Whitman," pp. 223-73. London: T. Fisher Unwin. "Walter Whitman," pp. 168-206.

Considered unclean, Whitman's poetry transgressed the rules of New England but not of New York. He revolted against false conventions, seeking to give total freedom to his partially free countrymen. His adverse critics misunderstood him, though he did err in being too open about private matters. He did not see clearly to resolve his intuitions consistently into adequate words, except in such poems as "Tears" and the Lincoln pieces; like all poets he wrote much bad poetry. Many of his memorable phrases "appeal instantly by their wonderful clearness and perfection," as do some "whole compositions of sustained beauty and splendour," in which no other style seems possible for expressing such thoughts. Whitman produces a sense of the cosmos in sympathetic readers. He "spoke for that large class which cannot speak for itself, and, indeed, is not conscious that it has anything to say." "The Good Gray Poet Gone" (1892.127) is reprinted.

12 MOULTON, CHARLES WELLS, ed. _The Library of Literary Criticism of English and American Authors_. Vol. 8. Buffalo, N.Y.: Moulton Publishing Co., pp. 129-53.

Biographical outline with list of works, followed by compendium of short extracts of critical commentary under the categories "Personal," "Leaves of Grass 1855," and "General," from a wide range of sources.

13 PAGE, CURTIS HIDDEN, ed. Whitman poems, bibliography, and biographical sketch in _The Chief American Poets: Selected Poems_. Boston: Houghton Mifflin Co., pp. 532-610, 647-50, 685-91.

Poems are arranged chronologically; extensive notes explain Whitman's purpose and present earlier versions or prose analogues. Bibliography lists editions, biographies and reminiscences, criticism, and tributes in verse. Biographical sketch relates Whitman's life to his works, explaining his themes and increasing recognition as a typical American poet expressing our whole life and character, even the cultured aspects typical of Longfellow and Lowell. Like no other poet, he embodies the American ideals of freedom and independence, individualism, and equality.

14 PERRY, RALPH BARTON. _The Approach to Philosophy_. New York: Charles Scribner's Sons, pp. 27-31, 36.

Though Whitman is sincere, "his truth is honesty and not understanding," for he shows "a marvelous ability to discover and communicate a fresh gladness about the commonest experiences" but fails to achieve unity or wisdom, in contrast to Shakespeare. Both poets, however, lack "any unitary construction upon human life and its environment."

15 SMILEY, JAMES B. _A Manual of American Literature_. New York, Cincinnati, Chicago: American Book Co. "Walt Whitman," pp. 239-45; also 255.

Whitman's two most important works, "quite dissimilar in form and character," are _Leaves_ (with vigor, freshness of thought, and coarseness) and _Drum-Taps_ (which proves him "the singer of the Civil War"). The Lincoln poems, "Brooklyn Ferry," "City Dead-House," "Cradle," "Come up from the Fields" are praised. His poetry expresses his love for the sea, nature, the common people. "He was gifted with feeling and imagination," and a surprising tenderness. Poems are suggested for reading.

16 STEVENSON, ROBERT LOUIS. _Essays in the Art of Writing_. London: Chatto & Windus. "Books Which Have Influenced Me," pp. 80-81. Reprint of 1887.44.

17 TRAUBEL, HORACE. _The Book of Heavenly Death by Walt Whitman Compiled by Horace Traubel_. Portland, Me.: Thomas B. Mosher. "Preface: Being an introductory note more or less in Whitman's own words," pp. xvii-xxiii.

An explanation, largely through Whitman's words from various sources, of Whitman's

1905

vision of individual immortality and
attitudes toward death.

18 TRIGGS, OSCAR LOVELL. The Changing Order: A
Study of Democracy. Chicago: Oscar L.
Triggs Publishing Co. "The Philosophic and
Religious Ground: Walt Whitman," pp. 262-
78; also passim, especially 295-300. No
index.
Leaves represents a modern theology
with a positive, democratic, and unifying
rather than negative, feudal, and alien-
ating basis, emphasizing "monism, or the
unitary nature of the universe," and seeking
"to establish man in undisputed mastery
over himself." Whitman balances Eastern
and Western thought. Whitman's primordial
rhythms and affinities with painter George
Inness are described.

19 TRIMBLE, W. H. Walt Whitman and Leaves of
Grass: An Introduction. London: Watts &
Co., 100 pp. No index.
1. "Early Years": Notes Whitman's
acquaintance with laborers.
2. "'Leaves of Grass'": Through his
appropriate rhythm, his poems "breathe a
sentiment of subdued melancholy." His
egotism is vicarious. His weak points are
compensated for by his excellent qualities,
including breadth of view, treatment of the
commonplace. Rossetti's titles (in 1868.2)
are preferable to Whitman's unfortunate
ones. His themes are human freedom, human
brotherhood, and death and immortality.
Particular sections and his corresponding
beliefs are explained: "Song of Myself"
(his most important poem); "Children of
Adam" (his start at changing common attitudes toward sex); "Democratic Vistas"
(equality but not uniformity, the importance
of work, individuality, love of comrades as
his ideal condition of society); "Religion"
(emphasizing the love of man, often seemingly blasphemous); "Prudence, Charity, and
Personal Force" (his redefinitions of
these); "Death and Immortality" (his "gateway to a fuller life").
3. "'Drum-Taps'": Whitman's war experience and its influence on his work.
4. "Whitman and Lincoln": Quotations
show Whitman's admiration for Lincoln.
5. "Whitman's Reception": The charges
of critics are usually true, but Whitman
remains uninjured. He has become recognized
"as a real, vital and permanent force in
literature," influencing most recent American verse.
6. "Conclusion": His later life and
work.
Appendix 1: Whitman's titles correlated
with Rossetti's (1868.2).
Appendix 2: Bibliography of Whitman's
works and secondary material, including
articles and incidental discussion.

PERIODICALS

20 CAFFIN, CHARLES H. "John W. Alexander."
World's Work 9 (January), 5695.
Incidentally notes the pronounced expression of character in Alexander's portraits of men, including Whitman (the
portrait reprinted, p. 5683).

21 CUNNINGHAM, CLARENCE. "A Defence of Walt.
Whitman's 'Leaves of Grass.'" Arena 33
(January), 55-59.
Defends Whitman against charge by Frank
McAlpine (source unspecified and unlocated).
Whitman's audience of "superior men and
women" is shifting attitudes on proper
themes for literature. Candor in literature
is necessary.

22 [FLOWER, B. O.] "Notes and Comments." Arena
33 (January), 112.
Cunningham's article (1905.21) deserves
careful consideration. Whitman, "a great,
free soul," typified a virile democracy
which is the antithesis of our present
reactionary, make-believe democracy.

23 NOYES, CARLETON. "Walt Whitman's Message to
a Young Man." Conservator 15 (January),
168-70.
Whitman affords the best education,
teaching the worth of the individual and
self-realization as success in life.
Whitman introduces one to true beauty, the
power of comradeship, and serene and vigorous optimism and joy in life.

24 T[RAUBEL, HORACE]. "An Early Whitman Poem."
Conservator 15 (January), 172.
Reprints poem from Brother Jonathan,
1843, on acceptance of death.

25 GARRISON, CHARLES G. "Walt Whitman, Christian
Science and the Vedanta." Conservator 15
(February), 182-85.
Whitman's philosophy, his egotism, is
that of the Hindu Vedanta. The one self is
expressed in individual men; man realizes
his identity by complete identification
with this self. This is the antithesis of
pantheism. Whitman's teachings are compared
with those of Christian Science.

26 WILLIAMS, TALCOTT. "With the New Books."
Book News Monthly 23 (February), 516-17.
Review of Platt (1904.12), a good introduction to Whitman, though neglecting the
sexual element in Whitman's life. Whitman,
so far the "most unique force in American
letters," has passages and aspects "which
will be read while men read English."
Beyond anyone in modern letters, he "is all
or nothing to those who read him, and to
many he has at the critical moment of a
reader's lifetime broken the bread and wine
of democratic faith."

27 ANON. "The Authorship of 'The Two Mysteries':
A Correction." Arena 33 (March), 318.
Cunningham (1905.21) incorrectly assigned
Mary Mapes Dodge's "The Two Mysteries"
(1876.69) to Whitman, as others have, be-
cause of the headnote quoting Whitman.

28 BRUÈRE, ROBERT W. "Walt Whitman." Reader
Magazine 5 (March), 490-94.
Whitman did not want his poems to support theories but sought to fill readers
"with vigorous and clean manliness and
religiousness." The first four lines of
"Myself" 48 epitomize all he wrote. "Adam"
appears increasingly valid. His expression
of human sympathy is unsurpassed. He looked ahead to an ideal democracy. "Cradle"
and "Lilacs" are "among the half dozen
superlative threnodies in the language."
Whitman's prose provides an excellent
introduction with its "transcripts from
nature more minutely faithful than the
painstaking descriptions of Thoreau" and
its evidence of his cultivated mind and
penetrating criticism.

29 B[URROWES], P[ETER]. Review of Traubel's
Chants Communal. Comrade 4 (March), 58.
This book is "not an echo of Whitman"
but "it is Whitman, just as Whitman was
himself the growing sense of the single
mindedness of all humanity, with a resultant
necessary protest against the mean and
little invoked by such a perception, and
also with a passionate and most knightly
appeal for justice and manliness and deep
moral breathing." Whitman and Traubel
represent contemporary "mental unrest"
producing "a struggle toward righteousness"
and they will continue to be heard.

30 T[RAUBEL, HORACE]. "Walt Whitman." Conservator 16 (March), 11-12.
Review of Burton (1904.5), which swings
"between yes and no" regarding Whitman and
misses the fact that Leaves "is not a book
of poems but one poem" that cannot be replaced by a selection.

31 NORTON, ALFRED. "The Man Walt." Conservator
16 (April), 21-22.
Praises Whitman, whom he loves from
personal acquaintance and whose work has
inspired him through its religious qualities.

32 T[RAUBEL, HORACE]. "The Book of Heavenly
Death." Conservator 16 (April), 27.
Impressionistic description of Whitman's
attitude toward death, based on 1905.17.
All of Leaves is about death, because it
is about life.

33 ANON. "Whitman Poem in Church." New York
Times (3 April), 9:4.
A church in Peoria under William
Hawley Smith used a Whitman poem in place
of the Scriptures.

34 EDWARDS, WARD H. "Walt Whitman, 1905."
William Jewell Student (May), 339-42.
Notes much recent commentary on
Whitman, which shows that the literature
surrounding his name will surpass in bulk
and volume that devoted to any other nineteenth-century writers, indicating that
his importance is recognized and he is
gaining ground.

35 T[RAUBEL, HORACE]. "Whitman." Conservator 16
(May), 44.
Review of Irwin (1905.10), correct in
recognizing the prevalence in Whitman of
neither sex.

36 WESCOTT, R. W. "'Chanter of Personality.'"
Yale Literary Magazine 70 (May), 304-11.
The pure contemplative wonder described
in "Cradle" is Whitman's habitual mood.
Fitted by patriotic temperament to feel as
well as depict the war, he writes his best
when dominated by the war spirit, revealing
both pathos and brilliance. His mixed
diction and lack of a sense of humor cannot
conceal his sincerity and fearlessness.
His virtues are all positive, not negative.
Whitman is quoted on expressing one's individuality; doing so gave Jesus so much
influence. Whitman's "rough, spontaneous
spirit-biography" gives us a chance to come
into contact with his ideal personality.

37 TRAUBEL, HORACE. "The Good Gray Poet at Home:
His Familiar Talks of Men, Letters and
Events." Saturday Evening Post 177 (13
May), 1-2. Illustrated.
Pre-publication extracts of 1906.22.
Continued 1905.44a.

*38 WOCKERS, JERRY. "No Tablet on Whitman's
House." Long Islander (19 May).
Reprinted: Whitman Supplement 1978.
The owner of the house where Whitman
dwelt at West Hills has refused to permit
a tablet to be erected on the property in
Whitman's memory, typical of many Long
Islanders then and now who fail to appre-
ciate him. A tablet will be erected, how-
ever, on the public highway.

39 ANON. "Won't Allow a Tablet on Poet's Birthplace. Owner of the House Refuses to Help
in Honoring Whitman." New York Times (29
May), 9:6.
Frank J. Rogers, owner of the birthplace,
is quoted, refusing to allow the women of
the Colonial Society of Huntington to place
a tablet on his property. It will be placed
on the highway instead.

40 PLATT, WILLIAM. "Wordsworth, Borrow, Whitman,
and Beethoven." Conservator 16 (June),
53-54.
Personal account of Platt's own progressing enthusiasms. Whitman regarded
every fellowman as a star, every star as a
fellowman. In comparison with Wordsworth,

Whitman has much greater power and emotional sympathy.

41 COMPENDIUM. "Some New Letters About Whitman." Conservator 16 (June), 54-57.
Letters addressed to Fellowship from Bazalgette, Walter Walsh (praising Heavenly Death [1905.17], calling Whitman second only to Jesus as singer of man's perfectness), Minot Savage, Eugene Debs, Bliss Perry, William Jennings Bryan ("Whitman's writings show great intellect, but they show a still greater heart"), F. B. Sanborn, Samuel Crothers, Wayland Hyatt Smith, F. H. Williams, Philip Hale (on Whitman, Poe, and Melville), Lucius D. Morse.

42 ANON. "Whitmanites Not Zoologic. Mr. Burroughs Resents Suggestion at Fellowship International Meeting." New York Times (1 June), 11:3.
Account of Fellowship meeting, noting various speakers and attendees, quoting Burroughs's response to letter from Perry, also quoted.

*43 ANON. Article. London (Ontario) Free Press (3 June).
Reported in Willard.
About the birthplace tablet (see 1905.38 and 1905.39).

44 E[DGETT], E. F. "Writers and Books." Boston Evening Transcript (3 June), 33:5.
Reprinted: 1905.49.
Review of Book of Heavenly Death (1905. 17), "one continuous paean of joy and glorification of the life hereafter." Explains Whitman's attitude toward death and immortality.

44a TRAUBEL, HORACE. "The Good Gray Poet at Home: His Intimate Talk of Men, Letters and Events." Saturday Evening Post 177 (3 June), 8-9. Illustrated.
Continues 1905.37. Concluded 1905.50.

*45 ANON. "Whitman, Editor Good Gray Poet [sic]." Long Islander (9 June).
Reprinted: Whitman Supplement 1978.
John Fleet, one of the oldest residents, presents his recollections of Whitman starting and working on the Long Islander in 1836, noting the men who took over the publication after he had ceased publishing.

46 ENDE, AMELIA von. "Walt Whitman and Arno Holz." Poet-Lore 16, no. 3 (Summer), 61-65.
Whitman's distinctive genius is in his view of life, not his form. Holz approaches Whitman in form and in his goal for German poetry, as reviewers have noted. Holz's tribute to Whitman (quoted) recognizes that "'although he broke the old forms, he did not give us new ones.'" Whitman sought rather "to give us new values of life," being "a poet for mankind," not for poets.

47 ANON. "Walt Whitman's Table Talk." Current Literature 39 (July), 37-38.
Whitman is quoted on various writers from Traubel's articles (1905.37 and 1905.44a) which give "an exceptionally vivid picture" of Whitman in Camden.

48 WENTWORTH, FRANKLIN. "The Breaker of the Seals." Conservator 16 (July), 69-71.
Whitman "breaks seals," emancipating like Christ; he will help us grow and open our minds to "a new morality, a new reverence for life, a new and nobler human religion."

49 EDGETT, E. F. "The Book of Heavenly Death." Conservator 16 (August), 92-93.
Reprint of 1905.44.

50 TRAUBEL, HORACE. "The Good Gray Poet at Home: His Intimate Talk of Men, Letters and Events." Saturday Evening Post 178 (19 August), 14-15.
Concludes 1905.44a.

51 T[RAUBEL, HORACE]. "Walt Whitman and Leaves of Grass." Conservator 16 (September), 107-8.
Review of Trimble (1905.19): Although so far away in New Zealand, Trimble is able to provide a "fair" introduction to Whitman, if such an introduction is needed.

52 S[ALT], H. S. "Thoreau and Walt Whitman." Manchester Guardian (6 October), 12:1.
Notes the friendship and mutual respect of Thoreau and Whitman, contrasted as "the thrifty, incisive intellect which so keenly criticised the sophisms of modern life, and the large catholic temperament which accepted and welcomed every phase of humanity." Thoreau's letters (1894.16) and Traubel's writings (1905.44a) are quoted. Whitman mistakenly attributed Thoreau's critical mind to superciliousness, but Thoreau did not yield even to Whitman in his love of healthy common life. Thoreau read Whitman better than Whitman read Thoreau. They have the most vitality in American literature.

53 TRAUBEL, HORACE. "With Walt Whitman in Camden." Century Magazine 71 (November), 82-98. Illustrated.
Pre-publication extracts of 1906.22, with occasional differences from the book but not in Whitman's words.

54 ANON. Paragraph under "Biography." Times Literary Supplement (London) (3 November), 374.
Announcement and brief description of Binns (1905.1).

55 ANON. "Tablet to Walt Whitman." New York Times (19 November), 4:1.
Account of birthplace tablet (see 1905.39), quoting it.

56 ANON. "Walt Whitman." Times Literary Supplement (London) (24 November), 401-2.
Reprinted: 1906.27.
Review of Binns (1905.1), informative
but long. Whatever Whitman's faults in
speech or thinking, he clearly speaks and
thinks out of his own experience; hence,
"his words have so much weight and consola-
tion for us." He is a good writer because
he can communicate the feeling of real
life, convincing as someone who has lived
and not merely written. His mysticism and
wonder at life are praised. He always
speaks personally, urging each to follow
his own way. Although much is not polished,
he occasionally produced true poetry, but
his true, unique art is in conveying himself fully.

57 ANON. "To Walt Whitman." Conservator 16
(December), 149.
Brief comment read at 19 December
dinner of Whitman friends, expressing hope
that Whitman has reached a joyous afterlife,
calling "Good-Bye" "one of the most touching
lyrics ever written by an American."

58 T[RAUBEL, HORACE]. "Whitman Editions." Conservator 16 (December), 157.
Warning that editions issued by Crowell
(1902.5) and Kerr of Chicago are reprints
of the 1860 edition, not containing later
pieces.

59 ANON. "A Walt Whitman Memorial." New York
Times (3 December), sec. 3, 7. Illustrated.
Describes and pictures the birthplace
tablet (see 1905.39); describes briefly
Whitman's early life around the Huntington
area, including his schoolhouse at Woodbury.

60 [HIGGINSON, T. W.] Review of Binns (1905.1).
Nation 81 (7 December), 469.
Binns frankly admits certain aspects of
Whitman which others have not so freely
exhibited (e.g., his illegitimate sons, his
self-reviews). Whitman was strangely unable to bear the strains which weaker men
lived safely through in the war, and his
death and old age cannot match the robust
old age of longer-lived American writers.
His pleasant personal habits are noted.
Binns has little to offer concerning
Whitman as poet beyond quoting the "ever
delightful" "Open Road." "He has not yet
discovered, that Whitman's poetry at its
loftiest takes us into an atmosphere far
above his general range, if not above that
attained by any American poet, as in this
cheering glimpse of human life's last
moment" ("Joy, Shipmate, Joy," quoted in
full).

1906

BOOKS

1 ALEXANDER, HARTLEY BURR. Poetry and the
Individual: An Analysis of the Imaginative
Life in Relation to the Creative Spirit in
Man and Nature. New York and London:
G. P. Putnam's Sons, pp. 12, 35.
Whitman, noted for his "expansive
freedom and full breath," is the "true
index to the poetic expression of the new
era," with "no ulcerous self-analysis, but
a quick susceptibility to all impressions."

2 BALFOUR, Lady BETTY, ed. Personal and Literary
Letters of Robert First Earl of Lytton.
Vol. 2. London: Longmans, Green, & Co.,
p. 373.
Letter of 1888 to Nichol regarding his
book (1882.7): "Your condemnation of Walt
Whitman is well deserved," but too merciful
for "an impudent, blatant impostor, who
deserves no serious consideration."

3 BELL, RALCY HUSTED. Words of the Wood.
Boston: Small, Maynard & Co. "Walt
Whitman," pp. 36-38.
Poem in nine rhymed stanzas about
Whitman's happy relation to nature.

4 BISLAND, ELIZABETH, ed. The Life and Letters
of Lafcadio Hearn. Boston and New York:
Houghton, Mifflin & Co. Vol. 1, pp. 271-
74, 292, 320, 432, 433; vol. 2, pp. 432,
512.
Letters to O'Connor cite the impossibility of praising Whitman "unreservedly in
the ordinary newspaper" as Hearn would have
liked to do, although Whitman's titanic
voice, praiseworthy for his "antique pantheism," earthiness, and "human animalism,"
remained only half articulated. Whitman
has something of Dionysus and a repellent
uncouthness. His democratic ideal is "a
generous dream" which is past.

5 CARPENTER, EDWARD. Days with Walt Whitman,
With Some Notes on His Life and Work.
London: George Allen & Unwin, 187 pp.
Illustrated.
Includes reprints of 1897.39, 1897.60, and
1902.32 (with minor changes and deletion of
introduction on importance of considering
any writer's personal relations).
"Whitman as Prophet": Whitman is part
of an ongoing tradition of prophecy, unique
in his universality and democratic scope.
He avoids the abstract, mental appeal,
seeking rather to reach the soul through
the senses. The appendix quotes passages
from early prophetic writings for purposes
of comparison with Leaves, to show them
coming from the same root.
"The Poetic Form of 'Leaves of Grass'":
Whitman's new literature appeals "to all
who deal with life directly," perfectly
matching expression to form. His mood and

theme, vast and inclusive, require a broad, flexible rhythm. He achieves artistic unity by such devices as the very long sentence, central symbols, recurrences, and a distinct mood or music (in short poems). "Lilacs" and "Cradle" are favorites for their "artistic effect and unity" but are less characteristic than "Myself," "Adam," and "Calamus," personal and prophetic utterances beyond art. His later poems show deficiency of inspiration and lapse into mannerisms. Various objections to Whitman's style are answered.

"Whitman and Emerson": Emerson's vision probably influenced Whitman before 1855, but his book depended much on what Emerson could not give him. Explanation of Emerson's difficulties with Whitman, their differences, Whitman's increased captiousness toward Emerson as a writer.

6 COYNE, JAMES H. "Richard Maurice Bucke--A Sketch." In Proceedings and Transactions of the Royal Society of Canada. 2d ser., vol. 12, sec. 2, pp. 159-96. References to Whitman, pp. 159, 175-76, 177-85, 190. Reprinted: 1923.3; in part: 1908.28.
    Biography of Bucke with bibliography of his writings, noting the impact of Whitman on Bucke, Bucke's efforts on Whitman's behalf, their relationship.

7 DAWSON, W[ILLIAM] J[AMES]. The Makers of English Poetry. New York, Chicago, Toronto: Fleming H. Revell Co., p. 403.
    "Whitman is a potential rather than an actual poet," in temperament and gift being "much more of a poet than either Longfellow, Whittier or Lowell," but having "a wholly mistaken conception of the nature and structure of poetry," lacking coordination with only an occasional perfect phrase. "Lilacs," despite its looseness of structure, has a noble sincerity which makes it one of the great elegies.

8 HENLEY, W. E. Views and Reviews: Essays in Appreciation. New York: Charles Scribner's Sons, pp. 151-52.
    To Whitman, the sea "has been 'the great Camerado' indeed, giving him that song of the brown bird bereft of its mate in whose absence the half of him had not been told to us."

9 MAITLAND, FREDERIC WILLIAM, ed. The Life and Letters of Leslie Stephen. New York: G. P. Putnam's Sons; London: Duckworth & Co., p. 464.
    Letter of 1901 to C. F. Adams responding to his disapproval of a recent consideration of Poe and Whitman as representative of American literature: "W. W. always seemed to me Emerson diluted with Tupper--twaddle with gleams of something better."

10 MORE, PAUL ELMER. Shelburne Essays. 4th ser. New York: G. P. Putnam's Sons. "Walt

Whitman," pp. 180-211.
Extract reprinted: Murphy.
    After a brief but favorable review of Traubel (1906.22) and Binns (1905.1), he discusses Whitman's flaws. However, comparison of "Whispers" with poems of death by Browning and Tennyson proves Whitman's ranking with the great and not the minor poets, revealing less egotism in the presence of death than the other two. His poetry is a poetry of movement, with a sensitivity to rhythm and the currents of life unlike that of other poets of his day. The war provided him with additional exalted vision. His concern was not with prescriptions for the problems of American democracy but with a "fraternal anarchy" of camaraderie (although the ordinary themes of exclusive love or friendship scarcely appear in Whitman). "He lacked the rare and unique elevation of Emerson from whom so much of his vision was unwittingly derived, but as a compensation his temperament is richer" and "his verbal felicity at its best more striking." Americans should accept him as one of their most original and characteristic poets.

11 PEEBLES, J[AMES] M[ARTIN]. The Spirit's Pathway Traced. Battle Creek, Mich.: Dr. Peebles Institute of Health, pp. 7, 10-20, 61.
    Quotes passages; recalls being introduced to Whitman's poetry by Eliza Farnham, who "knew how to elucidate his dark lines of mystery called poems." Whitman, "like nearly all inspired poets, believed in the human spirit's pre-existence." He looked for good and found it. Peebles recalls knowing Whitman and visiting him in Camden, appreciating "the spiritual wealth of his soul," "rugged as nature itself." "He was an all-around man," "radiating vigor and health, peace and good will." Whitman is quoted from Traubel (1906.22).

12 PENNELL, ELIZABETH ROBINS. Charles Godfrey Leland, A Biography. Boston and New York: Houghton, Mifflin & Co. Vol. 1, pp. 410-11; vol. 2, pp. 109-12, 191-95, 335.
    Leland's niece includes her memories of Whitman, George Boker, and her uncle; quotes from Leland's journal describing an 1881 meeting with Whitman; recalls other visits and memories, including William Wetmore Story's lack of admiration for Whitman.

13 PERRY, BLISS. Walt Whitman. Boston and New York: Houghton, Mifflin & Co., 318 pp. Index.
Revised: 1908.14. Extracts reprinted: Murphy.
    Biography. Traces Whitman's genealogy, personal development (noting some evidences of a neurotic tendency), unstructured movement toward literary expression, exuberant activity and interest in the city, probable

sexual experience in New Orleans. Amid the
social and intellectual ferment of the
1840s, he "seemed to be prolonging his
childhood indefinitely." In Leaves he
undertook to become America's representative
poet. As a poet's dissertation on poetry,
the 1855 Preface is unsurpassed for vigor
and passion. "Myself" is explicated, the
following pieces being variations on its
themes. He failed in wishing to be prophet
and philosopher as well as poet. Letters,
some previously unprinted, depict his
hospital work and Washington days. Drum-
Taps embodies "the very spirit of the civil
conflict, picturing war with a poignant
realism, a terrible and tender beauty, such
as only the great masters have been able to
compass." Whitman's various friends are
described. With Lowell's "Commemoration
Ode," "Lilacs" is "the finest imaginative
product of the Civil War period." Letters
from literary figures (including Matthew
Arnold [reprinted: Murphy]) to O'Connor
are printed regarding his book (1866.2).
Whitman's reputation is traced. Also
printed are extracts from Gilchrist's
letters to Rossetti, somewhat different
from the printed versions (1870.4), and
other letters to, from, or about Whitman.
Charles F. Richardson explains that
Whitman's Dartmouth visit was the result
of a joke students wished to play on the
faculty. Whitman's manuscript version of
the visit, intended for publication, is
printed. Whitman's personality, talk,
"critical tact" and perception, attitudes
toward various writers and subjects are
described. He was "a Mystic by temperament
and a Romanticist by literary kinship,"
with affinities to Rousseau and debts to
Transcendentalism. His international acceptance testifies to his largeness, power,
communicative emotion. His work is
"immodest" at worst, not erotic. His
exaltation of the athletic appealed to
"nervous invalids," not real athletes. He
regards human beings only in terms of the
individual and the mass, not in the intermediate groupings such as Whittier portrays.
His desire to glorify everything equally
is touching but futile, but his "grandiose
phrases and deep-heaving rhythms" suit his
depiction of the ideal life of America.
His positive political teachings are unaffected by his literary deficiencies or
personal faults. He is "the most original
and suggestive poetic figure since
Wordsworth." "No American poet now seems
more sure to be read, by the fit persons,
after one hundred or five hundred years."

14 RICKETT, ARTHUR. The Vagabond in Literature.
London: J. M. Dent & Co. "Walt Whitman,"
pp. 169-205; also passim. Woodcut portrait.
Whitman's total unconventionality makes
him "the supreme example of the Vagabond in
literature," "a spiritual native of the

woods and heath," "in touch with the elemental" in nature and in the multitude. In
art, he emphasized sincerity over mere
beauty, which he achieves at his best, as
in "On the Beach at Night," "Reconciliation,"
and "Lilacs" (comparable to Shakespeare,
Milton, and Shelley). His "sex cycle" has
worthy sentiments but weak art. His belief
in "absolute social equality" makes him
"the first genuine Poet of the People."
Whitman lacks profundity and an organized
philosophy but proclaims good health and
sanity.

15 RIETHMUELLER, RICHARD. Walt Whitman and the
Germans. Philadelphia: Americana Germanica
Press, 45 pp.
Reprints of 1906.25, 1906.32, and 1906.38.

16 ROSSETTI, WILLIAM MICHAEL. Some Reminiscences.
New York: Charles Scribner's Sons, pp. 219,
300, 378, 400-406, 484.
Traces his dealings with and for
Whitman and for his work, which was not un-
assailable in taste or form but praiseworthy
for its "majestic and all-brotherly spirit,
an untrammelled outlook on the multiplex
aspects of life, and many magnificent
bursts of sympathetic intuition allied to,
and strenuously embodying, the innermost
spirit of poetry." Explanation of his
brother's opinion of Whitman, Whitman's
extremist admirers, Watts-Dunton's incorrect
prediction in 1887 that Whitman would be
ignored in ten years.

17 SHERARD, ROBERT HARBOROUGH. Life of Oscar
Wilde. London: T. Werner Laurie, pp. 212,
214.
Quotes Wilde from an interview in the
Halifax (Nova Scotia) Morning Herald of
October 1882 (unlocated), expressing his
opinion of Whitman: "if not a poet, he was
a man who sounds a strong note, perhaps
neither prose nor poetry, but something of
his own that is grand, original and unique."
Their meeting in Camden is described briefly,
with Wilde's distress at Whitman's poverty
and the dust in his room. Whitman, "pri-
maevel, natural, aboriginal, would feel
little sympathy for the dandified Hellene."

18 STOKER, BRAM. Personal Reminiscences of Henry
Irving. New York and London: Macmillan
Co. Vol. 1, p. 214; vol. 2, "Walt Whitman,"
pp. 92-111.
Extract reprinted: Whitman Supplement 1979.
Recalls his acquaintance with Whitman
and his works, beginning at the university
shortly after publication of Rossetti's
selections (1868.2). Stoker first met
Whitman in company with Irving at Donaldson's
Philadelphia home, when Irving noticed
Whitman's resemblance to Tennyson. Description of Whitman's character and subsequent
visits to Camden in 1886 and 1887; Whitman's
reminiscences of the night of Lincoln's
assassination; the unfulfilled plan of St.
Gaudens to do a bust of Whitman.

1906

19 TAPPAN, EVA MARCH. A Short History of American
    Literature. New York and Chicago: Houghton,
    Mifflin & Co., pp. 116-18.
        Whitman's hospital work is praised.
    Though Whitman disregards conventions, he
    tends to use poetic rhythm in his best work.
    Much of his verse is prose, but when swept
    away by a poetic thought he is a "poet of
    lofty rank."

20 TRAUBEL, ANNE MONTGOMERIE. Preface to A
    Little Book of Nature Thoughts, by Walt
    Whitman. Portland, Me.: Thomas B. Mosher,
    pp. vii-viii.
        In the prose extracts comprising this
    volume, Whitman writes of objective nature
    but perceives its identity with human life.

21 TRAUBEL, HORACE. Foreword to Memories of
    President Lincoln and Other Lyrics of the
    War, by Walt Whitman. Portland, Me.:
    Thomas B. Mosher, pp. ix-xii.
        Impressionistic description of Whitman's
    treatment of Lincoln, who is not reduced to
    literature but is better understood.
    Whitman was literary, but first of all
    human. His conversation is quoted regarding
    Lincoln. A bibliographic note describes
    the poems' first publication. T. B.
    M[osher] adds a note saying that though we
    do not know whether Lincoln knew of Leaves
    or whether Whitman ever talked with him, we
    rejoice that both were in the world together,
    and "near in heart and brain." The dirge
    on Lincoln "will remain an everlasting
    masterpiece."

22 _____. With Walt Whitman in Camden (March 28-
    July 14, 1888). Boston: Small, Maynard &
    Co., 473 pp. Index. Illustrated.
    Reprinted: 1915.20. Extract reprinted:
    Murphy.
        Diary of conversations with Whitman
    transcribed by Traubel, noting visitors;
    Whitman's comments on writers, his critics,
    other people, and his past; letters to
    Whitman (some facsimiles) from various
    people; Whitman's literary efforts through-
    out this period. Continued 1908.17.

23 VINCENT, LEON H. American Literary Masters.
    Boston and New York: Houghton, Mifflin &
    Co. "Walt Whitman," pp. 485-506; also
    250-51.
        Contents: "His Life"; "The Growth of
    a Reputation"; "The Writer" (Whitman's
    creation of his own laws, actual cadence,
    inimitable catalogues); "Leaves of Grass"
    (Whitman counters brutality with benevolence
    and serene honesty; several extracts ex-
    plained to represent Whitman's ideas;
    Drum-Taps and Sequel considered his best
    gift to American literature, "Lilacs"
    representing "his supreme height");
    "Specimen Days and Collect" (revealing
    Whitman's character); "Whitman's Character"
    (though some words and ideas are unpleasant,
    like his images of comradeship, one cannot

help but like him; behind his poetry's
intensely personal element is true unself-
ishness).

PERIODICALS

24 HARNED, THOMAS B. "Walt Whitman in the Present
    Crisis of Our Democracy." Conservator 16
    (January), 167-68.
        Whitman's optimism about democracy will
    stand every test because it is through the
    common man that our civilization is to ad-
    vance.

25 RIETHMUELLER, RICHARD. "Walt Whitman and the
    Germans." German American Annals, n.s. 4
    (January), 3-15.
    Reprinted: 1906.15.
        Whitman, uniquely American, created an
    indigenous American literature. Whitman's
    German references, acquaintances, interests
    are enumerated. Continued: 1906.32.

26 T[RAUBEL, HORACE]. "Whitman Editions." Con-
    servator 16 (January), 173.
        Corrects note of December (1905.53):
    the Crowell and Kerr editions are titled
    not Leaves of Grass but "The Poetical Works
    of Walt Whitman."

27 ANON. "Walt Whitman." Living Age 248 (6
    January), 45-50.
    Reprint of 1905.56.

28 ANON. "'Walt.'" Saturday Review 101 (6
    January), 20-21.
        Review of Binns (1905.1), not bad,
    though a shorter book would have been
    better. Whitman must be accepted whole,
    even with his vulgarity, which can become
    inspiring and suggestive. He is only pre-
    mature, not unpoetic, in including what
    does not seem poetic. He is admirable for
    the heroism with which he followed his own
    logic. His mystical gift shows "an emo-
    tional receptiveness" to things. His
    theory could become his snare and he lacks
    selectivity, yet he is able to communicate
    lavishly a vision and a sense of life.

29 ANON. "New Light on Walt Whitman--Extracts
    from Horace L. Traubel's Diary of Conversa-
    tions and Opinions of 'the Good Gray Poet.'"
    Philadelphia Public Ledger (21 January), 4.
    Reprinted in part: 1906.30.
        Description of Traubel's work, probably
    "the most truthful biography in the lan-
    guage," actually Whitman's "unconscious
    autobiography." Most of the page is covered
    with illustrations and pre-publication ex-
    tracts from 1906.22 under various subject
    headings.

30 ANON. "With Walt Whitman in Camden." Con-
    servator 16 (February), 189.
    Reprint of editorial remarks in 1906.29.

30a ANON. "Walt Whitman." Fabian News 16, no. 2
(February), 6-7.
Summarizes Edgar Jepson's lecture of
January 26, to a full house, as part of a
literary series on "Prophets of the Past
Century." Whitman's "extravagant provin-
ciality . . . betrayed him into uneasy
self-assertion, lack of restraint, and
violent admiration of doubtful things" and
"marred the form of his poetry." "When he
rose above this fault, he attained to the
height of creative imagination and clothed
his creations in their fitting admirable
poetic form." Considering contemporary
America, Whitman's provincial prophecies
are nowhere nearer fulfillment, "based on
the fallacy that America is a young and
rising nation," while America's ideal is
simply money-making.

31 PLATT, ISAAC HULL. "Whitman's Superman."
Conservator 16 (February), 182-83.
Whitman was not a faddist, although
different groups find their own ideas in
him. Shaw's notion of the Superman was
preceded by Whitman's.

32 RIETHMUELLER, RICHARD. "Walt Whitman and the
Germans, II." German American Annals, n.s.
4 (February), 35-49.
Reprinted: 1906.15.
Continues 1906.25. Describes Whitman's
interest in Goethe and their similar ideas;
compares Whitman's poetic and philosophical
ideas with those of Herder, Schiller,
Heine; describes Whitman's personal acquaintance with Bertz and his small interest in
the plastic arts but love for music. Concluded 1906.38.

33 RITTENHOUSE, JESSIE B. "Walt Whitman. Horace
Traubel's New Revelations of the Poet's
Personality in a Diary--A Biography by
Henry Bryan Binns." New York Times Saturday
Review (24 February), 109-10.
Review of 1906.22 and 1905.1. Whitman's
conversation displays a rich mind and an
acute critical sense that penetrates to
the heart of a writer's works. The whole
of his liberating message "was lost sight
of by the Puritan vision." The beauty of
his spirit apparent in Traubel's book may
make converts. Binns overemphasizes the
political and historical context, for
Whitman was engrossed by "the universal
and not the particular aspect of things."

34 ANON. "Walt Whitman's Religion." Current
Literature 40 (March), 280-81. Photograph.
Quotes and summarizes Binns (1905.1)
on Whitman's religion as largely related
to sex.

35 BRUMBAUGH, ROSCOE. "At the Tomb of Walt
Whitman." Arena 35 (March), 278. Photograph, p. 297.
Whitman's tomb is described poetically,
personally.

36 HERRING, ALICE. "Whitman the Revealer."
Conservator 17 (March), 8-9.
Like Shakespeare, Whitman gives both
the universal, cosmic view and the minutest
detail of life; unlike Shakespeare, Whitman
addresses himself "to a new, and greater,
humanity to come."

37 IRWIN, MABEL MacCOY. "The Monism of Walt
Whitman." Triggs Magazine 2 (March), 8-13.
Whitman rejected the dualistic view of
life, believing in the unity of all things,
soul and body, even God and Satan. Leaves
is thus "the one superb symphony of literature, its different poem-parts contributing
to the resplendent beauty of the whole."

38 RIETHMUELLER, RICHARD. "Walt Whitman and the
Germans, III." German American Annals,
n.s. 4 (March), 78-92.
Reprinted: 1906.15.
Concludes 1906.32. Explains some of
Whitman's ideas, the extent of his acquain-
tace with the Kantian and Post-Kantian
idealistic school of philosophy. William
Ellery Leonard's sonnet on Whitman is re-
printed.

39 WILLIAMS, FRANCIS HOWARD. "What Walt Whitman
Means for Us All." Conservator 17 (March),
9-10.
Whitman impresses his personality on
different minds, radical or conservative.
He embodies an ultimate ideal yet to be
realized.

40 BICKNELL, PERCY F. "The Real and the Ideal
Whitman." Dial 40 (1 March), 144-46.
Review of Traubel (1906.22) and Binns
(1905.1): Traubel conveys a realistic impression of the poet and the man. Whitman's
justifications for his poetry's occasional
"'priapism'" cannot hold, for it cannot be
harmless to people in our fallen world.
Binns provides the best study of Whitman's
life and works yet, although ascribing
Whitman's development excessively to the
influence of a too vague, unknown Southern
woman.

41 A PERPLEXED SUBSCRIBER [A. M. Huger]. "What
Is Poetry?" New York Times Saturday Review
(3 March), 135.
Seeks to know the difference between
prose and poetry; asks readers for their
views "as to the poetic value of Whitman's
panoramic programmes."

42 BRASHEAR, WILLIAM H. "Further Contributions
to the Dispute About the Definition of
Poetry." New York Times Saturday Review
(17 March), 166.
Like nature, Leaves has "poetry in
solution," "a vast and manifold poetic
suggestion." Whitman's work is like "pages
of prose recited to the thrummings of the
lyre."

1906

43 McH., M. H. "Queries." New York Times
    Saturday Review (31 March), 202.
        Asks if Leaves contains all Whitman's
    poems, such as "Myself," if Whitman was
    married, if his private life was "justified
    in his works." Answer: Leaves, his first
    book, did not contain "I Celebrate Myself";
    his "private life was respectable; he never
    married."

44 AYNARD, M. JOSEPH. "Walt Whitman: As Re-
    flected in Recent French Criticism."
    Translated by William Struthers. Conserva-
    tor 17 (April), 21-23.
        Translated and excerpted by Struthers
    from an essay on Binns (1905.1) in Demain
    (Lyons): Whitman, a great poet, "composed
    a kind of poetic prose, rhythmic and fash-
    ioned according to the flight of thought";
    his themes, liberty, love, and personality,
    form the musical tissue of his book. His
    optimism is absolute. Though without ab-
    stract terminology or symbolism, Leaves is
    "a great metaphysical poem." Concluded
    1906.57.

45 PLATT, ISAAC HULL. "The Poet Who Could Wait:
    Contemporary Appreciations of Walt Whitman."
    Book News 24 (April), 545-49. Illustrated.
        Review of Binns (1905.1), Trimble
    (1905.19), Riethmueller (1906.15), Traubel
    (1906.22): Whitman was a prophet without
    honor in his own country. Binns lacks the
    picturesqueness and vigor his subject
    demands. Traubel's record of Whitman's
    correspondence and frank criticism is ex-
    cellent. Despite limited schooling, Whitman
    acquired much knowledge of literature and
    contemporary events, though not "an omniv-
    orous reader." His interest in applause
    was not inordinate but was indicative of
    his desire to know that his work was being
    accomplished.

46 WRIGHT, DAVID HENRY. "Whitman: the Inner
    Light of Quakerism." Conservator 17 (April),
    24-25.
        The "secrets" of Leaves and the Quaker
    inner light both reveal the secrets of the
    universe.

47 E., C. H. Letter responding to 1906.41. New
    York Times Saturday Review (7 April), 231.
        Mentions his aversion to Whitman in the
    short selections he has read.

48 HUGER, A. M. "The 'Perplexed Subscriber' Not
    Yet Wholly Enlightened as to Poetry and
    Prose." New York Times Saturday Review
    (7 April), 231.
        Questions responses (1906.42, 1906.47)
    to his letter (1906.41): "Whitman's Apo-
    theosis of Sweat" suggests the "mouthings
    of a mountebank"; his "'capitalized prose'"
    is easy to write.

49 ANON. "A Poet of the Cosmic Consciousness."
    Brotherhood 19 (14 April), 142-48.

Review of Binns (1905.1), which presents
Whitman as "a full-blooded sinner, with
strong passions." "Myself" dramatizes a
spiritual experience, but not an evangelical
conversion. Whitman's "passion for souls"
led to his war service.

50 HUGER, A. M. "Music, Poetry and Prose--Still
    Seeking a Definition of Poetry." New York
    Times Saturday Review (14 April), 246.
        The laurels accorded Whitman will not
    last.

51 BRASHEAR, WILLIAM H. "'Whitmaniacs.'" New
    York Times Saturday Review (21 April), 262.
        Letter in response to Huger (1906.48):
    he ignores much of Leaves, "one of the
    greatest of books; but to apprehend its
    real greatness and profound beauty it must
    be taken in its entirety," like nature.
    "Whitman had a profoundly philosophical and
    poetic soul, but was denied the gift of
    song." Nevertheless, his "chanted prose"
    expresses the highest truths. His book's
    greatness must be "apprehended of the soul,"
    not the mind.

52 SPHINX, LAMBKIN [pseud.?]. "Advice as to
    Poetry and Prose." New York Times Saturday
    Review (21 April), 262.
        Response to Huger (1906.48): "Let Walt
    Whitman live, and die yourself if need be!"
    One should suppress such distaste and prej-
    udice as harmful to oneself, not because
    Whitman has been placed among the immortals
    (an idea directly out of Carman [1905.4]).

53 [HIGGINSON, T. W.] Review of Traubel (1906.22).
    Nation 82 (26 April), 353.
        This is another of the Whitman cult's
    books which serve "to check his widening
    fame." Traubel takes too seriously
    Whitman's request to portray him honestly,
    even reproducing the coarsest words and
    Whitman's sense of superiority to New York
    and Boston literary men. The book says
    less of Whitman than of his intimate circle
    of second-rate men. The reader may doubt
    it as a faithful record of even the declin-
    ing years of the poet of "Captain" and "Joy,
    Shipmate, Joy."

54 CLOW, STEPHEN G. Letter. New York Times
    Saturday Review (28 April), 278.
        Whitman's soul lived "in the inner
    sanctuary of poetry," with "prophetic in-
    sight" seeing that "the message was all
    which mattered," style taking care of it-
    self. He climbed higher on Parnassus than
    any other American.

55 JAX [pseud.?]. "Poetry." New York Times
    Saturday Review (28 April), 278.
        A satirical poem on the perplexed reader
    who would say: "A pretty pass that 'Leaves
    of Grass' / Should stand for poetry!"

56 ANON. "Whitman's Place in the Hearts of His Contemporaries." Current Literature 40 (May), 507-8. Photograph.

Quotes from Traubel (1906.22) the high opinions of Whitman held during his lifetime by some of "his most eminent literary contemporaries" in Europe and America. He was "in contact and intimate touch with some of the greatest minds of his time."

57 AYNARD, JOSEPH. "Walt Whitman: As Reflected in Recent French Criticism, II." Conservator 17 (May), 37-39.

Concludes 1906.44. The Civil War brought Whitman a conflict of interests, doctrines, and principles, but his Quaker nonresistence led him to nursing. He recovered his moral equilibrium after the war and became accepted as a writer. Dressing like a workingman, he chose his friends from the working class. He has unwittingly founded an almost religious cult.

58 CALDER, ELLEN O'CONNOR. "William O'Connor and Walt Whitman." Conservator 17 (May), 42.

Corrects notions of Binns (1905.1) regarding Whitman's relationship with O'Connor; criticizes his overexplanation of some poems.

59 T[RAUBEL, HORACE]. "Nature Thoughts from Walt Whitman." Conservator 17 (May), 43.

Notice of Annie Traubel's volume (1906.20). Whitman's descriptions of nature are not decorative but "a matter of the soul." "His prose no less than his song incarnates and utters an imperishable forecast of the ultimate humanities."

60 ASTLEY, NORMAN. Letter in response to 1906.51. New York Times Saturday Review (5 May), 294.

Asks Brashear to point out truths original with Whitman or ones not expressed better and more spiritually than others. "Whitman was a great poetic animal, almost bursting at times with ideas he had not the power to express." "He was destitute of every form of aesthetic culture and expression" and of "the true spiritual inspiration necessary to and found in all great poetry." He was "rudely blunt in manner and method" as fit the "primitive poet" he considered himself.

61 HUGER, A. M. "Whitman. Various Views of the American Poet Who Wrote 'Leaves of Grass.'" New York Times Saturday Review (5 May), 294.

Response to Brashear (1906.51) and Sphinx (1906.52): defends his attitude toward Whitman, whose philosophy is simply the old "golden dream of fraternity, equality, and liberty," with the last converted into license. The question is not over his thoughts but whether his words are poetic. "I find Whitman's writings crude

in form, commonplace in thought, and coarse in sentiment." However, tastes vary.

62 BENEDICT, G. H. Letter. New York Times Saturday Review (12 May), 312.

Poetry involves words, not rhythm or form; hence, the title of poet cannot be denied Whitman because he rejects the latter.

63 CROSBY, ERNEST H. Letter in response to Astley (1906.60). New York Times Saturday Review (12 May), 312.

"Myself" 21, showing the poet as lover of the earth, is quoted as an original idea in Whitman; "Death Carol" is quoted as an idea no better expressed by anyone else.

64 E., C. H. Letter. New York Times Saturday Review (12 May), 312.

What he has read of Whitman offends his poetic taste. "There may be some original thoughts, but they are never beautifully expressed."

65 HILLARD, KATHARINE. Letter. New York Times Saturday Review (12 May), 312.

Too much concern is being paid to Whitman's poetry as related to standards of construction and beauty (which he often meets), when his unsurpassed "inspirational power" is of primary significance. She recalls knowing Whitman and his friends; he gave "no suggestion of a pose of any sort." Lowell discouraged Dickens, on his last trip to America, from visiting Whitman.

66 HUGER, A. M. "Poetry, Prose and Whitman." New York Times Saturday Review (12 May), 312.

Letter continuing the dispute: Whitman's verse must be regarded strictly as prose. In rejecting form, Whitman's mind was "distinctly immature, his ideas rudimentary."

67 BOLAND, HARRY. "The Dispute About Poetry." New York Times Saturday Review (19 May), 328.

Quotes lines from Tennyson which should appeal to those who fail to admire Whitman's poetry.

68 E., C. H. Letter responding to Crosby (1906.63). New York Times Saturday Review (19 May), 328.

Crosby's selections "seem crude, insincere, and false in conception," with objectionable and absurd phrasing. "One who has mastered Lowell will have all that is great in Whitman, with all the latter's coarseness and filth eliminated."

69 GLADIATORUM, MINIMUS [pseud.]. Letter responding to Crosby (1906.63). New York Times Saturday Review (19 May), 328.

Crosby has certainly selected passages which show Whitman's originality, but it is

eccentric and inappropriate. Lines from
Stephen Phillips are quoted as more successful with "the effect of rugged, fresh-air
enthusiasm" while retaining art.

70 HARBOE, PAUL. "Johannes Schlaf on Walt
Whitman." Conservator 17 (June), 58-59.
Review of Schlaf's monograph hailing
Whitman as leading Germany to "a new,
great modern religious sentiment." Whitman's
worth in the eyes of Europeans is contrasted
with "the inanity of most American popular
literature."

71 PLATT, ISAAC HULL. "A Correction." Conservator 17 (June), 61.
Corrects his biography (1904.12) which
wrongly suggested Whitman's relationship
to Zachariah Whitman.

72 T[RAUBEL, HORACE]. "Walt Whitman." Conservator 17 (June), 59-60.
Review of Binns (1905.1), the first
conclusive life of Whitman in English,
though speculating to little point on
Whitman's romances.

73 ANON. "Lemon Is Sour on the United States."
New York Tribune (1 June), 14:2.
Account of annual Whitman Fellowship
meeting, quoting Courtenay Lemon's criticisms of America, listing others present.

74 ANON. "Days with Whitman." New York Times
Saturday Review (16 June), 397.
Brief review of Carpenter (1906.5):
his opinion of Whitman is "that of a pupil
toward a chosen master." This book, which
describes Whitman's relations with women
and his children, "should please the ever-
widening circle" of his admirers.

75 ANON. "Walt Whitman--Three Notable Additions
to the Literature Concerning the 'Good
Gray Poet.'" Philadelphia Public Ledger
(25 June), 12:1.
Review of Carpenter (1906.5), Traubel
(1906.22), Binns (1905.1). Whitman may be
more popular abroad than at home because he
speaks of goals for Europeans which are
actualities in America. Carpenter gives a
reasonable view of Whitman's poetic form as
the only conceivable way he could convey
his themes. Views of Whitman may soon
balance out between his detractors and his
admirers.

76 ANON. "The 'Feminine Soul' in Whitman."
Current Literature 41 (July), 53-56.
Summary and commentary on Bertz's
analysis of Whitman as homosexual (in
"Jahrbuch für sexuelle Zwischenstufen,"
1905), which he and others have overstated.
The feminine trait of embracing sympathy
was Whitman's means of reconciling all
contradictions. Other feminine traits are
discussed. Schlaf's response to Bertz is
cited, refusing to see the abnormal in

Whitman, denying his presumed femininity,
asserting his virile manhood. Bertz discusses "to what extent his demands are
normal and healthy or abnormal and unhealthy," as should be known.

77 POTTER, GRACE. "Unfolded out of the folds of
the woman." Conservator 17 (July), 72-73.
Whitman's poem is merely used as the
opening text for comments on the full
development of man and woman through each
other.

78 [SERCOMBE, PARKER H.] "Whitman Fellowship
(?)." To-Morrow Magazine (July), 6.
Quoted in Knox.
The Chicago Whitman Fellowship should
not have missed meeting on his birthday,
the appropriate time to feel his influence.
However, for this writer, "all days are
Whitman days," enabling him to forget all
differences and wrongs.

79 TOWNE, WILLIAM E. "Walt Whitman. Poet--Proph-
et--Seer." Nautilus Magazine of New
Thought (July), 23-25.
Sketch of Whitman's life and personality.
His philosophy in Leaves is one with "New
Thought." His work was more individual
than that of his contemporaries and
"stronger, more rugged," being true to
nature, with the mysticism of nature, not
of "an aenemic brain." Though Burroughs
says that Whitman never had "an entanglement
of any sort with women," "Sometimes with
One I Love" shows that "Whitman was inspired
by a personal love, which was unrequited."

80 T[RAUBEL, HORACE]. "Days with Walt Whitman."
Conservator 17 (July), 75-76.
Review of Carpenter (1906.5): impressionistic comments on Carpenter's true
firsthand knowledge of Whitman and his
"distinct additions to Whitman history and
psychology." "Carpenter was an original
Whitman man because he was an original
Carpenter man."

81 CLOW, STEPHEN G. "From Readers. Some Further
Considerations of Horace Traubel's Book
About Whitman." New York Times Saturday
Review (14 July), 452.
Giving us a man, Traubel's book
(1906.22) is "a breath of fresh air" amid
currently popular books. Whitman was right
about poetry and about life; he is great as
the poet of naturalness, with the essence
and not the mere form of poetry, similar to
Milton in rejecting rhyme. His contemporaries' "indifference or studied contempt"
may be an indication of posterity's favor.

82 ANON. "Three Books on Walt Whitman." Independent 61 (19 July), 153-54.
Review of Traubel (1906.22), Carpenter
(1906.5), and Symonds (1893.9, recently
reissued), which present Whitman and his
works "sympathetically to a larger, saner

class of readers" than the usual abnormal people who extol him. Traubel's book is biographical in the spirit of Leaves, Whitman's "biography writ large in loose, bellowing poetic measures." Whitman touched the world like a lover; his comments are illuminating. Carpenter offers a more literary appreciation, describing Whitman's elemental forces and his search for the larger order, a deeper spirit. But Whitman could not be the whole thing, hence his incoherence. "He was the poet of democracy, and in democracy grandeur is always akin to vulgarity. Thus it suited Whitman's genius." His poetry presents us with what we are to be. However, he neglected the higher manifestations of mind and spirit. Symonds, because of his understanding of Greek literature, could tolerate "that feature of Whitman which is most offensive to the general reader."

83 ANON. "Walt Whitman. Records and Reminiscences by Two Followers." New York Tribune (22 July), sec. 2, 6:2-4. Illustrated.
Review of Traubel (1906.22) and Carpenter (1906.5): Traubel does Whitman a disservice in presenting the ailing poet's conversation with all its egotism and questionable opinions. Whitman's theory that modern poetry depends on thought more than on the lilt of the oral tradition, because of the increased importance of printing, is not worth disputing. Carpenter is another admirer reciting the seldom-varying litany.

84 ANON. Review of Traubel (1906.22). The Reader 8 (August), 320-21.
This book has made Whitman asked for even in Boston libraries.

85 BAZALGETTE, LEON. "To Whitman from the Whole World." Conservator 17 (August), 88.
Letter from Paris to the Whitman Fellowship congratulating Whitman's supporters, announcing his upcoming Whitman biography: "it is mostly in the old world now that Whitman and his cause are rapidly advancing."

86 CROSBY, ERNEST. "Walt Whitman's 'Children of Adam.'" Philistine 23 (August), 65-68.
Defense of the "Adam" poems against the charges of obscenity and exhibitionism. Whitman was ahead of his time in portraying sexuality unromantically.

87 GILDER, JEANNETTE L. "Whitman and His Boswell." Critic 49 (August), 185-87.
Review of Traubel (1906.22). She recalls her visits to Whitman's home: the litter seemed "something of a pose, for Whitman was a well-ordered, methodical man." As one of Whitman's early admirers, "I think he was a great poet--one of the greatest of his time--but I did not always take his poses seriously." Traubel is valuable for presenting Whitman's immediate

words, but Whitman would not have liked some of his careless comments on friends and contemporaries printed.

88 LESSING, O. E. "Horace Traubel: an American communist." Conservator 17 (August), 88-89.
Translated from the Munich Post. Traubel is no mere appendage of Whitman. Whitman, standing by existing American institutions, "had Socialistic ideas without being in fact a Socialist." Traubel goes farther.

89 MORGAN, MAY. "To Walt Whitman." Critic 49 (August), 148.
Reprinted: Legler.
Poem in two rhymed quatrains: "Tranquil as stars that unafraid."

90 WILLCOX, LOUISE COLLIER. "Walt Whitman." North American Review 183 (August), 281-96.
Describes Whitman's personality, nonpartisanship, democratic beliefs, faith in humanity, insistence on following the inner voice. He shifted emphasis from the perceived to the perceiver, seeking the hidden reality behind appearances. Analysis of his portraits. He was concerned with his prophetic message, not with mere art, but his use of the colloquial may grow in dignity, significance, and power with distance in time. Despite vast sympathy and selflessness, he does not reach the exalted level of the great religious leaders with whom his friends rank him, for his earlier life does not seem to have been above reproach.

91 ANON. "What Edward Carpenter Says About Walt Whitman in His Latest Book." Craftsman 10 (September), 737-46.
Review of Carpenter (1906.5), quoting extensively with favorable commentary. Carpenter "of all living men is perhaps best qualified to write with full understanding of the American prophet." Notes Whitman's interest in reform, his tremendousness, the importance of his mission to the world.

92 SHIPLEY, MAYNARD. "Walt Whitman's Message." Conservator 17 (September), 102-5.
Leaves represents Whitman's prophetic visions for humanity and "will abide through all time." His message appeals to the truly religious temperament, bridging the material and the spiritual, perceiving the divine in man. His religion is "based upon the needs and aspirations of an enlightened intelligence; upon the cravings of the human heart itself." Whitman has optimism and faith in the purpose of the universe.

93 ANON. "Walt Whitman: A Study." Philadelphia Public Ledger (29 September), 11:5.
Review of reprint of Symonds (1893.9), probably "the best criticism of the poetry

1906

of Whitman and the most remarkable explanation of the poet himself."

94 SMITH, GEORGE J. "Whitman's Reading of Life."
Poet-Lore 17, no. 4 (Autumn), 79-94.
Whitman's world is orderly, evolving,
beautiful. He is no mere materialist or
sensualist, for all is spiritual to him.
Explanation of Whitman's idea of equality,
glorification of the average, all-embracing
love (though Whitman does not seem to have
understood romantic love in its highest
reaches). Whitman reacts against puritanism but still recognizes evil as evil. He
views life as struggle and progress, believing fully in the individual's development. His views are "ampler, clearer,
saner, more satisfying" than those of other
significant poets.

95 ANON. "A Sober Life of Whitman." Nation 83
(11 October), 306.
Review of Perry (1906.13), welcome
after the Whitmania of other books. Perry
documents perhaps too much, while ignoring
more accessible material like Specimen,
"one of the most extraordinary pieces of
self-revelation" in English. Perry's defenses of Whitman against such interpretations as Symonds's are appropriate. He
shows ingenuity in explaining Whitman's
poetic and philosophical sources. The
debts to German philosophers might be pursued more fully.

*96 MACKAY, JESSIE. "Two Poets of the People's
Cause." Dunedin (New Zealand) Otago Witness
(24 October, 31 October, 7 November).
Reprinted without separation of the three
dates: McLeod.
Whitman and Bernard O'Dowd are compared
as democrats sharing "an all-penetrating
pity, a burning, leveling zeal for right."
Their national and social conditions are
contrasted; also temperaments (Whitman's
acceptance of all song material, optimism,
objectivity). Whitman's thought still inspires America with "a purer life and a
grander joy."

97 ANON. "Whitman's Sources." Literary Digest
33 (27 October), 589-90.
Discussion drawn from Perry (1906.13).

98 ANON. Paragraph review of Perry (1906.13).
Yale Literary Magazine 72 (November), 78-
79.
This biography of American literature's
"most unique character" is "sane and wholesome" and an "incisive and convincing"
essay.

99 PLATT, ISAAC HULL. "Walt Whitman's 'sin
against chastity.'" Conservator 17 (November), 137.
The relation which resulted in the
birth of children was "no casual liaison,"
from what Whitman told his friends in his

last illness, and therefore no sin against
chastity, as Perry (1906.13) suggests. He
felt it was "of a most earnest and spiritual
nature, profoundly influencing his whole
life, so deeply affecting him emotionally
that he was never able to tell the whole
story even to those who were closest to
him."

100 TRAUBEL, HORACE. "Questions for Bliss Perry."
Conservator 17 (November), 137-38.
Asks Perry for his source for statements regarding Whitman's finances (1906.
13).

101 T[RAUBEL, HORACE]. "Walt Whitman." Conservator
17 (November), 138-40.
Review of Perry (1906.13): his conclusions are unsupported; his new information is largely supplied by Ellen O'Connor.
Whitman was a man, preferable to the "gentlemen" Perry holds up for contrast; this
book, too, "is a gentleman's book."
Whitman continually emphasized that his
book "would live by its demonstration of
life." Perry's question of the ultimate
place of Whitman in contrast to Keats is
invalid: "The world may want Whitman for
one service and Keats for another."

102 ANON. "Walt Whitman--Bliss Perry's Critical
Study of the Poet a Valuable Addition to
the Growing Literature on the Subject."
Philadelphia Public Ledger (3 November),
10:5.
Favorable review of 1906.13, noting
the emphasis Perry puts on Whitman's wide
imaginative range. The large amount written
on Whitman indicates his assured place in
American literature, although people may
read less of his own work than works about
him.

103 CARY, ELISABETH LUTHER. "Mr. Perry's Whitman.
A New Study of the Eccentric Poet's Life
and Work by the Editor of the Atlantic
Monthly." New York Times Saturday Review
(3 November), 717-18.
Review of 1906.13. Perry's common
sense is preferable to the spirit of
rhapsody or depreciation usually offered
Whitman. Perry minimizes Whitman's "heroic
aspect" and explains the contradiction
"between the outspokenness of his verse
and the secretiveness of his mind." Whitman
failed as an artist because, unlike Blake,
he did not divide the essential from the
inessential. Similarities to Tupper and
Warren cannot detract from his essential
originality. He placed a clear value on
form.

104 SIMONDS, W. E. "Walt Whitman, Fifty Years
After." Dial 41 (16 November), 317-20.
Review of Perry (1906.13). Critical
concern about Whitman has shifted from
morality to technique. Perry's judgment is
sane and discriminating, always friendly

but avoiding the excessive enthusiasm of the Whitman cult which so adversely affected Whitman in his old age. Perry gives a vivid impression of "this free-hearted warm-blooded caresser of life."

105 ANON. "Whitman After Fifty Years." Current Literature 41 (December), 640-41.
Review of Perry (1906.13). Perry views Whitman as a true child of his age, a mystic, a romanticist, and an American. Changes over the years have brought greater acceptance of Whitman's form and "gospel of nudity."

106 HOWE, M. A. DeWOLFE. "The Spell of Whitman." Atlantic Monthly 98 (December), 849-55.
Review of Binns (1905.1), Perry (1906.13), Carpenter (1906.5), Traubel (1906.22). They reveal less pleasant aspects of Whitman, the existence of his children and the role of his egotism, which differs in real life from that in Leaves. The Whitman literature keeps expanding, but his spell is not universal, touching largely the scholar class he least expected to reach.

107 ANON. Review of Perry (1906.13). Christian Register 85 (27 December), 1443.
Perry presents a just view. Whitman's form, "that wonderful congeries of noble ideas,--some of the loftiest to be found in the writings of any American poet," is mixed with much that is tedious and trivial, sometimes prose-like, sometimes rhythmic.

1907

BOOKS

1 ADAMS, HENRY. The Education of Henry Adams. Washington: Privately published, p. 336.
Reprinted: 1918.1.
Among American writers, only Whitman insisted on sex as powerful rather than merely sentimental.

*2 BRIGHT, ANNIE. A Soul's Pilgrimage. Melbourne: n.p., pp. 79, 246-48, 251, 256, 275.
Reported in Saunders Whitman in Fiction.

3 COLUM, PADRAIC, ed. Preface to Whitman: Selected Poems. New Nation Booklets, no. 1. Dublin: New Nation Press, pp. 5-7.
Whitman's work has much to give an Irish public, for he "was very consistently a national poet," specifically for a country that "had a national unity to achieve." He anticipated and projected into literature the "emancipated individual" that America needed, as Ireland does.

4 JAMES, WILLIAM. Pragmatism: A New Name for Some Old Ways of Thinking. New York: Longmans, Green, & Co., pp. 274-78.

Reprints (with an error) "To You" and provides two alternative ways of reading this "fine and moving poem"--"the monistic way, the mystical way of pure cosmic emotion," and "the pluralistic way," both encouraging fidelity to ourselves.

5 KIRKHAM, STANTON DAVIS. The Ministry of Beauty. San Francisco and New York: Paul Elder & Co., pp. iii, 18.
Quotes "Open Road" as epigraph. Whitman is loved "for his great heart" and therefore forgiven for "his discordant twanging on the chord of sex." He worked for beauty, "the beauty of spiritual things, of comradeship in the truth, of broad mindvistas."

6 MICHAEL, HELEN ABBOTT. Studies in Plant and Organic Chemistry and Literary Papers. Cambridge, Mass.: Riverside Press. "Woman and Freedom in Whitman," pp. 370-92.
Reprint of 1897.56.

7 MORSE, W. F. "American Lectures." In The Writings of Oscar Wilde. Vol. 15. His Life with a Critical Estimate of His Writings. London and New York: A. R. Keller & Co., pp. 134-35.
Describes briefly two visits by Wilde to Whitman, accompanied by Joseph M. Stoddart, Wilde's American publisher. Wilde's high opinion of Whitman is cited. Whitman is quoted as basing his method on the compositor's stick.

8 OMOND, T. S. English Metrists in the Eighteenth and Nineteenth Centuries. London, New York, and Toronto: Henry Frowde, Oxford University Press, p. 148.
Reprinted: 1921.26.
In such poems by Whitman as "Lilacs" (quoted), "the rhythmic pulse beats strong." Whether or not irregular rhythms "ultimately oust the more regular" in favor of such "recondite harmonies of prose, often nobly illustrated by Whitman," some form of rhythmic expression will certainly continue.

PERIODICALS

9 E., C. "Some Random Thoughts about Walt Whitman." Ye Crank 1 (January), 48-52.
Impressionistic appreciation. Whitman is of the out-of-doors. "His sanity and breadth of vision, his glorious optimism and exultant joy in living, and above all his universality" seize those not put off by his rhythm. He has succeeded "in exactly and minutely portraying a man," a friend, with both good and evil, attraction and repulsion. His mystic sense is not cosmic consciousness in the sense of "comprehension of the whole cosmos."

10 FERM, ELIZABETH BURNS. "The Democracy of Walt Whitman." Mother Earth 1 (January), 23-31.
Whitman's democracy is a spiritual con-

cept grasped only by those who spiritually receive it. He calls us to introspection and "the evolution of a race consciousness." Concluded 1907.15.

11 PLATT, ISAAC HULL. "The Ethics of Biography." Conservator 17 (January), 173.
Perry (1906.13) would merit charges of libel if his claims about Whitman's finances were made of a living man. His book "has done incalculable harm." Platt also complains of a statement in More's otherwise fine essay (1906.10).

12 TRAUBEL, HORACE. "The Code of the Gentleman Referred to Bliss Perry." Conservator 17 (January), 168-72.
Traces his unsuccessful efforts to discover from Perry the source for his statements against Whitman (1906.13).

*13 [TRIMBLE, W. H.?] "The Message of Walt Whitman." Australian Herald (1 January), 176-79.
Reprinted: McLeod.
Impressionistic view of the feelings Whitman produces and his principal messages. Whitman seems intoxicated by nature and man. His message is the central importance of man in the universe, the significance of personality, evolution, faith in the future of the race, the religious basis of democracy. But "his optimism fails to take full account of what we call 'evil.'"

14 DENISON, FLORA MacD. "Burns and Whitman." Toronto Sunday World (27 January).
Burns and Whitman both stressed universal love and acceptance and opposed prejudice and privilege. Burns wrote lilting verse but Whitman's was flat, yet his thoughts were exalting and properly inspirational, to improve social conditions.

15 FERM, ELIZABETH BURNS. "The Democracy of Walt Whitman." Mother Earth 1 (February), 15-21.
Concludes 1907.10. Whitman is quoted to support her exhortations regarding the need for women's equality.

16 [HOWELLS, W. D.] "Editor's Easy Chair." Harper's New Monthly Magazine 114 (February), 482.
Whitman's new form at first appeared "something worth doing," for he seemed to be "bettering no man's instruction" as "richly beginning master, and not poorly beginning apprentice." However, he actually "like every other master had his instruction": the Psalms (with "passages like Whitman at his best, though with different subjects") and Song of Solomon.

17 KENNEDY, WILLIAM SLOANE. "On the Trail of the Good Gray Poet." Conservator 17 (February), 182-85.
Perry (1906.13) gives evidence of hard

work, but he is not qualified for his task, being a spokesman for the genteel class. He errs in tracing Whitman's literary influences, not recognizing when Whitman is original. Actual sources include Dickens, Plato, Montaigne, Sand, and Emerson, as shown in quotations, with Rousseau a negative influence.

18 MONTGOMERY, ALBERTA. "Walt Whitman and William Blake." Conservator 17 (February), 185-86.
Blake and Whitman share "titanic energy," positive spiritual optimism, affirmation of life, and biographical circumstances ("obscurity, poverty, neglect, often acute suffering").

19 ANON. "Mr. Perry's 'Whitman.'" Outlook 85 (2 February), 278-80.
Review of Perry (1906.13), welcome after "overheated accounts" by Whitman's friends. Whitman's strength and originality stem from his expression being so much a part of himself. He could not "see beyond the limits of his own horizons" due to his "colossal egotism." His greater inspirations, "Lilacs" and "Cradle," are American poetry's high-water mark. He was not the poet he thought himself to be, neither of the first order of creative genius nor the ultimate poet of democracy; but he is, however, a vital force in our literature, "an original and native voice."

20 ANON. Review of Bertz's Der Yankee Heiland (Dresden: C. Reissner, 1906). Nation 84 (21 February), 179-80.
Bertz's denunciations of Whitman are not justifiable. His theory is "that Whitman regarded himself as the Messiah of a new humanity, renascent in America, and by cunning, prevarication, and persistent self-advertisement, actually made himself the idol of a sect." Bertz accuses Whitman of a secret pessimism inconsistent with his public teaching, lack of originality in his democratic gospel, and pathological qualities in his ideal of comradeship. Bertz "admits that the 'over-force' of his language acts with a powerful suggestiveness upon susceptible souls," hence the hypnotic and demagogic danger of his art.

21 [FLOWER, B. O.] "Books of the Day." Arena 37 (March), 325-27.
Review of Traubel (1906.22) with extracts, valuable and interesting for the correspondence of the famous and the obscure, whom Whitman's "vigorous and unhackneyed thought" had helped, and for intimate revelations of Whitman, although its presentation might be improved.

22 KENNEDY, WILLIAM SLOANE. "Bliss Perry Not Disingenuous." Conservator 18 (March), 7-8.
Corrects some misquoting of Perry (1906.13).

23 LEE, GERALD STANLEY. "An Order for the Next Poet. For Outline: Walt Whitman. Details to be filled in, please, by Samuel Johnson and William Shakespeare." Putnam's Monthly 1 (March), 697-703.
 Poetry is best when read not merely as poetry: "A man who reads Walt Whitman for two hours feels like a poet. If he reads Tennyson for two hours, he feels that Tennyson is a poet." Whitman "best expresses the modern age because he is the first poet who has ever been matter-of-fact with a compost heap," even making it beautiful. He conceives of poetry as "working things through to their infinity" yet looking to even greater work, while Tennyson often looks to what has been done before. Whitman is a master of symbolism. Objections may be passed over, and he will eventually reach the reader. Concluded 1907.27.

24 BUTTON, W. E. "Walt Whitman." Outlook 85 (2 March), 528-29.
 Letter in response to review of Perry (1907.19), "the first really sane and critical article on Whitman" in a long time. Whitman's posing, "kindly disposition," and aid to workingmen are described from this writer's personal recollections of Whitman in Camden. "His moral character was as you state it, and my family say that he morally injured some young men that they knew." Much of his poetry was not thought inspired even by himself but "written to eke out an existence" from the demand in England "for something believed to be characteristically American." That the democracy he wrote for and about cared nothing for his poetry "shows the complete failure to strike the keynote of democratic feeling."

25 ECOB, JAMES H. Letter in response to review of Perry (1907.19). Outlook 85 (2 March), 529.
 The Outlook's review and Perry's book are wrong "to so slur over the foulness of that brute beast, Walter Whitman. Too idle and helpless to earn his own living, consorting with the toughs and bums of this city [Philadelphia] and Camden, spending all his last days with a 'buxom widow' as housekeeper, the father of six illegitimate children, the destroyer of two homes at least, not one honorable act or sentiment to his credit, it gives one a moral nausea to hear respectable periodicals and decent people mention his name with the least degree of allowance." His memory should be erased, like all "such brute beasts who happen to have some little smartness in trick literature!"

26 E[NDE], A. von. "Whitman in Germany: Edward Bertz Now an Apostate from the Whitman Cult--A Bitter Arraignment of the Camden Poet." New York Times Saturday Review (9 March), 146.
 Summary of Whitman's reputation in Germany. Review of Bertz's Der Yankee Heiland, which follows the new psychological school and regards Whitman as a degenerate, making many insinuations incompatible with serious criticism. Bertz criticizes Whitman's deceitfulness and intellectual shortcomings.

27 LEE, GERALD STANLEY. "An Order for the Next Poet. Details to be filled in, please, by Samuel Johnson and William Shakespeare." Putnam's Monthly 2 (April), 99-107.
 Concludes 1907.23. Shakespeare is of all moods, Whitman of only one; he could not laugh or cry, although he embraced the world more fully than Shakespeare; hence he is second-rate beside Shakespeare, though greater than any other poet in modern life. Whitman is "the ground-plan for the world's great modern poet, instead of the poet himself." His lack of humor was due to his largeness, his perception of sameness rather than difference. He lacked Johnson's skill of discrimination, seeing in each man the universal rather than the particular. Whitman is "a street poet" rather than a "private, personal poet." We await a combination of Whitman and Shakespeare.

28 MACDONALD, GEORGE E. "Unbidden Thoughts." Liberty 16 (April), 43.
 Incidental: during the crisis of capitalism in the 1870s, "forces were gathering as undissuadable as Walt Whitman vaunted himself to be, and we know how insistent he was."

29 PLATT, ISAAC HULL. "Bliss Perry's Whitman." Conservator 18 (April), 23-24.
 Perry (1906.13) is misleading in facts and in conclusions about and evaluations of Whitman and his friends and followers.

30 PUTNAM, FRANK. "Whitman and Traubel." Conservator 18 (April), 25-26.
 Review of Traubel (1906.22) reprinted from National Magazine (unlocated): Traubel's book furnishes a background for Leaves and a key to Whitman's philosophy.

31 TRIMBLE, WILLIAM H. "Surplusage or Shortage?" Conservator 18 (April), 24.
 Refutes Chadwick (1903.3) on Whitman's overuse of "luscious," "voluptuous," "delicious," by showing actual word counts for each.

32 H[OLLOWAY?], E[MORY?], and S., J. A. "Walt Whitman Again." Outlook 85 (13 April), 862.
 Response to Ecob (1907.25): asks for the authority for his assertions and presents evidence to contradict them. Whitman, like other prophets, was misunderstood by his fellowmen. Editors append a note: "It seemed to us that it was perfectly apparent that The Outlook certainly disagreed with Dr. Ecob's position."

1907

33 ROBINSON, VICTOR. "Walt Whitman." Altruria
    1 (May), 14-25.
        Text of an address delivered on several
    occasions listed: America has in Whitman
    "a poet who ranks with the Redeemers of the
    Race." Aristocratic readers do not appre-
    ciate him; he must be taken in a spirit
    like his own. To rank him with Shakespeare
    is not an honor but only justice. His
    approach to sex is healthy, though achieved
    through sentiment more than through science,
    and would improve relations between the
    sexes. His keynote is a limitless love.
    He has prepared the path for the liberation
    of woman as man's equal. He cannot be ex-
    pounded, his own attempts being sometimes
    ridiculous, but he must be read firsthand,
    preferably in the woods. Robinson's poem
    "Reading Walt" in five rhymed quatrains
    ends the essay, being addressed to a maiden
    with whom he has read Whitman under a tree.

34 WILLCOX, LOUISE COLLIER. "Mr. Bliss Perry's
    Walt Whitman." Conservator 18 (May), 41-42.
    Reprint of 1907.35.

35 ____. "Mr. Bliss Perry's 'Walt Whitman.'"
    North American Review 185 (17 May), 221-23.
    Reprinted: 1907.34.
        Review of Perry (1906.13), complaining
    of his tone and attitude toward Whitman.
    Contrary to Perry's suggestions, Whitman
    lived effectively, being "practical enough
    to hew out his own path, to live free and
    untrammelled, with plenty of leisure, and
    in full communion with himself," a great-
    souled man.

36 DUCLO, ESTELLE. "Walt Whitman." New York
    Times Saturday Review (25 May), 336.
        Tribute sonnet to Whitman, seeking to
    walk with him, remarking on the incongruity
    of her form for her subject.

37 CALDER, ELLEN M. "Personal Recollections of
    Walt Whitman." Atlantic Monthly 99 (June),
    825-34.
        O'Connor's widow recalls her acquain-
    tance with Whitman beginning in 1862: his
    hospital work, conversations at the O'Connor
    home, habits, personality, opinions (on
    book reviews, Emerson, "Free Love," mar-
    riage, the institution of the father,
    hatred of war, unfitness of blacks to vote),
    various anecdotes. As a protest against
    the double standard, he proclaimed the
    goodness and purity of all in nature. His
    tremendous optimism was uplifting, with
    faith in the triumph of right and justice.

38 ENDE, AMELIA von. "Whitman and the Germans
    Today." Conservator 18 (June), 55-57.
        Favorable description of the work of
    Lessing and Schlaf; Whitman's effect on
    German free verse and young poets. Bertz's
    work is unrepresentative, unscholarly.

39 ANON. "A Precursor of Whitman." North
    American Review 185 (21 June), 463-64.
        Thomas Traherne, whose poems have only
    recently been found and published, fore-
    shadows Whitman in his beliefs in the
    splendor and beauty of the universe, the
    sanctity of the body, the soul as a complete
    unity pervading the universe, the insepa-
    rability of essence and manifestation.
    Both have "the cataloguing habit." Passages
    from each are quoted.

40 COMPENDIUM. "About Walt Whitman." Conservator
    18 (July), 71-73.
        Quotes letters to Whitman Fellowship
    from Bazalgette, Debs, Louise Willcox,
    George Fred Williams, and Felix Schelling.

41 SWAN, TOM. "Walt Whitman: The Man." Open
    Road, n.s. 1 (July), 26-32.
        Biographical sketch, using quotations
    from Whitman, noting his early rapport with
    nature. Other descriptions of Whitman are
    quoted. Continued 1907.44.

42 TRAUBEL, HORACE. "Talks with Walt Whitman."
    American Magazine 64 (July), 281-88.
        Pre-publication extracts from 1908.17.
    Introduction briefly recounts Whitman's
    years in Camden, his impression on visitors.

43 ANON. "Did Whitman Borrow from the Orientals?"
    Current Literature 43 (August), 165-66.
        Précis of Elsa Barker's article in the
    Open Road (unlocated), suggesting Whitman's
    similarities to the Persians and Hindus.
    (The Open Road piece seems very similar to
    her Canada Monthly article, 1911.31.)

44 SWAN, TOM. "Walt Whitman: II. His Book."
    Open Road, n.s. 1 (August), 99-105.
        Continues 1907.41. Whitman avoided the
    usual niceties of expression not because he
    lacked literary culture "but because he
    believed they would stand as barriers be-
    tween him and his readers." Had he adopted
    the usual method, the loss would have out-
    weighed the gain in fame. He was "too
    staunch a democrat to be dominated by the
    past," although he did not ignore his debt
    to his predecessors. His work is "frankly
    didactic" but includes true poetry. Con-
    cluded 1907.57.

45 LEE, GERALD S. "This Round World." Mount Tom
    3 (9 August), 44-45.
        Incidental: Whitman is one of the
    recent literary figures now recognized who
    do not fit the expectations of the fastidious
    but appeal rather to "the literary outlaws
    and tramps." He "lifted the lid off the
    world."

46 TRAUBEL, HORACE. "Whitman in Old Age, from
    Horace Traubel's Record." Century Magazine
    74 (September), 740-55.
        Pre-publication extracts from 1908.17.
    Concluded 1907.50.

47 WIKSELL, PERCIVAL. "Peter Doyle." Conservator 18 (September), 103-4.
   Reminiscences of Whitman's friend Doyle, by a friend of his.

48 PLATT, ISAAC HULL. "Wounded in the House of Friends." Conservator 18 (October), 121-22.
   Response to Perry's implications of Whitman's dishonesty (1906.13).

49 TRAUBEL, HORACE. "Walt Whitman's Views." Appleton's Magazine 10 (October), 463-72. Photograph by Ulke.
   Pre-publication extracts of 1908.17. Editor's note explains that this represents an "arbitrary editorial selection of isolated paragraphs" on literary figures, Americans, "Captain," political and religious issues.

50 _____. "Whitman in Old Age: Third Paper from Horace Traubel's Record." Century Magazine 74 (October), 911-22.
   Concludes 1907.46.

51 ANON. "Whitman's Keen Literary Judgments." Current Literature 43 (November), 519-21. Photograph.
   Quotes Whitman's comments on other writers from recent Traubel installments (1907.42, 1907.46, 1907.49, 1907.50), which "witness to the depth and breadth, the enormous erudition, of Whitman's mind." He is no "literary vagabond," as hostile critics call him.

52 DE CASSERES, BENJAMIN. "Enter Walt Whitman." Philistine 25 (November), 161-72.
   Revised: 1926.7.
   Impressionistic appreciation: Whitman is about to be discovered as America's most significant figure, great because he was a rebel, was sincere, lived sublimely and naturally, embodied his philosophy. He believed in immortality through evolution, the soul of man as center of the universe, the democracy of the spirit, the wonder of life. His thirty years of composing Leaves "was one long majestic gesture, which translated a knowable universe into an unknowable fourth dimension that must forevermore claim our amaze."

53 PLATT, ISAAC HULL. "Some Later Reflections for Bliss Perry." Conservator 18 (November), 137-38.
   Reprint of 1907.54.

54 _____. "Resents Attack on Walt Whitman. Dr. Isaac Hull Platt Examines Reflections on Gray Poet's Character Made by Professor Bliss Perry." New York Times Saturday Review (2 November), 696.
   Reprinted: 1907.53.
   Compares accounts of Whitman by Traubel with Perry's charges against Whitman's honesty (1906.13.)

*55 ANON. "Walt Whitman as a Veteran Saw Him." Sand-Burr Magazine (December).
   Reported in CHAL.

56 HARNED, THOMAS B. "Slanderers of Whitman." Conservator 18 (December), 151-54.
   Response to Ecob (1907.25), citing tributes to Whitman's character.

57 SWAN, TOM. "Walt Whitman: III. His Message." Open Road, n.s. 1 (December), 290-98.
   Concludes 1907.44. Explains Whitman's message of religion, love, and democracy, and the quality of personality growing out of them. His religion "consists in joyfully recognising our relation to the Infinite" and "shaping our life in accordance." His optimism sees even evil as potentially producing good. Democracy can only be achieved by building up "grand individuals" and applying the principles of liberty and equality. His greatest glory is that his own life and person embodied his philosophy.

58 WINTER, WILLIAM. "Thomas Bailey Aldrich. Memories of an Old Comrade." Saturday Evening Post 180 (28 December), 12-13.
   Reprinted: 1909.15. Quoted in 1908.21.
   Whitman had impressed Winter as "a commonplace, uncouth and sometimes obnoxiously coarse writer, trying to be original by using a formless style, and by celebrating the proletarians who make the world almost uninhabitable by their vulgarity." Whitman's disparaging comments on Aldrich's and Winter's verse are quoted; his definition in conversation of a poet as a maker of poems is ridiculed.

1908

BOOKS

1 ALDEN, HENRY MILLS. Magazine Writing and the New Literature. New York and London: Harper & Bros., pp. 48-49.
   One-paragraph summary of Whitman's career in journalism.

2 BINNS, HENRY BRYAN. The Great Companions. London: A. C. Fifield, p. 58.
   Reprinted: 1915.10.
   Recalls Whitman's response to war's challenge, his healthy body shattered by the experience, yet a sign for all, "responsive to Love's lightest breath, a man for Love's most fierce demand patient, enduring."

3 BOWEN, EDWIN W. Whitman selections and bibliography in Makers of American Literature: A Case-Book on American Literature. New York and Washington: Neale Publishing Co., pp. 390-404, 409-10; "Walt Whitman," pp. 371-89.
   Whitman's reputation has suffered because he divided critics into two hostile schools. His style is unattractive, due to

1908

lack of adequate culture and a rich intellectual development, and he was found indecent, although his flaws are aesthetic
rather than moral. Lacking such faults,
<u>Drum-Taps</u> found a more cordial reception
than <u>Leaves</u>, being inspired by his "abiding
sympathy" and "absolute self-abandonment."
Without "the art instinct" or any "grand
and inspiring poem of sustained interest,"
he is still a poet for his "imagination,
passion, faith and the gift of utterance,"
being best in brief descriptive poems and
some extracts.

4 BURROUGHS, JOHN. <u>Leaf and Tendril</u>. Boston
and New York: Houghton, Mifflin & Co.,
pp. 211, 219-20, 226, 248, 263.
Incidental references and quotations
regarding Whitman's evolutionary beliefs.

5 BUTLER, NICHOLAS MURRAY. <u>The American As He
Is</u>. New York: Macmillan Co., p. 95.
Whitman stands apart from the New York
and Boston groups. He and Poe are the
poets most read and admired in other countries and have made a very respectable contribution to nineteenth-century literature
in English.

6 CARPENTER, EDWARD. <u>The Intermediate Sex</u>.
London: George Allen & Unwin, pp. 47, 75-
77, 117.
Describes Whitman as exemplar of the
love of comrades, in poetry and life.
Whitman insists on the social function of
this love, presumably aware of such passion
as alive around him. Carpenter answers
Bertz's objections that Whitman's democracy
is founded on a false basis.

7 GREENSLET, FERRIS. <u>The Life of Thomas Bailey
Aldrich</u>. Boston and New York: Houghton
Mifflin Co., pp. 38, 138-39, 140.
Quotes Aldrich's letters to Stedman in
response to his article (1880.35):
"Whitman's manner is a hollow affectation,
and represents neither the man nor the time.
As the voice of the nineteenth century, he
will have little significance in the twenty-
first," though outlasting most of his contemporaries. "Writing newspaper puffs of
himself" was despicable. His occasionally
admirable bits of "color and epithets and
lyrical outbreaks" are not enough to make
a poet.

8 HARTLEY, L. CONRAD. <u>The Spirit of Walt
Whitman (A Psychological Study in Blank
Verse)</u>. Manchester: J. E. Cornish, 36 pp.
Introduction calls Whitman the incarnation of sympathy. This blank-verse poem
presents the progress of Whitman's soul
toward his poetic mission, emerging from a
dramatic temptation by "Science," "Philosophy," and "Poetry" to teach "Love," without
which all is insignificant.

9 JAMES, HENRY. <u>Views and Reviews</u>. Boston:
Ball Publishing Co. "Mr. Walt Whitman,"
pp. 101-10.
Reprint of 1865.8.

10 KNOWLES, ROBERT E. <u>The Web of Time</u>. New
York: H. Revell Co., pp. 224-26.
Characters disagree whether Whitman's
work emulates Christ or belongs in the gutter.

11 LEE, VERNON [Violet Paget]. <u>Gospels of Anarchy
and Other Contemporary Studies</u>. London:
T. F. Unwin. New York: Brentano's (1909
issue), pp. 34-36, 53, 73.
Criticizes Whitman's view of all-equal-
izing divinity. "Emerson formulates what
has been blunderingly put into practice by
Whitman, and condenses into a few mystical
words what Whitman extends into grotesque
rhapsodies of mixed beauty and dirt."

12 MAYNARD, LAURENS, ed. Introduction to <u>The
Wisdom of Walt Whitman</u>. New York:
Brentano's, pp. xiii-xvi.
Extract reprinted: 1908.44.
This collection of passages selected to
reveal "the deep significance and rare
wisdom of Whitman's pregnant sentences" is
intended for readers unacquainted with
"this compelling master of the minds of
men." His main ideas, religion and democracy, are "subtly interdependent." The
individual is central. His attitude toward
death is noble and original. An index of
topics of the selections is included.

*13 MAYNE, XAVIER [Edward Irenaeus Prime
Stevenson]. <u>The Intersexes: A History of
Similisexualism as a Problem in Social Life</u>.
Privately printed. "Walt Whitman," pp. 377-
82.
Reprinted in facsimile: New York: Arno
Press, 1975.
Whitman's poetry reveals him as "one
of the prophets and priests of homosexuality,"
which is evident in various aspects of his
work and life. Convinced of its purity and
naturalness, he idealizes (but sensually)
man-to-man love, psychic and physical, and
translates this into a Socratic mission
and a Platonic notion of democracy.

14 PERRY, BLISS. <u>Walt Whitman</u>. Boston and New
York: Houghton Mifflin Co., 334 pp.
Appendix and index.
Revision of 1906.13.
Changes wording regarding several controversial matters. Notes in the appendix
explain the changes from the original version, quoting letters and other papers from
various people responding to his statements
in the earlier version.

15 RUSKIN, JOHN. <u>The Works of John Ruskin</u>. Vol.
34. London: George Allen; New York:
Longmans, Green, & Co., p. 727.
Reprint of 1880.7 with slight changes.

16 TOLLEMACHE, Hon. LIONEL A. Old and Odd
    Memories. London: Edward Arnold, p. 265.
        Quotes "what Tennyson said to a friend
    of mine" (Anna Swanwick) regarding Whitman:
    "The first requisite of a singer is that he
    should sing. Walt Whitman has not this
    first requisite; let him speak in prose."

17 TRAUBEL, HORACE. With Walt Whitman in Camden,
    II (July 16, 1888-October 31, 1888). New
    York: D. Appleton, 570 pp. Index. Illus-
    trated.
    Extracts reprinted: Murphy.
        Continues 1906.22. Continued 1914.16.

18 WILDE, OSCAR. Complete Works of Oscar Wilde.
    Vol. 9. Edited by Robert Ross. New York:
    Bigelow, Brown & Co. "The Gospel According
    to Walt Whitman," pp. 396-401.
    Reprint of 1889.18.

19 ZUEBLIN, CHARLES. The Religion of a Democrat.
    New York: B. W. Huebsch, pp. 173-74.
        Whitman's "pervasive force" is cited as
    exemplifying impersonal immortality; he
    "means more for humanity than many captains
    of industry."

PERIODICALS

20 JOHNSTON, J. H. "Half-Hours with Walt
    Whitman." Everywhere 21 (January), 212-14.
        Reminiscences of his acquaintance with
    Whitman. He only understood Leaves years
    after first reading, following which he
    wrote Whitman and then visited him in
    Camden, thus beginning many mutual visits.
    The Lincoln lecture of 1887 is described,
    with Lowell's moved response to it. Whit-
    man was "the purest minded man I ever met,"
    "the cleanest personality." George Waters
    is recalled painting Whitman's portrait.

21 ANON. "Topics of the Day." Providence Journal
    (26 January), sec. 2, 4:5.
        Editorial quoting Winter (1907.58)
    approvingly. His "sense of the 'brother-
    hood of man'" was due to his not taking a
    bath as often as most "desirable citizens"
    and to his sympathy for "tramps who have
    similar prejudices."

*22 JEPSON, EDGAR. "Walt Whitman." Fabian News
    (February).
        Reported in CHAL, but actually in 1906
    (see 1906.30a).

23 PLATT, ISAAC HULL. "Assailants and Defenders
    of Whitman." Conservator 18 (February), 183.
        Unpublished letter to Outlook attacking
    Ecob's slander (1907.25) and the Outlook's
    failure to cite Harned's credentials when
    printing his response (unlocated except
    in Conservator, 1907.56).

24 T[RAUBEL, HORACE]. "Walt Whitman: by Leon
    Bazalgette." Conservator 18 (February), 189.

        Notice of publication of Bazalgette's
    book in French. Traubel recalls his
    mother's warning against Whitman when he
    was young and is amused that this tribute
    now comes from abroad.

25 ANON. "Whitman and His Boswell. Horace
    Traubel's New Volume of Recollections of
    the Good Grey Poet an Interesting Illus-
    tration of Adoring Discipleship." New York
    Times Saturday Review (15 February), 81-82.
        Review of 1908.17: Whitman appears as
    "a monstrous (but amiable) egotist," with
    "naive self-complacency" due to his lack of
    a liberal education.

26 ANON. "Sixty Years of Newspaper Making."
    Brooklyn Times (29 February), Supplement
    Section, 4:3-4.
        Includes account of Whitman's editorship
    of the Times; quotes Frederick Huene on his
    early efforts to translate Leaves into
    German according to Whitman's wish; de-
    scribes Whitman's appearance. Whitman
    resigned his place because of articles
    criticized by church people.

27 BAZALGETTE, LEON. "Walt Whitman in France."
    Conservator 19 (March), 8-9.
        Notice of publication of his French
    translation of Whitman and hopes for its
    reception.

28 COYNE, JAMES H. "Richard Maurice Bucke VI."
    Conservator 19 (March), 5-7.
    Extract reprinted from 1906.6.

29 EASTMAN, MAX. "The Poet's Mind." North
    American Review 187 (March), 418, 424.
        "Whitman shows that the subject-matter
    of poetry is limited only by the power and
    enthusiasm of the poet; he demands that we
    should reconsider our definitions." "Isaiah
    and Whitman are of the same mental temper,
    where they kindle us, as Milton and
    Shelley," all of them being seers and
    "makers of vision."

30 FISKE, CHARLES HENRY. "The Story of American
    Painting: VI. Modern Portrait Painting."
    Chautauquan 50 (March), 86; Alexander por-
    trait, p. 71.
        Alexander's portrait of Whitman "speaks
    for itself."

31 SCOTT, FRED NEWTON. "A Note on Walt Whitman's
    Prosody." Journal of English and Germanic
    Philology 7, no. 2 (Spring), 134-53.
    Reprinted (with minor changes): 1910.41.
        Whitman has been regarded as either
    "falling below the standards of traditional
    art," a narrow-minded view, or rising above
    them and approximating nature, a false view.
    Tracing the development of particular poems
    reveals Whitman's artistry. He turned from
    the rhythm of beats to the prose rhythm of
    "pitch-glides," which "seemed nearer to the
    uncramped spirit of nature," particularly

1908

to "natural free motions" and "certain sequences of sounds." His wavelike lines are new to poetry, although akin to the Bible, Ossian, and Blake. Only Whitman of American poets can compare with the greatest British poets in his sense of artistry, but his beautiful passages, upon rereading, begin to sound commonplace, unlike Shakespeare's.

32 ANON. "Whitman's Vindication of His Literary Methods." Current Literature 44 (April), 399-400.
Quotes Whitman's various attitudes toward his work and comments on his purpose from Traubel II (1908.17), which "affords a vivid record of Whitman's conflicting moods during the years when the fate of 'Leaves of Grass' may be said to have hung in the balance." "Back of all else in Whitman's nature was feeling--emotional substance."

33 MARSH, EDWARD CLARK. "Mr. Traubel's 'With Walt Whitman in Camden.'" Bookman 27 (April), 164-67.
Reprinted: 1908.54.
Review of 1908.17, which transcribes "the daily life and talk of a man--and a man great enough, with all reservations made, to be representative." "The most unliterary of writers, Whitman was a catholic reader, and his judgments of men and books are often illuminating," although of Whitman more than of their subjects. His egotism is usually that of a big man, conscious of himself and the importance of his work.

34 PLATT, ISAAC HULL. "Bliss Perry and Walt Whitman." Conservator 19 (April), 23-25.
Reprint of 1908.35.

35 ____. "Mr. Bliss Perry and Walt Whitman. Dr. Platt Defends Poet's Memory from Animadversions in His 'Life' by Atlantic's Editor." New York Times Saturday Review (18 April), 232.
Reprinted: 1908.34.
"The second edition [1908.14] repeats and emphasizes the offenses of the first." Perry fails to give his authorities for many unwarranted statements regarding Whitman's finances and paternity.

36 CRONYN, GEORGE W. "The Idealism of the Real: Claude Monet and Walt Whitman." Columbia Monthly 5 (May), 237-51.
Monet and Whitman exemplify the idealist of the real, reconciling materialism and pure idealism, science and imagination, being similar in temperament and philosophy. Whitman displays true, not excessive, refinement, through his sympathy, affection, and spirituality. Though sometimes ridiculous, he splendidly adapts his means to his ends in "Brooklyn Ferry," "Lilacs," "Man-of-War-Bird," and "Cradle." He shares

qualities with Chaucer, Wordsworth, Goethe, Emerson, Stevenson. He substitutes goodness for mere morality. The poet of equality and human activity, he depicts the national life that other American poets have merely suggested. Monet and Whitman are "in harmony with the conditions that have produced them," and their work is important for "what it suggests to the future."

37 [FLOWER, B. O.] "Through the Closed Shop to the Open World." Arena 39 (May), 639.
Note on Traubel, contributor to this issue: he imbibed from Whitman "his broad spirit," love for democratic ideals, and "original, rugged and direct presentation of truth."

38 HOEBER, ARTHUR. "John W. Alexander." International Studio 34 (May), lxxxix, xcvii.
Incidental mention of Alexander's portrait of "the strong type of the thinker in riper years, Walt Whitman" (here reprinted).

39 WILLIAMS, FRANCIS H. "An Appreciation of Whitman." Columbia Monthly 5 (May), 254.
Recalls the increasing sense Whitman gave of "the enormous power of his personality and the originality of his genius." "Coarse only as Nature is coarse," rising above art, he is America's "only really cosmic poet."

40 COMPENDIUM. "More Letters about Walt Whitman." Conservator 19 (June), 56-57.
Letters from Ellen Glasgow (Whitman's spirit "is the spirit of the future"), Sarrazin, Truman Bartlett (personal reminiscence), Bazalgette (quoting anecdote of Tennyson calling Whitman "the only man worth knowing in America").

41 ____. "With Walt Whitman in Camden." Conservator 19 (June), 57-58.
Quotes comments on 1908.17: F. H. Williams appreciates this re-creation of Whitman's personality; the New York Evening Post (unlocated) finds Traubel unable to distinguish between Whitman's greatness and his fustian, although perhaps "Whitman himself never saw with the eye of the analyzing intellect the deep-seated sources of emotion and awe which feed his poetry at its best."

42 ANON. "Honor Genius of Whitman at Fellowship Meeting." New York Call (1 June).
Account of meeting. The speakers emphasized Whitman's popularity with the laboring class rather than the upper class.

43 COMPENDIUM. "With Walt Whitman in Camden." Conservator 19 (July), 74-75.
Notices of 1908.17: from Isaac Hull Platt and Frank Putnam.

44 MAYNARD, LAURENS. "The Wisdom of Walt Whitman." Conservator 19 (July), 72-73.

Extract reprinted from 1908.12.

45 HARTT, GEORGE M. "Whitman: An Inspiration to Democracy." Conservator 19 (August), 87-88.
    Whitman's message is democracy, meaning love-urgings toward humanity, which would solve social problems. Hartt relates Whitman to socialist ideals.

46 ANON. "Summer Visits to Walt Whitman--Shrines of Long Island." New York Herald (30 August), Magazine Section.
    Account of Whitman's life on Long Island, his editorial work, all while he was "formulating his creed--the celebration of man," and "exercising the magnetism which he realized he possessed to cheer the friendless and strengthen the weak."

47 ANON. "A Frenchman's Fervid Tribute to Walt Whitman." Current Literature 45 (September), 286-89.
    Traces Whitman's reception abroad, especially in France, where his indirect influence is appreciable. Bazalgette's biography, L'Homme et Son Oeuvre, is quoted, in English translation, on Whitman's greatness, nearness to the French, wonderful personality and life, and complex character with its contradictions, blended in harmony.

48 CAMPBELL, HELEN. "A Man and a Book." Arena 40 (September), 183-91.
    Biographical essay on Traubel with various considerations of his relations with Whitman and Whitman's influence on him.

49 COMPENDIUM. "With Walt Whitman in Camden." Conservator 19 (September), 104-6.
    Generally favorable notices of 1908.17 by Stedman, Ernest Crosby, Joaquin Miller, Paul Elmer More.

50 MEYER, ANNIE NATHAN. "Two Portraits of Whitman." Putnam's Monthly 4 (September), 707-10.
    The Eakins and Alexander portraits, here reproduced, are analyzed. Eakins presented the real Whitman because "he is more of Whitman than any other painter." Commentary on Eakins is quoted as equally applicable to Whitman.

51 ANON. "New England Nature Studies: Thoreau, Burroughs, Whitman." Edinburgh Review 208 (October), 343-66.
    These writers bring new vitality to the romantic return to nature, viewing the earth not as a veil or mirror but "in itself and for itself." Thoreau and Whitman are contrasted as intellect versus emotion, narrowness versus breadth. Whitman's "emotional mysticism" transcends even that of Lanier. Whitman in Specimen shows rather than tells, rarely allowing "reflexions" to intrude. He does not provide the close

studies of Thoreau and Burroughs, but his artistic prose reveals his skilled ear.

52 COMPENDIUM. "With Walt Whitman in Camden." Conservator 19 (October), 121.
    Notices of 1908.17, including pieces by George D. Herron and Charles Warren Stoddard, highly praising it.

53 ANON. "Letters of Walt Whitman to His Mother and an Old Friend." Putnam's Monthly 5 (November), 163-69. Illustrated.
    Helen Price presents these letters of the 1870s to Whitman's mother and her mother, Abby Price, whose biography is sketched; nowhere in print has Whitman been shown "'in so winning and attractive a light.'" Editorial comment notes the lack of the egotistical in these letters; his amiable egotism came only later. He was not a "'sponge'" as people have claimed. His mother's character is described.

54 COMPENDIUM. "With Walt Whitman in Camden." Conservator 19 (November), 137-38.
    Notices of 1908.17.

55 ANON. "Last of the Whitmans." Conservator 19 (December), 157.
    Item from Philadelphia Inquirer (unlocated) on the death of the last Whitman family member.

56 COMPENDIUM. "With Walt Whitman in Camden." Conservator 19 (December), 152-53.
    Notices of 1908.17.

1909

BOOKS

1 ALDEN, RAYMOND MacDONALD. An Introduction to Poetry for Students of English Literature. New York: Henry Holt & Co., pp. 15, 348.
    Brief references to Whitman's refusal to use a verse form "developed by natural literary evolution for the expression of poetical ideas." Quotes Courthope (1901.4).

*2 BOOTH, HEBER HEDLEY. Opalodes: Patriotic and Miscellaneous Verses. Brisbane: Powell. "In Memoriam. Walt Whitman," pp. 49-51. Quoted in Jones.
    Poem. Quotation from Whitman is used as epigraph of book.

3 BROWNELL, W. C. American Prose Masters. New York: Charles Scribner's Sons, p. 210.
    The true artist never loses sight of his effect, even if only subconsciously. Whitman is like Poe in this respect: "readers more sensitive to art than to poetry are deceived by the poetic disguise of that arrant artist, Walt Whitman, who achieved a fairly radiant degree of perfection in never yawping his commonplaces off the key, in spite of the variety of their modulations."

1909

4 CARPENTER, GEORGE RICE. <u>Walt Whitman</u>.
   English Men of Letters Series. New York:
   Macmillan Co., 175 pp. Index. No footnotes
   or bibliography.
        Emphasis on Whitman's personal develop-
   ment as related to his work. Perry (1906.
   13) is the uncredited source for much of
   the information. Whitman's early personality, intellectual development, early writing
   (which lagged behind his keenness of sensation and perception), valuable and stimulating criticism are characterized.
   Whitman's form is indebted not so much to
   the usually cited sources as to the speaking
   voice, as apparent in the style of his 1851
   Brooklyn Art Union lecture. His matter was
   unfamiliar to the upper-class background of
   other American literary men. His distinctive, "extraordinary mood" derives from his
   mystical experience, which provides the
   explanation for his catalogues that suffuse
   particulars with an impression of totality.
   The poems of 1855 (concentrating on "Myself"
   as providing the doctrine which the following poems merely reinforce) and 1856 (with
   diminished egoism and clearer altruism) are
   described. Whitman evolved for himself his
   ideas regarding the language of the people
   as appropriate for poetry, since such ideas
   were not then current in New York. The
   comradeship of 1860 is "no abnormality or
   perversion of feeling" but a latent and
   natural yearning and love between friends
   "that would be among the highest manifestations of the divinity within us." <u>Drum-</u>
   <u>Taps</u>, presenting the war in connection with
   past and future, offers "a subject-matter
   more simple and unified" and a "purified
   singer." Whitman's letters to Doyle reveal
   an amazing ability to lower "his threshold
   of consciousness." He is at his highest
   level of composition in the 1871 "Passage"
   group. The formlessness, sex, and egotism
   once considered so objectionable in Whitman
   are now accepted because of changed per-
   spectives. He may be the forerunner of
   poets who will reveal the unities of the
   universe in "a medium less mystical, more
   intellectual." He is to be compared less
   to other writers than to "great personalities" like St. Francis, George Fox, and
   oriental teachers, "the great accepters and
   unifiers of life."

5 COOPER, LANE. "The Poets." In <u>A Manual of</u>
   <u>American Literature</u>. Edited by Theodore
   Stanton. New York: G. P. Putnam's Sons,
   pp. 307-13; also 245, 292, 297.
        Whitman's belief in immortality and
   the value of each individual and thing
   constitutes his main permanent quality.
   Biographical sketch. Comparison of Rousseau
   and Whitman. More poetic than many conventional versifiers, he is a great poet,
   perhaps America's greatest, when he expresses what is true for all or many men,
   or for representative and typical men. He
   is most successful in regular metrical

form, as in "Captain." He has been overpraised as the poet of modern democracy,
for its literature does not require lack
of restraint. This volume also refers to
Whitman on pp. 341, 343, 413, 451, regarding
his journalism and prose (full of common
sense), mentioning him as one of the New
York <u>Evening Post</u>'s writers in Washington
during the first year of the Civil War.

6 HEYDRICK, BENJAMIN A. <u>One Year Course in</u>
   <u>English and American Literature</u>. New York:
   Hinds, Noble & Eldredge, pp. 221-25;
   Reading list, p. 227; lines to memorize,
   271.
        Biographical sketch. Whitman's uneven-
   ness leaves one in doubt as to whether he
   is one of our greatest poets or merely a
   writer of "incoherent prose with flashes of
   true poetry." Explanation of Whitman's
   democratic spirit in life and writings,
   comradeship stressed over love, hopeful
   spirit.

7 MOODY, WILLIAM VAUGHN; LOVETT, ROBERT MORSS;
   and BOYNTON, PERCY H. <u>A First View of</u>
   <u>English and American Literature</u>. New York:
   Charles Scribner's Sons, pp. 451, 456-61,
   463-65.
        Whitman is contrasted with Poe, both
   isolated from the literary community,
   Whitman more talked of than read. Whitman
   was interested in "a great social idea."
   He displays too little selectivity or argument. His individual style was "a result
   of frequent and painstaking revision." His
   meaning should be of more concern than
   whether his work is poetry. He follows
   transcendentalist thought but does not
   possess Emerson's balance. He lacks the
   features of popular literature.

8 PECK, HARRY THURSTON. <u>Studies in Several</u>
   <u>Literatures</u>. New York: Dodd, Mead & Co.,
   pp. 82-85, 90, 141-43.
        "If Americans were in reality a people
   of strident voice, of crass materialism,
   and of a thinly disguised brutality,"
   Whitman should be their poet, but actually
   his poetry tells only of surface national
   traits, although sometimes he is superb.
   His American is not the true American like
   Washington, Franklin, and Lincoln, though
   foreigners think so. Longfellow, his antithesis, is the true American laureate.
   Whitman "never saw the moral background of
   our daily life." Like Emerson he emphasized
   "an intense individualism," but Emerson
   strikes a higher though no less forcible
   note than Whitman's "intoxication of physical
   well-being."

9 SANBORN, MARY FARLEY. <u>The Canvas Door</u>. New
   York: B. W. Dodge & Co., pp. 100, 113, 114,
   120-22, 124-25, 127-30.
        Characters read Whitman (especially
   "Open Road"), with some explication and
   commentary.

10 SIMONDS, WILLIAM EDWARD. <u>A Student's History of American Literature</u>. Boston: Houghton Mifflin Co., pp. 295-302.

"A man of rich vitality, lustily greeting life in all its phases, emphasizing, perhaps needlessly, the physical side of life," Whitman was an innovator, violating conventionalities. Biographical sketch. His egotism and verse-form are becoming understood. His catalogues are "often picturesque, often musical, but often, too, unorganized and bewildering." The war led him to some of his finest compositions. Praised are "Cradle," "Man-of-War-Bird," sea poems, "Old Salt Kossabone," and the universally admired "Captain" ("Whitman's poetical power at its best") and "Lilacs." He grows upon the reader, who overlooks his flaws and responds to his spirit of comradeship. Reading him, preferably aloud, is "wholesome and invigorating." Secondary sources and selections (better as an introduction than a complete edition) are suggested.

11 STOCKER, R. DIMSDALE. <u>Personal Ideals, or Man As He Is and May Become</u>. London: L. N. Fowler & Co.; New York: Fowler & Wells. "Whitman's 'Song of Myself,'" pp. 1-21.

In Whitman "the new order became, for the first time, articulate." All of his poetry is full of "emotion kindled at the flame of life." He understood his time and synthesized ideas "to replace the current creed of his time." He represents the revolt from idealism and supernaturalism, to reveal the superman. His attitudes toward life, as depicted in "Myself," are explained: identification of the self with the whole cosmos, representative egotism, rejection of the supernatural in favor of the miraculous in the commonplace, perception of the role of evil without justification of its commission, faith in immortality.

12 THOMAS, EDWARD. <u>Richard Jefferies: His Life and Art</u>. Boston: Little, Brown & Co., pp. 189, 207, 313.

Sometimes Jefferies's phrasing and cadence recall Whitman, whose <u>Leaves</u> delighted him. He sent it to his father. He resembles Whitman "who eagerly embraces all life, not because it is all equally good, but because we may spoil all if we hastily condemn or destroy what has in it the goodness of fresh life; only the slothful and the imitative are bad."

*13 WEBLING, PEGGY. <u>The Story of Virginia Perfect</u>. London: Methuen, p. 270.
Reported in Saunders <u>Whitman in Fiction</u>.

14 WILLCOX, LOUISE COLLIER. <u>The Human Way</u>. New York and London: Harper & Bros., pp. 36, 42, 185, 246-49.
Whitman is quoted and used as example

of new spiritual perceptions, particularly regarding death and "the feeling of neighborliness."

15 WINTER, WILLIAM. <u>Old Friends: Being Literary Recollections of Other Days</u>. New York: Moffat, Yard & Co., pp. 29-31, 64, 88-92, 140-42, 154, 292-93.
Reminiscences and critical comments of Whitman: "That auctioneer's list of topics and appetites, intertwisted with a formless proclamation of carnal propensities and universal democracy," is not original in style or thought. Howells's recollections of meeting Whitman at Pfaff's are corrected. The material from 1907.58 is used.

16 YARNALL, ELLIS. <u>Wordsworth and the Coleridges</u>. New York and London: Macmillan Co., p. 193.
Charles Kingsley called some of the poetry Emerson favored "the product of a coarse sensual mind." Yarnall says that this is a reference to Whitman, but he had no defense to offer Kingsley in response.

PERIODICALS

17 NOGUCHI, YONE. "With Walt Whitman in Camden." <u>Conservator</u> 19 (January), 166-68.
Compares Whitman with Japanese poet Saigyo; comments on Whitman's statements regarding emigration laws.

18 STEELL, WILLIS. "Walt Whitman's Early Life on Long Island." <u>Munsey's Magazine</u> 40 (January), 497-502. Illustrated.
Describes Whitman's boyhood, young manhood, affectionate friendships, various incidents; recollections from old acquaintances.

19 BJERREGAARD, C. H. A. "The Inner Life." <u>The Word</u> 8 (February), 282, 288.
Quotes "Voices" by "our neglected poet" Whitman as text for this lecture.

20 SNYDER, JOHN EDWIN. "Walt Whitman's Woman." <u>Socialist Woman</u> 2 (February), 7.
Whitman "demanded not equality for woman but simply recognized it as her right and not in man's province to give." He caters to no preconceived social codes regarding women. He was a socialist, a universal lover, celebrating love, not lust. "Occupations" is his most revolutionary poem, placing the workman on top. <u>Leaves</u> will contribute to women's emancipation.

21 T[RAUBEL, HORACE]. "Walt Whitman." <u>Conservator</u> 19 (February), 188-89.
Favorable review of Carpenter (1909.4).

22 LODGE, HENRY CABOT. "'Our Best Senator.'" <u>Boston Evening Transcript</u> (6 February), sec. 3, 10:7.
Eulogy for Senator Allison, delivered in the U.S. Senate. Incidental: We shrank from Whitman until men like Symonds,

Stevenson, and Swinburne had spoken, and
then only slowly recognized him as a great
poet and "a real and original force in the
splendid annals of English verse."

23 DE CASSERES, BENJAMIN. "Walt Whitman." Fra
2 (March), 93-94.
     Whitman liberates us, urging us to find
our own directions and follow our highest
impulse. He is "the great poet of youth."
He returns us "to a sane, healthy egoism"
so that we may love others and urges us to
love our bodies. He was "the most significant man who has yet walked the earth."

24 EATON, CHARLOTTE. "What Walt Whitman Is to
Me." Conservator 20 (April), 23-26.
     Recollection of meeting Whitman in
New York; appreciation of his influence.

25 [MORE, P. E.] Review of Carpenter (1909.4).
Nation 88 (8 April), 364-65.
     This biography is "well-proportioned
and pleasantly written," with an original
explanation of the catalogues, though
Carpenter's version of Whitman's derivation
of form is to be questioned. Still un-
reconciled by Whitman commentators, however,
are Whitman's denial of all distinction,
acceptance of all as right, and rejection
of standards with "the vein of physical
puritanism expressed at times in his personal vows."

26 ANON. "Whitman Cult in France." New York
Times Saturday Review (17 April), 237.
     Bazalgette's efforts to bring Whitman
to working people are meeting with "rather
doubtful success," according to reports.

27 ANON. Review of Carpenter (1909.4). Living
Age 261 (8 May), 384.
     This book will be received well by
those who believe Whitman's work was written
by a poet. Whitman's language is criticized.
Carpenter and Perry (1906.13) neglect the
"abhorrence and contempt" in which Whitman
was held in his prime. "The hospital service which he chose to offer to his country,
instead of the military service for which
he was well qualified brought him more
readers than his verse attracted, his
abolitionist friends brought him others,
but until old age made him pitiable his
coarse volubility commanded as much and no
more respect in this country than England
gave to the inane volubility of Tupper."

28 ANON. "Other Recent Books." American Review
of Reviews 39 (June), 763.
     Paragraph review of Carpenter (1909.4):
most of the endless books on Whitman are
so tainted with prejudice for or against
Whitman that Carpenter's "sober, sedate,
and impartial appraisal" is refreshing.

29 KELLER, ELIZABETH LEAVITT. "Walt Whitman:
The Last Phase." Putnam's Monthly 6 (June),

331-37.
     Whitman's nurse during his last months
recalls meeting Whitman and Mrs. Davis,
describes his house and its disorder, his
physical condition, manner of speaking,
other habits, Mrs. Davis and Warren
Fritzinger, his leave-taking of her. (Much
of this material is used, rewritten, in her
book, 1921.19.)

30 ANON. "Stokes Rouses Whitmanites. Ideals Not
Enough, He Says, and Urges Fellowship Members to Action." New York Times (1 June),
8:7.
     J. G. Phelps Stokes, at the Fellowship
meeting, urges concern with living up to
Whitman's ideals, not mere reveling in his
poetry. Emma Goldman said Whitman is
claimed not by any creed but by the universe.

31 SIMONDS, W. E. "The Individuality of Walt
Whitman." Dial 46 (16 June), 404-5.
     Review of Carpenter (1909.4), which
makes Whitman "a more tangible personality
and a bigger man." The significance of
Whitman, one of America's most picturesque
writers, is being increasingly recognized.

32 L., ROSE. "Walt Whitman." Chicago Post (18
June).
     An interpretation of Whitman's beautiful
personality and ability to find beauty in
the commonplace, maintaining his joy and
love throughout the war, finding the men's
deaths not depressing but bracing.

33 ANON. "Walt Whitman." Chautauquan 55 (July),
289.
     Brief favorable review of Carpenter
(1909.4).

34 ANON. "The Latest Word on Whitman." Current
Literature 47 (July), 45-48. Caricature by
Snow of Whitman as Falstaff.
     Notes and quotes Carpenter (1909.4) and
other recent commentary on Whitman, including
William Aspenall Bradley's lengthy critique
in the Boston Herald (unlocated): Whitman's
fundamental weakness is his poetry's crudity;
he is "the poet of the intellectual middle
class"; his emphasis on sexual matters
shows his own actual experience to be very
limited; he may have invented the children
to appear philosophically consistent with
his preaching of perfect fatherhood.

35 HAMILTON, CLAYTON. "Walt Whitman as a Religious Seer." Forum 42 (July), 80-85.
     Review of Carpenter (1909.4), the most
satisfactory biography of Whitman yet. Like
the great religious masters, Whitman came
to be tolerated by the world at large only
after death. Carpenter realizes that
"Whitman must be considered primarily as a
religious seer."

36 JOHNSTON, BERTHA. "Walt Whitman and the
American Teacher, I." Conservator 20 (July),

70-73.
Whitman's concept of individualism may be the key to education in a democracy. Education must cultivate initiative and individuality but never forget the words "en masse." Continued 1909.38.

37 ANON. "Poets That Swinburne Didn't Like." Literary Digest 39 (3 July), 24.
Incidental: Whitman was the only American poet Swinburne thought well of, according to his letters to Stedman published in the London Times (unlocated) before the publication of Stedman's granddaughter's volume (1910.17).

38 JOHNSTON, BERTHA. "Walt Whitman and the American Teacher, II." Conservator 20 (August), 85-87.
Continues 1909.36. She explores the "pedagogical significance" of Whitman's writings. His concept of America as incorporating all races and cultures is also a message to the educational establishment, urging respect for laborers and all nationalities. Concluded 1909.39.

39 _____. "Walt Whitman and the American Teacher, III." Conservator 20 (September), 102-4.
Concludes 1909.38. Whitman's prose (quoted) includes comments on nature, evolution, culture.

40 TRIMBLE, A. E. "Concordance-Making in New Zealand." Atlantic Monthly 104 (September), 364-67.
Describes and defends making a concordance for Whitman, helpful in approaching his meaning. His prodigious vocabulary and use of compound words and various animal names are described.

41 VIOLLIS, ANDREE, and VIOLLIS, JEAN. "Walt Whitman's Works." Translated from French by William Struthers. Conservator 20 (October), 117-19.
Consideration of Bazalgette's translation, describing Whitman's energy, shocking style, sensuality. One may be disturbed at his mixed diction and disordered expression, but one is generally dazzled. His background and appearance are described. He has the voice of a Titan singing America and the earth.

42 ANON. "Whitman's Original Copy. Corrected MSS., on which He Helped to Set Type, to Go on Sale." New York Times (31 October), 6:1.
Description of the Two Rivulets manuscript, noting Whitman's markings, including changes made and a couplet addressed to the reader. Changes made indicate some dissatisfaction with the poems.

43 SMITH, WILLIAM HAWLEY. "A Visit to Walt Whitman." Conservator 20 (November), 136-37.

Account of visit with his wife to Whitman in 1889, describing Whitman's appearance, conversation, and gift to them of his complete works.

44 ANON. "Walt Whitman's Home Fails to Tempt Bidders." New York Herald (14 November), 8:2-3. Photograph.
Whitman's birthplace property is up for auction, but bidders would offer no more than $1250. The property and house are described as evidencing a lack of care.

1910

BOOKS

1 DOWNES, LOUISE. The New Democracy. Boston: Sherman, French & Co., passim, especially pp. 348-51, 360-62.
There are quotations from Whitman throughout the book, which uses him as symbol for "the scientific consciousness" and the union with law which must arise in America. He gave birth to national art, defining America. "He is not process but achievement." His is the true statesmanship.

2 FERGUSON, EMILY. Janey Canuck in the West. London: Cassell & Co., p. 34.
Quotes Whitman's words on Canada.

2a F[URNESS], H. H., ed. Records of a Lifelong Friendship, 1807-1882, Ralph Waldo Emerson and William Henry Furness. Boston and New York: Houghton Mifflin Co., p. 107.
Letter from Emerson to Furness of October 1, 1855, asks if Furness has "read that wonderful book--with all its formlessness & faults 'Leaves of Grass'?--"

3 GABLE, WILLIAM F. A Little Talk on People, Books and Autographs. Altoona, Pa.: n.p., pp. 10, 13-17.
Notes his collecting of Whitmania, because he believes Whitman is important; his acquaintance with Traubel. "Open Road" makes Whitman's critics look puny. The last line of "Prostitute" is "the biggest, broadest line in our language." Vistas reveals "the mind and mould of a great man."

4 GOLDMAN, EMMA. Anarchism and Other Essays. New York: Mother Earth Publishing Association, pp. 18, 27, 77.
Biographical sketch of Goldman by Hippolyte Havel notes her appreciation of Whitman and perception of him as expressing anarchist philosophy. She notes the rare appreciation the masses have for great figures such as Whitman.

5 HOBSON, J. A. A Modern Outlook: Studies of English & American Tendencies. Boston: Dana Estes & Co., pp. 146, 156, 170.

Incidental: "Most educated Americans
are ashamed of their own distinctive literary man, Walt Whitman." Holmes is contrasted with Whitman, who had "a far more
adventurous liberality of soul" than
possible to Holmes's guarded nature.
Whitman remains America's best interpreter.

6 KIRKHAM, STANTON DAVIS. Resources: An Interpretation of the Well-Rounded Life. New
York and London: G. P. Putnam's Sons,
pp. 144-45.
Whitman, "one of the most liberalising
influences in modern thought," "affects us
thru [sic] the elemental quality of his
idea, the breadth of his vision. He did
not so much write poems as gather the
material for them." However, the world is
larger and better to those who have read
him understandingly.

7 MARVIN, FREDERIC ROWLAND. The Excursions of
a Book-Lover: Being Papers on Literary
Themes. Boston: Sherman, French & Co.,
pp. 171-72, 284-85, 307.
Criticizes Nordau's comments on Whitman
(1895.8). Later discussion of modern attitudes toward death praises Whitman's wise
attitude in "Lilacs," which "will live in
our literature."

8 MAXIM, HUDSON. The Science of Poetry and The
Philosophy of Language. New York and
London: Funk & Wagnalls Co., pp. 252, 255,
256, 257, 268.
Poetry lies not in the thought or the
personality or the aspiration, as so many
claim in regarding all of Whitman's work
as poetry; although he occasionally wrote
excellent lines by accident (like "Myself"
44), it is usually "Whitman rag-time."

9 MEE, ARTHUR, ed. The Children's Encyclopaedia.
Vol. 8. London: Carmelite House. "Walt
Whitman: A Hero among Men: and a Singer
of Strange Songs," p. 5083.
Though many think poetry is made of
rhyme, regular meter, and carefully chosen
words, true poetry requires "thought, feeling, imagination," as found in Whitman. No
modern writer has better expressed the
thoughts and aspirations, feelings and
sympathies, "of a freedom-loving, fearless
son of Nature." Despite critical disagreement on his writing, he is admitted to be
"a great force in modern American thought,"
and his life (described) is admired.

10 MODJESKA, HELENA. Memories and Impressions of
Helena Modjeska, An Autobiography. New
York: Macmillan Co., pp. 371-72. 1872
portrait.
The actress recalls meeting Whitman at
Richard Gilder's home during a tour of
America in the 1870s. She describes his
appearance, fitting for King Lear, with "a
great deal of pessimism in the twinkle of
the lids" of his eyes. His speech was "like
his poems, deep and concise."

11 NOYES, CARLETON. An Approach to Walt Whitman.
Boston and New York: Houghton Mifflin Co.,
231 pp. No index.
1. "The Man": Summary of Whitman's
life as related to his work, which is incidental to his personality and sympathy.
He speaks for all; his poetry becomes our
own expression. His preparation as an
artist was haphazard, his greatest influence
coming from theater and opera.
2. "Whitman's Art": Difficult at
first, his work is poetry because of its
intensity of emotion. Leaves is new in
motive, material, and form. Whitman focuses
on the average man, represented in himself
and representing the universe, a new theme
needing a new form. He is a poet for his
phrasing, vision, and rhythm (examined in
"Cradle" along with its sounds). "A true
master of form," he writes with care, not
lazily. He lacks selectivity, but Leaves
is organic, poems achieving significance in
relation to others. Leaves is uneven but
has a suggestiveness that makes his poems
increasingly wonderful to the reader.
3. "The Human Appeal": Whitman emphasizes a personal relation with the
reader. Nature's processes and universal
laws speak through him. His attitudes to
life, learning, nature, fellowmen, woman
are described.
4. "The Soul's Adventure": Spiritual
meanings are central to Whitman, who seeks
to find God and succeeds. His religious
thought is compared to other religions.
His eidolons are dynamic versions of Plato's
Ideas. He emphasizes cosmic unity, recognition of law, optimistic faith, assertion
of immortality. Like Christ, he is "the
simple vehicle of the spirit of God."
5. "To You": True understanding of
Whitman reconciles his contradictions. He
must be tested by experience in life. He
is less a poet or teacher than an influence,
urging us to follow our own paths. He is
contrasted with Emerson and Thoreau regarding individualism. His high moral standards
are described.

12 POUND, EZRA. The Spirit of Romance. London:
J. M. Dent & Sons, n.d., pp. 163, 178-79.
Dante's expression of the cosmic consciousness is more convincing than
Whitman's. Villon, while singing the song
of himself, is free from Whitman's "horrible
air of rectitude" as if conferring a benefit
on the race "by recording his own self-
complacency," as in a parody here included:
"Lo, behold, I eat water melons" (reprinted:
Saunders).

13 SAINTSBURY, GEORGE. A History of English
Prosody from the Twelfth Century to the
Present Day. Vol. 3. London: Macmillan
& Co., pp. 22, 372, 383, 480, 490-92.
Extract reprinted: Miller.
Whitman's form is a genuine hybrid
between poetry and prose, but some of his

poetry is basically prose. Verse would
generally do better, but Whitman often
succeeds in truly matching form to matter.

14 SHARP, ELIZABETH. William Sharp (Fiona
Macleod): A Memoir. New York: Duffield &
Co., pp. 2, 193-94.
Account of Sharp's visit of January
1892 to Whitman, in whose fearless independence, mental outlook, joy in life, and
vigorous verse he found "incentive and
refreshment." Sharp's letter describing
the visit is quoted, along with his short
poem "In Memoriam" (1904.26) written for
Whitman's death.

15 SHUMAN, EDWIN L. How to Judge a Book. Boston
and New York: Houghton Mifflin Co., p. 194.
Incidental reference in discussion of
poetry as not dying: "There will be poets
of the future, and they will not be Walt
Whitmans, either."

16 SPARGO, JOHN. Karl Marx: His Life and Work.
New York: B. W. Huebsch, pp. 275-76.
Whitman's cosmic spirit, introduced to
Marx by W. Harrison Riley, appealed greatly
to him. He loved to repeat lines from
"Pioneers" and other poems.

17 STEDMAN, LAURA, and GOULD, GEORGE M., eds.
Life and Letters of Edmund Clarence Stedman.
New York: Moffat, Yard and Co. Vol. 1,
pp. 308-9, 535; vol. 2, pp. 98-99, 100,
101, 104-10, 114, 120-22, 202, 461.
Letter of January 1863 notes Whitman's
hospital work. The controversy over
Stedman's Scribner's article (1880.35) is
discussed, with Stedman's defense then and
at other times of Whitman as poet; letters
to Howells, Gilder, Curtis, R. G. White,
Aldrich, Kennedy, others, regarding the
article and response to it. Stedman's
critical standards are explained.

18 STEVENSON, BURTON E. A Guide to Biography for
Young Readers: American Men of Mind. New
York: Baker & Taylor Co., pp. 70-73, 82,
85.
Popular biographical sketch: "ferment-
ing inside the man and at last demanding
expression, was a strange new philosophy
of democracy" which needed a worthy poetic
form "stripped of conventions and stock
phrases." Lately "his fame has been established on a firmer basis than hysterical
adulation"; he will probably rank high as
"the first exponent of an original and
democratic literature," not merely imitative
of Europe.

19 THOMSON, JAMES. Walt Whitman, the Man and the
Poet. London: Published by the editor,
106 pp. Introduction by Bertram Dobell,
pp. v-xxxv.
Reprints of 1892.14; 1880.12, 1880.17,
1880.25, 1880.29, 1880.38.
Dobell provides a general estimate of

Whitman, who demands judgment by new
standards. He is "a part of ourselves,"
teaching a wholesome and much-needed message emphasizing mankind and the present.
Similarities to Traherne in ideas, poetics,
spirit are noted. Thomson and Whitman are
contrasted in their views of life, both
valid; they have some similarities.

*20 VAN DYKE, HENRY C. What is Art?, p. 7.
Quoted in Willard, but unable to verify
existence of this book.
Whitman was "a commonplace artist in
language" but an unusual thinker.

21 WHITING, LILIAN. Louise Chandler Moulton,
Poet and Friend. Boston: Little, Brown, &
Co., pp. 51, 66, 146, 258.
Moulton is quoted on Whitman (see
1888.24), with admiration for his sincerity
and large-heartedness. A diary entry describes further her delightful 1888 visit
to Whitman with Talcott Williams.

22 W[OODBERRY], G[EORGE] E[DWARD]. "American
Literature." Encyclopedia Britannica.
11th ed. Vol. 1. p. 840.
Paragraph on Whitman, who has received
attention in England and Germany on the assumption that he expressed the new and
original American, though Americans, not
interested in his naturalism, refuse to
consider him representative. Americans
know and value him chiefly "by those few
fine lyrics which have found a place in all
anthologies of American verse."

PERIODICALS

23 LESSING, O. E. "Whitman and German Critics."
Journal of English and Germanic Philology
9, no. 1 (Winter), 85-98.
Reprinted: 1926.72.
Whitman's reputation in Germany is
traced. His spiritual qualities, sympathy,
love for nature, and unity with the universe
have been praised. Bertz clarified
Whitman's gospel of friendship. Whitman
never found the synthesis of science and
religion he claimed. His religious views
are derivative. Like Nietzsche he fails in
logical consistency and places instinct
above reason. His form, like Wagner's, is
"enervating rather than invigorating."
"Nations that have produced a Goethe and an
Emerson need not and should not worship a
Whitman as one of their heroes."

24 ATKINSON, WILLIAM WALKER. "My Recollections
of Walt Whitman." New Thought 19 (January),
6-9.
Account of meeting Whitman in Camden,
physical description, ferry ride, Whitman's
friendship with all classes, anecdotes.

25 MOELLER, TYGE. "Walt Whitman." Translated
from the French by B. W. Thatcher. Conservator 20 (January), 165-68.

Essay by a Belgian critic on
Bazalgette's translation of Whitman: comparison of Whitman's philosophy with
Rousseau's. Whitman's "modernism was tempered by his born savagery on the one side
and his Quaker heritage on the other." His
teachings are affirmative; he is "the most
revolutionary of masters."

26 TALBOT, ETHEL. "Walt Whitman, Individualist."
Academy 78 (22 January), 88-89.
Whitman has the spirit and material of
poetry without the final form. His poetry
appeals for its intense masculinity, open-
air virility, and power. He was an egoist,
like any writer, but was honest about it,
and had an intense power of sympathy. He
achieves his own cadence. "Lilacs,"
"Cradle," and "Last Invocation" are
praised. He does not merely echo other
literature but is "the prophet of his land."

27 OPPENHEIM, JAMES. "The new poetry." Conservator 21 (March), 8-9.
Whitman's poetry is discussed as "a
true reflection of the age," like the music
of Wagner and Strauss, using discord deliberately. Younger writers must build on
Whitman, who has founded the new poetry.

28 T[RAUBEL, HORACE]. "An Approach to Walt
Whitman." Conservator 21 (March), 11-12.
Review of Noyes (1910.11), who approaches Whitman "through the great libraries"
but ends by accepting him.

29 MILNE, JAMES. "Drift of London Literary
Gossip. Mr. Frederic Harrison's Memories--
Walt Whitman in England." New York Times
Saturday Review (26 March), 166.
Suggests Harrison will include something
about Whitman in his book [but he apparently
did not]; notes growing popularity of
Whitman with ordinary English readers.

30 STRUTHERS, WILLIAM, trans. "The Life of Walt
Whitman." Conservator 21 (April), 22-23.
Translation of unsigned article in Les
Nouvelles: relates Whitman's life to his
style and philosophy; notes his superiority
to other poets.

31 MOUREY, GABRIEL. "Walt Whitman, I." Translated by Mildred Bain from Revue Bleue.
Conservator 21 (May), 37-40.
Whitman's interior and exterior lives
exist in harmony. He absorbs everything,
loves everything. He had read the classics
but preferred the inspiration of life. His
poetic material seems entirely original to
him. He is a superman with the faculty of
understanding all. Concluded 1910.35.

32 [MORE, P. E.] Paragraph review of Noyes
(1910.11). Nation 90 (26 May), 541.
Brief description of the ideas of this
"reverent exposition of Whitman's art and
philosophy."

33 ANON. "An Echo of Walt Whitman." New York
Times Saturday Review (28 May), 301.
Paragraph commenting on Traubel's
absorption of Whitman. His verse lacks
only "strength and imagination to make it
as good as Whitman's own."

*34 ANON. "Thoughts of Whitman." Theosophy in
Scotland (June), 25.
Reported in Saunders Supplement.

35 MOUREY, GABRIEL. "Walt Whitman, II." Translated by Mildred Bain. Conservator 21
(June), 53-54.
Concludes 1910.31. Whitman disdains
methods of ordinary composition and traditional rhetoric; he proceeds by enumeration
and accumulation, repeating himself on purpose. His technique is primitive but
superior in emotional impact to the "sentimental insipidities" of other poets.

36 JOHNSTON, J[OHN]. "Walt Whitman--the Poet of
Nature." Fortnightly Review 93 (1 June),
1123-36.
Whitman's profusion of life is rarely
equalled. Johnston praises his outdoor
quality, pregnant titles, health, love for
nature, "cinematographic fidelity of detail,"
"mastery of poetic expression," almost ex-
traterrestrial point of view. Like few
other poets, Whitman recognized "animal
kinship," "the complete identification of
the individual with the visible objects of
the universe," and the spirituality underlying all. The human heart and soul are
central to his work.

37 BAZALGETTE, LEON. "Some Sayings of Walt
Whitman Recorded by Horace Traubel." Con-
servator 21 (July), 73.
Praises Traubel; summarizes his work.

38 BINNS, HENRY BRYAN. "Whitman as the Poet of
Good Breeding." Eugenics Review 2 (July),
110-15.
Whitman was concerned with the body not
only for the "responsibility of Race-
building" but also because he regarded it
as part of the personality. Despite his
nonconformity in sexual standards (his
illegitimate children), his life was clean
and wholesome. Sex is for the production
of children, but America should also be
concerned with creating true manhood and
womanhood.

39 C., C. C. "Theosophy and Secular Literature,
II: Walt Whitman." Theosophical Quarterly
18 (July), 28-44.
Whitman recognized contemporary problems
but was no propagandist or reformer. The
road toward spiritual development is discovered by sympathy and spiritual expansion,
as dramatized by Whitman in "Myself." He
is often "startling and unintelligible" because of his "complete obedience to his own
precept." He is compared with Wordsworth,

St. Francis, the Bhagavad-Gita. He was
deficient in education and taste; he failed
to profit by conventions. He was "a genius
but not a gentleman."

40 MUFSON, THOMAS. "Walt Whitman, Poet of the
New Age." Twentieth Century Magazine 2
(July), 325-30.
Whitman "is of the living present,"
embodying the spirit of struggle toward a
new age. Life flowed through his veins in
his personal actions. "His is a new literature, a giant literature," requiring a
criticism that does not place art above
life. Life's suffering engaged him and his
understanding. His democratic art constructs
the future and seeks to eradicate suffering,
through emphasis on the individual, for
whom he urged freedom through brotherhood.
He is "the first Modern Man."

41 SCOTT, FRED NEWTON. "A Note on Walt Whitman's
Prosody, I." Conservator 21 (July), 70-72.
Revision of 1908.31.
Minor changes in style and wording,
not in content. Continued 1910.43.

42 [WILLCOX, LOUISE COLLIER.] "Not Without
Honor." Harper's Weekly 54 (16 July), 6.
Review of Bazalgette's French biography
of Whitman, superior to Perry's (1906.13).
Whitman's critical approval in Europe is
traced. America is last to recognize his
genius. Whitman was a careful craftsman;
he felt the "pulse of eternity." He lends
himself well to translation, "as only substantial work does."

43 SCOTT, FRED NEWTON. "A Note on Walt Whitman's
Prosody, II." Conservator 21 (August),
85-90.
Continues 1910.41; concluded 1910.44.

44 _____. "A Note on Walt Whitman's Prosody,
III." Conservator 21 (September), 102-4.
Concludes 1910.43.

45 ANON. "A Line-o'-Type or Two." Chicago Daily
Tribune (24 October), 10:5.
The Empory Gazette is mocked for saying
that "no involved, obscure poem ever became
popular with the masses, and none ever will":
Whitman and others "did not write with the
notion of becoming popular with the masses.
Thank heaven for that!"

46 ANON. "A Poet of Democracy." Chicago Daily
Tribune (24 October), 10:1.
Laudatory editorial. It was natural
that Whitman be criticized for denying all
aristocracies and claiming absolute equality
for all, but he is becoming better known
and will come to be appreciated for his
divine average. He has produced America's
"most arresting literature," but it is "his
manhood, his elemental sincerity, his heroic
nudity of ideas" that make him representative of us.

47 HENDERSON, ARCHIBALD. "The International Fame
of Mark Twain." North American Review 192
(December), 805.
America's three great original geniuses,
Poe, Whitman, and Twain, have won the
widest followings but still await full
critical appreciation. Whitman and Twain,
"the two great interpreters and embodiments
of America, represent the supreme contribution of democracy to universal literature,"
owing nothing to European literature.

1911

BOOKS

1 ALBREE, JOHN, ed. Whittier Correspondence.
Salem: Essex Book & Print Club, pp. 241-
44.
Letter from Holmes to Whittier (7 September 1885) suggests that they contribute
to Donaldson's subscription for Whitman
since "he served well in the cause of
humanity," though "some of his poems are
among the most cynical instances of indecent
exposure I recollect," outside of actual
obscene literature. Letter to Boston Transcript of 1885 (apparently withheld by
Whittier) defends his offer of money to
Whitman, whose war labors and "tender
tribute" to Lincoln are praised. However,
he does not wish to seem to be sanctioning
anything in Whitman's writings "of an evil
tendency," for his writings, "while indicating a certain virile vigor and originality, seemed to me often indefensible
from a moral point of view."

2 BU[RROUGHS], J[OHN]. "Walt Whitman." Encyclopaedia Britannica. 11th ed. Vol. 28.
pp. 610-11.
Biographical and character sketch.
Quotations from 1855 Preface show Whitman's
poetic intentions. Leaves "radiates democracy as no other modern literary work does,"
besides rendering other "fundamental human
qualities."

3 CARPENTER, EDWARD. Love's Coming-of-Age. New
York and London: Mitchell Kennerley, pp.
60, 69, 76-77.
Quotes Whitman on the currently demeaning
notions of the ideal woman and his contrasting ideal woman in "Woman Waits."

4 COLLES, RAMSAY. In Castle and Court House:
Being Reminiscences of Thirty Years. London:
T. Werner Laurie, n.d., pp. 25, 94-97, 119-
20, 122, 173-74, 178, 239, 304.
Quotes Swinburne's ideas on Whitman,
primarily opposed to his indiscriminate
admirers. Whitman was surely a singer as
well as "one of the most ardent among
liberators of the human-spirit from the
shackles of conventionality." W. E. Henley
is quoted: "Whitman at his best sang, and
sang clearly." A copy of Whitman selections

1911

sent to Tolstoy came "with obliterations made by the Press Censor on nearly every page!"

5 COLVIN, SIDNEY, ed. <u>The Letters of Robert Louis Stevenson</u>. New ed. New York: Charles Scribner's Sons. Vol. 1, pp. 64, 83, 86, 102, 106, 123-24, 167-68, 169; vol. 2, 95-97, 324.
Revision of 1899.5.

New letters mention Stevenson inspiring a friend to read more of Whitman, describe his early enthusiastic essay and his reading Whitman aloud. A letter to Trevor Haddon, a young art student who had read Whitman after reading Stevenson's essay and had written asking for further comment, is basically a response to questions on life rather than explication of Whitman.

6 CORSON, HIRAM. <u>Spirit Messages</u>. Rochester, N.Y.: Austin Publishing Co., pp. 67-72, 229-36; passim per index.

Records Whitman's messages from the spirit world to Corson, who knew Whitman for the last seven years of his life, having early recognized the greatness of his message and lectured on him to students. Whitman is presented as "diviner of hidden messages of life," deeply religious, misunderstood because he assumed that others realized the same things he knew.

7 GUMMERE, FRANCIS B. <u>Democracy and Poetry</u>. Boston and New York: Houghton Mifflin Co. "Whitman and Taine," pp. 96-148; also 95, 315-17.

Whitman's break from bonds of form and matter follows the poetic programs of Blake and André Chénier. He balances community and individual. His verse frequently has dignity and eloquence, tenderness, vigor, pathos of hope. His rhythm sometimes brilliantly breaks down the barrier between impassioned prose and verse. Passages from "Cradle" and Meredith's "Juggling Jerry" are compared. Whitman's refusal to submit to order in form and democracy is a major flaw, but "he interpreted certain phases of national life, notably the temper of our war-time, better than any one else." He is contrasted with Hardy.

8 HALLECK, REUBEN POST. <u>History of American Literature</u>. New York: American Book Co., pp. 381-91, 371-72, 392-95, 397.

Author's summary (p. 392): "Walt Whitman brings excessive realism into the form and matter of verse. For fear of using stock poetic ornaments, he sometimes introduces mere catalogues of names, uninvested with a single poetic touch. He is America's greatest poet of democracy. His work is characterized by altruism, by all-embracing sympathy, by emphasis on the social side of democracy, and by love of nature and the sea." His critical prose ranks only a little below that of Lowell

and Poe. The masses may find his poetry too difficult, but works like "Lilacs," "Cradle," and "Captain" are ignored. Suggested readings, study questions on the poems.

9 KALUZA, MAX. <u>A Short History of English Versification from the Earliest Times to the Present Day: A Handbook for Teachers and Students</u>. London: George Allen & Co. "Walt Whitman," pp. 335-37; also 326.

Whitman uses "merely the irregular rhythm of ordinary speech." Some of his enumerations are tiring, but in many poems his variation between types of metrical feet faithfully renders each change of mood, and he often falls into regularly constructed verses, as in "Locomotive."

10 MACDONALD, FREDERIC W. <u>Recollections of a Book-lover</u>. London: Hodder & Stoughton, p. 83.

Quotes some of Carlyle's flamboyant literary opinions, including his of Whitman: "It is as though the town bull had learnt to hold a pen."

11 MATTHEWS, BRANDER. <u>A Study of Versification</u>. Boston: Houghton Mifflin Co., pp. 40, 50, 94, 196-99, 255.

Whitman's form followed the precedents of Blake and the Bible, but many passages seem "little removed from prose." He is best when closest to shapely structure and flowing rhythm, as in "Lilacs" and "Captain" (which accepts poetic conventions but violates accent in rhyme).

12 MOULTON, RICHARD G. <u>World Literature and Its Place in General Culture</u>. New York: Macmillan Co., pp. 389-90.

Whitman is of another order than Tupper, using biblical parallelism to express the most modern thinking, giving trouble to critics who have become too distanced from "the Hebrew root of our culture." Whitman's spirit is "pan-anthropism" rather than pantheism.

13 TENNYSON, HALLAM Lord, ed. <u>Tennyson and His Friends</u>. London: Macmillan & Co., pp. 198, 203; also 193 in "Tennyson, Clough, and the Classics," by Henry Graham Dakyns.

Dakyns writes of Tennyson's appreciation of Whitman. Hallam writes that his father introduced Dakyns to Whitman: "the first passage he showed him was one of the most daring Whitman ever wrote."

14 TRIMBLE, ANNIE E. <u>Walt Whitman and Mental Science: An Interview</u>. Melbourne: Privately printed by W. H. Trimble, 15 pp. Reprinted: McLeod.

Questions are asked of Whitman concerning his views on the principles of "Mental Science" and "New Thought." Whitman's hypothetical answers are quotations from his poetry which show the similarity of his thought to those principles, regarding the unity and harmony of all, the conquest of death and evil.

15 UNDERHILL, EVELYN. Mysticism: A Study in the Nature and Development of Man's Spiritual Consciousness. London: Methuen & Co., pp. 232, 286, 299, 306.
   While not a pure mystic, Whitman is used as an example of those "acquainted, beyond most poets and seers, with the phenomena of the illuminated life."

PERIODICALS

16 NARODNY, IVAN. "The Experiences of a Russian Bookseller." Bookman 32 (January), 475.
   Incidental reference to the Russians' high regard for Whitman, among the most popular American writers there.

17 THORSTENBERG, EDWARD. "The Walt Whitman Cult in Germany." Sewanee Review 19 (January), 71-86.
   Reprinted: 1919.84.
   Whitman's reputation in Germany is traced, with quotations (in English translation). Whitman's fundamental spirit conflicted with German ideals (tradition, form, dual relationship between visible and invisible worlds). Now Whitman is frequently praised as a superman and for the vigor and energy of his language, his representation of the age and his country, affirmation of life, universality, break from European influence.

18 ANON. "Some Portraits and Autographs of Walt Whitman." Century Magazine 81 (February), 531-33. Illustrated.
   Hitherto unknown photographs are reprinted; facsimiles of opening page of Lincoln lecture, prewar manuscript poem used in part in "World Take Good Notice."

19 [RIVERS, W. C.] "Genius and Decadence." Hospital 49, n.s. 8 (11 February), 585.
   Whitman is considerably honored for his talent and his lack of preoccupation with himself, but beyond altruism and democracy he also preached "homosexualism," as many poems make clear. Expurgation would not be the answer, however; "these passages can only do harm to those predisposed to the tenets expressed in them."

20 ANON. "American Poetry--Mr. Augustin Duncan's Tribute to Walt Whitman." American Register (12 February).
   Quotes lecture by Duncan (Isadora's brother) on Whitman "as especially voicing America, an outcry of its civilization and development, as American as Homer was Greek and Shakespeare English."

21 ANON. "Musings without Method." Blackwood's Magazine 189 (March), 413.
   Whitman is the one experiment so far in democratic poetry, "an awful warning to those who would break the laws of literature." He is already forgotten, "a savage with a half-articulate voice," and will appear in anthologies only through "the best and the least characteristic of his works." His attempt proved "that there is no music without melody."

22 ANON. "The 'Higher Criticism' in Medicine." Interstate Medical Journal 18 (March), 267-69.
   Response to 1911.19, typical of the straining after effect to startle the fixed and placid views held about some geniuses. Why should suggestions made by certain lines in a literary work (as in Whitman) give rise to definite claims of abnormal sexuality?

23 OPPENHEIM, JAMES. "The New Poetry." Poet-Lore 22, no. 2 (Spring), 158-59.
   Whitman, "the first of the modern poets," made "a complete break with the past" appropriate to the new era, through self-expression. Modern poetry must build on Wagner and Whitman but not repeat them, achieving rather more order, structure, and compactness. Whitman based his poems on the line, not the stanza.

24 SCHINZ, A. "Léon Bazalgette's 'Walt Whitman.'" Bookman 33 (April), 199-201.
   In France the most highly regarded American writers are Whitman and Poe, though Whitman is inferior as an artist, except in a few great poems. Bazalgette neglects Whitman's defects, but because he presents Whitman "as humanity ought to see him," his biography should become classic. European criticism praising Bazalgette's work is quoted.

25 E[NDE], A. VON. "Walt Whitman in France--The French Will Be the First to Have Translations of All His Works." New York Times Review of Books (16 April), 231.
   Bazalgette's book brings the reader into the essential personal contact with Whitman. Henri Guilbeaux is quoted in translation from Portraits d'Hier, contrasting the individualism of Whitman and Nietzsche.

26 ANON. "Salut à la Jeunesse." Punch 140 (3 May), 320.
   Reprinted: Saunders.
   Parody.

27 S[MYTHE], A. E. "Crusts and Crumbs." Toronto Sunday World (7 May).
   Whitman is the greatest American example of a poet dealing with the perennial conflict between the material and spiritual senses. He is poorly regarded because he seeks the spiritual in the present rather than merely after death. Extracts are quoted extensively, since possible censorship of Whitman has been suggested.

1911

28 MENCKEN, H. L. "Novels for Hot Afternoons."
    Smart Set 34 (July), 158.
        Includes one-paragraph review of
    Traubel's Optimos, "dishwatery imitations"
    of Whitman, all of whose faults appear in
    his disciple, "the same maudlin affection
    for the hewer of wood and drawer of water,
    the same frenzy for repeating banal ideas
    ad nauseam, the same inability to distin-
    guish between a poem and a stump speech."
    But at least Whitman was "a poet at heart,"
    and whenever he avoided his "ethical and
    sociological rubbish, a strange beauty
    crept into his lines and his own deep
    emotion glorified them."

28a WHITE, ELIOT. "Walt Whitman's Significance to
    a Revolutionist." Conservator 22 (July),
    71-72.
        Whitman works to establish comradeship,
    the "fomenting element in all revolution."
    He is the "spiritual wound dresser" to
    revolutionists.

*29 ANON. Article. Providence Sunday Journal
    (23 July).
    Reported in Willard.
        O'Connor's widow points out the simi-
    larity of Charles Rann Kennedy's play The
    Servant in the House to "The Carpenter"
    (1868.5).

30 WALLACE, J. W. "Leaves of Grass and Optimos."
    Conservator 22 (September), 103-5.
        The religious influence of Whitman will
    outlast the artistic, for he can "revolu-
    tionize all your ideas and transform all
    your aims in life," as vital religions do.
    Traubel's Optimos poems continue Whitman's
    doctrine.

31 BARKER, ELSA. "What Whitman Learned from the
    East: Being a Study in Some Curious Simi-
    larities." Canada Monthly 10 (October),
    438-43.
        Whitman shares with oriental writers a
    meditative tendency, the resultant ecstasy,
    passiveness of soul in the power of God,
    great calm, simplicity, and frankness re-
    garding sex. These affinities do not suggest
    deliberate discipleship but are natural
    to him, though strange to his Western back-
    ground. His themes and poetic devices are
    examined for their similarities to those
    of Persian and Indian poets, through
    quotations.

32 TRAUBEL, HORACE. "With Walt Whitman in Camden."
    Forum 46 (October), 400-414.
        Pre-publication extracts from 1914.16.
    Editor's footnote explains that these ex-
    tracts show clearly "the range of the poet's
    mind, his grasp of large questions, his
    views of the great political and social
    movements of the time, and the mental
    vitality which outlasted bodily energy."
    Continued 1911.33.

33 _____. "With Walt Whitman in Camden." Forum
    46 (November), 589-600.
        Continues 1911.32. Continued 1911.35.

34 _____. "Estimates of Well-Known Men . . . by
    Walt Whitman from Horace Traubel's Memo-
    randa." Century Magazine 83 (December),
    250-56.
        Pre-publication extracts from 1914.16.

35 _____. "With Walt Whitman in Camden." Forum
    46 (December), 709-19.
        Continues 1911.33. Concluded 1912.23.

1912

BOOKS

1 BENNETT, ARNOLD. Your United States: Impres-
    sions of a First Visit. New York: George
    H. Doran Co., p. 166.
        Too often American dilettanti in the
    arts forget America's significant contri-
    butions to the world, including "one of
    the world's supreme poets--Whitman."

2 BURROUGHS, JOHN. Introduction to The Rolling
    Earth: Outdoor Scenes and Thoughts from
    the Writings of Walt Whitman, compiled by
    Waldo R. Browne. Boston and New York:
    Houghton Mifflin Co., pp. xvii-xxiv.
        Whitman "was the poet of the Earth con-
    sidered as an orb in the heavens, in a
    fuller sense than any other poet has been."
    He revels in thoughts of the whole scheme
    of things, in emotions akin to those of
    biblical writers rather than of modern
    science. His love of nature was evident on
    his visits to Burroughs's home at West Park.

3 _____. Time and Change. Boston and New York:
    Houghton Mifflin Co. "The Phantoms Behind
    Us," pp. 197, 202, 213; also 79.
        Borrowing his title from "Rise after
    Rise," Burroughs defines Whitman's belief
    in evolution, coming as an intuition of
    kinship with all life rather than specifi-
    cally a descent from the animals. He uses
    Whitman's "slumbering and liquid trees"
    line to describe Yosemite oaks.

4 CAIRNS, WILLIAM B. A History of American
    Literature. New York: Oxford University
    Press, American Branch, pp. 386-95.
    Reprinted: 1930.2.
        Life sketch. Whitman's contradictory
    nature, displaying egotism as well as
    "genuineness, simplicity, and unselfishness,"
    is apparent in his letters. His irregular
    rhythms reveal a subtle melody. His power
    comes from short suggestive phrases, pic-
    torial skill, optimism, and his broad free
    view, despite his defects. His chief idea
    is democratic, that nothing is to be de-
    spised; applied to sex, this idea may be
    displeasing in practice. His poetic theory
    has influenced recent poets in English.
    (Used in 1914.3.)

5 CLARE, MAURICE [May Clarissa Byron]. A Day
   with Walt Whitman. London and New York:
   Hodder & Stoughton, n.d., 48 pp. Illustrations of Whitman's poetry.
       Characterizes Whitman and his poetry
   while taking him through a midsummer day
   in 1877: his closeness to nature, hunger
   for adventure, perception of the divine in
   the human, the miraculous in the commonplace. His poems, if lacking in polish,
   share the vast harmony and symphonic movement of the noblest masters. He experienced
   much loneliness but did not lack "'the
   romantic attitude towards woman.'" His
   friendship with Gilchrist, as described,
   reveals his "child-like simplicity" and
   "woman-like tenderness."

6 COLLIER, WILLIAM FRANCIS. A History of English
   Literature. New ed. London: Nelson &
   Sons. "Walt Whitman," pp. 771-75; also
   785.
       Whitman, preeminent in American poetry,
   is "more typically American than any other
   writer." He raised the masses "well over
   the fences of exclusiveness." Brief sketch
   of his life, showing his range of friendship
   and experience. His critics may have found
   it harder "to forgive his uncouth diction,
   his trick of cataloguing, and his unmanage-·
   able rhythms, than even his daring egotism
   of thought. That, they were content to
   misunderstand." His later work "unconsciously pacified criticism by revealing a
   broader and more temperate outlook on life."
   He is now "universally accepted as a great
   and original poet," whose bracing message
   of freedom could have been spoken in no
   other way. He has no ordered philosophy,
   appealing to the emotions rather than the
   intellect, but "not unconscious of artistic
   effect."

7 CROTHERS, SAMUEL McCHORD. Humanly Speaking.
   Boston and New York: Houghton Mifflin Co.,
   pp. 6-9.
       Humorously quotes letter from Rev.
   Augustus Bagster praising Whitman's style:
   "There is no beating around the bush. The
   poet is perfectly fearless, and will not
   let any guilty man escape." Bagster offers
   his imitation of Whitman, "The Song of
   Obligations" (reprinted in Saunders).

8 FAIRCHILD, ARTHUR H. R. The Making of Poetry:
   A Critical Study of Its Nature and Value.
   New York and London: G. P. Putnam's Sons,
   pp. 44, 260.
       Quotes "There Was a Child" as "an ex-
   ceptional expression of this general idea"
   of the poet identifying with all he experiences.

9 GOLDSBOROUGH, F. C. Poems and Sonnets.
   London: David Nutt. "'The Personified
   Walt Whitmanesque,'" pp. 88-89.
   Reprinted: Saunders.
       Parody.

10 GUTHRIE, WILLIAM NORMAN. The Vital Study of
    Literature and Other Essays. Chicago:
    Charles H. Sergel & Co. "Walt Whitman the
    Poetic Artist," pp. 322-43; also 11, 12-13.
    Revision of 1898.55, 1898.63, and 1898.77.
        This essay, aiming "to suggest to the
    classically trained what angle of vision
    he might adopt towards Whitman for his own
    greater edification," has been revised to
    admit hostile critics' points and answer
    them. Whitman "protests by far too much"
    and is often inconsistent, even old-fashioned,
    but he has enough poetry to elicit admira-
    tion and delight, whatever may be thought
    of his aesthetic theories, no more erroneous
    than those of Browning or Wordsworth.

11 JACKSON, HOLBROOK. All Manner of Folk: Inter-
    pretations and Studies. New York: Mitchell
    Kennerley. "Walt Whitman," pp. 103-21.
        Whitman is "the most national product
    of American thought," discovering American
    characteristics by becoming them. The anti-
    thesis of European writers, he is closest
    to ancient bards. He democratically accepts
    all, sees life "evolving into permanency,"
    celebrates transience. His "poem is great
    because it is the poem of a great idea,"
    the "essential power of the average thought
    and the average emotion." His works are
    "romantic," but "their literary value is
    not their first value."

12 PERRY, BLISS. The American Mind. Boston and
    New York: Houghton Mifflin Co., pp. 34-35,
    79-80, 85, 115, 125, 126, 164, 217-18, 235,
    237-39, 241, 246.
        Incidental references to Whitman as
    exemplary of American movements toward in-
    dividualism and fellowship, and to the
    "magnificent Americanism" of Leaves.

13 RICKERT, EDITH. Introduction to American
    Lyrics, chosen by Edith Rickert and Jessie
    Paton. Garden City, N.Y.: Doubleday,
    Page & Co., pp. xvii-xxi.
        A "complete elasticity of verse form"
    was the only vehicle to make Whitman's
    "crude, chaotic, imperfectly formulated
    thought endurable," conveying his message
    and "gigantic personality." Whitman, "with
    all his glaring absurdities, his bottomless
    depth of crudity, in the ultimate primitive
    strength of his natural resources is more
    nearly typical of our national development
    than any other poet." He is the most ex-
    tensively represented poet in the anthology.

14 ROBERTS, MORLEY. The Private Life of Henry
    Maitland. New York: Hodder & Stoughton;
    George H. Doran Co., p. 299.
        This fictionalized biography of George
    Gissing notes: "The only very modern writer
    that he took to was Walt Whitman, and the
    trouble I had in getting him to see anything
    in him was amazing, though at last he suc-
    cumbed and was characteristically enthu-
    siastic."

1912

15 SAINTSBURY, GEORGE. A History of English
   Prose Rhythm. London: Macmillan & Co.,
   pp. 66, 343, 405, 470-72.
       Whitman's works would lose much if put
   into actual prose form, though they are
   "often very beautiful prose." Whitman aims
   at and achieves something quite different,
   through division into "individual staves."

16 TRAUBEL, HORACE. Introduction to Leaves of
   Grass (I) & Democratic Vistas. Everyman's
   Library. London and Toronto: J. M. Dent &
   Sons; New York: E. P. Dutton & Co., pp.
   vii-xiii.
       Emphasizes Whitman's radicalism, im-
   portance to contemporary thought, appeal to
   the first-rate men of England and America.
   His conversation is quoted. His Americanism
   was international because people came first.

17 TREDWELL, DANIEL M. Personal Reminiscences of
   Men and Things on Long Island. Part 2
   (copyright 1917). Brooklyn: Charles
   Andrew Ditmas, p. 212.
       Diary entry of 1848 notes his upcoming
   position on the Freeman under Whitman. He
   notes its appearance, his later surprise at
   finding Whitman acclaimed as humanitarian,
   moralist, and great poet. (Holloway 1921
   notes some errors.)

18 TRENT, W. P., and ERSKINE, JOHN. Great
   American Writers. New York: Henry Holt &
   Co. "Walt Whitman," pp. 212-28.
       Whitman is "the most thoughtful of
   American poets," with as much literary
   background as any. His break with poetic
   tradition has been overemphasized. His
   chief passion is social. His catalogues
   follow his poetic theory that every activity
   of man expresses emotion. His evolutionist
   philosophy, scientific spirit, wariness of
   the past are described. His free rhythms
   truly convey nature and the American spirit
   and are supported by Croce's aesthetics.
   "Captain" and "Lilacs" stand out, perhaps
   for different audiences, both "more full of
   echoes than he usually permits his work to
   be." His view of life is America's largest
   account of herself to the world.

PERIODICALS

19 BAZALGETTE, LEON. "Walt Whitman: Cosmic
   Consciousness." Translated with introductory
   note by Mildred Bain. Conservator 22 (Jan-
   uary), 166-67.
       Translation of portions of Bazalgette's
   Walt Whitman. Introductory note compares
   Bazalgette to Bucke on the nature of
   Whitman's inspiration.

20 ECCLES, CAROLINE A. "An Appreciation of Walt
   Whitman." Quest 3 (January), 349-59.
       "Cradle" and "Lilacs" contain the
   fullest expression of Whitman's great
   themes, love, death, and immortality. He
   has the music of nature. His coarseness
   and egotism are explained and justified.

His mystic qualities are noted. He is a
great literary artist "if truth to nature
and clarity of expression be characteristic
of high literary art," but he is emphasized
here as prophet.

21 HEYDRICK, BENJAMIN A. "As We See Ourselves.
   V. Poetry." Chautauquan 65 (January),
   185, 189. Portrait, p. 145.
       This survey of American poetry since
   1870 cites Whitman, "one of the chief poets
   of nationalism," who "delighted to celebrate
   democratic America, not only for its own
   greatness but as the consummation of all
   the past, and as carrying the hopes of
   humanity for the future," as in "Thou
   Mother" (quoted). The list of poems under
   various topic headings includes some by
   Whitman.

22 MONRO, HAROLD. "The Future of Poetry."
   Poetry Review 1 (January), 10-13.
       Modern poetry largely fails in its
   search for function and form, despite the
   experiments of Whitman and Carpenter, who
   "shirked the problem by simply dispensing
   with metre." Their work, "however fluent
   and rhythmical," cannot be called poetry.
   But their school holds more potential than
   the schools of Kipling or the poetasters
   who concentrate on their loves and troubles.

23 TRAUBEL, HORACE. "With Walt Whitman in Camden."
   Forum 47 (January), 78-89.
       Concludes 1911.35.

24 SWAIN, CORINNE ROCKWELL. "Song of the Manuscript." Century Magazine 83 (February),
   638.
   Reprinted: Saunders.
       Parody using many lines from Whitman.

25 ANON. "Optimos." Conservator 23 (March), 7-8.
       Review of Traubel's poems from Chicago
   Evening Post (unlocated): extensive com-
   parison with Whitman, whose best poems
   Traubel cannot approach.

26 BARTLETT, TRUMAN H. "Incidents of Walt
   Whitman." Conservator 23 (March), 8-9.
       Letter to Boston Globe in response to
   editorial here reprinted (unlocated) regarding Lowell's turning away an English
   nobleman from visiting Whitman, who today
   may have two or three times as many readers
   as Lowell. Incidents involving Whitman and
   the Boston writers and Whitman's 1881 visit
   are described.

*27 DIPSICUS [E. M. Wrong]. "Allons! Camaradoes
   [sic]!" Arbor (University Press, Toronto)
   (March).
   Reprinted: Saunders.
       Parody.

28 FANFAN [Grace Blackburn]. "On the Open Road
   with Walt Whitman." London (Ontario) Free
   Press (28 March).

Reprinted: 1919.244.

Long appreciation, urging readers to walk with Whitman. Description of Whitman's profound appreciation of the beauty of nature and the body, his vivid pictures (e.g., "his superbest poetry," "Myself" 21). He is not the "woman's poet" in the sense of writing traditional love-poems, but he gives woman an ideal to measure up to as man's equal. His love and brotherhood are immense. He finds God everywhere and accepts death.

29 KARSNER, DAVID FULTON. "Walt Whitman--Revolutonist." New York Call (7 April).

Impressionistic discussion of Whitman as supporter of the workers and opponent of the oppressive institutions of modern society. His daring and individualism make him "the very sage of obscenity."

*30 REED, JOHN. "The Tenement Clothes Line." Boston Evening Herald (25 April).
Reprinted: Saunders. See Addenda.
Parody (not located on this date).

31 T[RAUBEL, HORACE]. "Whitman Books." Conservator 23 (May), 45.

Mitchell Kennerley has taken over publishing Whitman's works. Spurious editions are complained of: they contain Whitman's poems but "are not Leaves of Grass."

32 ANON. "The Superman." Times Literary Supplement (London) (23 May), 210.

The end of this essay on Nietzsche contrasts him to Whitman, "an affirmer of the whole of life" who "had never heard of the Superman." Whitman "proclaimed the true Superman, and the Superwoman too," accepting the common man as Nietzsche did not, seeing greatness in all humanity.

*33 ANON. "Walt Whitman: A Reverie." Theosophy in Scotland (June), 23.
Reported in Saunders Supplement.

34 ANON. "Outdoor Scenes and Thoughts from Whitman." Dial 52 (1 June), 437-38.

Review of 1912.2, welcome because Whitman's attitude toward nature (here explicated) has rarely been stressed. This book reveals Whitman's "delicate and powerful sensuousness." In most of his greatest poems ("Lilacs," "Cradle," "Brooklyn Ferry," isolated passages like "Myself" 21), nature is more prominent than Whitman's insistent democratic propaganda.

35 BROMER, EDWARD S. "Is Walt Whitman the Best Representative of America's Independent Spirit in Poetry?" Reformed Church Review, 4th ser. 16 (July), 346-66.

Whitman's philosophy is "New England Transcendentalism writ large." Bromer recalls reading Whitman at first with prejudice, later responding to his themes of individualism, democracy, religion.

Whitman offers direct acquaintance with nature and oneself, "lays the foundations of democracy," brings the reader to a positive relationship with God. His problems are his failure to acknowledge the immaturity and sinfulness of the race and his equation of America with democracy. His "comradism" does not answer the problem of the workingman. He is not "the real poet of American Democracy" but gives "a vision of an impossible Utopia."

36 BURROUGHS, JULIAN. "Boyhood Days with John Burroughs: Part Second." Craftsman 22 (July), 367. Alexander portrait, facing p. 357.

Includes recollections of his parents' (John and Ursula Burroughs) attitudes toward and relations with Whitman, particularly his mother's disapproval of Whitman's "shiftless, care-free, Bohemian ways" and his father's loss on Notes (1867.1).

37 [CALVERT, BRUCE]. "Walt Whitman and His Commentators." Open Road: Official Organ of the Society of the Universal Brotherhood of Man 9 (July), 1-8.

Account of the New York Whitman birthday celebration on 31 May, disappointing because the emphasis was on the feast, rather inappropriate to "Walt of the open air," "of spare diet and abstemious habits." Professor George W. Herron was the only scheduled speaker there was time to hear. The meetings of the Chicago Whitman Fellowship have been more fitting to Whitman's messages.

38 [HOWELLS, W. D.] "Editor's Easy Chair." Harper's New Monthly Magazine 125 (July), 311.

This fictionalized argument over poetic form cites Whitman for his poetic prose. His poems "in their purely rhythmical movement revert to the Old Testament, though I am bound to say that they are not such good poetry as the Book of Job, which is frankly presented as prose."

39 NOBLE, JANE GRAVES. "Bliss Perry's Walt Whitman." Conservator 23 (July), 70-72.
She criticizes Perry on Whitman (1906.13) from a mother's point of view.

40 OSMASTON, F. P. "Discussion. The 'Coarseness' of Whitman." Quest 3 (July), 766-70.

Response to Eccles (1912.20), doubting whether Whitman is "coarse" as nature is. Even Emerson and Thoreau were repulsed. Equating Whitman's attitude with Christ's is heretical. Modesty and humility are the true Christian ideals, which Whitman misunderstood.

41 FANFAN [Grace Blackburn]. "Walt Whitman's Faces." London (Ontario) Free Press (15 July).

Describes the acuteness of Whitman's

1912

senses on the evidence of his poems; discusses "Faces" as an example, showing
Whitman's realization that something lies
behind the faces.

42 ABBOTT, LEONARD D. "Walt Whitman and His
Influence in American Poetry." Poetry
Review 1 (October), 473-75.
Whitman's value for American literature
lies in his influence as an emancipator in
message and manner. His "vitalizing
spirit" appears in several poets, but rarely
his form. "The radical movement" (Crosby,
Traubel, George D. Herron, J. William
Lloyd) reveals his influence most clearly.
He is "not so much Anarchistic as Socialistic." His individualism is most extreme
in his "utterly pagan" attitude toward sex.
He is "quoted even in pulpits" and cherished
by youth.

43 CHAPMAN, Dr. C. H. Article. Portland
Oregonian (19 October).
Whitman is America's only poet "of
supreme genius who is a continuing and
growing power in the literary world," im-
pregnating the mind of the world as Poe
did not.

44 ANON. "The Open Door." Poetry 1 (November),
63.
In discussing whether Poetry is presenting only minor poets, the writer notes
that Poe and Whitman were minor poets "to
the subjects of King Longfellow."

45 BREDVOLD, LOUIS I. "Walt Whitman." Dial 53
(1 November), 323-25.
Although "one feels the force of a
profound culture behind his written work,"
Whitman does not use it to make a criticism
of life but sets aside reason and taste to
present the very materials of life. He
broadens our outlook and sympathies when we
become too narrow; the cultivated reader
rather than the average man appreciates
what Whitman does.

46 ANON. "The Hospital." Life 60 (21 November),
2242.
Reprinted: Saunders.
Comic piece on hospitals, written in
paragraphs in diction similar to Whitman's.

47 CORBIN, ALICE. "America." Poetry 1 (December), 81.
Poem quoting and referring to Whitman.

48 H[ENDERSON], A[LICE] C[ORBIN]. "A Perfect
Return." Poetry 1 (December), 87-91.
Extracts reprinted: 1913.23; 1913.24.
Quotes Paul Scott Mowrer from Paris:
Whitman's influence in Europe is due to
"his acceptance of the universe as he found
it, his magnificently shouted comradeship
with all nature and all men," and "his
disregard of literary tradition"; perhaps
too his ideas are newer there than in

America. England recognizes Whitman's
spirit, France adopted his form, but America
looked at neither carefully. America should
accept her poets, not only after Europe's
recognition of them.

49 ANON. "Old Whitman Landmarks Are Fast Passing
Away." Brooklyn Daily Eagle (15 December),
3:1-2. Illustrated.
Describes Whitman's days in Brooklyn;
where he lived and worked.

1913

BOOKS

1 BAIN, MILDRED. Horace Traubel. New York:
Albert & Charles Boni, pp. 7-10, 27-31,
and passim. No index.
Whitman was an influence on Traubel but
Traubel is worthy of consideration in himself. The wide range of interests represented in the Fellowship indicates the
universality of Whitman's appeal. Extended
comparison of Leaves and Traubel's Optimos
contrasts Traubel's dynamic qualities with
Whitman's quietism. Traubel amplifies and
clarifies "the ideals of love and comradeship which Whitman left nebulous."

2 BRIGHAM, JOHNSON. James Harlan. Iowa City:
State Historical Society of Iowa, pp. 208-
10, 368-70.
Extract reprinted: 1927.54.
Harlan dismissed Whitman for purposes
of economy, not out of disapproval of
Leaves, as charged without substantiation
by O'Connor (1866.2). Harlan's letter of
1888 to DeWitt Miller is printed, explaining
the circumstances.

3 BROWNE, FRANCIS FISHER. The Every-Day Life of
Abraham Lincoln. Chicago: Browne & Howell
Co., pp. 263, 589-90, 597-98.
Quotes "Captain," "Lilacs," and
Whitman's account of the assassination,
which Whitman, who was present [sic], "de-
scribed with singular vividness."

4 BURROUGHS, JOHN. The Summit of the Years.
Boston and New York: Houghton Mifflin Co.,
pp. 34, 58, 62, 71, 73.
Incidental references to Whitman's
pre-Darwinian belief in evolution. He uses
science less than other poets but "has put
it more completely under his feet than
they." His lines about the animals ("Myself"
32) are appealing.

5 EASTMAN, MAX. Enjoyment of Poetry. New York:
Charles Scribner's Sons, pp. 71-81; also
19, 50, 65, 117, 135, 147, 189, 223.
Reprinted with index: 1939.3.
Illustrates discussion of figures of
speech with lines from Whitman, showing how
metaphoric language conveys the desired
impressions. Whitman varies between merely

naming things and vividly recreating them for his reader in "passages of supreme poetry."

6 EMERSON, EDWARD WALDO, and FORBES, WALDO EMERSON, eds. <u>Journals of Ralph Waldo Emerson</u>. Vol. 9. Boston and New York: Houghton Mifflin Co., pp. 401, 540.

Emerson explains Thoreau's fancy for Whitman (1862). Whitman should be thanked "for service to American literature in the Appalachian enlargement of his outline and treatment" (1863). Concluded 1914.9.

7 GEORGE, WALTER L. <u>Until the Daybreak</u>. New York: Dodd, Mead & Co., pp. 241-43. (In England: <u>Israel Kalisch</u>. London: Constable & Co., pp. 210-11.)

Israel describes reading Whitman.

8 JAMES, HENRY. <u>A Small Boy and Others</u>. New York: Charles Scribner's Sons, pp. 77, 78.

In James's youthful reading of contemporary writers, he found "the deep tone" only in the writings of Hawthorne, "till Walt Whitman broke out in the later fifties--and I was to know nothing of that happy genius till long after." "It was to be true indeed that Walt Whitman achieved an impropriety of the first magnitude; that success, however, but showed us the platitude returning in a genial rage upon itself and getting out of control by generic excess."

9 JERROLD, WALTER, and LEONARD, R. M. <u>A Century of Parody and Imitation</u>. London: Humphrey Milford, Oxford University Press, pp. 370-73, 377.

Reprints of 1881.21 and 1891.11.

10 LONG, WILLIAM J. <u>American Literature: A Study of the Men and the Books That in the Earlier and Later Times Reflect the American Spirit</u>. Boston: Ginn & Co., pp. 370-82; also 357, 443, 445.

Whitman's lack of "fine moral sense," his egotism, and his jarring diction all suggest the advantages of "a sternly abridged edition" so that "his undoubted power and originality" may be appreciated. One might start with "Captain" and "Pioneers," move to "Cradle" and his major works, "Lilacs" being perhaps the finest, his later works having a new "strength of spirit" and "deeper rhythm." His "glorification of self" was "an offshoot of transcendentalism," as was his superficially understood "orientalism," quite "out of place in America." Study questions are included.

11 MACY, JOHN. <u>The Spirit of American Literature</u>. Garden City, N.Y.: Doubleday, Page & Co. "Whitman," pp. 210-47; also 7, 8, 11, 13, 15, 32, 63-64, 97-99, 102, 116, 132, 144, 179, 191, 193, 302, 309, 310, 321.

Whitman looks toward the true democracy of the future for appreciation. His early work may be too aggressive but readers should read his work whole, not only his later poems. He blends all aspects of life in his work and "is the bravest of all poets of death." His verse's originality lies not in its difference from other poetry but "in the use he made of the metres he chose." His prose is less intensely serious and humorless, with the "accent of words spoken, not sung." Traubel (1906.22, 1908.17), more realistic and less selective than Boswell, reveals "a much greater, more original man" than Johnson, and "the richest intellect in America." Incidental references note Whitman's high place in American literature, as one of its great voices.

12 MASON, DANIEL GREGORY, ed. <u>Some Letters of William Vaughn Moody</u>. Boston and New York: Houghton Mifflin Co., pp. 12, 72, 154, 158.

Brief references suggest shifting attitudes toward Whitman, from Moody's early imitations to his opposition to but possible acceptance of "the Whitmanic verse-mode."

13 NICOLL, W[ILLIAM] ROBERTSON. <u>A Bookman's Letters</u>. London and New York: Hodder & Stoughton, pp. 33, 401.

Quotes Mark Rutherford [W. Hale White] on Whitman as "one of the very greatest of living poets," but peculiar.

14 NORTON, SARA, and HOWE, M. A. DeWOLFE, eds. <u>Letters of Charles Eliot Norton</u>. Vol. 1. Boston and New York: Houghton Mifflin Co., pp. 135, 441.

Extract reprinted: 1928.18.

Letter of 23 September 1855 recommends <u>Leaves</u> to Lowell, praising its original expression, vigorous and vivid writing, graphic description; noting its Emersonian basis; regretting its coarse (but not licentious) passages. (See 1894.9 for Lowell's response.) Journal entry for December 1872 describes an evening in London with Ruskin and Carlyle; Whitman is listed among the topics of conversation.

15 POWELL, F. G. MONTAGU. <u>Studies in the Lesser Mysteries</u>. London: Theosophical Publishing House, p. 62.

Quotes from "Myself" 45 on the meeting of God and man. "The more I read Walt Whitman the more I am convinced that his inspiration came both from the depths and the heights--a true seer."

16 RIVERS, W[ALTER] C. <u>Walt Whitman's Anomaly</u>. London: George Allen & Co., 70 pp. No index.

"The sale of this book is restricted to Members of the Legal and Medical professions."

1. "Introductory": Although homosexuality is apparent in "Calamus," hardly anyone but Bertz and this writer ("a medical man") admits it.

2. "The Prima-Facie Case": Passages from "Calamus" are compared with a similar personal account from a homosexual psychological patient.

3. "Whitman's Femininity": "In almost everything except outward form he was a woman": enjoyment of feminine activities, sexual indifference to women, affection for men.

4. "Evidence Mainly Indirect": Known homosexuals were attracted to Whitman. He knew he could only be appreciated thoroughly by the few. His entire physical organism was "erethistic," highly susceptible to sensation; hence he was oversexed.

5. "Objections": Notes mystic interpretation of particular passages, Whitman's claims of paternity, his lack of interest in homosexual literature.

6. "Further Examination, and Conclusion": Whitman's behavior suggests that he was the passive sort of homosexual. No one in modern times has exalted manly love over the love of woman with like genius.

17 SAINT-GAUDENS, HOMER, ed. The Reminiscences of Augustus Saint-Gaudens. Vol. 2. New York: Century Co., p. 113.
    Recalls his father, the sculptor, joining with R. W. Gilder to bring Whitman together with photographer George C. Cox for a series of pictures in 1887, to benefit both Cox and Whitman.

18 SANTAYANA, GEORGE. Winds of Doctrine: Studies in Contemporary Opinion. London: J. M. Dent & Sons; New York: Charles Scribner's Sons, pp. 202-3.
    Whitman is unpalatable to educated Americans because he is "the one American writer who has left the genteel tradition entirely behind," a needed first break, carrying democracy into psychology and morals. His pantheism was lazy and self-indulgent; his poetic genius fell to the lowest level, merely recording impressions.

19 SAWYER, ROLAND D. Walt Whitman, the Prophet-Poet. Boston: Richard G. Badger, 76 pp. No index.
    Reprinted in part: 1919.269.
    Being stirred by Whitman's poetry and then saturating himself in primary and secondary sources, Sawyer wrote this to fill "the need of a short, up-to-date, popular presentation of the poet, and his aims and philosophy." Quotations from critics and Whitman (not always accurate) are used throughout the book.
    1. "The Man": Biographical sketch, including Whitman's hidden romance.
    2. "His Message--Democracy": Commentators often discuss democracy as one of several themes rather than "mother of all Walt's ideas," embracing liberty, equality, and fraternity.
    3. "His Religion": Whitman believed in an immanent God, omnipresent revelation, and personal immortality; he opposed religious institutions.
    4. "The Nature Lover": He went beyond Bryant's rejection of rhyme for accurate transcription of the feelings evoked by nature, creating distinctly the outdoors style.
    5. "His Note of Joy": Whitman shows that joy comes "in the living out of our true selves" rather than in seeking what "an abnormal society says we must have."
    6. "The Poet Pioneer": He was a pioneer in form and in use of sex images. His artistry lay not in achieving technical perfection but in reproducing his emotions in the reader. His treatment of sex, though philosophically imperative, ignored too completely society's feelings.
    7. "His Place Among the Prophets": A brief Whitmanesque poem by Sawyer announces himself a follower of Whitman. Despite a certain egotism and arrogance, Whitman was large-souled, containing the graces of Christ as only St. Francis, Burns, and Tolstoy have done.

20 WATSON, ALBERT D. Love and the Universe: The Immortals and Other Poems. Toronto: Macmillan Co. of Canada. "Whitman," pp. 181-84.
    Poem written in Whitman's voice, describing his mystical enlightenment, with quotations from his work.

21 WHARTON, EDITH. The Custom of the Country. New York: Charles Scribner's Sons, p. 77.
    A young man of the leisure-class is wavering between being a poet and being a critic, but "it seemed likely that the critic would win the day, and the essay on 'The Rhythmical Structures of Walt Whitman' take shape before 'The Banished God.'"

PERIODICALS

22 TRENHOLM, HARRY. Review of Traubel's Optimos. Conservator 23 (January), 167-68.
    Optimos is but an echo, almost a theft, of Whitman's work and far inferior to it. It may "arouse the unthinking to fresh antagonism against Whitman." Traubel should have been content to be Whitman's errand boy and not tried to be a poet.

23 ANON. "Whitman's Siege of Europe." Literary Digest 46 (4 January), 20-21.
    Précis with quotation of 1912.48.

24 ANON. "Literature as Art." Current Opinion 54 (February), 140-41.
    Extracts from Poetry (1912.48) and Dial (1912.45).

25 BAIN, MILDRED. "A reply to Mr. Trenholm [1913.22]." Conservator 23 (February), 181-82.
    Optimos is no mere imitation of Leaves, though the two books are related in breadth, vision, and cosmic purpose.

*26 GIBSON, DAVID. "A Visit to Walt Whitman." Gibson's Magazine (February), 12-19.
Reported in Saunders Supplement.

27 MENCKEN, H. L. "The Burden of Humor." Smart Set 39 (February), 152.
Incidental: Twain "ranks well above Whitman."

28 MABIE, HAMILTON WRIGHT. "Makers of American Poetry: Whitman the Poet of Democracy." Mentor 1 (24 February), 9-10.
Whitman had little education; his resource was conversation, not books. Leaves contains much prose; it recalls the early bards. Whitman's best quality is "plastic imagination." It is too early to predict his final rank but he has already influenced younger poets.

29 RHYS, ERNEST. "Masterpiece of the Week: Walt Whitman's 'Leaves of Grass.'" Everyman 1 (28 February), 623.
Recalls his visit to Whitman the winter of 1888-89 and Whitman's interest in current affairs. Whitman came to temper his earlier notions that America must break with the past. "Myself" is "the most daring testament" of a man's personality in all its aspects "ever set down in a book," ignoring "the civil refinements, the niceties and beauties of language." Concluded 1913.31.

30 AUSTIN, Dr. B. F. "The Spiritualism of Walt Whitman." Reason 10 (March), 7-17.
Lecture delivered at the People's Church, Los Angeles: Whitman is "one of the greatest thinkers and noblest writers of our age--one of the few thoroughly illumined souls of the ages." He glorified himself as human, nature as divine, the ordinary as miraculous. "His views are nearly Spiritualistic--especially his Optimism, his knowledge (it is more than belief) of Immortality, his lofty scorn of Death, his conception of Man as Limitless, and his Wider Hope for the race." Poems most interesting for Spiritualists are "Trumpeter," "Captain," "Lilacs," "Myself," and "Open Road" (discussed as a song of abundant, unfettered human life, and inner life as well). Whitman believes, with "psycometrists," in the mutual inspiration of souls, objects, and places.

31 RHYS, ERNEST. "Walt Whitman's 'Leaves of Grass.'" Everyman 1 (7 March), 656-57.
Concludes 1913.29. The impulses behind Whitman's writings are "the idea of the race and the multitude, and the idea of the individual." His faith in his message led him to a form of expression new to our age. His book speaks for itself "as the living testament of a man," and is appropriate to the open air rather than the library.

32 S[MYTHE], A. E. "Crusts and Crumbs." Toronto Sunday World (9 March).

Whitman is one of the spiritual forces, social, intellectual, and moral, directed to helping humanity. Extensive quotations reveal his belief in the immortality of the soul and its reincarnations. He knew that democracy could not be realized through mere material equality but lay rather in the boundless human soul.

33 MOORE, CHARLES LEONARD. "All-America vs. All-England in Modern Literature." Dial 54 (16 March), 225.
Among various paralleled American and English nineteenth-century writers, Whitman and Browning are compared, the century's "two poetic puzzles," only barely succeeding in their poetry, though "Whitman's emotional gift, his oratorical exuberance, above all his profound belief in himself, might have made him a great religious power, the founder of a faith."

34 POUND, EZRA. "A Pact." Poetry 2 (April), 11-12.
Revised: 1916.13.
Poem on his relation as poet to Whitman: "I make a truce with you, Walt Whitman."

35 M'ARTHUR, PETER. "The Poets." Toronto Globe (26 April), 17:2.
Incidental: E. W. Thompson's poems on Lincoln surpass anything written on him by an American and do not take a second place even to "Captain" and "Lilacs."

36 FANFAN [Grace Blackburn]. "With Rodin in the Metropolitan Museum at New York." London (Ontario) Free Press (31 May).
Comparison of Rodin to Whitman, "his metaphysical brother," in their appreciation for the body and perception of the great soul within. Extracts from Whitman are quoted as suitable for describing Rodin's sculptures.

37 LAZENBY, CHARLES. "The Nineteenth Century Trimurti." American Theosophist 14 (June), 734-39.
Whitman represents the Brahma aspect of the trinity, expressing the creative ideal of democracy, projecting a vision for the future. "He was in himself Father-Mother, a splendid Uranian, a double-sexual nature."

38 ROBINSON, WILLIAM J. "Walt Whitman and Sex." Conservator 24 (June), 53-55.
Whitman was among the first in America to speak frankly and honestly of the body and sexual passion and to identify true modesty. He never repented these poems; he supported sex reform and women's independence.

39 SMITH, WILLIAM HAWLEY. "Whitman Needs No Advocate." Conservator 24 (June), 56-57.
Appreciation; humorous account of introducing a friend to Whitman's work.

1913

40 WHITLOCK, BRAND. "On Outgrowing Walt Whitman."
    Conservator 24 (June), 55-56.
        One cannot outgrow Whitman: he retains
    his effectiveness, "the most universal of
    our writers," with realistic pictures,
    true history, a statesman's sense of issues,
    vision.

41 HALL, HOLWORTHY [Harold Everett Porter].
    "Epithalamium." Life 61 (5 June), 1116.
    Reprinted: Saunders.
        Comic poem on weddings in the style of
    Whitman.

42 COMPENDIUM. "Horace Traubel: Walt Whitman's
    successor." Translated by Beatrice Manson
    and Adele Seltzer. Conservator 24 (July),
    69-71.
        Extracts from Die Lese of 15 February
    1913, issue honoring Traubel. Arthur
    Holitscher gives a rhapsodical appreciation
    of Whitman as "immortal," noting Traubel's
    debts to him. O. E. Lessing's and George
    Muschner's comments, briefly referring to
    Whitman, are also printed.

*43 ANON. "Walt Whitman's Mss." London Daily
    Telegraph (8 July).
    Quoted in Willard.
        Notes small price for which a collection
    of Whitman manuscripts was sold.

44 S[MYTHE], A. E. "Crusts and Crumbs." Toronto
    Sunday World (27 July).
        Whitman has much to offer contemporary
    readers. His national ideals and message
    of the new order overtaking the old are
    applicable equally to Canada, Britain, and
    the United States. Whitman was open in
    meeting life as well as death; we must live
    with the stars as he did.

45 SABEN, MOWRY. "Literature and Democracy."
    Forum 50 (August), 130, 134.
        Incidental: "Whitman sings his com-
    radeship into our heart of hearts," like
    other writers who fulfill some noble
    functions of literature. His democracy was
    not a hallucination merely because his
    appreciation came from people other than
    the common people he apotheosized.

46 SCHINZ, ALBERT. "Walt Whitman, A World's
    Poet?" Lippincott's Monthly Magazine 92
    (October), 466-74.
        Whitman's growing popularity in France
    is due to a reaction against the refinements
    of Symbolism. As poet of freedom he has
    precursors in French literature, his primary
    originality being his treatment of virile
    love. The work of Bazalgette and Sarrazin
    (freely translated by Morris in In Re) is
    examined. Together with Poe, Whitman is
    the most interesting American writer of the
    nineteenth century, showing "how a man
    having the soul of a great poet will react
    when thrown in the milieu of modern civili-

zation without having received in his
education the solid culture necessary to
understand our age," emerging anachronis-
tically as a bard.

47 WHITE, ELIOT. "Walt Whitman and the Living
    Present." Conservator 24 (October), 117-18.
        Whitman founded no school; he urged us
    to follow our own rather than his ideas.
    He has helped to overcome prudery and to
    open the way to "a renaissance of bodily
    beauty." His meaning is unique for each
    person.

48 ANON. "Does Walt Whitman Belong Among the
    World-Poets?" Current Opinion 55 (Novem-
    ber), 352.
        Précis of Schinz (1913.46).

49 T[RAUBEL, HORACE]. "Walt Whitman: the
    Prophet Poet." Conservator 24 (November),
    141.
        Review of Sawyer (1913.19), "ingratiat-
    ing" but adding nothing to our knowledge of
    Whitman, misquoting, borrowing from Traubel
    I and II without acknowledgement.

*50 LENT, E. B. Article on Whitman. Long
    Islander (7 November).
    Reported in Whitman Supplement 1978.
        Article from Brooklyn Daily Eagle on
    Whitman's life, theory of why he called
    Long Island Paumanok, interview with Mrs.
    Sammis about Whitman's poetry and preserva-
    tion of his birthplace.

51 BLACKBURN, GRACE. "Ibsen and the Woman
    Question." London (Ontario) Free Press (22
    November).
        Comparison of Ibsen to Whitman regarding
    women's equality, on which Whitman wrote
    some of literature's "clearest-eyed and
    most passionate poetry." Not feminists,
    both seem "even a bit brutal in their
    masculinity," and emphasize the married
    woman.

52 [PHILLIPS, STEPHEN.] "Walt Whitman's 'Leaves
    of Grass.'" Poetry Review 3 (December),
    273-76.
        Favorable review of Dent edition
    (1912.16). Whitman seems more popular in
    England than in America. In sometimes
    forcing coarseness upon the reader, he is
    perhaps affected. Nevertheless, he remains
    "an indubitable force," although some
    passages unfortunately recall Tupper, but
    with some grandeur. His poetry often lacks
    music, but not because of his rejection of
    blank verse and rhyme. At his best, however,
    as in "Cradle," he "never fails in rhythm
    which is adequate," becoming "the true
    mystic, the hushed interpreter."

53 POLLARD, MARGUERITE, F. T. S. "The Universality
    of Walt Whitman." Theosophist 35 (Decem-
    ber), 373-81.
        Whitman's poetry reveals "the Great

Plan of spiritual and intellectual evolution." He was aware of America's role in
the development of the new world to come
and as bard-prophet projects its nature,
much as Indian philosophy sees the universe
as a projection of "Universal Will." He
justifies the wholeness of the universe,
both present and future.

54 ZUEBLIN, CHARLES. "Walt Whitman Prophet and
    Democrat." Ford Hall Folks 2 (28 December),
    1-2, 4.
        Transcription by Miriam Allen de Ford
    of speech in Boston with the following
    questions and Zueblin's sensible answers:
    he describes Whitman's all-embracing
    philosophy, pantheism, appreciation of the
    body and motherhood, acceptance of all
    elements of life, identity with nature.
    He was "born again" to write Leaves, re-
    sembling Jesus in his thirty years of
    preparation.

1914

BOOKS

1 BARRUS, CLARA. Our Friend John Burroughs.
   Boston and New York: Houghton Mifflin Co.,
   passim per index.
        Many incidental references to Whitman,
   generally in relation to Burroughs, who
   offers some reminiscences in conversation
   with Barrus.

2 BROOKS, VAN WYCK. John Addington Symonds: A
   Biographical Study. New York: Mitchell
   Kennerley, pp. ix, 34, 66-67, 88, 144, 151,
   153, 160-69, 189, 201, 204, 205, 208, 211,
   214, 218, 221-23, 225, 227, 228, 229-30,
   231. No index.
        Discussion of Whitman's influence on
   and friendship with Symonds. Whitman's
   **adhesiveness was more spiritual than his
   amativeness.**

3 CAIRNS, WILLIAM B. American Literature for
   Secondary Schools. New York: Macmillan
   Co., pp. 212-19.
        Based on discussion in 1912.4.
   Whitman presents the American metropolis.
   Many of his passages are better than his
   theories.

4 CALL, WILLIAM TIMOTHY. A Plea for Shakespeare
   and Whitman. Brooklyn: W. T. Call. "Walt
   Whitman," pp. 31-62.
        Considers Whitman successively as man,
   crank, sensualist, seer, artist, poet.
   He was "an earnest self-centered poseur."
   His total freedom of speech was a means of
   attracting attention for his good ideas.
   He mistook "hysterical honesty and out-
   landish retchings for high thinking" but
   he should not be edited, being foolhardy,
   not weak. Many lines equal Shakespeare's
   as great quotations. "His style fits his

bumping notions," which sometimes touch
upon something amazing or grand. He displays "mastery of the elusive details of
the beautiful," as in many short pieces
cited here. The most important thing is to
read him fairly, not like his avid admirers
or detractors.

5 DE SELINCOURT, BASIL. Walt Whitman: A
   Critical Study. London: Martin Secker;
   New York: Mitchell Kennerley, 251 pp. No
   index.
   Extracts reprinted: Hindus, Murphy (chap.
   2); Miller, Bradley/Blodgett (ch. 3).
        1. "Biographical": Describes various
   influences of Whitman's life on his poetry;
   his early work. The presumed New Orleans
   romance would contradict the spirituality
   with which he invests sex, associated for
   him with the family, not with "irresponsible
   attachments." His works and life illustrate
   the "fusion of the physical and the spiritual." His postwar poetry lacks "the old
   unquenchable and intoxicating bravura of
   independence," showing rather "a continually
   deepening spiritual consciousness."
        2. "The Problem of the Form": Whitman
   succeeds when his rhythm contributes to the
   meaning but often fails when he yields to
   conventional rhythms and forms. He is most
   himself when his poem is most like a conversation. Discussions of "Prayer," "Universal," "Thou Mother," "Lilacs," "Broad-
   Axe," "As I Lay," "Terrible Doubt," "Tears."
        3. "The Form (ii) Constructive Prin-
   ciples": Every line must "contain his
   personality in the germ," line breaks being
   significant. His free verse is compared to
   that of Goethe and Arnold. His mature lines
   blend continuity and independence. Parallels
   to music and to actual experience are noted.
        4. "The Form (iii) The Question of
   Unity": Whitman sought to avoid appearances
   of artistry (see "Myself" 2). Leaves is
   essentially a study of various atmospheres,
   all part of a whole.
        5. "Style": Explanation of Whitman's
   diction, catalogues, participial sentences,
   omission of verbs. Whitman let language
   dictate to him rather than imposing his
   own meaning on language (see "Cradle").
   His style displays constant interplay
   between "his childlike objectivity and his
   magical suggestiveness." Mood and style in
   "Myself" are explicated.
        6. "Plan": The latter half of Leaves
   remains unfinished. All sections and major
   poems are discussed in relation to the
   whole. Only after "Song of Joys" is
   Whitman at less than his best. "Lilacs"
   is accepted incorrectly as typical of his
   work because of some nearly "sing-song"
   passages. "Drum-Taps" is an appropriate
   centerpiece.
        7. "Children of Adam": To reach a
   balanced view regarding sex, Whitman had to
   align himself with the progressives to
   correct the bias of the conservatives. He

portrays mutual responsibility in sex.

8. "Calamus": Wishing to praise love as distinguished from sex, Whitman used love between men rather than between the sexes "to divest this relationship of sexual associations." Only "Earth, My Likeness" "can be construed as an allusion to sodomy," as Whitman's acknowledgment of that human impulse. His longings for a true equal went unfulfilled in life, but were transferred to the reader of his poems.

9. "Democracy and the Individual": Whitman's ideals of "the growing man" and "the perfect state" cannot be bridged, as he supposes, by mere fraternal love. Whitman draws too facile a distinction between feudal Europe and democratic America regarding liberty.

10. "Conclusion: Whitman and America": Discussion of contrasting American and European receptions. Whitman emerges directly from the American spirit and need for poetic expression; he is the poet of the process of fulfillment rather than fulfillment itself.

6 DICKINSON, G. LOWES. Appearances: Being Notes of Travel. London and Toronto: J. M. Dent & Sons; New York: Doubleday, Page & Co., pp. 151-52, 217.

With America's lack of distinction, Whitman had nothing but the divine average to sing (or rather the all too human average). America has Whitman as her prophet of the native growth of the modern era. "In the coming centuries it is her work to make his vision real."

7 DOWDEN, ELIZABETH D., ed. Fragments from Old Letters E. D. to E. D. W. 1869-1892. London: J. M. Dent & Sons; New York: E. P. Dutton & Co. Vol. 1, pp. 28, 48, 54-55, 68, 74, 77, 89, 91; vol. 2, pp. 69, 76, 99, 146, 154; passim per index in vol. 2.

These letters from Edward Dowden to his student and future wife include much discussion of Whitman (chiefly during the 1870s) and his efforts to publish his article (1871.4), which he terms "rather wooden and dry" because it does not describe the pleasure Whitman's poetry gives him. Tennyson's attitude toward Whitman is described; likewise Burroughs's visit and discussion with Dowden of Whitman. Comparisons with Tennyson, Wordsworth, and Hugo are made.

8 DOWDEN, ELIZABETH D., and DOWDEN, HILDA M., eds. Letters of Edward Dowden and His Correspondents. London: J. M. Dent & Sons; New York: E. P. Dutton & Co., passim per index, especially pp. 52-64; also xii, 85, 152, 191, 215, 364, 396.

Letters discuss Dowden's attitudes toward Whitman and his writing and lecturing on Whitman. Letters to or from his brother John, J. B. Yeats, W. H. Trimble, and

Burroughs discuss Whitman, compare him with Wordsworth and Thoreau, note the appreciation of others, suggest ways of helping him during the 1876 controversy (including a pension from the U.S. Government). Burroughs claims that his appreciation for Whitman's work, as evident in the personal note of his book (1871.1), is due to his knowledge of the man, for "to know one is to know the other."

9 EMERSON, EDWARD WALDO, and FORBES, WALDO EMERSON, eds. Journals of Ralph Waldo Emerson. Vol. 10. Boston and New York: Houghton Mifflin Co., p. 147.

Concludes 1913.6. Emerson in 1866 entry suggests that the Welsh bard Taliessin may be a possible source for Whitman.

10 HIGGINSON, MARY THACHER. Thomas Wentworth Higginson: The Story of His Life. Boston and New York: Houghton Mifflin Co., pp. 336, 395.

An 1878 letter from Higginson, visiting the McCarthys in England, says: "Whitman among their set is the American poet." He quoted the lines of "Joy, Shipmate, Joy!" "with deep emotion, and he once said that he would like to have them engraved on his memorial stone."

11 JONES, P. M. "Whitman and Verhaeren." In Aberystwyth Studies. Vol. 2. Aberystwyth: University College of Wales, pp. 71-106.

The similarities of Whitman and Verhaeren are discussed: concern with the modern world, embodiment of their nations, belief in the average man, perception of beauty in energy and character, orator-like style, mastery of the universe, attitude toward science, pantheistic qualities, belief in altruism, man, and nature as their inspiration (though their nature is not Wordsworth's). Whitman treats these themes more fully (except for the modern city), but Verhaeren is the greater artist and seems to have answered Whitman's call for the new poet, though his work generally preceded his reading of Whitman.

12 METCALF, JOHN CALVIN. American Literature. Atlanta: B. F. Johnson Publishing Co. "Walt Whitman," pp. 357-66.

Describes Whitman's powerful, primitive personality, his love for people, egotism, lack of a sense of propriety or proportion. His verse should be heard, not merely seen. His theory requires inclusive catalogues. At his best he produced "Cradle," "Lilacs," "Pioneers," "Astronomer." He was a strong individualist, "a curious compound of realist, mystic, and egotist." He "greatly enlarged the sphere of American poetry."

13 MONAHAN, MICHAEL. At the Sign of the Van. New York and London: Mitchell Kennerley. "A Whitmanite," pp. 129-36.

Whitman was a true joiner and emphasized belonging to the human race. Humorous commentary on the cosmic birth, with reference to Bucke. This Fellowship perpetuates "the loving legacy of the world's Great Comrade."

14 SABEN, MOWRY. The Spirit of Life: A Book of Essays. New York: Mitchell Kennerley, pp. 26-27, 67, 143, 187, 231, 233.
    The higher affection includes the amatory, as in "Calamus."

15 SMITH, THOMAS KILE. Whitman's Leaves of Grass. Style and Subject-Matter with Special Reference to Democratic Vistas. Koenigsberg i. Pr.; Druck von Karg und Manneck, 69 pp.
    Emphasizes the close relation in Whitman between speculative and imaginative literature: Leaves puts into practice the ideas of Vistas as a treatise on the relation of such dichotomies as mind and matter. Whitman's philosophical similarities to both Plato and Aristotle reveal him as both idealist and scientist. He is related to his social and political background. He portrays and reconciles the conscious and unconscious self, and the concepts of democracy (or aggregation) and individualism (or separation). The thought-content of many specific poems is discussed, with section-by-section discussion of such longer poems as "Open Road" and "Broad-Axe." Other poems have a primarily aesthetic emphasis, with beautiful diction and imagery; their figures of speech are analyzed. Specific poems are examined to show Whitman's purposeful use of rhythm, regular and irregular, and figures of speech (especially "Captain," "Ethiopia," "Pioneers," "Beat! Beat! Drums!," "Joy, Shipmate, Joy!"). Other poems are examined for departures from metrical mechanism or the "harmonious adaptation of the words to the strong feeling permeating the verses." His word-order and rhetorical devices are discussed.

16 STODART-WALKER, A. The Moxford Book of English Verse 1340-1913. London: Eveleigh Nash Co. "Taxation," pp. 118-22.
    Reprinted: Saunders.
    Parody of "W*lt Wh*tm*n" using echoes from him in describing taxation.

17 TRAUBEL, HORACE. With Walt Whitman in Camden, III (November 1, 1888-January 20, 1889). New York: Mitchell Kennerley, 590 pp.
    Continues 1908.17.

PERIODICALS

18 BRADSHER, EARL L. "Walt Whitman and a Modern Problem." Sewanee Review 22 (January), 86-95.
    Whitman anticipated modern attitudes regarding the wholesomeness of the body and the act of sex, treating them openly rather

than by innuendo, like so many other writers. He even looks beyond the modern view, seeing the spiritual aspect of sex, as Gilchrist realized (1870.4).

19 O'LEARY, R. D. "Swift and Whitman as Exponents of Human Nature." International Journal of Ethics 24 (January), 183-201.
    To Swift man was a detestable animal; Whitman's contrasting view was just as "incapable of being lived out," being so defiant of convention. Whitman's monism is contrasted with Swift's dualism. Whitman's concept of evil is as close to materialism as to idealism. He was a "naturalist," not an "Emersonian." He has gone further than his readers can follow; Leaves might lead them to adopt Swift's philosophy.

20 ANON. "The Six Great Americans." Collier's Weekly 52 (10 January), sec. 1, 10.
    Irving Bacheller is quoted, including Whitman among the "six great men who had done all the big things accomplished in America since 1850." Do readers agree with him? What would the United States be like if they had "done all the big things" since 1850?

21 ANON. "A Message from Walt Whitman." Philadelphia North American (20 January).
    Presents Whitman as "apostle of democracy" for those unfamiliar with his work. Extensive quotations from Vistas show his keen but little-known analysis of the conditions and needs of democracy.

22 TRAUBEL, HORACE. "Walt Whitman on Paine." Truth Seeker 1 (7 February), 83.
    Account of Whitman's address at 1877 Paine Anniversary Meeting in Philadelphia.

23 HERSEY, HAROLD. "Walt Whitman and Lincoln's Assassination." Dial 56 (16 February), 136.
    Questions Browne's claim (1913.3) that Whitman was present at the assassination: in Specimen Whitman says he was in Brooklyn.

24 COURTNEY, W. L. "Books of the Day. Walt Whitman." London Daily Telegraph (18 February).
    Review of De Selincourt (1914.5). Describes Whitman's strong points and defects (in taste, ear, humor). His ideas are often vague and occasionally indefensible. His individualistic democracy is not the democracy practiced in America. Yet he is a great man, mostly by virtue of his war work and his personality in later years.

25 ANON. "A Futurist of the Sixties." Times Literary Supplement (London) (26 February), 97-98.
    Reprinted: 1914.31.
    Review of De Selincourt (1914.5) as "creative criticism," finding more order in Whitman's work than is indeed there, for Whitman often merely presents his immediate

1914

response to the world without the completeness of a more discriminating poetry, a
common characteristic of Impressionism.
He belongs also to Futurism, like such
contemporary poets as Marinetti who believe
in aggressive poetry. Most appealing in
Whitman are not his strength and expansive
qualities but rather "his pity and sorrow"
and faith in life, immortality, and the
human spirit.

*26 ANON. "Walt Whitman in the Stockyards."
Chicago Sun (1 March).
Reported in Willard.
Review of Sandburg's Chicago, noting
similarities to Whitman.

27 ANON. "An Idolised Iconoclast." Saturday
Westminster Gazette 43, no. 6477 (7 March),
22-23.
Review of De Selincourt (1914.5), extremely interesting but perhaps over-stress-
ing Whitman's artistry in his less successful poetry. "Whitman stands for the emancipation from all ties artificial, and some
natural, for unbounded youth, unbounded
enthusiasm." Whitman's best work can only
be compared with his worst, being "extremely
beautiful by comparison." Too often he
tries to express the inexpressible; his
catalogues are not mere record of fact but
are imbued with his personality. His greatness is "in the scope and comprehensiveness
of his intention even more strikingly than
in his actual accomplishment," presenting
himself as microcosm with ecstasy in ex-
periencing all things. His best work does
not differ from all true poetry, which
"never fails to kindle and evoke the best
and rarest self that is in us." Also in
the Westminster Gazette (proper), 43, no.
6477, p. 15.

*28 PENTECOST, H. O. "Walt Whitman's View of
Life." Truth Seeker (7 March).
Reported in CHAL but not located in this
issue.

29 ANON. "Walt Whitman's Chum Tells of Good Gray
Poet--J. H. Johnston, Who Recently Disposed
of Former Editor's Picture to the Eagle,
Recalls Many Interesting Facts About the
Life of the Famed Writer." Brooklyn Daily
Eagle (8 March).
Interview with Johnston, describing his
relations with Whitman and Leaves and
various incidents.

30 T[RAUBEL, HORACE]. "Walt Whitman." Conservator 25 (April), 28-29.
Review of De Selincourt (1914.5),
which would have been better if he had
dealt directly with Whitman and his life
and avoided explication.

31 ANON. "A Futurist of the Sixties." Living
Age 281 (18 April), 175-80.
Reprint of 1914.25.

32 SCOTT, DIXON. "Walt Whitman." London Bookman
46 (May), 81-82, 85.
Reprinted: 1923.14.
Review of De Selincourt (1914.5), who
rightly treats Whitman only as an artist,
avoiding the "free-and-easiness" with which
writers feel they must treat Whitman.
De Selincourt shows the "perfect attitude
for receiving the full force and swing of
the man's extraordinary powers," for
Whitman's poems are "a final product of
culture" rather than mere barbarism;
Whitman struggled against established
rhythms to produce his best music. An
oriental quality is apparent in Whitman's
juxtaposition of the general and the precise,
which renders the homeliest details significant. His message of making "the individual feel momentous" is "deeply stirring."

33 ANON. "Walt Whitman Honored." New York Times
(1 June), 10:7.
On Whitman Fellowship Celebration,
noting briefly various speakers and their
main ideas (Anna Strumsky Walling, Mrs.
Havelock Ellis, Gertrude Traubel, Max
Eastman, others). One woman always keeps
"Blades of Grass" beside her Bible.

34 CARMAN, BLISS. "Whitman in Camden. Third
Volume of a Biographical Work That Will
Apparently Take Forty or Fifty Years to
Complete." New York Times Review of Books
(14 June), 265.
Review of Traubel (1914.17), which is
too vast, giving "an immensely cumulative
sense of the actual man" but also printing
many trivial things and giving undue emphasis to Whitman's egotism. Whitman displays little knowledge or insightful criticism, little more than "an endless prattle
of personalities." But his work has
liberating power and value for English
poetry.

35 BICKNELL, PERCY F. "An Aged Poet in His Daily
Talk." Dial 56 (16 June), 493.94.
Review of Traubel (1906.22, 1914.17),
accurate biography but somewhat disjointed,
with occasional "flashes of truth and
gleams of beauty and poetry." Traubel's
portrait of Whitman is "richly human" and
"tenderly pathetic."

36 ANON. "Whitman and Friend Horace." Conservator
25 (July), 73-74.
Favorable review of Traubel (1914.17),
reprinted from New York Evening Globe (unlocated).

37 ANON. "'The Most Truthful Biography in the
English Language.'" Current Opinion 57
(July), 50-51. Photograph of Whitman
dressed for a walk.
Review with extensive quotation of
Traubel (1914.17), who has been honest with
his subject, despite his own differing
political views. Whitman appears "not as

the aged priest of a strange philosophy,
nor as an enemy or a savior of society,
but simply as a fine old gentleman, informed, patriotic, friendly and humorous."

38 T[RAUBEL, HORACE]. "Getting Whitman right and
    wrong." Conservator 25 (July), 77.
        Warns against Whitman editions which
    use Leaves of Grass as a title but are not
    the complete deathbed edition from
    Kennerley.

39 BREDVOLD, LOUIS I. "An English Study of Walt
    Whitman." Dial 57 (1 July), 17-18.
        Review of De Selincourt (1914.5),
    which answers a need in Whitman criticism,
    placing Whitman in relation with the past
    and estimating his significance for the
    future. "The poetic value of his work is
    secondary to its thought." Without his
    rough lines he would lose his power; the
    "grotesque and ugly" are needed to show
    his "undiscriminating sympathy." Spiritual
    growth is important to him for building a
    strong democracy.

40 [FOERSTER, NORMAN]. "Impromptu Confabs."
    Nation 99 (23 July), 107-8.
        Review of De Selincourt (1914.5),
    "which will please nobody," dealing half
    with sex, half with form. Its explanations
    do not explain, for Whitman's forms are so
    flexible they can hardly be said to exist.

41 THOMSON, W. R. "Masterpiece for the Week.
    Walt Whitman's 'Specimen Days in America.'"
    Everyman 4 (18 September), 616-17.
        Specimen strikes home today as we share
    a similar war experience. Whitman recog-
    nized the national will in wartime but did
    not glorify war for its own sake. His war
    work and writings are described; also his
    "exquisite soliloquisings on Nature, and
    wise, penetrating insights into men and
    books."

42 BOURNE, RANDOLPH S. "On Cultural Humility."
    Atlantic Monthly 114 (October), 507.
        Incidental: In Whitman's poetry, as
    in Edward MacDowell's and William James's
    work, is "a national spirit" as clear as
    anything Europe has recently offered, and
    "immensely more stimulating." Can Europe
    offer many greater than these and other
    major American talents?

43 M[ONROE], H[ARRIET]. Response to Pound (1914.
    44). Poetry 5 (October), 31-32.
        Whitman's quotation on the need for
    great audiences (motto for Poetry) signifies
    the need for wider audiences, so that genius
    may not stand alone.

44 POUND, EZRA. "The Audience." Poetry 5 (Octo-
    ber), 29-30.
        Complaint about the Whitman quotation
    on great audiences, used as Poetry's motto:
    "The artist is not dependent upon his

audience. This sentence is Whitman tired.
You have only to compare Whitman to my
mutton-headed ninth cousin, or to any other
American of his time who had the 'great
audience,' to see the difference of result."

45 HUNEKER, JAMES. "The Seven Arts. A Visit to
    Walt Whitman." Puck 76 (21 November), 8,
    20. Illustrated by C. B. Falls.
    Revised: 1915.12.
        Recalls his 1877 visit to Camden and
    "the immense impression" made by Whitman
    the man, who suggested "a feminine soul in
    a masculine envelope." Whitman had a poor
    reputation in Philadelphia. The "Adam"
    poems leave one cold, for he put more of
    his spirit into "Calamus," "the bible of
    the third sex." However, "the Whitman
    case" seems to be largely ignored despite
    our freedom in talking about Wilde or David
    and Jonathan. Despite flaws, his poetry
    displays "extraordinary sensitiveness to
    the sense of touch" and much skill at con-
    veying atmosphere. He does not really
    represent America. He took the easy way in
    rejecting blank verse, but had he not, we
    should have missed his true "salty tang."

1915

BOOKS

1 [ARMSTRONG, ANNIE.] The Seas of God. New
   York: Hearst's International Library Co.,
   pp. 64-65, 370-71, 379; frontispiece,
   quotation from Whitman.
       A young woman recalls passages from
   Whitman when her father dies. He allowed
   her to read Whitman, who continues to comfort her through the words of "Prostitute"
   and other poems, though her townspeople
   never dared speak of him aloud.

2 BENNETT, ARNOLD. These Twain. New York:
   George H. Doran Co., pp. 91-93.
       Reading "Myself" 32 shows two lovers
   that they have a common bond through their
   love for "the same varied forms of beauty."

3 BENSON, ARTHUR CHRISTOPHER. Escape and Other
   Essays. New York: Century Co. "Walt
   Whitman," pp. 63-88.
       Whitman is unique in trying to reveal
   himself with less reserve than any other
   human being, a program worthy of amazement
   and respect. He emphasized the harmonious
   cooperation of body and soul. Although
   "his form constantly collapses" and he has
   "ugly mannerisms" and some coarse, obscene
   passages, there are yet "countless passages
   of true and vital beauty" and "a magical
   thrill of passion." "Cradle" has "atmosphere and suggestiveness." "Lilacs" is
   "among the very greatest poems of the
   world." Both prove that the law of art
   "lies close to the instinct of suppression
   and omission," which Whitman did not always
   heed.

1915

4 BINNS, HENRY BRYAN. Walt Whitman and His
   Poetry. Poetry and Life Series. London:
   George G. Harrap & Co., 168 pp. No index
   or notes. Bibliography, p. 168.
   Reprinted: 1932.3.
      An "attempt to give an introduction
   only, a first not a final view." Significant poems or excerpts are printed and
   analyzed within appropriate chronological
   context to show the influence of Whitman's
   life on his poetry. His meaning is difficult to understand, not because of "inadequacy of expression" but because of
   complexity of theme--his invigorating personality and an America transcending the
   "existent nation." The 1855 Preface proves
   him "a master of words" although he could
   only offer a start toward his poetic program
   for America. "Myself" (summarized) is
   "symbolical rather than realistic."
   Whitman's self-complacency is regrettable.
   He most nobly fulfills his function when
   he expresses his inner realization, not
   merely abandoning himself to nature. Comradeship is his "prerequisite of social
   freedom." His hospital work provided
   needed discipline. "Lilacs" and "Cradle"
   are compared as Whitman's "most melodious
   achievements." His later work has a "less
   aggressive, more restrained tone," with a
   subsequent lapse of inspiration. Specimen
   is Whitman "at his mellowest, most spontaneous and most human," "with a quiet,
   wistful humor." Much of his work will
   endure because it urges readers in the
   direction of human evolution.

5 BROOKS, VAN WYCK. America's Coming-of-Age.
   New York: B. W. Huebsch. "The Precipitant,"
   pp. 109-29; also 11, 39, 99-10, 134, 182.
   Revised: 1934.3; Bradley/Blodgett.
      Whitman was the first writer to give
   "the sense of something organic in American
   life." He is oriented to action and the
   whole personality. He is "an old-fashioned
   Jacksonian democrat" in ideas, with the
   right instincts but lacking a strong intellectual equipment. The true Whitmanian
   tradition is not mere affirmation of all
   that is American.

6 BURROUGHS, JOHN. The Breath of Life. Boston
   and New York: Houghton Mifflin Co., pp.
   14, 48, 110-11, 256, 260.
      Incidental references and quotations
   on Whitman's beliefs regarding matter and
   evolution.

7 BYNNER, WITTER. The New World. New York:
   Mitchell Kennerley, pp. 27-29.
   Reprinted: 1919.291.
      Part of this long poem describes "a
   poet Celia loved," i.e., Whitman, who in-
   corporates Celia and the poet in his love
   and who represents unity with the dead and
   the future.

8 DART, WILLIAM KERNAN. "Walt Whitman in New
   Orleans." In Publications, Louisiana
   Historical Society (New Orleans). Vol. 7.
   pp. 97-112.
      Speculates on Whitman's "vagabond life,"
   describes Whitman's New Orleans experiences
   and journalism, which reveal little of importance but provide an interesting link in
   the chain of his life.

9 DAVIS, ELMER. The Princess Cecilia. New
   York and London: D. Appleton & Co.,
   p. 137.
      Whitman quotation heading Chapter 10.

10 ELLIOT, CHARLES N., ed. Walt Whitman as Man,
   Poet and Friend: Being Autograph Pages
   from Many Pens. Boston: Richard G. Badger,
   257 pp.
      Introduction explains his purpose of
   presenting in manuscript facsimile "anecdotes, reminiscences, or tributes to
   Whitman's memory" from those who knew him
   or wrote notably about him. The responses,
   presented in authors' alphabetical order,
   bear dates from the 1890s to 1915. Elliot
   writes of Whitman's "intrinsic manhood" and
   universally loving heart. Attempts to com-
   pile a companion volume of the reminiscences
   of ordinary men such as veterans and bus-
   drivers "have netted but meagre results."
   Some portraits and facsimiles of Whitman
   items are reproduced. The following list
   of contributors annotates only those items
   which are more than mere appreciative notes
   or material published elsewhere: Bazalgette
   (in French), Binns, Brinton (on Whitman's
   conversation), Bucke (on Whitman's personality), Burroughs (his last visit to
   Whitman), Ellen Calder, Andrew Carnegie,
   Edward Carpenter, Dowden (on the rejections
   of his article, 1871.4), Doyle, Annie Fields,
   Garland, Jeannette L. Gilder, R. W. Gilder,
   Harned, John Hay, Howells, Hubbard, John
   Newton Johnson (a Southern farmer who re-
   calls his visit to Whitman), Dr. J. Johnston,
   Alma Calder Johnston (revised: 1917.56),
   J. H. Johnston (extensive reminiscences in-
   corporating much of 1908.20, rewording
   Lowell's response to Whitman's Lincoln
   lecture; the background to Ingersoll's two
   addresses on Whitman; reminiscences of
   Charles A. Dana, Edwin Arnold, Burroughs,
   Bucke, all in relation to Whitman), Kennedy
   (on opinions of Trowbridge regarding
   Whitman's prewar and postwar work), Mabie,
   David McKay (Whitman's disregard for criticism), Laurens Maynard, Joaquin Miller
   (illegible account of Whitman at the Philadelphia Centennial Fair), Perry, Platt,
   Whitelaw Reid (recalling knowing Whitman in
   Washington and later), Theodore Roosevelt
   ("Of all the poets of the nineteenth century
   Whitman was the only one who dared use the
   bowery--that is, use anything that was
   strikingly and vividly typical of the
   humanity around him--as Dante used the
   ordinary humanity of his day."), Rossetti

(written at age 85), Saunders, Stedman,
Traubel, Triggs, A. E. and W. H. Trimble,
Trowbridge, Charles Dudley Warner.

11 ELLIS, HAVELOCK. Studies in the Psychology
of Sex. Vol. 2. Sexual Inversion. 3d ed.
Philadelphia: F. A. Davis Co., pp. 51-57,
339.
Revision of 1901.6.
    Additions discuss the background of
Whitman's letter to Symonds as published
in Traubel (1906.22) and the psychological
motivations for his eventual response.
Bertz and Rivers have overestimated
Whitman's feminine traits.

12 HUNEKER, JAMES. Ivory Apes and Peacocks. New
York: Charles Scribner's Sons. "A Visit
to Walt Whitman," pp. 22-31.
Revision of 1914.45. Reprinted: 1929.12.
    Minor changes, including some deletions
of homosexuality discussion.

13 KELLNER, LEON. American Literature. Translated from the German by Julia Franklin.
Garden City, N.Y.: Doubleday, Page & Co.
"The Subjective Writers: The Primitives:
Whitman," pp. 99-116.
    Whitman carried the revolt against
tradition further than his fellow noncon-
formists Emerson and Thoreau. His language
is not poetical, his rhythm only occasionally musical, but his treatment of standard
poetic subjects (love, patriotism) is distinctive, as is his astonishment at everyday
things. His self-absorption is wrongly
regarded as repellent, his frankness misinterpreted as immorality. His style is
traced back to the Psalms. His influence
is overestimated.

14 MASTERS, EDGAR LEE. Spoon River Anthology.
New York: Macmillan Co. "Petit, the
Poet," p. 78.
    Poem: Petit wrote "little iambics, /
While Homer and Whitman roared in the pines."

15 PACE, ROY BENNETT. American Literature.
Boston: Allyn & Bacon. "Walt Whitman,"
pp. 244-51.
    Whitman is unique but his place is
still not fixed. Sketch of his life is
given to help clarify his accomplishment.
Present criticism has become less negative
concerning his egotism, catalogues, comradeship.

16 PATTEE, FRED LEWIS. A History of American
Literature Since 1870. New York: Century
Co. "Walt Whitman," pp. 163-85; passim
per index.
    The current inadequate text of Whitman
should be replaced by one "with variorum
readings and chronological arrangement" to
reveal his poetic development and the
limitation of his condemned aspects to one
brief period. His impetus came from Transcendentalism, his vigor, passion, and in-

coherence from his lack of learning. He
gives "the first all American thrill in our
literature." His style was a spontaneous
discovery rather than "studied revolt."
From his earlier physical emphasis Whitman
became "the most positive singer of the
human soul in the whole range of English
literature," becoming "more metric with
every edition." His verse form may be
unique to himself but his influence has
been felt through his realism, "concrete
pictures," "swing and freedom," Americanism,
"insistence upon message, ethic purpose,
absolute fidelity to the here and now
rather than to books of the past."

17 POWRYS, JOHN COWPER. Visions and Revisions.
New York: G. Arnold Shaw; London: William
Rider & Son. "Walt Whitman," pp. 281-89.
Reprinted: Miller; Bradley/Blodgett.
    Whitman's genius for sheer poetry has
been slighted. His catalogues provide a
background full of life. His optimism is
less irritating than Browning's. His work,
expressing himself, is superior to modern
free verse, whose poets all write alike.
Whitman expresses "the magical ugliness of
certain aspects of Nature," the agony of
love ("Cradle").

18 SANBORN, KATE. Memories and Anecdotes. New
York and London: G. P. Putnam's Sons,
pp. 141-43.
Reprinted: Walt Whitman Newsletter 3
(March 1957), 7.
    Account of her visit to the Smiths
when Frances Willard (see 1889.10) and
Whitman were also present. Whitman attacked
Willard as advocate of temperance and then
left the room, while Willard chattered on
as if nothing unpleasant had occurred.
When he returned, he apologized and they
became friends. All pleaded with him to
leave out certain of his poems, but he
would not. The Smiths' daughter had raised
money at college for bed linen and blankets
for him.

19 THAYER, WILLIAM ROSCOE. The Life and Letters
of John Hay. Boston and New York: Houghton
Mifflin Co. Vol. 1, p. 46; vol. 2, p. 42.
    Hay notes his attendance at Whitman's
1889 lecture, "quite interesting as to
audience and accessories."

20 TRAUBEL, HORACE. With Walt Whitman in Camden
(March 28-July 14, 1888). New York:
Mitchell Kennerley, 473 pp.
Reprint of 1906.22.

PERIODICALS

21 BULLEN, HENRY LEWIS. "Biographies of Famous
Printers. No. 6--Walt Whitman, 'The Good
Gray Poet.'" American Bulletin, American
Type Founders Co., n.s. 4 (January), 5-7.
1876 photograph.
    Admiring biographical sketch drawn from

Whitman's own version, noting especially
his printing experiences. Whitman's works,
which "require much re-reading and pondering," are "intended to open minds narrowed
by class blindness, and to reinstate the
principles of elementary justice, equality
and brotherhood."

22 ERSKINE, JOHN. "With Walt Whitman in Camden."
Yale Review 4 (January), 415-20.
Reprinted: 1915.30.
Review of Traubel (1914.17), which
provides excellent commentary on Whitman's
poetry and insight into his personality.
He is "the truest and most insistent ex-
pounder of American democracy," never confusing "the issue between humanity and the
more selfish kinds of culture." The book's
length is justifiable for the sake of
veracity. Whitman's conversation may offend
some, but it is honest, showing keen intellect.

23 JONES, P. M. "Whitman in France." Modern
Language Review 10 (January), 1-27.
Whitman and the Symbolists developed
separately but along similar lines. Vers
libre was not indebted to Whitman, though
he now inspires the younger French poets.
His thought is embraced by common people
and radicals. His first translators and
critics are discussed; he is seen as a
primitive, spontaneously expressing his
singular nature. His later poems may reveal
a debt to Poe. List of translations and
studies in French.

24 SCHEFFAUER, HERMAN. "Whitman in Whitman's
Land." Fortnightly Review n.s. 97 (1
January), 128-37.
Reprinted: 1915.26.
Whitman is the property of a cult in
America, but vital and controversial in
Germany and France. His kind of democracy
no longer exists. His is "a poetry for
free spirits," unlike his contemporaries
or ours (the industrially oppressed). His
kind of socialism, robust and human, contrasts with today's primarily economic
version. The modern world's "universal
assertion of individuality" prevents the
achievement of a great personality such as
Whitman insisted on.

*25 [CHAPMAN, Dr. C. H.?] Article on Whitman.
Portland Oregonian (31 January).
Reported in Willard.
Whitman's life and current influence
are traced. His "pornographic passages"
are no longer so overemphasized, being not
"miasmatic" but far too realistic for his
early readers.

26 SCHEFFAUER, HERMAN. "Whitman in Whitman's
Land." North American Review 201 (15
February), 206-16.
Reprint of 1915.24.

27 ANON. "Great Poets' Lines Mark Fair Arches."
San Francisco Examiner (21 February).
Porter Garnett explains the Whitman
quotation (opening lines of "Facing West
from California's Shores") chosen to
represent America on one of the arches for
the Exposition: the poet is embodying the
westward-looking Aryan race. Whitman
"above all others represents the spirit of
the American people and the ideals of
democracy."

*28 RANDOM, JACK. "Admetus: A Poem with apologies
to the shade of Walt Whitman." The Railway
World (March).
Reprinted: Saunders.
Parody.

29 BAILEY, FRANCIS DANE. "Walt Whitman." New
York Sun (29 March), 6:7.
Defends Whitman against Hornor (see
Addenda, 1915.28a). He is one of the few
poets that currently "seem to have a healing
for the nations."

30 ERSKINE, JOHN. "With Walt Whitman in Camden."
Conservator 26 (April), 23-25.
Reprint of 1915.22.

31 [DE LA MARE, WALTER.] "Drum-Taps." Times
Literary Supplement (London) (1 April),
105-6.
Vistas remains applicable to the present
war. Whitman emphasized the dignity of the
common people, confidence, joy in life.
De la Mare imaginatively depicts Whitman
defending what he writes and ministering to
soldiers. With his theme being all of life,
Whitman often does not focus experience but
"merely transmits it," yet his verse is
always full of "things." Occasionally he
forces a moral in the otherwise excellent
"Drum-Taps," and he stumbles over rhyme in
"Captain." "Lilacs" is his best.

32 McGAFFEY, ERNEST. "'Imagistic' Cult Poetry."
Los Angeles Graphic 45, no. 23 (8 May), 3.
This discussion of current poets compares Whitman to his imitators, who never
match even his occasional rhythm.

33 FREILIGRATH, FERDINAND. "Walt Whitman--A
German Appreciation in 1868." New York
Call (16 May), Magazine Section.
Retranslation of 1868.36.

34 SANTAYANA, GEORGE. "Genteel American Poetry."
New Republic 3 (29 May), 94-95.
Only Whitman rebelled from the conventional poetry of the nineteenth century.
To the detriment of enervated contemporary
American poetry, his way did not take root,
possibly because he "renounced old forms
without achieving a new one," failing to
consider what was worthy from the past.

35 S[MYTHE], A. E. "Crusts and Crumbs." Toronto
    Sunday World (30 May).
        When the war is over, people may listen
    to Whitman's sane and profound message: he
    sees the real world, the real potential
    behind the actual, like Plato. His poetry
    is not for "mere intellectuality," but
    speaks to the human heart, in a deeper way
    than the conventional. For an introduction,
    read in order: "Open Road," "Answerer,"
    "Rolling Earth," "Universal," "Passage,"
    "To Think of Time," "So Long."

36 HERVEY, JOHN L. "The Growth of the Whitman
    'Legend.'" Dial 59 (June), 12-14.
        Letter complaining about the false
    information conveyed at the Chicago Fellow-
    ship meeting. The legend of Whitman's life
    is growing inordinately; his "fans" seem to
    be ignoring Leaves itself.

37 KILSPINDIE, VICTOR. "Communion with Nature."
    New York Times (6 June), sec. 1, 16:5.
    Reprinted: Saunders.
        Letter to editor in form of a free-
    verse poem expressing somewhat Whitmanesque
    sentiments but without reference to Whitman.

38 S[MYTHE], A. E. "Crusts and Crumbs." Toronto
    Sunday World (6 June).
        Incidental references to Whitman's
    perception of reconciliation of opposites
    and his prophetic powers (possessed by any
    who keep their eyes open wide enough), as
    evidenced in "Years of the Modern."

39 MOORE, AUBERTINE WOODWARD. "Walt Whitman's
    Vision of America Singing--The Poet as
    Prophet of His Country's Future Greatness
    in the Art of Music--His Call for 'A Higher
    Strain Than Any Yet'--'New Rhythms' Needed
    to Convey America's Mighty Message."
    Musical America 22 (12 June), 31. Illus-
    trated.
        Whitman had "an abiding faith in the
    future magnificent intellectual and spiri-
    tual output" of his country, seeking new
    forms for America's message. His ideas
    about music are expressed through quotations.

40 DELL, FLOYD. "Walt Whitman, Anti-Socialist."
    New Review 3 (15 June), 85-86.
        In contrast to the socialist movement's
    reliance on intelligence, Whitman believes
    in instinct and the senses (including those
    of sex and religion). His rejection of
    worry would be fatal to the socialist. Yet
    socialists should keep reading his "magni-
    ficent lines" as a means of experiencing
    and recognizing our instincts and emotional
    needs.

41 ANON. "Whitman's Unmitigated Self." Conser-
    vator 26 (July), 71.
        Review of Traubel (1914.17) reprinted
    from New York Evening Sun (unlocated): The
    work is a total "self-revelation" of Whitman,
    though the wheat should be separated from
    the chaff.

42 T[RAUBEL, HORACE.] "Walt Whitman and His
    Poetry." Conservator 26 (July), 72-73.
        Review of Binns (1915.4), who makes too
    many deductions, in contrast to Traubel's
    own inclusiveness, here defended.

43 TRAUBEL, HORACE. "With Walt Whitman in Camden."
    Forum 54 (July), 77-85.
        Pre-publication extracts of volume 4
    (not published until 1953). Continued
    1915.49.

44 ANON. "Song of the L.S.P.M. (After Walt
    Whitman.)" Life 66 (1 July), 16.
    Reprinted: Saunders.
        Parody of Whitman about the "Low Stan-
    dard of Public Morality."

45 ANON. "Walt Whitman as Muscial Prophet."
    Musical America 22 (3 July), 18.
        "The national epoch just concluded has
    produced no other prophetic voice" in the
    field of art and other general topics
    "equal to that of Whitman." His work must
    be revered "by all constructive artistic
    thinkers" as "a living fountain of creative
    energy and vision," his thought so universal
    "that all must find contact with it and
    stimulation from that contact." He is un-
    surpassed in his sense of America's future,
    including the future of an art appropriate
    to our land and time.

46 [HARTT, GEORGE.] Review of Traubel (1914.17).
    Passaic Daily News (16 July).
    Reprinted: 1915.50.
        Traubel's way is excellent for getting
    Whitman himself down in print. Several ex-
    tracts show Whitman "an accomplished and
    learned critic of literature." He seems to
    have lived the life he preached, speaking
    frequently of his philosophic themes but
    rarely mentioning Leaves.

47 ANON. "The Bellman's Book-Plate. The Whitman
    Legend." Bellman 19 (17 July), 78-79.
        To counteract the "grotesque assertions"
    and nebulous conceptions of "Whitman 'fans'"
    regarding him, the actual facts of his life
    are contrasted with the "legend" that Hervey
    (1915.36) pointed out.

48 CHAMBERS, JULIUS. "Was Walt Whitman a
    Baconian?" Conservator 26 (August), 86-87.
        Reprinted from Brooklyn Daily Eagle
    (unlocated): summary of Whitman's comments
    on Shakespeare as reported by Traubel.
    Chambers, a regular visitor to Whitman,
    testifies to Traubel's accuracy.

49 TRAUBEL, HORACE. "With Walt Whitman in Camden."
    Forum 54 (August), 187-99.
        Continues 1915.43. Concluded 1915.51.

50 HARTT, GEORGE. "With Walt Whitman in Camden."
    Conservator 26 (September), 102-3.
    Reprint of 1915.46.

51 TRAUBEL, HORACE. "With Walt Whitman in Camden."
    Forum 54 (September), 318-27.
         Concludes 1915.49.

52 MOORE, AUBERTINE WOODWARD. "Walt Whitman and
    Music. (Personal Reminiscences.)."
    Christian Register 94 (9 September), 851-
    53.
         Revised: 1926.49.
         Describes Whitman's use of music, love
    for and knowledge of it, belief in its
    value for America and the world. Recalls
    meeting Whitman at the Camden home of Col.
    Johnston in 1874, and later, at Whitman's
    request, playing Beethoven, upon whom he
    commented.

53 DE CASSERES, BENJAMIN. "From a Far Away
    Hippodrome." New York Call Magazine (12
    September), 9.
         Significant men from the past are
    imagined as looking at the war in Europe.
    Whitman calls to his "boys" in the trenches,
    loving them all; whatever their nation, they
    are what is truly important about the war.

54 HOLLOWAY, R. EMORY. "Walt Whitman in New
    Orleans." Yale Review n.s. 5 (October),
    166-83.
         Relates Whitman's experiences in New
    Orleans, including his brush with sex.
    Quotations from his contributions to the
    Crescent suggest his future themes. "The
    significance of the journey was mental and
    spiritual rather than artistic"; he gained
    "a new vision of the wealth and the destiny
    of the Union" and perhaps awareness of sex.

55 MENCKEN, H. L. "The Literature of a Moral
    Republic." Smart Set 45 (October), 151.
         Review of Kellner (1915.13), approving
    his general skepticism toward Whitman.
    Kellner admits "the sensuous character,
    the emotional appeal of some of those
    flamboyant dithyrambs," while recognizing
    "their general poverty of content" and
    frequent "descent into hollow jingling."
    Whitman's American influence has been
    slight, although he should be remembered
    as the only American writer of his day who
    stood firmly against puritanism, if with
    little result. Several recent commentators
    are mentioned, including Max Dauthendey.

56 HOLLOWAY, R. EMORY. "The Early Writings of
    Walt Whitman." Nation 101 (14 October),
    463.
         Announces his findings of published
    work by Whitman from the 1840s, asking for
    others that may be known in preparation for
    his study of early Whitman.

57 KARTOSHINSKY, OSCAR. "American Books in
    Russia." New York Evening Post (16
    October).
         Notes progress of Whitman's reputation
    in Russia, from scant about twenty-five
    years ago to wide at present, when readers

seem pleased with his spirit of democracy
and individualistic tendencies.

58 ANON. "The Poetry of War." Times Literary
    Supplement (London) (21 October), 361.
         Review of anthology of war poems, Pro
    Patria et Rege. Incidental discussion of
    "Dirge" as example of moving war poetry
    because it happened to Whitman, as "an
    event of his mind." The great poems of
    victory in war, like this, depict triumph
    in death rather than military success.

59 ROBINS, EDWARDS. "How Walt Whitman Looked to
    One Who Met Him Once." Philadelphia Public
    Ledger (7 November), sec. 2, 5:1-2.
         Reprinted in part: Whitman Supplement 1979.
         Recalls meeting Whitman in Philadelphia
    in the early 1880s, in the company of his
    uncle Charles G. Leland and his sister
    (later Elizabeth Pennell). Whitman is de-
    scribed, always a poseur, suggestive of
    King Lear. Whitman is quoted in response
    to a recent article of negative criticism.
    Wilde's visit to Leland shortly after
    visiting Whitman is recalled. Wilde and
    Whitman were different in all but their
    mastery of English and the art of dressing.

60 ANON. "Walt Whitman's Old Home Sold." New
    York Tribune (18 November), 14.
         Whitman's birthplace, sold at auction,
    is described, such a house as Whitman
    might have built for himself, "broad, un-
    gainly, stubborn of outline, tanned and
    weatherbeaten of hue." America has changed
    since his day, and the people as well have
    become different from Whitman's type.

61 ANON. "Walt Whitman's Americans." Philadelphia
    Evening Ledger (19 November).
         Editorial on Whitman's Americanism,
    which emphasized the brotherhood of human
    beings, not of a certain type of people, as
    implied in the account of his birthplace
    mourning the "fast-vanishing American
    farmers" (1915.60). Whitman would accept
    new-style farmers too.

62 McDONALD, BENNETT. "Genius Is a Merciless
    Obsession, Says Dreiser." New York Tribune
    (5 December), sec. 5, 5.
         Interview with Dreiser, who lists
    Whitman "among those who were possessed by
    genius, and could not have suppressed it
    had they so desired."

63 ANON. "Literary Notes. Walt Whitman on
    Camden's Index." Boston Herald (22 Decem-
    ber), 13:7.
         David Karsner tells that the Camden
    Public Library has barred Leaves from the
    open shelves as an obscene book. Camden
    considers Whitman "much of a poseur and a
    hypocrite," although many of its residents
    say, "He was a kind, but crazy, old man."

BOOKS

1 ANON. The Story of the Brothers of the Book.
Chicago: Brothers of the Book. "Walt
Whitman: Yesterday & Today," pp. 11-12.
Publisher's circular including a descriptive notice of Legler (1916.11), a
"scholarly contribution to Whitmaniana and
to American literature." Though today we
take Whitman and "his high place in American
literature" for granted, he was greeted
with much adverse criticism but "lived to
see unstinted appreciation accorded the
very works which had called forth such
torrents of abuse."

2 BURROUGHS, JOHN. Under the Apple-Trees.
Boston and New York: Houghton Mifflin Co.,
pp. 5, 79, 181-82, 193-95, 223, 229, 291,
299.
Incidental references: explanation of
Whitman's portrayal of the earth's sexuality; his synthetic, not analytic, scientific mind; his spiritualizing of the
modern world's materialism; his intuition
rather than logic; his "sense of limitless
space."

3 CARPENTER, EDWARD. My Days and Dreams: Being
Autobiographical Notes. London: George
Allen & Unwin, pp. 28, 30, 64-67, 86-89,
117-19, 144, 201, 250.
Recollection of his early joyous re-
sponse to Whitman's work, his treatment of
sex, his poems of comradeship. Leaves had
an intellectual effect before reshaping
Carpenter's "moral and artistic ideals."
The personality behind it became more sig-
nificant than ideas. Brief account of his
first visit to America, quoting Emerson and
Holmes on Whitman; his second visit; the
Bolton group of Whitman's admirers.

4 COLERIDGE, Hon. STEPHEN. An Evening in My
Library Among the English Poets. London
and New York: John Lane, pp. 34-38, 43.
Whitman has written one fine poem,
"Captain" (reprinted), "in spite of its
slipshod rhymes." His usual work is neither
poetry nor prose but "an idiotic catalogue
of words," "a literary impertinence" with
"no distinction of thought, and no felicity
of expression." Rather than sublimating
the passions, he "has approached them with
the mental attitude of a stud groom."

5 DUNLOP, ELINOR. "Walt Whitman and the American Civil War, 1861-1864." In Bibby's
Annual, edited by Joseph Bibby. Liverpool:
J. Bibby & Sons, pp. 11-12.
Popularized, slightly inaccurate version of Whitman's life from 1855. "Open
Road" is "vibrant throughout with the
consciousness of the divine destiny of the
human race." Whitman's outlook on life
made him "a natural nurse" who could con-

vince of "the soul's endurance" by his
presence alone.

6 ESENWEIN, J. BERG, and ROBERTS, MARY ELEANOR.
The Art of Versification. Rev. ed.
Springfield, Mass.: Home Correspondence
School, p. 60.
The chapter on the necessity of rhythm
quotes "Myself" 33 to show even Whitman's
"rude and impressive rhythm, produced by a
repetition of similar phrases." By means
of his insistent rhythms, "in his best
poems, he rouses our emotional excitement."

7 FERGUSON, JOHN DeLANCEY. American Literature
in Spain. New York: Columbia University
Press. "Prescott, Emerson, Whitman," pp.
170-201; also 241.
Whitman is more talked about than read
in Spain. Description with quotation of
the various Spanish studies and translations
of Whitman.

8 FITCH, GEORGE HAMLIN. Great Spiritual Writers
of America. San Francisco: Paul Elder &
Co. "Walt Whitman, The Prophet in His
Shirt-Sleeves," pp. 12-20.
Whitman is the most original of American
authors, a product of America, self-educated
(his development being "one of the curiosities of literature"), mystical. Leaves is
shown to correspond with Whitman's life.
Whitman is revealed most personally in
Drum-Taps and Specimen.

9 GEORGE, W[ALTER] L. The Strangers' Wedding.
Boston: Little, Brown & Co., pp. 380-81.
A young man tries reading Whitman and
other poetry to a young woman, but she
prefers humorous verse.

10 GILDER, ROSAMOND, ed. Letters of Richard
Watson Gilder. Boston and New York:
Houghton Mifflin Co., pp. 66, 92, 137-38,
186, 403-4, 408-13.
Gilder's letters explain that his "When
the True Poet Comes" was not written about
Whitman; praise him for his sense of form
and beauty, perhaps absorbed unconsciously
but present in his great work, if not in his
ranting theorizing; critically analyze what
Whitman does in his verse. For the reader,
Whitman "sets his whole being tingling."
Gilder recollects warmly Whitman's char-
acter.

11 LEGLER, HENRY EDUARD. Walt Whitman: Yesterday and Today. Chicago: Brothers of the
Book, 71 pp. No index.
Briefly traces Whitman's career and
reputation, quoting from many early negative
(and some positive) reviews, noting his
major biographers and commentators. Leaves
is "an extraordinarily candid" autobiography,
revealing his gentleness, brusqueness, egotism, humility, grossness, finer nature,
crudeness, eloquence, as "the attributes
of all mankind." The volume ends with an

1916

anthology of poetic tributes to Whitman,
including poems by Joseph W. Chapman,
Edward S. Creamer, Henry S. Bonsall, Max J.
Herzberg.

12 NADAL, B. H. Friendship and Other Poems.
New York: Robert J. Shores. "The Bliz-
zard--September 13, 1916. From Shark River
Anthology. A Horrible Example--a Long Way
after Whitman and Masters," pp. 39-41.
Reprinted: Saunders.
Parody.

13 POUND, EZRA. Lustra. London: Elkin Mathews.
"A Pact," p. 17.
Revision of 1913.34. Reprinted: 1928.2;
Rupp.

14 POWYS, JOHN COWPER. One Hundred Best Books.
New York: G. Arnold Shaw, p. 27.
Impressionistic explanation for the
inclusion of Whitman's "complete unexpurgated edition": for his style and "power
of restoring us to courage and joy."

15 QUILLER-COUCH, Sir ARTHUR. On the Art of
Writing. New York: G. P. Putnam's Sons;
Cambridge, England: University Press, pp.
64-65, 66, 68.
Incidental: Whitman is indeed a poet,
even though between the clearly marked
boundaries of verse and prose.

16 RANDALL, JOHN HERMAN. The Life of Reality.
New York: Dodge Publishing Co., pp. 13,
148, 153, 169-73, 339-40, 361-62.
Discusses Whitman as a new type of
mystic declaring "the nothingness of evil
as such, the righteousness of the flesh and
the holiness of love."

17 RANKIN, HENRY B. Personal Recollections of
Abraham Lincoln. New York and London:
G. P. Putnam's Sons, pp. 124-27.
Reprinted: 1916.41; Hindus. Extract reprinted: 1926.69.
Recalls Lincoln reading aloud passages
from Leaves in his law office, presumably
about 1857. He "commended the new poet's
verses for their virility, freshness, unconventional sentiments, and unique forms
of expression, and claimed that Whitman
gave promise of a new school of poetry."

18 RUSSELL, BERTRAND. Principles of Social Reconstruction. London: George Allen &
Unwin, pp. 35-36.
Reprinted: 1917.12.
Contrasts Carlyle's repugnance to
almost the entire human race with Whitman's
instinctive liking for the vast majority
of the race, upon which his philosophy was
based. "A world of Walt Whitmans would be
happier and more capable of realizing its
purpose than a world of Carlyles."

19 SARKAR, BENOY KUMAR. Love in Hindu Literature.
Tokyo: Maruzen Co., pp. 4, 62-64, 65, 71,

86.
Incidental references to Whitman's
similarities to Hindu and Western poets in
dealing with love and sex.

20 SHERARD, ROBERT HARBOROUGH. The Real Oscar
Wilde. London: T. Werner Laurie, p. 209.
Incidental: "Dour old Walt Whitman,
even, succumbed to the great charm of the
young Irish poet who visited him in his
dust-laden cabin."

21 STRONG, AUGUSTUS HOPKINS. American Poets and
Their Theology. Philadelphia: Judson
Press. "Walt Whitman," pp. 419-70; also
291, 410.
Whitman is judged from the points of
view of art, morality, and religion (from
the standard of "the evangelical faith,"
"modified Calvinism"). He wrote "an infantile and undeveloped kind of poetry."
The biographical sketch, based on Carpenter
(1909.4), emphasizes Whitman's indifference
to education and discipline. His philosophic
sources were Quakerism and Emerson. He
failed to realize that art copies not
merely nature but the higher nature. His
best works are most traditional; otherwise
his "naked individualism" corrupted his
art. His life was generally immoral. A
Camden pastor's letter is quoted deploring
Whitman's assumed influence in that town.
His idea of democracy is anarchy. His
religion of "affectionate comradeship" replaced God with materialistic ideas. His
"transient visitations of insight and of
conscience" reflected some musical influence
and an "instinct of immortality," but he
remains "a poet in the lower realms of
poetry." His failure to organize his material into pleasing form is the "necessary
outcome of a godless philosophy and a godless life."

22 WALLING, WILLIAM ENGLISH. Whitman and Traubel.
New York: Albert & Charles Boni, 145 pp.
"Walt Whitman," pp. 1-38; also passim. No
index.
Discussion of Whitman's philosophy pre-
cedes explanation of Traubel's development
and divergence from it. Whitman's poetry
and democratic stance, still relevant, are
interdependent. His Americanism is not
provincial or simply nationalistic. He
could have been more radical and socialistic,
but he generally regarded individual regen-
eration as the means to solving social
problems. He is "almost a believer in the
great man theory." He recognized material
considerations but underplayed economics
and failed to see the incongruities of his
metaphysical idealism with his social awareness.

23 WATTS-DUNTON, THEODORE. Poetry and the Rena-
scence of Wonder. New York: E. P. Dutton
& Co., n.d., pp. 69-70, 201-2.
Leaves, Tupper's "Proverbial Philosophy,"

Warren's "Lily and the Bee" are mere cari-
catures of biblical rhythm. Whitman's
mixture of Bible phraseology with the jargon
of the slums and "bad Spanish and worse
French" is a sacrilege, although one would
like to sympathize with his innovations.
His "marvellous pages," however, are "a
comfort" after the highly artificial forms
of poets of the 1880s.

PERIODICALS

24 BRADFORD, GAMALIEL. "Portraits of American
Authors: II--Walt Whitman." Bookman 42
(January), 533-48.
Revised: 1932.4.

Whitman's proclaimed break from tradition is itself traditional of "strong,
rising authors." His literary consciousness is greater than generally assumed.
Women dislike him not for making sex too
prominent but for not making it prominent
enough. Longfellow is more truly the poet
of democracy, with his spirit of aspiration
as opposed to Whitman's contentment with
the present. Whitman is praised as a man,
with his vigor, beautiful male friendships,
warm humor, positive and acceptable egotism.
His book is needed by the heart of man
"because it contains all the heart of man."

25 T[RAUBEL, HORACE]. "Drum-Taps." Conservator
26 (January), 171.

Review of London edition of Drum-Taps,
great war poems because they are great
peace and comrade poems. Whitman's work
should not be construed as supporting war
or mere nationalism; his America was "a
universalized America." He would approve
of the recent nonresistant attitude.

26 S[MYTHE], A. E. "Crusts and Crumbs." Toronto
Sunday World (16 January).

Report of reception at the Whitman Club
of Bon Echo. Describes James L. Hughes's
speech on Whitman's view of death and
Smythe's speech on Whitman's spiritual
perceptions attained through the war and
his mystical elements.

27 KILMER, JOYCE. "Free Verse Hampers Poets and
Is Undemocratic--Josephine Preston Peabody
Says That Nevertheless, the War Is Making
Poetry Less Exclusive and the Imagiste
Cult Will Be Swept Away." New York Times
Magazine (23 January), 14.

In this interview, Kilmer suggests
Whitman as the most democratic poet of his
day, but Peabody calls him "a democrat in
principle, but not in poetic practice,"
because his general lack of music limited
his audience.

28 OPPENHEIM, JAMES. "Democracy in Verse and
Art--James Oppenheim Disagrees with Some of
the Views Expressed by Josephine Preston
Peabody and Pleads for Every Form of Expression." New York Times (30 January),

sec. 3, 1:1-3.

Response to 1916.27, defending free
verse and Whitman, who found this medium
best suited to his needs. His influence
and acceptance are growing. His verse has
a dominant undercurrent of rhythm.

29 GARNETT, EDWARD. "A Gossip on Criticism."
Atlantic Monthly 117 (February), 177.

Incidental in this article on critical
standards, questioning why American reviewers apply their moral and idealistic shib-
boleths "when the poet--Whitman yesterday,
or Mr. Robert Frost to-day--shows us the
essential beauty or force of life, working
in the familiar scene, in the characteristic
human impulse."

30 HOLLOWAY, R. EMORY. "Early Poems of Walt
Whitman." Nation 102 (10 February),
Supplement, 15.

Whitman's biographers have neglected
his early work, which shows germs of his
later themes in several poems cited.

31 BRETHERTON, CYRIL H. "Our Hand-Picked Poets."
Los Angeles Graphic 49, no. 12 (19 February), 3.

Whitman is compared to Oppenheim. His
genius "is not seriously questioned" today,
but he certainly struck a blow to modern
poetry, transforming poets into preachers
and introducing "segmented prose."

32 KILMER, JOYCE. "How Does the New Poetry Differ
from the Old?" New York Times Magazine
(26 March), 8.

Interview with Amy Lowell, who notes
the partial derivation from Whitman of the
realistic school, notably Frost and Masters.
"America has produced only two great poets,
Whitman and Poe." Current poets surpass
all earlier American poets but these in
originality and the stuff of poetry.

33 CLARKSON, GROSVENOR B. "I Am the Poster."
Current Opinion 60 (April), 278.
Reprinted: Saunders.

These "Whitmanesque lines" on "the aim
of the modern poster," quoted from the
official catalogue for the Newark poster
contest, appear in an article on "The Poster
as an Artistic Ally in the Advertizing of
American Cities."

34 JONES, P. M. "Influence of Walt Whitman on
the Origin of the 'Vers Libre.'" Modern
Language Review 11 (April), 186-94.

The French development of vers libre
was not indebted to Whitman; the French
poets differ from him in spirit, thought,
and form. His first definite influence on
French literature came through the Belgian
poets, especially in the use of catalogues.
His principal appeal is "his brusque originality."

1916

35 BANNING, GEORGE HUGH. "To Walt Whitman."
Los Angeles Graphic 49, no. 18 (1 April),
2.
Poem of praise in five rhymed quatrains.

36 C[LOVER], S[AMUEL] T[RAVERS]. "Browsings in
an Old Book Shop." Los Angeles Graphic
49, no. 18 (1 April), 2.
Discussion of Drum-Taps as revealing
Whitman's universal sympathy, praising
especially "Pioneers," "Captain," "Dirge."
"His vignettes are admirable in their
sharpness, their fidelity to detail" (e.g.,
"Bivouac"). Vers librists are indebted to
Whitman, whose "total disregard for form"
was "the inevitable expression of his character."

37 HOLLOWAY, R. EMORY. "Some Recently Discovered
Poems by Walt Whitman." Dial 60 (13 April),
369-70.
Revised: 1916.66.
Announces significant discovery of early
poems of Whitman in Long Island Democrat
and Brooklyn Daily Eagle, which display
a "meditative, if not morbid" tone, with
themes of death and the vanity of life.

38 ANON. "Traubel Compared with Whitman in
Critical Analysis." Conservator 27 (May),
39-40.
Reprint of 1916.44.

39 EDINGTON, ARCHIE. "Whitman and Traubel."
Conservator 27 (May), 39.
Brief favorable review of Walling
(1916.22) from Montreal Star (unlocated),
noting Walling's opinions of Whitman's
greatness and social beliefs.

40 KARSNER, DAVID FULTON. "Whitman and Traubel."
Conservator 27 (May), 38-39.
Favorable review of Walling (1916.22)
from Wilmington (Delaware) Morning News
(unlocated): Walling's approach to Whitman
through social philosophy and economics is
new, revealing Whitman as "an idealist in
theory and an individualist in fact." But
Whitman's intellectual bulk and vital
poetic expression are not intended for
intricate theorizing.

41 RANKIN, HENRY B. "Lincoln and Leaves of
Grass." Conservator 27 (May), 40-41.
Extract reprinted from 1916.17.

42 [MONAHAN, MICHAEL.] "Smothering Walt."
Phoenix 5 (May-June), 30-32.
Reprinted: 1916.54; 1926.18.
All the material by Traubel has almost
buried Whitman and destroyed the chance of
a fitting legend for him, for in Traubel's
work Whitman is seen as failing utterly to
live up to the Leaves.

43 BROWN, Prof. J. MACMILLAN. "Shakespeare the
Man. A Day with Walt Whitman." Christchurch (New Zealand) Weekly Press (3 May).

Recalls visiting Whitman "some thirty
years ago" and discussing with him the controversy over the authorship of Shakespeare's
works. Whitman's arguments for Bacon's
authorship (quoted) lead into discussion of
Shakespeare.

*44 ANON. "Traubel Compared with Whitman in
Critical Analysis." Philadelphia Evening
Ledger (19 May).
Reprinted: 1916.38.
Review of Walling (1916.22), describing
his contrasting of Whitman and Traubel,
one the idealist, the other the realist.

45 KILMER, JOYCE. "City Bad for Writers, Says
John Burroughs--Distinguished Author and
Naturalist Thinks That Literature Cannot
Be Produced Where There Is No Atmosphere
of Repose." New York Times Magazine (21
May), 16.
In this interview Burroughs notes
Whitman's "country method" of writing about
the city; his love for its people; his
appeal for the younger poets, although
except for Frost they suggest Whitman in
little but their form; changes in literary
people's opinions of Whitman.

*46 ANON. Review of Helen Mackay's London, One
November. New York Evening Post Book
Section (27 May).
Quoted in Willard.
Incidental mention in this criticism
of contemporary free verse: a reformer
must not be judged by his earliest disciples, yet Whitman "has a good deal to
answer for."

47 KARSNER, DAVID FULTON. "Keeping Whitman's
Memory Green." New York Evening Post Book
Section (27 May), 1, 6.
Focuses on Traubel as exemplar of
Whitman's democratic spirit.

48 COMPENDIUM. "Whitman's Birthday." Conservator
27 (June), 54-57.
Quotes letters and articles on Whitman:
Bazalgette, Saunders, F. H. Williams,
Bynner, William Hawley Smith, Traubel,
Terre Haute Tribune (on Whitman dominating
all the poets of our land though little
known by the student or general reader),
Chicago Evening Post (on the religious
attitude of the Fellowship), Peoria Journal
(account of the talks at Peoria's Whitman
meeting, including those of the William
Hawley Smiths), and 1916.51.

49 T[RAUBEL, HORACE]. "Walt Whitman as Man Poet
and Friend." Conservator 27 (June), 60-61.
Review of Elliot (1915.10). Traubel
recalls gathering of friends after Whitman's
funeral. Whitman needs to be regarded less
as a god and more as a man.

50 ANON. "'Gray Poet's' Friends Hold Celebration."
New York Tribune (1 June), 6:7.

Account of New York Fellowship celebration and speakers, including Emma Goldman, Traubel, Garland, Kreymborg, J. B. Yeats.

51 ANON. "The Poet in His Own Country." New York Tribune (4 June), sec. 3, 2:2. Extract reprinted: 1916.48.

Whitman should be recognized by the common people for his timely messages and poems, giving the spirit of America its most perfect expression.

52 S[MYTHE], A. E. "Crusts and Crumbs." Toronto Sunday World (4 June).

Inauguration of a Whitman Fellowship in Toronto indicates Canada's growing interest in Whitman. Whitman begins with the self, but only as we all must begin with ourselves. We find ourselves in Leaves. Discussion of various dualities in Whitman, his inclusion of both philosophy and emotion. The ordinary reader need not concern himself with Whitman's occult side.

53 BOYNTON, PERCY H. "Whitman's Idea of the State." New Republic 7 (10 June), 139-41.

The America that Whitman loved and extolled was a community rather than a government. He emphasized healthy, active individuals and spiritual rather than material aspiration. His idea of the state, though "fragmentary and inarticulate," is "hope-inspiring" and sound.

54 MONAHAN, MICHAEL. "Smothering Walt." Conservator 27 (July-August), 70. Reprint of 1916.42.

55 BALDERSTON, JOHN LLOYD. "The Dusk of the Gods. A Conversation on Art with George Moore." Atlantic Monthly 118 (August), 165-66.

Moore is quoted on Whitman as the greatest American writer: "The best of Whitman's poems are among the grandest ever written."

56 RITTENHOUSE, JESSIE B. "Love as a Dominant Theme in Poetry." Forum 56 (September), 347-48.

Whitman "razed the Gothic structure of Romanticism" along with "the purely personal and romantic conception of love," which he seems not to have known. He gives man a wider freedom through his dominating democratic note which prepared America for Markham's "Man with the Hoe."

57 YARMOLINSKY, ABRAHAM. "The Russian View of American Literature." Bookman 44 (September), 45-46.

Whitman's popularity in Russia is growing due to Balmont's translation. The different aspects of Whitman which Russian critics praise are described. Balmont's essay "Polarity" is quoted on Whitman as representative of a positive movement to

"cosmical assertion of the Ego" and to democracy.

58 ANON. "American Poets in Russia." New York Times Review of Books (3 September), 344.

Editorial quoting Yarmolinsky (1916.57). Whitman moves, in contrast to Poe, from despair and sorrow to positive affirmation.

59 HOLLOWAY, R. EMORY. "Walt Whitman's History of Brooklyn Just Found--'Personal Chronicles and Gossip,' as Poet Calls Them, Were Written Long Before He Achieved Distinction in the Literary World." New York Times Magazine (17 September), 14-15.

Discusses and quotes Whitman's "Brooklyniana" sketches for the Brooklyn Standard (1861-62), of greater personal than historical value.

60 ANON. "Walt Whitman, Humorist." San Francisco Bulletin (30 September), 2:1-3.

Summarizes and quotes Whitman's writings from Holloway (1916.59).

61 FOERSTER, NORMAN. "Whitman as a Poet of Nature." Publications of the Modern Language Association 31, no. 4 (Autumn), 736-58.

Revised: 1923.5.

Whitman's romanticism is without the constraints of puritanism and embraces the whole of America. He generally makes only vague references to flora and fauna, being most interested in birds and the sea. His "unusual sensuous receptivity" resulted in his mystic experience. His senses, except for taste, were abnormally acute, as seen in his poetry. That love was the unifying force in the universe was vouched for by his senses. However, his excessive faith in his senses prevented his actually reaching spirituality.

62 DOS PASSOS, J. R., Jr. "Against American Literature." New Republic 8 (14 October), 270.

Incidental: Whitman, "our only poet," found his true greatness in dependence on the future rather than on the past, abandoning American writing's "vague genteelness" and founding his faith on himself, but failing to reach the people he intended to touch, arousing only "confused perturbation" and "moral flutter." But the future may prove his power.

63 KILMER, JOYCE. "A Talk with Sir Rabindranath Tagore." New York Times Magazine (29 October), 13.

Tagore, whom some critics see as influenced by Whitman, incidentally notes: "Whitman's poems, though strongly savoring of America, are yet deeply imbued with Eastern ideas and feelings."

64 MILLARD, BAILEY. "Rabindranath Tagore Discovers America." Bookman 44 (November),

1916

248-49.

Quotes Tagore's comments on Whitman,
"your greatest poet," "a voice--not an
echo," through whose pictures Tagore can
know America and "catch its heart-beat."

65 ROLLAND, ROMAIN. "America and The Arts."
Translated from the French by Waldo Frank.
Seven Arts 1 (November), 51.

This exhortation to American writers
to continue to defend liberty and carry
out America's mission concludes: "Behind
you, alone, the elemental Voice of a great
pioneer, in whose message you may well find
an almost legendary omen of your task to
come,--your Homer: Walt Whitman."

66 HOLLOWAY, R. EMORY. "Early Poems of Walt
Whitman." Nation 103 (21 December), Supplement, 5-6.

Reprint with minor revision of 1916.37.

1917

BOOKS

1 BROWN, WILLIAM THURSTON. Walt Whitman: Poet
of the Human Whole. Portland, Oreg.:
Modern School, n.d., 32 pp.
Reprinted in part: 1919.77.

Emerson recognized in Whitman "something
higher and greater than himself" (his
letter, 1855.12, is reprinted). Whitman's
poetry is exhilarating; his ideas were
revolutionary. Some of his lines have a
rhythm and power unsurpassed by other
poets, in a form appropriate for singing
the whole of humanity as no other poet has
done. He seeks freedom and knowledge regarding sex, denying dualism. His use of
the first person "enfolds the whole universe." Anyone who has been transfigured
by a human love will respond to Whitman and
find none of him impure. His greatness as
a poet is not individual but rather "the
inherent greatness of the common man." One
finds oneself in Whitman, in whom all sects
vanish.

2 BYNNER, WITTER. Grenstone Poems. New York:
Frederick A. Stokes Co. "The Highest
Bidder," p. 214.

Brief free-verse poem on the auction
of Whitman's birthplace.

3 CARPENTER, EDWARD. Ioläus: An Anthology of
Friendship. New York: Mitchell Kennerley,
pp. 188-92.
Reprint of 1902.7.

4 ELIOT, T. S. Ezra Pound: His Metric and
Poetry. New York: Alfred A. Knopf, pp. 9,
22.

Pound and Whitman are "antipodean" to
each other. Contrary to the opinion of
Mr. Scott-James (unlocated), Pound's work
is influenced by not "especially Walt

Whitman" but "least of all Walt Whitman,"
lacking any trace of him.

5 GOSSE, EDMUND. The Life of Algernon Charles
Swinburne. New York: Macmillan Co.,
pp. 94-95, 162, 243, 276.

Describes Swinburne's first acquaintance
with Leaves; quotes letters praising
Whitman's verse. His shift in "Whitmania"
(1887.63) indicates "the slow tyranny exer-
cised on Swinburne's judgment by the will
of Watts."

6 JOHNSTON, J[OHN], and WALLACE, J. W. Visits
to Walt Whitman in 1890-1891 by Two Lancashire Friends. London: George Allen &
Unwin, 279 pp. Index. Illustrated.
Reprinted: 1918.12.

"Walt Whitman's Friends in Lancashire"
(Wallace): Explains how the group began
reading Whitman in the late 1880s; their
correspondence with him.

"Notes of Visit to Walt Whitman in
July, 1890" (Johnston): Reprint of 1898.11,
with minor deletions and revision of "Supplementary Notes."

"Visits to Walt Whitman and His Friends,
Etc., in 1891" (Wallace): Account of Sep-
tember and October visits to Camden, to
Whitman scenes on Long Island, to Herbert
Gilchrist, and to Andrew Rome, who returns
with Wallace to see Whitman in Camden.
Whitman's conversation in quoted on his
book, the Gilchrists, America, Hicks,
Doyle, Washington days, opera, friends,
Carlyle, blacks. Account of visit with
Staffords and their reminiscences of
Whitman. Description of Whitman's person-
ality, a new type, combining the best values
of tradition and culture with new values of
the average workers.

"Whitman's Last Illness and Final
Messages" (Wallace): Reprinted from
1893.11.

"Copies of Letters and Post-cards from
Walt Whitman to J. Johnston and J. W.
Wallace": From May 1887 to February 1892.

7 LANUX, PIERRE de. Young France and New America.
New York: Macmillan Co., pp. 116-25; passim
per index.
Extract reprinted: 1917.44; 1917.57;
1919.82.

Young France has absorbed from Whitman
his spirit and the breadth of modern life,
not merely "a new resource in rhythm or
melody," although some poets use a verse
similar to his. The soldiers read "Drum-
Taps."

8 LOWELL, AMY. Tendencies in Modern American
Poetry. Boston and New York: Houghton
Mifflin Co., pp. 5, 154, 161, 183-84, 296.

Whitman and Poe were influential only
after their times. Whitman's "free, almost
rough, rhythmical prose" was appropriate to
portray a pioneer civilization. His connection with Masters and lack of influence
on John Gould Fletcher are noted.

9 MARTIN, G. CURRIE. Poets of the Democracy.
   London: Headley Bros. "Walt Whitman,
   'The Good Grey Poet,'" pp. 75-82.
       Recalls his own introduction to
   Whitman's poetry. Particular poems are
   cited as revealing Whitman's verse's melody
   and power, some being among "the most
   musical of all human songs." "Passage" and
   "Myself" 6 are compared with Tennyson poems.
   His war poems have messages of hope and comradeship for today. He always urges us "to
   more heroic effort." His poetry excludes
   nothing that is human. It is accessible
   because all can understand its language and
   his messages are full of love.

10 MORLEY, JOHN, Viscount. Recollections. Vol.
   2. New York: Macmillan Co., pp. 105, 107.
       Recalls "half a dozen saunters through
   the streets of Washington" with Whitman,
   who had genial ways but whose "doctrines
   of art without apparel did not at once conquer" Morley, who preferred Emerson and
   others who did not feel it necessary to
   seek entirely new thought and form.

11 NEWCOMER, ALPHONSO GERALD; ANDREWS, ALICE E.;
   and HALL, HOWARD JUDSON, eds. Preface,
   brief biography and forty-five selected
   Whitman poems in Three Centuries of American
   Poetry and Prose. Chicago, Atlanta, New
   York: Scott, Foresman & Co., pp. v, 748-
   74.
       Notes to the poems mention the "unflinch-
   ing realism" of Whitman's war writings,
   suggest questions and possible comparisons.

12 RUSSELL, BERTRAND. Why Men Fight. New York:
   Century Co., pp. 32-34.
   Reprint of 1916.18 (with new title for
   American edition).

13 SANBORN, F. B. The Life of Henry David
   Thoreau. Boston and New York: Houghton
   Mifflin Co., pp. 199, 308-11, 317, 336-37,
   382-86.
       Quotes Thoreau's impressions of Whitman,
   Cholmondeley's letters to Thoreau about
   Whitman, Alcott's diary; recalls Concord's
   responses to Whitman, various anecdotes.
   Whitman incorrectly termed Thoreau super-
   cilious. Thoreau seems to have thought
   Emerson overreacted to Whitman's use of his
   letter.

14 WATSON, WILLIAM. Pencraft: A Plea for the
   Older Ways. London and New York: John
   Lane, pp. 32-34.
       Although demanding to be considered
   "as the natural man addressing the natural
   man," Whitman reached only a "literary
   audience," providing "a novel stimulus for
   the jaded literary palates." Americans
   generally saw through "his truly magnificent pose." Swinburne's defection is explained.

15 WYATT, EDITH. Great Companions. New York and
   London: D. Appleton & Co. "With Walt
   Whitman in Camden, Volume III," pp. 158-76.
       Review of Traubel (1914.17) (original
   source unlocated): Traubel genuinely expresses Whitman and his sense of the dignity
   of life and its merging with death, although
   he overemphasizes Whitman's opinions, "of
   so much less value than his nature."
   Whitman is honest but not completely candid,
   lacking "the passion for absolute clarity,
   for directness." He had little interest in
   women. The music of his speech as a poet
   and of his existence as a man are almost
   inseparable, with buoyancy and happiness in
   his soul to the end.

16 YEATS, JOHN BUTLER. Passages from the Letters
   of John Butler Yeats: Selected by Ezra
   Pound. Churchtown, Dundram: Cuala Press,
   pp. 18, 59.
       Incidental references in letters of
   1915 to his son, W. B. Yeats: "Walt
   Whitman is a teacher in every line he wrote;
   and while Matthew Arnold concerned himself
   with teaching his own fellow-countrymen,
   Walt is a missionary, addressing all mankind
   and calling upon his own countrymen to
   arise and be a missionary nation." The
   Americans "interpret Whitman literally, as
   a few years ago they did the Bible, the
   same lunacy in another form."

PERIODICALS

17 MOORE, JOHN ROBERT. "Walt Whitman: a Study
   in Brief." Sewanee Review 25 (January),
   80-92.
       Relates Whitman's life to his poetry:
   his sensitivity, passivity, inability to
   understand or be understood by the American
   people because of his differences from
   them. His conception of poetical experience
   was false; he has the very faults he attributed to art (lack of definiteness, excess).
   However, he does have "something transcendent": "the splendid exultation of his manhood, the serene content of his old age,"
   his mystical experience. His works have
   "a subtle unity and interdependence."
   Groups favor him for different reasons.

18 RUSSELL, PHILLIPS. "Whitman and Traubel."
   Conservator 27 (January), 153.
       Review of Walling (1916.22), explaining
   differences and similarities between
   Traubel and Whitman; both must stand on
   their own feet.

19 T[RAUBEL, HORACE]. "Letters of Richard Watson
   Gilder." Conservator 27 (January), 155-56.
       Review of 1916.10, with reminiscences
   of Gilder and his sister Jennie, and his
   relations with Whitman, whom he accepted
   emphatically.

20 ANON. "Pests of the Metropolitan. After Walt
   Whitman." New York Sun (8 January).

1917

Reprinted: Saunders.
Parody on opera audiences in Whitmanesque lines and style.

21 ALEXANDER, COLIN CUTHBERT. "Walt Whitman."
Conservator 27 (February), 165.
Rhymed poem of tribute.

22 ANON. "Walt Whitman." London (Ontario)
Advertiser (5 March).
A consideration of Whitman and the
question of beauty, which he found in all
things, though ignoring at times the grada-
tions in what is beautiful or only potentially beautiful. What makes him great,
however, is the ardor and boldness with
which he wrote and which characterized the
man himself.

23 PRATT, JULIUS W. "Whitman and Masters: A
Contrast." South Atlantic Quarterly 16
(April), 155-58.
Contrasts their free-verse lines, their
moods (appropriate to their different
times). Masters is more objective, while
Whitman was "interested primarily in himself" where he found "the solution of the
cosmos."

24 ANON. "A War Poet." New York Times Review
of Books (15 April), 144.
"Drum-Taps" fulfills the need for a
patriotic poetry at this time of war. It
should be published apart from Leaves,
with "Memories of President Lincoln" and
"Ontario" as well, to depict America's
great spirit and destiny. "Banner" offers
a rebuke to pacifism.

25 O[PPENHEIM], J[AMES]. Editorial. Seven Arts
2 (May), 68-71.
Now that war is declared, he turns to
the "terrible martial music" and "national
heroism" of "Drum-Taps," quoting three
poems to show how Whitman's poetry can
provide spiritual help and inspiration
during the war.

26 OPPENHEIM, JAMES. "Memories of Whitman and
Lincoln." Seven Arts 2 (May), 8-12.
Free-verse poem echoing "Lilacs,"
praising Whitman's spirit.

27 [UNTERMEYER, LOUIS.] "The Fifth-Month Poet."
Seven Arts 2 (May), 117-19.
Whitman's form came from "his own inner
music." He followed the American traditions
of optimism, preaching, Jeffersonian democracy, Emersonian transcendentalism. His use
of the first-person gives his work "remarkable unity." His work has affinities with
both prophets and scientists. "Like most
realists, he is the most radical of idealists," with a vision which our un-self-
conscious life does not yet perceive.

28 ANON. "Fine Tribute Paid. John Cowper Powys
Lauds Walt Whitman." Portland Oregonian

(6 May).
Account of Powy's lecture on Whitman
which noted his growing acceptance and
deplored the narrow scope of the Whitman
clubs' version of him.

29 S[MYTHE], A. E. "Crusts and Crumbs." Toronto
Sunday World (27 May).
Defense of Whitman against Coleridge's
charges of obscenity (1916.4). His use of
catalogues is meant for meditation. "Broad-
Axe" has "superlative passages" and "a noble
conception of democratic life and ideals,"
"the true note of the Aquarian age, the
era of woman's consummation in purity and
in power."

30 ANON. "Whitman and Traubel." Conservator 28
(June), 54-55.
Favorable review of Walling (1916.22)
from Philadelphia Press (unlocated).

31 ANON. "Walt Whitman's Americanism." New York
Tribune (3 June), sec. 3, 2:2.
Whitman exemplifies the individualist,
the nationalist, and even the internationalist, appropriately for today. He "understood the living soul of America in nearly
all its aspects." He was no pacifist and
"too broadly national" to be adopted by
social radicals.

32 WYATT, EDITH. "A Peace-Lover's War-Epic."
New Republic 11 (30 June), 242-44.
Whitman's prose and poetry are valuable
now for his portrayal of the struggle of
war, our democratic purpose, and the primary
significance of our national character.
Specimen is quoted to show Whitman's wisdom
and love.

33 BROWN, HARVEY DEE. "An Adult Appreciation of
Whitman." Conservator 28 (July), 71-72.
We need not read Whitman only for a
definite message or spiritual stimulation;
we should rather find encouragement in him
to live our own lives.

34 DEBS, EUGENE V. "Whitman and Traubel." Conservator 28 (July), 77.
Review of Walling (1916.22), describing
its ideas. Traubel's socialism is the
natural outcome of his following Whitman's
concept of democracy.

35 LEONARD, MARY HALL. "Walt Whitman to His
Followers." South Atlantic Quarterly 16
(July), 222-26.
The imagists follow but do not surpass
Whitman in using free verse, but they
should also follow his concern for the
moral purpose behind poetry and should not
denigrate the poetry of the past.

36 SHUSTER, GEORGE NAUMAN. "Our Poets in the
Streets." Catholic World 105 (July), 434-
35, 436, 442.
Incidental: Longfellow, not Whitman,

was the true democratic poet, but both belong to a time that is past. Whitman was "a Homeric barbarian," who "reveled in the divine freshness of life, and felt keenly the pulsations of creation." He read himself into others; the working class could not understand him and his pagan recognition of the body's beauty. "His songs, however crude or imperfect, mirrored the great zest of dawn." Current practitioners have shown the validity of his form. He is compared with Lindsay.

37 BROWN, HARVEY DEE. "Whitman and the America of Today." Conservator 28 (August), 86-88.
      Whitman understood the soul of America, foreseeing future national developments. We need today his message of spiritual growth for America. "Ontario" should be adopted as our national poem.

38 T[RAUBEL, HORACE]. "Walt Whitman's New Publishers." Conservator 28 (August), 92-93.
      Whitman's official publishers now are Doubleday, Page and Co. His relations with publishers are traced. He tried to destroy "what he considered useless manuscript" in order that his discarded or immature work not be brought out after his death.

39 MORDELL, ALBERT. "Whitman, Democrat, Not a Pacifist. Francis Howard Williams Talks About the Poet and Other Literary People He Has Known." Philadelphia Record (12 August).
      Extract reprinted: 1917.47.
      Interview with Williams, who deplores the way the free verse poets and the socialists have appropriated and misinterpreted Whitman, who was neither pacifist nor anarchist. Williams recalls Whitman telling him about "his early personal affairs," including his encounter with a "married woman he met in his sojourn in New Orleans," to whom he refers in "Once I Pass'd."

40 McNICOLL, THOMAS STEWART. "Three Teachers." Reedy's Mirror 26 (17 August), 528.
      Legler (1916.11) is one of the books reviewed. Whitman's reputation, as presented in Legler, is traced.

41 O'NEIL, DAVID. "Walt Whitman." Poetry Journal 7 (September), 202.
      Brief free-verse poem describing Whitman: "An arrogant oak," "Fusing the immediate / With the infinite."

42 T[RAUBEL, HORACE]. "Visits to Walt Whitman." Conservator 28 (September), 108-9.
      Announcement of 1917.6, quoting opinions of the first edition (1890.7) by Symonds, Dowden, Rossetti.

43 TRAUBEL, HORACE. "With Walt Whitman in Camden." Seven Arts 2 (September), 627-37.

Pre-publication extracts from volume 4, published 1953.

44 LANUX, PIERRE de. "The New Poets of France." Dial 63 (27 September), 257-60.
      Extract reprinted from 1917.7.

45 WALLACE, J. W. "Keir Hardie and Walt Whitman." Manchester Labour Leader (27 September).
      Reprinted: 1917.50.
      Reports his correspondence with Hardie about Whitman, noting passages that particularly appealed to him (on service and the importance of activity, the heroic note, human tenderness and comradeship).

46 FIRKINS, O. W. "Poetry Insurgent and Resurgent." Atlantic Monthly 120 (October), 500-501.
      Incidental: Whitman's meager contribution to the renovation of poetry begun by Wordsworth is due more to his inability than to "the breakdown of the tradition before his powers." He has only scattered inspirations.

47 MORDELL, ALBERT. "Whitman, Democrat." Conservator 28 (October), 120-21.
      Extract reprinted from 1917.39.

48 SARKAR, BENOY KUMAR. "Walt Whitman." Conservator 28 (October), 116.
      Blank-verse poem, "Englished from the original by the author."

49 T[RAUBEL, HORACE]. "Leaves of Grass." Conservator 28 (October), 125.
      Review of Doubleday edition, which prints Whitman as he wanted to be published.

50 WALLACE, J. W. "Keir Hardie and Walt Whitman." Conservator 28 (October), 118-19.
      Reprint of 1917.45.

*51 ANON. "Songs for the Civil Service. By What Whichman. 1. 'To the Leaden Leaves they Turned.'" Public Service Journal (Wellington, New Zealand) (20 October).
      Reprinted: Saunders.
      Parody.

52 TRAUBEL, HORACE. "Walt Whitman's America." Conservator 28 (November), 134-36.
      Records Whitman's conversation regarding what he wanted America to be; his spiritual goals. America gave the crowd the best chance. "He didn't object to education because it was education but because it wasn't."

53 WILLIAMS, WILLIAM CARLOS. "America, Whitman, and the Art of Poetry." Poetry Journal 8 (November), 27-36.
      Analysis of the current state of the art of poetry in America, which Whitman created and which must now be carried beyond him. "Whitman aside from being the foremost analyst was above all a colorist--a mood

1917

man." "His poems fall apart structurally
but the sweep of his mood, the splendor of
his pigment blends his work into some
semblance of unity without which no work
of art can be said to exist." Poetry needs
his breadth of vision. "The only way to be
like Whitman is to write unlike Whitman"
and be one's self.

54 ANDERSON, SHERWOOD. "An Apology for Crudity."
Dial 63 (8 November), 438.
   Incidental: America today is different
from that of Twain and Whitman, when the
dominant note was "the noisy, swaggering
raftsman and the hairy-chested woodsman."

*55 COOKE, M. B. "Harrigan." Pearson's Magazine
(December), 456-57.
   Reported in Saunders Whitman in Fiction,
but not located in this issue.

56 JOHNSTON, ALMA CALDER. "Personal Memories of
Walt Whitman." Bookman 46 (December), 404-
13. Illustrated.
Revision of 1915.10.
   Recalls the gradual power Leaves gained
in her mind, impelling her to write Whitman
and then visit him in 1876; records anecdotes from their acquaintance, conversations
regarding his poetry, death, expurgation,
his attitudes toward education and socialism.

57 LANUX, PIERRE de. "Walt Whitman in France."
Conservator 28 (December), 152.
Extract reprinted from 1917.7.

58 MAYNARD, LAURENS. "Walt Whitman and Elbert
Hubbard." Conservator 28 (December), 151-
52.
   Corrects the inaccuracies in Hubbard's
story (1902.37). A letter from Doyle
denies certain details.

59 RUSSELL, BERTRAND. "Carlyle and Whitman."
Conservator 28 (December), 152-53.
Extract reprinted from 1916.18.

60 WATTLES, WILLARD. "I Now, Walt Whitman."
Midland 3 (December), 353-55.
   Poem in Whitmanesque free verse, ex-
tolling Whitman's influence and proclaiming
Whitman's philosophy.

61 HOLLOWAY, EMORY. "Whitman's First Free
Verse." Nation 105 (27 December), 717.
Reprinted: 1918.38.
   Whitman had already written free verse
by 1850, when three poems were published
in the New York Tribune under the editorship of Horace Greeley. Greeley was thus
one of the first to recognize him as a
new force in literature, even championing,
"in a lecture in the 1850's, 'Walt
Whitman's rare poetic genius.'"

1918

BOOKS

1 ADAMS, HENRY. The Education of Henry Adams.
Boston and New York: Houghton Mifflin Co.,
p. 385.
Reprint of 1907.1.

2 ANDERSON, SHERWOOD. Mid-American Chants.
New York and London: John Lane. "Song of
Industrial America," p. 16.
Quoted in 1933.3.
   Describes America's rugged, biblical
old men: "We got Walt and Abraham out of
that lot."

3 ANDREWS, C[LARENCE] E[DWARD]. The Writing and
Reading of Verse. New York and London:
D. Appleton & Co., pp. 65-66, 317, 318, 319,
323-24, 327.
   Incidental references to Whitman as a
master of free verse, which has its own
standards. His type "gains its variety
through changes in the rhythm itself," as
shown in a passage from "Trumpeter" (analyzed), revealing a fine sense of artistic
effect.

4 BOYNTON, PERCY H., ed. Selected Whitman poems
and commentary in American Poetry. New
York: Charles Scribner's Sons, pp. 473-
541, 676-80.
   Whitman adopted his verse form because
of his program, not because of lack of
success with conventional forms. His free
verse reverts to the effects of the Psalms
and the Anglo-Saxon "Seafarer." His best
verse reveals melodic beauty and his skill
in rhythmic regularity and variation, as in
examples analyzed. His democracy was not
governmental or merely nationalistic, for
his outlook was idealistic although devoid
of an international sense. "His mind seemed
to entertain no concepts between his tangibly concrete surroundings and the most
distantly vague abstractions." But his
ideas are hope-inspiring, his influence
great. His poems are indexed by subject in
a subject index for the volume's poems.

5 DANE, CLARENCE [Winifred Ashton]. First the
Blade: A Comedy of Growth. New York:
Macmillan Co. Frontispiece.
   Quotation from "Rolling Earth" as epi-
graph.

6 EASTMAN, MAX. Colors of Life. New York:
Alfred A. Knopf. "American Ideals of
Poetry: A Preface," pp. 13-39.
Reprint of 1918.51 and 1918.52.

7 GOSSE, EDMUND, and WISE, THOMAS JAMES, eds.
The Letters of Algernon Charles Swinburne.
London: William Heinemann. Vol. 1, pp. 58,
180, 201, 237; vol. 2, pp. 103, 153-54.
   Letters to Houghton, Stedman, Gosse,
others, showing praise for Whitman, dis-

approval of some of his later "rubbish"
and his growing "habit of vague and flatulent verbiage." Gosse notes some of
Whitman's animadversions upon Swinburne
during Gosse's visit, later telling
Swinburne in a friendly report. However,
the atmosphere then surrounding Swinburne
was fatal to a continued appreciation for
Whitman.

8 HAKE, THOMAS, and COMPTON-RICKETT, ARTHUR, eds.
The Letters of Algernon Charles Swinburne
with Some Personal Recollections. London:
John Murray, p. xviii.
While Gosse (1917.5) suggests that
Watts-Dunton influenced Swinburne's change
in attitude toward Whitman, Watts-Dunton
attributed it "to a pathological study
published on Whitman the man, which both he
and Swinburne read."

9 HARNED, THOMAS B., ed. Preface and introduction to The Letters of Anne Gilchrist and
Walt Whitman. Garden City, N.Y.:
Doubleday, Page & Co., 242 pp. Illustrated.
Whitman's preservation of these letters
implies that he intended them to be included in his complete biography. The
relationship is sketched (based on 1887.6).
Whitman's refusal to reciprocate is explained by the 1864 romance Holloway describes (1918.10). Gilchrist's articles
(1870.4, without headnote, and 1885.14) are
reprinted. Letters trace Gilchrist's
feeling for Whitman, with occasional comments on his work. There are a few from
Whitman to her, and from Herbert or Beatrice
Gilchrist to Whitman.

10 HOLLOWAY, EMORY. "Whitman." In The Cambridge
History of American Literature. Vol. 2.
Edited by William Peterfield Trent, John
Erskine, Stuart P. Sherman, and Carl Van
Doren. New York: G. P. Putnam's Sons,
pp. 258-74.
Reprinted: 1922.9.
This biography presents only established
facts, says Holloway, rather than doubtful
incidents. Whitman's shoolteacher's opinion of him is quoted. His romance with a
married woman in 1864 produced "Rolling
Ocean." Whitman is compared to Emerson.
The chronology of his publications reveals
how "a heroic and loving soul gradually
freed itself from the passions of a very
human and earthly body." In the early part
of the war, he seemed to be saying "farewell
to the light-hearted irresponsibility of
his protracted youth" before becoming the
serious and noble hospital worker. He has
various appeals for different readers.
Other references to Whitman in this volume
(especially to his war poetry), passim per
index.

11 HOLLOWAY, EMORY, and SAUNDERS, HENRY S.
"Bibliography for Whitman." In The Cambridge History of American Literature.

Vol. 2. Edited by William Peterfield Trent,
John Erskine, Stuart P. Sherman, Carl Van
Doren. New York: G. P. Putnam's Sons,
pp. 551-81.
1. Bibliographies; 2. Separate Works
(descriptive); 3. Collections and Selections (descriptive); 4. Contributions to
Periodicals (a) Verse, (b) Prose; 5. Letters; 6. Biography and Criticism; 7.
Translations.

12 JOHNSTON, J[OHN], and WALLACE, J. W. Visits
to Walt Whitman in 1890-1891 by Two Lancashire Friends. New York: Egmont Arens,
279 pp.
Reprint of 1917.6.

13 JUPP, WILLIAM J. Wayfarings: A Record of
Adventure and Liberation in the Life of
the Spirit. London: Headley Bros., pp.
56, 67-68, 69, 89, 110-15, 138-48, 150-52,
155-57, 185, 210.
This spiritual autobiography explains
the influence of Whitman, among others,
upon the writer. Whitman has not only "a
vigorous realism," "full-blooded sensuousness," and broad comradeship, but also
perception of the spiritual significance of
life, with which he strengthens religious
feeling. Through his war work and his
poems' impassioned words, his personality
becomes a living presence. He and his
poems are like nature. He is compared with
Thoreau and Carpenter (who is no mere imitator of Whitman). He calls for more from
his readers than they can always give.

14 O'GRADY, STANDISH. Selected Essays and Pas-
sages. New York: Frederick A. Stokes Co.,
n.d. Dublin: Talbot Press; London: T.
Fisher Unwin, n.d. "Walt Whitman: The
Poet of Joy," pp. 269-90.
Reprint of 1875.16.

15 PERRY, BLISS. The American Spirit in Literature: A Chronicle of Great Interpreters.
Vol. 34. The Chronicles of America Series.
New Haven: Yale University Press; Toronto:
Glasgow, Brook & Co.; London: Humphrey
Milford, Oxford University Press. "Poe and
Whitman," pp. 187-205; also 90, 108, 255,
265, 266.
Poe and Whitman were both egotists,
romanticists, and acquainted with the literature of the European movement only at
secondhand. Whitman's mind is "fundamentally religious." He is an individualist,
part of Transcendentalism. A more serious
defect than his frankness is his "imperfect
transfusion" of material. He emphasizes
human divinity and love, America's newness,
unity, and solidarity with other nations.

16 WHITMAN, WALT. Poems of Walt Whitman: Selections for Stirring Times. Old South Leaf-
lets no. 216, n.d. Boston: Old South
Association.
The anonymous introduction says:

1918

Whitman might well be proud; he "succeeded better than any of his contemporaries in transmitting the spirit of those stirring times to these stirring times." His purpose is described, with the background of his political poems and their view into the future. His prophecies are fulfilled, including hopefully that of the League of Nations to save mankind from war.

PERIODICALS

17 ANON. "Visits to Walt Whitman." Times Literary Supplement (London) (3 January), 7.
    Review of Johnston (1917.6), which sheds light upon a new type of hero with naturalness and sympathy. Whitman's capacity for pleasure in his old age is contrasted with Carlyle's growling.

18 T[RAUBEL, HORACE]. "Visits to Walt Whitman." Conservator 28 (February), 188-89.
    Review of Johnston (1917.6). Recalls Whitman's opinions of the written version of Arnold's visit, his reactions to Johnston and Wallace. The Bolton group is praised.

19 SYMONS, ARTHUR. "A Note on Walt Whitman." Bellman 24 (9 February), 154-55.
    Whitman is "one of the voices of the earth," excluding nothing. Symons recalls Whitman's influence on him regarding the need to paint the world truly and exploit one's personality. Whitman has flaws in meter, syntax, treatment of the body, but "Cradle" has imagination, evoking "almost primitive elements." Whitman is compared to contemporary French poets. Whitman confesses himself loudly but never seems to apprehend the spiritual reality.

20 ANON. Brief review of Johnston (1917.6). New York Times Review of Books (3 March), 86.
    This "entertaining little book" presents a picture of Whitman worth preserving, revealing the favor granted Whitman in England before American recognition; he was in fact "a sort of supplemental hero with the Pre-Raphaelites."

*21 ANGLO-FRENCH [pseud.]. "Walt Whitman on France." Everyman (20 April).
    Quoted in Saunders Supplement.
    Whitman is cited as a whole-hearted admirer of France. "O Star of France" is currently pertinent.

22 ANON. "Walt Whitman's Poems." New York Herald (20 April), sec. 2, 10;5.
    Review of Patriotic Poems of Walt Whitman, a timely publication from Doubleday, Page. Although Whitman "must always have a sure place well to the forefront of American poets the present volume will appeal only to the few who long ago learned to love him."

23 ANON. "Walt Whitman's Vogue in Europe. Admirers of 'Leaves of Grass' Are Helping to Unite the Old and the New Worlds." Current Opinion 64 (May), 349-50.
    Review of Johnston (1917.6), "a story of hero-worship that is creditable both to the hero and to his worshippers," and Lanux (1917.7).

24 T[RAUBEL, HORACE]. "Whitmania." Conservator 29 (May), 40-42.
    Robert M. Wernaer's recent book has been called an echo of Whitman, who was "the first to decide that it did not matter how you wrote at all, if only you had something worth while to say." Whitman, however, "is not a safe model," for one can write his form badly. He was influenced by others and free verse preceded him, so it may be used by anyone.

25 VRCHLICKY, JAROSLAV. "Walt Whitman." Poetry Review 9 (May-June), 151.
    Sonnet (from New Sonnets of a Recluse, 1891) by a Czech poet, defining Whitman through questions and responses.

26 ANON. "The American Soldiers' March Past." Manchester Guardian (13 May), 4:4.
    If Whitman had seen "his 'tan-faced children' go by" in the march today, he would have given "the appropriate full-blooded comment" as in "Pioneers."

27 T., G. K. "In the Realm of Music--Walt Whitman Showed Love of Music." Pittsburgh Gazette Times (13 May).
    Several prose passages from Whitman show Whitman's love of music. America's foremost poet, he furthered democracy, as is becoming realized.

*28 ANON. Article on the Occult. Light (18 May).
    Quoted in Saunders Supplement.
    Incidental: Whitman perceived that all he experienced was part of himself, though he saw into life more deeply than he could clearly describe.

29 LOVE, BERT. "Whitmania." Reedy's Mirror 27 (24 May), 309.
    Reprinted in part: 1918.33.
    Regrets the lack of any true lovers of Whitman, even among the Fellowship. So many people reject him because of the sex poems. A publisher should bring out a book of condensed (but not expurgated) Whitman, to delete the drivel and "cataloguish agonies" and give "the true Walt," his profundity, lyric swing, "epic sweep and soul-surge."

30 VRAN-GAVRAN, R. A. "Communion of the Saints." New Age 23 (30 May), 71-72.
    Questions Whitman's glorification of democracy, since his "soul was not for numbers but for qualities." Whitman's soul was musical, yet he "wrongly thought

that the bigger the orchestra the more
beautiful the music."

31 BEFFEL, JOHN NICHOLAS. "Dinner Honors Birthday
of Whitman." Chicago Herald-Examiner (1
June).
Account of Chicago Fellowship meeting,
with speeches by George Burnam Foster and
Harriet Monroe quoted on Whitman's emphasizing the worth of the everyday and of the
plain man and on American colonialism in
letting Europe determine Whitman's significance.

32 S[MYTHE], A. E. "Crusts and Crumbs." Toronto
Sunday World (2 June).
Discusses Whitman's attitude toward
Lincoln, quoting his prose and "Lilacs,"
which should be in school readers to famil-
iarize children "with the majestic rhythm
of the long rolling lines" of his new form.
"Hush'd be the Camps To-day" is quoted,
with praise for its "transmuting power."

33 ANON. "A Lonely Whitmanite." Literary Digest
57 (15 June), 29-30.
Précis of 1918.29 with quotations.

34 ANON. "Before the Red Cross." New York Times
Review of Books (16 June), 282.
Commends Whitman's service and spirit
in the war, which present-day hospital
workers might emulate. He vividly conveyed
scenes of the war in "historical documents
of permanent value" like Specimen.

35 ANON. "Walt Whitman's Songs of Democracy. A
Collection of 'Patriotic Poems' in Which the
'Good Grey Poet' Celebrates the Ideals for
Which America is Fighting Today." New York
Times Review of Books (16 June), 277, 285.
Reprinted: 1918.44.
Review of Doubleday's Patriotic Poems
and Complete Prose Works: Whitman's poems,
appropriate for today, recognize the necessity of fighting to combat the powers of
evil, urging faith in the democratic ideals.
Though his verse is better, his prose conveys his war experiences vividly and directly. The medical profession has recognized
that he was ahead of his time in insisting
on hygiene. Americans should honor his
centenary by turning to him for inspiration.

36 ANON. "With Authors and Publishers." New
York Times Review of Books (16 June), 286.
Paragraph announcing the publication
of "The Love Letters of Walt Whitman and
Anne Gilchrist" (1918.9), giving a brief
(inaccurate) sketch of their relationship.

37 SMITH, L[OGAN] PEARSALL. "Miscellany:
Montaigne." New Statesman 11 (29 June),
253.
Incidental: It is odd that only
Whitman and Montaigne have really tried to
describe themselves and their consciousness,
though "Myself" is "a mere sketch compared
with Montaigne's life-size picture."

38 HOLLOWAY, EMORY. "Whitman's First Free Verse."
Conservator 29 (July), 74-75.
Reprint of 1917.61.

*39 ANON. "Walt Whitman--Ideals of Today."
London Sunday Times (21 July).
Quoted in Saunders Supplement.
Patriotism in America found a new inspiration in Whitman's poems, never so
popular as they are today, because now the
same goals move all Anglo-Saxons. He is
recognized as "the great poet and prophet
of democracy."

*40 ANON. Two paragraphs. London Weekly Dispatch
(21 July).
Quoted in Saunder Supplement.
Announces publication of "Love Letters
of Walt Whitman and Anne Gilchrist" (1918.9).

41 HIER, FREDERICK. "The Whitman Fellowship
Meeting." Conservator 29 (August), 89-91.
Account of speeches at the meeting in
New York, showing Whitman's universality:
Roy Mitchell (Whitman's prophet-like
teachings), Duncan Macdougall (comparison
of Whitman's poetry and the theater),
Everett Martin (Whitman's individualistic
humanism as more significant than his
bourgeois humanitarianism), Thomas Libbin
(psychoanalytical reading of the trouble
Whitman had making readjustments in his
life), Anna Strunsky Walling (Whitman's
sympathy and faith in society), Smith
(1918.43), White (1918.48), Keller (1918.42);
other speeches and readings briefly noted.

42 KELLER, HELEN. "The Poet of All Poets." Conservator 29 (August), 87-88.
Pays homage to the "poet of all poets
whom I love the best." Common love for
Whitman can unite all radicals. She recalls
reading him from raised letters. He brought
light into her world, "the eager, turbulent
tramp of life," encouraging her "to prove
my spiritual equality to that world." "His
imagination has foothold as well as wings."
She describes the aspects of the world she
experiences with Whitman. "Many are blind
to his vision, deaf to his message" (love
and joy, needed during the war).

43 SMITH, WILLIAM HAWLEY. "Walt Whitman's Contribution." Conservator 29 (August), 89.
Whitman's contribution has staying
power, measureless value. Smith describes
his and his wife's love for Whitman's
poetry. Whitman's key phrase, "How long
have we been fooled!," awakens us to the
desire for wisdom.

44 ANON. "Walt Whitman Speaks Again to the
United States." Public Opinion (London)
114 (2 August), 74.
Reprint of 1918.35.

1918

*45 ANON. Paragraph. London Weekly Dispatch (4 August).
Quoted in Saunders Supplement.
Grace Gilchrist Frend's letter is quoted in response to 1918.40: Gilchrist's letters were not love letters but "were the fruit solely of my mother's profound admiration and reverence" for Leaves and its author.

46 ANON. "Whitman, Traubel and Democracy." Conservator 29 (September), 107.
Review of Walling (1916.22) from Christian Science Monitor (unlocated): brief explanation.

47 LYCHENHEIM, MORRIS. "Vicious Circle Still Bars Whitman." Conservator 29 (September), 104-5.
Reprinted from Chicago Examiner (unlocated): Americans are ignorant of Whitman's writings because they fear the sex poems and because the average schoolteacher, unacquainted with Whitman, does not teach him.

48 WHITE, ELIOT. "Walt Whitman After Twenty Four Years." Conservator 29 (September), 103-4.
Recalls his first reading of Whitman in 1894; explains enthusiastically Whitman's magnetism and the meaning of some of his words and phrases.

49 de CASSERES, BENJAMIN. "Excursions Into the Ego of Walt Whitman." New York Sun Books and the Book World (1 September), 11.
Review of Johnston (1918.12). Whitman was "the St. John who foresaw and glorified in canticles of fire the American People," who "carried within himself the psychological and physical interpretations of Greater America," who spoke about America "with an uncanny insight" in several prophetic poems. He took philosophy "and made it walk and talk and live," embodying philosophy rather than teaching it. "In singing of himself he sang of a Whole," not merely a single man, making the individual the center of the universe. "In evolution he found the secret of immortality," and not a mere personal kind. "His democracy was a spiritual concept," the only aristocracy being one of character. He considered himself an evolved variant of the criminal. He always perceived the wonder of the world. Johnston and Wallace's book is of great interest to those who feel Whitman's greatness, because it shows "the daily life of a god--a very human god," "the sanest and humanest seer that has walked the planet."

50 WHITMAN, WALT. "Unpublished Letter of Walt Whitman." New York Evening Post (7 September), sec. 3, 1.
Through the courtesy of Louis I. Haber, this letter from Whitman to Nat and Fred Gray (19 March 1863) is published for the first time.

51 EASTMAN, MAX. "American Ideals of Poetry. I." New Republic 16 (14 September), 190-92. Reprinted: 1918.6.
Extended contrast of Poe and Whitman, "the two American poets of unique distinction," with the strongest influence on modern poetry. Poe regarded the poem objectively, Whitman subjectively. Whitman's poetry, though its emotions are those of simple people, is not humble enough to be social and consider others and is therefore not popular, as Poe's is. Concluded 1918.52.

52 _____. "American Ideals of Poetry. II." New Republic 16 (21 September), 222-25. Reprinted: 1918.6.
Concludes 1918.51. Unlike his contemporary free-verse followers, Whitman realized that his form discarded subtlety but attained the presence of a man, the source of his influence on the literature of democracy and of all lands. He achieves "the carved concentration of image and emotion" only in occasional passages (quoted) and once for the whole poem ("When I Heard at the Close of Day").

53 ANON. "Whitman and Traubel." Conservator 29 (October), 123-24.
Reprinted from New York Evening Post (unlocated): Whitman is being discredited by attempts to hitch Traubel's reputation to his. Traubel's poetry has Whitman's irregularity "without Whitman's eloquence, richness and sonority." Fortunately Whitman's own social philosophy did not develop into what Traubel holds now.

54 BAIN, MILDRED. "A Few Words to Morris Lychenheim." Conservator 29 (October), 124.
Response to 1918.47, denying that Whitman wrote sex poems because he was the poet of both good and evil. Rather, he glorified sex. Issued separately, these poems would have been "secretly hugged to the breast of the average repressed, sexually furtive member of society." Whitman is really rejected because he was on a plane different from the majority.

55 LAW, JAMES D. "Walt Whitman: Some Personal Remarks." Conservator 29 (October), 117-19.
Rhymed poem of tribute.

56 SMITH, GEORGE JAY. "Whitman's Children of Adam." Conservator 29 (October), 120-21.
The sex poems are the keystone of Whitman's poetic structure, for he meant to represent all of life. They may not need to be reread, because once their message works on the mind their purpose is achieved.

57 FREND, GRACE GILCHRIST. "'Love Letters of Walt Whitman.'" Nation (London) 24 (5 October), 16.
Corrects misconceptions regarding Harned's Letters (1918.9): they are not

"love letters," as 1918.36 termed them; the feeling was rather a high esteem. She owns Whitman's letters herself.

58 T[OMLINSON], H. M. "The World of Books." Nation (London) 24 (12 October), 46.
Reprinted: 1922.25.
Picking up Drum-Taps after learning that soldiers are reading it, Tomlinson finds it an eternally valid depiction of war. British writers have made nothing from their experiences to compare with Whitman's range, understanding, metrical ardor, and humanity in these poems. At his best he conveys our inner emotions "like a miraculous voice."

59 ANON. "'Abraham Lincoln.'" Manchester Guardian (14 October), 4:5.
Incidental quotation of Whitman's address on Lincoln in this review of John Drinkwater's play, Abraham Lincoln.

*60 ANON. "Mr. John Drinkwater on Poetry and Tradition." Leeds Yorkshire Post (21 October).
Quoted in Saunders Supplement.
Report of Drinkwater's address to Yorkshire Dialect Society: every poet of distinction has worked in forms of recognizable parentage while the rebels achieved nothing. "Whitman was the only possible exception, and his value was in spite of, and in no way because of, his manner."

61 ANON. "Poems of the Sea." Times Literary Supplement (London) (24 October), 508.
Incidental reference in this review of Lady Sybil Scott's A Book of the Sea: Whitman's roving mind and spirit were at home in and on the sea. "Its might and its suggestion of freedom alike called to him as to a brother."

62 CROSS, CAREL. "By the Way." Dunedin (New Zealand) Evening Star (24 October).
The latter part of this column presents Whitman as a poet with much to say for modern America, especially the America which just participated in the war. His poetry is full of patriotic feeling and the great soul that is America's, as quotations show.

63 LAWRENCE, D. H. "Introduction to Studies in Classic American Literature. I. The Spirit of Place." English Review 27 (November), 319.
Incidental: Whitman is listed among the "familiar American classics." "We have not wanted to hear the undertone, the curious foreign, uncouth suggestion, which is in the over-cultured Hawthorne and Poe or Whitman." (This comment does not appear in the book version, 1923.9.)

*64 VAUGHAN WILLIAMS, R[ALPH]. Article on Sir Hubert Parry. The Musical Student (Novem-

ber).
Quoted in Saunders Supplement.
Incidental: "Walt Whitman says: 'Why are there men and women that while they are nigh me sunlight expands my blood.' Parry was one of these."

65 ANON. "Modern American Poetry." Cambridge Magazine 8 (2 November), 89-90.
Discussion of Eastman (1918.51), quoting his ideas on Whitman and Poe extensively. Whitman and Poe "are the foundations of the two strongest influences in all modern poetry of the occident," though if Whitman had written as few pages of poetry as Poe he would hardly have been remembered.

66 PERRY, BLISS. "Walt Whitman's Complex Love Affairs--Letters Between the Poet and Anne Gilchrist That Reveal an Unknown Chapter in Whitman's Life." New York Times Review of Books (3 November), 2.
Review of Harned (1918.9), tracing the relationship.

67 ABBOTT, LEONARD D. "Anne Gilchrist and Walt Whitman." Modern School 5 (December), 380-82.
Review of Harned (1918.9), a tragic story of unreciprocated love.

68 ANON. "Walt Whitman and His 'Noblest Woman-Friend': A Story of Unreciprocated Love Which Ended in Loyal Comradeship." Current Opinion 65 (December), 394-95.
Review of Harned (1918.9), tracing the relationship with quotations.

69 ANON. "The Poets." New York Sun Books and the Book World (1 December), 8:2.
Incidental note that Amy Lowell's Con Grandee's Castle "is the biggest thing since Walt Whitman."

70 de CASSERES, BENJAMIN. "Outstanding Books of the Fall and Year Choices of Books and Book World." New York Sun Books and the Book World (1 December), 11:2.
Among de Casseres's choices is Harned (1918.9), presenting "the soul of a woman revealed in all its nakedness--as interesting a human document as has ever appeared in English."

71 _____. "Tristan-Whitman and Isolde-Gilchrist." New York Sun Books and the Book World (15 December), 7. Illustrated.
Review of Harned (1918.9), "among the most poignantly beautiful love letters in any language," "the calls of an Isolde for her Tristan." Gilchrist's life and relationship with Whitman are described. The passion is gone from her letters after she meets Whitman; perhaps she should have left him "unseen and unteaed."

1918

*72 ANON. "Making a Splendid Race." <u>Dundee
     Evening Telegraph</u> (21 December).
     Quoted in Saunders Supplement.
          "For You O Democracy" is quoted: once
     smiled at by Whitman's readers, these
     dreams of a great city are now becoming
     materialized as America's president travels
     to Europe "preaching the creed of Whitman."

73 UNTERMEYER, LOUIS. "Whitman, Poe, and Max
     Eastman." <u>Dial</u> 65 (28 December), 611-12.
          Review of Eastman (1918.6). Eastman's
     preface seeks to prove Poe to be more demo-
     cratic than Whitman. Whitman indeed would
     never have appealed to the masses, who
     "prefer prettiness to splendor," "tinsel to
     truth." His unpopularity was a matter not
     of his form but of his message.

1919

BOOKS

1 AIKEN, CONRAD. <u>Scepticisms: Notes on Contem-
    porary Poetry</u>. New York: Alfred A. Knopf,
    pp. 86, 93, 148, 172, 188, 263.
         Includes reprints of 1919.43 and 1919.158.
         Other essays incidentally relate
    Whitman, one of America's only poetic pio-
    neers, to contemporary poets.

2 BEERS, HENRY A. <u>Four Americans</u>. New Haven:
    Yale University Press. "A Wordlet about
    Whitman," pp. 85-90.
         Whitman's fame has come of age. His
    poetry is imperfect, devoid of humor; the
    common reader still prefers Longfellow and
    Riley. Whitman was a man of genius but the
    Whitmanites are humbugs.

3 BOYNTON, PERCY H. <u>A History of American Lit-
    erature</u>. Boston: Ginn & Co. "Walt
    Whitman," pp. 362-79; passim per index;
    bibliography, 379.
         Whitman and Twain are the distinctively
    American authors for the rest of the world.
    Whitman's form was not the result of lazi-
    ness or inability but offered vital rhythms
    in a true relation between form and content,
    unlike similar experiments by some of
    Whitman's contemporaries. His rhythm and
    diction were generally most effective when
    dealing with "definite aspects of natural
    and physical beauty" as in "Cradle." Dis-
    cussion ends with material reprinted from
    1919.240 and includes study questions.

4 BROWN, GEORGE E. <u>A Book of R. L. S.</u> New
    York: Charles Scribner's Sons, pp. 278-80.
         Describes background of Stevenson's
    essay (1878.17), whose restraint Symonds
    explained (1893.9). The essay "outlived
    its subject. Whitman's ideal of a world
    democracy is much with us in these days
    (1919), but Whitman is remembered by a
    very few." Others have expressed his ideas
    "as vigorously and with infinitely more in-
    telligibility and grace."

5 BURROUGHS, JOHN. <u>Field and Study</u>. Boston and
    New York: Houghton Mifflin Co., pp. 225-
    32; passim per index.
         Perry (1906.13) fails to reveal
    Whitman's all-inclusive democratic spirit,
    unique to him. His lack of selection was
    part of his desire not to prettify anything.
    His work is too intimate and prophetic to
    be called prose. He speaks in the spirit
    of nature, not distilled as in Wordsworth.
    Unlike Emerson, Whitman is not a product of
    culture. He gives "the soul and suggestion
    of poetry" rather than "finished poetry."
    He is "tender, yearning, motherly," rather
    than "'robust,' 'athletic,' 'masculine.'"

6 BUTCHER, Lady [ALICE]. <u>Memories of George
    Meredith</u>. New York: Charles Scribner's
    Sons, pp. 96-97.
         Describes a conversation with Meredith
    in which she noted the importance of
    Whitman's poems, especially "Myself" 18,
    to people at crucial times in their lives.
    Meredith said his "Orson of the Muse"
    (1883.6) was intended for Whitman, many of
    whose poems he admired; but he felt that
    Whitman's "language and style were too un-
    couth and undisciplined to carry his
    thoughts safely through the ages."

7 FRANK, WALDO. <u>Our America</u>. New York: Boni &
    Liveright. "The Multitudes in Whitman,"
    pp. 202-21; also 222, 231.
         Reprinted: 1922.6.
         Four stanzas from "Paumanok" are used
    as epigraph. Whitman saw the relations of
    men to all worldly life and to an Infinite
    Beign. His form is necessary for his vision.
    He can be reduced to no one label. His spirit
    contributes to making Americans a chosen
    people. <u>Vistas</u> is our greatest book of social
    criticism, <u>Leaves</u> our greatest poem. Emerson
    pales beside Whitman's immediacy. Description
    of the lack of development in the multitudes
    Whitman had examined in 1871.

8 JOHNSON, LIONEL. <u>Some Winchester Letters of
    Lionel Johnson</u>. London: George Allen &
    Unwin; New York: Macmillan Co., pp. 127-
    29, 131, 135, 139, 181, 182, 190, 198, 202,
    203-4, 206, 207, 209, 210.
         Many admiring references to Whitman and
    quotations in these letters of 1884-85,
    which record Johnson's first reading of
    Whitman, a nobler poet than Shelley. Con-
    tists have inappropriately claimed Whitman
    for their priest. "Jesus and Shelley and
    Whitman, they are steadfast in faith, never
    wavering."

9 JOHNSTON, MARY. <u>Michael Forth</u>. New York and
    London: Harper & Bros., pp. 282, 284.
         The narrator, with affinities for
    Whitman, Shelley, Blake, and others, is
    urged to do an article on Whitman about the
    "Continuity of Pioneering."

10 KING, BASIL. <u>The City of Comrades</u>. New York
     and London: Harper & Bros., p. 174.

"I Dream'd in a Dream" is quoted as title-page epigraph. A character's friends were knit to him "in the bonds of the 'robust love' which was the atmosphere of brave old Walt Whitman's City of Friends."

11 KARSNER, DAVID. _Horace Traubel: His Life and Work_. New York: Egmont Arens. "With Walt Whitman," pp. 59-77; also 28-29, 105-9, passim. No index.

Describes Traubel as biographer, his relations with Whitman; compares _Leaves_ and _Optimos_, both "bibles of labor," as to their authors' styles and qualities. Whitman merely gives hints, with optimism looking toward the future, while Traubel's optimism rejoices in the present and puts Whitman's philosophy into practical application.

12 LIBRARY OF CONGRESS. Report of the Librarian of Congress for the Fiscal Year Ending June 30, 1919. Washington, D.C.: Government Printing Office, p. 42.

Harned has added to his Whitman deposit twenty-four volumes of Whitman notebooks and seventy-two letters from Gilchrist.

13 LOWES, JOHN LIVINGSTON. _Convention and Revolt in Poetry_. Boston and New York: Houghton Mifflin Co., pp. 42, 190, 256, 280, 303-304, 345.

Incidental references to Whitman and his poetry for examples of various qualities of poetry, like the use of language in "Myself" 21. His free-verse descendants lack his Titanic voice. He brings the truth of actual things into his poetry but sometimes loses the poetic illusion.

14 M., B. Introduction to _Songs of Democracy_, by Walt Whitman. Philadelphia: David McKay, pp. 7-18.

Explains the reason for this selection of Whitman's poetry (though basically contrary to Whitman's intention of keeping his work whole): "to show how truly Whitman is the poet of the hour," not to delete the sex poems, regarding which "America has not yet grown up to Walt Whitman." The influence of the "merely literary" is gradually lifting so the ideas of _Leaves_ may now be appreciated. His poetry has influenced Europe in form and spirit, even though his ideas are directed to America. But his great service to America was to "evoke a principle of unity" out of diversity. Modern poets have not followed this, being regional. The imagists too are not cosmic. Quoted passages show the similarity of President Wilson's ideals to Whitman's, whose "constructive optimism" is needed.

15 MAXWELL, W[ILLIAM] B[ABINGTON]. _A Man and His Lesson_. London: Hutchinson & Co., p. 197.

Parody reprinted: Saunders.

In London during World War I, the leading character experiences thoughts "like the poetry of that colossal humbug of an easily humbugged age, the late Mr. Walt Whitman." He inwardly sings "the Song of Himself," a series of Whitman-like lines and sentiments of brotherhood.

16 MENCKEN, H. L. _The American Language_. New York: Alfred A. Knopf, pp. 73, 320.

Whitman and Lowell were the first literary men to use the great changes in language between the War of 1812 and the Civil War. Whitman, quoted on American speech and his purpose in using it, moved toward a new tongue with "many daring (and still undigested) novelties" of foreign words and coinages, but he "made a half-attempt and then drew back" from fully presenting the American dialect in poetry.

17 _____. _Prejudices_. 1st ser. New York: Alfred A. Knopf. "Memorial Service," pp. 249-50; also passim per index. Reprinted: 1927.13.

We should commemorate the day in 1865 that brought together America's greatest poet and "the damndest ass" (Harlan).

18 MORDELL, ALBERT. _The Erotic Motive in Literature_. London: Kegan Paul Trench Trubner & Co., pp. 134, 146-47, 185, 188, 240, 248.

"Calamus" is an example of literature revealing the "homosexualism" of the author's unconscious. Whitman exemplifies the sublimation of "infantile narcisstic [sic] sex life" into valuable emotions, especially individualism, as in passages quoted. His individualism appeals to "the young man who does not fit into the social order."

19 MORLEY, CHRISTOPHER. _Mince Pie: Adventures on the Sunny Side of Grub Street_. New York: George H. Doran Co. "Walt Whitman Miniatures," pp. 272-91. Reprinted: 1925.12; 1925.13; 1928.16.

Describes Camden ferries, the current condition of Whitman's home, his tomb. We need a Whitman today "who can catch the heart and meaning of these grevious bitter years, who can make plain the surging hopes that throb in the breasts of men." Morley narrates an imaginary contemporary meeting with Whitman, wise and kindly, who looks at the modern world and stresses his ideals, particularly the individual's value.

20 PATTEE, FRED LEWIS, ed. Notes to Whitman selections in _Century Readings for a Course in American Literature_. New York: Century Co., pp. xxv-vi, 476.

Headnote to selections from prose and poetry places Whitman in spirit and influence with the post-mid-century group, characterizes his two distinct periods (youth and age), describes his Americanism ("equality pressed to the extreme"). His America is bound "only by the boundless soul of

1919

man." Notes explain background and vocabulary of the selections.

21 PAYNE, LEONIDAS WARREN, JR. History of American Literature. Chicago and New York: Rand McNally & Co., pp. 118-26, 142, 212, 237, 322, 356, 358, 359, 360, 373-74, 378, 395, 402-3. Illustrated.

Sketch of Whitman's life and its influence on his work. His great themes are described; "he was intensely human." His only serious weakness is that his poetry is "not always inspired," occasionally burdened with vague logic, mere catalogues, and topics "utterly foreign to his purpose." "One of the largest-brained, biggest-hearted men of his century," he may never be a popular poet because his work "offers too strong a meat and is too fundamental and cosmic for the general public," but "he may be placed next to Emerson in his power of stimulating other minds," with a profound influence and no question as to his genius and "elemental purity." He is elsewhere related to other writers. He was the only early writer "to strike a peculiarly original American note." His work will "have a tonic and invigorating effect" on the reader. Study questions.

21a _____. Explanatory notes to selections from Whitman in Selections from American Literature. Chicago and New York: Rand McNally & Co., pp. 503-12.

Explains background, vocabulary, philosophy. Suggestive questions and exercises provide for a thorough explication of each poem, particularly the long ones, in matters of form and content.

22 UNTERMEYER, LOUIS. Including Horace. New York: Harcourt, Brace & Howe. "Walt Whitman Rhapsodizes About It," pp. 22-23. Reprinted: Saunders.

Parody based on Horace's "Integer Vitae," echoing many of Whitman's lines.

23 _____, ed. Modern American Poetry: An Introduction. New York: Harcourt, Brace & Howe, pp. vii-viii. Revised: 1921.33.

Whitman "was the greatest of the moderns who showed the grandeur of simplicity, the rich poetry of everyday." Many new poets follow him.

24 _____. The New Era in American Poetry. New York: Henry Holt & Co., pp. 10-13, 15-16; passim per index.

Whitman challenged the prurient Puritans and aesthetic formalists of his day. He "broke the fetters of the present-day poet and opened the doors of America to him." His emotional and energetic power are described. He had no immediate followers; Oppenheim and Sandburg came only later.

25 WATSON, ALBERT DURRANT. The Twentieth Plane: A Psychic Revelation. Philadelphia: George W. Jacobs & Co., pp. 34, 46, 95-96, 129, 193, 220, 271.

This series of messages from the spirits of various writers of the past includes messages from Whitman, who terms his last work his best, favors "Lilacs" above his other poems, comments on his work, advises humility, praises concentrated thought and style. Watson notes his own high regard for Whitman.

26 WILKINSON, MARGUERITE. New Voices: An Introduction to Contemporary Poetry. New York: Macmillan Co., pp. 28, 215.

Whitman achieves symmetry of design in "Lilacs" by using interwoven images to tie his threads together. He is valued most for his long poems, their breadth of vision and spirit of democracy, rather than for his craftsmanship, though it shows "certain shining powers." As the "tidal wave of democracy," he swept away "the refuse of old preferences."

PERIODICALS

27 ANON. "The Letters of Algernon Charles Swinburne." Blackwood's Magazine 205 (January), 139.

Review of 1918.7. Swinburne's appreciation and depreciation of Whitman have been misunderstood. He witnessed the decay of Whitman's power and said so. His opinions of Whitman are quoted.

28 ANON. Paragraph. Poetry 13 (January), 231.

Requests poems honoring Whitman's centenary for the May issue.

29 BUNKER, JOHN. "Nationality and the Case of American Literature." Sewanee Review 27 (January), 83.

America's contribution to literature "hardly extends beyond the names of Emerson, Hawthorne, Poe, Whitman, and Longfellow," and the poets could not be listed with the major poets of English literature, Whitman because he "lacks art."

30 EDWARDS, WARD. "I'm so glad Horace Traubel was born." Conservator 29 (January), 171-72.

Describes his own interest in Whitman formed by the negative attitudes toward Whitman of two professors, one of whom became converted.

31 SMITH, GEORGE JAY. "When Helen Keller Spoke." Conservator 29 (January), 167-68.

Free-verse poem on Keller's talk (1918.42), including her comments on Whitman.

*32 SLOCOMBE, G. E. "The Love of Comrades. Dreams of Home-Coming Islanders." London Daily Chronicle (1 January).

Quoted in Saunders Supplement.

In discussing the proud and hopeful homecoming of British soldiers, the writer asks readers to cry with Whitman the opening lines of "For You, O Democracy."

33 SALEEBY, C. W. "The Pleasures of Quotation." Times Literary Supplement (London) (2 January), 10.

Quotes lines from "Years of the Modern" as "indeed prophecy--the human utterance of the Divine."

34 ANON. "At the Dangerous Age." Nation 108 (4 January), 22-23.

Review of Harned (1918.9). Gilchrist's great passion for Whitman is described, her eloquent language quoted. Hers are the most tragic love-letters in the world. It is to Whitman's credit that he could retain her friendship while rejecting her love. Though the letters are valuable, Gilchrist's daughter should perhaps have been consulted before their publication.

35 ANTHONY, KATHARINE. "A Normal Madness." Dial 66 (11 January), 15-16.

Review of Harned (1918.9), tracing the Whitman-Gilchrist relationship.

36 BRAGDON, CLAUDE. "An Educated Heart." Dial 66 (11 January), 14-15.

Review of Johnston (1918.12), which presents the real love felt for Whitman. We go to Whitman not for pleasure or instruction, but for inspiration.

37 RIDGE, LOLA. "Kreymborg's Marionettes." Dial 66 (11 January), 29.

Incidental discussion: "Whitman and not Poe was the true pioneer of American poetry," with his "grandly nihilistic gesture," "wholly a democrat," with a declaration of independence which is the guide for truly American poets such as those of today.

38 KAUFMAN, NATHAN. "Walt Whitman--Poet and Original Welfare Worker." Afloat and Ashore (14 January).

Describes Whitman's great humanitarianism during his war experiences, with quotations; his prophetic voice; his message of love and comradeship.

39 T[OMLINSON], H. M. "The World of Books." Nation (London) 24 (18 January), 462.

Incidental references, including the statement that one might drop all else "if one could create anything half so good as 'Drum-Taps' about this war."

40 ANON. "With Authors and Publishers." New York Times Review of Books (19 January), 30.

Paragraph wondering what were the conditions in the first two decades of the nineteenth century that produced so much American talent, as evidenced by the year's centenaries, including Whitman's.

*41 ANON. "The Poets on the 'War-Time Match.'" Bystander (22 January).
Reprinted: Saunders.

Parody of Whitman (among others).

42 PRICE, LAWRENCE MARSEN. "English > German Literary Influences: Bibliography." University of California Publications in Modern Philology 9 (22 January), 102-3.

Includes several articles in German and English on Whitman in relation to Germany, including a paper for the Modern Language Association by Trangott Böhme, "Whitman's Influence on German Poetry" (1917), with the topics covered and specific German figures discussed. The survey accompanying this bibliography follows in 1920.63.

43 AIKEN, CONRAD. "The Literary Abbozzo." Dial 66 (January), 83.
Reprinted: 1919.1.

Incidental: the "abbozzo" (a sketch or unfinished work) is exemplified by Whitman's catalogues, which would be even worse if "written as conscientiously in heroic couplets." Success in a more elaborate style would have required deletion, to Whitman's improvement.

44 RANDALL, ALEC W. G. "German Literary Chronicle: 1914-1918." New Statesman 12 (25 January), 352.

Incidental mention of Max Dauthendey and Franz Werfel as poets of the Whitmanian school.

45 DEUTSCH, BABETTE. "Realists and Orators." Bookman 48 (February), 753.

Incidental note of recent Hindu poems deriving from Whitman.

46 FLETCHER, JOHN GOULD. Review of Chinese Poems, translated by Arthur Waley. Poetry 13 (February), 274.

Incidental: the modesty in these poems is a contrast to Whitman.

47 T[RAUBEL, HORACE]. "Reminiscences of Lafcadio Hearn." Conservator 29 (February), 185-86.

Review of book by Setsuko Koisimi, Hearn's widow. Incidental reference to Traubel's own treatment of Whitman--deleting nothing, despite the objections of others.

48 ANON. "Manhattan." Times Literary Supplement (London) (6 February), 68.

Review of The Book of New York Verse, edited by H. F. Armstrong, who rightly gives Whitman the prelude and final piece. He may be "an imperfect genius," but it is better to stress the genius than the imperfection. Full of contradictions, "he sought to catch the under-melody and rhythms, not only of New York but of 'These States' at large." "Brooklyn Ferry" is

1919

missed here, so suggestive "of his prophetic
delivery, of his mingled subjectivity and
universality."

49 ANON. "The Romance of Walt Whitman and Anne
Gilchrist." Graphic 99 (8 February), 194.
Illustrated.
      Review of Harned (1918.9), describing
the Whitman-Gilchrist relationship. Her
letters have "a literary touch that gives
striking power to their human touch."

50 ANON. Review of Harned (1918.9). Literary
Digest 60 (8 February), 49.
      One-paragraph description of this
interesting book.

51 GIOVANNITTI, ARTURO. "A Lance for Max
Eastman." Dial 66 (8 February), 146.
      Criticizes Untermeyer's review (1918.73)
of Eastman's book (1918.6). Untermeyer
slighted Eastman's poetry in favor of discussing his opinions of Poe, Whitman, and
free verse, not Eastman's main concern in
publishing the book.

52 ANON. "Whitman and Anne Gilchrist--Passionate
Love Letters of a Literary Woman to a Great
Poet." San Francisco Chronicle (9 February),
8:7-8. Illustrated.
      Review of Harned (1918.9). The letters
are valuable, as Whitman realized, "as an
interpretive and beautiful tribute to his
life and work."

53 FLETCHER, JOHN GOULD. "The Wrong End of Modern
American Poetry." Nation (London) 24 (15
February), 586, 588.
      Review of Roma Claire's anthology
Modern American Verse. The ground was well
prepared in America for free verse by the
time Whitman wrote it, because of the rest-
less, impatient American temperament. He
was long "a voice crying in the wilderness
to his countrymen," however, because they
sought to be as English as possible in
their tastes. His "real inheritors," the
present generation of true poets who write
in more or less irregular forms, are noted
as being unrepresented in this anthology.

54 BOYNTON, PERCY H. "Lowell in His Times." New
Republic 18 (22 February), 112-14.
      This centenary consideration of Lowell
opens with a comparison with Whitman: "we
regard the tardy and eccentric Whitman in
the light of current developments, but we
estimate the timely and centripetal Lowell
almost wholly with reference to his own
generation."

*55 MASTERS, EDGAR LEE. "The Tie." Toronto World
(23 February).
      Reported in Saunders Supplement.
      Reference to Whitman.

56 ANON. "New Books Reviewed." North American
Review 209 (March), 425-26.

      Review of Harned (1918.9). Gilchrist
could fall in love with Whitman through his
work because it contains the whole man,
"virile personality, warm affection, democratic bluster, along with the great thought."
His "insistent humanity, his personal intru-
sions" bother some, but the power of his
thought to uplift is proven by this cultivated woman's response to him as "a moral
and intellectual liberator," "object of
deep affection," and more.

57 BUCKRAM, ELIOT. "The Romance of American Walt
Whitman and English Anne Gilchrist." Book
Monthly 14 (March), 253-56.
      Review of Harned (1918.9), tracing the
relationship.

58 LINDSAY, VACHEL. "A Doughboy Anthology."
Poetry 13 (March), 329-30.
      Review of Yanks--A Book of A. E. F.
Verse. The truly American idiom of this
poetry "delivers us from Whitman, thank
God!"--with his "Brobdignagian tyrannies
and over-distensions." "It contains an invisible writing which appears on the fourth
reading, and which was never in Whitman,
even on the tenth reading."

59 M[ONROE], H[ARRIET]. "A Radical-Conservative."
Poetry 13 (March), 323-24.
      Review of Eastman (1918.6). The
aesthetic principles of Whitman and Poe are
far from irreconcilable, as Eastman believes
they are. Can Eastman find more form and
"structural modelling" in "The Raven" than
in the glorious "Lilacs," which is of the
school of Rodin?

60 NOGUCHI, YONE. "Whitmanism and Its Failure."
Bookman 49 (March), 95-97.
      Having attempted to revive her spiritual
past, Whitman does not provide appropriate
guidance for a different America. "He expressed understandably his mighty power of
literary destruction; he showed no formula
of construction," such as America needs.
His "prophetic idealism" was too dreamy.
But he is a great personage, representative
of that period of the common man.

61 T[RAUBEL], H. "Collect." Conservator 30
(March), 1-6.
      Extensive recollections of Whitman from
his boyhood in Camden, when neighbors warned
Traubel's parents against his associating
with Whitman. They "were natural comrades,"
even before he had read Whitman's works.
Whitman made him revise all ideas of greatness because "he was just usual." Whitman
had a keen knowledge of his own emotions.

62 WYATT, EDITH FRANKLIN. "Adventures of a
Poetry-Reader." North American Review 209
(March), 404-15.
      Whitman is dealt with, among others.
The imagists lack his musical imagination.
Sexual and metrical controversies have dis-

tracted attention from "his skill in an enormous free-hand drawing of the spirit of a people during a great social and military crisis." Whitman's unique vision produced unmatched patriotic poetry.

63 HIER, FREDERICK P. "Walt Whitman and Mr. J. Russell Lowell." Playboy 1 (March-April), 30-31.

Deplores acclaim for Lowell rather than Whitman by the American Academy of Arts and Letters; describes Lowell's turning an English nobleman away from visiting Whitman. "Whitman was the real and great democrat of American literature." Perhaps his patriotism "is too humane and full of pity" for today. Whitman and Traubel are quoted on Lowell.

64 ANON. "Where There Is No Use For Men of Letters." Literary Digest 60 (8 March), 29.

Quotes E. W. Howe in E. W. Howe's Monthly (unlocated): people learn lessons better from parents and neighbors than from such writers as Whitman.

*65 ANON. "Some Psychic Experiences." Toronto Telegram (10 March).

Reported in Saunders Supplement and Willard.

On Flora MacDonald Denison, who suggests that a bas-relief of Whitman be made on Gibraltar Rock at Bon Echo.

66 H., F. "The American Spirit." New Republic 18 (15 March), 221.

Review of Perry (1918.15), noting his appreciation of Whitman's greatness, largesse, "continental expanse and inclusion," and his out-of-date balking at "Whitman's unashamed sexuality."

67 BOYNTON, PERCY H. "The American Note." Dial 66 (22 March), 306.

Review of Perry (1918.15), noting his "cautious deference" when discussing Whitman.

68 UNTERMEYER, LOUIS. "A Whitman Centenary." New Republic 18 (22 March), 245-47.

Whitman has strengthened, clarified, democratized most tendencies in American letters, challenging New England's literary aristocracy, proclaiming the glory of the commonplace to become "our first American poet," leading to most of the significant writers of today.

69 ANON. Editorial paragraph. New York Times Review of Books (23 March), 144.

Though he may not gain the English and American acclaim that Lowell's centenary won him, Whitman owes his recognition to English admirers. The fame of his verse is now more widespread than that of any other American poet except possibly Poe.

70 ANON. "With Authors and Publishers." New York Times Review of Books (23 March), 154.

Untermeyer's book (1919.24) is coming out in commemoration of Whitman's death day, "an attempt to estimate how American poets during the last generation have answered Whitman's challenge to 'Poets to Come.'"

71 LOWELL, AMY. "The Early Years of the Saturday Club." New York Times Review of Books (23 March), 147.

Review of Edward Emerson's book. Whitman is mentioned as not known by the New England school.

72 ANON. "American Letters." New York Times Review of Books (30 March), 160.

Cites Bunker (1919.29); notes that Whitman had to be recognized abroad before America recognized him.

73 BOWEN, EDWIN WINFIELD. "The Poet of Democracy." Methodist Quarterly Review 68 (April), 246-60.

Whitman's "new evangel" presented a complete picture of typical humanity, emphasizing America's "untold possibilities." His treatment of sexuality was well-meant. More culture might have given him a proper appreciation of good form. Leaves, stronger emotionally than intellectually, cannot be described as literature. His typical flaws in language and clarity do not appear in his best poems (listed). He is most significant as poet of democracy. His religious nature, while pantheistic and evolutionary, retains belief in free moral agency and the individual's freedom.

74 GILFORD, FRANKLIN KENT. "The Only Democracy." Open Court 33 (April), 204, 217.

Incidental references in this article presenting a dialogue on metaphysics: one "could learn a thing or two" from Whitman on democracy.

75 M[ONROE], H[ARRIET]. "The Glittering Metropolis." Poetry 14 (April), 31, 32.

Remarks on the Lowell centenary celebration, at which Masters read his poem, whose "smooth quatrains of rhymed eloquence led up to Whitman's name instead of Lowell's." Many wondered whether "the greater bard" would be so honored at his centenary in New York.

76 ABBOTT, LEONARD D. "Whitman as a Revolutionary." Modern School 6 (April-May), 138-41.

Whitman is revolutionary in form and subject matter, especially in treating sex and friendship. He was an internationalist and pantheist who "staked all on fundamental change."

77 BROWN, WILLIAM THURSTON. "Whitman and Sex." Modern School 6 (April-May), 144-47.

Excerpt reprinted from 1917.1.

1919

78 BURROUGHS, JOHN, and GILDER, RICHARD WATSON.
   "Letters about Whitman by John Burroughs
   and Richard Watson Gilder." Modern School
   6 (April-May), 114-25.
      Letters to each other, to Perry, to
   Barrus, commenting on Whitman, his influence, self-evaluation, impressions of
   literary men, friends.

79 COLUM, PADRIAC. "Whitman's Influence in
   Ireland." Modern School 6 (April-May),
   128-29.
      Traces Whitman's influence on Irish
   thought and his critics in Ireland.

80 COOMARASWAMY, ANANDA. "Whitman as Prophet."
   Modern School 6 (April-May), 98-102.
      Whitman is a great visionary, uniquely
   revealing the nature of love. He is nearer
   than other Western writers to Chuang-tzu
   and the Upanishads. His poetry represents
   a monistic philosophy, a social order, and
   a moral system. In his thought, "East and
   West may meet."

81 HARNED, THOMAS B. "The Good Grey Poet in
   Camden." Modern School 6 (April-May),
   112-14.
      Recollections of Whitman, his friend-
   ships with persons of all classes and ages.
   He died "confident that he was to be heard."
   (Harned's Conservator article, 1919.279,
   uses the same material.)

82 LANUX, PIERRE de. "Two Generations of Whitman
   in France, II." Modern School 6 (April-
   May), 132-34.
   Extract reprinted from 1917.7.

83 O'GRADY, STANDISH JAMES. "Whitman the Poet of
   Joy." Modern School 6 (April-May), 106-11.
   Reprint of 1875.16.

84 THORSTENBERG, EDWARD. "Whitman in Germany."
   Modern School 6 (April-May), 149-54.
   Reprint of 1911.17.

85 TRAUBEL, HORACE. "Walt and Freedom." Modern
   School 6 (April-May), 105.
      Recalls Whitman's statements on freedom,
   his desire that others lead an unobstructed
   life; comments on "Whitmanism" and "Traubel-
   ism."

86 WAGENVOORT, MAURITS. "Walt Whitman. A Dutch
   View." Translated by J. Van Gogh. Modern
   School 6 (April-May), 155-56.
      Translated from introduction to Dutch
   translation of Leaves. Whitman's work is
   not ordinary poetry but closer to Beethoven's
   music and to primeval poetry like the Iliad
   and the Vedas.

87 WALLACE, J. W. "The Letters of Anne Gilchrist
   and Walt Whitman." Modern School 6 (April-
   May), 136-37.
      Gilchrist's devotion is worthy but she
   misinterpreted Whitman's univeral message
   as personal.

88 WALLING, ANNA STRUNSKY. "Walt Whitman and
   Russia." Modern School 6 (April-May),
   142-43.
      Whitman of all poets comes nearest the
   Russian concept of democracy. He is read
   enthusiastically by young revolutionaries.
   Perhaps his message of revolution came from
   Russia, "aware as he was of the Nihilist
   movement."

89 WHITMAN, WALT. "Unpublished Letters of Walt
   Whitman to John Burroughs." Modern School
   6 (April-May), 126-27.
      Brief notes written 1877-89 to
   Burroughs and Harned, on meetings with
   Joaquin Miller, Longfellow, Holmes, the
   elder Henry James.

90 WYSEWA, T. de. "Two Generations of Whitman
   in France, I." Modern School 6 (April-
   May), 130-32.
      Extracted from Revue Bleue. All inno-
   vations in form and thought in French
   poetry for the last twenty-five years are
   traceable to Leaves: vers libre, glorification of the self, naturalism. Whitman's
   inner life "is a slow and gradual recon-
   quest of civilization by nature."

91 [ZIGROSSER, CARL.] "Editorial Note and Comment." Modern School 6 (April-May), 157-60.
      Whitman's aims are similar to those of
   modern educators: internationalism, freedom.
   A letter from John Butler Yeats is quoted,
   declining to contribute to this issue,
   calling Whitman "scarcely an artist,"
   though "a picturesque figure."

*92 ANON. "The Walt Whitman Centenary." Teachers'
   World (3 April).
   Reported in Saunders Supplement.

93 ANON. "Current News." Dial 66 (5 April), 374.
      Notes Harned's gift to the Library of
   Congress of many of Whitman's literary
   remains.

94 ANON. "With Authors and Publishers." New
   York Times Review of Books (13 April), 202.
      Paragraph on plans for Whitman celebra-
   tion at the Brooklyn Institute, listing
   English and American figures asked to attend
   or send messages, including Shaw, H. G.
   Wells, Galsworthy, Kipling, Amy Lowell,
   E. A. Robinson.

95 HALL, FLORENCE HOWE. "The Saturday Club."
   New York Times Review of Books (13 April),
   196.
      Letter in response to 1919.71: the
   New England school did know Whitman. Hall
   (daughter of Julia Ward Howe) recalls her
   first acquaintance with Leaves, when her
   elders' conversation led her to believe it
   was coarse. The phrase "barbaric yawp"
   (the origin of which she claims not to
   know) fits Whitman about as aptly as the
   phrase "the still small voice."

96   ANON. "Modern Armenian Literature." Christian
Science Monitor (17 April), 3:5-6.
Incidental: among other Armenian
writers, Siamanto is discussed, "an ardent
disciple of Whitman," with whom "his mental
kinship" is "easily felt."

97   ANON. "Current News." Dial 66 (19 April),
436.
Notes Whitman's appearance in Regis
Michaud's Mystiques et Realistes Anglo-
Saxons, indicative of the natural French
interest in Whitman.

98   ANON. "French Studies in Anglo-Saxon Literature." Nation 108 (19 April), 614.
Review of Michaud (see 1919.97), which
comments on Whitman as the realization of
Emerson's ideal national poet and which
gives sympathetic and insightful treatment
to Whitman's philosophy of nature, his
nationalism, and his art.

99   UNTERMEYER, LOUIS. "'Poetry Has Sounded, for
the First Time, A Homogeneous and Truly
National Note.'" Philadelphia Press (19
April), 16:5.
The real American poetry that springs
from our own soil dates from Whitman, an
emancipator in form and ideas (triumphant
democracy, beauty in the common and the
present, use of direct rather than dead
language). Modern American verse has
responded to his "combined challenge and
invitation," as in several contemporary
poets Untermeyer describes.

100 ANON. "Autobiographies." New York Times
Review of Books (20 April), 208.
Incidental references to Traubel's
volumes as being close to autobiography,
since the words are Whitman's and Traubel
no doubt discussed his work with Whitman.

101 ANON. "Notable Books in Brief Review." New
York Times Review of Books (20 April), 230.
Review of Eastman (1918.6), noting his
discussion of the ironically reversed reputations of Whitman and Poe.

102 ANON. "Walt Whitman's Odyssey." Philadelphia
Press (20 April), sec. 2, 8:3-4.
Summary of Whitman's long foreground,
careful craftsmanship. Like Wordsworth,
Whitman lacked critical ability regarding
his own work.

103 BELSHAW, ALEXANDER. "The Whitman-Lowell Case."
Chicago Post (25 April).
In response to a previous article (un-
located), Belshaw verifies that Lowell in-
sulted Whitman, with reference to Traubel
III (1914.17).

104 E[LIOT], T. S. "American Literature."
Athenaeum, no. 4643 (25 April), 236-37.
Review of CHAL (1918.10). Incidental
references: Whitman, Poe, and Hawthorne,

"the three important men" of their age, are
pathetic because their environment prevented
their becoming as great as they might have
been. Whitman was more original and shocking than Browning.

105 ANON. "Poe and Philadelphia." New York Times
(27 April), sec. 3, 1:4-5.
Editorial on the extension to cities of
the perpetual battle between the respective
admirers of Poe and Whitman as representatives of order and chaos, form and matter.
Greenwich Village poets, though they borrow
Whitman's meter and ideas, scorn him and
his city, Brooklyn, yet he is greater than
any of them.

106 ANON. "Field and Study." New York Times
Review of Books (27 April), 248.
Review of Burroughs (1919.5), quoting
his "timely remarks on Whitman."

107 ANON. "Walt Whitman's Triumph." Philadelphia
Press (27 April), sec. 2, 6:3-4.
Account of the publication and reception
of 1855 Leaves, the misunderstanding of his
"mystical theory," the justification for
his self-reviewing.

108 TURNER, EMORY S. "Barbaric Yawp." New York
Times Review of Books (27 April), 247.
Explains that phrase as Whitman's own,
in response to 1919.95.

109 ANDREWS, GERTRUDE NELSON. "Walt Whitman."
Sunset of Bon Echo 1 (May), 3.
Brief tribute to Whitman's openness,
understanding, companionship.

110 ANON. "Anne Gilchrist." Sunset of Bon Echo
1 (May), 35.
Note praising the letters (1918.9).

111 BAIN, MILDRED. "A Lighthouse by the Sea."
Conservator 30 (May), 36-37.
Same as 1919.112.
Poem for Whitman.

112 _____. "A Lighthouse by the Sea." Sunset of
Bon Echo 1 (May), 6.
Same as 1919.111.

113 BANKS, J. LINDSAY. "Walt Whitman." Sunset of
Bon Echo 1 (May), 6.
The sculptor of the Gibraltar Rock bas-
relief of Whitman praises Whitman's love
for nature and humanity and the inspiration
of his writings.

114 BENGOUGH, J. W. "Walt Whitman." Sunset of
Bon Echo 1 (May), 21.
Poem praising Whitman's sturdiness,
fitly represented by the bas-relief.

115 BINNS, HENRY BRYAN. "Walt and the New World
Order." Conservator 30 (May), 45.
Praises Whitman's challenge and his
"creative, freedom-giving power of love."

1919

116 BRUNO, GUIDO. "Snapshots of 'People of Importance.'" Pearson's Magazine 40 (May),
312-14.
Reprinted: 1921.3; 1921.19; 1930.1.
Records conversations with two Camden
men who knew Whitman: William Kettler who
reports scandal about him, and Dr. McAlister
who praises Whitman's character, spiritual
aspirations, and democratic attitude.

117 BURROUGHS, JOHN. "Is Nature without Design?"
North American Review 209 (May), 671.
Incidental quotation of Whitman.

118 BYNNER, WITTER. "This Man." Poetry 14 (May),
80-81.
Poem wondering how Whitman would praise
the contemporary American man of destiny.

119 CARNEVALI, EMANUEL. "Walt Whitman." Poetry
14 (May), 60.
Short poem.

120 CROSBY, ERNEST. "Centenary of Walt Whitman."
Conservator 30 (May), 43.
Whitman brings "a new era in the life
of Humanity." His purpose of expressing
his deepest self is briefly explained.

121 DELL, FLOYD. "Books. The Road to Freedom."
Liberator 2 (May), 42, 43. Woodcut of
Whitman by J. J. Lankes.
Review of Bertrand Russell's Prepared
Roads to Freedom. Incidental mention of
Whitman among those who have the attitude
of individual revolt against the timid
democracy of the herd.

121a DENISON, FLORA MacDONALD. "The Twentieth
Plane." Sunset of Bon Echo 1 (May), 13-17.
Quotes her conversation with Whitman's
spirit at a session run by Dr. Albert
Watson; Whitman commends Denison's work
for him and Traubel's nobility. Also quotes
tributes to Whitman from the spirits of
Lincoln, Emerson, Bryant, Ingersoll, and
Bucke.

122 ELLIS, HAVELOCK. "Still the Same." Conservator 30 (May), 45.
Brief testimony to his persisting love
and reverence for Whitman.

123 ERSKINE, JOHN. "American Character." Fortnightly Review 105 (May), 713, 719, 722.
Incidental references to Whitman,
"truly American in his expression of diffuse and indiscriminate amiability."

124 GABLE, WILLIAM F. "Lincolnism or Whitmanism."
Conservator 30 (May), 42-43.
Brief testimony to his enthusiasm for
both Lincoln and Whitman.

125 GILMAN, CHARLOTTE PERKINS. "Walt Whitman."
Sunset of Bon Echo 1 (May), 28.
Appreciation of Whitman, who has beauty,
music and feeling.

126 GILMAN, LAWRENCE. "The Book of the Month.
The American Language." North American
Review 209 (May), 703.
Review of Mencken (1919.16). Inciden-
tal: the average American "would willingly
chuck Walt Whitman any day for Longfellow."

127 HARNED, THOMAS B. "How I Met Walt Whitman."
Sunset of Bon Echo 1 (May), 25-26.
Brief recollection of first acquaintance
with Whitman in Camden, 1873, Whitman's
popularity there, and "spiritual acceptance
of the Universe."

128 HARRIS, FRANK. "Walt Whitman: the Greatest
American." Pearson's Magazine 40 (May),
305-311.
Reprinted: 1920.13.
Whitman is "the most characteristic
American and thereby the most original,"
large like his land, surpassing Emerson
because of his appreciation of the body.
Harris recalls hearing Whitman speak in
Philadelphia. Whitman had doubts about
democracy; he failed in his critical pronouncements, diction, unmusical verse form,
but he should not be so unpopular in America.
He is great because "he speaks to the soul,"
as in "Prayer," America's noblest poem.

129 HIER, FREDERICK. "Walt Whitman's Mystic Catalogues." Conservator 30 (May), 39-42.
Mysticism is omnipresent in Leaves.
Whitman's method followed laws of psychology, presenting many images flashing
through the mind as at peak moments of
consciousness. Suggestiveness pervades
some of his shorter poems and appears also
in his catalogues. The objects listed are
always dynamic and important in their context. Three types of catalogues are listed
and described.

130 HOLMES, JOHN HAYNES. "Walt Whitman." Sunset
of Bon Echo 1 (May), 35-36.
Compares Whitman and Lincoln as American
and more than American. Whitman is the
universal man, foreseeing a future of love.

131 H[OYT], H[ELEN]. "Three Whitman Books."
Poetry 14 (May), 106-8.
Review of Johnston (1918.12), Harned
(1918.9), Doubleday Page's Patriotic Poems
of Walt Whitman. Johnston reveals "hero-
worship in its most exalted form," conveying
a fine sense of Whitman's personality and
glamor. The Gilchrist letters are accompanied by her estimates of Whitman, analyzing him from a scientific outlook; her
appreciation of him was early and uncommon.
The patriotic poems are appropriately
issued at this time, calling attention to
Whitman as patriot and democrat.

132 HUGHES, JAMES L. "To Walt Whitman." Sunset
of Bon Echo 1 (May), 28.
Rhymed poem of tribute.

133 KARSNER, DAVID FULTON. "Walt Whitman." Conservator 30 (May), 43-44.
Tribute to Whitman, who stood his
ground against adverse reactions; praise
for his vast love and democracy. His day
is come.

133a MacDONALD, FLORA. "Bon Echo." Sunset of Bon
Echo 1 (May), 2-3.
Describes work of the Whitman Club and
announces Centenary convention at Bon Echo
at the scene of Banks's bas-relief.

133b _____. "John Burroughs." Sunset of Bon Echo
1 (May), 22-24.
Describes visit to Burroughs, with his
comments on Whitman.

133c _____. "Walt Whitman." Sunset of Bon Echo 1
(May), 1.
Brief tribute to Whitman, her "Great
Teacher," whose "Democratic Ideals" she
seeks to propagate through this journal.

134 McCARTHY, JOHN RUSSELL. "Come Down, Walt!"
Poetry 14 (May), 59-60.
Reprinted: 1919.328.
Free-verse poem.

136 M[ONROE], H[ARRIET]. "Walt Whitman." Poetry
14 (May), 89-94.
Reprinted: 1926.19.
Leaves ranges from "prosy moralizing"
and bombast to work which reveals Whitman's
"power as a colorist, as a draughtsman of
immense and revolutionary rhythms, as a
democrat and lover of men, and as a serious-
minded thinker." Explanation of his limitations and excesses, his major contributions
to poetry, including the conception of the
poet as prophet. Commentary on the qualities of particular poems.

136 PAULL, HERBERT G. "Comrade Ave." Sunset of
Bon Echo 1 (May), 33-34.
Whitmanesque poem, seeking words from
Whitman, who replies only, "Comrade."

137 RHYS, ERNEST. "The Ever-Living Poet." Conservator 30 (May), 45.
Brief paragraph of tribute.

138 _____. "Walt Whitman--1819-1892." Bookman
(London) 61 (May), 66-68.
Whitman is very modern, with an impact
on current poetry. He is to be recognized
for his imaginative, not his aggressive
elements. Rhys recalls his impressions of
Whitman and Whitman's adventurous mental
quality. Whitman's idiom appears similar
to that of the letter of Rahel von Ense
quoted by Carlyle. Whitman found a style
to suit his vision.

139 RUSSELL, PHILLIPS. "Whitman's Shiftlessness."
Conservator 30 (May), 44.
Testimony to Whitman's appeal for him:
he earlier thought Whitman's poetry must

have been wrong because it was so pleasant,
not stuffy and moralizing.

140 SALTER, WILLIAM M. "The Great Side of Walt
Whitman." Standard 5 (May), 201-7.
Abridged from 1899.68.

141 SAUNDERS, HENRY S. "Whitman's Vitality Today."
Sunset of Bon Echo 1 (May), 25.
Whitman is vital because of his fear-
lessness, in contrast to Stevenson's and
Emerson's hesitancy.

142 SMYTHE, ALBERT E. S. "Walt Whitman." Sunset
of Bon Echo 1 (May), 27. Photograph of
Banks's bas-relief.
Sonnet comparing Whitman with other
great prophets.

143 _____. "Whitman in Canada." Sunset of Bon
Echo 1 (May), 4-5.
On Whitman's revolution from the Victorian era, embrace of the whole universe
in his consciousness, possible knowledge
of "the Great Indian Philosopher" Kanada,
and "harmony of innocence and knowledge"
for which Canadians and all should strive.

144 TRAUBEL, HORACE. "As I Sit at Karsners' Front
Window." Conservator 30 (May), 37-38.
Poem of reminiscences of Whitman.

145 T[RAUBEL], H. "Collect." Conservator 30
(May), 33-36.
Whitman's year should make us remember
that it is our year as well. He emphasized
love for all humanity. He remained an out-
law. We must judge ourselves by the standards he meant to arouse in us as a living
force.

146 TRAUBEL, HORACE. "Horace Traubel on Walt
Whitman." Sunset of Bon Echo 1 (May), 7-8.
Whitman cannot be owned by any one
group but must be kept alive, "wide open,
unclassified," by all new readers, however
they may interpret him. Nellie O'Connor
and John Swinton are quoted on new interpretations of Whitman.

147 WALLACE, J. W. "The Walt Whitman Birthday
Centennial." Conservator 30 (May), 38-39.
Examines current civilization and
Whitman's vision for the new order; describes Whitman's experience of illumination,
which he saw possible for all and which required new forms and himself as theme.
Whitman has no creed or philosophy but ranks
with the loftiest scriptures. Leaves is
"the most revolutionary of modern books,"
universal in its sympathies.

148 _____. "Whitman's Personality." Bookman
(London) 56 (May), 68-69.
Democratic ideas reached their fullest
state in Whitman. He lived his philosophy
of love and oneness with all others and
with the spirit of the universe. Wallace

1919

recalls meeting Whitman and being impressed by his common humanity, loving nature, and lofty spirit.

148a WALLINGTON, EDWARD. Extract of letter. Sunset of Bon Echo 1 (May), 8.
    Queen Mary's private secretary writes the Whitman Club of Bon Echo indicating the Queen's interest in the publication of the club's centenary tributes to Whitman.

148b WATSON, ALBERT DURRANT. "Walt Whitman." Sunset of Bon Echo 1 (May), 17.
    Praises Whitman's various ideals, his spirit, and his illumination.

149 WYATT, EDITH FRANKLIN. "The Answerer: Walt Whitman." North American Review 209 (May), 672-82.
    Whitman has proved valuable during the war as the defender of democracy, which he embodied in life and books. His expression of democracy in sex is a great contribution to civilization and to poetry.

150 ANON. Whitman Issue. Brooklyn Institute of Arts and Sciences Bulletin 22 (3 May).
    "Whitman's Rank," p. 237: Many regard him as "the most powerful and catholic, the most natural and real, a poet and prophet speaking through the average man." The ever more democratic world becomes ever more ready to respond to him.
    "Whitman's School at Woodbury, L.I.";
    "Whitman's Birthplace," p. 239: Short notes with illustrations.
    "Whitman as an Editor," p. 240: Short article.
    "Whitman Bibliography," p. 241: Note with short book list.
    "The Pilgrimage," p. 241: Outline of May 31 trip.
    "Who's Who on the Whitman Centennial Program," p. 243: Short article with illustration.
    "Whitman's Friends," p. 245: While Whitman responded to people of all levels of society, he most liked those of the laboring class.

151 ANON. "'Maud' and Tears." New York Times Review of Books (4 May), 256.
    Discusses Emerson's retreat from early admiration of Whitman, and the kind of poetry the nineteenth century preferred ("more or less melodramatic expression of sentiment"), now displaced by the "genuine, healthful realism" Whitman represented.

152 ANON. "With Authors and Publishers." New York Times Review of Books (4 May), 266.
    Paragraph on the planting of memorial trees in Whitman's honor, under the auspices of the American Forestry Association.

153 LOWELL, AMY. "The Saturday Club. Miss Lowell Replies to Mrs. Florence Howe Hall" [1919.95]. New York Times Review of Books

(4 May), 253, 261-62, 264.
    The Brahmins remained deaf to Whitman's true worth, as quotations show, while posterity prefers him.

*154 TRAUBEL, HORACE. "What Walt Whitman Thought of Whitman Celebrations." Philadelphia Press (4 May).
    Reported in Saunders Supplement but not located in this issue.

155 ANON. "Mr. Burroughs' Vital Truths." Christian Science Monitor (7 May), 16:4.
    Review of 1919.5. This book's appreciation of Whitman "will be savored by those who have learned to love Whitman not for the expression of beauty alone, but for his universality."

156 ROMIG, EDNA DAVIS. "Walt Whitman: 1819-1919." Outlook 122 (7 May), 34-37.
    Critical overview. Whitman presents three kinds of ego (the autobiographical, the ego which identifies with all it sees, the transcendental ego which is part of God), but does not always indicate or explore the distinctions. Discussion of Whitman's irresponsibility in grammar and proofreading; his sympathy, virility, optimism, gospel of naturalness.

157 STEWART, JANE A. "Walt Whitman, the Teacher." Journal of Education 89 (8 May), 513-14.
    Relates Whitman's experiences as a teacher; presents his themes, love of nature and books, interest in human nature, patriotic emphasis, intensive child study, appreciation of scholarship (in misquoted lines).

158 AIKEN, CONRAD. "The Ivory Tower--I." New Republic 19 (10 May), 59.
    Reprinted: 1919.1.
    Review of Untermeyer (1919.24). Incidental: "Is Poe to be judged, as an artist, inferior to Whitman because he is less nationalistic or less preoccupied with social consciousness?"

159 ANON. "The Story of Radicalism in American Literature." Appeal to Reason (10 May).
    Review of Macy (1913.11). Paragraph on his discussion of Whitman, which demonstrates not only the "humanitarian import of his poetic message" but also his "gloriously appropriate cadences." Whitman was "conspicuously in advance of his time."

160 ANON. "Walt Whitman Centenary Observed at Notable Academy Meeting." Brooklyn Daily Eagle (10 May), 4-5.
    Summarizes and quotes in part the following addresses at the celebration by the Brooklyn Institute of Arts and Sciences: Arthur M. Howe, editor of the Eagle (printed in full: 1919.253); Harned (quoted extensively), on reminiscences of Whitman, defending him against accusations

of lawlessness, defining his aim; Dr. Samuel McChord Crothers on Whitman's effect on him, Whitman's message of equality and America's mission; Untermeyer on Whitman's contemporary influence, as "father of the American language (see 1919.273)"; William Lyon Phelps on Whitman's reputation and the qualities that gave him permanence, "a splendid imagination, absolute universality of feeling, a personality of extraordinary power that breathed into all he wrote unbounded vitality, and the art to express himself at intervals in perfect words."

161 ANON. "Whitman a Hundred Years After." Brooklyn Daily Eagle (10 May), 6:1.
   The celebration indicates Whitman's recognition as founder of free verse. His book has been "a firebrand in English literature," but all his work is not good just because written "by the man of the greatest poetic vision whom America has produced." A second centennial will find him notable not for creating free verse but for breaking with "an outworn tradition."

162 BURROUGHS, JOHN. "John Borroughs [sic], Early Champion of Whitman, Gives Personal Recollections and Tells How Gray-Poet, Pioneer, Has Been Vindicated by Time." Brooklyn Daily Eagle (10 May), 4-5.
   Text of paper for Whitman celebration. Poets are measured by their opinions of Whitman. Whitman's unnoticed visit to Vassar some forty years ago is contrasted with the recent tribute there at which Masters spoke, denying any spiritual inheritance from Whitman. Burroughs defends Whitman against Masters's criticisms (see 1919.262); describes Whitman's personality, so much a part of his work; recalls his failure to interest Theodore Roosevelt in Whitman.

163 GARLAND, HAMLIN. "Whitman Greatest Optimist I Ever Knew--Garland." Brooklyn Daily Eagle (10 May), 4:4-5.
   Text of address at Whitman celebration, recalling the 1889 dinner, his first meeting with Whitman, Whitman's personality and appearance.

164 M., H. J. "The World of Books." Nation (London) 25 (10 May), 172.
   Incidental mention of "Whitman's great song of the widowed song-sparrow" along with other literary birds.

165 MARKHAM, EDWIN. "Edwin Markham's Estimate of Walt Whitman as Poet." Brooklyn Daily Eagle (10 May), 4:4-5.
   Text of address at Whitman celebration. Whitman is unique among American poets. Moved by his country, he "confronts the world with the passion and daring of youth." He "undertook to give us a cosmic vision," but his philosophy is not completely sound.

166 UNTERMEYER, LOUIS. "The Ivory Tower--II." New Republic 19 (10 May), 60-61.
   Response to Aiken (1919.158). Incidental mention of Whitman among other poets, including Shakespeare, Wordsworth, and Shelley, whose work may be "imperfect and far from elaborate" yet surpasses "poetry that is merely 'perfectly formed.'"

167 ANON. "Growth of Whitman's Fame." Philadelphia Press (11 May), sec. 2, 6:3-4.
   It is wrong to say that the great majority of Americans rejected Whitman. His increasing reputation parallels that of other innovators such as Wordsworth, in many ways similar to Whitman but less "conscious of the cosmic unity of men and the universe." "Prayer" is praised.

168 [CHAMBERLIN, JOSEPH EDGAR?] "The Listener." Boston Evening Transcript (14 May), sec. 2, 2:5-6.
   Informal column on different aspects of Whitman's career: the 1882 suppression, Harlan, Civil War deeds, British recognition.

169 ANON. "With Authors and Publishers." New York Times Review of Books (18 May), 291.
   Paragraph on Whitman celebrations, including Brooklyn's (see 1919.160).

170 ANON. "Tho' Dead He Lives." Portland Oregon Journal (18 May).
   Editorial on Whitman's achievement of freeing poetry from its conventions, based on Monroe (1919.135), briefly commenting on Whitman's ideas of liberty, justice, service, and "dynamic peace."

171 ANON. "Whitman's Later Life." Philadelphia Press (18 May), sec. 2, 6:3-4.
   Notes the negative criticisms and the defenses of Whitman. His fame has outlived destructive criticism. His influence is now profound.

172 VAN CLEVE, FLORENCE. "'When Lilacs Last in the Dooryard Bloom'd.'" New York Times (18 May), sec. 3, 1:8.
   Blank-verse poem of tribute to the "Good Gray Poet of Democracy," whose faith in America has been justified by those who died in the war.

173 EDWARDS, WARD. "Alan Seeger and Walt Whitman." William Jewell Student 25 (22 May), 7.
   "Myself" 45 may be the source for Seeger's poem "I Have a Rendezvous with Death."

174 EVERETT, M. S. "Editorial. The Great Revolutionist." William Jewell Student 25 (22 May), 6, 10.
   Describes the reader's gradual appreciation of Whitman; Whitman's quest for true individuality and equality; his aesthetic revolution.

1919

175 HERVEY, J. L. "Walt Whitman and His Centenary." Reedy's Mirror 28 (22 May), 322-24.
Recalls his own favorable responses to
Leaves. Many movements use Whitman's name
as a rubber stamp; his followers hardly
know his actual work and spirit. Traubel's
portrayal of Whitman's egotism and little-
ness of soul is regrettable, as is Whitman's
secretiveness. Whitman criticism is evaluated; his portraits described. We cannot
take him uncritically.

176 PALMER, RAYMOND H. "Whitman and the Untamed."
William Jewell Student 25 (22 May), 7.
Describes his personal experience of
Leaves. The young should be allowed to
evaluate Whitman because they are willing
to sacrifice form for substance, and
Whitman has a great message.

177 TAKAYAMA, R. "A Japanese Estimate of Walt
Whitman." Translated from Japanese by
Yasutate Fukumura and Rinyu Yamamoto with
introduction by Ward Edwards. William
Jewell Student 25 (22 May), 5, 9-10.
Whitman is a corrective for a superficial, insincere civilization with his
natural law, national spirit, healthy
attitude toward the flesh, and value for
the present.

178 WHITE, GEORGE H. "Life of Walt Whitman."
William Jewell Student 25 (22 May), 8.
Brief sketch of Whitman's life.

179 ANON. "Walt Whitman. 'The Gray Old Poet's'
Centenary." Manchester City News (24 May).
Consideration of Whitman's main themes
based on Romig (1919.156).

180 E[DGETT], E. F. "Pictures in Little--IV.
Walt Whitman." Boston Evening Transcript
(24 May), sec. 3, 11:4.
Reprinted: Willard.
Short free-verse poem commemorating
Whitman as perhaps not the greatest but "a
giant," "individual and unique."

181 JOHNSON, H. H. "Walt Whitman--Centenary
Article." Inquirer, no. 4012, n.s. 1115
(24 May), 163-64.
Whitman's work is autobiographical,
representative of our modern world, but he
was hardly a typical American. He could
write so much truth without a formal education "simply by being true to himself."
He is "a cosmic impressionist," opening up
vistas of the eternal, perceiving unity and
purpose.

182 SUTCLIFFE, EMERSON GRANT. "Whitman, Emerson
and the New Poetry." New Republic 19 (24
May), 114-16.
New poets should acknowledge debts not
only to Whitman but to his forebear
Emerson. Whitman also links the new poets
to puritanism. Unlike some of the new
poets, Whitman evokes distinct situations

in swift order "not only to give pleasure
to the visual imagination, but more because
he feels in each situation something illustrative of his creed."

183 ANON. Brief paragraph. New York Sun Books
and the Book World (25 May), 7:4.
"A page of Whitmanesque tribute to
Walt Whitman by living American poets will
be published in Books and the Book World's
next issue." (Several issues were searched
but these tributes were not located.)

184 ANON. "Walt Whitman." New York Times (25
May), sec. 3, 1:3-4.
Whitman is to be admired not as founder
of a religion but as poet, with splendor
and perfection in his own form. He was
bourgeois, with a progressive view of life.

185 ANON. "Walt Whitman's Centenary." Philadelphia Press (25 May), 8:3-4.
Whitman's "rhymeless rhapsodies" are
becoming appreciated, as is his word magic.
He preached individualism to a government
and society that have since become more
socialized, making much that he wrote lose
its significance. His poems on war and
Lincoln place him high in American literature's ranks.

186 BRAITHWAITE, WILLIAM STANLEY. "Walt Whitman,
1819-1919--His Rank as America's Poet."
New York Tribune (25 May), sec. 7, 4.
Whitman is the poet of American democracy, "the curious blend of the mystical
and romantic" which is American idealism,
but the people have hardly reacted to him.
Only intellectuals "had the intellect to
understand him, and the moral generosity to
sympathize with the tremendous purpose he
had in view." His self-reviews may be seen
now as "less a case of audacious egotism
than practical self-preservation," in
search of understanding, particularly
1855.10, a "remarkable document." His
acceptance in England is due to "the intrinsic substance and sincerity of the
poems." Youth will turn to him "to tell it
the law of romantic individualism and
illumine for it the social vision of American democracy." But his social significance has been overemphasized, at the expense of his deeper impulses of spiritual
faith and the growth of the individual.

187 HALL, FLORENCE HOWE. "The Saturday Club."
New York Times Review of Books (25 May),
297, 302.
Response to Lowell (1919.153): incidental references to Whitman, to whom the
New England group may have been deaf in
terms of "underrating his reputation."

188 HENDERSON, DANIEL. "Walt Whitman." New York
Sun Books and the Book World (25 May), 6.
The time is come for the poets Whitman
prophesied, but even if there come no new

bards like Whitman, at least his songs are "entirely adequate" for the new age, transcribing accurately the feelings of the recent war and the "note of world fraternity" in poems quoted.

189 HERVEY, JOHN L. "Emerson, Whitman, and the Saturday Club." New York Times Review of Books (25 May), 297.
    Response to Lowell (1919.153): presents further facts of Emerson's friendly relations to Whitman, not just the cooling that Lowell emphasizes; notes Longfellow's visit to Whitman in Brooklyn.

190 MICHAUD, REGIS. "France Re-energized from America." New York Times Magazine (25 May), 14.
    Whitman is included in this tracing of American influences on France: "a real dynamo to send American energy and strenuous life circulating through France," preceding Bergson in heralding the "'élan vital' and 'evolution créatrice.'" The Unanimistes have adopted him.

191 SHILLITO, Rev. EDWARD. "Peace and the Poets." London Sunday Times (25 May), 9.
    Incidental: "Whitman cried boastfully, but truly" that "Democracy rests finally upon us" (three lines quoted but not located in Leaves).

192 S[MYTHE], A. E. "Crusts and Crumbs." Toronto Sunday World (25 May).
    Discusses the importance to Whitman of the Quaker inner light, his symbolism, directness, lack of obscenity, daring in breaking conventions.

193 STRATTON-PORTER, GENE. "Whitman." New York Sun Books and the Book World (25 May), 7.
    Free-verse poem echoing Whitman's lines and images, describing the fresh perspectives on the world that she and others have gained "because of him."

194 WYATT, EDITH FRANKLIN. "Walt Whitman." Chicago Sunday Tribune (25 May), sec. 7, 5. Reprinted in part: 1919.322.
    Appreciation of the varied aspects of Whitman's poetry. His great achievements include breaking away from early nineteenth-century melancholy to "the intentional pursuit of happiness"; recognizing sex; including in his work the breadth of the continent. He does not merely loaf but can face evils "with a magnificent clarity." His verse is musical and vivid.

*195 ANON. Article. Boston Evening Transcript (26 May).
    Reported in Willard but not located on this date.
    We no longer criticize Whitman's substance but we desire fewer imitators. "Only a genius with a profound poetic insight could hope to overcome, as he has

done, the monstrous handicap of an utterly chaotic form."

196 [HIND, C. LEWIS.] "A Bookman's Memories--Walt Whitman." Christian Science Monitor (27 May), 3:1-2. Reprinted: 1921.15.
    Recalls enjoying Whitman's work, his refreshing ideas and vast sense of brotherhood, in London during the 1880s. His purpose was to startle, to make American poetry truly American, thus leading to the free-verse movement. His debt to Emerson is clear.

197 ANON. "The Librarian." Boston Evening Transcript (28 May), sec. 3, 7.
    Other poets need not be derided for one to recognize Whitman as an American poet of the first rank and to appreciate the excellence of some (not all) of his work. "Six or seven of his long poems are among America's finest contributions to art," sincere, revealing pride in America.

*198 ANON. "Whitman Centenary." Christian Commonwealth (28 May).
    Reported in Saunders Supplement.
    Short article.

199 ANON. "Whitman Centenary to Be Celebrated." Christian Science Monitor (28 May), 2:7.
    Brief announcement of Whitman celebration to be held on 29 May at London's City Temple with an address by Dr. Fort Newton (see 1919.316).

200 CHAMBERLIN, JOSEPH EDGAR. "Whitman's Name and Fame at His Centenary." Boston Evening Transcript (28 May), sec. 3, 2-3. Reprinted: 1937.2.
    Whitman is "probably the greatest poet of America, because of the splendid audacity and breadth of his utterance, and the startling originality of his style, as well as the freshness and force of his message, the American origin and substance of his matter, and finally the fascination of his rhythm." Extended biographical sketch, tracing the influence on his poetry of his childhood environment, newspaper work, war experience. A major flaw is his lack of a great relationship with a woman.

201 ANON. "Walt Whitman." Times Literary Supplement (London) (29 May), 285-86.
    Whitman seems to be shouting to put himself into a "willed cheerfulness." He does not adequately demonstrate his assertions. His poetry often seems "a mere release," a makeshift way of writing. When he is most musical he most tells the truth about himself and life, not merely his creed. His war poems express his true faith as he finally faced the fact of evil. He is compared with Poe and Browning.

1919

202 BODGENER, J. H. "Walt Whitman--A Centenary Tribute." Methodist Times 35 (29 May).
Praises Whitman's religious spirit, great-hearted love, wise recognition of the connection of body and soul. Methodists might read him for enlightenment, for he has the love of God, if no clear creed.

203 CHASE, AUDRIE ALSPAUGH. "Walt Whitman Poems Among Best Sellers--People Buying and Reading Great Poet's Works During His Centenary Week." Chicago Herald and Examiner (29 May), 13:4.
Book sales indicate Whitman's popularity this week, but he should be read throughout the year and the future; he is surely coming into his own.

204 MITCHELL, CHARLES B. "America and Whitman." Reedy's Mirror 28 (29 May), 340-31.
Whitman's poor reception in America is "a serious indictment of American democracy." His radical qualities in form and actual brotherhood are described. He was the pioneer of many of the encouraging new social, philosophical, and political movements. He brought Emerson's dreams down to earth. New social programs carry on his beneficent spirit while Lowell will be forgotten.

205 WALLACE, J. W. "The Walt Whitman Centennial-- The Man and His Message." Manchester Labour Leader 16 (29 May), 9.
Whitman was the exemplar of the true democracy our civilization needs. His message is religious and social, emphasizing unity with God and with one's fellows. He relies on the silent influence speaking between his lines. His character grew in greatness.

*206 ANON. "Whitman Centenary--World Famed Poet." Church Family Newspaper (30 May). Reported in Saunders Supplement. Long article.

207 ANON. "Nature's Great Revealer." Long Islander (30 May).
An appreciation describing Whitman's themes and praising his command of language and flights of imagination, his cosmic vision of unity, democratic sympathy, unfettered religious belief, faith in immortality.

208 JONES, LLEWELLYN. "The Whitman Centenary." Chicago Evening Post Literary Review (30 May).
Whitman must be looked at objectively now that he has become sufficiently accepted to eliminate the need for a defensive attitude.

209 RATLIFFE, S. K. "The Centenary of Walt Whitman." London Daily News (30 May). Reported in Saunders Supplement. Long article.

210 ALLISON, W. T. "Walt Whitman, the Good, Grey Poet." Calgary Daily Herald (31 May).
General favorable overview of Whitman's life and works. His break with tradition was appropriate for a poet of the people. He is now coming into his proper recognition as a major figure. "Captain" is the greatest poem ever written in Lincoln's praise. The reader should seek Whitman's "buffalo strength" in "Myself" and "Open Road."

211 ANON. "Patriotic Poetry, and Walt Whitman." Boston Evening Transcript (31 May), sec. 3, 2:4.
Praises Whitman's patriotic feeling in life and poetry. Recent more extraordinary productions have made the once radical Whitman seem to stand among the poetic conservatives. His true worth may take another century to determine; he may be ranked above Tennyson or Wordsworth by the next century.

212 ANON. "Brooklyn's Many Whitman Landmarks." Brooklyn Daily Eagle (31 May), Walt Whitman Section, 5. Illustrated.
Describes Whitman's various residences over the years.

213 ANON. "Poet's Birthplace Now in Good Hands." Brooklyn Daily Eagle (31 May), Walt Whitman Section, 2. Illustrated.
Describes current state of Whitman's birthplace.

214 ANON. "Walt Whitman." Brooklyn Daily Eagle (31 May), 6:1-2.
Whitman is now assured a place with Poe and Emerson as one of the three nineteenth-century American writers who will live. His all-inclusive mind led to his "wearisome catalogues." Description of his democratic faith, breadth of view, and sturdy manliness needed today.

215 ANON. "A Walt Whitman Poem Written in Brooklyn." Brooklyn Daily Eagle (31 May), Walt Whitman Section, 9.
Introductory note to a facsimile of an early version of "Passage" 5 written about 1849 explains the background of the manuscript.

216 ANON. "Whitman as Lawyer Won His Own Case." Brooklyn Daily Eagle (31 May), Walt Whitman Section, 2.
Account of assault case from Whitman's youth.

*217 ANON. Article. Chicago News (31 May). Quoted in Willard.
Whitman is called "the original poet of the league of nations."

*218 ANON. "The Religion of Walt Whitman." Christian Life 45 (31 May), 172. Reported in Saunders Supplement.

219 ANON. "Walt Whitman, a Poet of America."
Christian Science Monitor (31 May), 6:1-5.
Illustrated.
Describes Whitman's broad humanity,
representative egotism, love of nature,
brotherhood, potential internationalism.
Longfellow's and Whittier's poems of childhood are compared with "There Was a Child,"
which is "wider and freer in conception
and form." Whitman fails in attempting to
express the spirit in terms of the flesh.
His debt to the East is explained; Specimen
is praised.

220 ANON. Centenary editorial. Dial 66 (31 May),
566.
Whitman seems more nearly our contemporary than his fellow centenarians. He represents the general canvas of life rather
than his own particular segments. We look
to him as a prophet for enduring ideals and
community of purpose.

221 ANON. "Walt Whitman." Glasgow Herald (31
May), 4.
Whitman, America's one great writer,
was revolutionary in form and in theme.
His poetry is praised. He wrote of the
vast possibilities of "the earth's first
democracy."

*222 ANON. "Walt Whitman Centenary." London Globe
(31 May).
Reported in Saunders Supplement.

223 ANON. "Walt Whitman." London Times (31 May),
15:4.
Informal look at Whitman's life,
personality, reputation. He is not popular
with the people despite his themes. Though
"full of primal energy and even originality," he is deficient in intellectual force.
Many disapproved of him for his lack of
religion, "the nudity of his style," or the
"nauseous drivel" of his verses. He was "a
great prophet, if not a sublime poet"--"but
what did he teach?"

*224 ANON. "Walt Whitman and the Press." Mainly
about Newspapers (31 May).
Reported in Saunders Supplement.
Short article.

225 ANON. "Walt Whitman." Montreal Gazette (31
May), 10.
General estimate. Whitman's art as
well as his thought is important. He
ranks with Emerson and Thoreau as one of
the three greatest figures in American
literature. He is a figure of the present
and the future.

226 ANON. "Life and Letters--The Voice of
America." Nation (London) 25 (31 May),
260-61.
Whitman alone is a true American
writer, but he recognized modern life and
what was wrong with his country. His ideal
was man in nature, his democracy more than
political equality. He emphasized the fulfillment of the individual soul. His great
poems are listed.

227 ANON. "In the Driftway." Nation (New York)
108 (31 May), 868.
Note on Whitman's centenary, coming at
an appropriate time. His work is the best
anodyne for the fever and madness of the
present.

228 ANON. "200 on Pilgrimage to Birthplace of
Walt Whitman--Celebration of Poet's Centenary." New York Evening Post (31 May),
7:1-3.
Quotes Richard D. Burton's address at
birthplace celebration: on Whitman's great
personality, aspiration, self-reliance,
artistic blemishes as part of his largeness.
Quotes Mansfield (1919.261), Bennett (1919.
236), and Masters (1919.262).

229 ANON. "Walt Whitman's Centenary." New York
Sun (31 May), 8:2-3.
Reprinted in part: 1919.322.
Whitman may wonder why his work continues to be debated. Some of his lines
are unwelcome, though they may be "Great
Truths." Most readers of him "find the
greatest pleasure in his rough strength."
But some poems disappoint because he does
not sustain the perhaps unconscious meter
with which he begins. Parts of "Cradle"
printed unidentified today might be accepted
as translated from "a fairly good Japanese
poet." His work might be divided into
books for his separate themes and audiences.
The man in the street knows only "Captain,"
his poem "most likely to live forever."
Whitman cannot be held responsible for the
current "mess of free verse."

230 ANON. "Put Whitman Bust in Hall of Fame."
New York Times (31 May), 10:2.
Describes the prank of some anonymous
writers who smuggled a bust of Whitman into
the Hall of Fame and presented an appropriate
ceremony.

231 ANON. "Current Topics of the Town." Philadelphia Public Ledger (31 May), 8.
Quotes Whitman and others on Whitman,
including Harned and Burroughs on Whitman's
habits and activities, particularly during
the war; G. K. Chesterton in the London
Daily News, 1904 (unlocated), called
Whitman America's ablest man and the greatest man of the nineteenth century.

232 ANON. "Today's Walt Whitman." Philadelphia
Public Ledger (31 May), 8.
Whitman is an influence in England but
not America. If as a poet he will be
remembered "by a loyal few at least," he
will never be forgotten as a humanist. He
will retain his permanent place in our
literature and our life.

1919

233 ANON. "The Teacher Whitman." Schoolmaster 95
(31 May), 862.
"There is no poet whose words are more
instinct with the spirit of good cheer,
whose message is more inspiriting, whose
outlook on life is more manly and invigorating." Whitman and others are quoted on
his early days and his teaching experience.
He is the poet of absolute equality and
vast sympathy, poet of the earth and the
ordinary man. He regards sex as natural.

234 ANON. "This Is Walt Whitman's Centenary."
Toronto Mail (31 May).
Denies the vast claims made for Whitman
but recognizes him as a great soul and
unique poet, with some passages of song and
a profound method in composition. His life
is inaccurately sketched. He is compared
to Carlyle.

*235 ANON. "Centenary of the 'Good Gray Poet.'"
Westminster Gazette (31 May).
Reported in Saunders Supplement.

236 BENNETT, ARNOLD. "Arnold Bennett's Tribute."
Brooklyn Daily Eagle (31 May), Walt Whitman
Section, 9.
Letter to Brooklyn Institute: "America
has produced no greater writer"; Whitman is
"one of the greatest teachers that ever
lived."

237 BLACK, JOHN. "John Burroughs' Whitman
Memories." Brooklyn Daily Eagle (31 May),
Walt Whitman Section, 1.
Chatty reminiscences: Burroughs was
disappointed that none of America's poets
attended the funeral; the tomb was a tribute
to Whitman's mother; Whitman did not get
excited by negative criticism.

238 BOYD, JOHN. "A Canadian's Tribute to the
Poet of Democracy." Brooklyn Daily Eagle
(31 May), Walt Whitman Section, 12.
Long poem of appreciation.

239 BOYNTON, PERCY H. "Walt Whitman--A Centenary
View." Nation 108 (31 May), 866-67.
Traces changing views of Whitman from
his beginning to the present.

240 _____. "I, Walt Whitman." New Republic 19
(31 May), 141-43.
Reprinted: 1919.3.
Explanation of Whitman's different uses
of the first person singular (personal,
typical, mystical). Whitman emphasizes
"the generating of life" and the importance
of democracy. He may be regarded "as a
Puritan stripped of his dogma." His
current influence and acceptance of science
are explained.

241 BROWN, Professor J. MACMILLAN. "Special
Article--Walt Whitman at Home (1885)."
Christchurch (New Zealand) Press (31 May).
Account of his visit to Whitman, their

conversation on rhythm and subject matter.
A prophet-like faith saturates Whitman's
poems and life.

242 BUSS, KATE. "Anne Gilchrist to Walt Whitman."
Boston Evening Transcript (31 May), sec. 3,
5:1-4. Illustrated.
Account of Whitman-Gilchrist relationship. Whitman should have destroyed his
private correspondence; reading it will not
enhance the Whitman legend. Proffered explanations for Whitman's failure to respond
are unnecessary; he was "neither for one
woman, nor a fender for convention," and he
simply sought repose. A New England
acquaintance of Gilchrist has told the
writer that they rarely spoke of each other.

*243 COCKS, GEORGE F. M. "The Good Gray Poet."
Globe Turnover (31 May).
Reported in Saunders Supplement.

244 FAN FAN [Grace Blackburn]. "Centenary of Walt
Whitman." London (Ontario) Free Press (31
May), 11.
Reprint of 1912.28.

245 FARLEY, BELMONT. "Whole Nation Pays Honor to
'Good Grey Poet'--Walt Whitman Looms Up as
Leader in Literature of the Past Century."
Kansas City Post (31 May).
Whitman's prophecies are coming true.
He believed in America but insisted she
destroy the spirit of caste. He had great
moments ("Captain," "Cradle") as well as
commonplace periods with "prosy repetition
of mere words that have no poetic signif-
cance." Explanation of his themes, beliefs,
Eastern-derived religious views, realistic
concerns, democratic spirit, Old Testament
prophet's voice. He may be coming into his
own.

246 FIRKINS, O. W. "Walt Whitman." The Review
(New York) 1 (31 May), 56-58.
Whitman had great capacity for pleasure,
affection, and moral courage, but his
ethics were ordinary. His method and language were flawed, despite "the poetic
throb." His gospel (consisting chiefly of
equalizations, optimisms, and selfhoods)
suited his time. He fails in completely
achieving any of the ways of presenting a
state of life: simply embodying it (because
he was too self-conscious), drawing it like
an artist, or upholding it like a teacher
(for he lacked a system).

247 GOLLOMB, JOSEPH. "Would Whitman Be Bolshevist?
An Interview with Horace Traubel." New
York Evening Post Book Review (31 May), 1,
8. Illustrated.
Traubel stresses that Whitman would not
be bound by any "ism," although he certainly
sympathized with the workers. He was an
"anarch in art of his time" and "prophet of
world revolution."

248 GREY, ROWLAND. "The Centenary of Walt Whitman."
Great Thoughts 7, 8th ser. (31 May), 106-8.
Illustrated.
   Whitman is a figure of controversy,
especially for "the unnecessary coarseness"
of "Adam," but he holds favor with many.
His life is described, especially his
hospital experiences, through which "he
lived one poem more beautiful than any he
ever wrote." The war provided material for
some of his best work in the "fearful
realism" of the poems of "Drum-Taps," some
of them misquoted here.

249 H., F. "Books and Things." New Republic 19
(31 May), 154.
   The contemporary pantheon already holds
"most of the ancient deities," including
Whitman. "I marvel at men who understand
and forgive all," "as generous and many-
sided as Walt Whitman."

250 HARNED, THOMAS BIGGS. "Walt Whitman and His
Publishers." Brooklyn Daily Eagle (31
May), Walt Whitman Section, 4.
   History of the editions (including
posthumous ones) and their publication
problems. Whitman's patriotic poems are of
great value now. Facsimile of Whitman
postcard to Burroughs.

251 HERFORD, C. H. "Walt Whitman." Manchester
Guardian (31 May), 7:2-3.
   Whitman is in no danger of being
forgotten, as Lowell is. Whitman brought
energy to Emerson's ideas. His lack of
constraint and indiscriminate comradeship
offended New England. He gave life to his
principles in the war.

252 HOOCKLEY, ALBERT HERMAN. "Whitman in Camden."
Brooklyn Daily Eagle (31 May), Walt Whitman
Section, 10.
   Brief reminiscences of Whitman's
activities, good nature, and friends in
Camden.

253 HOWE, ARTHUR M. "Walt Whitman as an Editor."
Brooklyn Daily Eagle (31 May), Walt Whitman
Section, 3.
   Text of address at Whitman celebration
(1919.160). Describes background of contemporary journalism, Whitman's editorial
career and enthusiasm, showing "sincerity
and courage, but without noticeable distinction of thought or style."

*254 HURST, MAURICE. "Walt Whitman: the Poet of
Comradeship." Auckland New Zealand Herald
(31 May).
   From typed copy in Saunders Supplement.
   Whitman's poetry is proving of more
influence than other nineteenth-century
poetry. He is recognized "as one of the
voices of the earth--a writer of unique
achievement, of genuine originality and
strength." His purposes are described, as
picturing all of nature and human life "in

a manner more natural and direct" than ever
before, "plain, full of vigour, so simple
that anyone can read and understand."

255 IRWIN, MABEL. "To Walt Whitman." Brooklyn
Daily Eagle (31 May), Walt Whitman Section,
11.
   Poem of tribute.

256 KIRKLAND, WINIFRED. "Americanization and Walt
Whitman." Dial 66 (31 May), 537-39.
Reprinted: 1920.16.
   Whitman "is preeminent in expressing
what America means to an American." His
patriotism, pioneer vitality, breadth of
hospitality, pride of place are ideals that
his book helps to clarify for the teacher
of Americanization, but he may be too
strong for those just becoming citizens.

257 KRIGSMAN, ANITA L. "Whitman's International
Creed." New York Times (31 May), 12:6.
   Cites Whitman's belief in the interdependence of nations, all striving toward
the same goals.

*258 M., C. "Walt Whitman Centenary Today."
Glasgow Evening Citizen (31 May).
Reported in Saunders Supplement.
Two-column article.

259 MacKAYE, PERCY. "On Walt Whitman's 'Leaves of
Grass.'" Brooklyn Daily Eagle (31 May),
Walt Whitman Section, 4.
   Blank-verse poem of tribute.

*260 MARSDEN, JAMES W. "Walt Whitman's Centenary."
Blackburn Weekly Telegraph (31 May).
Reported in Saunders Supplement.
Two-column article.

261 MASEFIELD, JOHN. "John Masefield Calls
Whitman America's First Real Voice."
Brooklyn Daily Eagle (31 May), Walt Whitman
Section, 10.
   Letter to Brooklyn Institute: Whitman
was "your first real voice." He liked men
and women, conveyed welcome to them, a
message for all the world.

262 MASTERS, EDGAR LEE. "Edgar Lee Masters Says
Whitman 'Justified the Ways of God to Man.'
A Centenary Summation on Walt Whitman,
Written by Mr. Masters for the Brooklyn
Institute's Celebration of the Whitman
Centenary." Brooklyn Daily Eagle (31 May),
Walt Whitman Section, 8.
   Whitman, lacking humor, dramatic genius,
and argument, is "a chanter, a panoramic
observer, a rhapsodist." His program of
depicting America is sound, but not his
rejection of classics as feudal, for they
too portray the human heart. More than any
other American writer, Whitman justified
life to men. He looks forward to the
American Homer who will make an epic of our
Civil War.

1919

263 MORGAN-POWELL, S. "Walt Whitman, Prophet."
Montreal Daily Star (31 May), 2.
Whitman is praised as proponent of a
sane Americanism, though at his worst he
was but a strident proclaimer, going to
excesses. He was unheeded in his time,
only to be heard by later generations
approaching a new age of brotherhood. His
verse has power, with occasional failings.

*264 NEVINSON, HENRY W. "The People's Poet."
Derby Herald (31 May). Illustrated.
Reported in Saunders Supplement.
Long article.

265 PRICE, HELEN E. "Reminiscences of Walt
Whitman." New York Evening Post Book
Review (31 May), 2.
Recalls meeting Whitman when she was
fifteen, about 1856; anecdotes of Whitman's
visits to her family. His religious sentiment is his chief characteristic. He was
generally reserved, despite his self-reveal-
ing poems. His character is described,
with his sense of humor.

266 RASCOE, BURTON. "Casual Remarks on the Centenary of Walt Whitman." Chicago Tribune
(31 May), 13:1.
Whitman is nationally recognized but
rarely read by those about whom he wrote.
His book would probably be denounced if
published today. He and Poe are "the two
glories of our national literature," both
with schools of followers in French poetry,
to whom Amy Lowell is indebted, as well as
indirectly to Whitman.

267 RUNNYMEDE, RALPH. "The Walt Whitman Centenary." Derby Daily Telegraph (31 May).
Whitman's philosophy comes from the
long line of puritanism. He and Thoreau
rejected the intellectual side in favor of
the passion for nature and the care of the
body. Whitman's "grand descriptive passages," "vigorous style," strong personality, and large soul are praised.

268 RUSSELL, A. J. "Song of the Rough-Barked
Tree." Bellman 26 (31 May), 598.
Poem in free verse in honor of Whitman,
presenting a tree with Whitman's qualities.

269 SAWYER, ROLAND D. "Walt Whitman, the Prophet-
Poet." Brooklyn Daily Eagle (31 May), Walt
Whitman Section, 8.
Extracts reprinted from 1913.19.

270 SHERMAN, STUART P. "Walt Whitman and These
Times." New York Evening Post Book Review
(31 May), 4-5.
Revised: 1922.22.
Whitman lives in the present through
his personality and looks toward the future
of America. He reconciled the one with the
many, stressed the greatness possible for
the divine average, disliked doctrinaire
political schemes, qualified his support

for democracy. He raises man to an awareness of himself as a moral being and of his
great destiny. Whitman's work must be seen
as a whole.

271 SMITH, HYACINTH STODDART. "Walt Whitman."
Survey 42 (31 May), 327.
Poem of tribute in six rhymed quatrains.

272 T[RIMBLE], W. H. "Walt Whitman." Dunedin
(New Zealand) Evening Star (31 May).
Cites and quotes various critics to
show the range of Whitman criticism. Final
judgment cannot be rendered until a century
after his work appeared.

273 UNTERMEYER, LOUIS. "Whitman and the American
Language." New York Evening Post Book
Review (31 May), 3.
Whitman was "the father of the American
language," for he "not only sensed the
richness and vigor of the casual word, the
colloquial phrase--he championed the vitality of slang, the freshness of our quickly
assimilated jargons, the indigenous beauty
of vulgarisms." He led to such current
poets as Frost, Sandburg, and Masters.

*274 WATSON, A. D. "Walt Whitman." Toronto Globe
(31 May).
Reported in Saunders Supplement.
Poem to Whitman.

275 WHITMAN, WALT. "Editorials Written by Walt
Whitman as Editor of the Eagle 1846-47."
Brooklyn Daily Eagle (31 May), Walt Whitman
Section, 6-7.
Editorials reprinted for the first time
from the Eagle. Introductory note describes
them and Whitman's "varied and voluminous"
writing for the Eagle, revealing "the
beginning of his poetic conceptions and
abundant evidence of his imaginative powers,"
though immature in style.

*276 WHITMORE, ALICE J. "Prometheus Unbound."
Yorkshire Observer (31 May).
Reported in Saunders Supplement.
Three-column article on Whitman.

277 ANON. "Walt Whitman: A Bibliographical
Survey." Bulletin of the Brooklyn Public
Library 11 (June), 153-66.
A "representative and well-rounded,"
though not complete, bibliography, listing
the library's holdings of primary and
secondary Whitman material, with many annotations, some inaccuracy. Introduction
quotes Stedman and Bucke on Whitman's
reputations, with "suggestions on how to
get acquainted" with Whitman from 1894.66
and 1898.13. The first three editions of
Leaves, "issued at the high-tide of the
poet's vigor," are described as the explication of Whitman's theory of a democratic
literature, radiating "personal force to a
degree wholly unprecedented in literature."

278 ANON. "Celebrating Walt Whitman as a Liberator." Current Opinion 66 (June), 392-93.
Compendium of current commentary,
quoting or citing 1919.5, 1919.128, 1919.68,
1919.135, 1919.156, 1919.149, 1919.145;
Masters interview (unlocated).

279 HARNED, THOMAS B. "Walt Whitman's Personal-
ity." Conservator 30 (June), 54-55.
Personal reminiscences; anecdotes;
Whitman's comments on religion, Lincoln.
Uses material from 1919.81.

280 H[ENDERSON], A. C. "On 'The Movement.'"
Poetry 14 (June), 162.
Review of Untermeyer (1919.24), which
errs in making Whitman chiefly responsible
for the new poetic impulse. Frost owes far
less to Whitman than to the New England
poets, who are perhaps "as racial in
quality as Whitman."

281 LESSING, O. E. "Horace Traubel." Translated
from Die Neue Zeit by David Cumings.
Conservator 30 (June), 58-61.
Tribute to Traubel with comparisons to
Whitman. "Optimos has the advantages of
Leaves of Grass in its unified, experienced,
well thought out world view."

282 NAGANUMA, SHIGETAKA. "Whitman's Influence in
the Orient." Conservator 30 (June), 55-58.
Cites Whitman's references to Japan;
traces his introduction into Japan, the
growth of his reputation there, including
influence on Japan's free-verse movement.
Whitman's "faith in the supremacy of the
individuality as well as in 'en masse' will
guide Japan to the realization of her
dreams."

283 THAYER, WILLIAM ROSCOE. "Personal Recollections of Walt Whitman." Scribner's Magazine
65 (June), 674-87.
Reprinted in part: 1926.5.
Recalls visit to Whitman in Camden,
printing a letter recounting details of the
visit, including Whitman's comments on
Dante and Darwin; records impressions from
later visits. Whitman, "not an orderly
thinker," usually did not admit his sources,
particularly Emerson. He was irresponsible
toward his children, "a poseur of truly
colossal proportions" regarding money.

284 WIKSELL, PERCIVAL. "If All." Conservator 30
(June), 61.
This article closes the last issue of
the Conservator. If all scriptures were
destroyed, Leaves would fill their place.
As biography of a man, Leaves is "the
biography of God."

285 ANON. "Chicagoans Laud Whitman." Chicago
Herald and Examiner (1 June).
Account of Whitman celebration, quoting
Horace J. Bridges, Llewellyn Jones, Walter
Macpherson on Whitman's faith in democracy,

individualism, and patriotic importance.
Jones and Harriet Monroe spoke of Whitman's
technical aspects.

286 ANON. "The Gray Prophet Honored." New York
Sun Books and the Book World (1 June), 6.
Describes the tributes Whitman has been
receiving, including those in the schools.
His strangeness, not obscenity or indecency,
has retarded the public's appreciation of
him; America is no longer prudish about
him. He and Poe are recognized as our
first poets, but the question remains
whether he has come into his own in terms
of who reads him.

287 ANON. "Go on a Pilgrimage to Whitman's House."
New York Times (1 June), 17:2-3.
Describes Long Island Whitman tributes,
particularly addresses by Dr. Richard
Burton and Dr. Mabel Irwin (see 1919.228).

288 ANON. "Viereck Breaks Up Whitman Tribute."
New York Times (1 June), 17:1-2.
George Sylvester Viereck disrupted the
Whitman celebration with his pro-German
speech; other addresses are noted, including
the remarks of James Fawcett, Helen Keller,
and Emma Goldman.

289 ANON. "Whitman Bust Vanishes." New York
Times (1 June), 17:3.
The bust of Whitman mysteriously placed
in the Hall of Fame (see 1919.230) has just
as mysteriously vanished.

290 ANON. "Walt as a Cult." New York Times
Review of Books (1 June), 308.
Whitman should be regarded as a poet,
universal in appeal, rather than as a
teacher appropriated by various causes.
Compared to Browning, he has simplicity and
is one of the "elemental poets."

291 ANON. "U. C. Observes W. Whitman's Anniversary." San Francisco Examiner (1 June),
sec. 2, 6:1-4.
Account of Whitman celebration arranged
by Witter Bynner, whose students read poetic
appreciations of Whitman, upon which J. C.
Powys commented; Powys also described
Whitman as most original of the great poets;
his life is traced. Poems are printed by
Bynner (1915.7), Stanton A. Coblentz ("To
Walt Whitman," praising Whitman in free
verse as founder of that form), and William
Maxwell ("A Salute to Walt Whitman," praising Whitman and seeking his voice for today,
in free verse).

292 GOSSE, EDMUND. "World of Books. Gossip in a
Library." Walt Whitman." London Sunday
Times (1 June), 7:2-3.
Reprinted: 1919.342.
Whitman remains "the unsolved problem
of literature." The apparently neglected
1855 Preface merits attention. Whitman's
influence on the pre-Raphaelites is described.

1919

Once he became fashionable, however, his
influence declined. But he is <u>not</u> respectable and must be approached "at his uncompromising centre," not in his more innocuous
poems. The 1876 subscription for Whitman
is described.

293 LOWELL, AMY. "Emerson and Whitman." <u>New York
Times Review of Books</u> (1 June), 312.
Response to 1919.187: Emerson and
Whitman treated each other politely, re-
garding each other's work with "not too
exuberant interest."

*294 SECCOMBE, THOMAS. "Walt Whitman--Centenary of
the Great American Writer." London <u>Daily
Chronicle</u> (1 June).
Reported in Saunders Supplement.

295 UNDERWOOD, GEO. "The Centenary of Walt
Whitman (1819-1892)." <u>Freethinker</u> 39 (1
June), 264-65.
Whitman's democratic spirit and poetry
of death came from actual experience, not
abstractions. His poetic theory and work
derived from his pantheism, a conscious
attempt to return to nature, skilled
artistry rather than the artlessness of a
child. His early admirers are noted.

*296 ANON. "Walt Whitman." <u>Liverpool Post</u> (2
June).
Reported in Saunders Supplement.

297 ANON. "Walt Whitman Again." New York <u>Herald</u>
(2 June).
Editorial on Whitman bust episode (see
1919.289). However radical those responsible may be, Whitman remains important "in
this period of international sloppiness,
because of the intensity of his nationalism."

298 ANON. "Art and Courage." <u>New York Times</u> (2
June), 14:4-5.
Satiric editorial on the bust (see
1919.289): Whitman has come along well
enough without being in the Hall of Fame.

*299 ANON. "Whitman Devotees Honor His Memory."
Toronto <u>World</u> (2 June).
Reported in Saunders Supplement.
Account of meeting.

300 BROWN, J. MACMILLAN. "Special Article. Walt
Whitman, the American." Christchurch (New
Zealand) <u>Press</u> (2 June).
Whitman might have been more successful
had he written in prose and omitted the sex
poems and catalogues. His poetic spirit
appears especially in "Drum-Taps" and all
the sections following, and in <u>Specimen</u>.
But his theory of poetry with its over-
whelming nationalism destroyed his poetry.
His rhythms lately are being adopted.

*301 S., R. C. "Walt Whitman, the Poet of the New
Democracy." <u>Birmingham Post</u> (2 June).

Reported in Saunders Supplement.
Three-column article.

*302 WALBROOK, H. M. "An Unconventional Poet."
<u>Sussex Daily News</u> (2 June).
Reported in Saunders Supplement.

303 ANON. "Writers and Books." <u>Boston Evening
Transcript</u> (4 June), sec. 2, 7:1-2.
Paragraph pointing out the widely differing lengths of the first edition and a
current edition of <u>Leaves</u>, "one of the most
original and most notable collections of
poetry in the entire history of world literature."

304 ANON. "The Collector." <u>Christian Science
Monitor</u> (4 June), 16:6-7.
Describes Whitman editions and the
current prices. Prints letter from Whitman
on the publication and pirating of the 1860
<u>Leaves</u>.

305 ANON. "Walt Whitman." St. John (New Brunswick)
<u>Weekly Globe</u> (4 June).
Editorial. Slightly inaccurate life
sketch. Whitman is possibly the greatest
poet of democracy, especially important at
this time of democracy's triumph. His
birthday is more deserving of commemoration
than Lowell's, for he had the broader vision,
as lines from "Trumpeter" 8 show.

306 OSLER, WILLIAM. "Walt Whitman's Message. The
Glory of the Day's Work." London <u>Times</u> (4
June), 8:4.
Whitman's physician responds to 1919.
223 quoting from Whitman to show what he
taught.

307 P., G. P. "Walt Whitman's Message." London
<u>Times</u> (4 June), 8:4.
Response to 1919.223: Whitman "taught
the wonderful value of comradeship, the
love of nature, the joy of a healthy body
and a free and open-air life." His character and use of first person are defended;
his originality, wide horizon, full portrayal of the average man, "almost feminine
power of sympathy" are praised. His defects
are slight when compared to his inspiration,
derived from emotion and not mere intellect.

308 ANON. "Whitman No Boudoir Bolshevik." <u>New
York Times</u> (5 June), 12:5.
Deplores the radical sentiments voiced
at the Whitman tribute (see 1919.288).
Whitman would probably have disapproved, for
he was patriotic. He was a revolutionist
of a different sort from those today--that
is, in his poetry, which should be admired
as such rather than for ideologies.

309 J., E. "Walt Whitman." <u>Times Literary Sup-
plement</u> (London) (5 June), 313.
Response to 1919.201: Whitman's poetry,
the expression of a mystical faith, is not
rationally explainable. It appeals not to

"shallow optimists" but to those who have
sought to create a new God out of their own
hearts.

310 ANON. "The Whitman Celebration." Chicago
Evening Post Literary Review (6 June).
Whitman's radicalism is really individualism, which is actually conservative. He
was optimistic about humanity's ability to
transcend the faults he clearly saw; he is
consequently well worth reading today.

311 ANON. "Visit Whitman Haunts. Big Party Came
Out from Brooklyn to Celebrate the Centenary
of the 'Good Gray Poet.'" Long Islander
(6 June).
Account of Long Island celebration,
quoting Richard Burton's address on what
constitutes Whitman's great personality,
also letters from Bennett, Masters, and
Masefield (see 1919.228).

312 ANON. "The Prose Writings of Walt Whitman."
Spectator 122 (7 June), 724-26.
To give the reader an idea of the richness of Whitman's prose, several extracts
are printed as examples of his "highest and
best work," showing the value of his ideas
for today.

313 THE BOOKMAN. "A Reader's Notes." Winnipeg
Manitoba Free Press (7 June).
Quotes various critics of Whitman,
particularly recommending Stevenson (1878.
17). This writer prefers "Captain" to
"Lilacs."

314 ANON. "Did Not Attend Whitman Dinner." New
York Times (8 June), sec. 2, 1:7.
Jessie B. Rittenhouse says that she was
not at the Whitman dinner, although her
name was on the program as a speaker.

315 ANON. "Teachers' Union Protests. Objects to
Board Inquiry into Conduct of George J.
Smith." New York Times (9 June), 16:2.
The teachers' union protests a Board of
Education inquiry into the conduct of
George J. Smith as toastmaster at the
Whitman dinner.

316 NEWTON, J. FORT. "Walt Whitman: Universalist."
Christian World Pulpit 95 (11 June), 280-
82.
Reprinted in part: 1919.341.
Sermon preached in the City Temple
considering Whitman's poetry (or poetic
prose) as ministering to the human spirit,
explaining Whitman's mysticism, faith in
God or a cosmic consciousness, emphasis on
love as "the sovereign reality of the
universe." He is unique in praising the
beauty and benignity of death. He presented
the ideal mixed with the real. His life is
described. He is compared with other great
men and poets. He believed in the national
religion of democracy.

317 COLUM, PADRAIC. "The Poetry of Walt Whitman."
New Republic 19 (14 June), 213-15.
In Whitman's poetry, "the Becoming seems
not only to be realized, but to be participated in." His verse "creates a new and
special norm" toward which his revisions
were directed. His vast vocabulary, "epic
multiplicity," vivid lines, "epic majesty,"
and spiritual vigor are praised. His great
themes of "affection, reconciliation,
death" are depicted in his greatest poems
(here named). His democracy is a prophecy,
not a program.

318 RASCOE, BURTON. "Data in Pursuit of a Fallacy."
Chicago Tribune (14 June), 13:2.
Mencken is wrong in saying that the new
poetry did not start in America, for Leaves
was "the first flouting of fixed rhythms
and conventional rhyme schemes to appear in
Europe or in America. Whitman furnished
not only the impetus but the actual model
for the free verse poets of France."
French poets and critics are quoted concerning Whitman's influence upon them:
they developed his methods, and from them
some modern American poets drew upon
Whitman at second hand.

319 ANON. "With Authors and Publishers." New
York Times Book Review (15 June), 333.
Paragraph on the stimulated interest in
Whitman's works due to his centenary,
according to bookstore sales.

320 S[MYTHE], A. E. "Crusts and Crumbs." Toronto
Sunday World (15 June).
Describes Rev. J. C. Hodgin's Unitarian
Church address, "The Religion of Walt
Whitman," emphasizing Whitman's purity and
discovery of beauty in nature's processes,
his profound religion, and his belief in
liberty. "Song of Prudence" is an exposition of the law of Karma.

321 R., Q. "Comrades." Christian Science Monitor
(16 June), 16:1-2.
Incidental quotation of "I Hear It Was
Charged" in praise of the soldiers who have
died recently.

322 ANON. "Walt for Our Day." Literary Digest 61
(21 June), 28-29. Portraits.
Prints extracts from recent articles on
Whitman, including one from the Philadelphia
North American (unlocated).

323 MARY. "A Few Remarks Addressed to the Ghost
of Walt Whitman." New York Sun (21 June).
Reprinted: Saunders.
Presents a parody under "The Sun Dial"
column, since all views of Whitman are
interesting. This poem reacts against the
current celebration of Whitman. The poem
notes his contradictions; only in war did
he speak like "plain people."

1919

324 T[OMLINSON], H. M. "The World of Books."
Nation (London) 25 (21 June), 356.
Incidental: great writers like Whitman
do not need to consult theories of art but
mock such criteria.

325 ANON. "Salvation by Poetry." New York Times
(22 June), sec. 3, 1:5-6.
Incidental in this editorial: "The
enthusiasm with which our Bolsheviki have
read into Walt Whitman doctrines which that
strong-hearted democrat--who was not a
pacifist in the great war of his time--
would have thrown out of the window is
another indication of the danger of making
your poet the custodian of the public
conscience."

326 ANON. "With Authors and Publishers." New
York Times Book Review (22 June), 344.
Paragraph: Percy MacKaye and Harry
Barnhardt, the community singing leader,
are planning to lead a group in the chanting of poetry, including pieces by Whitman
like "Captain."

327 ANON. "Whitman and His 'Song.'" Musical
Leader, no. 26 (26 June), 716.
Presents article on Whitman's feeling
for music, reprinted from New York Globe
(unlocated): Whitman seems to have "viewed
all things and all ideas in a musical way."
Many specific references prove his extensive knowledge of music. "What greater
work is there in all literature than 'Proud
music of the storm'?" "And among musical
prophets who is greater than Whitman?"

328 SQUIRE, J. C. "Life and Letters by J. C.
Squire--Walt Whitman." Land and Water,
no. 2981 (26 June), 23.
Reprinted: 1920.28.
Whitman has little influence, being
generally "a bad artist" in his long lists
and mere statements of his gospel. But he
will survive because of his personality
and courageous thought. His successful
poems (such as "Cradle," "Lilacs," "Dirge")
are written from the heart, use description
clearly and words appropriately, and communicate emotion.

329 ROSSETTI, W. M. "The Author of 'Leaves of
Grass.'" Christian Science Monitor (28
June), 15:3-4.
Extract reprinted from 1868.2.

330 ANON. "The Gossip Shop." Bookman 49 (July),
632-33; also 639.
Whitman's centenary recognition is
evidence of his significance and possibly
growing public acceptance. Account of
Brooklyn Institute celebration (see 1919.
160): a clear portrait of Whitman was
difficult to obtain because of his personality's many "contradictory sidelights."

331 ANON. "Voices of Living Poets." Current
Opinion 67 (July), 54.
Notes recent discussions and celebrations of Whitman, "a trail-maker," more
contemporary than Lowell. Recent poetry
has followed him in lack of restraint,
although a countertrend seems to be developing. McCarthy's poem (1919.134) is reprinted as the most successful centenary
poetic tribute.

332 ANON. Editorial. The New Music Review and
Church Music Review 18 (July), 199-201.
Traces Whitman's appreciation of music
through quotations from his poetry and
prose, noting English and American composers
who have written music based on Whitman's
work.

333 BROWNELL, BAKER. "Five Poems to Walt Whitman."
Open Court 33 (July), 394-97.
Free-verse expressions of several of
Whitman's moods.

334 CAIRNS, WILLIAM B. "Walt Whitman." Yale
Review, n.s. 8 (July), 737-54.
Whitman's philosophy is inconsistent,
indebted to transcendentalism but more
aggressive in its individualism. His
poetic aversions are forgotten in moments
of inspiration. The care he took is
evident in his revisions. His treatment of
sex was hampered by his period's assumption
that any mention of sex was licentious and
by the lack of appropriate vocabulary.
Working classes have difficulty with his
work because his philosophy came from a
higher intellectual plane. His greatness
in nineteenth-century literature is clear,
not for his ideas but for his poetry.

335 GREY, ROWLAND. "Walt Whitman, Patriot: A
Centenary Note." The Englishwoman 42
(July), 162-68.
Whitman was convinced of the greatness
of his own work and of his country, imper-
vious to shocks and opposition, "before all
things a patriot." Various critics are
cited. He still awaits proper recognition.

336 HULT, GOTTFRIED EMANUEL. "Whitman Once More."
Quarterly Journal of the University of
North Dakota 9 (July), 309-30.
Whitman's vocabulary and prosody are
artistically suited to his purpose. Leaves
is a "resolute grappling with totality,"
not just biography or "the expression of a
merely perceptual mind in a state of
Bacchanalian sense activity." It is a
counterpart of modern society in its individualism, political stance, and healthy
realism. Whitman has vast potential significance, representing the poetry of the
future.

*337 McFADDEN, JAS. P. "A Word for Whitman." The
World of Books 1 (July), 8.
Reported in Saunders Supplement.
Short article.

338 MIMNERMUS. "Book Chat. The Centenary of Walt Whitman." Literary Guide and Rationalist Review, n.s. 277 (July), 102.
   Praises Whitman, his permanence, personality, philosophy, war and slavery poems.

339 PIERCE, FREDERICK E. "New Poets in a New Age." Yale Review 8 (July), 804.
   Incidental: thanks to Whitman's greatness and Dreiser's smallness, we are getting conventional immorality in poetry, worse than conventional morality.

340 SHIPLEY, MAYNARD. "Democracy as a Religion." Open Court 33 (July), 385-93.
   Whitman's idea of democracy, founded upon love, leads to a new religion based on enlightened intelligence and the needs of the heart, affecting one's whole life with sympathy and a Gospel-like spirit. Whitman is "the most powerful and convincing exponent" of transcendentalism, a monist, a pantheist, with optimism and faith for the scientific age. His poems on death provide excellent comfort.

341 ANON. "Walt Whitman, Universalist: A Commemoration Address by Dr. Fort Newton." Poetry Review 10 (July-August), 222-24.
   Account of commemorative service at London's City Temple. Besides Newton's address on Whitman (1919.316), here summarized and quoted, the service included a reading of "Trumpeter," appropriate for peace celebrations, especially in its musical setting by Hamilton Herty.

342 GOSSE, EDMUND. "The Whitman Centenary." Living Age 302 (5 July), 41-43.
   Reprint of 1919.292.

343 R., J. "Appeals to Readers." New York Times Book Review (20 July), 379.
   Asks where some lines of poetry that Whitman quoted several times can be found. Answer in 1919.349.

344 REEDY, WILLIAM MARION. "Father Wilbur's 'Roosevelt.'" Reedy's Mirror 28 (24 July), 492.
   Incidental: Rev. Russell J. Wilbur is quoted, addressing Theodore Roosevelt: "Whitman and Nietzsche are thy focal points."

345 JACKSON, HOLBROOK. "The Poetry of A. E. Housman." To-day 5 (August), 207.
   Housman's view of death is similar to Whitman's.

346 LESSING, O. E. "Walt Whitman's Message." Open Court 33 (August), 449-62.
   Extract reprinted: 1919.361.
   Despite his wish to reconcile religion and science, Whitman's mind was unscientific. His message of love is "identical in spirit with the Sermon on the Mount." He was a poet rather than a consistent or original thinker, being derived from Emerson. Vistas emphasizes "the harmony of the individual with the collective spirit." His impressionistic and subjective literary criticism has four criteria: "the democratic, the cosmic, the suggestive, the healthy and naked." He failed to perceive how his ideals were realized in Goethe. A less academic criticism is needed to respond to Whitman's ideals and depiction of actual life, and not only to his verse form.

347 ANON. "Gloucestershire Group." Christian Science Monitor (9 August), 14:1-2.
   Incidental: Ralph Vaughan Williams "seems to have a remarkable affinity" for Whitman, whose poems he has set in "Sea Symphony" and "Toward the Unknown Region."

348 DUDLEY, DOROTHY. "Made in America." Reedy's Mirror 28 (14 August), 551.
   Incidental: America's few immortal names include Whitman, "tolerated possibly for a single strain of sentimentality in a nature made otherwise of the elements--his faith in that most consummate abstraction of all, democracy."

349 WALSH, HENRY C. "Lines Whitman Quoted." New York Times Book Review (24 August), 435.
   Responds to 1919.343, identifying the poet.

350 ANON. "Kinship of Music and Poetry." Christian Science Monitor (30 August), 14:3-4.
   Last paragraph focuses on Whitman, second only to Browning "in his appreciation of the power of music and its deeper influences." He did not fulfill his "inborn poetic gifts," choosing to disregard the laws of prosody and the value of restraints, although musical phrasing is present in much of his poetry, "a rhythmical balance and an antiphonal cadence."

351 ANON. "American University Criticism." Nation 109 (30 August), 309.
   Review of CHAL (1918.10). Unfortunately, the concentration is on the life and character rather than the poetry of Whitman and Poe, "the two poets whose influence has extended furthest beyond the United States."

352 ANDERSON, MARGARET. "D. H. Lawrence." Little Review 6 (September), 39-40.
   Incidental: Lawrence reveals "the Whitman feeling, intellectualized." How can Whitman be considered a voice on love? He is in effect sterile.

353 ANON. "Signs of the Times." Liberator 2 (September), 40.
   Whitman's centenary was celebrated in Paris "not at the French Academy, but at the Labor Temple," an appropriate setting for "the great comrade of all men and of

1919

all women," according to La Vie Ouvriere.

354 CARNEVALI, EMANUEL. "The Day of Summer."
Poetry 14 (September), 324.
Free-verse poem with Whitmanesque
qualities: reference to Whitman as once
living in Manhattan.

355 D[ELL], F. "A Prison Magazine." Liberator 2
(September), 49.
On the Kansas Wire City Weekly, a
Bolshevik paper produced by political
prisoners: its first issue included notice
of Whitman centenary celebration in Wire
City. Whitman is one of their most-read
authors.

356 FISCHER, RAYMOND P. "Our Motto." Poetry 14
(September), 347.
Quotes Poetry's motto (Whitman's line
about great audiences) and discusses its
idea.

357 MODERWELL, HIRAM K. "The Blood of Munich."
Liberator 2 (September), 13.
Description of Gustav Landauer, a
devoted admirer of Whitman, whose work he
made known to Germany; his German revolution sought to realize "Whitman and Tolstoy,
never Marx and Lassalle."

358 WYATT, EDITH. "Whitman and Anne Gilchrist."
North American Review 210 (September),
388-400.
Describes Whitman-Gilchrist relationship, their similar spiritual outlooks, his
qualities precluding passionate involvement.

359 HUNEKER, JAMES GIBBONS. "Recollections:
Theodore Roosevelt and Georg Brandes." New
York Times (14 September), sec. 4, 8:2-3.
Brandes was interested in Emerson, Poe,
and Whitman, "though not as iconoclasts and
pathfinders," since they were "made-over
Europeans," "Walt's rugged speech a windy
parody" of Ossian.

360 ANON. "Essays on My Favorite Author."
Bookman (London) 57 (October), 18.
Among the authors dealt with in the
entries for this competition, Whitman
appears with those represented by two to
six essays apiece.

361 ANON. "New Light on Whitman's Contradictory
Gospel: An Effort to Relate 'Leaves of
Grass' to Its Spiritual Progenitors."
Current Opinion 67 (October), 246-47.
Illustrated.
Long abstract with quotation of Lessing
(1919.346).

362 ANON. "Whitman." Delineator 95 (October), 5.
A poem like "Pioneers" impresses by its
"sheer beauty of imagery" and Whitman's
"wonderful conception of democracy" such as
no other American had expressed. Had he
put music in his verse, he would have been
one of the great poets of all time.

363 BALDENSPERGER, FERNAND. "Walt Whitman and
France." Columbia University Quarterly 21
(October), 298-309.
Describes Whitman's affinity to French
thought and genius, interest in French
writers, early and current reputation in
France, influence.

364 BANHAM, ARTHUR. "Walt Whitman." Holborn
Review, n.s. 10 (October), 433-43.
Whitman was "the pioneer to a high
spiritual conception of life," "the child
of America" with a Hebrew prophet's vision.
His themes are personality (development of
the individual, regard for the body), love
(though ignoring spiritual love between the
sexes), democracy (faith in the common
people, well-depicted in his poetry),
religion (materialism as part of his
spiritualism). He achieved cosmic consciousness not by suppressing life but by
its highest expression.

365 EASTMAN, CRYSTAL. "The Workers of the Clyde."
Liberator 2 (October), 33.
Article on William Gallacher, Scottish
labor leader, who quotes "Pioneers" as his
message to the workers of America.

366 M[ONROE], H[ARRIET]. "What Next?" Poetry 15
(October), 34.
Quotes Burton Rascoe from Chicago
Tribune regarding poetry as "a succession
of revitalizations," noting particularly
"the eruption of Whitman."

*367 SMITH, H. J. "Walt Whitman in Paris." Chicago
News (8 October).
Reported in Saunders Supplement.

*368 B., W. H. "A Song of the Road, by a temporary
tramp (after Walt Whitman)." The Passing
Show (18 October).
Reprinted: Saunders.
Parody.

369 FAWCETT, JAMES WALDO. "Horace Traubel: A
Tribute. Personal Memories." Modernist 1
(November), 11-14.
Incidental references to Whitman in
comparison with Traubel, whose "message is
a development of Whitman's" and whose
affection for people surpasses Whitman's.

370 BELL, CLIVE. "Fine Arts: Order and Authority.
II." Athenaeum, no. 4672 (14 November),
1192.
Incidental references to the French
studying Whitman in translation and then
plunging into a "morass of sentimentality."

371 ANON. "With Authors and Publishers." New
York Times Book Review (16 November), 666.
The Franklin Inn Club is preparing a
medal of Whitman (described); the proceeds
on sales will go to a Whitman memorial.
The American and English members of the
honorary committee for the memorial are
named.

*372 ANON. "The Translation of Poetry." New Age (20 November).
Quoted in Saunders Supplement.
Notes the high average of excellence in the French translation of Whitman but criticizes several renderings of details.

373 [HUBBELL, JAY.] "De Tocqueville and Whitman." Nation 109 (22 November), 655.
Quotes passages from Democracy in America as prophetic of Whitman: on the loose style of democratic literature, rejection as poetic themes of past legends and supernatural beings in favor of "the destinies of mankind."

*374 ANON. Article on the songs of Frank Bridge. The Referee (30 November).
Quoted in Saunders Supplement.
Analysis of Bridge's setting of "The Last Invocation."

375 HARTLEY, MARSDEN. "The Business of Poetry." Poetry 15 (December), 155.
Incidental: "No one finds Whitman brutal," for he simply presents the picture. But his effect on some is brutal because "his simple frankness hurts," though he is right to remove the loincloth.

376 M[ONROE], H[ARRIET]. Review of John Drinkwater's Abraham Lincoln, A Play. Poetry 15 (December), 161.
Incidental: "Whitman was lifted by Lincoln's martyrdom to the sublime height of a great elegy."

377 ANON. "The Year's Achievement in Books." New York Times Book Review (7 December), 727, 732.
Cites Untermeyer (1919.24); notes the year's failure to meet the centenaries of Whitman and others with biographies.

378 RICE, CALE YOUNG. "What Is the New Poetry?" New York Times Book Review (7 December), 737.
Browning and Whitman are mentioned as the two great nineteenth-century poets who tended toward realism while clinging to the romantic spirit. Browning's psychological reality and Whitman's free-verse reality were the antecedents of the new twentieth-century poetry.

379 ANON. "Snow Birds." Times Literary Supplement (London) (18 December), 762.
Review of the book by Sri Ananda Acharya. Incidental: "Rhetoric where it occurs in Whitman is generally the vigour of spiritual emptiness."

1920

BOOKS

1 ANON. Twenty-fifth Annual Report of the American Scenic and Historic Preservation Society. Albany: J. B. Lyon Co. "Walt Whitman Landmarks," pp. 179-85.
Describes the poet's birthplace, with its changes since the time of his birth; surrounding scenery; his grandfather's home; family history; the Whitman school; the site of Whitman's printing office. Current photographs of the birthplace and school appear facing p. 264.

2 BAZALGETTE, LEON. Walt Whitman: The Man and His Work. Translated from the French by Ellen FitzGerald. Garden City, N.Y.: Doubleday, Page & Co., 355 pp. No index or bibliography, but references in footnotes.
Translator's preface explains her abridgement of certain episodes, so that Bazalgette's book may help bring about "a right reading of Whitman." Bazalgette's introduction (dated October 1907) praises Whitman as among the world's sovereign geniuses and acknowledges debts to earlier writers on Whitman.
Part One: "Origin and Youth: Long Island (1819-1841)."
Part Two: "The Multitudinary Life: New York (1841-1855)": Whitman's literary beginnings are less important than his life experiences in forming his later self. Reading (particularly periodicals) was only part of his education, for his was not a writer's or journalist's temperament, but demanded open air and companionship. His trip South aroused his consciousness of the continent and of himself, and he probably fell in love with a French or Spanish woman in New Orleans, although "a whole sentimental drama" is not needed to explain his departure from the South. His person and habits are described.
Part Three: "'Leaves of Grass': Brooklyn (1855-1862)": Whitman's new religious sense of life came about as a gradual, not a sudden, transformation, contrary to earlier theories. The power of his book is due to the presence in it of his personality. He was consistently motivated by his message and his achievement of American themes. The 1856 edition is praised for its "tremendous beauty," "passion, superabundance, torrential violence." Regarding his debt to Emerson, it may be assumed that he must have been familiar with at least some of Emerson's work, though his poetry derives primarily from the life around him. The 1860 edition (described) is "an organic whole," the most challenging and audacious edition.
Part Four: "The Wound Dresser: Washington (1862-1865)": His wartime service revealed his "reserve of latent femininity" and proved his ideal of comradeship (ex-

1920

plained). His war poems "immortalized the purest and most intimate emotion of the Civil War and of all war."

Part Five: "The Good Gray Poet: Washington (1865-1873)": His friendships (e.g., with Burroughs, O'Connor, Doyle) are described. His "imperious penchant for intimate comradeship," especially with young men of the common people, does not make him "a sexual anomaly." Rather, he "was a law unto himself." Vistas and the Passage collection are described.

Part Six: "The Invalid: Camden (1873-1884)": The more intimate Walt, touched by physical suffering, proved the culmination of the earlier Walt, "alive and sauntering, so glorious in his triumphant health." His loneliness as an invalid and lack of recognition from America are described; his faith in nature and in the future of America; his travels; Specimen Days and the culminating 1881 edition.

Part Seven: "The Sage of Camden: Camden (1884-1888)": Being "deprived of expanding in space," he "deepened within himself," becoming "filled with thoughts of eternity." His soul is described, full of contrasts, "close to the common run of man," yet "formidably isolated by his superhuman proportions." His methods of composition and reading demonstrate his own kind of mental discipline.

Part Eight: "The Setting Sun: Camden (1888-1892)": His friendships, growing reputation, activities, and spiritual endurance are described.

3 BIRRELL, AUGUSTINE. Frederick Locker-Lampson: A Character Sketch. New York: Charles Scribner's Sons, pp. 135-36.
Prints a letter of 26 May 1880 from Whitman to Locker.

4 BISPHAM, DAVID. A Quaker Singer's Recollections. New York: Macmillan Co., pp. 15, 50, 198.
Incidental references: Whitman's courageous proclamation of Americanism; recollection of Whitman walking past Bispham's family's business in the Philadelphia area.

5 BROCKLEHURST, J. H. "Walt Whitman." In Papers of the Manchester Literary Club. Vol. 46. Manchester: Sherratt & Hughes, pp. 318-37.
Whitman rarely masters his philosophy sufficiently "to expound it clearly and convincingly." Despite "a certain crudity of thought," he has much poetry of a high order, with an optimistic religious feeling and a spiritual outlook. He could hardly have written "Adam" and "Calamus" for advertising purposes, as is sometimes claimed, "for they have considerably restricted his popularity"; his conclusions, moreover, are inevitable from his premise concerning the relations of men and women.

His personal character reveals lapses (illegitimate children), although his plain-spoken treatment avoids the glamor more recent works have given to vice, being primal and passional rather than romantic, sentimental, or spiritual. He is best read from beginning to end. He lacks the profound philosophy and poetical beauty of the great nineteenth-century English poets, with much plain prose and no humor, though sometimes a fine rhythm. His debts to other writers are noted. He preferred the role of prophet but was "not a trained thinker." If his poetry survives, "it will not be because of his depth, and subtlety, and artistic elaboration of his themes." He is best when writing about America, the individual's importance, and democracy, but his talk of comradeship, "too often physical," is somewhat "mawkish and unhealthy." Many of his poems will live, particularly those of "Drum-Taps," which no poet of the recent war has equalled. He challenges, stirs the blood, but does not soothe like many poets. "He might have been a better poet had there been more receptive and sympathetic hearers."

6 BURROUGHS, JOHN. Accepting the Universe. Boston and New York: Houghton Mifflin Co. "The Poet of the Cosmos," pp. 316-28; also 13, 52, 73, 77, 85, 110, 200, 202, 242, 249, 284, 291, 294.
Whitman is the greatest personality the Christian era has known, and the only poet of the cosmos. Lovers of Whitman go to him for contact with his spirit rather than for poetry, for he incarnates his philosophy and is understood through contact not with literature but with nature, from which he draws his attitude toward good and evil. Burroughs recalls Whitman's character and walks with him. In contrast with other poets (Tennyson, Wordsworth, Emerson, others), Whitman perceives nature as a whole, putting us "in touch with primal energies." Incidental references and quotations throughout the volume.

7 BYNNER, WITTER. A Canticle of Pan and Other Poems. New York: Alfred A. Knopf. "Whitman," pp. 154-55.
Free-verse poem on Whitman's touching all men with his prophetic presence.

8 DELL, FLOYD. Moon-Calf. New York: Alfred A. Knopf, p. 195.
A hard-laboring man in this novel goes home to read "a volume of strange-looking poems which had intrigued him in previous glances at its pages" (Leaves).

9 De SELINCOURT, ERNEST, ed. Introduction to Leaves of Grass, Selected. London: Oxford University Press, pp. v-xxxiii.
Not fully recognized in his own country, Whitman rather gave America and her democratic spirit to the world. Leaves records

"the daring adventures of his spirit," his "rich and stimulating personality," which comes through more than a sense of him as artist or thinker. Biographical sketch, noting the central influence of nature, his quest to be a national poet, leading to his own natural style, which his best work justifies, though sometimes he is too conscious of theory, "employing a jargon as different from the picturesque and arresting colloquialism of his best poems as from that language of the plain people he sought to represent." Leaves is "the passionate expression of the ideal spirit of democracy as he conceived it," calling all to join the struggle for freedom through his ideals of equality, the potential greatness of individuals, the evolution of religion. Dealing with the body, "he fails less in moral than in artistic perception." If the most offending works are left out (as in this edition), "his true message stands out more clearly than in his full text." His central emotion is "a glowing love for humanity," which he seeks to inspire in us. His war experience and its effect on him are described. His principles of faith in human destiny, optimism, acceptance of death, struggle for emancipation are necessary today.

10 DREISER, THEODORE. Hey Rub-a-Dub-Dub. New York: Boni & Liveright, pp. 57, 257, 271, 276.
  Incidental references to Whitman as a figure Americans have rejected, though one of America's "few genuine thinkers." This rich country, since Whitman, has produced only one poet, Masters.

11 EAGLE, SOLOMON [J. C. Squire]. Books in General. 2d ser. New York: Alfred A. Knopf; London: Heinemann. "Mutual Compliments," pp. 75-76.
  Short note quoting Ernest Rhys on Whitman's comments on Swinburne, which may have prompted Swinburne's attack (1887.63). (However, Whitman made his statements after Swinburne's attack.)

12 ELTON, OLIVER. A Survey of English Literature 1830-1880. London: Edward Arnold. Vol. 1, pp. 32, 293; vol. 2, pp. 81, 125, 127.
  Incidentally notes the opinions held of Whitman by Carlyle, Symonds, Swinburne, others.

13 HARRIS, FRANK. Contemporary Portraits. 3d ser. New York: Published by the author. "Walt Whitman," pp. 211-33. Portrait. Reprint of 1919.128.

14 HUNEKER, JAMES GIBBONS. Steeplejack. New York: Charles Scribner's Sons. Vol. 1, pp. 5, 56, 57, 90, 100, 117, 195-98; vol. 2, pp. 6, 12, 123, 134, 142, 169, 171, 175, 176, 232, 233, 241.
  Recollection of his youthful admiration of Whitman, his first visit to him in 1877, taking him to concerts. Whitman's "Bowery Boy Emersonianism, his anarchic defiance of the ordinary decenies of life completed the disruption of my character." But Twain should outlive Whitman's "swaggering humbuggery." Whitman's preoccupation with sex was a necessary reaction against the New England school. Thoreau was a truer American and prose stylist than Whitman, who does not picture our national feeling. Opinions of Whitman are cited from Brandes (see 1919.359) and George Moore (regarding Whitman as superior because "he writes with his whole body, not alone with the hand"). Frequent quotations of Whitman throughout.

15 JAMES, HENRY [William's son], ed. The Letters of William James. Vol. 2. Boston: Atlantic Monthly Press, p. 123.
  Letter of 2 April 1900 regarding Santayana (1900.14): "Give me Walt Whitman and Browning ten times over" rather than mere concern for "Dramatic unities," "laws of versification," and "scholastic doctrines."

16 KIRKLAND, WINIFRED. View Vertical and Other Essays. Boston: Houghton Mifflin Co. "Americanization and Walt Whitman," pp. 236-43.
  Reprint of 1919.256.

17 LAWRENCE, D. H. Preface to New Poems. New York: B. W. Huebsch, pp. v-vii, x. Reprinted: 1920.69; Murphy; 1936.18.
  Whitman's poetry is the best example of the poetry of "the urgent, insurgent Now," revealing his appreciation of the present moment. He "pruned away his clichés," of rhythm as well as of phrase, and showed what poetry could do through free verse.

18 LEWIS, SINCLAIR. Main Street. New York: Harcourt, Brace & Howe, p. 339.
  Two characters discuss whether Whitman used "Brooklyn back-street slang, as a boy": "Not Whitman. He's Keats--sensitive to silken things."

19 MENCKEN, H. L. Prejudices. 2d ser. New York: Alfred A. Knopf. "Prophets and Their Visions," "The Answering Fact," pp. 9-18 (reprinted: Hubbell); also 53, 56, 57, 59, 61-65, 96-98.
  Vistas is quoted as typical of American prophetic visions which the country has not fulfilled. Only Whitman and Poe of America's "four indubitable masters" (including Hawthorne and Emerson) "have been sufficiently taken into the consciousness of the country to have any effect upon its literature," though only at second-hand. Whitman's reception is described and deplored. Neither he nor Poe yielded to the dominant taste of his time, but each followed his own inner necessity, heedless of his temporal welfare. Whitman's democracy was

1920

what "not one actual democrat in a hundred thousand could so much as imagine." Twain is "a much greater artist" than Poe or Whitman, but "a good deal lower as a man."

20 MORDELL, ALBERT, ed. The Function of the Poet and Other Essays by James Russell Lowell. Boston and New York: Houghton Mifflin Co., pp. viii, 143n, 148-49.
     Includes reprints of 1866.21 and 1868.40.
     Mordell points out the Whitman references.

21 MORLEY, CHRISTOPHER. Travels in Philadelphia. Philadelphia: David McKay Co. "Market Street: As Certain Eminent Travelers Might Have Described It. III. Walt Whitman," pp. 127-28 (reprinted: Saunders); "The Whitman Centennial," pp. 135-40 (reprinted: 1928.16); "Anne Gilchrist's House," pp. 141-46.
     "Market Street" is a parody. "Centennial" describes his visit to Mickle Street and Harleigh Cemetary on the occasion of Whitman's hundredth birthday; Whitman's value for the reader is that he "sends you your own soul." "Gilchrist" describes her house in Philadelphia, the street, and her relationship with Whitman.

22 MOSHER, THOMAS BIRD. Introduction to Leaves of Grass by Walt Whitman, Facsimile Edition of the 1855 Text. Portland, Me.: Thomas Bird Mosher, William Francis Gable, pp. 9-16.
     Recalls his first knowledge of Whitman's work in 1866 and his view of Whitman in St. Louis later. The bibliographical history of the 1855 Leaves is described, and several copies' ownership traced. Rankin (1916.17) is reprinted, on Lincoln reading Whitman; also Emerson's letter (1855.12). Some of Whitman's debts are noted.

23 PAINE, WILLIAM. A New Aristocracy of Comradeship. London: Leonard Parsons, p. 54.
     Whitman, Tennyson, and Carpenter have given "word of the new spirit" of love between man and man, the higher comradeship of this book's concern: close comradeship between young men of different classes.

24 PERRY, BLISS. A Study of Poetry. Boston: Houghton Mifflin Co., pp. 61, 71, 72, 206-7, 213-15.
     Whitman's work is not mere prose but follows biblical rhythms in "a unique embodiment of passionate feeling" between declamation and song, showing his extraordinary natural rhythmic endowment. Examples are quoted.

25 POWELL, CHARLES. The Poets in the Nursery. London and New York: John Lane. "Goosey, Goosey, Gander," pp. 52-56.
     Parody of Whitman.

26 RODGERS, CLEVELAND, and BLACK, JOHN, eds. The Gathering of the Forces. New York and London: G. P. Putnam's Sons. Vol. 1, 272 pp.; vol. 2, 394 pp. Illustrated.
     Collection of Whitman's writings for the Brooklyn Daily Eagle in 1846-47, arranged topically. Black's foreword describes Whitman as speaking through his book, "the unique composite of world citizen and nationalist." Rodgers writes on "Whitman's Life and Work 1846-1847." This volume goes beyond the stock data about his early years and reproduces Whitman's own long-neglected writings, "the product of the mature Whitman immediately before he evolved a different form of expression," showing that his departure from convention was deliberate, for he appears able to write in ordinary style. The recollections of William Henry Sutton, printer's devil when Whitman was editor of the Eagle, are noted. Whitman's political ideas are traced and explained (also in introductions to the various sections). He introduced literary columns to the Eagle. The development of the ideas of Leaves, Vistas, and his religion of democracy are traced, with notice of his occasionally prophetic vision, the presence of humor, his clear perspective on America and Europe.

27 SHAY, FRANK. The Bibliography of Walt Whitman. New York: Friedmans,' 46 pp. Photograph.
     Extract reprinted: 1920.74.
     Descriptive bibliography of Whitman's works, with some background of certain editions. The foreword traces the publishing history of Leaves and Whitman's growth with his book. His careful overseeing of the production of his books and frequent tampering with the plates resulted in many curious imprints.

28 SQUIRE, J. C. Life and Letters. London: Hodder & Stoughton, n.d. "Walt Whitman," pp. 180-86.
     Reprint of 1919.328. Reprinted: 1921.32.

29 WALLACE, J. W. Walt Whitman and The World Crisis. Manchester: National Labour Press, n.d., 26 pp. Photograph.
     Text of a lecture to the Bolton W. E. A. [Workers' Educational Association?]. Whitman is the "supreme prophet and exemplar" of the new democratic era, although his book, simply presenting a living man, is free from doctrine. Religion is the basis of his democracy, spiritual illumination the basis of Leaves. Whitman wants his readers to develop, through association with him, pride in self and an out-going, all-including sympathy. His vision of a new, world-wide order is based on this identity with others, the equality and divinity of all. Selections from his conversations with Traubel (1906.22) suggest that he would have rejoiced in current

liberating movements. He will be increasingly recognized as the greatest pioneer of the age of "human brotherhood and international solidarity."

30 WALSH, WALTER. _The Endless Quest: Spoken Reviews of Men and Books_. London: C. W. Daniel. "Walt Whitman: His Religion," pp. 119-31.

Whitman's prose "admits us to the workshop of his interior being," "in language compact, analytic, detached, definitive," "marking him a prose-writer of the first order," with power, vision, and audacity like that of Theodore Parker and Carlyle. His religion is explained, based on democracy and the importance of the individual rather than divinity and the church. Literature for him is inseparable from a religious purpose, evident in _Leaves_, "a veritable Evangel." His theology is a kind of pantheism, following Hegel. Whitman's strong belief in immortality was sensed when Walsh visited Whitman's tomb. Whitman's "virile and prophetic religion" is Walsh's own faith, equivalent to his "Free Religious Movement towards World-Religion and World-Brotherhood."

31 WILLIAMSON, CLAUDE C. H. _Writers of Three Centuries, 1789-1914_. London: Grant Richards. "Walt Whitman as a Herald of Revolt," pp. 222-24.

Whitman's faults were of breeding rather than of art--volubility, indiscretion, "a lust for description rather than suggestion." He looked into the future with a boundless gaze, with faith in democracy. "Whitman was ahead of the taste of his time; and he was not a good enough artist to enforce the beauty and the possibilities of his experiment upon the world."

PERIODICALS

32 ANON. "Grub Street Gossip." _Book Monthly_ 15 (January), 6.

Description of bronze medallion of Whitman designed by Tait MacKenzie.

33 CLUTTON-BROCK, A. "On Blake as a Prophet." _London Mercury_ 1 (January), 283.

Whitman is used incidentally to exemplify the prophet's relation to his audience: "Who are you, says Whitman, that wanted a book to encourage you in your nonsense?"

34 LESSING, O. E. "Horace Traubel." _Open Court_ 34 (January), 49-62.

This critical estimate of Traubel discusses his debts to Whitman. Traubel is not to blame for "Whitmania" for he regarded Whitman as "a great human being, a comrade, not a saint or a demigod." Whitman's verse differs from its formal models "in its inner form," with its "melody and rhythm, color and tone" deriving from his own soul.

Traubel fuses poet and prophet in himself, like Whitman, whose hopes he carries out for an American literature and its social ideals, though surpassing Whitman's "emotional impressiveness" with keenness of perception, and differing from Whitman's transcendentalism. Concluded 1920.35.

35 _____. "Horace Traubel." _Open Court_ 34 (February), 87-97.

Concludes 1920.34. Discusses Traubel's poetry and Whitman's influence on its form and spirit. Whitman's mysticism involves "the soul's solidarity with all other entities" rather than "the total absorption of indidivual existence by 'God.'" Traubel "turned from Whitman's indiscriminate universalism and sentimental spiritualism to the logical monism of Spinoza." Traubel stated Whitman's ideas on the body and sexual equality with more restraint; Whitman's "brutality" and "anatomical wordlists" offended aesthetic as well as ethical tastes. Traubel uses "friend" and "comrade" without Whitman's "sense of morbid 'adhesiveness.'"

36 BELSHAW, ALEXANDER. "France to America." Chicago _Daily News_ (11 February).

Brief favorable review of Bazalgette (1920.2).

37 E[DGETT], E. F. "Writers and Books. The Literary World of Today." _Boston Evening Transcript_ (11 February), sec. 2, 7:1.

Review of Bazalgette's "appreciative volume" (1920.2), regretting the translator's censor-like liberties.

38 ANON. "Criticism and the Tradition." _Times Literary Supplement_ (London) (26 February), 137.

Review of Mme. Duclaux's _Twentieth-Century French Writers_. Incidental: Whitman is listed among the divergent influences on Claudel, blending with others "to produce a peculiar thirst for the infinite" typical of early twentieth-century literature.

39 ANON. "Whitman in France." _Times Literary Supplement_ (London) (26 February), 134.

Review of Bazalgette's translation of Whitman, which "does not always convey the ruggedness and descriptiveness" of the original. The French admire Whitman the man and the spirit, while they admire Poe strictly as an artist. Whitman has become influential among the young French poets, sharing their concern with men and humanity. Charles Vildrac's poetry is compared with Whitman's as more intimate and artistic.

40 DALY, TOM. "Two Genial Gentlemen Before Us." _Bookman_ 51 (March), 105.

Review of Morley (1919.19). Incidental: notes his own futile efforts to appreciate Whitman's poetry, "a monumental false

1920

alarm" because "we cannot banish the
thought of the closeup we've had of his
personality" as "a vainglorious old
blatherskite." Hence he has found few
"four-leaf clovers" in his work.

41 ANON. Paragraph. Freeman 1 (17 March), 23.
Quotes Karsner's comparison of Whitman
and Traubel from 1919.11. Traubel is "the
connecting link between Whitman and
latter-day socialism."

42 ANON. "Our Writers--Sherwood Anderson."
Christian Science Monitor (24 March), 22:6.
Incidental: "Walt Whitman in verse,
and Winslow Homer in painting, stand apart,
above, fixed--two dynamic forces. They are
racial: they are American," in contrast to
New England's English tradition. The
twentieth-century writers of the West and
Middle West are akin to Whitman and Homer,
but are rougher and more confused.
Anderson's Mid-America Chants (1918.2) are
in the Whitman tradition.

43 B[ROOKS], V. W. "A Lost Prophet." Freeman 1
(24 March), 46-47.
Traubel is described as a shadow of
Whitman, having lived with him too long.
Surprisingly, neither Whitman nor Twain
mentioned each other in letters or talk.

44 JOURNEYMAN [pseud.]. "Miscellany." Freeman
1 (24 March), 43.
Paragraph notes Whitman's paper also
called the Freeman and mentions his political and social interests at that time.

45 B[ROOKS], V. W. "A French View of Whitman."
Freeman 1 (31 March), 68-69.
Review of Bazalgette (1920.2), a
"classical panegyric," "the first adequate
version of the great legend," although an
acceptable psychological study of Whitman
is still needed.

46 ANON. Paragraph on Traubel and Whitman.
Sunset of Bon Echo 1 (April-May), 11.
Whether Traubel is considered ahead of
Whitman or "miles behind," "they will ever
be companions and symbolize for all time
the highest type of friendship," Whitman's
ideal.

47 MacDONALD, FLORA. "Walt Whitman." Sunset of
Bon Echo 1 (April-May), 1.
Praises Whitman's exaltation of friendship, faith in immortality, and view of
life as a miracle. He was "the great
positive spiritualizing force," making
matter and spirit identical.

48 TRAUBEL, HORACE. "O My Dead Comrade." Sunset
of Bon Echo 1 (April-May), 23.
Poem about Whitman's death and his own
experience of it.

49 ____. "Walt at Bon Echo." Sunset of Bon
Echo 1 (April-May), 11-13.
Poem addressed to Whitman, describing
Traubel's addresses on Whitman in New York
and Bon Echo, recalling his experiences of
Whitman and people's responses to Whitman.

50 BLACK, JOHN. "Walt Whitman: Fiction-Writer
and Poets' Friend." Bookman 51 (April),
172-74.
Whitman's Eagle editorials reveal a
bias toward poetry. As editor he received
daily contributions from poets and published
many of them with enthusiasm. In his
reviews, he was antagonistic to current
schools of poetry and praised Longfellow.
Bazalgette (1920.2) neglected Whitman's
editorial phase. Whitman's prose sketches
in the Eagle are prophetic of his later
poetic style.

51 AIKEN, CONRAD. "Letters from America. IV.
The American Scene, 1840-1920." Athenaeum,
no. 4692 (2 April), 450-51.
Incidental references to Whitman, once
scarcely noticed in England, now regarded
as the typical American and distinctly
alien to the English standard: "A noble
mountain, a droll monstrosity."

52 ANON. "Bibliographical Notes." Athenaeum,
no. 4692 (2 April), 452.
Incidental reference to Whitman, very
fully represented in the recently sold
library of H. Buxton Forman.

53 ANON. "Arno Holz." Athenaeum, no. 4693 (9
April), 490.
Incidental reference to the considerable
influence Whitman has had on Holz's poetry.

54 ANON. Paragraph. Liberator 3 (May), 42.
Calls attention to Whitman's birthday
and the portrait by Boardman Robinson on
p. 4 of this issue.

55 OPPENHEIM, JAMES. "One of Our Sun-Gods."
Dial 68 (May), 633-36.
Review of Bazalgette (1902.2). "Myself"
is praised as "the discovery of a new
continent." Whitman's passages bear up
even under intellectual scrutiny.
Bazalgette's celebration of Whitman is unnecessary, Whitman doing better himself.
Whitman is "last of the great revealers,"
having preceded the psychological stance
prevalent now. Too many merely follow his
footsteps, but we must overcome him to find
ourselves. However, Whitman did contribute
to the mythologizing of himself.

56 DICKINSON, SIDNEY E. "On a Drawing of
Whitman." New York Times (5 May), 10:6.
Letter praising Robinson's portrait
(1920.54), which matches certain passages
in Whitman (quoted).

57 ANON. "Modern American Poetry." Times Literary Supplement (London) (6 May), 277-78.
     America has not produced a new poetic
era, except partially in Whitman, "so
genuinely American, so wholly new and
mainly great in spirit." His influence is
chiefly felt through the free-verse movement, his lesser theoretical side, rather
than through his true poetic inspirations,
when he becomes "a poet and a classic in
spite of himself," most musical and least
free when he deals with "things intimate,
mysterious, and profound." He is "probably
the greatest stirrer of the world's poetic
waters during the last fifty years," but
his poetic liberties may not survive.

58 De CASSERES, BENJAMIN. "Walt Whitman as a
French Critic Sees Him." New York Times
Book Review (9 May), 239.
     Favorable review of Bazalgette (1920.2).
Whitman belongs with the great names, not
as a mythic, miraculous genius but as intensely human, drawing his inspiration from
crowds rather than solitude, not seeking
the admiration of a cult. The French
appreciate Whitman as an American colossus,
part of the elements. Leaves will stand
with Zarathustra as a major monument of the
nineteenth century.

59 ANON. "Parodies." Times Literary Supplement
(London) (20 May), 317.
     Review of Powell (1920.25), quoting
from the admirable Whitman parody.

60 ANON. "To Honor Famous Bard." Chicago Leader
(21 May).
     Account of Whitman fellowship meeting,
quoting letter from Burroughs on Whitman's
qualities as easier found among working men
than among intellectuals; yet he had an
uncommon spirit.

61 M., A. N. "New Books. Fun with the Poets."
Manchester Guardian (24 May), 3:1.
     Review of Powell (1920.25), praising
and quoting the Whitman parody, which
"gains by the wider scope" afforded by
book form than in its earlier published
version (unlocated).

62 ANON. "Whitman Again." Chicago Evening Post
Literary Review (28 May).
     Review of Bazalgette (1920.2), the
definitive book on Whitman. The foreign
perspective conveys "a greater sense of the
reality of Whitman's message" than possible
with an American perspective, which can
perceive the contrast between America as it
is and the America of Whitman's "glowing
postulates and prophecies."

63 PRICE, LAWRENCE MARSEN. "English > German
Literary Influences: Survey." University
of California Publications in Modern
Philology 9 (29 May), 571-76, passim.
     Whitman alone of American poets had a
cult in Germany, although "his admirers
advertised him not wisely but too well."
Freiligrath's endorsement was premature,
since the Germans lacked an acceptance of
Darwinism and socialist ideas, necessary
antecedents to an appreciation of Whitman.
Whitman's major commentators in Germany are
noted. Accompanying bibliography in
1919.42.

64 ALDINGTON, RICHARD. "The Approach to M.
Marcel Proust." English Review 30 (June),
492.
     Incidental: Proust's "sensitiveness,
that habit of mind which can only be described by the misused 'cultured,' is so
intimate, so unforced, and yet so controlled
that the personality disengaged from books
becomes something typical and representative,
an ideal presentation of the best in the
old world, as Whitman, in another sense,
was of the new."

65 ANON. "Hail Walt Whitman as Red." New York
Times (1 June), 26:2.
     Account of Whitman celebration.
Speakers hailed Whitman as "the apostle of
motherhood, universal democracy, true
Americanism and modern radicalism," and as
a probable supporter of Emma Goldman and
Eugene Debs.

*66 NICHOLS, ROBERT. "The League of Friends."
London Daily Herald (10 June).
Reported in Saunders Supplement, but not
located in this issue.
     Review of Paine (1920.23), noting
Whitman's inspiration of the Unanimistes of
France in their encouragement of "unanimity
as humans first between a man and his own
heart's friend, next between a man and a
group, and finally between nation and
nation."

67 [DODDS, M.] "The People's Poet." Toronto
Industrial Banner (11 June).
     Editorial on Whitman as a poet of the
working people, with quotations from his
prose. "Open Raod" is of significance
greater than a mere physical journey for
working people, who can best appreciate his
ideal of a classless society.

*68 ANON. "The Future of British Music: The Need
for Simplicity." Sheffield Independent (16
June).
Quoted in Saunders Supplement.
     Incidental reference to Percival
Garrett's musical setting of "Last Invocation," which attempts more than he can
manage.

*69 ANON. "Music." Cambridge Review (18 June).
Quoted in Saunders Supplement.
     Review of concert performance of Vaughan
Williams's "Sea Symphony," his music "sweeping the gaunt verse of Walt Whitman into
greater heights and further distances."

1920

70 LAWRENCE, D. H. "The Poetry of the Present."
New York Evening Post Book Review (19 June).
Reprint of 1920.17.

71 LOVING, PIERRE. "The Tragedy of Horace
Traubel." New York Evening Post Book
Review (19 June), 6.
Review of Karsner (1919.11), noting
what Traubel has done for Whitman, including
exposing Whitman's "generous budget of
foibles and creaking humanness," to the
displeasure of some Whitman enthusiasts.

72 POWYS, JOHN COWPER. "The Actual Walt Whitman."
New York Evening Post Book Review (19 June),
3.
Emphasis on Whitman's "democratic
humanism" should be placed instead on his
strong sense of individuality, a movement
away from all institutions but the dear
love of comrades. His absolute individualism, apparent in his poetic technique, leads
into a chaos that is "polytheistic and
pluralistic" rather than a pantheistic all-
embracing unity. His verse is no mere
escape from poetic difficulties but is a
complicated system of harmonies with their
own rhythmic law, all elements fitting in.
Whitman is far from demonstrating complete
openness; "that strange mixture of chastity
and passion that characterizes all his
emotional work" remains unexplained. "The
same aristocratic remoteness," "spiritual
anarchy," "suspicion of the authority of
governments," "contempt for the prejudices
of public opinion" appears in all the other
really great Americans and thus may represent the American character more truly than
the assumed "gregarious docility."

73 KUEFFNER, LOUISE M. "The Poet and the City--
A Characteristic Tendency of the Modern
Muse." New York Evening Post Book Review
(19 June).
Whitman was "the first to recognize and
extol the city's larger life," in its
various aspects, particularly its evolutionary inevitability. Later poets, also
discussed, owe their affirmation to Whitman,
but embody only one of these aspects; "no
one has understood the comprehensiveness
of Whitman's scheme."

74 SHAY, FRANK. "Walt Whitman's Publishers."
New York Evening Post Book Review (19 June),
3.
Reprint of 1920.27, Foreword.

75 MONAHAN, MICHAEL. "Re-Readings and Revisions."
Freeman 1 (23 June), 351.
Reprinted with minor changes: 1926.18.
Whitman "is one of the few Immortals
this country has produced," but Traubel
(1906.22, etc.) "has projected a Whitman
who fails utterly to live up to the best
and highest" in Leaves, with "vast ignorance, provincial narrowness, amazing lack
of taste, puerile prejudices and finally,

his inordinate, even fetid, self-conceit."
Monahan hopes that the appreciation of
Whitman's work will not consequently be
hurt.

76 ANON. "Emerson and Whitman. Comparison of
One with the Other Brings Out Interesting
Facts." New York Times (4 July), sec. 1,
8:4.
From Minneapolis Journal (unlocated):
Emerson, though "highbrow," is read by the
people, while "lowbrow" Whitman has an
audience of "'intellectuals,' 'longhairs,'
superior women, English cranks, American
faddists--but nary a lowbrow on his list."

77 ANON. "Our Poets--Robert Frost." Christian
Science Monitor (7 July), 12:6.
Frost carries out Whitman's program as
a poet, his "reticence" contrasted with
Whitman's "loud inclusiveness." Both write
of their familiar country.

78 ANON. "Walt Whitman Home Sold for $600." New
York Times (28 July), 4:4.
Whitman's Camden home was sold to the
city by his heirs for a museum.

79 ANON. "Whitman and Traubel as Prophets
Rejected." Current Opinion 69 (August),
233-36.
We are asked too vehemently to accept
Traubel as well as Whitman, although both
need "not adoration but revaluation."
Translator FitzGerald's need to abridge
Bazalgette (1920.2) exemplifies Whitman's
conflict with the American people.

80 DONOSO, ARMANDO. "The Free Spirit of Walt
Whitman." Inter-America (Eng. ed.) 3
(August), 340-46.
Impressionistic appreciation of Whitman,
presenting him and his work in relation to
his life, emphasizing his exaltation of the
human spirit, his simple life, his fresh
qualities. The war brought out his "epic
accent." American poetry contains nothing
better than "Captain," and his last songs
are perhaps his most stirring.

81 WINTER, JEFFERSON. "As I Remember. Part Two."
Saturday Evening Post 193 (7 August), 38,
40.
These reminiscences of his father,
William Winter, describe his negative
attitudes toward Whitman because of his
indecent treatment of sex and pretentious
use of language. Winter's parody (1860.47)
is printed, according to Jefferson, for the
first time.

82 EMERY, GEORGE M. "Walt Whitman's Ugly Home a
Shrine." Boston Evening Transcript (14
August), sec. 3, 4. Illustrated.
Reprinted in part: 1920.87.
Description of the Camden house in
Whitman's lifetime and now. Whitman's
poetic aim was not mere social and political

democracy, but a "democratic interest in all things human." His treatment of sex cannot cause dismay when taken with his work as a whole, but Anglo-Saxon readers have greater difficulties with the physical contact described in the comradeship poems. His Quaker background led him to trust his intuition and have faith in man as a spiritual being. Whitman remains "the one powerfully original element in American poetry," measuring up to the greatest European poets during his period.

83 ANON. "Latin Praise of Whitman." New York Times (22 August), sec. 2, 2:5.
Editorial on the "lyric enthusiasm, the almost religious fervor" demonstrated by Bazalgette (1920.2) and Donoso (1920.80) in treating Whitman. Much of Whitman must be lost in translation, however, because he is so thoroughly American and colloquial. His rich vocabulary sometimes transcends even the understanding of Americans.

84 HARTWICK, F. GREGORY. "Chant Pagan." Life 76 (26 August), 359.
Reprinted: Saunders.
Parody: "I sing the summer resort."

85 ANON. "Dedicate Giant Rock to 'Walt.'" Toronto Globe (2 September), 20:2.
Account of dedication of Whitman bas-relief on Gibraltar Rock at Bon Echo; quotes the inscription; notes Traubel's appearance there and death.

86 [BROOKS, VAN WYCK.] "A Reviewer's Note-Book." Freeman 2 (15 September), 22.
Paragraph on Whitman, revealed by Traubel (1906.22, etc.) to be "a product of conditions, a victim of complexes," although these do not appear in his work. His personal character, pompous, trivial, complacent, has undergone "a singular transmutation" from life to art, in "a self that has become universal."

87 ANON. "Whitman's Home to Be Preserved as a Literary Shrine." Current Opinion 69 (October), 527-29. Illustrated.
Précis of 1920.82. People persisted in believing Whitman poor despite the claims of his acquaintances that he had enough for his simple tastes. His Camden years are described.

88 HOLLOWAY, EMORY. "Walt Whitman's Love Affairs." Dial 69 (November), 473-83.
Reprinted in part: 1921.16.
A poem written when he was twenty prefigures Whitman's later sexual stance and "Narcissian 'egotism.'" The manuscript change in gender in "Once I Pass'd" prevents its use for supporting the New Orleans romance theory. Whitman is unique among the great poets, with the possible exception of Shakespeare, in his power to shift back and forth between man's and woman's point

of view, like the great religious teachers. But he realized "that such a nature as his would be misunderstood by most men, and that it might even prove dangerous to him." He did experience a major emotional struggle in some love affair in the 1860s, according to various evidence, which is, however, rather conflicting. After this period of struggle, Whitman "has less to say in praise of untrammelled natural impulses," but more to say of democracy, immortality, and the soul.

89 ANON. "Fame." New York Times (9 November), 14:4.
Editorial on why Whitman is not yet in the Hall of Fame: he put his unconventionality on paper rather than merely living it like some of the figures honored there. But he is fairly widely appreciated at home, and much more so abroad than "some of the most distinguished American mediocrities" who have never been heard of in Europe.

90 MARQUIS, DON. "The Sun Dial." New York Sun (10 November), 14:4.
Whitman and Twain do not need the respectable Hall of Fame, which can do nothing for them, "the two most essentially American writers that America has produced, and the two biggest ones."

91 PROHME, WILLIAM. "Walt Whitman and America's Hall of Fame." San Francisco Examiner (12 November), 22.
Having been accepted by the people, Whitman will eventually be recognized by the learned critics for his truly American writing, a "virile verse" distinctly American, with "abundant life" rather than form, like America herself. He pushed beyond mere nonconformity to literary conventions toward a broader nonconformity with the genteel tradition and its puritanical taboos.

92 FLETCHER, JOHN GOULD. "The Puritan Whitman." Literary Review 1 (20 November), 1-2.
Leaves typifies more than any other American work "the fusion of the consciously ethical purpose with the unconscious search for beauty," derived from Whitman's Quaker background, reform-oriented journalism, and aesthetic interests. His poems reveal this perpetual conflict. The sex poems are prime examples of his didacticism, which is greater than Wordsworth's, "because the beauty that he does achieve is obtained without consciously searching for it." The ethical element in Whitman is now the least important.

93 BECKER, MAY LAMBERTON. "Reader's Guide." Literary Review 1 (27 November), 13.
H. S. A. is looking for poems about spiders; the answer notes Whitman's "Spider" as "the most beautiful poem ever written

1920

about a spider, and one of the most beautiful poems ever written."

94 DEUTSCH, BABETTE. Review of Sandburg's Smoke
and Steel. Literary Review 1 (27 November), 6.
Sandburg's similarities to Whitman are
pointed out: "generous sympathy for all
kinds and conditions of men," internatial-
ism, "a Whitmanesque sentimentalism,"
"certain emotional gestures, certain echoing rhythms."

95 CHESTERTON, G. K. "Old King Cole (After Walt
Whitman)." New Witness 16 (10 December), 577.
Reprinted: Saunders.
Parody.

96 KENNEDY, W. S. "Walt Whitman Never Used
Tobacco." Boston Evening Transcript (14
December), 12.
Letter setting the record straight on
Whitman's non-use of tobacco.

97 E[DGETT], E. F. "Masquerades. LX. The
Moralists." Boston Evening Transcript (18
December), sec. 6, 5:4.
Reprinted: Willard.
Brief poem: how will the moralists
respond to the inclusion of Leaves on a
list of books worth reading compiled by the
New York Public Library?

98 BLACK, JOHN. "The Manhattan He Prophesied."
New York Herald Magazine and Books (19
December), 9:6-7.
Enthusiastic personal account of Black's
work with the files of the Eagle preparing
1920.26; how impressed he was with Whitman's
manner of writing exactly as he felt; the
changes in New York since Whitman's time.

99 ROGERS [sic], CLEVELAND. "Walt Whitman's
Prose Issued as a New Book--Poet ad Editor
Before Civil War." New York Herald Magazine and Books (19 December), 9:2-5.
Description of Whitman's journalistic
work as presented in 1920.26, which demonstrates his democratic sentiments and
strong moral sense.

100 ANON. "Whitman in Journeyman Stage." New
York Sun (24 December), 7:3-4.
Review of Gathering (1920.26), which
demonstrates Whitman's fine intelligence,
reasoning ability, and intense awareness of
rights and wrongs, as examples show, and
which makes comprehensible his development.

101 EDGETT, EDWIN FRANCIS. "Walt Whitman as Newspaper Editor." Boston Evening Transcript
(24 December), sec. 4, 4:1-4. Illustrated.
From Gathering (1920.26), traces
Whitman's career with the Eagle, various
factors foreshadowing his later-expressed
democratic interests. But his reading of
great novelists in terms of his democratic
principles is "a false theory of poetry or
of any form of literature."

102 McKILLOP, ALAN D. "The Puritan Whitman."
Literary Review 1 (24 December), 14.
Illustrated by John Storrs, p. 7.
Response to 1920.92: Whitman owes
much of his philosophy to the transcendentalists, who came out of the puritan tradition, but his version of it is vague.

*103 ANON. Article. New York Call (28 December).
Reported in Willard.
Notes George J. Smith reading Emma
Goldman's telegram to the Fellowship.

1921

BOOKS

1 BENSON, E[DWARD] F[REDERIC]. Lovers and
Friends. London: T. Fisher Unwin, pp. 45,
255.
Characters in this novel quote Whitman
and perceive a sculpture head as a symbol
of "that which Whitman sought in his 'Lover
divine and perfect comrade.'"

2 BROWN, STEPHEN J. The Realm of Poetry: An
Introduction. London: George G. Harrap &
Co., pp. 26-27, 35.
Incidental: Whitman is not denied the
name of poet but his work is "hybrid prose."

3 BRUNO, GUIDO. The Sacred Band: A Litany of
In gratitude. New York: Guido Bruno.
"Walt Whitman" Twenty Years After," pp. 25-
30; "Walt Whitman: a German Appreciation
in 1868," pp.42-44.
Reprints of 1919.116 and 1897.84.

4 BURROUGHS, JOHN. Under the Maples. Boston
and New York: Houghton Mifflin Co., pp. 9-
10, 193.
Incidental quotations of Whitman: his
expression "slumbering and liquid trees"
represents "the words of a poet who sees
hidden relations and meanings everywhere"
and "knows how fluid and adaptive all
animate nature is."

5 CHAMBERS, JULIUS. News Hunting on Three Con-
tinents. New York: Mitchell Kennerley,
pp. 303-5.
Chambers published Whitman's "The First
Violet of Spring" (i.e., "The First Dandelion") in the New York Herald on the day of
the 1888 blizzard; Whitman was solicitous
of the ridicule bestowed on Chambers because
of the powers of nature. "No Violets for
Him," a parody by John Russell Young (reprinted: Saunders) from a contemporary
paper, is quoted. A facsimile of a letter
from Whitman about his inability to send
more poems (3 July 1888) is printed.

6 CHARNWOOD, Lord [GODFREY]. "Walt Whitman and
America." In Essays by Divers Hands:
Transactions of the Royal Society of Liter-
ature. n.s. 1. London: Oxford University

Press, pp. 103-23.

Whitman is not the great characteristic American poet English admirers have claimed. He contains much that is adverse to poetry. Although passages display melody, his true poetic sensibility, his observant eye, in general he lacks the poet's requisite of a passion directed to someone besides the "vaguely beloved crowd." "His semirhythmical form is ineffective, tiresome, and absurd." His emphasis on the body and male comradeship is quite unmanly and appeals to those with little actual bodily vigor. After a section dealing with America's essential conservatism and lack of great literary figures, Charnwood presents a postscript dated 1919 to suggest the value still in "Cradle" and "Lilacs," and to correct Whitman's emphasis on American democracy as new. Whitman's contribution lies rather in his love for his country's soul and his vast charity.

7 CLUTTON-BROCK, A[RTHUR]. More Essays on Books. London: Methuen & Co. "Walt Whitman," pp. 1-13.

Whitman differs from "writers of the first order" since one cannot "separate his art from his doctrine." He aims at beauty and philosophy but descends to explanations. His cheerfulness is typically American; beneath the optimism is a great grief which often bursts forth. He is best when honest about himself; then his poems are "nearest in rhythm to ordinary verse." He is "most serious when most musical." "Myself" is an "interesting essay" in which he makes a fool of himself; however, when touched by death, his verse conveys real values. The war poems are best.

8 DAWSON, A. M. P. "Whitman: A Poet of the New Life." In New Life: A Scheme of Study for the Year 1921 for Adult Schools. London: National Adult School Union, pp. 118-34, including bibliography.

Lessons for three Sundays, focusing on the messages of Whitman's poetry. "Biographical Foreword" notes the courage of the committee in devoting these lessons to Whitman rather than to "a poet of less virility, though, doubtless, a sweeter singer," who would not arouse feelings of dislike upon first reading.

1. "The Poet of Personality": Explains Whitman's belief in himself, his predestination theories, his estimate of the personalities which produce national greatness.

2. "The Poet of Comradeship": Friendship for Whitman was not exclusive but directed toward the whole human race, yet still deep and emotional, so vital that he appropriates language "ordinarily confined to 'lovers.'" "There is nothing decadent about Whitman's passionate friendship for his fellows."

3. "The Poet of the Wonder of Life": Whitman's Quaker connections, recogni-

tion of the perpetual wonder of life, democratic sympathies, enthusiastic acceptance of life, belief in perennial inspiration, attitude toward death, joy in a religious aspect, conception of man as pioneer.

Each lesson includes Bible readings, references to Whitman's poetry and other readings and allied subjects, and discussion questions to help incorporate Whitman's teachings into one's life.

9 DELL, FLOYD. The Briary-Bush. New York: Alfred A. Knopf, pp. 192-93, 196.

A clergyman's daughter describes her conversion to paganism through Leaves, which she found on a forbidden books shelf in a library. "Body Electric" 8 with its "uncouth, wonderful lines" was not so much poetry to her as a revelation of her body.

10 GOSSE, EDMUND. Books on the Table. New York: Charles Scribner's Sons. "A Poet among the Cannibals," p. 65.

Records of the Anthropological Society describe a paper read on 17 March 1868, with the subsequent debate in which Swinburne joined, praising Poe and Whitman, the latter "still high in his favour."

11 HARTLEY, MARSDEN. Adventures in the Arts: Informal Chapters on Painters Vaudeville and Poets. New York: Boni & Liveright. "Whitman and Cézanne," pp. 30-36.

Whitman and Cézanne, the "two most notable innovators" in poetry and painting, "the giants of the beginning of the twentieth century," share similar ideals and attitudes toward aesthetic principles, liberating the artist from characteristics not his own, seeking "direct expression out of direct experience." Their attitudes toward life, open and closed respectively, are diametrically opposed. Whitman's inclusiveness was both his virtue and his defect. A Cézanne still-life or landscape reveals "the same gift for life" as Whitman's best pieces, with their "majestic line with its gripping imagery."

12 HARTMANN, SADAKICHI. A Note on the Portraits of Walt Whitman. New York: At the Sign of the Sparrow, 4 pp.

Describes painted and other artistic representations of Whitman, the best likenesses being in the photographs, since the only real painters to depict him produced a portrait inappropriately "genteel and debonair" (Alexander) and "a well painted study head," "a prosaic vision of cheerful stubborness [sic]" (Eakins).

13 HAYES, WILL. Walt Whitman: The Prophet of the New Era. London: C. W. Daniel, n.d., 194 pp. No index.

This explication of Whitman's message as something to be followed uses many quotations and makes frequent reference to other prophets and founders of world religions, especially Christ.

1. "The Christ of Our Age": Whitman
acknowledges the past in advocating a universal, non-ritualistic religion with a
message of love, "a personal and passionate
attachment of man to man, of woman to
woman--and of man to woman."

2. "The Carpenter of Brooklyn": Like
other prophets, Whitman came from humble
people and spoke only after living through
practical existence.

3. "A Sermon on the Mount--of Vision":
Whitman delivers his message from the
heights, as in "Myself."

4. "A Prophet in His Own Country":
Only Thoreau and Lincoln realized Whitman's
greatness; those who criticized him "are
withdrawing to the background." The common
people loved him despite the critics; they
read his poems not on the page but in his
actions.

5. "The City of Friends: Whitman's
'Kingdom of God'": Whitman released
Emerson's gospel from the prison of culture.
He sought to show love as the only religion
necessary.

6. "A Friend of Publicans and Sinners":
Whitman dedicated his work to the unre-
pressed common people whom he understood,
even sinners; they are his true disciples,
though they may not read him.

7. "Many Things--in Parables": Many
of his poems use stories and facts from
nature to convey deeper truths; Hayes re-
titles them in biblical parable fashion.
They emulate nature in their lack of regularity.

8. "The Thought of God": Whitman
found his nobler idea of God in "the Great
Comrade" of "Passage," "the Parable of
Divine Unity."

9. "Signs from Heaven": Whitman saw
God's messages and miracles everywhere.

10. "The Disciples--and the Dinner
Basket": Whitman's disciples quibble over
details when they should be concerned with
his gospel, greater than Christ's.

11. "Yourself, For Ever and Ever!":
Like Christianity, Whitman stresses the
kingdom within rather than without, urging
that one be true to oneself.

12. "The Wound-Dresser": Like the
great miracle-makers, Whitman provided a
healing influence through his life as well
as his poetry, recognizing the reconciliation in death.

13. "The World View": His poetry
embraces the whole world, viewing it as
one, with a glowing future. America in
"Thou Mother" symbolizes the world.

14. "The Flag of Man: Hours Prophetic":
He combines individual equality with comradeship as the basis of the new democracy.

15. "Changes of Garments": His ability to put himself in another's place enabled him to write of the inner life of a
vast diversity of people. He saw beneath
the surface.

16. "The Least of These My Brethren":
His sympathy extended to animals, children,
lunatics, sinners, and "the younger races."

17. "The Veiled Glory": He saw the
body's necessity for the whole life: sexual matters may be veiled, as Whitman himself has done "behind much beautiful
imagery," "but let that veiling be because
of their transcendent glory, not as in the
past because of some fancied ugliness."

18. "Ye Downcast Hours: A Soul Ex-
ceeding Sorrowful": Despite moments of
doubt, like other prophets, he always renewed his faith in himself.

19. "Sailing the Seas of God: The
Task Eternal": He is a pioneer and "in-
spirer of pioneers," urging on "to newer,
better worlds."

20. "Songs of Parting": His spirit of
comradeship will ever remain with the world.

14 HECHT, BEN. Erik Dorn. New York and London:
G. P. Putnam's Sons, p. 340.
In this novel, Landerdauer "the Whitman
translator" is announced as minister of
education in Germany.

15 HIND, C. LEWIS. Authors and I. London and
New York: John Lane. "Walt Whitman,"
pp. 312-17.
Reprint of 1919.196.

16 HOLLOWAY, EMORY, ed. Preface and introduction
(biographical and critical) to The Uncollected Poetry and Prose of Walt Whitman.
Garden City, N.Y., and Toronto: Doubleday,
Page & Co., pp. ix-xcii.
Biographical section emphasizes
Whitman's early years, placing the early
poetry, fiction, and journalism in appropriate context. Included are recollections
of Whitman from Ellen Calder (an unpublished
passage from her article, 1907.37, regarding
his love for a married woman in Washington)
and the daughter-in-law of James Brenton,
on whose paper Whitman worked as a young
man and with whose family he lived. His
political, religious, and journalistic
ideas are explained. His style was "fresher
and dealt with more important journalistic
matter than was to be found in the pages of
any Brooklyn contemporary." Evidence for
his Southern romance is examined; "Once I
Pass'd" was originally written about a man.
His poetry requires a slipping back and
forth between the man's and the woman's
point of view. The development of his
ideas and literary style and skill is
traced; Leaves was the inevitable outcome
of his poetic progress and journalistic
style, with "great increase of terseness
and rhythm" from his early notes. Influences are described; likewise his view of
the editor's function, his subjects, criticism, poetic mission. Material from 1920.
88 is reprinted. Extensive notes throughout the two volumes indicate original publication place and date, provide identifi-

cations, and suggest parallels with his later work.

17 HUNEKER, JAMES GIBBONS. Variations. New York: Charles Scribner's Sons, pp. 13, 24, 59, 61, 127, 134.

People read Leaves for the erotic element. Huneker's visit to Whitman in 1877 and his change from being "an ardent Whitmaniac" are described. Whitman is a "disruptive force" and remains so, as evident in the "lascivious caterwaulings" of the new school, which are due to Whitman's initiative in "Adam." (Includes material from 1919.359.)

18 JOHNSON, LIONEL. Reviews and Critical Papers. New York: E. P. Dutton & Co., p. 108.

Le Gallienne's poetry has "a frank zest and lust of life in it, the better spirit of Whitman."

19 KELLER, ELIZABETH LEAVITT. Walt Whitman in Mickle Street. New York: Mitchell Kennerley, 227 pp. Illustrated. Index. Includes reprint of 1919.116.

Editor's note by Charles Vale describes Mrs. Keller. She sketches Mrs. Davis's early life and acquaintance with Whitman, who neglected to pay for household expenses and insisted on his own way, although always treating Mrs. Davis as an equal, unlike many of his later friends. His last illness, nursed by Mrs. Keller and Warren Fritzinger, is described. In concentrating on the domestic rather than literary aspects of Whitman's life, she attempts to correct certain misconceptions promulgated in print, especially regarding Mrs. Davis. The book expands upon her article, 1909.29.

20 MATHEWS, GODFREY W. Walt Whitman: Being the Substance of Three Lectures Delivered to the Liscard Adult School. Liverpool: Daily Post Printers, 57 pp.

"Walt Whitman": He is a universal rather than endemic writer. His poetry accurately records his environment and experience. Account of his life; the Civil War was its turning-point, though not apparent in his poetry, which does not reveal his mental development.

"Method and Style": Specimen is his best prose. His greatest fault is erratic punctuation, though it works well in the poetry. Close examination of his prose style reveals the secret of his poetic form. His purpose was to arrest public attention; his avoidance of conventions was effective, harmonizing method and manner. No poet "ever sought beauty less" and still achieved it. He appeals chiefly to the intellect, therefore losing the masses.

"Prophet": He was not a logical thinker and probably did not himself understand his reasoning, yet he remains scientific rather than emotional. Transcendental influence on Whitman is hard to determine.

"Sex Poems": With a wider range of subjects than any poet, Whitman is never immoral but "sometimes indecent." He writes of "healthy sex," showing that evil exists only in relation. His own sex life was probably active. He deserted his six children because he was involved "with a highly placed lady of New York," whose people insisted that the paternity of her children not be known. "Calamus" made critics arraign him for sodomy; his subject is a dangerous one; his pictures of contact between men are his means of portraying affection between men; the general interpretation is that he was trying to spiritualize the love of man for man. The ideas of Carpenter's Intermediate Sex (1908.6) are "entirely foreign to Whitman's thought." He does not deal with female comradeship but implies it.

"Religion": Many sects claim Whitman. His philosophy has two poles: law applies to natural phenomena; love is "the regenerating force of the human race, the motive power of Democracy" dramatized in Whitman's poetry but never explained or related to the concept of law. He is more poet than philosopher.

"Democracy": In Leaves, democracy seems close to anarchy, although Whitman only means equality of opportunity. In his prose, democracy is related to his religious philosophy as the working out of a universal law. He never pretended to construct a social philosophy, though his poetry glorifies industry, portrays woman as man's equal, urges physical fitness.

"Self": Whitman's egotism is never divorced from imagination or sympathy. The role of the poet is to lift men to higher levels; thus Whitman is not a "leveller." His lack of direct influence is "the price of the method he adopted." He will probably not rank among the immortals.

21 MORDELL, ALBERT. The Literature of Ecstasy. New York: Boni & Liveright, pp. 12, 15, 23, 31, 44, 45, 63, 65, 79-80, 114, 116, 117-18, 124, 142, 154, 159, 164, 165, 175, 176, 178.

Whitman is among the greatest critics of poetry in English. "He brought poetry back to rhythmical prose, and is the greatest liberator poetry has ever had." He fathered modern free verse but did not claim to have originated it, merely restoring an older form. He overdid his demand for distinctly American poetry; a great idea from "Myself" or the sympathetic note of "Cradle" is human, universal, rather than merely American. But he was the first to embody American political ideals in poetry.

22 MORLEY, CHRISTOPHER. Plum Pudding. Garden City, N.Y.: Doubleday, Page & Co. "Fulton Street, and Walt Whitman," pp. 57-62.

Record of visits to Brooklyn scenes associated with Whitman's life, with quotations from his prose, "one of the most neglected of American classics." His judgments on literature revealing "complacent naïveté, " he needs to be forgiven more than any other great writer. Examples of his humor are noted.

23 NEVINSON, HENRY W. Essays in Freedom and Rebellion. New Haven: Yale University Press; London: Humphrey Milford, Oxford University Press. "The Voice of America," pp. 100-107.

Whitman alone of American writers has fulfilled the expectation of a fresh and vital revelation coming out of America, instead of Old World views. His vision of America emphasized nature and man in nature. He recognized modern life, the reality of war (the first poet to do so, in Drum-Taps). He combined democracy, "an equality of spirit," with individuality, "the fulfillment of the personal soul."

24 NEWTON, A. EDWARD. A Magnificent Farce and Other Diversions of a Book-Collector. Boston: Atlantic Monthly Press. "Walt Whitman," pp. 140-59; also 37-39. Illustrated.

Whitman, whom anyone in Philadelphia of any literary taste used to affect to know, "has not yet come into his own," but he shall, although the controversy is still evident in a denigrating letter quoted. A poet only in the sense that he was a prophet, Whitman lacked taste, humor, aptness of phrase. Personal reminiscences of Whitman; description of first edition and other bibliographic items and their later histories. A Whitman manuscript about the 1860 edition and Worthington's reissue of it is printed. Whitman was interested in the future rather than the past. "His literary judgments and pronouncements were frequently foolish." Newton prints a facsimile of a Whitman manuscript which he used as a Christmas card in 1907.

25 NOGUCHI, YONE. Japan and America. Tokyo: Keio Universtiy Press; New York: Orientalia, pp. 29, 40, 51-59, 68, 75-76.

Notes Japanese appreciation of Whitman. The Declaration of Independence, Lincoln, and Whitman represent the country's inner vision. Whitman sang idealism, as an individual yet also as one of the divine average, whose right America may now be denying. He perhaps followed the idealism of the past "too reminiscentically." Whitman, "that extraordinary personage of contradiction, that interesting mixture of dreamer and propagandist," exemplifies the best of America's men. His European fame rests on "his universal idealism touched to distinction by his provincialism."

26 OMOND, T. S. English Metrists: Being a Sketch of English Prosodical Criticism from Elizabethan Times to the Present Day.

Oxford: Oxford University Press, pp. 168-69, 308.
Includes reprint of 1907.8.
Adds chronological listing at back, including Whitman.

27 OVERTON, GRANT. The Answerer. New York: Harcourt, Brace & Co., 373 pp.
Novelization of Whitman's life.
"Part One: A Miracle in Fifth Month": In the spring of 1840 Whitman is shown in relationship with young men to whom he feels an attraction which includes the physical; with a girl he considers marrying after much intellectual consideration of love; with Melville, met by chance, with whom he talks about love and finding one's self; with Margaret Fuller, also met by chance, with whom he discusses Emerson. He appears as an incipient poet, expressing his ideas, impressions, and experiences in phrases and lines from his poems. The birth of "Cradle" is described.
"Part Two: Gulf Stream": In New Orleans, 1848, Whitman forms a relationship with a married Creole woman; learns of Hegel's ideas from a German named Traubel; carefully composes the passages dealing with the runaway slave and the black team-driver ("Myself"); discovers his true poetic form after writing "The Mississippi at Midnight," leaving New Orleans because he has discovered his poetic mission, writing "Once I Pass'd" for the woman left behind.
"Part Three: Dark Mother": In December 1862 Whitman learns of his brother's wound while spending the evening at the O'Connors' home in Washington. He is seen in the hospitals, again attracted to young men. Through his friendship with John Hay, he meets Lincoln who tells him about reading Leaves in his law office (as in Rankin, 1916.17) and narrates a dream about being on a ship. In a second conversation, they exchange stories about the women they early loved and were parted from.
"Part Four: The Answerer": In 1865 Whitman learns about Lincoln's death while in Brooklyn. The composition of "Lilacs" is described as memorializing Lincoln as well as the long-ago moment when Whitman lost the woman he was hoping to marry.

28 RICHARDSON, DOROTHY M. Deadlock. New York: Alfred A. Knopf, p. 22.
A Russian in this novel says: "I know also of course their great poet, Vitmann."

29 SALT, HENRY S. Seventy Years Among Savages. London: George Allen & Unwin, pp. 96, 106-7, 111, 113.
Notes Rossetti's introduction of Whitman to England; Swinburne's negative criticism and Whitman's indignation; Bertram Dobell's strange plan "to re-write Whitman's poems in the Omar Khayyám stanza."

30 SANDBURG, CARL. Introduction to Leaves of
Grass. The Modern Library. New York:
Boni & Liveright, pp. iii-xi.
Abridged: 1926.74.
 Leaves is "the most peculiar and noteworthy monument" in American literature in
regard to style, critics' treatment, personality, scope, literary rank abroad, influence in America, Americanism. The first
two editions are described, with critical
response. Whitman is a challenger, his
most vital work being done during "America's
most stormily human period." The qualities
of his major poems are described; title
changes are noted. Some poems like "Myself"
rank with the masterpieces of world literature. His lines (quoted) speak to the
simplest understanding.

31 SAUNDERS, HENRY S., ed. Introduction to A
Whitman Controversy: Being Letters Published in Mercure de France 1913-1914.
Toronto: Henry S. Saunders, 48 pp. Index.
Limited typed edition.
 Prints letters and responses, as translated by a friend, regarding the question
of Whitman's homosexuality, difficult to
resolve since there is a partial basis in
fact, although those who want to prove homosexuality in him rely on one-sided interpretations. The controversy begins with a
letter by Apollinaire (1 April 1913) quoting
an anonymous eyewitness at Whitman's funeral,
to which "pederasts came in crowds," with
much rowdy activity described. Stuart
Merrill retorts, defending Whitman as "the
most normal man in the world." The subsequent controversy involves Benjamin
De Casseres, Bazalgette, and Merrill denying
Whitman's homosexuality; Harrison Reeves
and Bertz citing Whitman's work and testimony from unnamed people who knew Whitman,
asserting his homosexuality. Other letters
are included from Apollinaire and Schinz.

32 SQUIRE, J. C. Life and Letters: Essays by
J. C. Squire. London: William Heinemann;
New York: Doran, n.d. "Walt Whitman,"
pp. 196-202.
Reprint of 1920.28.

33 UNTERMEYER, LOUIS. Modern American Poetry.
Rev. and enlarged ed. New York: Harcourt,
Brace & Co. "Walt Whitman," pp. xx-xxiv;
passim throughout introduction.
Revision of 1919.23. Reprinted: 1925.14.
Revised: 1930.21; 1936.28.
 Whitman is "our great poetic emancipator" in form and in "a wider aspect of
democracy" and of nature, with a great
belief in life, celebrating not so much
himself but rather the ordinary man. The
qualities of Whitman's major poems are
described. He did not scorn the past. His
influence on recent poets is noted.

PERIODICALS

34 CLARK, GRACE DELANO. "Walt Whitman in Germany."
Texas Review 6 (January), 123-37.
 Survey of the wide range of German
appreciation and interpretation of Whitman.
Germans regard his philosophy as fundamentally German, in its subjective genius and
its specific derivation from Kant and
Hegel. Appreciation of him grew slowly
until the increase in realism of the 1890s.
Comments on translations, critics, imitators. Most follow Schlaf's nonscholarly
enthusiasm. Bertz's view, not widely
accepted, "robs him of all virility"
through pathological analysis; an acceptance
of Bertz would mean relinquishing belief in
Whitman as a human brother with deeper insight into our common humanity.

35 SHERMAN, STUART P. "The National Genius."
Atlantic Monthly 127 (January), 8, 9.
Reprinted: 1923.15; Hubbell.
 Incidental references to the importance
for Whitman of the influence of an "environ-
ing spirit" of "profound moral idealism,"
and his overstated "hate" of literature.

36 WEEKS, RUTH MARY. "Phrasal Prosody." English
Journal 10 (January), 11-19.
 Examination of Whitman's work reveals
the basis of free-verse prosody. His
style is purposeful, as evident in the two
styles of "The Singer in Prison"; his
mannerisms may be ignored. "His rhythmic
unit is the vocal wave," sometimes over the
course of parallel stanzas ("The Last
Invocation"), more commonly in phrases
which reveal his fusion of the pitch
patterns of prose with the stress patterns
of poetry. Analysis of the metrics of
"Whispers," "As a Strong Bird," "Brooklyn
Ferry."

37 EGAN, MAURICE FRANCIS. "When Whitman Was
Editor." New York Times Book Review and
Magazine (2 January), 2, 15. Illustrated.
 Review of Gathering (1920.26). The
usual criticisms have a share of truth, but
Whitman is becoming an important figure.
Whitman "was compact of prejudices, but
these prejudices were founded on his love
of liberty." The early works in Gathering
"reveal his soul as it grew" and present
him in a more conventional mode than usual.
His opinions are analyzed from these newspaper writings. Rodger's introduction is
more reasoned than Black's impressionistic
praise.

38 JOURNEYMAN [pseud.]. "Miscellany." Freeman
2 (5 January), 398-99.
 Photographs at the National Arts Club
in New York could serve as appropriate
illustrations for "Song for Occupations,"
exemplifying a Whitmanesque spirit, "his
belief in a free democracy, with his quench-
less faith in joy and health and that far

1921

off divine event toward which his whole
creation moved."

39 ANON. "Answers. From Walt Whitman." Montreal
Star (15 January), 12.
 Letter from reader asks for the significance of the number twenty-eight in
"Myself" 11. Mildred Bain replies: Leaves
has many hidden meanings, but the surface
cannot be separated from what is underlying; in this instance, the number is
either to present a clear-cut picture or
to report an actual scene.

40 ANON. "Walt Whitman as Journalist." New York
Tribune (23 January), sec. 7, 9.
 Review of Gathering (1920.26). These
writings express Whitman's "big, generous,
warm-hearted personality," his "tonic and
exhilarating" faith in America and democracy, his sense of justice and optimism,
his earnestness. His sympathies and idea
of American democracy (not excluding im-
perialism) are described. "His theory of
government is libertarian in the extreme."
Much of his editorial comment is "amazingly
up to date."

41 ANON. "An Artist Who Celebrates Wright and
Whitman." Current Opinion 70 (February),
245-47. Illustrated.
 On artist John Storrs, printing his
illustration for "Myself."

42 ERVINE, ST. JOHN. "American Literature: Now
and To Be, Part One." Century Magazine
101 (February), 460-66.
 Incidental: America has produced one
poet, Whitman, "who is very nearly on the
level of supreme genius." He may be to
America what Chaucer was to England, "the
great forerunner of a great race of giants."
The America of Whitman's day was more homogeneous than today's; major writers had a
common Anglo-Saxon background. Concluded:
1921.47.

43 WOLFENSTEIN, ALFRED. "The New German Literature." Literary Review 1 (5 February), 7.
 Incidental reference in discussion of
Stefan George: "A manly love, of the
noblest and most intellectual sort, ir-
radiates his work; an emotion, not robust,
cosmic, unrestrained as in Walt Whitman,
whose democratic instinct loved all humanity
in each individual, but the fine flower of
a highly individualistic talent."

44 ANON. "Phoebus with Admetus." Times Literary
Supplement (London) (10 February), 88.
 Review of Gathering (1920.26), of value
only "for the light it throws on the
psychology of the artist, for Whitman
became an artist only when he escaped from
his editorship." His literary criticisms
are feeble, his political stances chauvin-
istic and sometimes inconsistent, as any
editor's often are. Fortunately he broke

away to proclaim his independence of
thought and form. His predominant virtue,
generosity, is evident here, but "not expressed yet in language worthy of it."

45 O., S. "The Great Railway Ramp." Nation and
Athenaeum 28 (19 February), 689.
 Reprinted: Saunders.
 A five-line parody on railway abuses,
"Profiteers, O profiteers!," ends this
article.

46 ANON. "Walt Whitman as an Old-Fashioned Conservative." Current Opinion 70 (March),
383-85. Illustrated.
 Review of Gathering (1920.26).
Whitman's Eagle editorials are "surprisingly
old-fashioned," coming not from a revolutionary but from "a hundred per cent.
American." Evidences of Whitman's warm
heart and libertarian sentiment are noted;
also his ideas on morality and literature.

47 ERVINE, ST. JOHN. "American Literature: Now
and To Be, Part Two." Century Magazine
101 (March), 575.
 Concludes 1921.42. Incidental: Given
that "a work of genius is both the expression of a rich and rare individuality and
the expression, through that rich and rare
individuality, of a great race," Whitman's
poems could only have been written by him,
and only by him as an American.

48 WOOLCOTT, ALEXANDER. "Walt Whitman--Dramatic
Critic." Bookman 53 (March), 75-77.
 Review of Gathering (1920.26). The
editors fail to mention two reasons for the
neglect of this material: "that the stuff
was hardly worth the labor involved in its
exhumation or, more positively, that its
republication would be a distinct disservice
to the reputation of a great name." There
is occasional writing here "that was wholesome and brave and characteristic and
prophetic," but Whitman is largely a typical
newspaperman of the day, not too praiseworthy. His dramatic criticism is cited as
evidence of the theater's state several
generations ago.

49 HARRIS, LYNN H. "Walt Whitman as Artist and
Teacher." South Atlantic Quarterly 20
(April), 120-36.
 Thorough consideration of Whitman's
style and themes. He seldom shows "sustained powers of diction," but his music
and diversified, subtle rhythms sometimes
surpass the poetry of his precursors.
"Cradle" and "Lilacs," his highest artistry,
solve death's mystery by means of the
"intimate and spiritual use of Nature."
Unlike other poets, who are less modest
though not usually considered egotistical,
Whitman's frank use of the first person
"openly announces that his views are personal merely," while imagining in himself
all other people, as in "One Hour," his

one example of "moral revolt." His treatment of death, more acceptable to modern readers than to those of his day, transcends that of other modern poets; also strong are his view of all men's divinity, equality, and brotherhood, the necessity of evil, and the reciprocal relations of body and soul. His war service atones for any personal frailties. As an artist, he is great in spirit but imperfect in expression, though this is mainly intentional. His noble teachings surpass those of other American poets. Though failing to reach the proletariat because of his form, he remains "America's truest interpreter."

50 BRIGHAM, JOHNSON. "Johnson Brigham Recalls Meetings and Correspondence with John Burroughs." Des Moines Sunday Register (10 April).

Prints his correspondence with Burroughs, concerning Whitman and Brigham's own early objections to Whitman's "inexcusably frank glorification of animal passion" until he appreciated Whitman for his soul's qualities. He describes his attempts to discover from Burroughs Whitman's attitude toward Harlan, against whom Burroughs continued to feel resentment.

51 ATKINSON, J. BROOKS. "Walt Whitman's Democracy." Freeman 3 (13 April), 106-8.

American critics have merely echoed foreign estimates of Whitman as "the poet of democracy," a title more appropriate to Bryant, Riley, or Longfellow; American democracy has not risen to Whitman's breadth of vision, tolerance, and sympathy. He favored the average over the cultivated, not realizing that they too could share "the stouter qualities of manhood." His followers imitate, while Whitman created. He was a poor journalist with little understanding of the classics, but he had the rare qualities of being "untamed, courageous, observant, honest."

52 ANON. Brief review of Gathering (1920.26). Dial 70 (May), 593.

This book is poorly put together, by journalists, not scholars. But the Whitman material presented will be welcomed by students of him and of various aspects of American history and culture.

53 FLETCHER, JOHN GOULD. "Walt Whitman's Beginnings." Freeman 3 (4 May), 188.

Review of Gathering (1920.26). Whitman is accepted internationally but still unappreciated in America. His era provided no justification for his optimism and faith, yet Leaves remains a "monument to great religious faith" like other major poems. Another Whitman is unlikely to arise. His journalism reveals little that is new but may revive interest in his poetry's message of individual faith and individual rebellion against law. In literary theory he followed

Poe, in self-reliance Emerson, in rebellion Thoreau. Leaves was produced because Whitman was ripe for the times and the times were ripe for him.

54 [BROOKS, VAN WYCK.] "A Reviewer's Notebook." Freeman 3 (18 May), 238-39. Reprinted: 1932.5.

Though great, Whitman has produced a negative influence, like other great artists. His diagnosis of our society and description of our literature in Vistas remain true. Present literature "takes its character largely from him," though not progressing to the results he desired. His refusal to make distinctions sets a disastrous precedent. If he had not been stricken by paralysis, he might have passed to a second stage, providing our literature with greater depth and elevation to join its ample spontaneity.

55 HIER, FREDERICK P. "The Sources of Walt Whitman." New York Call Magazine (29 May), 6.

A fanciful account of Whitman's escape to Long Island after publishing 1855 Leaves, "different from all other books in the world, the combined complete expression of Adamic man and a cosmic dream." He questioned his poetic enterprise during his three-month stay at Peonic Bay, coming back reassured and confirmed by his "recontact with the earth-mother." His personality, as evidenced in his work, is described. He was not always the hearty comrade but was often lonely and self-contained.

56 FOERSTER, NORMAN. "Whitman and the Cult of Confusion." North American Review 213 (June), 799-812. Reprinted: 1923.5.

Whitman was a necessary breath of fresh air, fittingly recognized first by the transcendentalists, though Whitman's unity differed from that of Emerson. While Emerson helps us transcend our inner confusion, Whitman accepts and worships it. His "romantic dualism of conformity and individualism, externality and inwardness," is sound but does not reveal the innermost self. He responded to nature with wonder, reverie, and love. His devotion to the soldiers is not quite spiritual but "merely gregarious sympathy in a human form." He lacked the discipline necessary for spiritual vision. Adhesiveness is his means to the ultimate goal of individuality, which he could not reconcile with his gospel of solidarity. His religion is "a mass of ill-sorted ideas," thus making him less valuable for today than Emerson or Lincoln. His energy and drive breathe into our literature "the sanity of nature like no one else since Wordsworth."

57 THOMAS, PHILIP. "Walt Whitman's America." Positivist Review 29 (June), 121-24.

1921

Whitman is "a mendicant of the ideal," like St. Francis's followers. He turned the world's prose into poetry, as in his hospital work, though many call him a materialist. His splendid vision of the future is clear, as in "Thou Mother." His feeling for America, permeating his works, is in "the true Positivist spirit." Positivists must recognize him and his philosophy.

58 ANON. "Walt Whitman Dinner." New York Times (1 June), 16:7.

Speakers at the Whitman Society dinner are quoted on Whitman's greatness, though he is ignored by the Hall of Fame, and on his influence abroad.

59 ANON. "The Whitman Dinner." Chicago Evening Post Literary Review (3 June).

Whitman is emphasized today as democrat rather than poet, with a gospel of "letting everyone have a fair chance" without spiritual or fiscal restrictions. Charles Edward Russell's letter, read at the Chicago dinner, named "Captain" the closest thing to a good poem Whitman wrote. This editorial writer disagrees: it is far from being in the same class with Whitman's best poems.

60 ANON. "Book Chat." Freethinker 41 (5 June), 363.

Paragraph review of Hayes (1921.13), "an enthusiastic, if a little over-strained, study of the poet's message to humanity." Whitman does not need to be made a proponent of an actual religion to be appreciated; the feelings he arouses can be reached through the poetry itself without "his so-called ethical message" revealed by his expounders.

61 BECKER, MAY LAMBERTON. "Reader's Guide." Literary Review 1 (9 July), 13.

In response to a letter from R. C. asking for good descriptions of music in literature, three lines from "Occupations" are cited as the second best description. "Whitman's long poem, 'Proud Murmurs [sic] of the Storm,' is peculiarly good for impressions of tone-color."

62 LAWRENCE, D. H. "Whitman." Nation and Athenaeum 29 (23 July), 616-18. Reprinted: Miller; Murphy; Bradley/ Blodgett.

"Whitman is the greatest of the Americans," having "gone further, in actual living expression, than any man." His vast sense of oneness and identity with all fails to acknowledge the necessary opposite movement, away from merging. He opens a new field of living in portraying "the pure sensual body of man." He reduces woman to the maternal function, choosing rather to penetrate beyond race continuance to "sheer, ultimate being, the perfection of life,

nearest to death," in the polar relationship between man and man, which Whitman alone of all moderns has known positively. He depicts this mystery gravely, hesitantly, in "Calamus," revealing his deepest self. This is his cohering principle for "the men of a pure creative nation," with marriage and comradeship equal in his new era. Americans have not yet accepted his truth. His verse springs "from the spontaneous sources of his being" portrayed in its wholeness. (Only a small portion of this article is used in Studies, 1923.9.)

63 ANON. "Visit to Walt Whitman's Birthplace." State Service 5 (August), 372-76. Illustrated.

Describes extensively, from a visit on 31 May 1919, Whitman's birthplace house, the surrounding region, his grandfather's house, the Woodbury schoolhouse where he taught in 1838, the Rome printing office site in Brooklyn.

64 ANON. "'The Good Grey Poet.' Walt Whitman: The Man and His Message." Workers at Home and Abroad 17 (August), 123-24.

Enthusiastic appreciation covering Whitman's major themes: universal function of first person, democratic message, Christlike sympathy, comradeship, religion centered on life and man with death "but an episode in life," beautiful as in "that exquisite poem," "Lilacs."

65 CARRINGTON, C. E. H. "New Life. Whitman: A Poet of the New Life." One and All 32 (August), 119-20.

Defends the reading of Whitman's poetry as part of the Adult School program for this summer; explains the lessons in Dawson (1921.8). He should be judged not by individual lines or by his "crude mannerisms," but by his cumulative influence on one's inner life. He invests the word "friendship" with a noble, virile meaning; he asks people not to stifle affection. His spirit of joy and wonder will be imbibed by readers.

66 HAYES, WILL. "Quaker Traits in Walt Whitman." One and All 32 (August), 110, 121.

Whitman's Quaker elements included his belief that all were his equals, "essentially divine" and with purpose; love of simplicity; freedom from passionate grief; unconventionalism; belief in free speech; rejection of religious authority; deep religious feeling; condemnation of war; insistence on the authority of the inner light.

67 PORTERFIELD, ALLEN WILSON. "Foreign Notes and Comment: What Makes a Translation?" Bookman 53 (August), 561-63.

Includes favorable comment on Max Hayek's German translation of Leaves, although he has difficulties with some of Whitman's strange words and colloquialisms.

68 WILLIAMS, GWEN. "Walt Whitman. The Laureate of Democracy." One and All 32 (August), 109-10. Photograph.

An introductory appreciation, describing Whitman's themes and method, based on inspiration as is biblical poetry. His poetry reveals himself and the reader's self. He emphasized the importance of the individual's personality, identified with all. His religion and democracy are explained. Those having difficulty with his form should first read "Lilacs."

69 FIRKINS, O. W. "Whitman Journalist." Weekly Review 5 (6 August), 127.

Review of Gathering (1920.26), which disproves the accounts of Whitman's laziness as a journalist. The ordinariness of these writings and of Whitman as a man at that time suggests the size of the jump he made into originality. He wrote "a nefarious English." The spirit of help these editorials offer for social problems seems more moving than the broad, "rather fulsome benevolence" of Leaves. Whitman's attitudes are explained. The editors have been careless in transcribing from the originals.

70 O'LONDON, JOHN. "London Book Talk." New York Times Book Review and Magazine (28 August), 27:1.

Discussion of Lawrence (1921.62), who is apparently uncomfortable with Whitman's passion for all things and his "radiating sympathy with the universe," because Lawrence believes in the individuality of every soul.

71 SHERMAN, STUART P. "What Is a Puritan?" Atlantic Monthly 128 (September), 355.
Reprinted: 1923.15.

Incidental: "Emerson hailed Walt Whitman because Whitman had sought to make splendid and beautiful the religion of a Puritan democracy."

72 DAVENPORT, W. E. "Dante and Whitman." Brooklyn Daily Eagle (14 September), 6:5.

Poem to Whitman's latter-day admirers, on the anniversary of Dante's death, in rhymed quatrains: both poets were rejected while alive but are now accepted in each other's countries after death.

73 LANUX, PIERRE de. "As a Frenchman Sees It." Literary Review 2 (24 September), 33-34.

Incidental discussion, in this examination of the future of American literature, of Vistas and the contemporary quality of Whitman's criticisms and prophecies.

74 BENET, WILLIAM ROSE. "Amy Lowell and Other Poets." Yale Review 11 (October), 177.

Review of books by Lowell and by Fletcher, who admires Whitman. Benét claims never to have been able to read or tolerate Whitman, "a great, intensely talkative personality."

75 [HARTWELL, RICHARDSON, and DRIVER, architects.] "Whitman Memorial, Mount Auburn Cemetary, Cambridge, Mass." Architectural Forum 35 (October), 151, Plate 57.
Reported in Allen.

This memorial has nothing to do with Walt Whitman.

76 HOLLOWAY, EMORY. "Whitman as Journalist." Yale Review 11 (October), 212-15.

Review of Gathering (1920.26), refusing to comment on its editorial craftsmanship because of his own volumes in the press discussing Whitman's journalism. It is "a helpful source-book" for discovering the poetry's long foreground. The many aspects of life Whitman observed as a newspaper man contributed to his poetry and quickened his "humanitarian sympathy for all classes of men." Having to write about what he observed with his insatiable curiosity "developed in him that sense of the real which serves so well to balance his otherwise too transcendental mysticism."

77 RODGERS, CLEVELAND. "Old Notebook, Just Discovered, Shows Walt Whitman Began 'Leaves of Grass' While Editor of The Eagle in 1847." Brooklyn Daily Eagle Magazine (6 November), 2. Photograph.

Favorable review of Uncollected (1921.16), tracing Whitman's early career, noting the unpromising nature of his early prose and poetry and his "indolent, self-centered" character at that time.

78 BOYNTON, H. W. "A Story of Whitman and His World." Independent and Weekly Review 107 (26 November), 218-19.

Review of Overton (1921.27). Having assimilated Whitman's character and experience, Overton conveys the "Whitmanian mood of mystical exaltation" in his style, not stooping to "the jaunty vernacular or the conscientious humdrum of current usage."

79 [BROOKS, VAN WYCK.] "A Reviewer's Notebook." Freeman 4 (14 December), 334-35.
Revised: 1932.5.

Vistas remains a contemporary message, though Whitman failed to foresee America's developments in urban and other directions. We cannot share today his notions of manifest destiny and shallow utopianism. The value of Vistas lies in Whitman's "incomparable style" and "feeling for the creative life." The state of America since his writing has not advanced, nor have Whitman's "heroic bards" arrived.

80 PERRY, BLISS. "Whitman Under the Searchlight." New York Times Book Review (25 December), 8. Illustrated.

Review of Uncollected (1921.16), which clears up many unknown areas. These works do not add to Whitman's literary reputation, but the editorials help to show his attitudes toward American life in the 1840s and

1850s. He celebrated the future destiny of America in "high, astounding terms." There is little trace of literary distinction or mastery of prose. There is material here for the "pathologist" also, in the note-books' portrayal of a "'sick soul,' struggling lamentably for mastery over itself."

81 [BROOKS, VAN WYCK.] "A Reviewer's Notebook." *Freeman* 4 (28 December), 382-83.

Review of Bazalgette (1920.2), Keller (1921.19), *Uncollected* (1921.16), Overton (1921.27). *Uncollected* is more interesting than *Gathering* (1920.26), revealing Whitman as "far more of a literary man" than supposed, with evidence of Whitman's wide reading. Keller's "extraordinary picture" of Whitman in his old age shows "the greatest writer of the Western hemisphere" "reduced to knocking for his breakfast"; though not sentimental, it brings the reader to "a higher opinion of Whitman than ever."

1922

BOOKS

1 BAILEY, ELMER JAMES. *Religious Thought in the Greater American Poets*. Boston: Pilgrim Press. "Walt Whitman," pp. 183-228; also 6, 230, 232-33, 238, 240, 241, 246, 249, 252, 253-54.

Whitman, unique in American and perhaps all literature, cannot be evaluated like other poets. He contains much that is repulsive, for obscenity is weak, not virile. With an "exuberant intellect," he lacked a sense of "relative values." His use of the first person, often misconstrued, is illuminating, not repugnant. He separated himself from creeds in order to reach true religion, an enactment of one's principles. He reconciled physical and spiritual reality as equally important. Incidental lines and the George Fox essay better convey God's nature than philosophical poems like "Square Deific" and "Eidólons." "To Him that Was Crucified" is not intentionally irreverent though in "the very worst taste." Whitman believes in the Quaker inner light but does not associate it with the Holy Ghost. He carried democracy to extremes with which his countrymen were not comfortable, though equivalent to Christ's true gospel, which Whitman sought to revive in its true sense of an "intense personal regard," a "strong active affection." His religion included his passion for America. His attitude toward good and evil was shocking but not immoral. His virile lines on personal immortality, increasingly a dominant theme for Whitman (as in "Passage"), carry a conviction which more beautiful lines of other poets cannot. Incidental references compare Whitman with other poets; note that though not antagonistic to science

like Arnold, he looked to something beyond it.

2 BLACK, ALEXANDER. *The Latest Thing and Other Things*. New York and London: Harper & Bros. "The Desk," pp. 163-67.

Personal reminiscences about his work at the *Brooklyn Times*, where Whitman's old desk was pointed out to him (1891). He quotes his letter to Whitman and Whitman's reply about his inability to identify the desk. It fell apart the next year, at almost the same time Whitman's voice ceased.

3 BURROUGHS, JOHN. *The Last Harvest*. Boston and New York: Houghton Mifflin Co., pp. 17, 25, 34, 94, 100, 111-12, 179, 202, 208-9, 222, 227, 250, 251, 253-54, 278, 285.

Incidental references and quotations. Speaking with Burroughs in 1871 or 1872, Emerson "wished Whitman's friends would 'quarrel' with him more about his poems." It is Whitman's "tremendous and impassioned philosophy suffusing his work" that keeps *Leaves* "forever fresh." Whitman emphasizes criticism of his country and times as one of a poet's functions. Burroughs judges young poets according to their opinion of Whitman; he notes the opinions of Whitman from various writers and his own early recognition of Whitman. Though some contemporary poets claim to get their charter from Whitman, Whitman would probably not "be enough interested in them to feel contempt toward them."

4 CARPENTER, EDWARD. *Towards Democracy*. New York and London: Mitchell Kennerley. "A Note on *Towards Democracy*," pp. xxiv-xxv (reprint of 1894.31); "Edward Carpenter" (introduction), by Charles Vale, pp. ii-vi.

Vale discusses Whitman's influence on Carpenter: Whitman sought to enlarge the boundary of human expression, with a democratic feeling and form, making Carpenter's form inevitable. Whitman's expression was more real than Shelley's.

5 CHESTERTON, G. K. *What I Saw in America*. London: Hodder & Stoughton, pp. 60, 172.

In response to an interviewer's question as to the greatest American writer, Chesterton had replied, "The greatest natural genius and artistic force was probably Walt Whitman," "'your one real red-blooded man.'" "Whitman's truly poetic vision of the beautiful old women suffers a little from that bewildering multiplicity and recurrence that is indeed the whole theme of Whitman" and suggests "the green eternity" of *Leaves*.

6 FRANK, WALDO. *The New America*. London: Jonathan Cape. "The Multitudes in Whitman," pp. 220-40.
Reprint of 1919.7.

7 GRAHAM, STEPHEN. Tramping with a Poet in the
Rockies. New York: D. Appleton & Co.,
p. 156.
Vachel Lindsay "did not care for
Whitman" but "loved Longfellow."

8 HARRIS, FRANK. My Life and Loves. Vol. 1.
Paris: Privately printed, pp. xv, 111,
171, 267-72.
Reprinted: 1925.6.
Whitman on sex is better than many
rather foul poets, "though often merely
commonplace." Whitman's 1877 Paine lecture
in Philadelphia is described, with Harris's
impressions of him then as "a new type of
personality." Harris was introduced to
Whitman's poetry by Byron Caldwell Smith,
who valued Whitman's "transparent simplicity
and sincerity." Whitman was right to speak
about sex, though abused for it and wrongly
suspected of "perverse tastes."

9 HOLLOWAY, EMORY. "Whitman." In A Short
History of American Literature, edited by
William Peterfield Trent, John Erskine,
Stuart P. Sherman, and Carl Van Doren. New
York: G. P. Putnam's Sons, pp. 225-41;
also passim per index.
Reprint of 1918.10.
Minor changes indicate recent publica-
tions. Minor references elsewhere in the
volume include comparisons with Bryant and
Twain.

10 HUBBELL, JAY B., and BEATY, JOHN O. An Introduction to Poetry. New York: Macmillan
Co., pp. 12, 374-79, 401-3, passim per
index.
The chapters mentioning Whitman are by
Hubbell. Whitman is preeminently the poet
of American democracy, turning his back on
traditional subject-matter, form, and
diction in an endeavor to translate into
poetry American life and ideals. He is a
pioneer in introducing into poetry such
American themes as the city and machinery.
He "often wrote wretched stuff," but "when
he wrote spontaneously of what he knew and
felt, he produced great and original poetry,"
his later poems being "much less uneven in
merit than his earlier verse." Several
poems are reprinted, with brief comments.

11 HUNEKER, JOSEPHINE, ed. Letters of James
Gibbons Huneker. New York: Charles
Scribner's Sons, p. 202.
Letter to John Quinn (6 November 1915):
The English have seized on Whitman as a
seer, rather than on Emerson, Whitman's
source. Zangwill rebels at the Whitman
story; perhaps Nordau's description of him
is not so bad.

12 J[AYNE], H. H. F., ed. The Letters of Horace
Howard Furness. Vol. 1. Boston and New
York: Houghton Mifflin Co., pp. xxxiii,
234, 345-46.
Letter to S. Weir Mitchell (30 September

1885): Whitman is in no need; he gives
Furness strength through "his grand imper-
turbable paucity." An 1897 letter to his
sister discusses the editing of Whitman's
works, which should be expurgated (though
then they might not sell); recalls pleading
with Whitman for expurgation, which Whitman
said "'would break the ensemble of my
nature.'" He was a poseur all his life,
regarding his financial status, his learning, the effortlessness of his poetic
utterance (contradicted by manuscripts
which Furness has). The best thing about
him was "his godlike face and mien," for
which Furness complimented him, to his
honest acceptance.

13 [LOWELL, AMY.] A Critical Fable. Boston and
New York: Houghton Mifflin & Co., pp. 6-7,
44, 81.
The narrator-spokesperson for contemporary poetry remarks that Poe and Whitman
are ranked together by the moderns, while
the old-man-interlocutor (J. R. Lowell)
ridicules him for writing the same book
"every two or three years," and without
rhyme.

14 MACY, JOHN. The Critical Game. New York:
Boni & Liveright. "Biographies of Whitman,"
pp. 203-11.
The only fault with Traubel (1914.17)
is that there is too much of it, yet
Whitman emerges as able to stand up against
such exhaustive records because "he was a
great talker, full of experience and endowed with the gift of speech." Though all
his conversation is not valuable, "he is
never a bore," but "for once, a literary
man as big as his literary work." This is
material for a great biography of "our one
magnificent American poet," such as Perry
(1906.13) and De Selincourt (1914.5) have
not provided. "Whitman does not stand for
America" but is rather "in revolt against
the American fact and celebrating a possible
American future"; hence he is welcomed by
"literary and revolutionary spirits" rather
than official or conventional America.
England has produced more minds capable of
appreciating him.

15 MERRILL, STUART. Walt Whitman (à Leon
Bazalgette). Translated by "Aeon." Ltd.
ed. Toronto: Henry S. Saunders, 10 pp.
Photograph.
Reprinted: Walt Whitman Newsletter 3
(December 1957), 55-57.
Translated by Saunders's friend "Aeon"
from Le Masque, ser. 2, nos. 9-10, pp. 303-
7. Recalls meeting Whitman at his New York
Lincoln lecture (see 1887.32), having
looked forward to hearing "the voice of a
prophet, who moved in advance of his race
and beyond his own time." His narrative
was gripping. His appearance is described:
the unmatched beauty of his old age,
"physical harmony" equalling that of the

soul. Merrill presented to Whitman a copy of Vogue with Laforgue's translation of "Adam" in it; Whitman smiled, saying, "I was certain that a Frenchman would hit upon those poems."

16 PAPINI, GIOVANNI. Four and Twenty Minds. Translated by Ernest Hatch Wilkins. New York: Thomas Y. Crowell Co. "Walt Whitman," pp. 125-62.

Translated from the 1912 Italian version written upon the appearance of Gamberale's translation of Leaves, which Papini had read as his discovery of poetry. He loves Whitman, "a soul childlike and great, inebriate with joy and heavy with sadness," whose life matched his poems. He is a universal poet, yet also intensely individual, a prophet rather than a poet, adoring the self "because he adores the all," reflected in the self. "His constant insistence on particular things," and many of them, "suggests amplitude and universality more effectively" than philosophers' abstractions. He is no mere optimist but rather a passionate lover and worshipper who transcends evil. In ideas he is a percursor of Nietzsche, Dostoevsky, and Tolstoy. His religion is not eclectic but universal, not polytheistic but unitarian, a Christian pantheism. His poetry is not a coherent system but includes all and should inspire readers to move away from current over-refinement.

17 POPE, BERTHA CLARK, ed. The Letters of Ambrose Bierce. San Francisco: Book Club of California, pp. 44, 122.

Letters of 1901 and 1906 reveal Bierce's "loathing of the Whitmaniacal 'form,'" although many others think Whitman great.

18 PRESCOTT, FREDERICK CLARKE. The Poetic Mind. New York: Macmillan Co., pp. 59, 239, 240, 241-42.

Incidental references to Whitman as representing "poets of a primitive or strongly individual kind" who feel the emotion "in something like its native wildness and force."

*19 REINHART, MARY R. The Breaking Point. New York: Doran, p. 288.
Reported in Saunders Whitman in Fiction.

20 RODD, Sir JAMES RENNELL. Social and Diplomatic Memories 1884-1893. Vol. 1. London: Edward Arnold & Co., pp. 28-30.

Swinburne's attack (1887.63) aroused the youthful indignation of Rodd, "a sincere if discriminating admirer" of Leaves and Drum-Taps, "which contained a genuine burst of natural song, a roughhewn art developing under elemental conditions." His response of praise for Whitman and belittling of Swinburne in hexameter couplets is printed: "To Walt Whitman. After

reading a recent article in the 'Fortnightly Review.'" (Also printed in Traubel III, 1914.17.)

21 SHERMAN, STUART P. Americans. New York: Charles Scribner's Sons. "Walt Whitman," pp. 153-85; also 22, 101, 111, 219, 229, 237, 241, 242.
Reprint of 1922.22.

Includes incidental references to Whitman in connection with Emerson and Joaquin Miller.

22 _____. Introduction to Leaves of Grass. New York: Charles Scribner's Sons, pp. vii-xxvii.
Revision of 1919.270. Reprinted: 1922.21.

Adds commentary on Whitman's method of "imaginative contemplation of the object," his importance as poetic interpreter of America's social and political ideals, his chief theme of the reconciliation of the individual with society, his early life and influences, his belief in man rather than political mechanisms, his faith in the Union and not pacifism in the war, his recognition of the truly heroic.

23 SQUIRE, J. C. Books Reviewed. New York: George H. Doran Co. London: Heinemann. "A Supplement to Whitman," pp. 252-59.

Review of Uncollected (1921.16), from Observer (unlocated). It is a disservice to Whitman to resurrect such feeble writings, with interest only in some fragments of literary criticism and the papers on Brooklyn. Leaves is the most worthy of our attention, as "an achievement, a revelation, and a warning," with some of the noblest and some of the flattest of modern poetry. Though much of his verse is merely free prose, at its best it is truly free verse: "as he rises to poetry, he tends to write like other poets, in rhythms more repetitive than those of prose." However, because other poets before him abstained from rhyme and uniform line lengths, his deliberate originality led to nothing, in contrast to his genuine poet's imagination when dealing with things not previously treated in poetry.

24 STEAD, ROBERT. Neighbours. Toronto: Hodder & Stoughton, p. 292.

The narrator is surprised that an acquaintance he had thought shallow has a copy of Whitman, from which he quoted copiously.

25 TOMLINSON, H. M. Waiting for Daylight. London, New York, Toronto, Melbourne: Cassell & Co. "News from the Front," pp. 80-85.
Reprint of 1918.58.

26 WEBSTER, HENRY K. Mary Wollaston. London: Eveleigh, Nash, pp. 32, 80-81, 83-84, 89, 173, 220, 346.

This novel concerns the romances of a

singer and a composer, who sets passages of "Cradle" to music in a song in which "Whitman's free unmetered swing, the glorious length of his stride, fell in with March's rhythmic idiom." The song becomes a recurring motif representing the characters' feelings. "Cradle" is "one of the supreme lyric expressions in the English language of the passion of love."

27 WELLS, CAROLYN, and GOLDSMITH, ALFRED F. A Concise Bibliography of the Works of Walt Whitman. Boston and New York: Houghton Mifflin Co., 107 pp. Reprinted: Trent.
    Descriptive bibliography of works of Whitman (no translations), selections, books about Whitman (significant books, most dealing entirely with Whitman).

28 YEATS, W. B. The Trembling of the Veil. London: T. Werner Laurie, pp. 111, 127.
    Incidental: "through some influence from an earlier generation, from Walt Whitman, perhaps, I had sat talking in public bars"; Whitman and Emerson are "writers who have begun to seem superficial precisely because they lack the Vision of evil."

PERIODICALS

29 LE GALLIENNE, RICHARD. "James Huneker, Steeplejack of the Seven Arts." New York Times Book Review and Magazine (29 January), 31.
    Review of Huneker (1921.17), quoting his opinions on Whitman and his imitators. But "a great man is not diminished by his idiotic imitators." The author of "Open Road" and "Lilacs" neither stands nor falls by "Adam," target of Huneker's criticism, though in its time it was a needed protest.

30 HOLLOWAY, EMORY. "Childhood Traits in Whitman." Dial 72 (February), 169-77.
    A Freudian discussion of Whitman's development from childhood will help understanding him. He lived a romance, with trouble distinguishing between fiction and reality. The catalogues represent his impressionable nature, unified only by his constant joy. He relied on inspiration, not reason. Nature became the object of his sexual emotion, thwarted due to unreturned affection; his outlet was not his attachment to his mother or romantic attraction to other men, but rather a narcissistic egotism which he offers to the reader. His comprehension of both sexes allows him to interpret one sex to the other. If he lacks a sense of humor, he has the greater sympathy. His sexuality was sublimated to extend to all humanity, part of his democratic theory. His idea of comradeship was mutual loafing rather than labor. He actually preferred working alone--like a child.

31 HYDE, FILLMORE. "Whitman the Apprentice." Bookman 54 (February), 585-86.
    Favorable review of Uncollected (1921.16). The deep feeling inspired in his friends has furthered Whitman's reputation more than his own words and the eulogies of his champions. He is, from beginning to end, "a partner with his expression and an instrument by which fluent experience could be transformed into comprehensible and changeless language." "His book is his life." He expresses the "kinship of the universe and man" such as most people realize at adolescence, but only inarticulately.

32 EASTMAN, MAX. "Books: Suggesting a Biography." Liberator 5 (March), 27-29.
    Review of Uncollected (1921.16). The great biography of Whitman remains to be written to explain his duality, capable of producing his fine poetry and this feeble prose, occasionally bigoted in its opposition to free love and abolitionism. His diary reveals "a powerful homosexual passion" that his "Puritan schoolmaster's restraint" kept him from acting upon; it led to his "achievement of serene and lonely communion with universal life." His fabricated children should be recognized as a joke. He repressed "his inmost experience of sex" because it could not be discussed "from the standpoint of social acceptability." Out of his repressed nature he made poetry, "personal and expressive of his sublime self-love."

33 ANON. "Book of the Day. Whitmania." London Morning Post (2 March).
    Review of Uncollected (1921.16). Whitman, like Lincoln and Twain, is representative of the period of American adventure and exuberance, but a puritanical few have kept him from being fully accepted as a representative American voice, because of certain elements of his unconventionality. This book's pieces should not have been exhumed, though there is some interesting, if imitative, matter, with the real Whitman glimpsed only in some of the notebooks. Fortunately, Holloway "cannot throw fresh light on his mysterious love-affairs."

34 ANON. "Literature. Essays on Books. A Stimulating Critic." Adelaide Advertiser (4 March).
    Review of Clutton-Brock (1921.7), especially his commentary on Whitman, who "alone of the great American writers is wholly American," epitomizing the young spirit of the nation.

35 HAWK, AFFABLE [pseud.?]. "Books in General." New Statesman 18 (4 March), 620.
    Review of Uncollected (1921.16), material generally not worth reprinting except for "queer, emphatic entries" from Whitman's notebooks which shed light on his

character, showing how he paid for his
great gift of loving, which produced "the
finest modern war-poems and noble poems on
death."

36 VAN DOREN, CARL. "The Roving Critic." Nation
114 (8 March), 288.
Reprinted: 1923.16.
Whitman's newspaper work in Gathering
(1920.26) is unexceptional. His notebook
jottings in Uncollected (1921.16), though
coming out of "his very tissue," do not
reveal his vast personal change as do
passages in his poetry ("Myself" 5,
"Cradle," "Proud Music").

37 ANON. "Budapest Bans Whitman's Works." New
York Times (11 March), 3:5.
Brief item on the Hungarian government's
ban.

38 REGER, REES R. "A Prophet Is Not Without
Honour." Freeman 5 (15 March), 17-18.
Letter deploring Whitman's neglect in
America and the impossibility of finding
his books on sale in Camden. He is granted
merely passing mention in school, at most
the reading of one or two "minor fragments
picked out by our all-mighty and well-
meaning but nevertheless too delicately
moraled school-system"

39 ANON. "A Sentimental Democrat." Times Literary Supplement (London) (16 March), 164.
Review of Uncollected (1921.16), not
very valuable, showing Whitman a "mediocre
journalist" without the "pure abandonment"
and "instinctive energy" of his best poetry.
These volumes do present his principal
ideas of naturalness and spirituality and
reveal his debts to Poe, Hawthorne, Emerson,
and Carlyle. His literary judgments reveal
inability to distinguish the great and rare
from what is worthy but mediocre. Subtleties of thought are lost in Whitman, but he
does convince us of his experience of the
"mystical apprehension of the huge harmony
of the universe." He is at his best casti-
gating the particular abuses in artistic
form, in manners, and in government.

40 [ROBERTS, CECIL.] "Walt Whitman as Critic."
Liverpool Daily Courier (20 March).
Whitman was "a journalist much above
the average in intelligence and industry."
His book reviewing and often astute critical remarks on writers past and present are
discussed.

41 ANON. "The New Order of Literary Values."
Vanity Fair 18 (April), 40-41.
A chart shows how ten contemporary
critics rank many figures of art and thought
along a scale of +25 (complete approval) to
-25 (complete disapproval). Whitman ranks
fifteenth of the many people, with a generally high average (+15.3).

42 ANON. "The Library. The Literary World. A
Fresh Volume of Walt Whitman." Bazaar
Exchange and Mart (1 April).
Review of Uncollected (1921.16),
Whitman's "pot-boiling," of no intrinsic
value. Leaves remains a milestone, expressing "his country's newly-found creative
energy and genius," even though his country
wasn't able then to approve it.

43 STRACHEY, J. ST. LOE. "Books. The Uncollected
Poetry and Prose of Walt Whitman." Spectator 128 (8 April), 430-31.
Review of 1921.16. While many carp at
the publication of this work, it is important that a great writer's early work be
put in print, so that everyone may judge
its merits; it has biographical interest
also. The verse here shows "a curious
counter-instinct, unconscious, no doubt,"
against meter; yet once he took to unrhymed,
unmeasured verse, he showed "a masterly ear
for the wider verbal harmonies." The 1855
Preface shows him to be a fine prose
writer.

44 ROBERTS, CECIL. "Walt Whitman. Collection of
Uncollected Work." Liverpool Daily Courier
(18 April).
Review of Uncollected (1921.16), with
description of Whitman's life and obscure
romance with a woman, suspected by every
reader of Whitman's verse, especially of
"Once I Pass'd."

45 HOLLOWAY, EMORY. "Books. Whitman in Extremis."
Nation 114 (19 April), 471.
Review of Keller (1921.19), "the most
connected story" of Whitman's last years
yet published. Holloway explains Whitman's
problematic dealings with Mrs. Davis, noting
his tendency to accept attentions paid him
"as a welcome tribute to himself."

46 SCOTT-JAMES, R. A. "Walt Whitman as Journalist. Early Writings of the Poet." London
Daily Chronicle (21 April).
Review of Uncollected (1921.16), which
will hardly enhance Whitman's reputation.
An attempt to read these writings as they
would have been read then, without a knowledge of Whitman's poetry, reveals an earnest,
clever, brilliant reporter, cursory reviewer of books, socialistically oriented
moralist. Occasional glimpses of his
future greatness in poetry appear, though
these could not be seen if we weren't
already familiar with his work.

47 YOUNG, STARK. "Forward and Backward." New
Republic 30 (10 May), 316.
Account of a theatrical presentation of
"Salut," "an attempt to build a festival
around Whitman's poem and its theme of the
brotherhood of the world and of all races
and all centuries."

48 CLARK, THOMAS CURTIS. "To Walt Whitman."
        <u>Unity</u> 89 (25 May), 199.
        Poem in blank verse.

49 BOOTH, EDWARD TOWNSEND. "The Intellectuals
        and Religion." <u>Literary Review</u> 2 (27 May),
        681-82.
            Religion is not acceptable to modern
        intellectuals; hence, as a prime example,
        they ignore Whitman's mysticism while
        recognizing <u>Leaves</u> as "the completest ex-
        pression of the American genius that has
        been given to the world." Every page is a
        revision of reality from a standpoint
        reached only by something akin to a reli-
        gious experience. <u>Leaves</u> is "the first
        maturity of our Puritan culture," with Dutch
        and transcendentalist roots. Whitman fuses
        "the moralist, the artist, and the mystic,"
        who are now distinct; we need someone to
        follow Whitman and fuse them again.

50 ERSKINE, JOHN. "Whitman, Poet-Prophet."
        <u>Literary Review</u> 2 (27 May), 685.
            Review of Bazalgette's <u>Le 'Poeme-
        Evangile' de Walt Whitman</u>. Because of
        Latin acceptance of the body and of the
        idea of liberty as related to responsibility
        to society, Whitman now enjoys in France
        the reputation for "a clarity and distinc-
        tion of thought which he did not enjoy at
        home." This is due to Bazalgette, who dis-
        cusses Whitman's poem "as a work of art, as
        a philosophy turning upon democracy, love,
        and religion, and as a national expression
        of America," describing the poem's language
        and rhythm more faithfully than anything
        written in English. Whitman tried to
        develop a mass aesthetic, to express things
        in terms of themselves and of their own
        rhythm. "His genius lay in guessing
        accurately what was typical of the mass in
        his own personality." Bazalgette empha-
        sizes Whitman's passion for others, which
        equals his pride of personality. <u>Leaves</u> is
        "an actual picture of us--in its disengage-
        ment from the past, in its confidence in
        our modernness." Its dream of democracy
        makes it "our national epic."

51 FOERSTER, NORMAN. "Genesis of 'Leaves of
        Grass.'" <u>Literary Review</u> 2 (27 May), 685-
        86. Illustration.
            Review of <u>Uncollected</u> (1921.16) and
        <u>Gathering</u> (1920.26), which "reveal in
        detail the ill-related sentimentalism and
        didacticism and the conventionalism and
        radicalism of the early Walt Whitman, which
        were destined to be transformed into the
        romantic morality of the prophet of idiocy-
        racy and adhesiveness." His early work is
        examined for prefigurations of <u>Leaves</u>,
        moralism, transcendental influence, includ-
        ing the influence of Carlyle and Bryant,
        slighted by Holloway. <u>Gathering</u> is "a
        reasonably complete record of his writing
        during two important years."

52 MORLEY, CHRISTOPHER. "The Powerful, 'Cute
        Mind." <u>Literary Review</u> 2 (27 May), 683.
        Illustration.
            Review of Overton (1921.27), "a gallant
        attempt to reconstruct, in fictional form,
        some of the aspects" of Whitman's life,
        with some chronological shifts and melo-
        dramatizing, showing some of the vitality
        associated with anything concerning Walt,
        capturing his personality, even in its
        "exasperating jargon" and "absence of humor."
        Whitman "will always remain the great Amer-
        ican paradox."

53 FRANK, SEP. Unpublished etching of Whitman.
        <u>New York Times Book Review and Magazine</u>
        (28 May), 7.

54 ANON. "Walt's Birthday." <u>Hamilton Spectator</u>
        (31 May).
            Whitman cannot be criticized for his
        form; his message is primary, dealing not
        with things temporal but with things eternal
        and their temporal manifestation. He is
        compared to Queen Victoria. His thought
        demands such rhythms. The poems of sex are
        "as high-minded as the Song of Solomon."

55 GRAFLY, DOROTHY. "Whitman Lovers Join the
        City of Camden in Plans for Making His
        House a Memorial." <u>Christian Science
        Monitor</u> (7 June), 7:1-3. Illustrated.
            The "battered condition" of Whitman's
        old house is "symbolic of his passionate
        understanding of all men and women."
        Description of his personality (vast capac-
        ity for life, philosophy of human tolerance)
        and its projection forever beyond the limit
        of a single state or nation. He was dis-
        liked during life for his departure from
        conventions.

*56 KARSNER, DAVID F. Article. New York <u>Call</u>
        (18 June).
        Reported in Willard.
            Camden is criticized for waiting until
        Whitman's commercial value was assured
        before making a shrine of his house, which
        had been various things since his death.

57 AUSTIN, MARY. "Native Rhythms." New York
        <u>Herald Literary Review</u> (1 July).
            Whitman is presented as forebear of
        later attempts to find a rhythm appropriate
        to America rather than as the fulfillment,
        since his form remained inchoate, his
        rhythms occasionally imitative. But he
        showed later poets "of what stuff the
        poetry of America should be made."

58 BOYNTON, PERCY H. "Soil Preparation and Grass
        Seed." <u>New Republic</u> 31 (19 July), 225-26.
            Review of <u>Uncollected</u> (1921.16). Al-
        though Whitman's early life is not unknown,
        this volume has "the surprising freshness
        of an ante-bellum daguerreotype." Whitman's
        early poetry is sometimes laughable, but he
        gradually developed his prose and poetic

styles, similar in their use of rhythmic patterns. More important is his growth in convictions; his 1848 travels rid him of "peevishness and excitability," increasing his humor and tolerance. The source of the mysticism of Leaves remains undiscovered.

59 RUSSELL, PHILLIPS. "American Literature in France." Freeman 5 (16 August), 539-40.
Discusses the French appreciation of American writers. Whitman made no great impression until Bazalgette's complete translation of Leaves. The article focuses on Bazalgette and his ideas on Whitman and other Americans. He admires the character, courage, and untamed quality of the great American writers, and the way they have returned to the earth, as Europeans must.

60 LOVING, PIERRE. "Towards Walt Whitman." Double Dealer 4 (September), 139-42.
Sandburg, Lindsay, and Frost exhibit the "tenacious virility of the indigenous American vein" of poetry originated by Whitman. Pound, Lowell, and Fletcher also show a debt. The best American poetry will, for some time at least, sway toward Whitman, "the true guardian spirit of authentic American poetry."

61 POUND, EZRA. "Paris Letter." Dial 73 (September), 335.
Comments on Eliot's complaint in Tyro about American writers: "He cannot mean that there has been no American contribution to international letters, for there remain Poe, Whitman, and may we say Hawthorne."

62 STANTON, THEODORE. "The Poet of the Stacks." Freeman 6 (13 September), 16.
Letter deploring the fact that Whitman's work is kept in the stacks of the New York Public Library, not on the general reading-room shelves.

63 _____. "Literature Abroad--Walt Whitman in Germany." Literary Review 3 (30 September), 68.
Review of Reisiger's Walt Whitman's Werke. Whitman attracted Reisiger by his "proclamation of the magnificence of Self in Body and Soul." Whitman, once he became better known in Germany, was seen to embody the American voice, leading toward new regions of humanity, increasingly recognized as "the most powerful, purest, and most virile embodiment of a truly cosmo-demo-crat." Whitman successfully blended the contrast between individuality and the mass. His literary and personal influence is noted in quotations from Zweig, Mann, and Fritz Schwiefert.

64 ELY, CATHERINE BEACH. "Whitman and the Radi-cals as Poets of Democracy." Open Court 36 (October), 594-601.
The verse of the new "radical poets," though they claim to follow Whitman, differs from that of Whitman in its national and political aspects. Passages from Pound, Sandburg, Lindsay, Eliot, and Kreymborg are compared with Whitman's to reveal his greater belief in democracy, the war, the progress of the race. He expressed America's spiritual mission and what became America's goal in the World War, a wholesome, con-structive patriotism as well as love of the soil and the masses. The "radical poets" only have an "affectation of Whitmanism," with too much pessimism.

65 HAYES, WILL. "The Birth of a Bible." Texas Review 8 (October), 21-31.
Leaves is becoming "the Bible of Democ-racy"; the early writings in Uncollected (1921.16) are a welcome key to its develop-ment with hints of its beauty and freshness. Leaves was produced not by Bucke's notion of one moment of revelation but by "a grad-ual evolution of ideas," as shown by pas-sages from notebooks and early drafts. In-fluences from his reading are noted, partic-ularly that of Emerson before 1855.

66 WOOD, JAMES N. "'Democratic Vistas.'" Open Court 36 (October), 575-85. Photograph, facing p. 575.
This article, listed in Allen, makes no reference to Whitman beyond using his title as its own.

67 LANUX, PIERRE de. "Notes from France." Bookman 56 (November), 372-73.
Paragraph précis of Dominique Braga's article in L'Europe Nouvelle (19 August) concerning Bazalgette's translation and biography of Whitman, both of which are full of freedom and health. Whitman is bringing back to Europe the synthesis it needed.

68 ANON. "Hull Literary Club. The Gospel of Walt. Whitman." Hull (England) Daily News (5 December), 3:5.
Summary of W. E. Walker's paper on Whitman's gospel, which is democracy, with explanation of his spirit of identity with others, "the essential fraternity of human-ity." His "cosmic politics" implied "an immanentist philosophy, enormous breadth of association, and simple faith in personal-ity." His democratic and extra-democratic (death, a creedless religion) values are described, his gospel compared to Christ's.

69 CASCA [W. H. Trimble]. "Walt Whitman, Demo-crat." Woman and Home 1, no. 9 (11 Decem-ber), 10-11.
Brief explanation of Whitman's philos-ophy: democracy depends on liberty, equal-ity, and primarily "the huge obligations of Fraternity." For us to attain the demo-cratic ideal, Whitman urges us to realize "our own inherent nobleness," each individual guided by his or her own conscience.

BOOKS

1 BROWN, HORATIO F., ed. Letters and Papers of John Addington Symonds. London: John Murray, pp. 13, 20, 31, 48, 50, 113, 161-62, 170, 216, 230, 245, 252, 253.

   Incidental remarks on Whitman and his impact on Symonds, who had initial difficulties with him. Some of the letters (chiefly to Brown and Henry Sidgwick) are presented in more complete form than in 1895.2.

2 BUCKE, RICHARD MAURICE. Cosmic Consciousness: A Study in the Evolution of the Human Mind. Philadelphia: Innes & Sons, 384 pp. "Walt Whitman," pp. 215-37; also passim. No index.
   Reprint of 1901.3.

3 COYNE, JAMES. Richard Maurice Bucke: A Sketch. Rev. ed. Toronto: Henry S. Saunders. "Walt Whitman and Dr. Bucke," pp. 51-59; also 7, 40, 45, 47-48, 50, 69-70. Reprint of 1906.6, adding chapter headings and updating the bibliography.

4 DELL, FLOYD. Janet March. New York: Alfred A. Knopf, pp. 443-45, 449, 456.

   The title character is unable to see poetry in Whitman; her future husband reads to her "Woman Waits" as Whitman's prophecy of her, which she later appreciates.

5 FOERSTER, NORMAN. Nature in American Literature. New York: Macmillan Co. "Whitman," pp. 176-220; also passim per index. Revision of 1916.61 and 1921.56.

   Slight changes, deletions, and additions, notably discussion of Whitman's Dutch ancestry as contributing to his keen sensitivity to nature.

6 HANEY, JOHN LOUIS. The Story of Our Literature. New York: Charles Scribner's Sons. "Walt Whitman," pp. 140-44; list of major works, p. 371. Photograph.

   Brief life sketch. Whitman's work includes prosaic lists but also much of worth, including his "fine elegy," "Lilacs." He has been denounced for his egotism and defiance of rules of art and decency, and praised as "manly, vigorous, sympathetic, and intensely American." Most Americans today "recognize his stimulating and refreshing qualities," without accepting the British verdict of him as "our most characteristic genius."

7 HASTINGS, WILLIAM T. Syllabus of American Literature. Chicago: University of Chicago, pp. 41-44; also 15.
   Outline form introduction to Whitman: biographical sketch with interpretations of his personality ("consciously violent and pagan" youth, "harmless egotism and affection, with essential charm and sincerity"); significant poems grouped by subjects and described ("Autobiographical poems," "Poems of democracy," "Poems of the war," "Nature poetry"), which include vivid descriptions; central ideas outlined (self-assertion, science, democracy); his art (new form and literary relationships); "general estimate" balancing his virtues and defects (such as inability to sustain poetic continuity). Whitman is powerful, "individual and essentially dignified, with a limited but genuine poetic endowment."

8 JOHNSON, ROBERT UNDERWOOD. Remembered Yesterdays. Boston: Little, Brown, & Co. "Walt Whitman," pp. 332-39; also 329, 341, 353, 358, 363.

   Johnson, former editor of the Century, classifies Whitman's poetry, much of it really eloquence rather than poetry; Whitman, not an artist, had a power of imagination and ability to convey elemental qualities. The Lincoln poems are his highest achievement in expressing sincere emotion. Account of his first Lincoln lecture in New York. Though always a poseur, Whitman had penetrating opinions on most subjects, as in 1879.41, quoted. Letter from Holland to Gilder is printed regarding Whitman's indecency: "A good brain with all its energies wasted on a style so irredeemably vicious that no man can ever imitate it without disgrace." Despite his naturalism, "he sounds no note of hopelessness." Johnson quotes his conversation with Lowell, who terms Whitman's work not poetry at all or even anything between poetry and prose, because there is no such thing.

9 LAWRENCE, D. H. Studies in Classic American Literature. New York: Thomas Seltzer. "Whitman," pp. 241-64; also viii, ix. Reprinted: Pearce; in part: Rupp.

   "Walt was really too superhuman," mechanical in his overgeneralized, all-inclusive aching with amorous love. He loses his individual self in absorbing and identifying with all. Whitman moves from love of woman to love of man to merging with death. He is a great poet of "the transitions of the soul as it loses its identity." He has "meant so much" to Lawrence. He stands alone, the first to smash the old idea that the soul is superior to the flesh. He portrays the soul on the open road, calling for true sympathy, giving "a morality of actual living, not of salvation." But he errs in transforming sympathy into love, the merging into one identity, for he fails to feel with the actual feelings of others, which may include evil. "But the exultance of his message still remains." (Only a few sentences and words regarding "Calamus" are incorporated from 1921.62.)

10 MORLEY, CHRISTOPHER. <u>Inward Ho!</u> Garden City,
N.Y.: Doubleday, Page & Co. "Moby Walt,"
pp. 21-28.
Revision of 1923.24. Reprinted: 1925.12;
1925.13.
Deletes comparison with Lawrence.

11 OVERTON, GRANT. <u>American Nights Entertainment</u>.
New York: D. Appleton & Co., George H.
Doran Co., Doubleday, Page & Co., Charles
Scribner's Sons, pp. 124-25, 263, 322.
Whitman speaks to the thousands and
therefore does not receive the attention
given to those poets with intimate personal
appeal. Significant books to be familiar
with on Whitman are mentioned.

12 SAUNDERS, HENRY S., comp. <u>Parodies on Whitman</u>.
New York: American Library Service, 171 pp.
Preface by Christopher Morley.
Reprints in chronological order many
parodies (some unlocated because undated).
Morley suggests that Whitman would have
been pleased by the attention these parodies
gave him, but only Bunner's (1881.21) would
capture him. Whitman might have parodied
himself but apparently felt that he had
made his contribution to humor in training
Traubel, with "his zealous affectionate
spirit." A little humor when dealing with
Whitman is acceptable and necessary.
Whitman emerges from this ordeal "practically unscathed."

*13 SAUNDERS, HENRY S. <u>Whitman Portraits, with
Note</u>. Toronto: Henry S. Saunders, 114
leaves.
Reported in Allen.

14 SCOTT, DIXON. <u>Men of Letters</u>. London:
Hodder & Stoughton. "Walt Whitman," pp.
307-13.
Reprint of 1914.32.
This book was originally published in
1916, without the Whitman essay.

15 SHERMAN, STUART P. <u>The Genius of America:
Studies in Behalf of the Younger Generation</u>.
New York and London: Charles Scribner's
Sons, pp. 2, 24, 26-27, 71, 170, 198, 234,
261.
Includes reprints of 1921.35 and 1921.71.
Incidental references and quotations.

16 VAN DOREN, CARL. <u>The Roving Critic</u>. New
York: Alfred A. Knopf. "Whitman in His
Crises," pp. 40-44; also 125-27.
Reprint of 1922.36.
Includes incidental comparion with
Burroughs, who lacked Whitman's "cosmic
reach" and "prophetic lift."

17 WHARTON, EDITH. <u>A Son at the Front</u>. New
York: Charles Scribner's Sons, title page.
This novel has an epigraph from
Whitman: "Something veil'd and abstracted
is often a part of the manners of these
beings."

18 WILLIAMS, WILLIAM CARLOS. <u>Spring and All</u>.
Contact Publishing Co., n.d., pp. 38, 84.
The vigor of Whitman's imaginative life,
evident in his democratic identity with all
about him, is one with the modern trend.
Contemporary discussions of differences
between prose and poetry help to explain
"why some work of Whitman's is bad poetry
and some, in the same meter is prose."

19 WOOD, MILDRED MARY CUMMER, and WOOD, CLEMENT.
<u>For Walt Whitman</u>. Toronto: Henry S.
Saunders, 25 pp. 100 copies.
Includes poems "The Good Gray Rebel"
and "The Sound of the Gong" by Clement, and
"Prophets Honour" by Mildred, and brief
essay, "Walt Whitman: The Good Red Poet,"
by Clement: Whitman's color is not gray
but red, like his "burning words" and "flush
of love." He sounds the trumpet for comradeship and equality in the spirit of
Jefferson and Paine but cannot be placed in
one political creed. He sought equal
opportunity for all. He saw himself as
forerunner of greater poets. He is "an
ever-living part of us" and will lead an
awakened society.

PERIODICALS

20 ANON. "Proscribes Walt Whitman." <u>New York
Times</u> (1 January), 10:3.
The Hungarian government has banned the
works of Whitman and others as being "of a
destructive tendency."

21 ANON. "Whitman in Hungary." <u>New York Times</u>
(2 January), 12:5.
The destructive tendency for which
Whitman's works have been banned in Hungary
is apparent only in the way he has destroyed
the placidity of young men who have followed
his course in being a free-verse poet,
founding many schools upon him. His ideas
have been taken up by differing political
ideologies; concerning ideas, he "is a
regular department store."

22 ANON. "Walt Whitman. Professor de Selincourt's
Lecture." Hanley (England) <u>Staffordshire
Sentinel</u> (29 January).
Summary of Ernest de Selincourt's
lecture for the Workers' Educational Association: Whitman interpreted the common
man, writing in a manner expressive of his
spirit; he was poet of equality and the
divinity in one's self; he inspires many;
he shares a great spirit with Burns, who
was the better artist.

23 ANON. "Recent Books in Brief Review." <u>Bookman</u>
56 (February), 772.
Brief review of Merrill (1922.15),
which may appeal as "one more glimpse of
this great American."

24 MORLEY, CHRISTOPHER. "Moby Walt." <u>New York
Evening Post</u> (9 February), 8:4.

Revised: 1923.10.

Whitman remains "the youngest, the most modern, the most generously daring and terribly inscrutable of them all." Lawrence has no "truth that had not been sped with infinitely greater velocity, kinetics, and accurate aim by old Walt." Whale-like, "he jets poem-stuff"--"Moby Walt!" A preacher could base a sermon on "Paumanok," "Answerer," or "Myself" (which reveals "what America really means--or might mean"). Leaves is "a dangerous book" with "a hard lesson," tossing away "natural and defensive instinct." Whitman's flaws may be allowed, for he is a "triumphant, rigorous spirit." His prose is "the least known American classic."

25 ZAREK, OTTO. "Walt Whitman and German Poetry." Living Age 316 (10 February), 334-37.
    Translated from Die Neue Rundschau (December 1922): Whitman is "the poet of the American race," a corrective to contemporary German literature's "effeminacy," though German poetry cannot copy Whitman's form or ideals.

26 ADAMS, GEORGE MATTHEW. "George Matthew Adams." London (Ontario) Free Press (26 February).
    This inspirational column uses Whitman as an example of the right way to live.

27 L[IVINGSTON], F[LORA] V. "Whitman." Harvard Library Notes, no. 11 (May), 237-38.
    Early Harvard cataloguers reflected contemporary confusion over Whitman in their treatment of his works. Harvard's copies of Whitman's early editions, owned by Norton, Longfellow, Lowell, Aldrich, Charles Sumner, are described.

28 ANON. "Whitman, the Prophet." Hamilton Spectator (31 May).
    Whitman conveyed his consciousness of God and saw a place for everything in the world, including sex without overemphasis. He writes not as an ordinary but as the typical man, and therefore as a prophet. Quotation from Triggs (1898.17).

29 ANON. "Whitman's Fame Growing. Out of 200 Writers Only Three Report Poet's Influence Waning." New York Times (1 June), 8:2.
    Report of James Fawcett's speech announcing results of his survey asking if Whitman's popularity was increasing.

30 ANON. "Whitman as Prophet." New York Times (3 June), sec. 2, 4:4.
    Reprinted: 1923.34.
    Since the people mentioned in published reports of Fawcett's survey (see 1923.33) are all English or French, it seems "Whitman is still the great American poet of Europe." If growing slowly among the lower intellectual strata, his reputation is increasing yearly "in the only class whose opinion is able to carry him into immortality." He

may come to be regarded as more representative of our culture than he really was. Yet he opened windows in the soul which have not been locked since. "We are gradually growing up to him, and that is about as much as a people can do for any prophet."

31 ADAMS, A. M. "Whitman Appreciated. The Poet Found to Be the 'Patron Saint' of Bolshevist Circles." New York Times (6 June), 20:6.
    Letter complaining of speaker at this year's Whitman dinner who praised Russia, recalling a similar disgrace five years ago (see 1919.288).

32 MORTON, JAMES F., Jr. "Whitman Celebrates. Bolsheviki and Others Who Do Honor the Poet." New York Times (9 June), 10:6.
    Letter responding to Adams (1923.31): Whitman is embraced by propagandists of various sorts because he was out of the commonplace, intensely individualistic. This is the fault of the conservatives, who do not grant Whitman the recognition he deserves to bring him into the mainstream of society's ideals rather than let him be claimed "as an apostle of chaos and turbulent revolution."

33 FAWCETT, JAMES WALDO. "One Hundred Critics Gauge Walt Whitman's Fame." New York Times Book Review (10 June), 6, 14. Portrait.
    Favorable sales reports of Whitman are cited from publishers. Leaves is one of the bibles of the race, as indicated by the responses (many quoted) from G. B. Shaw, Jean de Quirielle, Havelock Ellis, G. K. Chesterton, Lord Dunsany, Sidney Dark, Gilbert Frankau, Lady Augusta Gregory, Will Hayes, Edmond Holmes, W. B. Maxwell, Ernest Rhys, Eden Phillpotts, Hugh Walpole, Haldane Macfall, M. P. Willcocks, Romain Rolland, Herbert Trench, H. de Vere Stacpoole, Coulson Kernahan, Sir William Robertson Nicoll, Sir Gilbert Parker, Cuthbert Grundy, Sir Henry Newbolt, Millicent Garrett Fawcett, Frederic Harrison, Henry W. Nevinson. Some tell their own personal experiences and appreciation of Whitman, some examine his influence and reputation. Many regard him as a "fixed star," beyond the need for popularity.

34 ANON. "Influence of Whitman Is Steadily Increasing." Toronto Mail (16 June).
    Reprint of 1923.30.

35 H[OPKINS], F[REDERICK] M. "Rare Books, Autographs and Prints." Publishers' Weekly 103 (16 June), 1839.
    Fawcett's survey (1923.33) attests to the popularity of Whitman already observed in the auction room. Whitman first editions and manuscripts will continue to increase in value.

1923

36 SHANKS, EDWARD. "American Literature." The
Queen 153 (28 June), 884.
Incidental: Whitman and Twain are "the
first of great and distinctively American
authors."

37 BRESLOW, M. M. "American First Editions.
No. 38. Walt Whitman 1819-1892." Publishers' Weekly 103 (30 June), 1929-30.
Descriptive bibliography of editions of
Leaves and other Whitman works, with brief
introduction: "Whitman's important literary effort was expressed in his own unique
poetic form; his prose work was mostly
incidental, or connected with newspaper
work."

38 CESTRE, CHARLES. "Walt Whitman, Poet of Self."
University of California Chronicle 25
(July), 318-43.
Whitman's qualities were typically
American, focusing on the self. His animal
exhilaration emulated the Romantics as well
as the pioneers, but his metaphors of
"defiant pan-sexualism" were unique. His
work moves toward restraint and more artistry. His vital and buoyant treatment of
nature appeals to contemporary French poets.
He renders beauty like a painter, adding
music to the visual. A few recognized in
him "a breath from a saner climate" than
Baudelaire's. Despite debts to the Romantics, Whitman stands alone in creating new
art forms, interpreting new aspects of
human nature, expressing the self, yet
transcending individual consciousness to
become mouthpiece of the race. Whitman is
a precursor of modern art in discovering
the beauty of laborers. Instinct rather
than intellect is for him "the mainspring
of personality." He is interested in action
and active love rather than neurotic romantic conquest. His verse has "the direct
impact of a magnetic individuality" with
its own "rugged forms of beauty." He provided liberation for Old World writers.
"His faith in progress is subdued by a
gentle creed of resignation," making his
later mysticism acceptable to the French.

39 ERSKINE, JOHN. "A Note on Whitman's Prosody."
Studies in Philology 20 (July), 336-44.
Whitman's "originality is more for the
eye than for the ear," for his rhythms are
clear and familiar. Like readers of blank
verse, he ended where a reader would end
rather than use enjambment. Without the
essential pauses at the close of lines, the
verse of Shakespeare and Milton would pale
beside Whitman's best, basing its rhythm
on the accent of the words.

30 HOLLOWAY, EMORY. "Whitman as Critic of
America." Studies in Philology 20 (July),
345-69.
Whitman "had the wrong sort of humor
and too much mystical humanitarianism to be
a typical satirist." Leaves challenges

average American readers to measure themselves against Whitman. His early boasting
was a protection against possible rejection
but it decreased. He was led to encourage
his country and chide it (for the spirit of
its government, religion, attitude toward
sex). He praised athletics and health as
important for "independence of spirit" as
well as work and sought women for such men,
considering sex "a dominating power in
civilization." "Exposition" uses "parody
on his own style" to suggest that crude
experimenting in self-expression is better
than polished imitation. Vistas provides
the most searching examination ever made
of the state of American literature by a
contemporary. The movement from "Respondez"
to "So Long" suggests that "America lost a
great satirist" because of his faith: "he
remains the most discerning, the most courageous, the most loving critic America has
ever had."

41 _____. Review of Wells (1922.27). Studies in
Philology 20 (July), 371-73.
Compiling a bibliography for Whitman is
a difficult task. This one is flawed but
valuable.

42 RICHTER, MILO C. "Walt Whitman and Wisconsin."
Wisconsin Magazine 1 (July), 21-22. Drawing
by Richter.
Describes Whitman's brief 1848 visit to
Wisconsin, unnoted by Milwaukee papers.
His western journey changed him, with an
increased sense of Americanism and an urge
to write a book for the New World. His
references to Wisconsin are quoted. For
him "poetry was a passionate movement, the
rhythm of progress, the march of humanity,
the procession of Freedom."

43 RIDLEY, H. M. "Great Friendships. IX.--Anne
Gilchrist and Walt Whitman." Canadian
Magazine 61 (July), 251-58.
Reprinted: 1932.24.
Traces the Gilchrist-Whitman relationship, quoting their letters. She "came
into his life at least ten years too late,"
for at that time "his love was of the cosmic order" and could not be exclusive,
especially for a woman.

44 FAWCETT, JAMES WALDO. "America Judges Walt
Whitman. A Symposium of Opinion." New
York Herald Books (15 July), 1, 4.
Quotes responses of American writers,
critics, and scholars to the question: "Is
Whitman's popular acceptance increasing or
decreasing?" Some say he is becoming more
popular; others doubt it but note his growing influence. Much of his nation is awak-
ing to appreciation of his message and to
understanding of America's soul. Respondents
quoted are: Samuel Hopkins Adams, Leonard
D. Abbott, Katharine Lee Bates, William
Rose Benét, Harry Weir Boland, Gamaliel
Bradford, William Stanley Braithwaite,

Canby, Dr. Frank Crane, Dr. Wilbur Cross,
Floyd Dell, De Casseres, Dr. W. E. B.
Du Bois, Eastman, Erskine, Firkins, Zona
Gale, Garland, Dr. Franklin H. Giddings,
Mrs. Charlotte Perkins Gilman, Dr. Isaac
Goldberg, Guthrie, Dr. John Haynes Holmes,
Clark Howell, Dr. David Starr Jordan,
Miss Bertha Johnston, Dr. Willis Fletcher
Johnson, Charles Rann Kennedy, Dr. Louise
M. Kueffner, Sen. Henry Cabot Lodge, John
Macy, Morley, Harriet Monroe, Dr. John
Howard Melish, George Jean Nathan, Dean
Roscoe Pound, Chester C. Platt, Phelps,
Perry, Rascoe, Repplier, Dr. Joel E.
Spingarn, Dr. Thomas Wood Stevens, Rev.
Mrs. Anna Garlin Spencer, Dr. George Jay
Smith, Booth Tarkington, Untermeyer, Carl
Van Doren, John V. A. Weaver, William Allen
White, Clement Wood.

45 B., C. F. "Walt Whitman in His Second
    Century." Christian Science Monitor (17
    July), 15:1-2.
    Reprinted: 1923.50.
        A century after first startling his
    readers, Whitman can now be considered as
    a poet, not merely a prophet. His long
    line expresses his ideas well, but its
    lack of classic finish may keep him from
    the ranks of the greatest. He occasionally
    glorifies the means at the expense of the
    end (for example, singing "athletic democ-
    racy," whose place may not be in poetry).
    While he may be glorifying all humanity in
    singing himself, he still "grates upon our
    sensibilities." Many like him best when
    he is impersonal, as in "some delightful
    little vignettes" (quoted) prefiguring the
    imagists. His writings on Lincoln and
    friendship are praised. His idea of com-
    radeship is associated with internationalist
    feelings. "Lilacs" allows us to forgive
    him anything.

*46 LE GALLIENNE, EVA. List of her ten best
     books. Toronto Star (22 August).
     Reported in Willard.
         Leaves is third only to Les Misérables
     and Gilbert Murray's translation of the
     Greek drama.

47 ANON. "Edwin Markham, Poet, Deplores Sex
    Writing. Criticizes Walt Whitman for Un-
    sound Philosophy on Virtue." Toronto Daily
    Star (28 August), 20:1.
        Though resembling Whitman in appearance,
    Markham is more spiritually akin to J. W.
    Riley. Markham's estimate of Whitman is
    quoted extensively: "brilliant in spots,"
    with a "great influence on the morals of
    America, but some times in evil ways." "He
    is frequently a poor thinker." The writer
    says Whitman's influence might not be so
    great if many did not confuse him with
    Walt Mason.

48 PHELPS, WILLIAM LYON. "Makers of American
    Literature. Walt Whitman--The American

Optimist." Ladies' Home Journal 40 (September), 23, 172, 175. Alexander portrait.
Revised: 1924.18.
    Prints a manuscript letter of 1880 from
the Yale Library, showing Whitman as cheerful optimist. He shared Twain's faith in
democracy but not his pessimism or humor.
He cannot be considered a greater poet than
Tennyson because his poetry is not as good.
Life sketch, noting his deliberate assumption of his unconventionalities and the
revolutionary changes in his attitude
toward life and art. He wrote "poems of
amazing originality and beauty" and "passages which never should have been printed,"
included perhaps to gain attention; they
have helped sell the book, then and now.
He was a man of genius but lacked humor,
taste, and a sense of proportion. He is at
last a popular poet, having created the
demand for his style, being helped by the
current poetic renaissance. The 1872
Preface (quoted) has become even more important because of the World War. He was
unconventional rather than original,
shocking in "literary etiquette" rather
than in thought. He dealt with universal
rather than timely questions and was no
political revolutionist, believing intensely
in individualism. His free verse remains
unique and unsurpassed. A list of titles
reveals his genius for expressing a universal idea in "a permanently beautiful
phrase." Such poems as "Prayer," "Lilacs,"
"Man-of-War-Bird" speak for us all. To
Europe he interpreted America; "to America
he tried to interpret the universe."

49 RODGERS, CLEVELAND. "Walt Whitman Poet of
    Democracy." The Mentor 11 (September),
    3-14.
        Whitman has not yet reached the masses
    and must be rescued from possessive cliques.
    He was a simple man without literary pre-
    tensions, a patriot, a self-educated poet.
    For him democracy is religion. He is "the
    first real American propagandist" to sell
    America, yet he is also an internationalist.
    Readers should study his work, especially
    Vistas, which proves him "an informed
    critic." His poetry represents his total
    personality. Account of his war service
    and old age.

50 [B., C. F.] "Walt Whitman." Melbourne Leader
    (1 September), 60:3-4.
    Reprint of 1923.45.

51 SMITH, LEWIS WORTHINGTON. "Walt Whitman and
    Natural Democracy." Dearborn Independent
    23 (15 September).
        Ridicules the idea of absolute equality
    and the absence of discriminations in
    Whitman as being not what American democracy
    is about. Although at his highest he gave
    us "the wonderful threnody" "Lilacs,"
    Whitman's legacy has been naturalism, which
    has produced mere "wallowing in the slime."

52 BLATCHFORD, ROBERT. "Walt Whitman." Clarion
(21 September).

Personal account of first reading
Whitman, his shock at Whitman's "naked
talk on sexual mysteries," uncouth versification, strident conceit. Later he became
excited reading "Open Road," discovering
Whitman as "a man and a brother." He resents the overpraise of Whitman's disciples.
Whitman's philosophy is summed up in preparation for a further analysis of his
claims to greatness (not located).

53 RODGERS, CLEVELAND. "Walt Whitman, the Politician." Literary Review 4 (22 September),
57-58.

Traces Whitman's political concerns
and involvements from his newspaper
writings and activities, until he became
disillusioned and turned to poetry, "a new
way in which to deliver his message."

54 ANON. "City Today Makes Memorial Shrine of
Whitman Home. Eminent Scholars Join Personal Friends Here in Honoring Great Poet.
Pilgrimage to Tomb. His Physician, Students
of His Works, Speakers at Mickle Street
House." Camden Courier (17 November), 1:1,
5:1-6. Illustrated.

Detailed account of the dedication of
the Mickle Street home as a shrine.
Harrison Morris describes how the memorial
was set up, quoting from his Italian book
on Whitman in Mickle Street (see 1929.17)
and his own memories of visits with Whitman,
Whitman's sense of humor, birthday dinners,
disagreement with Ingersoll. Duncan Spaeth
termed Whitman the poet of the whole sweep
of the country rather than a single area;
some of his best and most mature works were
produced in Camden; he has had great influence abroad; we are just beginning to
catch up with some of his ideas; "he was
less an interpreter of the past to the
present than a diviner of the future in the
present." Dr. MacAlister cleared Whitman's
name of atheism and materialism. He was a
natural, no "pompous pretender," with
limitless sympathy.

55 ANON. "Walt Whitman." Camden Courier (17
November), 4:1.

Editorial on Camden's welcome dedication
of the Mickle Street house as a shrine "to
the memory of its most distinguished citizen." Whitman broke away from English convention to express himself freely with the
"sturdiness of spirit" we admire, having
come to accept him as has the rest of the
world. Camden will be remembered in time
to come only because of Whitman's residence
here.

56 ANON. "City Dedicates Whitman's Humble Home
as Memorial to the 'Good Gray Poet.'"
Camden Post-Telegram (17 November), 1:2.
Illustrated.

Announces dedication of tablet at
Mickle Street house, "where the poet penned
many of his lines that have become classic,"
while "sponsored by an ever-growing cult."

57 ANON. "A Prophecy Fulfilled." Camden Post-
Telegram (17 November).

Quotes Bonsall's obituary article
(1892.66) to show that, now that Whitman's
home is restored, it is a place of pilgrimage, with his fame and influence widespread.

58 ANON. "Whitman of 'The Camden Post.'" Camden
Post-Telegram (17 November), 1.

Whitman wrote pieces for the Post on
various matters, often making abrupt transitions characteristic of him and his wide
range of interests.

59 ANON. "Walt Whitman's House: Its Various
Meanings." Philadelphia Public Ledger (17
November).

Impressionistic account of Whitman's
life on Mickle Street. With his simplicity
of heart and greatness of mind, democratic
spirit and closeness to the earth, he was
an ideal for all to look to.

60 QUERIST [pseud.]. "Literature and Life. Free
Song." Irish Statesman 1 (17 November),
303-4.

Considers whether free-verse poets can
really soar or else fall flat, as Whitman
occasionally did, though he was "the first
considerable poet to attempt sustained
flight in song, discarding traditional
metrical formulae." Because its soaring
power is intermittent, Leaves fails as
song, however exciting in idea or emotion,
except for about three hundred lines, including "Death Carol."

61 ANON. "Camden Dedicates Home of Whitman."
New York Times (18 November), sec. 1, 14:1.
Account of dedication ceremonies and
addresses.

62 ANON. "The Paumanok Puritan." New York Times
(18 November), sec. 2, 6:5.
Response to Jean Catel's article in
Mercure de France, "Walt Whitman, Puritan":
It is startling to consider Whitman as a
puritan, though he is certainly moral and
didactic, qualities which should not be
part of literature. But now who can be
considered the anti-puritan American poet?

63 ANON. "Camden Dedicates Whitman Shrine."
Philadelphia Public Ledger (18 November),
sec. 2, 1:5. Illustrated.

Describes the "democratic celebration,"
"such as Whitman himself, the first poet to
voice in literature the full reverberation
of America's rich and varied life, would
have desired." Describes speeches and
Mrs. Weda Cook Addicks's rendition of
"Captain," which she often sang to Whitman.

64 SPENCER, LILIAN WHITE. "To Walt Whitman."
     <u>Lyric West</u> 3 (December), 23.
         This poem describing a tree is intro-
     duced by a reference to Whitman's descrip-
     tion of a tree in "I Saw in Louisiana."

65 LINDSAY, VACHEL. "Walt Whitman." <u>New Republic</u>
     37 (5 December), Views of American Poetry
     Supplement, 3-5.
     Reprinted with minor changes: 1929.16.
         Whitman is "as big a poet as his most
     emphatic admirer makes him out to be," but
     he is no hero. He has the grand style,
     with all its attendant fatalities for imi-
     tators. He claims a personal devotion,
     especially through his followers, yet we
     have "no interesting details" about his
     actual life. He cannot fill the needs of
     the American people for a hero because he
     lacks chivalry toward women, so he "will
     always survive outside the main line of
     tradition as a gigantic lonely individual."

1924

BOOKS

1 BAUDOUIN, CHARLES. <u>Contemporary Studies</u>.
    Translated from the French by Eden and
    Charles Paul. London: George Allen &
    Unwin. New York: E. P. Dutton (1925).
    "Whitmanesque Realism," pp. 174-94; also
    60, 202, 217-20, 224, 232, 249, 271, 283.
        A lecture delivered in 1921. Whitman
    is "the most typical of realist poets" in
    his emphasis on tangible reality, his pre-
    sentation of material in sequences "deter-
    mined by bursts of feeling" rather than
    "natural order," and his "impetus towards
    mankind." The <u>Unanimistes</u>, French realists,
    follow him but transform his acceptance of
    all as good into much "condemnation of
    extant reality." They lack Whitman's
    robustness because of the difference between
    French and American environments. Symbol-
    ists like Verhaeren and Claudel also follow
    Whitman, with many poets using his "quasi-
    biblical versification."

2 BIANCHI, MARTHA DICKINSON. <u>The Life and
    Letters of Emily Dickinson</u>. Boston and New
    York: Houghton Mifflin Co., p. 239.
        Includes reprint from 1891.47 of
    Dickinson's letter mentioning Whitman.

3 BULLETT, GERALD. Biographical and critical
    essays in <u>Walt Whitman: A Study and A
    Selection</u>. London: Grant Richards, pp. 3-
    24, 27-48.
    Reprinted: 1925.2.
        Novelistic narrative of Whitman's life,
    based on <u>Specimen</u>, Binns (1905.1), and
    Perry (1906.13), notes the impact of his
    experience on his writing, without overem-
    phasizing environment. His less than
    frank use of anonymous reviews and of
    Emerson's letter was reprehensible. He was

not a great artist, though he took care in
revising his work. His defects include
sentimentalism and tediousness. "Myself"
displays "not an offensive egotism" but
"only a noble arrogance." His occasional
faults do not invalidate his claim to real
greatness. His convictions are sometimes
so overstated as to suggest a doubt behind
his faith. "Adam" becomes ridiculous only
when he fails to choose the right words;
"Calamus" is "gushing and mawkish," the
phrase "manly love" being "grotesquely mis-
applied." <u>Leaves</u> shows little trace of
development, intellectual or artistic. The
war and old age led Whitman to express "a
tender, reflective note, a pensive beauty"
that was rare in his prior work. <u>Drum-Taps</u>,
unlike the poems of the World War, exhibits
only verbal blemishes, not spiritual ones.
Twelve poems are printed. (Used in part in
1934.4.)

4 CABELL, JAMES BRANCH. <u>Straws and Prayer-
    Books: Dizain des Diversions</u>. New York:
    Robert M. McBride & Co., pp. 19, 248.
        Longevity "induces us to cherish our
    Longfellows and Bryants, and even to toler-
    ate our Whitmans." Whitman is one of "ten
    'established' authors endowed with 'cults'
    whose masterpieces once appeared to me the
    most violently uninteresting and ill
    written."

5 CARPENTER, EDWARD. <u>Some Friends of Walt
    Whitman: A Study in Sex-Psychology</u>. Pub-
    lication no. 13. London: British Society
    for the Study of Sex Psychology, 16 pp.
        Discussion of Whitman's homosexual pas-
    sion, unacknowledged by the world but
    "burning fiercely within him and pressing
    for deliverance," expressed in "Calamus"
    and explaining his responses to Symonds's
    letters and Gilchrist's love. Other critics
    fail to recognize or accept this aspect of
    Whitman's personality. His combination of
    feminine and masculine characteristics may
    indicate a superior rather than pathological
    type of humanity.

6 CRAWFORD, NELSON ANTRIM, ed. <u>Poems of Walt
    Whitman, with Introduction and Notes</u>.
    Girard, Kans.: Haldeman-Julius Co. "The
    Life of Walt Whitman," pp. 7-15; "The Poetry
    of Walt Whitman," 16-24.
        Life sketch, noting "the conflict be-
    tween the Puritan and the liberal in his
    nature" as the basis for his work's
    "breadth, serenity, and wisdom." His later
    days in Washington were "troubled both by
    an unhappy love affair, and by emotional
    attachment to his own sex, the two showing
    the apparent erotic duality" seen in many
    of his poems. His physical characteristics
    are described. He represented, as no one
    else has, "the various attributes of the
    ideal America which he envisioned." His
    poetic development is traced, following his
    own nature, leading to "the rhythms of

1924

external nature set against the rhythms of living humanity" accompanied by "the personal rhythm of the poet." His poetic position comes from the emotional and intellectual factors which produced his rhythms: his fusion of body and spirit, his representative egocentrism. The "erotic implications" of his emphasis on same-sex comradeship "form a problem for the psycologist more than for the literary critic." His patriotism may seem idealistic and sentimental today, but is realism necessary from a poet? His influence is growing, not upon contemporary verse form but with regard to democratic ideals and through his readers ("among the most intelligent and discerning people").

6a CRONWRIGHT-SCHREINER, S[AMUEL] C., ed. The Letters of Olive Schreiner 1876-1920. Boston: Little, Brown, & Co., pp. 17, 21, 96, 103, 129, 243, 389.

Letters (particularly to Havelock Ellis) note Olive Schreiner's early laughter at Whitman's work, changed to warm appreciation when she read him for herself; "one needs to be strong and in overpowering health really to enjoy him." His moving power is Faust's desire to know and to be all things.

7 DELL, FLOYD. Looking at Life. New York: Alfred A. Knopf. "Walt Whitman and the American Temperament," pp. 193-99.

Whitman exemplifies the tendency of the American people to be self-contradictory and to remain blithely unconscious of it, as in his conflicting attitudes toward war and his alternate faith in and doubts about America, seen in passages in which he "speaks for us all."

8 DRINKWATER, JOHN. The Outline of Literature. Vol. 3. New York and London: G. P. Putnam's Sons. "Walt Whitman," pp. 862-66; also 843. Illustrated.

Sketch of Whitman's life for young readers. "No poet has ever more persistently sung himself," to compel "recognition of his own individuality." "He loved himself because he loved life" and all creatures on earth. For his time he was "almost outrageously masculine." He emphasizes respect for the mass and for the individual. Without being "'suggestive,'" he acclaims the pleasures of the body as well as of the mind and spirit. He was American without "narrow nationalism." Though "an unequal poet," at his best he found exactly the right way to say what he wanted to say.

9 FRANK, WALDO. Salvos: An Informal Book about Books and Plays. New York: Boni & Liveright. "A Letter to the Annual Whitman Celebration," pp. 276-79; also 17, 38, 41, 65, 191, 208, 209, 249, 265, 269.

Whitman, "our greatest poet," is not read because he offers no help with our immediate problems; he would "drag us into grips with the entire, uneasy problem." America should not be complacent about producing him, perhaps the nineteenth century's deepest and most creative spirit, for he is as alone in 1923 America as in 1860. His work remains unassimilated in this country, though influential in Germany and France. He challenges our literature and society to "grow up to his own universal Norm." The Whitman Fellowship might enlarge its function to help make Whitman part of America by sponsoring an annual award for the most significant work on Whitman by an American.

10 HAMBLEN, EMILY S. Walt Whitman: Bard of the West. Little Blue Book no. 529. Girard, Kans.: Haldeman-Julius Co., 64 pp.

Whitman set himself up as would-be bard for America, standing for the spirit of the West, differing from Homer in projecting the future. His book's arrangement is explained with comments on poems and sections. "Eidólons" is "one of the most perfect poems in the language," deeply characteristic of him. Whitman uses science but sees beyond it. The theme of "Myself" is "personality in its widest scope--commensurate with the universe." His sex poems are unrestrained, not merely symbolic of general ideas but part of his total philosophy of life, the aftermath of his Southern love affair. He was assuredly a husband and father, hence the "two deep emotional springs in the poet, desire for the one true mate and the passion of paternity." "Calamus" is confusing, using "lover" while "Adam" does not, showing Whitman certainly troubled by feelings he "knew must be restrained." He does not answer the question whether relationships can be bifurcated, thus not giving women their due. Biographical sketch emphasizes his sensitivity, the spiritual autobiography of "Sea Drift," his personal magnetism, love for music, racy and vital conversations recorded by Traubel, unflagging optimism with later concern for America's immediate future, similarities to Nietzsche but differing attitude toward democracy.

11 HOLLOWAY, EMORY, ed. Editorial note to Leaves of Grass, Inclusive Edition. Garden City, N.Y.: Doubleday, Page & Co., pp. vii-viii.

Explains inclusion of additional poems, prose, and variorum readings (compiled by Triggs [1902.25]). Whitman's stylistic idiosyncrasies, part of this "record of an original personality," are retained. Dates are included to indicate Whitman's growth.

12 KENNEDY, WILLIAM SLOANE. The Real John Burroughs: Personal Recollection and Friendly Estimate. New York and London: Funk & Wagnalls Co., pp. 43-45, 49, 66-67, 75-76, 81-86, 190, 193, 211, 233, 239-41.

Quotes letters about Whitman, comments

on books about Whitman. Whitman was "too big for Burroughs to handle," for Whitman's critic "should be built on as large a model as Walt himself," as Bazalgette and Sarrazin are. He did not fully comprehend "the more profound Hegelian features of Walt's works." "Burroughs loved Walt like a woman; but so did I." Extract is reprinted from 1866.26.

12 MENCKEN, H. L. <u>Prejudices</u>. 4th ser. New York: Alfred A. Knopf, pp. 15, 17-19, 40-41, 279-80.
Extract reprinted: 1937.21.
    References to Whitman as example of the writers some refuse to accept as representative of America, in favor of genteel poets; Whitman as product of the war.

14 MITCHELL, EDWARD P. <u>Memories of an Editor: Fifty Years of American Journalism</u>. New York and London: Charles Scribner's Sons, pp. 269-72.
    Whitman thanked Mitchell for his review (1881.45), "some rather callow observations" which he had thought "sufficiently conservative to be obnoxious to Walt." Reasons are suggested. Whitman's letter is printed in facsimile, as is another paragraph.

15 MORLEY, CHRISTOPHER. <u>One Act Plays</u>. Garden City, N.Y.: Doubleday, Page & Co. "Walt," pp. 105-42.
Reprint of 1924.41.

16 O'HIGGINS, HARVEY, and REEDE, EDWARD H. <u>The American Mind in Action</u>. New York: Harper & Bros. "In Walt Whitman and Mark Hanna," pp. 202-25.
    Describes George Fox's Quaker doctrines as "the backbone of Whitman's philosophy." Whitman's personal development is traced from his own account. Eventually he turned from "the current American reality" and began to "exploit his personality in a sort of exhibitionism." His early poems have two distinct strains, the surface assumption of himself as representative American and the deeper drift of the sexual undercurrents. Both themes are deceptive, for he was hardly representative and was nearer homosexuality than heterosexuality. "A Narcissan egotist," he created a role for himself.

17 PAUL, ELLIOT H. <u>Imperturbe</u>. New York: Alfred A. Knopf, pp. 286, 307.
    Uses "Me Imperturbe" in full as epigraph. A character reads and rereads <u>Leaves</u>, "feeling a new integrity and self-respect as the significance of the poems grew upon him."

18 PHELPS, WILLIAM LYON. <u>Howells, James, Bryant and Other Essays</u>. New York: Macmillan Co. "Whitman," pp. 31-65. Alexander portrait. Revision of 1923.48. Reprinted: 1924.19.
    Some rewording, some additions. More of a sensationalist than a thinker, Whitman

seldom stimulates the mind. His present popularity is due to the general preference for the animal attitude toward life over the spiritual. His was a religion of nature. His best lines have "superb rolling music," more impressively fitting some of his subjects than conventional forms.

19 _____. <u>The Poetry of Walt Whitman</u>. New York: Macmillan Co., 45 pp. Paper.
Reprint of 1924.18.

20 RANKIN, HENRY B. <u>Intimate Character Sketches of Abraham Lincoln</u>. Philadelphia and London: J. B. Lippincott Co. "Lincoln and Walt Whitman," pp. 85-94; also 12, 54-57, 319, 336.
Extract reprinted: 1933.20.
    Recollection in greater detail than in 1916.17 of Lincoln reading <u>Leaves</u> aloud in his Springfield law office. Account of his presumed words on Whitman, going by the White House. Description of Whitman's character ("splendid optimism," "benign faith in his fellowmen") and hospital work; his diary remarks on Lincoln quoted, likewise some poetry. Few men of the nineteenth century will be so well-remembered as Whitman.

21 SAUNDERS, HENRY S. <u>Illustrations to Walt Whitman's Leaves of Grass Gathered from Various Sources Including Many Original Photographs</u>. Selected, mounted, and bound by Henry S. Saunders. Over 330 pictures. In manuscript only.

22 SINCLAIR, MAY. <u>Arnold Waterlow</u>. New York: Macmillan Co., pp. 324-27, 397.
    A young man borrows from a young woman a copy of Whitman, which he loves for its "strange new beauty," "large, stretching rhythm," "undecorated, naked phrase," "passionate adoration of life." Poems are quoted, including "Last Invocation," which he remembers when he is dying.

23 SULLIVAN, LOUIS H. <u>The Autobiography of an Idea</u>. New York: Press of The American Institute of Architects, pp. 25, 37, 236, 249, 271, 275, 284. Foreword by Claude Bragdon, p. 5.
    Sullivan quotes "There Was a Child" and uses it as a motif; cites Whitman's "deep insight"; uses term "Democratic Vistas." Bragdon compares Sullivan to Whitman: they share Americanism and "lusty faith in the ultimate emergence into brotherhood and beauty of the people of 'these states.'"

24 WEIRICK, BRUCE. <u>From Whitman to Sandburg in American Poetry: A Critical Survey</u>. New York: Macmillan Co. "Walt Whitman," pp. 1-37; primary and secondary readings, pp. 226-28; also ix-x, passim per index.
    Whitman, our greatest poet, is "the most stimulating influence in contemporary

poetry," as shown in comparisons with recent poets, especially Sandburg, his most notable follower. He saw America as "amorphic, fluid, aspiring," and not static as did the New England poets. His treatment of things American "is realistic and at the same time national and imaginative." His mysticism is a new sort of transcendentalism, an acceptance rather than rejection of earthly things. He emphasizes love for friends, nature, and democracy, but he is a poet of scenes, processions, and people as well as ideals, and thus, with his inclusiveness, "the authentic voice of a national spirit." His form of ideal friendship, as strong as love yet of wider applicability, seems unattainable to human nature as now known but is an ideal worthy of men's aspirations. His artistic renovations as well as ideals have been upheld, notably "the desire to eliminate the dead abstractions from poetry," to cling to the live image itself. His style suits his moods, "with beauty and force in perfect equipoise."

25 WHARTON, EDITH. <u>Old New York: The Spark (The 'Sixties)</u>. New York: D. Appleton & Co., pp. 70, 80-83, 87, 92, 101-9.
     A recurrent motif in this novella is Hayley Delane's recollection of "a sort of big backwoodsman" who spoke with him in the hospital during the Civil War: "he taught me Christian charity." The story concludes when Delane finds his picture and the narrator tells him that the man is Whitman, whose poems he reads aloud. Although the narrator feels "the oft-read lines" as he has never felt them before, Delane prefers the poetry he knew when young and wishes he had not been told that the "great chap" wrote "all that rubbish."

26 WILSON, FRANCIS. <u>Francis Wilson's Life of Himself</u>. Boston and New York: Houghton Mifflin Co. "Walt Whitman and 'Leaves of Grass,'" pp. 228-42. Photograph, facsimile.
     Recollection of his boyhood impressions of Whitman in Philadelphia, "the proud old man with the market-basket," which was full of his books, generally regarded as "the filthiest old rascal in Philadelphia" because of his writings about women. But young Wilson liked Whitman's poetry; he describes his visit with Whitman in 1891, noting Whitman's fondness for actors and critical comment on Poe. The values of his philosophy and poetry are being recognized.

PERIODICALS

27 ANON. "Song of the Universe. The Philosophy of Walt Whitman." <u>Yorkshire Observer</u> (24 January).
     Summary of lecture by Percy Lund to the Bradford English Society on Whitman's universal ideal. Whitman reached for a univer-

sal synthesis in his work, "the Bible of modern times."

28 HOLLOWAY, EMORY. "Walt Whitman as an Editor Fought All, Including His Boss." <u>Brooklyn Daily Eagle</u> (27 January), sec. B, 4:7-8. Excerpt from 1924.29.

29 _____. "More Light on Whitman." <u>American Mercury</u> 1 (February), 183-89.
     Discusses Whitman's work for Brooklyn <u>Evening Star</u>, 1845-46, a Whig paper though Whitman was a Democrat; cites material attributed to Whitman. Comments by <u>Star</u>'s publishers show Whitman as politically argumentative. He was devoted to the theater, though reviews show him opinionated, often caustic; his music reviews were more positive. His editorials support nonviolence in politics, oppose corporal punishment in education. The <u>Star</u> writings show Whitman absorbed in his society; this period prepared him for poetry and for wider editorial responsibility.

*30 MARKHAM, EDWIN. Comments on Whitman. Winter Park (Florida) <u>Herald</u> (28 February). Reported in Kennedy (1926).

31 FLETCHER, JOHN GOULD. "Walt Whitman." <u>North American Review</u> 219 (March), 355-66.
     Whitman was "the only democratic poet the world has ever possessed," the one "authentically great American poet." He had to "contain multitudes" because he has been among them. He is the poet not of individuality but of personality; he subordinates his individuality to the crowd. Mere originality such as later poets have stressed is not enough; for Whitman, revolt must satisfy the emotional and physical as well as intellectual needs of man. He has a sense of life continually transcending itself and is probably "the only death-poet who attempted such a feat as accepting death on the same terms as life." He is religious, even Christian. He was unique, as a product of his specific period.

32 HUTCHINSON, PERCY A. "American Poetry in an Extensive Critical Survey." <u>New York Times Book Review</u> (2 March), 11, 25.
     Review of Weirick (1924.24). Most now grant that Whitman was our greatest poet, but he should be called humanitarian, not democratic as Weirick narrowly uses the term, for he was not concerned merely with government. Quoted passages showing Whitman's pantheism indicate a great poet's and teacher's voice. As a philosopher he was less a dynamic than a potential force. His synthesizing power is more significant than his overemphasized passion for humanity, which is secondary, though the major influence on many lesser poets.

33 HIER, FREDERICK P., Jr. "The End of a Literary Mystery." <u>American Mercury</u> 1 (April), 471-78.

Much of Burroughs's Notes (1867.1) was written by Whitman, as suggested by such **evidence as its wide difference** from Burroughs's Study (1896.2), its similarity to some of Whitman's prose, and correspondence from Traubel indicating Notes' origin.

34 MACK, LAURENCE. "The Good Gray Poet." Book Notes Illustrated 2 (April-May), 139.
       Modernist American poets ignore the significant influence of Whitman, perhaps because of his "very real sense of music." People will always return to his naturalness and sanity, his affinity for the common people making him "America's greatest elemental force in letters." His poetry expresses a strong individuality; the only qualifications of its purity are certain salient passages (especially in "Calamus") requiring some expurgation for American youth, although understandable in one so intoxicated with life. A true idealist, he recognized men's duty to relieve suffering, yet always saw beauty in the world.

35 ANON. "The Godfather of Rough-necks." Literary Digest 81 (12 April), 31-32.
       Quotes and summarizes Weirick (1924.24) regarding Whitman's impact on contemporary poets.

36 [SMYTHE, A. E. S.] "Walt Whitman's Day." Hamilton (Ontario) Spectator (31 May).
       Presents Whitman's teaching, so often forgotten among the controversies: he is the poet of the soul's immortality yet also recognizes elements of life that are not purely spiritual; his refusal to be a hypocrite about them makes many object to him.

37 ANON. "One of Whitman's Secrets Revealed--A Story Involving John Burroughs' First Book." Current Opinion 76 (June), 791.
       Quotes and summarizes Hier (1924.33).

38 MABBOTT, THOMAS OLLIVE. "Walt Whitman and the Aristidean." American Mercury 2 (June), 205-7.
       Describes Whitman's hitherto overlooked contributions to the Aristidean.

39 PATTEE, FRED LEWIS. "Call for a Literary Historian." American Mercury 2 (June), 134-40.
       Reprinted: 1928.10.
       Several incidental references to Whitman's shifted place in American literature.

40 TRAUBEL, HORACE. "Whitman on His Contemporaries." American Mercury 2 (July), 328-32.
       Pre-publication extracts of Traubel IV: comments on Lowell, Emerson, Howells.

41 MORLEY, CHRISTOPHER. "Walt. A One-Act Portrait." Bookman 59 (August), 646-62.
       Sketch by Jo Mielziner.

Reprinted: 1924.15.
       Vivid recreation of a November 1888 afternoon in Whitman's Mickle Street living room, with Mrs. Davis and Dr. Osler talking about him, followed by a visit from Traubel, Logan Pearsall Smith, and Richard Harding Davis, to whose questions about literature and marriage Walt warmly responds with comments largely drawn from his works and Traubel's recorded conversations. Alone, he throws old letters and a photograph into the fire, saying "Good-bye. . . . My Fancy," which he tells the returning Traubel will be the title for the last section of his book. Traubel should further inform a "school marm" correspondent from Australia that "I wrote my book for lonely people."

42 TRAUBEL, HORACE. "Walt Whitman on Himself." American Mercury 3 (October), 186-92.
       Pre-publication extracts from Traubel IV.

43 HOLLOWAY, EMORY. "A Whitman Manuscript." American Mercury 3 (December), 475-80.
       Description of Whitman notebooks of 1840s and 1850s, donated by Bucke to Library of Congress.

44 ANON. "Mr. Middleton Murry's Essays." Times Literary Supplement (London) (11 December), 844.
       Review of two books by J. Middleton Murry, who "has no right to quote Whitman's beautiful apostrophe" of the "Death Carol" as though it bore out his own disbelief in personal immortality, for Whitman believed in it as well as in the individual's many stages of development through different lives.

1925

BOOKS

1 BARRUS, CLARA. The Life and Letters of John Burroughs. Boston and New York: Houghton Mifflin Co., passim per index.
       Many references, quoting letters between Whitman and Burroughs on the writing of Notes (1867.1), Whitman's opinions, Burroughs's ideas on him, anecdotes.

2 BULLETT, GERALD. Walt Whitman: A Study and a Selection. Philadelphia: J. B. Lippincott Co., 166 pp.
       Reprint of 1924.3.

3 CUSHING, HARVEY. The Life of Sir William Osler. Oxford: At the Clarendon Press. Vol. 1, pp. 264-66; vol. 2, pp. 130, 631, 666.
       Quotes Osler's fragmentary reminiscences (quoted in 1939.21) of Whitman at 64, visited on Bucke's request. Though Whitman was "a fine old man, full of common sense and kindly feelings," his poetry did not

appeal to Osler, who was more interested in Bucke's fervid discipleship. Osler's impressions of Perry's book (1906.13) are quoted. At the end of his life, Osler was **working on a lecture on Whitman.**

4 FOERSTER, NORMAN. Whitman selections and notes in American Poetry and Prose: A Book of Reading 1607-1916. Boston: Houghton Mifflin Co., pp. 635-712, 1035-38; also iii, iv, v, vi, 1058.

Notes explain ideas, sources, background, especially for "Myself." Introduction describes Emerson and Whitman as the pivotal figures in our literary evolution. Whitman, directly indebted to Emerson, is "a more complete romanticist" than he, though both point toward the realistic school. Does their optimism spring more from the eighteenth-century doctrine of natural goodness or from the vision of a land of opportunity?

5 GOSSE, Sir EDMUND. "Walt Whitman." In Selected Modern English Essays. 1st ser. Edited by Humphrey Milford. N.p.: Oxford University Press, pp. 77-92. Reprint of 1894.28.

6 HARRIS, FRANK. My Life. Vol. 1. New York: Frank Harris Publishing Co., pp. 106, 174, 234-40. Reprint of 1922.8 (sections of the book are expurgated for American audiences).

7 _____. My Life. Vol. 2. Nice: Privately printed for subscribers only, pp. x, 272-73, 422.

Continues 1922.8. Brief references, including Edwin Arnold's comments on Whitman. Continued 1927.8.

8 KREYMBORG, ALFRED. Troubadour: An Autobiography. New York: Liveright, pp. 120, 148-49, 150, 156, 162, 210, 294, 372, 401.

Describes Whitman's appeal to him "as the first original, the one true democrat and cosmopolitan on American soil." No Americans have approached him with "so passionate a stride, such enchantment of song, so powerful a reality of vision, or with an individuality radiating all the points of the human circumference." Though so often deplored in America, he was needed by the youth. He was "a demigod in Paris."

9 LE GALLIENNE, RICHARD, ed. The Le Gallienne Book of American Verse. New York: Boni & Liveright, pp. xxviii.

With Emerson, Longfellow, and Poe, Whitman is a world-poet, yet also distinctly American. "The spiritual element in Whitman's broader, grosser, more specifically national genius, comes largely from Emerson, as from Whitman has come the new energy, the revolutionary freedom, which vitalizes all modern poetry written in the English language." "He is pre-eminently the poet of the modern world." He is the best-represented in this anthology.

10 LINDSAY, VACHEL. "Walt Whitman's Spirit--White-hot." In Percy MacKaye: A Symposium on His Fiftieth Birthday. Hanover, N.H.: Dartmouth Press, pp. 31-32.

Tribute to MacKaye, for whom Lindsay would read "Pioneers" if he were present at the symposium. Besides title, no other reference to Whitman.

11 MACY, JOHN. The Story of the World's Literature. New York: Boni & Liveright, pp. 552, 557-59.

Brief account of Whitman and Leaves, "the youngest, most audacious and challenging book of verse published in this country," "a curious mixture of crudity and beauty." Of American poets, only Whitman is truly American, but his greatness lies not in his originality but in the splendor and beauty of his best work. "Lilacs" is "undoubtedly the high mark of American poetry."

12 MORLEY, CHRISTOPHER. Forty-Four Essays. New York: Harcourt, Brace & Co. "Moby Walt," pp. 204-7; "Walt Whitman Miniatures," 240-55. Reprints of 1923.24 and 1919.19.

13 _____. Safety Pins and Other Essays. London: Jonathan Cape. "Moby Walt," pp. 201-4; "Walt Whitman Miniatures," pp. 233-47; also 180. Reprints of 1923.24 and 1919.19.

Additional incidental remark: Whitman may be the only writer great enough for New York.

14 UNTERMEYER, LOUIS, ed. Modern American Poetry: A Critical Anthology. 3d rev. ed. New York: Harcourt, Brace & Co. "Walt Whitman," pp. 5-8. Revision of 1921.33. Revised: 1930.21.

The Whitman discussion is the same as in 1921.33.

15 VAN DOREN, CARL, and VAN DOREN, MARK. American and British Literature Since 1890. New York and London: Century Co., pp. 3, 29, 36, 68, 126. Revised: 1939.14.

The American imagists have turned away from Whitman and his vague generalities. Wharton's and Masters's uses of Whitman are noted. Whitman and Mencken are both thoroughly American in sending their imaginations over the continent.

16 WAHL, JEAN. The Pluralist Philosophies of England & America. Authorized translation by Fred Rothwell. London: Open Court Co., pp. 31, 36-37, 100, 101, 121, 126, 127, 132, 178, 186-87, 197.

Whitman is considered throughout as a forerunner of William James. His monism includes pluralism, involving the "might of the individual and the incessant change of the world," engagement in the storm of life, and a transcendentalist religion of democracy like Emerson's.

17 WILLCOCKS, M. P. Between the Old World and
the New: Being Studies in Literary Personality from Goethe and Balzac to Anatole
France and Thomas Hardy. London: George
Allen & Unwin. "The Builders: III. Walt
Whitman and Edward Carpenter," pp. 315-30.
Richard Jefferies was forerunner of
Whitman and Carpenter, sharing their principal ideals of the completeness of personality through joining mind and soul and
the recognition of a vast universal being,
familiar and comfortable except when
Whitman shouts it. Whitman and Carpenter
look toward a change in consciousness
although they do not achieve it fully since
they retain their power of speech. Whitman
gives "an electric shock" in his emphasis
on the body, his attitudes to life, and his
natural rhythm. Carpenter differs in expressing the new consciousness as related
to a new social order. Both "are loved by
the people, mainly because both chose the
life of the toiler." Working people are
nearer these writers' ideal of the whole
man than the intellectuals.

18 WOOD, CLEMENT. Poets of America. New York:
E. P. Dutton & Co. "Walt Whitman: A
Mystic Volcano," pp. 35-55; also passim
per index.
Whitman was the first poet to present
actual contact with America and its soil.
Life sketch. O'Connor should not have
suggested Whitman's "kinship to decadent
embroiderers of sexual themes," for his
relationships were probably continuing, not
promiscuous. His sickness "may have been
an unconscious flight from further conflict
with the harshness of material life, while
still leaving him free to serve his singing." He has only recently been established
as America's leading poetic voice. His
greatness as poet rests upon "peak moments
of lyric intensity and beauty," "constant
fragments of exquisite phrasing," and "the
liberating sweep of his vision and method."
A lyric rather than narrative or dramatic
poet, he is unmatched in recent times.
His rhythms, rooted in the spoken word, lie
between prose and "lockstep verse," which
is less successfully adapted to different
content than Whitman's style, as shown in
a metric analysis. Whitman's view is that
of an eagle, never looking at specific
details, singing only himself, not other
individuals like Shakespeare. His depiction
of sex was a necessary corrective. His
universality has not quite reached the ear
of the people, but he would be pleased at
his academic recognition and poetic influence. His vocabulary was made up mostly
of the words of standard written speech.

19 YEATS, WILLIAM BUTLER. A Vision. London:
Privately printed for subscribers only,
T. Werner Laurie, pp. 46-47, 105.
Revised: 1937.19.
Phase six of Yeats's cycle is explained

with Whitman as the example, with note of
"his interest in crowds, in casual loves
and affections, in all summary human experience," his cataloguing, the basis of
his thought.

PERIODICALS

20 ANON. Paragraph review of Carpenter (1909.4).
Bookman 60 (January), 642.
The subject becomes real and powerful
because the book, "quiet and unassuming in
style," focuses on Whitman, from within and
from without (avoiding the ecstacy of Bucke
and his cosmic consciousness).

21 BUTTS, NELLIE DOTY. "Walt Whitman's Sister."
Bookman 60 (January), 590-92.
Account of visit with Whitman's sister,
Mrs. Hyde, in Burlington, Vermont, where
Whitman spent many summers. The fact that
"Walt never lived in the country" explains
what many find contradictory in his poetry;
"my brother never depicts nature save incidentally as it leads to greater truths."
She worries about people thinking her
brother had no message. Butts ends the
article by asserting that he did leave a
message about democracy.

22 KETLER, WILLIAM H. "Walt Whitman--'The Good
Gray Poet.'" Camden First 2, no. 1 (January), 7, 18.
City librarian presents Whitman's ideas,
themes, poetic qualities, influences. "One
does not usually get Whitman at the first
reading, but in repeated readings the
student absorbs Whitman and then realizes
how elemental, and close to nature, he was."
Three careful readings of "Open Road" will
give such a vision as "never before en-
chanted the soul." His religious quality
centered on a belief in love as the basis
of life.

23 LUCE, MORTON. "Poetry and Prose. Part III.
'Leaves of Grass,' by Walt Whitman."
Church Quarterly Review 99 (January), 313-
23.
An examination of "Ox-Tamer" reveals
correspondence between the emotion and its
setting, but nothing to distinguish the
words from prose. In Whitman the thought
or emotion moulds the form, while in verse
the emotion is moulded by a definite form.
Whitman may decide upon some formal require-
ments (e.g., for the sake of contrast), but
none is necessarily demanded by his form.

24 POUND, LOUISE. "Walt Whitman and the Classics."
Southwest Review 10 (January), 75-83.
Whitman's rejection of Europe and the
past did not extend to vocabulary, for he
borrowed not only from the Romance languages
but also from Greek and Latin, both of which
literatures he admired. Many examples are
cited to point out classical borrowings.

25 LUCAS, F. L. "Enfant Terrible: Enfant Gâté."
    New Stateman 24 (17 January), 420-21.
    Revised: 1926.16.
         Review of Bullett (1924.3) followed by
    review of Swinburne's collected poetry.
    Whitman's great spirit does not necessarily
    make his poetry worth reading, but without
    personality there is no great writing.
    Literary men alone could appreciate his
    defiance of literary tradition and his free
    spirit. Now we see Whitman as "no philos-
    opher, only a light-hearted, incoherent
    mystic" with many inconsistencies, yet an
    appealing naïveté about his newness and a
    courageous awareness of what questions to
    ask, with "an ear and an imagination" and
    a Flaubertian interest in the right word.
    Whatever his less worthy qualities, his
    death was noble. This book is worthy of
    him, though it might have been enlarged to
    contain the best passages from poems not
    worth quoting as a whole. Whitman had the
    "touch of human greatness" that Swinburne
    lacked.

26 K., P. "The Question of an American Rhythm."
    Christian Science Monitor (20 January),
    11:1-2.
         Discussion opens with a consideration
    of Whitman, perhaps the originator of a
    "distinctive American rhythm." Can his
    "long, trailing series and catalogues" be
    regarded as rhythmical merely because of
    typographical arrangement? Lines from "As
    a Strong Bird" and "Pioneers" are con-
    trasted to show true rhythm.

27 ANON. "Walt Whitman." Times Literary Supple-
    ment (London) (22 January), 52.
         Favorable review of Bullett (1924.3),
    who looks at Whitman from "a common-sense
    standpoint" rather than a mystical point of
    view. His selections are the choice reading
    from Whitman, including "Myself," the "core
    of his message." Although he was no artist
    in a poetic tradition, his motivating ideas
    marked him a true artist, "defying rules
    and conventions for the sake of a vision of
    a reconstituted life." Though little read
    in America, he represents the soul of the
    American people, so different from that of
    Europeans.

28 POUND, LOUISE. "Walt Whitman's Neologisms."
    American Mercury 4 (February), 199-201.
         Whitman borrowed much from European
    languages. He invents "agent nouns," with
    fondness for feminine formations and suf-
    fixes. He shortens loan-words to create
    new forms, coins abstract nouns by addition
    of common suffixes, changes common spellings
    to create rhythm, invents adjectives through
    truncation. He rarely coins verbs. His
    diction is more reflective of twentieth
    than of nineteenth-century usage.

29 COOK, HOWARD WILLARD. "Whitman Collections."
    Mentor 13 (March), 51. Photograph.

         Describes Hier's collection of editions
    of Leaves (as in photograph); other collec-
    tions, appreciated by lovers of Whitman
    for "preserving these intimate recollections
    of his life and work," which gain in value
    with time.

30 BULLETT, GERALD. "Whitman: Our Elemental
    Poet." New York Sun (28 March), 7:1-2.
         Review of Holloway's edition of Leaves
    (1924.11). Much that Whitman writes is
    ridiculous, sometimes his declaiming does
    not ring true, he is sometimes arrogant and
    vain, he always lacks humor. Yet his
    tremendous enthusiasm for life can only be
    admired and emulated, along with his per-
    vasive emphasis on universal charity. The
    1855 Preface, happily included by Holloway,
    states his aspirations clearly, in "suffi-
    ciently eloquent prose."

31 HEMINGWAY, ERNEST. "Homage to Ezra." This
    Quarter 1 (Spring), 222.
         Eliot, in contrast to Pound, is a minor
    poet; "Whitman, on the other hand, if a
    poet, is a major poet."

32 STEWART, GEORGE R., Jr. "Whitman and His Own
    Country." Sewanee Review 33 (April), 210-
    18.
         Survey of Whitman's critical reception
    in American and England. He was more ac-
    claimed in England because of the presence
    of a more liberal class in revolt against
    established conditions, not objecting like
    Americans to Whitman's free verse and liking
    the very qualities of which Americans feared
    they possessed too much. The greater suc-
    cess of the 1881 edition in America and his
    subsequent wider recognition were largely
    due to Stedman's review in the established
    magazine Scribner's (1880.35) and to the
    censorship incident.

33 WOOD, CLEMENT. "The Jack and Jiliad." Literary
    Review 5 (4 April), 8.
         Among the parodies retelling the nursery
    rhyme in various styles is "Walt Whitman's
    Auro Radios This Gusty Yawp," adapting
    lines from "Myself."

34 DREISER, THEODORE. "America and the Artist."
    Nation 120 (15 April), 423.
    Reprinted: Pizer.
         Whitman is listed among the geniuses
    American conditions have already produced.

35 ANON. "The Snap-Bean Sage." Saturday Review
    of Literature 1 (2 May), 721.
         Incidental: Twain and Whitman "have
    assumed heroic proportions in our pantheon"
    but should be joined as great American
    writers by Joel Chandler Harris.

36 SHERMAN, STUART. "O Camerado!" New York
    Herald-Tribune Books 1 (3 May), 5. Illus-
    trated.
         Favorable reviews of Holloway Leaves

(1924.11), Bullett (1925.2), and "Broad-Axe" edition with illustrations (examples reprinted). Bullett lists Whitman's faults without considering that "Whitman wished to mirror all the faultiness of the world and that he wished even his art to remain in a sense faulty and unfinished," so Bullett includes only the least faulty portions, thus providing a good introduction to Whitman for such people as "ought to know something of Whitman, but ought not to know everything of him."

37 SEAVER, EDWIN. "A Real Contribution Toward a Critical Estimate of Whitman." Literary Review 5 (29 May), 2.
    Review of Bullett (1925.2), who recognizes Whitman's flaws and strengths but suggests he was not primarily an artist. Seaver disagrees about Whitman's "little trace of development, either intellectual or artistic," for he developed, like every artist, toward the clear definition of his vision. This book is welcome to an America which has not really provided the expected critical commentary on Whitman; it is a start (though limited) in that direction. It fails to relate Whitman to the American scene, explain his contribution to American poetry, treat his prose, or determine what is derivative and what new in his poetic vision.

38 ANON. "New York's Own Neglected Poet." Brooklyn Daily Eagle (2 June), 6:3.
    Editorial. The time has come that the masses appreciate Whitman, "whose works are among the most potent factors in assuring the continuance of democracy." He has been unrecognized by them because of his form and because of the schools and libraries, but he is truly a poet of the people, not of his "narrow cults" from whom he must be rescued.

39 ANON. "Too Many Statues of Nobodies, He Says, but None of Whitman." New York Times (2 June), 1:2.
    At Whitman celebration, Holloway said that the foreigner approaching American shores might prefer to see "the paternal hand of Whitman extended him in welcome" rather than the Statue of Liberty.

40 ANON. "Walt Whitman." New York Times (7 June), sec. 2, 4:3-4.
    Editorial on Holloway's drive for a Whitman statue. Views of Beers and Symonds on Whitman are contrasted. Whitman will get his statue because he will become appreciated. He may be more accessible at first in his prose. His devotion to the soldiers is touching, as evident in a letter to a bereaved mother.

41 CHESTERTON, G. K. "Our Notebook." Illustrated London News 166 (13 June), 1146.
    Reprinted in part: 1925.50.

Whitman is probably no more appreciated or understood today than when he first appeared. "That sincere though sometimes muddled and misguided sense of comradeship and the joy of life, that really were in Whitman's poems, has not really been successfully revealed by Whitman's poems." He can be appreciated only by artists; his refined readers hardly share his mood. Free-verse writers, though influenced by him in form, have adopted a mood quite the opposite of his enlarging spirit of love, rejoicing, and acceptance. Whitman, like other innovative artists, "is less important now than he was then," because such artists "exaggerate some mode or manner which is less eternal than tradition." Because he tried to be too original in style, "the world does not know how original he really was in spirit."

42 FAWCETT, JAMES WALDO. "Monument to Whitman." New York Times (14 June), sec. 9, 14:3.
    Agrees with Holloway and editorial (1925.40) on the need for a statue of Whitman in New York.

43 ANON. "Authors' Club Takes Lead in Project for Whitman Memorial." New York Herald-Tribune (17 June), 10:5.
    Holloway announced a campaign by the Authors' Club to raise $40,000 for a public memorial in New York City, probably a statue in a park. Committee members are listed.

44 DAVENPORT, WILLIAM E. "Walt Whitman Memorial Should Be Placed in Old Fort Greene Park." Brooklyn Daily Eagle (18 June), 6:6.
    Letter on Brooklyn's duty in honoring Whitman, who as a citizen of Brooklyn took great interest in it, even in his later years. The general recognition of his genius is evidenced by the remarks of a leading New York bookseller, contrasting him to other nineteenth-century poets.

45 GORMAN, HERBERT S. "Whitman Etched New York in Verse. Proposal That Statue Honoring Him Be Erected Stirs Memories of the Poet's Life Here." New York Times Magazine (21 June), 13.
    The statue would be appropriate on the Battery, where Whitman so often watched the pageantry of the city and the ships. Appropriate passages from Whitman's poetry and prose illustrate different aspects of the city that he knew and observed.

46 ANON. "A Statue to Walt Whitman." New York Herald-Tribune (22 June), 12:2-3.
    Approves the idea of a statue. Though the debate over form goes on, "the greatness of Whitman's lines is incontrovertible, and none more clearly so than some of his gorgeous and prophetic passages upon his city."

47 HOLLOWAY, EMORY. "Whitman's Embryonic Verse." Southwest Review 10 (July), 28-40.

Reprinted: 1927.10.

After an introduction, prints for the first time Whitman's "Pictures" from what is probably Whitman's second oldest notebook, with notes pointing out later uses of specific passages. This poem's value lies chiefly in biographical significance rather than in poetic effect, like other catalogue poems, each being "a microcosm of the whole Leaves," "a picture of himself in all his cosmopolitan diversity."

48 ANON. "Seek Whitman Memorial." New York Times (5 July), sec. 2, 10:4.

Notes Holloway's drive to get a Whitman memorial.

49 JOHNSON, ROSSITER. "Concerning Monuments." New York Herald-Tribune (11 July), 8:7.

Letter ridiculing the enthusiasts who advocate a monument to Whitman, hardly a poet except in half a dozen pages, the rest of him being "rubbish, and incidentally some indecenter indecencies than can be found elsewhere in our literature--so far as I know it." He lived off the money of his supporters.

50 ANON. "Pioneering in Art and Missing Fire." Literary Digest 86 (18 July), 28.

Précis of Chesterton (1925.41).

51 HOLLOWAY, EMORY. "Now, My Idea Is This! Daily Talks with Thinking New Yorkers on Subjects They Know Best. New York's Lack of Memorial to the Poet Whitman." New York Evening Post (20 July), 10:1-2.

A full statue of Whitman should be erected, since he celebrated the whole man. He is gaining in familiarity and appreciation; his words are heard on the radio. Perhaps he was not recognized sooner because "he was too profoundly like us, so unlike our idealizations of ourselves." Modern audiences are more open to free verse, no longer concerned about "that particular sort of innocence" nineteenth-century readers extolled.

52 MORLEY, CHRISTOPHER. "The Bowling Green." Saturday Review of Literature 1 (25 July), 928, 931.

Revised: 1926.21.

Comments on Emerson's appreciation of Whitman seventy years ago and the many vicissitudes for Leaves from then until now when it "really begins to be absorbed into the actual tissue of American life." The 1855 Preface is "one of the most precious documents in American ink," "a masterpiece of noble prose" with only minor flaws. Whitman's life up to 1855 is traced. Not knowing any other nation, Whitman could hardly judge American characteristics properly. The real miracle is this Preface, "so long smuggled away (perhaps because it damaged the stereotype of the untutored child of Adam)." Whitman reveals "a lonely

and massive mind" with "manly tread." The Preface is, "within human limits, immortal," comparable to other great poets' statements on poetry.

53 WOOLF, VIRGINIA. "American Fiction." Saturday Review of Literature 2 (1 August), 1-3. Reprinted: Collected Essays. Vol. 2. New York: Harcourt, Brace & World, 1967.

Incidental: Because English readers want to find in American literature something different, Whitman is the one American writer they "whole-heartedly admire," representing "the real American undisguised," thus making it difficult for England to appreciate other American authors. Both the Jamesian tendency to overrefine social distinctions and that of "the simpler and cruder writers" like Whitman, Anderson, and Masters to support America rather self-consciously are unfortunate and "delay the development of the real American literature itself."

54 MILLAR, A. H. "Alleged Walt Whitman Hoax." Edinburgh Scotsman (24 August), 5.

Letter describing the collusion of Rossetti, Buchanan, Dowden, and Swinburne "to foist an inferior literary man upon the public, and test the gullibility of the public by lauding his productions," choosing Whitman as their man. Bayne (1875.15) charged them with this plot. How can Whitman be representative of an American that has produced Irving, Longfellow, Cooper, Bryant, Lowell?

55 MARWICK, W. "Alleged Walt Whitman Hoax." Edinburgh Scotsman (27 August).

Letter challenging Millar (1925.54): the theory is impossible; by whom was it recently revealed?

56 LEWIS, WILFRID. "Alleged Walt Whitman Hoax." Edinburgh Scotsman (29 August).

Letter citing other admirers of Whitman. "It is a poor test of poets to ask if their lucubrations are worthy of a place in a child's reader, and to that happy, if conditional, immortality Dr. Millar's cohort of of 'great literary heroes' have certainly attained."

57 MILLAR, A. H. "Alleged Walt Whitman Hoax." Edinburgh Scotsman (29 August).

Letter responding to Marwick (1925.55), bringing further proof from Bates (1883.1).

58 HOLLOWAY, EMORY. "Belated Tribute to Be Paid to Whitman, Long Neglected by City He Loved Most." Brooklyn Daily Eagle Sunday Magazine (30 August), 7. Portrait.

Whitman alone of our major poets has sung the city, having experienced so much of New York in his youth, especially its people. "Manhattan and Brooklyn, whose praise his poetry has carried around the world," should honor "the greatest of our bards" with a statue, perhaps in Battery Park.

59 ANON. "Walt Whitman Hotel Edition." Camden First 2, no. 9 (September). Illustrated.
    Pictures and description of the hotel named for Whitman, with no discussion of Whitman himself.

60 POUND, LOUISE. "Walt Whitman and Italian Music." American Mercury 6 (September), 58-63.
    Music is more worthy of attention as an influence on Whitman than the overemphasized literary influences, affecting "his manner of expression and his general attitude toward his poetic utterance and his public." Prose and poetry demonstrate his interest in opera and use of musical terminology, which constitutes most of his borrowings from Italian, generally "less far-fetched and much more poetical" than his use of French. He liked to consider himself as singing rather than writing, abandoning himself to poetry as he did to music. To him "poetry is something uttered," not written as with most nineteenth-century poets. His poems are constructed similarly to symphonies, although not intentionally as are Lanier's.

61 MARWICK, W. "Alleged Walt Whitman Hoax." Edinburgh Scotsman (1 September).
    Letter calling attention to American critical comments on Whitman, questioning the use of Bates by Millar (1925.57).

62 A LOVER OF TRUTH. "Alleged Walt Whitman Hoax." Edinburgh Scotsman (3 September).
    Quotes Buchanan's poem on Whitman's death (1892.143) to show he could not have been part of any hoax.

63 CALDER, JOHN COOPER. "Alleged Walt Whitman Hoax." Edinburgh Scotsman (3 September).
    Quotes Swinburne's later attack on Whitman; notes Burroughs's praise.

64 MILLAR, A. H. "Alleged Walt Whitman Hoax." Edinburgh Scotsman (3 September).
    Response to Marwick (1925.61), correcting the typographical error in the Bates date, asking why Americans have not adopted Whitman's "ultra-democratic and anti-social proposals."

65 R., A. "Alleged Walt Whitman Hoax." Edinburgh Scotsman (3 September).
    Defends Whitman for his comradeship and haunting rhythm. Whitman's "deep sense of humour" would have enabled him to laugh at Millar (1925.54).

66 J., B. "Whitman on Evolution." New York Times (6 September), sec. 7, 12:3.
    Letter quotes "Whitman's remarkable epitome of the cosmic process" from "Myself" 44, to help and strengthen many readers in the controversy over evolution.

67 MARWICK, W. "Alleged Walt Whitman Hoax?" Edinburgh Scotsman (7 September).
    Points out more errors in Millar (1925.57).

68 ANON. "Whitman Exhibition in Library Opens Nov. 1." New York Times (9 September), 25:4.
    Describes New York Public Library exhibition; notes the collectors represented.

69 BARRUS, CLARA. "Whitman and Burroughs As Comrades." Yale Review, n.s. 15 (October), 59-81.
    History of relationship of Burroughs and Whitman, quoting from Burroughs's notebooks, including some unpublished anecdotes, comparing theirs with famous literary friendships, demonstrating that Notes (1867.1) was not written by Whitman except for one brief section, title and subtitles, and supplementary notes for second edition (1871.1). Charges against Whitman regarding financial matters are answered. (This article is expanded into her book, 1931.1.)

70 SEAVER, EDWIN. "Is Walt Whitman an American?" Guardian (Philadelphia), 2 (October), 409-11.
    Eli Siegel's recent poem in the Nation, "Hot Afternoons Have Been in Montana," is clearly in the Whitman tradition, but American critics ignored this fact. The America Whitman sang was one of potentialities, not the actual country he lived in; but in so singing he was a great poet. He must be assimilated into our individual and national consciousness to become our poet, a literary tradition we can build upon and develop.

71 GORMAN, HERBERT S. "World Literary History in a Hop, Skip and Jump." New York Times Book Review (25 October), 4. Illustrated.
    Review of Macy (1925.11), mentioning Whitman incidentally, praising Onorio Ruotolo's portrait of him from the book, here reprinted.

72 HOLLOWAY, EMORY. "The Walt Whitman Exhibition." Bulletin of the New York Public Library 29 (November), 763-66.
    Lists collectors contributing to the public library exhibition of Whitman; describes items on display, including various editions. Specimens of his journalism help one understand his work's "strange merging of poetry and journalism." This exhibition verifies his growing recognition.

*73 CLEMENS, WILLIAM MONTGOMERY. "A Whitman Letter Brings a Small Price." Biblo 5 (November-December), 855-56.
    Reported in KTO.

74 ANON. "To Open Exhibition of Whitman MSS." New York Times (8 November), sec. 1, 12:1.
    Describes extensively the library exhibition opening tomorrow.

1925

75 ANON. "Notes on Rare Books." New York Times
       Book Review (8 November), 16.
       Quotes 1872 Whitman letter to Dowden,
       one of the items at the Isaac Doonan sale.

76 ANON. "Open Door for Whitman." Outlook 141
       (18 November), 422, 424. Illustrated.
       Describes exhibition, quoting from
       Holloway (1925.72).

77 BOYD, ERNEST. "The Father of Them All."
       American Mercury 6 (December), 451-58.
       Reprinted: 1927.4.
       Writers in contemporary reviews display
       the defective influence of Whitman's ob-
       scure and pedestrian prose, just as his
       influence is seen on the contemporary
       poetry of "typographical eccentrics." His
       "essentially illiterate" mind is apparent
       in his letters. He was deceptively a lit-
       erary man, with a premeditated rather than
       unconscious way of working, although he
       perpetuated the legend of himself as "quin-
       tessential he-man," attracting "sedentary
       scholars in English libraries" rather than
       common people. If he had only lacked "that
       embryonic sense of poetry," younger poets
       would have ignored his influence.

78 HEARTMAN, CHARLES F. "The Untimeliness of the
       Walt Whitman Exhibition at the New York
       Public Library. An Open Letter to the
       Trustees." Americana Collector 1 (Decem-
       ber), 83-85. Photograph of Whitman and
       Doyle.
       The library's exhibition is "glorifying"
       a "pervert" whose works reveal "a clear
       case of contra-sexuality," as do the facts
       of his life, including his war work, "a
       repulsive action if analyzed." Many people
       in New Jersey "will spit when you mention
       his name." The "Whitman hero-worship will
       disappear" if he is "properly labelled."
       He may have produced "lines of pure poetic
       gold," but "his New Democratic Ideals" are
       "Bunk." Someone with an "abnormal psycho-
       logical and physical complex" could never
       "become the creator of a new creed." He
       must be placed in a class apart with such
       artists as Wilde, Verlaine, Voltaire,
       Michelangelo.

79 HICHENS, ROBERT. "The Unearthly." Ladies'
       Home Journal 42 (December), 52.
       Reprinted: 1926.11.
       The first installment of this novel
       includes a description of a character as
       being "a touch of what I imagine Walt
       Whitman may have been."

80 ANON. "Whitman in Bronze, Ten Feet Tall."
       Literary Digest 87 (12 December), 30-32.
       Illustrated.
       "It is often stated by intelligent
       foreigners that it is Walt Whitman, more
       than any other literary worthy, who puts
       us and keeps us on the world's literary
       map." Various periodicals are quoted on

the New York Public Library exhibition and
Jo Davidson's statue design.

81 MABBOTT, THOMAS OLLIVE. "Notes on Walt
       Whitman's 'Franklin Evans.'" Notes and
       Queries 149 (12 December), 419-20.
       Notes sources for mottos in Franklin
       Evans; comments briefly on other parts of
       the novel.

1926

BOOKS

1 BAILEY, JOHN. Walt Whitman. English Men of
      Letters Series. New York and London:
      Macmillan & Co., 220 pp.
      1. "Introductory": Whitman's newness
      lies in his treatment of New York and
      America. Such faults as triviality, the
      "mixture of grandiosity and banality," his
      unpoet-like refusal to submit to the limi-
      tations of words are transcended by his
      native genius.
      2. "The Life of Whitman": His life's
      influences on his poetic development are
      traced. Of the two great needs of any
      poet, experience and peace, the second was
      more powerful. His refusal to volunteer
      was due not to the stronger call of his
      writing but to Quaker "'conscientious
      objection,'" his aversion to discipline,
      and his age. His magnetism with the
      wounded is compared with Henry James's help
      of a dying man in 1915. His hospital work
      produced his greatest poetry, with recol-
      lections of the Greek Anthology. Vistas
      presents his qualifications of democracy as
      well as his faith. His rather small output
      is due to his unproductive later years.
      3. "Characteristics and Comparisons":
      His work has more unity than that of most
      poets. He did not develop as a poet: he
      and his poems were the same at the end as
      at the beginning, except for the deepening
      of human tenderness the war produced. He
      is concerned with the unity of himself, the
      average man, and the universe, his three
      principal subjects, emphasizing the uni-
      versality of love. Flaws include "purely
      intellectual" poems, tedious catalogues,
      vulgar jargon (influenced by journalism and
      politics), which are absent from his best
      work, poems on war, sea, and death. He is
      compared extensively with Milton and
      Wordsworth. Few have had "the nature and
      genius of a poet" more than Whitman.
      4. "Whitman's Language and Metre":
      Whitman brought to his generation the
      familiar literary "return to Nature," but
      often failed to make the distinction
      "between art and photography." His rejec-
      tion of meter has been abandoned by most of
      his contemporary successors. His often
      flat, ordinary language disappears when he
      is really moved and uses "language of
      greater beauty and finer associations."

But his career does not reveal an increasing
sense of artistry. His successful poems
have "a sense of echo." Comparisons are
made with poems by Shelley, Browning, Hood.
He "suffers from the monotony produced by
the unit of his verse being the statement,"
yet he gains in having no need to say anything he does not exactly mean because of
the demands of rhyme.

    5. "A Walk Through 'Leaves of Grass'":
Leaves is examined, section by section, to
give an overview of Whitman's thought. His
new notes, notes such as even Thoreau and
Emerson did not strike, are described.
"Myself," "one of the most astonishing expressions of vital energy ever got into a
book," is summarized. "Calamus" and "Adam"
are discussed and found not so diametrically opposed as often suggested, for
"Calamus" is not without "a physical side,
however innocent." "Cradle" is "one of the
finest lyrics of the nineteenth century."
"Tears" may be "the most entirely unalloyed
piece of imagination that ever came from
him." "Death Carol" is "one of the great
lyrics of the world." His later work is
generally much weaker, more prosaic.

    6. "The Ultimate Remainder": Whitman
is "the genius of America," a great voice
of the democratic ideal, though his exuberance is a defect. Full of contradictions, Whitman reveals the greatness of his
spirit in his prose, although it cannot
match his poetry.

2 BECK, L. ADAMS. Dreams and Delights. New
    York: Dodd, Mead & Co., p. 247.
        Brief quotation from "Lilacs" with no
    reference to Whitman.

3 BULLITT, WILLIAM C. It's Not Done. New York:
    Harcourt, Brace & Co., pp. 20-22.
        A boy and his father visit Whitman at
    his home in Camden, where he speaks out
    against "mummified snobbery," saying "the
    people who work with their hands" will
    bring about America's growth. The father
    later explains Whitman's "mystical ideas"
    about democracy and common people and his
    belief that people are as kind as himself,
    although the father disagrees. Alone the
    boy reads "O Tan-Faced Prairie-Boy," finding
    it descriptive of his own friend.

4 BURROUGHS, JOHN. "Leaves of Grass. Standard
    of the Natural Universal." In Century
    Readings in the English Essay, edited by
    Louis Wann. New York: Century Co., pp.
    412-15; brief note, 517.
    Extracts reprinted from 1867.1 (pp. 37-42,
    45-49).
        Burroughs's work is significant "as an
    early defense of a much-maligned poet of
    the 'Natural.'"

5 CHUBB, EDWIN WATTS. Stories of Authors,
    British and American. New York: Macmillan
    Co. "Mr. Thayer Visits Walt Whitman,"

pp. 385-92. Photograph.
Includes extract reprinted from 1919.283.
    Brief account of Whitman's career.
"His poetry is most unusual, his personality
most striking, and yet his life rather commonplace."

6 DEACON, WILLIAM ARTHUR. Poteen: A Pot-Pourri
    of Canadian Essays. Ottawa: Graphic Pub-
    lishers. "The Cult of Whitman," pp. 97-
    101; also 42, 65-67, 69-70.
        Address delivered to Whitman Fellowship
    of Toronto, 31 May 1925. Today Whitman is
    being calmly embraced by people alien to
    his radical spirit. Such acceptance could
    lead to the dilution of his ideal, which
    must be preserved by those who truly under-
    stand it: "tolerance, candor, independence
    of thought and action, liberty of conscience,
    the exaltation of the flesh as well as the
    soul, love--physical, mental and spiritual--
    the essential divinity of man and the re-
    fusal to bow to 'outside authority' unless
    preceded by 'inside authority', and a faith
    in life itself."

7 DE CASSERES, BENJAMIN. Forty Immortals. New
    York: Joseph Lawren. "Walt Whitman," pp.
    223-32; also passim.
    Revision of 1907.52.
        Minor changes and deletions. Whitman
    is referred to throughout the book, gener-
    ally as a revolutionary figure.

8 DICKSON, MARGARETTE BALL. Tumbleweeds. New
    York: Harold Vinal. "Good Gray Poet
    (Whitman)," p. 23.
    Reprinted: 1927.34.
        Sonnet on the positive shift in Whitman's
    reputation.

9 FORNELLI, G[UIDO]. Four American Writers:
    Longfellow--Whitman--Emerson--Poe.
    Livorno: Raffaello Giusti. "Walt Whitman,"
    pp. 157-61.
        This American literature text for
    Italian students includes selections with
    notes in Italian (including some errors).
    The introduction, in English, includes a
    brief biographical sketch and discusses
    Whitman's poetry as freeing American liter-
    ature from European influence, having "the
    air of the New Continent" and "the modern
    vision of society," showing transcendental-
    ist influence in his belief in individualism
    but also revealing love of mankind, the
    basis of his championship of democracy. He
    is compared to Nietzsche and related to
    European influences (especially Rousseau).
    He has accomplished much for American and
    universal literature, presenting America as
    it should always be, though democracy need
    not reject artistic traditions.

10 HAZEN, CHARLES DOWNER, ed. The Letters of
    William Roscoe Thayer. Boston and New York:
    Houghton Mifflin Co., pp. 32-36, 168, 359,
    369-70, 409.

1926

Letter to Isabella Coolidge (1885) describes his visit to Whitman (earlier printed in 1919.283). Letter to C. E. Norton (1906) praises Perry's biography and Whitman's frequent reaching of the elemental, as in "Cradle," which has "the quintessence of love and grief." Whitman loses little in Italian translation. Letter to Henry Van Dyke (1919) comments on Thayer's article (1919.283), objecting to Whitman's lack of moral sense and his usual failure to achieve poetry. Letter to Mrs. Michael Foster (1921) agrees with her appreciation of Whitman's apostrophes to death.

11 HICHENS, ROBERT. *The God Within Him*. London: Methuen & Co., p. 57.
Reprint of 1925.79.

12 HOLLOWAY, EMORY, ed. Preface and introduction to *Leaves of Grass by Walt Whitman: Abridged Edition with Prose Selections*. Garden City, N.Y.: Doubleday, Page & Co., pp. v-vii, xv-xxiv.
There remains disagreement over the value of Whitman's work, with much of it unaccepted or ignored as is understandable because his plan of presenting his whole growth necessitated the inclusion of moments of "early banality and formless experimentalism." This selection presents to general readers Whitman without his defects, containing "all the great poetry he wrote" and some of his best prose, with none of the passages and poems which have offended "sensible but sensitive critics." Dating of poems is explained (as in 1924.11). Whitman is our only truly national poet, identifying himself with more than one region, with nature as well as books. He presented the details of American life and translated their qualities "into the language of mystic and enduring art." He had masculine and feminine qualities and could appeal to all types of people, with a diversity appropriate to his role as mystical prophet in his book, "the slowly evolving autobiography of himself and of nineteenth-century America." The powerful image of his "average man" is described. His book has been a significant influence and inspiration. The ideals he pointed toward are very much with us today. He became a poet rather than a satirist because of his hopes for the future. He creates beauty not through perfection of form but with a humility that inspires original perception in the reader, appealing more to the imagination than to reason, making the reader provide his own synthesis.

13 HOLLOWAY, EMORY. *Whitman: An Interpretation in Narrative*. New York and London: Alfred A. Knopf, 330. No references cited. Illustrated.
This book, the story of Whitman's life rather than of his book and directed to the general reader rather than to the scholar,

includes "nothing which is not, as I believe, provable fact or a logical deduction from the facts." It begins with Whitman's editorship of the *Eagle*, his literary, theatrical, recreational, political, and social interests. His trip south produced a strong effect on him, especially his presumed romantic involvement for which he may have returned south. Emerson influenced him. His mystical experience stemmed from America's religious background and his own. After early efforts to express his feelings and political convictions, he now wrote poetry to fulfill a personal ambition for individual independence and a national purpose related to independence and union. *Leaves* had "an epic purpose" and "lyric point of view." "Artistically Whitman's first book was his worst," though with fresh mystical inspiration and robust optimism. The various editions and poems are described, noting the development of his poetic purpose, the revelations of his thought through his writings, biographical sources of some work, psychological insights. Whitman tried to sublimate his overweening, not quite normal affection for men in longing for fulfillment after death, until his hospital work gave him an outlet. *Drum-Taps* revealed a decrease in self-consciousness and an increase in lyricism and careful construction. His relationships are described, including those with his mother, Mrs. Davis, Doyle, and a married woman; some admirers turned to Whitman out of their own needs. "Passage," "Prayer," and "Trumpeter" represent his swan song. His last years were perhaps the most picturesque, "as if his nature had at once bared itself of superfluities the better to reveal its fundamental qualities, and at the same time had irresistibly called to its own."

14 JACOBSON, ARTHUR C. *Genius: Some Revaluations*. An Adelphi Publication. New York: Greenberg Publishers, pp. 5, 28-29, 135, 138, 148.
Various abnormalities in Whitman, as in other geniuses, are noted: family history, slightly immature love of ease, outlook on life, use of alcohol after age thirty as contributing to his sudden transformation into "a creative Titan." His homosexual nature and relinquishment of conventional life account for much of *Leaves*.

15 KENNEDY, WILLIAM SLOANE. *The Fight of a Book for the World: A Companion Volume to Leaves of Grass*. West Yarmouth, Mass.: Stonecroft Press, 304 pp.
Part 1. "Story of the Reception of 'Leaves of Grass' by the World": Bibliographic essay discussing the criticism and providing anecdotes about Whitman and his commentators, tracing Whitman's publishing career and responses to his work during his lifetime and up to the present, based on

Kennedy's extensive collection of references
to Whitman, not strictly in chronological
order because this volume has been in
preparation since 1886. The conflicting
attitudes toward Whitman from such figures
as Emerson and Lanier indicate the mastering
of their original "unsophisticated instinct"
by "the marring intellect, the artificial
man."

Part 2. "(Reader's Vade-Mecum of Aids):
I. The Growth of 'Leaves of Grass' as a
Work of Art": Rambling but perceptive
notes on Whitman's excisions, additions,
changes, corrections, apt coinages, revealing a general movement toward improvement.
II. "Elucidations and Analyses of Difficult
Poems": In alphabetical order, many poems
are explicated, most extensively "Passage,"
"Ontario," "Myself," "Eidólons," "Come,
said my Soul." Notes include historical
allusions, mystical and philosophical meanings, development from earlier versions,
idiosyncratic word definitions. III.
"Index of Dates of the Poems": Alphabetical
list of varying titles for "all the poems
of all the editions" of Leaves, with the
page number in the 1897 edition, the year
first published, and the final title. IV.
"The Titles of Walt Whitman's Poems (A
Variorum Collation of Changes)": List of
Whitman's poems by final titles, noting
corresponding titles (or untitled position)
in earlier editions.

Part 3. "A Bibliography of Walt
Whitman's Writings": Descriptive bibliography, including information about particular copies, publishing history; includes
foreign editions.

Appendix 1. "Index of Important
Whitman Articles in the Conservator":
Annotated, with some critical commentary.
Appendix 2. "A Conspectus of Friends and
Foes": The list given here of Whitman's
hostile commentators appears small and in-
significant now, in comparison with that
given of his admirers. Appendix 3. "Walt
Whitman's Last Will and Testament."

16 LUCAS, F. L. Authors Dead & Living. London:
Chatto & Windus. "Enfant Terrible: Enfant
Gâté," pp. 115-23.
Revision of 1925.25.
Minor changes and additions.

17 MENCKEN, H. L. Prejudices. 5th ser. New
York: Alfred A. Knopf, "The Critic and
His Job," pp. 202-8; also passim per index.
Whitman has taken "two generations to
make his way," the change of opinion representing "a triumph of external forces
over criticism." Political forces rather
than literary criticism brought about the
shift from furtive scuffling over "Woman
Waits" and "Calamus" to the radicals'
praise and use of his "sonorous strophes to
an imaginary and preposterous democracy."

18 MONAHAN, MICHAEL. Nemesis. New York: Frank-
Maurice. "Walt Whitman--Two Notes," pp.

184-89. Photograph.
Reprints of 1916.42; 1920.75.

19 MONROE, HARRIET. Poets & Their Art. New
York: Macmillan Co. "Walt Whitman."
pp. 179-84.
Revision of 1919.135.
Minor verbal changes.

20 MORDELL, ALBERT, ed. Introduction to Notorious
Literary Attacks. New York: Boni &
Liveright, pp. xi, xiv, xli-xliv; "Walt
Whitman," 214-20.
Includes reprint of 1876.32.
Introduction discusses some of the
early abuse of Whitman, although he was
also praised by others; recounts the 1876
controversy over him; notes the background
of the first Saturday Review criticism
(1856.9).

21 MORLEY, CHRISTOPHER. Introductory note to
Two Prefaces by Walt Whitman. Garden City,
N.Y.: Doubleday, Page & Co., pp. vii-xx.
Revision of 1925.52. Reprinted: 1928.16.
Besides verbal changes and deletions,
several paragraphs are added, noting that
Whitman's prose is worthy of study, partic-
ularly his "amazing musical effects" and
effective sentence endings. William Rose
Benét's poem on reading Whitman is quoted.
The 1855 Preface will serve as guide into
Whitman's poetry.

22 MUMFORD, LEWIS. The Golden Day: A Study in
American Experience and Culture. New York:
Boni & Liveright. "High Noon," pp. 121-37;
also 68, 89, 92, 93, 94, 106, 142, 144,
146, 153, 173-76, 182, 204, 229, 262, 276-
79, 283.
Extract reprinted: 1930.14; Bradley/
Blodgett.
Whitman, in his greatness justifying
Emerson's genius, is one of the five figures
of American literature's "golden day," who
"answered the challenge of American experience," with a vision we need today. His
development showed the same strands of
influence as the nation--the puritan, the
republican, the pioneer--combined into a
new essense, along with the quaker and the
cosmopolitan. "Not a democrat, in the
sense of being a popular mediocrity," but
a man of genius, he added to the possibilities of American life, whose flaws he was
quite capable of recognizing. He was kept
from completing his plan for the new sacred
literature which would help satisfy the
American people's need for rootedness because of the war, ill health, and the decline of his powers after Drum-Taps.

23 NICOLSON, HAROLD. Swinburne. New York:
Macmillan Co., pp. 161, 193, 195.
Swinburne repudiated Whitman "under the
dictation of Watts-Dunton." "Whitmania"
(1887.63) is written in deplorable prose.

1926

24 ROGERS, CAMERON. The Magnificent Idler.
    Garden City, N.Y.: Doubleday, Page & Co.,
    312 pp. Illustrations by Edw. A. Wilson.
        This fictionalized biography begins
    with the marriage of Whitman's parents,
    focusing on the feelings of his mother
    until the time of his boyhood, when his
    sensitivity begins to appear, with his
    inclinations to loaf and enjoy life as
    shown through his occupations. His writing
    ambitions and early unsatisfying efforts,
    when his style was indebted to Poe and
    Henry Ward Beecher, are shown. His rela-
    tions with women include a New Orleans
    affair with a beautiful Creole who bore
    him a child. The train of thought that
    convinced him to write poetry particularly
    American is traced. His kind and affec-
    tionate ministrations in the war revealed
    the womanliness in his nature, as did his
    warm friendship with Doyle. In his old
    age he "was becoming a cult." He could be
    selfish and ungrateful, but his poems are
    what is important and have nothing to do
    with his personality as such.

25 ROSSETTI, W. M., ed. Prefatory notice to
    Poems by Walt Whitman. London: Chatto &
    Windus, pp. 1-22.
    Reprint of 1886.8.

26 SHERLOCK, CHESLA C. Homes of Famous Persons.
    Vol. 2. Des Moines: Meredith Publications.
    "The Home of Walt Whitman," pp. 129-38.
    Photograph of birthplace.
        Whitman's home in Camden was cramped,
    but it was the people of the town, not the
    architecture, that made him feel at home.
    His strength is that he is unorthodox, "a
    singer of the universe" with "great,
    majestic sweep and breadth of vision." His
    is the voice of mature manhood in love and
    in democracy. "He will, doubtless, live,
    and as he lives, he brings more sympathy
    and understanding to those who read him."
    Minor factual errors.

27 SHERMAN, STUART. Critical Woodcuts. New York
    and London: Charles Scribner's Sons, pp.
    10, 12, 23, 37-38, 67, 240, 256.
        Incidental references to contemporary
    writers (Anderson, Lawrence, Cather,
    Mencken, Ben Hecht, Barrett Wendell) and
    their attitudes or similarities to Whitman.
    A college friend of Sherman told of Cather
    "sitting every morning on a bench in Wash-
    ington Square" reading Leaves.

28 STRACHEY, J. ST. LOE. American Soundings.
    New York: D. Appleton & Co. "Walt Whitman,"
    pp. 216-31.
        Whitman provides the book's epigraph.
    America has few better expositors than
    Whitman, although the ordinary American
    might not admit it. He believed that
    America would lead in the necessary re-
    alignments of human energy in accord with
    scientific discoveries and social changes.

He loved the literature of the past but
was wholly a modernist. He was an optimist
and humanist, although he recognized difficulties. He interprets America well in
the great prose of "Backward Glance," and
even better in his poetry, which has many
great moments any poet might envy.

29 SWINBURNE, ALGERNON CHARLES. Complete Works.
    Vol. 15. Edited by Sir Edmund Gosse and
    Thomas James Wise. London: William
    Heinemann; New York: Gabriel Wells.
    "Whitmania," pp. 307-18.
    Reprint of 1894.18.

30 TATE, ALLEN. Foreword to White Buildings:
    Poems by Hart Crane. New York: Boni &
    Liveright, pp. xiv-xv.
        Describes Crane's major debt to Whitman
    and their differences.

31 UNTERMEYER, LOUIS, ed. Walt Whitman. The
    Pamphlet Poets. New York: Simon &
    Schuster. "Walt Whitman," pp. 5-6; "How to
    Know Walt Whitman," p. 31.
        Introduction to these selections gives
    a brief biography. Whitman's universality
    draws different emphases from the philos-
    ophers, the psychologists, the craftsmen
    (who emphasize "his flexible sonority, his
    orchestral timbre and tidal rhythms, his
    piling up of details into a symphonic
    structure"). His "spirit's breadth" has
    established him "as the foremost genius
    which this country has yet produced," like
    Homer and Shakespeare, his medium being
    elements, not words. Significant secondary
    sources are listed; selection process and
    use of extracts are justified.

PERIODICALS

32 MOORE, JOHN B. "The Master of Whitman."
    Studies in Philology 23 (January), 77-89.
        Analysis of Whitman's debts to Emerson,
    "the primary external source" of Whitman's
    new impulse and vision, as seen in passages
    from Whitman's early prose. His short
    essay "Emerson's Books, (The Shadows of
    Them)," "one of the most indispensable ever
    written upon Emerson," shows Whitman's
    "profound comprehension of Emerson, and of
    Emerson's mastership over him." Their
    ideas vary regarding friendship, the physi-
    cal, self-assertion, death, and nature.
    Whitman ironically praises Emerson for not
    taking on disciples while addressing himself
    to his own disciples.

33 MURRY, JOHN MIDDLETON. "An Englishman Pre-
    sumes." Saturday Review of Literature 2
    (9 January), 473-74.
        Incidental references about the English
    appreciating Whitman as exemplar of "an
    autochtonous American literature." He and
    Melville are regarded so highly by English
    readers because of the creative heights
    they reach.

34 ANON. "Sees Price Tag Put on College Degree."
New York Times (14 January), 8:1.
    Among the speakers at the National
Lutheran Educational Conference, John A. W.
Haas "attacked Walt Whitman as 'the curse
of America, because of his infernal doc-
trine of naturalism.'"

35 SHUSTER, GEORGE N. "Whitman and the Wayside."
Commonweal 3 (20 January), 298.
    Some of the planned statues of Whitman
travesty him as a barbarian rather than
commemorate what is great and abiding in
him. As moralist and poet, he was the
creature of leisure. He has not been understood or forgiven because "he was tall
enough to reach stars" and "was not one of
us," being related to the great European
romantics. His magnificence is his humble
wonder, his weakness a childish ignorance
of the world about him and a lack of
realism. His poem burying Lincoln "as a
woman might bury her lover is his own best
and firmest literary portrait," which
Lincoln himself would not have understood,
for Whitman represented "the true revolution
against America."

36 ANON. "Walt Whitman." Saturday Review of
Literature 2 (23 January), 505.
    Whitman deserves a fitting memorial but
is still rejected by the Hall of Fame. He
was "the last of his race, not the first,"
since most of what he prophesied and stood
for has failed to come to pass in America.
But "like Lincoln, he showed what democracy
could do, and therefore can do again."
Many readers who are not poetry lovers
respond to his poetry not for its literary
qualities, which puzzle them, but for his
personality, which sets up a goal to which
all may aspire. He was what he preached.

37 ANON. "Louis Keila, Sculptor, Sees Walt
Whitman as Ideal American." Brooklyn Daily
Eagle (28 February), Sect. A, 12:1-2.
    Quotes Keila at length on Whitman, com-
paring the success of his poetry to that of
sculpture, in which what is left out is as
significant as what is put in, praising
his vivid description of the black teamster
("Myself" 13), urging that Americans know
him as a figure of Americanism and prophet
of nature. Illustrated.

38 ANON. "The Voice of Whitman." New York Herald-
Tribune (3 March), 22:3.
    Editorial finding Whitman worthy of
memorialization: his is "one of the few
major voices this country has produced."
The world as well as America will always
turn to him "in those great moments to
which his soul belonged" (rather than to
"the routine hours of life"). Despite
some "egostistic and empty" passages which
lead many readers to find him boring and
disgusting, "his irregular lines have, at
their best, the strength and beauty of
classic fragments."

39 MABBOTT, THOMAS OLLIVE. "Early Quotations
and Allusions of Walt Whitman." Notes and
Queries 150 (6 March), 169-70.
    Brief explanatory notes for early
writings in Uncollected (1921.16).

40 JACOBSON, ANNA. "Walt Whitman in Germany
Since 1914." Germanic Review 1 (April),
132-41.
    Whitman's following has increased in
Germany since Thorstenberg's discussion
(1911.17): now "he has become a living
force," especially for the working class.
His ideas and ideals are appropriate for
the period after the war, including his
belief in brotherhood, his appreciation of
ordinary soldiers, and a positive attitude
toward death. Critical articles, translations, and poets influenced by him are
noted and discussed. His popularity is
shown by public readings, quotations used
on calendars, many centenary articles.
Thomas Mann is among the latest to be inspired by Whitman's spirit, especially
regarding his conception of death.

41 FOERSTER, NORMAN. "American Literature."
Saturday Review of Literature 2 (3 April),
677-69.
Reprinted: 1928.10.
    Incidental discussion of Whitman, in
whom "the frontier background of Emerson's
idealism becomes foreground." He witnessed
"the flowering and fading of the pioneer
spirit." Among America's leading romantics,
Whitman guided the development into realism,
although its bitterness contrasts with his
optimism.

42 ROBINSON, LANDON. "Magnificent Youth and
'Good Gray Poet.'" Literary Review 6 (24
April), 2.
    Review of Rogers (1926.24) and Morley
(1926.21): Rogers makes some omissions and
gives too light a treatment. Whitman certainly entertained the sexual feelings he
expressed so freely, but covered his tracks
too carefully for us to determine whether
he acted upon them. The 1855 Preface is an
explanation of the poems, occasionally displaying a similar "rhythmic beat." "Backward Glance" reveals a significant "development in emotional richness and intellectual
grasp" in "a moving piece of sustained
poetic prose."

43 GORMAN, HERBERT S. "Walt Whitman, 'Starting
from Fish-Shape Paumanok'--Cameron Rogers
Writes a New Biography in the New Fictional
Manner." New York Times Book Review (25
April), 7, 23.
    Review of Rogers (1926.24). The real
Whitman, the greatness of soul which comes
through in his work, largely the creation
of his poetry, eludes Rogers. The "mystery
concerned with the almost feminine facets
of his personality" may be explainable with
the material existing now, but Rogers's

1926

Whitman is incomplete with its New Orleans
assumptions and emphasis on loafing (though
this is the Whitman of many readers).

44 WHICHER, GEORGE F. "The Ariel Jazz." New
York Herald-Tribune Books 2 (25 April),
4-5. Illustrations from Rogers (1926.24).
Review of Rogers (1926.24) and Morley
(1926.21). Whitman's effort in Leaves, "to
tilt his unbalanced generation back to a
sane joy of the senses, led to no tangible
result." Rogers captures some of Whitman's
qualities, but Leaves "remains Whitman's
best biography." The prefaces are important
for all Whitman lovers, the first a "great
prose rhapsody," "Backward Glance" a "calmer
and clearer statement of his poetic aims"
and "a startling anticipation of recent
aesthetic theory," ranking with Poe's
"Philosophy of Composition."

45 ANON. "Hardly Fair to Walt." Chicago News
(28 April).
Review of Rogers (1926.24), "more mush"
than is quite fair to Whitman, although
"Whitman himself combined a good deal of
mush and blah with undeniable greatness."

46 POUND, LOUISE. "Walt Whitman and the French
Language." American Speech 1 (May), 421-
30.
Whitman always admired France and
French republicanism. The French words he
uses are discussed. Whitman "had unusual
linguistic consciousness," admiring the
English language but freely using loan-words
from Old World languages, words which are
generally "clear in meaning and attractive
in sound" and "hardly seem affected or out
of place" when the reader surrenders to
Whitman's "catholicity of diction," so important to the effect of his poetry.

47 ANON. "Walt Whitman Not a Mere Revoltist."
Toronto Star (1 May).
Whitman's poetry was "really a leap
back to the freedom of Homer over the artificial and new fangled strait-jackets of
more modern authorship." He was "not a
mere modern," but "an everlasting pagan who
managed to get his city and the critic back
to the sensations of Homer." His life is
traced with admiration, along the lines of
Rogers (1926.24).

48 ANON. "Whitman and His Story." Christian
Science Monitor (12 May), 9:1-3.
Review of Rogers (1926.24) and Morley
(1926.21), which complement each other.
Whitman has emerged from unpopularity
during his life into current greatness,
"glorifying not the common man, but that so
different thing which is common humanity."
Rogers's narrative is pleasant, with "sympathetic insight" into Whitman's "tenderness" and "bumptiousness," although Edward
Wilson's illustrations are "truer essentially to the genius of Whitman" than Rogers's

prose. Morley's illustrator also bears
witness to Whitman's greatness of spirit.
Posterity seems to have agreed with
Whitman's self-evaluation of future importance.

49 MOORE, AUBERTINE WOODWARD. "Walt Whitman and
American Music: Personal Reminiscences."
Musical Leader 5 (20 May), 5.
Revision of 1915.52.
Recalls her introduction to Whitman's
work through "Redwood" and "Prayer," both
described; her meetings with Whitman; his
conversation. Concluded 1926.51.

*50 ANON. Account of Whitman celebration.
Chicago News (26 May).
Reported in Willard.
Sandburg dubbed the celebration "The
Whitman Follies."

51 MOORE, AUBERTINE WOODWARD. "Walt Whitman and
American Music: Personal Reminiscences."
Musical Leader 5 (27 May), 22.
Concludes 1926.49. Describes the images
Whitman's descriptions of music arouse in
her. His love of music included that in
nature and in such art as Sand's Consuelo.
He told her his hopes for American music.
Huneker's letter to her is quoted on
Whitman's attendance at Philadelphia con-
certs in 1880. Earlier articles on Whitman
and music are cited.

52 CANBY, HENRY SEIDEL. "Introducing Whitman."
Saturday Review of Literature 2 (29 May),
819.
Review of Rogers (1926.24) and Morley
(1926.21). Whitman needs to be read, not
praised, but most readers need an introduction to him. He was both "behind his age"
(regarding artistic knowledge) and ahead of
it (regarding belief in "the coming domi-
nance of the plain human man"). He gave
poetry a new rhythm and then decided to
make himself the subject of his verse, as
typical man. The reader who fails to understand Whitman and his America will appreciate only his most familiar poems, not
always the best. Rogers offers perhaps the
best introduction so far, though failing to
explain adequately what "soul conflicts"
and "prophetic visions" led Whitman to
write this poetry. The prefaces make him
intelligible as poet and should be read
after learning about Whitman the man and
before moving into Leaves. The 1855 Preface
"is one of the remarkable documents of
American history," "a theory of poetry, a
theory of democracy, a theory of the American
idealism which Whitman professed," with a
religious spirit less common recently.

53 ANON. "Community Church Gets Whitman Bust."
New York Times (31 May), 18:3.
Account of dedication of the Whitman
bust by Louis Mayer, with his comments on
Whitman's vision, and Rev. John Herman
Randall's address on Whitman's ideals.

54 ROMIG, EDNA DAVIS. "The Paradox of Walt Whitman." University of Colorado Studies 15 (June), 95-132.
Whitman remains prophetic, ahead of our time, with his faith in democracy and the potency of freedom. His "Whitmanese" (mixed, unaesthetic language) will keep him from the highest ranks, although the beauty and completeness of the Lincoln poems, "Cradle," "Brooklyn Ferry," "Proud Music," "Passage," and certain excerpts will never die. His catalogues fail at their presumed mystic purpose. Paradoxes of Whitman's personality, systemless philosophy (adhesiveness vs. individualism, materialism vs. idealism), and religion (unclear, shifting from youth to age) are described. He has force but does not come close to the human heart. His contradictions may be part of his claim as "a figure and a force to be reckoned with" and much studied.

55 S., G. S. "A Poet 'With the Face of an Angel'-- And the Joyous Rush of Spring in All His Work." London Daily Herald (2 June).
Review of Bailey (1926.1) and Augustan Books' selection of Whitman. Whitman was great in conveying the excitement of life, as the selections reveal. Bailey concentrates too much on Whitman's defects, which are present but should not be dwelt upon in such a great writer.

*56 ANON. Article. Chicago Post (11 June).
Reported in Willard.
Describes plans for Whitman Fellowship festivities, including a dance group pursuing "soul rhythms."

57 SHERMAN, STUART. "A Reluctant Witness Testifies for Whitman." New York Herald-Tribune Books 2 (13 June), 1-3.
Review of Bailey (1926.1). The Hall of Fame's snub of Whitman is hardly worth notice, for his immortality as a first-rate, original voice is spread throughout Europe as well as America. People should begin reading him in his prefaces rather than in "Adam," that "they might respond to him with their imaginations rather than with their sensuality." Bailey's limited ideas of America do not allow him to appreciate perhaps "the most significant aspects of Whitman's form, substance and feeling." He prefers to admire Whitman's genius in universal qualities shared with the classical Greek, Latin, and English poets. But Whitman's role as a poet speaking for his country is not so reprehensible as Bailey makes it appear; it is largely for his portrayal of American life and the American ethos that Sherman, along with other Americans, responds to Whitman.

58 ANON. "Walt Whitman." Times Literary Supplement (London) (17 June), 411.
Review of Bailey (1926.1), which presents a controlled and clearly reasoned attitude toward Whitman, no less ardent for coming from a scholar of more traditional writers. While "Sea Drift," "Drum-Taps," and "Memories of President Lincoln" have certainly been accepted into the mainstream of English literature, "Whitman as a whole is still a challenge to a clear-headed and constructive critic" like Bailey, who recognizes that Leaves is all of a piece by looking at Whitman's lesser work as well. Whitman "never clearly saw the difference between the two worlds in which he lived-- the world in which the equality of men is nothing but a foolish phrase, and the world of another order, where all men are alike," in which world he was "a matchless poet."

59 HOLLOWAY, EMORY. "Walt Whitman at Thirty-One." New York Evening Post (26 June).
Describes the poem and five letters Whitman contributed to the Post in 1850-51, under Bryant's editorship, including excellent examples of his musical and art criticism and revelations of his mystical side and his keen interest in nature and the people of the city.

60 ANON. "The All-Star Literary Vaudeville." New Republic 47 (30 June), 163.
Incidental reference in this examination of the status of contemporary American writers: "Emerson, Whitman, Poe; Walden and Moby Dick: they are all independent one-man turns."

61 YORKE, DANE. "Whitman in Camden." American Mercury 8 (July), 355-62.
Camden has finally accepted Whitman, though most residents are still unaware of his greatness. Traubel's version of Whitman as a saint surrounded by disciples is untrue; he was less well-known than currently presented. His early Camden years, up to 1881, found him center of a semiliterary discussion group, a major figure of which was Dr. Regnell Coates who did not respect Whitman and quarreled openly with him. During the later years, his fame grew; residents remained indifferent. Anecdotes are cited.

*62 ANON. Article. Hartford Courant (1 July).
Quoted in Willard.
Even years ago there were many who believed Whitman a genius; that number has increased with time.

63 ANON. "The Listener." Boston Evening Transcript (3 July), sec. 3, 2:4-5.
Favorable review of Kennedy (1926.15), citing various opinions on Whitman.

64 ANON. "Plans of Fauntleroy Memorial in Central Park Rejected by Board, but May be Resubmitted." New York Times (16 July), 1:7.
Final paragraph notes the rejection of

1926

the proposal to place Jo Davidson's statue
of Whitman in Battery Park because of the
unfitting location.

65 READ, HERBERT. "Walt Whitman." Nation and
Athenaeum 39 (17 July), 447.
Review of Bailey (1926.1), whose scale
of values is inadequate when applied to
Whitman. Whitman is not really a free-
verse poet, having no interest in poetic
technique but writing "instinctively and in
vague imitation of Biblical phrasing." His
real significance is literary only in being
antiliterary, destroying the literary
categories. He is more important for his
message, which Bailey fails to cover successfully: his timely revival of the
masculine ideal and creation of "a humane
democratic ideal." Bailey tends to "ethe-
rialize or platonize" the implications of
"Calamus" and "Adam." He should have
"delved deeper into the records of Whitman's
life" and "assembled the evidence for the
interpretation of the poet's message" on a
psychological basis.

66 THE PHOENICIAN [pseud.]. "The Phoenix Nest."
Saturday Review of Literature 2 (24 July),
960.
Paragraph comment wondering at Whitman's
inclusion in the English Men of Letters
series (1926.1).

67 MUMFORD, LEWIS. "Walt Whitman." New Republic
47 (28 July), 288-89.
Review of Bailey (1926.1), Rogers
(1926.24), Morley (1926.21). Bailey cannot
cope with Whitman's verse or see "that
Whitman turned aside from the English
tradition for a deep inner reason, and not
out of a harsh contempt for the best that
was thought and written in the past."
Bailey prefers "Pioneers" to "the sonorous
sweep of the longer poems, which achieve
their effect partly through repetition and
length." The Welsh can appreciate Whitman's
poetry better than the English. Rogers
"has turned an epic life into a pedestrian
novel," a let-down after "Bazalgette's
glowing and hearty biography" (1920.2).
Whitman seems to defy restatement in biographies. The prefaces reveal that Whitman
did not want to destroy the past but merely
sought to "put his own great bulk in the
foreground," though others regarded his
"large self-discipline" as "a sprawl." His
"tough and knotty and juicy prose" is "one
of the genuine glories of American literature."

68 SNOW, WILBERT. "Walt Whitman." Book Notes
Illustrated 4 (August-September), 211-13,
218. Woodcut illustration by James Britton.
Whitman fulfilled Emerson's quest for
an American literature. Leaves "is primarily a document and only secondarily a book
of poems," his ideas of more importance to
him than the polish of his lines; yet his

catalogues are often attractive with
brilliant lines; his first lines are
beautiful. Though generally writing on
levels too high (abstractions) or too low
(catalogues), he achieves the successful
middle path in "Lilacs," "Cradle," "Passage,"
"Proud Music." His attitude toward sex,
no longer out of place, was needed by his
time; so was his real faith in democracy
and in the vitality of the world. Significant contemporary poets show the influence
of Whitman, "the one figure of our literature who has taken on world significance."

69 ANON. "Lincoln Admired 'Leaves of Grass.'"
New York Times Book Review (1 August), 4.
Favorable review of Kennedy (1926.15),
with quotation from Rankin (1916.17).

70 STRACHEY, J. ST. LOE. "Walt Whitman Survives
a Trial by Ordeal. John Bailey's Study of
the Poet Tempers Admiration With Discerning
Criticism." New York Times Book Review
(1 August), 4, 17.
Review of Bailey (1926.1), "one of the
best pieces of literary criticism of recent
years," applying to Whitman's work the
standards Whitman himself demanded, with
Whitman coming through "on the whole unscathed." It is relieving that Bailey
absolves Whitman from the "disturbing accusations of moral depravity" aroused by
"Calamus." Strachey defends Whitman against
some of Bailey's criticisms, such as the
vulgarity of Whitman's use of the vernacular.
Much of Whitman's poetry has "lilt," although he professed to have eliminated it.
"Good-Bye, My Fancy" and "Broad-Axe" are
discussed as successful poems. Whitman
owed his "metrical artifice" to the Hebrew
poets, "though no doubt unconsciously."

71 ALLISON, W. T. "Walt Whitman, Greatest of All
Democrats." Calgary Daily Herald (14
August).
Review of Bailey (1926.1), emphasizing
Whitman as great voice of democracy and his
country. It is odd that Bailey considers
"Lilacs" much greater than "Captain," though
"Death Carol" is "one of the great lyrics
of the world." Bailey absolves Whitman of
immorality, although Whitman "had no tact
in the use of language." He regarded everything in the universe with wonder, reverence,
acceptance, and love.

72 LESSING, O. F. [sic]. "Whitman and his German
Critics Prior to 1910." American Collector
3 (October), 7-15.
Reprint of 1910.23.

73 GORMAN, HERBERT S. "Whitman as Poet, Prophet
and Egotist. Emory Holloway's Study Is
Concerned Chiefly With His Middle Period."
New York Times Book Review (10 October), 5.
Review of Holloway (1926.13), which
may regard Whitman the man as too great,
for his personal and philosophical flaws

can be forgiven only if he is regarded as
among the finest of poets and teachers.
Some readers may find no more than "half a
dozen extraordinary and beautiful poems"
in Whitman. This book represents sound
study and gives a good picture of the
American mind. Whitman's "inconsistencies
were more the weakness of a mind that
surged forth from atavistic reasonings"
than from an intellect that comprehended
and accepted all. Holloway is reticent on
the feelings toward men evidenced in
"Calamus," which must be "fairly considered."

74 SANDBURG, CARL. "Walt Whitman." World Review
3 (11 October), 57.
Abridged from 1921.30.

75 ANON. "The Book Column. A New Interpretation
of Old Walt. Mr. Holloway's Whitman." New
York Sun (13 October), 28:7.
      Favorable review of Holloway (1926.13),
with references to Overton's "dignified
and imaginative" presentation of Whitman
(1921.27) and Rogers's "intelligent and
sympathetic portrait" (1926.24). The significant problems in Whitman's life are
described, although Holloway's purpose "is
to stress all that was noble and creative
in the man and the poet" in this "vivid
and well rounded portrait" of one whose
work "seems to gain power with the years."

76 MORLEY, CHRISTOPHER. "The Bowling Green.
The Whitman Shelf." Saturday Review of
Literature 3 (16 October), 195.
      "A brief digest" of recent treatment of
Whitman. Holloway's Popular Authorized
Edition of Leaves (1926.12) presents poems
"carefully sifted and abridged," for Whitman
"must be edited for the tender reader." It
includes the welcome Vistas as a voice
different from the poetry, "violently contemporary" and powerful if at times a bit
absurd, demanding to be better known among
"its possible beneficiaries." Contrasting
current opinions on Whitman in the periodicals are noted. Bailey (1926.1) justly and
sympathetically balances Whitman's pros and
cons. "Nothing that concerns either Walt
the poet or Whitman the too-little read
artist in prose is wholly unimportant."

77 MUMFORD, LEWIS. "'Here Is Whitman the Man.'"
New York Herald-Tribune Books 3 (7 November), 5-6. Illustrated.
      Review of Holloway (1926.13), in which
"the man emerges from the myth," "free from
conjecture and romantic improvisation."
Holloway is "faint-hearted" when dealing
with "Adam" and "Calamus." Modern psychology has "widened the concept of homosexuality" so that a biographer may recognize
such strands in a subject like Whitman,
even if these elements are sublimated and
allow him a "healthy development" and
"normal, full" heterosexual experience, as
shown by the evidence.

78 SAWYER, PHILIP. "A Motto for the Wets." New
York Times (8 November), 18:6.
      Quotes as appropriate for the anti-
Prohibitionists the lines Whitman addressed
to the states: "Resist much, obey little."

79 ANON. Paragraph. Outlook 144 (10 November),
343-44.
      Brief review of Holloway (1926.13) and
Rogers (1926.24).

80 EASTMAN, MAX. "Menshevizing Walt Whitman."
New Masses 2 (December), 12.
      Review of Holloway (1926.13), which
lacks the vast life which is Whitman's and
fails to discuss candidly the fact that
Whitman "was strongly homosexual, and at
certain periods of his life very passion-
ately in love with himself," as in the
"rapturous love-songs" of some of his
anonymous articles on himself. "His was a
revolt against the negation and the limitation involved from the beginning in the
very fact of civilization itself, a declaration of animal and cosmic independence."
His lines make Christian culture's "tight
little negative moralisms" dwindle away.
Though not a definitive biography, this
book clearly raises the questions for a
future biographer of "the interior and
exterior cause and the significance of his
pronounced doubleness of character" and how
he developed from the early "over-grown
literary lout."

81 VAN DOREN, MARK. "First Glance." Nation 123
(15 December), 641.
      Review of Kennedy (1926.15) and
Holloway (1926.13). Kennedy's excitement
leads to his confused presentation.
Holloway goes only a little way toward explaining the great mystery of how Whitman
suddenly broke loose and achieved the freedom to write Leaves.

82 ELIOT, T. S. "Whitman and Tennyson." Nation
and Athenaeum 40 (18 December), 426.
Reprinted: Murphy. Excerpt reprinted:
Miller.
      Review of Holloway (1926.13), "as good
a biography of Whitman as has been written,
or is likely to be," because it takes into
consideration Whitman's time and place. He
was primarily "a 'man with a message,' even
if that message was sometimes badly muti-
lated in transmission," rather than "the
inventor of a new technique of versification."
Whitman and Tennyson, both "born laureates,"
were similar in being conservative rather
than reactionary or revolutionary: "they
believed explicitly in progress, and believed implicitly that progress consists in
things remaining much as they are." They
transmuted the real into an ideal. Whitman
is not only "a great representative of
America" (although of one different from
that of Fitzgerald, Hemingway, and Dos
Passos), for "behind all the illusions

1926

there is another vision. When Whitman
speaks of the lilacs or of the mocking-
bird, his theories and beliefs drop away
like a needless pretext."

1927

BOOKS

1 AUSLANDER, JOSEPH, and HILL, FRANK ERNEST.
   The Winged Horse: The Story of the Poets
   and their Poetry. Garden City, N.Y.:
   Doubleday, Page & Co. "'I Sing Democracy,'"
   pp. 348-62.
   Extract reprinted: 1934.26.
        Introduction for young people, tracing
   Whitman's life, purpose, belief in America,
   the power of his poetry (praising especially
   "Passage," "Proud Music," "Cradle"), his
   contributions to poetic tradition through
   his "message of vitality and generosity."
   "Our not having an exact place to put him,"
   unlike other great poets, proves him great.

2 BEARD, CHARLES A. and BEARD, MARY R. The Rise
   of American Civilization. New York:
   Macmillan Co. Vol. 1, pp. 776-78, 779,
   786, 791-92, 793; vol. 2, pp. 435-36.
        "Whitman celebrated a whole-souled and
   jubilant faith in democracy, accepting and
   loving the masses as he found them, good,
   bad, or indifferent." "Singing of America,
   he sang of himself, a spokesman of a pushing
   and defiant working class," and became
   recognized at home and abroad as democracy
   incarnate. Later, in "Passage," he questioned "the rush and roar" of industrial,
   capitalist America. He is compared with
   other American poets.

3 BENNETT, JAMES O'DONNELL. Much Loved Books:
   Best Sellers of the Ages. New York: Boni
   & Liveright. "Whitman's 'Leaves of Grass,'"
   pp. 339-44; "Whitman and Certain Curiosities
   of Criticism," 345-51; brief bibliography,
   460-61.
        Whitman is the liveliest reading in
   seventy years. He is compared to a Greek
   god and a blackguard. Passages are quoted
   to show his great sanity. He is the servant
   and celebrant of natural law and human
   liberty. His life illustrates his devotion
   to comradeship. Criticism on Whitman is
   quoted. Bennett reveres Whitman but finds
   in him "things appalling and grotesque."
   Nevertheless, his contradictions and boundless variety are stimulating. It is "the
   less portentous Whitman, the Whitman of
   the fleeting things of life" that shows
   beauty and eloquence. "Captain," quoted,
   is "the perfect threnody of American
   poetry."

4 BOYD, ERNEST. Literary Blasphemies. New
   York and London: Harper & Bros. "Walt
   Whitman," pp. 186-212; also 13-14.
   Reprint of 1925.77.

Notes the blind objections of Whitman's
admirers to the opinions expressed in the
1925 article, here reprinted.

5 CHARLESWORTH, HECTOR. The Canadian Scene.
   Sketches: Political and Historical.
   Toronto: Macmillan Co. "Walt Whitman in
   Canada: Marginalia," pp. 200-207.
        Discusses Whitman in relation to
   Canada. He would have appreciated the
   Western Rockies. Charlesworth questions
   whether Whitman's form was due to the
   surge of emotion or to mere laziness. He
   had more talent as a writer of prose.
   Bucke is commented upon as Whiman's defender.

6 DUNCAN, ISADORA. My Life. New York: Boni &
   Liveright, pp. 3, 31, 78, 80, 217, 233,
   252, 339-40, 341.
        Calling herself "the spiritual daughter
   of Walt Whitman," she seeks a dance and a
   music for dance worthy of the song he heard
   when he wrote "I Hear America Singing."
   She notes the disapproval his writings
   faced, though he was "at heart a Puritan."

7 GOSSE, Sir EDMUND. Leaves and Fruit. New
   York: Charles Scribner's Sons. "Walt
   Whitman," pp. 205-11.
        It is characteristic of Whitman that
   his readers react differently to him in
   different moods or stages of life, as
   Emerson did. Bailey's book (1926.1) describes Whitman clearly, with simultaneous
   infatuation and clear-sightedness, the
   proper spirit in which to approach Whitman.
   The 1855 Leaves is probably the best, because Whitman does not break up his text
   into fragments with fortuitous titles,
   although one would not like to miss "the
   beautiful and mystic 'Calamus,' which no
   one has been daring enough to fathom, or a
   few of the 'Drum-Taps.'" Whitman's one
   subject is "the masculinity of other men,"
   illustrated by his own body. One should
   not be misled by "Adam" or "the subterfuges
   of his alarmed correspondence" with Symonds.
   He should be appreciated for his candor,
   zest for life, and the "beauty and originality of his strange unshackled rhapsody."

8 HARRIS, FRANK. My Life. Vol. 3. Nice:
   Privately printed for subscribers only,
   pp. 45, 124, 219, 325, 380.
        Continues 1925.7. Brief references:
   notes Symonds's surprise at "Whitman's
   passionate repudiation of abnormal desires";
   wonders at Whitman's praise of death, since
   life is so good.

9 HAZARD, LUCY LOCKWOOD. The Frontier in American
   Literature. New York: Thomas Y. Crowell
   Co. "Walt Whitman: The Afterglow of the
   Golden Age," pp. 170-77; brief bibliography,
   180; also xvi, xix, 147, 151, 156, 157,
   163, 253.
        The history of American literature is
   a fulfillment of Whitman's vision of the

singer of these states. Though "the self-proclaimed prophet of a new era," he was actually "singing the swan song of the old," his death coinciding with the disappearance of the frontier. His ideas have much in common with Old World Liberalism: passionate faith in the New World, the "essentially Old World relationship" between men (whether phallic or purely spiritual), the perfectibility of human nature. His spiritual pioneering consists of deifying democracy without defining it.

10 HOLLOWAY, EMORY. Introduction to <u>Pictures:</u> <u>An Unpublished Poem of Walt Whitman. With</u> <u>an Introduction and Notes by Emory Holloway</u>. New York: The June House; London: Faber & Gwyer, 37 pp., pp. 7-11. Reprint with minor changes of 1925.47.

11 KENNEDY, WILLIAM SLOANE. <u>An Autolycus Pack or</u> <u>What You Will</u>. West Yarmouth, Mass.: Stonecroft Press. "Walt Whitman's Indebtedness to Emerson," pp. 45-51. Reprint of 1897.123.

12 MABBOTT, THOMAS OLLIVE, ed. Introduction and notes to <u>The Half-Breed and Other Stories</u> by Walt Whitman. New York: Columbia University Press, pp. 11-19, 117-29.
   Traces history of <u>Aristidean</u>, in which several of these stories appeared; comments upon the stories and their historical and biographical sources; explains the texts used here.

13 MENCKEN, H. L. <u>Selected Prejudices</u>. New York: Alfred A. Knopf. "In Memoriam," pp. 57-58. Reprint of 1919.17.

14 MITCHELL, LANGDON. <u>Understanding America</u>. New York: George H. Doran Co. "Walt Whitman," pp. 159-82.
   Whitman exerts the most powerful influence upon America's younger poets, having freed them from much that would have retarded their progress and enabled them to impart new life to American literature. He was unpopular during his lifetime because critical doctrine was not interested in a poet's attitude to life; hence only his poetic beauties were admired. He was actually not like the common people but set apart by genius and his ideals. He was destroyer as well as creator. <u>Leaves</u> has its origin in the conflict between his Christian (Quaker) influence and his non-Christian qualities; his appreciation for life and the body contrasts with the world-weary sentiments of popular religion, while "Adam" protests against contemporary attitudes, perhaps too self-consciously, though necessarily so. He unfortunately appeals too much to weaklings and eccentrics. His physical presence (recollected from Mitchell's personal acquaintance) revealed him as one of those rare men of "an amazing-

ly perfected humanity." He was "a great maker and molder of language," a philosophical poet writing "a Hymn of the Perfection of Things." He will come into his own as science gives rise to a new religion.

15 MORROW, HONORÉ WILLSIE. <u>Forever Free</u>. New York: William Morrow & Co., pp. 66-67, 389-90.
   This novelized biography of Lincoln describes Lincoln's admiration for Whitman's poetry, considering him the prophet of democracy with helpful ideas on government. John Hay is presented introducing them.

16 NIVEN, FREDERICK. <u>Wild Honey</u>. New York: Dodd, Mead & Co., pp. 187, 191, 195.
   A quotation from "Lilacs" comes into the narrator's mind as he listens to lake sounds. Though appropriate to the open air, "Whitman's joyous chant of death" is not quoted aloud, since it would not fit a friend's mood. At the mention of Whitman's name, a Western fellow places him as a "plug with a soft hat and long beard like Moses," similar to Joaquin Miller.

17 O'CONNOR, WILLIAM DOUGLAS. <u>The Good Gray</u> <u>Poet: A Vindication</u>. Toronto: Henry S. Saunders, 75 pp. Introduction by Ellen M. O'Connor-Calder, pp. i-ix. Ltd. ed. of 125 copies. Reprint of 1866.2.
   O'Connor's widow describes him and his relationship with Whitman.

18 PARRINGTON, VERNON LOUIS. <u>Main Currents in</u> <u>American Thought</u>. Vol. 2. <u>The Romantic</u> <u>Revolution in America 1800-1860</u>. New York: Harcourt, Brace & Co., p. i and passim per index.
   Various incidental references in comparison with other writers, especially Melville. Continued 1930.17.

19 ROBERTS, MORLEY. Introduction to <u>Thyrza: A</u> <u>Tale</u>, by George Gissing (Reprint of 1887.7). New York: E. P. Dutton & Co., n.d., pp. vii-viii; in novel, 420, 423-26, 439.
   Roberts recalls introducing Whitman to Gissing by reading him aloud; Gissing responded to "the big-breathed Whitman."

20 ROURKE, CONSTANCE MAYFIELD. <u>Trumpets of</u> <u>Jubilee</u>. New York: Harcourt, Brace & Co., pp. 173-75; passim per index.
   Whitman in the 1850s is described, proclaiming the great idea, "urging the life of instinct and impulse." He and Henry Ward Beecher shared similar experiences in New York, similar idiom and use of rhapsodic discourse. Whitman was perhaps influenced by Beecher, who called on him after the publication of <u>Leaves</u>. Victoria Woodhull may have been influenced by Whitman. Horace Greeley scored him in a public address on poetry.

1927

21 SAUNDERS, HENRY S. Portrait Gallery of
Whitman Writers with Quotations. Toronto:
Henry S. Saunders. Manuscript only.
Photographs of various writers, each
captioned by his or her comment on Whitman.

22 THORNSBURGH, ZADA, ed. Introduction, notes,
and bibliography to Selections from Whitman.
New York: Macmillan Co., pp. xv-xxxvii,
265-76, 277.
Introduction to this selection for high
school students traces Whitman's life and
explains his ideas on democracy. In America
he sees the opportunity for reconciling
liberty and union, emphasizing the individual's importance and recognizing the facts
of inequality, urging spiritual growth.
His two ideals are the growing man and the
perfect state. Though he is so American
that his own did not appreciate him, his
democracy transcends Americanism. He looks
to literature, not government, for the
effective voice of the nation. He identifies himself with our lives, encouraging
his reader to be a man and get at the value
of life rather than to be a writer and wit
as other poets do. He is a teacher and
prophet, "the life-giver of our time," who
"gave America to the world." Several poems
are scanned to reveal Whitman's various
metrics ("Captain," "Pioneers," "Beat!
Beat! Drums!," "Joy, Shipmate, Joy!"), and
specific literary devices are pointed out
in other poems. His free verse has affected
modern free verse but is better than most
of it. Uses material from Pattee (1915.16).
Notes explain certain words, provide background for some poems, and ask questions
(extensively for Vistas) about meaning and
use of words.

23 WATSON, E. H. LACON. Lectures on Dead Authors.
London: Ernest Brown. "The Poetry of
Democracy," pp. 105-28.
Reprint of 1901.50.

24 WILSON, DAVID ALEC. Carlyle at His Zenith
(1848-53). London: Kegan Paul, Trench,
Trubner & Co., p. 296.
Whitman was "one of the best of the
later writers who discussed the politics
of Carlyle," as in a passage quoted from
Specimen.

PERIODICALS

25 JONES, E. Review of Two Prefaces (1926.21).
Sewanee Review 35 (January), 124-25.
Reading Whitman can restore to us today
some of the optimism of that golden age.
These prefaces (described) account for him
better than biographies or criticism. The
1855 Preface is an "astonishing document,"
"beautiful, superb, shining, incomparable."

26 LAFOURCADE, GEORGES. "Swinburne and Walt
Whitman." Modern Language Review 22 (January), 84-86.

Traces Swinburne's comments on Whitman
from unpublished letters to his "Whitmania"
(1887.63) to show that his doubts grew
gradually.

27 ALLEN, HERVEY. "Whitman in His Works."
Saturday Review of Literature 3 (29 January), 546.
Review of Holloway (1926.13). Though
excellent, this is not quite the ultimate
examination of the difficult subject of
Whitman, concentrating as it does on
Whitman's life as reflected in his work.
It emphasizes Whitman's urge toward equality, the spiritual significance of his
imagery, his debt to Emerson, who gave his
philosophy unity. Holloway is too delicate
in dealing with his abnormality, for "the
supreme fact of his life" is the loving
"paternal-maternal spirit" which came from
his "feminine soul in a man's body."

28 MORLEY, CHRISTOPHER. "The Bowling Green."
Saturday Review of Literature 3 (29 January), 547.
Quotes letter punning with printer
terminology from Bruce Rogers on his ambition to print, among other items, "an
edition of Leaves of Grass on esparto
paper."

29 ANON. "School in Which Walt Whitman Taught
to Go; Woodbury, L.I., to Auction Building
Today." New York Times (26 February),
17:4-5.
The school building in whose one room
Whitman taught in 1836 is to be sold at
auction or else torn down. It is described;
likewise previous efforts to have it moved.

30 ANON. "Walt Whitman Schoolhouse Bid in at
$18, to Be Scrapped." New York Times (27
February), sec. 1, 1:2.
Describes the auction of the schoolhouse
and Whitman's association with it. A carpenter won and will use the schoolhouse for
building material.

31 ANON. "Admirers Raise Fund to Save Walt
Whitman's Schoolhouse." New York Times
(28 February), 6:3.
Describes fund contributed to by
several figures in literature and the arts,
to buy the schoolhouse from the carpenter
and have it moved and eventually placed
somewhere permanently.

32 WEBER, OSCAR F. "Walt Whitman: the Mystic."
English Journal 16 (March), 222-23.
Whitman, for whom life was eternal and
all experience unified, was truly a mystic,
radiating "an angelic presence." The
"abandoned at-oneness with his God" expressed in "Myself" (quoted) and much of
Whitman's verse is more exalted than the
experience of many mystics. Every word
might have been uttered by Christ.

33 ANON. "Saving Whitman's Schoolhouse." New
York Times (1 March), 26:5.
Editorial on the last-minute salvation
from destruction of Whitman's schoolhouse,
a needed testimonial to the respect now
granted him and due "a poet indigenous to
American soil, representative of America's
vigor and rugged strength."

34 ANON. "Current Poetry." Literary Digest 92
(5 March), 32.
Includes reprint of Dickson's sonnet
(1926.8), a "tribute to the poet whose life
sums up the strangest contrasts of public
appreciation."

35 ANON. "Whitman School Moved." New York Times
(9 March), 19:7.
Account of the saving of the schoolhouse
and today's plans to move it.

36 LOWELL, AMY. "Walt Whitman and the New
Poetry." Yale Review 16 (April), 502-19.
Reprinted: 1930.12; Murphy.
Whitman fell into his form through
ignorance, not through "a high sense of
fitness." His development was toward "a
greater preoccupation with form": witness
his changes in lines and titles (away from
their early clumsiness). He could use
rhyme but did not find it appropriate to
most of his poetry because looking for it
would stop the poem's movement. He had
little rhythmical sense, unlike the moderns,
whose vers libre relies on cadence. But
he is a great poet (only after the propagandist), because he has "the poetic point
of view": the use of a recurring "basic
emotional symbol," as in "Cradle," "Passage," and "Tears" which demonstrate a
superb use of rhythm representing his finest
work. He was a man of his time, not a
pacifist; his theories would be acceptable
to Longfellow and Tennyson. The moderns
owe to him not their form but an attitude,
his aim to give America "autochthonous
song," largely achieved by him. He occasionally writes imagistic pieces and uses
a type of suggestion like that of the
moderns, but his sentimentality is absent
in poets like Sandburg who are closest to
him.

37 MABBOTT, THOMAS OLLIVE. "Some Account of
Sojourner Truth." American Collector 4
(April), 18-20.
Prints a letter to Whitman from Elisa
Seaman Leggett of Detroit (1881), concerning Sojourner Truth, the black abolitionist,
upon which Whitman made no known comment
and of which his biographers have been unaware.

*38 JEFFERS, ROBINSON. "Poetry and True Poetry."
The Advance (1 April).
Reprinted: 1933.2.
Review of James Rorty's Children of the
Sun and Other Poems: Rorty is akin to both

Thoreau and Whitman, "the two polarities
of American life, the secret austerity
under the national expansiveness."

39 WING, JAMES G. "Whitman Again." Saturday
Review of Literature 3 (2 April), 706.
Letter: "Whitman was not strictly
original" but followed a poetic tendency to
"untrammeled verse" available even to
children, as shown humorously by a poem
Wing wrote as a child. But Whitman "did
bring forth his inhibitions," though preceded in this by the Song of Solomon.

*40 ANON. Article. Book News Brevities (Columbia
University Press) (5 April).
Reported in Willard.
On a press clipping service and its
many articles on Whitman.

41 ANON. "New Site for Whitman School; Relics
of Poet Gathered for It." New York Times
(10 April), sec. 2, 1:2.
The schoolhouse has been moved to
Jericho, Long Island.

42 ELIOT, T. S. "Israfel." Nation and Athenaeum
41 (21 May), 219.
Review of books on Poe. Incidental:
"In England the romantic cult was transformed
by the enormous prestige of Tennyson; in
America by Tennyson also and later by
Whitman, the American Tennyson."

43 ANON. Brief review of Half-Breed (1927.12).
Saturday Review of Literature 3 (28 May),
869.
This "handsome collector's item" shows
evidence of scholarship but adds little to
our knowledge of Whitman the poet. The
title story shows that "Whitman had improved his handling of melodramatic themes
since his bizarre 'Franklin Evans.'" His
themes and style conformed to the fashion
of his day.

44 ANON. "Plan College to Aid Writers As a
Tribute to Whitman." New York Times (1
June), 1:4.
Notes the plan announced at a Camden
birthday dinner, at which Christopher
Morley spoke, to establish a college in
memory of Whitman. According to Dr.
Alexander McAlister, the college will help
get American writers published.

45 McNULTY, J. H., and ELIOT, T. S. "Tennyson
and Whitman." Nation and Athenaeum 41 (4
June), 302.
McNulty's letter asks, in response to
1927.42: "What is there in common between
the perfect verse of Tennyson and the wild
formless writing, neither verse nor prose,
of the American?" Eliot responds by referring him to 1926.82, citing their similar
attitudes toward their societies. Whitman's
gifts, though not of the same kind or
reliability as Tennyson's, show him "a

1927

great master of versification," for which he should be remembered rather than for his intellect, inferior to Tennyson's: "His political, social, religious, and moral ideas are negligible."

46 HIER, FREDERICK P., Jr. "When Boston Censored Walt Whitman--Official Disapproval of His 'Leaves of Grass' Finds a Parallel in the Recent Book Suppressions." New York Times Magazine (19 June), 7, 19.
Account of the 1882 suppression.

47 FREND, GRACE GILCHRIST. "Walt Whitman as I Remember Him." Bookman (London) 72 (July), 203-5. Illustrated.
Despite all attempts to explain Whitman, "no man wrote more without set purpose; he wrote impelled by the tumult of elemental forces within him." Frend recalls "his Titanic personality" when visiting her family in Philadelphia, noting his Socrates-like love for young disciples. Letters of 1878 to Herbert Gilchrist (with one facsimile) are quoted, regarding his ordinary daily experiences. His later years are summarized.

48 HARTMANN, SADAKICHI. "Salut au Monde: A Friend Remembers Whitman." Southwest Review 12 (July), 262-67.
Reprinted: Knox.
Reminiscence of Whitman in the mid-1880s and the last years of his life, from Hartmann's visits to Camden. He used to sit by his front window, although passersby were rare. He often was silent during conversations. He kept putting off explaining his children, despite many queries.

49 ANON. "Whitman Shrine Damaged." New York Times (29 July), 20:1.
A storm has damaged the schoolhouse in Woodbury.

50 KALTENBORN, OLGA. "Walt Whitman Looks at Today." Brooklyn Daily Eagle Sunday Magazine (23 October), 11.
Imagines Whitman in the Alexander portrait (reproduced) talking to her in the Metropolitan Museum, responding to her questions about contemporary American problems in words from his prose and poetry.

51 ANON. "'The Good Gray Poet.'" Nation 125 (2 November), 468.
Brief review of O'Connor (1927.17), with a description of its background and argument, which is particularly modern.

52 WINTERICH, JOHN T. "Romantic Stories of Books: I. Leaves of Grass." Publishers' Weekly 112 (19 November), 1869-73. Illustrated.
Revised: 1929.29.
A popular history of the editions of Leaves, especially the first, noting physical formats, problems with publishers,

critical response, the monetary value of early editions. Whitman's campaign to sell his book included printing a few copies of the Emerson letter "'for the convenience of private reading only.'"

53 ANON. "Whitman Great Poet Says Emma Goldman." Toronto Star (2 December).
Report of Goldman's address on Whitman, praising "his unbiased view of life and his sterling character." He was in advance of his age in perceiving the importance of sex; "Woman Waits" alone would have given him "an undying place in history as a great liberator of the mind and body." She emphasizes his vitality and energy, which many people cannot accept.

53a ANON. "Walt Whitman's Home in 1848 Now Being Razed in Brooklyn." New York Times (10 December), 17:2.
Notes the history of the house, now being destroyed.

54 BRIGHAM, JOHNSON. "Why Harlan Dismissed Walt Whitman." Nation 125 (14 December), 685.
Letter quoting 1913.2 to set matters straight regarding Whitman's dismissal.

55 BULLIET, C. J. "Faggi Springs Magnificent American." Chicago Evening Post Art World Magazine (27 December), 1.
Praises Alfeo Faggi's sculpture of Whitman, which depicts him as "the one magnificent embodiment in literature of Americanism," great like the powerful Hebrew prophets, and which conveys the spirit of "his own rugged, athletic poetry."

56 BENÉT, WILLIAM ROSE. "A Distinguished Poet." Saturday Review of Literature 4 (31 December), 483.
Review of Lola Ridge's Red Flag. Social theory does not create great art, for though Whitman and Shelley, both ahead of their times, saw through their world's conventions and worked for a new order, their main hold upon posterity is their ability "to express themselves in amazing verbal music," Whitman's "the vast undertones of the teeming earth."

1928

BOOKS

1 ACOSTA, MERCEDES DE. Until the Daybreak. New York and London: Longmans, Green & Co., pp. 172, 299.
A character calls Whitman the only American "big enough" to stand alone.

2 BARRUS, CLARA, ed. The Heart of Burroughs's Journals. Boston and New York: Houghton Mifflin Co., pp. x, 32-33, 40-44, 48-49, 51, 54-57, 61n, 62-63, 69, 72, 77-80, 101-2, 118-19, 128, 137-41, 152-53, 164, 166-67, 170-71, 173, 191-92, 200, 221, 226,

236-38, 296, 305, 311-12, 323-24, 337.
Extracts reprinted: Whitman Supplement
1979.

Journal entries describe Whitman's
personality, physical qualities, effect on
Burroughs; experiences and conversations
with Whitman, including his comments on
Bryant and Joaquin Miller; his impressions
of Whitman's work, including some shock and
"the impression that the poet is sometimes
putting on airs, and is wilfully perverse
and defiant"; Emerson's opinions of Whitman.

3 BARTON, WILLIAM E. Abraham Lincoln and Walt
Whitman. Indianapolis: Bobbs-Merrill Co.,
277 pp. Illustrated. Index.

Barton's initiating motive was to discover the truth about Whitman in relation
to Lincoln by looking at firsthand, contemporary information, including Whitman
manuscripts. These, particularly a notebook Whitman kept on his trip to find his
brother in December 1862, reveal him as
less than honest in his later accounts
exaggerating the extent of his hardship and
work. His hospital work is described,
begun when he was a paid delegate of the
United States Christian Commission, which
he never credited after he went off on his
own. He seems to have built up his otherwise praiseworthy volunteer efforts in
order to get a comfortable government job.
His fatness and poor living habits make his
breakdown understandable. Rankin's memories
of Lincoln and Leaves (1916.17; 1924.20)
are largely imaginary, since there is no
evidence to corroborate his stories, which
he published only after those who might
verify them were dead. The source of
O'Connor's story in 1866.2 of Lincoln
saying about Whitman, "Well, he looks like
a man!" (often misquoted), is shown as a
letter, reprinted in facsimile, apparently a
joke or forgery. Lincoln seems never to have
known or known of Whitman. Whitman's Lincoln
lecture, reprinted here in various forms
beginning with the New York Sun version of
12 February 1876, based its narrative of the
assassination on Peter Doyle's eyewitness
account; contrary to the usual estimate,
evidence exists only for nine deliveries of
it. Whitman and Lincoln shared many similar
qualities, most notably their faith in democracy and love for the nation. In Lincoln,
Whitman saw the incarnation of the America he
had been singing. He transformed his earlier
material emphasis into a notion of spiritual
progress for America. (Despite Barton's
claim to accuracy and careful research, some
errors occur, not all sources are identified,
and he perpetuates without evidence the
accusations of i-responsible paternity, involvement with prostitutes, and celebration
of himself over Burroughs's name in 1867.1
and his 1890s writings.)

*4 BIANCO, GIUSEPPE. On the Sixth Day. Indiana-
polis: n.p., pp. 92, 280.
Reported in Saunders Whitman in Fiction.

5 BURROUGHS, JOHN. "Walt Whitman." In Great
Short Biographies of the World, edited by
Barrett H. Clark. New York: Robert M.
McBride & Co., pp. 1329-55.
Extract reprinted from 1896.2 (pp. 23-72).

6 CORBETT, ELIZABETH. Walt: The Good Gray Poet
Speaks for Himself. New York: Frederick
A. Stokes Co., 331 pp.

Fictionalized biography of Whitman in
the form of dialogues involving or concerning Whitman, from childhood to the funeral,
with brief scene-setting stage directions.
Actual incidents and quotations are used
along with hypothetical ones, real people
as well as fictional ones (including family,
newspaper associates, Poe, Emerson, the
O'Connors, the Gilchrists, Traubel,
Burroughs, Carpenter, Doyle, and a hypothetical sweetheart, potential father-in-law,
and grandson), emphasizing his curiosity,
growing interest in creativity, independence,
literary ambitions, peculiarity, confidence
in his poetry, the development of his ideas
and moods from edition to edition, his
opposition to the war, love for nature and
human beings, talks on poetry.

7 DEEPING, WARWICK. Old Pybus. New York:
Alfred A. Knopf, p. 50.
Among the "solid books" the title
character tells his grandson he reads is
Whitman.

8 ELIOT, T. S. Introduction to Selected Poems,
by Ezra Pound. London: Faber & Gwyer,
pp. viii-ix, xi.
Includes reprint of 1916.13.

Pound owes nothing to Whitman. Eliot
recalls his first reading of Whitman.
Whitman's originality is genuine in being
a logical development of certain English
prose; he was a great prose writer, but his
assertion that "his great prose was a new
form of verse" is spurious. "The large
part of clap-trap in Whitman's content" is
here ignored.

9 FOERSTER, NORMAN. American Criticism: A
Study in Literary Theory from Poe to the
Present. Boston and New York: Houghton
Mifflin Co. "Whitman," pp. 157-222; also
v, xiii-xvi, 83n, 104n, 110, 111, 121, 149,
150n, 223-28, 232, 261.

Though no professional critic, Whitman
expounds a consistent theory of literature
throughout his career. He had originality
and wide acquaintance with music, drama,
and literature. Lacking the usual critical
qualities of humor, common sense, and
reasoning power, he substituted abandon,
believing that the work of art must be
organic and combine the almost contradictory
qualities of power and delicacy or suggestiveness. The poet must have an ethical
purpose, although not narrowly so. Whitman's
poetic and critical faiths rested on science
and democracy. His new vision of man re-

quired both expansive pride or selfhood and
expansive sympathy. As a prophetic critic,
Whitman must not be judged on the failure
of the current age to fulfill his expectations. He was last of the romantics and
precursor of twentieth-century realists,
although they neglect his optimistic religion and democracy in favor of his criticisms of America. He came to realize the
importance of recognizing the past, represented by Europe.

10 FOERSTER, NORMAN, ed. The Reinterpretation of
American Literature. New York: Harcourt,
Brace & Co., pp. 3, 4, 7, 11, 19, 25, 29-
30, 32, 34, 35-36, 38, 40, 47, 48, 49, 52,
63, 79, 81, 113, 115, 123, 134-36, 146, 150,
195.
Includes reprints of 1924.40; 1926.41.
Incidental references in other essays
by Jay B. Hubbell ("The Frontier": notes
the influence of Jacksonian democracy on
Whitman); Howard Mumford Jones ("The
European Background": Whitman's failure to
perceive the wrongs of exploitation);
Kenneth B. Murdock ("The Puritan Tradition"); Paul Kaufman ("The Romantic Movement": Whitman as the fullest American
culmination of all the elements of romanticism); Vernon Louis Parrington ("The
Development of Realism": Whitman's "formless enthusiasms" expressing the broad
democratic movement); Harry Hayden Clark
("American Literary History and American
Literature").

11 FURNESS, CLIFTON JOSEPH, ed. Introduction to
Walt Whitman's Workshop: A Collection of
Unpublished Manuscripts. Cambridge, Mass.:
Harvard University Press; London: Humphrey
Milford, Oxford University Press, pp. 3-24.
The value of these unpublished manuscripts is explained for clarifying the
purpose and growth of Leaves. Whitman's
notebooks indicate the evolution of his
political, social, and philosophical ideas.
His mode of expression also develops,
closer to meditation than inspiration:
Whitman works from a trance, alert and
aware, then revises extensively. The manuscripts are divided into the following
sections, with introductory notes pointing
out historical and biographical background:
"Notes for Lectures," "Anti-Slavery Notes"
(which remained undeveloped by Whitman),
"The Eighteenth Presidency," "Introductions
Intended for American Editions of 'Leaves
of Grass,'" "Introduction to the London
Edition," "To the Foreign Reader," Appendix
(miscellaneous fragments), Notes (Furness
provides bibliographical information).
Facsimiles are printed.

12 GOSSE, EDMUND. "Walt Whitman." In Contemporary Essays, edited by William Thomson
Hastings. Boston: Houghton Mifflin Co.,
pp. 158-73.
Reprint of 1894.28.

13 HOWELLS, MILDRED, ed. Life in Letters of
William Dean Howells. Garden City, N.Y.:
Doubleday, Doran & Co., p. 116.
Letter to Stedman (5 December 1866):
"The small but enthusiastic admirers of
Walt Whitman could not make him a poet, if
they wrote all the newspapers and magazines
in the world full about him. He is poetical
as the other elements are, and just as
satisfactory to read as earth, water, air
and fire. I am tired, I confess, of the
whole Whitman business."

14 HUXLEY, ALDOUS. Point Counter Point. New
York and London: Harper & Bros.; Garden
City, N.Y.: Doubleday, Doran & Co., pp.
194-95.
Philip Quarles has moments when, in
the company of Carlyle, Whitman, or
Browning, he "believed in strenuousness for
strenuousness' sake."

15 JESSE, F. TENNYSON. Many Latitudes and Other
Stories. New York: A. A. Knopf. "The
Two Helens," pp. 17, 21.
Narrator feels delicacy about lending a
lady his copy of Whitman.

16 MORLEY, CHRISTOPHER. Essays. Garden City,
N.Y.: Doubleday, Doran & Co., pp. 318-36,
435-41, 694-707.
Reprints of 1919.19, 1920.21, 1926.21.

17 MORROW, HONORE WILLSIE. With Malice Toward
None. New York: William Morrow & Co.,
p. 280.
Chapter twenty-one of this fictionalized
biography of Lincoln is titled "Starting
from Paumanok." Mary reads to Lincoln from
the Whitman volume borrowed from John Hay,
from which he memorizes passages.

18 MURDOCK, KENNETH BALLARD, ed. A Leaf of Grass
from Shady Hill. Cambridge, Mass.:
Harvard University Press.
Includes reprint of 1855.6.
Murdock's explanatory essay presents
evidence for Charles Eliot Norton's authorship of the Putnam's review of the 1855
Leaves: he would seem "too close to Boston"
to appreciate Whitman, but he caught
Whitman's strength. His letter to Lowell
(1913.14) and Lowell's response (1894.9)
are reprinted; a letter to E. P. Gould;
Murdock also prints Norton's imitation of
Whitman, "A Leaf of Grass," showing similarities in thought and form.

19 NEWTON, A. EDWARD. The Book-Collecting Game.
Boston: Little, Brown & Co., pp. 274-75,
282, 291, 293, 306.
The collector should secure anything in
Whitman's writing and his early editions,
though his merit is that of the prophet,
not the poet. He should be judged by his
best, not his worst, work. He usually
found the right word. He is ranked at the
top of American literature with Twain (but
Newton admits he cannot read Whitman).

20 PETERSON, HOUSTON. <u>Havelock Ellis, Philosopher</u>
    <u>of Love</u>. Boston and New York: Houghton
    Mifflin Co., pp. 124-25, 183-84, 205, 209-
    10, 212-13, 362.
        Incidental references to Ellis's admira-
    tion for Whitman and writings about him,
    noting the validation Symonds received for
    his homosexuality from Whitman's work.

21 UMPHREY, GEORGE W., and PRADA, CARLOS GARCÍA,
    eds. <u>Selections from Prose and Poetry of</u>
    <u>Rubén Darío</u>. New York: Macmillan Co.,
    p. 189.
        Note to Darío's sonnet in Spanish,
    "Walt Whitman," pp. 114-15: Darío admired
    Whitman's poetry greatly and was probably
    influenced by it, particularly in his
    metrical innovations and "the effort to
    present the ideals and aspirations of his
    race with something of the vigor with which
    Whitman expressed the achievements and
    aspirations of the U.S."

22 VALENTE, JOHN, ed. Introduction to <u>Leaves of</u>
    <u>Grass</u>. New York: Macmillan Co., pp. xix-
    xxx.
        Detailed biographical sketch showing
    the development of the poet, stressing the
    universality of Whitman's expression of
    personality. He emphasized love in its two
    manifestations in "Adam" and "Calamus," the
    latter being more spiritual and all-encom-
    passing, representing his "large friendli-
    ness for individuals and for mankind," a
    feeling for community indigenous to the
    young, expanding country he grew up in. He
    also sought to reconcile physical and
    spiritual, past and present. His war ex-
    perience produced <u>Drum-Taps</u> and "Lilacs,"
    its "austere beauty" unmatched in the
    elegiac poetry of the English language.

23 WELLS, CAROLYN, and GOLDSMITH, ALFRED F.
    Forward to <u>Rivulets of Prose: Critical</u>
    <u>Essays by Walt Whitman</u>, New York:
    Greenberg, pp. vii-xviii.
        Most of Whitman's prose is "effortless-
    ly written, and seldom revised or amended."
    It should be read by all Whitman students,
    though not necessarily for inherent value
    in itself. <u>Leaves</u> presents Whitman him-
    self; the prose gives a more objective
    viewpoint. These critical essays are
    "limited to the actual opinions of Whitman
    regarding men and letters." Perhaps his
    greatest limitations were the lack of a
    sense of humor and of schooling, but
    against these are placed many excellent
    qualities.

PERIODICALS

24 ANON. "Offers Whitman Relics." <u>New York</u>
    <u>Times</u> (29 January), sec. 1, 19:2.
        Whitman's niece Jessie is donating
    Whitman material to the Camden house.

25 BABBITT, IRVING. "The Critic and American
    Life." <u>Forum</u> 79 (February), 170-71.
    Reprinted: 1932.1; 1937.21.
        Incidental: "It would be possible to
    base on technical grounds alone a valid
    protest against the present preposterous
    overestimate of Walt Whitman." Along with
    the French Symbolists he is noted as an
    influence on modern poetry.

26 ANON. "The Book Column--More (and Different)
    Truth About the Good Gray Walt." <u>New York</u>
    <u>Sun</u> (10 February), 24:7.
        Review of Corbett (1928.6), generally
    authentic as to Whitman's tone, quality,
    bulk, and meaning, although sentimentalizing
    him by linking him up with various women
    and somewhat ignoring "the Peter Doyle
    element in his life and his verses."

27 ANON. "Whitman Lends Himself to a Dramatic
    Biography." <u>New York Times Book Review</u>
    (19 February), 5.
        Review of Corbett (1928.6). She makes
    Whitman's character consistent, even if she
    has not gone strictly by the record. She
    might have included more poetry, though
    that is not dramatic.

28 ANON. "Backs Creed of Whitman." <u>New York</u>
    <u>Times</u> (20 February), 24:4.
        Quotes Hubert C. Herring's address at
    the Community Church, urging knowledge of
    Whitman's philosophy of the "Open Road,"
    holding him up as the true exponent of
    religion.

29 ANON. "Whitman Relics Sent to Shrine at
    Camden." <u>New York Times</u> (25 February),
    17:2.
        Describes articles which have arrived
    at Whitman's Camden house, including a
    contract for the tomb which reveals the
    true price paid.

30 ANON. "Lincoln and Walt Whitman." <u>Brooklyn</u>
    <u>Daily Eagle</u> (26 February), sec. B, 4:2-3.
        Editorial deploring Barton's discredit-
    ing of Whitman in 1928.3. The names of
    Lincoln and Whitman are coupled because
    both represented the spirit of American
    democracy, broad human sympathy, and marked
    individuality.

31 BOYNTON, H. W. "Debunking Whitman." <u>New York</u>
    <u>Sun</u> (17 March), 7:1-2.
        Review of Barton (1928.3), a sorely
    needed realistic view of Whitman. Though
    he is "somewhat rudely removed from his
    oversized pedestal," "there is a good deal
    left."

32 CURTI, MERLE EUGENE. "Walt Whitman, Critic of
    America." <u>Sewanee Review</u> 36 (April), 130-
    38.
        Whitman's early patriotic excesses were
    appropriate to his youthfulness and America's
    expansive, optimistic 1840s and 1850s.

1928

With the 1870s he realized America's flaws and the importance of international solidarity, but even his prewar poems reveal international sentiments, albeit somewhat vague. America became a symbol for the future as he concentrated on her promise rather than her current failures. He did not, as claimed, identify spiritual with physical grandeur. He feared "the new dominion of wealth" which disappointed him more than his own reception. His faith in America's mission may have been unjustified, as later events suggest, but it was sincere and intelligent.

33 MORLEY, CHRISTOPHER. "The Bowling Green." Saturday Review of Literature 4 (19 May), 886.
    Paragraph on "the extraordinary greatness" of Whitman's title for his book, showing genius "to take as his emblem this commonest, humblest, most disregarded and yet most satisfying of all earth's generosities."

34 WELLER, ALANSON. "Walt Whitman, Schoolmaster." English Journal 17 (June), 503-5.
    Notes the conversion of the Woodbury schoolhouse into a Whitman museum. He was a successful teacher, as many former pupils have recalled, because he abandoned "primitive methods of instruction and discipline." His early poem "An Ideal School" reveals his advanced ideas; a later poem "An Old Man's Thoughts of School" (reprinted) reveals his happy memories. While teaching, he began to feel the poetic impulse which would produce Leaves, "more than a literary masterpiece--it is a man's life with all its strength and weakness, its virgin simplicity, born of the soil, and its all pervading, all-embracing love of humanity and brotherhood." America is just beginning to realize his worth and to understand his supposedly indecent poems as not indecent at all.

35 ANON. "Whitman Biographers Clash in Deft Satire." Camden Evening Courier (1 June).
    At a banquet celebrating Whitman's birthday, Holloway criticized biographers like Corbett (1928.6) who romanticize Whitman, like many who worship him without really getting at the truth. Other speakers are quoted on Whitman's "rare combination of the egotist and the altruist," the importance of exploring one's own spirit to counterbalance American commercialism.

36 FURNESS, CLIFTON JOSEPH. "Walt Whitman Looks at Boston." New England Quarterly 1 (July), 353-70.
    Whitman manuscript notes and other documents, here published for the first time, dispel the popular conception that Whitman had little love or respect for New England and its writers. Whitman describes the town, its treatment of blacks as equals. His letters to brother Jeff and to Abby Price are quoted. He retained happy impressions of Boston.

37 MEREDITH, RICHARD. "The Red Page. The Whitman Legend." Sydney Bulletin (25 July).
    Demonstrates via quotations that Whitman was a poetic craftsman, using poetic rhythms, inversions, diction, even if all his work does not demonstrate this. Two quatrains of "Death Carol" are scanned.

38 HOLCOMB, ESTHER LOLITA. "Whitman and Sandburg." English Journal 17 (September), 549-55.
    Whitman as prophet finds an answering voice in Sandburg, who was influenced by Whitman, though no mere copy. Both express the actual life around them, with vivid pictures, American vigor and freedom, in similar style. Whitman gives "a great moving panorama," with "biblical sweep and power"; Sandburg focuses on compact pictures. Sandburg makes artistic use of contrast; Whitman sings more primitively, without Sandburg's subtlety in offering compassionate or satirical glimpses, thus falling at times into the sentimentality Sandburg avoids. Sandburg is more sensitive to "the difference between dirt and divinity." Whitman is superior in his portrayal of the sea.

39 LAMBART-TAYLOR, MAUDE. "Robert Browning and Walt Whitman." Personalist 9 (October), 263-75.
    Both "deal with the life of the soul and its desire to know truth." "Whitman depicts the soul of humanity through his own personality," Browning through that of others. They differ in their relations to nature and social equality, but both perceive the necessity of evil and the ultimate triumph of good. Quotations show their belief in the connection between soul and body, but Browning retains the body's mystery while Whitman occasionally is coarse. "Whitman always seeks the spiritual through the material." He expresses "superb egotism." Both see "the higher vision" as they move from perfection to perfection, as in "Passage."

40 WELLER, ALANSON. "Here and There in New York--Walt Whitman and Music." Jacobs' Orchestra Monthly (October).
    Account of Whitman's acquaintance with and love for music, which "did much to develop his powerful imagination and peculiarly beautiful style of poetry." His music poems are noted; "Proud Music" may be his "most beautiful and vivid description of music," "certainly one of the great poems of all time." Weller wonders "what Whitman might have written had he heard the music of Debussy, Stravinsky, Richard Strauss or (I breathe this quietly) the jazz idiom of this age."

41 ANON. "The Sea in Whitman." Christian Science Monitor (22 November), 9:6.
    The sea, the lilac bush, and the grass are Whitman's three great poetic affinities.

His view of the sea from the shore contrasts with Conrad's experience of it as a sailor, but Whitman had the advantage of growing up with it. His poetry of the sea displays appropriate diction, as quoted lines show. Much of his poetry also demonstrates his attraction to night. "Cradle" and "Lilacs," the two poems which ensure his literary immortality, are compared as "the offspring of night wandering."

42 GREGORY, HORACE. "New Walt Whitman Manuscripts Are Revealed." New York Evening Post (1 December), sec. 3, 8.

Review of Furness (1928.11), "valuable background" which may lead to "an honest revaluation of Whitman and his work." His medium became poetry rather than lectures as "a by-product of his enthusiasm for his cause," "his only chance of becoming fully articulate." While his poetry underwent many changes, his attempts to put forth his ideas in prose were made with much more difficulty. His democratic principles appear in his lecture notes, as does his eloquent style, known through his poetry.

43 ANON. "Flotsam and Jetsam for the Whitmaniacs." New York Times Book Review (9 December), 8, 22.

Review of Furness (1928.11). Furness's scholarship is impeccable but produces no new discoveries, only a reaffirmation of Whitman's sturdy personality and an illustration of his mind moving toward the convictions that made him Walt Whitman.

44 ANON. "Whitman Enjoyed City Auctions--Penciled Note Says Scenes Best Revealed American Manners and Characteristics. Manuscript to Be Sold--Part of Wyman Collection, Which Also Includes Works of Other Authors." New York Times (16 December), sec. 3, 6:7.

Quotes note by Whitman, apparently unpublished, written 20 February 1878, revealing his disinclination to caricature the average America.

45 ANON. "Topics of the Times. Whitman on Auctions." New York Times (17 December), 24:5-6.

Quotes Whitman on auctions (see 1928.44), noting the difference in the auction to be held tomorrow. Whitman did not like to focus on the greed present at such events.

1929

BOOKS

1 BABCOCK, BERNIE. Lincoln's Mary and the Babies. Philadelphia and London: J. B. Lippincott Co., pp. 81, 83-84, 210-11, 307-9.

As in Rankin (1916.17), Lincoln reads Leaves after hearing the office dispute over "the big nature poet." At home, Mrs. Lincoln calls his work disgraceful. Lincoln, later telling her of Whitman's hospital work, terms him "'one of the greatest voices ever lifted up for Democracy,'" his writings the expressions of a great soul, in touch with the soul of the universe. After Lincoln's death, a maid reads "Captain"; Mrs. Lincoln is shocked that it is by Whitman, whom she would not let her husband bring to the house.

2 BLAVATSKY, HELENA PETROVNA. Some Unpublished Letters of Madame Blavatsky. London: Rider & Co., n.d., pp. 19, 70.

Whitman had cosmic consciousness "with but little wandering, though he too had to suffer some." She quotes Whitman's "outburst over the self-sufficiency and complacency of his time, and of its lack of spiritual intuition."

3 CANBY, HENRY SEIDEL. American Estimates. New York: Harcourt, Brace & Co. "Walt Whitman," pp. 94-96.

Whitman "was capacious even without his books," but not great as he supposed himself to be, as "prototype of a new race of Western man," but rather as "the last of his race," for after him came "the standardization of the American type." People are generally moved not by his poetry's literary qualities but by his personality, fullness of living, and response to his continent; it takes a poetry lover to admire his greatness. He was "Emerson's man (as far as he could be any one's)." His monument is his very person.

4 C[ANBY], H. S. "American Literature." Encyclopaedia Britannica. 14th ed. Vol. 1. p. 788.

Paragraph on Whitman, who embodied the great forces that climaxed in the 1850s, regarding himself as prophet of a democratic brotherhood. Leaves is "a commentary on life as interpreted by a child of the Enlightenment, with a transcendental faith in the goodness of man, and a robust scorn of all feudal and aristocratic cultures." He shocked his contemporaries by his frank paganism and music based on phrase rhythms but has become American poetry's chief figure.

5 CHAPMAN, J. A. Papers on Shelley, Wordsworth, and Others. London: Oxford University Press. "Walt Whitman," pp. 115-27.

Whitman, appropriately for a poet, divided his life between crowds and solitude to gain experience and to understand himself. Friendship for him was as receptive and uncritical as a person's reactions to nature; to it he offered "something of the feeling of a lover, and got something of the feeling of the lover in return." He was a pioneer in freeing the human spirit. "Myself" 5 reveals his mission. He had "a

1929

mystic's sense of the significance of
things." "If he did not write the fully
revealing poetry that he meant to write,
the poetry which should reveal man's
estate to men, well he knew what it should
be."

6 DOBREE, BONAMY. *The Lamp and the Lute*.
Oxford: Clarendon Press, pp. 104, 117.
Lawrence's ideas on Whitman are noted.
Eliot's turn away from the doctrine of
passion for passion's sake is a relief
"after the cult of the Whitmanesque 'barbaric yawp'!"

7 ELLIOT, G. R. *The Cycle of Modern Poetry*.
Princeton: Princeton University Press;
London: Humphrey Milford, Oxford University
Press. "The Whitmanism of Browning," pp.
83-90.
Revision (minor) of 1929.43.

8 FRANK, WALDO. *The Re-discovery of America:
An Introduction to a Philosophy of American
Life*. New York and London: Charles
Scribner's Sons, pp. 139, 140, 157-58, 167,
196, 200, 212, 218-21, 313.
Whitman projected an art created <u>from</u>,
and not in spite of, chaos. He is among
"the prophetic giants of the Romantic era,"
among American mystic voices. <u>Leaves</u> is a
vision rather than a thought-out plan like
Emerson's, yet is "solid enough to draw
the eyes of the world." However, these
American writers are thwarted, lacking "a
clear way into America's past from which to
issue, clear, into America's future"; yet
it is their vision rather than the "practical
tradition" of their more popular contemporaries which we should follow. A Whitman
quotation is the epigraph.

9 HEARN, LAFCADIO. *Essays on American Literature*. Edited by Sanki Ichikawa. Kanaa,
Tokyo: Hokuseido Press. "Leaves of Grass,"
(reprint of 1882.80), pp. 91-95. Introduction by Albert Mordell, pp. xvi-viii.
Hearn's attack "was unfair, ill-
tempered and unworthy of the writer who
had much in common after all with Whitman
in his attacks on puritanism, bourgeois
civilization and devotion to pantheistic
ideas." Hearn's review is explained, with
quotations from later correspondence
(1906.4) regarding his secret admiration
for Whitman; he also liked the <u>Conservator</u>.

10 HOLLOWAY, EMORY, ed. Introduction to <u>Franklin
Evans by Walter Whitman</u>. New York: Random
House, pp. v-xxiv.
Discussion of the novel and its faults,
its composition and publication. Whitman
was temperate but not a teetotaler. This
book seems almost a parody of his future
self. The story's dream-like quality,
resembling "The Sleepers," is more appropriate to poetry than to fiction. Reprint
of <u>New World</u> announcement (1842.8). This

is one of the earliest temperance novels.
The influence of Dickens, whom Whitman
admired, is more apparent in his poetry.

11 HOL[LOWAY], E[MORY]. "Walt Whitman."
<u>Encyclopaedia Britannica</u>. 14th ed. Vol.
23. pp. 582-84.
Traces Whitman's life, influences,
newspaper concerns, literary career.
<u>Leaves</u> was his attempt to record himself,
discarding conventional poetics for "the
direct address of rhythmical declamation."
The war taught him "mature idealism" and
"laid the foundation for his influence as
an international force" seeking a world
united in peace. His later sickness kept
"the sweet reasonableness of his maturity"
from being as fully represented as "the
hopeful self-reliance, the exuberant spirit
of his youth." His character is described:
love of nature and sense enjoyments,
"womanly sensitiveness," "courageous
imagination," "quest of ideal beauty" without turning away from reality. Through
his "fundamentally religious" purpose, he
widened our conception of literature's
function, though not always joining propaganda and his artistic instinct with success. His art shows various influences
yet is checked against the experience of
American life. His ideals remain contemporary. Bibliographic paragraph.

12 HUNEKER, JAMES. *Essays by James Huneker*.
Selected with an Introduction by H. L.
Mencken. New York: Charles Scribner's
Sons. Introduction, p. xiv; "A Visit to
Walt Whitman," pp. 416-23 (reprint of
1915.12).
Mencken notes Huneker's rendition of
"the authentic last words of Whitman,
gasped into poor Horace Traubel's solicitous
ear, and too horrible, almost, to be remembered in a Christian land."

13 KREYMBORG, ALFRED. *Our Singing Strength: An
Outline of American Poetry (1620-1930)*.
New York: Coward-McCann. "Whitman and the
Democratic Cosmos," pp. 206-30; also 74,
274, 512, passim per index.
Reprinted: 1934.7.
Whitman is set in context. Though
failing with the average American, he has
a strong influence with the current free-
verse movement, which lacks his nationalistic spirit, not appreciated in his lifetime
either. His egoism is "the reflection of
genius," a projection of himself into other
experience and into the future. He had to
create his own tradition and a language
indigenous to America. He shaped his
poems "out of his inner passion and outer
serenity." He believed in equality, not
the survival of the fittest. "Myself" has
some humor. "Adam" recreates a Garden-of-
Eden kind of love, without the subtleties
of modern courtship. The "Calamus" poems
are richer in texture and contrasting moods

than preceding groups. Whitman's debts to
his Puritan and Dutch forebears are noted.
Descriptions of "Broad-Axe" ("in some
respects his greatest"), "Cradle" (showing
that Whitman might have mastered the mechanics of his poetic scheme if not handicapped
by economic needs, the war, and health),
"Lilacs" (fitting the Greek-like tragedy of
Lincoln's death), "Ontario." The war
"mellowed rather than impaired his faith in
the American destiny." Other references
use Whitman as a touchstone for later poets.

14 LANDIS, PAUL, and ENTWISTLE, A. R. The Study
of Poetry. New York: Thomas Nelson &
Sons, pp. 223-24, 226.
Brief discussion, placing Whitman in
context of the history of English poetry
as "the first distinctively American note."

15 LEISY, ERNEST ERWIN. American Literature: An
Interpretive Survey. New York: Thomas Y.
Crowell Co. "Walt Whitman: Prophet of
American Democracy," pp. 151-61; passim per
index.
Whitman, "obedient to both the romantic
and the realistic impulses," gave the impetus which made the new literature possible.
His use of the "I" represents his glorification of the divine average, although his
somewhat theatrical swagger seems due to a
lifelong sense of inferiority and the need
"to assert a masculinity he felt lacking."
His patriotism represents genuine concern
that Americans live up to their opportuni-
ties and each citizen develop his personality to achieve a true democracy. His formlessness is "the diversified regularity in
nature," the idea governing the form. His
prefaces and Vistas "constitute perhaps the
most important literary document since
Wordsworth's Preface to the Lyrical Ballads." A reading order is suggested.
Whitman was a prophet, fulfilling Emerson.
His ultimate weakness is that the individual's importance may be reduced in favor of
a superior order.

16 LINDSAY, VACHEL. The Litany of Washington
Street. New York: Macmillan Co. "The
Loneliness of Whitman, Statesman-Poet,"
pp. 54-64.
Reprint with minor changes of 1923.65.
Abridged: 1929.52.
At end of essay, adds the idea that
Whitman will come to be recognized as a
statesman, like Jefferson. Throughout the
book, Lindsay intersperses extended poetic
"Quotations from Walt Whitman" with appro-
priate headings for a context of American
nationalism.

17 MORRIS, HARRISON S. Walt Whitman: A Brief
Biography with Reminiscences. Cambridge,
Mass.: Harvard University Press; London:
Humphrey Milford, Oxford University Press,
122 pp. Index.
Whitman is set in social and political

context, a forerunner whose ideas are still
current. His life is traced, with Morris's
own recollections of him in Camden, including conversations and his description
of his poetic method and mission. He owes
much to hereditary, natural, and Quaker
influences. His work centers on the soul.
His philosophy is not a system but a profound penetration into the soul. His inspiration sometimes flags in his catalogues,
though his purpose is sure. "Myself" conveys "the essense of a youthful giant
America," fresh and free. In the war he
put "into practice the potency of comradeship" and made many friends, including
"some very queer ones" (like Doyle). His
fame increased due to his uncommon personality, the wrongs done to him, and especially the illumination of his message.
Vistas indicates that he "saw where democracy led." Letter from Herbert Gilchrist
is quoted on Lowell's comment, "There is
something in the man!" Rumors are reported
that "two of Whitman's sons wished to visit
him on his death bed, but were refused."
He has a little humor but took his disciples' words too seriously. His additions,
changes, and underscorings in Morris's
translation of Sarrazin (in 1893.11) reveal
his vanity and desire to make his message
known. His appearance at Ingersoll's
lecture (see 1890.52) is described. The
thought and method of Leaves, both of which
will make Whitman live, are discussed at
the end. As "a rebel's utterance," his
book required irregular style, though "he
had a standard of technical perfection,"
as in poems here cited.

18 MUMFORD, LEWIS. Herman Melville. New York:
Harcourt, Brace & Co., pp. 4, 5.
Melville shares with Whitman "the
distinction of being the greatest imaginative writer that America has produced."
Melville's exploration of the substratum
of life must precede such a response as
Whitman's embracing the world's "mingled
good-and-evilness."

19 NEALE, WALTER. Life of Ambrose Bierce. New
York: Walter Neale, pp. 176, 241, 362.
Quotes Bierce on Whitman, whose technique is not substantially different from
David's, though Whitman crassly violates
laws of versification. Bierce disapproved
of Whitman largely because he wrote prose
that he falsely labeled verse.

20 NOYES, ALFRED. The Opalescent Parrot.
London: Sheed & Ward. "Walt Whitman and
American Individualism," pp. 155-67.
The identification of man and state is
a common fallacy of modern thought, exemplified by English regard for Whitman as the
typical American, neglecting highly civilized figures. Whitman's catalogues present
"a harmonious adjustment of the various
claims" and he is not wholly to blame for

1929

the simplistic identification of his traits
as American.

21 _____. *The Sun Cure*. New York: Cosmopolitan
Book Corp., pp. 7, 109, 154.
A character dips into Whitman as part
of "the 'Return-to-Nature' literature,"
and observes that in Whitman "reaction had
run wild; and, through the desire to make
things better, there was an obvious desire
to startle and offend."

22 PENNELL, ELIZABETH ROBBINS. *The Life and
Letters of Joseph Pennell*. Boston: Little,
Brown, & Co. Vol. 1, pp. 118-20; vol. 2,
pp. 239, 240.
Describes visits in England with
William Rossetti and the Gilchrists and
their Whitman worship. A letter from
Pennell to Saunders discusses Pennell's
drawings of the Whitman house and burial
grounds.

23 POWYS, JOHN COWPER. *The Meaning of Culture*.
New York: W. W. Norton & Co., pp. 2, 51,
84, 101, 122, 162, 190, 211.
Incidental references to Whitman as a
representative great writer, noting his
polytheistic tendencies and invigorating
qualities. The current open-air cult has
no connection with Whitman's cosmic qualities.

24 QUINN, ARTHUR HOBSON; BAUGH, ALBERT CROLL; and
HOWE, WILL DAVID, eds. *The Literature of
America: An Anthology of Prose and Verse*.
Vol. 2. New York: Charles Scribner's
Sons. "Walt Whitman," pp. 773-818 (including selections); notes, pp. N34-35.
"Whitman must be studied not as a
departure from the development of our
literature but as one element in its
progression" through his expressing the
principles of democracy. He was a conscious
artist, to be understood through his prefaces and *Vistas*, which reveal the need for
individual development in democracy. His
ideas were not new; his contribution lay
in combining them, insisting on their
importance, and expressing them in his
personal manner. He is "a powerful thinker
who expressed the aspirations of humanity
in his own way, and made of himself a symbol" of his ideal for America. Many
writers have been influenced by him in more
than form, his work's "least important
element," which many have adopted unsuc-
cessfully. He is best when "the concrete-
ness of his subject has helped him to
achieve simplicity" as in "Lilacs," with
traditional rhythmic utterance. Notes
give a biographical sketch and suggested
bibliography.

25 van DYKE, HENRY. *The Man Behind the Book:
Essays in Understanding*. New York and
London: Charles Scribner's Sons. "A
Greater Comet," pp. 59-90. Alexander

portrait.
Explores the reason behind the paradox
of Whitman's desired and acquired audiences.
Biographical sketch with slight errors.
The Civil War produced his best verse. He
took in impressions but did not participate
actively in the strenuous world of democracy; hence "he became one of the best
recorders of American scenes, and one of
the poorest interpreters of the American
spirit." Exemplifying the poet as preacher,
he carries "Transcendentalism to an extreme," producing "original and vivid"
writing. Most of his work is "not poetical"
because it lacks art and rarely distills
"the finer essense of life" which the
ordinary reader seeks. He is best when he
ignores his theory. His three real services
to American poetry are enlarging the range
of metrical forms, expressing the spirit of
nature, and presenting a powerful patriotism, as in his finest poem, "Captain."

26 WAGNER, HARR. *Joaquin Miller and His Other
Self*. San Francisco: Harr Wagner Publish-
ing Co., pp. 91-92.
Quotes Miller's article from San
Francisco *Chronicle* (1892.212), unlocated.

27 WELLS, CAROLYN. Introduction to *Leaves of
Grass*. 1855 ed. reprint. New York:
Limited Editions Club, pp. ix-xviii.
Brief life sketch. Wells notes her
many editions of *Leaves*. Whitman's friends
did not always agree with him or comprehend
his poems. His lines may "grate on the
senses" and "repel the lover of softly
flowing verse," but he has rhythm and a
genius for selecting the right word. The
reader must supply receptivity to his
verse; like the proletariat, scholars too
may be ordinary people.

28 WHARTON, EDITH. *Hudson River Bracketed*. New
York: D. Appleton & Co., pp. 63, 73, 175.
A character recalls the simple verse
he was nurtured on, including "Pioneers"
("good, too, but rather jiggy"). Another
character recalls knowing Whitman, who
once visited his home on the Hudson.

29 WINTERICH, JOHN T. *Books and the Man*. New
York: Greenberg. "Walt Whitman and *Leaves
of Grass*," pp. 1-17. Illustrated.
Revision of 1927.52. Reprinted: 1929.30.
Abridged: 1929.50.
Expands the scene-setting, physical and
biographical, for the first edition; the
description of Fowler and Wells; Whitman's
introduction into England.

30 _____. *The Romance of Great Books and Their
Authors*. New York: Halcyon House. "Walt
Whitman and *Leaves of Grass*," pp. 1-17.
Reprint of 1929.29.

PERIODICALS

31 ANON. Editorial. <u>Poet's Magazine</u> (January),
    2-3.
        Describes Whitman's claims to our
    praise: his melody (Keatsian), humor (a
    deep knowledge of proportion), purity of
    thought and expression, and intense sin-
    cerity. He will rank as the poet most
    representative of our aims today.

32 GOHDES, CLARENCE L. F. "Whitman and Emerson."
    <u>Sewanee Review</u> 37 (January), 79-93.
        Traces the Whitman-Emerson relationship
    and influence. Early references to Emerson
    suggest that Whitman's 1856 letter to him
    "was prompted as much by a sentimental
    gratefulness for a flattering expression of
    esteem delivered by a revered idol, as by
    the charlatanism of a self-constituted
    press agent." Whitman later minimized his
    indebtedness for fear of being considered
    not his own man, as Emerson himself urged
    men to be; yet he always retained love for
    him.

33 WARE, LOIS. "Poetic Conventions in <u>Leaves of
    Grass</u>." <u>Studies in Philology</u> 26 (January),
    47-57.
        After discarding the more obvious
    poetic devices (regular stanza forms, meter,
    rhyme), Whitman "unconsciously adopted the
    less obvious conventions, such as allitera-
    tion, assonance, repetition, refrain,
    parallelism, and end-stopped lines."
    Examples and lists of all of these are
    provided, along with examples of internal
    and end rhymes, familiar rhythms, use of
    word inversion to improve rhythm, and
    poetic diction.

34 HOLLOWAY, EMORY. "Some New Whitman Letters."
    <u>American Mercury</u> 16 (February), 183-88.
        Quotes letters of the 1860s from
    Whitman to his family, revealing his char-
    acter, donated by Jessie Whitman to the
    Mickle Street Memorial.

*35 ANON. "First Edition and MSS Sold at W. Cohen
    Sale." <u>New York Times</u> (7 February), 20:6.
    Reported in Allen and <u>New York Times</u> index
    but not located.

36 ANON. "Walt Whitman Finds Hellas." <u>New
    Statesman</u> 32 (9 February), 572, 574.
        Review of Jeffers's <u>Roan Stallion, Tamar
    and Other Poems</u>. Whitman knew nothing but
    himself; "his vast occupation with his own
    Parnassus does rather detract from its
    beauty." He distrusted the classics, which
    Jeffers knows, showing writing here "as
    vigorous and unashamed as Whitman's, but
    more controlled, less vain, and full of
    subject."

37 DOLE, NATHAN HASKELL. "In the Workshop of
    Walt Whitman." <u>Boston Evening Transcript
    Book Section</u> (9 February), 3:3-5. Photo-

graph.
        Favorable review of Furness (1928.11),
    noting a few apparent errors in Furness's
    transcription of Whitman's manuscripts.
    Whitman's methods of composition are de-
    scribed, which often lost him "the grace of
    inspiration." This volume will contribute
    to Whitman's "rapidly extending fame."

38 C., S. C. "Whitman at Work." <u>Christian
    Science Monitor</u> (13 February), 7:7.
        Review of Furness (1928.11), an inter-
    esting volume that casts much light on
    Whitman's thought and ways of work.

39 ANON. "Whitman's Workshop." <u>Times Literary
    Supplement</u> (London) (21 February), 136.
        Favorable review of Furness (1928.11),
    examining the probable development of
    Whitman's poetic style and theme. His
    passion for oratory is a clue to Whitman's
    psychology and his poetics. "His poems
    were to be an extension of himself." His
    adulation of man seems an extension of his
    egotism; he may have turned to nature when
    tired on occasion of man. He preferred to
    see all men as undistinguished from himself.

40 MORLEY, CHRISTOPHER. "The Bowling Green."
    <u>Saturday Review of Literature</u> 5 (23
    February), 705.
        Prints "Walt's memorandum of his
    symptoms after his paralytic stroke in
    1873," courtesy of Dr. Alfred P. Lee,
    noting particularly "Walt's finely accurate
    description of his own mind: pondering and
    lambent."

41 BARDHAN, NIRANJAN MOHAN. "The Modernity of
    Whitman's Poetry." <u>Modern Review</u> 45
    (March), 309-12.
        In celebrating nineteenth-century
    America, which gave birth to the modern man,
    Whitman made his complete portrait in both
    mundane and spiritual aspects. Similarities
    to Keats and Tagore are noted. He replaced
    old doubts with faith and hope. The quality
    of his personality and his internationalism,
    also modern, are noted.

42 FURNESS, CLIFTON JOSEPH. Letter. <u>Boston
    Evening Transcript Book Section</u> (9 March),
    6:2.
        Response to Dole (1929.37): what he
    considered errors were not.

43 ELLIOT, G. R. "Browning's Whitmanism."
    <u>Sewanee Review</u> 37 (April), 164-71.
    Revised: 1929.7.
        Whitman and Browning cultivated similar
    emotions and rejection of tradition.
    Browning is more the grandfather of the new
    poetry, successfully rebelling against
    heavier weights of tradition than Whitman
    knew and thus "even more Whitmanian than
    Whitman," more a "truly spiritual man" who
    reached a wider audience, interweaving body
    and soul, while Whitman stayed with the

body. Browning was more intellectual and
well-read. Whitman's creed was Emerson's
plus "genial materialism." Both sought to
simplify the growing complexity of thought
in their time, appealing to natural feelings.
Both failed to control "dramatic zest" and
tended to become repetitive. Often
Browning's monologues read like "developed
nodes of the Whitmanian soliloquy." Unfortunately, later poets merely "reproduce
their vast lack of understanding," not their
"superb temperamental quality."

44 FURNESS, CLIFTON JOSEPH. "Walt Whitman's
    Politics." American Mercury 16 (April),
    459-66.
         Describes Whitman materials still un-
    published: scrapbooks of clippings with
    annotations that reveal "habits so studious
    that Whitman himself wished to conceal
    them," evidence that his ideas "were the
    logical outgrowth of sustained and detailed
    study." His comments on various political
    questions (the Constitution, the Fugitive
    Slave Law, political equality, emancipation
    and education, regulation of industry) are
    cited and discussed. There is no evidence
    that Whitman's response to exercise of
    federal powers would ever be "violent
    protest."

45 BLODGETT, HAROLD. "Whitman and Dowden."
    American Literature 1 (May), 171-82.
    Revised: 1934.1.
         Traces history of Dowden's appreciation
    for Whitman through published comments,
    letters. Dowden was drawn to Whitman by
    his own "fortified idealism" and "the zest
    with which he exercised his keen faculty
    for comprehending the central or structural
    idea behind a new work."

46 CAMPBELL, KILLIS. Review of Murdock (1928.18)
    and Furness (1928.11). American Literature
    1 (May), 204-6.
         Praises and describes both books,
    evidence that the recently reawakened
    scholarly interest in Whitman is not waning.
    The Eighteenth Presidency seems the most
    valuable of these new documents, revealing
    "how powerfully Whitman was stirred up over
    the abolition movement." Furness emphasizes
    correctly Whitman's religious purpose.

47 KEMMERER, JOHN. Review of Wells (1928.23)
    and Furness (1928.11). Bookman 69 (May),
    327-28.
         Critical works of such earlier American
    writers as Whitman begin to have for us
    "appreciable form, simplicity, permanence,
    authority." Whitman's ideas of Emerson
    may be seen in his critical essays, which
    show his "very simple but powerful criterion
    for literature" (described). The new prose
    pieces in Furness make his biography better
    known, though they are less important as
    literature than as literary history.

48 O'HIGGINS, HARVEY. "Alias Walt Whitman."
    Harper's Monthly Magazine 158 (May), 698-
    707.
    Reprinted: 1930.15.
         Describes the poor quality of Whitman's
    early work in journalism and fiction; his
    affected change of costume. He sought
    publicity through his anonymous reviews and
    his concealed part in Burroughs's Notes
    (1867.1). He was not the person he pro-
    claimed himself to be, "neither sensual,
    nor rough and rugged, nor truly healthy,
    nor lusty, nor even very masculine," but
    "a Narcissan, in love with himself,"
    "arrested in his sexual development very
    near the homosexual level," despite auto-
    biographical suggestions to the contrary.
    He advocated freedom and equality because
    of "his own colossal egotism," which re-
    quired him to feel the equal of any man.
    He also "accepted financial dependence,"
    and turned his back on the country's eco-
    nomic aspirations. He voiced few "normal
    emotions" and hence remains unaccepted in
    America.

49 WILEY, AUTREY NELL. "Reiterative Devices in
    Leaves of Grass." American Literature 1
    (May), 161-70.
         Examines and enumerates Whitman's ex-
    tensive use of epanaphora (initial repeti-
    tion), epanalepsis (repetition within the
    line), and terminal repetition, and their
    various purposes, especially for achieving
    poetic form and lyric effectiveness.

50 WINTERICH, JOHN T. "Walt Whitman and Leaves
    of Grass." Golden Book Magazine 9 (May),
    78-81. Illustrated.
    Abridged from 1929.29.

51 MORLEY, CHRISTOPHER. "Granules from an Hour
    Glass: II. Across Camden Bridge."
    Saturday Review of Literature 5 (11 May),
    997.
         Describes Camden Bridge and Whitman's
    grave, a "pagan, palaeolithic" cave.
    "Whitman was called a loafer because he
    liked to watch others work," while no one
    could witness his work at writing. Though
    termed a "yawp" or "shout," his work has
    "a core of quiet." He is recognized as "a
    great terrene creator" if not "a precise
    artist in detail," "yet even his catalogues,
    much reproached, are often marvels of
    cinematic portraiture and studio technique."

52 LINDSAY, VACHEL. "Loneliness of Whitman,
    Statesman-Poet." World Review 8 (27 May),
    247. Illustration of 1872 caricature.
    Abridged from 1929.16.

53 GALE, Major R. J. "Walt Whitman Speaks for
    Himself." Education 49 (June), 618-25.
         Whitman's "lusty philosophy" of free
    choice and courage overpowers his occasional
    lack of beauty. However, he often does ex-
    press emotions beautifully, for example,

"his favorite theme," "the companionship of strong men." Passages are quoted to depict Whitman's various ideas, occasionally like propaganda, but inspired and encased in excellent poetry, making a worthy philosophy stressing a new determination, fellowship, and brotherhood.

54 ANON. "Durant Lauds Walt as 'Modern Homer.'" Camden Courier (1 June).
      Account of birthday banquet program. Will Durant spoke of Whitman's opposition to the feudal spirit as represented by Shakespeare and his equality to the Hebrew prophets in greatness. His poetry should not be read merely by the elite, as represented by this well-dressed banquet audience, but by the common people.

55 ANON. "Edward Carpenter." Manchester Guardian Weekly 21 (5 July), 18.
      Obituary article noting incidentally Whitman's influences on Carpenter in style, thought, life.

56 BOATRIGHT, MODY C. "Whitman and Hegel." University of Texas Bulletin Studies in English 9 (8 July), 134-50.
      Whitman found much of Hegel in Emerson but tried to master him on his own. Whitman's habitual point of view is in accord with Hegel's absolute idealism, regarding the universe as in eternal process of becoming and as exhibiting at once the greatest possible unity and diversity. Whitman uses the Hegelian triad as in "Square Deific." His egotism was democratic. Whitman and Hegel had different theories of knowledge, Whitman using intuition, Hegel logic. Whitman knew Hegel probably as early as 1854 from Joseph Gostwick's book; his thought did not materially change after 1855.

57 BLODGETT, HAROLD. "Walt Whitman in England." American Mercury 17 (August), 490-96. Reprinted: 1930.28. Revised: 1934.1.
      English praise of Whitman is contrasted with American rejection, although the praise remained that of a minority, "among whom luckily the doctrinaires and the faddists have been outnumbered by men of education and intelligence," such men being more common in England than in America during the nineteenth century. He was generally accepted more as a moralist than as an artist, and mostly by social radicals. His English admirers are listed.

58 GARLAND, HAMLIN. "Roadside Meetings of a Literary Nomad. III. Early Stories-- Meetings with Walt Whitman--Sidney Lanier." Bookman 70 (December), 392-406. Revised: 1930.8.
      Account of his acquaintance with Whitman and his work, "its deeply patriotic spirit, its wide sympathy with working men and women and especially its faith in the destiny of 'these States'." He prints his letter of 1886 to Whitman, describing his successful use of Whitman in teaching and the public's failure to discover Whitman's power because they have been misled. Account of his first visit to Whitman in October 1888, noting his conversation which has been misinterpreted because interviewers have failed to record Whitman's style and humorous intonation. Whitman spoke on his work, his desire that things take their course regarding his reputation and that friends not defend him, his ideas on American authors, including his disapproval of the emphasis contemporary realists place on abnormal characters. Account of 1889 birthday dinner; quotation from Garland's review of November (1888.74) and poem (1893.3). The later discussion of Lanier compares him to Whitman: both were "poets of cosmic sympathy"; although doing different things with verse form, "each was striving for a newer, freer form, a greater and broader poetic art."

59 HARRISON, RICHARD CLARENCE. "Walt Whitman and Shakespeare. I. Whitman's Knowledge of Shakespeare. II. Echoes of Shakespeare in Whitman's Works." PMLA 44 (December), 1201-38.
      After Harrison's death, Killis Campbell prepared this paper for final publication. Whitman, American literature's "most outstanding individualist," drew much from earlier literature. He is quoted on his reading philosophy and his acquaintance with Shakespeare's work. His perception of Shakespeare as feudal motivated him to write the poetry of democratic ideals. The tabulation of Shakespeare quotations from Whitman's prose reveals his absorption of Shakespeare's content and style, in vocabulary and allusions. Whitman's allusions are listed by play with the parallel passage from Whitman, compiled from Harrison's notes by Robert Adger Law.

60 HOLLOWAY, EMORY. "Whitman As His Own Press Agent." American Mercury 18 (December), 482-88.
      Whitman constantly served as his own critic by direct writings, insertions, quotations from friends. Many pieces from Washington papers are quoted as inspired or written by Whitman, as are other reviews using information or phraseology from Whitman. The 1876 controversy is described. Whitman was always "trying to launch the idea that only prejudice and bad luck prevented him from being a literary lion," but he was unsuccessful.

61 McAREE, J. V. "Walt Whitman Boosted His Own Writings." Toronto Mail and Empire (4 December), 8:4.
      While Whitman is "easily the most important" poet of America, he deserves less respect as a man, being a bit of an ingrate,

living off the world and his friends, and **being his own press agent, as Holloway re-**veals (1929.60), although genius may be allowed some disagreeable habits. Whitman's misinterpretation of the facts of his reading at the American Institute Fair is noted. He considered the price paid for his poetry by a paper as equivalent to its value, but high prices paid for manuscripts can hardly be regarded a literary judgment.

1930

BOOKS

1 BRUNO, GUIDO. "A Letter Written in Camden on the Twenty-Seventh Anniversary of His Death." In One Precious Leaf from the First Edition, Leaves of Grass. New York: Bennett Book Studios. 47 copies. Reprint of 1919.116.

An actual leaf is included from a defective copy of the 1855 Leaves.

2 CAIRNS, WILLIAM B. A History of American Literature. Rev. ed. New York: Oxford University Press, pp. 386-95; also 510, passim per index. Revision of 1912.4.

The Whitman article remains the same; **additional minor Whitman references accord-**ing to index.

3 CAPPON, JAMES. Bliss Carman and the Literary Currents and Influences of His Time. New York & Montreal: Louis Carrier & Alan Isles. "The Tradition of Emerson and Whitman in American Literature," pp. 257-312; "New Systems of Verse: Whitman and Claudel," 313-33; passim in Part 1, especially Chapters 1 and 10.

Part 1 notes Whitman's influences on Carman. The essay on Emerson discusses his doctrine of "free ecstatic expression" which Whitman transformed into license. Whitman's poems reflect Fourier's ideas. "Calamus" represents not "perversions" but his form of the Christian love-feast, his new basis of society. His phrases "have the large defining power, the comprehensive inclusiveness of the best prose but not quite the visualizing completeness and the emotional touch of poetry." More concerned with his message, he lacks constructive ability and reaches poetic form rarely (as in "Captain"). Drum-Taps "does not rise above a tragic realism." He seems to idealize men's primitive instincts over reason, yet his moral attitude demands some spiritual discipline. He narrowly rejects the past, viewing spiritual progress in its **external aspect only. He is full of contra-**dictions, changing from earlier encouragement of disrespect for law and the social system to conservative economic views. He leaves synthesis up to the reader. His "uncompromising form of expression" is

illuminating, but not like the "steady light" shed on "the place of things in a whole" by Kant, Goethe, or Wordsworth. The Claudel essay notes his germ of a free-verse theory, which influenced American poets only in conjunction with French Symbolists. His utterances rise to oracular, biblical sublimity, "the language of the mystic religious consciousness." He relies largely on dactylic hexameter. French free verse has more direction. "Whitman remains the great stimulus both by the breadth of his work and an afflatus which often gave his line the soar of great poetry."

4 CARPENTER, FREDERIC IVES. Emerson and Asia. Cambridge, Mass.: Harvard University Press, pp. 129, 247, 250, 252.

Briefly discusses Whitman's oriental qualities, due to Emerson's influence. "A complete study of Whitman's Orientalism should reveal much; for, like Emerson, he is one of the most 'original' of the great American writers."

5 CRANE, HART. The Bridge: A Poem. Paris: Black Sun Press. "IV. Cape Hatteras." Reprint of 1930.30. Reprinted: 1933.5.

6 FERBER, EDNA. Cimarron. New York: Grosset & Dunlop, p. 153.

An Oklahoma preacher speaks from the pulpit quoting "Paumanok" as his text, calling Whitman "a poet with real blood in him, and the feel of the land, and a love of his fellow beings."

7 FLETCHER, JOHN GOULD. The Two Frontiers: A Study in Historical Psychology. New York: Coward-McCann, pp. 226-46; also 94, 124, 125, 175, 190, 192-93, 251, 272, 273, 275, 283.

In their great mid-century crises, American and Russia produced their four greatest geniuses: Whitman and Tolstoy, Melville and Dostoevsky. Whitman and Tolstoy were both completely part of their country in outlook, "divinely gifted ama-**teurs," with immense vitality and range of** experience, itching for self-expression, combining the mystical, elemental savage and the modern scientific philanthropist, differing in sexual nature (Whitman being fundamentally feminine, tending toward "mawkish morbidity"). They perceived both **idealistic and materialistic sides, with** fragmentary intellectual development. Similar passages are suggested as presenting nature itself. They gave us our "most supreme war documents," seeing war as part of the spectacle of nature; Whitman was not aware of the complex, harsh realities behind the proclaimed purposes. He won only rejection from his country, wrongly assuming that poetry could affect life. His "glorification of the average American," the mere common denominator, developed a race of Babbitts rather than "the rare exception."

8 GARLAND, HAMLIN. Roadside Meetings. New York: Macmillan Co. "Walt Whitman Old and Poor," pp. 127-43; also 147-50, 154-56, 164. Revision of 1929.58.

Adds commentary on Whitman's manner of speech; notes from Whitman to Garland; discussion of Whitman's corrections and commentary on Garland's manuscript. Lanier essay adds to 1929.58 paragraphs on Lanier and Whitman sharing a faith in science and in the miracle of the common, a sympathy for men, and an unbounded love for nature. Essay on Burroughs quotes him on Whitman and on Garland's espousal of Whitman's cause.

9 JONES, RUFUS M. Some Exponents of Mystical Religion. New York, Cincinnati, Chicago: Abingdon Press. "The Mystical Element in Walt Whitman," pp. 176-208; 218.

Jones has only recently come to appreciate Whitman's thought, poetic genius, and attempt to save America from materialism. Whitman's mystical element derives in part from Hicks and the Quakers. Whitman's belief in identity or mystical union fitted him for his hospital service. His transcending experiences (as in "Myself" 5) made him a poet. His conception of the universe and life was pantheistic. "Passage" and "Prayer" are discussed as revealing aspects of his mystical experience. Whitman's triumphant attitude in the face of all that confronted him was due to "his absolute certainty of an inner spiritual World of Life and Love."

10 JOSEPHSON, MATTHEW. Portrait of the Artist as American. New York: Harcourt, Brace & Co., pp. 23-26, 147-54; also xvii, xix, xxii, 18, 27, 33, 35, 145, 146, 155, 163, 173, 187, 293, 299.

Whitman embodies his period's libertarian impulses, taking upon himself a mission of leadership through prophecy, basing his intense patriotism on young America's free institutions. As an outcast, he is typical of the great mad artists of nineteenth-century America. While chiding his country in Vistas, he sought also to inspire America through an optimism and nationalism the flaws of which he did not recognize, sentimentalizing the pioneers. This patriotism, however, did not prevent his being rejected by his country.

11 KREYMBORG, ALFRED. Lyric America: An Anthology of American Poetry (1630-1930). New York: Coward-McCann, p. xxxv.

Whitman sought the theory after the performance rather than vice versa. His poems "contain an intrinsic esthetic standard for self-judgment, and imply or inspire criticism of all other poetry." Twenty pages of his poetry are included in this anthology.

12 LOWELL, AMY. Poetry and Poets. Boston and New York: Houghton Mifflin Co. "Walt Whitman and the New Poetry," pp. 61-87. Reprint of 1927.36.

13 MABBOTT, THOMAS OLLIVE, and SILVER, ROLLO G., eds. A Child's Reminiscence by Walt Whitman. Seattle: University of Washington Book Store, 44 pp. Includes reprints of 1860.3, 1860.18, 1860.40, 1860.2.

Mabbott's introduction describes the biographical background of "Child's Reminiscence" (first published version of "Cradle"), "not of great textual significance" because its revised version is merely smoothed out with a slight increase of the subjective. The authorship of 1860.3 is established as Whitman's. Includes an incomplete list of other Whitman items in the Saturday Press.

14 MUMFORD, LEWIS. "Whitman." In Modern Writers at Work, edited by Josephine K. Piercy. New York: Macmillan Co., pp. 178-83. Reprint of 1926.22 (pp. 128-37).

14a MURRY, JOHN MIDDLETON. Discoveries. London: Jonathan Cape, pp. 184, 231, 246, 150-52.

Incidental references: "There is far more 'impassioned simplicity' in the 'barbaric' Whitman than in all the English poetry of the eighteenth century before Blake." Unlike Whitman, "the greatest of American poets," Poe, the other great American poet, belongs to the English tradition. Behind Whitman's courage is the same fear that characterizes other poets of the United States. Nevertheless, he is the first American poet "native to his continent," breaking away from the puritan tradition though still a moralist. His succession is not yet apparent in American literature. (First published 1924.)

15 O'HIGGINS, HARVEY. Alias Walt Whitman. Newark: Carteret Book Club, 49 pp. Reprint of 1929.48.

16 OSBORNE, CLIFFORD HAZELDINE. The Religion of John Burroughs. Boston and New York: Houghton Mifflin Co. "'The Breath of Life,'" pp. 22-29; also 6, 12, 13, 14, 15, 17, 19, 31, 47, 51, 52, 73-74, 78.

"In Whitman, young Burroughs found life, abundant, free, daring, and unashamed." Whitman embodied the theory of life that Burroughs believed in. He came to regard Whitman as a contemporary Christ. Account of the extent of Burroughs's appreciation of Whitman and first acquaintance with Whitman's work.

17 PARRINGTON, VERNON LOUIS. Main Currents in American Thought. Vol. 3. The Beginnings of Critical Realism in America, 1860-1920. New York: Harcourt, Brace & Co. "The Afterglow of the Enlightenment--Walt Whitman,"

pp. 69-86; passim per index.
Abridged: Bradley/Blodgett; Miller.

Whitman was the complete embodiment of
the Enlightenment but lived in an age be-
traying those ideals. A pagan, romantic,
transcendentalist, mystic, he is contrasted
to writers of Puritan heritage; he is American literature's "most deeply religious
soul." He began as a dandy, became involved
in politics, later became an evolutionist
in sympathy with all rebels. Leaves was
influenced by "the fervid emotionalism of
the fifties," with the radical utopians his
forebears. He added to the philosophical
tradition of optimism and fraternity. War
strengthened his faith in the common man.
His debts to Emerson, Hegel and German
idealism, and Herbert Spencer are noted.
He had two duties as poet, to criticize
America's failure to establish democracy
and to revive faith. Most successful as a
critic, he projected democracy into the
future. His twin ideals were the growing
man and the perfect state, both mocked by
the Gilded Age. He is the greatest figure
in our literature.

18 PATTEE, FRED LEWIS. The New American Literature 1890-1930. New York: Century Co.,
pp. 7, 180, 195, 196, 201, 211, 215, 272,
274, 278-82, 285, 286, 361, 362, 366, 367,
375-77, 382-83, 388-89, 410, 439-40, 441,
452.

Whitman, Melville, and Lowell are contrasted in background, being coevals. More
of Lowell's Harvard quality might have
given Whitman's poetry a wider appeal, but
probably not, considering what the mixture
did to Melville. Whitman is a product of
New York, not of New England at all. Passages from Melville's Mardi are examined as
possible sources for Whitman. Unlike
Melville, he had the patience and "the gift
of totality" to make Leaves a unity. The
war enabled him to surpass mere Transcendentalism.

19 ROLLAND, ROMAIN. Prophets of the New India.
Translated by E. F. Malcolm-Smith. New
York and London: Albert & Charles Boni,
pp. 337-50.

This discussion of the nineteenth-
century Vedantist Vivekananda notes his
contact with Ingersoll and reading of
Leaves. Whitman's poems are full of nature
as the mother. Whitman's religious thought
has been neglected due to concentration on
love and democracy. "Paumanok" should not
be so overshadowed by "Myself," which
earlier opened the book in a "much starker
and more virile form." His religion is
based on identity, by which he means either
"an immediate perception of Unity" or "the
permanence of the Ego throughout the eternal
journey and its metamorphoses." Whitman
sometimes feels despair but his faith in
identity never varies. He reached this
faith by some illumination of his own,

prepared by his Quaker background, and not
through knowledge of Indian thought.
Emerson may have intellectualized his intuition. Quotations show Whitman's ecstasy
and intuition akin to Vendantism. Whitman's
spirit announced that America was ready to
listen to Indian thought, but he has no
influence in America.

20 SAYLER, OLIVER M., ed. Revolt in the Arts.
New York: Brentano's, pp. 50, 86; "Nature,
Teacher of the Dance," by Elizabeth Duncan,
p. 247; "Modern Poetry," by Hart Crane,
297-98 (reprinted: 1933.5).

Sayler mentions Whitman among figures
America did not recognize as great. Duncan
(Isadora's sister) notes the responses at
their dancing school of "the grown body to
older music, to words of greater depth,
such as Walt Whitman's or an ancient Greek
poet's." Crane praises Whitman's "expression of the American psychosis" and success
in fusing the forces of America into a universal vision, despite technical flaws:
"his bequest is still to be realized in all
its implications."

21 UNTERMEYER, LOUIS. Modern American Poetry:
A Critical Anthology. 4th rev. ed. New
York: Harcourt, Brace & Co. "Walt
Whitman," pp. 5-8.
Revision of 1925.14. Revised: 1936.28.
Adds a paragraph to 1925.14 describing
the various capacities in which Whitman is
regarded.

PERIODICALS

22 FRANKEL, DORIS. "Walt Whitman." Poet's Magazine (January), 5.
Poem of tribute in five rhymed stanzas.

23 POUND, LOUISE. "Note on Walt Whitman and Bird
Poetry." English Journal 19 (January),
31-36.
Whitman discarded the Romantics'
assumptions of birds as joyful and as
material for moral lessons in favor of
learning from them "what can be expressed
in song" and the meaning of death. "Cradle"
is explicated as one of poetry's "most
devastating love elegies," transcending
poetic convention, with note of Whitman's
phonetic and rhythmic skills. His genuine
feeling for the birds (in "Lilacs" also)
"accentuates the falsity of the earlier
bird poems," revealing him as "more in key
with coming generations than with his own."

24 ROLLINS, CARL PURINGTON, and TROXELL, GILBERT
M. "The Compleat Collector. The Limited
Editions Club." Saturday Review of Literature 6 (11 January), 644.
Describes Wells's 1855 reprint (1929.27),
set in "thin, lithe type" contrary to our
expectations of "a bold, crude type" as
appropriate for Whitman's verse.

25 HOLLOWAY, EMORY. "Whitman on the War's
Finale." Colophon, pt. 1 (February), 37-43.
Describes Whitman and his writings at
the end of the war; reprints his letter on
Lincoln and the capture of Davis from the
Armory Square Hospital Gazette (20 May
1865), similar in feeling and imagery to
the Lincoln poems.

26 ANON. Editorial. New York Times (9 February),
sec. 3, 4:4.
Incidental: Scott's works are "'feudal,' as Whitman loved to bellow."

27 WOODRUFF, E. H. "Whitman and Scott. Venerable
Poet Preferred Him Over Other Fiction
Writers." New York Times (12 February),
22:7.
Response to 1930.26, recalling his
visit to Whitman in 1884. Whitman appreciated Scott, despite his use of the epithet
"feudal"; because he was great, he may be
permitted such an idiosyncrasy on the basis
of national pride.

28 BLODGETT, HAROLD. "Walt Whitman in England:
The Magnification Here of the Man and His
Message." The World Today 55 (March),
371-78.
Reprint of 1929.57.

29 ANON. "New Names for the Hall of Fame?"
Publishers' Weekly 117 (8 March), 1334-36.
Illustrated.
Article on the Hall of Fame election
process, noting and printing portraits of
the authors likely to be considered, including Whitman, "whose omission has been
very widely commented on."

30 CRANE, HART. "Cape Hatteras." Saturday Review
of Literature 6 (15 March), 821-22.
Reprinted: 1930.5; 1933.5.
This poem, later incorporated into The
Bridge (1930.5), is addressed to Whitman,
used as a contrast with the modern scene,
and includes many phrases from Whitman.

31 ANON. "Whitman Oratorio Given." New York
Times (21 March), 30:6.
Johanna Mueller Hermann's work based
on Whitman's poem in memory of Lincoln is
briefly described as premiered in Vienna.

32 BLODGETT, HAROLD. "Whitman and Buchanan."
American Literature 2 (May), 131-40.
Reprinted: 1934.1.
Traces course of Buchanan's attitudes
toward Whitman and his efforts on Whitman's
behalf, as an English O'Connor of superior
talent.

33 HOLLOWAY, EMORY. Review of Morris (1929.17).
American Literature 2 (May), 185-87.
Morris's biographical section will be
found "repetitious if not platitudinous."
The most important section is Morris's
reminiscences, with welcome details.

Morley's explanation of the title of Good-
Bye in 1924.42 is not so helpful as Morris's
note of a book of verse called Halloo My
Fancy (see also 1935.38).

34 SPEIRS, RUSSELL F. "A Note on Whitman."
Education 50 (May), 568-70.
"Faces," exemplifying Whitman's poetry
and philosophy, does not encourage complacency in its recognition of all souls as
equal, for their equality lies in their
potential for development. The reader of
"Faces" is shamed and exalted, encouraged
to reject the trivial and to realize "his
own finer powers."

35 RODGERS, CLEVELAND. "Walt Whitman Still an
Outsider! Why Isn't America's Greatest
Poet in the Hall of Fame?" Brooklyn Daily
Eagle Sunday Magazine (25 May), 1-2. Illustrated.
Perhaps electioneering is necessary to
agitate for Whitman's inclusion in the Hall
of Fame, yet Whitman was "the first super-
salesman of American democracy," with indigenous writing. A radical in form, he
held the patriotic democratic ideal of his
time. The best of the new literature
derives from him. Vistas should be better
known. Early political defeat led him to
express his ideas in poetry, which drew its
vitality from this "sociological-political
background." Facsimile of Whitman's letter
to Lowell offering "1861" for twenty dollars.

36 ANON. "Walt Whitman's Notes of His Western
Trip." Biblia (Friends of the Princeton
Library) 1 (June), 3.
Describes and prints ten fragments of
paper recently purchased for Princeton's
library, Whitman's memoranda embryonic "of
a poem then intended but never written--a
poem descriptive of America's West."

37 ROSS, E. C. "Whitman's Verse." Modern Language Notes 45 (June), 363-64.
Whitman's verse differs from prose more
than traditional verse does, for traditional
verse is "composed in sentences" like prose,
"whereas Whitman's verse is composed in
lines," some even containing two or three
sentences. Leaves is not prose poetry
either, but is rather like the chant.

38 WINTERS, YVOR. "The Progress of Hart Crane."
Poetry 36 (June), 153-65.
Review of The Bridge (1930.5), which
reveals Whitman as Crane's master. Crane's
poem has no more unity than "Myself" but
extends the basically Whitmanian theme.
Whitman's sense of destiny is vague, unlike
that of the classical epic heroes, and he
merely accepts all things. Crane demonstrates
"the impposibility of getting anywhere with
the Whitmanian inspiration."

39 DREISER, THEODORE. "The New Humanism."
Thinker 2 (July), 8-12.

Reprinted: Pizer.
　　Mentions Whitman among the great, powerful writers of all time.

40　ANON. "Lariats for Pegasus." New York Times (6 July), sec. 3, 1:3-4.
　　Editorial on the publication in Biblia (1930.36) of Whitman's notes for a never-written epic poem on the West, demonstrating that literature does not spring full-blown, although a number of phrases had already formed themselves in his notes.

41　HOWARD, LEON. "Walt Whitman and the American Language." American Speech 5 (August), 441-51.
　　Whitman sought to revolt against the foreign elements of the English language in favor of an American language, for example, in his preference for the aboriginal in place names, without substituting artifical names for legitimate ones. Popular speech provided a source of linguistic revitalization, as did the vocabularies of various professions. Anglo-Saxon remains pale next to Whitman's lusty ideal, but there has been a tendency to more freedom in the use of words, as Whitman sought in American Primer (1904.17).

42　CRANE, NATHALIA. "Walt Whitman." Brooklyn Daily Eagle Sunday Magazine (28 September), 3.
　　Poem in eight rhymed quatrains.

43　PAUL, LYDIA. "Whitman Isn't in the Hall of Fame." Brooklyn Daily Eagle Sunday Magazine (28 September), 3.
　　Statements from Untermeyer, Mencken, Markham, Canby, Lindsay, Suzanne La Follette, Helene Mullins, Carl Van Doren call for Whitman's inclusion in the Hall of Fame, important not for Whitman's sake but for the credibility of the Hall of Fame. Markham points out Whitman's poetic and philosophical imperfections. Seward Collins suggests that his inclusion would "reduce his present fantastic overestimation," especially for his philosophy and martyrdom.

44　ANON. "Four Names Added to the Hall of Fame." New York Times (26 October), sec. 2, 1:1.
　　Describes the voting of new names into the Hall of Fame, including Whitman; notes previous attempts to get him elected.

45　ANON. "To Auction Rare Books." New York Times (26 October), sec. 2, 2:2.
　　Among the items to be auctioned tomorrow is a first edition of Leaves.

46　RODGERS, CLEVELAND. "Walt's Enshrinement Ends Long Agitation." Brooklyn Daily Eagle (26 October), sec. A, 3:2-3; also 3:1.
　　Traces the history of Whitman's treatment by the Hall of Fame. A few years ago his inclusion would have been shocking but now it may lead to greater acceptance for

him and greater acquaintance with his work by those Americans who should find inspiration therein.

46a　ANON. "Fame's Recruits." New York Times (27 October), 20:2.
　　Editorial commenting upon the ascent to permanent fame of the four people just elected into the Hall of Fame.

47　MONROE, WILL S. "Recent Walt Whitman Literature in America." Revue Anglo-Américaine 8 (December), 138-41.
　　Review of Barton (1928.3) and O'Higgins (1930.15), critical; of O'Connor (1927.17), Kennedy (1926.15), Morris (1929.17), Furness (1928.11). Commentary on the state of Whitman's reputation. The work in progress of several people is noted, including Monroe's own on Walt Whitman and His Contemporaries.

48　ANON. "Collectors Unearth Early Whitman Prose." New York Times (7 December), sec. 2, 3:2-4.
　　Notice of Mabbott (1930.13), describing contents.

49　ANON. "$2,100 Paid for a Whitman." New York Times (13 December), 2:2.
　　Describes first edition sold at auction.

50　LEWIS, SINCLAIR. "Text of Sinclair Lewis's Nobel Prize Address at Stockholm." New York Times (13 December), 12:2-7.
　　Lewis, first American to win the Nobel Prize for literature, discusses American literature past and present, incidentally mentioning Whitman among the "outcasts" but "authentic fellows" "who insisted that our great land had something more than teatable gentility."

1931

BOOKS

1　BARRUS, CLARA. Whitman and Burroughs Comrades. Boston and New York: Houghton Mifflin Co., 392 pp. Illustrated. Index.
　　A record of Whitman's life and contemporary reception, largely in relation to Burroughs and his life, quoting extensively from letters and journals, many unpublished. Barrus notes and corrects previous errors of fact or interpretation. This book expands earlier article (1925.69).
　　Introduction: Whitman's notion of comradeship, often misunderstood in "Calamus," was mystical, exemplified in his life. Burroughs's background, described, prepared him for his response to Whitman and Leaves. Whitman's wholesome life and praiseworthy hospital work are vouched for by many.
　　1. "The Call to Comradeship (1861-1865)": Burroughs's introduction to Leaves and later to Whitman by E. M. Allen;

Whitman's life in Washington.

2. "'The Good Gray Poet' Vindicated
(1865-1866)": Harlan's letter (1913.2) is
evasive. Other letters discuss the dismissal, including one from Ashton regarding
his interview with Harlan.

3. "Burroughs Enters the Lists (1866-
1870)": He wrote the Galaxy piece (1866.26)
when Whitman was in New York, so Whitman
saw it first in print. Correspondence
between Higginson and Burroughs differing
over Whitman.

4. "Appreciation Abroad and at Home
(1871-1876)": Correspondence of Burroughs,
Dowden, Rossetti (proposing readings by
Whitman).

5. "'The Voyage Balk'd' (1873-1875)":
Whitman's health; "Prayer" is his "real
swan song," for he never reached such sublimity again.

6. "O'Connor and Whitman Estranged
(1872-1882)": Explained through Burroughs's
recollections and various letters.

7. "Whitman Pulled and Hauled (1874-
1882)": Answers criticisms; reprints
Whitman's manuscript response to the Nation's
criticism (1881.53), written for Burroughs
to submit. Burroughs received some help
from Whitman in his writings but not as
much as some writers suggest.

8. "A Great Succoring Love (1876)":
Letters by Gilchrist and others regarding
support for Whitman and the 1876 controversy.

9. "'Love Me, Love Walt' (1876-1877)":
Letters by O'Connor and Burroughs defending
Whitman; comments from Whitman on Burroughs.

10. "Whitman's Noblest Woman Friend
(1869-1885)": Unpublished letters from the
Gilchrists to Burroughs and Whitman; comments on the publication of the Gilchrist-
Whitman letters (1918.9); Burroughs's
defense of Whitman's response to her;
citation of unpublished manuscript by Grace
Gilchrist Frend; Carpenter's letter to
Burroughs regarding conversations with
Holmes, Lowell, Longfellow, Emerson (more
extensive than in 1916.3).

11. "Birds and Poets (1877)": Whitman's
emendations to 1877.1; Myron Benton's comments on Whitman's true artistry--"interpretation instead of photography."

12. "'After the Dazzle of Day' (1877-
1881)": Whitman's visits to Burroughs;
background of "Dalliance"; the Parton debt;
literary borrowings from Burroughs;
Stedman's correspondence with O'Connor and
Burroughs; the pirated 1860 edition; letter
by Kennedy analyzing Whitman's qualities;
letters from Whitman on his visit to Boston
and Emerson; letters from O'Connor to Bucke
regarding the biography (1883.3).

13. "The Suppression of 'Leaves of
Grass' (1882)": Unpublished defenses by
O'Connor and Gilchrist; Burroughs's con-
versations in England regarding Whitman;
Comstock's underhanded tactics; Wilde's
visits to Whitman and Burroughs; the

Authors' Club and Whitman; Burroughs's explanation of "Prostitute."

14. "'As I Ebb'd with the Ocean of
Life' (1883-1888)": Background of "With
Husky-Haughty Lips"; Stedman's letter
praising Whitman's sea poetry and Homeric
traits; Whitman's friendship with the
Smiths; the Bolton group; Jessie Whitman's
description of Whitman's brother Ed's condition.

15. "November Boughs (1888-1891)":
Camden relationships. Burroughs suggests
Traubel overused oaths in transcribing
Whitman's conversation. Traubel and Bucke
made funeral plans in 1888.

16. "'This is Thy Hour, O Soul' (1891-
1892)": His death and responses to it;
Burroughs's great loss.

17. "The Old Guard and New Recruits
(1892-1897)": Charles Eldridge notes the
West Coast press's friendliness to Whitman;
his preparation of recollections of
Whitman (unpublished, the notes never found),
some of which "might shock a rigid moralist," although Whitman's relations with
women were noble. Whitman's comments on
some people would not be included, for fear
of hurting their feelings. Eldridge rejects
Symonds's perception of "sodomy" in "Calamus."
A page of proof from unpublished Burroughs
article, not used in 1896.2, is printed,
summarizing Whitman's significant ideas.
Donaldson's book (1896.3) is faulty.

18. "The Embers that Still Burn (1897-
1922)": Burroughs, Kennedy, and Eldridge
reject the story of the six children, fig-
ments of a possibly weakened mind or refutation of Symonds's inferences. Harned's
letters discuss the tomb; Burroughs and
others comment on Traubel's and Perry's
book. Summary of Brooklyn centenary
addresses (see 1919.160). Barrus records
her acquaintance with various friends of
Whitman.

Bibliography of Burroughs on Whitman.

2 BLANKENSHIP, RUSSELL. American Literature as
an Expression of the National Mind. New
York: Henry Holt & Co. "Walt Whitman,"
pp. 348-67; also viii, x, passim per index.
Whitman expressed Emerson's individualism
and cultural independence and Rousseau's
reverence for the natural man in a startling
and original way. He is to be considered
"as the last and the most fluent of the
transcendentalists and as the epitome of
the Golden Day of American romanticism."
His poems "vacillate between praise of
Whitman, the individual, and triumphal
paeans to democracy." Biographical sketch,
commenting on his political sympathies.
With a large debt to Emerson, his spirit is
even closer to Thoreau's. His mysticism,
with Quaker and transcendentalist bases,
emphasized delight in nature and the inter-
linking of soul and body. His optimism is
not excessive but a transcendental idealism,
faith in goodness, an antidote for today's

pessimism. His belief in his own significance was extended into a rich humanitarianism. He epitomized "the spirit of the
western frontier," recognizing also the
frontier of the cities. "Captain," long
"a favorite of all classes of Americans"
for "its simplicity, directness, and note
of personal grief," and "Lilacs," one of
the nineteenth century's "superlative literary productions," are fitting tributes to
a great American leader by "our greatest
poet." His natural rhythm is effective.
His reputation relies on "the fundamental
poetry in the amplitude of his imagination
and in the sustained majesty of his utterances." The 1855 Preface is one of the
most significant in literature. Vistas
has "an imaginative grasp and a grandeur of
utterance equaled only by his best poetry."
His strong influence is described. Secondary sources are suggested, with critical
comments.

3 BOND, F. FRASER. Mr. Miller of "The Times."
The Story of an Editor. New York and
London: Charles Scribner's Sons, p. 16.
    Biography of Charles Ransom Miller,
who was introduced to Whitman's voice
through periodicals and persuaded his class-
mates at Dartmouth to ask him to address
their graduating class, though "the choice
had its chief inspiration in a desire to
outrage the faculty."

4 BUCK, PHILO M., Jr. Literary Criticism: A
Study of Values in Literature. New York
and London: Harper & Bros., pp. 82, 187-
88, 333.
    Notes Whitman's later mannerism.
Examines "Captain" as inferior to "Lilacs"
in expressing grief, giving too easy a
response, sentimental. Whitman may write
lyrics that are not singable, as in Drum-
Taps at his best, since lyric poetry need
not be so.

5 BURKE, KENNETH. Counter-Statement. New York:
Harcourt, Brace & Co., p. 118.
Reprinted: 1937.21.
    Incidental: Gide's work suggests "a
kind of morbid Whitmanism."

6 CANBY, HENRY SEIDEL. Classic Americans: A
Study of Eminent American Writers from
Irving to Whitman. New York: Harcourt,
Brace & Co. "Walt Whitman," pp. 308-351;
bibliography, 359-60; also passim per index.
    Whitman's electric quality is clearer
in "Myself" than in his conversations with
Traubel. His first readers were disturbed
more by his "intolerable assurance" than
by his coarseness, although this was
chiefly in his poetry, his life being
characterized by sympathy and affection.
His treatment of form, sex, and egoism
makes his status still difficult to determine; he was nevertheless "the Great Personality he celebrated in his work," his

qualities closer to the people than they
realized. He made a religion of democracy
through combining Emerson's idealism,
spiritual enthusiasm, and democratic ideals.
His utopian America may be true in a deeper
sense if not in actuality. His philosophy,
an "expansionist romanticism," despite
questionable elements, "gave form to his
intentions" and "made him an artist on the
grand scale." He is a major influence upon
the modern imagination. He wrote for individuals rather than classes. In avoiding
artifice, like the Quakers, his free verse,
not free at all, tends toward monotony,
lacking the variety and restraints of form,
moving as the opera sounded to him, a non-
musician. He follows Carlyle in being
heroic and oracular. His style, if not
always poetry, was "exactly suited to description" and to his time and society,
which he pictured accurately. The early
attacks on his verse hardened Whitman into
persisting in this method, shutting himself
off from further experiment by considering
this method "utterly and irrevocably him."
His depiction of sex reacts against
Victorian prudery and expresses himself and
the whole human being; the homosexuality of
"Calamus" and the heterosexuality of "Adam"
are inevitable parts of the complete Leaves.
Whitman must be recognized not as a systematic philosopher but as a poet and
prophet, his flaws those of taste, not
thought. His "unbridled egoism" "wearies
the reader," although also part of his
greatness and balanced by moments of self-
doubt and humility. He cannot be ranked
with the greatest poets because of defects
in form and philosophical insight, but he
is great for his sense of human significance,
raising his vision into an art, the culmination of a period in American literature and
history.

7 CHARTERIS, EVAN, The Hon., K. C. The Life and
Letters of Sir Edmund Gosse. New York and
London: Harper & Bros., pp. 169-71, 300,
453.
    Gosse's admiring letter to Whitman of
1873; record of his "enchanting visit to
Camden" in January 1885; letter to Perry
praising the biography (1906.13), denying
belief in existence of Whitman's children,
noting Whitman's interesting psychology,
its keynote perhaps "a staggering ignorance,
a perhaps wilful non-perception, of the
real physical conditions of his nature,"
though apparent on almost every page.

8 CROFFUT, WILLIAM A. An American Procession
1855-1914: A Personal Chronicle of Famous
Men. Boston: Little, Brown, & Co., pp.
108-10.
    Reminiscences of Whitman, with whom he
boarded in the same house in Washington;
some inaccuracies. He was "greatly overestimated, especially as a poet," though
"an agreeable companion." He despised art.

Anecdote of Whitman being charged with wearing a mask. His casual reactions to being dismissed by Harlan. He was "the most expert interpreter" of the thieves' argot when a group that met in the Treasury Department was translating the proofs in French of Les Misérables.

9 CRUM, RALPH B. Scientific Thought in Poetry. New York: Columbia University Press, pp. 192, 197-203.

Whitman, like Tennyson, resorted to mysticism in dealing with science, not recognizing a disparity between the emotional nature of the poet and the intellectual nature of the scientist, untroubled by science's materialistic aspects but lacking the scientific temperament. His philosophy and use of science are explained. In conveying a conception of infinite space and time, Whitman succeeds better than other poets of his time.

10 CURRIE, BARTON. Fishers of Books. Boston: Little, Brown, & Co., pp. 52, 229, 273, 274, 276, 300, 314. Illustrations of 1st ed., 239 and facing 230.

Describes a first edition Whitman sent to W. Morton Fullerton with a letter (quoted) thanking him for a flattering critique in the Boston Advertiser. The praise of Whitman by Sinclair Lewis, Mencken, and their ilk to the denigration of most other earlier American writers does not detract from his worth.

11 DE MILLE, GEORGE E. Literary Criticism in America: A Preliminary Survey. New York: Dial Press, pp. 123, 128, 147-49, 229, 232, 235, 246, 257, 280.

Praises Stedman's daring act, as a conventional and recognized critic, of appreciating "an excellence of a new and disturbing kind." Notes later critics writing on Whitman.

12 FERRANDO, GUIDO. "Edward Carpenter as I Knew Him." In Edward Carpenter: In Appreciation, edited by Gilbert Beith. London: George Allen & Unwin, pp. 63-73.

Records his discovery of Carpenter's message through his interest in Whitman. Both believed "in the infinite possibilities of man, and in the absolute reality of love." Whitman's boisterous, pagan, and typically American qualities, his crudeness as an artist, differed from Carpenter's "finesse of mind," sense of proportion, and "meditative habit." "Whitman sensualized nature, Carpenter spiritualized it."

13 GOLDMAN, EMMA. Living My Life. New York: Alfred A. Knopf, pp. 140, 145, 224, 378, 474, 528, 568, 979, 991, 992.

Incidental references to her appreciation of Whitman, the suppression of an anarchist paper for printing "Woman Waits," her acquaintance with Traubel, Carpenter, Saunders.

14 LANZ, HENRY. The Physical Basis of Rime: An Essay on the Aesthetic of Sound. Stanford University: Stanford University Press, pp. 321-23, 325.

Whitman regarded rime as inadequate for important themes, as explained in a prose quotation.

15 LEWIS, B. ROLAND. Creative Poetry: A Study of Its Organic Principle. Stanford University: Stanford University Press; London: Humphrey Milford, Oxford University Press, pp. 3, 44, 52-53, 54, 64, 65, 155, 186, 205-6, 226, 327.

Whitman is quoted and used as example for different elements of poetry (particularly "The Last Invocation" and "Captain").

16 MONROE, WILL S. "Walt Whitman and other American Friends of Edward Carpenter." In Edward Carpenter: In Appreciation, edited by Gilbert Beith. London: George Allen & Unwin, pp. 144-54.

Cites and quotes various of Carpenter's writings on and to Whitman, and comparisons of Carpenter and Whitman by American socialist writers.

17 MORLEY, CHRISTOPHER. John Mistletoe. Garden City, N.Y.: Doubleday, Doran & Co., pp. 75, 93, 137, 169-70, 221, 273-77, 422-23.

Describes visit to Whitman's birthplace on Whitman's birthday. Davidson's "fine striding open-air statue" of Whitman should be placed in Prospect Park, Brooklyn. "Walt was able to take some of the morbid anxieties of life and show us their health and honor." References to Whitman's value throughout.

18 OPPENHEIM, JAMES. "Whitman." In American Writers on American Literature, edited by John A. Macy. New York: Horace Liveright; Tudor Publishing Co., pp. 258-73; also passim per index.

Whitman's vision of industrial democracy contrasts with Russian depersonalization and current American standardization. Leaves completes the activist message of Longfellow and Emerson but adds sensuality. Whitman is his book. A brief life sketch demonstrates continuing idealism. Leaves is unique in subject and style. Whitman spent his life polishing it, "vainly trying to make it more musical." His failure is in fact a triumph, his inspiration being greater than control. Whitman was not tragic. Comradeship and sociability are his themes, though overly so, creating too much sunshine. He is contrasted with Melville. Whitman was "awestruck by the commonplace," while we are hungry for deeper things. Modern America leaves us unsatisfied as Whitman does. Young writers must turn to European models or seek American depth.

19 RHYS, ERNEST. Everyman Remembers. New York: Cosmopolitan Book Corp., pp. 24-25, 46, 85, 94, 116, 121-26, 128-29, 131, 279.

Recalls conversations about Whitman

with Bucke and Olive Schreiner; his visit with Whitman, Whitman's conversation on Swinburne, <u>Franklin Evans</u> (which Rhys considers "super-excellent," considering how it was written, according to Whitman's own testimony), use of rhyme. He could be humorous when telling his own experiences, though humor did not enter into his ordinary attitude toward life.

20 ROURKE, CONSTANCE. <u>American Humor: A Study of the National Character</u>. New York: Harcourt, Brace & Co., pp. 168-79, 204-5, 277, 278, passim per index.
Extract reprinted: Murphy.

Whitman's poetry approaches the soliloquy, sometimes moving toward modern stream-of-consciousness and delving into the mind, sometimes following the tradition of the backwoodsman monologue in shifting from the personal to the "generic and inclusive 'I' who embraces many minds and many experiences." Whitman's imagery and feelings of vastness and good humor derive from the West, its tall tales and self-mockery. He uses language as a "plastic and even comical medium," as in native folklore. He remains "an improviser of immense genius," often on the verge of achieving the sustained heroic tone. His reconciling attitude to death is almost that of the higher comedy.

21 UNTERMEYER, LOUIS. General preface and introduction to selected Whitman poems in <u>American Poetry from the Beginning to Whitman</u>. New York: Harcourt, Brace & Co., pp. 56-62; also 582-98 (reprinted with deletions: 1936.28); passim per index.

Preface presents the violent reactions Whitman aroused, due partly to misinterpretation of his praise for the body, partly to his deceptive formlessness, partly to his spirit, which is what assures him permanence, being both sensual and mystical, optimistic, loving, affirming. "With Whitman early American poetry ends and modern American poetry begins." The introduction to eighty-seven pages of his poems traces his life, following recent scholarship. His self-praise protests his maleness too vehemently, out of insecurity. Untermeyer explains Whitman's attempts at being representative, his democracy, language, the power of "Myself," his rhythm, magnitude, inclusiveness, adhesiveness (a less possessive and therefore finer love, as in his reactions with Symonds and Gilchrist). His contradictions resist complete synthesis but somehow he attains unity, transcending his defects and retaining the effect.

PERIODICALS

22 CARPENTER, FREDERIC I. "The Vogue of Ossian in America: A Study in Taste." <u>American Literature</u> 2 (January), 405-17.

This discussion of American authors and their comments on Ossian culminates with Whitman, his regard for Ossian as a classic though without the credulity Thoreau gave this poet. A passage from Ossian is compared with the opening of "Lilacs." Through Whitman, the Ossian poems influenced American literature profoundly, their rhythms and spirit translated into the method of an authentic poetry of an entirely new and American type.

23 HUNGERFORD, EDWARD. "Walt Whitman and his Chart of Bumps." <u>American Literature</u> 2 (January), 350-84.

Traces Whitman's involvement with phrenology to explain some difficult aspects of Whitman's writings, including his notebook entries about "164." His interest is apparent in reviews of related books in the <u>Eagle</u>, 1846, here reprinted for the first time. The role of Fowler and Wells in selling <u>Leaves</u> is described. The chart analyzing his bumps is reprinted, important in his conception of himself and his description of the greatest poet in the 1855 Preface. His terms must be understood, sometimes differing from their modern meanings. Adhesiveness (no more than the "'disposition to attachment'") and amativeness (physical love), with related excesses, are described. He later deleted some passages dealing with phrenology.

24 ANON. "A Whitman Item." <u>New York Herald Tribune Books</u> 7 (18 January), 16.

Review of Mabbott (1930.13), valuable for the early text of "Cradles," later revised generally for the better. Whitman, though praising himself in the <u>Saturday Press</u> articles, erred less than his condemning critics; he is "a warning to all those who set out to damn their contemporaries."

25 MONROE, WILL S. "Swinburne's Recantation of Walt Whitman." <u>Revue Anglo-Américaine</u> 9 (April), 347-51.

Explains Swinburne's recantation from his earlier high opinion of Whitman, largely due to Watts's influence. Monroe recalls a morning spent with Whitman in May 1885 and Whitman's comments on Bayard Taylor.

26 CAIRNS, W. B. "Swinburne's Opinion of Whitman." <u>American Literature</u> 3 (May), 125-35.

Swinburne's feeling toward Whitman, not his estimate of his qualities, was what changed, as seen through letters and other writings. He came to find Whitman less musical, his political and critical ideas less sound than at first; he was irritated that his "enemies compared his treatment of sex to that of Whitman with praise of the latter." Watts-Dunton exerted some influence, but he might have written "Whitmania" (1887.63) without ever meeting him.

27 GLICKSBERG, CHARLES I. "A Whitman Letter. A Criticism of Exemption From Military Service Found." New York Times (1 May), 26:8.

Glicksberg quotes letter and article from New York Times of March 1863. Whitman registered for the draft and would have gone. This letter shows his commitment to the war effort and does not support the idea that he did not enlist because of Quakerism.

28 ANON. "Noted Sculptors Design Fame Busts." New York Times (3 May), sec. 2, 2:1.

Account of the busts of the Hall of Fame honorees: Chester Beach designed Whitman's, as a gift of the Eagle, to be unveiled by Mrs. Traubel.

29 BIGELOW, POULTNEY. "Whitman's Best Monument." New York Times (4 May), 18:7.

Whitman would have cared little for the Hall of Fame tribute; "his godlike verses" are sufficient memorial; the money for the bust should have gone to Burroughs's grandchildren.

30 JOHNSON, ROBERT UNDERWOOD. "Whitman Deficit." New York Times (4 May), 18:7.

The director of the Hall of Fame requests aid for expenses in installing the bust of Whitman, "one of the most American figures of our history, the laureate of Lincoln and the prophet of democracy."

31 ANON. "Hall of Fame Gets 4 Busts Thursday." New York Times (10 May), sec. 2, 4:1.

Announces program for the unveiling ceremony and the quotations to accompany the busts. Honoring Whitman will be Harrison S. Morris and Edwin Markham, reading a new poem.

32 ANON. "Hoover Hails Honor for Monroe at N.Y.U." New York Times (15 May), 1:4, 3:3-4.

Quotes President Hoover's message on the "recognition of the enduring quality of the works" of the four honorees; describes the ceremony; quotes last verse of Markham's poem of tribute (1932.16).

33 FINNEGAN, J. A. "A Critic of Whitman." Philadelphia Public Ledger (22 May), 12:6.

Commentary stemming from Morris's remarks at Hall of Fame ceremony. Whitman is remembered by locals "as a picturesque, lovable loafer." He was a poser and shirked responsibility. The only valuable thing he did was to serve as a nurse in the Civil War. Others are just as worthy of such an honor.

34 HOUSE, JAY E. "On Second Thought." Philadelphia Public Ledger (23 May), 10:7.

Incidentally notes his inability to understand the honor rendered Whitman, asking what Whitman did as the basis of his fame to discover some reason "for Mr. Whitman's post-mortem pre-eminence."

35 QUAERO [pseud.]. "Exemption of Quakers Suggests Questions." New York Times (24 May), sec. 3, 2:8.

Letter about conscientious objection, incidentally mentioning Whitman in response to 1931.27.

36 CHEYNEY, RALPH. "Whitman Defended." Philadelphia Public Ledger (26 May), 14:5-6.

Response to Finnegan (1931.33): Whitman created a shrine for the world, "a birthplace for a better future." A dreamer to be proud of, he expressed the truth and pointed toward new poets, who also need to be read and published today.

37 HOUSE, JAY E. "On Second Thought." Philadelphia Public Ledger (26 May), 14:7.

A. B. responded to query in 1931.34, terming Whitman "a tramp printer who afterward wrote free verse." House calls that quite enough but notes Whitman's peculiar punctuation and capitalization and "choppy" style.

38 ANON. "The Week." New Republic 67 (27 May), 30.

Paragraph on Whitman's admittance to the Hall of Fame, recalling Lowell's epithets for him, the earlier incident of his bust being placed there (1919.230). Justice triumphs with this official, if belated, recognition of his talent.

39 ANON. "A Gesture in Cranberry Street." Brooklyn Daily Eagle (1 June), 18:1-2.

Editorial on the worthy memorial to Whitman at the site of the 1855 printing of Leaves. He believed American democracy could work, despite inherent evils in the democratic system, for it allowed individuals to live "with the maximum of freedom to develop their potentialities."

40 ANON. "Walt Whitman Acclaimed as Peerless Poet." Brooklyn Daily Eagle (1 June), 17:1-3. Illustrated.

On dedication of memorial plaque at 1855 printing site: the speakers' comments on Whitman's love for the city and democratic spirit; list of places in Brooklyn associated with Whitman's life.

41 ANON. "Brooklyn Unveils Plaque to Whitman." New York Times (1 June), 19:4.

Describes dedication of memorial plaque by Alexander Finta (reproduced), with addresses by John Erskine and Holloway (1931.45).

42 ANON. "Authors Honor Advent of 'Leaves of Grass.'" Philadelphia Public Ledger (1 June), 2:8.

Brief account of Brooklyn memorial to the first printing of Leaves, copies of which now bring five thousand dollars.

43 ANON. "Fete Honors Birth of Walt Whitman." Philadelphia Public Ledger (1 June), 2:7.

1931

Brief account of tribute to Whitman at Mickle Street.

44 FINNEGAN, J. A. "A Critic 'Apologizes.'" Philadelphia Public Ledger (1 June), 12:6.
Response to Cheyney (1931.36): Finnegan grants that Whitman wrote something worthy-- "Captain"--but will be forgotten before true poets like Tennyson and others. Leaves is not poetry in the accepted sense.

45 HOLLOWAY, EMORY. "Prof. Holloway's Tribute at Whitman Plaque Unveiling. Whitman the Pioneer." Brooklyn Daily Eagle (1 June), 18:4-6.
Appreciative explanation of Whitman's thematic content. His idea of the role of the poet broke down old definitions and categories, transcending distinctions of romanticism and realism, good and evil, in "the paradoxical complexity of modern thought and life." He was a poet of America and all her causes, but his poetry transcended particular causes. He was not a strict philosopher but a poet who spoke to the spirit. He looked forward to much of what America was to experience in the future, yet he also looked to the world. This memorial should be but a symbol of a truer memorial, in common words and deeds.

46 DUFFUS, R. L. "Burroughs and the Whitman Cult--A Study by Clara Barrus Which Adds Measurably to Our Understanding Of a Notable Chapter in Our Literary History." New York Times Book Review (7 June), 2.
Review of Barrus (1931.1). Whitman became a cause because of his personality and his work. His cult "came near killing his genius" with their worship. His personality was more open and unrestrained than that of Burroughs, who emphasized Whitman's wholesomeness and sanity. The view of Whitman's later life given through the letters here is "so much saner and calmer" than that given by Traubel. This book's information may not add to our opinion of the work but so it adds to the stature of the man, so closely related to the poetry.

47 GARRETT, ERWIN CLARKSON. "'Whitman Was Not a Poet.'" Philadelphia Public Ledger (12 June), 12:6.
Response to Finnegan (1931.44): Whitman's poems are indeed negligible, and even "Captain" is faulty. A reader might enjoy them as great literature but not as poetry. They are too careless, like those of many modern poets.

48 BLACK, IVAN. "'Whitman Was a Poet.'" Philadelphia Public Ledger (16 June), 10:5-6.
Response to Garrett (1931.47): Whitman is still hard to accept for some, being ahead of his time and acclaimed as "one of the really great modern poets." Black explains Whitman's sane view of his

work, his conscious choice of method. His only fault was his originality. Adult readers prefer "Lilacs" to "Captain," famous chiefly through schoolboy readers. Garrett misses Whitman's soul.

49 [GRATTAN, C. HARTLEY.] "Log-Rolling Whitman-- How Burroughs and Others Championed the Giant of Free Verse in Effort to Get 'Leaves of Grass' Accepted." New York World Telegram (17 June), 24:1-2.
Review of Barrus (1931.1), which, in describing techniques used by early admirers to get Whitman recognized, "might be taken as the basis for a code of rules on what not to do." Whitman needed "calm, collected critical handling," as he does today, when the time has come to evaluate him properly.

50 ANON. "Government Paid Walt Whitman $1,600 a Year, Payroll Shows." New York Times (19 June), 4:3.
A document has been found recording Whitman's salary in the Attorney General's office.

51 ANON. "Whitman's Fame Brightening with the Years." Literary Digest 109 (20 June), 16, 43. Illustrated with Finta tablet.
Quotes Erskine's unveiling speech at Brooklyn plaque dedication; the Eagle interview with Mrs. Leader Young, daughter of Whitman's sister Mary (unlocated); abrupt and snide remarks on the unveiling from Philadelphia Public Ledger (unlocated).

52 MAXWELL, WILLIAM. "Some Personalistic Elements in the Poetry of Whitman." Personalist 12 (July), 190-99.
Defines Whitman's philosophy of life, vague but positive. His independence of mind was both strength and defect. Whitman's common sense helped him to conceive ideas immediately. His ideas on a personal relation with God, death, good, and evil are described. His beliefs, though clear to himself, lack clarity for readers. His religious thought would suit a contemporary orthodox pulpit. His notion of the soul was vague. He can never achieve true abstract thought. Yet he is "a great voice in American thought," especially in his respect for humanity.

53 STEVENSON, LIONEL. "Mute Inglorious Whitman." University of California Chronicle 33 (July), 296-316.
Beyond the title, this article on colonial poets refers to Whitman only in noting a "Whitmanesque catalogue" in a William Bradford poem.

54 BIRSS, JOHN HOWARD. "O Captain! My Captain!" Notes and Queries 161 (26 September), 233.
Notes musical versions of "Captain."

55 MILLER, FRED R. "Post-Mortem Effects." Rebel Poet, 1 (October-December), 4.

Poem addressed to Whitman in Whitmanesque lines about the negative effects of
his philosophy, which have betrayed the
American average.

56 SPIER, LEONARD. "What We Need." Rebel Poet 1
(October-December), 9.
Whitman is "the dawning consciousness
of the masses," with growing importance for
workers; but his words were more adequate
for his times.

57 ARVIN, NEWTON. "Individualism and American
Writers." Nation 133 (14 October), 391-92.
Reprinted: 1937.21.
Incidental references to Whitman,
Thoreau, and Emerson as representing the
meridian of our individualism. The individualistic revolt of the 1910s, "unlike
theirs, was radically personal and anti-
social."

58 POWELL, LAWRENCE CLARK. "Leaves of Grass and
Granite Boulders." The Carmelite 4 (22
October), 8-9.
Contrast of Whitman and Jeffers, showing
their divergence from an original agreement.
From looking across the Pacific as the
eventual end, Whitman "sends man packing
back onto himself" while Jeffers "bundles
him off to the stars" as a twentieth-
century man. Specific poems are cited.
Whitman became static, Jeffers less sure of
the future and more convinced of the failure
of empire-building. Used in 1934.12.

59 HICKS, GRANVILLE. "Letters to William Francis
Channing." American Literature 3 (November), 294-98.
Includes a letter of 1868 from Whitman
to Channing, responding to Channing's invitation. Channing knew Whitman from the
1855 Leaves.

60 MABBOTT, THOMAS OLLIVE. "'Whitman's' Lines on
Duluth." American Literature 3 (November),
316-17.
The poem on Duluth (1892.89) which
Holloway includes in Uncollected is revealed
as a joke by reprinting from the Duluth
Daily News the original letter including
the poem, signed "Mendax."

1932

BOOKS

1 BABBITT, IRVING. On Being Creative and Other
Essays. Boston and New York: Houghton
Mifflin Co. "The Critic and American Life,"
pp. 220, 222.
Reprint of 1928.25.

2 BELL, RALCY HUSTED. Memoirs & Mistresses:
The Amatory Recollections of a Physician.
New York: William Faro. "Drab Love,"
pp. 89-99.

Quoted in "Mrs. Davis's 'Drab Love,'" by
Harold Aspiz, WWR 22 (December 1976).
Account of Mary Davis's life with
Whitman and after, when she served as maid
to friends of Bell. Whitman took advantage
of her faithful love, but such is the way
of genius; Traubel and Bucke have no such
excuse. She claimed that "Whitman did not
take kindly to Traubel, personally," being
usually bored by him. Bell notes discrepancies between Keller's account (1921.19)
and Mary's stories; describes his own
appreciation of Whitman's works, to which
Mrs. Frank Leslie introduced him, and
Whitman's influence on his own poetry.
Whitman's godlike indifference to calumny"
is his most admirable trait, showing his
self-respect. He had beautiful intuitions.

3 BINNS, HENRY BRYAN. Walt Whitman and His
Poetry. Poetry and Life Series. London:
George G. Harrap & Co., 168 pp.
Reprint of 1915.4.

4 BRADFORD, GAMALIEL. Biography and the Human
Heart. Boston and New York: Houghton
Mifflin Co. "Walt Whitman," pp. 63-93.
Photograph.
Revision of 1916.24. Reprinted: 1938.3.
Includes brief chronology; makes only
minor changes and additions, noting recent
Whitman volumes, but nothing can appear to
alter Whitman's fundamental character as
here delineated.

5 BROOKS, VAN WYCK. Sketches in Criticism.
New York: E. P. Dutton & Co. "The Influence of Whitman" (reprint of 1921.79),
178-83; "Whitman: Sixty Years After"
(reprint of 1921.54), 184-89; "The Critical
Movement" (reprinted 1937.21), 11, 14, 16;
also 26, 27, 32, 82, 85, 108, 132-33, 142,
190, 218, 244, 260, 266.
The 1921 articles are only slightly
revised stylistically. Incidental references throughout: the long infancy of
great writers like Whitman and Thoreau,
America's most original writers although
indebted to Emerson; Whitman's vastness,
optimism, transfiguration of personal
characteristics into the universal in his
poetry (from 1920.86); his knowledge of
literature; J. B. Yeats's attitudes toward
him.

6 BUSH, DOUGLAS. Mythology and the Renaissance
Tradition in English Poetry. Minneapolis:
University of Minnesota Press, pp. 3, 137.
Incidental: "Exposition" is quoted as
example of the break from mythology, yet
much of Whitman "is a close parallel to
the Homeric catalogue of the ships."
Marlowe "must sing of the body electric."

7 CALVERTON, V. F. The Liberation of American
Literature. New York: Charles Scribner's
Sons. "The Frontier Force," pp. 275-98.
Whitman was "the first genuine force in

the creation of an American art," transforming "the individualistic revolt of the
frontier into poetic form." His egotism was
"absorbed from the environment rather than
created in himself." His contempt for
traditional literature is intrinsic to the
psychology of the West. It was the impact
of the West as a spiritual reality, not a
place visited, that influenced Emerson and
Whitman. Whitman describes life as lived
on the prairies and in the new cities. He
was the first writer "to escape the bondage
of the colonial complex." He is now accepted because of "freer morals" and a new
attitude toward traditional writing. He is
not a prophet of social revolution but a
"petty bourgeois individualist" who believed
in private property and tolerated slavery.
His message is not for this day, offering
no inspiration to modern workers.

8 DICKINSON, THOMAS D. The Making of American
   Literature. New York: Century Co. "Walt
   Whitman," pp. 530-41; also 414, 516, 520,
   521, 522, 609.
       Whitman brought to literature many
   frontier qualities, a new subject-matter,
   "a fresh and renovating point of view," new
   verse forms. Life sketch shows his preparation for a life of literature on a plane of
   actual life and experience, avoiding the
   literary traditions earlier writers emphasized. He mystified his career; whether
   a recorded event is real or fanciful is not
   always clear. The war brought him, earlier
   "something of a poseur," a deeper note.
   "Myself" is one of the world's great poems.
   His work is based on the "germinal principle," praising all things, believing that
   "oneself was all that one could know."
   With his passion for democracy, he felt
   that literature should express the common
   man's life. He became the war's outstanding
   poet, later "the poet of the liberated soul"
   as in "Prayer," one of his greatest poems.
   His formal innovation is the least important
   part of his originality.

9 DOUGLAS, LLOYD C. Forgive Us Our Trespasses.
   Boston and New York: Houghton Mifflin Co.,
   p. 246.
       A character quotes Whitman to describe
   his own feeling of unity with all.

10 GOHDES, CLARENCE, ed. Uncollected Lectures by
   Ralph Waldo Emerson. New York: William
   Edwin Rudge. "Books," p. 41.
   Reprint of 1864.5.

11 HOLLOWAY, EMORY, and SCHWARZ, VERNOLIAN, eds.
   Introduction and notes to I Sit and Look
   Out: Editorials from the Brooklyn Daily
   Times by Walt Whitman. New York: Columbia
   University Press, pp. 3-30, 201-32. Index.
   Includes reprints of 1859.7; 1856.27.
       Holloway's introduction traces Whitman's
   newspaper career up through his editorship
   of the Brooklyn Daily Times, its history,

his reasons for leaving it (probably two
articles he wrote taking a liberal attitude
toward sex). His editorial topics are
described, revealing his "detached yet
sympathetic spirit" regarding political and
economic problems, his concern with reform,
his interests in science and literature.
His frankness in treating sex was due to
"his desire to increase the number of happy
marriages by teaching a modern pride in
oneself" and to decrease the degradation of
sex by attacking the silence surrounding it.
Notes to the editorials reprinted explain
background, subjects, allusions.

12 HOWE, M. A. DeWOLFE, ed. New Letters of James
   Russell Lowell. New York and London:
   Harper & Bros., pp. 101-2, 115-16.
       In 1861 Lowell forwards to James T.
   Fields, his successor as Atlantic editor,
   poems by Whitman, noting the prices Whitman
   asks. Letter to Rev. W. L. Gage in 1863
   responds to Gage's comments on Leaves, "a
   book I never looked into farther than to
   satisfy myself that it was a solemn humbug";
   however, every book should be included in
   a college library, to which he believes he
   sent his copy of Leaves. He thanks Gage
   for calling his attention to a part of the
   book of which he knew nothing and which he
   will keep "out of the way of students."
   However, less harm is done "by downright
   animality" than "by a more refined sensuousness" as in Byron.

13 HUXLEY, ALDOUS, ed. The Letters of D. H.
   Lawrence. New York: Viking Press, passim
   per index.
       Incidental references to Whitman's use
   of rhythm, other qualities; "sometimes
   Whitman is perfect" in his rhythm.

14 KNIGHT, GRANT C. American Literature and
   Culture. New York: Ray Long & Richard R.
   Smith. "Walt Whitman," pp. 271-85.
       Whitman at first does not seem like
   poetry but must be understood on his own
   terms. Sketch of his life, including early
   failures, growth of democratic philosophy,
   change in the 1850s, positive responses to
   him. Emerson's plea for literary independence in "The American Scholar" underlies
   Leaves. American literature must follow
   Whitman's literary and poetic theory and
   celebrate the material, common life. The
   American is still not free enough from an
   imposed culture to accept him. The "arch-
   romantic" of America, he belongs to the
   future and has not been equaled.

15 LEWISOHN, LUDWIG. Expression in America. New
   York and London: Harper & Bros., pp. 198-
   213; also xxviii, 85, 115, 196, 217, 339,
   363, 380, 422, and passim per index.
       Whitman is the "most strange and dif-
   ficult figure in all our letters and perhaps
   the greatest, certainly the most far-reaching, far-echoing poetic voice." Failure to

acknowledge him openly as "a homosexual of the most-pronounced and aggressive type" lies behind the misinterpretations and the discrepancy between his actual and his desired audience. "Calamus" with "amazing outspokenness" reveals much of the homosexual mind. One must conquer the "slightly repellent impression" given by his work and life in order to perceive and enjoy his great qualities of "authentic genius." His form is remote "from all tradition and normal instinct" but "frequently great and noble" with occasional regular rhythm, perhaps unconscious. Vistas provides a background for his poems, which may display looseness of logic and too much glowing optimism, counteracted by the shadows in Vistas. His poetry is great in fragments. Although his "theme of universal acceptance" is a "type of communistic passion" due to "abnormal channeling of erotic impulses" and he proposes no new principle of guidance, all may respond to his "tonic note of individualism." (See Addenda.)

16 MARKHAM, EDWIN. New Poems: Eighty Songs at Eighty. Garden City, N.Y.: Doubleday, Doran & Co. "Walt Whitman," pp. 95-98.
Poem addressed to Whitman on the occasion of his entry into the Hall of Fame (see 1931.32), criticizing his portrayals of the average man and of women, his contradictions, his emphasis on the ego, and then praising "Cradle" and "Lilacs," his singing of democracy, comrade-love, faith, and joy.

17 MORLEY, CHRISTOPHER. Ex Libris Carissimis. Philadelphia: University of Pennsylvania Press, pp. 26, 27-29, 103, 133.
Quotes a letter to the Philadelphia Public Ledger (1931.33) criticizing Whitman upon his entry into the Hall of Fame. Morley recalls finding Whitman's work in a Russian bookstore in New York. His prose is "one of the greatest American testimonies," "certainly as important as his poetry, a book that we neglect at our intellectual peril."

18 RASCOE, BURTON. Titans of Literature from Homer to the Present. New York: Blue Ribbon Books. "Whitman the Prophet," pp. 391-94; also 226, 322, 421.
Whitman is certainly a poet, maintaining faith in democracy despite its degradation, inventing a form and poetic expression entirely new and individual. At its best, his poetry is "an exalted song of a healthy and hearty enjoyment of life." Life sketch. Many believe Whitman's boasts of love affairs and children were meant to cover up his homosexuality. "Much of the distaste which we feel for some of the 'friendship' poems of Whitman is due to his abnormality." Yet his tendencies may have been "wholly unknown to him," sublimated into poetry, impossible to accept because of his puritanical background and contemporary mores. He never became the poet of the people as he had hoped, because the people

still hold "the eighteenth and nineteenth century inclination to regard literature as something like wax flowers under glass."

19 SHERMAN, STUART P. The Emotional Discovery of America and Other Essays. New York: Farrar & Rinehart. "The Emotional Discovery of America," pp. 20-29.
Whitman, Thoreau, and Emerson are presented as the three great explorers whose emotional discovery of America revealed the importance of the here and now, in their "essential unamity of theory, of feeling, of purpose, and of courage." The ideas Whitman expressed were probably shaped by Thoreau or Emerson before him; what he added was "the exuberant richness and fecundative ardor of his emotional nature." This trio's principles remain relevant, as does their concern for the advancement of letters. (See Addenda.)

20 WARD, A. C. American Literature, 1880-1930. New York: Lincoln Macveagh, Dial Press. "Walt Whitman," pp. 33-41.
Whitman's preparation as a poet included writing in traditional meters, eventually rejected because of his "passion for the exact renderings of experience." Both civilized and primitive, he introduced frankness and virility into American verse. He is unique because universal. America provided "a suitably extensive environment" for poetry on a heroic scale. His temperament was "akin to natural forces." He established free verse by using it consistently, though his is both good and bad. He is great because he revitalized literature.

21 _____. Landmarks in Literature. London: Methuen & Co. "Whitman," pp. 170-76.
Whitman, "the New Man" who gives the reader a blood transfusion, is "Adam reborn," rediscovering the natural world and the self. His poetry presents problems because of this new vision and his all-inclusiveness. His work confounds the puritan, although sex is not "disproportionately stressed." His verse is musical, not formless but patterned on larger, natural models.

22 WILLIAMS, WILLIAM CARLOS. A Novelette and Other Prose. Toulon, France: TO. "Marianne Moore," p. 61.
Incidental reference: Only poems "shall separate the good Whitman from the bad."

PERIODICALS

23 FURNESS, CLIFTON JOSEPH. "Walt Whitman's Estimate of Shakespeare." Harvard Studies and Notes in Philology and Literature 14 (1932), 1-33.
Whitman approached Shakespeare from a scholarly as well as an appreciative and

1932

purely literary standpoint. He favored the
chronicle plays for displaying Shakespeare's
oratory and the "decaying social fabric."
He gradually reconciled his contradictory
statements about the place in literature
merited by Shakespeare, whom he regarded as
a rival.

24 RIDLEY, HILDA. "Walt Whitman and Anne
Gilchrist." Dalhousie Review 11 (January),
521-26. Illustrated.
Reprint of 1923.43.

25 CROCKER, LIONELL. "The Rhetorical Influence of
Henry Ward Beecher " Quarterly Journal of
Speech 18 (February), 32-37.
Incidentally cites parallel between
Beecher and Whitman from Rourke (1927.20).

26 HOWARD, LEON. "For a Critique of Whitman's
Transcendentalism." Modern Language Notes
47 (February), 79-85.
Whitman's message of the individual's
limitless potential is similar to that of
transcendentalism, though different in conception of man's ultimate realization.
"Myself" 5, describing an experience resembling that in Emerson's Nature, differs
in the importance given the body.

27 MABBOTT, THOMAS OLLIVE, and SILVER, ROLLO G.
"Mr. Whitman Reconsiders." Colophon 9
(February), 1-8.
Reprint of 1879.41.
Notes changes Whitman made when including
part of this interview in Prose Works as
"An Interviewer's Item." He deleted his
negative appraisals of American authors,
which the notes compare with his criticisms
of them elsewhere.

28 STOVALL, FLOYD. "Main Drifts in Whitman's
Poetry." American Literature 4 (March),
3-21.
Whitman's development falls into three
periods, marked off by four key-poems which
are most characteristic of their respective
periods. "Myself" stresses love of freedom
with a materialistic rather than religious
emphasis. "Cradle" and "Lilacs" perfect
artistic works, suggest an emotional crisis,
perhaps the loss of a lover; death for
Whitman became the consoler. "Calamus"
depicts two types of love which can be
explained without reference to "sexual abnormality." "Lilacs" fuses this period's
great themes: love, death, and nationalism.
"Passage," his "most profound and characteristic work," has multiple levels and
international tendencies. In depicting the
progress of a specific, nontypical personality, Whitman moves from interest in life
through thought of death to hope of immortality. His poetic career follows the
major drifts of his time: political,
philosophical, religious. Used in 1934.16.

29 ANON. "$1,100 for Whitman Book." New York
Times (10 March), 19:6.
Notes sale at auction of a first
edition.

30 GLISKSBERG [sic], CHARLES I. "Walt Whitman in
the Civil War." Revue Anglo-Américaine 9
(April), 327-31.
Corrects misinformation about events
and chronology in Jean Catel's article (in
French) in Revue Anglo-Américaine (June
1926).

31 HOLLOWAY, EMORY. "Whitman as Journalist."
Saturday Review of Literature 8 (23 April),
677, 679-80.
Quotes and comments on Brooklyn Times
articles (see 1932.11), in which Whitman
"writes with a detachment which measures
the restraint imposed upon the journalist
by the philosopher and the artist." These
articles contain "the germination of various
poems" and Whitman's modern reaction to
certain problems. His political, literary,
and social beliefs are described.

32 BIRSS, JOHN HOWARD. "Whitman on Arnold: an
Uncollected Comment." Modern Language
Notes 47 (May), 316-17.
Reprints from New York Herald (April
1888) Whitman's comment on Arnold's death;
quotes other comments showing Whitman's
rejection of Arnold as significant for the
modern world.

33 ZUNDER, T. A. "Walt Whitman and Nathaniel
Hawthorne." Modern Language Notes 47
(May), 314-16.
Reprints commentary on Hawthorne from
Eagle, including a "hitherto unreprinted
editorial" of 1846. Hawthorne has left no
reference to Whitman.

34 ANON. "$1,000 for 'Book of Hours.'" New York
Times (12 May), 17:5.
Notes sale at auction of 1855 Leaves
for $540.

35 ALLINSON, ANNE C. E. "The Distaff--In View Of
A Poetic Event At The College On The Hill--
A Personal Selecting From Walt Whitman."
Providence Evening Bulletin (18 May).
On the occasion of the Saunders collection coming to Brown University. She could
forego Whitman's "most characteristic verse,
ringing the changes on soul and body, on
'physiology from top to toe,' on 'I' and
'Self,'" but not the three poems she selects
and quotes as Whitman's greatest, with comments: "Captain," "Lilacs" ("one of the
most beautiful creations in the English
language"), "Passage" (eloquent of past
and present achievements, inspiring the
soul). The latter two are summarized.

36 ANON. "Walt Whitman at Brown." Providence
Journal (20 May), 12:3-4.
Editorial on Brown's acquisition of the

Saunders collection of Whitman material:
Whitman is no mere figure of the past, for
"his sturdy individualism and hearty comradeship" are still needed for successful
human life. The democracy he celebrated,
though largely changed in form, still
exists in the lives and ideals of the mass
of Americans, whose voice he remains,
"still potent for inspiration and manly
cheer."

37 ANON. "$610 for Whitman Volume." New York
Times (26 May), 30:2.
Notes sale at auction of 1855 Leaves.

38 BIRSS, JOHN HOWARD. "Nicknames of the States--
a Note on Walt Whitman." American Speech
7 (June), 389.
Reprints a list of names for various
states' inhabitants from 1845 Broadway
Journal as possible source for Whitman's
list in "Slang in America," noting Whitman's
changes and omissions; however, a newspaper
clipping found among Whitman's scrapbooks
and papers may be the direct source.

39 CURTI, MERLE EUGENE. "Poets of Peace and the
Civil War." World Unity 10 (June), 150,
156-59.
Whitman had celebrated more exuberantly
than other American poets "the beauties of
peace and international solidarity," yet
had also expressed "ardent cultural patriotism" and given hints that he would glorify
war. The poetry he wrote during the war,
after some early exultation, showed him a
friend of peace, writing the only Civil War
poetry to rank with that of the greatest
poets who have condemned war. He emphasized
the sacredness of human life. His pacifism
is more virile and universal than that of
Emerson, Whittier, Lowell, and Longfellow,
since he knew the inhumanity of battle.
Though in the last war he was quoted in
support of pacifists, he was actually confused, being loyal and patriotic.

40 ANON. "Whitman Verse Lovers Visit Poet's Old
Haunts To Mark 113th Birthday." Camden
Courier-Post (1 June).
Birthday celebration took place at
Laurel Springs on Timber Creek, with Dr.
MacAlister speaking impressionistically of
Whitman's being favored by nature, whom he
sang in poetry which "instantly appeals"
and carries the mind beyond.

41 ANON. "A Whitman Dogwood." New York Times
(5 June), sec. 2, 1:4-5.
Describes tree planted by Whitman's
admirers at Timber Creek; describes the
time he spent there.

42 DUFFUS, R. L. "Walt Whitman, Editorial
Writer--A Few Traces of the Poet of 'Leaves
of Grass' May Be Found in His Collected
Contributions to The Brooklyn Times." New
York Times Book Review (5 June), 2. Illustrated.
Review of Holloway (1932.11). The
surprising conservatism of some of these
editorials is hard to reconcile with the
already published Leaves, although some of
his ideas do appear, regarding nature,
Emerson, "the great national song," "filthy
modesty." Perhaps the stereotyped opinions
are those of the paper's owner rather than
of Whitman. A poet "so thoroughly conscious
of what he intended to say and preserve as
Whitman was" would not care to have such
material published, though it is ably edited
except for the nonchronological ordering,
which does not allow insight into the
growth of Whitman's mind.

43 CALVERTON, V. F. "Leftward Ho!" Modern
Quarterly 6 (Summer), 29, 32.
Incidental references: American intellectuals need such a renewed faith as
Emerson and Whitman had. Whitman believed
that American democracy "had elevated the
poor man into the lord of creation." But
their faith is of the past since it falsely
praised man "as an individualist and not as
a collectivist."

44 DOS PASSOS, JOHN. "Whither the American
Writer (A Questionnaire)." Modern Quarterly
6 (Summer), 12.
Incidental reference in his response to
the questionnaire: "Walt Whitman's a hell
of a lot more revolutionary than any Russian
poet I've ever heard of."

45 SMITH, BERNARD. "The Literary Caravan."
Modern Quarterly 6 (Summer), 100-101.
Review of Lewisohn (1932.15) discussing
his comments on Whitman, valid regarding
aesthetics but overemphasizing the effects
of his homosexual content and neglecting to
study him in full relation to his age.

46 BENSON, ADOLPH B. "Walt Whitman's Interest in
Swedish Writers." Journal of English and
Germanic Philology 31 (July), 332-45.
Whitman as editor of the Eagle gave
Fredrika Bremer much attention, in commentary
quoted. Some American biographers like
Holloway have noted similarities in their
views or qualities, particularly with "her
moral and religious family philosophy." He
did not care for Jenny Lind. An account of
Swedenborg, reprinted in part, indicates
Whitman's interest in him, an influence yet
to be analyzed.

47 ARVIN, NEWTON. "Whitman's Individualism."
New Republic 71 (6 July), 212-13.
Review of Holloway (1932.11). Though
liberal critics present Whitman's message
as "acceptable to Herbert Hoover," Whitman's
roots are in American radicalism. He was
sympathetic with Tolstoy. Though too old
to make the transition from Paine to Marx,
in his Camden conversations "he spoke far
more in the manner of a Marxian than a

1932

Jacksonian." His early editorials reveal more concern for workers as an oppressed class than for race or other considerations. Vistas describes the shifting basis of democracy and opposition to capitalism. Whitman today would support the revolutionary labor movement.

48 BURKLUND, CARL EDWIN. "A Chant for America." Rebel Poet, no. 17 (October), 8.

Parody in Whitmanesque verse, celebrating America's having become "greatest in everything--radios, automobiles and souplines."

49 BIRSS, JOHN HOWARD. "Notes on Whitman." Notes and Queries 163 (29 October), 311-12.
"A Note on Whitman Bibliography": Quotes Laurence Maynard's editorial note inside an advance copy of Platt (1904.12) on a typographical error. "Whitman and the Armoury Square Hospital": Notes a description of the hospital in the Northern Monthly (December 1864) which will fill in knowledge of where Whitman worked.

1933

BOOKS

1 ADAMS, JAMES TRUSLOW. The Epic of America. Boston: Little, Brown, & Co., pp. v, 325, 326.
Quotation from "As a Strong Bird" as epigraph. "Whitman, as no one else before or after, caught a vision, so vast he could not master it, of the whole of America and of its tumultuous democratic dreams." He made "a clear attempt to put into winged and singing words the authentic American dream," of the perception of the uncommon in the common man.

2 ALBERTS, S. S. A Bibliography of the Works of Robinson Jeffers. New York: Random House, pp. 140, 207, 216, 234-35.
Includes reprint of 1927.38.
The common practice of criticizing Jeffers in terms of Whitman is absurd because of their dissimilar philosophy. "Una Jeffers writes that: R. J. says he owes less to W. W. than to most other poets of his era and sees no reason to link W. W. and R. J."

3 ANDERSON, SHERWOOD. Introduction to Leaves of Grass, Selected and Illustrated by Charles Cullen. New York: Thomas Y. Crowell, pp. v-vii.
Whitman is in the bones of America, and America must return to him. Anderson recalls finding copies of Leaves in middle-class homes "with the so-called ugly lustful passages cut out with scissors," although Whitman is "the most delicate and tender of all American singers." He, like the blacks,

brought song to America. He is the "singer of the great land" that Americans forget and to whom they must return, before finding the needed "brother to brother love" described by Whitman.

4 BRENNER, RICA. Twelve American Poets Before 1900. New York: Harcourt, Brace & Co. "Walt Whitman," pp. 229-66.
Traces Whitman's life, career, style, ideas, emphasizing his various contradictions as part of the democratic inclusiveness upon which his poetic theory is based: his predominating theme of human personality; his discovery of a free new form appropriate to America; his development of a "democratic comradeship"; at his best the excellence of his rhythm, language, and pictorial qualities, though some catalogues fail to move because lacking in detail. His significance lies more in his message than in his craftsmanship, emphasizing acceptance of the body, development of the individual, unity and identity with the deity, and an optimistic sense of continuity. He is "outstandingly the poet of America and of the nineteenth century." At its noblest, Leaves is both poetry and prophecy.

5 FRANK, WALDO. Introduction to The Collected Poems of Hart Crane. New York: Liveright Publishing Co., pp. vii-xxix, passim.
Notes influence on Crane of Whitman as a major American poet. Whitman's poetry is founded on the old order and on Jeffersonian politics. "Whitman gives the vision; Poe, however vaguely, the method." The volume includes reprints of "The Bridge" (1930.5) and "Modern Poetry" (1930.20).

6 GLICKSBERG, CHARLES I., ed. Walt Whitman and the Civil War: A Collection of Original Articles and Manuscripts. Philadelphia: University of Pennsylvania Press, 201 pp. Index.
Introduction: Whitman was involved in the war effort before going to Washington, as shown by these articles on his visits to New York hospitals in 1862. Barton's often unsubstantiated claims (1928.3) are answered. The war's profound influence on Whitman produced a stronger notion of the Union, developed his patriotism, strengthened his book's nationalistic purpose, although his health seemed to prevent his completing a true book about the war and his experience of it; his fragmentary accounts are nevertheless immediate, emotionally intense, vivid and honest.
Part 1. Original Writings--City Photographs: Articles signed Velsor Brush in the New York Leader, 1862, here reprinted, are probably written by Whitman, as shown here, and reveal his activities in hospitals and New York life. Manuscript notes, poem drafts, unpublished letters (to soldier Lewis Brown, Trowbridge, his mother, Abby

Price), Brooklyn <u>Daily Union</u> article are printed, with discussion, revealing his personality, concerns, style.

Part 2. Manuscript Material, Diary for 1863: Whitman's notes on various aspects of the war, hospitals, and Lincoln are printed and discussed; some fragments throw light on Whitman's method of composition.

Appendix: List of newspaper clippings Whitman made, evidence of "the nature of Whitman's interest and his reactions to many phases of the Civil War," possible source material for him as well.

7 HICKS, GRANVILLE. <u>The Great Tradition: An Interpretation of American Literature Since the Civil War</u>. New York: International Publishers, Macmillan Co., pp. 20-31; also 14, 17, 32, 57, 89, 90, 130, 131, 155, 237, 242, 291, 293, 305; bibliographic note, 308. Revised: 1935.6.

Whitman led the way to "the new American literature, the literature of the industrial era," by recognizing in his poetry all the elements of life making up the chaos that was contemporary America, even though he can be faulted for his lack of form and discipline. He provided no second step to improving the quality of American life beyond the initial effort of understanding, perceiving, and recording the reality as his earlier and later contemporaries did not choose to do. He hardly knew that his two beliefs, "unlimited expression of the individual will" and "the progress of the cohered mass," might conflict, yet he increasingly saw, "despite his deep-seated individualism," that "these men he admired must organize themselves for the conquest of power." Whitman and Dickinson are presented as complementary (he expansive and broad, she intensive and narrow, the future lying with him).

8 MORDELL, ALBERT. <u>Quaker Militant: John Greenleaf Whittier</u>. Boston and New York: Houghton Mifflin Co., pp. xvii, xviii, 160, 242, 267-70, 302.

Traces connections of Whittier and Whitman. In throwing <u>Leaves</u> into the fire, a story that may be believed, Whittier "confessed that he could not conceal his own inner thoughts and desires from Whitman." He resented Whitman's open treatment of sex, being somewhat repressed himself. They were similar, Quaker (though Whitman was Hicksite), interested in reform and love for the common people; however, "Whitman was more independent, more original, more masculine," with "the greater mind," but "not heroic like Whittier." Whitman was always fairer than Whittier in estimating the other poet.

9 NEWTON, A. EDWARD. <u>End Papers: Literary Recreations</u>. Boston: Little, Brown, & Co. "Carolyn Wells and Her Books," pp. 209-12.

Newton encouraged Wells to collect Whitman, "destined to take an important place" as a "yelper--of the brotherhood of man." Her collection became outstanding. He prophesies that the first edition of <u>Leaves</u> "will reach a higher figure than any other important book published in the nineteenth century."

10 WINWAR, FRANCES. <u>Poor Splendid Wings: The Rossettis and their Circle</u>. Boston: Little, Brown, & Co., pp. 125, 199, 224, 306-9, 318, 384.

Notes Scott's introduction of <u>Leaves</u> to the Rossettis, Whitman's not going to war because he opposed the taking of life, Watts's instrumentality in Swinburne's rejection of Whitman; traces the relationship with Gilchrist, whom Whitman could not love because of his hopeless love for a married lady, being also "anxious only for stockinged comfort in his emotional life." Before her support of him he had few defenders in England.

PERIODICALS

11 CAMPBELL, KILLIS. Review of Barrus (1931.1). <u>American Literature</u> 4 (January), 398-99.

This "extraordinarily full" record sheds much light on Whitman, giving the fullest commentary on his early reputation yet assembled.

12 ZUNDER, THEODORE A. "Whitman Interviews Barnum." <u>Modern Language Notes</u> 48 (January), 40.

Reprints an uncollected item from the <u>Eagle</u> (23 May 1846) quoting Barnum's comments on the differences between Europe and America, shortly after his arrival in New York.

13 BIRSS, JOHN HOWARD. "A Satire on Whitman." <u>Notes and Queries</u> 164 (7 January), 6-7.

Quotes with brief comment the Whitman passages of <u>The Obliviad</u> (1879.6).

*14 BLODGETT, HAROLD W. "Walt Whitman's Dartmouth Visit." <u>Dartmouth Alumni Magazine</u> 25 (February), 13-15.

Reprinted: Whitman Supplement 1972.

Account of Whitman's being asked to address the graduating class and feeling honored, not knowing that his invitation was in part due to students' desires to annoy the more conservative members of the faculty, although other students, especially Charles Ransom Miller, were eager to hear him.

15 HOLLOWAY, EMORY. "Walt Whitman's Visit to the Shakers." <u>Colophon</u> 13 (February), 110-19.

Prints Whitman's notebook descriptions with introductory explanation and editorial notes; a facsimile page is bound in.

1933

16 BRADLEY, SCULLEY. "'Mr. Walter Whitman.'"
Bookman 76 (March), 227-32.
When Whitman went to Camden, he "was
destined still to live a score of years and
write much of his best poetry and all of
his best prose." Timber Creek and the old
Stafford house are described, with directions. Bradley records a conversation with
John Rowan, who as a young man working on
the Stafford farm knew and liked Whitman
when he visited. He describes Whitman's
nude mud-bathing, which caused people to
talk; his knowledge of birds, flowers,
farming; his talk about Lincoln. Such
recollections are typical of the impression
Whitman made "upon a simple people when he
lived and moved among them." (Some of this
article is used in 1933.31.)

17 MABBOTT, THOMAS O., and SILVER, ROLLO G.
"William Winter's Serious Parody of Walt
Whitman." American Literature 5 (March),
63-66.
Winter said many harsh things about
Whitman, perhaps having forgotten his
imitation of Whitman (1860.64), here re-
printed.

18 MONROE, WILL S. "Whitman and the Professors."
American Mercury 28 (March), 377-78.
Few American professors discussed
Whitman before 1910, Hiram Corson being the
notable exception; students recall hearing
him mention Whitman favorably in lectures
as early as 1859. English and Irish professors, especially Dowden, show a finer
record.

19 D[AVIS], W[ILLIAM] H[ARPER]. "Walt Whitman
Walks Into the Grolier Club." American
Book Collector 3 (April), 221-22.
Parody presenting Whitman addressing
books, authors, and scholars.

20 RANKIN, HENRY B. "Lincoln Savors Walt
Whitman." Christian Science Monitor (1
April), 9:2-3.
Extract reprinted from 1924.20.

21 BIRSS, JOHN HOWARD. "Whitman and Herman
Melville." Notes and Queries 164 (22
April), 280.
Reprints Whitman's brief and hurried
notice of Melville's Omoo for the Eagle
(5 May 1847), "not to be read as a well-
considered judgment, despite Whitman's
ability (shown here to some extent) to form
spontaneous and incisive critical opinion."

22 HOLLOWAY, EMORY. "Notes from a Whitman
Student's Scrapbook." American Scholar 2
(May), 269-78.
Quotes a Whitman manuscript about the
war. Through Whitman's interest in the
common soldier rather than heroic battle
action, he discovered his concepts of the
average man as the state's concern and of
adhesiveness as the cement of democracy

rather than "a purely personal emotion."
In a note written before the 1855 Leaves,
Whitman urges himself to emphasize the
reader. An essay on the soul reveals
similarities to later poetry. A passage
from Carlyle which Whitman found applicable
to himself is noted.

23 NEUMANN, HENRY. "Walt Whitman." American
Scholar 2 (May), 260-68. Portrait.
Whitman's hopeful spirit is not quite
appropriate in today's world of mass production and big business. He was unsurpassed
"in putting into music the spirit of the
frontier." But complete self-reliance is
no longer possible. He was not a great
thinker, "but some pages throb with a life
which may continue to disturb" future
American readers. He has much sympathy,
with faith in man's worth; even his love
for himself did not detract from his love
for others. Advocacy of the common did not
mean conformity. His love for America may
help America "achieve a truer self-aware-
ness," even if his work may fail to accord
with the temper of a particular decade.

24 ANON. "Say Whitman Saw 'Place for All Kinds.'"
Brooklyn Daily Eagle (1 June), 5.
At local celebration of Whitman's
birth, John Erskine took issue with the
interpretation placed on his social philosophy by communists, citing the broad range
of individual differences Whitman extolled.
Cleveland Rodgers spoke on political concerns of Whitman.

25 ANON. "Walt Whitman Honored." New York Times
(1 June), 17:2.
Account of birthday celebration at the
Camden house.

26 D., J. B. "Rediscovering Walt Whitman."
Christian Science Monitor (26 July), 7:1-2.
Reading Leaves again is invigorating,
with Whitman's voice speaking directly to
the reader. Whitman perceived "the gran-
duer, the fluid beauty, the unplumbed
splendor of creation," although at times
only glimpses of it emerge in his poetry.
His times are described, important for
understanding him and his concept of democracy. He became a symbol of his times, of
America's vastness and virility. His role
as prophet occasionally makes him difficult
to read, but he is rewarding. Whether
America's greatest poet or not, he is
definitely "her first autochthonous one,"
providing the key to all who have come
after him.

27 ALLEN, GAY W. "Biblical Analogies for Walt
Whitman's Prosody." Revue Anglo-Américaine
10 (August), 490-507.
The line is the basic unit of rhythm in
biblical verse and in Whitman, with various
types of parallelism (including the device
of the "envelope") and reiteration, used to

provide structure. Whitman's rhythm may be a phenomenon of nature or intuitive thinking but is probably based at least partly on the Hebraic rhapsodists. Whitman makes use of grammatical rhythm (repetition of parts of speech), as Jannaccone and Catel note. Whitman uses parentheses to change or suspend the rhythmic pattern. He repeats words not merely for emphasis but mainly for their rhythmical effects, thus showing his art. (This material, omitting biblical analyses, is largely used in 1935.2.)

28 ZUNDER, THEODORE A. "William B. Marsh: The First Editor of the Brooklyn Daily Eagle." American Book Collector 4 (August), 93-95.
    Whitman helped to raise money for Marsh's family after his death, when Whitman succeeded him as editor; he called attention in print to Marsh's literary performances.

29 STARKE, AUBREY. "Lanier's Appreciation of Whitman." American Scholar 2 (October), 398-408.
    Lanier's praise of Leaves is quoted from letters to Taylor, from whom he had borrowed the book. Although in his lectures ("The English Novel") he defended Whitman from charges made against him, such friendly allusions were deleted when Browne edited the lectures for publication (1883.5), though restored by Mrs. Lanier later (1897.14). The prevailing impression has emphasized his disapproval of Whitman, but he recognized in Whitman beauty, prophecy, and manhood and shared his ideals of personal liberty, independence from mere tradition and orthodoxy, a purer national **life, and interest in new forms of verse.** Whitman's comments on Lanier are not unfriendly.

30 HOLLOWAY, EMORY. "Whitmania." New York Herald-Tribune Books 10 (8 October), 15.
    Review of Glicksberg (1933.6), which corrects Barton's errors and throws light on Whitman's war experience.

31 BRADLEY, SCULLEY. "Walt Whitman on Timber Creek." American Literature 5 (November), 235-46.
    The discovery of the actual location of Whitman's Specimen description serves to substantiate at least part of his autobiographical notes, upon which much doubt has recently been cast. Members of the Stafford family still living testify to his record, recalling Whitman as "a serene, quiet, thoughtful man, gentle and sympathetic." "It has seldom fallen to the lot of a philosophical poet to be put so thoroughly to the test of his theory and to survive the ordeal so successfully," greatly assisted by his love of nature and the capacity for observation. The Stafford family testify to his working on his writing in the outdoors. Nature's realities

had always persisted in his consciousness, even in city life. The area's people knew him as one who loved them and whom they loved. (This article uses some of the material in 1933.16.)

32 GOHDES, CLARENCE. Review of Glicksberg (1933.6). American Literature 5 (November), 290-91.
    Describes contents; praises the scholarship.

33 ANON. "$18,413 Paid for Books." New York Times (8 December), 21:6.
    Notes sale at auction of 1855 Leaves for $450.

34 CHESTERTON, G. K. "The Great Loafer." Chicago Herald and Examiner (9 December).
    Discussion of Hicks (1933.7) who tries to "remould everything upon the Communist model." Whitman hardly fits in with modern Communism. His great love for all of humanity has nothing in common with the modern version of human sympathy, as found in Dreiser.

35 ANON. "L. C. Leiter Books Sold." New York Times (16 December), 16:4.
    Notes sale at auction of 1855 Leaves for $360.

1934

BOOKS

1 BLODGETT, HAROLD. Walt Whitman in England. Ithaca: Cornell University Press. London: Humphrey Milford, Oxford University Press, 244 pp. Bibliography, pp. 223-34. Includes reprints of 1929.45; 1930.32; 1929.57 (revised as introduction and conclusion).
    Examination of Whitman's critical reception in England by concentrating on major figures and the development of their relationships, critical and personal, with Whitman, using quotations from letters, biographies, criticism. Chapters are devoted to Rossetti; Dowden; Symonds; Buchanan; Gilchrist; Swinburne; Tennyson; "Other Poets" (Morris, Browning, Austin, Houghton, Locker-Lampson, Lionel Johnson, Noel, Wilde, Thomson, Edwin Arnold, Richard Hengist Horne, Watson, Barlow); "The Major Prophets" (Ruskin, Carlyle, Matthew Arnold, Eliot, Stevenson); "The Professors and the Journalists" (especially O'Grady, Rolleston, York Powell, Forman, Rhys, Gosse); Carpenter, Ellis, and the "Bolton College."

2 BODKIN, MAUD. Archetypal Patterns in Poetry. London, New York, Toronto: Geoffrey Cumberlege, Oxford University Press, pp. 130-31.
    Whitman's branch of lilac in "Lilacs" is a parallel to Virgil's golden bough.

1934

Here it is contrasted as a romantic treatment with the classical treatment of the
mystery of death in the Aeneid, Book 6.

3 BROOKS, VAN WYCK. Three Essays on America.
New York: E. P. Dutton & Co. "The Precipitant," pp. 77-89; also 201, 202, 203, 212.
Reprint with minor changes and deletions
of 1915.5.

4 BULLETT, GERALD. "Walt Whitman." In Great
Democrats, edited by A. Barratt Brown.
London: Ivor Nicholson & Watson, pp. 651-
62; also 106-7, 111, 114, 702-3.
Revision of 1924.3.
    Biographical sketch. Leaves is "either
more or less than a piece of literature."
Believing in divinity attainable by anyone,
Whitman rejects "the crude dualism of the
puritan." All he includes, "tedious or
not," is "germane to his purpose." Despite
possibly false notes or unclear expressions,
Leaves is "a work of great cumulative
power" with important ideas. Specimen is
"a real complement" to Leaves. With "a
greatness that was personal rather than
intellectual, and spiritual rather than
literary," Whitman was "a great lover,"
with an incalculable influence on and
attraction for "the passionate, the affectionate, the turbulent, the preachers of
an all-inclusive charity." Minor references
to Whitman in Brown's conclusion and Henry
Nevinson's essay on Carpenter.

5 GOHDES, CLARENCE, and BAUM, PAULL FRANKLIN,
eds. Letters of William Michael Rossetti
Concerning Whitman, Blake, and Shelley to
Anne Gilchrist and Her Son Herbert
Gilchrist. Durham, N.C.: Duke University
Press, 201 pp.
    Rossetti's letters printed here usually
concern Whitman, disagreeing with Gilchrist
over Whitman's bluntness in physical matters
and flaws in diction. Preparation and publication of her article (1870.4) are discussed, as well as efforts to assist
Whitman financially, beginning with her
suggestion in 1873. Whitman is compared
with Homer, Shakespeare, Christ, and
praised for his great personality and
boundless fellowship. Excerpts from some
of the letters have appeared in 1887.6 and
1918.9. Appendix includes Rossetti's
letter to President Cleveland seeking
recognition for Whitman as a great American,
considered "by many of the best minds in
Europe" to be "the poet of largest scope,
strongest initiative, and widest future,
alive in the world"; a Whitman circular
(letter from Whitman of 1886 with list of
contributors); Rossetti's letters to Charles
Aldrich, generally concerning the subscription for Whitman.

6 HARTLEY, L. CONRAD. "Walt Whitman." Papers
of the Manchester Literary Club. Vol. 10.
Manchester, Eng.: n.p. pp. 182-203.

Hartley says he has nothing to add to
his earlier interpretation of Whitman
(1908.8). Whitman, in his quest for self-
understanding, found doubts and sufferings.
He is full of contradictions, so many fail
to see his true unity. His life, illuminating criticisms, and connections with
other writers are described. Vistas and
the 1855 Preface are praised. Traubel's
book (1906.22), with "pitiless" accuracy,
is an excellent aid to studying Whitman.
A more logical presentation was beyond
Whitman for he wrote in moments of inspiration, driven by the idea of unity which was
part of his belief in immortality. Words
were inadequate "to express the knowledge
born of faith." Leaves is pervaded by the
Greek philosophy of acquiescence and by an
emphasis on love.

7 KREYMBORG, ALFRED. A History of American
Poetry: Our Singing Strength. New York:
Tudor Publishing Co. "Whitman and the
Democratic Cosmos," pp. 206-30.
Reprint of 1929.13.

8 LUCCOCK, HALFORD E. Contemporary American
Literature and Religion. Chicago and New
York: Willett, Clark & Co., pp. 71, 175.
    Whitman is an outstanding exception to
the usual conventional apprenticeship of
most earlier American authors. His complaint
that American literature did not furnish
any heroic models is pertinent today.

9 PARRY, ALBERT. Garrets and Pretenders: A
History of Bohemianism in America. New
York: Covici-Friede. "Walt at Pfaff's--
and the King of Bohemia," pp. 38-43; also
passim per index.
    Describes Whitman and his relationships
with people at Pfaff's, especially Henry
Clapp, Ada Clare, and George Arnold, with
whom he quarreled.

10 PHELPS, WILLIAM LYON. What I Like in Poetry.
New York and London: Charles Scribner's
Sons, pp. 135, 524-35.
    Anthologizes poems with brief introduc-
tory comments: If Whitman could have
spoken "Captain" over the radio, "the
effect and the response could not have been
more immediate." Even Whitman would be
astonished at his future fame and influence.
There is no finer "apologia in verse" than
his famous lines, "Spirit."

11 POUND, EZRA. ABC of Reading. New Haven:
Yale University Press, pp. 65, 163, 181.
    Pound cannot now find the thirty pages
he once thought were well-written in
Whitman. However, Whitman's faults are
superficial, for "he does convey an image
of his time," more than poets who limited
themselves to what was considered suitable
for literary expression. "The only way to
enjoy Whitman thoroughly is to concentrate
on his fundamental meaning." His flaw is

that he sporadically conforms to regular
meter or literary language.

12 POWELL, LAWRENCE CLARK. <u>Robinson Jeffers:</u>
<u>The Man and His Work</u>. Los Angeles:
Primavera Press, pp. 31, 110-11, 116, 178,
182, 191, 202.
    Incidental comparisons of Jeffers to
Whitman are based on 1931.58.

13 POWYS, JOHN COWPER. <u>Autobiography</u>. New York:
Simon & Schuster, pp. 163, 263, 275, 343,
432, 495-96, 525, 542.
    Describes his mania for Whitman, the
"bold individualism" of whose poetry
satisfied the cravings of his nature like
no other, though Whitman's optimism seemed
extravagant. The creative wave that came
with the World War was a return to Whitman's
spirit. His "gigantic sense of well-being"
suited the English from the start. Powys
describes the muscular young men of America,
"super-normal pillars of society," about
whom Whitman wrote "his lovely and passionate 'Calamus' poems."

14 REINHARDT, AURELIA HENRY. Introduction to
<u>Song of the Redwood Tree by Walt Whitman</u>.
Mills College, Calif.: Eucalyptus Press,
4 pp.
    Traces background of "Redwood" (here
printed with illustrations), its "primal
forces," with description of its glimpse
of creation.

15 SAUNDERS, HENRY S. <u>An Introduction to Walt</u>
<u>Whitman</u>. Toronto: Henry S. Saunders.
Ltd. ed. in typescript, 25 pp. Two
portraits.
    Biographical sketch. Quotations from
others show Whitman's magnetic personality.
"Backward Glance" explains his poetry's
purpose; <u>Specimen</u> gives a different view of
the man. Most literary leaders of America
consider Whitman their greatest poet.
Though sometimes denied as poetry, his work
remains a powerful and convincing force.
Sixteen poems are listed as likely "to make
a favorable impression" on those unfamiliar
with Whitman. "Salut" provides an example
of Whitman's catalogues: "if they are read
carefully they build up, by suggestion, a
force which could not be obtained in any
other way."

16 STOVALL, FLOYD, ed. <u>Walt Whitman: Representa-</u>
<u>tive Selections, with Introduction, Bibliog-</u>
<u>raphy, and Notes</u>. New York: American Book
Co. Introduction, pp. xi-lii; selected bibliography, liii-lx; chronological table,
lxi-lxiii; notes, 405-18.
Revised: 1939.12.
    Whitman, as the culmination of romantic
idealism in America and the beginning of
scientific realism, was never popular
because he was suspected by both factions.
He attempted to forestall the error of the
usual attempts to discover a writer's per-

sonality in his biography rather than in
his work "by recreating his essential self
in his poems and consciously suppressing
all else." He chose to demonstrate the
individual's potential for all human qualities through himself. He is "a true primitive, the archetypal man, simple, universal,
bisexual," desiring independence and unity,
the eternal dilemma of democracy and humanity. He developed from the prevailing
philosophies of his day, moving into the
future with an anchor in the past. His
early life is traced: his political thought,
weak early writings, intellectual development into the poet of <u>Leaves</u>. The 1855
Preface is explained, emphasizing the qualities of the American character which pre-
dominate in Whitman's own personality. His
primary attributes, egotism, sensuousness,
and sentiment, are the basis for his book's
dominant themes, democracy, love, and religion, traced through his poetry in a discussion largely based on 1932.28. His
later prose has a "cautious and conservative
tone," indicating a preference for evolution
over revolution. He had critical acumen in
appraising his own work and that of his
contemporaries, coming to realize that pure
realism must be transcended to spiritualize
the material. He founded his new verse
form as more appropriate to America, its
unit of rhythm the phrase, its unit of
thought the line, its features being repetition, parallelism, and a high rhetorical
tone. Notes to the poems (here printed in
chronological order) include explications,
background, information on the original
appearance or form.

17 WHARTON, EDITH. <u>A Backward Glance</u>. New York
and London: D. Appleton-Century Croft,
p. 186.
    Title from Whitman. Description of
Henry James regarding Whitman's poetry
beautifully, his talk with her about
Whitman, whom they both thought the greatest
of American poets: "Oh, yes, a great genius; undoubtedly a very great genius! Only
one cannot help deploring his too-extensive
acquaintance with the foreign languages."

18 WILSON, DAVID ALEC, and MacARTHUR, DAVID
WILSON. <u>Carlyle in Old Age (1856-1881)</u>.
London: Kegan Paul, Trench, Trubner & Co.,
pp. 240, 261.
    Allingham found Carlyle reading <u>Vistas</u>
on 3 October 1872; though he had earlier
compared Whitman to "the town-bull" (see
1911.10), "on this occasion he praised him
somewhat."

PERIODICALS

19 HARRISON, JOSEPH B. "Modernity and Walt
Whitman." <u>Frontier and Midland</u> 14 (January),
101-9.
    "Whitman's right to speak for his Amer-
ica must be examined on other grounds" than

psychological. He may be termed a modern because he recognizes the failures in democracy and other ideals, even while believing in ideals we have since rejected. He "believed chiefly in the creative life," the world's readiness for some "human constructive effort." His affirmation, no mere resignation, is grounded in reality; thus perfection is the very process of becoming and not some lost state to which becoming will lead us, as in Emerson. For Whitman, democracy is a driving force rather than an established fact.

20 SILVER, ROLLO G. "Whitman and Dickens." American Literature 5 (January), 370-71.
    Identifies the source of an undated Whitman manuscript in Uncollected (1921.16) as an 1880 Dickens biography.

21 RUKEYSER, MURIEL. "The Committee-Room" (from a long poem, "Theory of Flight"). Dynamo: A Journal of Revolutionary Poetry 1, no. 2 (March-April), 7.
    Whitman is among several other revolutionary literary figures deplored by modern authority figures.

22 FRUMP, TIMOTHY. "A Whitman Manuscript." Notes and Queries 166 (24 March), 206.
    Announces New York Public Library's acquisition of an early manuscript draft of "Cradle," containing some excellent variants which should be examined carefully.

23 REED, HARRY B. "The Heraclitan Obsession of Walt Whitman." Personalist 15 (April), 125-38.
    Discussion of the reasons for Whitman's "ceaseless and indiscriminate motion." He followed the contemporary spirit of free inquiry regarding religion. His pantheism and his belief in personality and progressive integration are described. His work does not attain the unity he intended because he could not "rise above the infinite variety of concrete things." Although he sees beyond the maelstrom, what is important for him is "the cosmic flight" through many kinetic images.

24 O'CONNOR, W. D. "Walt Whitman in 1866 and 1867. Three Letters by W. D. O'Connor." Book Hunter (May), 3-9.
    A brief introduction describes O'Connor's courageous support for Whitman, whom most Americans failed to recognize as "the only truly American writer" and one of the greatest poets of all time. Three long letters from O'Connor to Conway are printed, from May 1866 and February and May 1867: Whitman needs not the money Conway offers but rather recognition as a poet, through "exhaustive analysis" and clear interpretations of his poems. Such criticism has been published in England but not in America, where magazines remain hostile to him. English articles, however (Conway,

1866.22; Strangford, 1866.13; and Swinburne's comparison of Whitman to Blake, later published in 1868.3); are wrong-headed in emphasizing Whitman's eccentricity, since he is universal, and in noting parallels with past and foreign writers, for he is primarily American. O'Connor has high hopes for Symonds's article planned for the Edinburgh Review. Leaves must not be expurgated for England, because everything in it is included for a deeply religious purpose, and its scope and spirit merit a high place. O'Connor praises Burroughs's book (1867.1); notes Professor Newman's response to Good Gray Poet (1866.2) and praise for Whitman; predicts that his good choice of epithet for Whitman will last; describes Whitman's appearance and personality incidentally.

25 ADIMARI, RALPH. "Leaves of Grass--First Edition." American Book Collector 5 (May-June), 150-52.
    Presents evidence for Leaves being put on sale on 4 July; discusses number of copies printed, advertising, sales, "first impartial printed review" (1855.2) by Dana, who probably did not know Whitman and who did not consider his poetry worthy to include in his 1858 anthology.

26 AUSLANDER, JOSEPH. "Walt Whitman: His Neighbors Thought Him Smart But Lazy." Chicago Herald and Examiner (14 May), 11:6.
    Extract reprinted from 1927.1.
    Continued 1934.27.

27 _____. "Walt Whitman." Chicago Herald and Examiner (16 May), 11:2-3.
    Continues 1934.26. Continued 1934.28.

28 _____. "Walt Whitman: 'Leaves of Grass' Bewildered Critics and Editors." Chicago Herald and Examiner (17 May), 13:6.
    Continues 1934.27. Concluded 1934.29.

29 _____. "Walt Whitman: He Was the First True American Singer." Chicago Herald and Examiner (21 May), 15:6.
    Concludes 1934.28.

30 GLICKSBERG, CHARLES I. "Walt Whitman and Heinrich Zschokke." Notes and Queries 166 (2 June), 382-84.
    Prints Whitman's notes and quotations from Zschokke, a mystic who adumbrated many of Emerson's ideas, with sentiments similar to Leaves.

31 CAMPBELL, KILLIS. "Miscellaneous Notes on Whitman." University of Texas Bulletin: Studies in English 14 (8 July), 116-22.
    "Bibliographical Notes": Notes variant versions of some poems; rejects "New Year's Day, 1848" (1892.69) as uncharacteristic in style of any Whitman work. "Literary Echoes in Leaves of Grass": Cites verbal borrowings from Shakespeare and other

allusions. "Coinages and Other Rare Words in Leaves of Grass": Cites examples. "Textual Errors in Leaves of Grass": Notes possible misprints or misspellings. "Whitman's Use of the Figure Metanoia": Cites nine examples from Leaves of metanoia, "making an assertion and then taking it back or modifying it," a figure appropriate to Whitman's contradictory impulse.

32 COOKE, Mrs. ALICE LOVELACE. "Whitman's Indebtedness to the Scientific Thought of His Day." University of Texas Bulletin: Studies in English 14 (8 July), 89-115.
"Whitman's Knowledge of Science": "A staunch believer in science," the most revolutionary movement of his day, Whitman was interested in most branches, with several scientific friends. "Whitman's Use of Contemporary Revelations in Astronomy": Examples from his poetry show his scientific ideas; sources are noted. "Whitman's Use of Contemporary Revelations in Geology": Whitman accepted the theory of evolution, current in America before Darwin. "Whitman's Use of Other Sciences": Phrenology, physiognomy, physiology. "Whitman's Conception of the Conflict Between Science and Religion": He always tried to reach beyond the mere concrete fact. He believed in a divine force, not a precise idea of God. He believed that the poet could reconcile science and religion.

*33 ANON. "Walt Marches On." Toronto Mail (14 July).
Quoted in Willard.
Whitman's current acceptance makes him "crowned and neglected," while before, "the fights between Whitmaniacs and the jeerers used to keep the question of his merit to the fore, and his lines in the mouths of supporters and detractors."

34 SILVER, ROLLO G. "Concerning Walt Whitman." Notes and Queries 167 (11 August), 96.
Notes two articles by Whitman in Life Illustrated which are being edited for publication.

35 ADMARI [sic], R. "Unknown Whitman Material." Saturday Review of Literature 11 (18 August), 56.
Letter noting his discovery of Whitman's hitherto unreprinted work in Life Illustrated as well as "a remarkable tribute by Fanny Fern," and announcing the preparation of his book with Holloway (1936.15).

36 VIRBIUS [pseud.?]. "Walt Whitman's Death [from a contemporary bulletin]." Notes and Queries 167 (18 August), 116.
Describes handwritten bulletin posted outside Whitman's house at the time of his death, its details agreeing with other accounts.

37 SILVER, ROLLO G. "Interviews with Walt Whitman." Notes and Queries 167 (25 August), 133.
Lists several newspaper interviews.

38 PARRY, ALBERT. "Walt Whitman in Russia." American Mercury 33 (September), 100-107.
Whitman's poetry in translation is popular in Russia and has played a part in the Soviets' struggles. Korney Chukovsky's original translations were rejected by editors until he rhymed some of them. Turgenev was interested in translating Leaves in 1872 but nothing has turned up. Tolstoy disapproved of Whitman's lack of a clear philosophy of life. Konstantin Balmont's advocacy and erroneous translations of Whitman were more harmful than beneficial, emphasizing mystic rather than democratic qualities. Other Russian misunderstandings and commentaries are cited. Acclaimed earlier for his mysticism, parallel to Russian philosophers, Whitman is now hailed as a revolutionary and imitated by class-conscious poets.

39 ALLEN, GAY WILSON. "Walt Whitman Bibliography, 1918-1934." Bulletin of Bibliography 15 (September-December), 84-88.
Revised: 1943. Reprinted: 1935.3.
Introduction explains sources for items. Part 1. Bibliography; Part 2. Editions and Reprints; Part 3. Books about Whitman. Concluded 1935.19.

40 SILVER, ROLLO G. "A Parody of Walt Whitman." Notes and Queries 167 (1 September), 150.
Notes Urner's "Grant" (1885.28), which does not equal Whitman's "Death of General Grant."

41 SAMUEL, RUTH A. "Walt Whitman: Democracy's Laureate." Fantasy 4 (Autumn), 39-41.
Impressionistic appreciation by a nineteen-year-old of Whitman's democratic, religious, and moral ideas. He stood on his own, while earlier American poets represented old rather than fresh thought. Some of his verse is not poetry by any stretch of the imagination and his efforts at conventional verse ("Captain") are unfortunate, but these lapses may be overlooked in view of the "wealth of the authentic Whitman."

42 ALLEN, GAY W. "Biblical Echoes in Whitman's Works." American Literature 6 (November), 302-15.
Whitman drew most of his biblical inspiration from the New Testament, next from the prophets. Biblical influence became deeper and more abstract in his mature work. The bulk of this article is lists: biblical allusions, paraphrases, and quotations (identifying specific biblical parallels for passages in his work); general or inclusive biblical allusions; index to the numbered items in the first list by book of the Bible.

1934

43 BAKER, PORTIA. "Walt Whitman and The Atlantic
Monthly." American Literature 6 (November),
283-301.
    Traces the coolness of the Atlantic's
various editors to Whitman and its few
mentions of him during his lifetime. If
they were influenced not only by personal
taste but by a knowledge of their audience,
one may judge that Whitman was never acceptable during his lifetime "to this conservative, select, but fairly large group."

44 BLODGETT, HAROLD. Review of Gohdes (1934.5).
American Literature 6 (November), 357-58.
    Describes contents of this "substantial
contribution" to the record of Whitman's
English connections.

45 CAMPBELL, KILLIS. "The Evolution of Whitman
as Artist." American Literature 6 (November), 254-63.
    "In mere animal vigor, in rude
strength," the 1855 and 1856 poems exceed
anything Whitman ever wrote, but they
represent also "the very peak of his formlessness." His later revisions on most of
his poems "testify to his deep concern for
his art" and enable us to trace his development as an artist. He gained in taste, "in
picturesqueness and in loveliness of
phrase," and "in the control of his verse
effects," with a tendency toward a brief
line and an iambic rhythm.

46 GLICKSBERG, CHARLES I. "Walt Whitman in
1862." American Literature 6 (November),
264-82.
    Describes and quotes jottings from
Whitman's 1862 notebook in the Library of
Congress, explaining his activity in this
hitherto-obscure year of Whitman's life.
Categories include memoranda of books to
read; fragments intended for elaboration
into poems; notes dealing with New York
history; notes that express concretely his
gospel of adhesiveness (recording meetings
and acquaintance with common men, mostly
stage-drivers, interest in whom should be
regarded not as homosexually based but as
evidence of his "bouyant, loving nature"
and as part of his "conception of the
democratic function of literature," the
basis of "Calamus"). The notebooks offer
"a vivid, panoramic view of life in New
York."

47 GOHDES, CLARENCE. Review of Blodgett (1934.1).
American Literature 6 (November), 355-57.
    Blodgett should have concentrated not
only on key figures but also on lesser-
known reviews. He lacks adequate explanation of the English interest in Whitman:
"that Emerson and others had prepared a
good many English writers for Whitman and
that not only do rebels like rebels but
that mystics find pleasure in mystics even
though they write free verse, howl praises
of America, and believe that sex is as im-

portant as friendship in the life of a
normal man." Blodgett should pay more
attention to these writers' sympathy with
Taine's theories, to the democratic movement (looking at Whitman's reputation in
the lower classes), and to the spread of
foreign interest in America after the Civil
War and the opening of the West.

48 MYERS, HENRY ALONZO. "Whitman's Conception of
the Spiritual Democracy, 1855-1856." American Literature 6 (November), 239-53.
Abridged: Bradley/Blodgett.
    Whitman is usually seen as poet of
political democracy and sexual emancipation,
his spiritual democracy ignored, although
the inner world and eternal law are his
major concerns. His poetry is a direct
consequence of his two principles, the unlimited individual and the equality of individuals. The 1855 Leaves poems are explicated in order; they reveal Whitman's
notion of spiritual democracy which was
never again presented in its entirety,
although at no time did he contradict any
of these principles. He always tried to
see his inner principle in relation to the
surface problems of society. He attacked
conventions only when they stood in the
way of his vision of reality. The continua-
tion of his vision in "Unfolded," "Brooklyn
Ferry," and "Salut" is briefly noted.

49 GLICKSBERG, CHARLES I. "Whitmaniana."
Saturday Review of Literature 11 (1 December), 324.
    Letter noting his discovery of three
articles by Whitman for a Brooklyn newspaper in 1860 and 1862, containing some
autobiographical passages.

50 SILVER, ROLLO G. "Walt Whitman's Letters."
Saturday Review of Literature 11 (8 December), 338.
    Letter requesting letters and postcards
of Whitman for his census.

1935

BOOKS

1 ABBOTT, CLAUDE COLLEER, ed. The Letters of
Gerard Manley Hopkins to Robert Bridges.
London: Oxford University Press, pp. 154-
58; 311-16 (reprint of 1874.10).
Reprinted: Miller; Hindus; Murphy.
    Hopkins's letter of 18 October 1882
notes similarities between Whitman's style
and his own and discusses him in terms of
meter (with an error in quotation). He
read Whitman selections in a review (the
Saintsbury one here reprinted), discovering
"Whitman's mind to be more like my own than
any other man's living. As he is a very
great scoundrel this is not a pleasant confession."

2 ALLEN, GAY WILSON. <u>American Prosody</u>. New
York: American Book Co. "Walt Whitman,"
pp. 217-43; also vii, xli, xliii, xliv,
100, 107, 132, 247, 270, 310, passim per
index; brief annotated bibliography, 242-43.
   Whitman's pronouncements on poetry are
generally ambiguous in reference, applying
either to his versification or to his content, although he believed that thought and
form should coincide. Discussion of his
prosody is based on 1933.27. Whitman's
persistent use of concrete objects demonstrates his concept of indirection, or
suggestion via metaphor, as the best way to
reproduce the actual imaginative response
in the reader, although it has confused
some readers. Except for his change from
conventional meter and rhyme around 1851,
his versification reveals no chronological
development, although the poems of his later
life, necessarily shorter because of his
physical condition, are more compact. Many
examples are used for illustration or
analysis, particularly from "Lilacs."

3 _____. <u>Walt Whitman Bibliography 1918-1934</u>.
Bulletin of Bibliography Pamphlets, no. 30.
Boston: F. W. Faxon Co. 33 pp.
Reprint of 1934.39 and 1935.18. Revised:
1943.

4 BENET, STEPHEN VINCENT. <u>Burning City: New
Poems</u>. New York: Farrar & Rinehart. "Ode
to Walt Whitman," pp. 26-41.
Reprint of 1935.24.

5 DEUTSCH, BABETTE. <u>This Modern Poetry</u>. New
York: W. W. Norton & Co., passim per index.
   Whitman sought to identify himself as
completely as possible with his place, time,
and people, celebrating life and America.
For him poetry had a religious, not a
pleasure-giving function. He is presented
throughout as a central point of comparison
with and influence on the modern poets in
form, spirit, and content.

6 HICKS, GRANVILLE. <u>The Great Tradition: An
Interpretation of American Literature Since
the Civil War</u>. Rev. ed. New York: International Publishers, Macmillan Co., pp. 20-
31, passim per 1933.7; also 328-29, 332.
Revision of 1933.7.
   The revisions are simply a reworking
of the original final chapter and the addition of a new final chapter, with minor
reference to Whitman.

7 KILGORE, MANLEY WOODBURY, and WOODBURY, GEORGE
FRANK, eds. <u>Personal Recollections of
English and American Poets</u>. Patten, Me.:
Privately printed. "Emerson in His Home,"
by Frank B. Sanborn (reprint of 1895.83),
pp. 30-36; "Conversations with Walt
Whitman," by Horace L. Traubel (reprint of
1896.24), 108-14; "The Religion of Walt
Whitman's Poems," by M. J. Savage (reprint
of 1894.48), 114-35.

8 ORAGE, A. R. <u>Selected Essays and Critical
Writings</u>, edited by Herbert Read and Denis
Saurat. London: Stanley Nott. "Whitman
in Short," p. 73.
   Whitman may be regarded either as a
man, with his writings mere documents of
self-revelation, or as a writer, his personal life being of no concern. He is important "as the anti-Euphues of English
style," as dangerous to read as Euphues,
"as mannered, and as much off the highway
of English letters," although "a draught of
Whitman now and then is a tonic." His
prose, however, was excellent, some of the
best America has produced; he should have
written only prose.

9 PERRY, BLISS. <u>And Gladly Teach: Reminiscences</u>.
Boston and New York: Houghton Mifflin Co.,
pp. 59, 75, 188-91, 194, 195, 211, 231-32.
   Recalls his early reading of Whitman,
the writing of his <u>Whitman</u> (1906.13), its
sources, the controversy over it, Burroughs's
admiration of this book, Josiah Phillips
Quincy's visit to Emerson the day the 1856
<u>Leaves</u> arrived, and Emerson's dissatisfaction
with the use of his name.

10 POUND, LOUISE, ed. Introduction and selected
bibliography to <u>Specimen Days, Democratic
Vistas, and Other Prose</u>. Garden City, N.Y.:
Doubleday, Doran & Co., pp. ix-xlvi, xlvii-
lii. Portrait.
   Whitman was influenced by the prevalent
nationalistic and romantic thought of his
day and particularly by transcendentalism,
which he expressed in a more original way
than his contemporaries, with a faith in
the masses and an emotional intensity that
Emerson lacked. "His greatest debt was to
himself." His reading and life are traced.
He brought into poetry American subject
matter, but his greatest subjects remained
universal. His new literary form came from
oral delivery rather than Ossian or the
Bible, emphasizing music and direct address.
His poems reveal descriptive power, "unusual
effects of amplitude and mass movement" (as
in his catalogues), reliance on intuition,
power of identification. His mannerisms
usually convey his meaning effectively;
contemporary diction has largely followed
his direction. He was not a prose master,
but his prose, distinctive and mannered, is
important for understanding his poetry.
<u>Specimen</u> has more sympathy, tenderness,
courage, wonder, and understanding of the
pathos and glory of the death of the young
soldier than other nineteenth-century American literature. <u>Vistas</u> is "a stirring
statement of his democratic convictions."
His faith in democracy extends beyond
Wordsworth and Byron, moving toward internationalism. His belief "in the intense
personal attachment of man to man" should
not be given "too private an interpretation."
Science affected his outlook, but he retained
a pre-Darwinian nature, with faith in human

1935

goodness and nature's beauty, much like Wordsworth. His poetry had a pantheistic faith in the unity of life, with a tonic attitude toward death. The World War placed him at the height of his influence and prestige as "a liberator of the language, the creator of American free verse, the apostle of American cultural independence, and the spokesman of American democracy." "His successors owe more to his spirit of independence than they do to his manner of expression." His major influence was in the direction not of a new race but of new literary methods and a freer spirit.

11 SANTAYANA, GEORGE. The Last Puritan: A Memoir In the Form of a Novel. London: Constable & Co., pp. 221-24, 238-39, 278, 381.
      Characters discuss Whitman, one calling him the best American poet, another disapproving because he is not religious, although he later wonders about Whitman. Some found that Whitman could "liberate them from moral cramp."

12 STEIN, GERTRUDE. Lectures in America. New York: Random House, pp. 51, 241.
      American writers (including Whitman) knew that there is a "separation between what is chosen and from what there is the choosing." Whitman "wanted really wanted to express the thing and not call it by its name," especially through his title, which he wanted "to be as little a well known name to be called upon passionately as possible."

13 van DYKE, TERTIUS. Henry van Dyke: A Biography. New York and London: Harper & Bros., pp. 160, 415-16.
      Whitman's appreciation for Tennyson is cited. Henry van Dyke's letter of October 1932 to Nicholas Murray Butler is quoted, regarding the choice of six outstanding names in American literature: he would include Whitman, though most of his work "outruns his undoubted genius," occasionally dull or indecent; for he brought some "a larger freedom, not from metre (for everyone of his best poems has a subtle metrical structure of its own) but from the bondage of monotony in the use of metre," with "many superbly beautiful lyrics and lyrical passages."

14 ZILLMAN, LAWRENCE JOHN. The Elements of English Verse: A Manual and Workbook for Students of Poetry and Verse Writing. New York: Macmillan Co., pp. 5, 63-64, 102, 110, 125-27.
      Describes "the Whitman type" of free verse: it has "no basic norm line"; "the feeling of appropriate rhythmical relationship between form and content largely determines the shortness or length of verses." "This increased freedom" can produce "many magnificent effects" such as "strong climaxes" due to a cumulative

effect as in "Cradle" and "Lilacs." Modern free verse has been an adaptation of Whitman's and Arnold's types rather than direct imitation. Several poems and passages are printed.

PERIODICALS

15 DANIEL, LEWIS C. "Two Etchings For Walt Whitman's 'Song of the Open Road.'" Forum 93 (January), 32-33.
      Reprints stanzas from "Open Road" under two illustrations, from new edition of the poem illustrated by Daniel.

16 GLICKSBERG, CHARLES I. "A Walt Whitman Parody." American Literature 6 (January), 436-37.
      Notes first reprinting of Winter's poem (see 1933.17) in Nichols's book (1864.2), quoted; his remarks "seem to indicate that the parody was not as serious in intent as the writers of the article in question would have it appear."

17 SILVER, ROLLO G. "A Note About Whitman's Essay on Poe." American Literature 6 (January), 435-36.
      Reprints original article (1875.11) which Whitman included in his essay "Edgar Poe's Significance," noting the changes Whitman made.

18 ALLEN, GAY WILSON. "Walt Whitman Bibliography, 1918-34." Bulletin of Bibliography 15 (January-April), 106-9.
      Reprinted: 1935.3. Revised: 1943.
      Concludes 1934.39: Part 4. Periodical Literature.

19 GLICKSBERG, CHARLES I. "A Friend of Walt Whitman." American Book Collector 6 (March), 91-94.
      Whitman was acquainted with both Charles Godfrey Leland and his brother Henry P., who sent Whitman an early encouraging letter and wrote "an eloquent and energetic defence" of Whitman (1860.35, quoted). A poem is also quoted, "perhaps the first serious and, on the whole, fairly successful imitation of the poet's loose-jointed, loping style."

20 SILVER, ROLLO G. "Oscar Makes a Call." Colophon, pt. 20 (March), 85-88.
      Reprint of 1882.21.

21 _____. "Seven Letters of Walt Whitman." American Literature 7 (March), 76-81.
      Prints unpublished letters with annotations and introductory explanations.

22 GOHDES, CLARENCE. "The 1876 English Subscription for Whitman." Modern Language Notes 50 (April), 257-58.
      The Rossetti letters (1934.5) reveal that help for Whitman was considered in England before 1876. Two further letters

of 1873 and 1875 from Gilchrist to Rossetti are printed.

23 METZDORF, ROBERT F. "A Whitman Letter." Saturday Review of Literature 11 (6 April), 598.
   Quotes letter from Whitman to Nat Bloom, from the University of Rochester's collection; Holloway agrees that it is "very important."

24 BENET, STEPHEN VINCENT. "Ode to Walt Whitman." Saturday Review of Literature 12 (4 May), 7-10.
   Reprinted: 1935.4.
   Free-verse re-creation of Whitman in his old age, his feeling toward death, with allusions to lines of his poetry and prose. The speaker replies to his own questions about the contemporary state of the country that tyranny remains and democracy is unfulfilled, but Whitman and his land endure.

25 MABBOTT, T. O. "Walt Whitman and William Motherwell." Notes and Queries 168 (4 May), 314.
   Notes that Motherwell's poem "Hollo, my Fancy" may be the source for title Good-Bye My Fancy, since Whitman included Motherwell in a list of poets in Notes and Fragments (1904.11).

*26 ANON. Account of sale of Bucke's collection of Whitman letters. Washington News (16 May).
   Reported in Willard.

27 WHITE, VIOLA C. "Thoreau's Opinion of Whitman." New England Quarterly 8 (June), 262-64.
   Reprints with discussion a partial rough draft of Thoreau's letter to Blake of 19 November 1856, indicating the changes from the version Emerson printed (1865.1), which deletes Thoreau's reference to the printing of Emerson's letter to Whitman. This fragment with its reworkings indicates that "Thoreau found Whitman an important but difficult phenomenon."

28 ANON. "Walt Whitman Honored." New York Times (1 June), 13:5.
   Account of birthday celebration at Laurel Springs, where admirers (including Dr. MacAlister) gathered at the Stafford home.

29 VAN DOREN, MARK. "Walt Whitman, Stranger." American Mercury 35 (July), 277-85.
   Whitman's homosexuality is now recognized; "Calamus" includes real love poems, not mere "work of the dramatic imagination." Love for Whitman was inseparable from death, because his love could not be satisfied in life. Leaves is "drenched with longing." Even among his friends, Whitman displayed a "sense of separateness" and "a certain impersonality." His best poetry came out of his contradictions and efforts to resolve or remove them. His democratic dogmas cannot be valid, being based on homosexual love. His disciples have pushed him the wrong way. His poetry is great "because he was not primarily interested in it," caring more for what he had to say. The value of Whitman and his poetry is that he wrote "at once about himself and about the man he wanted to be." (Much of this article is based on material from Rivers, 1913.16, unacknowledged.)

30 MORLEY, CHRISTOPHER. "The Bowling Green." Saturday Review of Literature 12 (6 July), 15-16.
   Prints passage from diary of Thomas Chalkley Palmer regarding Whitman's funeral and his own ideas of Whitman: While Whitman's verse construction will be long remembered, "even if only as an anomaly," his matter is of more value, "as showing the workings of a perfectly unbiased and free mind." He was "a conscious agent of the 'inner light.'"

31 COOKE, Mrs. ALICE LOVELACE. "Whitman's Background in the Industrial Movements of His Time." University of Texas Bulletin: Studies in English 15 (8 July), 76-91.
   Whitman as editor took part in discussions of problems of labor, as he did later in life, but he generally followed his social instincts and faith in democracy rather than economic theories. Though not associated with any particular group, he opposed labor abuses but saw the narrowness of trade unionism. His comments on socialist ideas reveal some influence and some demurring. He brought machinery into his poetry in the interest of the poet explaining the meaning, not as a mere reporter. The similarity of his ideas to those of socialism have led socialists to regard him as their poet. His internationalism was long with him.

32 SPIER, LEONARD. "Walt Whitman." International Literature, no. 9 (September), 72-89.
   Whitman's own times were not ripe for socialism but his self-education and idealism made him a "social revolutionist," opposing the status quo, though vestiges of middle-class psychology remained with him. He was Hegelian, believing in social evolution. Leaves is a "politico-philosophic epic," dominated by Whitman's optimistic fatalism. His "petty bourgeois fashion" of supporting minor movements like feminism and tariffs was due to his faith in Hegel rather than Marx. Nevertheless he was closer than any American poet to "formulating a militant working-class ideology." He is held in high esteem in Russia. His only fault was adherence to Hegel's "pseudo-dialectic."

1935

33 ANON. "Grass Roots." <u>New York Times</u> (7 September), 14:2-3.
    Editorial on grass growing in the city quotes and comments on Whitman's appropriate words.

34 BUNCE, ROBERT. "Protective Grass." <u>New York Times</u> (15 September), sec. 4, 9:2.
    Response to editorial (1935.33) mentions its use of Whitman.

35 SHULMAN, J. L. "Victor." <u>New York Times</u> (15 September), sec. 4, 9:6.
    Calls attention to a Whitman quotation: "He only wins who goes far enough."

36 GLICKSBERG, CHARLES I. "A Whitman Discovery." <u>Colophon</u>, n.s. 1 (Autumn), 227-33.
    The notebook quoted in 1933.6 was used for an article in <u>Harper's New Monthly Magazine</u> (July 1857), as parallel passages and details show. The index ascribes the article to B. J. Lossing, an illustrator and historian whose name may have been more desirable than Whitman's and who probably did the illustrations for the article.

37 _____. "Whitman and Bryant." <u>Fantasy</u> 5 (Autumn), 31-36.
    Presents what each writer had to say about the other, from Bryant's earliest mentions of Whitman in the <u>Evening Post</u> (1842.2). Bryant's traditional stance in literary and moral matters contrasts sharply with Whitman's, although both shared faith in American and democratic ideals.

38 ADKINS, NELSON F. "Walt Whitman and William Motherwell: 'Good-Bye My Fancy.'" <u>Notes and Queries</u> 169 (12 October), 268-69.
    Response to 1935.2: other poets have used the phrase, "Hallo, My Fancy," notably Charles Henry Lüders, shortly before the appearance of Whitman's volume.

39 BAKER, PORTIA. "Walt Whitman's Relations with Some New York Magazines." <u>American Literature</u> 7 (November), 274-301.
    Survey of New York literary magazines from 1860s to Whitman's death reveals neither neglect (except possibly from 1871 to 1875) nor persecution, "though many stupid and prejudiced remarks were made, and probably some malicious ones." Extensive references are presented to commentary on Whitman and acceptance of his writings in the <u>Nation</u> and <u>Independent</u> (both hostile); <u>Harper's</u>, <u>Round Table</u>, and <u>Scribner's/Century</u> (through which a view of Whitman as not quite a monster entered many homes); and the <u>Saturday Press</u> and <u>Critic</u> (the only periodicals giving Whitman consistent approval).

40 SILVER, ROLLO G. "Whitman." <u>New York Times</u> (3 November), sec. 4, 9:2.
    Announces discovery of a file of the <u>New York Weekly Graphic</u>, for which Whitman wrote six articles in 1874.

41 GOLD, MIKE. "Ode to Walt Whitman." <u>New Masses</u> 17 (5 November), 21.
    Reprinted: 1935.42.
    Long free-verse poem. Whitman's loafing and "a lazy poet's lies" are not appropriate for an oppressed world. Whitman's dream America and dream democracy shall be born only through strikes.

42 _____. "Change the World! Ode to Walt Whitman." <u>Daily Worker</u> (New York) (6 November), 5:1.
    Reprint of 1935.41.

43 ANON. "Morgan Partner Buys Rare Book." <u>New York Times</u> (22 November), 21:3.
    Notes $875 paid for 1855 <u>Leaves</u> copy containing a copy of Emerson's letter.

44 JONES, HOWARD M. "Letters to the Editor: Whitman and the Immigrant. Salut au Monde." <u>Saturday Review of Literature</u> 13 (30 November), 9.
    The juxtaposition of quotations from "Salut" and from Pound's introduction (1935.10) reveals the differences between his true attitude toward immigrants and the one she ascribes to him.

1936

BOOKS

*1 ALDRICH, DARRAGH. <u>Earth Never Tires</u>. New York: H. C. Kinsey & Co.
    Reported in Saunders <u>Whitman in Fiction</u>. Quotations from Whitman.

2 BEACH, JOSEPH WARREN. <u>The Concept of Nature in Nineteenth-Century English Poetry</u>. New York: Macmillan Co. "Whitman," pp. 370-94; notes, 602-5.
    Whitman is perhaps the culminating point in the romantic concept of nature. His deism and idealism show the influence of Emerson, Carlyle, Hegel, Schelling. Idealism for Whitman is the key to understanding man, nature, and God. Whitman, never a systematic thinker, is intuitive and enthusiastic, an "ensemblist." His religious doctrine is universal harmony, with faith in progress, immortality, struggle. His concept, identical to Emerson's, reflects his times. His idea of social democracy is militant. He celebrates sex as part of the identification of the soul with all processes of nature but is not obsessed with it, being concerned with all human activities. He justifies evil by reference to universal harmony and acceptance of reality. He regarded himself as a nature-poet and the out-of-doors as the appropriate background of man's life, though most of his poems are too didactic to admit extensive nature-study. His transcendentalism places him with Emerson and Carlyle, but in seriousness and con-

creteness he is closer to Goethe and
Wordsworth. His "democratic passion" links
him with Shelley. His evolutionism is more
Hegelian than Darwinian. Less naturalistic
than preceding romantics, he represents the
end of a phase in English poetry.

3 BOYNTON, PERCY H. Literature and American
  Life. Boston: Ginn & Co. "Walt Whitman,"
  pp. 477-98; bibliography, 513-15; biographical sketch, 903; also passim per index.
      This critical overview of Whitman in-
  corporates material from 1918.4, 1919.54,
  1919.239, 1919.240, with references to
  recently published writings by and about
  Whitman. Despite unpromising literary
  work, the early Whitman reveals symptoms
  of his later self: "an ambition to become
  a public speaker affected his style, steer-
  ing him away from elegance toward force and
  clearness; and the desire to say something
  that men would listen to led him from
  pleasant nothings in the direction of
  bardic and prophetic utterance." Although
  his seemingly improvised lines have branded
  him "a slovenly, hasty writer," scholarship
  has revealed his painstaking processes of
  composition. His sexual theme was the
  largest obstacle to his popularity but not,
  as Lewisohn (1932.15) suggests, homosexuality, which was hardly a concern of a
  naive American public, though explicit in
  "Calamus."

4 BROOKS, VAN WYCK. The Flowering of New Eng-
  land 1815-1865. New York: E. P. Dutton &
  Co., pp. 269, 440, 520, 521, 524, 531.
      Brief mentions of Whitman as a major
  American writer, noting Thoreau's and
  Lowell's opinions of him.

5 BRYANT, ARTHUR. The American Ideal. London,
  New York, Toronto: Longmans, Green & Co.
  "Emerson and Whitman," pp. 106-38; also
  260, 261, 274.
      Whitman, the American bard Emerson
  looked for, was largely self-taught, familiar with the life of the American people,
  an ordinary man telling the truth about
  himself, entirely American unlike his
  poetic predecessors. Looking inward, he
  widened the frontier of the human soul.
  His faults include hasty work and crudeness.
  His portrayal of war is unmatched since
  Homer, with a sense of more than its horror.
  "Lilacs," discussed and quoted, is great
  because of its suggestiveness. No one has
  better expressed American aspirations or
  understood her history. Because he has
  made poetic America's creed, he is her
  greatest poet.

6 BUCK, PHILO M. The World's Great Age. New
  York: Macmillan Co. "A Vociferous Faith--
  Whitman," pp. 113-41.
      Whitman's poetry represents America
  before the war and the pioneer's ideals.
  He "ignores the primitive and admires com-

plexity and variety." His poetry is "a
response to the sheer ecstacy of living,"
each verse based on "actual experience."
He was influenced by John Stuart Mill, in
revolt against asceticism, and drawn to
Emerson's transcendentalism as a basis from
which to seek the unknown. Whitman, both
mischievous and serious, represents "the
individualism of adolescent America." He
lacks discrimination, overuses foreign
words, flaunts sensuality and egotism.
Unlike proponents of modern naturalism, he
is not morbid or concerned with aberrations.
Not a pacifist, he was inspired to write
his best poetry by the war, which did not
change his basic idealism. His life is "an
allegory of America." As critic he urged
responsibility. True democracy based on
law and solidarity is still a worthy ideal;
Whitman remains the poet of the New America.

7 CANBY, HENRY SEIDEL. Seven Years' Harvest:
  Notes on Contemporary Literature. New York:
  Farrar & Rinehart, pp. 7, 9, 13, 19, 47,
  60, 69, 73, 74, 92, 99, 116-17, 118-19, 164,
  165, 167, 169, 184, 202-3, 206, 229, 231,
  255, 293.
      Incidental references to Whitman, his
  treatment of America, his value for today,
  his influence on Thomas Wolfe. He invented
  "the language for one of the most stirring
  poems of Utopia ever written," an approach
  to the kind of literature which can open
  the way to peace.

8 CHESTERTON, G. K. The Autobiography of G. K.
  Chesterton. New York: Sheed & Ward, p. 90.
      Chesterton's way of looking at things
  "with a sort of mystical minimum of gratitude" was assisted by those few writers who
  were not pessimists, especially Whitman.

9 CLARK, HARRY HAYDEN. Whitman selections,
  chronology, bibliography, and notes in
  Major American Poets. New York: American
  Book Co., pp. 651-732, 914-28.
      Whitman's poems should be read in
  chronological order, as presented here, to
  recognize both "his earlier radical work"
  and "later conservative work" and his aim
  of presenting a representative personality.
  Various critics are quoted and cited.
  Whitman's later work is superior to "Myself"
  in artistry and soundness of thought, for
  his first philosophic period emphasized
  sensation, freedom, self-love, arrogant
  pride, and equalitarianism, with some purpose of shocking. "Myself" centers on the
  ideas of universality in himself and equality of all people, things, and experiences.
  Notes include explications, suggesting how
  his poems illustrate his ideas and prosody.

10 DOS PASSOS, JOHN. The Big Money. New York:
   Harcourt, Brace & Co., p. 150.
       In this stream-of-consciousness section
   on political ponderings, "Camera Eye 46,"
   the speaker wonders what might "bring back

1936

(I too Walt Whitman) our storybook democracy."

11 DOUGLAS, LLOYD C. White Banners. New York: P. F. Collier & Son Corp., pp. 98-100.
Philip Raymond, though dying, shares with his beloved some readings from Leaves which release his soul through "good old Walt's challenge."

12 ECCLES, CAROLINE A. James William Wallace, An English Comrade of Walt Whitman. London: C. W. Daniel Co., 45 pp.
Wallace, mentioned in Bucke's Cosmic Consciousness (1901.3), was humble and unassuming. He introduced Leaves to his friends and opened correspondence with Whitman. His specifically Christian spiritual experience is contrasted to Whitman's. Letters to Whitman and addresses to Whitman Fellowship are quoted, with appreciative anecdotes on and tributes to Wallace by his friends. Wallace's references to Whitman concentrate on his broad spiritual principles. Eccles includes an account of her brother's vision the night of Whitman's death, her own conversion to Whitman's philosophy, and her acquaintance with Wallace and Traubel.

13 FREEMAN, JOSEPH. An American Testament: A Narrative of Rebels and Romantics. New York: Farrar & Rinehart, pp. 84-85, 239-41, 291.
Incidental references to the effect of Whitman's "revolutionary message" on American artists and workers.

14 HARTWICK, HARRY. "Walt Whitman." In A History of American Letters, by Walter Fuller Taylor (Boston: American Book Co., 1936), pp. 536-41.
Bibliography of works, texts, biography, criticism, bibliography.

15 HOLLOWAY, EMORY, and ADIMARI, RALPH, eds. Introduction and notes to New York Dissected by Walt Whitman: A Sheaf of Recently Discovered Newspaper Articles. New York: Rufus Rockwell Wilson, 257 pp. Index. Includes reprints of 1855.2, 1856.12-.14, 1856.18, 1856.21-.23, 1860.19, 1860.24, 1860.68.
Traces Whitman's career in the late 1850s, particularly his relationship with the Fowler and Wells paper, Life Illustrated. The background of each article printed is described. Notes explain factual matter, parallels to other Whitman writings.

16 HUBBELL, JAY B., ed. American Life in Literature. New York and London: Harper & Bros. Vol. 1, pp. xxiii, xxiv, 296, 302, 303, 305, 327, 495; vol. 2, pp. 8, 11, 14, 15, 37-38, 40, 47, 59-113 (selections), 210, 268, 400, 421, 429, 447, 451, 479, 480, 481, 536.
Includes reprints in toto or in part of

1904.7, 1895.39, 1891.47, 1855.12. 1860.18, 1865.1, 1920.19, 1921.35.
"The Poet of American Democracy," introduction to selections from Whitman's poetry and prose, provides sketch of his life, the context for the 1855 Leaves, his reception, his use of first person, his influence, his similarities to Emerson. His work "seems the logical literary sequel" to Jacksonian democracy. "He is generally recognized as one of the two or three most important American writers." Bibliographic paragraph. Commentaries on Whitman throughout the volumes note his significance and influence.

17 LEWIS, LLOYD, and SMITH, HENRY JUSTIN. Oscar Wilde Discovers America. New York: Harcourt, Brace & Co., pp. 65, 73-77, 88, 118-19, 164, 276, 343-44, 347-38, 404.
Various newspaper interviews (including 1882.21, in full, and 1882.29) are quoted to show Wilde's admiration for Whitman, describing their meeting and Whitman's opinions of Wilde. A second visit to Whitman early in May 1882 is noted.

18 McDONALD, EDWARD D., ed. Phoenix: The Posthumous Papers of D. H. Lawrence. New York: Viking Press, pp. 23-24, 61, 91, 206, 220, 221, 319, 699, 704, 705, 709, 713, 722, 740. Includes reprint of 1920.17.
Incidental references include criticism of Whitman's conflicting notions of democracy, particularly the nullification of individual identity.

19 MILLIN, SARAH GERTRUDE. General Smuts. Boston: Little, Brown, & Co. Vol. 1, pp. 17, 22, 35-49, 180, 234; vol. 2, pp. 51, 97.
This biography of Jan Christian Smuts discusses and summarizes his book, Walt Whitman: A Study in the Evolution of Personality (not to be published until 1973). George Meredith and others felt the time was not right for publishing it, since English interest in Whitman had waned, although the book actually only uses Whitman as a vehicle for exploring Smuts's idea of Holism, studying him as a biological specimen, using Leaves to trace "the development of his Personality through his impulse towards anarchy, progress, comradeship, democracy and equality."

20 MORLEY, CHRISTOPHER. Streamlines. Garden City, N.Y.: Doubleday, Doran & Co. "Notes on Walt," pp. 284-90.
Reprint of 1936.45.

21 RAINS GALLERIES. First Editions, Autograph Letters and Manuscripts of Outstanding Importance. New York: Rains Galleries, pp. 70-85.
This description of items to be auctioned lists Whitman items: copies of his works, his will; letters, manuscripts, described in laudatory terms.

22 SCHWARTZ, Dr. JACOB. <u>Manuscripts, Autograph
Letters, First Editions and Portraits of
Walt Whitman</u>. New York: American Art
Association, Anderson Galleries, 127 pp.
"Strong Sensual Germs" (foreword), by
Christopher Morley, 5 pp.

Morley describes this catalogue of
Bucke's Whitman collection of "miscellaneous
personalia" as a vivid biography of Whitman
through its multiplicity of material. His
best writing "represents humanity at large
singing in its tub--a kind of frank booming
improvisation--grave, innocent, and clean."
Whitman's notes for poems reveal him as
"the patient reconsiderer of the word,"
continuing to revise. He is wise, to be
cherished in every scrap. The catalogue's
prefatory note calls each scrap of paper
listed "a link in the great chain of
thought that finally established a new
literature," here presented in approximate
chronological arrangement. The sections,
with many items quoted or summarized, are
as follows: "Building the Man: Genealogy
and Biography of the Whitman Family and its
Influence on the Poet"; "The Gestation
Years"; "Building the Poet: Preparatory
Reading and Thought"; "Building 'Leaves of
Grass'"; "'Leaves of Grass': The Poetic
Interpretation of America through a Personality" (early drafts of 1855 <u>Leaves</u>, many
fine passages not appearing in the published
work; through his natural attitude toward
the human being and religion Whitman broke
the bonds of a stilted and hypocritical era
of literature); "Big Brother to the Boys in
Blue and Gray" (letters from and to soldiers); "The Character of Walt Whitman Revealed in Letters from His Family" (Bucke's
work, 1883.3, is actually Whitman's autobiography, since he supplied the information
and revised the book; character of family
members is described); "Walt Whitman's
Autobiography" (emendations to 1883.3, in
manuscript); "Contemporary Opinion of Walt
Whitman"; "The Second Preparatory Period";
"Maturity and Fame"; "The Edifice Completed"
(notes change of punctuation and capitalization in 1881 <u>Leaves</u>, perhaps under Boston's
influence); "The Final Revision of 'Leaves
of Grass'" (revisions of major poems and
groups noted); "The Last Phase" (including
a note by Bucke asking Whitman about his
children, a query Whitman dismissed as
being no problem, 23 December 1891).

23 SHEPHARD, ESTHER. <u>The Thread of Ariadne:
Walt Whitman as Poet (The record of a
search)</u>. Seattle: McNeil Press, 39 pp.
Revised: 1938.17.

Her study of Whitman began as an
examination of his coined words. She cites
her reading list, notes her impressions of
Whitman's attitude toward language. His
idea of the translation of music into language led to her search for a particular
remembered quotation, which turned out to
be taken from George Sand's <u>Consuelo</u>.

Seeking out the source, she discovered
further passages suggesting Whitman in its
sequel, <u>The Countess of Rudolstadt</u>, the
epilogue (quoted) to which reveals "most of
the important words which Whitman coined
from the French" as well as "his most
characteristic ideas, themes, and moods."
Other Sand novels cited as offering suggestions to Whitman for his poetic persona
include <u>Spiridion</u>, <u>The Journeyman Joiner</u>,
and <u>The Mosaic Workers</u>. Reading Sand gave
Whitman the idea for the poem that Margaret
Fuller had called for earlier. (This book
is expanded and extensively revised, with
more quotations, more consideration of
Whitman's subterfuge, and some deletion, to
become Chapter 2 of 1938.17.)

24 SILVER, ROLLO G., ed. Introductory note to
<u>Letters Written By Walt Whitman To His
Mother 1866-1872</u>. New York: Alfred F.
Goldsmith, At the Sign of the Sparrow,
pp. 1-2.

Biographical sketch of Whitman's mother,
whose influence, "emotional and not intellectual, was one of the most important
forces of his life." He found the typical
American family and "the 'perfect mother'"
in his own home. Her qualities come
through in Whitman's letters to her, with
"occasional touches of humor."

25 STEVENS, WALLACE. <u>Ideas of Order</u>. New York:
Alfred A. Knopf. "Like Decorations in a
Nigger Cemetery, I," p. 45.

The sun is described "Like Walt Whitman
walking along a ruddy shore," singing the
things that are part of him.

26 TATE, ALLEN. <u>Reactionary Essays on Poetry and
Ideas</u>. New York and London: Charles
Scribner's Sons, pp. 24, 32.

Incidental references: Dickinson, like
Hardy and Whitman, "must be read entire."
Essay on Crane (reprint in 1937.21) describes his use of Whitman in "The Bridge"
(1930.5).

27 TAYLOR, WALTER FULLER. <u>A History of American
Letters</u>. Boston: American Book Co.
"Toward Modern America: Walt Whitman,"
pp. 225-38; also passim per index;
Hartwick's bibliography (1936.14), 536-41.

Whitman's preparation was based on experience, political activity, and reading.
He is still difficult to appraise. He is a
transcendentalist through Emerson, mystically
affirming truths, and a romanticist as well.
His verse swings between individualism and
common humanity. He is more optimistic and
sensual than Emerson. His nationalism includes definition of a new race and celebrates fraternal love as an unstructured
religion. His democracy is a product of
romanticism, his verse the peak of American
romanticism. Like Emerson's essays, his
verse stimulates and suggests rather than
explains or finishes. His best are "Pas-

1936

sage" and the elegies, investing particular
events with universal significance. He is
the precursor of modern writing, comparable
to Wordsworth in achievement and vision.

28 UNTERMEYER, LOUIS. Modern American Poetry:
A Critical Anthology. 5th rev. ed. New
York: Harcourt, Brace & Co. "Walt
Whitman," pp. 31-38, followed by selections;
also 4-7, passim per index.
Revisions of 1930.21 and 1931.21.
Preface is reprinted from 1930.21 with
two paragraphs added from preface to 1931.
21 on Whitman's permanence through his
spirit. Introduction to the thirty-seven
pages of selections is reprinted from
1931.21 with deletions, including the re-
placement of a discussion of Whitman's
adhesiveness and claims of paternity by a
paragraph based on Van Doren (1935.29).

29 YEATS, W. B. Dramatic Personae 1896-1902.
New York: Macmillan Co., p. 94; London:
Macmillan & Co., 87-88.
One notices a tendency to pose in
active natures, as in "some modern who has
tried to live by classical ideas," like
Wilde or, less obviously, Whitman.

PERIODICALS

30 WERNER, W. L. "Whitman's 'The Mystic Trumpeter' as Autobiography." American Literature 7 (January), 455-58.
Analyzes the last five sections of
"Trumpeter" as representing five periods
in Whitman's life: (4) his early fondness
for Walter Scott's feudalism; (5) his
celebration of love; (6) the war; (7) postwar despair; (8) his final optimism and
ecstacy.

31 HOLLOWAY, EMORY. "Notes for Bibliophiles:
Schoolmaster Whitman." New York Herald
Tribune Books 12 (5 January), 18.
Describes Whitman's school-teaching;
manuscript minutes taken by Whitman for the
Smithtown Debating Society of 1837, "brief
and formal in style" with careful handwriting; Whitman's attitudes toward slavery
and the Indians; the Smithtown school
shortly before he taught there; his school
routine.

32 ANON. "Dr. Damrosch, at 74, to Offer New
Work." New York Times (30 January), 21:2.
Walter Damrosch will introduce his
musical setting of "Captain," which he describes, noting the poem's susceptibility
to "wonderful musical treatment."

33 BERNARD, EDWARD G. "Some New Whitman Manu-
script Notes." American Literature 8
(March), 59-63.
Presents notes from Dr. Samuel W.
Bandler's collection, with annotations.
Some "bear significantly upon Emerson and
the Orient as sources of Whitman's thought,

and afford revealing glimpses of uncompleted
poems in the earliest stages of germination."

34 SILVER, ROLLO G. "Walt Whitman's Lecture in
Elkton." Notes and Queries 170 (14 March),
190-91.
Reprint of 1886.26.

35 ANON. "'Whitman Inn' Opposed." New York
Times (6 April), 2:5.
Whitman's birthplace may be sold to
become an inn, to the chagrin of the
Huntington citizens who are unable to pay
the asking price.

36 HOPKINS, FREDERICK M. "Dr. Bucke Whitmaniana."
Publishers' Weekly 129 (11 April), 1537-39.
Describes Bucke's collection and the
catalogue (1936.22), praising the arrangement of material, reprinting some items; an
unequalled collection for an author.

37 BROOKS, PHILIP. "Notes on Rare Books." New
York Times Book Review (12 April), 20.
Describes the upcoming auction of the
Bucke collection and its excellent catalogue
(1936.22), with quotations.

38 MACKALL, LEONARD L. "Notes for Bibliophiles:
Whitman and Bucke." New York Herald
Tribune Books 12 (12 April), 23.
Quotes Osler (1925.3) on his first
visit to Whitman and Bucke's admiration for
him; describes the catalogue of the Bucke
collection (1936.22).

39 ANON. "Rare Whitman Book Brings $500." New
York Times (17 April), 19:4.
Notes sale of autograph presentation
copy of Memoranda.

40 ANON. "Plea Sent to President To Save
Whitman's Home." New York Times (23 April),
21:2.
William Watt of Huntington has asked
the federal government to buy Whitman's
birthplace, since it is dear to the local
people and they cannot buy it.

41 ANON. "Birthplace of Whitman Surveyed for a
Shrine." New York Times (5 May), 17:2.
The federal government is being asked
to save Whitman's birthplace from becoming
an inn by buying it for a shrine.

42 ANON. "Road Named for Whitman Proposed on
Long Island." New York Times (6 May),
13:2.
"Walt Whitman Highway" is the name
proposed for the new highway running by
Whitman's birthplace.

43 MORLEY, CHRISTOPHER. "The Bowling Green."
Saturday Review of Literature 14 (9 May),
15-16.
Quotes his catalogue preface (1936.22)
and a letter from W. E. Davenport in response, noting that Whitman used "an

immense tin or pewter bath tub" kept under
the bed, which he was recently shown on a
visit to the Camden house where he had
earlier visited Whitman in 1889.
Davenport's Whitmanesque poem, "The Whitman
Sale," is printed, commenting on his being
bought up in these various parts while his
whole self is available to everyone
through reading.

44 HOPKINS, FREDERICK M. "The Last Month's Book
Sales." Publishers' Weekly 129 (16 May),
1971-72.
Describes auction of items in catalogue
(1936.22), noting various items sold and
the prices they brought.

45 MORLEY, CHRISTOPHER. "Notes on Walt."
Saturday Review of Literature 14 (30 May),
12, 16.
Reprinted: 1936.20.
Whitman makes himself so much our own
"that even his gaffes are part of the fun."
He failed to notice many of the truly
American writers writing at his time.
Vistas shows him in a gloomy mood but with
hopes for the future, including "a more
generous womanhood," perhaps due to his
knowledge in New Orleans of women different
from the period's stereotype. He lost his
dark mood at Timber Creek. Specimen is
unsurpassed as "good outdoor reading," with
acute observation. His "naif superlativism"
assumed "that what happened to him or was
seen by him was the greatest, most important,
most significant anywhere."

46 TRAUBEL, GERTRUDE. "Philadelphians Remember
Charm of Walt Whitman's Personality."
Philadelphia Record (31 May), 7:2-4.
Traubel's daughter records interviews
with Dr. S. Burns Weston, Dr. Daniel
Longaker, Harrison S. Morris, Dr. Calvin B.
Knerr, and Annie Traubel on their impres-
sions of Whitman in Camden.

47 OLIVER, EGBERT S. "Walt Whitman in the High
Schools." English Journal (High school ed.)
25 (June), 461-67.
Whitman's "broad, all-enveloping personality" appeals to high school students,
with experience and heritage broader than
any other major American writer and an unparalleled unity throughout his work. His
poetic theory is described. "Come Up from
the Fields" is explained as a good poem for
introducing students to Whitman; also
"Wound Dresser," "To Think of Time," and
"Lilacs," his finest writing, for which
preparation is necessary. Some high school
students would enjoy "Myself." "Whitman,
surely one of our greatest poets, if not
our greatest, deserves a better, more fitting consideration in the high schools than
he has received." Thus he could win "a
sympathetic reading public."

48 TAGGARD, GENEVIEVE. "Night Letter to Walt
Whitman." New Frontier 1, no. 3 (June), 11.
Free-verse poem about the current de-
based state of the world.

49 ANON. "Drive for a Shrine to Whitman Begun."
New York Times (1 June), 21:6.
Cleveland Rodgers announced a committee
to raise money to make Whitman's birthplace
a memorial. Other speakers at this Whitman
birthday celebration included Holloway.
Mrs. Charles Hawkins and Bertha Johnston
recalled knowing Whitman when children.

50 ANON. "Honor Poet's Memory." New York Times
(1 June), 21:6.
Account of Whitman birthday celebration
at Stafford home in Laurel Springs. Camden's
Mayor Frederick von Nieda explained how
Whitman's home came to be a shrine.

51 GLICKSBERG, CHARLES I. "Walt Whitman, the
Journalist." Americana 30 (July), 474-90.
Brief sketch of Whitman's career as
journalist. He was trained in studying the
urban scene and reading for himself, "a
born newspaperman," maintaining scrapbooks
and notes, "indefatigable in his quest of
original and indigenous material," successful as his own press agent. Journalistic
influence is evident in his style and
habits of composition. Through jottings
for an 1862 Brooklyn City News article and
the published form, Glicksberg discusses
Whitman's mode of composition, which shows
much rewriting.

52 COY, REBECCA. "A Study of Whitman's Diction."
University of Texas Bulletin: Studies in
English 16 (8 July), 115-24.
Characteristic of Whitman's early
period are forceful colloquialisms, Americanisms (dealing with particularly American
things), terminology from the trades.
Archaisms were more common after 1865 and
more "deliberately conventional" as an indication that Whitman "had made his peace
with the past." He "made no radical changes
in conventional poetic diction"; Leaves is
"not the rich depository of colloquial language and Americanisms which might reason-
ably been expected." At his best, without
a theory, his poetry has "a formal beauty
of diction comparable only to the greatest
in English poetry. At his worst, he produced, not the great representative American
speech of which he dreamed, but only a
Whitmanesque dialect which will remain forever personal and inimitable."

53 DUGDALE, CLARENCE. "Whitman's Knowledge of
Astronomy." University of Texas Bulletin:
Studies in English 16 (8 July), 124-37.
Whitman had considerable knowledge of
astronomy, evident in his prose and poetry,
identifying heavenly bodies, reading articles, being aware of scientific theories
although his interest was more from the

point of view "of a poet whose imagination demanded a whole universe for its operation."

54 MORLEY, CHRISTOPHER. "The Bowling Green: Walt's French." Saturday Review of Literature 14 (11 July), 12.
   French words and Whitman's transcribed pronunciations of them are listed from Holloway (1936.15). His mistakes provide "harmless chuckles."

55 G[OHDES], C[LARENCE]. "Walt Whitman And the Newspapers of His Day." Library Notes (Duke University Library) 1 (October), 3-4.
   Describes scrapbooks of newspaper clippings dealing with Whitman, collected by Bucke, now at the Duke University Library, with the different points of view they take toward Whitman and the increasing recognition of Whitman's poetical worth they show.

56 Z[ABEL], M[ORTON] D. "Sandburg's Testament." Poetry 49 (October), 33-45.
   Reprinted: 1937.21.
   Review of Sandburg's The People, Yes, extensively comparing Sandburg, as historian, with Whitman, as prophet. Sandburg is saved from some of Whitman's diffuse and inflated flaws. It is doubtful whether any poet could write on Whitman's premises, "since that tradition represents an immense exploration and discovery of poetic resources, but not their proof and mastery as poetry."

57 BLANCK, JACOB. "News from the Rare Book Shops." Publishers' Weekly 130 (31 October), 1792.
   Describes the second binding of the 1855 edition.

58 MYERS, HENRY ALONZO. "Whitman's Consistency." American Literature 8 (November), 243-57.
   Whitman took transcendentalism's conclusions for granted and thus was never aware what he was doing. He is consistent in accepting both war and peace, good and evil, death and equality, individual and state, for he could reconcile them through his perception of eternal laws. His imaginative rather than intellectual insight will be part of all subsequent American philosophy.

59 STOVALL, FLOYD. Review of Holloway (1936.15). American Literature 8 (November), 323-24.
   The book gives glimpses of the long foreground of Leaves: Whitman's acquaintance with all types of life, knowledge of man's intellectual achievements, confidence.

60 ANON. "News of Art." New York Times (4 December), 22:4.
   Paragraph on Lewis Daniel's etching-illustrations of "Open Road" now on exhibit.

61 JEWELL, EDWARD ALDEN. "Graphic Art in a Long Perspective." New York Times (6 December),

13:4.
   Paragraph on exhibit of Daniel's illustrations of "Open Road."

BOOKS

1 BLACK, ALEXANDER. Time and Chance: Adventures with People and Print. New York and Toronto: Farrar & Rinehart, pp. 28, 54, 72-74, 75, 101.
   Recalls working at Whitman's desk in Brooklyn Times office; facsimile of Whitman's note to him regarding it. Account of Arthur Stedman's story of William Sharp's visit to Whitman. Grace Channing Stetson, who knew Whitman in her childhood, testifies to his human proportions rather than "tumultuous personality."

2 CHAMBERLIN, JOSEPH EDGAR. Nomads and Listeners. Edited by Samuel W. Waxman. Cambridge, Mass.: Privately printed at Riverside Press. "Walt Whitman," pp. 118-44.
   Reprint of 1919.200.

3 COLUM, MARY M. From These Roots: The Ideas That Have Made Modern Literature. New York and London: Charles Scribner's Sons, pp. 296-301; passim per index.
   Of all American writers, Poe, Whitman, and James "left behind them the most penetrating influences." Whitman absorbed all the ideas of his age, literary, political, and philosophic, aiming to be "an American national poet." "He was both realist and romantic, national and universal," and more mystical and oracular than even Emerson. He disregarded private emotions in favor of those of man as a member of society. His invention of free verse was inevitable because the other forms were "locked up with the purely personal experiences." He was the only poet to make his readers collaborators in the composition. The high plane of memorable expression, though rarely reached in his long poems, "was as memorable as that of any poet who ever lived." His vitality and originality continue to affect world literature.

4 ECKERT, ROBERT P. Edward Thomas: A Biography and a Bibliography. New York: E. P. Dutton & Co., pp. 79, 90, 106, 109, 118.
   Incidental references to Thomas's admiration for Whitman and his perception of men's divinity, after an early disagreement with Edward Garnett.

5 HAMMERTON, Sir J. A. Outline of Great Books. New York: Wise & Co. "Leaves of Grass: Walt Whitman," pp. 781-87. Alexander portrait.
   Whitman was "an ardent prophet" of democracy, with poetry of optimism, breadth,

serenity, tenderness. Critics are quoted; poems and extracts are presented to let him be judged on his best work. "Sea Drift" is his "most intimate" work. Whitman is full of echoes, as in the "Elizabethan texture" of "Lilacs" 7. The catalogues are flawed but can attain a cumulative power. His muses are from the present, not the past. Leaves is "a monumental epitome of life-in-action" with "the busy hum of humanity" as well as "a quiet fugue of life and death."

6 HART, HENRY, ed. The Writer in a Changing World. n.p.: Equinox Cooperative Press. "Toward the Forties," by Joseph Freeman, pp. 12-14, 20; "The Democratic Tradition," by Newton Arvin, 42, 43.

Freeman terms Whitman "the greatest poetic voice of American democracy." Most of us now know only Poe and Whitman among older American writers; they are not, however, exceptions but "the perfect flower of the American literary tradition." Arvin quotes Whitman and cites the democratic spirit "that broke out so grandly and musically in the chants" of Leaves.

7 LANDAUER, BELLA C. Leaves of Music by Walt Whitman. New York: Privately printed. Paper, no page numbers.

List of 244 compositions based on Whitman's poems, in alphabetical order by composer; bibliographic description for some. Includes facsimiles of Whitman documents and an index of Whitman's titles and the composers.

8 LUCAS, E. V. All of a Piece: New Essays. London: Methuen & Co. "A Carpenter's Son," pp. 55-60.

Informal discussion of Whitman, on the occasion of finding two manuscript fragments from 1855 on sale at a secondhand bookseller. We go to him not for "sententiae" but "for what is elemental and big." Whitman formed "his plans for the democratic manifesto" during his various activities. No one could have written Leaves but "the large, reflective carpenter." Emerson's commendation aroused interest in Leaves "as a living virile thing that could not be neglected." Whitman's personality is worthy of emulating.

9 MASTERS, EDGAR LEE. Whitman. New York: Charles Scribner's Sons, 342 pp. Photograph.

This biography, with some errors, has no notes or bibliography but cites its references in the text, frequently quoting Whitman on his experience and ideas. His varied influences made him America's national poet. His devotion to his mother was not a mother-fixation. His early life seemed lived in a lethargy. His philosophy is based on Jeffersonian democracy. His national, social, and political milieu is described, as are the various editions,

with special praise given the 1856 edition. The war was shattering to him, though his exact position as nurse is unclear. The Calamus letters of 1897.2 (which Bucke or Doyle may have carefully selected) reveal a love with "few parallels in literary annals." His "masculine love" (discussed) had other objects as well. The disapproval of Whitman's housekeeper and others kept Doyle from Mickle Street. Whitman seemed not to realize that homosexuality did not necessarily involve sex. He was simply not interested in romantic involvement with women, which would have detracted from his philosophy. "Passage" represents "the purest heights of his art," Vistas an excellent appraisal of America. His home and Camden environs are described from visits Masters made in 1909 and 1936. People in Camden consider Keller's book (1921.19) "not entirely trustworthy." As a critic, Whitman is unsurpassed in America. Despite the country's corruption, which he failed to trace to the war, Whitman "became more lofty and spiritual." Religiously inconsistent, Whitman failed to perceive Christ and the Bible as responsible for the attitudes he opposed. "Sleepers" is explicated. Closely interrelated are his cosmic consciousness, belief in unity (exemplified in his catalogues), belief in immortality, Uranian love, sexual nature. His being "flaccid, effeminate, dull, slack, and perhaps impotent" suggests his possible inheritance of family weaknesses. "No other poet entered with such loving sympathy into the hearts of every description of people." Whatever his poetic failings, including a lack of dramatic talent, he is "more important than his English compeers" because of his "richness of feeling," "suggestiveness," "moral fervor," and vision for America. "His worship of nature is earthly and rich," not idyllic like that of earlier pastoral writers. He was the pioneer and father of American poetry, suggesting the spirit in which American poems should be written, treating the seen, not the unseen; the poem of America is still to be written.

10 MULLER, HERBERT J. Modern Fiction: A Study of Values. New York and London: Funk & Wagnalls Co., pp. 213, 409, 411, 416.

Whitman is compared to Dreiser and Wolfe, who carry further the tendencies he initiated.

11 NEVINS, ALLAN. "The Newspapers of New York State, 1783-1900." In History of the State of New York. Vol. 9. Edited by Alexander C. Flick. New York: Columbia University Press, p. 292.

Whitman was the Eagle's "most illustrious editor--expounding democracy with both the small and the large D, enthusiastically backing the Mexican War, and then with equal enthusiasm demanding enactment of the Wilmot Proviso; a somewhat inconsistent, hot-headed journalist."

1937

12 NICHOLS, THOMAS LOW. Forty Years of American
Life: 1821-1861. New York: Stackpole
Sons, p. 409.
Reprint of 1874.1.

13 OVERTON, JACQUELINE; LONG, CHARLES W.; and
DAVIS, WILLIAM T. "Long Island and Staten
Island Since the Revolution." In History
of the State of New York. Vol. 10. Edited
by Alexander C. Flick. New York: Columbia
University Press, pp. 142, 150; also
"Scenic and Historic Possessions," by
Edward Porter Alexander, 261.
        Notes Whitman's journalistic career,
the school where he taught. Alexander
notes Whitman's birthplace.

14 V[AN]-D[OREN], M[ARK]. "Walt Whitman." In
Dictionary of American Biography. Vol. 20.
Edited by Allen Johnson and Dumas Malone.
New York: Charles Scribner's Sons, pp.
143-52.
        Thorough, up-to-date biographical
sketch, discounting the exaggerated impact
New Orleans was said to have on Whitman's
work. Whether he had a mystic experience
or not, he discovered a way of justifying
to the world his nature, which he realized
was different (as described from 1935.29).
He was indebted to Goethe, Carlyle, Emerson.
He perhaps never "understood how excellent
he was merely as a poet," being concerned
with being a prophet. The power of 1855
Leaves is described, with the development
of his writing and reputation. Criticism
now ranks him higher as a poet, emphasizing
him less "as man and moralist" than earlier
writers. His is "certainly the most original work yet done by any American poet,"
perhaps "the most passionate and best."
His prose is also a permanent contribution.
Bibliography of significant primary and
secondary sources.

15 WARFEL, HARRY R.; GABRIEL, RALPH H.; and
WILLIAMS, STANLEY T. Introduction to
Whitman selections in The American Mind:
Selections from the Literature of the
United States. New York: American Book
Co., pp. 833-34.
        Leaves is "one of America's great
original contributions to world literature," "a spiritual autobiography of middle
nineteenth-century America," stressing "an
underlying religious purpose," demanding
active virtues (rebellion against wrong,
athletic individualism, cooperation).
Whitman moved from nationalism to internationalism.

16 WELLS, CAROLYN. The Rest of My Life. Philadelphia and New York: J. B. Lippincott
Co., pp. 111, 242-44, 248-50, 252-60.
Extract reprinted: 1937.47.
        Describes her experience of collecting
Whitman books: "He is not my favorite
poet; I don't know who is, but he is America's foremost and greater singer." After

collecting his books, she sought "something
personal" and decided upon a necktie, only
to discover that he never wore one.

17 WILLIAMS, STANLEY THOMAS. "The Literature of
New York." In History of the State of New
York. Vol. 9. Edited by Alexander C.
Flick. New York: Columbia University
Press, pp. 252-56, 258, 259, 261, 265-66;
Cox photograph, facing p. 248.
        Biographical sketch. Whitman's career
is "New York's greatest contribution to
American literature." Extracts show his
debt and closeness to mid-century New York.
His actual experiences led to his enduring
convictions concerning life. His passionate
love of life made him break with restrictions
of form. He had few original ideas, drawing
much from Carlyle and Emerson. His mysticism, monism, glorification of a spiritually
based democracy are described. When inspired, he produced moving and sublime
poetry on these themes. As a romantic, he
never failed to capture America's spirit,
picturing the America he wished for, yet
with a realistic recognition of suffering.

18 WINTERS, YVOR. Primitivism and Decadence: A
Study of American Experimental Poetry. New
York: Arrow Editions, pp. 16, 38, 51, 80-
82, 96.
        Criticizes Whitman's "lax and diffuse"
form, his faulty belief in "the fallacy of
imitative form." He is "a second-rate poet"
with vague poetic and expository language,
at which Crane surpasses him. Pound surpasses him as well, though the Cantos have
a structure similar to Whitman's work.

19 YEATS, WILLIAM BUTLER. A Vision. London:
Macmillan & Co., pp. 113-14, 171-72.
Revision of 1925.19.
        Only language, not content, is revised
in these passages.

20 YUTANG, LIN. The Importance of Living. New
York: Reynal & Hitchcock, pp. 66, 89-90,
124, 128-30, 150, 420.
        Whitman is quoted and cited as "the
greatest literary champion of American individualism," "one of the wisest and more
far-seeing of Americans," with a sensible
and human philosophy ("I am sufficient as
I am") and emphasis on the importance of
the senses. A passage from Specimen is
quoted in comparison with ideas from the
Chinese.

21 ZABEL, MORTON DAUWEN, ed. Literary Opinion in
America. New York and London: Harper &
Bros., pp. xv-xvi, xix, xx, xxxiv, xlviii,
liii, 39, 41, 43, 60, 61, 97, 210-11, 408,
409, 410-11, 414-15, 484, 515, 517-18, 525,
527.
Includes reprints of 1932.5, 1928.25,
1924.13, 1936.56, 1936.26, 1931.5, 1931.57.
        Incidental references to Whitman in
Zabel's introduction (Whitman as related to

criticism and its methods, particularly
the necessity of a social principle in
criticism) and Horace Gregory's "D. H.
Lawrence" (comparing Whitman and Lawrence).

PERIODICALS

22 MIRSKY, D. S. "Walt Whitman: Poet of American Democracy." Translated from Russian by
Bernard Guilbert Guerney. Dialectics, no.
1 (1937), 11-29.
Reprinted: Murphy.
     Whitman, "the last great poet of the
bourgeois epoch of humanity," represents
the strength and antirevolutionary limitations of America's democratic capitalism
(explained). His passive mystic pantheism
and optimism, including the "debasement of
politics before 'higher values,'" though
democratic, are typical of America's tendency to construct religious systems.
Whitman's is, in fact, a religious system,
its discrepancies being part of it. His
view of things is dependent on his belief
in America rather than in the class struggle,
although he is "a precursor of the poetry
of socialism" in his break with romanticism
to affirm actuality and what was "valuable
and progressive--democracy, toil, the conquest of nature," and human dignity. He is
actually "the impersonal type of poet,"
stronger as poet than as prophet, his great
poems being those of the 1850s and 1860s,
using concrete images without philosophical
utterances and being free from stylization
and aestheticism. His language is new not
in being colloquial but in dealing with
new subjects. His form achieves energy and
flexibility. He "spoke for, and not to the
masses." "Broad-Axe" is examined as an ode
to toil, using "carpentry as a symbol of
the democratic constructiveness of America."

23 BURKE, KENNETH. "Acceptance and Rejection."
Southern Review 2 (Winter), 600-606, 609,
610, 630.
     Whitman, William James's "poetic
replica," accepted all, resorting to a
Jamesian pluralism "as a way of seeing an
organized unity of purpose behind diversity,"
and regarding the good element as the
essence of the pair. He transfigures death
through his rhapsodic style. "Brooklyn
Ferry" is a vision of the city akin to
Wordsworth's sonnet written on Westminster
Bridge. Whitman can only affirm the certainty and excellence of things by a
transcendental bridging. Later poems perceiving the negative aspects of the world
seem "an almost painful burlesque of
Whitman's healthy appetite."

24 SILVER, ROLLO G. "For the Bright Particular
Star." Colophon 2 (Winter), 197-216.
     Prints, with her consent, Whitman's
letters to Mary Whitall Smith Costelloe
Berenson and other members of the Smith
family, from 1884 to 1890, providing "a
close record of Walt's last years."

25 ALLEN, GAY WILSON. "Walt Whitman--Nationalist
or Proletarian?" English Journal 26 (January), 48-52.
     Whitman came to realize the failure of
his intention to record the life of the
average nineteenth-century American and
projected his voice into the future. His
mysticism, effeminacy, and submissiveness
repelled the American mind. Comments from
Jensen and Tagore show the positive oriental
response to "the 'Calamus' phenomenon"
which shocked Americans. The American environment colored his content and utterance; however, his philosophy, democratic
ideal, and style derive from India and
Europe (particularly Goethe, Thorild,
Michelet, Nekrassow, Hugo). German writers
in turn have felt his influence, which
American writers do not acknowledge. Whitman
should be studied not as exemplary of American phenomena but "as a configuration of
a world-proletarian movement."

26 GLICKSBERG, CHARLES I. "Walt Whitman in New
Jersey, Some Unpublished Manuscripts."
Proceedings of the New Jersey Historical
Society 55 (January), 42-46.
     Describes Whitman's nineteen years in
Camden, his publishings in local papers,
including possibly some anonymous articles
which have not been discovered.

27 SILVER, ROLLO G. "Thirty-one Letters of Walt
Whitman." American Literature 8 (January),
417-38.
     Prints unpublished letters to various
people from 1863 to 1890, with introductory
and explanatory notes on sources and biographical background.

28 GEIS, JOHN F. "The Times-Union Begins 90th
Year." Brooklyn Times-Union (28 February),
1A.
     Traces history of Brooklyn Times,
particularly noting Whitman's association
with it, as "first a reporter and then,
later, managing editor." Quotes 1937.1,
reproducing from it a facsimile of Whitman's
letter to Alexander Black.

29 VAN DOREN, MARK. "Plowing Through Whitman."
New York Herald Tribune Books 13 (28 February), 7. Illustrated with reprint of
Beerbohm (1904.3).
     Review of Masters (1937.9). Masters,
slouching through his subject, fits Whitman,
with the rare virtues in Whitman commentary
of balance and common sense, providing "the
best general account of the poet to date,"
piercing through the Whitman legend though
with some interpretive error. Masters
appreciates "the superb work Whitman did
at his best" and "the potential poet who
has perhaps exerted more influence than the
actual one has."

30 JACK, PETER MONRO. "Walt Whitman's Fresh
Vision of a Pioneer America. Edgar Lee

Masters's Biography Stresses the Poet's Political and Prophetic Role." New York Times Book Review (7 March), 5. Eakins portrait.

Review of 1937.9. Whitman is compared to Lindsay. Masters concentrates on Whitman's prophetic nationalism, regretting the loss of that vision in modern America. Whitman's poetry transcends political or national creed; to perpetuate his chauvinism is no justice to him. His extreme statements on America and the past came "partly from ignorance, partly from spleen, but mostly from the need to justify himself." His poetry has survived, despite the failure of his prophecies, with influence on Masters, Sandburg, and Hart Crane.

31 WALTON, EDA LOU. "Whitman Reconsidered." Nation 144 (20 March), 330-31.

Review of Masters (1937.9), "the most comprehensive life that has yet appeared," with much factual material to "prove Whitman's general humanity." Masters acknowledges Whitman's faults and shows him as "subnormal sexually," his passions flowing "into tender and imaginative channels only." Whitman's myth was possible only because of the expansive nature of his time, which saw no contradictions between the principles of complete democracy and those of complete individualism.

32 FURNESS, CLIFTON JOSEPH. "Spokesman of America." Saturday Review of Literature 15 (27 March), 7.

Review of Masters (1937.9), "honest, reverent, even grateful," "an ideal introduction" to Whitman, though lacking scholarly apparatus, clarifying some matters and treating the sex element sanely, offering excellent literary criticism, revealing his mysticism.

33 MALONE, DUMAS. "Who Are the American Immortals?" Harpers Magazine 174 (April), 547.

Whitman is listed fourth among nine men of letters included in this list of forty greatest Americans; he is seen to be gaining ground.

34 [DeVOTO, BERNARD.] "At the Cannon Mouth." Saturday Review of Literature 15 (3 April), 8.

Editorial on Malone's selection (1937.33): Whitman's place on the list "shows how great his reputation was at its crest" fifteen or so years ago, when he would have been considered first, as "a sacred symbol of revolution," though the America he projected was actually past. His reputation now is waning; few people have read more than the anthologized pieces. DeVoto would place Whitman seventh on his list.

35 ARVIN, NEWTON. "Whitman as He Was Not." New Republic 80 (14 April), 301-2.

Review of Masters (1937.9), a disappointment, with errors, curious assumptions impossible to verify, and a failure to dig below the surface for Whitman's historical roots or a distinctive psychological interpretation.

36 WHIPPLE, T. K. "Life in the Doldrums." New Republic 90 (21 April), 311.

Incidental: "Whitman thought he was a rooster crowing at dawn, but actually he was singing the swan song of the once triumphant ante-bellum democracy." He, Melville, and Emerson lingered on into a world to which they did not belong.

37 O'FAOLAIN, SEAN. "The Good Gray Poet." Spectator 158 (23 April), 769-70.

Review of Masters (1937.9). "Whitman sang the poetry of native America," and "much more than America." He has the vastness of Carlyle. "Myself" is "a song of all times." Masters seeks to compass him only in America, "as an apostle of Jeffersonianism," but this fresh, vigorous nationalist criticism places Whitman in his times and contributes to the sympathetic understanding of him, whose poetry "will always be a matter of personal choice, or rejection."

38 ALEXANDER, COLIN C. "A Note on Walt Whitman." American Literature 9 (May), 242-43.

Prints Whitman's postcard of 14 January 1880 to John P. Usher of Lawrence, Kansas, to supplement Silver's letters (1937.27).

39 ALLEN, GAY W. "Walt Whitman and Jules Michelet." Etudes Anglaises 1 (May), 230-37.

An Eagle review reveals Whitman's familiarity with Michelet's works. A passage from Michelet was the basis of "Man-of-War-Bird." Michelet's The People "contains every major idea of Whitman's philosophy of democracy, religion and art." Whitman's poetry reveals similarities to Michelet's writing in phrasing, identification of book with writer and of writer with the people, "indifference to artistic conventions." Both sought an "ethical democracy" based on the people. Reading Michelet may have contributed to Whitman's "spiritual and intellectual rebirth" around 1849, though the similarities may be due to their common background in Hegel and Rousseau.

40 RUBIN, JOSEPH JAY. "Whitman in 1840: a Discovery." American Literature 9 (May), 239-42.
Reprint of 1840.1.

Reprints with explanation of the political background newspaper items of 6 October 1840: the Long Island Farmer criticism of Whitman's political remarks and his response, "A Card" from Long Island Democrat. These represent "the earliest signed Whitman prose yet discovered" and "the earliest published critical commentary upon Whitman."

41 SIXBEY, GEORGE L. "'Chanting the Square Deific'--A Study in Whitman's Religion." American Literature 9 (May), 171-95.
    Explication of the poem, with the development of its ideas traced from Whitman's notebooks, published prose, and other poetry, and from Hegel. The feminine Santa Spirita mystically resolves the eternal conflict of the three other sides, representing aspects of American idealism.

42 GLICKSBERG, CHARLES I. "Walt Whitman and Bayard Taylor." Notes and Queries 173 (3 July), 5-7.
    Taylor early endorsed Leaves but caricatured Whitman in his novel John Godfrey's Fortunes (1864.3); "Taylor's growing antagonism towards Whitman may have been prompted by the realisation that they represented different traditions, different social and moral points of view."

43 EMERSON, DOROTHY. "Poetry Corner: Walt Whitman." Scholastic 31 (25 September), 21-E, 24-E.
    Popular sketch for high school youth of Whitman's life and early activities, varied experiences, belief in America and individual importance, fathering of modern poetry and free verse. Whatever he expresses in his poems, "we always sense their sincerity and realness," as in the simple ponderings of extracts which follow.

44 EAKINS, THOMAS. Portrait of Whitman. Magazine of Art 30 (November), Supplement, 21.
    This collection of American portraits juxtaposes Eakins's portrait of Whitman with his "expansive spirit" against a photograph of Whitman from the same period.

*45 FURNESS, CLIFTON JOSEPH. "Walt Whitman and Music." Boston Chapter Special Libraries Association News Bulletin (November). Reprinted in offset, single-page; seen in Saunders Supplement.
    Transcribed from David Goodale's manuscript notes of Furness's lecture: Whitman's poems are "essentially verbal music," as seen in the works of many American composers who have adapted his work and whose ideas of its musicality are cited. Hitherto unknown manuscript notes on a poem, "An Opera," are quoted. With Henry Saunders and David Goodale Furness is preparing a complete bibliography of Whitman.

46 SMITH, LOGAN PEARSALL. "Friendly City." Atlantic Monthly 160 (November), 568-72. Reprinted: 1939.11.
    Reminiscences. Smith's sister Mary introduced him to the writings of Whitman, "a great American poet and prophet" neglected by America, living not far from their neighborhood. Though Whitman's reputation was not good in Philadelphia, their father, Robert Pearsall Smith, agreed to their visiting him; once there, he invited Whitman to visit their home, as he often did later, as related, with descriptions of his character, serenity, lack of literary vanity. An anecdote of Mary meeting Gosse on his way to see Whitman conflicts with Gosse's account (1894.28). Whitman explains how he came to write "With Husky-Haughty Lips." Logan Smith's generation came to regard Leaves as a sacred book that revealed and rejoiced in feelings and affections which an older generation had ignored or treated as shameful; it spoke also of Whitman's broad affection for humanity and exultant pride in democracy, with some splendid passages of great poetry.

47 WELLS, CAROLYN. "Tie Collector." The Digest 1 (Literary Digest 124) (6 November), 28. Extract reprinted from 1937.16.

1938

BOOKS

1 ANON. An Outline of American Literature. Pt. 2. Boston: Student Outlines Co. "Walt Whitman," pp. 49a-54.
    Biographical outline. Summaries of Whitman's philosophy as poet of transcendentalism and democracy, his theory of poetry, major poems including "Myself" ("triumphant, egotistical, and sympathetic with mankind and nature"), Vistas (its prose "rivals, if not excels, his poetry"). His paradoxical position is that he is not appreciated by the masses for whom he wrote, while "the bookish" consider him America's "most powerful and original" poet.

2 ARVIN, NEWTON. Whitman. New York: Macmillan Co., 320 pp. Bibliographic notes at end. Extract reprinted: Murphy.
    1. "The Main Concern": Although Whitman cannot be categorized under one label, this book will consider to what extent he may be considered a socialist poet.
    2. "The Tenor of Politics": Young Whitman supported Jeffersonian and Jacksonian democracy, enjoying the political processes but disliking partisan fighting and becoming disillusioned. He had some radical prejudice but supported the anti-slavery cause, though most interested in saving the Union, not seeing the advantage the rich took of the poor. After the war he was divided between acceptance and repudiation, often blind to presidents' faults, finding it difficult to change his way of thinking to accord with a corrupt, more industrialized America, being unfamiliar with leftist parties. He perceived larger forces behind mere political issues.

3. "Wealth and Illth": His family background favored the virtues of industry and self-help, hence his approval of **capitalists and material prosperity. He** ignored much poverty and struggle. Yet his early journalism indicates an aversion to acquisition of wealth and a perception of working-class oppression.

4. "Science and the Unseen": The eighteenth-century rationalism of Paine, Volney, and Frances Wright was instrumental in his being open, to a greater degree than most American writers of his generation, to the many scientific developments of his time. He believed in the Quaker inner light and was attracted to European senti-mentalism, being drawn to Scott, Sand, Coleridge, Carlyle, Channing and other **Transcendentalists, especially Emerson, and** later the German metaphysicians, especially **Hegel. His "naturalistic credo," though** retaining his anticlericalism, gave way to "an intuitionalist theism." **His spiritual world had a materialist basis. He** followed the ideas of flux and evolution but was "too good a romantic" for the dif-ficult discipline of science. He moved from an early insistence on absolute clarity of expression to a deliberate obscurantism as he became increasingly mystical and obsessed with death and immortality, his idea of God becoming "more personal, more Biblical," with a "mental flaccidity" in later verse like "Passage."

5. "For Purposes Beyond": Whitman disliked trade-unionism and was not attract-ed by the socialist ideas current in his earlier years. Labor problems would have disrupted the prevailing optimism of Leaves. In his later years he tended toward the **spirit if not the theory of socialism. More fully than his fellow-writers, Whitman** in Leaves reaches toward "an equalized and **unified society" and a natural approach to** life untinged by the supernatural. With its emphasis on action, Leaves can remain valid under socialism, speaking for the future as well as its own time. Whitman's sympathies, imagination, creative sensibility "were quite as proletarian as they were bourgeois." **He came to subordinate individualism to** unity for the mass, achieved through com-radeship, still valuable as an ideal for all despite its basis in Whitman's homo-sexuality because Whitman elevates his **tendencies, latent in everyone as "warm** fraternal emotions," into the symbol for the drive toward true fraternity. No other American poet has so risen to this con-ception of a free and wholesome communality. As he became increasingly internationalistic, he made Leaves unparalleled in its antici-pation of "a democratic and fraternal humanism."

3 BRADFORD, GAMALIEL. "Walt Whitman." In America Through the Essay: An Anthology for English Courses, edited by A. Theodore

Johnson and Allen Tate. New York: Oxford University Press, pp. 387-406. Reprint of 1932.4.

4 CHADWICK, JOHN WHITE. "Walter Whitman." In Chambers's Cyclopaedia of English Litera-ture. Vol. 3. Edited by David Patrick, **revised and expanded by J. Liddell Geddie** and J. C. Smith. Philadelphia and New York: J. B. Lippincott Co., pp. 806-11. Reprint of 1903.3, with additional updated bibliography.

5 ERSKINE, JOHN. The Start of the Road. New York: Frederick A. Stokes Co., 344 pp. Novelizes Whitman's life, from the trip to New Orleans to his dismissal by Harlan, introducing for him an octoroon mistress who urges him to write of his actual exper-ience in the words of real conversation, but whose family and racial background prevent their marriage. Whitman's politi-cally liberal attitudes and disregard for convention get him into trouble. The birth of several poems (like "Brooklyn Ferry") is shown. His subsequent actions are seen as largely motivated by his love for Annette; his concern for his Southern son keeps him from fighting; in his hospital work he finds a boy whom he believes to be his son and for whom he cares, watching his death with despair. The book ends with Whitman meeting Annette again and discovering their son's whereabouts. Whitman meets Harlan first on his journey to New Orleans and regards him highly.

6 HOLLOWAY, EMORY, ed. Editor's preface, bio-graphical and bibliographical chronology, and notes to Walt Whitman: Complete Poetry & Selected Prose and Letters. London: Nonesuch Press, pp. xxv-xxxix, 1062-116. Readers find various emphases in Whitman; therefore it is important that he be presented fairly complete for readers to perceive him for themselves. The chrono-logical presentation of everything except the poetry is explained; for each poem the date of composition or first publication is noted. Notes cite some of Whitman's com-mentary on the poetry, earlier periodical publication, factual background for the prose and letters.

7 KOUWENHOVEN, JOHN A. Adventures of America 1857-1900: A Pictorial Record from Harper's Weekly. New York and London: Harper & Bros. Preface notes that Whitman sent his mother a copy of Harper's Weekly in 1867 with a picture he claimed was "tip-top." Picture 172 uses an extract from "Exposi-tion" as its caption.

8 KUNITZ, STANLEY J., and HAYCRAFT, HOWARD. American Authors, 1600-1900, A Biographical Dictionary of American Literature. New York: H. W. Wilson Co., pp. 807-10, includ-

ing bibliography.

Biographical: Whitman's early environment was appropriate for a poet of nature and the city. His stances in the 1840s were both conformist and reformer. A romance and paternity are "most improbable," stories to the contrary of twins in Camden and of a silent movie actor who called himself Walt Whitman and looked like him. He probably had no deep emotional interest in any human being except a few younger men and above all, himself. "The gradual mellowing and 'spiritualizing' of his later works" suggest his instinctive admission of the difficulty his contemporaries had with his work. He did not attain his ambition of exerting influence as prophet of democracy, being rejected by the people. He fathered free verse, although his lines are not always of high quality. He was a child in his sentimental egotism and lack of taste, but a child of genius. His cosmic shouts cover "the voice of a lonely man who felt his lack of kinship with humanity," and so all the more strenuously proclaimed identity of feeling with it. This "strain of neuroticism" may have transformed "the dull, orthodox editorial writer" into "the great poet."

9 LONG, HANIEL. Walt Whitman and the Springs of Courage. Santa Fe: Writers' Editions, 144 pp. No index.

Introduction: In following his own way to live, Whitman sought corroboration from various sources, as this book explains.

1. "Whitman and Phrenology": Phrenology furnished him a picture of a balanced life, means for understanding himself, and encouragement for his chosen course.

2. "Emerson": Whitman was more reliant on Emerson than his 1856 letter suggested. To Emerson's doctrine that the individual is unlimited, Whitman added the idea that all individuals are equal.

3. "Whitman's Sensitiveness to Criticism": Various critical commentaries are reviewed, with Whitman's hopes for reassurance.

4. "Whitman's Americanism": He was self-educated. He was right to object to New England's hostility to him as a substitute for honest criticism. His poetry offers affirmation.

5. "Mrs. Gilchrist": Along with Quaker independence, Whitman's work reveals mystical leaning. Gilchrist perceived what Leaves lacked and tried to bring Whitman to "a wiser description of the bonds between man and woman."

6. "Whitman's Idea of Culture": Whitman's utterances on death gained in power from his hospital contacts. Unlike Matthew Arnold, Whitman sought a culture that emphasized human relations without separating body from spirit.

7. "The Strength of Thought, the Leaven of Soul": Whitman provides answers for questions about human relations, emphasizing the importance of feeling as well as thought and the acceptance of one's self. He portrays the reality and mystery of sex, using parenthood merely "to appease Mrs. Grundy," realizing that "the problems of sexuality cannot be separated from those of love." In "Calamus" he "suggests his own sexual temperament, a remarkable and epoch-making thing to do." He emphasizes self-unification and is worth more attention than such contemporaries as Howells, who shunned Whitman for his sexual openness.

8. "The Blunder": "Adam" rings false in its physical emphasis, for we need more the exaltation of feelings in "Calamus," "an incomparable work of art" "spun out of depths which Whitman knew."

9. "Peter Doyle": Doyle's nature was sweeter than Whitman's. Their love for each other gave Whitman support. Whitman found good company among the uneducated because of their sense of values and life, their recognition of him for himself alone.

10. "The Triumph of the Leaves": Whitman offers the idea that one should be what one's nature, rather than society, demands, as do later writers like Lawrence and Gide.

11. "Whitman and Religion": The voice of religion grows more dominant in Whitman's later years. He could not transform the invisible into human terms. He allowed his ego to dominate him. One should read his prose first and then approach Leaves aware of the anxiety in his heart so that the poems will seem not "the utterances of an unchained optimism" but his "suggestions for a far-flung campaign against our chaos and futility." His attitudes toward Hicks reveal how he feels about his parents, perhaps indicating the deepest source of his courage. He provides a guide for us into a new sense of life.

10 MacLEISH, ARCHIBALD. Land of the Free. New York: Harcourt, Brace & Co., p. [14].

In this book combining Depression photographs with poetry, the "elder races" stanza of "Pioneers" is quoted.

11 MONROE, HARRIET. A Poet's Life: Seventy Years in a Changing World. New York: Macmillan Co., pp. 250, 257, 294, 365, 366, 430.

Incidental: Whitman did not found a school or gain much attention from American intellectuals or his fellow countrymen during his lifetime, though he made "his own way into the wilderness, and up to the heights" in his free verse, which only later came to be used by poets with any success.

12 MORLEY, CHRISTOPHER. Preface to Walt Whitman in Camden: A Selection of Prose from Specimen Days. Camden: Haddon Craftsmen,

1938

5 pp. Photographs of Camden by Arnold Genthe.

Examines Camden's current recognition of Whitman. His "Timber Creek passages are among the most moving he ever wrote" with some of the noblest simplicity in American writing. The Mickle Street home is described. Philadelphia has changed from the time when John Wannamaker would not sell Leaves. Whitman has had grotesque memorials and, during his lifetime, "abominable" printing. "He had one characteristic of a really great poet, that his prose (at its best) was better than his verse." Whitman must be recognized as a great artist, with "a core of wise and unanswerable quiet" behind "all his often ill-chosen lingo" and his "ejaculating, promulging, effusing."

13 POWYS, JOHN COWPER. Enjoyment of Literature. New York: Simon & Schuster. "Whitman," pp. 342-64; passim per index. Photograph. Same as 1938.14.

Whitman's optimism is "heathen and profane," physical and mystical. His universe is based on a "mystical pluralism" rather than on God, a "sovietization of the Absolute." He is one of the greatest poets in English because "he has a 'secret' to communicate": "the emotional extension of our personal ego" into the inner identity of every object around it. He reveals and exalts what other poets omit. He uses "dignified simple traditional words" with "staggering appropriateness." He worships his own inner spirit, his self-assertion surpassing even Nietzsche's. His sexuality is all-inclusive, his elements of romance "certainly of a homosexual character." He makes the "traditional psychological differences between normal and abnormal" seem unimportant, transfigured. He could see what the average man does not see in himself; hence his appeal chiefly to the sophisticated. His acceptance of evil is in error or susceptible to misunderstanding. A "pluralistic anarchist," he will continue to inspire with his ideas, despite possible totalitarian reactions. Incidental comparisons elsewhere with Goethe, Rabelais, Wordsworth.

14 _____. The Pleasures of Literature. London, Toronto, Melbourne, Sydney: Cassell & Co. "Whitman," pp. 440-78; passim per index. Same as 1938.13, with some changes in accidentals.

15 SANDBURG, CARL. A Lincoln and Whitman Miscellany. Chicago: Holiday Press. "A Sketch of Walt Whitman," pp. 26-33. Photograph.

A vigorous sketch of Whitman's life. "He becomes a permanent, looming ghost of American art and literature." Facsimile of his "Autobiographic Note," which now exists only in one copy of Leaves, although it may have been included in many others.

Whitman's letter to J. P. Kirkwood requesting money for the soldiers is printed.

16 SHEPARD, ODELL, ed. The Journals of Bronson Alcott. Boston: Little, Brown & Co., pp. vii, 278-79, 281n, 286-87, 289-91, 293-94, 387, 391, 423, 468, 527-28. Extracts reprinted: Hindus.

Account of visits to Whitman in late 1856, one made with Thoreau and Mrs. Tyndall, which Shepard notes was given a "grotesquely false rendering" in Sanborn's edition of Thoreau letters (1894.16). Alcott describes Whitman, "an extraordinary person, full of brute power, certainly of genius and audacity, and likely to make his mark on Young America." The scant communication between Thoreau and Whitman may have been due to a mutual literary jealousy. Other visits and meetings with Whitman are described; some critical comments on his work ("Personalism," "Exposition"). Only Thoreau, Emerson, and Whitman can represent the New World.

17 SHEPHARD, ESTHER. Walt Whitman's Pose. New York: Harcourt, Brace & Co., 453 pp. Illustrated. Revision of 1936.23.

1. "The Paradox of Walt Whitman": Whitman's character is full of contradictions, with a tendency toward concealment. He was influenced by Goethe's autobiography, Margaret Fuller's "American Literature," Schlegel's Philosophy of Life and Philosophy of Language.

2. "The Thread of Ariadne (The record of a search)": His use of Sand's Countess of Rudolstadt is explained, showing him motivated less by a "wish-to-create" than by a "wish-to-be-great-by-creating." Though with some poetic sensitivity, he lacked a great poet's imagination and mastery over his material, with a furtiveness due to his belief in originality and American cultural independence. His ideals of democracy and universal brotherhood are simplistic and borrowed.

3. "The Pattern": Reprints the Countess of Rudolstadt epilogue from the Francis G. Shaw translation, which Whitman read.

4. "In Character (Whitman and Emerson)": Whitman combined both characters from the Sand epilogue. The question of the Emerson debt may be resolved by the suggestion that Whitman was familiar with Emerson's ideas before writing Leaves but only read him extensively after Emerson's letter. Whitman's paradox is that "while posing as an original and natural musician-poet of man he produced some original poems and some finely true natural lines and some beautiful word-music." His method may be justifiable but it remains despicable, his criticism of his contemporaries not ringing true.

18 SPRING, HOWARD. My Son, My Son! New York:
    Grosset & Dunlap, pp. 267-69. (Published
    in England as O Absalom.)
        Rev. Wintringham is about to give a
    lecture on "The Message of Whitman," which
    he interprets as "just brotherly love."

19 THOMAS, HENRY [H. T. Schnittkind]. The Story
    of the United States: A Biographical
    History of America. New York: Doubleday,
    Doran & Co. "Walt Whitman, Dreamer of the
    Great American Dream," pp. 239-50; also
    305, 360, 367, 385, 408.
        Whitman retained his sense of direction
    for democracy during the country's troubled
    years, emphasizing everyone's potential for
    development and perceiving "the miracle of
    common things," thus striking a new note
    in literature. His life is traced, noting
    his New Orleans romance whose vast influence
    is evident in the "fervid simplicity" of
    "Rolling Ocean." Emerson, disapproving of
    Whitman's "disconcerting realism," thus
    failed to understand his universality.
    Leaves is founded on the principles of
    equality, pity, religion, and love. Whitman
    created death in his own image, "a kindly
    and beautiful elderly brother." He looks
    to a new era of human dignity and unity.
    He was one of America's "most healthy-
    minded men," seeing life clearly because he
    saw it whole. His "perfect mental vision"
    was deceived only in some of his poems
    favoring the war, although he generally
    abhorred it. "Reconciliation" is one of
    "the very few things in literature which
    attain to the simple grandeur of the
    Sermon on the Mount."

PERIODICALS

20 JOHNSON, MAURICE O. "Walt Whitman as a Critic
    of Literature." University of Nebraska
    Studies in Language, Literature and Criti-
    cism, no. 16, 73 pp.
        Explanation of Whitman's literary back-
    ground, noting the few literary allusions
    in his writings, the many in his conversa-
    tion. Account of his attitudes toward
    Shakespeare, Tennyson, Scott, Dickens,
    Carlyle, Burns, Emerson, Longfellow,
    Bryant, and Whittier, with reservations
    toward almost all writers but Hegel and
    Dickens. Whitman himself fulfills his own
    requirements for literature.

21 BOZARD, JOHN F. "Horace Traubel's Socialistic
    Interpretation of Whitman." Furman
    Bulletin 20 (January), 35-45.
        Brief biographical sketch of Traubel,
    summarizing his relationship with Whitman
    and his strained version of Whitman's life,
    philosophy, and conversations, which has
    hurt Whitman's popularity. Whitman was an
    individualist, not a "social revolutionist."
    The Conservator lacked popularity because
    of Traubel's socialistic orientation.

22 SILVER, ROLLO G. "Whitman's Earliest Signed
    Prose: A Correction." American Literature
    9 (January), 458.
        The 1840 piece reported in 1937.40 was
    preceded by the minutes of the Smithtown
    Debating Society as Whitman's earliest
    signed prose (see 1936.31).

23 ____. "Whitman Interviews Himself." American
    Literature 10 (March), 84-87.
        Prints a manuscript from the Charles A.
    Raymond collection of "Walt Whitman in
    Denver," which Whitman says was printed
    (1879.35), although it has not been
    located.

24 ANON. "Rogers Sculptor Here." New York Times
    (5 March), 19:8.
        Brief interview with Jo Davidson, who
    is working on a nine-foot statue of Whitman
    for W. Averell Harriman.

25 ENGLEKIRK, JOHN E. "Notes on Whitman in
    Spanish America." Hispanic Review 6
    (April), 133-38.
        Poe is more popular than Whitman with
    Spanish readers, who prefer "romantic"
    writing. Whitman was not translated until
    1901; later translations are noted. Only
    twelve books or articles discussing Whitman
    have appeared in Spanish, though many
    references to Whitman are made in prose and
    poetry. Bibliography with some annotations.

26 THOMPSON, RALPH. "Books of the Times." New
    York Times (7 April), 21:2-3.
        Review of Shephard (1938.17), a con-
    vincing book but rambling and over-
    elaborate. "Even if Whitman did 'pose' and
    deliberately 'hide' the source of his in-
    spiration, he still managed to write--by
    himself--some of the greatest poetry ever
    written by an American."

27 CANBY, HENRY SEIDEL. "Grains of Sand and
    'Leaves of Grass.'" Saturday Review of
    Literature 17 (9 April), 3-4. 1855 portrait
    on cover.
        Review of Shephard (1938.17), which
    explains an important source but not
    Whitman's true poetic power and originality.
    The Sand passage contains "too little about
    love to sound more than ten per cent
    Whitmanesque." This discovery provides
    another example which we can enjoy of
    Whitman's faking, and does not detract from
    his "ample genius."

28 JACK, PETER MONRO. "A New Light on Walt
    Whitman. Esther Shephard Establishes Among
    Other Things His Great Indebtedness to a
    Novel by George Sand." New York Times Book
    Review (17 April), 2. Illustrated.
        Review of Shephard (1938.17). Some of
    Whitman's poses are already familiar: his
    costume as the carpenter poet, each edition's
    changes in his "spontaneous" poetry, his
    awareness of literary tradition despite

1938

claims to being merely "natural," tales of **illegitimate sons, his self-reviews.** Shephard's idea is valid but her book is not well written and she does not like his poetry much. Whatever its source, Whitman's work remains "the first expression of a militantly emergent America, bent on its own course."

29 GOODALE, DAVID. "Some of Walt Whitman's Borrowings." <u>American Literature</u> 10 (May), 202-13.
    Notes Whitman's use in poems and notebooks of material from various sources, citing parallel passages from "Myself" 35 and John Paul Jones's letter to Franklin. Frances Wright and Volney provided him with concepts, phrases, and patterns that may indicate the origins of his characteristic poetic idiom but do not account for the underlying genius.

30 McCUSKER, HONOR. "Leaves of Grass: First Editions and Manuscripts in the Whitman Collection." <u>More Books</u> (Bulletin of the Boston Public Library) 13 (May), 179-92. Illustrated with facsimiles.
    Only recently has criticism of Whitman achieved any real compromise between heroic myth and snobbish contempt. Through tracing the Boston Library's Whitman collection, started by Bucke, the history of <u>Leaves</u> is followed from the 1855 Preface, "a vital contribution to criticism," through the second edition (more artistic than the first) to his tamed exuberance and strengthened mysticism after the war. His revisions for "Locomotive," "Eidólons," "Out from Behind This Mask," "Come, said my Soul," are explained. Letters to and from Whitman in the collection are quoted, revealing an old man's "pathetic weariness and melancholy." Whitman's principles were "clearness and simplicity," along with an appreciation for "values of rhythm and tone."

31 RUBIN, JOSEPH JAY. "Whitman and Carlyle: 1846." <u>Modern Language Notes</u> 53 (May), 370-71.
    Reprints short review of Carlyle's book on Cromwell from the Brooklyn <u>Evening Star</u>, antedating Whitman's previously supposed earliest mention of Carlyle in print.

32 _____. "Whitman and the Boy-Forger." <u>American Literature</u> 10 (May), 214-15.
    Presents the factual background for the fourth of Whitman's "Fact-Romances" from the December 1845 <u>Aristidean</u>, here reprinted.

33 SAMMIS, Mrs. IRVING S. "Whitman Collection of Huntington Historical Society." <u>Long Islander</u> (6 May).
    Early biographical information on Whitman as related to Long Island and the <u>Long Islander</u> and the items in the society's collection. Continued 1938.35.

34 MUMFORD, LEWIS. "Sand in the Shephard's Pie." <u>New Republic</u> 95 (11 May), 23-24.
    Review of Shephard (1938.17). Academicians see Whitman as "a negation of their accepted scheme of values." Shephard fails to understand the growth of an original mind, for the Sand passage is quite different, impossible to accept as the source for Whitman's personality and poetry. His ideas on the poet and artist were common among nineteenth-century artistic pioneers. She fails "to grasp the inevitable contradictions between the private and the public personality of the artist," for great writers create their own personae. Whitman actually displays harmony between his life and his work.

35 SAMMIS, Mrs. IRVING S. "Whitman Collection of Huntington Historical Society. Part II." <u>Long Islander</u> (13 May).
    Continues 1938.33, concentrating on period beginning 1855. Continued 1938.36.

36 _____. "Memorial Day--An Approach to the Day with Walt Whitman. Part I." <u>Long Islander</u> (20 May).
    Continues 1938.35. Biographical information about Whitman's Civil War experiences, quoting letters. Concluded 1938.38.

37 MABBOTT, T. O. "Walt Whitman's Use of 'Libertad.'" <u>Notes and Queries</u> 174 (21 May), 367-68.
    "Libertad" was printed on "the usual silver coinage of the Mexican Republic," legal tender in the United States until 1857.

38 SAMMIS, Mrs. IRVING S. "Memorial Day--An Approach to the Day with Walt Whitman. Part II." <u>Long Islander</u> (27 May). Illustrated.
    Concludes 1938.36, on the latter part of Whitman's life.

39 PIERRA [pseud.?]. "Lines About Leaders--Walt Whitman." <u>Christian Science Monitor</u> (31 May), 13:6. Illustrated.
    A free-verse sketch of Whitman, his life and artistic development, emphasizing his ideals and aspirations.

40 ANON. "100 Admirers of Walt Whitman Mark Poet's Natal Anniversary." <u>Camden Courier-Post</u> (1 June).
    Quotes some personal reminiscences and **Sculley Bradley's remarks on reading** <u>Leaves</u>: its changing facets (like a person), the gradual discovery of harmony. Whitman's poetry is full of progress, love, wisdom, and humor.

41 COBLENTZ, STANTON. "Walt Whitman as a Lover of Life." <u>New York Times Book Review</u> (12 June), 4.
    Review of Long (1938.9). All attempts to explain Whitman leave him an enigmatic

figure. He appears differently in different lights. Long's book is summed up, its main idea being "that Whitman went back to fundamental and natural things." It provides half glimpses of Whitman.

42 STEVENSON, PHILIP. "Walt Whitman's Democracy." New Masses 27 (14 June), 129.
    Marxist interpretation. Whitman's democracy is "the dialectical unity of the individual and the masses." His ideal "was completely identified with the mass character and mass aspiration," opposing the American ruling class, seeing fruition in the future. Though not a socialist, he supported labor struggles. He represents the transition between revolutionary middle-class democracy and working-class democracy.

43 SPENDER, STEPHEN. "In Praise of Whitman." New Statesman and Nation, n.s. 15 (18 June), 1030.
    Review of Nonesuch edition (1938.6). Whitman's poetry, though uneven, dates less than that of greater nineteenth-century poets. Leaves, "the most moving and complete personal confession since Rousseau," "the only successful contemporary epic of modern times," deals with "hunks of material reality." Whitman fit his historic moment. His comradeship, poetry, and war service gave him a fortunate "outlet for homosexual tendencies which in other circumstances might have left him unhappy and neurotic." He remains a pioneer, his discoveries in verse little exploited or analyzed. His verse attains power through creating in an unforgettable image "the vast and magnificent subject of the whole of his poetry." Lawrence's attack (1923.9) ignores his own similarity to Whitman whose root was in universal sympathy while Lawrence's was in personal frustration. Whitman's ideals have "extraordinary vitality" for today, when people appear shoddy compared with his pioneers. He was not a dreamer but a realist; his poetry reminds us of "tremendous opportunities lost."

44 MERRITT, JEAN. "Walt Whitman and Long Island Quakerism." Long Islander (24 June).
    Chiefly quotations from Whitman on Hicks.

45 GLICKSBERG, CHARLES I. "Charles Godfrey Leland and Vanity Fair." Pennsylvania Magazine of History and Biography 62 (July), 311, 315-16.
    According to Burroughs in the National Cyclopaedia (1898.4), Whitman wrote for Vanity Fair, although nothing has been identified as his work. However, he "was frequently the object of satiric comment," as in items quoted (see Vanity Fair in the 1860s).

46 WANN, LOUIS. "Robinson Jeffers--Counterpart of Walt Whitman." Personalist 19 (July),

297-308.
    Describes Jeffers's ideas, particularly those in contrast with Whitman's: self-abnegation vs. exaltation of the individual, doubt and disillusion vs. faith in America and in reconciliation. Jeffers is more naturalistic than Whitman. "Whitman has resolved the conflicts of life. Jeffers has not yet done so."

47 BROPHY, JOHN. "The Walt Whitman Legend. Did He Impose on His Generation?" John o' London's Weekly 39 (15 July), 560-61.
    Sketch of Whitman's life. He is largely responsible for the current "confusion between the purposes and methods of prose and of poetry." "Captain" is "more suitable for recitation before an enthusiastically uncritical audience than for its place in the Oxford Book of English Verse." Whitman saw himself as a prophet and savior, as Shephard (1938.17) shows, acknowledging "a high estimation of his poetry which I for one cannot share." She exposes his pose and borrowing, not a fault provided something enduring is produced, but his work has no lasting value, his poetry being mere "prose vitiated by rhetoric."

47a ANON. "Whitman Box Yields Unpublished Poems. Other Material Is Found in Library of Congress." New York Times (21 August), 27:1.
    Joseph Auslander describes findings in package bought from Whitman's estate when he died, including papers which have been erased and reused, clippings, notes.

48 STRAUCH, CARL F. "The Structure of Walt Whitman's 'Song of Myself.'" English Journal (College ed.) 27 (September), 597-607.
    Reprinted: Whitman's 'Song of Myself'--Origin, Growth, Meaning, edited by James E. Miller, Jr. New York: Dodd, Mead & Co., 1964.
    Whitman's architectonics are excellent but neglected, although "Lilacs" has long been held "the high-water mark of American poetry." People have approached Whitman through his religion and biography but seldom through his significance as an artist. Discovering the structure of "Myself" leads to "a new realization of the greatness of this greatest American poet." Avoiding discussion of its different versions or its ideas, Strauch explicates the five large divisions of "Myself": 1-18 ("the Self; mystical interpenetration of the Self with all life and experience"); 19-25 ("definition of the Self; identification with the degraded, and transfiguration of it; final merit of Self withheld; silence; end of first half"); 26-38 ("life flowing in upon the Self; then evolutionary interpenetration of life"); 39-41 ("the Superman"); 42-52 ("larger questions of life--religion, faith, God, death; immor-

1938

tality and happiness mystically affirmed").
Despite occasional indifference to minor
details, Whitman is "one of the great
artists in poetry," "conscious of the movement and direction of his ideas."

49 ANON. "Two Long Islanders Get Niches at Fair."
New York Times (19 September), 21:2.
Theodore Roosevelt and Whitman will
represent Long Island in the New York State
exhibit at the World's Fair. Cleveland
Rodgers's praise of Whitman as "the first
authentic voice of American democracy" is
quoted.

50 ANON. "Long Island's Sons." New York Times
(20 September), 22:4.
Editorial praising the choice of
Whitman and Roosevelt (see 1938.49),
figures of whom any island would be proud
to boast. The devoted Whitmanite
Christopher Morley would be an ideal choice
to speak at the dedication.

51 THOMPSON, RALPH. "Books of the Times." New
York Times (25 October), 21:2-3.
Review of Erskine (1938.5) and Arvin
(1938.2). Erskine's book is useless as an
interpretation of Whitman, with its un-
Whitman-like love affair. Arvin is excellent and deep, not confining the complex
Whitman to a single label. Whitman is
"our great and abiding genius" because he
gave expression to the ideals this country
stands for.

52 McCOY, CHARLES G. "A Walt Whitman Memorial."
New York Times (31 October), 14:6.
As spokesman for the Brroklyn Printers
Group, he urges the naming of a park in
Brooklyn after Whitman to remind people
"that one of America's great men lived and
worked here."

53 SILVER, ROLLO G. "Walt Whitman: First
Appearance of 'Virginia--The West.'" Notes
and Queries 175 (12 November), 348-49.
It first appeared in Kansas Magazine,
March 1872.

54 UNTERMEYER, LOUIS. "Doubtful Socialist."
Saturday Review of Literature 19 (19
November), 10.
Review of Arvin (1938.2), "plausible
rather than compelling": Whitman contains
too many contrasting statements to support
any single label. The book gives valuable
background. In comparison with Erskine
(1938.5) and Shephard (1938.17), this is
"the least exciting but the most important."
Whitman's contradictions are noted between
his "excessive male assertiveness and his
inverted but obvious homosexuality, his
broad humanitarianism and his narrow sec-
tionalism," "his vaunted freedom from
cliques and his uncritical adherence to
party politics," his championship of American words and use of foreign hybrids.

55 FOLLETT, WILSON. "Walt Whitman as the Poet of
Socialism--Newton Arvin's Study Is Focused
on That Aspect of the Man and the Writer."
New York Times Book Review (27 November),
2. Illustrated.
Review of Arvin (1938.2). Its misleading title suggests that the socialist
aspects of Whitman represent the whole man.
Arvin has limited Whitman, although he
argues impressively against Dell and Canby
who see him opposed to socialism and concerned purely with individuals. His
brotherhood is better grasped "as a spontaneous and unifying necessity in that
whole complex, perverse, incalculable ego
than it could ever be in the rootless
idealized form" of dedication to a kind of
future that may never arrive.

56 COAD, ORAL SUMNER. "A Walt Whitman Manuscript."
Journal of the Rutgers University Library
2 (December), 6-10.
Discusses and prints the four different
versions of "Hush'd be the Camps Today,"
from a manuscript at Rutgers. Facsimile
of first two stanzas. Whitman's careful,
laborious craftsmanship is revealed, making
changes for the better.

57 ANON. "Bronx Postoffice Mural Assailed By
Father Cox as Insult to Religion. He Terms
Its Whitman Lines 'Government Propaganda'
and Urges Catholic Protest. Artist Offers
to Omit Them." New York Times (12 December), 3:3.
Rev. Ignatius Cox opposes the use on a
public mural of the opening six lines of
"Thou Mother" 3, in which "the note of
religious skepticism is quite clearly conveyed, and some sort of an absolute faith
in the living present is indicated." One
postal clerk admitted learning the poem in
school.

58 ANON. "Artist Halts Work on Postoffice Mural."
New York Times (13 December), 22:6.
After Cox's criticism (1938.57), the
artist assents to a change of quotation if
necessary.

1939

BOOKS

1 BROOKS, CLEANTH. Modern Poetry and the
Tradition. Chapel Hill: University of
North Carolina Press, pp. 71, 76n, 131, 233.
Though Whitman thought he resolved the
two extremes of concentration on local
color and detachment from America, "the
diverse elements in all but his best
poetry tend to stay apart" (i.e., the par-
ticularity of the catalogues and the vague
generalities about democracy and progress).
In celebrating formlessness he becomes
nebulous in "thin and diluted" poetry.

2 DOUGLAS, LLOYD C. Disputed Passage. Boston:
    Houghton Mifflin Co., frontispiece.
        Uses quotation from "Stronger Lessons"
    as epigraph.

3 EASTMAN, MAX. Enjoyment of Poetry with Other
    Essays in Aesthetics. New York and London:
    Charles Scribner's Sons, passim per index;
    also pp. 185-86.
        Includes reprint of 1913.5 with index added.
        Essay on "The History of English Poetry"
    notes Whitman's influence on Sandburg.

4 FURNESS, CLIFTON JOSEPH, ed. Introduction to
    Leaves of Grass by Walt Whitman (1855 fac-
    simile). New York: Columbia University
    Press, pp. v-xviii.
        Account of first edition (its printing,
    sales, influences for its title and binding,
    number of issues). Specific remaining
    copies are noted. Whitman's title may come
    from the printer's slang "grass" for a
    person who does casual work at printshops.
    A newspaper clipping from Hugh Farmer
    McDermott (not dated or identified) is
    quoted, interviewing Whitman on his memories
    of this time.

5 GARCIA LORCA, F. Poems. With English Trans-
    lation by Stephen Spender and J. L. Gili.
    London: Dolphin. "Ode to Walt Whitman,"
    pp. 76-81; Introduction by R. M. Nadal,
    p. xx.
        The ode, presented in parallel texts
    of Spanish and English, contrasts modern
    New York with Whitman's ideal of unity with
    nature and contemporary homosexuals with
    Whitman's homoerotic ideal. Nadal notes
    that Lorca had Whitman translated to him
    when he was in New York (1929-30).

6 GREENBIE, MARJORIE BARSTOW. American Saga:
    The History and Literature of the American
    Dream of a Better Life. New York and
    London: Whittlesey House, pp. 336, 368-69,
    515-16, 600, 621-22.
        Quotations from Whitman are used to
    exemplify moments of American history or
    American life. He sang the new gospel of
    adhesiveness, a vast love to which he saw
    man advancing from "earlier skulking affec-
    tions."

7 HERRON, IMA HONAKER. The Small Town in Amer-
    ican Literature. Durham, N.C.: Duke
    University Press, pp. 113, 193, 221, 260,
    355, 362, 372, 376, 399, 424, 425.
        Minor mentions including comparisons of
    Whitman with Masters, Garland, Anderson,
    Wolfe.

8 JOYCE, JAMES. Finnegans Wake. New York:
    Viking Press, pp. 263, 551.
    Reprinted: Miller.
        Passing allusions to Whitman: "I said
    to the shiftless prostitute; let me be your
    fodder; and to rodies and prater brothers;
    Chau, Camerade!: evangel of good tidings,
    omnient as the Healer's word," etc.

9 MOORE, JOHN. The Life and Letters of Edward
    Thomas. London: William Heinemann, p. 37.
        Thomas "was utterly repelled by Walt
    Whitman, whom he believed to be 'an added
    fiend to Hell.'"

9a RUSK, RALPH L., ed. The Letters of Ralph
    Waldo Emerson. Vols. 1, 4-6. New York:
    Columbia University Press, passim per
    index in Vol. 6.
        Several letters from Emerson to others
    praise Whitman and Leaves. His later
    silence on Leaves was probably due to the
    "dismay of a number of his personal
    friends," such as J. P. Lesley and Bennett
    H. Nash, whose letters on Whitman are
    cited. In 1869 Emerson gave a series of
    readings in Concord, which included
    Whitman. Emerson notes Whitman's appear-
    ance at Emerson's Baltimore lecture in
    1872. Letters to Emerson from William
    Swinton and Emma Lazarus are cited, men-
    tioning Whitman.

10 SMITH, BERNARD. Forces in American Criticism:
    A Study in the History of American Literary
    Thought. New York: Harcourt, Brace & Co.
    "Democracy and Realism, II. The Romance of
    Reality: Whitman," pp. 143-57; also 158
    and passim per index.
        Whitman was recognized for his romantic
    qualities, particularly his transcendental-
    ism, evidenced in the 1855 Preface; however,
    he pointed toward realism in "his cry for
    plain speech" and "dogmatic contemporane-
    ity," his "will to deal with facts," and
    his love for the masses. Vistas shows his
    basic theory retained, with added anger,
    fear, and bitterness; its predictions were
    mistaken, for fiction, not poetry, has
    dominated, as have the critical and pessi-
    mistic moods. Whitman grew more critical
    of America and more confused, never quite
    accepting or understanding socialism, be-
    coming internationalist. He failed to
    acknowledge that readers might love poetry
    of the past yet remain able to judge its
    archaic values. His value as critic is not
    as guide or interpreter but as prophet, for
    his estimates of individuals (cited) were
    romantic. Followers must be selective
    regarding his ideas. His experimentation,
    sexual frankness, and allegiance to the
    masses make him a forerunner of modern
    literature.

11 SMITH, LOGAN PEARSALL. Unforgotten Years.
    Boston: Little, Brown, & Co. "Walt
    Whitman," pp. 92-108.
    Reprint of 1937.45.

12 STOVALL, FLOYD, ed. Introduction, bibliography,
    and notes to Walt Whitman: Representative
    Selections. New York: American Book Co.
    Revision of 1934.16.
        Vistas is added to the selections;
    some notes are revised, particularly with
    updated bibliographic references.

1939

13 UNITED STATES, LIBRARY OF CONGRESS. A List of
    Manuscripts, Books, Portraits, Prints,
    Broadsides, and Memorabilia in Commemora-
    tion of the One Hundred and Twentieth
    Anniversary of the Birth of Walt Whitman
    [May 31, 1819-1939] from the Whitman
    Collection of Mrs. Frank Julian Sprague of
    New York City Exhibited at the Library of
    Congress 1939.
        Lists and describes items of the
    collection, including letters, editions of
    Whitman, secondary material. Many copies
    are from personal libraries of figures
    significant in Whitman biography and
    criticism. Preface by Harriet Sprague
    announces her desire to assemble "a Whitman
    reference library."

14 VAN DOREN, CARL, and VAN DOREN, MARK.
    American and British Literature Since 1890.
    New York and London: Century Co., pp. 3,
    31, 38, 82.
    Revision of 1925.15.
        Deletes the comparison of Whitman and
    Mencken.

15 WHITMAN, WALT. A Whitman Manuscript from the
    Albert M. Bender Collection of Mills
    College. Oakland: Bibliophile Society of
    Mills College, 21 pp.
        Foreword by Oscar Lewis: The manu-
    script first draft (here reprinted) of
    Whitman's "Waves in the Vessel's Wake"
    (here reprinted), later developed into
    "After the Sea-Ship," reveals much about
    Whitman's method of working, showing ex-
    tensive revision as the poem takes shape
    before our eyes. The poem's history is
    traced. "Whitman's Revisions" by Sidney L.
    Gulick, Jr.: Gulick describes the various
    changes made in the manuscript, as Whitman
    may have justified them.

PERIODICALS

16 ALLEN, GAY WILSON. "Walt Whitman's 'Long
    Journey' Motif." Journal of English and
    Germanic Philology 38 (January), 76-95.
        Whitman's notes reveal a plan to write
    an epic work on human progress through the
    ages. He diverted his scheme to make life
    as a journey the major motif of Leaves,
    incorporating "a scientific theory, a
    metaphysics, a religious faith, and a
    personal philosophy," which saw America as
    a culmination but not a final one and
    viewed death as part of an eternal journey.
    Whitman was not a great hiker but enjoyed
    nature more passively, so the journey is
    largely allegorical in "Open Road."
    Whitman anticipated interior monologue as
    part of the process occurring within him,
    his catalogues being part of his meditative
    process. His style is compared to Hans
    Christian Andersen's use of association of
    ideas, with the same "sympathetic identifi-
    cation of author and subject and desire to
    feel in one's own self the unity of the

universe." Henrik Wergeland, writing in
the decades before Whitman, displays "a
Whitmanesque cosmic lyricism" and similar
philosophical basis. Johannes Jensen has
recently used Whitman in his novels. The
journey and cosmic motif, part of a nineteenth-century movement in world literature,
are important to the message, genesis, and
style of Leaves (although Whitman lacks
Wergeland's and Jensen's structural sense).

17 BRADLEY, SCULLEY. "The Fundamental Metrical
    Principle in Whitman's Poetry." American
    Literature 10 (January), 437-59.
        Whitman's form has not been successfully
    explained. He founded his poetic principle
    on organic form, with similarities to
    English poetry, matching his verse and
    lines to the content. Several poems
    ("Tears," "Spider," "Lo, Victress") are
    examined for their use of wave-like crests,
    a similar movement occurring in consecutive
    stanzas.

18 HOLLOWAY, EMORY. Review of Long (1938.9).
    American Literature 10 (January), 507-9.
        "Product of the nineteenth century,
    Whitman is still more an influence in the
    twentieth century because he has something
    to say concerning the reconciling of
    thought and feeling, the body and the soul,
    in the reintegration of the individual,"
    beyond authority. The flaws in "Adam" are
    due to failure in art, not a defect in
    Whitman's emotional nature. Long is in
    error regarding adhesiveness, for at times
    Whitman found it a spring of anything but
    courage, causing him almost to renounce
    poetry. Shephard (1938.17) is guilty of
    hasty writing, failing to balance other
    influences against Sand. Though not
    scholarly, Long's book is worth reading as
    commentary on personal development.

19 FLETCHER, JOHN GOULD. "Whitman--Without and
    Within." Poetry 53 (February), 273-79.
        Review of Arvin (1938.2) and Long
    (1938.9). Whitman, his work intended as a
    gospel, "possessed the fiery drive, the
    concentration, the multiplicity in unity,
    the persistence that belongs to the world's
    greatest men." He moved in the direction
    of "revolutionary socialism" but halted
    halfway in favor of a quasi-religious
    approach to the world. Arvin's assumption
    that Whitman's "gospel of fraternalism"
    pointed the way "to possible human solidar-
    ity under socialism" is largely denied by
    many critics with regard to Whitman's own
    psychology. Arvin admits Whitman's homo-
    sexual aspects, arguing that Whitman's
    viewpoint is valid and worthy of respect,
    while ignoring him as a poet. Long regards
    Whitman "as an abiding spiritual force,"
    accepting the later poems on death and
    immortality as more than the anticlimax
    Arvin sees. Long's Whitman "made the myth
    of himself as the perfect democrat interfuse

with and illuminate the America of his day." Long's Whitman is closer to the real Whitman, "a democrat of more religious than political import."

20 ANON. "Gift for Dearborn Inn." New York Times (20 February), 19:2.

Long Island citizens presented a map of Long Island to the colonial village in Dearborn, Michigan, for use in the reproduction of the Whitman homestead. Many will visit the original during the World's Fair.

21 FURNESS, CLIFTON JOSEPH. Review of Arvin (1938.2) and Shephard (1938.17). American Literature 11 (March), 95-101.

"Arvin answers his self-imposed questions neatly," showing Whitman's socialism as a pose but leaving one no nearer the poetry. Whitman's genius lay, as no biographer has yet realized, "in the commonplaces of the heart," being little affected by contemporary events, likely to have reacted the same in other times. Shephard's thesis is valid. Furness corrects her errors regarding cost of the tomb and the Parton debt. An expression of Whitman "based on his really significant 'ensemble'" is needed rather than dissection of him.

22 WHITE, WILLIAM. "Walt Whitman and Sir William Osler." American Literature 11 (March), 73-77.

Prints fragmentary manuscript reminiscences of Whitman by Osler, expanding upon those in 1925.3, describing a visit to Mickle Street when Whitman was sixty-four. Whitman's complaints and pessimism about his health are noted.

23 RUBIN, JOSEPH JAY. "Whitman on Byron, Scott and Sentiment." Notes and Queries 176 (11 March), 171.

Reprints comment on Whitman's editorial writing from Yankee Doodle (1847.1), criticizing his doting on Byron and Scott. A later editorial in the Eagle is apparently a refutation of this attack.

24 BRUMSBAUGH, ROSCOE. "For a Walt Whitman Park in Brooklyn." Publishers' Weekly 135 (18 March), 1129.

Letter encourages support for adopting the name "Walt Whitman Park" and providing a suitable monument.

25 PHILLIPS, WILLIAM. "Whitman and Arnold." Partisan Review 6 (Spring), 114-17.

Review of Arvin (1938.2) and Trilling's Matthew Arnold. Far apart in training, Whitman and Arnold each epitomized his national culture and recognized the economic challenge to his libertarian ideals, though Whitman was more optimistic. Their contributions have been obscured by their legends, Whitman having become "the god-

father of every populist crank." Arvin's book is scholarly but seems "more intent on bringing Whitman up to date." Whitman's meaning is to be found in his poetry, not his opinions. In his poetry his "plebeian instincts and personal optimism merged with the social currents that shaped the thought of his time," combining equalitarian longings and self-reliance with scientific materialism and the multitude. His poetry's energy came from the projection of his being into the various impulses of American life. He fused the individual's expansive ego with society's urgent tasks.

26 WILLIAMS, WILLIAM CARLOS. "Against the Weather. A Study of the Artist." Twice a Year, no. 2 (Spring-Summer), 70-71, 77-78.

Incidental: "Whitman was never able fully to realize the significance of his structural innovations," falling back to "overstuffed catalogues" in later poems "and a sort of looseness that was not freedom but lack of measure." He broke through the dead copied forms, but he "was a romantic in a bad sense," lacking structural form, being a model for us today only to a degree.

27 HOLLOWAY, EMORY. "Commemorating Whitman." Saturday Review of Literature 19 (15 April), 9.

Letter on naming a park in Brooklyn for Whitman. Other current commemorations indicate increasing appreciation of him and should help to "impress the young with the ideals of democracy of which he is our most influential voice." The new Whitman collection at Queens College should be built up.

28 RUBIN, JOSEPH JAY. "Whitman's New York Aurora." American Literature 11 (May), 214-17.

A complete file for the Aurora during Whitman's editorship has been found. Two new poems recognizably Whitman's are reprinted.

29 ANON. "Walt Whitman Collection at Penn State Contains Material Shown for First Time." New York Times (14 May), sec. 3, 1:4-5.

Joseph J. Rubin's collection on exhibit at Penn State is described.

30 ANON. "Walt Whitman Items Added." New York Times (16 May), 18:3.

Notes items added to Long Island display at World's Fair.

31 WILLIAMS, RICHMOND B. "Highway Name Suggested." New York Times (24 May), 22:7.

The new highway around Brooklyn and Queens should be named after Whitman to "honor a distinguished son of the region."

32 POORE, CHARLES. "Books of the Times." New York Times (26 May), 21:5.

Describes Miss P. E. Levison's prize-winning poem for the World's Fair as gaining from its kinship with the verse of Whitman, Hart Crane, and Pare Lorentz.

33 ANON. "Topics of the Times." New York Times (28 May), sec. 4, 8:4.
Commends the suggested highway name (1939.31). Extension of Poore's conjunction of Whitman and Lorentz (1939.32), comparing Lorentz's "The River" to Whitman, who lacks Lorentz's dominant note of defeat, common to so many contemporary American writers.

34 TINKER, EDWARD LAROCQUE. "Our 'Good Gray Poet.'" New York Times Magazine (28 May), 7, 19. Illustrated.
Popular sketch of Whitman's life, noting the exhibit of the Sprague Whitman collection at the Library of Congress. Whitman dignified the common and paved the way for Frost, Jeffers, Robinson, and other regional writers, reviving American literature. The "loudspeaker of democracy," he exemplifies love for America and humanity.

35 RAHV, PHILIP. "Paleface and Redskin." Kenyon Review 1 (Summer), 251-56.
The American dissociation between experience and consciousness, suggesting the dichotomy of "Redskin" and "Paleface," is best represented by Whitman and James, "who as contemporaries felt only disdain for each other," no mere "mutual repulsion between the two major figures in American literature" but having "a profoundly national and social-historical character," followed up in modern figures. The need to choose between them has created a break in American literary tradition without parallel in any European country. Will they ever be reconciled; "will they finally discover and act upon each other?"

36 ANON. "Whitman Tributes Paid at His Statue." New York Times (1 June), 23:4. Illustrated.
Account of dedication of Davidson's bronze statue of Whitman at World's Fair, quoting addresses of Will Durant, John Erskine, Holloway, reprinting Garland's poem (1893.3).

37 ANON. "Walt Whitman." New York Times (2 June), 22:3.
Editorial. Whitman was a prophet but the optimistic mood of his life and era, though much needed now, has largely disappeared. He is not popular but is universally recognized as "the most original of American poets both in form and matter." He is stronger as poet than as propagandist and should not be made representative of a single ideology.

38 POORE, CHARLES. "Books of the Times." New York Times (2 June), 27:5.
Describes statue dedication (see 1939.36). Though Whitman was denounced in his time as "half-baked," it is other

poets who are "over-baked," with their humanity cooked out.

39 QUERCUS, P. E. G. "Trade Winds: An Insurance Policy." Saturday Review of Literature 20 (10 June), 21.
Describes Whitman's insurance policy and examination for it in May 1847, the documents having been lately on display at an insurance company's office.

40 COMPENDIUM. "The Situation in American Writing: Seven Questions." Partisan Review 6 (Summer), 25-51.
The responses of several authors to a questionnaire are printed. The first question ends asking if "Henry James's work is more relevant to the present and future of American writing than Walt Whitman's." Authors responding (with a brief note on their comments on Whitman) are: John Dos Passos, 26 (Twain, Melville, Thoreau, and Whitman are the best immediate ancestors for today's American writing); Allen Tate, 28 (disapproves of the national school stemming from Whitman); James T. Farrell, 30-32 ("Whitman should always have a profound and salutary moral value," though too all-inclusive and undiscriminating, with an ideology no longer valid; his current admission into the Communist Party is "an abortion on both history and literary criticism"); Kenneth Fearing, 34-35 (Whitman is more important to the present and future of American writing than James); Katherine Anne Porter, 36 (James and Whitman, as world figures, are both relevant, but James is the better workman and thinker; Whitman has had disastrous effects on some American writers); Wallace Stevens, 39 (neither means anything to him); William Carlos Williams, 41-42 (neither is necessarily more relevant for today); John Peale Bishop, 45 (Whitman carries conviction not when he is conscious of nothing but his Americanism, but when he is unconsciously American and sings of love and death; neither writer is particularly relevant to the future of American writing); Harold Rosenberg, 48 (Whitman and others are relevant, but the major contemporary American poets surpass "Whitman's private lingo" for "aural accuracy and literary associations"); Henry Miller, 50 (Whitman "is more alive than any American ever was" and will live forever, because he is more than just a writer). Concluded 1939.46.

41 PAINE, GREGORY. "The Literary Relations of Whitman and Carlyle with Especial Reference to Their Contrasting Views on Democracy." Studies in Philology 36 (July), 550-63.
Discusses their exchange in Galaxy (1868), their knowledge and opinions of each other. Whitman's revisions of Vistas for his complete works are described. Vistas is, "because of the way it was put together, a composite of half-conflicting ideas, representing developing stages in

Whitman's thought concerning democracy."
Carlyle and Whitman seemed to be coming to
understand each other. Carlyle may have
been "as important a spiritual force to
Whitman in his latter years as Emerson had
been in his early life."

42 MATHEWS, JOSEPH CHESLEY. "Walt Whitman's
Reading of Dante." University of Texas
Bulletin: Studies in English 19 (8 July),
172-79.
Quotes Whitman's comments on reading
Dante and the comments of others on
Whitman's knowledge of Dante. He failed to
appreciate Dante fully, disliking his
theology and sternness, because he read the
Inferno but not the Paradiso and seems to
have been unaware of the Purgatorio.

43 MERTINS, LOUIS. "Walt Whitman Talks to Ed
Poe." Southern Literary Messenger 1
(August), 533-36.
Blank-verse poem presenting Whitman
addressing Poe at Poe's grave, noting their
similarites as rejected poets, each evolving "a school of writing without peer."

44 ANON. "Whitman Lore Going to Shrine." New
York Times (21 August), 3:6.
Gustav P. Wiksell's Whitman collection
is going to the Library of Congress.

*45 ANON. Portrait. Christian Science Monitor
Magazine (2 September), 14.
Reported in Reader's Guide to Periodical
Literature.

46 COMPENDIUM. "The Situation in American
Writing: Seven Questions. (Part Two)."
Partisan Review 6 (Fall), 103-23.
Concludes 1939.40. The writers and
their comments are: Sherwood Anderson, 104
(Whitman's work has more of the earth in
it than James's); Louise Bogan, 105 (having
read Whitman with enthusiasm when young,
she does not return to him, for James's
writing is more relevant to present and
future American writing than Whitman's
"naive vigor and sentimental 'thinking'");
Lionel Trilling, 110 (James's is the
healthier influence, though "Whitman is a
very great poet and subtler and more
beautifully modulated than most people care
to discover," but his influence encourages
simplified emotions and nationalism);
Robert Penn Warren, 112 (on the technical
side, Whitman's work has "been exercising
a very destructive influence"); Robert
Fitzgerald, 114-15 ("I'm damn well tired
of hearing the two of them built up into
Antithetic Forces in American literature.
That isn't what they wrote for."); R. P.
Blackmur, 117-18 ("James got more of his
intention on the page than Whitman did.");
Horace Gregory, 121 (the relevance of
James and Whitman depends on how the
writer uses them).

47 GARLAND, HAMLIN. "'Let the Sunshine In.'"
Rotarian 55 (October), 8-9.
Includes reprint of 1893.3.
Account of his 1888 visit to Whitman
in Camden (slightly expanded from 1929.58).
Garland takes off from their discussion of
recent American authors to discuss negative
tendencies in modern American fiction, not
democratic in Whitman's sense. Whitman's
advice should be followed: "Don't let
evil overshadow your books," but "somewhere
in your play or novel, let the sunshine in."

Appendix

DOCTORAL DISSERTATIONS

BAKER, PORTIA. "The Development of Walt Whitman's Literary Reputation in the United States and in England from 1855-1892." University of Chicago, 1934. (See 1934.43, 1935.39.)

BLODGETT, HAROLD WILLIAM. "Walt Whitman in England." Cornell University, 1929. (See 1934.1.)

BOOTH, BATES. "The Education and Educational Views of Walt Whitman." School of Education, University of Southern California, 1927.

BOZARD, JOHN F. "Whitman in America: 1855-1892." Cornell University, 1937.

BURKE, CHARLES BELL. "The Open Road, or the Highway of the Spirit: An Inquiry into Whitman's Absolute Selfhood." Cornell University, 1901.

COOKE, ALICE LOVELACE. "Whitman's Backgrounds in the Life and Thought of His Time." University of Texas at Austin, 1933. (See 1934.32, 1935.31.)

GLICKSBERG, CHARLES IRVING. "Walt Whitman and the Civil War." University of Pennsylvania, 1932. (See 1933.6.)

HOWARD, PERCY LEONIDAS [Leon Howard]. "Whitman's Evangel of Democracy." Johns Hopkins University, 1929.

MERCER, DOROTHY FREDERICA. "Leaves of Grass and Bhagavad Gita." University of California, 1933.

PETROVITCH-NIEGOSCH, Mrs. H. G. [S.]. "Whitman's Verse Form and Influence on the Free Verse Movement." University of Southern California, 1933.

POSEY, MEREDITH N. "Whitman's Debt to the Bible with Special Reference to the Origins of His Rhythm." University of Texas at Austin, 1938.

PRESSLEY, RUTH PEYTON. "Whitman's Debt to Emerson." University of Texas at Austin, 1930.

SHEPHARD, ESTHER [Lofstrand]. "Walt Whitman's Pose." University of Washington, Seattle, 1938. (See 1938.17.)

SWAYNE, MATTIE. "Structural Unity in Leaves of Grass." University of Texas at Austin, 1938.

WARNER, ELLA PARDEE. "A History of Walt Whitman's Reception in the British Isles." Yale University, 1916.

WILD, HENRY DOUGLAS. "Democratic Idealism in American Literature from Penn to Whitman: A Study of the Origins and Elements of This Thought in American Life and Letters." University of Chicago, 1924.

MASTER'S THESES

BREW, VIRGINIA W. "Tabulated Analysis of the Philosophy of Walt Whitman." University of Maryland, 1927.

HUDSON, RICHARD BRADSHAW. "The Conflict Between the Materialistic and the Idealistic in the Poetry of Walt Whitman." University of Southern California, 1938.

THOMAS, BEE COTTON. "An Analysis of the Influence of Ralph Waldo Emerson on Walt Whitman." University of Southern California, 1932.

Addenda

References Cited in Addenda

Boswell, Jeanetta. Walt Whitman and the Critics: A Checklist of Criticism, 1900-1978. Scarecrow Author Bibliographies, No. 51. Metuchen, N.J., and London: Scarecrow Press, 1980.

Bergman, Herbert. "Whitman and Tennyson." Studies in Philology 51 (July, 1954), 492-504.

Francis, Gloria A., and Lozynsky, Artem. Whitman at Auction 1899-1972. Detroit: Bruccoli Clark, Gale Research Co., 1978.

Hench, Atcheson L. "Walt Whitman Recollected." American Notes and Queries 1 (October, 1962), 22.

Kaplan, Justin. Walt Whitman: A Life. New York: Simon & Schuster, 1980.

Kennedy, X. J. An Introduction to Poetry. 3rd ed. Boston: Little, Brown & Co., 1974.

1852

*1 ANON. Headnote to "Visit to the People's Bath and Wash House--A New Era." Williamsburg Times (4 May).
Quoted in Rubin.
The article following is "from the pen, we judge, of our friend Walter Whitman."

1884

*24a LOVEJOY, GEORGE NEWELL. "Walt Whitman." Baldwin's Monthly 29 (July), 1.
Reported in Bergman.

1887

*29a ANON. On Whitman and Tennyson. Toronto World (26 March).
Reported in Bergman.

*30a ANON. On Whitman and Tennyson. Cincinnati Enquirer (2 April).
Reported in Bergman.

1889

*46a JOHNSTON, CHARLES. "A Poet Theosophist." Theosophist 10 (June), 535-38.
Reported in CHAL.

57a ANON. "Crossing Brooklyn Ferry." New York World (23 June).
In honor of Whitman's birthday, the paper prints a poem which years ago was much discussed as either magnificent or utter nonsense.

1892

1a ARNOLD, Sir EDWIN. Death--and Afterwards, with a Supplement. 13th ed. London: Kegan Paul, Trench, Trübner, & Co., pp. 21, 60.
Revision of 1889.1.
Quotations from Whitman are used with praise.

*65a ANON. Account of funeral. Philadelphia Evening Bulletin (30 March).
Reported in Kaplan.

*177a ANON. On Whitman and Tennyson. New York Sun (22 May).
Reported in Bergman.

1896

*2a DAVENPORT, WILLIAM E. Poetical Sermons: a Thank Offering of Song. Brooklyn.
Reported in Francis, p. 409.
Many of the poems are in Whitman's style; some refer to him.

10a PATTEE, FRED LEWIS. A History of American Literature. Since 1870. Boston: Silver, Burdett & Co. "Walt Whitman," pp. 376-84.
Revised: 1903.11.
This earlier version is more negative in statements on Whitman's egotism and use of the body, which "bar him from the company of the great masters of song," for he has "a few good things amid a disgusting mass of rubbish." Besides tempering these criticisms, the 1903 version adds a brief bibliography in place of the opening

quotation from Whitman and adds a quotation from Burroughs (1896.2); otherwise the two versions are identical.

1898

*17a WESTLAKE, J. WILLIS. Common-school Literature, English and American, with Several Hundred Extracts to be Memorized. Philadelphia. Quoted in Kennedy.
　　　Brief estimate of differing views on Whitman: "Most of his so-called poems are mere catalogues of things," but in a few lines and more regular poems like "Captain," "he is grandly poetical."

47a ANON. Review of Chapman (1898.7). Christian Register 77 (24 March), 330-31.
　　　The Whitman essay has "cheap smartness." Whitman "attracts him by his revolt against the placid mediocrity of our habitual life."

1899

*75a FARNSWORTH, EDWARD G. "Walt Whitman." Universal Brotherhood 14 (November), 398-402.
　　　Reported in CHAL.

1900

26a TRIGGS, OSCAR L. "American Literature." Unity 44 (1 March), 872.
　　　Review of Fisher (1899.7), rejecting her idea of Whitman, regarding whom they have "no common ground even for dispute." He also questions William Salter's negative notion of Whitman (1899.74), whose ideas of good and evil are those of today.

1905

*30a IRWIN, FRANCES JOSEPH. "The Religion of Walt Whitman." Truth Seeker (11 March), 147.
　　　Reported in CHAL.

1907

26a ANON. "The Rev. Dr. Crothers Talks of Walt Whitman." Brooklyn Daily Eagle (12 March), 9:6.
　　　Extensively quotes Crothers's address at the Brooklyn Art Gallery regarding "Whitman's conception of the new democracy and his marvellous realization of the infinite."

1908

*19a ANON. "Walt Whitman and his Disciples." Fair Play (New York) (January).
　　　Reported in Francis, p. 36, Item No. 1353.

1910

12a SAINTSBURY, GEORGE. Historical Manual of English Prosody. Lodnon and New York: Macmillan, 33n, 315.
　　　Summarizes Whitman's verse as pushing farther and more successfully than anyone "the substitution, for regular metre, of irregular rhythmed prose, arranged in versicles something like those of the English Bible, but with a much wider range of length and rhythm, the latter going from sheer prose cadence into definite verse."

1912

*29a REED, JOHN. "The Tenement Clothes Line." New York Mail (24 April).
　　　Reprinted: 1913.15a. Same as 1912.30. Reported in Hicks (1936.14a, addenda).

1913

15a REED, JOHN. The Day in Bohemia or, Life among the Artists. New York: Printed for the author. "The Tenement Clothes-Line; A Series of Excellent Parodies . . . Walt Whitman," p. 18; also 26, 43.
　　　Parody reprinted from 1912.29a; reprinted (with errors): Saunders.
　　　Other poetic references to Whitman include a character's referring to his "Hardware cataloguing by the yard" and the broad field of vocabulary "That loud Walt Whitman ruled as his demesne."

1914

25a ANDERSON, MARGARET C. "The Poetry of Rupert Brooke." Little Review 1 (March), 31.
　　　Though Swinburne would have loved Brooke, "the significant thing is that Whitman would, too. There are several poems . . . that Whitman would have loved."

29a ANDERSON, SHERWOOD. "More About the 'New Note.'" Little Review 1 (April), 16.
　　　"Why do we so prize the work of Whitman, Tolstoy," and others? Because the book is true and a man of flesh and blood "has lived the substance of it."

29b SOULE, GEORGE. "Rupert Brooke and Whitman." Little Review 1 (April), 15-16.
　　　Response to Anderson (1914.25a): Whitman would not like all of Brooke, because, as in "Open Road" (quoted), "Whitman was frank about the whole world, dirt and all, and he accepted it enthusiastically," unlike Brooke.

31a ANON. One-paragraph favorable review of De Selincourt (1914.5). Little Review 1 (May), 49.

32a WING, DE WITT C. "On Behalf of Literature." Little Review 1 (May), 2-4.
　　　In opposition to the idea of a national

literature, he cites Whitman, whose poetry
was "cosmic," unlike imitative English
verse. He is one of the true poets,
"chanter of the earth's major note."

40a _____. "Horace Traubel's Whitman." Little
Review 1 (September), 50-51.
Review of 1914.17. There is much
personality and interpretive value in some
of Whitman;s most commonplace utterances.
His "kinship with common clay" led to
Leaves. He was first "a big, magnificent
animal-man" and second "a powerful poetic
instrumentality." His work expresses "the
bio-economic democracy." Each page has
value in "this extraordinary autobiography
of the most outstanding figure in American
literature."

1915

23a POUND, EZRA. "Webster Ford." Egoist 2 (1
January), 11.
Ford is a poet America has discovered,
while most American poets since Whitman
have had to follow his pattern and get
their acceptance abroad first.

28a HORNOR, C. G. "Walt Again." New York Sun
(22 March), 6:7.
Whitman's verse is not crude but shows
"extraordinary literary quality" and revision despite its abandoned appearance,
with the 1860 edition "perfect in form."
His cult is made up of dilettantes. His
writings are of interest "in a literary
point of view and worthless in any other,"
with no new ideas, teaching only "idleness,
sensuality and vagabondage."

30a ALDINGTON, RICHARD. "Decadence and Dynamism."
Egoist 2 (1 April), 57.
"The formula for Dynamism is energy,
electrically illuminated cities, action,
frenzy, 'the rape of negresses,' Prussian
egoism wedded to American vulgarity, Walt
Whitman."

31a MONRO, HAROLD. "The Imagists Discussed."
Egoist 2 (1 May), 78.
Americans had been coming to "admire
a new kind of literary fungus," "the Cosmic
Poet," with his vague notions of modern
ideas discussed "in an inflated manner."
But "the Imagists did not bother much about
Whitman," who "was too artless."

58a RANDALL, ALEC W. G. "Notes on Modern German
Poetry. V. Walt Whitman in Germany;
(a) Arno Holz." Egoist 2 (1 November),
172-73.
Whitman was a key influence on German
literature in the late nineteenth century
and "has produced classics," influenced
chiefly by his personality and doctrine.
Holz is his key follower, though chiefly as
democrat and writer of prose-poetry.

61a _____. "Notes on Modern German Poetry. V.
Walt Whitman in Germany. (b) Johannes

Schlaf." Egoist 2 (1 December), 187.
Schlaf "came under the two most powerful
influences in modern German poetry--Verhaeren
and Walt Whitman." Holz "never absorbed
Whitman" as Schlaf did in technique and
philosophy.

1917

11a PECKHAM, H. HOUSTON. Present-Day American
Poetry and Other Essays. Boston: Richard
G. Badger; Toronto: Copp Clark Co., pp. 11,
13, 22, 36, 44, 65, 76, 99.
Incidental references to Whitman as a
major American poet.

*23a ANON. "Walt Whitman as Musical Prophet."
Musical America 16 (15 April), 12-14.
Reported in Boswell, but not located on
this date; Vol. 16 is another year but does
not include April.

58a POUND, EZRA. "Editorial on Solicitous Doubt."
Little Review 4 (December), 53.
Ford Maddox Hueffer's "On Heaven" is
"the first successful long poem in English
vers libre, after Whitman."

1918

11a HUMPHREYS, CHARLES A. Field, Camp, Hospital
and Prison in the Civil War, 1863-1865.
Boston: Geo. H. Ellis Co.
Reported in Boswell, but no Whitman references were found in this book.

1920

13a HARTLEY, L. CONRAD. "The Function of Parody."
Papers of the Manchester Literary Club, 46
(1920), 95.
Incidental: Quotes 1868.45 as the only
parody which has captured Whitman, whose
"strong manner provokes the parodist."

87a BROCKLEHURST, J. H. "Walt Whitman." Manchester Quarterly 39 (October), 318-37.
Reported in Allen. Same as 1920.5.

1921

28a ROMM, CHARLES. Collection of First Editions,
Manuscripts and Inscribed Copies of
Esteemed English and American Authors. New
York: American Art Association.
Items 626-701 of this auction catalogue
are Whitman books and manuscripts, here
described.

1922

16a PATTEE, FRED LEWIS. Side-Lights on American
Literature. New York: Century Co., p. 248.
In contrast to Longfellow, "Whitman is
our prophet of to-day, and his influence
is spreading and deepening."

1923

1a AUSTIN, MARY. _The American Rhythm._ New York: Harcourt, Brace & Co., pp. 17-19. Reprinted with additions to other parts of the text in 1930.

Uses material from 1922.57. Whitman mistood "the bigness of things" for universality and "was unclear in his conclusions; the American type." He chanted "mere unpatterned noises of the street," "seldom far from the rutted pioneer track." Only in his solitude does his verse show the true American strain of "goal consciousness, and pattern attained by balance and a system of compensating phrases." He had an adolescent intelligence. He is chiefly used now to justify "the urge and recovery of the democratic experience." His method resembles Indian verse but with less "emotional affectiveness [sic]."

4a ELLIS, HAVELOCK. _The Dance of Life._ Boston and New York: Houghton Mifflin Co., pp. 172, 254.

Incidental references to Whitman.

5a GABLE, WILLIAM F. _The Renowned Collection of the Late William F. Gable of Altoona, Pennsylvania: First Editions, Autograph Manuscripts and Letters of English and American Authors._ New York: American Art Association.

Auction catalogue with many Whitman items: Part One (1923), Items 861-950; Part Three (1924), Items 610-627; Part Four (1924), Items 1104-1159; Part Five (1925), Items 960-981; Part Six (1925), Items 1049-1076.

37a BYNNER, WITTER. Note to "A Hitherto UnPublished [sic] Walt Whitman Letter." _Laughing Horse_ 1, No. 7 (July), n.p.

This 1870 letter (to a young man Whitman knew at the end of the war) was a gift to Bynner from one who had several Whitman letters but whose name Bynner has forgotten. Whitman's "large and simple human kindness which informs and illuminates his poems" is shown in these few words.

1924

33a NOTT, G. WILLIAM. "Walt Whitman in New Orleans." _The Reviewer_ 4 (April), 183-87.

Describes the importance to Whitman of New Orleans, especially for "his first great passion for woman." Quotes his _Crescent_ writings to indicate his thoughts and interests.

33b OPPENHEIM, JAMES. "Free Verse Is Dying Out." _The Reviewer_ 4 (April), 188-89.

Whitman was unique, achieving the new Americanism Emerson merely looked for. The Whitman tradition was carried on in the movement of 1914. Even if it is waning now, the tide will continue.

1925

37a VOIGT, GILBERT PAUL. "The Religion and Ethical Element in the Major American Poets." _Bulletin of the Graduate School of the University of South Carolina_ (1 June), 124-34.

This chapter traces Whitman's new religion combining the Greek view of the body and acceptance of life with Christianity's "sustaining power in sickness" and death; notes Whitman's view of God and Christ; belief in the divinity and evolution of man; emphasis on science and democracy; belief in moral law; influence from Hicks, Emerson, and Hegel. Voigt's bibliography cites _The Mind of Whitman: A Study of His Fundamental Religious Ideas_, 1904, by Chauncey J. Hawkins, but this should be _The Mind of Whittier._

1926

27a SHERMAN, STUART PRATT. "The Emotional Discovery of America." In _Four Addresses in Commemoration of the Twentieth Anniversary of the Founding of the American Academy of Arts and Letters._ Academy Publication No. 54, pp. 169-81; also, "The Relations of American Literature and American Scholarship in Retrospect and Prospect," by Paul Shorey, pp. 30, 32-55; "Kinship and Detachment from Europe in American Literature," by Bliss Perry, pp. 110, 111-14.

Sherman's essay is the same as reprinted in 1932.19. Shorey questions whether Whitman and Twain are the only key to future American literature. Whitman shows that we are dependent on what we read; his message is not original, for he could not help but borrow. He has "a sometimes exquisite ear for rhythm," with "genius in spots" but "no unflawed poem." Shorey notes reasons suggested for "his trailing participles." Perry notes that Whitman realized that American literature "should express the unique experience of a unique people," though one can't be only national.

27b SMUTS, J. C. _Holism and Revolution._ New York: Macmillan Co., p. vi.

This book's basis was an unpublished study on "Walt Whitman: A Study in the Evolution of Personality" (see 1936.19), though this book does not refer to Whitman.

1929

24a RUSSELL, CHARLES EDWARD. _An Hour of American Poetry._ Philadelphia and London: J. B. Lippincott Co., pp. 89-91.

Whitman "had the soul of a poet," writing "the greatest rhapsodical prose ever written," though some deny that it's poetry. "Captain" is poetry, but many lines are not, however "vibrant with feeling, power, beauty." He is generally admired for his human sympathies and faith, not really for his works.

1930

5a CURLE, RICHARD. <u>Collecting American First
Editions: Its Pitfalls and Its Pleasures</u>.
Indianapolis: Bobbs-Merrill Co., passim
per index, also p. 200. Illustrated.
Describes different states of several
Whitman works and how to verify whether one
actually has the distinguishing features of
an actual first edition.

8a HESSELTINE, WILLIAM B. <u>Civil War Prisons--A
Study in War Psychology</u>. Columbus: Ohio
University Press, p. 229.
Incidnetal mention of Whitman's letter
to <u>New York Times</u> of December 27, 1864.

18a RILEY, [ISAAC] WOODBRIDGE. <u>The Meaning of
Mysticism</u>. New York: Richard R. Smith,
pp. 64, 86, 98-102.
Germanic mysticism led to Whitman, one
of America's great "seers of symbolism,"
"enamored of nature," a mystic whose theory
of cosmic consciousness "insisted upon the
unity and all-comprehensiveness of true
being," as quotations show.

47a ANON. "Walt Whitman Likenesses Are Carved in
Wood." <u>Brooklyn Daily Eagle</u> (7 December).
Illustrated.
Interview with sculptor Adam Dabrowski
on his carvings of Whitman.

1931

53a LEWISOHN, LUDWIG. "Whitman." <u>This Quarter</u> 4
(July-September), 75-87.
Reprinted: 1932.15.
This is the same article, with changes
in accidentals, as in his later book.

1932

15a LUCAS, E. V. <u>Reading, Writing and Remembering</u>.
New York and London: Harper & Bros., p. 39.
Burroughs (1877.1) led him to Whitman.
He still returns to <u>Leaves</u> and used "The
Open Road" as title for an anthology, though
he never tried to write like Whitman.

50 BRAGMAN, LOUIS J., M. D. "Walt Whitman,
Hospital Attendant and Medical Critic."
<u>Medical Life</u>, 39 (November), 606-15.
Traces Whitman's career as hospital
attendant (through many quotations), his
interest in the body and proper patient
care, and descriptions of his health
(largely from Osler).

1933

*4a COOKE, ALICE LOVELACE. <u>Studies in Walt
Whitman's Backgrounds</u>. Austin: University
of Texas Press.
Reported in Boswell (presumably her dissertation; see Appendix).

7a LAWRENCE, D. H. <u>Last Poems</u>. Edited with an
introduction by Richard Aldington. London:
Martin Secker. "Retort to Whitman," p.
134; also 11.
Response to "Myself" 48: "And whoever
walks a mile full of false sympathy/walks
to the funeral of the whole human race."
Aldington's introduction calls these posthumous poems sometimes "like the utterances
of a little Whitman, but without Walt's
calm <u>sostenuto</u> quality."

*25a McKINSEY, FOLGER. "Good Morning." Baltimore
<u>Sun</u> (11 July), 8:7.
Reported in Hench.
Includes discussion of Whitman. Hench
also notes McKinsey columns referring to
Whitman on 5 September, 4:7 and 6 December,
12:7 for 1933; and for 1934, 16 May; 30
May, 8:7; 15 August, p. 7; 25 October, 10:5.

1935

4a CRUSE, AMY. <u>The Victorians and Their Reading</u>.
Boston and New York: Houghton Mifflin Co.,
pp. 150, 258-59.
Misquotes Lytton (1906.2); the index
implies this is Edward Bulwer-Lytton rather
than Robert Lytton.

8a PATTEE, FRED LEWIS. <u>The First Century of
American Literature 1770-1870</u>. New York
and London: D. Appleton-Century Co.,
pp. 16-17, 394-95, 594-95, passim per index.
Incidental quotations of Whitman or
comparisons with other American writers of
this period, noting Whitman's ability to
rise above his period's flaws; unlike most
of his contemporaries, he moved ahead into
the 1860s and beyond, and he voiced the new
spirit.

1936

14a HICKS, GRANVILLE. <u>John Reed: The Making of a
Revolutionary</u>. New York: Macmillan Co.,
pp. 49-50, 75, 79, 227, 300-302, 341.
Quotes Reed's comments on and quoting
from Whitman; notes his similar style and
thought; quotes Charles Erskine Scott
Wood's letter to Reed on Whitman's poetry.

31a ANON. "Walt Whitman Notes To Be Sold to
Public." <u>Brooklyn Daily Eagle</u> (12 January).
Notes and quotes letters from Whitman
to Harry Stafford, from the Abel Carey
Thomas collection, to be sold at the
Anderson Galleries. They are "filled with
the advice of a father to a beloved son."

34a ANON. "Villagers Fear Whitman Home May Be
Sold for Roadhouse." <u>Brooklyn Daily Eagle</u>
(6 April).
Same story as 1936.35.

34b ANON. "Long Islanders Protest Sale Of Walt
Whitman's Birthplace." <u>New York Herald
Tribune</u> (6 April).
Same story as 1936.35.

35a ANON. "Walt Whitman's Newspaper." Brooklyn
   Daily Eagle (8 April).
   　　　Editorial on the discovery of a copy
   of the Freeman, noting Whitman's early
   newspaper experiences and the political
   reasons behind his starting a new paper.

38a ANON. "Walt Whitman Items Bring $6,568 at
   Sale." New York Herald Tribune (16 April).
   　　　Notes the first day's sales from the
   Bucke collection (1936.22).

39a ANON. "Whitman Manuscripts Bring Total of
   $13,489." New York Herald Tribune (17
   April).
   　　　Notes sales from Bucke collection
   (1936.22).

*46a COOKE, ALICE LOVELACE. "American First
   Editions at the University of Texas
   (Austin)." University of Texas Library
   Chronicle 2 (June), 95-105.
   Reported in Boswell.

54a TRAUBEL, ANNA M. "Education in Our Schools.
   A Fragment by Walt Whitman." Brooklyn
   Daily Eagle (12 July).
   　　　Foreword to this extensive manuscript,
   here printed for the first time, describes
   it as "a few consecutive pages and a series
   of disjointed paragraphs," representing "a
   summation of the dreams, desires and practical attempts of those early years" when
   he taught. Found among Traubel's papers by
   his wife, this was titled "Intended School
   Address 1872," apparently for a new public
   school building.

1937

*1a ANON. First Editions, Autograph Letters,
   Manuscripts, Standard Sets . . . Willetts
   . . . Gould . . . Paine . . . Armour . . .
   New York: American Art Association, p.
   180, Item No. 432.
   Reported in Bergman.

13a SHEPARD, ODELL. Pedlar's Progress: The Life
   of Bronson Alcott. Boston: Little, Brown
   & Co., pp. 463-66, passim per index.
   　　　Notes Whitman's influence on Alcott's
   prose style after he read the first edition
   of Leaves. Describes Whitman's impact on
   Alcott, especially as an American, with
   praise for Whitman's "magnificent roughhewn
   forthright songs for a national mourning"
   (i.e., the Lincoln poems).

*32a McKINSEY, FOLGER. "Good Morning." Baltimore
   Sun (19 February), 10:5.
   Reported in Hench.
   　　　Includes remarks on Whitman. Hench
   also cites this column of 14 February
   1936, 10:5; 25 June 1937, 12:8; 8 April
   1939, 6:5.

1938

22a LORCH, FRED W. "Thoreau and the Organic Prin-

ciple in Poetry." PMLA 53 (March), 286,
293, 297.
　　　Brief references to Whitman's philosophy
and poetic ideas.

27a ANON. "Admirer of Whitman Chides Attack on
   Him." Brooklyn Daily Eagle (10 April).
   　　　Interview with Holloway, who criticizes
   Shephard's book (1938.17).

33a ANON. "Whitman Enthusiasts Deplore Statue
   Shift." Brooklyn Daily Eagle (8 May).
   　　　Holloway and Cleveland Rodgers regret
   the removal of Davidson's statue from Long
   Island; the statue's background is traced;
   perhaps William O. Partridge's statue of
   Whitman could be used; Joseph Pennell's
   etchings for a Whitman volume are noted.

47b ANON. "New Whitman Gems Revealed at Capital."
   Brooklyn Daily Eagle (21 August).
   　　　Auslander explains his discovery of
   Whitman manuscripts and clippings at Library
   of Congress; notes tobacco cuttings and
   apple peels in the box of manuscripts and
   Whitman's erasures.

59 BRUMBAUGH, ROSCOE. "Convincing Proof That
   Brooklyn Park Should Bear Walt Whitman's
   Name." Printing News (31 December).
   Illustrated.
   　　　Urges that Whitman be honored and the
   Rome Brothers print shop saved; explains
   Whitman's importance. (A note from
   Brumbaugh in the Long Island Historical
   Society scrapbook notes his error about
   the Rome Brothers print shop, which had
   already been torn down.)

1939

18a SIDNEY, WALTER. "Whitman Reinterpreted."
   Brooklyn Daily Eagle (1 January).
   　　　Favorable, explanatory review of Arvin
   (1938.2).

23a ANON. "Reveals Whitman's Difficulty in
   Selling 'Leaves of Grass.'" Brooklyn Daily
   Eagle (12 March).
   　　　Describes Furness (1939.4).

24a ANON. "Walt Whitman Statue on Way to Fair."
   Brooklyn Daily Eagle (30 March).
   　　　Traces background of Davidson's statue.

30a ANON. "Whitman, Free Soul." Brooklyn Daily
   Eagle (24 May).
   　　　Editorial praising Davidson's statue
   as appropriate to Whitman's free spirit.

34a ANON. "Walt Whitman Statue To Be Unveiled at
   Last." Brooklyn Daily Eagle (29 May).
   　　　Announces ceremony of unveiling of
   Davidson's statue at World's Fair.

Introduction to the Index

Indexed here are all the authors of items and the periodicals in which articles appeared. Each number following a name consists of the year of the item, followed by a period and the number of the item within that year: 1855.7 means the seventh item in 1855. Only the first appearance of a piece will be listed, since reprints and revisions are cited under the entry indexed. Likewise, only the first item in a series is indexed, since that item will refer to continuations.

This index serves as a subject index as well. To differentiate persons as authors from persons as subjects dealt with in items annotated, I have placed brackets around any item which discusses the indexed name. Figures such as Burroughs who both wrote about Whitman and who are discussed in items included here will have two listings after their name: one for pieces they wrote, and the second, completely bracketed, for pieces in which they are discussed. Many names will have no bracketed items, many (such as Shakespeare and Beethoven) will have only bracketed items.

A problem I have faced as indexer was whether to list an interview with a person under items by that person. Unless the interview consists almost entirely of a particular person's words, it will be listed in brackets along with the other items about that person. The same holds true for items presenting speeches: even though the speech is extensively quoted, the item will usually be listed under items about that person.

For additional ease of reference, bracketed items are included in some of the primary listings themselves to indicate items responding to or discussing that item. It is in this position, under the author rather than subject listing, that book reviews will be listed, following the item number of the book.

In the case of pseudonymous works, when the author's real name is known, the reader will be referred from the pseudonym to the real name and all entry numbers will be listed under the author's real name. The author's name will be followed by the pseudonym either in parentheses when it is the habitual pseudonym or in brackets when it is nonhabitual.

Subjects dealt with, such as democracy, education, modern poetry, are also indexed. In a few of the subject listings, asterisks will be used to indicate key discussions of figures or subjects whose listings are quite long. However, those subject specified as Whitman's, such as family, journalism, style, are indexed under Whitman himself, in alphabetical order after the author item, along with a list of his works. In addition, the reader seeking discussion of any subject, work, or person is advised to consult the key books listed under Analyses of Whitman's Work and under Biographies, since it would have been quite redundant to continue listing these same items under almost every significant subject heading (although if the discussion is particularly noteworthy or extensive, it will be listed under that subject). Similarly, the indexes of Traubel's With Walt Whitman in Camden (see References Cited in Text), although they list only names of people, are also an important source to consult, either for Whitman's opinions about individuals or for their relations with him.

Because of the lateness of the additions represented by the Addenda, the items therein could not be included in the index except in a few cases where the word "Addenda" could fit into an already present entry. If one is looking up a particular name or subject, therefore, one should not omit going over the Addenda for any possible items.

Index

A., A. 1884.12
A., H. S. 1920.93
A., W. W. See Astor, W. W.
Abbey, Charlotte 1895.52; 1896.65; 1897.149; 1900.
    43
Abbott, Claude Colleer 1935.1
Abbott, Edward 1882.55
Abbott, Leonard D. 1902.28, 43, 58; 1912.42; 1918.
    67; 1919.76; 1923.44
Abernethy, Julian W. 1902.1; 1904.1
Aberystwyth Studies 1914.11
Academia 1868.13
Academy 1874.10; 1875.13; 1876.63; 1880.32; 1882.
    127-128; 1883.35; 1885.23,27; 1887.53; 1888.
    41; 1889.23; 1890.15; 1891.37, 52; 1892.107;
    1893.40; 1897.116, 136, 148; 1901.64; 1910.26
Acharya, Sri Ananda [1919.379]
Acosta, Mercedes De 1928.1
Adams, A. M. 1923.31 [1923.32]
Adams, C. F. [1906.9]
Adams, George Matthew 1923.26
Adams, Henry 1907.1
Adams, James Truslow 1933.1
Adams, Oscar Fay 1884.1; 1897.1
Adams, Robert Dudley 1876.58
Adams, Samuel Hopkins 1923.44
Adams, W. Davenport 1878.1
Addicks, Mrs. Weda Cook [1923.63]
Adelaide (South Australia) Advertiser 1922.34
Adhesiveness. See Comradeship; Homosexuality;
    Phrenology
Adimari, Ralph 1934.25, 35; 1936.15
Adkins, Nelson F. 1935.38
Adler, Felix 1889.9
Admari, Ralph. See Adimari, Ralph
Advance, The 1927.38
Aeon [pseud.] 1922.15
Afloat and Ashore 1919.38
Agnostic [pseud.] 1882.92
Agnostic Annual (London) 1903.9
Aiken, Conrad 1919.1, 158 [1919.166]; 1920.51
Airey, Peter (P. Luftig) 1902.38
Aitken, Robert M. 1883.12
Alberts, S. S. 1933.2
Albion, The (New York) 1855.8; 1860.22; 1866.20
Albree, John 1911.1
Alcott, Amos Bronson 1894.16; 1938.16
    [1866.2; 1895.83; 1917.13; Addenda]
Alden, Henry Mills 1882.13; 1883.37; 1908.1
Alden, Raymond MacDonald 1904.2; 1909.1
Alden, William L. 1898.44, 80; 1899.65
Aldington, Richard 1920.64; Addenda
Aldrich, Charles 1892.148
    [1934.5]

Aldrich, Darragh 1936.1
Aldrich, Thomas Bailey 1889.9; 1892.15; 1908.7
    [1882.134; 1907.58; 1910.17; 1923.27; 1934.43]
Alexander, Colin Cuthbert 1917.21; 1937.38
Alexander, Edward Porter 1937.13
Alexander, Hartley Burr 1906.1
Alexander, John W. [1887.32; 1889.66, 74; 1905.20;
    1908.30, 38, 50; 1921.12; 1927.50]
Alger, William Rounseville [1904.24]
Allen, E. M. [1931.1]
Allen, Rev. Frederick Baylie [1895.13; 1927.46]
Allen, Gay Wilson 1933.27; 1934.39, 42; 1935.2-3;
    1937.25, 39; 1939.16
Allen, Hervey 1927.27
Allgemeinen Zeitung 1868.36
Allibone, S. Austin 1872.1
Allingham, William 1897.9
    [1896.57; 1934.18]
Allinson, Anne C. E. 1932.35
Allison, Senator [1909.22]
Allison, W. T. 1919.210; 1926.71
Altruistic Review 1894.44
Altruria 1907.33
Amativeness. See Sex; Phrenology
America 1888.37, 42
America and Americanism [1847.1; 1860.30, 38;
    1866.2, 19, 27; 1867.8, 17, 19; 1868.6, 37;
    1871.6; 1872.12; 1873.4; 1876.5; 1892.155,
    165, 178; 1900.18; 1903.41; 1906.30a; 1908.36;
    1909.8, 38; 1911.20; 1912.11-12, 16, 21;
    1915.5, 60; 1916.22, 53, 65; 1917.6, 31, 37,
    52, 54; 1918.62; 1919.7, 20, 60, 128, 204,
    256, 263; 1921.6, 23; 1923.40; 1924.7; 1926.57;
    1927.22; 1928.32; 1929.16, 20; 1930.10;
    1932.19; 1933.1, 3; 1937.25; 1939.40]
American, The (Philadelphia) 1881.8; 1882.87-88;
    1883.29; 1888.31, 38-39, 46, 48, 54, 56, 75;
    1889.35, 72; 1890.18; 1897.145 [1897.140];
    1898.26
American Art Journal 1887.79
American Book Collector 1933.19, 28; 1934.25;
    1935.19
American Bulletin (American Type Founders Co.)
    1915.21
American Collector. See also Americana Collector
    1926.72; 1927.37
American Institute Fair (New York, 1871) [1871.11-17,
    22, 25; 1929.60-61]
American Journal of Psychology 1896.23
American language [1904.17; 1919.16, 273; 1930.41;
    1936.52]
American Literature 1929.45-46; 1930.32; 1931.22-
    23, 26, 59-60; 1932.28; 1933.11, 17, 31-32;

1934.20, 42-48; 1935.16-17, 21, 39; 1936.30,
    33, 58-59; 1937.27, 38, 40-41; 1938.22-23, 29,
    32; 1939.17-18, 21-22, 28
American literature (histories and interpretations).
    See also Textbooks [1882.7; 1888.4; 1898.2;
    1899.7, 18; 1900.1, 3, 11, 18; 1901.13;
    1902.1; 1903.11, 14a; 1904.18, 21; 1905.15;
    1906.19; 1911.8; 1912.4; 1913.10; 1914.12;
    1915.13, 15-16; 1918.10; 1919.3, 21; 1923.6;
    1926.22; 1927.9, 18; 1929.15; 1930.17-18;
    1931.2, 21; 1932.7-8, 14-15, 20; 1933.7;
    1936.3, 5, 27; 1939.10]
American Magazine 1887.86; 1907.42
American Mercury 1924.29, 33, 38-40, 42-43; 1925.28,
    60, 77; 1926.61; 1929.34, 44, 57, 60; 1933.18;
    1934.38; 1935.29
American Phrenological Journal 1855.11
American Register 1911.20
American Review [1847.3]
American Review of Reviews. See also Review of
    Reviews 1909.28
American Scenic and Historic Preservation Society,
    Annual Report 1920.1
American Scholar 1933.22-23, 29
American Speech 1926.46; 1930.41; 1932.38
American Theosophist 1913.37
Americana 1936.51
Americana Collector. See also American Collector
    1925.78
Andersen, Hans Christian [1939.16]
Anderson, Margaret 1919.352; Addenda
Anderson, Sherwood 1917.54; 1918.2; 1933.3; 1939.46
    [1920.42; 1925.53; 1926.27; 1939.7; Addenda]
Andrews, Alice E. 1917.17
Andrews, C[larence] E[dward] 1918.3
Andrews, Gertrude N. 1919.109
Anglo-French [pseud.] 1918.21
Anthony, Katharine 1919.35
Apollinaire, Guillaume 1921.31
Appeal to Reason 1919.159
Appletons' Journal 1870.6; 1871.24; 1876.21, 42, 53.
Appletons' Magazine. See also Booklover's Magazine
    1907.49
Apuleius [1856.7]
Arbor (Toronto) 1912.27
Arcadia 1892.172
Architectural Forum 1921.75
Arena 1892.18, 206; 1894.48; 1895.83; 1896.24;
    1902.47; 1905.21-22, 27; 1906.35; 1907.21;
    1908.37, 48
Argus [pseud.?] 1892.175 1892.178 , 189
Aristidean (New York) 1924.38; 1927.12; 1938.32
Aristides 1848.6
Aristotle [1914.15]
Armory Square Hospital Gazette [1930.25]
Armstrong, Annie 1915.1
Armstrong, Judge E. Ambler 1889.9
    [1889.52, 54]
Armstrong, H. F. [1919.48]
Arnold, Sir Edwin 1887.1; 1889.67; 1891.2 [1891.52];
    1899.24 [1889.62-66; 1890.41; 1892.27; 1900.13;
    1915.10; 1918.18; 1925.7; 1934.1]
Arnold, George [1882.10, 135; 1934.9]
Arnold, Matthew 1867.17; 1906.13
    [1871.21; 1879.42; 1888.45, 62; 1890.57a;
    1892.96; 1894.60; 1897.72; 1898.75; 1900.13;
    1914.5; 1917.16; 1922.1; 1932.32; 1934.1;
    1935.14; 1938.9; 1939.25]
Art (based on Whitman or his works, including
    photography). See also Whitman Memorials;
    John Alexander, Jo Davidson, Eakins, Saint-

Gaudens [1860.24; 1871.20; 1887.39, 68;
    1889.47; 1892.31, 53; 1897.36; 1920.32, 55;
    1921.12; 1922.53; 1924.21; 1925.81; 1926.35,
    37, 53, 64; 1927.55; 1929.22; 1931.28, 41;
    1935.15; 1936.60-61; 1938.57-58; Addenda]
Art News 1897.84
Artsman 1904.29
Arvin, Newton 1931.57; 1932.47; 1937.6, 35; 1938.2
    [1938.51, 54-55; 1939.19, 21, 25]
Ashtabula (Ohio) Sentinel 1860.52
Ashton, J. Hubley 1931.1
Ashton, Winifred (Clarence Dane) 1918.5
Astley, Norman 1906.60 [1906.63]
Astor, W. W. 1894.42
Astronomy [1934.32; 1936.53]
Atchison (Kansas) Champion 1879.27
Atchison (Kansas) Globe 1879.40
Athenaeum. See also Nation and Athenaeum 1868.22
    [1868.27]; 1876.22; 1880.6; 1885.29; 1887.28;
    1892.109, 133, 137 [1892.173]; 1919.104, 370;
    1920.51-53
Atkinson, J. Brooks 1921.51
Atkinson, William Walker 1910.24
Atlanta Constitution 1898.84
Atlantic Monthly 1867.26; 1872.8, 10, 17; 1876.70;
    1877.11, 16; 1878.10, 15; 1882.14; 1883.26;
    1886.12; 1887.61; 1890.36, 43; 1891.47;
    1892.180, 183; 1893.48; 1894.25; 1896.58, 70;
    1897.24, 67, 69, 72, 74, 77; 1899.30; 1901.31;
    1902.34, 40; 1903.48-49; 1904.30; 1906.106;
    1907.37; 1909.40; 1914.42; 1916.29, 55;
    1917.46; 1921.35, 71; 1937.46
    [1860.11; 1869.2; 1932.12; 1934.43]
Atlantis [pseud.] 1882.135
Auckland New Zealand Herald. See New Zealand Herald
Aurora (New York) 1842.3, 5-6, 14
    [1842.4; 1893.2; 1901.21; 1939.28]
Auslander, Joseph 1927.1
    [1938.47a]
Austin, Alfred 1869.4; 1876.30
    [1887.11; 1896.35; 1934.1]
Austin, Dr. B. F. 1913.30
Austin, Mary 1922.57; Addenda
Australia [1899.51]
Australian Herald (Melbourne) 1892.201, 209a;
    1893.4; 1907.13
Aynard, M. Joseph 1906.44
Aytoun, W. E. [1856.25]

B. 1881.32
B., A. 1931.37
B., C. F. 1923.45
B., J. B. 1886.40
B., P. See Burrowes, Peter E.
B., V. W. See Brooks, Van Wyck
B., W. H. 1919.368
Babbitt, Irving 1928.25
Babcock, Bernie 1929.1
Bacheller, Irving 1914.20
Backus, Truman J. 1884.2
Bacon, Sir Francis [1864.5; 1886.45; 1894.51;
    1897.26, 59; 1901.3, 44; 1915.48; 1916.43]
Bagster, Rev. Augustus 1912.7
Bailey, Elmer James 1922.1
Bailey, Francis D. 1915.29
Bailey, John 1926.1 [1926.55, 57-58, 65-67, 70-71,
    76; 1927.7]
Bain, Mildred 1910.31; 1912.19; 1913.1, 25;
    1918.54; 1919.111; 1921.39
Bain, R. M. 1893.11
Baker, Brownell 1919.333

Baker, I. Newton 1892.15
Baker, May Cole 1883.14
Baker, Portia 1934.43; 1935.39; Appendix
Bakewell, Charles M. 1899.42
Baldensperger, Fernand 1919.363
Balderston, John Lloyd 1916.55
Baldwin, James 1882.1
Balfour, Lady Betty 1906.2
Balfour, Graham 1901.1
Ball, B. W. 1882.19
Ball, M. V. 1898.60; 1903.36
Ballou, William H. 1885.18
Balmont, Konstantin [1916.57; 1934.38]
Baltimore American and Commercial Advertiser
      1877.8-9
Baltimore News 1897.133
Balzac, Honoré de [1895.34]
Bandler, Dr. Samuel W. [1933.22; 1936.33]
Banham, Arthur 1919.364
Banks, J. Lindsay 1919.113, 142
      [1919.114, 133a]
Banner of Light (New York and Boston) 1860.23
Banning, George Hugh 1916.35
Barber, Edward 1901.32
Bardeen, C[harles] W[illiam] 1898.1
Bardhan, Niranjan Mohan 1929.41
Barker, Elsa 1904.32; 1907.43; 1911.31
Barlow, George 1876.12; 1890.2
      [1934.1]
Barnhardt, Harry [1919.326]
Barnum, P. T. [1933.12]
Barron, Elwyn A. 1892.111
Barrows, Samuel J. 1886.38
Barrus, Clara 1914.1; 1925.1, 69; 1928.2; 1931.1
      [1931.46, 49; 1933.11]
      [1919.78]
Bartlett, Truman H. 1908.40; 1912.26
Bartol, Rev. Dr. Cyrus A. 1887.48 [1887.47]
Barton, William Eleazor 1928.3 [1928.30-31;
      1930.47; 1933.6, 30]
Bates, Katharine Lee 1898.2; 1923.44
Bates, William 1883.1 [1892.132; 1925.57, 61, 64]
Bathgate, Herbert J. 1879.12
Baudelaire [1875.17; 1897.132; 1923.38]
Baudouin, Charles 1924.1
Baugh, Albert Croll 1929.24
Baulsir, John Y. [1890.7]
Baum, Paull Franklin 1934.5
Bauser, Whartin 1897.145 [1897.140]
Baxter, Sylvester 1881.15, 38; 1887.77; 1889.9, 14;
      1892.15, 199; 1903.42
Bayne, Peter 1875.15 [1876.7a, 9, 49; 1925.54]
Bazaar Exchange and Mart 1922.42
Bazalgette, Léon 1905.41; 1906.85; 1907.40; 1908.27,
      40; 1910.37; 1912.19; 1915.10; 1916.48; 1920.2
      [1920.36-37, 45, 50, 55, 58, 62, 83; 1921.81;
      1926.67]; 1921.31
      [1908.24, 47; 1909.26, 41; 1910.25, 42; 1911.
      24-25; 1913.46; 1920.39; 1922.50, 59, 67;
      1924.12]
Beach, Chester [1931.28]
Beach, Joseph Warren 1936.2
Beach, Juliette H. 1860.26 [1860.25, 32, 37]
Beach, Mr. 1860.26
Beard, Charles A. and Mary R. 1927.2
Beardshear, W. M. 1900.30
Beaty, John O. 1922.10
Beck, L. Adams 1926.2
Becker, May Lamberton 1921.61
Beckett, Reginald A. 1888.43
Beecher, Henry Ward [1888.42; 1926.24; 1927.20;

1932.25]
Beerbohm, Max 1904.3
Beers, Henry A. 1887.2; 1919.2
      [1925.40]
Beethoven [1901.48; 1905.40; 1919.86; 1926.49]
Beffel, John Nicholas 1918.31
Beith, Gilbert 1931.12, 16
Bell, Clive 1919.370
Bell, Ralcy Husted 1906.3; 1932.1
Bell, William Henry [1900.27, 52]
Bellew, Frank 1884.24
Bellman 1915.47; 1918.19; 1919.268
Belshaw, Alexander 1920.36
Benedict, G. H. 1906.62
Benét, Stephen Vincent 1935.24
Benét, William Rose 1921.74; 1923.44; 1926.21;
      1927.56
Bengough, J. W. 1919.114
Bennett, Arnold 1912.1; 1915.2; 1919.236
Bennett, D. M. 1882.121 [1882.130], 129
      [1888.15]
Bennett, James O'Donnell 1927.3
Bensel, James Berry 1884.18 [1884.19], 22
Benson, Adolph B. 1932.46
Benson, Arthur Christopher 1904.4; 1915.3
Benson, E[dward] F[rederic] 1921.1
Benson, Eugene 1866.19; 1867.8; 1868.42
Benton, Joel 1877.4; 1898.46; 1900.49; 1901.38;
      1903.20 [1887.32]
Benton, Myron B. 1867.22; 1931.1
Bentzon, Mme. Thérèse 1872.18 [1872.20]
Berenson, Mary W. Smith Costelloe. See Costelloe,
      Mary W. Smith
Bergson, Henri [1919.190]
Bernard, Edward G. 1936.33
Bertz, Eduard 1889.9; 1921.31
      [1906.32, 76; 1907.20, 26, 38; 1908.6;
      1910.23; 1913.16; 1915.11; 1921.34]
Best, St. George 1901.29
Bhagavad-Gita. See Oriental thought and reli-
      gion and Appendix
Bianchi, Martha Dickinson 1924.2
Bianco, Giuseppe 1928.4
Bibby, Joseph 1916.5
Bibby's Annual 1916.5
Bible (including specific books, especially Psalms,
      Song of Solomon, Isaiah) [1858.1; 1866.2, 27;
      1868.31; 1874.10; 1876.55; 1879.12; 1880.35;
      1881.45; 1883.14; 1890.6; 1891.5; 1892.16, 39,
      99, 100; 1894.17, 48; 1895.48; 1898.26, 34;
      1907.16; 1908.29; 1911.11-12; 1912.2, 38;
      1915.13; 1916.23; 1918.4; 1919.245; 1921.68;
      1922.54; 1926.70; 1927.39; 1929.19, 54;
      1933.27; 1934.42; 1935.10]
Biblia (Friends of the Princeton Library) 1930.36
      [1930.40]
Bibliographie Impériale [1860.65]
Biblo 1925.73
Bicknell, Percy F. 1906.40; 1914.35
Bierce, Ambrose 1922.17
      [1929.19]
Bigelow, Poultney 1931.29
Billings, Josh [1892.130]
Binns, Henry Bryan 1905.1 [1905.54, 56, 60;
      1906.10, 28, 33, 40, 44-45, 49, 58, 72, 75,
      106]; 1908.2; 1910.38; 1915.54 [1915.42], 10;
      1919.115
Birds [1873.8; 1930.23]
Birmingham (England) Post 1919.301
Birrell, Augustine 1920.3

Birss, John Howard. 1931.54; 1932.32, 38, 49;
    1933.13, 21
Bishop, John Peale. 1939.40
Bisland, Elizabeth. 1906.4
Bispham, David 1920.4
Bjerregaard, C. H. A. 1909.19
Black, Alexander 1922.2; 1937.1
Black, George D. 1892.200
Black, Ivan 1931.48
Black, John 1919.237; 1920.26 [1921.37; See Rodgers
    for reviews.], 50, 98
Black and White 1892.85
Blackburn, Grace (Fanfan) 1912.28, 41; 1913.36, 51;
    1919.244
Blackburn (England) Weekly Telegraph 1919.260
Blackmur, R. P. 1939.46
Blacks and slavery. [1848.5, 6; 1895.50; 1897.76,
    80; 1907.37; 1917.6; 1928.11, 36; 1929.44;
    1936.31; 1938.2]
Blackwood, John [1885.2]
Blackwood's Magazine 1911.21; 1919.27
Blaine, James Gillespie [1884.25, 27; 1890.41]
Blake, H. G. O. [1865.1; 1935.27]
Blake, William [1868.3, 8, 31-32; 1874.8; 1875.3;
    1893.12; 1898.55, 102; 1906.103; 1907.18;
    1908.31; 1911.7, 11; 1919.9; 1920.33; 1930.14a]
Blanck, Jacob 1936.57
Blankenship, Russell 1931.2
Blatch, Harriet Stanton 1889.44
Blatchford, Robert 1923.52
Blavatsky, Helena Petrovna 1929.2
Blind, Mathilde 1883.2
Bliss, Dr. D. W. 1887.13
Block, Louis James 1893.38
Blodgett, Harold William 1929.45, 57; 1930.32;
    1933.14; 1934.1 [1934.47], 44; Appendix
Bloom, Nat [1935.23]
Boatright, Mody C. 1929.56
Bocock, John Paul 1885.36
Bodgener, J. H. 1919.202
Bodkin, Maud 1934.2
Boehme, Trangott [1919.42]
Bogan, Louise 1939.46
Boker, George H. 1889.9, 49
    [1890.10; 1906.12]
Boland, Harry Weir 1906.67; 1923.44
Bolshevism. See Socialism
Bolton group. See also Dr. J[ohn] Johnston; J. W.
    Wallace [1916.3; 1931.1; 1934.1]
Bolton Journal 1892.100
Bon Echo. See also Sunset of Bon Echo [1916.26;
    1919.65; 1920.85]
Bond, F. Fraser 1931.3
Bonsall, Harry [Henry L.] 1888.26; 1889.9, 48;
    1892.15, 66
    [1889.52, 54]
Bonsall, Henry S. 1916.11
Book Buyer 1888.16; 1889.11; 1897.36-37, 63;
    1899.47
Book Hunter 1934.24
Book-Lover 1901.29, 40, 61; 1902.52, 61; 1903.41
Book Monthly 1919.57; 1920.32
Book News. See Book News Monthly
Book News Brevities (Columbia University Press)
    1927.40
Book News Monthly (also called Book News) 1893.24;
    1905.26; 1906.45
Book Notes Illustrated 1924.34; 1926.68
Booklovers' Magazine. See also Appleton's Magazine
    1903.44
Bookman, The [pseud.] 1919.313
Bookman (London) 1892.157; 1914.32; 1919.138, 148,

360; 1927.47
Bookman (New York) 1895.31; 1897.40, 138; 1898.23;
    1908.33; 1911.16, 24; 1916.24, 57, 64; 1917.56;
    1919.45, 60, 330; 1920.40, 50; 1921.48, 67;
    1922.31, 67; 1923.23; 1925.20-21; 1929.47, 58;
    1933.16; 1924.41
Books and the Book World. See New York Sun
Booth, Bates. See Appendix
Booth, Edward Townsend 1922.49
Booth, Heber Hedley 1909.2
Born, Helena 1895.55; 1896.31; 1897.157; 1899.71;
    1902.2 [1902.50]
Borrow, George [1905.40]
Boston. See also New England; specific writers
    [1881.43; 1912.26; 1928.36]
Boston Advertiser. See Boston Daily Advertiser
Boston Chapter Special Libraries Association News
    Bulletin 1937.45
Boston Commonwealth 1864.6; 1866.9, 14, 24; 1868.38;
    1882.30, 49, 96 [1882.100], 101, 105
Boston Cosmopolite 1860.56
Boston Courier 1859.2
Boston Daily Advertiser 1881.10, 36; 1882.37, 46;
    1887.57, 71-72; 1897.91
    [1931.10]
Boston Daily Globe 1882.38, 51
    [1912.26]
Boston Evening Herald. See also Boston Herald
    1912.30
Boston Evening Transcript 1866.3; 1876.39, 51;
    1881.11, 16, 37, 40, 43; 1882.39; 1887.64, 66;
    1888.19, 45, 64, 74; 1889.27, 31, 44; 1890.17;
    1891.23; 1892.23-24, 56-57, 211; 1895.21, 22,
    22a, 24; 1897.88, 90; 1901.24; 1902.62;
    1903.19, 33, 47; 1905.44; 1909.22; 1919.168,
    180, 195, 197, 200, 211, 242, 303; 1920.37,
    82, 96-97, 101; 1926.63; 1929.37
Boston Evening Traveller. See also Boston Traveller
    1881.12
Boston Globe. See Boston Daily Globe
Boston Herald. See also Boston Evening Herald,
    Boston Morning Herald, Boston Sunday Herald
    1881.15; 1882.47, 56, 112; 1885.33; 1887.47-48;
    1889.14; 1890.45; 1892.44; 1909.34; 1915.63
Boston Index. See Index
Boston Intelligencer 1856.16
Boston Journal 1868.44; 1871.5, 25, 27; 1873.3;
    1875.12; 1881.13; 1897.96, 112
Boston Literary Review 1898.97
Boston Morning Herald. See also Boston Herald
    1897.87
Boston Pilot. See also Pilot 1897.97
Boston Post 1887.55
Boston Saturday Evening Gazette 1860.14, 19
Boston Sunday Herald. See also Boston Herald
    1881.38; 1882.52; 1888.24
Boston Transcript. See Boston Evening Transcript
Boston Traveller. See also Boston Evening Traveller
    1889.16, 67
Boston Weekly Transcript 1883.27
Boston Wide World 1860.68
Boswell, James [1891.28; 1908.25; 1913.11]
Botta, Anne C. Lynch 1899.1
Boughton, Willis 1892.206
Bourne, Randolph S. 1914.42
Bowen, Edwin Winfield 1908.3; 1919.73
Boyd, Ernest 1925.77; 1927.4
Boyesen, H. H. [1887.32]
Boynton, Henry Walcott 1903.5; 1921.78; 1928.31
Boynton, Percy H. 1909.7; 1916.53; 1918.4; 1919.3,
    54, 239-240; 1922.58

Bozard, John F. 1938.21; Appendix
Brace, Maria [1888.11]
Bradford, Gamaliel 1916.24; 1923.44
Bradford, William [1931.53]
Bradford, Sculley 1933.16, 31; 1939.17
    [1938.40]
Bradley, William Aspenall 1909.34
Bradsher, Earl L. 1914.18
Braga, Dominque [1922.67]
Bragdon, Claude 1919.36; 1924.23
Brainerd, Erastus 1885.36
Braithwaite, William Stanley 1919.186; 1923.44
Brandes, Georg [1919.359; 1920.14]
Brann's Iconoclast 1898.93
Brashear, William H. 1906.42 [1906.48], 51
    [1906.60-61]
Bredvold, Louis I. 1912.45; 1914.39
Bremer, Fredrika [1932.46]
Brenner, Rica 1933.4
Brenton, James J. 1849.4; 1850.1 [1849.9]
    [1921.16]
Brereton, J. Le Gay 1894.41, 46
Brereton, J. Le Gay, Jr. 1899.2
Breslow, M. M. 1923.37
Bretherton, Cyril H. 1916.31
Brew, Virginia W. See Appendix
Bridge, Frank [1919.374]
Bridges, Horace J. [1919.285]
Bridges, Robert [1935.1]
Brigham, Johnson 1899.28; 1913.2; 1921.50; 1927.54
Bright, Annie 1907.2
Bright, Charles 1883.13
Bright, John 1892.94
Brinton, Daniel G. 1889.9; 1892.15; 1894.64;
    1895.25; 1896.46; 1898.61; 1899.77; 1915.10
    [1894.55]
Brisbane, Albert [1893.1]
Brisbane, Redelia 1893.1
Bristol Times and Mirror 1892.68
British Weekly 1887.44; 1892.75
Britton, James 1926.68
Broadway Journal 1845.1-3
    [1932.38]
Broadway Magazine 1867.23; 1868.31
Brocklehurst, J. H. 1920.5
Bromer, Edward S. 1912.35
Bronson, Walter C. 1900.1
Brooke, Stopford A. 1900.3
Brooklyn [1898.29a; 1900.40; 1912.49; 1916.59;
    1919.105, 212; 1921.22; 1925.44, 58; 1931.39-
    42; 1938.52; 1939.24, 31; 1927.53a]
Brooklyn Advertiser. See also Brooklyn Daily
    Advertiser 1846.3-4, 6; 1847.2-3; 1848.9;
    1849.1, 6, 8
    [1848.10]
Brooklyn Citizen 1892.127
Brooklyn City News 1859.6; 1860.62
    [1936.51]
Brooklyn Daily Advertiser. See also Brooklyn
    Advertiser 1851.1
Brooklyn Daily Eagle 1842.4, 13; 1846.1-2; 1847.4;
    1848.4, 7-8, 10; 1849.3, 7; 1850.2; 1855.9;
    1856.3; 1897.94; 1900.40; 1912.49; 1913.50;
    1914.29; 1915.48; 1919.160-163, 165, 212-216,
    236, 250, 252-253, 255, 259, 261-262, 269,
    275; 1921.72, 77; 1924.28; 1925.38, 44, 58;
    1927.50; 1928.30; 1930.35, 42-43, 46; 1931.39-
    40, 51; 1932.34; 1933.12, 21, 24
    [1846.5; 1847.1-2; 1848.1-3, 5; 1850.3;
    1864.4-5; 1870.2; 1894.10; 1916.37; 1920.26,
    50, 98-101; 1931.23, 28; 1932.46; 1937.11;
    1939.23]

Brooklyn Daily Times. See also Brooklyn Times;
    Brooklyn Times-Union 1855.10; 1856.27;
    1859.7
    [1864.5; 1908.26; 1932.11, 31]
Brooklyn Daily Union 1865.10
Brooklyn Eagle. See Brooklyn Daily Eagle
Brooklyn Evening Star. See also Brooklyn Star
    1849.2; 1854.1
    [1924.28-29; 1938.31]
Brooklyn Freeman [1848.12; 1849.2, 4, 10; 1850.1;
    1864.5; 1870.2; 1912.17; 1920.44; Addenda]
Brooklyn Institute of Arts and Sciences Bulletin
    1919.150 [1919.94, 160, 330]
Brooklyn Standard 1860.67; 1863.1-2; 1864.4-5
    [1916.59]
Brooklyn Star. See also Brooklyn Evening Star
    [1848.2]
Brooklyn Times. See also Brooklyn Daily Times
    1908.26
    [1922.2; 1937.1, 28]
Brooklyn Times-Union. See also Brooklyn Times
    1937.28
Brooks, Cleanth 1939.1
Brooks, Philip 1936.37
Brooks, Van Wyck 1914.2; 1915.5; 1920.43, 45, 86;
    1921.54, 79, 81; 1932.5; 1934.3
Brophy, John 1938.47
Brother Jonathan 1842.1, 11; 1843.1
    [1905.24]
Brotherhood (London) 1906.49
Brown, A. Barratt 1934.4
Brown, George E. 1919.4
Brown, Harvey Dee 1917.33, 37
Brown, Horatio F. 1895.2; 1923.1
Brown, Prof. J. Macmillan 1916.43; 1919.241, 300
Brown, John (abolitionist) [1881.42]
Brown, John Henry 1890.25
Brown, Lewis [1933.6]
Brown, Sandford [1890.7]
Brown, Stephen J. 1921.2
Brown, William Thurston 1917.1
Brown University 1932.35-36
Browne, Francis Fisher 1882.16; 1913.3 [1914.23]
Browne, Waldo R. 1912.2 [1912.34]
Browne, Dr. William [1883.33; 1933.29]
Brownell, W. C. 1909.3
Browning, Robert [1867.10; 1870.3; 1871.21;
    1872.9; 1876.20; 1886.13; 1889.64; 1891.12,
    54; 1892.210; 1893.12, 25; 1895.70; 1898.83,
    87; 1899.4, 38; 1900.14; 1901.51; 1903.4, 6;
    1904.13; 1905.1; 1906.10; 1912.10; 1913.33;
    1915.17; 1919.104, 201, 290, 350, 378;
    1920.15; 1926.1; 1928.14, *39, *43; 1934.1]
Bruère, R. W. 1905.28
Brumbaugh, Roscoe 1906.35; 1939.24; Addenda
Bruno, Guido 1919.116; 1921.3
Bryan, William Jennings 1905.41
Bryant, Arthur 1936.5
Bryant, William Cullen 1842.2
    [1878.11, 12, 16; 1879.4; 1880.5; 1882.19;
    1885.18; 1887.48; 1888.57; 1889.37; 1892.13,
    60, 145, 180; 1897.17, 67; 1899.12; 1900.16;
    1901.14; 1913.19; 1919.121a; 1921.51; 1922.9,
    51; 1924.4, 30; 1925.54; 1926.59; 1928.2;
    *1935.37; 1938.20]
Buchanan, Robert William 1867.23; 1868.1; 1872.2;
    1876.1, 24 [passim throughout 1876], 29, 31;
    1880.10; 1885.27; 1887.3 [1887.45]; 1889.43;
    1892.143 [1925.62]; 1899.79
    [1876.66; 1903.6; 1925.54; 1930.32; 1934.1]
Buck, Philo M., Jr. 1931.4; 1936.6

Bucke, Richard Maurice 1879.1; 1880.13, 15; 1882.36,
     45; 1883.3 [1883.17, 21-22, 29, 31, 32, 35;
     1894.23]; 1889.9, 12; 1890.20, 49; 1892.15,
     211; 1893.11 [for reviews see Traubel], 44;
     1894.30, 33, 47 [1894.51]; 1895.33, 59
     [1895.71]; 1896.20, 42, 47, 62; 1897.2 [for
     reviews see Whitman--Letters], 38, 59, 71;
     1898.3 [for reviews see Whitman--Letters], 27,
     51, 74-75; 1899.3 [1899.69], 38, 61; 1901.3;
     1902.12-13, 25-26, 55; 1915.10
     [1881.27, 29, 40; 1887.49; 1891.35-37;
     1894.49; 1901.49; 1902.37; 1903.25; 1904.11,
     22; 1906.6; 1912.19; 1914.13, 1919.121a;
     1923.3; 1924.43; 1925.3, 20; 1927.5; 1931.1,
     19; 1932.3; 1935.26; 1936.22, 55; 1938.30]
Buckeye [pseud.?] 1840.1
Buckram, Eliot 1919.57
Buddha and Buddhism [1895.33; 1901.25]
Buffalo Morning Express 1892.32
Bullen, Henry Lewis 1915.21
Bulletin of Bibliography 1934.39
Bulletin of the Brooklyn Public Library 1919.277
Bulletin of the New York Public Library 1925.72
Bullett, Gerald 1924.3 [1925.25, 27, 36-37];
     1925.30; 1934.4
Bulliet, C. J. 1927.55
Bullitt, William C. 1926.3
Bulwer-Lytton 1898.29; Addenda
Bunce, Robert 1935.34
Bunker, John 1919.29 [1919.72]
Bunner, H. C. 1881.21 [1923.12]
Burke, Charles Bell. See Appendix
Burke, Kenneth 1931.5; 1937.23
Burkland, Carl Edwin 1932.48
Burns, Robert [1874.8; 1876.49; 1898.82; 1907.14;
     1913.19; 1923.22; 1938.20]
Burroughs, John 1866.24, 26; 1867.1 [1867.10-12,
     22; 1894.23; 1924.33, 37; 1925.1; 1926.4;
     1928.3; 1934.24]; 1868.17; 1870.6; 1871.1;
     1873.8; 1875.1 [1876.19]; 1876.13, 47
     [1876.54], 65; 1877.1 [1877.11-12]; 1879.2
     43; 1881.1, 25; 1882.104; 1884.5 [1885.24];
     1885.20; 1886.1; 1887.22; 1889.2, 9, 57;
     1892.15, 26, 29 [1892.30], 95, 96, 161, 203;
     1893.11, 20, 28, 45; 1894.1, 21 [1894.57], 26,
     58; 1895.3, 34, 53, 60 [1895.71], 68; 1896.2
     [1896.86-87; 1897.23, 30-35, 37, 40, 46-48,
     104], 39, 48, 56, 70; 1897.3, 72, 95; 1898.4,
     37, 87; 1900.2; 1902.5-6; 1903.12; 1905.2
     [1905.58; 1906.26], 3; 1908.4; 1911.2; 1912.2
     [1912.34], 3; 1913.4; 1915.6, 10; 1916.2;
     1919.5 [1919.106, 155], 78, 117, 162, 237;
     1920.6, 60; 1921.4; 1922.3; 1925.1; 1928.2
     [1870.7; 1877.4; 1887.32; 1890.7; 1895.6;
     1897.124; 1899.37; 1900.8; 1901.59, 65;
     1902.37; 1903.15, 21; 1905.42; 1906.79;
     1908.51; 1912.36, 69; 1919.133b; 1928.6;
     1930.8, 16; 1931.1, 29; 1934.43; 1935.9]
Burroughs, Julian 1912.36
Burrowes, Peter E. 1904.39; 1905.29
Burton, Dr. Richard D. 1896.75; 1903.1; 1904.5
     [1905.30]
     [1919.228, 287, 311]
Bush, Douglas 1932.6
Bush, Harry D. 1889.9; 1892.15
Buss, Kate 1919.242
Butchart, Reuben 1894.43; 1923.12
Butcher, Lady Alice 1919.6
Butler, George F. 1899.4
Butler, Nicholas Murray 1908.5
     [1935.13]
Button, W. E. 1907.24

Butts, Nellie Doty 1925.21
Bynner, Witter 1915.7; 1916.48; 1917.2; 1919.118;
     1920.7
     [1919.291]
Byron, George Lord [1847.1; 1889.37; 1892.147;
     1896.39; 1932.12; 1935.10; 1939.23]
Byron, May Clarissa (Maurice Clare) 1912.5
Bystander (London) 1919.41
C. (Nation) 1892.148
C. (Round Table) 1867.4, 6
C., C. C. 1910.39
C., J. E. See Chamberlin, Joseph Edgar
C., J. F. 1886.42
C., L. C. 1892.97
C., P. See Carus, Paul
C., S. C. 1929.38
C., S. T. See Clover, Samuel Travers
C., V. S. 1888.29
Cabell, James Branch 1924.4
Cable, George Washington [1898.80]
Cade, Jack [1888.42]
Caffin, Charles H. 1905.20
Cairns, William B. 1912.4; 1914.3; 1919.334;
     1930.2; 1931.26
Calder, Alma. See Johnston, Alma Calder
Calder, Ellen M. O'Connor 1892.15; 1906.58; 1907.37;
     1915.10; 1921.16; 1927.17 [1927.51; 1930.47]
     [1906.101; 1911.29; 1919.146; 1928.6]
Calder, John Cooper 1925.63
Calgary Daily Herald 1919.210; 1926.71
Californian 1880.9, 22, 30; 1881.9
Californian Illustrated Magazine 1892.158; 1893.21-
     22
Call, William Timothy 1914.4
Calvert, Bruce 1912.37
Calverton, V. F. 1932.7, 43
Cambridge Fortnightly 1888.10
Cambridge Magazine 1918.65
Cambridge Meteor 1882.61
Cambridge Review 1920.69
Camden. See also Whitman--Activities; Visits to
     [1885.10; 1888.49; 1892.121; 1893.16, 19;
     1897.24; 1900.19; 1909.29; 1919.19; 1920.21,
     78, 82, 87; 1921.19; 1922.38, 55-56; 1923.54-
     57, 59, 61, 63; 1926.26, 61; 1928.24, 29;
     1929.51; 1931.43; 1933.25; 1936.43, 50;
     1937.9, 26; 1938.12]
Camden Coast Pilot 1886.31
Camden Courier. See also Camden Courier-Post;
     Camden Evening Courier 1887.46; 1888.34;
     1923.54-55; 1929.54
Camden Courier-Post. See also Camden Courier;
     Camden Post 1932.40; 1938.40
Camden Daily Post. See Camden Post
Camden Evening Courier. See also Camden Courier
     1928.35
Camden First 1925.22, 59
Camden Mirror 1883.23
Camden New Republic 1876.40
Camden Post. See also Camden Post-Telegram 1877.10,
     14; 1880.3, 11, 16; 1882.43; 1884.15; 1885.8-
     9, 22, 32; 1888.26, 84; 1889.42, 48, 76;
     1890.31-32; 1891.21, 30; 1892.63, 66
     [1923.58]
Camden Post-Telegram. See also Camden Post
     1923.56-58
Campbell, Helen 1908.48
Campbell, Killis 1929.46, 59; 1933.11; 1934.31, 45
Campbell, W. W. 1892.98
Canada. See also Bon Echo [1911.27; 1919.143;
     1927.5]

Canada Monthly 1911.31
Canadian Journal 1856.25
Canadian Magazine 1923.43
Canadian Monthly and National Review. See also
    Rose-Belford's Canadian Monthly and National
    Review 1872.9
Canby, Henry Seidel 1923.44; 1926.52; 1929.3-4;
    1930.43; 1931.6; 1936.7; 1938.27
    [1938.55]
Cappon, James 1930.3
Carleton, Will 1889.9
Carlill, H. F. 1901.20 [1901.23]
Carlyle, Thomas [1856.10; 1860.46; 1867.28, 30;
    1868.7, 27, 30; 1876.53, 56; 1877.1; 1881.3;
    1882.131; 1883.4; 1886.45; 1892.104; 1895.5;
    1897.65, 164; 1898.29, 49; 1899.38; 1905.1;
    1911.10; 1913.14; 1916.18; 1917.6; 1918.17;
    1919.138, 234; 1920.12, 30; 1922.39, 51;
    1927.25; 1928.14; 1931.6; 1933.22; 1934.1,
    18; 1936.2; 1937.14, 17, 37; 1938.2, 20, 31;
    *1939.41]
Carman, Bliss 1897.88; 1900.31; 1904.6; 1905.4;
    1914.34
    [1930.3]
Carmelite, The 1931.58
Carnegie, Andrew 1915.10
    [1887.36, 42]
Carnevali, Emanuel 1919.119, 354
Carpenter, Edward 1889.9, 32; 1892.15; 1894.31;
    1896.71; 1897.39, 60; 1902.7, 32; 1904.22;
    1906.5 [1906.74-75, 80, 82-83, 91, 106];
    1908.6 [1921.20]; 1911.3; 1915.10; 1916.3;
    1922.4; 1924.5; 1931.1
    [1886.34; 1896.31; 1900.8; 1901.5, 66;
    1912.22; 1918.13; 1920.23; 1925.17; 1928.6;
    1929.55; 1931.12-13, 16; 1934.1, 4]
Carpenter, Frederic Ives 1930.4; 1931.22
Carpenter, George Rice 1898.6; 1900.3; 1903.2;
    1909.4 [1909.21, 25, 27-28, 31, 33-35; 1925.20]
Carrington, C. E. H. 1921.65
Carus, Paul 1900.20 [1900.38]
Cary, Elisabeth Luther 1906.103
Casca. See Trimble, William H.
Catel, Jean [1923.62; 1932.30; 1933.27]
Cather, Willa 1896.26
    [1926.27]
Catholic World 1882.25; 1917.36
Catullus [1867.4]
Cauldwell, William 1901.21
Cavazza, E. 1892.131
Cecil Democrat (Elkton, Maryland) 1886.18-19, 21,
    26
Cecil Whig (Elkton, Maryland) 1885.41-42; 1886.15,
    17, 22-25, 27
Century Magazine. See also Scribner's Monthly
    1882.118; 1883.16; 1885.30; 1889.40; 1893.44;
    1895.17; 1897.124; 1905.53; 1907.46; 1911.18,
    34; 1912.24; 1921.42
    [1888.55, 60; 1935.39]
Cestre, Charles 1923.38
Cezanne [1921.11]
Chadwick, Rev. John White 1882.53 [1882.63, 68];
    1889.9; 1893.47; 1897.34, 108 [1897.112];
    1903.3 [1907.31]
Chainey, George 1881.22-23; 1882.34, 62 [1882.66],
    70; 1885.21
    [1882.92, 97, 113; 1896.67]
Chamberlin, Joseph Edgar 1892.56-57; 1895.21, 22,
    22a, 24; 1897.24; 1919.168; 200; 1937.2
Chambers, Julius 1889.9; 1915.48; 1921.5
Chambers, Robert 1903.3

Chambers's Journal of Popular Literature, Science,
    and Art 1868.37
Champneys, Basil 1900.4
Chandos-Fulton, W. A. 1863.1; 1864.4-5
Channing, William Ellery [1938.2]
Channing, William Francis [1931.59]
Chap-Book 1897.107, 115, 129-132, 143; 1898.32,
    36, 87
Chapman, Dr. C. H. 1912.43; 1915.25
Chapman, J. A. 1929.5
Chapman, John Jay 1897.115 [1897.105, 129-131, 134,
    143]; 1898.6 [1898.46]
Chapman, Joseph W. 1916.11
Charlesworth, Hector 1927.5
Charlton, Jay 1882.10
Charnwood, Lord [Godfrey] 1921.6
Charteris, Evan, The Hon., K. C. 1931.7
Chase, Audrie Alspaugh 1919.203
Chase, Secretary Salmon [1903.15]
Chaucer, Geoffrey [1908.36; 1921.42]
Chautauquan 1887.30; 1892.181; 1908.30; 1909.33;
    1912.21
Cheney, John Vance [Anthony Thrall] 1880.22
    [1880.30]; 1893.21
Chénier, André [1911.7]
Chesterton, Gilbert K. 1902.8; 1903.4; 1905.5;
    1919.231; 1920.95; 1922.5; 1923.33; 1925.41;
    1933.34; 1936.8
Cheyney, Ralph 1931.36 [1931.44]
Chicago Daily News. See also Chicago News 1920.36
Chicago Daily Tribune. See Chicago Tribune
Chicago Evening Post. See also Chicago Post
    1897.89; 1912.25; 1916.48; 1919.208, 310;
    1920.62; 1921.59; 1927.55
Chicago Examiner. See also Chicago Herald-Examiner
    1918.47
Chicago Herald. See also Chicago Herald-Examiner
    1882.113; 1890.48
Chicago Herald-Examiner. See also Chicago Examiner;
    Chicago Herald 1918.31; 1919.203, 285;
    1933.34; 1934.26
Chicago Inter-Ocean. See Inter-Ocean
Chicago Leader 1920.60
Chicago News. See also Chicago Daily News 1888.52;
    1919.217, 367; 1926.45, 50
Chicago Post. See also Chicago Evening Post
    1909.32; 1919.103; 1926.56
Chicago Republican 1866.5
Chicago Sun 1914.26
Chicago Sunday Record-Herald 1902.54
Chicago Sunday Tribune. See Chicago Tribune
Chicago Tribune 1881.46; 1892.113; 1896.87;
    1910.45-46; 1919.194, 266, 318, 366
Children and young people, Books for. See Textbooks
    and books for young people
Childs, George W. 1889.9
    [1887.42; 1888.24; 1900.33]
Chilton, Mary A. 1860.31 [1860.35]
Cholmondeley, Thomas 1893.48
    [1894.16; 1917.13]
Chopin, Kate 1894.20
Christ and Christianity [1878.17; 1885.27; 1886.4;
    1887.3; 1888.43; 1892.80; 1895.34; 1897.64;
    1898.92; 1899.38; 1901.25, 56; 1903.18;
    1905.36, 41, 48; 1910.11; 1912.40; 1913.19,
    54; 1919.8, 346; 1921.13; 1922.1, 33, 68;
    1924.32; 1927.14, 32; 1930.16; 1934.5; 1937.9;
    1938.19, 57]
Christchurch (New Zealand) Press. See also
    Christchurch Weekly Press 1919.241, 300

Christchurch (New Zealand) Weekly Press. See also
    Christchurch Press 1916.43
Christian Commonwealth 1919.198
Christian Examiner 1856.24
Christian Leader 1892.28; 1893.35
Christian Life 1919.218
Christian Register 1876.68; 1886.38; 1893.47;
    1896.64, 66; 1897.139; 1898.52, 76; 1906.107
Christian Science [1905.25]
Christian Science Monitor 1918.46; 1919.96, 155,
    196, 199, 217, 304, 321, 329, 347, 350;
    1920.42, 77; 1922.55; 1923.45; 1925.26;
    1926.48; 1928.41; 1929.38; 1933.20, 26;
    1938.39
Christian Science Monitor Magazine 1939.45
Christian Spiritualist 1856.3
Christian Union. See also Outlook 1888.17; 1892.95,
    103
Christian World Pulpit 1919.316
Christie, John 1892.2
Chubb, Edwin Watts 1926.5
Chubb, Percival 1892.15
Chukovsky, Korney [1934.38]
Church Family Newspaper 1919.206
Church Quarterly Review 1925.23
Churches [1905.33; 1926.53; 1928.28]
Cincinnati Commercial. See also Cincinnati Daily
    Commercial 1871.9; 1873.5
Cincinnati Daily Commercial. See also Cincinnati
    Commercial 1859.8
Cincinnati Post 1892.156
Cities. See also specific cities [1920.73; 1937.23]
City and State (Philadelphia) 1902.44
Claire, Roma [1919.53]
Clapp, Henry 1860.18, 32
    [1934.9]
Clare, Ada 1860.4
    [1934.9]
Clare, Maurice. See Byron, May Clarissa
Clarion (London) 1898.52; 1899.23; 1923.52
Clark, Barrett H. 1928.5
Clark, Grace Delano 1921.34
Clark, Harry Hayden 1928.10; 1936.9
Clark, Thomas Curtis 1922.48
Clarke, Helen A. See also P. A. C. 1894.34, 66;
    1895.19, 22b [1895.24a], 30; 1896.59; 1899.57;
    1900.34
Clarke, William 1892.3 [1892.189, 194, 196, 206,
    207; 1894.23]
Clarkson, Grosvenor B. 1916.33
Classics. See also Greek [1925.24; 1930.38]
Claudel [1920.37; 1924.1; 1930.3]
Clear, Claudius [pseud.] 1892.75
Clemens, Samuel (Mark Twain) 1889.9, 50; 1896.3
    [1873.4; 1892.73; 1910.47; 1913.27; 1917.54;
    1919.3; 1920.14, 19, 43, 90; 1922.9, 33;
    1923.48; 1925.35; 1928.19; 1939.40]
Cleveland, Grover [1883.23, 27; 1884.25, 27; 1934.5]
Cleveland, Mrs. Grover [1888.24]
Cleveland, Paul R. 1888.51
Cleveland Leader 1868.39; 1885.18; 1897.95
Clifford, John Herbert 1889.9; 1892.15; 1895.35,
    36
    [1889.54]
Clifford, William Kingdon 1877.15
Clive, Arthur. See O'Grady, Standish James
Close, Stuart 1897.61
Clover, Samuel Travers 1916.36
Clow, Stephen G. 1906.54, 81
Clutton-Brock, Arthur 1920.33; 1921.7 [1922.34]
Coad, Oral Sumner 1938.56

Coates, Dr. Reginald [1926.61]
Coblentz, Stanton A. 1919.291; 1938.41
Cockrill, John A. 1889.9
Cocks, George F. M. 1919.243
Cog, I. N. See Porter, Charlotte
Coleridge, Samuel [1938.2]
Coleridge, Hon. Stephen 1916.4 [1917.29]
Colles, Ramsay 1911.4
Collier, William Francis 1912.6
Collier's Weekly 1897.164; 1898.45; 1914.20
Collins, John Churton 1904.28
Collins, Seward 1930.43
Collinson, Joseph 1892.132
Colophon 1930.25; 1932.27; 1933.15; 1935.20, 36;
    1937.24
Colum, Mrs. Mary G. M. 1937.3
Colum, Padraic 1907.3; 1919.79, 317
Columbia Monthly 1908.36, 39
Columbia University Quarterly 1919.363
Columbus, Christopher. See also Whitman--Works--
    "Prayer of Columbus"
    [1895.23; 1901.7]
Columbus Daily Ohio State Journal 1860.12
Columbus Morning Journal 1866.12
Colvin, Sidney 1899.5; 1911.5
Commercial Advertiser 1891.40
Commonweal 1926.35
Communism. See Socialism
Compton-Rickett, Arthur. See Rickett, Arthur
Comrade 1901.55, 65; 1902.28, 43; 1903.24, 38, 45;
    1904.39, 43; 1905.29
Comradeship. See also Homosexuality; Whitman--
    Works--"Calamus" [1874.10; 1875.16; 1893.9,
    40; 1897.86; 1898.16; 1900.39; 1901.5; 1902.7;
    1906.23; 1909.4; 1911.28; 1913.46; 1916.3, 24;
    1920.5, 23, 35, 66, 82; 1921.6, 8, 27, 62, 65;
    1922.30; 1931.21, 23; 1934.46; 1935.10]
Comstock, Anthony [1882.51, 79, 85, 94; 1931.1]
Comte, Auguste [1868.20; 1919.8]
Con Amore [pseud.] 1882.83
Concert Goer 1901.60; 1902.35
Cone, Helen Gray 1882.118
Conrad, Joseph [1928.41]
Conservative Review (Washington) 1899.34
Conservator 1890.20, 38, 49; 1891.17, 43; 1892.80,
    82, 162, 184, 194; 1893.18; 1894.29-30, 33,
    36-37, 49, 53, 58, 65; 1895.12-13, 15, 20, 22,
    24-25, 30, 35-40, 42-48, 51-58, 61-64, 66, 69,
    73, 78, 80-82; 1896.19-22, 27-28, 31-36, 38-
    50, 56, 58, 65-69, 72-74, 76-79, 81-86;
    1897.25-26, 28-29, 38, 41-42, 48-53, 59, 61-
    62, 64-65, 68, 70, 73, 80-81, 85-86, 101-106,
    123, 125-127, 139-141, 149-152, 157-158;
    1898.22, 24, 27-28, 29a, 39-43, 52-53, 55,
    56a, 57-58, 60-63, 74, 76-78, 84-86, 90-91,
    93-94, 97-99, 101-102, 104-105; 1899.24-26,
    29, 31-33, 39-41, 44, 46, 49, 53, 55, 57-64,
    66-67, 69, 72, 77; 1900.21-27, 29, 31-32, 34-
    37, 39, 41-44, 47-48, 50; 1901.18, 22, 25-26,
    30, 32, 34-35, 41-44, 46, 48, 54, 56, 58;
    1902.29, 33, 36, 39, 41, 44-45, 49-51, 58, 60;
    1903.18, 22, 25-27, 30, 33a, 36, 43, 50;
    1904.23-24, 27, 37-38, 40, 42, 44, 47; 1905.23-
    25, 30-32, 35, 40-41, 48-49, 51, 57-58;
    1906.24, 30-31, 36, 44, 46, 57-59, 70-72, 77,
    88, 92, 99-101; 1907.11-12, 17-18, 29-31, 34,
    38, 40, 47-48, 53, 56; 1908.23-24, 27-28, 34,
    40-41, 43-45, 49, 52, 54-56; 1909.17, 21, 24,
    36, 38-39, 41, 43; 1910.25, 27-28, 30-31, 35,
    37, 41, 43-44; 1911.28a, 30; 1912.19, 25-26,
    31, 39; 1913.22, 25, 38-40, 42, 47, 49; 1914.30,

36, 38; 1915.30, 41-42, 48, 50; 1916.25, 38-
  41, 48-49, 54; 1917.18-19, 21, 30, 33-34, 37-
  38, 42, 47-50, 52, 57-59; 1918.18, 24, 38,
  41-43, 46-48, 53-56; 1919.30-31, 47, 61, 111,
  115, 120, 122, 124, 129, 133, 137, 139, 144-
  145, 147, 281-282, 284
  [1926.15; 1929.9; 1938.21]
Contemporary Review 1872.16; 1875.15; 1886.35;
  1894.60
Conway, Moncure Daniel [Monadnock] 1860.54; 1866.17,
  22; 1867.7; 1868.8; 1875.13; 1881.3; 1882.2;
  1892.4, 58, 119; 1904.7
  [1903.12; 1934.24]
Cook, Clarence 1882.26
Cook, George C. 1897.30 [1897.32, 55], 43 [1897.54]
Cook, Howard Willard 1925.29
Cook, Joseph [1893.11]
Cook, Kenningale 1903.12
Cooke, Mrs. Alice Lovelace 1934.32; 1935.31;
    Appendix; Addenda
Cooke, George Willis 1881.4
Cooke, M. B. 1917.55
Coolidge, Isabella [1926.10]
Coomaraswamy, Ananda 1919.80
Cooper, James Fenimore [1842.12; 1925.54]
Cooper, Lane 1909.5
Cooper, Capt. Simon [1887.17]
Copeland, Arthur 1899.66, 75
Cope's Tobacco Plant 1875.14; 1880.12
Corbett, Elizabeth Frances [1928.6] 1928.26-27, 35
Corbin, Alice. See Henderson, Alice C.
Corelli, Marie 1887.4
Corning, J. Leonard, U.S. Consul 1895.54
Corot, Jean Baptiste [1902.46]
Corson, Hiram 1911.6
  [1933.18]
Cosmopolis 1897.161; 1898.75
Cosmopolitan 1888.51; 1892.216; 1893.15; 1902.37
Costelloe, Mary D. Smith (Mary Smith) 1886.32, 56;
  1889.9
  [1915.18; 1937.24, 46]
Cotterill, H. B. 1882.3
Courthope, William John 1901.4
Courtney, W. L. 1914.24
Cox, George C. [1887.40; 1897.79; 1913.17]
Cox, Rev. Ignatius [1938.57-58]
Coy, Rebecca [1936.52]
Coyne, James H. 1906.6
Craftsman 1906.91; 1912.36
Crane, Dr. Frank 1923.44
Crane, Hart 1930.5 [1930.38], 20; 1936.2
  [1926.30; 1933.5; 1937.9, 18; 1939.32]
Crane, Nathalia 1930.42
Crane, Stephen [1895.31; 1901.45]
Crawford, Annie Laziere 1892.78
Crawford, Nelson A. 1924.6
Crayon 1856.5; 1860.41
Creamer, Edward S. 1916.11
Crinkle, Nym. See Wheeler, Andrew Carpenter
Criterion (New York) 1855.14
Criterion (New York) 1898.76, 84, 99, 104; 1899.29
Critic (London) 1856.11; 1860.49
Critic (New York) 1881.24-25, 29, 33, 40a, 49;
    1882.4, 57-58, 68, 102-104, 109; 1883.9, 18,
    20, 22, 24; 1884.19, 22; 1886.29, 37, 39-40,
    58; 1887.17, 21, 24, 31, 36-37, 40, 43, 45,
    49-50, 59-60, 65, 68, 70, 73, 78, 87-88;
    1888.8, 12, 15, 23, 28, 30, 36-37, 47, 60-62;
    1889.17, 41, 45, 57, 66, 68, 74, 75; 1890.12,
    14, 19, 23, 27, 35, 46-47, 53, 58; 1891.15,
    19, 27a, 32-33a, 39, 44, 48, 62; 1892.19, 26,

29-30, 96, 101, 122-123, 130, 140, 145-146,
  149-151, 153, 174-175, 178, 186-189, 192, 208,
  213, 225; 1893.16, 23, 27, 33-34, 37; 1894.26-
  27, 40; 1895.29, 48, 58; 1898.25, 37, 47, 100;
  1902.55; 1904.33; 1906.87, 89
  [1882.69; 1890.40; 1935.39]
Croce, Benedetto [1912.18]
Crocker, Lionel 1932.25
Crockett, S. R. 1893.35
Croffut, William A. 1931.8
Cronin, David Edward 1896.49
Cronwright-Schreiner, Samuel C. 1924.6a
Cronyn, George W. 1908.36
Crosby, Ernest H. 1896.81; 1897.150; 1899.60; 1901.5,
  30, 65; 1904.44; 1906.63 [1906.68-69], 86;
  1908.49; 1919.120
  [1912.42]
Cross, Carel 1918.62
Cross, John W. 1885.2
Cross, Dr. Wilbur 1923.44
Crothers, Dr. Samuel McChord 1899.30; 1905.41;
  1912.7; Addenda
  [1919.160]
Crum, Ralph B. 1931.9
Cullen, Charles 1933.3
Cumings, David 1919.281
Cuningham, Clarence 1905.21 [1905.22, 27]
Current Literature. See also Current Opinion
  1888.44; 1900.51; 1901.53; 1905.47; 1906.34,
  56, 76, 105; 1907.43, 51; 1908.32, 47; 1909.34
Current Opinion. See also Current Literature
  1913.24, 48; 1914.37; 1916.33; 1918.23, 68;
  1919.278, 331, 361; 1920.79, 87; 1921.41, 46;
  1924.37
Currie, Barton 1931.10
Curti, Merle Eugene 1928.32; 1932.39
Curtis, George W. 1860.60; 1865.11; 1876.61;
  1889.9
  [1910.17]
Curtis, William O'Leary 1891.20
Cushing, Harvey 1925.3
Custer, Mrs. General [1887.32]
Cyril, Grand Duke of Russia 1899.24

D. 1892.217
D., F. See Dell, Floyd
D., J. B. 1933.26
D., N. G. 1901.39
D., N. H. See Dole, Nathan Haskell
Daily Worker 1935.42
Dakyns, Henry Graham 1911.13
Dalhousie Review 1932.24
Dalton, Joseph G. 1880.1; 1885.3
Daly, Tom 1920.40
Dalziel [1891.31]
Damrosch, Walter [1936.32]
Dana, Charles A. 1855.2 [1934.25]; 1876.3, 33, 55
  [1915.10]
Danbury News 1882.10
Dane, Clarence. See Ashton, Winifred
Daniel, Lewis C. 1935.15
  [1936.60, 61]
Dante [1866.2, 27; 1895.34; 1898.71, 102; 1910.12;
  1915.10; 1919.283; 1921.72; 1939.42]
Darío, Rubén 1928.21
Dark, Sidney 1923.33
Darrow, Clarence S. 1899.6
Dart, William Kernan 1915.8
Dartmouth Alumni Magazine 1933.14
Dartmouth College. See Also Whitman--Works--"Thou
  Mother" [1872.13; 1906.13; 1931.3; 1933.14]

Darwin, Charles. See also Evolution [1888.57; 1919.283; 1920.63; 1934.32]
Daskam, Josephine Dodge 1901.31
Dauthendey, Max [1915.54; 1919.44]

Davenport, W[illiam] E. 1900.40; 1903.21; 1904.42; 1921.72; 1925.44; 1936.43; Addenda
Davidson, James Wood 1888.1
Davidson, Jo [1925.80; 1931.17; 1938.24; 1939.36, 38; Addenda
Davis, Elmer 1915.9
Davis, Jefferson [1930.25]
Davis, Mrs. Mary [1892.59; 1894.24; 1900.19; 1907.25; 1909.29; 1921.19; 1922.45; 1924.41; 1926.13; 1932.2]
Davis, Rebecca Harding 1897.63
Davis, Richard Harding [1924.41]
Davis, Sam 1880.30
Davis, William Harper 1933.19
Davis, William T. 1937.13
Dawson, A. M. P. 1921.8
Dawson, Polly Ernestine 1901.18
Dawson, W[illiam] J[ames] 1906.7
Deacon, William Arthur 1926.6
Dearborn Independent 1923.51
Death and immortality. See also Whitman--Death and funeral 1886.32; 1890.10, 28-30; 1893.11; 1896.51, 59; 1897.100; 1899.17; 1902.6, 14; 1905.17, 24; 1909.14; 1910.7; 1913.32; 1916.26, 37; 1917.56; 1919.316; 1921.49; 1924.45; 1926.40; 1927.8; 1931.20
De Bonhélier [1899.21]
Debs, Eugene V. 1905.41; 1907.40; 1917.34 [1920.65]
Debussy, Claude [1928.40]
De Casseres, Benjamin 1907.52; 1909.23; 1915.52; 1918.49, 70-71; 1920.58; 1921.31; 1923.44
Deeping, Warwick 1928.7
De Kay, Charles 1889.61; 1897.162
De la Mare, Walter 1915.31
Delineator 1919.362
Dell, Floyd 1915.40; 1919.121, 355; 1920.8; 1921.9; 1923.4, 44; 1924.7 [1938.55]
Del Vecchio, James 1860.68
Demain (Lyons) 1906.44
De Mille, A[lban] B[ertram] 1900.6
De Mille, George E. 1931.11
Democracy (Whitman's qualities of and ideas about) 1867.28, 30; 1868.7, 42; 1871.23; 1881.9, 23, 35; 1883.5; 1884.8; 1890.8; 1892.50, 95, 119, 161, 181, 202; 1893.12; 1894.35, 61, 66; 1895.21a, 70; 1896.58, 71; 1897.11; 1898.14, 16; 1899.71; 1900.9, 14; 1902.47, 58; 1903.37; 1905.18, 22; 1906.24; 1907.10, 24; 1908.45; 1909.5; 1910.1, 40; 1913.19, 37; 1914.5, 15, 21, 24; 1915.24; 1916.22, 27-28, 47; 1917.27, 32; 1918.4, 27, 30, 35; 1919.14, 121, 148-149, 186, 191, 204-205, 317, 340, 373; 1921.20, 51; 1923.48-49, 51; 1931.6, 18, 39; 1934.19, 48; 1937.22
Democratic Review. See also United States Review [1842.2, 7]
Denison, Flora MacDonald (Flora MacDonald) 1907.14; 1919.121a, 133a-c; 1920.47 [1919.65]
Dennett, J. R. 1868.6
Dent, John C. 1873.4
Denver Daily Tribune 1879.35
Denver Rocky Mountain News 1879.34
de Quirielle, Jean 1923.33

Der arme Teufel 1896.30
Derby Daily Telegraph 1919.269
Derby Herald 1919.264
de Salamanca, Felix 1879.4
De Selincourt, Basil 1914.5 [1914.24-25, 27, 29-30, 32, 39-40; 1922.14]
De Selincourt, Ernest 1920.9 [1923.22]
Des Moines Sunday Register 1921.50
Detroit Free Press 1882.17; 1888.40
Deuceace [pseud.?] 1882.71
Deutsch, Babette 1919.45; 1920.94; 1935.5
Deutsche Press 1889.9
DeVoto, Bernard 1937.34
Diack, William 1901.66
Dial (Chicago) 1882.16; 1885.40; 1892.16, 182, 207, 214; 1893.20, 36, 45, 49; 1896.75, 80; 1897.30, 32, 43 [1897.52], 44-45; 1901.51; 1902.30; 1906.40, 104; 1909.31; 1912.34, 45; 1913.33; 1914.23, 35, 39; 1915.36; 1916.37; 1917.44, 54; 1918.73; 1919.35-37, 43, 67, 93, 97, 220, 257; 1920.55, 88; 1921.52; 1922.30
Dial (Cincinnati) 1860.55
Dialectics 1937.22
Dickens, Charles [1842.1; 1897.17; 1899.79; 1906.65; 1907.17; 1929.10; 1934.20; 1938.20]
Dickinson, Emily 1891.47 [1905.4; 1933.8; 1936.26]
Dickinson, G. Lowes 1914.6
Dickinson, Sidney E. 1920.56
Dickinson, Thomas H. 1932.8
Dickson, Margarette Ball 1926.8
Digest, The. See also Literary Digest 1937.47
Diogenes [1876.28]
Dipsicus. See Wrong, E. M.
Dircks, Will H. 1865.1
Dixon, Thomas 1892.9; 1903.12 [1892.134]
Dobell, Bertram 1910.19 [1921.29]
Dobrée, Bonamy 1929.6
Dodds, M. 1920.67
Dodge, Mary Mapes 1876.69 [1905.27] [1905.9]
Dole, Nathan Haskell 1891.25; 1898.62; 1929.37 [1929.42]
Donaldson, Thomas 1892.217; 1896.3 [1896.87; 1897.23, 30-35, 37, 44; 1931.1] [1885.34; 1889.52, 54; 1906.18; 1911.1]
Donnan, May W. 1897.98
Donoso, Armando 1920.80 [1920.83]
Doonan, Isaac [1925.75]
Dos Passos, John [R., Jr.] 1916.62; 1932.44; 1936.10; 1939.40 [1926.82]
Dostoevsky, Fyodor [1922.16; 1930.7]
Double Dealer 1922.60
Douglas, Lord Alfred 1892.217
Douglas, Lloyd C. 1932.9; 1936.11; 1939.2
Dowden, Edward 1871.4; 1875.2; 1878.3 [1878.13]; 1881.5; 1882.128; 1883.35; 1884.3; 1886.35; 1889.9; 1903.12; 1914.7-8; 1915.10 [1875.15; 1917.42; 1925.54, 75; 1929.45; 1931.1; 1933.18; 1934.1]
Dowden, Elizabeth D. 1914.7-8
Dowden, Hilda M. 1914.8
Dowden, John 1914.8
Downes, Louise 1910.1
Doyle, Peter 1897.2 [for reviews see Whitman--Letters]; 1915.10 [1902.37; 1905.1; 1907.47; 1917.6, 58; 1920.2; 1926.13, 24; 1928.3, 6; 1929.17; 1937.9; 1938.9]

Drake, A. B. 1898.53
Drake, Francis S. 1872.3
Draper, J. W. 1895.25
Dreiser, Theodore (The Prophet) 1896.52, 63;
    1901.67; 1915.61; 1920.10; 1925.34; 1930.39;
    1933.34
    [1919.339; 1937.10]
Drinkard, Dr. 1885.10
Drinkwater, John 1924.8
    [1918.59-60; 1919.376]
Dublin Evening Telegraph 1889.69
Dublin University Magazine 1876.5; 1878.13
Dublin University Review 1886.34
Du Bois, Dr. W. E. B. 1923.44
Duclaux, Mme. [1920.38]
Duclo, Estelle 1907.36
Dudley, Dorothy 1919.348
Duer, Caroline and Alice 1896.4
Duffus, R. L. 1931.46; 1932.42
Dugdale, Clarence 1936.53
Duluth Daily News 1931.60
Duncan, Augustin [1911.20]
Duncan, Elizabeth 1930.20
Duncan, Isadora 1927.6
    [1911.20; 1930.20]
Duncan, James G. 1892.100
Dundee Evening Telegraph 1918.72
Dunedin (New Zealand) Evening Star 1918.62;
    1919.272
Dunlop, Elinor 1916.5
Dunsany, Lord 1923.33
Durant, Will [1929.54; 1939.36]
Duse, Eleonora [1897.79]
Dusenbury, V. Hugo 1880.37
Dutch. See Whitman--Dutch traits
Dwight, Timothy 1900.15
Dyer, Adalena F. 1901.46
Dyer, Louville H. 1902.59
Dynamo. A Journal of Revolutionary Poetry 1934.21

E., A. von See Ende, Amelia von
E., C. 1907.9
E., C. H. 1906.47 [1906.48], 64, 68
E., E. F. See Edgett, Edwin Francis
E., T. S. See Eliot, T. S.
E. W. Howe's Monthly 1919.64
Eagle, Solomon. See Squire, J. C.
Eagle See Brooklyn Daily Eagle
Eakins, Thomas 1892.194; 1937.44
    [1892.53; 1908.50; 1921.12]
East, The. See Oriental thought and religion
Eastman, Crystal 1919.365
Eastman, Max 1908.29; 1913.5; 1918.6 [1918.65, 73;
    1919.51, 59, 101]; 1922.32; 1923.44; 1926.80;
    1939.3
    [1914.33]
Eaton, Charlotte 1909.24
Eaton, Wyatt 1889.40
    [1887.32]
Eccles, Caroline A. 1912.20 [1912.40]; 1936.12
Echo (London) 1889.19; 1892.143
Eckert, Robert P. 1937.4
Eclectic Magazine 1883.10; 1887.82; 1898.54
Eclectic Review 1892.167, 170
Ecob, Dr. James H. 1907.25 [1907.32, 56; 1908.23]
Edgar, Pelham 1892.133
Edgett, Edwin Francis 1905.44, 49; 1919.180;
    1920.37, 97, 101
Edinburgh Review 1908.51
    [1934.24]
Edinburgh Scotsman. See Scotsman

Edington, Archie 1916.39
Education 1929.53; 1930.34
Education [1909.36; 1917.52, 56; 1918.10, 47;
    1919.91, 233; 1928.34; 1929.44]
Edwards, Ward H. 1901.33; 1905.34; 1919.30, 173,
    177
Egan, Maurice Francis 1921.37
Eldridge, Charles Wesley 1896.33, 43; 1902.42;
    1931.1
Eliot, George 1876.2; 1884.2
    [1883.2; 1887.6; 1934.1]
Eliot, T. S. 1917.4; 1919.104; 1926.83; 1927.42,
    45; 1928.8
    [1922.61, 64; 1925.31]
Elkton (Maryland) Appeal 1886.20, 28
Elliot, Charles N. 1915.10 [1916.49]
Elliott, G. R. 1929.43
Ellis, [Henry] Havelock 1882.33; 1888.1a; 1890.3
    [1890.15]; 1901.6; 1915.11; 1919.122a; 1923.33
    [1924.6a; 1928.20; 1934.1]
Ellis, Mrs. H. Havelock [1914.33]
Elmina. See Slenker, Elmina D.
Elmira, "the Quaker Infidel" [pseud.] 1882.125
Elmira Daily Gazette and Free Press 1892.116
Elshemus, Louis M. 1898.72
Elton, Oliver 1890.15; 1920.12
Ely, Catherine Beach 1922.64
Emerson, Dorothy 1937.43
Emerson, Edward Waldo 1889.3; 1913.6
    [1919.71]
Emerson, Ralph Waldo 1885.12; 1864.6; 1865.1
    [1935.27]; 1883.4 [1883.11]; 1904.9; 1910.2a;
    1939.9a
    [1855.2-3, 14-15; 1856.10; 1860.38, 45;
    1865.3; 1866.22, 26; 1867.7, 14; 1868.17, 37;
    1871.10; 1874.7; 1875.7; 1876.13, 35, 56;
    1880.5, 12; 1881.4, 55; 1882.2, 20, 25-26, 35,
    37, 48, 53, 63, 64-65, 68, 94, 104, 131;
    1883.16, 28; *1884.24; 1885.4, 18; 1886.13, 41;
    1887.6, 59; 1888.4, 9, 1889.3, 37; 1890.3, 9,
    41; 1892.16, 20, 27, 58, 100, 140, 201;
    1893.11-12; 1894.17, 34, 58, 67; 1895.5, 17,
    18, 34, *83; 1896.36, 43, 59, 69; 1897.8, 26,
    40, 43, 59-60, 65, 72, *123, 162, 164; 1898.15,
    78, 85; 1899.12, 48; 1900.3, 16; 1901.13;
    1902.16, 19, 34, 53; 1903.9, 12, 15, 33-33a,
    36, 42; 1904.6, 44; 1905.1, 4; 1906.5, 9-10;
    1907.17, 38; 1908.11, 36; 1909.7-8, 16; 1910.2a,
    11, 23; 1912.40; 1913.6, 14; 1914.9, 19;
    1915.13; 1916.3, 21; 1917.1, 10, 13; 1918.10;
    1919.5, 7, 21, 29, 98, 121a, 128, 141, 151,
    182, 189, 196. 204, 214, 225, 251, 283, 293,
    346, 359; 1920.6, 19, 76; 1921.13, 27, 53,
    56, 71; 1922.3, 11, 21, 28, 39, 65; 1924.40;
    1925.4, 9, 16, 52; 1926.1, 22, *32, 41, 60, 68;
    1927.7, 27; *1928.2, 6; 1929.8, 15, *32, 43, 47,
    56; 1930.3-4, 17, 19; 1931.1-2, 6, 18, 57;
    1932.5, 7, 14, 19, 39, 42-43; 1934.30; 1935.9;
    1936.2, 5-6, 27, 33; 1937.3, 14, 17, 36;
    1938.2, 9, 16-17, 20; 1939.41; Appendix]
Emery, George M. 1920.82
Empory Gazette 1910.45
Ende, Amelia von 1903.27; 1904.23, 27; 1905.46;
    1907.26, 38; 1911.25
England [1867.21; 1868.25; 1872.1; 1876.7a, 42, 46
    and passim; 1887.61; 1888.19, 45, 55; 1889.9;
    1891.49; 1892.9, 61, 112, 114, 129, 140, 146,
    175; 1894.67; 1896.61; 1897.115, 143, 153;
    1898.44; 1903.47; 1910.29; 1918.20; 1919.69,
    186, 232; 1920.51; 1925.32; 1926.33; 1929.57;
    1933.18; *1934.1; 1926.19; Appendix]

Englekirk, John E. 1938.25
English Journal 1921.36; 1927.32; 1928.34, 38;
    1930.23; 1936.47; 1937.25; 1938.48
English Review 1918.63; 1920.63
Englishwoman 1919.335
Ense, Rahel von [1919.138]
Entwhistle, A. R. 1929.14
Epictetus [1891.23]
Era. See also Literary Era 1903.33
Erskine, John 1912.18; 1915.22; 1918.10; 1919.123;
    1922.50; 1923.39, 44; 1938.5 [1938.51, 54]
    [1931.41, 51; 1933.24; 1939.36]
Ervine, St. John 1921.42
Esenwein, J. Berg 1916.6
Ethical Addresses 1899.68, 74
Ethical Record 1903.29
Ethics. See Whitman--Philosophy
Etudes Anglaises 1937.39
Etymologist [pseud.] 1887.88
Eugenics Review 1910.38
Europe. See also specific countries [1872.20;
    1892.189; 1910.22, 42; 1912.48; 1915.24;
    1918.23; 1919.14; 1923.30; 1924.9; 1937.25]
Europe Nouvelle, L' [1922.67]
Evening Tattler [1842.6]
Everett, M. S. 1919.174
Every Saturday 1866.25; 1868.11
Everyman (London) 1913.29; 1914.41; 1918.20
Everywhere 1908.20
Evolution. See also Darwin 1897.149; 1908.4;
    1912.3, 18; 1913.14; 1915.6; 1925.66; 1934.32;
    1936.2
Ev'ry Month 1896.52, 63
Examiner (London) 1856.10; 1868.20; 1876.71
    [1876.66]
Eyre, Lincoln L. 1889.9

F., W. A. C. See Chandos-Fulton, W. A.
Fabian News 1906.30a; 1908.22
Faggi, Alfeo [1927.55]
Fairchild, Arthur H. R. 1912.8
Fairchild, Elizabeth 1892.15
Faithfull, Emily 1884.7
Falls, C. B. 1914.45
Family Circle 1882.36
Fanfan. See Blackburn, Grace
Fanfulla 1881.37
Fantasy 1934.41; 1935.37
Farley, Belmont 1919.245
Farnelli, G. See Fornelli, Guido
Farnham, Eliza W. 1864.1
    [1906.11]
Farrell, James T. 1939.40
Fawcett, Edgar 1880.9 [1880.22]; 1895.56 [1895.59-
    60, 77; 1896.20], 71; 1897.164; 1898.45
    [1898.74]
    [1888.11; 1898.42]
Fawcett, James Waldo 1919.369; 1923.33, 44; 1925.42
    [1919.288; 1923.29-30]
Fawcett, Millicent Garrett 1923.33
Fearing, Kenneth 1939.40
Federn, Karl [1904.27]
Fellows, Col. [1892.4]
Fenollosa, Ernest 1895.24a
Feraud, A. 1885.12
Ferber, Edna 1930.6
Ferguson, Emily 1910.2
Ferguson, John DeLancey 1916.7
Ferm, Elizabeth Burns 1907.10
Fern, Fanny. See Parton, Sarah Payson Willis
Ferrando, Guido 1931.12
Fichtor, L. C. 1899.27

Fields, Annie (Mrs. James T.) 1895.17; 1915.10
Fields, James T. [1932.12]
Findlater, Jane Helen 1904.10
Finley, Kate Barclay 1890.47
Finnegan, J. A. 1931.33 [1931.36], 44 [1931.47]
Finta, Alexander [1931.41, 51]
Firkins, O. W. 1917.46; 1919.246; 1921.69; 1923.44
Fischer, Raymond P. 1919.356
Fisher, Mary 1899.7
Fiske, Charles Henry 1908.30
Fiske, John 1889.7; 1894.2
    [1887.32; 1900.22]
Fitch, George Hamlin 1916.8
FitzGerald, Ellen 1920.2 [1920.79]
Fitzgerald, F. Scott [1926.82]
Fitzgerald, Robert 1939.46
Fleet, John [1905.45]
Fletcher, A. E. 1898.92
Fletcher, John Gould 1919.46, 53; 1920.92 [1920.102];
    1921.53; 1924.31; 1930.7; 1939.19
    [1917.8; 1921.74; 1922.60]
Flick, Alexander C. 1937.11, 13, 17
Flower, B. O. 1905.22; 1907.21; 1908.37
Foerster, Norman 1914.40; 1916.61; 1921.56;
    1922.51; 1923.5; 1925.4; 1926.41; 1928.9-10
Follett, Wilson 1938.55
Foley, P. K. 1897.5
Foote, George W. See also Foote's Health Monthly
    1893.2
    [1876.7]
Foote's Health Monthly 1882.67, 81, 82, 95, 107
For Ide og Virkelighed [1872.20]
Forbes, Waldo Emerson 1913.6
Ford, Miriam Allen de 1913.54
Ford Hall Folks 1913.54
Forman, Alfred 1893.11
Forman, H. Buxton 1871.2 [1872.9]; 1887.5; 1889.9;
    1892.15, 59
    [1920.52; 1934.1]
Fornelli, G[uido] 1926.9
Forney, Col. John W. 1879.8, 20-21, 26, 32; 1881.20
Fortnightly Review 1866.22; 1868.8; 1872.19;
    1879.42; 1887.63; 1910.36; 1915.24; 1919.123
    [1881.24]
Forum 1893.42; 1901.19; 1909.35; 1911.32-33, 35;
    1913.45; 1915.43; 1916.56; 1928.25; 1935.15
    [1889.35]
Foss, Sam Walter 1892.5; 1895.63
Foster, George Burnam [1918.31]
Foster, Mrs. Michael 1926.10
Fountain, Lucy 1871.8
Fourier, Charles [1930.3]
Fourteen Thousand Miles Afoot 1859.1
Fowler and Wells [1855.1, 4; 1856.20; 1929.29;
    1931.23; 1936.15]
Fox, George. See also Whitman--Works--Prose--
    "George Fox" [1905.1; 1909.4; 1924.16]
Fox, William J. 1856.8
    [1882.94]
Fra 1909.23
France. See also French language [1860.64; 1896.47;
    1897.143; 1899.21; 1908.27, 47; 1909.26;
    1911.24-25; 1913.46. 1915.23; 1916.34; 1917.7;
    1918.19, 21; 1919.90, 98, 190, 266, 318, 353,
    363, 367, 370, 372; 1920.38, 57, 65; 1922.50,
    59; 1923.38; 1924.1; 1930.3; 1931.8]
Francis of Assisi, St. [1909.4; 1910.39; 1913.19]
Frank, Sep 1922.53
Frank, Waldo 1916.65; 1919.7; 1924.9; 1929.8;
    1933.5

Frank Leslie's Illustrated Newspaper 1876.41, 45
    [1876.53]
Frank Leslie's Illustrated Weekly 1892.136
Frank Leslie's Popular Monthly 1892.193
Frankau, Gilbert 1923.33
Frankel, Doris 1930.22
Franklin, Benjamin [1896.62; 1909.8; 1938.29]
Franklin, Julia 1915.13
Frederic, Harold 1892.112
Free verse. See Modern Poetry; Whitman--Style
Freeman, Joseph 1936.13; 1937.6
Freeman (Brooklyn) See Brooklyn Freeman
Freeman (New York) 1920.41, 43-45, 75, 86; 1921.38,
    51, 53-54, 79, 81; 1922.38, 59, 62
Freethinker (London) 1919.295; 1921.60
Freiligrath, Ferdinand 1868.36
    [1882.94; 1920.63]
French language. See also France 1892.105;
    1925.60; 1926.46; 1936.23, 54
Frend, Grace Gilchrist. See Gilchrist, Grace
Fritzinger, Warren 1893.11
    [1909.29; 1921.19]
Frontier, The American. See West, The
Frontier and Midland 1934.19
Frost, Robert [1916.29, 32, 45; 1919.273, 280;
    1920.77; 1922.60; 1939.34]
Frothingham, O. B. 1882.108
Frump, Timothy 1934.22
Fukumura, Yasutate 1919.177
Fuller, George [1889.61]
Fuller, Henry B. 1900.21
Fuller, Margaret [1921.27; 1936.23; 1938.17]
Fullerton, W. Morton [1931.10]
Fulton, W. A. Chandos. See Chandos-Fulton, W. A.
Fun (London) 1868.10
Furman Bulletin 1938.21
Furness, Clifton Joseph 1928.11 [1928.42-43,
    1929.37-39, 46-47; 1930.47], 36; 1929.42, 44;
    1932.23; 1937.32, 45; 1939.4, 21
Furness, Horace Howard 1889.9; 1910.2a; 1922.12
Furness, William Henry   1910.2a

G. 1882.122
G., A. E. 1882.100
G., C. See Gohdes, Clarence
G., E. P. 1903.24
Gable, William F. 1910.3; 1919.124; Addenda
Gabriel, Ralph H. 1937.15
Gage, Rev. W. L. [1932.12]
Galaxy 1866.19, 26; 1867.8; 1868.17, 32, 42;
    1871.8; 1876.13, 65; 1877.5
    [1867.18, 27; 1868.24, 30; 1939.41]
Galbraith, J. A. 1882.90
Gale, Major R. J. 1929.53
Gale, Zona 1923.44
Gallacher, William [1919.365]
Galsworthy, John [1919.94]
Gamberale, Luigi 1904.42
    [1922.16]
Gannett, William C. 1889.9
Garcia Lorca, Federico 1939.5
Garfield, James [1892.117; 1897.15; 1904.35]
Garland, Hamlin 1888.74; 1889.9; 1892.15; 1893.3,
    42; 1894.3; 1895.37; 1901.42; 1915.10;
    1919.163; 1923.44; 1929.58; 1930.8; 1939.47
    [1889.54; 1916.50; 1939.7]
Garnett, Edward 1916.29
    [1937.4]
Garnett, Porter [1915.25]
Garrett, Edwin Clarkson 1931.47 [1931.48]
Garrett, Percival [1920.68]

Garrison, Judge Charles G. 1889.9; 1896.34;
    1897.50; 1905.25
    [1889.52, 54]
Garrison, J. F. 1889.9
Garrison, William H. 1892.163
Gautama. See Buddha
Gay, William 1892.201, 209a; 1893.4; 1894.4;
    1895.5 [1896.45]; 1896.21
Geddie, J. Liddell 1938.4
Geis, John F. 1937.28
Genthe, Arnold 1938.12
Gentleman's Magazine 1875.16; 1892.167
Genung, John Franklin 1900.7
Geology [1934.32]
George, Stefan [1921.43]
George, Walter L. 1913.7; 1916.9
Gere, Thomas A. 1882.59
German American Annals 1906.25
Germanic Review 1926.40
Germany [1860.38, 61; 1871.1; 1887.24; 1888.63;
    1893.11, 30; 1903.27; 1904.23; 1905.46;
    1906.15, 95; 1907.26, 38; 1908.26; 1910.23;
    1911.17; 1919.42, 44, 357; 1920.63; 1921.34,
    43, 67; 1922.63; 1923.25; 1926.40; 1930.17;
    1937.25]
Gibson, David 1913.26
Gibson's Magazine 1913.26
Giddings, Dr. Franklin H. 1923.44
Gide, André [1931.5; 1938.9]
Gilchrist, Anne 1870.4 [1903.12]; 1885.14; 1906.13;
    1918.9 [see Harned for reviews]; 1931.1;
    1935.22
    [*1887.6; 1897.39; 1900.8; 1912.5; 1914.19;
    1917.6; 1919.12; 242, 358; 1920.21; 1923.43;
    1924.5; 1928.6; 1929.22; 1931.21; 1933.10;
    1934.1, 5; 1938.9]
Gilchrist, Beatrice (daughter) 1918.9
Gilchrist, Grace (Grace Gilchrist Frend; daughter)
    1898.29 [1898.34]; 1918.45, 57 [1918.68];
    1927.47
    [1919.34; 1931.1]
Gilchrist, Herbert Harlakenden (son) 1887.6
    [1887.28, 51, 61]; 1889.9; 1892.15; 1918.9;
    1929.17
    [1877.14; 1885.29; 1889.52, 54; 1890.7;
    1892.31; 1898.29; 1917.6; 1927.47; 1931.1;
    1934.5]
Gilder, Jeannette Leonard 1882.4; 1885.22; 1886.37,
    58; 1887.40, 43, 59, 60, 68, 70; 1888.6, 30,
    61; 1889.9, 66, 68, 74; 1890.19; 1891.15, 33a,
    39, 53, 62; 1892.26, 30, 101, 185, 212;
    1906.87; 1915.10
    [1887.32; 1917.19]
Gilder, Joseph B. (Jeannette's brother) 1888.6
    [1887.32]
Gilder, Richard Watson (Jeannette's brother) 1886.3;
    1889.9; 1892.15; 1896.3; 1915.10; 1916.10
    [1917.19]; 1919.78
    [1889.52, 54; 1891.29; 1910.10, 17; 1913.17;
    1923.8]
Gilder, Mrs. Richard Watson [1887.32]
Gilder, Rosamond (Richard's daughter) 1916.10
    [1917.19]
Gilford, Franklin Kent 1919.74
Gili, J. L. 1939.5
Gilman, Arthur 1879.7
Gilman, Mrs. Charlotte Perkins 1919.125; 1923.44
    [1901.37]
Gilman, J. H. 1889.9
Gilman, Lawrence 1919.126
Gilman, Nicholas P. 1894.35

Giovannitti, Arturo 1919.51
Gissing, George 1887.7
    [1912.14; 1927.19]
Gladiatorum, Minimus [pseud.] 1906.69
Glasgow, Ellen 1908.40
Glasgow Evening Citizen 1919.258
Glasgow Herald 1895.79; 1896.19; 1919.221
Glasier, J. Bruce 1904.43
Glicksberg, Charles Ives [Charles I. Glisksberg]
    1931.27; 1932.30; 1933.6 [1933.30, 32];
    1934.29, 46, 49; 1935.16, 19, 36-37; 1936.51;
    1937.42; 1938.45; Appendix
Glisksberg, Charles I. See Glicksberg, Charles I.
Globe Turnover (London) 1919.243
Gnostic, The 1885.21
Godey's Magazine 1892.223; 1893.46
Goethe [1892.147; 1904.13, 27; 1906.32; 1908.36;
    1910.23; 1914.5; 1919.346; 1924.6a; 1930.3;
    1936.2; 1937.14, 25; 1938.13, 17]
Gohdes, Clarence 1929.32; 1932.10; 1933.32; 1934.5
    [1934.44], 47; 1935.22; 1936.55
Gold, Michael 1935.41
Goldberg, Dr. Isaac 1923.44
Golden Book Magazine 1929.50
Golden Era 1860.53
Goldman, Emma 1910.4; 1931.13
    [1909.30; 1916.50; 1919.288; 1920.65, 103;
    1927.53]
Goldsborough, F. C. 1912.9
Goldsmith, Alfred F. 1922.27; 1928.23
Gollomb, Joseph 1919.247
Goodale, David 1937.45; 1938.29
Goodale, Mrs. Dora H. Read 1886.33; 1888.83
Goose-Quill 1902.56
Gordon, T. Francis 1882.88
Gorman, Herbert S. 1925.45, 71; 1926.43, 73
Goss, Charles F. 1899.25
Gosse, Sir Edmund 1876.63; 1894.28 [1895.53;
    1897.153; 1898.34]; 1917.5 [1918.8]; 1918.7;
    1919.292; 1921.10; 1926.29; 1927.7; 1931.7
    [1885.8-9; 1889.35; 1893.45; 1897.72; 1934.1;
    1937.46]
Gostwick, Joseph [1929.56]
Gould, Elizabeth Porter 1887.50; 1889.4 [1890.14,
    36]; 1898.29a; 1900.8 [1900.37, 45; 1901.61;
    1928.18]; 1903.24
Gould, George M. 1900.46; 1910.17
Grafly, Dorothy 1922.55
Graham, Stephen 1922.7
Grant, U. S. [1876.17; 1885.16, 25, 28; 1934.40]
Graphic, The (London) 1892.86; 1919.49
Grattan, C. Hartley 1931.49
Gray, Nat and Fred [1918.50]
Great Thoughts 1890.57a; 1892.143; 1894.22;
    1919.248
Greek literature and thought [1871.10; 1873.1;
    1880.35; 1888.43; 1890.3; 1892.100, 200;
    1894.25-27; 1895.47; 1897.132, 153; 1898.16;
    1900.48; 1925.24; 1926.1]
Greeley, Horace 1848.3, 12
    [1871.14; 1886.18, 20-21; 1917.61; 1927.20]
Green, David Bonnell 1875.6
Green, H. M. 1903.35
Greenbie, Marjorie 1939.6
Greene, Henry C. 1898.38 [1899.46]
Greenough, Chester Noyes 1904.21
Greenslet, Ferris 1908.7
Greg, Thomas T. 1888.2
Gregory, Lady Augusta 1923.33
Gregory, Horace 1928.42; 1937.21; 1939.46
Grey, Rowland 1919.248, 335

Grey, Samuel H. 1889.9
    [1889.52, 54]
Gridley, C[harles] Oscar 1884.8
Grindrod, James [1892.9]
Griswold, Rufus W. 1855.14 [1855.15]
Grundy, Cuthbert 1923.33
Guardian (London) See London Guardian
Guardian (Philadelphia) 1925.70
Guerney, Bernard Guilbert 1937.22
Guilbeaux, Henri 1911.25
Gulick, Sidney L., Jr. 1939.15
Gummere, Francis B. 1911.7
Gurowski, Adam 1866.1
    [1887.6]
Guthrie, Kenneth S. 1905.7
Guthrie, William Norman 1890.21; 1897.7 [1897.81,
    141; 1899.41]; 1898.55; 1912.10; 1923.44
Gutekunst, Frederick 1889.68

H., A. C. See Henderson, Alice Corbin
H., E. 1907.32
H., F. 1919.66, 249
H., F. M. See Hopkins, Frederick M.
H., H. See Hoyt, Helen
H., Miss 1883.21
H., P. See Hale, Philip
Haas, John A. W. [1926.34]
Habberton, John 1889.9; 1892.113, 223; 1893.46
Haddon, Trevor [1911.5]
Hafiz [1895.64, 65; 1911.31]
Hager, J. C. 1876.68
Haight, B. H. 1892.79
Hake, Thomas 1918.8
Hale, Edward Everett 1856.6
    [1879.26]
Hale, Edward E., Jr. 1897.129
Hale, Philip 1874.11; 1897.96, 112; 1898.33;
    1905.41
Halifax (Nova Scotia) Morning Herald 1906.17
Hall, Florence Howe 1919.95 [1919.108, 153];
    1919.187 [1919.293]
Hall, Rev. George 1888.77
Hall, Holworthy. See Porter, Harold Everett
Hall, Howard Judson 1917.11
Hall of Fame [1919.230, 289, 297-98; 1920.89-91;
    1921.58; 1926.36, 57; 1930.29, 35, 43-44, 46,
    46a; 1931.28-33, 38]
Halleck, Reuben Post 1911.8
Halsey, Francis Whiting 1901.7; 1902.10, 45
Halsey, John J. 1892.16
Hamblen, Emily S. 1924.10
Hamilton, Clayton 1909.35
Hamilton, Walter 1888.3
Hamilton (Ontario) Spectator 1922.54; 1923.28;
    1924.36
Hammerton, Sir J. A. 1937.5
Haney, John Louis 1923.6
Harboe, Paul 1906.70
Hardie, Keir [1917.45]
Harding, Edward J. 1888.62
Hardy, Thomas 1889.4
    [1894.5; 1898.72; 1911.7; 1936.26]
Harlan, Secretary James. See also Whitman--
    Dismissal 1913.2 [1931.1]
    [1865.2; 1866.2, 6, 8-10; 1892.58; 1919.17;
    1921.50; 1927.54; 1938.5]
Harleigh Cemetery. See also Whitman--Death and
    funeral [1889.76; 1890.35, 37; 1892.59;
    1895.21, 22, 22a, 24; 1900.19; 1906.35;
    1919.19, 237; 1920.21, 30; 1928.29; 1929.51;
    1931.1; 1939.21]

Harned, Thomas Biggs 1889.9; 1892.15; 1893.11, 44;
   1895.38, 80; 1899.54; 1902.11, 13, 25-26;
   1906.24; 1907.56 [1908.23]; 1915.10; 1918.9
   [1918.36, 40, 45, 57, 66-68, 70-71; 1919.34-
   35, 49-50, 52, 56-57, 87, 110, 131]; 1919.81,
   127, 250, 279; 1931.1
   [1889.52, 54; 1893.39; 1895.6; 1903.26;
   1919.12, 89, 93, 160, 231]
Harper, Francis P. 1897.44
Harper, Olive 1875.10
Harper's Bazar 1887.26, 29, 38
Harper's New Monthly Magazine 1860.60; 1865.11;
   1876.61; 1882.13; 1883.37; 1888.9, 72-73;
   1889.20; 1890.13; 1891.49; 1895.39; 1904.26;
   1907.16; 1912.38; 1929.48; 1937.33
   [1892.59, 123; 1935.36, 39]
Harper's Weekly 1876.62; 1879.10; 1887.39; 1892.20,
   105, 108; 1910.42
   [1938.7]
Harriman, W. Averell [1938.24]
Harris, Frank 1919.128; 1902.13; 1922.8; 1925.6-7;
   1927.8
Harris, Joel Chandler 1893.11
   [1925.35]
Harris, Lynn H. 1921.49
Harrison, Benjamin [1890.41, 45]
Harrison, Clifford 1892.6
Harrison, Frederic 1923.33
   [1910.29]
Harrison, Joseph B. 1934.19
Harrison, Mary St. Ledger (Lucas Malet) 1891.8
   [1897.50]
Harrison, Richard Clarence 1929.59
Harrison, Prof. W. H. or W. M. 1889.17
Hart, Henry 1937.6
Hart, John S. 1872.4
Harte, [Francis Brett] 1860.53
   [1873.4; 1898.44]
Harte, Walter Blackburn 1892.202; 1895.29; 1896.56;
   1897.83
Hartford Courant 1926.62
Hartley, L. Conrad 1908.8; 1934.6; Addenda
Hartley, Marsden 1919.375; 1921.11
Hartmann, C. Sadakichi 1889.37; 1892.191; 1893.17,
   19; 1895.6 [1895.57]; 1897.84; 1921.12;
   1927.48
   [1887.57, 60, 71; 1889.34]
Hartswick, F. Gregory 1920.84
Hartt, George M. 1908.45; 1915.46
Hartwell, Richardson, and Driver, architects
   1921.75
Hartwick, Harry 1936.14
Harvard Library Notes 1923.27
Harvard Monthly 1888.7; 1890.22; 1892.164-165
Harvard Studies and Notes in Philology and Literature
   1932.23
Haskell, E. B. 1882.52
Hastings, William Thomson 1923.7; 1928.12
Hatton, Joseph 1884.9
Havel, Hippolyte 1910.4
Haweis, Rev. Hugh R., M. A. 1886.13 [1886.16, 40];
   1896.7
Hawk, Affable [pseud.?] 1922.35
Hawk, The 1892.153
Hawkins, Mrs. Charles 1936.49
Hawthorne, Julian 1888.37; 1889.9; 1891.5 [1896.79,
   85]; 1896.82; 1900.15, 21
   [1889.52, 54]
Hawthorne, Nathaniel [1889.38; 1903.25; 1913.7;
   1918.63; 1919.29, 104; 1920.19; 1922.39, 61;
   1932.34]

Hay, John 1889.9; 1915.10
   [1921.27; 1927.15; 1928.17]
Haycraft, Howard 1938.8
Hayek, Max [1921.67]
Hayes, Will 1921.13 [1921.60]; 66; 1922.65;
   1923.33
Hazard, Lucy Lockwood 1927.9
Hazen, Charles Downer 1926.10
Hearn, Lafcadio 1882.80; 1906.4
   [1919.47; 1929.9]
Heartman, Charles F. 1925.78
Hecht, Ben 1921.14
   [1926.27]
Hegel, George Wilhelm Friedrich [1860.61; 1886.7;
   1893.11; 1895.5; 1896.45; 1897.23; 1898.38;
   1900.9, 24; 1901.64; 1904.13, 19; 1920.30;
   1921.27, 34; 1924.12; 1921.56; 1930.17;
   1935.32; 1936.2; 1937.39, 41; 1938.2, 20]
Heine, Heinrich [1874.8; 1882.33; 1898.29; 1906.32]
Hemingway, Ernest 1925.31
   [1926.82]
Hempstead (New York) Enquirer 1838.2
Henderson, Alice Corbin (Alice Corbin) 1912.47-48;
   1919.280
Henderson, Archibald 1910.47
Henderson, Daniel 1919.188
Hendry, Hamish 1898.95
Henley, W. E. 1906.8; 1911.4
   [1888.72; 1894.60; 1897.164]
Herder [1906.32]
Herford, C. H. 1919.251
Hermann, Johanna Mueller [1930.31]
Hermes (University of Sydney) 1894.41; 1903.35
Herne, James A. 1899.61
Herrick, Anson 1842.3, 5-6; 1860.43
Herring, Alice 1906.36
Herring, H. C. 1928.28
Herringshaw, Thomas William 1890.4; 1901.8
Herron, George D. 1904.40; 1908.52
   [1912.37, 42]
Herron, Ima Honaker 1939.7
Hersey, Harold 1914.23
Herty, Hamilton [1919.341]
Hervey, John L. 1915.36 [1915.47]; 1919.175, 189
Herzberg, Max J. 1916.11
Heydrick, Benjamin A. 1909.6; 1912.21
Heywood, Angela 1882.12
Heywood, Ezra H. 1882.12
   [1882.115, 121, 129-130]
Hibbert Journal 1904.22
Hichens, Robert 1925.79
Hicks, Elias See also Whitman--Works--Prose--
   "Elias Hicks" [1887.29, 36; 1888.57, 66;
   1892.4; 1917.6; 1930.9; 1938.9, 44]
Hicks, Granville 1931.59; 1933.7 [1933.34]
Hicks, Mrs. Mary Dana [1895.78]
Hier, Frederick P., Jr. 1918.41; 1919.63, 129;
   1921.55; 1924.33 [1924.37]; 1927.46
Higginson, Mary Thacher 1914.10
Higginson, Thomas Wentworth 1867.26; 1881.53;
   1882.27; 1887.26, 30; 1891.47; 1892.60
   [1892.130, 137, 157]; 1897.8, 74; 1898.8;
   1899.8; 1902.31; 1903.5, 19, 31; 1906.53;
   1931.1
   [1892.104; 1898.85, 86; 1914.10]
Hill, A. S. 1867.2
Hill, Frank Ernest 1927.1
Hill, George Birkbeck 1896.57; 1897.9
Hill, S. McCalmont 1891.52
Hillard, Katharine 1866.65
Hiller, J. H. 1882.123 [1882.130, 133]

Hind, C. Lewis 1919.196
Hinduism. See Oriental thought and religion
Hinton, Howard 1892.67
Hinton, Richard J. 1866.11; 1868.12; 1871.9;
    1872.20; 1873.5; 1889.9, 38; 1899.35
Hispanic Review 1938.25
Histories of American literature. See American
    literature--histories
Hitchcock, Ripley 1903.14
Hobby Horse (London) 1889.13
Hobson, J. A. 1910.5
Hodgins, Rev. J. C. [1919.320]
Hodgson, Geraldine 1900.9
Hoeber, Arthur 1908.38
Holborn Review 1919.364
Holbrook, M. L. 1898.101
Holcomb, Esther Lolita 1928.38
Holitscher, Arthur 1913.42
Holland, J. G. 1876.56 [1876.48, 55]; 1878.16;
    1881.34; 1923.8
    [1876.33]
Holloway, [R.] Emory 1907.32; 1915.54, 56; 1916.30,
    37, 59; 1917.61; 1918.10-11 [1919.104, 351];
    1920.88; 1921.16 [1921.77, 80-81; 1922.23,
    31-33, 35-36, 39, 42-44, 46, 51, 58, 65], 76;
    1922.9, 30, 45; 1923.40-41; 1924.11 [1925.30,
    36], 28-29, 43; 1925.47, 51, 58, 72; 1926.12
    [1926.76], 13 [1926.73, 75, 77, 79-82];
    1927.27], 39, 59; 1929.10-11, 34, 60; 1930.25,
    33; 1931.45; 1932.11 [1932.42, 47]; 1933.15,
    22, 30; 1936.15 [1934.35, 1936.59], 31;
    1938.6 [1938.43]; 1939.18, 27
    [1925.39-40, 42-43, 48; 1928.35; 1931.41;
    1935.23; 1936.49; 1939.36]
Holmes, Edmond 1902.14 [1901.64; 1902.30-31, 36];
    1923.33
Holmes, Dr. John Haynes 1919.130; 1923.44
Holmes, Oliver Wendell 1885.4; 1890.43; 1896.3;
    1911.1
    [1881.6; 1887.41; 1889.37; 1890.13; 1895.17;
    1897.39; 1898.85; 1910.5; 1916.3; 1919.89;
    1931.1; Addenda]
Holz, Arno [1905.46; 1920.53]
Homans, Nathalie W. 1896.66
Home Journal. See New York Home Journal
Home Magazine 1898.99
Homer [1879.12; 1886.2, 26-27, 45; 1892.179;
    1894.17; 1895.82; 1911.20; 1915.14; 1916.65;
    1917.36; 1919.86, 262; 1924.10; 1926.31, 47;
    1929.54; 1932.6; 1934.5; 1936.5]
Homer, Winslow [1920.42]
Homiletic Review 1901.47
Homosexuality. See also Comradeship; Whitman--
    Works--"Calamus" 1896.17; 1898.1; 1901.6;
    1906.76; 1908.6, 13; 1911.19, 22; 1913.16;
    1914.5, 45; 1915.11-12; 1919.18; 1921.20, 31,
    34; 1922.32; 1924.5, 16; 1925.78; 1926.13-14,
    73, 77, 80; 1927.7, 27; 1928.20, 26; 1929.48;
    1930.7; 1931.1, 6; 1932.15, 18, 45; 1935.29;
    1936.3; 1937.9; 1938.2, 13, 43; 1939.5
Hoockley, Albert Herman 1919.252
Hood, Thomas [1926.1]
Hoover, Herbert 1931.32
    [1932.47]
Hopkins, Frederick M. 1923.35; 1936.36, 44
Hopkins, Gerard Manley 1935.1
Hopps, Rev. John Q. 1880.28, 31
Horace [1919.22]
Horne, Richard Hengist 1875.3
    [1934.1]
Horton, George 1890.48

Horton, Rev. Robert F. 1894.22
    [1897.153]
Hospital 1911.19
Hotten, John Camden 1903.12
Houghton, Lord. See Milnes, Richard Monckton
Hour, The 1876.18
House, Jay E. 1931.34, 37
Housman, A. E. [1919.345]
Hovey, Richard [1899.29]
Hovey, Mrs. Richard [1901.37]
Howard, [Percy] Leon[idas] 1930.41; 1932.26;
    Appendix
Howe, Arthur M. 1919.253 [1919.160]
Howe, E. W. 1919.64
Howe, Julia Ward [1919.95]
Howe, Mark A. De Wolfe 1898.23; 1906.106; 1913.14;
    1932.12
Howe, Will David 1929.24
Howell, Clark 1923.44
Howells, Mildred 1928.13
Howells, William Dean 1860.12, 52; 1865.7; 1866.4;
    1876.20; 1888.9 [1888.19], 71; 1889.9, 20, 49;
    1891.49 [1892.29, 205]; 1895.39 [1909.15];
    1901.7; 1907.16; 1912.38; 1915.10; 1928.13
    [1866.21, 1887.35, 43; 1910.17; 1924.40;
    1934.43; 1938.9]
Howitt, William 1856.8; 1870.3
Hoyt, Helen 1919.131
Hubbard, Elbert 1896.8; 1900.28, 46; 1901.59;
    1902.37 [1917.58], 46; 1915.10
Hubbell, Jay B. 1919.373; 1922.10; 1928.10; 1936.16
Hudson, Richard Bradshaw. See Appendix
Huene, Frederick 1908.26
Huger, A. M. (A Perplexed Subscriber) 1906.41
    [1906.47], 48 [1906.51-52], 50, 61, 66
Hughes, Harry D. 1886.45; 1887.23
Hughes, James L. 1919.132
    [1916.26]
Hughes, Thomas, Q. C. 1888.8
    [1894.15]
Hugo, Victor [1872.19; 1880.1a; 1886.2, 45;
    1898.29; 1914.7; 1923.46; 1931.8; 1937.25]
Hull (England) Daily News 1922.68
Hult, Gottfried Emanuel 1919.336
Human Nature 1876.12
Huneker, James Gibbons 1887.79; 1889.46; 1891.26,
    50; 1898.89; 1900.52; 1914.45 [1929.12];
    1919.359; 1920.14; 1921.17 [1922.29]; 1922.11
    [1926.51]
Huneker, Josephine 1922.11
Hungary [1922.37; 1923.20, 21]
Hungerford, Edward 1931.23
Hunt, Theodore W. 1887.8; 1902.61
Hurst, Maurice 1919.254
Huston, Paul Griswold 1898.102
Hutchison, Percy A. 1924.32
Hutton, Laurence 1905.9
    [1887.32; 1902.10]
Huxley, Aldous 1928.14; 1932.13
Hyde, Fillmore 1922.31
Hyde, Mrs. Hannah Whitman (Whitman's sister)
    [1925.21]

Ibsen, Henrik [1888.1a; 1890.15; 1894.25; 1896.13;
    1913.51]
Ichikawa, Sanki 1929.9
Iconoclast (Indianapolis) 1882.125
Illustrated American 1892.21, 141, 185
Illustrated Australian News 1892.173
Illustrated London News 1889.71, 73; 1892.87, 106;
    1925.41

Image, Selwyn 1889.13

Imagism. See Modern poetry

Immortality. See Death and immortality

Independent (New York) See also Independent and
   Weekly Review 1867.3; 1876.57, 64; 1881.55;
   1888.14, 20, 55, 76; 1891.45; 1892.70, 118,
   155; 1895.28; 1897.155; 1906.82

Independent and the Weekly Review. See also
   Independent; Weekly Review 1921.78

Index, The (Boston) 1882.19, 65; 1883.38

Indianapolis Journal 1897.98

Indians (American) [1849.8; 1860.38; 1895.75;
   1919.143; 1936.31]

Infidel Pulpit 1881.22-23

Ingersoll, Robert G. 1889.9; 1890.6 [1891.27a];
   1892.15 [1892.126, 135]
   [1880.14; 1890.28-32, 49-57, 58; 1892.175;
   1895.71; 1901.47; 1915.10; 1919.121a; 1923.54;
   1930.19]

Ingersoll Chronicle and Canadian Dairyman 1885.26

Inness, George. See also Whitman--Works--Poetry--
   "Death's Valley" [1905.18]

Inquirer 1919.181

Inter-America 1920.80

International Journal of Ethics 1895.63; 1899.42;
   1914.19

International Literature 1935.32

International Review 1882.26

International Studio 1897.58; 1908.38

Internationalism [1917.31; 1919.29, 76, 91, 219,
   257; 1920.94; 1923.49; 1929.41; 1935.10, 31;
   1937.15; 1938.2, 42; 1939.10]

Inter-Ocean (Chicago) 1890.56; 1892.111

Interstate Architect and Builder 1901.28

Interstate Medical Journal 1911.22

Ireland [1882.90; 1907.3; 1919.79; 1933.18]

Irish Statesman 1923.60

Irving, Henry 1889.9
   [1884.9; 1885.11; 1906.18]

Irving, Washington [1925.54]

Irwin, Dr. Mabel MacCoy 1905.10 [1905.35]; 1906.37;
   1919.255
   [1919.287]

Italy, [1881.37a; 1898.88; 1925.60; 1926.9-10]

Ives, Ella Gilbert 1901.24

J., B. 1925.66

J., E. 1919.309

J., H. H. F. See Jayne, H. H. F.

J., S. B. 1886.46

Jack, Peter Munro 1937.30; 1938.28

Jackson, Edward Payson 1895.12; 1897.64 [1897.80],
   75

Jackson, Holbrook 1912.11; 1919.345

Jacobs' Orchestra Monthly (Boston) 1928.40

Jacobson, Anna 1926.40

Jacobson, Arthur C. 1926.14

James, Henry (the elder) [1919.89]

James, Henry (the younger) 1865.8; 1898.59, 69;
   1913.8
   [1887.6; 1925.53; 1926.1; 1934.17; 1937.3;
   1939.35, 40]

James, Henry (William's son) 1920.15

James, William 1875.9; 1879.11; 1895.63; 1897.10;
   1899.9; 1902.15; 1903.33; 1907.4; 1920.15
   [1914.42; 1925.16; 1937.23]

Jannaccone, Pasquale [1898.39, 88; 1900.29;
   1933.27]

Japan [1909.17; 1919.177, 282; 1921.25]

Jarves, James Jackson 1881.37a

Jax [pseud.?] 1906.55

Jay, Harriett 1903.6

Jayne, H. H. F. 1922.12

Jefferies, Richard [1893.12; 1909.12; 1925.17]

Jeffers, Robinson 1927.38
   [1929.36; 1931.58; 1933.2; 1934.12; 1938.46;
   1939.34]

Jeffers, Una 1933.2

Jefferson, Thomas [1923.19; 1929.16; 1933.5;
   1937.9; 1938.2]

Jensen, Johannes V. [1937.25; 1939.16]

Jepson, Edgar 1908.22

Jerrold, Laurence 1897.143

Jerrold, Walter 1913.9

Jesse, F. Tennyson 1928.15

Jesus. See Christ

Jewell, Edward Alden 1936.61

John o' London. See O'London, John

John o' London's Weekly 1938.47

John Swinton's Paper 1885.28

Johnson, A. Theodore 1938.3

Johnson, Allen 1937.14

Johnson, Charles F. 1898.10; 1900.11

Johnson, Col. (of Camden) [1915.52; 1926.49]

Johnson, Farmer (Ohio Valley) 1892.156

Johnson, H. H. 1919.181

Johnson, H. Harold 1897.11

Johnson, John Newton 1915.10
   [1887.46; 1893.11]

Johnson, Lionel 1894.5; 1919.8; 1921.18
   [1934.1]

Johnson, Maurice O. 1938.20

Johnson, Robert Underwood 1923.8; 1931.30

Johnson, Rossiter 1925.49

Johnson, Dr. Samuel [1901.30; 1907.27; 1913.11]

Johnson, William H. 1892.80

Johnson, Dr. Willis Fletcher 1923.44

Johnston, Alma Calder (wife of John H., Bertha's
   mother) 1878.2; 1915.10; 1917.56
   [1901.37]

Johnston, Bertha (daughter) 1909.36; 1923.44
   [1936.49]

Johnston, George (Quilp) 1886.18-19
   [1886.27]

Johnston, Dr. J[ohn]. See also Bolton group
   1890.7; 1892.15; 1898.11 [1898.91]; 1910.36;
   1915.10; 1917.6 [1917.42; 1918.17-18, 20, 23];
   1918.12 [1918.49; 1919.36, 131]
   [1891.36; 1892.141]

Johnston, J[ohn] H. (husband of Alma) 1892.15;
   1908.20; 1915.10
   [1877.7; 1886.50; 1887.32; 1889.52, 54;
   1895.75; 1914.29]

Johnston, Mary 1919.9

Jones, E. 1927.25

Jones, Howard Mumford 1928.10; 1935.44

Jones, John Paul [1896.62; 1938.29]

Jones, Llewellyn 1919.208
   [1919.285]

Jones, P. M. 1914.11; 1915.23; 1916.34

Jones, Rufus M. 1930.9

Jones, Mayor Samuel M. 1899.61; 1901.9
   [1899.52; 1901.37]

Jordan, Dr. David Starr 1923.44

Josephson, Matthew 1930.10

Journal of Education 1919.157

Journal of English and Germanic Philology 1908.31;
   1910.23; 1932.46; 1939.16

Journal of Hygiene and Herald of Health 1898.31

Journal of the Rutgers University Library 1938.56

Journeyman [pseud.] 1920.44; 1921.38

Joyce, James 1939.8

Judy 1884.26
June, Jennie 1877.8-9
Jupp, William J. 1918.13

K. See Kennedy, William Sloane
K., E. 1871.20
K., P. 1925.26
Kaltenborn, Olga 1927.50
Kaluza, Max 1911.9
Kansas [1879.13-39; 1895.75]
Kansas City Daily Journal 1879.15, 21
Kansas City Journal 1879.23, 28
Kansas City Post 1919.245
Kansas City Times 1879.13-14, 18, 22, 26, 29, 39
Kansas Magazine 1872.20
    [1938.53]
Kansas Tribune 1879.30
Kansas Wire City Weekly [1919.355]
Kant, Immanuel [1860.39; 1896.45; 1906.38; 1921.34;
    1930.3]
Karsner, David Fulton 1912.29; 1916.40, 47; 1919.11
    [1920.70], 133; 1922.56
    [1915.63]
Kartoshinsky, Oscar 1915.57
"Katinka" [pseud.] 1856.1
Kaufman, Nathan 1919.38
Kaufman, Paul 1928.10
Keats, John [1888.72; 1906.101; 1920.18; 1929.31,
    41]
Keila, Louis 1926.37
Keller, Elizabeth Leavitt 1909.29; 1921.19 [1921.81;
    1922.45; 1932.2; 1937.9]
Keller, Helen 1918.42 [1918.41; 1919.31]
    [1919.288]
Kelley, William V. 1897.153; 1901.47 [1901.56]
Kellner, Leon 1915.13 [1915.55]
Kemmerer, John 1929.47
Kempe, Edward 1903.23
Kennedy, Charles Rann 1923.44
    [1911.29]
Kennedy, Walker 1884.21 [1895.20]
Kennedy, William Sloane 1881.9; 1883.20; 1886.2
    [1888.54]; 1887.65; 1888.28, 64; 1889.9;
    1890.38; 1891.17; 1892.15, 24; 1895.13, 22a
    [1895.24]; 1896.9 [1896.74, 78; 1897.23], 50,
    72, 77; 1897.12, 26 [1897.59], 65, 85, 123;
    1898.30, 39, 82; 1899.31; 1900.24, 26; 1903.37;
    1904.11, 24; 1907.17, 22; 1915.10; 1920.96;
    1924.12; 1926.15 [1926.63, 69, 81; 1930.47];
    1927.11; 1931.1
    [1888.12; 1892.187; 1910.17]
Kent, Charles 1868.19
Kent, Charles A. 1902.54
Kenyon Review 1939.35
Kernahan, Coulson 1923.33
Kerr, Orpheus C. 1873.6
Ketler (or Kettler), William H. 1925.22
    [1919.116]
Kilgore, Manley Woodbury 1935.7
Kilmer, Joyce 1916.27 [1916.28], 32, 45, 63
Kilspindie, Victor 1915.37
King, Basil 1919.10
Kingsley, Charles [1909.16]
Kipling, Rudyard [1897.57; 1898.72; 1912.22;
    1919.94]
Kirkham, Stanton Davis 1907.5; 1910.6
Kirkland, Winifred M. 1919.256
Kirkwood, J. P. [1938.15]
Knapp, Adeline 1904.33
Knerr, Dr. Calvin B. [1936.46]
Knight, Grant C. 1932.14

Knorr, Helena 1898.96
Knortz, Karl 1893.11
    [1887.24; 1888.63]
Knowles, Frederic Lawrence 1897.13
Knowles, Robert E. 1908.10
Knoxville (Tennessee) Tribune 1897.92
Koisimi, Setsuko [1919.47]
Kottabos 1877.2
Kouwenhoven, John A. 1938.7
Kreymborg, Alfred 1925.8; 1929.13; 1930.11
    [1916.50; 1919.37; 1922.64]
Krigsman, Anita L. 1919.257
Kruell, G. 1892.96
Kueffner, Dr. Louise M. 1920.72; 1923.44
Kunitz, Stanley J. 1938.8

L. 1892.152
L., Rose 1909.32
Labor. See also Socialism [1912.35, 38; 1919.353,
    365; 1920.29, 67; 1923.22; 1932.47; 1935.31;
    1936.13]
Labour Leader (Manchester) 1892.219; 1904.43;
    1917.45; 1919.203
Labour Prophet 1894.31; 1895.16
Lacey, Margaret 1903.49
Ladies' Home Journal 1923.48; 1925.79
Lafayette, Marquis de [1905.2]
La Follette, Suzanne 1930.43
LaForgue, Jules [1922.15]
Lafourcade, Georges 1927.26
Lambart-Taylor, Maude 1928.39
Lancaster, Albert Edmund 1893.11
Lancet (London) 1860.44
Land and Water 1919.328
Landauer, Bella C. 1937.7
Landauer, Gustav [1919.357]
Landerdauer [1921.14]
Landis, Paul 1929.14
Lanier, C. D. 1892.180
Lanier, H. W. 1899.10
Lanier, Mary Day (Mrs. Sidney) 1883.33; 1899.10
    [1933.29]
Lanier, Sidney 1883.5 [1883.18, 37], 33; 1884.10;
    1893.11; 1896.73; 1897.14; 1899.10
    [1887.30; 1892.13; 1896.69; 1908.51; 1925.60;
    1926.15; 1929.58; 1930.8; 1933.29]
Lankes, J. J. 1919.121
Lanman, Charles 1866.8
    [1866.10-11]
Lanux, Pierre de 1917.7 [1918.23]; 1921.73; 1922.69
Lanz, Henry 1931.14
Larminie, William 1894.60
Lathrop, George Parsons 1877.16; 1886.3, 43
    [1934.43]
Latin America [1920.80; 1928.21; 1938.25]
Law, James D. 1893.5; 1903.7; 1918.55
Law, Robert Adger 1929.59
Lawrence, D. H. 1918.63; 1920.17; 1921.62 [1921.70];
    1923.9 [1938.43]; 1932.13; 1936.18; Addenda
    [1919.352; 1923.24; 1926.27; 1937.21; 1938.9]
Lawrence (Kansas) Daily Journal 1879.16, 24
Lawton, William Cranston 1902.16
Lazarus, Emma [1939.9a]
Lazenby, Charles 1913.37
Leader (London) 1856.19; 1860.39
    [1875.6]
Le Baron, Marie 1873.9
Lee, Dr. Alfred P. [1929.40]
Lee, Gerald Stanley 1897.40; 1907.23, 45
Lee, Vernon See Paget, Violet
Lee & Shepard [1885.16]

Leech, Dr. William 1879.6 [1933.13]
Leeds (England) Yorkshire Post 1918.60
Lees, Henry A. 1846.3-4; 1848.9; 1850.3
Le Gallienne, Eva 1923.46
Le Gallienne, Richard 1893.6; 1898.40 [1898.42,
    56a]; 1922.29; 1925.9
    [1895.79; 1898.28, 72; 1921.18]
Leggett, Elisa Seaman 1927.37
Legler, Henry Eduard 1916.11 [1916.1; 1917.40]
Leigh, Arran 1877.1
Leighton, Walter 1902.47
Leisure Moments 1886.45; 1887.23
Leisy, Ernest Erwin 1929.15
Leland, Charles Godfrey 1882.6; 1893.7
    [1906.12; 1915.59; 1935.19]
Leland, Henry P. 1860.35
    [1893.7; 1935.19]
Lemmon, Leonard 1891.5 [1896.79, 82, 85]
Lemon, Courtenay [1906.73]
Lent, E. B. 1913.50
Leonard, Mary Hall 1917.35
Leonard, R. M. 1913.9
Leonard, William Ellery 1906.38
Lesley, J. P. [1939.9a]
Leslie, Mrs. Frank [1932.2]
Lese, Die 1913.42
Lessing, Otto Edward 1906.88; 1910.23; 1913.42;
    1919.281, 346; 1920.34
    [1907.38]
Levison, Miss P. E. [1939.32]
Lewes, George Henry 1856.19
Lewin, Walter 1887.53, 74; 1888.41; 1889.23;
    1893.40
Lewis, B. Roland 1931.15
Lewis, E. C. 1902.17
Lewis, Lloyd 1936.17
Lewis, Oscar 1939.15
Lewis, Sinclair 1920.18; 1930.50
    [1931.10]
Lewis, Wilfrid 1925.56
Lewisohn, Ludwig 1932.15 [1932.45; 1936.3]
Libbin, Thomas [1918.41]
Liberator 1919.121, 353, 357, 365; 1920.54; 1922.32
Liberty 1881.32, 47; 1882.50, 78, 93, 100, 116;
    1890.57; 1891.27, 34; 1892.191, 209; 1899.24;
    1907.28
Libraries [1882.90; 1887.86; 1888.42; 1892.83;
    1897.12; 1906.84; 1915.63; 1920.97; 1922.62;
    1923.27; 1925.38; 1932.12]
Library Magazine 1887.62, 81
Library Notes (Duke University Library) 1936.55
Library of Congress 1919.12; 1939.13
    [1924.43; 1938.47a; 1939.44]
Liddell, Mark H. 1902.18
Life (London) 1882.135
Life (New York) 1903.47; 1912.46; 1913.41; 1915.44;
    1920.84
Life Illustrated (New York) 1855.3-4, 13, 15;
    1856.12, 18, 20-23
    [1934.34-35; 1936.15]
Light 1918.28
Lin Yutang. See Yutang, Lin
Lincoln, Abraham. See also Whitman--Lectures;
    Works--"O Captain!," "When Lilacs," and
    "Hush'd Be the Camps" [1866.2, 12, 22; 1881.42;
    1886.40; 1888.4; 1889.9; 1892.98, 117; 1893.12;
    1899.33; 1901.13, 45, 62-63; 1903.12; 1905.19;
    1906.18, 21; 1909.8; 1911.1; 1914.23; *1916.17;
    1917.26; 1918.32, 59; 1919.124, 185, 279, 376;
    1921.13, 25, 27, 56; 1922.33; 1923.8, 45;
    *1924.20; 1926.35-36, 69; *1928.3; 1930.25,
    31; 1933.6, 16]
    Fictionalized: [1927.15; 1928.17; 1929.1]
Lincoln (Nebraska) Sunday State Journal 1896.26
Lind, Jenny [1887.6; 1932.46]
Lindsay, Vachel 1919.58; 1923.65; 1925.10; 1929.16;
    1930.43
    [1917.36; 1922.7, 60, 64; 1937.30]
Linton, W[illiam] J[ames] 1878.4; 1894.6
Lippincott's Monthly Magazine 1884.24; 1886.33;
    1887.15, 22, 80, 84; 1889.25; 1891.18, 34a-
    35; 1892.163, 169; 1893.28; 1913.46
    [1891.19]
Literary Digest. See also Digest 1892.102;
    1896.29; 1897.46, 121, 134, 163; 1906.97;
    1909.37; 1913.23; 1918.33; 1919.50, 64, 322;
    1924.35; 1925.50, 80; 1927.34; 1931.51
Literary Era. See also Era 1901.27
Literary Gazette 1860.45
Literary Guide 1919.338
Literary News 1880.4, 24; 1881.39; 1885.20;
    1889.40; 1890.37; 1891.40, 42; 1892.76, 215
Literary Opinion 1892.81, 166
Literary Review (from the New York Evening Post)
    1920.92-94, 102; 1921.43, 61, 73; 1922.49-52,
    63; 1923.53; 1925.33, 37; 1926.42
Literary World (Boston) 1881.18-19, 44, 48;
    1882.55, 119; 1884.23; 1885.38-39; 1887.25,
    56, 58; 1888.78; 1891.25, 46; 1892.31, 124-
    126, 131, 197, 205, 218; 1897.35, 144, 156
Literary World (London) 1892.190; 1893.26
Literature 1898.34, 45, 59, 69, 88; 1899.29;
    1901.20, 23, 50
Literature and Life 1885.13
Littell's Living Age. See Living Age
Little Journeys to the Homes of Eminent Artists
    1902.46
Little Review 1919.352; Addenda
Liverpool Daily Courier 1922.40, 44
Liverpool Labour Chronicle 1899.29
Liverpool Post 1919.296
Living Age 1868.23, 33-34; 1876.6; 1894.32;
    1906.27; 1909.27; 1914.31; 1919.342; 1923.25
Livingston, Flora V. 1923.27
Livingston, Luther S. 1898.103
Lloyd, J. William 1895.7; 1902.19; 1903.18
    [1892.209; 1902.43; 1912.42]
Lloyd, Rev. William [1888.11]
Lloyds Weekly London Newspaper 1868.21
Locker-Lampson, Frederick [1920.3; 1934.1]
Lockwood, DeWitt C. 1893.22
Lodge, George Cabot 1902.20
Lodge, Henry Cabot 1909.22; 1923.44
Lombroso, Cesare 1891.6
London, Jack 1901.62
London 1897.116
London Chronicle. See London Daily Chronicle
London Daily Chronicle 1867.13; 1892.59; 1897.48,
    109; 1899.29; 1919.32, 294; 1922.46
London Daily Herald 1920.66; 1926.55
London Daily Mirror 1904.45
London Daily News 1876.23-25, 27-28 [1876.31, 47],
    29-31; 1886.47, 49; 1887.52; 1892.205;
    1919.209, 231
London Daily Telegraph 1913.43; 1914.24
London Globe 1919.222
London Guardian 1901.53
    [1901.32]
London Mercury 1919.32
London Morning Post 1922.33
London Morning Star 1868.18
London News 1900.27

London Review 1866.18; 1868.14
London Society 1892.224
London Standard 1892.60
London Sun 1868.19
London Sunday Times 1866.7; 1868.16; 1918.39;
    1919.191, 292
London Times. See also Times Literary Supplement;
    London Sunday Times 1866.16; 1878.11; 1882.32;
    1892.45; 1919.223, 306-307
London Weekly Dispatch 1856.8; 1918.40, 45
London (Ontario) Advertiser 1880.18; 1917.22
London (Ontario) Free Press 1880.19; 1890.33;
    1905.43; 1912.28, 41; 1913.36, 51; 1919.244;
    1923.26
Long, Charles W. 1937.13
Long, Haniel 1938.9 [1938.41; 1939.18-19]
Long, William J. 1913.10
Long Island. See also Whitman--Birthplace
    [1881.27; 1902.23; 1905.59; 1908.46; 1909.18;
    1913.50; 1917.6; 1920.1; 1921.55, 63; 1937.13;
    1938.33, 49-50; 1939.20]
Long Island Democrat 1849.4
    [1839.1; 1916.37; 1937.40]
Long Island Farmer 1839.1; 1840.1
Long Island Star 1838.1; 1849.5
Long Islander (Huntington) 1848.13; 1849.9; 1851.2;
    1858.1; 1881.27-28; 1883.19, 36; 1888.85;
    1905.38, 45; 1913.50; 1919.207, 311; 1938.33,
    44
    [1838.1-2; 1883.19; 1905.45]
Longaker, Daniel 1892.15; 1893.11
    [1936.46]
Longfellow, Henry Wadsworth [1860.60; 1868.39;
    1876.29; 1878.6, 16; 1880.5, 23;
    1881.7, 24; 1882.32, 58; 1884.18-19, 22;
    1885.18; 1892.27, 126, 145, 158; 1895.17;
    1897.15, 17, 39; 1898.85, 89; 1900.41; 1905.13;
    1906.7; 1909.8; 1912.44; 1916.24; 1917.36;
    1919.2, 29, 89, 126, 189, 219; 1920.50;
    1921.51; 1922.7; 1923.27; 1924.4; 1925.9, 54;
    1927.36; 1931.1, 18; 1932.39; 1938.20]
Longman's Magazine 1884.16
Loomis, Charles Battell 1899.11
Lorca. See Garcia Lorca, Federico
Lorentz, Pare [1939.32-33]
Los Angeles Graphic 1915.32; 1916.31, 35-36
Lossing, B. J. [1935.36]
Louisiana Historical Society, Publications 1915.8
Love, Bert 1918.29
Lover of Truth, A [pseud.] 1925.62
Lovering, H. B. [1887.13, 18]
Lovett, Robert Morse 1909.7
Loving, Pierre 1920.71; 1922.60
Lowell, Amy 1917.8; 1919.71 [1919.95], 153
    [1919.187, 189], 293; 1922.13; 1927.36
    [1916.32; 1918.69; 1919.94, 266; 1921.74;
    1922.60]
Lowell, James Russell 1866.21; 1868.40; 1894.9;
    1932.12
    [1876.29; 1882.134; 1887.59; 1889.37; 1890.13;
    1892.16-17, 96, 104, 158-159; 1893.12; 1894.35;
    1895.17, 23, 35; 1897.12, 39, 72; 1898.85;
    1901.13; 1902.34, 54, 61; 1903.20; 1905.13;
    1906.7, 13, 65, 68; 1908.20; 1911.8; 1912.26;
    1913.14; 1915.10; 1919.16, 54, 63, 69, 75, 103,
    204, 251, 305, 331; 1920.20; 1922.13; 1923.8,
    27; 1924.40; 1925.54; 1928.18; 1929.17; 1930.18;
    1931.1, 38; 1932.39; 1934.43; 1936.4]
Lowes, John Livingston 1919.13
Lucas, E. V. 1937.8; Addenda
Lucas, F. L. 1925.25

Luccock, Halford E. 1934.8
Luce, Morton 1925.23
Luders, Charles Henry 1888.54
    [1935.38]
Luftig, P. See Airey, Peter
Lund, Percy [1924.27]
Lychenheim, Morris 1918.47 [1918.54]
Lynch, Arthur 1891.7
Lynn (Massachusetts) Saturday Union 1884.18
    [1884.19]
Lyric West 1923.64
Lytton, Robert First Earl of 1906.2; Addenda

M., A. N. 1920.61
M., B. 1919.14
M., C. 1919.258
M., D. S. 1892.164
M., E. J. See McPhelim, Edward J.
M., E. P. See Mitchell, Edward P.
M., G. E. 1882.22
M., H. See Monroe, Harriet
M., H. J. 1919.164
M., W. E. 1897.147; 1898.49
Mabbott, Thomas Ollive 1924.38; 1925.81; 1926.39;
    1927.12 [1927.43], 37; 1930.13 [1930.48;
    1931.24]; 1931.60; 1932.27; 1933.17 [1935.16];
    1935.25 [1935.38]; 1938.37
Mabie, Hamilton Wright 1892.8, 103; 1897.124;
    1903.42 [1903.50; 1905.10]; 1913.28; 1915.10
MacAlister, Dr. Alexander. See McAlister, Dr.
    Alexander
MacArthur, David Wilson 1934.18
Macaulay, G. C. 1882.132
MacCracken, Henry M. 1902.21
MacCulloch, J. A. 1899.76
MacDonald, Flora. See Denison, Flora MacDonald
Macdonald, Frederic W. 1911.10
Macdonald, George E. 1907.28
Macdougall, Duncan [1918.41]
MacDowell, Edward [1914.42]
Mace 1882.31, 131
Macfall, Haldane 1923.33
Mack, Laurence 1924.34
Mackall, Leonard L. 1936.38
Mackay, Helen [1916.46]
Mackay, Jessie 1906.96
MacKaye, Percy 1919.259
    [1919.326; 1925.10]
MacKenzie, Tait [1919.31]
Maclean, Mrs. Kate Seymour 1880.20 [1880.21]
MacLeish, Archibald 1938.10
Macleod, Norman [1872.16]
MacMechan, Archibald 1899.73
Macphail, Sir Andrew 1905.11
Macpherson, Walter [1919.285]
Macy, John 1913.11 [1919.159]; 1922.14; 1923.44;
    1925.11 [1925.71]; 1931.18
Maeterlinck, Maurice [1895.8, 48; 1896.81; 1900.34]
Magazine Internationale, Le [1896.30]
Magazine of Art 1889.61; 1937.44
Magazine of Poetry 1889.12
Mainly About Newspapers (London) 1919.224
Maitland, Frederic William 1906.9
Malcolm-Smith, E. F. 1930.19
Malet, Lucas. See Harrison, Mary St. Leger
Malone, Dumas 1937.14, 33 [1937.34]
Man 1882.97
Man of Letters, A [pseud.] 1892.97
Manchester City News 1919.179
Manchester Guardian 1892.58; 1897.110;
    1905.52; 1918.26, 59; 1919.251; 1920.61

Manchester Guardian Weekly 1929.55
Manchester Labour Leader. See Labour Leader
Manchester Literary Club, Papers 1920.5; 1934.6
Manhattan [1881.43; 1886.43; 1898.29a, 105;
    1901.30; 1902.35; 1903.5; 1919.48; 1920.98;
    1925.13, 39, 42-43, 45-46, 58; 1934.46;
    1937.17]
Mann, Thomas [1922.63; 1926.40]
Manson, Beatrice 1913.42
Marietta (Ohio) Register 1885.17
Marinetti, Filippo T. [1914.25]
Markham, Edwin 1902.27; 1919.165; 1923.47; 1924.30;
    1930.43; 1932.16
    [1901.36-37, 62-63; 1902.28; 1916.56; 1931.31-
    32]
Marlowe, Christopher [1932.6]
Marlowe, Julia 1899.61
Marquis, Don 1920.90
Marr, James H. 1882.77
Marsden, James W. 1919.260
Marsh, Arthur Richmond 1900.15
Marsh, Edward Clark 1908.33
Marsh, William B. [1933.28]
Marston, Attorney General of Massachusetts
    [1882.38, 40, 51, 54, 78, 90, 93]
Marston, Philip Bourke [1888.23]
M'Arthur, Peter [Peter McArthur] 1913.35
Martial [1876.49]
Martin, Everett [1918.41]
Martin, G. Currie 1917.9
Marvin, Frederic Rowland 1910.7
Marvin, Joseph B. 1877.13
Marwick, W. 1925.55 [1925.57], 61 [1925.64], 67
Marx, Karl. See also Socialism [1903.45; 1910.16;
    1919.357; 1932.47]
Mary 1919.323
Mary, Queen to George V of England 1919.148a
Masefield, John 1919.261
Mason, Daniel Gregory 1913.12
Mason, H. L. 1901.11
Mason, Walt [1923.47]
Masque, Le 1922.15
Masters, Edgar Lee 1915.14; 1919.55, 262 [1919.162],
    278; 1937.9 [1937.29-32, 35, 37]
    [1916.12, 32; 1917.8, 23; 1919.75, 273;
    1920.10; 1925.15, 53; 1939.7]
Matador [pseud.] 1873.11
Mathews, Cornelius [1842.12]
Mathews, Godfrey William 1921.20
Mathews, Joseph Chesley 1939.42
Matthews, Brander 1896.10; 1911.11
Matthews, Horace B. 1903.47
Maude, Aylmer 1902.22
Maupaussant, Guy de [1882.80]
Maurel, Victor 1895.58
Maxim, Hudson 1910.8
Maxwell, William 1919.291; 1931.52
Maxwell, W[illiam] B[abington] 1919.15; 1923.33
Mayer, Louis [1926.53]
Mayer, S. R. Townshend 1875.6
Maynard, Laurens 1895.41; 1896.78; 1897.86;
    1898.85; 1908.12; 1915.10; 1917.58; 1932.49
Maynard, Mrs. Mila Tupper 1903.9 [1902.60; 1903.24]
Mayne, Xavier. See Stevenson, Edward Irenaeus
    Prime
Mazzini, Giuseppe [1905.1]
McAlister (or MacAlister), Dr. Alexander [1919.116;
    1923.54; 1927.44; 1932.40; 1935.28]
McAlpine, Frank [1905.21]
McAree, J. V. 1929.61
McArthur, Peter See M'Arthur, Peter

McCarthy, J. H. 1876.71
McCarthy, John Russell 1919.134 [1919.331]
McCarthy, Justin 1899.12
    [1914.10]
McClure's Magazine 1897.79; 1901.67
McCoy, Charles G. 1938.52
McCulloch, H., Jr. 1892.165
McCusker, Honor 1938.30
McDermott, Hugh Farmer 1939.4
McDonald, Bennett 1915.62
McDonald, Edward D. 1936.18
McFadden, James P. 1919.337
McGaffey, Ernest 1915.32
McGovern, Mr. [1893.11]
McH., M. H. 1906.43
McIlwraith, Jean N. 1902.40
McKay, David 1915.10
McKillop, Alan D. 1920.101
McKinsey, Folger 1885.41-42; 1886.24-27; Addenda
McNicoll, Thomas Stewart 1917.40
McNulty, J. H. 1927.45
McPhelim, Edward J. 1888.42
Mead, Leon 1900.41
Mee, Arthur 1910.9
Melbourne Australian Herald. See Australian Herald
Melbourne Leader 1923.50
Melish, Dr. John Howard 1923.44
Melville, Herman [1866.20; 1867.3; 1874.8; 1889.43;
    1899.65, 73; 1905.41; 1921.27; 1926.60;
    1927.18; 1929.18; 1930.7, 18; 1931.18;
    1933.21; 1937.36; 1939.40]
Mencken, H. L. 1911.28; 1913.27; 1915.55; 1919.16
    [1919.126], 17; 1920.19; 1924.13; 1926.17;
    1929.12; 1930.43
    [1919.318; 1925.15; 1926.27; 1931.10]
Mendax [pseud.] 1931.60
Menken, Adah Isaacs 1860.27
    [1888.1]
Mentor, The 1913.28; 1923.49; 1924.30
Mercer, Dorothy Frederica. See Appendix
Mercer, Edmund 1890.57a
Mercure de France 1921.31
    [1923.62]
Meredith, George 1883.6; 1892.159
    [1911.7; 1919.6; 1936.19]
Meredith, Richard 1928.37
Merlin [pseud.?] 1891.14
Merrill, Stuart 1921.31; 1922.15 [1923.23]
    [1887.32]
Merritt, Jean 1938.44
Mertins, Louis 1939.43
Merwin, Henry Childs 1897.77
Mesdag, H. W. [1897.58]
Metcalf, John Calvin 1914.12
Methodist Quarterly Review 1919.73
Methodist Review 1897.47, 153
Methodist Times 1919.202
Metzdorf, Robert F. 1935.23
Meyer, Annie Nathan 1908.50
Michael, Helen Abbott 1897.56
Michaud, Regis 1919.190
    [1919.97-98]
Michelangelo [1905.9; 1925.78]
Michelet, Jules [1904.33; 1937.25, 39]
Middleton, Lamar 1897.27
Midland, The 1917.60
Midland Monthly Magazine 1899.28
Mielziner, Jo 1924.41
Milford, Humphrey Sumner 1925.5
Mill, John Stuart [1936.6]
Millar, A. H. 1925.54 [1925.55-56, 65], 57

[1925.61, 67], 64
Millard, Bailey 1901.63; 1916.64
Miller, Charles Ransom [1931.3; 1933.14]
Miller, DeWitt [1913.2]
Miller, Florence Hardiman 1904.25
Miller, Fred R. 1931.55
Miller, Henry 1939.40
Miller, Joaquin 1875.14; 1877.5; 1892.212; 1897.15;
    1898.62; 1908.49; 1915.10
    [1873.4; 1876.5; 1881.7; 1885.41; 1887.6;
    1890.41; 1898.44; 1900.8, 41; 1919.89;
    1922.21; 1927.16; 1928.2; 1929.26]
Miller, John 1897.16
Miller, Kelly 1895.50
Millett, Jean François [1881.20; 1889.40; 1890.8;
    1893.12; 1896.71; 1897.77]
Millin, Sarah Gertrude 1936.19
Mills, Benjamin Fay 1899.52
Milne, James 1910.29
Milnes, Richard Monckton (Lord Houghton) [1876.35;
    1903.25; 1918.1; 1934.1]
Milton, John [1872.1; 1882.33; 1886.45; 1887.86;
    1890.26; 1896.9; 1898.55; 1906.14, 81;
    1908.29; 1923.39; 1926.1]
Milwaukee Sentinel 1866.11
Mimnermus [pseud.] 1903.10; 1919.338
Mind (London) 1879.11
Mind: Science, Philosophy, Religion, Psychology,
    Metaphysics (New York) 1900.28
Minneapolis Journal 1920.76

Minto, W. 1892.9
Mirsky, D. S. 1937.22
Mitchell, Charles B. 1919.204
Mitchell, Edward P. 1881.45; 1924.14
Mitchell, Langdon 1927.14
Mitchell, Roy [1918.41]
Mitchell, S. Weir 1894.7; 1900.12
    [1890.30; 1922.12]
Modern Language Association, Publications. See
    Publications
Modern Language Notes 1930.37; 1932.26, 32-33;
    1933.12; 1935.22; 1938.31
Modern Language Review 1915.23; 1916.34; 1927.26
Modern Poetry [1910.27; 1911.23; 1912.22, 42;
    1915.23; 1915.32, 34; 1916.27-28, 31-32, 34,
    36, 46; 1917.8, 35-36, 39, 53; 1918.24, 51-52;
    1919.1, 13-14, 23-24, 26, 37, 53, 62, 90, 99,
    105, 135, 138, 160-61, 182, 188, 196, 209,
    229, 318, 331, 378; 1920.17, 57; 1921.54;
    1922.3, 64; 1923.21, 45; 1924.24, 34; 1925.15,
    41, 77; 1927.22, 36; 1928.25; 1929.13, 43;
    1935.5; 1937.18; 1939.1]
Modern Quarterly 1932.43-45
Modern Review 1929.41
Modern School (Stelton, New Jersey) 1918.67;
    1919.76-91
Modern Thought 1882.33, 98
Modernist 1919.369
Moderwell, Hiram K. 1919.357
Modjeska, Helena 1910.10
Moeller, Tyge 1910.25
Molloy, Fitzgerald 1882.98
Momus 1860.19
Monadnock. See Conway, Moncure Daniel
Monahan, Michael 1904.34, 41; 1914.13; 1916.42;
    1920.75
Monck, Emily Christiana 1895.48, 82
Monet, Claude [1908.36]
Monro, Harold 1912.22; Addenda
Monroe, Harriet 1892.145 [1892.175]; 1914.43;

1919.59, 75, 135, 366, 376; 1923.44; 1926.19;
    1938.11
    [1918.31; 1919.285]
Monroe, Will S. 1930.47; 1931.16, 25; 1933.18
Montaigne [1907.17; 1918.37]
Montclair, John W. [1867.19]
Montgomery, Alberta 1907.18
Month, The 1891.20
Monthly Magazine (Barnsley, England) 1888.77
Monthly Review 1903.28
Monthly Trade Gazette 1856.4
Montreal Daily Star. See also Montreal Star
    1919.263
Montreal Gazette 1919.225
Montreal Star. See also Montreal Daily Star
    1916.39; 1921.39
Moody, William Vaughn 1901.12; 1909.7; 1913.12
Moore, Aubertine Woodward 1915.39, 52; 1926.49
Moore, Charles Leonard 1901.51; 1913.33
    [1888.72]
Moore, George [1888.63; 1898.72; 1916.55; 1920.14]
Moore, Isabel 1905.9
Moore, John 1939.9
Moore, John B. 1926.32
Moore, John Robert 1917.17
Mordell, Albert 1917.39; 1919.18; 1920.20;
    1921.21; 1926.20; 1933.8
More, Paul Elmer 1906.10 [1907.11]; 1908.49;
    1909.25; 1910.32
More Books (Bulletin of Boston Public Library)
    1938.30
Morgan, May 1906.89
Morgan-Powell, S. 1919.263
Morley, Christopher 1919.19 [1920.40]; 1920.21;
    1921.22; 1922.52; 1923.12, 24, 44; 1924.41
    [1930.33]; 1925.12-13, 52; 1926.21 [1926.42,
    44, 48, 52, 67; 1927.25], 76; 1927.28;
    1928.33; 1929.40, 51; 1931.17; 1932.17;
    1935.30; 1936.22, 43, 45, 54; 1938.12
    [1927.44; 1938.50]
Morley, John, Viscount 1917.10
Morrill, Justin S. 1887.9
Morris, Charles 1887.10; 1888.39 [1888.56]
Morris, Harrison Smith 1888.46 [1888.56]; 1889.35,
    72; 1892.15, 31, 105; 1893.11 [1913.46];
    1894.8; 1929.17 [1930.33, 47]
    [1923.54; 1931.31, 33; 1936.46]
Morris, Lewis 1891.33
Morris, William 1889.9
    [1900.28; 1905.1; 1934.1]
Morrow, Honoré Willsie 1927.15; 1928.17
Morrow, Rev. James 1882.74-75, 82, 94
Morse, Lucius Daniel 1899.46, 61, 77; 1905.41
Morse, Sidney H. 1866.15; 1889.9; 1891.43; 1892.15;
    1893.11
Morse, W. F. 1907.7
Morton, James F., Jr. 1923.32
Mosher, Thomas Bird 1906.21; 1920.22
Mother Earth 1907.10
Motherwell, William [1935.25, 38]
Moulton, Charles Wells 1905.12
Moulton, Louise Chandler 1888.24
    [1910.21]
Moulton, Richard G. 1911.12
Mount Tom 1907.45
Mountain, William 1899.61; 1901.25
Mourey, Gabriel 1910.31
Mowrer, Paul Scott 1912.48

Mufson, Thomas 1910.40
Muller, Herbert J. 1937.10

Mullins, Helene 1930.43
Mulvany, Charles Pelham 1880.21
Mumford, Lewis 1926.22, 67, 77; 1929.18; 1938.34
Mumford, Morrison 1879.13-14, 18, 22, 26, 39
Munger, Rev. T. T. 1888.17
Munich Post 1906.88
Munsey's Magazine 1895.75: 1909.18
Murdock, Kenneth Ballard 1928.10, 18 [1929.46]
Murger, Henri [1891.33a, 48; 1894.54]
Murray, John 1892.178 [1892.189]
Murray, Samuel A. [1892.53]
Murray's Magazine 1887.74; 1891.33
Murry, John Middleton 1926.33; 1930.14a
    [1924.44]
Muschner, George 1913.42
Music 1894.34
Music (including musical settings of Whitman's
    works) See also Opera
    [1845.3; 1846.1-2; 1894.34, 65; 1900.27, 42,
    52; 1901.60; 1902.6; 1906.32; 1914.5; 1915.39,
    45, 52; 1918.27; 1919.332, 341, 347, 350, 374;
    1920.68-69; 1921.61; 1922.26; 1923.63; 1925.60;
    1926.49; 1928.40; 1930.31; 1931.54; 1936.32;
    1937.7, 45]
Musical America 1915.39, 45
Musical Courier 1891.26; 1897.142; 1898.33, 89;
    1900.52
Musical Leader 1926.49
Musical Student 1918.64
Muzzey, David Saville 1903.29
Myers, Henry Alonzo 1934.48; 1936.58
Mysticism [1898.102; 1902.13; 1911.15; 1912.20;
    1913.16; 1916.16, 26, 61; 1919.129; 1920.35;
    1922.58; 1924.24; 1927.32; 1931.2]

Nadal, B. H. 1916.12
Nadal, E. S. [1887.32]
Nadal, R. M. 1939.5
Naganuma, Shigetaka 1919.282
Narodny, Ivan 1911.16
Nash, Bennett H. [1939.9a]
Nathan, George Jean 1923.44
Nation (London) See also Nation and Athenaeum
    1919.39, 53, 164, 226, 324
Nation (New York) 1865.8; 1866.6; 1867.14, 18, 27,
    29; 1868.6; 1875.9, 17; 1876.7a, 8; 1881.53
    [1931.1]; 1883.30-31, 1885.24; 1887.51;
    1888.81; 1892.120; 1897.34, 108; 1902.31;
    1903.31; 1905.60; 1906.53, 95; 1907.20;
    1909.25; 1910.32; 1914.40; 1915.55; 1916.30,
    66; 1917.61; 1918.57; 1919.34, 98, 227, 351,
    373; 1922.36. 45; 1925.34; 1926.81; 1927.51;
    1931.57; 1937.31
    [1925.70; 1935.39]
Nation and Athenaeum See also Nation 1921.45, 62;
    1926.65, 82; 1927.42, 45
National Magazine 1898.51; 1904.35; 1907.30
National Observer 1891.1
National Reformer 1874.3-9
Nationalism. See American and Americanism
Naturalism [1910.22; 1914.19; 1923.8, 51; 1926.34]
Nature. See also Birds; Sea [1870.6; 1879.43;
    1881.25, 35; 1882.104; 1891.14; 1892.111;
    1893.12; 1901.24; 1903.9; 1904.33; 1906.20,
    79; 1908.51; 1910.11, 36; 1912.2, 28, 34;
    1913.19; 1915.17; 1916.61; 1920.6; 1936.2]
Nautilus Magazine of New Thought 1906.79
Neale, Walter 1929.19
Negroes. See Blacks.
Nekrassow [1937.25]
Nencioni, Enrico [1881.37a]
Neue Rundschau, Die 1923.25

Neue Zeit, Die 1919.281
Neumann, Henry 1933.23
Nevins, Allan 1937.11
Nevinson, Henry W. 1919.264; 1921.23; 1923.33;
    1934.4
New Age 1898.92; 1918.30; 1919.372
New Eclectic 1868.9, 35-36
New England. See also Boston [1898.85; 1919.71,
    95, 153, 187, 189, 251, 280; 1920.14, 42;
    1924.24, 30; 1928.36]
New England Magazine 1891.22; 1892.199-200, 202;
    1899.38
New England Quarterly 1928.36; 1935.27
New Era 1841.1
New Frontier 1936.48
New Jersey Historical Society Proceedings 1937.26
New Masses 1926.80; 1935.41; 1938.42
New Music Review and Church Music Review 1919.332
New Orleans [1915.8, 53; 1917.39; 1920.88; 1921.27;
    1936.45]
New Orleans Crescent [1848.8; 1915.53]
New Orleans Delta 1860.50
New Orleans Item 1892.89
New Orleans Sunday Delta 1860.67
New Orleans Times-Democrat 1882.80
New Orleans Weekly Mirror 1860.29
New Poetry See Modern Poetry
New Quarterly Magazine 1878.17
New Republic (Camden) See Camden New Republic
New Republic (New York) 1915.34; 1916.53, 62;
    1917.32; 1918.51-52; 1919.54, 66, 68, 158,
    166, 182, 240, 249, 317; 1922.47, 58; 1923.65;
    1926.60, 67; 1931.38; 1932.47; 1937.35-36;
    1938.34
New Review (New York) 1915.40
New Review (London) 1894.28
New Stateman 1918.37; 1919.44; 1922.35; 1925.25;
    1929.36
New Statesman and Nation 1938.43
New Thought 1910.24
New Unity 1897.117
New Voice 1899.35, 60
New Witness 1920.95
New World (Boston) 1894.35; 1898.38
New World (New York) 1842.8
New York. See Manhattan; Brooklyn
New York Atlas 1848.6; 1860.43
New York Aurora. See Aurora
New York Call 1908.42; 1912.29; 1915.33, 53;
    1920.103; 1921.55; 1922.56
New York Citizen 1867.16
New York Commercial Advertiser 1871.11; 1888.18;
    1891.40; 1892.99
New York Constellation 1859.3
New York Criterion. See Criterion
New York Daily Globe. See also New York Globe
    1848.1 1848.4, 5
New York Daily Graphic 1873.6, 9-11; 1875.10;
    1885.12; 1888.29
New York Daily Times. See also New York Times
    1856.26
New York Daily Tribune. See New York Tribune
New York Evangelist 1882.23
New York Evening Globe. See also New York Globe
    1914.36
New York Evening Mail 1870.7
New York Evening Post. See also Literary Review
    1841.3; 1842.2; 1848.11; 1855.5; 1867.11;
    1871.12-13, 20; 1881.54; 1886.49, 51; 1892.60;
    1897.111; 1908.41; 1915.57; 1916.46-47;
    1918.50. 53; 1919.228, 247, 265, 270, 273;

1920.70-74; 1921.43; 1923.24; 1925.51; 1926.59;
1928.42
[1909.5]
New York Evening Sun. See also New York Sun
1887.32; 1915.41
New York Evening Telegram 1892.46-47, 64-65
New York Examiner 1882.20
New York Globe. See also New York Daily Globe and
New York Evening Globe 1871.14
[1842.1]
New York Herald. See also New York Sunday Herald
1841.4; 1842.9, 12; 1865.2; 1872.13, 15;
1876.43-44; 1888.21-22, 57, 58 [1888.61], 82;
1889.28, 34, 36-37; 1892.33; 1895.57; 1898.28;
1908.46; 1909.44; 1918.22; 1919.297; 1920.98-
99; 1922.57; 1923.44; 1932.32
[1888.15; 1921.5]
New York Herald Tribune. See also New York Herald
Tribune Books 1925.43, 46, 49; 1926.38
New York Herald Tribune Books 1925.36; 1926.44, 57,
77; 1931.24; 1933.30; 1936.31, 38; 1937.29
New York Home Journal 1888.59, 67; 1889.31, 46;
1892.67, 69; 1898.52
New York Illustrated News 1860.15, 20, 23, 33
New York Leader 1860.8; 1862.2
[1933.6]
New York Ledger 1856.13, 17
New York Mail and Express 1896.53
New York Mirror 1846.5
New York News 1892.147
New York Recorder 1891.50; 1892.34
New York Saturday Press 1859.5; 1860.2-7, 10, 17,
24-26, 30-32, 35-37, 39-40, 46, 49, 53, 56-
58, 63-64, 66; 1866.7
[1930.13; 1935.39]
New York Spectator and Weekly Commercial Advertiser
1872.18
New York Sun. See also New York Evening Sun
1871.21; 1876.33; 1878.12; 1881.45; 1882.47;
1885.18a; 1887.33; 1892.35; 1897.114; 1899.66;
1915.29; 1917.20; 1918.49, 69-71; 1919.183,
188, 193, 229, 286, 323; 1920.90, 100; 1925.30;
1926.75; 1928.26, 31
New York Sunday Mercury 1860.27
New York Sunday Times 1847.5
New York Times. See also New York Daily Times
1860.17; 1865.9; 1866.27; 1867.7, 9, 15;
1868.41; 1870.5, 8; 1871.15; 1872.11; 1873.7;
1876.26; 1880.26; 1881.14, 37a; 1882.22, 28,
35, 40, 54, 72-73, 89, 134; 1885.31, 34;
1886.36, 50; 1887.34, 55, 67; 1888.11, 13,
32-33, 35, 50, 63; 1889.49, 62, 65; 1890.10,
16, 28, 34, 44, 51; 1891.29, 56-61, 63-65;
1892.36-37, 48-49, 71, 110, 112, 115, 121,
176; 1893.31; 1894.24; 1897.128, 162; 1898.44,
46, 72, 79-81; 1899.27, 36, 65; 1900.49;
1901.21, 37-39, 45, 57; 1902.42, 48; 1904.31;
1905.33, 39, 42, 55, 59; 1906.33, 41-43, 47-
48, 50-52, 54-55, 60-69, 74; 1907.26, 36, 54;
1908.25, 35; 1909.26, 30, 42; 1910.29, 33;
1911.25; 1914.33-34; 1915.37; 1916.27-28, 32,
45, 58-59, 63; 1917.24; 1918.20, 34-36
[1918.57], 66; 1919.40, 69-72, 94-95, 100-
101, 105-106, 108, 151-153, 169, 172, 184,
187, 189-190, 230, 257, 287-290, 293, 298,
308, 314-315, 319, 325-326, 349, 359, 371,
377; 1920.56, 58, 65, 76, 78, 83, 89; 1921.37,
58, 70, 80; 1922.29, 37, 53; 1923.20-21, 29-
33, 61-62; 1924.32; 1925.39-40, 42, 45, 48,
66, 68, 71, 74-75; 1926.34, 43, 53, 64, 69-70,

73, 78; 1927.29-31, 33, 35, 41, 44, 46, 49;
1928.24, 27-29, 43-45; 1929.35; 1930.26-27,
31, 40, 44-45, 46a, 48-50; 1931.27-32, 35, 41,
46, 50; 1932.29, 34, 41-42; 1933.25, 33, 35;
1935.28, 33-35, 40, 43; 1936.32, 35, 37, 39-
42, 49-50, 60-61; 1937.30; 1938.24, 26, 28, 41,
47a, 49-52, 55, 57-58; 1939.20, 29-34, 36-38,
44 [1860.43]
New York Times Book Review. See New York Times
New York Times Saturday Review of Books and Art.
See New York Times
New York Tribune 1841.2; 1842.7, 10; 1848.3, 12;
1855.1, 2, 12; 1859.2; 1865.4; 1867.10;
1868.27; 1871.16, 19; 1874.12; 1875.8, 14;
1876.11, 14-15, 17, 34-38, 46-47, 52, 66;
1877.6-7; 1879.9, 17; 1880.6, 33, 36; 1881.17,
43a; 1882.24, 41, 48, 53, 63-64, 74, 85, 90-
91, 94, 111; 1883.17, 21; 1887.18, 35, 54;
1888.79; 1889.50; 1890.40 [1890.47]; 1891.38;
1892.38, 72, 114, 117, 154; 1893.32; 1894.39,
50-51, 55-56; 1896.37; 1897.33, 146; 1898.35,
73; 1900.33; 1901.36; 1902.53, 63-64; 1906.73,
83; 1915.60 [1915.61], 62; 1916.50-51;
1917.31; 1919.186; 1921.40
[1917.61]
New York Weekly Graphic [1935.40]
New York World 1871.17-18; 1876.59; 1882.59, 109;
1884.27; 1885.15; 1887.17; 1889.38; 1891.51;
1892.39, 171; 1898.93
New York World Telegram 1931.49
New Zealand Herald (Auckland) 1919.254
New Zealand Illustrated 1903.23
Newbolt, Sir Henry 1923.33
Newcastle (England) Weekly Chronicle 1892.88, 132,
139
Newcomer, Alphonso Gerald 1901.13; 1917.11
Newell, Robert Henry 1860.28
Newhall, James Robinson 1897.17
Newman, Prof. [1934.24]
Newspapers. See Whitman--Journalism
Newton, A. Edward 1921.24; 1928.19; 1933.9
Newton, Dr. J. Fort 1919.316 [1919.199, 341]
Nichol, John 1875.4; 1882.7 1906.2
Nichols, Robert 1920.66
Nichols, Dr. Thomas L. 1864.2 [1935.16]; 1874.1
Nicoll, Sir W[illiam] Robertson 1913.13; 1923.33
Nicolson, Harold 1926.23
Nieda, Mayor Frederick von [1936.50]
Nietzsche, Friedrich [1897.162; 1899.42; 1901.47;
1903.26; 1905.1; 1910.23; 1911.25; 1912.32;
1919.344; 1920.58; 1922.16; 1924.10; 1926.9;
1938.13]
Nineteenth Century 1877.5; 1882.132
Niquell [pseud.?] 1892.177
Niven, Frederick 1927.16
No Name Magazine 1891.13
Noah, Mordecai 1847.5
Noble, Charles 1898.12
Noble, Jane Graves 1912.39
Noel, Hon. Roden 1871.23; 1886.4; 1887.84
[1934.1]
Noguchi, Yone 1909.17; 1919.60; 1921.25
Nordau, Max 1895.8 [1895.29, 33, 44; 1899.48;
1910.7; 1922.11]
Norman 1903.3
Norris, Homer A. 1901.60
Norristown Herald 1884.8
North, Ernest Dressel 1899.47
North American (Philadelphia) See Philadelphia North
American

North American Review 1856.6; 1866.21; 1867.2;
    1868.40; 1882.108; 1884.21; 1892.161; 1900.21;
    1906.90; 1907.35, 39; 1908.29; 1910.47;
    1915.26; 1919.56, 62, 117, 126, 149, 358;
    1921.56; 1924.31
    [1881.8; 1887.67; 1890.60; 1891.19]
North British Review 1892.177
Northern Monthly Magazine 1867.20
    [1932.49]
Norton, Alfred 1905.31
Norton, Charles Eliot 1855.6; 1894.9; 1913.14;
    1928.18
    [1887.41; 1903.12; 1923.27; 1926.10]
Norton, Sara (Charles's daughter) 1913.14
Notes and Queries 1925.81; 1926.39; 1931.54;
    1932.49; 1933.13, 21; 1934.22, 30, 34, 36-37,
    40; 1935.25, 38; 1937.42; 1938.37, 53;
    1939.23
Nouvelles, Les 1910.30
Noyes, Alfred 1929.20-21
Noyes, Carleton 1905.23; 1910.11 [1910.28, 32]

O., J. See Oppenheim, James
O., S. 1921.45
Observer 1922.23
O'Connor, Ellen (William's wife) See Calder, Ellen
O'Connor, William Douglas 1866.2 [1866.3-6, 9, 11-
    12; 1873.2; 1913.2], 10, 27; 1867.5; 1868.5
    [1867.29; 1911.29; 1928.3]; 1876.52 [1876.54];
    1882.48 [1882.53, 64, 67], 63 [1882.68], 94;
    1883.3; 1891.9 [1890.58]; 1893.11; 1896.67;
    1903.12; 1931.1; 1934.24
    [1860.69; 1876.38; 1892.20, 209; 1896.72;
    1897.114; 1900.8; 1902.34, 42; 1903.15;
    1906.4, 13, 58; 1920.2; 1925.18; 1927.17;
    1928.6; 1930.32]
O'Donovan, William R. [1892.53]
O'Dowd, Bernard 1899.51
    [1906.96]
O'Faoláin, Seán 1937.37
O'Grady, Standish James (Arthur Clive) 1875.16
    [1876.9]
    [1934.1]
O'Higgins, Harvey 1924.16; 1929.48 [1930.47];
    1930.15
O'Leary, R. D. 1914.19
Oliver, Egbert S. 1936.47
Ollier, Charles 1875.6
Ollier, Edmund 1856.19 [1875.6]
O'London, John (John o'London) 1921.70
Omar Khayyám [1902.40; 1921.29]
Omond, T. S. 1907.8; 1921.26
Once a Week (London) 1868.45; 1872.12
Once a Week (New York) 1892.198
Onderdonk, James L. 1894.44; 1901.14
One and All 1921.65-66, 68
O'Neil, David 1917.41
Open Court 1891.23a [1891.34], 33a-b; 1892.118;
    1900.20, 38; 1919.74, 333, 340, 346; 1920.34;
    1922.64, 66
Open Road (London) See also Ye Crank 1907.41, 43
Open Road: Official Organ of the Society of the
    Universal Brotherhood of Man (Griffith,
    Indiana) 1912.37
Opera [1860.3; 1895.77; 1898.33; 1910.11; 1917.6,
    20; 1925.60; 1931.6; 1937.45]
Oppenheim, James 1910.27; 1911.23; 1916.28;
    1917.25-26; 1920.55; 1931.18
    [1916.31; 1919.24]
Orage, A. R. 1935.8
Oregon Journal 1919.170
Oregonian. See Portland Oregonian

O'Reilly, John Boyle 1881.31
    [1887.55; 1890.41]
Oriental thought and religion [1866.13, 22;
    1868.3; 1886.46; 1892.200; 1897.149; 1898.30,
    43, 66, 98; 1905.25; 1906.5; 1907.43; 1909.4;
    1910.39; 1911.31; 1913.10, 53; 1914.32;
    1916.19, 63; 1919.45-46, 80, 86, 219, 245,
    320; 1930.4, 19; 1936.33; 1937.20, 25]
Osborne, Clifford Hazeldine 1930.16
Osgood, James H. [1882.38, 41, 49; 1895.80;
    1927.46]
Osler, William 1919.306; 1925.3; 1939.22
    [1924.41; 1936.38; Addenda]
Osmaston, F. P. 1912.40
Ossian [1867.7, 20; 1876.55; 1878.15; 1881.45, 53;
    1882.20; 1892.60; 1908.31; 1919.359; *1931.22;
    1935.10]
Ostrander, Stephen M. 1894.10
Otago Witness (Dunedin, New Zealand) 1906.96
Ottawa (Kansas) Gazette 1879.38
Outlook. See also Christian Union 1895.21;
    1902.65; 1903.42; 1907.19, 24-25, 32;
    1919.156; 1925.76; 1926.79
    [1908.23]
Overland Monthly 1892.160; 1904.25
Overton, Grant Martin 1921.27 [1921.78, 81;
    1922.52; 1926.75]; 1923.11
Overton, Jacqueline 1937.13
Oxford Magazine 1890.2

P. See Porter, Charlotte
P., C. C. 1860.38
P., G. P. 1919.307
P. A. C. (Charlotte Porter and Helen A. Clarke)
    1894.66; 1895.23, 26, 32; 1896.59
Pace, Roy Bennett 1915.15
Pacific Monthly 1901.49
Page, Curtis Hidden 1905.13
Paget, Violet (Vernon Lee) 1908.11
Pain, Barry E. O. 1888.10
Paine, Gregory 1939.41
Paine, Thomas [1877.6; 1892.4; 1914.22; 1922.8;
    1923.19; 1932.47; 1938.2]
Paine, William 1920.23 [1920.66]
Painter, F. V. N. 1897.18
Pall Mall Budget 1886.14; 1888.69; 1892.174
Pall Mall Gazette 1866.13; 1867.17; 1882.37, 69
    [1882.73]; 1886.13, 16, 48, 51-57; 1887.20,
    42, 52, 73; 1888.65; 1889.18; 1891.31, 55;
    1892.50-51, 97, 134, 143
Pall Mall Magazine 1894.42
Palmer, Raymond H. 1919.176
Palmer, Thomas Chalkley 1935.30
Pancoast, Henry S. 1898.13
Papers for the Times (London) 1879.12; 1880.2;
    1886.32
Papers of the Manchester Literary Club. See
    Manchester Literary Club
Papini, Giovanni 1922.16
Papyrus 1904.41
Parke, Walter 1882.8
Parker, Gilbert 1892.81; 1923.33
Parker, Theodore [1867.17; 1882.12; 1920.30]
Parrington, Vernon Louis 1927.18; 1928.10; 1930.17
Parry, Albert 1934.9, 38
Parry, Sir Hubert [1918.64]
Partisan Review 1939.25, 40, 46
Parton, Sarah Payson Willis (Fanny Fern) 1856.13,
    17
    [1934.35]
Parton family [1882.135; 1892.99; 1931.1; 1939.21]

Passaic (New Jersey) Daily News   1915.46
Passing Show   1919.368
Path, The   1886.46
Patmore, Coventry   1900.4
Paton, Jessie   1912.13
Patrick, David   1903.3
Patriotism. See also America and Americanism;
    Whitman--Works--Patriotic Poems   [1918.39
    1919.211, 250, 335]
Pattee, Fred Lewis   1896.80; 1903.11; 1915.16;
    1919.20; 1924.39; 1930.18
Patterson, James   1892.134
Paul, Eden and Charles   1924.1
Paul, Elliot H.   1924.17
Paul, Lydia   1930.43
Paull, H. G.   1919.136
Payne, Leonidas Warren, Jr.   1919.21, 21a
Payne, William Morton   1889.33; 1892.182; 1893.49
Peabody, Josephine Preston   1916.27 [1916.28]
Pearson's Magazine   1917.55; 1919.116, 128
Peck, Harry Thurston   1895.31; 1909.8
Peebles, J[ames] M[artin]   1906.11
Pellew, George   1883.7 [1883.30]
Pennell, Elizabeth Robins   1892.166; 1906.12;
    1929.22
    [1915.59]
Pennell, Joseph   1929.22 [Addenda]
Pennybacker, Isaac R.   1880.5
Pentecost, H. O.   1914.28
Peoria Journal   1916.48
Perplexed Subscriber, A. See Huger, A. M.
Perry, Bliss   1905.41-42; 1906.13 [1906.95, 98-107;
    1907.11-12, 17, 19, 22, 24-25, 29, 35, 48, 54;
    1909.4, 27; 1912.39; 1919.5; 1922.14; 1925.3;
    1926.10; 1931.1, 7]; 1908.14 [1908.35];
    1912.12; 1915.10; 1918.15 [1919.66-67], 66;
    1920.24; 1921.80; 1923.44; 1935.9; Addenda
    [1919.78]

Perry, Jennette Barbour   1898.37 [1898.47]
Perry, Nora   1876.53
Perry, Ralph Barton   1905.14
Perry, Thomas Sergeant   1876.7a, 70
Persian poetry   [1866.13; 1907.43; 1911.31]
Personalist   1928.39; 1931.52; 1934.23; 1938.46
Peterson, Houston   1928.20
Petitt, Maud   1897.19
Petrovich-Niegosch, Mrs. H. G. [S.]. See Appendix
Pfaff's   [1895.39; 1896.16, 49, 53; 1897.51; 1903.14;
    1934.9]
Pfleiderer, Edmund   [1875.9]
    1892.104
Phelps, William Lyon   1919.160; 1923.44, 48; 1924.18;
    1934.10
Philadelphia Call   1886.50
Philadelphia City Item   1860.36
Philadelphia Evening Bulletin   1888.71; 1897.113
Philadelphia Evening Ledger   1915.61; 1916.44
Philadelphia Evening Star   1892.22
Philadelphia Evening Telegraph   1896.54, 69
Philadelphia Inquirer   1889.51-52; 1890.30; 1892.40,
    52, 73, 84, 90; 1908.55
Philadelphia Ledger. See also Philadelphia Evening
    Ledger; Philadelphia Public Ledger   [1903.26]
Philadelphia News   1885.36
Philadelphia North American   1888.68; 1889.53-54;
    1900.42; 1914.21; 1919.322
Philadelphia Press   1880.5, 13-15; 1881.41; 1882.21,
    42, 44, 75-76, 83-84, 86, 99; 1883.11; 1884.25;
    1885.25, 35, 37; 1886.30; 1888.49, 66, 80;
    1889.29-30, 55, 58, 63, 70; 1890.29, 35, 41,

50, 52; 1892.41-42, 53, 74; 1897.135, 137;
    1917.30; 1919.99, 102, 107, 154, 167, 171,
    185
    [1882.102]
Philadelphia Public Ledger. See also Philadelphia
    Evening Ledger; Philadelphia Ledger   1876.67;
    1897.99; 1906.29, 75, 93, 102; 1915.59;
    1919.231-232; 1923.59, 63; 1931.33-34, 36,
    42-44, 47-48, 51
Philadelphia Record   1893.27; 1917.39; 1936.46
Philadelphia Telegraph. See also Philadelphia
    Evening Telegraph   1887.69
Philadelphia Times   1876.16; 1881.50; 1882.18;
    1884.20; 1888.27, 70; 1889.21, 22, 56, 64;
    1890.41; 1893.39; 1901.52
Philistine, The   1900.30, 46; 1901.59; 1906.86;
    1907.52
Phillips, Barnet   1892.105
Phillips, George S. (January Searle)   1860.1, 16, 21
Phillips, Melville   1888.66
Phillips, Stephen   1913.52
    [1906.69]
Phillips, William   1939.25
Phillpotts, Eden   1923.33
Phoenician, The [pseud.]   1926.66
Phoenix   1916.42
Phrenology   1891.22; 1931.23; 1934.32; 1938.9
Physical Culture   1903.40
Piatt, John James   1866.12; 1892.215
    [1868.40]
Pier, Arthur Stanwood   1899.13 [1899.64]
Pierce, Frederick E.   1919.339
Piercy, Josephine K.   1930.14
Pierra [pseud.?]   1938.39
Pilot, The (Boston)   1881.31
Pioneer Press   1881.52
Pittsburgh Gazette Times   1918.27
Plato   [1856.7; 1890.59; 1907.17; 1908.13; 1910.11;
    1914.15; 1915.35]
Platt, Chester C.   1923.44
Platt, Dr. Isaac Hull   1894.29, 36; 1895.51;
    1901.34; 1902.41, 57; 1903.26; 1904.12
    [1904.46-47; 1905.26; 1906.45; 1932.49];
    1906.31, 45, 71, 99; 1907.11, 29, 48, 54;
    1908.23, 35, 43; 1915.10
    [1894.55; 1901.37]
Platt, William   1899.63; 1901.48; 1905.40
Playboy   1919.63
Poe, Edgar Allan   1845.1-3
    [1875.11; 1878.16; 1882.69; 1889.37; 1892.27,
    91, 181; 1893.45; 1896.69; 1897.8, 13, 162;
    1899.7; 1900.16; 1901.10, 19; 1904.15; 1905.41;
    1906.9; 1908.5; 1909.3, 7; 1910.47; 1911.8,
    24; 1912.43-44; 1913.46; 1915.23; 1916.32, 58;
    1917.8; 1918.15, 51, 63, 73; 1919.29, 37, 59,
    69, 104-105, 158, 201, 214, 266, 286, 351,
    359; 1920.19, 39; 1921.10, 53; 1922.13, 39,
    61; 1924.26; 1925.9; 1926.24, 44, 60; 1927.42;
    1928.6; 1930.14a; 1933.5; 1935.17; 1937.3, 6;
    1938.25; 1939.43]
Poet Lore   1889.24, 59; 1890.39; 1891.54; 1892.17,
    77, 159, 203-204, 210, 222; 1893.25, 29-30,
    38, 43; 1894.21, 23, 52, 54, 57, 63, 66;
    1895.18, 23, 47, 65, 81; 1896.30, 51, 59;
    1897.22-23, 55-57, 100, 147; 1898.20-21, 49,
    81a, 82-83, 96; 1899.22-23; 1905.46; 1906.94;
    1911.23
Poetry   1912.44, 47-48; 1913.34; 1914.43-44;
    1919.28, 46, 58-59, 75, 118-119, 131, 134-135,
    280, 354, 356, 366, 375-376; 1930.38; 1936.56;
    1939.19

Poetry Journal 1917.41, 53
Poetry Review 1912.22, 42; 1913.52; 1918.25;
    1919.341
Poet's Magazine 1929.31; 1930.22
Politics and political philosophy. See also Democ-
    racy; Socialism [1840; 1841; 1846.3; 1847.2-
    3; 1848.1-6, 9-12; 1849.2, 5-6, 8; 1850.1, 3;
    1890.41; 1895.6; 1899.22, 59; 1902.42; 1914.15;
    1916.53; 1918.16; 1920.25; 1923.19, 21, 32,
    53; 1924.29; 1928.11; 1929.44; 1930.35;
    1933.7, 24; 1937.40; 1938.2]
Pollard, Marguerite, F. T. S. 1913.53
Pollock, Frederick 1879.3
Pond, Major J. B. 1900.13
    1887.32
Poore, Ben: Perley 1868.44; 1871.5, 25, 27;
    [1873.3]
Poore, Charles 1939.32 [1939.33], 38
Pope, Alexander [1882.104; 1904.6, 16]
Pope, Bertha Clark 1922.17
Popoff, Dr. P. 1883.24
Popularity polls [1893.33; 1922.41; 1923.29-30, 33,
    44; 1937.33-34]
Porter, Charlotte [I. N. Cog]. See also P. A. C.
    1889.24; 1893.25, 29; 1894.23; 1895.19, 22
    [22a, 24], 64, 65, 70; 1896.58-59; 1897.23,
    57; 1898.21, 83
Porter, Harold Everett (Holworthy Hall) 1913.41
Porter, Katherine Anne 1939.40
Porterfield, Allen Wilson 1921.67
Portland Oregon Journal. See Oregon Journal
Portland Oregonian 1912.43; 1915.25; 1917.28
Portraits d'Hier 1911.25
Posey, Meredith N. See Appendix
Positivist Review 1921.57
Posnett, Hutcheson Macaulay 1886.5
Potter, Grace 1906.77
Pound, Ezra 1910.12; 1913.34; 1914.44 [1914.43];
    1917.16; 1922.61; 1934.11; Addenda
    [1917.4; 1922.60, 64; 1925.31; 1928.8; 1937.18]
Pound, Louise 1925.24, 28, 60; 1926.46; 1930.23;
    1935.10 [1935.44]
Pound, Dean Roscoe 1923.44
Powell, Charles 1920.25 [1920.59, 61]
Powell, F. G. Montagu 1913.15
Powell, Lawrence Clark 1931.58; 1934.11
Powell, York [1934.1]
Powers, Horatio N. 1885.40
Powers, L. M. 1902.44
Powys, John Cowper 1904.13; 1915.17; 1916.14;
    1920.72; 1929.23; 1934.13; 1938.13
    [1917.28; 1919.291]
Prada, Carlos Garcia 1928.21
Praed, Winthrop [1865.9]
Pratt, Julius W. 1917.23
Presbyterian Journal 1888.52
Prescott, Frederick Clarke 1922.18
Pressley, Ruth Peyton. See Appendix
Price, Abby (mother of Helen) [1908.53; 1928.36;
    1933.6]
Price, Helen 1883.3; 1919.265
    [1908.53]
Price, Lawrence Marsen 1919.42; 1920.63
Primitive Methodist Quarterly Review 1894.38
Proceedings of the New Jersey Historical Society.
    See New Jersey
Proctor, Thomas 1893.31
Progress 1879.8; 1880.10; 1881.20; 1882.124;
    1887.13
Progressive Review 1896.71; 1897.39, 60, 122
Prohme, William 1920.91

Pro Patria et Rege [1915.58]
Prophet, The See Dreiser, Theodore
Proust, Marcel [1920.64]
Providence Evening Bulletin 1932.35
Providence Journal. See also Providence Sunday
    Journal 1899.60; 1908.21; 1932.36
Providence Sunday Journal. See also Providence
    Journal 1911.29
Prowell, George R. 1886.6
Public Opinion (London) 1867.9; 1868.29; 1918.44
Public Opinion (Washington and New York) 1887.16,
    27, 42, 69, 83; 1888.53; 1890.56; 1892.90,
    127, 185, 196, 221; 1897.119-120, 154;
    1898.48, 68
Public Service Journal (Wellington, New Zealand)
    1917.51
Publications of the Modern Language Association
    1916.61; 1929.59
Publishers (Whitman's) See also Whitman--Advertising;
    Suppression [1875.13; 1876.10, 17, 61 (and
    passim)]; 1881.30-31, 36; 1885.16; 1888.15;
    1895.80; 1896.33; 1897.126; 1912.31; 1917.38,
    49; 1919.250]
Publishers' Weekly 1923.35, 37; 1927.52; 1930.29;
    1936.36, 44, 57; 1939.24
Puck 1880.34, 37; 1885.5; 1914.45
"Puck" [pseud.] 1885.5
Punch 1856.15; 1887.76; 1890.54; 1892.128; 1911.26
Puritanism [1905.1; 1906.94; 1915.55; 1916.61;
    1919.182, 240, 267; 1920.92, 102; 1921.71;
    1922.49; 1923.62; 1927.6; 1928.10; 1929.13;
    1930.17; 1932.18]
Putnam, Frank 1907.30; 1908.43
Putnam's Magazine 1868.5
Putnam's Monthly 1855.6; 1907.23; 1908.50, 53;
    1909.29
Pythian Journalists' Club (Elkton, Maryland)
    [1885.41; 1886.15]

Q. See Quiller-Couch, Sir Arthur T.
Q. 1901.6
Quaero [pseud.] 1931.35
Quakerism. See also Hicks, Elias [1890.38;
    1897.7; 1905.1; 1906.46; 1910.25; 1916.21;
    1919.192; 1920.82, 92; 1921.8, 66; 1922.1;
    1924.16; 1929.17; 1930.9, 19; 1931.6, 27;
    1933.8; 1938.2, 9]
Quarterly Journal of Speech 1932.25
Quarterly Journal of the University of North Dakota
    1919.336
Quarterly Review 1886.41
Quartier Latin 1897.27
Queen 1923.36
Queen's Quarterly 1899.73
Quercus, P. E. G. 1939.39
Querist [pseud.] 1923.60
Quest 1912.20, 40
Quick, Tom 1862.2
Quiller-Couch, Sir Arthur T. 1890.1; 1916.15
Quilp See Johnston, George
Quincy, Josiah Phillips [1935.9]
Quinn, Arthur Hobson 1894.61; 1929.24
Quinn, John [1922.11]

R. See Raper, R. W.
R. 1892.106
R., A. 1925.65
R., C. F. 1888.23
R., H. J. See Hinton, Richard
R., J. 1919.343
R., J. G. 1904.46

R., Q. 1919.321
R., T. W. See Rolleston, T. W. H.
Rabelais [1860.17; 1867.7; 1882.33; 1904.3; 1938.13]
Radical 1866.15; 1867.22; 1870.4
Radical Review 1877.13; 1892.142
Raffalovich, André 1892.153
Rahv, Philip 1939.35
Railway World 1915.28
Rains Galleries, New York 1936.21
Randall, Alec W. G. 1919.44; Addenda
Randall, John Herman 1916.16
     [1926.53]
Random, Jack 1915.28
Random, Roderick [pseud.] 1890.26
Rankin, Henry B. 1916.17; 1924.20 [1928.3]
Rankin, Prof. J. E. 1892.155
Raper, R. W. 1890.1
Rascoe, Burton 1919.266, 318, 366; 1923.44; 1932.18
Ratcliffe (or Ratliffe), S. K. 1901.23; 1919.209
Raymond, Charles A. [1938.23]
Raymond, George Lansing 1893.8; 1894.11-12
Read, Herbert 1926.65; 1935.8
Reader, A 1892.139
Reader Magazine 1905.28; 1906.84
Realism [1887.63; 1894.25; 1896.71; 1901.19;
     1902.1, 6; 1911.8; 1915.16; 1916.32; 1917.11,
     27; 1919.151, 378; 1924.1; 1925.4; 1926.41;
     1928.9-10; 1929.58; 1936.2; 1939.10]
Reason 1913.30
Rebel Poet 1931.55-56; 1932.48
Read and Blue, The (University of Pennsylvania)
     1849.61
Reed, Harry B. 1934.23
Reed, John 1912.30; Addenda
Reede, Edward H. 1924.16
Reedy, William Marion 1919.344
Reedy's Mirror 1917.40; 1918.29; 1919.175, 204,
     344, 348
Rees Welsh & Co. [1882.102, 110]
Reeves, Harrison 1921.31
Referee 1919.374
Reformed Church Review 1912.35
Reformer, The 1902.32
Reger, Rees R. 1922.38
Reid, Whitelaw 1874.12; 1915.10
Reinhardt, Aurelia Henry 1934.14
Reinhart, Mary R. 1922.19
Reisiger, Hans [1922.63]
Reitzel, Robert 1896.30
Religion. See also Christ and Christianity;
     Christian Science; Churches; Mysticism;
     Quakerism; Puritanism; Oriental thought and
     religion [1878.17; 1886.46; 1890.3; 1892.28;
     1893.9, 11; 1894.48, 66; 1895.13, 67; 1896.2;
     1897.7, 11; 1901.3, 34; 1903.22; 1906.34, 92;
     1909.35; 1910.11; 1911.30; 1913.19; 1916.21;
     1919.73, 202, 216, 279, 320, 340; 1920.30;
     1921.8, 13; 1922.1, 16, 49; 1928.28; 1930.9,
     19; 1931.52; 1934.32; 1937.41; 1938.2, 9]
Renan, Ernest [1893.11]
Repplier, Agnes 1888.47; 1923.44
Republic, The 1883.14-15
Review, The (New York) 1919.246
Review of Reviews. See also American Review of
     Reviews 1890.60; 1891.16, 28, 41; 1892.193
Revista d'Italia 1904.42
Revue Anglo-Américaine 1930.47; 1931.25; 1932.30;
     1933.27
Revue Bleue 1892.205; 1910.31; 1919.90
Revue des Deux Mondes 1872.18 [1872.20]
Reynolds, Stephen M. 1899.61; 1903.38

Rhav, Philip See Rahv, Philip
Rhys, Ernest 1886.7 [1886.32]; 1889.9, 47;
     1892.106; 1894.13; 1913.29; 1919.137, 138;
     1923.33; 1931.19
     [1888.11, 14, 19; 1889.27, 31; 1920.11;
     1934.1]
Rice, Allen Thorndike 1886.6
Rice, Cale Young 1919.378
Richardson, Charles F. 1876.64; 1878.5; 1884.11;
     1888.4
     [1906.13]
Richardson, Dorothy M. 1921.28
Richter, Milo C. 1923.42
Rickaby, John, S. J. 1889.5
Rickert, Edith 1912.13
Rickett, Arthur (Arthur Compton-Rickett) 1898.16;
     1906.14; 1918.8
Ridge, Lola 1919.37
     [1927.56]
Ridley, Hilda M. 1923.43
Riethmueller, Richard 1906.15 [1906.45]
Riley, James Whitcomb [1893.11; 1896.77; 1899.37;
     1919.2; 1921.51]
Riley, W. Harrison 1903.45
     [1910.16]
Ripley, George 1876.3
Rittenhouse, Jessie B. 1906.33; 1916.56
     [1919.314]
Ritter, Professor [1887.32]
Rivers, W[alter] C[ourtenay] 1911.19 [1911.22];
     1913.16 [1915.11]
Roberts, Cecil 1922.40, 44
Roberts, Charles G. D. 1884.17; 1888.5
Roberts, Harry 1904.14
Roberts, Mary Eleanor 1916.6
Roberts, Morley 1912.14; 1927.19
Robertson, J[ames] Logie 1894.14
Robertson, John MacKinnon 1884.12
Robins, Edward 1915.59
Robinson, Boardman 1920.54 [1920.56]
Robinson, Charles 1893.15
Robinson, Edwin Arlington 1896.11
     [1919.94; 1939.34]
Robinson, Landon 1926.42
Robinson, Victor 1907.33
Robinson, William J. 1913.38
Rochester Evening Express 1868.12
Rockell, Frederick 1899.48
Rodd, Sir James Rennell 1922.20
Rodgers, Cleveland 1920.26
     [1920.100-101; 1921.37, 40, 44, 46, 48, 52-53,
     69, 76, 81; 1922.36, 51]; 1921.77; 1923.49, 53;
     1930.35, 46; 1933.24
     [1936.49; 1938.49]
Rodin, Auguste [1913.36; 1919.59]
Roe, Charles A. 1895.27
     [1902.33]
Rogers, Bruce 1927.28
Rogers, Cameron 1926.24 [1926.42-45, 48, 52, 67,
     75, 79]
Rogers, Cleveland See Rodgers, Cleveland
Rogers, Frank J. [1905.38, 39, 43, 55]
Rogers, George 1888.68
Rolland, Romain 1916.65; 1923.33; 1930.19
Rolleston, T. W. H. 1877.2; 1884.15; 1889.9;
     1892.15, 107; 1893.11
     [1888.63; 1889.31; 1890.58; 1934.1]
Rollins, Carl Purington 1930.24
Romanticism [1881.45; 1894.61; 1906.13; 1916.56,
     61; 1918.15; 1919.378; 1923.38; 1925.4;
     1926.41; 1928.9-10; 1929.8; 1930.17, 23;

1931.2, 6; 1932.14; 1936.27; 1937.22; 1939.10]
Rome, Andrew (and his printing shop) [1890.7;
    1917.6; 1921.63; 1931.39-42]
Romig, Edna Davis 1919.156; 1926.54
Roosa, Dr. D. B. St. John 1896.53
Roose, Pauline W. 1892.168
Roosevelt, Theodore 1915.10
    [1919.162, 344; 1938.49]
Ropes, John F. 1842.3, 5, 6
Rorty, James [1927.38]
Rose, Ray Clarke 1901.15
Rose-Belford's Canadian Monthly and National Review.
    See also Canadian Monthly and National Review
    1880.20, 21
Rosenberg, Harold 1939.40
Ross, E. C. 1930.37
Ross, Peter 1902.23
Ross, Robert 1908.18
Rossetti, Dante Gabriel 1895.9; 1896.57
    [1872.2; 1886.16; 1904.4; 1906.16]
Rossetti, William Michael 1867.13 [1867.14];
    1868.2 [1868.13-14, 16, 18-22, 26, 29, 37;
    1905.19]; 1870.4; 1872.5; 1876.27; 1878.6;
    1887.6, 64; 1889.9; 1892.9, 15; 1895.9;
    1899.14; 1903.12; 1906.16; 1915.10; 1931.1;
    1934.5 [1935.22]
    [1875.15; 1882.91; 1883.1; 1885.16; 1888.24;
    1889.64; 1900.8; 1906.13; 1917.42; 1921.29;
    1925.54; 1929.22; 1933.10; 1934.1]
Rotarian 1939.47
Rothwell, Fred 1925.16
Round Table 1865.5, 7; 1866.4, 8, 10, 17, 23;
    1867.4-6, 21, 28, 30; 1868.7, 15, 24, 25, 30,
    43
    [1935.39]
Rourke, Constance Mayfield 1927.20; 1931.20
Rousseau, Jean Jacques [1876.28; 1889.37; 1894.28;
    1895.76; 1896.47; 1906.13; 1907.17; 1909.5;
    1910.25; 1926.9; 1931.2; 1937.39; 1938.43]
Rowan, John [1933.16]
Rowlandson, H. 1886.34
Royal Society of Canada, Proceedings and Transactions
    of 1906.6
Rubens, Peter Paul [1882.33]
Rubin, Joseph Jay 1937.40; 1938.31-32; 1939.23
    [1939.29]
Rukeyser, Muriel 1934.21
Runnymede, Ralph 1919.267
Ruotolo, Onorio [1925.71]
Ruskin, John 1908.15
    [1880.4, 7; 1882.94; 1900.28; 1903.45;
    1913.14; 1934.1]
Russell, A. J. 1901.16; 1919.268
Russell, Bertrand 1916.18
    [1919.121]
Russell, Charles Edward [1921.59]; Addenda
Russell, Mary Annette 1899.15
Russell, Phillips 1917.18; 1919.139; 1922.59
Russia [1911.16; 1915.57; 1916.57; 1919.88; 1930.7;
    1931.18; 1932.17; 1934.38; 1935.32]
Rutherford, Mark See White, W. Hale
Rutherford, Mildred 1894.15

S. 1892.135
S., A. E. See Smythe, A. E. S.
S., G. S. 1926.55
S., G. W. See Smalley, G. W.
S., H. S. See Salt, Henry S.
S., J. See Spargo, John
S., J. A. 1907.32
S., J. F. 1876.59

S., J. K. See Stephen, James Kenneth
S., J. M. See Scovel, Col. James Matlack
S., R. C. 1919.301
Saben, Mowry 1913.45; 1914.14
Saerasmid [pseud.?] 1860.6-7, 11
Saigyo [1909.17]
Saint-Gaudens, Augustus [1887.38; 1906.18; 1913.17]
Saint-Gaudens, Homer 1913.17
Saint James's Gazette 1887.78; 1892.62
Saint James's Magazine 1875.6
Saint John (New Brunswick) Weekly Globe 1919.305
Saint Louis Globe-Democrat 1879.19, 25; 1882.29,
    71; 1897.93
Saint Louis Hesperian 1899.39
Saint Louis Missouri Republican 1879.20
Saint Louis Post-Dispatch 1879.41
Saintsbury, George 1874.10 [1935.1]; 1876.8;
    1904.15; 1910.13; 1912.15; Addenda
    [1875.17]
Saleeby, C. W. 1919.33
Salmon, Edward 1892.224
Salt, Henry S. 1886.44; 1896.12-13; 1897.104;
    1905.52; 1921.29
Salter, William Mackintire 1889.9; 1899.16
    [1900.20, 22, 24]; 1900.26
Saltus, Francis [1879.6]
Sammis, Mrs. Irving S. 1938.33
    [1913.50]
Samuel, Ruth A. 1934.41
San Francisco Bulletin 1916.60
San Francisco Chronicle 1889.15; 1892.43, 54, 212;
    1897.118; 1919.52
    [1884.22]
San Francisco Examiner 1901.62-63; 1915.27;
    1919.291; 1920.91
Sanborn, F[rank] B. 1866.14; 1876.49; 1881.6;
    1882.9 [1883.12]; 1889.9; 1893.48; 1894.16
    [1938.16]; 1895.83; 1897.78 [1897.80];
    1899.59; 1905.41; 1917.13
    [1898.85]
Sanborn, Kate 1886.9; 1915.18
Sanborn, Mary F. 1909.9
Sand, George [1876.70; 1887.6; 1898.29; 1900.8;
    1907.17; 1926.51; 1936.23; 1938.2, 17]
Sand-Burr Magazine 1907.55
Sandburg, Carl 1921.30; 1938.15
    [1914.26; 1919.24, 273; 1920.94; 1922.60, 64;
    1924.24; 1926.50; 1927.36; 1928.38; 1936.56;
    1937.9; 1939.3]
Sanders, Lloyd C. 1887.5
Santayana, George 1890.22; 1896.14; 1898.14;
    1900.14 [1900.31; 1920.15]; 1913.18; 1915.34;
    1935.11
Sappho [1887.69]
Sarkar, Benoy Kumar 1916.19; 1917.48
Sarony, Napoleon 1892.86-87
Sarrazin, Gabriel 1889.9; 1893.11 [1913.46;
    1929.51]; 1908.40
    [1889.72; 1890.58; 1924.12]
Saturday Evening Post 1900.21; 1905.37, 44a;
    1907.58; 1920.81
Saturday Night. See Toronto Saturday Night
Saturday Press. See New York Saturday Press
Saturday Review (London) 1856.9 [1926.20]; 1860.46;
    1867.19 [1867.21]; 1868.26; 1876.32; 1889.26;
    1892.91 [1892.152]; 1898.70, 95; 1906.28
Saturday Review of Literature 1925.35, 52-53;
    1926.33, 36, 41, 52, 66, 76; 1927.27-28, 39,
    43, 56; 1928.33; 1929.40, 51; 1930.24, 30;
    1932.31; 1934.35, 49-50; 1935.23-24, 30, 44;
    1936.43, 54; 1937.32, 34; 1938.27, 54;
    1939.27, 39

Saturday Westminster Gazette 1914.27
Saunders, Henry S. 1915.10; 1916.48; 1918.11;
    1919.141; 1921.31; 1923.12-13; 1924.21;
    1927.21
    [1922.15; 1929.22; 1931.13; 1932.35-36;
    1937.45]
Saurat, Dennis 1935.8
Savage, Minot Judson 1877.3; 1894.48 [1894.52];
    1898.104; 1899.17; 1905.41
Savage, Philip Henry 1897.62
Sawyer, Philip 1926.78
Sawyer, Roland Douglas 1913.19 [1913.49]
Sayler, Oliver M. 1930.20
Scheffauer, Herman 1915.24
Schelling, Felix 1907.40
Schelling, Friedrich von [1936.2]
Schiller, Friedrich von [1906.32]
Schinz, Albert 1911.24; 1913.46; 1921.31
Schlaf, Johannes [1904.27; 1906.70, 76; 1907.38;
    1921.34; Addenda]
Schlegel, Friedrich von [1938.17]
Schmidt, Rudolf 1889.9; 1892.15; 1893.11
Schnittkind, H. T. (Henry Thomas) 1938.19
Scholastic 1937.43
Scholes, C. W. 1901.49
Schoolmaster 1919.233
Schools. See Universities and Schools; Education;
    Textbooks; Whitman--Schoolteaching
Schopenhauer, Arthur [1875.9]
Schreiner, Olive 1924.6a
    [1888.59; 1931.19]
Schumaker, J. G. 1892.117
Schwartz, Dr. Jacob 1936.22 1936.36-38
Schwarz, Vernolian 1932.11
Schwiefert, Fritz 1922.63
Science. See also Astronomy; Evolution [1890.20;
    1893.20, 30; 1894.44; 1895.5, 25; 1896.2, 45;
    1919.240; 1931.9; 1934.32; 1935.10; 1936.53;
    1938.2]
Scotsman (Edinburgh) 1925.54-57, 61-65, 67
Scott, Colin A. 1896.23
Scott, Dixon 1914.32
Scott, Fred Newton 1908.31
Scott, Lady Sybil [1918.61]
Scott, Sir Walter [1847.1; 1887.6, 39; 1898.29;
    1930.26, 27; 1936.30; 1938.2, 20; 1939.23]
Scott, William Bell 1892.9; 1899.14
    [1868.2; 1871.2; 1933.10]
Scott-James, R. A. 1922.46
    [1917.4]
Scottish Art Review 1889.32, 47
Scottish Review 1882.117; 1883.34; 1889.60
Scovel, Col. James Matlack 1875.7; 1885.16; 1904.35
    [1889.54]
Scribner's Magazine 1919.283
Scribner's Monthly. See also Century Magazine
    1873.8; 1876.19, 56, 69; 1877.11; 1878.16;
    1879.43; 1880.35; 1881.21, 34-35
    [1935.39]
Scudder, Horace E. 1887.61; 1892.183 [1892.192,
    203 ; 1903.12]
    [1934.43]
Scudder, Vida 1898.15
Sea [1886.1; 1909.10; 1918.61; 1928.38, 41]
Seaman, Owen 1896.15
Searle, January. See Phillips, George S.
Sears, Lorenzo 1899.18
Seaver, Edwin 1925.37, 70
Seccombe, Thomas 1919.294
Secular Review 1880.8
Secularist 1876.7

Sedgwick, A. G. 1878.14
Sedgwick, Henry D., Jr. 1897.67
Seeger, Alan [1919.173]
Self Culture 1899.75
Seltzer, Adele 1913.42
Selwyn, George [pseud. for Walt Whitman] 1885.10;
    1888.6
Sempers, Charles T. 1888.7
Sercombe, Parker H. 1906.78
Seven Arts 1916.65; 1917.25-27, 43
Sewanee Review 1911.17; 1914.18; 1917.17; 1919.29;
    1925.32; 1927.25; 1928.32; 1929.32
Sex. See also Homosexuality; Woman; Whitman--
    Children, Immorality, Works--"Children of
    Adam," "To a Common Prostitute," "A Woman
    Waits for Me" [1866.2; 1872.2; 1887.74-75;
    1888.4; 1892.60; 1893.9, 40; 1896.39, 46;
    1898.16; 1899.4, 74; 1902.32; 1903.9; 1905.10,
    26; 1906.34, 99; 1907.1; 1909.34; 1910.38;
    1913.38; 1914.5, 18; 1915.54; 1916.19, 24;
    1918.29, 47, 54; 1919.14, 18, 66, 149, 334;
    1920.5, 14, 88, 92; 1921.13, 20; 1922.8, 30,
    54; 1924.16; 1925.18; 1927.53; 1931.6, 23;
    1932.11; 1938.9]
Shakespeare, William [1864.5; 1866.2; 1872.1;
    1875.2, 16; 1877.3; 1881.5; 1886.45; 1887.6;
    1888.42; 1890.6; *1890.39; *1891.54; 1892.147;
    1894.17, 51; 1895.33; 1897.26, 30, 59; 1898.29,
    34, 55; 1899.76; 1900.15; 1901.3, 44; 1905.14;
    1906.14, 36; 1907.27, 33; 1908.31; 1911.20;
    1914.4; 1915.48; 1916.43; 1919.166; 1920.88;
    1923.39; 1925.18; 1926.31; 1929.54, *59
    *1932.23; 1934.5, 31; 1938.20]
Shanks, Edward 1923.36
Sharp, Elizabeth A. (William's wife) 1910.14
Sharp, R. Farquharson 1898.15a
Sharp, William 1889.6; 1898.88; 1904.26
    [1910.14; 1937.1]
Shaw, Francis G. [1938.17]
Shaw, George Bernard 1923.33
    [1906.31; 1919.94]
Shay, Frank 1920.27
Sheffield (England) Independent 1920.68
Sheffield (England) Weekly Independent 1892.92-94
Shelley, Percy Bysshe [1874.9; 1880.1a; 1892.16;
    1894.22, 36; 1896.13, 31, 51; 1903.35;
    1906.14; 1908.29; 1919.8-9, 166; 1922.4;
    1926.1; 1927.56; 1936.2]
Shepard, George 1858.1
Shepard, Odell 1938.16; Addenda
Shepard, William See Walsh, William Shepard
Shephard, Esther 1936.23; 1938.17 [1938.26-28, 34,
    47, 54; 1939.17, 21; Appendix]
Sherard, Robert Harborough 1906.17; 1916.20
Sherlock, Chesla C. 1926.26
Sherman, Stuart Pratt 1918.10; 1919.270; 1921.35,
    71; 1922.21-22; 1923.15; 1925.36; 1926.27, 57;
    1932.19; Addenda
Shillito, Rev. Edward 1919.191
Shipley, Maynard 1906.92; 1919.340
Shoemaker, W. L. 1881.51
Shotover Papers (Oxford) 1874.2
Shulman, J. L. 1935.35
Shuman, Edwin L. 1910.15
Shuster, George Nauman 1917.36; 1926.35
Siamanto [1919.96]
Sidgwick, Henry [1923.1]
Sidney, Sir Philip [1888.81]
Siegel, Eli [1925.70]
Sigma (New York Daily Tribune) See Stoddard, Richard
    Henry

Sigma [pseud.?] (New York Evening Mail) 1870.7
Silver, Rollo G. 1930.13; 1932.27; 1933.17 [1935.16];
    1934.20, 34, 37, 40, 50; 1935.17, 20-21, 40;
    1936.24, 34; 1937.24, 27 [1937.38]; 1938.22-
    23, 53
Simonds, Arthur B. 1894.17 [1894.63]
Simonds, William Edward 1906.104; 1909.10, 31
Sinclair, May 1924.22
Sixbey, George L. 1937.41
Skinner, Charles M. 1903.49
Slavery. See Blacks
Slenker, Elmina D. (Elmina) 1882.66, 114 [1882.123],
    126, 133
Slocombe, G. E. 1919.32
Small, Herbert 1897.83
Smalley, G. W. 1868.27; 1876.34; 1892.114
Smart Set 1911.28; 1913.27; 1915.55
Smiley, James B. 1905.15
Smith, Bernard 1932.45; 1939.10
Smith, Byron Caldwell [1922.8]
Smith, Elizabeth Oake [1899.27]
Smith, George James (Dr. George Jay Smith) 1891.10;
    1898.65, 105; 1902.49; 1903.33a; 1906.94;
    1918.56; 1919.31; 1923.44
    [1919.315; 1920.103]
Smith, H. J. 1919.367
Smith, Henry Justin 1936.17
Smith, Hyacinth Stoddart 1919.271
Smith, J. C. 1938.4
Smith, Joseph [1882.8]
Smith, Lewis Worthington 1923.51
Smith, Logan Pearsall 1918.37; 1937.46
    [1924.41]
Smith, Mary (Logan's sister). See Costelloe
Smith, Robert Pearsall (Logan's and Mary's father)
    1889.9
    [1884.7; 1887.32; 1889.10; 1915.18; 1931.1;
    1937.24, 46]
Smith, Thomas Kile 1914.15
Smith, Wayland Hyatt 1898.66; 1905.41
Smith, William, F. S. A. S. 1892.10
Smith, William Hawley (and Mrs.) 1909.43; 1913.39;
    1916.48; 1918.43 [1918.41]
    [1905.33; 1922.33]
Smuts, General Jan Christian Addenda [1936.19]
Smyth, Albert E. 1896.16 [1897.41]
Smythe, A. E. S. 1911.27; 1913.32, 44; 1915.35, 38;
    1916.26, 52; 1917.29; 1918.32; 1919.142-143,
    192, 320; 1924.36
Snow (caricaturist) 1909.34
Snow, Wilbert 1926.68
Snyder, John Edwin 1909.20
Socialism [1887.86; 1888.43; 1891.13; 1895.16;
    1898.60; 1899.71; 1900.39; 1902.58; 1906.88;
    1908.45; 1909.20; 1912.42; 1915.24, 40;
    1916.22; 1917.34, 39, 56; 1919.247, 308,
    325, 355; 1920.63, 65; 1923.31; 1931.16;
    1932.7; 1933.34; 1935.31-32; 1937.22; 1938.2,
    21, 42; 1939.10, 40]
Socialist Woman 1909.20
Socrates [1885.27; 1887.3; 1893.37; 1899.17;
    1908.13; 1927.47]
South Atlantic Quarterly 1917.23, 35; 1921.49
Southern Field and Fireside 1860.30
Southern Literary Messenger 1939.43
Southern Review (Baltimore) 1871.6
Southern Review (Baton Rouge) 1937.23
Southwest Review 1925.24, 47; 1927.48
Southwick, Albert P. 1883.8
Spaeth, Duncan [1923.54]
Spain [1916.7]
Spargo, John 1901.55; 1903.24, 45; 1910.16

Spaulding, Mrs. A. H. 1889.9
    [1888.19; 1889.27]
Speaker, the Liberal Review (London) 1892.104
Spectator 1860.51; 1883.28; 1891.24; 1892.195;
    1898.71; 1919.312; 1922.43; 1937.37
Spedding, W. 1894.38
Speight, Ernest Edwin 1899.19
Speirs, Russell F. 1930.34
Spencer, Rev. Mrs. Anna Garlin 1923.44
Spencer, Herbert [1899.79; 1900.14; 1930.17]
Spencer, Lilian White 1923.64
Spender, Stephen 1938.43; 1939.5
Spenser, Edmund [1872.1; 1898.102]
Sphinx, Lambkin [pseud.?] 1906.52 [1906.61]
Spier, Leonard 1931.56; 1935.32
Spingarn, Dr. Joel E. 1923.44
Spinoza, Baruch [1856.7; 1874.8; 1888.7; 1920.35]
Spirit Lamp 1892.216, 219
Spirit of the Times 1859.4
Spiritual Magazine 1870.3
Spiritualism [1870.3; 1911.6; 1913.30; 1919.25,
    121a]
Spooner, Alden 1838.1
Sprague, Harriet [Mrs. Frank Julian Sprague]
    1939.13
Sprague, Leslie Willis 1903.13
Sprague, Mrs. Frank Julian. See Sprague, Harriet
Spring, Howard 1938.18
Springfield (Massachusetts) Daily Republican
    1860.35; 1871.10; 1875.7; 1876.9, 49;
    1880.27; 1881.42; 1882.45, 106; 1885.16;
    1887.19, 77; 1888.83; 1892.55; 1899.24
Squire, J. C. (Solomon Eagle) 1919.328; 1920.11, 28;
    1922.23
Stacpoole, H. de Vere 1923.33
Stafford family. See also Timber Creek [1877.14;
    1897.39; 1917.6; 1933.16, 31; 1935.28;
    1936.50; Addenda]
Staffordshire (Hanley, England) Sentinel 1923.22
Standard 1919.140
Stanton, Theodore 1909.5; 1922.62, 63
Starke, Aubrey 1933.29
Starkweather, Chauncey C. 1900.15
State Service 1921.63
Stead, Robert 1922.24
Stead, W. T. 1892.135; 1895.10 [1896.25]
Stedman, Arthur 1892.11 [1892.214-215, 218, 221,
    233], 12 [1892.154, 182, 188, 196; 1898.57];
    1900.16
    [1887.32; 1937.1]
Stedman, Edmund Clarence 1875.5; 1876.38; 1880.35
    [1881.35, 38; 1895.53; 1908.7; 1910.17;
    1925.32], 1881.26, 35; 1883.16; 1885.6
    [1885.40; 1886.12], 30; 1889.9; 1892.13, 15,
    118; 1900.16 [1901.19, 51]; 1901.42; 1908.49;
    1910.17; 1915.10; 1931.1
    [1876.37; 1882.134; 1887.32, 59; 1888.61;
    1889.37; 1891.29; 1892.32; 1895.6; 1909.37;
    1918.7; 1928.13; 1931.11]
Stedman, Laura 1910.17 [1909.37]
Steell, Willis 1909.18
Stein, Gertrude 1935.12
Stephen, James Kenneth 1891.11 [1891.24]
Stephen, Leslie 1879.3; 1906.9
Stepniak (Russian Nihilist) [1889.44]
Sterling (Kansas) Rice County Gazette 1879.36
Sterling (Kansas) Weekly Bulletin 1879.37
Stetson, Grace Channing [1937.1]
Stevens, District Attorney [1882.62, 78, 93]
Stevens, Dr. Thomas Wood 1923.44
Stevens, Wallace 1936.25; 1939.40

Stevenson, Burton E.　1910.18
Stevenson, Edward Irenaeus Prime (Xavier Mayne)
　　1908.13
Stevenson, Lionel　1931.53
Stevenson, Philip　1938.42
Stevenson, Robert Louis　1878.17; 1882.11 [1887.56;
　　1900.44]; 1887.44; 1899.5; 1911.5
　　[1901.1; 1902.8; 1908.36; 1909.22; 1919.4,
　　141; 1934.1]
Stewart, George R., Jr.　1925.32
Stewart, Jane A.　1919.157
Stiles, Henry R.　1870.2
Stillman, W. J.　1903.12
Stocker, R[ichard] Dimsdale　1909.11
Stockton, Frank R.　[1887.32]
Stodart-Walker, A.　1914.16
Stoddard, Charles Warren　1908.52
Stoddard, Richard Henry　1866.4; 1876.42; 1881.7;
　　1882.64; 1888.55; 1896.53; 1900.15; 1903.14
　　[1882.134; 1889.37; 1890.13; 1893.43]
Stoddart, Joseph M.　[1907.7]
Stoddart, Mary　1897.68
Stoker, Bram　1906.18
Stokes, J. G. Phelps　[1909.30]
Storrs, John　1920.102; 1921.41
Story, William Wetmore　[1906.12]
Stovall, Floyd　1932.28; 1934.16; 1936.59
Strachey, J. St. Loe　1922.43; 1926.28, 70
Strahan, Alexander　1872.16
Strangford, Viscount　1866.13 [1934.24]
Strangford, Viscountess　1869.1
Stratton-Porter, Gene　1919.193
Strauch, Carl F.　1938.48
Strauss, Richard　[1910.27; 1928.40]
Stravinsky, Igor　[1928.40]
Stronach, A. L.　1891.12
Strong, Augustus Hopkins　1916.21
Struthers, William　1899.26, 61; 1900.29; 1901.26,
　　35; 1906.44; 1909.41; 1910.30
Student Outlines Company　1938.1
Studies in Philology　1923.39-41; 1926.32; 1929.33;
　　1939.41
Sturgis, Julian　1884.16
Sullivan, Louis H.　1901.28; 1924.23
Summers, William, M. P.　1888.65
Sumner, Charles　[1923.27]
Sunday State Journal.　See Lincoln Sunday State
　　Journal
Sunday Times.　See London Sunday Times
Sunset of Bon Echo　1919.109-110, 112-114, 121a,
　　125, 127, 130, 132, 133a-c, 136, 141-143, 146,
　　148a-b, 1920.46-49
Survey　1919.271
Sussex Daily News　1919.302
Sutcliffe, Emerson Grant　1919.182
Sutton, William Henry　[1920.26]
Swain, Corinne Rockwell　1912.24
Swain, Dr. J. H.　[1882.12]
Swan, Tom　1907.41
Swanwick, Anna　[1908.16]
Swayne, Mattie.　See Appendix
Sweden　[1932.46]
Swedenborg, Emanuel　[1868.2, 20; 1932.46]
Swift, Benjamin　1897.161
Swift, Jonathan　[1914.19]
Swinburne, Algernon Charles　1868.3 [1868.8, 31-32;
　　1874.8; 1934.24]; 1871.3; 1872.6, 19; 1887.63
　　[1887.59, 67-68, 70, 72-73, 75, 77, 80, 85;
　　1892.96; 1922.20]; 1918.7 [1919.27]
　　[1868.2; 1870.3; 1871.2, 8; 1872.2; 1875.5;
　　1876.7, 44, 49; 1878.14; 1881.37; 1882.20;

1887.79; 1892.114; 1896.39; 1909.22, 37;
　　1911.4; 1917.5, 14; 1918.8; 1920.11-12;
　　1921.10, 29; 1925.25, 54, 63; 1926.23;
　　1927.26; 1931.19, *25-26; 1933.10; 1934.1]
Swinton, John　1897.114
　　[1898.79; 1901.37; 1919.146]
Swinton, William　1856.26
　　[1939.9a]
Sydney Bulletin　1902.38; 1903.32; 1928.37
Sydney Evening News　1876.58; 1883.13
Sydney Morning Herald　1892.61
Sydney Town and Country Journal.　See Town and
　　Country Journal
Symbolism　[1913.46; 1915.23; 1924.1; 1928.25;
　　1930.3]
Symington, Andrew James　1889.7
Symonds, John Addington　1873.1; 1878.7; 1879.42;
　　1890.8 [1894.35, 61]; 1892.15; 1893.9
　　[1893.26, 37, 40, 46; 1894.23; 1906.82, 93],
　　11; 1895.2 [1897.70]; 1896.17; 1897.2;
　　1903.12; 1923.1
　　[1892.130; 1897.72, 135, 137; 1898.29; 1899.5;
　　1906.95; 1909.22; *1914.2; 1915.11; 1917.42;
　　1919.4; 1920.12; 1924.5; 1925.40; 1927.7-8;
　　1928.20; 1931.1, 21; 1934.1, 24]
Symons, Arthur　1904.16; 1918.19

T.　See Traubel, Horace L.
T., G. K.　1918.27
T., H. L.　See Traubel, Horace L.
T., H. M.　See Tomlinson, H. M.
T., S.　1897.126
T., W. H.　See Trimble, William H.
Tabb, John B.　1892.118
Taggard, Genevieve　1936.48
Tagore, Sir Rabindranath　[1916.63-64; 1929.41;
　　1937.25]
Taine, Hippolyte　[1911.7; 1934.47]
Takayama, R.　1919.177
Talbot, Ethel　1910.26
Taliessin (Welsh poet)　[1914.9]
Tappan, Eva March　1906.19
Tarbell, Ida M.　1897.79
Tarkington, Booth　1923.44
Tate, Allen　1926.30; 1936.26; 1938.3; 1939.40
Taylor, Bayard　1864.3; 1871.19; 1872.10, 17;
　　1876.35 [1876.40], 37, 46, 54
　　[1880.5; 1896.16; 1899.10; 1931.25; 1933.29;
　　1937.42]
Taylor, Mrs. Fanny　1889.9
Taylor, Father　[1888.76]
Taylor, Walter Fuller　1936.27
Teachers' World　1919.92
Temple Bar　1869.4; 1873.4; 1886.44; 1893.41;
　　1898.29
Temps, Le　1895.59
Tennyson, Alfred Lord　1887.87; 1892.15; 1897.12
　　[1855.11; 1856.5; 1860.12; 1864.6; 1866.2;
　　1867.10; 1868.10; 1870.5; 1871.21, 25;
　　1875.7; 1880.5, 23; 1883.15; 1884.9; 1885.18
　　1886.13; 1887.6; 1889.64; 1890.18, 41;
　　1891.29, 44; 1892.20, 27, 100, 114, 211-212;
　　1893.7, 20; 1894.22; 1896.3; 1897.30, 55,
　　125, 151; 1898.29; 1899.17, 37, 38; 1902.6;
　　1903.12; 1904.42; 1906.10, 18, 67; 1907.23;
　　1908.16, 40; 1911.13; 1914.7; 1917.9; 1919.151,
　　211; 1920.6, 23; 1923.48; 1926.82; 1927.36,
　　42, 45; 1931.9, 44; 1934.1; 1935.13; 1938.20]
Tennyson, Hallam Lord (Alfred's son)　1889.9;
　　1897.21; 1911.13
　　[1892.211]

Terre Haute <u>Tribune</u> 1916.48
<u>Texas Review</u> 1921.34; 1922.65
Textbooks and books for young people. <u>See also</u>
    American Literature histories 1872.4, 7;
    1878.5; 1882.1, 3; 1883.8; 1884.1-2, 11;
    1887.2; 1889.1; 1891.5, 10, 12; 1894.14-15;
    1896.10; 1897.18; 1898.12-13; 1899.1, 19;
    1901.11; 1902.3, 16; 1908.3; 1909.5-7, 10;
    1912.6; 1914.3; 1917.11; 1919.21a; 1923.7;
    1924.8; 1925.4; 1927.1, 22; 1929.24; 1936.9,
    16; 1937.43; 1938.1
Thabab, Babbaga [pseud.?] 1860.33
Thatcher, B. W. 1910.25
Thatcher, T. D. 1879.30, 38
Thatcher, T. R. [1846.2]
Thayer, Rev. T. B. [1846.2]
Thayer, William Roscoe 1883.29; 1899.20; 1915.19;
    1919.283; 1926.10
Theater. <u>See also</u> Opera; Shakespeare [1846.3-5;
    1918.41; 1921.48]
<u>Theatre, The</u> (London) 1885.11
<u>Theosophical Quarterly</u> 1910.39
<u>Theosophical Review</u> 1903.39
<u>Theosophist</u> 1913.53; Addenda
<u>Theosophy in Scotland</u> 1910.34; 1912.33
Therrell, Dan MacLaughlin 1892.147
<u>Thinker</u> 1930.39
<u>This Quarter</u> 1925.31; Addenda
<u>This World</u> 1882.34, 62, 70
    [1882.97]
Thomas, Bee Cotton. <u>See</u> Appendix
Thomas, Prof. Calvin 1892.137
Thomas, Edward 1909.12
    [1937.4; 1939.9]
Thomas, G. Walter R. 1883.38
Thomas, Henry. <u>See</u> Schnittkind, H. T.
Thomas, Joseph 1885.7
Thomas, Philip 1921.57
Thompson, E. W. [1913.35]
Thompson, Maurice 1888.20; 1893.10; 1894.25
    [1894.26], 27; 1897.130, 132
    [1893.11]
Thompson, Ralph 1938.26, 51
Thompson, Vance 1898.76, 84; 1899.21
Thompson, William 1886.16
Thomson, James [B. V.] 1874.3-9; 1876.7; 1880.12
    [1910.19; 1934.1]
Thomson, W. R. 1914.41
Thoreau, Henry David 1865.1 [1935.27]; 1894.16
    [1866.2; 1871.10; 1878.16; 1881.6; 1882.9,
    11, 94; 1886.44; 1887.6, 53; 1890.3, 10, 26;
    1892.100, 214; 1893.12, 48; 1895.83; 1896.12;
    1897.8; 1898.85; 1899.48; 1900.3, 28; 1902.2,
    19; 1903.23; *1905.1, 28, 52; 1908.51; 1910.11;
    1912.40; 1913.6; 1914.8; 1915.13; 1917.13;
    1918.13; 1919.225, 267; 1920.14; 1921.13, 53;
    1926.1, 60; 1927.38; 1931.2, 57; 1932.5, 19;
    1936.4; 1938.16; 1939.40; Addenda]
<u>Thorild</u> [1937.25]
Thornsburgh, Zada 1927.22
Throstenberg, Edward 1911.17
Thrall, Anthony. <u>See</u> Cheney, John Vance
Thurnam, Rowland 1895.42
Ticknor & Fields [1885.16]
Tilling, A. E. 1892.68
Tilton, Theodore 1898.93
Timber Creek. <u>See also</u> Stafford family [1877.14;
    1887.47; 1900.19; 1932.40-41; 1933.16, 31;
    1936.45; 1938.12]
<u>Time</u> 1887.85; 1888.25
<u>Time and the Hour</u> 1897.82

<u>Times Literary Supplement</u> (London) 1905.54, 56;
    1912.32; 1914.25; 1915.31, 57; 1918.17;
    1919.33, 48, 201 [1919.309], 309, 379;
    1920.38-39, 57, 59; 1921.44; 1922.39; 1924.44;
    1925.27; 1926.58; 1929.39
Tinker, Edward Larocque 1939.34
Titherington, Richard H. 1895.75
Titian [1887.69]
Tocqueville, Alexis de [1919.373]
<u>To-day</u> 1888.43; 1919.345
Todhunter, John 1877.2; 1880.1a
Toke, Leslie A. St. L. 1898.16
Toledo <u>Journal</u> 1882.15
Tollemache, Hon. Lionel A. 1908.16
Tolstoy, Leo [1888.9, 20; 1890.15; 1894.25;
    1895.12, 21a; 1897.150; 1898.92; 1900.28;
    1901.66; 1902.8, *22, 59; 1905.1; 1911.4;
    1913.19; 1919.357; 1922.16; 1930.7; 1932.47;
    1934.38]
Tomlinson, H. M. 1918.58; 1919.39, 324
<u>To-Morrow Magazine</u> 1906.78
Topeka <u>Commonwealth</u> 1879.31
Topeka <u>Daily Blade</u> 1879.32-33
<u>Torch of Reason</u> (Silverton, Oregon) 1902.44
Toronto <u>Daily Star</u>. <u>See</u> Toronto <u>Star</u>
Toronto <u>Globe</u> 1892.98, 152; 1919.274; 1920.85
Toronto <u>Industrial Banner</u> 1920.67
Toronto <u>Mail</u>. <u>See also</u> Toronto Mail and Empire
    1880.23; 1892.25, 133; 1919.234; 1923.34;
    1934.33
Toronto <u>Mail and Empire</u>. <u>See also</u> Toronto <u>Mail</u>
    1929.61
Toronto <u>Saturday Night</u> 1894.43; 1923.12
Toronto <u>Star</u> 1923.46-47; 1926.47; 1927.53
Toronto <u>Sunday World</u>. <u>See also</u> Toronto World
    1907.14; 1911.27; 1913.32, 44; 1915.35, 38;
    1916.26, 52; 1917.29; 1918.32; 1919.192, 320
Toronto <u>Telegram</u> 1919.65
Toronto <u>World</u> 1883.32; 1919.55, 299
Torrey, Bradford 1897.69
<u>Town and Country Journal</u> (Sydney) 1892.129
Towne, William E. 1906.79
Townsend, George Alfred 1868.39
Townshend, E. C. 1895.14
Traherne, Thomas [1907.39; 1910.19]
Traill, H. D. 1892.62
Transcendentalism [1846.3; 1860.39, 51; 1866.13;
    1892.160; 1898.38; 1899.76; 1903.14a; 1906.13;
    1909.7; 1912.35; 1915.16; 1917.27; 1918.15;
    1919.334, 340; 1920.102; 1921.20, 56; 1922.49,
    51; 1924.24; 1926.9, 25; 1931.2; 1932.26;
    1935.10; 1936.2, 27, 58; 1938.2]
Traubel, Anne Montgomerie (Horace's wife) 1906.20
    [1906.59; Addenda]
    [1931.28; 1936.46]
Traubel, Gertrude (Horace's daughter) 1936.46
    [1914.33]
Traubel, Horace L. 1884.15; 1889.9; 1890.42; 1891.18
    [1891.28], 22, 33a [1891.33b, 34]; 35-36, 48;
    1898.56a; 1892.15 [1892.225], 17, 82, 194, 198,
    204; 1893.11 [1892.213, 222; 1893.47, 49;
    1894.23], 18, 43-44; 1894.37, 49, 53-54, 64;
    1895.27, 43, 54; 1896.24-25, 60, 74, 79, 84-
    86; 1897.28, 41, 52, 70, 80-81, 105, 137, 140-
    141, 151; 1898.24, 42-43, 57, 78, 86, 91;
    1899.33, 41, 64, 69; 1900.22, 37, 42, 44;
    1902.13 [1902.63], 25-26, 33, 36, 48, 50, 60;
    1903.34, 40; 1904.29-30, 38, 47; 1905.1, 17
    [1905.32, 41, 59], 30, 35, 37 [1905.47], 44a,
    51, 53, 58; [1906.21, 22] 1906.10, 29, 33, 40,
    45, 53, 75; 81-84, 87, 106; 1907.21, 30; 1913.11;

1920.75, 86], 26, 59, 72, 80, 100–101; 1907.12,
42, 46, 49–50; 1908.17 [1908.25, 32–33, 41,
43, 49, 52, 54, 56], 24; 1909.21; 1910.28;
1911.32–35; 1912.16 [1913.52], 31; 1913.49;
1914.17 [1914.34–37; 1915.22, 41, 46; 1917.15;
1919.100; 1922.14], 22, 38; 1915.10, 42–43;
1916.25, 48–49; 1917.19, 38, 42–43, 49, 52;
1918.18, 24; 1919.47, 61, 85, 144–146, 154,
247; 1920.48–49; 1924.40, 42
[1888.64; 1892.209; 1893.39; 1894.55; 1898.81a;
1899.66; 1900.19; 1903.26; 1905.29; 1906.88;
1908.37, 48; 1910.3, 33, 37; 1911.28, 30;
1912.25, 42; 1913.1, 22, 25, 42; 1915.48;
1916.22, 42, 47, 50; 1918.53; 1919.11, 30,
121a, 175, 281, 369; 1920.34, 41, 43, 46, 79,
85; 1923.12; 1924.33, 41; 1926.61; 1928.6;
1931.1, 13, 46; 1932.2; 1936.12; 1938.21
Tredwell, Daniel M. 1912.17
Tree, Ellen [1846.5]
Trelawney, Edward John [1882.91, 120]
Trench, Herbert 1923.33
Trench, Archbishop Richard Chenevix 1868.4
Trenholm, Harry 1913.22 [1913.25]
Trent, William Peterfield 1903.14a; 1904.18;
1912.18; 1918.10
Trevor, John 1897.62
Triggs, Oscar Lovell 1892.210; 1893.12 [1893.23,
25, 36], 30; 1895.44–45, 77; 1896.45, 68;
1897.32 [1897.43–45, 55], 54, 117, 127, 131;
1898.17 [1898.57, 81, 96, 100; 1899.29], 94
1901.19; 1902.25–26; 1905.18; 1915.10
Triggs Magazine 1906.37
Trilling, Lionel 1939.46
[1939.25]
Trimble, A[nnie] E. (William's wife) 1909.40;
1911.14; 1915.10
Trimble, William H. [Casca] 1900.38; 1905.19
[1905.51; 1906.45]; 1907.13, 31; 1915.10;
1919.272; 1922.69
[1914.8]
Trowbridge, John Townsend 1896.36 [1896.40, 43];
1902.34; 1903.15; 1915.10
[1885.16; 1890.13; 1933.6]
Troxell, Gilbert M. 1930.24
Trumbull, General M. M. 1891.23a [1891.27, 33a],
33b [1891.34]
Trumbull, Jonathan 1890.39; 1891.54
Truth, Sojourner [1927.37]
Truth (London) 1900.27
Truth Seeker (New York) 1882.60, 66, 77, 92, 114,
120–123, 126, 129–130, 133; 1890.55; 1914.22,
28; Addenda
Truthseeker (London) 1880.28
Tucker, Benjamin 1882.50, 78 [1882.95], 93; 1890.57;
1891.27 [1891.33a], 34; 1892.209; 1899.24
[1882.12]
Tucker, John Foster 1898.58
Tufts, Helen 1902.2
Tupper, Martin Farquhar 1886.10
[1856.10; 1860.39, 46, 49, 62; 1865.8; 1877.3;
1880.21; 1890.36; 1892.60; 1895.9; 1906.9,
103; 1909.27; 1911.12; 1913.52; 1916.23]
Turgenev, Ivan [1934.38]
Turner, Emory S. 1919.108
Turner, J. M. W. [1868.14]
Twain, Mark. See Clemens, Samuel
Twentieth Century Magazine 1910.40
Twice a Year 1939.26
Tyndall, Mrs. [1938.16]
Tyro 1922.61

Ulke (photographer) 1907.49
Umos [pseud.?] 1860.5
Umphrey, George W. 1928.21
Unanimistes (French Realists) [1919.190; 1920.66;
1924.1]
Underhill, Evelyn 1911.15
Underwood, U.S. Consul at Glasgow [1886.47]
Underwood, Francis H. 1872.7; 1893.13
Underwood, Geo. 1919.295
United Ireland 1894.62, 67
United States Congress, House Report 1887.13
[1887.18, 19, 26]
United States Library of Congress. See Library of
Congress
United States Review 1855.7
[1894.9]
Unity 1890.42; 1900.27; Addenda
Universal Brotherhood Path 1901.68; Addenda
Universal Review 1889.43
Universalist Leader 1902.44
Universities and schools, Whitman in. See also
Dartmouth; Education; Whitman--Schoolteaching
[1895.37, 45; 1919.30, 286, 291; 1922.38;
1925.38; 1929.58; 1933.18; 1934.1; 1936.47;
1938.57]
University Magazine and Free Review 1899.48
University of California Chronicle 1923.38;
1931.53
University of California Publications in Modern
Philology 1919.42; 1920.63
University of Colorado Studies 1926.54
University of Nebraska Studies in Language, Liter-
ature and Criticism 1938.20
University of Texas Bulletin: Studies in English
1929.56; 1934.31–32; 1935.31; 1936.52–53;
1939.42
University of the South Magazine 1890.21
Untermeyer, Louis 1917.27; 1918.73 [1919.51];
1919.22–24 [1919.70, 158, 280, 377], 68, 99,
166, 273; 1921.35; 1923.44; 1925.14; 1926.31;
1930.21, 43; 1931.21; 1936.28; 1938.54
[1919.160]
Urner, Benj. 1885.28 [1934.40]
Usher, John P. [1937.38]

V., B. See Thomson, James
Vale, Charles 1921.19; 1922.4
Valente, John 1928.22
Valentine, Edward A. Uffington 1899.34
Van Anden, Isaac 1848.4
Van Cleve, Florence 1919.172
Van Doren, Carl 1918.10; 1922.36; 1923.16, 44;
1925.15; 1930.43
Van Doren, Mark 1925.15; 1926.81; 1935.29; 1937.14,
29
van Dyke, Henry C. 1910.20; 1929.25; 1935.13
[1926.10]
van Dyke, Paul 1900.15
van Dyke, Tertius 1935.13
Van Gogh, J. 1919.86
Vanity Fair 1860.9–10, 13–14, 48, 61, 66; 1862.1;
1922.41
Vassar Miscellany 1892.78–79
Vaughan Williams, Ralph 1918.64
[1919.347; 1920.69]
Vedantism [1930.19]
Verhaeren [1899.21; 1914.11; 1924.1]
Verlaine, Paul [1889.8; 1925.78]
Victoria, Queen [1922.54]
Vie Ouvrière, La 1919.353
Vielé-Griffin, Francis [1899.21]

Viereck, George Sylvester [1919.288]
Vildrac, Charles [1920.39]
Villon, François 1910.12
Vincent, Leon H. 1906.23
Viollis, Andrée and Jean 1909.41
Virbius [pseud.?] 1934.36
Virgil [1934.2]
Vivekananda [1930.19]
Vogue 1894.20
Volney, Constantin [1938.2, 29]
Voltaire [1925.78]
Vran-Gavran, R. A. 1918.30
Vrchlicky, Jaroslav 1918.25

W. (Round Table) See O'Connor, William Douglas
W. (Universal Brotherhood Path) 1901.68
W., D. 1856.25
Wagenvoort, Maurits 1919.86
Wager-Fisher, Mrs. Mary E. 1878.9
Wagner, Harr 1929.26
Wagner, Richard [1868.36; 1873.6; 1884.12; 1886.13;
    1888.40; 1892.120; 1893.12, 30, 43; 1895.8;
    1896.9, 71; 1897.27; 1910.23, 27; 1911.23]
Wahl, Jean 1925.16
Walbrook, H. M. 1919.302
Waley, Arthur [1919.46]
Walford, Mrs. L. B. 1892.146 [1892.175]
Walker, E. C. 1882.130
Walker, W. E. [1922.68]
Wallace, Henry 1904.19
Wallace, James William. See also Bolton group
    1892.15, 219; 1893.11; 1894.37; 1895.46;
    1896.61; 1911.30; 1917.6 [for reviews See
    Dr. J. Johnston], 45; 1918.12; 1919.87, 147-
    148, 205; 1920.29
    [1891.36; 1897.137; 1936.12]
Walling, Anna Strunsky 1919.88
    [1914.33; 1918.41]
Walling, William English 1916.22 [1916.39-40, 44;
    1917.18, 30, 34; 1918.46]
Wallington, Edward 1919.148a
Walpole, Hugh 1923.33
Walsh, Henry C. 1919.349
Walsh, Walter 1905.41; 1920.29
Walsh, William Shepard [William Shepard] 1882.10;
    1889.25; 1892.169
Walt Whitman Fellowship [1894.37, 39-40, 55;
    1895.36, 49, 78; 1896.37, 55; 1898.20, 40, 73,
    79; 1899.61; 1900.39; 1901.36-37, 42; 1902.42;
    1903.30, 36-37, 43; 1904.39, 41; 1905.41-42;
    1906.78. 85; 1907.40; 1908.42; 1909.30;
    1912.37; 1913.1; 1914.13, 33; 1915.36; 1916.48,
    50, 52; 1917.28; 1918.29, 31, 41; 1920.60,
    103; 1921.58-59; 1923.31; 1924.9; 1926.56;
    1936.12]
Walt Whitman Fellowship Papers 1894.45, 47, 59, 64;
    1895.19, 27, 66, 68, 69, 72-74, 77; 1896.55;
    1897.66, 71, 75; 1898.50, 56, 64-68; 1899.45,
    50, 54, 56; 1904.32, 34, 36
Walters, Frank 1880.2
Walton, Eda Lou 1937.31
Wanamaker, John [1938.12]
Wann, Louis 1926.4; 1938.46
War and war poetry. See also Whitman--Works--Drum
    Taps [1904.29; 1915.52, 57; 1916.25; 1917.24-
    25; 1917.32; 1918.10, 58; 1919.188, 201, 262;
    1930.7, 25; 1931.27; 1932.30, 39; 1933.6, 22;
    1936.5]
Ward (artist) [1865.6]
Ward, A. C. 1932.20-21
Ward, Artemus [1892.130]

Ward, Sam 1882.109 [1882.116]
Ward, William Haynes 1884.10
Ware, Lois 1929.33
Warfel, Harry R. 1937.15
Warner, Charles Dudley 1915.10
Warner, Ella Pardee. See Appendix
Warren, Robert Penn 1939.46
Warren, Samuel [1860.39; 1892.172; 1906.103;
    1916.23]
Washington, D. C. See Whitman--Dismissal; Hospital
    service
Washington, George [1909.8]
Washington Chronicle. See also Washington Sunday
    Morning Chronicle 1871.22
Washington Daily National Intelligencer 1856.7
Washington Evening Star 1868.28; 1870.5; 1872.14;
    1875.11; 1877.14
Washington News 1935.26
Washington Post 1881.54; 1882.115
Washington Sunday Capital 1882.79
Washington Sunday Chronicle. See also Washington
    Chronicle 1869.3
Washington Sunday Morning Chronicle. See also
    Washington Chronicle and Sunday Chronicle
    1867.25
Waters, George [1877.8; 1908.20]
Watrous, A. E. 1892.108
Watson, Albert Durrant 1913.20; 1919.25, 148b, 274
    [1919.121a]
Watson, E. H. Lacon 1901.50
Watson, J. 1897.45 [1897.55]
Watson, William 1884.13; 1917.14
    [1934.1]
Watson's Weekly Art Journal 1865.6
Watt, William [1936.40]
Wattles, Willard 1917.60
Watts, D. G. 1892.18
Watts, Theodore. See Watts-Dunton, Theodore
Watts-Dunton, Theodore (Theodore Watts) 1892.109
    [1892.97, 152]; 1906.16; 1916.23
    [1917.5; 1918.8; 1926.23; 1931.25-26; 1933.10]
Waxman, Samuel M. 1937.2
Wayne [pseud.?] 1867.30; 1868.7
Weaver, John V. A. 1923.44
Weber, Oscar F. 1927.32
Webling, Peggy 1909.13
Webster, Henry K. 1922.26
Week, The (Toronto) 1884.17; 1890.24-25; 1891.14
Weekly Review (Boston) 1893.17, 19
Weekly Review (New York) 1921.69
Weeks, Ruth Mary 1921.36
Weirick, Bruce 1924.24 [1924.32, 35]
Weller, Alanson 1928.34, 40
Wells, Carolyn 1904.20; 1922.27 [1923.41]; 1928.23
    [1929.47]; 1929.27 [1930.24]; 1937.16
    [1933.9]
Wells, H. G. [1919.94]
Wendell, Barrett 1893.14; 1900.18 [1901.32, 53, 57;
    1902.49, 57]; 1904.21
Wentworth, Franklin 1905.48
Werfel, Franz [1919.44]
Wergeland, Henrik [1939.16]
Wernaer, Robert M. 1918.24
Werner, W. L. 1936.30
Wescott, R. W. 1905.36
West, The [1879 passim; 1899.28; 1923.42; 1924.10;
    1927.9; 1930.40; 1931.1, 20; 1932.7-8]
West Jersey Press (Camden) 1876.10, 60; 1878.8
Westminster Gazette 1914.27; 1919.235
Westminster and Foreign Quarterly Review. See also
    Westminster Review 1860.61

Westminster Review. See also Westminster and
    Foreign Quarterly Review 1871.4; 1883.25;
    1895.14; 1899.76; 1901.66
Weston, Dr. S. Burns [1936.46]
Wharton, Edith 1913.21; 1923.17; 1924.25; 1929.28;
    1934.17
    [1925.15]
Wheeler, Andrew Carpenter (Nym Crinkle) 1892.99
Wheeler, Leonard 1883.3; 1885.21
Whicher, George F. 1926.44
Whipple, Edwin Percy 1866.3; 1887.14
Whipple, T. K. 1937.36
White, Eliot 1911.28a; 1913.47; 1918.48 [1918.41]
White, George H. 1919.178
White, Richard Grant 1860.21; 1868.32; 1883.26;
    1884.14
    [1910.17]
White, Viola C. 1935.27
White, W. Hale [Mark Rutherford] 1880.8; 1913.13
White, William 1939.22
White, William Allen 1923.44
Whitelock, William Wallace 1902.27
Whiting, Lilian 1910.21
Whitlock, Brand 1913.40
Whitman family. See Whitman--Biographies; Family for
    the various family members
Whitman, Edward (brother) [1931.1]
Whitman, George (brother) 1893.11
    [1900.19]
Whitman, Hannah (sister). See Hyde, Hannah
Whitman, Jefferson (brother) 1889.9
    [1928.36]
Whitman, Jessie (Jefferson's daughter) [1928.24;
    1929.34; 1931.1]
Whitman, Louisa (mother) [1908.53; 1926.13, 24;
    1933.6]
Whitman, Mary (sister) [1931.51]
Whitman, Walt 1855.7, 10 [1919.186], 11; 1856.2,
    23; 1859.5; 1860.3, 18, 63; 1862.1; 1869.2;
    1872.14, 20; 1875.11; 1876.10, 60; 1877.10, 14;
    1879.35; 1880.3; 1884.20; 1885.10; 1887.20;
    1888.6 [1889.41], 83; 1890.17, 30, 32; 1891.15-
    16, 21, 30; 1892.69, 89; 1893.11; 1904.11;
    1919.275; 1937.40
-Activities and appearance. See also Reminiscences;
    Visits [1848.9; 1850.2; 1855.10; 1856.13, 23;
    1859.2-4; 1860.8, 15, 43, 68; 1862.2; 1863.1;
    1864.5; 1866.2, 11-12; 22; 1867.1; 1868.12,
    39, 41, 44; 1869.3; 1870.7; 1871.5, 9, 14, 20,
    25, 27; 1872.15, 20; 1873.7, 10; 1875.7, 13;
    1876.9-11, 45, 60, 62, 66; 1877.7-10, 14;
    1878.9, 12; 1879.13-40; 1880.3, 27, 32;
    1881.15, 18, 20, 27, 29, 31, 33, 36-37, 49;
    1882.135; 1884.20; 1885.10, 12-13, 15; 1886.6,
    17-18, 20, 36, 42, 50, 58; 1887.27, 39-41, 46,
    49, 54, 67, 84; 1888.27, 29-30, 49, 57-58, 63-
    64, 85; 1889.21-22, 29, 66; 1890.17, 34, 46,
    52, 58; 1891.21-22; 1892.24, 184, 209;
    1898.19, 94; 1900.33; 1901.59; 1902.37;
    1903.34; 1914.22; 1920.96; 1934.24; 1936.43]
-Advertising [1855.1, 4; 1860.40; 1865.4; 1882.102,
    106, 110]
-Analyses of Whitman's work
--Books. 1866.2; 1867.1; 1871.1; 1883.3; 1884.12;
    1886.7; 1889.9; 1890.6; 1892.3, 15; 1893.9,
    11; 1896.2, 9; 1897.7, 11; 1899.16; 1900.9;
    1902.13-14; 1903.9; 1904.19; 1905.10, 19;
    1906.5; 1910.11; 1913.19; 1914.5, 15; 1915.4;
    1916.11; 1917.1, 6; 1920.26; 1921.13, 16, 20;
    1924.3, 6, 10; 1926.1, 15; 1934.16; 1935.10;
    1938.2, 9, 17

--Articles. See also Reviews of specific editions
    of Leaves, under Works 1858.1; 1860.63;
    1867.13; 1868.36; 1871.21, 23; 1872.4, 7;
    1873.11; 1894.9, 11; 1875.6, 15-16; 1877.1,
    13; 1878.17; 1879.12; 1880.2, 9, 12, 20-22,
    28, 35; 1881.9; 1883.14, 35; 1884.21; 1885.21,
    42; 1886.41, 45; 1887.63, 74; 1888.7, 30, 41,
    45, 76; 1889.39, 46, 71; 1890.3, 57; 1891.1,
    7, 13, 20; 1892.16, 18, 20-21; 1893.2, 21, 28,
    30, 41, 43; 1894.28, 41-42, 44-45, 61;
    1897.115; 1898.1, 16, 17, 23, 38; 1899.6, 37,
    75-76; 1900.14; 1901.23, 38, 49-50, 68;
    1902.59; 1903.1, 3, 35, 42; 1904.10, 14, 42;
    1905.11, 18, 28, 36; 1906.10, 14, 23, 90;
    1907.13, 33, 43, 52; 1910.19, 26, 31, 36, 40;
    1911.7; 1912.11, 18, 20, 28, 35; 1913.11, 29;
    1914.4; 1915.3; 1916.8, 21, 24; 1917.9, 17,
    27; 1918.4, 15; 1919 (passim); 1920.5, 9, 29-
    30, 72; 1921.6-8, 23, 30, 49, 62, 64, 68;
    1922.1, 16, 22, 50, 68; 1923.9, 19, 24, 38,
    40, 45, 48-49, 52, 65; 1924.16, 24, 31, 34;
    1925.18, 22; 1926.9, 12, 22, 26, 28, 54, 68;
    1927.14; 1928.9; 1929.3, 5, 13, 25, 31, 41, 48;
    1930.3, 7; 1931.6, 18; 1932.18, 21; 1933.4, 23;
    1934.4, 6; 1936.6, 45; 1937.3, 5, 14, 22;
    1938.8, 13, 19, 43
-Ancestors [1881.27; 1891.18; 1905.1]
-Appearance. See Activities and appearance
-Art (on Whitman and his work). See Portraits;
    also general index)
-Auctions and sales of early editions. See also
    Prices of early editions [1930.45, 49;
    1932.29, 34, 37; 1933.33, 35; 1935.43;
    1936.21-22, 36-37, 39, 43-44]
-Autographs. See Handwriting
-Bibliographical description. See also Bibliog-
    raphies [1920.22; 1921.24; 1923.27; 1927.52;
    1931.10; 1932.12; 1936.57; 1939.4; Addenda]
-Bibliographies 1897.5, 138; 1898.16; 1899.47;
    1902.25; 1903.16; 1904.12; 1905.13, 19;
    1918.11; 1919.3, 42, 150, 277; 1920.27;
    1922.27; 1923.37; 1926.15; 1931.1; 1934.1;
    1935.3, 10; 1936.9, 14; 1937.7, 14-15; 1938.8,
    25; 1939.13
    [1937.45]
-Biographies
--Books 1867.1; 1883.3; 1896.2, 3; 1905.1; 1906.13;
    1909.4; 1918.10; 1920.2; 1926.13; 1929.17;
    1931.1; 1937.9
--Fictionalized 1921.27; 1926.24; 1928.6; 1938.5
--Shorter pieces with biographical information
    1850.1; 1864.4-5; 1882.28, 135; 1886.6; 1889.7;
    1892.28; 1895.76; 1902.13, 32; 1904.12;
    1905.13; 1919.216; 1921.19; 1922.30; 1929.60;
    1934.46; 1939.39. See also particular events
    and locations; Activities; Interviews;
    Reminiscences; Visits
-Birthday dinners [1888.25; 1889.9, 42, 45, 48-59;
    1890.27-32, 42; 1891.29-33, 35, 37; 1929.58]
-Birthplace. See also Long Island [1890.7; 1894.53,
    55, 64; 1905.38-39, 43, 55, 59; 1909.44;
    1913.50; 1915.60; 1917.2; 1919.150, 213, 228,
    287; 1920.1; 1921.63; 1926.26; 1931.17;
    1936.35, 40-42, 49]
-Caricatures and cartoons 1860.10; 1904.3; 1909.34;
    1929.52
-Catalogues. See also Style; reviews of early
    editions [1871.8; 1872.6; 1874.10; 1882.33,
    117; 1888.44; 1889.3; 1894.41; 1895.83;
    1897.61; 1900.49; 1907.39; 1909.4; 1912.18;
    1914.5, 12, 27; 1915.17; 1917.29; 1919.43,

129; 1922.30; 1925.47; 1926.54, 68; 1929.20, 51; 1931.53; 1932.6; 1933.4, 15; 1935.10; 1937.5; 1939.16]

-Cemetery. See Death and funeral; also general index, Harleigh Cemetery

-Censorship. See also Suppression; also general index, Libraries [1892.108; 1903.40; 1911.27]

-Character analysis [1860.8; 1891.17-18; 1895.34; 1897.60; 1898.31, 75, 94; 1907.56; 1909.32; 1917.6; 1918.41; 1919.279; 1920.88; 1922.30; 1926.14; 1931.7]

-Children (Whitman's claims to having) [1902.32; 1905.1; 1906.99; 1907.25; 1913.16; 1919.283; 1920.5; 1921.20; 1929.17; 1931.1; 1936.22; 1938.8]

-Civil War experience. See Hospital service; Works-- Drum Taps; also general index, War and war poetry

-Collections of Whitman materials [1910.3; 1919.12, 93; 1925.29; 1928.19; 1929.27; 1933.9; 1935.26; 1936.22, 36-38, 43-44; 1937.16; 1938.30, 33; 1939.13, 29; Addenda]

-Comic poems. See Parodies

-Composing process [1873.9; 1888.16; 1896.9, 50; 1897.38; 1898.23; 1899.77; 1902.26; 1919.317, 334; 1928.11; 1930.40; 1933.6; 1936.22, 51; 1938.29, 56]

-Context, Whitman's literary and sociopolitical [1894.44; 1903.13; 1914.15; 1917.27; 1926.22; 1928.10; 1929.13, 17; 1933.26]

-Critical reception surveys. See also particular countries [1883.3; 1884.4; 1893.11; 1916.11; 1920.19; 1925.32; 1926.15, 20; 1930.47; 1931.1; 1934.43; 1935.39; 1936.55]

-Criticism, Whitman's [1846.3-5; 1904.15; 1908.33; 1909.4; 1919.346; 1920.101; 1923.40; 1928.9, 23, 32; 1932.27; 1933.21; 1938.20; 1939.10]

-Death and funeral. See also general index, Harleigh Cemetery [1892.15 (and passim, especially 1892.32-74); 1894.47; 1905.1; 1916.49; 1919.237; 1921.31; 1931.1; 1934.36; 1935.30]

-Degeneracy. See also Immorality; Indecency [1895.8, 33; 1896.49; 1898.61]

-Department of Interior. See Dismissal

-Dismissal from Department of Interior. See also James Harlan [1865.2-3; 1866.2, 8, 11-12, 17; 1873.2; 1874.5; 1876.37; 1931.8]

-Drama, Whitman in 1924.41

-Dutch traits [1891.17; 1899.31; 1922.49; 1923.5; 1929.13]

-Early work [1915.56; 1916.30, 37; 1917.61; 1920.26; 1921.16; 1926.39, 59; 1939.28]

-Earnings. See Finances

-Education. See Schoolteaching; also general index

-Egotism [1842.4; 1849.8; 1860.21; 1892.202; 1894.58; 1895.10, 55; 1898.46; 1899.71; 1900.41; 1901.48; 1902.53; 1908.33, 53; 1912.20; 1916.24; 1917.27; 1918.49; 1919.156, 186, 240; 1921.49; 1931.6, 20]

-Exhibits of Whitman material [1925.68, 72, 74, 76, 78, 80; 1939.29, 34]

-Facsimiles [1883.9; 1887.20; 1889.4; 1891.16; 1892.106; 1902.26; 1903.16; 1904.7, 25, 29; 1911.18; 1915.10; 1919.215, 250; 1921.5, 24; 1924.14, 26; 1927.47; 1928.11; 1930.35; 1933.15; 1936.31; 1937.1, 7; 1938.15, 56; 1939.15]

-Family. See also Ancestors; Biographies; partic- ular individuals [1876.67; 1892.116; 1893.11; 1908.55; 1925.21; 1936.22; 1938.9]

-Fiction, Whitman in. See also Biographies-- Fictionalized 1864.3; 1868.5; 1878.2; 1883.26; 1884.16; 1887.4, 7; 1888.72; 1891.8; 1894.7; 1897.19; 1899.13, 15; 1900.12; 1901.67; 1902.19; 1907.1; 1908.10; 1909.9, 13; 1910.2; 1912.14; 1913.7, 21; 1915.1, 9; 1916.9; 1917.55; 1918.5; 1919.9-10; 1920.8, 18; 1921.1, 9; 1922.19, 24, 26; 1923.4, 17; 1924.17, 22, 25; 1925.79; 1926.2-3; 1927.15-16; 1928.1, 4; 1928.7, 14-15, 17; 1929.1, 21, 28; 1930.6; 1932.9; 1935.11; 1936.10-11; 1938.18; 1939.2, 8

-Fiction by Whitman. See Works

-Finances. See also Sales; Subscriptions; Will [1846.6; 1885.16; 1888.51; 1889.30; 1906.100; 1907.11; 1908.35; 1925.69; 1931.50; 1932.12]

-First editions. See Auctions; Prices of early editions; Bibliographical description

-Foreign editions and translations. See specific countries

-Funeral. See Death and funeral

-Genealogy and family history. See Family

-George Selwyn [pseud.] 1885.10; 1888.6

-Handwriting. See also Facsimiles [1879.4; 1889.4; 1891.16; 1936.31]

-Health, Whitman's. See also Activities [1873.3; 1876.9; 1882.112, 124; 1887.13; 1888.31-35, 49, 79, 83; 1890.16, 27, 33; 1891.56-65; 1892.19, 23, 25-26; 1893.11; 1897.71; 1929.40; 1939.39; Addenda]

-Health, Whitman's ideas about [1899.54; 1903.40; 1910.38; 1918.35]

-Hoax, reputed (in England) [1883.1; 1892.132; 1925.54-57, 61-65, 67]

-Homes. See Brooklyn; Camden; Birthplace [1927.53a]

-Hospital service during Civil War. See also Pension [1865.7; 1866.2, 14, 22, 26; 1867.1; 1868.5; 1871.9-10; 1873.5; 1874.4, 12; 1876.30, 43; 1887.50; 1891.27, 34; 1892.216; 1893.44; 1894.6; 1896.3; 1898.3 (See Letters for reviews); 1906.57; 1907.55; 1910.17; 1916.5; 1918.34-35; 1919.38; 1924.25; 1928.3; 1932.49; Addenda]

-Humor [1889.29; 1896.68; 1902.62; 1907.27; 1916.24; 1919.265; 1921.22; 1923.12, 40; 1928.23; 1929.13, 17, 31; 1931.19-20]

-Immorality. See also Degeneracy; Indecency; Suppression; also general index, Sex [1882.108; 1907.24-25; 1916.21; 1919.339; 1928.3]

-Indecency. See also Immorality; reviews of specific editions of Leaves, under Works [1860.46; 1892.109; 1903.40]

-Influence upon others. See also general index, Modern poetry [1887.22; 1894.31; 1896.56, 61; 1897.3, 124, 160; 1901.19-20, 23; 1904.23; 1907.38; 1911.23, 30; 1912.4, 42, 48; 1913.1; 1914.2; 1915.16, 23, 32, 55; 1916.28, 31-32, 34, 36; 1917.4, 7-8, 36, 53; 1918.13, 19, 24, 51; 1919.21, 23-24, 42, 44, 53, 96, 99, 135, 138, 160, 190, 232, 254, 282, 318, 328, 331, 363; 1920.34, 38-39, 42, 53, 57, 66, 77; 1921.33-34, 54; 1922.4, 60, 63-64; 1923.33, 44, 47; 1924.6, 24, 34; 1925.77; 1926.40; 1927.6, 14, 20, 22; 1928.21, 25, 38; 1929.13, 24, 55; 1930.3, 38; 1936.7-8; 1939.18, 34-35, 40; Appendix]

-Influences upon Whitman. See Sources

-Interviews 1868.39; 1875.7, 10-11; 1876.16, 49, 59; 1879.19, 41; 1880.5, 18-19; 1881.30, 41,

43; 1882.18, 21, 38; 1884.27; 1885.15, 17–18,
  25; 1886.49; 1887.32; 1889.64; 1890.10, 16,
  41; 1892.33; 1939.4
–Journalism [1838.1–2; 1842.3–6, 9; 1846.3–6;
  1848.1–10; 1849.1–10; 1850.1; 1852.1; 1854.1;
  1864.4–6; 1883.19; 1901.52, 57; 1903.49;
  1905.45; 1908.1, 26, 46; 1909.5; 1912.17;
  1915.8; 1916.59; 1919.150, 253, 275; 1920.1,
  26, 44, 50, 92, 98–101; 1921.16; 1922.2;
  1923.57; 1924.28–29; 1925.72; 1926.59;
  1929.60; 1931.23; 1932.11, 31; 1933.6, 28;
  1935.36; 1936.15, 51; 1937.11, 13, 26, 28;
  1938.2; 1939.23, 28]
–Language. See Style; Vocabulary; also general
  index, American language
–Lectures
––Brooklyn Art Union [1851.1; 1900.40]
––Lincoln [1876.71; 1879.9–10; 1880.11; 1881.10–15,
  18, 20; 1886.17, 21, 24–28, 30–31, 36; 1887.31–
  37; 1890.17, 19, 23; 1892.28; 1903.21; 1908.20;
  1911.80; 1913.3; 1915.19; 1922.15; 1923.8;
  1928.3]
–Letters 1872.12; 1883.36; 1885.16, 29, 41; 1886.15,
  37; 1887.20; 1891.15–16; 1892.106, 186; 1893.11,
  44; 1895.81; 1896.3, 9; 1897.2 [1896.84 ;
  1897.82, 85, 87, 99, 102, 107–114, 117–118,
  122, 133, 135–37, 144–147, 155, 161; 1898.25,
  59; 1899.34; 1909.4]; 1898.3 [1898.24, 33, 36,
  48–49, 61, 69–71, 100, 104; 1899.34]; 1902.11;
  1904.25; 1906.13; 1908.53; 1917.6; 1918.9, 50,
  57; 1919.89, 250, 304; 1920.3; 1921.5, 24;
  1922.2; 1923.48; 1924.14; 1925.73, 75; 1927.47;
  1928.36; 1929.34; 1930.8, 35; 1931.10, 27, 59;
  1933.6; 1934.50; 1935.21, 23, 26; 1936.21–
  22, 24; 1937.24, 27, 38; 1938.15, 30, 36;
  1939.13; Addenda
–Manuscripts [1898.81a; 1909.42; 1913.43; 1917.38;
  1922.12; 1924.43; 1928.11, 44–45; 1929.37, 40,
  44; 1931.1; 1933.6, 22; 1934.20, 22; 1936.21–
  22, 31, 33; 1937.8, 26, 45; 1938.23, 47a, 56;
  1939.15; Addenda]
–Memorials [1919.371; 1925.39–40, 42–46, 48–49, 51,
  58; 1926.36, 38, 64; 1931.39–42, 51; 1936.49]
–Metrics. See Style
–Musical settings of Whitman's works. See general
  index, Music
–Novels, Whitman in. See Fiction, Whitman in
–Parodies and comic poems 1846.5; 1856.10; 1860.6–
  7, 10–11, 19–20, 22, 33, 48, 50, 53, 61, 64,
  67; 1862.1; 1868.10, 45; 1871.19; 1872.17;
  1873.6; 1874.2; 1877.2; 1880.34, 37; 1882.8,
  61, 109, 116; 1884.8, 16, 26; 1885.3, 5, 26,
  28, 36–37; 1886.38; 1887.76, 86; 1888.3, 10,
  18, 21–22, 52; 1890.1; 1891.11; 1892.89, 118,
  135; 1894.42–43; 1896.15, 18; 1897.116;
  1899.11, 23, 25; 1901.17; 1902.38, 40;
  1903.28, 32, 47; 1904.20, 45; 1906.55; 1910.12;
  1911.26; 1912.7, 9, 24, 27, 30, 46; 1913.41;
  1914.16; 1915.28, 37, 44; 1916.12, 33; 1917.20,
  51; 1919.15, 22, 41, 323, 368; 1920.21, 25,
  84, 95; 1921.5, 45; 1923.12; 1925.33; 1932.48;
  1933.19
–Pension [1887.13, 18–19, 26; 1891.23a, 27, 33a–b,
  34]
–Personality. See Character analysis
–Phaeton (gift to Whitman) [1885.32–37]
–Philosophy [1888.43; 1889.5; 1894.29, 49; 1895.5,
  30, 38, 43, 51; 1896.2, 45, 65; 1897.7;
  1898.65; 1899.16, 48, 57; 1902.15, 48;
  1903.29, 39; 1904.13; 1906.37, 94; 1907.20,
  39, 57; 1908.12, 36; 1909.11; 1911.14;
  1913.30, 53–54; 1914.11, 15, 19; 1916.2, 22,

52; 1918.41, 49; 1925.16; 1931.9, 52;
  1934.23; 1936.58]
–Photographs. See Portraits
–Poems to Whitman and referring to Whitman 1860.1;
  1871.3; 1877.1–2, 5; 1881.16, 31, 51; 1883.3,
  6, 38; 1884.12–13; 1885.27; 1886.33; 1887.15;
  1889.4, 9; 1890.2, 25, 48; 1891.14, 25, 36;
  1892.5, 15, 68, 111, 128, 131, 143, 209a,
  216; 1893.3, 5, 11, 38; 1894.4, 8, 13, 19, 53;
  1895.7, 35, 46, 62; 1896.11, 21; 1897.68,
  1898.58; 1901.12, 15, 29, 35, 46; 1902.20;
  1903.18; 1904.26, 32; 1906.3, 38, 89; 1907.33,
  36; 1908.8; 1909.2; 1912.47; 1913.19–20, 34;
  1915.7, 14; 1916.11, 35; 1917.2, 21, 26, 41,
  48, 60; 1918.2, 25, 55; 1919.28, 55, 111, 114,
  118–119, 132, 132, 136, 142, 144, 172, 180,
  183, 193, 255, 259, 268, 271, 274, 291, 333,
  354; 1920.7, 48–49, 97; 1921.72; 1922.20;
  1923.19, 64; 1926.8, 21; 1930.5, 22; 1931.55;
  1932.16; 1934.21; 1935.19, 24, 41; 1936.25,
  43, 48; 1938.39; 1939.5, 43
–Poetic development [1897.127; 1905.13; 1915.16;
  1919.277; 1921.16; 1924.11; 1926.15; 1928.11;
  1932.28; 1933.22; 1934.45; 1936.22, 33;
  1938.30]
–Poetics. See Style
–Portraits (printed or discussed) [1860.24;
  1889.47; 1891.16, 18, 22; 1897.36; 1898.94;
  1899.38; 1906.90; 1911.18; 1919.175; 1920.56;
  1921.12; 1923.13; 1925.17; 1936.22; 1937.44]
–Prices of early editions. See also Sales
  [1919.304; 1923.35; 1927.52; 1929.35;
  1931.42; 1933.9]
–Prose. See Works
–Prosody. See Style
–Psychological interpretations. See Character
  analysis
–Reading. See Sources
–Reminiscences of Whitman (also quotations of his
  conversation) 1871.9; 1873.5; 1882.6, 10, 59;
  1883.3; 1885.21; 1892.4, 22, 57, 96, 99, 113,
  117, 119, 124, 163, 166, 176, 180, 198–199,
  212; 1893.1, 7, 11, 22, 43; 1894.2, 6, 47, 64;
  1895.6, 24, 39, 83; 1896.3, 9, 24, 49, 53, 56;
  1897.2, 15, 17, 59, 71, 74, 78; 1898.29, 31,
  45, 51, 74, 89; 1899.35, 38, 77; 1900.8, 12–
  13, 40; 1901.21, 27, 44, 49, 65; 1902.13, 34,
  42; 1903.7, 14, 21; 1904.29, 35; 1905.2, 9,
  31, 37, 45, 53; 1906.11–12, 18, 22, 29, 39,
  65, 87; 1907.24, 37, 42, 46, 49–50, 58;
  1908.20, 24, 26, 40; 1909.15, 18, 24, 29;
  1910.10, 24; 1911.32–35; 1912.2, 16–17, 26,
  36; 1913.17, 29; 1914.1, 29; 1915.10, 18, 43,
  48, 52, 59; 1916.3, 10, 21; 1917.6, 10, 13,
  39, 43, 52, 56; 1918.18; 1919.61, 78, 81, 85,
  116, 127–128, 138, 144, 148, 154, 160, 162–
  163, 231, 252, 265, 279; 1920.4, 6, 14, 22,
  26, 48–49; 1921.5, 16–17, 19, 24, 31; 1922.2,
  8, 12, 15; 1923.54; 1924.14, 26, 40, 42;
  1925.1, 3, 21, 69; 1926.49; 1927.14, 47–48;
  1928.2; 1929.17, 58; 1930.8, 27; 1931.7–8, 19,
  25, 33; 1933.16, 31; 1936.46, 49; 1937.1, 46;
  1939.22
–Reviews. See Works, Critical reception; also W. M.
  Rossetti, reviews of 1868.2
–Revision. See Composing process
–Revolutionary qualities. See also general index,
  Politics; Socialism [1896.27, 71; 1911.28a;
  1912.16, 29; 1919.76, 174, 204, 221, 308,
  310; 1922.14; 1923.48; 1931.57; 1932.47;
  1934.38; 1936.13]

-Sales. See also Auctions; Prices [1864.5; 1882.85, 95, 127; 1885.38-39; 1886.36-37, 50; 1888.29; 1919.203, 319; 1923.33; 1925.44; 1939.4]
-Schoolteaching. See also general index, Education; Woodbury School [1895.27; 1918.10; 1919.157, 233; 1936.31]
-Sources. See also Bible, Carlyle; Emerson; Hegel; Kant, Michelet; Opera; Sand; Shakespeare [1894.17; 1896.42, 62; 1897.56, 65; 1898.17, 38; 1899.76; 1904.24; 1910.11; 1915.23; 1919.283; 1920.5; 1921.16, 55; 1922.39, 51, 65; 1925.60; 1926.9, 22, 32; 1929.11, 32, 56; 1930.17-19; 1931.22; 1932.19; 1934.30-32, 42; 1935.10; 1936.2, 6, 23-24, 51; 1937.14, 25, 39; 1938.2, 29, 32; 1939.18; Appendix]
-Style. See also Catalogues; Vocabulary; general index, American language; Modern poetry [1872.2, 17; 1876.56; 1877.16; 1880.35; 1886.2, 34, 39; 1888.1, 38-39, 48, 54; 1890.14; 1891.33; 1893.30; 1894.21, 60; 1895.24, 76; 1896.2, 9, 71, 73; 1898.55, 56a, 88; 1899.21, 76; 1900.7, 29; 1901.51; 1902.6, 18; 1904.2; 1906.5, 41-68 (passim), 83; 1907.23; 1908.29, 31; 1909.1, 3-4; 1910.11, 13, 30, 35; 1911.9, 11; 1912.38; 1913.5, 52; 1914.5, 15, 45; 1916.4, 6, 10, 23; 1917.23; 1918.3-4, 19; 1919.3; 128, 135, 138, 195, 241, 285, 317, 335, 350; 1920.24; 1921.20, 36, 49; 1922.57-58; 1923.39, 60; 1925.18, 23, 26, 60; 1926.1, 15; 1927.22, 36; 1928.37; 1929.17, 33, 49; 1930.3, 37; 1931.6, 14-15, 19-22, 37; 1933.27; 1934.16, 31; 1935.1, 10, 13-14; 1936.23, 52; 1938.48; 1939.17, 26]
-Subscriptions (chiefly from English supporters) [1885.23, 29; 1886.47-56; 1887.16; 1892.31; 1911.1; 1919.342; 1931.1; 1934.5; 1935.22]
-Suppression (Boston). See also Censorship; general index, Libraries [1882.12, 38 (and passim); 1895.13, 80; 1896.36, 67; 1904.35; 1927.46]
-Teaching. See Schoolteaching
-Textual errors [1934.17]
-Titles [1868.20, 37; 1902.26; 1905.19; 1924.11; 1926.15; 1927.36]
-Tomb. See general index, Harleigh Cemetery
-Tributes. See Poems to Whitman; Birthday dinners; Memorials
-Visits to Whitman [1865.1; 1866.22; 1867.1; 1873.9; 1884.7-9; 1885.8-9, 11, 18, 27, 42; 1886.13, 19, 54; 1887.3, 86; 1888.24, 65; 1889.9, 32, 37-38; 1890.7, 45; 1891.2, 51, 53; 1892.10, 28, 58, 93, 101, 104, 106, 173; 1894.16, 28; 1895.11; 1896.8; 1897.39, 60; 1899.12; 1900.41; 1902.61; 1903.12; 1907.7; 1909.43; 1910.10, 14, 21; 1914.45; 1916.43; 1917.6; 1919.241, 283; 1930.27; 1936.17; 1938.16; 1939.47]
-Vocabulary. See also Style [1907.31; 1909.40; 1918.48; 1919.16, 20, 317; 1920.83; 1925.24, 28; 1926.46; 1932.38]
-Will. See also Finances [1892.115, 121, 140; 1926.15; 1936.21]
-Works
--Criticism. See Criticism
--Fiction [1864.5; 1927.12; 1938.32]
    -"Army of Tears, The" [1842.7]
    -"Death in a School Room" [1850.1]
    -Franklin Evans [1842.8, 10-14; 1864.4-5; 1892.117; 1898.103; 1925.81; 1927.43; 1929.10; 1931.19]
    -"Last of the Sacred Army" [1842.2]
    -"Richard Parker's Widow" [1845.1]
    -"Shirval" [1847.5]
    -"Tomb Blossoms, The" [1850.1]

--Poetry (particular poems, sections, and editions)
    -"After All, Not to Create Only." See "Song of the Exposition"
    -"After the Sea-Ship" [1897.58; 1939.15]
    -"As a Strong Bird on Pinions Free." See "Thou Mother"
    -"As I Ebb'd with the Ocean of Life" [1860.12; 1896.9]
    -"As I Lay with My Head in Your Lap, Camerado" [1914.5]
    -"Ashes of Soliders" [1886.3]
    -"Autumn Rivulets" [1899.37]
    -"Bardic Symbols." See "As I Ebb'd with the Ocean of Life"
    -"Beat! Beat! Drums!" [1865.11; 1914.15; 1927.22]
    -"Broadway Pageant, A" [1860.43, 60; 1899.22]
    -"By Blue Ontario's Shore" [1881.47; 1917.24, 37; 1926.15; 1929.13]
    -"By the Bivouac's Fitful Flame" [1916.36]
    -"Calamus" [1866.24; 1870.4; 1871.26; 1881.5; 1883.3; 1886.4; 1889.47; 1893.9, 11; 1894.17, 61; 1897.92, 107, 147; 1898.89; 1903.3; 1906.5; 1913.16; 1914.5, 45; 1919.18; 1920.5; 1921.20, 62; 1924.3, 5, 10, 34; 1926.1, 17, 65, 70, 73, 77; 1927.7; 1928.22; 1929.13; 1930.3; 1931.1, 6; 1932.15, 28; 1934.13, 46; 1935.29; 1936.3; 1937.25; 1938.9]
    -"Carol for Harvest, for 1867, A." See "Return of the Heroes"
    -"Chanting the Square Deific" [1893.9; 1895.52; 1897.11; 1922.1; 1929.56; 1937.41]
    -"Child's Reminiscence, A." See "Out of the Cradle"
    -"Children of Adam" [1860.26; 1866.24; 1867.6, 23; 1874.3; 1882.17, 22, 25, 54, 80; 1889.46; 1892.87, 130, 206; 1893.11; 1897.86; 1899.37; 1900.38; 1904.10; 1905.10, 19, 28; 1906.5, 86; 1914.5, 45; 1918.56; 1919.248; 1920.5; 1921.17; 1922.15, 29; 1924.3, 10; 1926.1, 57, 65, 77; 1927.7, 14; 1928.22; 1929.13; 1931.6; 1938.9; 1939.18]
    -"City Dead-House, The" [1899.63; 1905.15]
    -"Come, said my Soul" [1896.50; 1902.26; 1926.15; 1938.30]
    -"Come Up from the Fields Father" [1868.4; 1899.7; 1905.15; 1936.47]
    -"Crossing Brooklyn Ferry" [1866.24; 1914.5; 1919.48; 1921.36; 1926.54; 1934.48; 1937.23; 1938.5]
    -"Dalliance of the Eagles, The" [1931.1]
    -"Darest Thou Now O Soul" [1892.60]
    -"Dead Emperor, The" [1892.209]
    -"Dead Tenor, The" [1899.42]
    -"Death Carol." See "When Lilacs Last in the Dooryard Bloom'd"
    -"Death of General Grant" [1885.16; 1934.40]
    -"Death of the Nature-Lover" [1843.1]
    -"Death's Valley" [1892.59, 123]
    -"Dirge for Two Veterans" [1900.32, 35; 1903.48; 1915.57; 1916.36; 1919.328]
    -Drum-Taps (book and section) [1865.4-11; 1866.7, 14-16, 18, 24, 26-27; 1867.1-2, 23; 1870.4; 1871.23; 1872.20; 1875.4; 1881.53, 55; 1882.22, 27; 1887.63; 1892.37, 96, 100, 224; 1894.17; 1898.2; 1899.43; 1900.38; 1902.34; 1903.11, 22; 1904.12; 1905.15, 19; 1906.13, 23; 1908.3; 1909.4; 1914.5; 1915.31; 1916.8, 25, 36; 1917.7, 24-25; 1918.58; 1919.39, 248, 300; 1920.5; 1921.23; 1922.20; 1924.3; 1926.58; 1927.7; 1930.3; 1931.4]
    -"Earth, My Likeness" [1914.5]

-"Eidólons" [1876.63; 1886.3; 1892.159; 1896.9; 1897.11; 1900.32, 35; 1922.1; 1924.10; 1926.15; 1938.30]
-"Enfans d'Adam." See "Children of Adam"
-"Ethiopia Saluting the Colors" [1882.16; 1894.45; 1904.1; 1914.15]
-"Faces" [1930.34]
-"Facing West from California's Shores" [1915.27]
-"Fallen Angel, The" [1899.36]
-"First Dandelion, The" [1888.21-22; 1889.28; 1921.5]
-"For You O Democracy" [1901.55; 1918.72; 1919.32]
-"Gods" [1901.61]
-Good-Bye My Fancy [1890.58, 61; 1891.34a, 37-38, 40-41, 43-46, 55]
-"Good-Bye My Fancy" [1905.57; 1924.41; 1926.70; 1930.33; 1935.25, 38]
-"Grand Is the Seen" [1897.28; 1902.26]
-"House of Friends, The" [1850.3]
-"Hush'd Be the Camps To-Day" [1918.32; 1938.56]
-"I Hear America Singing" [1927.6]
-"I Hear It Was Charged against Me" [1919.321]
-"I Saw in Louisiana a Live-Oak Growing" [1923.64]
-"I Sing the Body Electric" [1856.11; 1882.80; 1896.52; 1921.9]
-"Ideal School, An" [1928.34]
-"In Cabin'd Ships at Sea" [1892.155]
-"Isle of La Belle Rivière" [1892.156]
-"Italian Music in Dakota" [1881.38]
-"Joy, Shipmate, Joy!" [1899.17; 1905.8, 54; 1906.53; 1914.10, 15; 1927.22]
-"Last Invocation, The" [1910.26; 1919.374; 1920.68; 1921.36; 1924.22; 1931.15]
-"Last of Ebb, and Daylight Waning" [1897.162]
-"Leaf for Hand in Hand, A" [1914.5]
-Leaves of Grass, 1855. See also Auctions; Sales [1855.2-3, 6-7, 9-12, 14; 1856.3-11, 16-17, 19, 24-26; 1882.26; 1886.37; 1889.38; 1896.36; 1898.103; 1909.4; 1919.107; 1920.22; 1921.55; 1927.7, 52; 1930.1; 1931.39-42; 1934.25, 48; 1939.4]
-Leaves of Grass, 1856 [1856.24, 26-27; 1898.103; 1920.2; 1937.9]
-Leaves of Grass, 1860 [1860.3, 15-18, 20-32, 34-35, 37-40, 42-46, 49, 51-52, 55-56, 62, 69; 1882.123; 1888.28; 1896.33; 1905.58; 1919.304; 1920.2; 1921.24]
-Leaves of Grass, 1867 [1866.24, 27; 1867.1, 23]
-Leaves of Grass, 1871 [1870.8; 1871.4; 1874.10]
-Leaves of Grass, 1876 [1892.55; 1897.156]
-Leaves of Grass, 1881-82 [1881.38, 40a, 42-47, 50, 52-53, 55; 1882.13-17, 20, 22, 25-26, 31, 38 (See also Suppression), 80, 87-88, 96, 99, 132; 1920.2; 1925.32]
-Leaves of Grass, 1897 [1897.156, 160, 162; 1898.21, 25-26, 32; 1899.34]
-Leaves of Grass, 1900 Variorum [1900.49]
-Leaves of Grass, 1902 [1902.62-65; 1903.31; 1904.38]
-"Lo, Victress on the Peaks" [1939.17]
-"Long, Long Hence" [1891.40]
-"Memories of President Lincoln." See also poems in this group; general index, Lincoln [1892.109]
-"Midnight Visitor, The" [1891.33a, 48; 1892.32, 105; 1894.54]
-"Mississippi at Midnight, The" [1921.27]
-"Mystic Trumpeter, The" [1875.7; 1887.27;

1894.44; 1895.5; 1899.34; 1901.11; 1904.1; 1913.30; 1918.3; 1919.305, 341; 1936.30]
-"Native Moments" [1914.5]
-"New Year's Day 1848" [1892.69; 1934.31]
-"Noiseless Patient Spider, A" [1892.206; 1900.49; 1904.24; 1920.93; 1939.17]
-November Boughs [1886.6; 1888.27, 30, 49, 57, 64, 66-68, 70-71, 74-76, 78-79, 81-83; 1889.11, 13, 15-20, 23-26, 32-33, 60]
-"O Captain! My Captain!" [1865.11; 1866.14, 22; 1868.20; 1876.60, 64; 1877.5; 1879.10; 1881.12, 38, 44, 53; 1882.7, 16, 20, 26; 1883.28, 33; 1884.1-2, 12; 1886.24, 30; 1887.48, 63, 86; 1888.42; 1889.1; 1890.15, 19; 1891.5, 33a; 1892.28, 32, 43, 60, 103, 126, 169, 183, 196, 224; 1896.10; 1898.12, 45; 1899.7, 33, 43, 68; 1900.6, 11, 49; 1901.1, 8, 11, 23, 33, 62-63; 1903.2, 11, 14a; 1904.1; 1905.15; 1906.53; 1907.49; 1909.5, 10; 1911.8, 11; 1912.18; 1913.3, 10, 30; 1914.15; 1915.31; 1916.4, 36; 1919.210, 229, 245, 313, 326; 1920.80; 1921.27, 59; 1923.63; 1926.54, 58, 71; 1927.3, 22; 1929.1, 25; 1930.3; 1931.2, 4, 15, 44, 47-48, 54; 1932.35; 1934.10, 41; 1936.32; 1938.47; Addenda]
-"O Star of France" [1872.19; 1918.21]
-"O Tan-Faced Prairie-Boy" [1926.3]
-"Of Him I Love Day and Night" [1860.7]
-"Of the Terrible Doubt of Appearances" [1914.5]
-"Old Age Echoes" [1897.160; 1904.38]
-"Old Age's Lambent Peaks" [1888.55]
-"Old Ireland" [1872.12; 1892.39]
-"Old Man's Thoughts of School, An" [1928.34]
-"Old Salt Kossabone" [1909.10]
-"On the Beach at Night" [1906.14]
-"Once I Pass'd through a Populous City" [1902.32; 1905.1; 1914.5; 1917.39; 1920.88; 1921.16, 27; 1922.44]
-"One Hour to Madness and Joy" [1921.49]
-"Out from Behind This Mask" [1938.30]
-"Out of the Cradle Endlessly Rocking" [1859.5-8; 1860.4-5; 1868.3, 19, 22; 1871.8; 1873.8; 1882.14, 20, 26; 1883.34; 1886.41, 45; 1887.27; 1888.24, 54; 1890.6; 1891.1; 1892.21, 33, 37, 39, 76, 103, 126, 132, 155, 180, 202, 206; 1894.22, 45; 1895.5, 11, 16; 1896.51; 1899.34; 1900.11; 1901.1, 11, 24; 1902.18, 30; 1903.1, 35; 1904.1, 18, 28; 1905.15, 28, 36; 1906.5, 8; 1907.19; 1908.36; 1909.10; 1910.11, 26; 1911.7-8; 1912.20, 34; 1913.10, 52; 1914.5, 12; 1915.3, 4, 17; 1918.19; 1919.3, 229, 245, 328; 1921.6, 21, 27, 49; 1922.26, 36; 1926.1, 10, 54, 68, 82; 1927.1, 36; 1928.41; 1929.13; 1930.13, 23; 1932.16, 28; 1934.22; 1935.14]
-"Out of the Rolling Ocean the Crowd" [1918.10; 1938.19]
-"Ox-Tamer, The" [1876.63; 1887.4; 1892.181; 1925.23]
-"Passage to India" [1870.8; 1893.1; 1894.44; 1895.22a, 24a; 1897.57; 1899.68; 1902.30; 1904.18; 1914.5; 1915.35; 1917.9; 1919.215; 1921.13; 1922.1; 1926.15, 54, 68; 1927.1-2, 36; 1928.39; 1930.9; 1932.28, 35; 1936.27; 1937.9; 1938.2]
-Patriotic Poems, 1918 [1918.22, 35, 44; 1919.131]
-"Patroling Barnegat" [1886.3; 1904.1]
-"Pictures" [1925.47]

-"Pioneers! O Pioneers!" [1865.6; 1882.14; 1883.24; 1888.73; 1893.35; 1900.32; 1903.48; 1910.16; 1913.10; 1914.15; 1916.36; 1918.26; 1921.45; 1925.10, 26; 1926.67; 1927.22; 1929.28; 1938.10]
-"Prayer of Columbus" [1876.63; 1880.8; 1890.59; 1892.50, 96; 1895.23; 1899.34; 1914.5, 12; 1919.128, 167, 362, 365; 1923.48; 1926.49; 1930.9; 1931.1; 1932.8]
-"Proud Music of the Storm" [1869.2; 1894.34; 1921.61; 1922.36; 1926.54, 68; 1927.1; 1928.40]
-"Punishment of Pride, The" [1902.33]
-"Reconciliation" [1882.7; 1906.14; 1938.19]
-"Respondez!" [1923.40]
-"Return of the Heroes, The" [1867.18, 20]
-"Sail Out for Good, Eidôlon Yacht!" [1892.39]
-"Salut Au Monde!" [1866.24; 1893.11; 1897.86; 1903.38; 1922.47; 1934.15, 48]
-"Sands at Seventy." See also November Boughs [1894.17]
-"Sea-Drift" [1892.183; 1897.149; 1914.5; 1924.10; 1926.58; 1937.5]
-"Sea-Shore Memories" [1889.26]
-"Singer in the Prison, The" [1881.44; 1892.103; 1896.7; 1921.36]
-"Sleepers" [1929.10; 1937.9]
-"So Long" [1915.35; 1923.40]
-"Sometimes with One I Love" [1906.79]
-"Song at Sunset" [1900.2]
-"Song for Occupations, A" [1899.7; 1909.20; 1921.38, 61]
-"Song of Joys, A" [1887.7; 1914.5]
-"Song of Myself" [1855.9; 1856.7, 9; 1860.38, 46, 49; 1866.24; 1867.23; 1868.26; 1873.4; 1874.11; 1876.63, 65; 1880.5; 1881.38; 1882.1, 20, 22, 66; 1883.3, 14; 1884.21; 1885.12; 1887.48; 1888.1; 1892.32, 183, 206; 1893.11; 1894.28; 1895.5; 1896.62; 1898.88; 1900.18, 47; 1901.3, 61; 1903.3; 1905.19, 28; 1906.5, 13, 43, 49, 63; 1909.4, 11; 1910.8, 39; 1912.28, 34; 1913.4, 15, 29-30; 1914.5; 1915.2, 4; 1916.6; 1917.9; 1918.37; 1919.6, 13, 173, 210; 1920.55; 1921.7, 13, 21, 27, 30, 39, 41; 1922.36; 1923.24; 1924.3, 10; 1925.4, 27, 33, 66; 1926.1, 15, 37; 1927.32; 1929.5, 13, 17; 1930.9, 19, 38; 1931.6, 21; 1932.8, 26, 28; 1936.9, 47; 1937.37; 1938.1, 29, 48]
-"Song of Prudence" [1919.320]
-"Song of the Answerer" [1915.35; 1923.24]
-"Song of the Banner at Daybreak" [1882.26; 1892.22; 1893.29; 1914.5; 1917.24]
-"Song of the Broad-Axe" [1882.3; 1883.24; 1888.1a, 4; 1892.100; 1894.44; 1898.27; 1900.52; 1902.38; 1914.5, 15; 1917.29; 1925.36; 1926.70; 1929.13; 1937.22]
-"Song of the Exposition" [1871.11-19, 21-22, 24-25; 1872.8; 1894.44; 1898.82; 1901.68; 1914.5; 1923.40; 1932.6; 1938.7, 16]
-"Song of the Open Road" [1866.24; 1900.7, 38; 1901.66; 1904.45; 1905.54; 1910.3; 1913.30; 1914.5, 15; 1915.35; 1916.5; 1919.210; 1920.67; 1922.29; 1923.52; 1925.22; 1935.15; 1939.16]
"Song of the Redwood-Tree" [1876.63; 1887.10; 1892.96; 1899.7; 1901.68; 1926.49; 1934.14]
-"Song of the Rolling Earth, A" [1915.35]
-"Song of the Universal" [1892.16; 1914.5; 1915.35]
-"Spirit that Form'd this Scene" [1881.38; 1882.1; 1886.3; 1934.10]

-"Starting from Paumanok" [1923.24; 1930.19]
-"Stronger Lessons" [1939.2]
-"Tears" [1905.11; 1914.5; 1926.1; 1927.36; 1939.17]
-"There Was a Child Went Forth" [1912.8; 1919.217, 219; 1924.23]
-"This Compost" [1900.2, 38]
-"Thou Mother with Thy Equal Brood." See also general index, Dartmouth [1872.13-15; 1903.28; 1904.1; 1912.21; 1914.5; 1921.13, 36; 1925.26; 1938.57]
-"Thought of Columbus, A" [1892.198]
-"To a Common Prostitute" [1867.4-6; 1882.62, 121, 133; 1899.37; 1910.3; 1915.1; 1931.1]
-"To a Locomotive in Winter" [1876.56, 63, 71; 1882.14; 1897.57; 1900.49; 1911.9; 1938.30]
-"To Him that Was Crucified" [1922.1]
-"To the Man-of-War-Bird" [1882.14; 1898.12; 1900.11; 1903.11, 14a; 1904.33; 1908.36; 1909.10; 1923.48; 1937.39]
-"To Think of Time" [1915.35; 1936.47]
-"To You" [1907.4]
-"Twilight Song, A" [1892.32]
-Two Rivulets [1875.13; 1876.9, 15, 23, 63, 71; 1880.8; 1909.42]
-"Unfolded Out of the Folds" [1906.77; 1934.48]
-"Vigil Strange I Kept on the Field One Night" [1892.220; 1914.5]
-"Virginia--The West" [1938.53]
-"Vocalism" [1909.19]
-"Voice of the Rain, The" [1897.12]
-"Voices." See "Vocalism"
-"Warble for Lilac-Time" [1898.63]
-"Weave in, My Hardy Life" [1900.35]
-"When I Heard at the Close of Day" [1918.52]
-"When I Heard the Learn'd Astronomer" [1914.12]
-"When Lilacs Last in the Dooryard Bloom'd" [1866.2, 26; 1867.1-2, 23; 1868.3, 19-20; 1871.8, 23; 1873.8; 1874.9; 1875.4; 1876.63-64; 1877.5; 1882.7, 14, 16, 20; 1883.34; 1884.12; 1886.41, 45; 1887.86; 1888.38, 42, 54; 1889.26, 38; 1890.6; 1891.1; 1892.22, 60, 67, 75-76, 103, 132, 155, 224; 1893.2, 12; 1895.5, 11; 1896.9, 51, 59; 1897.11, 115; 1898.34, 38, 45, 89; 1899.30, 33-34, 43; 1900.11, 47, 49, 52; 1901.11, 31, 33, 45, 66; 1902.30; 1903.1, 9; 1904.1, 12, 28; 1905.15, 28; 1906.5, 7, 13-14, 23, 63; 1907.8, 19; 1908.36; 1909.10; 1910.7, 26; 1911.8, 11; 1912.18, 20, 34; 1913.3, 10, 30; 1914.5, 12; 1915.3-4, 31; 1917.26; 1918.32; 1919.25-26, 59, 313, 328; 1921.6, 27, 49, 64, 68; 1922.29; 1923.6, 45, 48, 51, 60; 1924.44; 1925.11; 1926.1, 35, 54, 59, 68, 71, 82; 1927.16; 1928.22, 37, 41; 1929.13, 24; 1930.23; 1931.2, 4, 48; 1932.16, 28, 35; 1934.2; 1935.14; 1936.5, 47; 1937.5; 1938.48]
-"Whispers of Heavenly Death" [1886.13; 1903.48; 1906.10; 1921.36]
-"With Antecedents" [1860.6, 51]
-"With Husky-Haughty Lips, O Sea!" [1931.1; 1937.46]
-"Woman Waits for Me, A" [1896.40, 43; 1905.10; 1923.4; 1926.17; 1927.53; 1931.13]
-"World Take Good Notice" [1911.18]
-"Wound-Dresser, The" [1878.4; 1936.47]
-"Years of the Modern" [1915.38; 1919.33]
-"Yonnondio" [1887.88]
-"Youth, Day, Old Age and Night" [1898.88]
--Prose. See also Works--Fiction [1887.23;

1892.11; 1898.14; 1905.28; 1908.51; 1912.15; 1919.312; 1928.8, 23; 1935.8, 10; 1937.40; 1938.22]
  –"American Primer" [1904.17, 30-31; 1930.41]
  –"Army Hospitals and Glimpses" [1888.60]
  –"Art-Singing and Heart-Singing" [1845.3]
  –"Backward Glance O'er Travel'd Roads, A." See also November Boughs; Christopher Morley, for reviews of 1926.21 [1889.39; 1899.34, 75; 1926.21, 28]
  –"Boz and Democracy" [1842.1]
  –Complete Prose Works [1898.71, 95; 1918.35]
  –"Democracy." See also "Personalism" [1867.27-28, 30; 1868.7]
  –Democratic Vistas [1868.41, 43; 1870.8; 1871.4; 1872.19; 1886.4; 1888.41; 1892.32, 50, 55, 206; 1893.11; 1901.3, 51; 1902.7; 1903.37; 1904.18; 1905.1, 19; 1910.3; 1914.15, 21; 1915.31; 1919.7, 346; 1920.2, 19, 25; 1921.54, 73, 79; 1923.40, 49; 1924.23; 1926.1, 76; 1929.15, 17; 1930.10, 35; 1931.2; 1932.15, 47; 1934.18; 1935.10; 1936.45; 1937.9; 1938.1; 1939.10, 41]
  –"Edgar Poe's Significance." [1935.17]
  –"Eighteenth Presidency, The" [1928.11; 1929.46]
  –"Elias Hicks." See also November Boughs; general index, Hicks [1887.29, 36; 1888.56, 65]
  –"Emerson's Books, (The Shadows of Them)" [1926.32]
  –"George Fox (and Shakspere)." See also November Boughs; general index, Fox [1922.1]
  –"Interviewer's Item, An" [1932.27]
  –Memoranda During the War [1875.13; 1876.63; 1880.29; 1936.39]
  –November Boughs. See Poetry––November Boughs
  –"Old Man's Rejoinder" [1890.40, 47]
  –"Old Poets" [1890.60]
  –"Personalism." See also "Democracy" [1868.24, 30; 1938.16]
  –"Poetry of the Future, The" [1881.8]
  –Prefaces. See also "Backward Glance"
  ––1855 [1855.2-3, 6, 9; 1856.6; 1882.56; 1883.14; 1888.41; 1892.183; 1893.41; 1898.100; 1900.15; 1901.26; 1906.13; 1915.4; 1919.342; 1922.43; 1925.30, 52; 1926.21 (See Christopher Morley for reviews); 1929.15; 1931.2, 23; 1934.16; 1938.30]
  ––1872 [1923.48]
  –"Slang in America" [1932.38]
  –Specimen Days [1882.111-112, 119, 128, 131, 134; 1883.9, 25, 28, 36; 1887.50, 53; 1888.77; 1892.50; 1897.107; 1898.95; 1899.7; 1901.26, 45, 50; 1904.18; 1905.8; 1906.23, 95; 1908.51; 1914.41; 1915.4; 1916.8; 1917.32; 1918.34; 1919.219, 300; 1920.2; 1921.20; 1933.31; 1934.1; 1935.10; 1936.45; 1937.20]
  –Two Rivulets. See Poetry––Two Rivulets
Whitman, Zachariah (reputed ancestor) [1906.71]
Whitmore, Alice J. [1919.276]
Whittier, John Greenleaf 1889.9, 49; 1896.3; 1911.1 [1868.39; 1879.4; 1880.5, 35; 1885.18; 1890.13, 41; 1891.44; 1892.60, 126, 158, 178; 1894.35; 1897.67; 1898.85; 1901.13; 1903.2; 1906.7, 13; 1919.219; 1932.39; *1933.8; 1938.20]
Wide Awake 1878.9
Wiksell, Gustav P. 1898.67 [1939.44]
Wiksell, Percival 1907.47; 1919.284

Wilbur, Rev. Russell J. [1919.344]
Wild, Henry Douglas. See Appendix
Wilde, Oscar 1889.18 [1882.18, 21, 26-27, 29, 56, 118; 1895.28; 1897.153; 1906.17; 1907.7; 1914.45; 1915.59; 1916.20; 1925.78; 1931.1; 1934.1; 1936.17, 29]
Wiley, Autrey Nell 1929.49
Wilhelm, Emperor [1892.209]
Wilkie, James 1886.11
Wilkins, Ernest Hatch 1922.16
Wilkinson, Marguerite 1919.26
Willard, Cyrus Field 1887.86
Willard, Frances E. 1889.90 [1915.18]
Willcocks, M[ary] P. 1923.33; 1925.17
Willcox, Louise Collier 1906.90; 1907.35, 40; 1909.14; 1910.42
William Jewell Student 1901.33; 1905.34; 1919.173-174, 176-178
Williams, Francis Howard 1887.15; 1888.31 [1888.39, 46], 56; 1889.9; 1893.11; 1894.19, 45 [1894.50]; 1895.20; 1896.40; 1897.100; 1900.39; 1901.56; 1903.30; 1905.41; 1906.39; 1908.39, 41; 1916.48; 1917.39 [1889.52, 54; 1892.15; 1894.15]
Williams, George Fred 1907.40 [1903.47]
Williams, Gwen 1921.68
Williams, Richmond B. 1939.31
Williams, Stanley Thomas 1937.15, 17
Williams, Talcott 1905.26 [1888.24]
Williams, William Carlos 1917.53; 1923.18; 1932.22; 1939.26, 40
Williamsburgh (New York) Times 1849.10; 1852.1
Williamson, Claude C. H. 1920.31
Williamson, George M[iller] 1903.16
Willis, N. P. [1872.10]
Wilmington (Delaware) Morning News 1916.40
Wilshire's Magazine 1902.59; 1903.21
Wilson, David Alec 1927.24; 1934.18
Wilson, Edward A. 1926.24 [1926.48]
Wilson, Francis 1924.26
Wilson, James Grant 1889.7
Wilson, Woodrow [1918.72; 1919.14]
Wing, James G. 1927.39
Winnipeg Manitoba Free Press 1919.313
Winter, Jefferson 1920.81
Winter, William 1860.48, 64 [1864.2; 1933.17; 1935.16]; 1883.17; 1888.45; 1907.58; 1909.15 [1860.4; 1920.81]
Winter Park (Florida) Herald 1924.30
Winterich, John T. 1927.52
Winters, Yvor 1930.38; 1937.18
Winwar, Frances 1933.10
Wisconsin Magazine 1923.42
Wise, Thomas James 1918.7; 1926.29
Wit and Wisdom 1890.26
Wockers, Jerry 1905.38
Wolfe, Theodore F. 1895.11; 1898.19; 1899.36; 1900.19
Wolfe, Thomas [1936.7; 1937.10; 1939.7]
Wolfenstein, Alfred 1921.43
Woman. See also Sex [1864.1; 1883.18; 1892.108; 1896.34; 1897.56; 1900.43; 1901.37; 1905.10; 1906.77; 1907.15; 1909.20; 1911.3; 1913.51]
Woman and Home (Auckland) 1922.69
Woman's Journal 1882.27
Wood, Clement 1923.19, 44; 1925.18, 33
Wood, James N. 1922.66
Wood, Mrs. Mildred Mary Cummer 1923.19
Woodberry, George Edward 1903.17; 1910.22 [1881.24; 1896.59]

Woodbury, Charles J. 1890.9 [1890.41]
Woodbury, George Frank 1935.7
Woodbury School (where Whitman taught) [1905.59;
     1919.150; 1920.1; 1921.63; 1927.29-31, 33,
     35, 41, 49; 1928.34]
Woodhull, Mary G. 1901.27
Woodhull, Victoria C. 1873.2
     [1927.20]
Woodhull & Claflin's Weekly 1873.2
Woodruff, E. H. 1930.27
Woodward, F. L. 1903.39
Woolcott, Alexander 1921.48
Woolf, Virginia 1925.53
Woolson, Constance Fenimore 1888.73
Word, The [1882.12]
Word, The (New York) 1909.19
Wordsworth, William [1867.1; 1873.4; 1875.16;
     1879.42; 1883.5; 1885.14; 1888.46; 1890.3;
     1892.107, 139, 180, 220; 1895.77; 1897.27;
     1900.9; 1901.53; 1902.21; 1904.13; 1905.40;
     1906.13; 1908.36; 1910.39; 1912.10; 1914.7-8;
     1917.46; 1919.5, 102, 166-167, 211; 1920.6,
     92; 1921.56; 1926.1; 1929.15; 1930.3; 1935.10;
     1936.2, 27; 1937.23; 1938.13]
Workers at Home and Abroad 1921.64
World of Books 1919.337
World Review 1926.74; 1929.52
World Today, The 1930.28
World Unity 1932.39
World's Work 1905.20
Wright, David Henry 1906.46
Wright, Frances [1938.2, 29]
Wright, Silas [1847.3]
Writer 1892.83
Wrong, E. M. (Dipsicus) 1912.27
Wyatt, Edith Franklin 1917.15, 32; 1919.62, 149,
     194, 358
Wyzega (or Wyzewa), M. de 1892.205; 1919.90

X. X. X. 1894.41
Y., J. W. See Young, James Walter
Yale Literary Magazine 1874.11; 1886.42; 1904.46;
     1905.36; 1906.98
Yale Review 1915.22, 54; 1919.334, 339; 1921.74,
     76; 1927.36
Yamamoto, Rinyu 1919.177
Yankee Doodle 1847.1 [1939.23]
Yarmolinsky, Abraham 1916.57
Yarnall, Ellis 1909.16
Ye Crank. See also Open Road 1907.9
Yeats, John Butler 1917.16; 1919.91
     [1914.8; 1916.50; 1932.5]
Yeats, William Butler 1894.62, 67; 1922.28;
     1925.19; 1936.29
     [1917.16]
Yorke, Dane 1926.61
Yorkshire Observer 1919.276; 1924.27
Yorkshire Post. See Leeds Yorkshire Post
Youmans, Edward Livingston [1894.2]
Young, Harry De M. [1896.27]
Young, James Walter 1897.92, 106
Young, John Russell 1892.22 [1892.30]; 1901.17;
     1921.5
     [1900.13]
Young, Mrs. Leader [1931.51]
Young, May D. Russell 1901.17
Young, Stark 1922.47
Youth's Companion 1900.33
Yutang, Lin 1937.20

Z., M. D. See Zabel, Morton Dauwen

Zabel, Morton Dauwen 1936.56; 1937.21
Zagranichny Viestnik 1883.24
Zangwill, I[srael] 1895.48; 1896.18
     [1922.11]
Zarek, Otto 1923.25
Zigrosser, Carl 1919.91
Zillman, Lawrence John 1935.14
Zola, Emile [1880.19; 1882.20, 80; 1883.7, 30, 37;
     1887.63; 1888.20, 25; 1895.14]
Zschokke, Heinrich [1934.30]
Zubof, Roman I. 1892.83
Zueblin, Charles 1908.19; 1913.54
Zunder, Theodore A. 1932.33; 1933.12, 28
Zweig, Stefan [1922.63]